A TOPOGRAPHICAL LIST OF THE INSCRIPTIONS OF THE MADRAS PRESIDENCY

A TOPOGRAPHICAL LIST
OF THE
INSCRIPTIONS OF THE MADRAS PRESIDENCY

(Collected till 1915)

WITH NOTES AND REFERENCES

BY

V. RANGACHARYA, M.A., L.T.

ASSISTANT PROFESSOR OF HISTORY, PRESIDENCY COLLEGE, MADRAS.

VOLUME II.

GYAN

Published by

Gyan Publishing House
5, Ansari Road
Daryaganj, New Delhi-110002
Phone: 011-47034999, 9811692060
E-mail: books@gyanbooks.com

Distribution Network
gyanbooks.com
India, USA, Canada, UK, Australia, France

ISBN : 978-81-212-4129-8 (Set)
ISBN : 978-81-212-4903-4 (PB)
First Published, 1919

2nd Impression 2020

Printed at: Gyan Press, Delhi.

Inscriptions of the Madras Presidency Vol. II
Author: V. Rangacharya

A TOPOGRAPHICAL LIST

OF THE

INSCRIPTIONS OF THE MADRAS PRESIDENCY

(Collected till 1915)

WITH NOTES AND REFERENCES

BY

V. RANGACHARYA, M.A., L.T.,

ASSISTANT PROFESSOR OF HISTORY, PRESIDENCY COLLEGE, MADRAS.

VOLUME II.

MADRAS:

PRINTED BY THE SUPERINTENDENT, GOVERNMENT PRESS.

1919.

CONTENTS TO VOL. II.

GŌDĀVARI DISTRICT.

GUNTŪR DISTRICT.

SOUTH KANARA DISTRICT.

KISTNA DISTRICT.

TOPOGRAPHICAL INSCRIPTIONS.

VOLUME II.

GŌDĀVARI DISTRICT.

GENERAL COPPER PLATES.

1. *C.P. 76 of Mr. Sewell's List.*—(Telugu.) In the Collector's office. Records a grant of land to a Brahman in Ś. 1606 (A.D. 1684), Raktākshi, by a chief styling himself "Mahārāja Śrī Rāja Gaṇapati Rāja Jagannātha Rāja."

2. *C.P. 77 of Mr. Sewell's List.*—In the same place. Records a grant by a descendant of the Eastern Chāḷukya kings. [An examination of the contents of this inscription shows that it was issued by a chief of the Bēṭa Vijayāditya line, referred to in the third Piṭhāpuram inscription. The donor was Śrīsēna Sārathi, between whom and Mallappa III there were four chiefs named . . . Bhūpa, Pratāpa Bhūdara, Vishṇuvardhana (IV) and Mahādēva. The inscription thus carries the genealogy five generations further. Mr. Sewell confounds this line with the E. Chāḷukyan line proper, considering it to be subsequent to Vikrama Chōḷa. He is of course wrong.]

3. *C.P. 78 of Mr. Sewell's List.*—In the Collector's office. Records that in the twenty-fifth year of his reign, a chief named Śrī Prithivīmula Rāja, son of Prabhākara Viśruta Mahārāja, granted the village of Chuyipāka to his household priest and the members of the latter's gōtra as an agrahāram, after having assembled the Rāshṭrakūṭa and other families of the district of Tārupāka. The order is issued from the city of Kāndāḷi. No date of any kind is given. The characters of the plates are similar to those of the E. Chāḷukya plates.

4. *C.P. 191 of Mr. Sewell's List.*—Records grant of lands to a Brahman in Ś. 1500 (A.D. 1578) by "Rāja Śrī Vitaraṇa Rāya." It is very badly executed, much damaged, and dated in Durmati, which is inconsistent.

4-A. The Korumilli Plates of Rājarāja I, the Eastern Chāḷukyan sovereign (1022—63), the son of Vimalāditya and Kuṇḍavā Dēvi, the daughter of the Chōḷa Rājarāja the Great (985—1013). The record is important for the fact that it mentions the date of the king's coronation as Thursday, August 16, A.D. 1022. See *Ind. Antq.*, Vol. XIV, p. 56; *Ibid.*, Vol. XXIII, p. 131, No. 110 and Kielhorn's *Southern List*, No. 569.

5. Naḍupūru grant of Anna Vēma Reḍḍi (which is included here as the exact topography of Naḍupūru is not known). A record of Anna Vēma of the Koṇḍavīḍu Reḍḍis, dated in a day of lunar eclipse, Kārttika, Ś. 1296 (A.D. 1374). It records the grant to 20

Brāhmaṇas of the village of Naḍupūru or Vēmāpuram by the king for the merit of his sister Vēmasāni (stated to be the queen of a certain Nallanūṅka). The place was in Kōnasthala (the Delta) The grant gives the Reḍḍi genealogy as it is in the Vānapalli grant. [See *Ep. Ind.*, Vol. III, pp. 286—92. The dates are not quite consistent as lunar eclipse did not, according to Dikshit, fall on that year. This is Kielhorn's *Southern List*, No. 593.]

6. The Nagpur Museum Inscription of Sōmēśvara. A Telugu record dated Ś. 1130, discovered at Sironcha in Upper Gōdāvari district, recording that Gaṅga mahādēvi, the chief queen of Sōmēśvara dēva, gave the village of Kēramaruka to two temples of Śiva she built. The date of consecration of these was Sunday, 12th *tithi*, of the bright fortnight of Phalguna, Ś. 1130, which corresponds to the 7th February, A.D. 1210. (It should however be Ś. 1231.) Sōmēśvara has the titles of Jagadēkabhūshaṇa Mahārāja, descendant of the race of Nāga, Lord of the city of Bhōgavati, of the Kāśyapa gōtra. Mr. Krishna Sastri suggests that he might belong to the Sinda family. See *Ep. Ind.*, Vol. III, pp. 314—8.

7. The Nandampūṇḍi grant of Rājarāja I (Sanskrit and Telugu). At first in the Collector's office and now in the Madras Museum. Records a grant by king Rājarājadēva (I) of the E. Chāḷukyan family, the son of Vimalāditya and Kuṇḍavādēvi, in the thirty-second year of his reign, during a lunar eclipse (probably according to Kielhorn, on November 28, A.D. 1053). It is addressed to the cultivators (headed by the Rāshṭrakūṭas) in the Reṇḍērulu-nadimivishaya (the district between the two rivers) in the presence of the Mantrin, Purōhita, Sēnāpati, Yuvarāja, Dauvārika and Pradhāna. The object of the grant is the village of Nandampūṇḍi. The donee is Nanni Nārāyana Kavirājaśēkhara (evidently the celebrated translator of the *Mahābhārata*) whose birudas and genealogy are given. The date of the king's coronation was Thursday, 16th August, A.D. 1022. See *Ep. Ind.*, Vol. IV, pp. 300—9. Kielhorn draws attention to the resemblance of the epigraph to Gd. 4-A and Gd. 48 in the introductory, legendary and historical parts. Was Nandampūṇḍi the same as Nandanpūḍi in Amalāpuram taluk? See also Kielhorn's *Southern List*, No. 570.

8. The Raṇastepūṇḍi grant* of Vimalāditya [included here owing to the uncertain topography of the village]. (Sanskrit and Telugu.) A grant of the E. Chāḷukyan Vimalādityan Mummuḍi Bhīma to his minister Vajra, of the Kauṇḍinya gōtra, a resident of Kāremchēdu (nine miles west of Bāpaṭla in Kistna district). The epigraph gives the date of the king's coronation which corresponds, with some correction, according to Kielhorn, to Thursday, 10th May, A.D. 1011. See Kielhorn's *Southern List*. No. 567 and *Ep. Ind.*, Vol. VI, pp. 347—361, where Venkayya edits it. See also *Ep. Rep.*,

* The plates were originally discovered at Amalāpuram taluk and "are now in possession of Valavala Jagganna who lives at Amalāpuram." *Ep. Ind.*, Vol. VI, p. 347.

1900, pp. 14-15, where it is pointed out that between 1011 and 1015 Vimalāditya should have been a prisoner in the Chōḷa court and that his real accession, as other records show, should have been after his return from there about A.D. 1015.

AMALĀPURAM TALUK.

Palivēla.

Mr. Sewell gives thirteen inscriptions in this place, but he is not sure as to their accuracy. His suspicion seems to be well grounded as 12 of the 13 cannot be identified with any in the following list. No. 10 of his list is the same as the first of this. For an account of the place see *Local Records*, Vol. II, p. 204 f., and *Gōdāvari Gazr.*, pp. 203-4.

9. 498 *of* 1893.—(Sanskrit.) On a slab lying in the Koppēśvara temple. Records in Ś. 1094 the grant of land by a minister of Velanānṭi-Chōḍa.

10. 499 *of* 1893.—(Telugu.) On a pillar in the Asthānamaṇṭapa of the same temple. A record in Āṅgirasa refers to a certain Vamanālaka-Oḍeya, who conquered the fort of Rājamahēndravara, and to two Mussalman officers.

11. 500 *of* 1893.—(Telugu.) On the east wall of the shrine in the same temple. Records in Ś. 1345, Śubhakrit, a gift by a queen of Vīrabhadra to the Koppēśvara temple at Palivēla.

12. 501 *of* 1893.—(Telugu.) On the same wall. Belongs to the reign of the Kākatīya king, Pratāpa-Rudradēva. Records in Ś. 1239, Piṅgaḷa, a gift. Mentions the minister Annaya-Preggaḍa.

13. 502 *of* 1893.—(Telugu.) In the Kalyāna-Maṇṭapa of the same temple. A record of Vishṇuvardhana-Ballahādēva. Mentions the king's son, Bhīmadēva. [Do these refer to Ammarāja I and his son Bhīma II?]

14. 503 *of* 1893.—(Sanskrit and Telugu.) On a pillar of the same maṇṭapa. The Reḍḍi king, Allāḍa, son of Doḍḍaya-Reḍḍi (servant and successor of Kāṭaya Vēma of Rājahmundry), records in Ś. 1338, Durmukhi, the building of the maṇṭapa.

15. 504 *of* 1893.—(Telugu.) On the "Kanakadurga stone." A record dated in Ś. 1345, Śōbhakrit. Mentions Vēma-Reḍḍi, son of Kāṭama-Reddi, and Allāḍa-Reḍḍi (the son of Doḍḍaya). See the above No.

16. 505 *of* 1893.—(Telugu.) On the wall of the garden of the temple. Dated in the time of the Koṇḍavīḍu Reḍḍi king Ana-Vēmaya-Reḍḍi. Records in Ś. 1299, a gift of land for a garden. See No. 18.

Tottaramuḍi.

17. A C.P. grant of Kāṭaya Vēma of Rājahmundry dated in Ś. 1333, Khara, Kārttika Paurṇami. It records a grant by Kāṭaya Vēma, the minister of Kumāragiri of Koṇḍavīḍu, who received from nis master the eastern country of Rājahmundry for his distinguished services. The genealogies of both Kumāragiri and Kāṭaya Vēma are given and the inscription is thus of great value in connecting the two Reḍḍi lines. The object of the grant was the village of Mallāvaram (named after his wife Mallāmbika, who was sister of Kumāragiri) on the Vriddha-gautami, in the vicinity of Muktīśvara in Kōṇadeśa, to Narisimha, son of Ahōbala and grandson of Appayārya, of the Kāśyapa gōtra and Kaṇva Śākha. [The genealogies are the same as in Gd. 5 and 18 and in Kāṭaya Vēma's commentary on Kāḷidāsa's *Śākuntaḷa* called *Kumāra-girirājījayam*. See *Ep. Ind.*, Vol. IV, pp. 318–27, where Mr. Ramayya Pantulu edits the inscription See also Gd. 50, 60 and 66 and Kielhorn's *Southern List*, No. 596.]

Vānupalli.

18. A C.P. grant (now in the Madras Museum) of Anna-Vēma of the Koṇḍavīḍu Reḍḍi dynasty, dated 14th tithi of the dark fortnight of māgha, in year Siddhārthin, Ś. 1300, corresponding, according to Mr. Dīkshit, to Monday, the 6th February A.D. 1380. The king granted the village of Anna-Vēmapura or Immaḍi-Laṅka as an agrahāra to a certain Immaḍi of the Lōhita gōtra, the son of the minister Mallaya, and apparently the spiritual preceptor of the king. See *Ep. Ind.*, Vol. III, pp. 59—66, where Dr. Hultzsch edits it. The inscription quotes from Hēmādri's *Dāṇakhaṇḍa*. It is No. 594 in Kielhorn's *Southern List*.

COCANADA TALUK.

Bhimavaram.

Mr. Sewell mentions three epigraphs in this place. Two of * them are the same as 20 and 22 below. The other is stated to be a private record in Ś. 1336. For an account of the place see *Gōdāvari Gazetteer*, pp. 207–8.

19. 460 *of* 1893.—(Sanskrit and Telugu.) On a pillar in the maṇṭapa in front of the Bhīmēśvara temple. Records in Ś. 1348, Parābhava, consecration of an image of Pārvati by the minister Sūrya or Sūraṇa. [The temple is famous for its architectural beauty, its sanctity and its huge liṅgam.]

20. 461 *of* 1893.—(Sanskrit and Telugu.) (No. 1 of Mr. Sewell's three local inscriptions.) On another pillar in the same maṇṭapa. Records in Ś. 1356, Ānanda, a gift of land by the queen of Vēma Reḍḍi, son of Allāḍa of Rājahmundry. [Bhīmavaram is called Skandārāma and its temple Chāḷukya Bhīmēśvara, which

---

* Some inscriptions of private nature are given in *Mack. MSS.* (*Local Records*, Vol. II, pp. 213—30). They also give a C.P. grant of Kāṭama Vēma Reḍḍi to the Nārāyanasvāmi temple in A.D. 1393. See *Gōdāvari Gazetteer*, p. 208.

enables us to identify it with the temple built, according to the third Pithāpuram pillar inscription, by the E. Chāḷukyan Chāḷukya-Bhīma I. See No. 26 below and 15 above.

21. 462 *of* 1893.—(Sanskrit and Telugu.) On a pillar in the lower verandah of the same temple. Records in Ś. 1344, Śubhakrit, the construction of a maṇṭapa by the minister Sūrya or Sūraṇa.

22. 463 *of* 1893.—(Sanskrit and Telugu.) (No. 2 of Mr. Sewell's local list.) On a pillar near the same verandah. Records in Ś. 1416, Ānanda, the digging of a channel from the river Yela by Yerama-Nāyaka.

23. 464 *of* 1893.—(Telugu and Sanskrit.) On a pillar in the upper verandah of the same temple. Records in Ś. 1346, Krōdhin, the construction of a maṇṭapa by the minister Sūraṇa or Sūrya.

24. 465 *of* 1893.—(Sanskrit.) On a pillar of the Vīrabhadra shrine in the same temple. Records in Ś. 1366, Raktākshi, the consecration of an image of Śiva by the minister Pegaḍa.

25. 466 *of* 1893.—(Tamil language and in Telugu characters.) On the south wall of the same temple. A record of the Chōḷa king, Rājēndra-Chōḷadēva (I). An incomplete, usual historical introduction.

26. 467 *of* 1893.—(Sanskrit.) On a pillar lying in the same temple. A record mentioning Allāḍa, son of Doḍḍaya. See No. 14 above.

27. 468 *of* 1893.—(Telugu.) On the Bhairava shrine in the same temple. A record of Vishṇuvardhana-Mahārāja (VII or Kulōttuṅga I?) in his forty-second year.

28. 469 *of* 1893.—(Telugu.) On a pillar in a maṇṭapa in the garden of the same temple. A record of the Western Chāḷukya king Tribhuvanamalladēva (Vikramāditya VI). (Date doubtful.)

29. 470 *of* 1893.—(Telugu.) On a pillar in the same maṇṭapa. A record in Ś. 1009, referring to a Mahāmaṇḍalēśvara of the Nāgavaṁśa. (An incomplete record.)

30. 471 *of* 1893.—(Telugu.) On a buried stone near the same temple. A record in very archaic characters. Mentions a certain Kēdārarāśi Paṇḍita. [Evidently different from Kēdārabhaṭṭa, the author of the *Vrittaratnākara*. See Hultzsch's *Rep.*, *Sans. MSS.*, III, No. 1775 and II, No. 847.]

31. 472 *of* 1893.—(Telugu.) On a pillar in the maṇṭapa in front of the Nārāyaṇasvāmin temple. Mentions Vishṇuvardhana Mahārāja and the Rājanārāyaṇa-Viṇṇagara temple, founded by a certain Maṇḍaya in the time of Rājanārāyaṇa Kulōttuṅga I. [See *S.I.I.*, Vol. I, p. 59, verse 12.]

32. 473 *of* 1893.—(Sanskrit and Telugu.) On another pillar in the same maṇṭapa. Records in the reign of the Chāḷukya-Chōḷa king Vishṇuvardhana Mahārāja (Kulōttuṅga I) in his forty-fifth year and Ś. 1037, the gift of a lamp by Mādhava, minister of Parāntaka, to the temple of Nārāyaṇa, founded by the Vaiśya Maṇḍaya. See *Ep. Ind.*, Vol. VI, pp. 219–20.

33. 474 *of* 1893.—(Sanskrit.) On the same pillar. A record of Narēndra, son of Vijayāditya of Veṅgi, son of Malla, in Ś. 1098, describing the gift of two lamps to Rājanārāyaṇa. [Dr. Hultzsch believes that Narēndra was the son of Vijayaditya III and brother of Mallappa III. See the genealogy of the Bēṭa Vijayāditya branch.]

34. 475 *of* 1893.—(Telugu.) On the same pillar. Records in Chāḷukya-Vikrama year 46, Plava, a gift of land to the Rāja-nārāyaṇa-Viṇṇagara temple.

35. 476 *of* 1893.—(Telugu.) On another pillar in the same maṇṭapa. A record of Vishṇuvardhana-Mahārāja (Kulōttuṅga I) in his thirty-seventh year and Ś. 1019, regarding the gift of two lamps by a minister of Tribhuvanamalladēva. See No. 32 above.

36. 477 *of* 1893.--(Sanskrit.) On the same pillar. A record containing a *praśasti* of a certain Mallāchāri.

37. 478 *of* 1893.—(Telugu.) On another pillar in the same maṇṭapa. A record of Vishṇuvardhana-Mahārāja in his thirtieth year.

38. 479 *of* 1893.—(Telugu.) On another pillar in the same maṇṭapa. Records in the tenth year Vishṇuvardhana-Mahārāja and Ś. 1105, a gift by the daughter of a Nāyaka. [This Vishṇu-vardhana came to the throne in A.D. 1173. It is difficult to say who he was.]

39. 480 *of* 1893.—(Telugu.) On the same pillar. A record of the Western Chāḷukya king Bhūlōkamalladēva (i.e., Sōmēśvara III) in Chāḷukya-Vikrama year 9 (for 59?), Rākshasa, concerning a gift by the Daṇḍanāyaka Lakshmarasa.

40. 481 *of* 1893.—(Sanskrit.) On the same pillar. A record of Vīra-Chōḍa. (Date doubtful.) See No. 48-A below.

41. 482 *of* 1893.—(Telugu.) On another pillar in the same maṇṭapa. A record of Vishṇuvardhana-Mahārāja. Records a number of different dates without the corresponding Śaka years.

42. 483 *of* 1893.—(Telugu.) On another pillar in the same maṇṭapa. [A record of Vishṇuvardhana-Mahārāja in Ś. 1145 (A.D. 1223). The chief has not been identified.] See No. 103.

43. 484 *of* 1893.—(Sanskrit.) On another pillar in the same maṇṭapa. A record giving a genealogy of the Chāḷukya from Taila to Tribhuvanamalla (Vikramāditya VI). (An incomplete record.)

44. 485 *of* 1893.—(Telugu.) On the same pillar. Records in the ninth year of Vishṇuvardhana Mahārāja, the gift of a lamp by the granddaughter of a Nāyaka.

45. 486 *of* 1893.—(Telugu.) On another pillar in the same maṇṭapa. A record of Vishṇuvardhana-Mahārāja *alias* Mallapadēva in his third year and Ś. 1099. [See No. 38 where the same chief is referred to. Was he a prince of the Bēṭa Vijayāditya line ?]

46. 487 *of* 1893.—(Telugu.) On the south enclosure of the same temple. Records in the third year of Vishṇuvardhana-Mahārāja, Ś. 1098, the gift of a lamp by Mallapadēva. [See Nos. 38 and 48.]

47. 488 *of* 1893.—(Telugu.) In the same place. Records in the thirteenth year of Rājarāja, the gift of a lamp.

48. 489 *of* 1893.—(Sanskrit.) In the same place. An incomplete record mentioning Mallapadēva, son of Vijayāditya. [Was he Mallappa III of the Bēṭa Vijayāditya line ? 1124.]

Chellūr.

48-A. A C.P. grant of Vishṇuvardhana Vīrachōḍa (now in the Madras Museum). An abstract of this has been published by Sir W. Elliot in his *Coins* of *S. Ind.*, pp. 88 and 150, and in *Ep. Rep.*, July 1888, p. 2. It is a very important inscription as it throws light on the connexion between the E. Chāḷukyas and the Chōḷas. Records that Vīrachōḍa, the son of Kulōttuṅga I (1070—1118) and Viceroy of Veṅgi, issued an order to the inhabitants of the Guḍḍivāḍu vishaya that he gave a village (name indistinct) to the Vishṇu temple at Chellūr, founded by his Brahman Sēnāpati Mēḍamārya, or Guṇḍa ratnabhūshaṇa in his twenty-first year. Among the executors were the five pradhānis (*Panchā pradhānis*). The plates have been edited in *S.I.I.*, I, No. 39, pp. 49—62, and in *Ind. Antq.*, Vol. XIX, pp. 423-36, by Dr. Fleet. The latter fixes from the details of the date given that Thursday, 23rd August A.D. 1078, was intended. See also Kielhorn's *Southern List*, No. 573.]

48-B. The Chellūr plates of the E. Chāḷukya Kulōttuṅga II (now in the British Museum). Records a grant by his Daṇḍādhinātha Kāṭa or Kolaṇi Kāṭama Nāyaka (i.e., Kāṭama Nāyaka of Kolanu) in Ś. 1056 (1065 ?) ārdra, pūrvapaksha, etc. See *Ind. Antq.*, XIV, p. 56, and Kielhorn's *Southern List*, No. 574, where it is shown that the date regularly corresponds to 24th March A.D. 1143. See also *Ep. Ind.*, Vol. VII, pp. 9—107. See No. 109 below.

Sarpāvaram.

This place was in Prolunāṇḍu, a subdivision of Gaṅgaikoṇḍachōḷavaḷanāḍu. In his *Antiquities* Mr. Sewell gives twenty-five inscriptions in this place. Of these Nos. 3 and 17 seem to be the same as Nos. 50 and 49 below. The others are not either identifiable or copied. The other inscriptions of Mr. Sewell are not included in this list because it is impossible to say how many of the "undated" and "private" grants of his are the same as those of the following list. For an account of the place see *Gōdāvari Gazetteer*, pp. 214–5 and *Mack. MSS.*, No. 686 (No. 8, C.M. 690), section I.

49. 452 *of* 1893.—(Sanskrit.) On a stone behind the Bhāvanārāyaṇa temple. A record of Goggayadēva in Ś. 1321. [The temple is called Vīrachōḍa-viṇṇahar and was evidently founded by him.]

50. 453 *of* 1893.—(Sanskrit and Telugu.) At the entrance to the same temple. A record of the Reḍḍi king Vēma Reḍḍi, son of Kāṭama Reḍḍi, in Ś. 1336, Jaya. [This chief was the founder of the Rājahmundry Reḍḍi line. He was the author of a learned commentary on the dramas of Kāḷidāsa. See Gd. 17.]

51. 454 *of* 1893.—(Tamil.) On a pillar in the maṇṭapa in front of the same temple. A Tamil record of Kulōttuṅga-Chōḷadēva (I) in his forty-sixth year.

52. 455 *of* 1893.—(Telugu.) On the same pillar. A record of Vishṇuvardhana Mahārāja in his ninth year and Ś. 1123. [Was he identical with Vishṇuvardhana IV of the Bēṭa Vijayāditya line?]

53. 456 *of* 1893.—On another pillar in the same maṇṭapa. Records in the twenty-seventh year of Vishṇuvardhana Mahārāja, the gift of a lamp by Mīnavanmahādēvi. See No. 52.

54. 457 *of* 1893.—(Telugu.) On the same pillar. Records in the twenty-seventh year of Vishṇuvardhana Mahārāja, the gift of a lamp by Chōḍamahādēvi. See No. 52.

55. 458 *of* 1893.—(Telugu.) On the same pillar. Records in the twenty-seventh year of Vishṇuvardhana-Mahārāja, the gift of a lamp by a queen of Vīra-Chōḍadēva. See No. 52.

56. 459 *of* 1893.—(Telugu.) On the same pillar. Records in the twenty-seventh year of Vishṇuvardhana-Mahārāja, the gift of a lamp by a queen. See No. 52.

57. A C.P. mentioned by Mr. Sewell. It is said to be in the temple and record a grant of lands to it by a private person in Ś. 1319.

PEDDĀPURAM TALUK.

Tirupati.

Mr. Sewell gives twenty inscriptions in this place of which Nos. 7, 15 and 17 are evidently the same as 60, 59 and 58 of the list below. The remaining inscriptions are yet to be copied and have been however included here under Nos. 62-A—Q.

58. 494 *of* 1893.—(Telugu.) On a pillar at the entrance of the Śriṅgarāraya temple. A record of Kapilēśvara in Bahudhānya showing that that a minister of his was governing Rājamahēndra vara (Rājahmundry).

59. 495 *of* 1893.—(Telugu.) On a pillar in the Mukha-Maṇṭapa of the same temple. Dated in the reign of Pratāpa-Vatsarāya-Ayyapadēva-Mahārāja. Records in Ś. 1364, Dundubhi, a gift of land.

60. 496 *of* 1893.—(Telugu.) On a pillar in the Āsthāna-Maṇṭapa of the same temple. Records in Ś. 1330, Sarvadhārin, a gift by a relation of Vēma Reḍḍi, son of Kāṭama Reḍḍi, to the Śriṅgārarāya temple at Komāragiripura (i.e., Tirupati). See Nos. 50 and 17 above.

61. 497 *of* 1893.—(Śōbhakrit in Telugu.) On another pillar in the same maṇṭapa. Records in Ś. 1347 a gift for the merit of Allāḍa-Reḍḍi and his family. See No. 14 above.

62. A—Q. 1—6, 8—14, 16 *and* 18—20 *of Mr. Sewell's list.*—Except one or two all these are said to record private grants, and range from Ś. 1322 to Ś. 1566. Nos. O and Q are undated and record grants by Raghudēva Mahēndramahādēva of Rājahmundry (then under the rule of Kapilēśvara Mahārāya) and by Veṅkaṭapati Rāya Narēndra Mahārayaluṅgaru. No. 62-P is dated K. 4955 (A.D. 1854). All the others are private grants. See *Antiquities*, I, p. 23.

PITHĀPURAM DIVISION.

Piṭhāpuram.

That Piṭhāpuram is a very ancient place is proved by the fact that it is mentioned in Samudrāgupta's inscription at Allahabad and that it was captured by the W. Chāḷukyan Satyāśraya, the elder brother of Kubja Vishṇuvardhana in A.D. 584. *Ind. Antq.*, Vol. V, p. 67. Mr. Sewell refers to three inscriptions and these are identical with 63, 64 and 65. See also *Local Records*, Vol. II and Vol. XIX and *Gōdāvari Gazetteer*, pp. 233—9.

63. 490 *of* 1893.—(Sanskrit and Telugu.) On a pillar in the Kuntimādhava temple. Records in the reign of Velanāṇḍu Prithivīśvara grant of a village in the district of Prolunāṇḍu in Ś. 1108 by his mother Jayāmbikā. The inscription traces the genealogy from the mythical Indrasēna and the first historic figure Malla I to Prithivīśvara, the twelfth of the line and the present donor. See *Ep. Ind.*, Vol. IV, pp. 32—54 and Kielhorn's *Southern List*, No. 582.

64. 491 *of* 1893.—(Sanskrit and Telugu.) On the same pillar. A record of the Kōṇa (Haihaya) kings Mallidēva and Manma Satya II in Ś. 1117 describing the grant of Oḍiyūru (near Drākshārāma) to the Piṭhāpuram temple. [Gives a genealogy of the Eastern Chāḷukyas and of the Kōna chiefs who profess to be the descendants of Kārtavīrya. See *Ep. Ind.*, Vol. IV, pp. 83—97 and Kielhorn's *Southern List*, No. 583.]

65. 492 *of* 1893.—(Sanskrit in Telugu.) On the same pillar. A record of the Eastern Chāḷukya feudatory king Mallappa III in

Ś. 1124. [Gives the genealogy of the Eastern Chāḷukyas down to Vikramachōḍa Tyāgasamudra and then the genealogy of the Bēṭa-Vijayāditya branch descended from the seventeenth of the line (i.e., Vijayāgaditya V) up to Mallappa III, the son of Vijayāditya III, whose coronation was on January 11, A.D. 1158. The object of the record is the grant of the village of Guḍivāḍa in the district of Prolunāḍu to the temple. See *Ep. Ind.*, Vol. IV, pp. 226—42, and *Southern List*, Nos. 575–6. Kielhorn fixes the date on Sunday, the 16th June, A.D. 1202.]

66. 493 *of* 1893.—(Sanskrit and Telugu.) On the same pillar. A record of the Reḍḍi king, Vēma-Reḍḍi, son of Kāṭama Reḍḍi in Ś. 1313, Prajāpati, regarding the building of an enclosure of the temple. The record gives the genealogy of the Rājahmundry Reḍḍis as in Gd. 17. Kielhorn calculates the date of the inscription (Ś. 1313, *Prajāpati*, *Makarasaṅkrānti*) to be Thursday, the 29th December, A.D. 1391. See *Ep. Ind.*, Vol. IV, pp. 328–29 and Kielhorn's *Southern List*, No. 595. Also Nos. 50 and 17 above.

67. The Dōnepūṇḍi grant of Piṭhāpuri Nāmaya Nāyaka. (Sanskrit and Telugu.) Records a grant on Sunday, full moon, of Bhādrapada in Ś. 1259, by Sāmanta Nāmaya Nāyaka of Piṭhāpuri (Piṭhāpuram). The object of the grant was Dōnepūṇḍi, called after his father Prōlōra, as an agrahāra, with the eight enjoyments and powers, to one Gaṇapati of the Bhāradvāja Gōtra. [The date is irregular. Sunday, the 30th August, A.D. 1338, is the probable date but, says Kielhorn, the Śaka date should be 1260. See *Ep. Ind.*, Vol. IV, pp. 356—360, and *Ibid.*, Vol. V, pp. 265—66, for Kielhorn's note on the alphabet of the grant. See also *Southern List*, No. 601.]

68. The Piṭhāpuram plates of Vīrachōḍa (Sanskrit and Telugu.) A grant of Vīrachōḍa, the son of Kulōttuṅga Chōḷa I, who ruled at Jananāthanagari (which has been identified with Rājahmundry) and who was, for some time, recalled by his father after his rule of five years (1078—83). The object of the grant was the village of Vīrachōḍachaturvēdimaṅgalam, in the twenty-third year of the king's reign. [Mr. H. Krishṇa Sastri who edits the inscription in *Ep. Ind.*, Vol. V, pp. 70—96, compares this with Gd. 48-B of the same ruler. See also *Ep. Rep.*, 1890, October, p. 2; Burnell's *S. Ind. Palæ.*, second edition, Plate XXIX and Kielhorn's *Southern List*, No. 573. Vīrachōḍa's vassal Vedura II is referred to in the Velanāṇḍu and Kōṇa genealogies.]

RĀJAHMUNDRY TALUK.

Korukoṇḍa.

Mr. Sewell mentions two inscriptions in this place, which are identical with 70 and 69. In the latter, however, he gives the wrong date of Ś. 1371. The local temple is said to have been built by a Nāyaḍu in 1353. For the traditional account see *Local Records*, II,

231 and XIX, 75 f. and *Gōdāvari Gazetteer*, pp. 242–3, where the inscriptions given by Mackenzie are summarized.

69. 43 *of* 1912.—(Śrīmukha in Telugu.) On a pillar set up in front of the Raṅgarājasvāmin temple. Records in Ś. 1375, the gift of lands at Koḍukulūru and other villages, to the temple of Śrīraṅgarāja, by two merchants who had constructed (or repaired) certain portions of it.

70. 44 *of* 1912.—(Sanskrit in Telugu.) On a pillar set up in the courtyard of the Lakshmi-Narasimhasvāmin temple on the hill, in the same village. Records in Ś. 1275, a genealogical account of a certain Mummaḍi-Nāyaka, ruler of Kōrukoṇḍa, subduer of the kingdoms of Panara, Kōna, etc., and refers to the foundation of the temple of Nrisimha by a courtesan (dāsi). [Tradition is that his teacher Parāśara Bhaṭṭa incarnated as the God at his death. See *Ep. Rep.*, 1912, p. 87, for details. This is confirmed by C.P. 21 of 1906 at Śrīraṅgam. The inscription is thus of great interest in the history of Śrīvaishṇavism. See No. 71-A below.]

71. 45 *of* 1912.—(Prabhava in Telugu.) On a slab set up in the same place. Records in Ś. 1370, a gift by a certain Lakkhasāni of Rājamahēndravaram, to the temple of Narasimha on the Parāśara-giri. (A damaged record.)

71-A. C.P. 2 of 1912–13 or Akkalapūṇḍi grant of Śiṅgaya Nāyaka, dated in Ś. 1290, Śrāvaṇa, solar eclipse. It is a grant which belongs to the time of Mummuḍi Nāyaka (referred to in 70 above). The genealogy of his line is as follows :—

Kēśava, N.,
of the Manchikoṇḍa gōtra.
|
Gaṇapati
|
Kūṇabhūpala
|

Mummuḍi Nāyak ruled at Kōrukoṇḍa. Married the niece of Kāpaya Nāik, the Āndhrasuratrāṇa.	Śiṅgaya, N., occupied Kōṭipuri. Founded Mummuḍivīḍu on the Pampa and made it his capital.	Gaṇṇaya, N., occupied Tāḍipāka.

The inscription records that Śiṅgaya Nāik gave the village of Akkalapūṇḍi to a doctor named Parihitāchārya. See *Ep. Rep.*, 1913, p. 129. [Mr. Krishna Sastri believes that his chief was probably the contemporary and admirer of Vēdānta Dēśika for whose sake he wrote the *Subhāshitanivi* and other works. See my article on Vēdānta Dēśika in the *Journal of the Bombay Branch of the Royal Asiatic Society, 1915–16.*]

Rājahmundry.

For the traditional account of Rājahmundry, see *Antiquities*, I, p. 22, and *Local Records*, II, 210 ff., XIX, 75 and LX, 1 f., and for a historical account, *Gōdāvari Gazr.*, pp. 243—6.

72. 506 *of* 1893.—(Telugu.) On a pillar in the compound of the residence of the Sessions Judge. Dated in the reign of the Kākatīya king Gaṇapatidēva in Ś. 1170. Records a gift to a liṅga called Mahādēvēśvara (after the king's father).

73. 507 *of* 1893.—(Sanskrit and Telugu.) At the east entrance of the Gōpālasvāmin temple. Records in Ś. 1742, that a certain Veṅkaṭarāya performed the *tulārōhaṇa* ceremony at Rājamahēndrapaṭṭaṇa and constructed three shrines of Vēṇugōpāla, Nṛisiṁha, and Vēṅkaṭēśvara.

74. 36 *of* 1912.—(Telugu.) On a pillar lying near the godown in the Municipal Museum. Records in the time of the Velanāḍu king, Gōkarāja of Veṅgi, lord of the Shaḍsahasra country (Guṇṭūr district) in Ś. 1102, a gift of 30 buffalo cows for a lamp to the temple of Vīrabhadrēśvara-Mahādēva. [This Gōkarāja, says Mr. Krishna Sastri, was either identical with Prithvīśvara of the Piṭhāpuram inscription or a feudatory of his ruling the 16,000 country of Guṇṭūr.]

75. 37 *of* 1912.—(Telugu.) On the same pillar. Records in Ś. 1117, a gift of 25 cows for a lamp to the same temple by a certain Teliki merchant of Penugoṇḍa.

76. 38 *of* 1912.—(Sanskrit.) On the same pillar. Records in Ś. 1065, a gift by a certain Rāyanripa, to the temple of Vīrabhadrēśvara at Paṭṭīśa.

77. 39 *of* 1912.—(Sanskrit and Telugu.) On the same pillar. Records in Ś. 1065, a gift of lamp to the same temple.

78. 40 *of* 1912.—(Telugu.) On the same pillar. Records in Ś. 1071, the gift of 25 cows for a lamp to the same temple by Dattanapeggaḍa-Sōmaṇa, minister of Nārāyaṇadēva, who was the son of the Mahāmaṇḍalīka Boddaṇa. The inscription also registers gifts of lamps made by the same chief to different temples in the Telugu country, comprising the Gōdāvari, Kistṇa and Guṇṭūr districts. See Mr. Sewell's *Antiquities*, I, pp. 48 and 56. Mr. Krishna Sastri believes that Boddaṇa was probably a *Maṇḍalika* subordinate to Kulōttuṅgachōḍa Goṅka III who, in his turn, was a subordinate of Kulōttuṅgachōḍa II.

79. 41 *of* 1912.—(Sanskrit and Telugu.) (This is No. 8 in Mr. Sewell's local list.) On the same pillar. A record of the Eastern Chāḷukya king Sarvalōkāśraya Vishṇuvardhana-Mahārāja in Ś. 1067 and twenty-first year, relating to a gift of 25 cows for a lamp by a certain Prōli-śeṭṭi, son of Madi-śeṭṭi of Penuṅgoṇḍa, to the temple of Vīrabhadrēśvara-Mahādēva of Paṭṭisapu-nāṇḍu. [The king should have succeeded in A.D. 1123-4. Mr. Krishna Sastri thinks that, as his name is not found in the usual lists, he was probably an ancestor of Mallappa III of the Piṭhāpuram epigraph. See *Ep. Ind.*, Vol. IV, p. 229.]

80. 42 *of* 1912.—(Telugu.) On a granite stone in the house of the pūjārin of the Mārkaṇḍēśvara temple, in the same village. A record in Ś. 1098, mentioning a Mahāmaṇḍalēśvara who was "the elevator of the Chāḷukya-Rājya" and recording a gift of land to the potter Kamaṇa by the trustees (Sthānādhipathi) and the worshippers in the temple of Vīrabhadrēśvara Mahadēva. [The chief seems to be Velanāṇṭi Prithvīśvara, one of whose ancestors, Goṅka II, boasted of being the supporter of the Chāḷukyan dynasty. See *Ep. Ind.*, Vol. IV, p. 38.]

81. *C.P.* 8 *of* 1912-13.—A record of a local chief Chōḍa Annadēva, recording the gift of the village of Uttamagaṇḍachōḍannadēvavaram in Viśarināṇḍu on the banks of the Gaṅga river at a spot called Piṅnanisaṅga to Brahmans. [The plates disclose a line of local chiefs about whom no other records are available and who, says Mr. Krishna Sastri, evidently flourished after the Reḍḍi kings of Rājahmundry. See *Mad. Ep. Rep.*, 1912, p. 86, for details.]

82. On the door of the local mosque. (Persian.) Records that it was erected by Sharif Salar Ulvi in the reign of Emperor Mahomed Toglak and in the time of Humayun Gajjar on the 20th day of Ramzān, H. 724, i.e., A.D. 1324 (*Antiquities*, I, p. 22). [See also *Gōdāvari Gazr.*, p. 244.]

83. In the Mārkaṇḍēya temple. Records that the wife of Kāṭaya Vēmā Reḍḍi, minister of Kumāragiri, son of Anapōta Reḍḍi, made a grant to the temple. [*Ibid.*, p. 22.] Kumāragiri Vēmā ruled from 1381 to 1395. See Gd. 17 above.

84. An inscribed slab unearthed at the District Jail. A grant by a private person in Ś. 1350 and erection of a Kalyāṇa-manṭapam.

84-A. In a slab in the Judge's residence. A grant by Gaṇapatidēva to a temple in Ś. 1170 (A.D. 1248). [The donor evidently was the Kākatīya king of that name.]

85-A—G. On stone fixed in front of the District Jail. Eight inscrptions, dated Ś. 1115, 1100, 1100 (one undated), 1060, 1050, 1112 and 1067, all recording private grants. [*Ibid.*, p. 22. The last of these belonged to the twenty-first year of a Vishṇuvardhana.]

RĀMACHANDRAPURAM TALUK.

Drākshārāma.

The place has been so called because it was, according to the local tradition, the Dakshatapōvana or Dakshavāṭika. It was in the Guḍḍivāḍināṇḍu, a subdivision of Gaṅgaikoṇḍachōḷavaḷanāḍu, of which Prolunāṇḍu was a subdivision. The Piṭhāpuram inscriptions refer to the local temple. Mr. Sewell gives 216 inscriptions based on Elliott's collection in this place but he himself acknowledges that they are inaccurate. The department has copied 271 inscriptions. Mackenzie's collections are reproduced in *Local Records*, Vol. II, 27 f. See also *Gōdāvari Gazr.*, pp. 250—2.

86. 181 *of* 1893.—(Sanskrit and Telugu.) On one of eight slabs lying in the storehouse of the Bhīmēśvara temple. A record of Vishṇuvardhana-Mahārāja (Kulōttuṅga I?) in Ś. 1002. Records the gift of a lamp to Bhīmēśvara by Padmāvati, wife of Rājēndra, minister of Rājarājadēva (II, son of Kulōttunga I) and Viceroy of Veṅgi from 1077 to 1078.

87. 182 *of* 1893.—(Sanskrit and Telugu.) On the second of the same. Records in Ś. 987, the gifts to Bhīmēśvara by Sōmaḷādēvi, granddaughter of Rājamārtāṇḍa (unidentified).

88. 183 *of* 1893.—(Sanskrit and Telugu.) On the third of the same. A record of the Eastern Chāḷukya king Vishṇuvardhan-Mahārāja *alias* Rājarājadēva (I, 1022—63) in his twenty-sixth year and in Ś. 969.

89. 184 *of* 1893.—(Telugu.) On the fourth of the same. A record of Vishṇuvardhana-Mahārāja in his twenty-third year. The gift of a lamp by a Tamiḷa.

90. 185 *of* 1893.—(Sanskrit and Telugu.) On the fifth of the same. Records in the reign of the Western Chāḷukya king Trailōkyamalladēva (I) in Ś. 977, the gift of a lamp by Kupamā, daughter of the minister Nārāyaṇa-Bhaṭṭa.

91. 186 *of* 1893.—(Sanskrit and Telugu.) On the sixth of the same. A record of Vishṇuvardhana-Mahārāja in his thirteenth year, in Ś. 995. Records the gift of a lamp by a queen of Kīrtirāja of the Haihaya race. [As the king came to the throne in A.D. 1060 we may identify him with Vijayāditya VII, the rival of Kulōṭtuṅga I.]

92. 187 *of* 1893.—(Telugu.) On the seventh of the same. A record of Vishṇuvardhana Mahārāja in his eighth year and in Ś. 990, regarding the gift of a lamp by a merchant of Viśākhavaṭṭana (Vizagapatam). See the above epigraph.

93. 188 *of* 1893.—(Sanskrit and Telugu.) On the eighth of the same. Records in the third year of Vishṇuvardhana Mahārāja, in Ś. 986, the gift of a lamp by the Brāhmaṇa Suppa-Nāyaka. See No. 91.

94. 189 *of* 1893.—(Telugu.) On a slab lying in the same temple. Records in Ś. 960, some gifts to Bhīmēśvara.

95. 190 *of* 1893.—(Telugu.) On a slab lying in the *maṭha* within the same temple. A record of Vishṇuvardhana Mahārāja in his fifteenth year and in Ś. 1006. Records gifts by the daughter of an officer of Kulōttuṅga-Chōḍadēva (I) Vishnuvardhana was probably Vīrachōḍa, Viceroy of Veṅgi, from 1078 to 1084 and 1089 to 1093.

96. 191 *of* 1893.—(Telugu.) On the east wall of the same temple, right wing, between the first and second pillars, fourth slab from bottom. Records the gift of a lamp by Maḍapaḷḷi-Nūṅkaya, son of Piṭṭama.

97. 192 *of* 1893.—(Telugu.) On the same slab. Records in the sixth year of Vishṇuvardhana Mahārāja (unidentified) the gift of a lamp by a merchant.

98. 193 *of* 1893.—On the same slab. A Telugu inscription of Rājadhirājadēva in his seventy-second year and in Ś. 1211. [So the king came to the throne in A.D. 1217. See No. 111.]

99. 194 *of* 1893.—(Sanskrit and Telugu.) In the same place, sixth slab. A record of the Chāḷukya-Chōḷa king Rājakēsarivarman *alias* Saptama-Vishṇuvardhana *alias* Kulōttuṅga-Chōḷadēva (I) in his forty-ninth year and in Ś. 1040. Endows gift of a lamp by Nūṅkaya, son of Nelupuni-Bhīmarāja.

100. 195 *of* 1893.—(Telugu.) In the same place, third slab. Dated in the reign of the Chāḷukya-Chōḷa king, Saptama-Vishṇuvardhana *alias* Kulōttuṅga Chōḍadēva in his thirty-first year. Records a gift of land.

101. 196 *of* 1893.—(Tamil.) On the same slab. A record of the Chāḷukya-Chōḷa king, Rājakēsarivarman *alias* Kulōttuṅga-Chōḍa-dēva (I) in his thirty-first year; Tamil version of the above epigraph.

102. 197 *of* 1893.—(Tamil.) On the same slab. A record of the Chāḷukya-Chōḷa king, Rājakēsarivarman *alias* Kulōttuṅga-Chōḍadēva (I) in his fortieth year, relating to the gift of a lamp.

103. 198 *of* 1893.—(Sanskrit and Telugu.) In the same place, second slab. Udayachandradēva, son of Vishṇuvardhana-Mahārāja *alias* Gonaga, records in Ś. 1147, the gift of a lamp. [See No. 42.]

104. 199 *of* 1893.—(Telugu and Tamil.) On the same slab. Records the gift of a lamp.

105. 200 *of* 1893.—(Tamil.) On the same slab. A fragmentary record.

106. 201 *of* 1893.—(Telugu.) On the same slab. Records in the reign of Vishṇuvardhana-Mahārāja the gift of a lamp.

107. 202 *of* 1893.—(Telugu.) In the same place, first slab. Records a gift in the forty-sixth year of the Chāḷukya-Chōḷa king, Rājakēsarivarman *alias* Saptama-Vishṇuvardhana *alias* Kulōttuṅga Chōḷadēva (I).

108. 203 *of* 1893.—(Tamil.) On the same slab. A fragmentary record.

109. 204 *of* 1893.—(Sanskrit and Telugu.) In the same place, first pillar from left. Records in Ś. 1062, a gift by Kāṭama-Nāyaka. Dr. Hultzsch identifies this chief with the one of Kolanu (Ellore) who issued a copper plate grant in the time of Kulōttuṅga (II). See *Ind. Antq.*, XIV, p. 55, and Gd. 48-B above.

110. 205 *of* 1893.—(Sanskrit.) In the same place, second pillar. A record opening with the genealogy of a dynasty of the Chaturtha-kula. (The Koṇḍavīḍu Reḍḍis ?)

111. 206 *of* 1893.—(Telugu.) In the same place, first tier from bottom. A record of Rājādhirājadēva in his thirty-seventh year and in Ś. 1175. [The king came to the throne in A.D. 1216–17. See Nos. 98 and 116 for the same chief.]

112. 207 *of* 1893.—(Sanskrit and Telugu.) In the same place, fifth slab from bottom. A record of the Western Chāḷukya king Tribhuvanamalladēva recording in Chāḷukya-Vikrama year 45, the gift of a lamp by a merchant. [The king was Vikramāditya (VI) who was in possession of Veṅgi from 1120 to 1124, in consequence of Vikrama Chōḷa's departure to the south.]

113. 208 *of* 1893.—(Sanskrit.) On the same slab. A record in Ś. 1037, referring to "Chāḷukya Pąrāntaka."

114. 209 *of* 1893.—(Sanskrit.) On the same slab. Records in Ś. 1037, the gift of a lamp.

115. 210 *of* 1893.—(Telugu.) On the east wall of the same temple, left wing, between the first and second pillars, fourth slab from bottom. Records the genealogy of some chief.

116. 211 *of* 1893.—(Sanskrit and Telugu.) In the same place, second tier from bottom. A record of Rājādhirājadēva in his thirty-sixth year and Ś. 1174, regarding the gift by Sūramādēvi, daughter of a Vīrapa-Nāyaka. See No. 111 above.

117. 212 *of* 1893.—(Telugu.) In the same place, second pillar. A record of Kulōttuṅga-Chōdadēva (I or II ?) in his sixteenth year.

118. 213 *of* 1893.—(Telugu.) In the same place, first pillar. A record of Rājādhirājadēva mentioning Kākatīya Gaṇapatidēva-Mahārāja. See No. 111 above.

119. 214 *of* 1893.—(Telugu.) On the west wall of the same temple, first pillar, from left. Kōṇa-Bhīmarāja records the gift of a lamp. [We are not able to say which of the three Bhīmas is referred to.]

120. 215 *of* 1893.—(Telugu.) On the same pillar. A record, dated in Ś. 1175, Pramādin.

121. 216 *of* 1893.—(Sanskrit and Telugu.) On the same wall, between the first and second pillars, fourth slab. A record of Rājarāja in his twentieth year and Ś. 1087, concerning the gift of a lamp by Koṇḍapaḍumati-Bhūdarāja. [The epigraph shows that Rājarāja came to the throne in A.D. 1145.] See No. 122.

122. 217 *of* 1893.—(Sanskrit and Telugu.) In the same place, fifth slab. A record of Rājarājadēva in his twentieth year and Ś. 1087, regarding the gift by an officer of Kulōttuṅga-Rājēndra-Chōḍayarāja. [Was he the Velanāṇṭi king who ruled from 1180 was Rājarāja, the son of the Eastern Gaṅja king Anantavarman Chōḍagaṅga, 1075—1146 ? It is doubtful.]

123. 218 *of* 1893.—(Telugu.) In the same place, second slab. An inscription of Kulōttuṅga Rājēndra-Chōḍayarāja. See the above epigraph.

124. 219 *of* 1893.—(Sanskrit and Telugu.) In the same place, second pillar. A record of Ś. 1075.

125. 220 *of* 1893.—(Telugu.) On the same wall between the second and third pillars, first slab from bottom. Records the gift of a lamp in the reign of the Kākatīya king Gaṇapati-Mahādēva.

126. 221 *of* 1893.—(Sanskrit and Telugu.) In the same place, second slab. A record of Ś. 1156.

127. 222 *of* 1893.—(Sanskrit and Telugu.) On the same slab. Records in Ś. 1021, the gift of a lamp. Mentions Tribhuvanamalla. [Vikramāditya (VI) of the Western Chāḷukyan dynasty.]

128. 223 *of* 1893.—(Sanskrit and Telugu.) In the same place, third slab. A record, dated in Ś. 1071.

129. 224 *of* 1893.—(Telugu.) In the same place, fourth slab. Bhoddaṇa-Bhīmaṇa records in Ś. 1071, the gift of a lamp.

130. 225 *of* 1893.—(Sanskrit and Telugu.) In the same place, fifth slab. A record of Rājarāja in his twentieth year and Ś. 1087, mentioning Kulōttuṅga-Rājēndra Chōḍayarāja. See No. 122 above.

131. 226 *of* 1893.—(Telugu.) In the same place, third pillar. Records in the seventh year of Rājarājadēva, the gift of a lamp by Gaṅga-Chōḍa-Mallirāja. [With whom this chief is to be identified it is difficult to say. He might be Rājarāja II, the son of Anantavarman Chōḍagaṅga (1075—1146).]

132. 227 *of* 1893.—(Sanskrit and Telugu.) On the same wall between the third and fourth pillars, second slab from bottom. Records in Ś. 1071, the gift of lamps by a relation of Kulōttuṅga-Chōḍa-Goṅkarāja (II, 1133—57).

133. 228 *of* 1893.—(Sanskrit and Telugu.) In the same place, third slab. Kulōttuṅga Chōḍa-Gaṅgarāja records in Ś. 1075 (Goṅka II ?, 1133—57), the gift of a lamp.

134. 229 *of* 1893.—(Sanskrit and Telugu.) In the same place, fourth slab. Rājarāja records in Ś. 1085, the gift of a lamp. See note to 122 above.

135. 230 *of* 1893.—(Telugu.) In the same place, fifth slab. Records in S. 1071, the gift of lamps by a Nāyaka.

136. 231 *of* 1893.—(Telugu.) In the same place, sixth slab. Kulōttuṅga Rājēndra-Chōḍayarāja records the gift of a lamp. (Date not clear.) See No. 122 above.

137. 232 *of* 1893.—(Sanskrit and Telugu.) In the same place, fourth pillar. An incomplete record of a gift of a lamp.

138. 233 *of* 1893.—(Telugu.) On the same pillar. A record of Rājarāja in Ś. 1085. See No. 122 above.

139. 234 *of* 1893.—(Sanskrit and Telugu.) On the same wall, between the fourth and fifth pillars, second slab from bottom. A record of the Kōṇa (Haihaya) king Satya (I), younger brother of Rājēndra-Chōḍa, and joint ruler with Mummudi Bhīma (II), dated in Ś. 1057 and Chāḷukya-Vikrama year . . . Records gift of a lamp. [See the genealogy of the Kōṇa chiefs.]

140. 235 *of* 1893.—(Sanskrit and Telugu.) In the same place, third slab. Dated in the reign of Kōṇa (Haihaya) king, Mallarāja. Records in Ś. 1077 and Chāḷukya-Vikrama year . . . the gift of a lamp by Gaṅgādēvi. [The Mallarāja of this epigraph was evidently Mallidēva, the joint ruler with Vallabha. See the genealogy of the Kōṇa chiefs.]

141. 236 *of* 1893.—(Sanskrit and Telugu.) In the same place, fourth slab. Records in the twentieth year of Rājarāja and Ś. 1087, the gift of a lamp by a minister ot Kulōttuṅga-Rājēndra-Chōḍayarāja (1163—1180). See No. 122 above.

142. 237 *of* 1893.—(Sanskrit and Telugu.) In the same place, fifth slab. A record, dated in Ś. 1148.

143. 238 *of* 1893.—(Sanskrit and Telugu.) In the same place, sixth slab. Records in the eighteenth year of Rājarāja, in Ś. 1085, the gift of a lamp in the time of Kulōttuṅga-Velanāṇṭi-Rājēndra-Chōḍayarāja (1163—80). See No. 122 above.

144. 239 *of* 1893.—(Telugu.) In the same place, fifth pillar. Rājarāja records, in his twelfth year, the gift of a lamp.

145. 240 *of* 1893.—(Telugu.) On the same wall, between the fifth and sixth pillars, first slab, from bottom. A record of Kulōttuṅga-Chōḍa-Goṅkarāja (Goṅka II?) regarding the gift of a lamp by the son of a minister.

146. 241 *of* 1893.—(Sanskrit and Telugu.) In the same place, second slab. Records in Ś. 1065, the gift of a lamp.

147. 242 *of* 1893.—(Telugu.) On the same slab. Dated in the reign of Kulōttuṅga-Chōḍadēva *alias* Rājarājadēva. Records in his fourth year, the gift of a lamp by a merchant.] The word *alias* makes it impossible to identify him with either of the sons of Kulōttuṅga.]

148. 243 *of* 1893.—(Sanskrit and Telugu.) In the same place, third slab. Records in Ś. 1119, the gift of a lamp by the wife of a Reḍḍi.

149. 244 *of* 1893.—(Telugu.) In the same place, fourth slab. A record mentioning Kākatīya-Rudradēvarāja (I or II?).

150. 245 *of* 1893.—(Sanskrit and Telugu.) On the same wall, sixth pillar. Records in Ś. 1079, the gift of a lamp.

151. 246 *of* 1893.—(Sanskrit and Telugu.) On the same wall, between the sixth and seventh pillars, first slab from bottom. Dated in the reign of Rājarājadēva. Records in his ninth year and Ś. 1075, the gift of a lamp by Bhīmarāja (i.e., Bhīma III), son of Kōṇa-Satyarāja. [This Bhīma was joint ruler with Lōkamahīpāla. See the genealogy of the Kōṇa chiefs and No. 122 above.]

152. 247 *of* 1893.—(Telugu.) In the same place, second slab. Records in the thirty-first year of Rājādhirājadēva the gift of a lamp in the time of Kulōttuṅga Prithīśvaradēva Mahārāja. (*Circa* A.D. 1186.)

153. 248 *of* 1893.—(Telugu.) On the same slab. Records in the twenty-fifth year of Kulōttuṅga-Chōḍadēva the gift of a land.

154. 249 *of* 1893.—(Telugu.) In the same place, third slab. Records in the fourth year of Rājarāja-Chōḍadēva and Ś. 1072 the establishment of a *sattra*. See No. 122 above.

155. 250 *of* 1893.—(Telugu.) In the same place, fourth slab. A record of Kulōttuṅga Chōḷadēva in his seventeenth year and Ś. 1078 relating the gift to a *sattra*. [The king therefore came to power in 1139.]

156. 251 *of* 1893.—(Sanskrit.) In the same place, seventh slab. A fragment of a record mentioning Trinayana-Pallava and Buddhavarman.

157. 252 *of* 1893.—(Telugu.) On the same wall, seventh pillar from left. Records in his thirteenth year of Rājarājadēva and Ś. 1080 the gift of a lamp. [As the chief came to the throne in 1145, he may be identified with his namesake in No. 122.]

158. 253 *of* 1893.—(Sanskrit and Telugu.) On the same wall between the seventh and eighth pillars, first slab from bottom. Kulōttuṅga-Chōḍa-Goṅkarāja (Goṅka II, 1133—57) records in Ś. 1072, the gift of a lamp.

159. 254 *of* 1893.—(Sanskrit and Telugu.) In the same place, second slab. Records in Ś. 1055 and Chāḷukya-Vikrama year . . . the gift of a lamp by the Daṇḍanāyaka Kēśimayya, son of Siddhirāja.

160. 255 *of* 1893.—(Telugu.) On the same slab. A record of the western Chāḷukya king, Tribhuvanamalladēva (Vikramāditya VI) recording in Chāḷukya-Vikrama year 17, the gift of a lamp.

161. 256 *of*. 1893.—(Sanskrit and Telugu.) In the same place, third slab. Dated in the reign of Rājarāja (II), probably the son of the Gaṅga king Anantavarman.] Records in his eighteenth year and Ś. 1085 the gift of a lamp by an Officer of Kulōttuṅga-Rājēndra-Chōḍarāja (1163—80). See No. 122 above.

162. 257 *of* 1893.—(Sanskrit and Telugu.) In the same place, fourth slab. A record of Rājarāja (II), 1146—78, in Ś. 1085, detailing the gift of a lamp by Paṇḍāmbika, queen of Rājēndra Chōḍayarāja, i.e., Vīrarājēndra Chōḍa (1163—80), son of Kulōttuṅga-Chōḍa-Goṅkarāja II (1133—57).

163. 258 *of* 1893.—(Telugu.) On the same slab. Records gift in the time of Kulōttuṅga-Rājēndra-Chōḍayarāja (1163—80).

164. 259 *of* 1893.—(Sanskrit.) In the same place, fifth slab. A record mentioning Kulōttuṅga-Rājēndra-Chōḍa (son of Goṅka II (1163—80).

165. 260 *of* 1893.—(Sanskrit.) On the same wall, eighth pillar. Malla, son of the lord of Veṅgi, records the gift of two lamps. (Date not clear.)

166. 261 *of* 1893.—(Sanskrit and Telugu.) On the same wall first tier from bottom. Records in Ś. 1124 the gift of a lamp by a Nāyaka.

167. 262 *of* 1893.—(Sanskrit and Telugu.) In the same tier. A record of the king Rājādhirājadēva in his sixth year and Ś. 1144. Records the gift of a lamp by a merchant. [See No. 98 for this king.

168. 263 *of* 1893.—(Sanskrit and Telugu.) On the north wall first pillar from right. Records in Ś. 1182 a gift by Nāyaka.

169. 264 *of* 1893.—(Sanskrit and Telugu.) On the same wall between the first and second pillars, first slab from bottom. An epigraph of Kulōttuṅga-Chōḍa-Goṅkarāja II (1133—57) in Ś. 1073, recording the gift of lamps by merchants.

170. 265 *of* 1893.—(Telugu.) In the same place, second slab. Dated in the reign of Kulōttuṅga Chōḍadēva in his seventh year and Ś. 1061. Records the gift of a lamp by an officer of Kulōttuṅga-Chōḍa-Goṅka (1133—57).

171. 266 *of* 1893.—(Telugu.) In the same place, third slab. A record of Nambirāja, lord of Kollipākapura, recording gift of a lamp in Ś. 1053. The exact date was the occasion of Vyatipāta on Monday, full moon tithi of Viśākha, i.e., 13th April, A.D. 1131. See *Ep. Ind.*, Vol. VI, pp. 224-5.

172. 267 *of* 1893.--(Telugu.) On the same slab. A record of Trailōkyamallarāja, son of Nambirāja (the scent-elephant of Namba), recording in Ś. 1081 the gift of a lamp. Kielhorn says that the date should be either Tuesday, 12th May, A.D. 1159 or Saturday, 30th April 1160 as the Śaka date is current or expired. See *Ep. Ind.*, VI, pp. 225-6. The chief is one of the numerous local rulers who came into existence in the twelfth century in the Veṅgi country.]

173. 268 *of* 1893.—(Sanskrit and Telugu.) In the same place, fourth slab. A record of Kulōttuṅga-Chōḍa-Goṅkarāja II (1133—57) of Sanadavrōlu in Velanāṇḍu recording in Ś. 1079 the gift of a lamp by a Nāyaka.

174. 269 *of* 1893.--(Sanskrit and Telugu.) In the same place, fifth slab. A record of Kulōttuṅga-Chōḍa-Goṅkarāja II (1133—57). Gift of a lamp by a merchant. (Date not clear.)

175. 270 *of* 1893.--(Sanskrit and Telugu.) On the same slab. A record of Kulōttuṅga-Chōḍa-Goṅkarāja II (1133—57) in Ś. 1077. Gift of a lamp by a Nāyaka.

176. 271 *of* 1893.—(Sanskrit and Telugu.) In the same place, sixth slab. A record in Ś. 1077.

177. 272 *of* 1893.—(Telugu.) On the same wall, second pillar from right. A record of Kulōttuṅga-Chōḍadēva. Records the gift of a lamp by a merchant in the time of Kulōttuṅga-Chōḍa-Goṅkarāja II (1133—57).

178. 273 *of* 1893.—(Sanskrit.) On the same wall, between the second and third pillars, second slab from bottom. The son of Goṅka records the gift of four lamps.

179. 274 *of* 1893.—(Sanskrit and Telugu.) In the same place, third slab. The Velanāṇṭi Goṅkaya (II) records in Ś. 1055 the gift of a lamp.

180. 275 *of* 1893.—(Telugu.) On the same slab. An epigraph of Kulōttuṅga-Chōḍa-Gāṅgēya-Goṅkarāja II (1133—57) in Ś. 1060. Records the gift of a lamp by a merchant.

181. 276 *of* 1893.—(Sanskrit and Telugu.) In the same place, fourth slab. Records in the reign of Velanāṇṭi Kulōttuṅga-Chōḍa-Goṅka II (1133—57) the gift of a lamp.

182. 277 *of* 1893.—(Sanskrit.) In the same place, fifth slab. A record of Rājēndra Chōḍa (1163—80), son of Goṅka II and Sabbāmbika.

183. 278 *of* 1893.—(Telugu.) In the same place, sixth slab. Kulōttuṅga-Chōḍa-Goṅkarāja II (1133—57) records in Ś. 1064 the gift of golden bracelets.

184. 279 *of* 1893.—(Telugu.) On the same wall, third pillar from right. Velanāṇṭi Goṅkarāja records the gift of a lamp.

185. 280 *of* 1893.—On the same pillar. A gift of lamp by Kulōttuṅga-Chōḍadēva Gāṅgēyarāya *alias* Goṅkarāja II (1133—57).

186. 281 *of* 1893.—On the same wall, between the third and fourth pillars, second slab from bottom. A record of Kulōttuṅga Chōḍadēva (1133—57) in his seventeenth year and Ś. 1071 relating the gift of a lamp by a merchant from Penugoṇḍa.

187. 282 *of* 1893.—(Sanskrit and Telugu.) In the same place, third slab. A record of Kulōttuṅga Chōḍadēva in his fourth year and Ś. 1072. Records the gift of a lamp by a Nāyaka. So the king came to the throne in 1145. See No. 122.

188. 283 *of* 1893.—(Sanskrit.) On the same slab. A record of the Kōṇa (Haihaya) king Chōḍa *alias* Vikramarudra, son of Rājaparēṇḍu, recording in Ś. 1050, the gift of a lamp. [The king referred to was evidently Rājēndra Chōḍa. See genealogy of the Kōṇa chiefs as given in the second Piṭhāpuram inscription.]

189. 284 *of* 1893.—(Sanskrit and Telugu.) In the same place, fourth slab. A record of Kulōttuṅga Chōḍadēva. Details the gift of a lamp by the Mahāmaṇḍalēśvara Bhīmaya of Kaṇḍravāḍi.

190. 285 *of* 1893.—(Telugu.) On the same slab. A record of Rājādhirājadēva in his twenty-fifth year. Mentions Kākatīya Rudradēva Mahārāja (I or II ?). See No. 198.

191. 286 *of* 1893.—(Sanskrit.) In the same place, fifth slab. A fragment of record. Refers to Kōna-Pōta of Kaṇḍravāḍi, who conquered Rājēndra-Chōḍa of Trikaliṅga.

192. 287 *of* 1893.—(Telugu.) On the same wall, fourth pillar from right. A record of Kulōttuṅga Chōḍadēva in his seventh year. Mentions the gift of a lamp by a merchant in the time of the Mahāmaṇḍalēśvara Velanāṇṭi Kulōttuṅga-Chōḍa-Goṅkarāja (II).

193. 288 *of* 1893.—(Telugu.) On the same wall, between the fourth and fifth pillars, first slab from bottom. Records in the reign of Vishṇuvardhana-Mahārāja (unidentified) the gift of a lamp in the time of the Mahāmaṇḍalēśvara Kākati-Rudradēva (I or II ?) of Ammakoṇḍa. See No. 190.

194. 289 *of* 1893.—(Sanskrit and Telugu.) In the same place, second slab. A record of Kōṇa (Haihaya) Mummaḍirāja (i.e., Mummuḍi Bhīma II) in Ś. 1057 and Chālukya Vikrama year 60, relating the gift of a lamp by Rājadēvi.

195. 290 *of* 1893.—(Sanskrit and Telugu.) In the same place, third slab. Records the gift of a lamp by the wife of Bhīmarāja and mother of Pōta.

196. 291 *of* 1893.—(Telugu.) On the same slab. Records in the thirteenth year of Kulōttuṅga-Chōḍadēva the gift of a lamp by Pōtarāja.

197. 292 *of* 1893.—(Telugu.) On the same slab. Records the gift of a lamp by the daughter of Kōṇa Mummaḍirāja. (Date not clear.) [There were three Mummuḍi Bhīmas in the line and it is uncertain as to which of them is referred to here.]

198. 293 *of* 1893.—(Sanskrit and Telugu.) In the same place, fifth slab. Rājādhirājadēva records in his twentieth year and Ś. 1186, the gift of a lamp. [So the king came to the throne in A.D. 1244.]

199. 294 *of* 1893.—(Sanskrit.) On the same slab. A record mentioning Prōlamāmbika, the wife of Goṅka.

200. 295 *of* 1893.—(Sanskrit and Telugu.) In the same place, sixth slab. Kulōttuṅga Chōḍa-Goṅkarāja records the gift of a lamp. [The donor was evidently Goṅka II (1133—57) of the Velanāṇḍu dynasty.]

201. 296 *of* 1893.—(Sanskrit and Telugu.) On the same wall, fifth pillar from right. Baṇṭarāja records in Ś. 1065, the gift of a lamp. [Baṇṭa must have been the contemporary of Goṅka II.]

202. 297 *of* 1893.—(Sanskrit and Telugu.) On the same wall, between the fifth and sixth pillars, first slab from bottom. A record of Vishṇuvardhana. (Unidentifiable.) Date doubtful.

203. 298 *of* 1893.—(Telugu.) In the place, second slab. A record of Velanāṇṭi Goṅka (I, II or III ?).

204. 299 *of* 1893.—(Sanskrit and Telugu.) In the same place, third slab. Vishṇuvardhana-Mahārāja records in Ś. 1051, the gift of a lamp. [This ruler was not improbably Kulōttuṅga II.]

205. 300 *of* 1893.—(Telugu.) In the same place, fifth slab. A record mentioning Mahāmaṇḍalēśvara Kulōttuṅga Rājēndra chōḍayarāja (who was the Velanāṇḍu chief who ruled from 1163 to 1180).

206. 301 *of* 1893.—(Sanskrit and Telugu.) On the same wall, between the sixth and seventh pillars first slab. Records in Ś. 1069, the gift of a lamp.

207. 302 *of* 1893.—(Telugu.) In the same place, third slab. Chōḍachakravartin records in his fifth year and Ś. 1059, the gift of cows. [The donor was evidently Goṅka II, 1133—57.]

208. 303 *of* 1893.—(Sanskrit and Telugu.) On the same slab. Vishṇuvardhana-Mahāraja records in Ś. 1051, the gift of a lamp. See note to 204.

209. 304 *of* 1893.—(Sanskrit and Telugu.) On the same slab. Dated in the reign of Rājādhirājadēva. Records in Ś. 1174, the gift of a lamp by Bhīma-Reḍḍi. See No. 198.

210. 305 *of* 1893.—(Telugu.) In the same place, fourth slab. Records in Ś. 1085, in the reign of Rājarāja, the gift of a lamp by a minister.

211. 306 *of* 1893.—(Sanskrit.) In the same place, fifth slab. Chōḍa, son of Goṅka (I ?) and Sabbāmbika, records the gift of a village. [Chōḍa received the charge of the Veṅgi 16,000 from Kulōttuṅgachōḍa I.]

212. 307 *of* 1893.—(Sanskrit.) In the same place, sixth slab. A record mentioning Satya.

213. 308 *of* 1893.—(Sanskrit.) In the same place, seventh slab. A record of Rājēndra-Chōḍa (1163—80), son of Goṅka (II) and Sabbāmbika.

214. 309 *of* 1893.—(Telugu.) On the same wall, seventh pillar from right. Records the gift of a lamp by a queen.

215. 310 *of* 1893.— (Telugu.) On the same wall, between the seventh and eighth pillars, second slab from bottom. Records in the reign of the Chāḷukya-Chōḷa king, Rājakēsarivarman *alias* Kulōttuṅga-Chōḍadēva (I) the gift of a lamp. (Date doubtful.)

216. 311 *of* 1893.—(Telugu.) On the same slab. A record of Kulōttuṅga-Chōḍadēva (II) in his eleventh year and Ś. 1065.

217. 312 *of* 1893.—(Sanskrit and Telugu.) In the same place, third slab. An epigraph of the Gaṅga king, Anantavarmadēva (1075—1146) in Ś. 1050, regarding the gift of a lamp by a queen. See *Ind. Antq.*, Vol. XVIII, p. 161 ff. See also No. 227 below.

218. 313 *of* 1893.—(Telugu.) On the same slab. Records in the reign of the Gaṅga king Anantavarmadēva (1075—1146). The gift of a lamp by a queen.

219. 314 *of* 1893.—(Sanskrit and Telugu.) In the same place, fourth slab. Records in the reign of Vishṇuvardhana-Mahārāja, in his second year and Ś. 1050, the gift of a lamp by Līlāvati, a queen of the Gaṅga king Anantavarmadēva (1075—1146).

220. 315 *of* 1893.—(Sanskrit and Telugu.) On the same slab. Dated in the second year of Vishṇuvardhana-Mahārāja, Ś. 1050. Records the gift of a lamp by the mother of the same queen.

221. 316 *of* 1893.—(Sanskrit and Telugu.) In the same place, fifth slab. Records in the second year of Vishṇuvardhana-Mahārāja, Ś. 1050, the gift of a lamp by Rājalādēvi, a queen of the Gaṅga king Anantavarmadēva (1075—1146).

222. 317 *of* 1893.—(Telugu.) On the same slab. Records the gift of a lamp by Padmaḷādēvi, a queen of the Gaṅga king Anantavarmadēva Chōḍagaṅga (1075-1126).

223. 318 *of* 1893.—(Sanskrit and Telugu.) On the same slab. An inscription of Vishṇuvardhana in Ś. 1050, recording the gift of a lamp.

224. 319 *of* 1893.—(Telugu.) On the same wall, eighth pillar from right. Records in the reign of Kulōttuṅga-Chōḍadēva the gift of a lamp by a son of the Gaṅga king Anantavarmadēva (1075—1146). (Date doubtful.)

225. 320 *of* 1893.—(Sanskrit and Telugu.) On the north wall of the maṇṭapa at the entrance of the same temple, first slab from bottom. A record of Vishṇuvardhana Mahārāja in Ś. 1101.

226. 321 *of* 1893.—(Telugu.) In the same place, second slab. A record of Kulōttuṅga-Chōḍadēva (I ?) mentioning Chōḍagaṅgadēva of Kaliṅga (probably Anantavarman, 1075—1146).

227. 322 *of* 1893.—(Sanskrit and Telugu.) In the same place, third slab. A record of Rājarājadēva, mentioning Kulōttuṅga Rājēndra-Chōḍayarāja (evidently the Velanāṇḍu chief ruling from 1163 to 1180).

228. 323 *of* 1893.—(Sanskrit.) In the same place, fourth slab. A record mentioning Chōḍa, son of Velanāṇṭichōḍa.

229. 324 *of* 1893.—(Sanskrit and Telugu.) In the same place, sixth slab. An epigraph of Rājarāja in Ś. 1091. See No. 122.

230. 325 *of* 1893.—(Sanskrit and Telugu.) On the north wall of the same temple, first tier from bottom. A record of the Mahāmaṇḍalēśvara Kolani (i.e., Ellore) Maṇḍalīka Kēśavadēvā in Ś. 1122. See Ellore inscriptions for other epigraphs of this chief.

231. 326 *of* 1893.—(Telugu.) On the south wall of the same temple, first pillar from left. Records the gift of a lamp by a garland-maker.

232. 327 *of* 1893.—(Telugu.) On the same pillar. Dated in the reign of Rājarāja. Records in his seventeenth year and Ś. 1084, the gift of a lamp by a Nāyaka. So Rājarāja came to the throne in 1145. Was he the successor of Anantavarman Chōḍa-gaṅga? See No. 122 above.

233–234. 328 *of* 1893.—(Telugu.) On the same wall, between the first and second pillars from the left, first slab from bottom. Records in Ś. 1079, the gift of a lamp by the wife of the Mahāmaṇḍalēśvara Bāyyarāja of Bīragōtta.

235. 329 *of* 1893.—(Telugu.) On the same slab. A record of Ś. 1079, mentioning the same Mahāmaṇḍalēśvara.

236. 330 *of* 1893.—(Kanarese.) On the same place, second slab. Dated in the reign of the Western Chāḷukya king Tribhuvanamalladēva (Vikramāditya VI). Records in his forty-fifth year, a gift by a wife of the Daṇḍanāyaka Anantapāla. [See Fleet's *Dynas., Kanar. Dts.*, p. 51, for a reference to this officer. Also No. 264 below.]

237. 331 *of* 1893.—(Telugu.) On the same slab. Dated in the reign of the Western Chāḷukya king Tribhuvanamalladēva (Vikramāditya VI). Records in Chāḷukya-Vikrama year 45, the gift of a lamp by the Daṇḍanāyaka Āditya.

238. 332 *of* 1893.—(Telugu.) On the same slab. Dated in the reign of the Western Chāḷukya king Tribhuvanamalladēva (Vikramāditya VI). Records a gift in Chāḷukya-Vikrama year 46 and Ś. 1043.

239. 333 *of* 1893.—(Sanskrit.) In the same place, third slab. Records in Ś. 1038, that the king Parāntaka set up images of Śiva and Pārvati and granted villages to them.

240. 334 *of* 1893.—(Sanskrit and Telugu.) On the same slab. Records in Ś. 1123, the gift of a lamp by a merchant.

241. 335 *of* 1893.—(Telugu.) On the same slab. Dated in the reign of the Western Chāḷukya king, Tribhuvanamalladēva (Vikramāditya VI). Records in Chāḷukya-Vikrama year 46, the gift of a lamp by a queen of Mahāmaṇḍalēśvara Eruva-Toṇḍayarāja.

242. 336 *of* 1893.—(Sanskrit and Telugu.) In the same place, fourth slab. Records in Chāḷukya-Vikrama year and Ś. 1054, the gift of a lamp by a merchant.

243. 337 *of* 1893.—(Sanskrit and Telugu.) On the same slab. A record of Veṅgi Goṅka *alias* Mānyasimha, son of Mallaparāja, recording in Ś. 1118, the gift of a lamp by a queen. [One of the numerous local chiefs, unidentified.]

244. 338 *of* 1893.—(Sanskrit and Telugu.) In the same place, fifth slab. Records in Chāḷukya-Vikrama year (57?) and Ś. 1054, the gift of a lamp by the wife of Bāyyarāja of Bīragōtta. See 233–4.

245. 339 *of* 1893.—(Telugu.) On the same wall, second pillar from left. The Pallava king, Bāyyarāja of Bīragōtta, records the gift of ornaments. See the above epigraph.

246. 340 *of* 1893.—(Telugu.) On the same wall, between the second and third pillars, first slab from bottom. A record of Rājādhiraja in Ś. 1185. See No. 190.

247. 341 *of* 1893.—(Sanskrit and Telugu.) In the same place, second slab. Dated in the reign of Vishṇuvardhana Mahārāja. Records the gift of a golden bracelet by Subbamā, wife of Velanānṭi-Goṅka (II?).

248. 342 *of* 1893.—(Tamil and Grantha.) On the same slab. Records the gift of a lamp.

249. 343 *of* 1893.—(Telugu.) In the same place, third slab. A record of Kulōttuṅga Chōḍadēva (I?) in his forty-ninth year.

250. 344 *of* 1893.—(Tamil.) On the same slab. A record of Kulōttuṅga-Chōḷadēva.

251. 345 *of* 1893.—(Sanskrit and Telugu.) In the same place, fourth slab. Dated in the reign of the Western Chāḷukya king Tribhuvanamalladēva (Vikramāditya VI). Records in Chāḷukya-Vikrama year 45 and Ś. 1042 the gift of a lamp by Nārāyaṇa, minister of Vēlānāṇṭi Rājēndra-Chōḍa. [The latter cannot be, owing to chronological difficulty, the son of Goṅka II. Was he the same as Chōḍa, the son of Goṅka I?].

252. 346 *of* 1893.—(Sanskrit and Telugu.) On the same wall, third pillar from left. Dated in the reign of Kulōttuṅga-Chōḍadēva II. Records in Ś. 1063, the gift of a lamp.

253. 347 *of* 1893.—(Telugu.) On the same wall, between the third and fourth pillars from left, first slab from bottom. A record in Ś. 1070 of the Mahāmaṇḍalīka Kāṭama-Nāyaka. See No. 109 above and note thereon.

254. 348 *of* 1893.—(Sanskrit.) In the same place, second slab. A record dated in Ś. 1030.

255. 349 *of* 1893.—(Sanskrit.) In the same place, third slab. A record of Rājēndra-Chōḍa (unidentified).

256. 350 *of* 1893.—(Telugu.) In the same place, fourth slab. Vishṇuvardhana (unidentified) records the gift of a lamp.

257. 351 *of* 1893.—(Sanskrit and Telugu.) In the same place, fifth slab. A record of Rājarājadēva in Ś. 1091, mentioning the Mahāmaṇḍalēśvara Chōḍayarāja (evidently Velanāṇṭi Kulōttuṅga Rājēndra, 1163—80).

258. 352 *of* 1893.—(Telugu.) In the same place, seventh slab. An epigraph of Vishṇuvardhana Mahārāja in his second year, mentioning the country (dēśa) of Vijayāditya.

259. 353 *of* 1893.—(Sanskrit and Telugu.) On the same wall, fourth pillar from left. Records in Ś. 1062, the gift of a lamp by

Sōmaṇa-Pregaḍa, minister of Rājēndra-Chōḍayarāja (evidently the Velanāṇṭu chief who ruled from 1163—80 before he became ruler ?)

260. 354 *of* 1893.—(Tamil.) On the same wall, between the fourth and fifth pillars, second slab from bottom. A record of Kulōttuṅga-Chōḷadēva. (Date indistinct.)

261. 355 *of* 1893.—(Telugu.) On the same slab. Records a gift in the reign of the Chāḷukya-Chōḷa king, Rājakēsarivarman *alias* Saptama-Vishṇuvardhana *alias* Kulōttuṅga-Chōḍadēva (I). (Date indistinct.)

262. 356 *of* 1893.—(Telugu.) On the same slab. Records a gift in the reign of the Western Chāḷukya king Tribhuvanamalladēva (Vikramāditya VI) in Chāḷukya-Vikrama year 46 and Ś. 1044.

263. 357 *of* 1893.—(Telugu.) In the same place, third slab. Records in the reign of the Western Chāḷukya king Tribhuvanamalladēva in Ś. (?), the gift of a lamp and of ornament.

264. 358 *of* 1893.—(Telugu.) In the same place, fifth slab. A record of the Western Chāḷukya king Tribhuvanamalladēva (Vikramāditya VI) mentioning the minister Anantapāladaṇḍanāyaka. [See Fleet's *Dynas., Kanar. Dts.*, p. 51, for a reference to this officer. See No. 236 above.]

265. 359 *of* 1893.—(Telugu.) In the same place, seventh slab. A record of the Western Chāḷukya king Tribhuvanamalladēva in Chāḷukya-Vikrama year 48 and Ś. 1045. See No. 262 above.

266. 360 *of* 1893.—(Sanskrit and Telugu.) On the same slab. Records in Ś. 1035 in the reign of Rājādhirājadēva, the gift of a lamp. The chief has not been identified.

267. 361 *of* 1893.—(Telugu.) On the same wall, fifth pillar from left. Records in Ś. 1056 the gift of a lamp by a Daṇḍanāyaka.

268. 362 *of* 1893.—(Telugu.) On the same wall, between the fifth and sixth pillars, first slab from bottom. A record of the Chāḷukya-Chōḷa king Rājakēsarivarman *alias* Saptama-Vishṇuvardhana *alias* Kulōttuṅgachōḍadēva (I, 1070—1118) recording in his thirty-second year the gift of a lamp.

269. 363 *of* 1893.—(Sanskrit and Telugu.) On the same slab. A record of Vishṇuvardhana-Mahārāja (unidentified) in his second year and Ś. 1101, relating to the gift of a lamp.

270. 364 *of* 1893.—(Telugu.) In the same place, second slab. Dated in the reign of the Chāḷukya-Chōḷa king Rājakēsarivarman *alias* Saptama-Vishṇuvardhana *alias* Kulōttuṅga-Chōḍadēva (I, 1070—1118). Records in his thirty-eighth year, the gift of a lamp.

271. 365 *of* 1893.—(Sanskrit and Telugu.) On the same slab. Dated in the reign of the Chāḷukya-Chōḷa king Rājakēsarivarman *alias* Saptama-Vishṇuvardhana *alias* Kulōttuṅga-Chōḍadēva (I, 1070—1118). Records in his thirty-first year and Ś. 1022, the gift of a lamp.

272. 366 *of* 1893.—(Telugu.) In the same place, third slab. Dated in Chāḷukya-Vikrama year 50. Records the gift of a lamp by a merchant.

273. 367 *of* 1893.—(Telugu.) On the same slab. A record of Vishṇuvardhana-Mahārāja relating to the gift of a lamp. (Date indistinct.)

274. 368 *of* 1893.—(Telugu.) On the same slab. Records in the forty-seventh year of the Chāḷukya-Chōḷa king Rājakēsarivarman *alias* Saptama-Vishṇuvardhana *alias* Kulōttuṅga-Chōḍadēva (I) the gift of lamp for a garden.

275. 369 *of* 1893.—(Telugu.) In the same place, fourth slab. A record of Vishṇuvardhana-Mahārāja containing an agreement between the king and a certain Parāntakadēva.

276. 370 *of* 1893.—(Telugu.) On the same wall, sixth pillar from left. An epigraph of Kulōttuṅgachōḍadēva recording the gift of a lamp.

277. 371 *of* 1893.—(Telugu.) On the same wall between the sixth and seventh pillars, first slab from bottom. A record dated in Ś. 1244, Dundubhi, mentioning a certain Maṅgi Nāyaka.

278. 372 *of* 1893.—(Sanskrit and Telugu.) On the same slab. A record of Rājādhirājadēva in Ś. 1123. See No. 111 above.

279. 373 *of* 1893.—(Sanskrit and Telugu.) In the same place, second slab. Records in the thirty-fourth year of the Chāḷukya-Chōḷa king Rājakēsarivarman *alias* Saptama-Vishṇuvardhana *alias* Kulōttuṅga-Chōḍadēva (I, 1070—1118) the gift of land for a *maṭha* by the Śūdra Śīrāḷa.

280. 374 *of* 1893.—(Telugu.) On the same slab. Records in the forty-fifth year of the Chāḷukya-Chōḷa king Vishṇuvardhana-Mahārāja (Kulottuṅga I), Ś. 1036, the gift of a lamp. See *Ep. Ind.*, VI, p. 279, where Kielhorn discusses the date of the inscription and fixes it on Wednesday, 9th December, A.D. 1114.

281. 375 *of* 1893.—(Telugu.) In the same place, third slab. Dated in the reign of the Chāḷukya-Chōḷa king Rājakēsarivarman *alias* Saptama-Vishṇuvardhana *alias* Kulōttuṅga-Chōḍadēva (I, 1070—1118). Records in his forty-sixth year the gift of a lamp.

282. 376 *of* 1893.—(Telugu.) On the same slab. Dated in the reign of the Chāḷukya-Chōḷa king Rājakēsarivarman *alias* Saptama-Vishṇuvardhana *alias* Kulōttuṅga-Chōḍadēva (I). Records in his forty-fifth year a gift of land.

283. 377 *of* 1893.—(Tamil.) On the same slab. Records in the reign of the Chāḷukya-Chōḷa king Rājakēsarivarman *alias* Kulōttuṅga-Chōḷadēva (I) gift of land. (Date indistinct.)

284. 378 *of* 1893.—(Telugu.) On the same slab. Records the gift of a lamp by the son of a minister of Kulōttuṅga-Chōḍa Goṅka. (Date indistinct.)

285. 379 *of* 1893.—(Telugu.) In the same place, fourth slab. A record of the Chāḷukya-Chōḷa king Rājakēsarivarman *alias* Saptama-Vishṇuvardhana *alias* Kulōttuṅga-Chōḍadēva (I).

286. 380 *of* 1893.—(Tamil.) On the same slab. Fragment of a record.

287. 381 *of* 1893.—(Telugu.) In the same place, sixth slab. An epigraph of the Chāḷukya-Chōḷa king Rājakēsarivarman *alias* Saptama-Vishṇuvardhana *alias* Kulōttuṅga-Chōḍadēva (I) in his forty-eighth year.

288. 382 *of* 1893.—(Telugu.) On the same slab. A record of the Chāḷukya-Chōḷa Rājakēsarivarman *alias* Saptama-Vishṇuvardhana *alias* Kulōttuṅga-Chōḍadēva (I) in his forty-eighth year.

289. 383 *of* 1893.—(Tamil.) On the same slab. A record of Kulōttuṅga-Chōḷa. (Date indistinct.)

290. 384 *of* 1893.—(Sanskrit and Telugu.) On the same wall, seventh pillar from left. Records in Ś. 1061, the gift of a lamp by a minister of the Mahāmaṇḍalēśvara Kulōttuṅga-Chōḍa-Goṅka Rāja (i.e., Goṅka II, 1133—57).

291. 385 *of* 1893.—(Sanskrit.) On the same pillar. Records in Sarvajit, the gift by a Nāyaka.

292. 386 *of* 1893.—(Telugu.) On the same wall, between the seventh and eighth pillars, first slab from bottom. Belongs to the reign of the Chāḷukya-Chōḷa king Saptama-Vishṇuvardhana *alias* Kulōttuṅga-Chōḍadēva (I). Records in his thirty-seventh year and Ś. 1029, the gift of a lamp.

293. 387 *of* 1893.—(Telugu.) In the same place, second slab. An epigraph of the Western Chāḷukya king Tribhuvanamalladēva recording in Chāḷukya-Vikrama year 46, the gift of a lamp. See No. 262.

294. 388 *of* 1893.—(Telugu.) On the same slab. Records the gift of a lamp by the Sēnāpati Rājarāja Brahma mārāya.

295. 389 *of* 1893.—(Sanskrit and Telugu.) In the same place, third slab. Belongs to the reign of the Chāḷukya-Chōḷa king Rājakēsarivarman *alias* Saptama-Vishṇuvardhana *alias* Kulōttuṅga-Chōḍadēva (I, 1070—1118). Records in his thirty-seventh year and Ś. 1029 the gift of a lamp.

296. 390 *of* 1893.—(Telugu.) On the same slab. Records in the thirty-eighth year of the Chāḷukya-Chōḷa king Rājakēsarin *alias* Saptama-Vishṇuvardhana *alias* Kulōttuṅga-Chōḍadēva the gift of a lamp.

297. 391 *of* 1893.—(Telugu.) On the same slab. An epigraph of the Chāḷukya-Chōḷa king Rājakēsarivarman *alias* Saptama-Vishṇu-vardhana *alias* Kulōttuṅga-Chōḍadēva (I) recording in his thirty-seventh year the gift of a lamp.

298. 392 *of* 1893.—(Sanskrit and Telugu.) On the same slab. A record of Rājādhirājadēva in Ś. 1215. See No. 111 above.

299. 393 *of* 1893.—(Sanskrit and Telugu.) In the same place, fourth slab. Dated in the reign of the Western Chāḷukya king Tribhuvanamalladēva. Records in Chāḷukya-Vikrama year 45 and Ś. 1043, the gift of a lamp. [The king referred to is Vikramāditya, VI.]

300. 394 *of* 1893.—(Sanskrit and Telugu.) On the same slab. A record of the Western Chāḷukya king Tribhuvanamalladēva recording in Chāḷukya-Vikrama year 46 and Ś. 1043, the gift of a lamp. See the above epigraph.

301. 395 *of* 1893.—(Sanskrit and Telugu.) On the same wall eighth pillar from left. Dated in the reign of Kulōttuṅga-Chōḍadēva. Records in his ninth year and Ś. 1063, the gift of a lamp by a minister of Goṅka (Goṅka II, 1133—57).

302. 396 *of* 1893.—(Telugu.) On the south wall of the maṇṭapa at the entrance of the same temple, right pillar. Records in Chāḷukya-Vikrama year 5, the gift of lamps by a doorkeeper of the temple.

303. 397 *of* 1893.—(Telugu.) In the same place, first slab from bottom. Records a gift in the reign of Kulōttuṅga-Chōḍadēva by a queen. See the next epigraph.

304. 398 *of* 1893.—(Telugu.) In the same place, second slab. An inscription of the Chāḷukya-Chōḷa king Saptama-Vishṇuvardhana *alias* Kulōttuṅga Chōḍadēva (I, 1070—1118). Records in his thirty-second year, the gift of a lamp by a merchant.

305. 399 *of* 1893.—(Telugu.) On the same slab. Records in the reign of Vishṇuvardhana-Mahārāja *alias* Vīra-Chōḍadēva, the gift of a lamp. See Gd. 48-A.

306. 400 *of* 1893.—(Telugu.) On the same slab. A record of the Chāḷukya-Chōḷa king Rājakēsarivarman *alias* Saptama-Vishṇuvardhana *alias* Kulōttuṅga-Chōḍadēva (I) in his forty-eighth year.

307. 401 *of* 1893.—(Telugu.) In the same place, third slab. An incomplete record, mentioning some geographical names.

308. 402 *of* 1893.—(Sanskrit and Telugu.) On the same slab. A record of the Chāḷukya Chōḷa king Rājakēsarivarman *alias* Saptama-Vishṇuvardhana *alias* Kulōttuṅga Chōḍadēva (I) recording in his forty-third year and Ś. 1034, the gift of a lamp.

309. 403 *of* 1893.—(Sanskrit aud Telugu.) On the same slab. A record of the Chāḷukya-Chōḷa king Rājakēsarivarman *alias* Saptama-Vishṇuvardhana *alias* Kulōttuṅga-Chōḍadēva (I, 1070—1118) in his forty-fifth year relating to the gift of a lamp.

310. 404 *of* 1893.—(Telugu.) In the same place, fourth slab. A record of the Chāḷukya-Chōḷa king Rājakēsarivarman *alias* Saptama-Vishṇuvardhana *alias* Kulōttuṅga-Chōḍadēva (I, 1070—1118) in his forty-eighth year relating to the gift of a lamp.

311. 405 *of* 1893.—(Telugu.) On the same slab. Dated in the reign of the Chāḷukya-Chōḷa king Rājakēsarivarman *alias* Saptama-Vishṇuvardhana *alias* Kulōttuṅga-Chōḍadēva (I, 1070—1118). Records in his forty-third year the gift of a lamp in the time of the Mahāmaṇḍalēśvara-Śūraparāja of Bīragōtta.

312. 406 *of* 1893.—(Telugu.) In the same place, fifth slab. Records the gift of a lamp.

313. 407 *of* 1893.—(Telugu.) In the same place, left pillar. Records in the eighth year of the Gaṅga king Aniyaṅka-Bhīmadēva-Ravatu, son of Anantavarman (1075—1146) *alias* Rājarājadēva of Trikalinga, the gift gold. [See Nos. 217—21 above.]

314. 408 *of* 1893.—(Telugu.) In the same place, first tier from bottom. A record of Rājādhirājadēva in his forty-ninth year and Ś. 1137, mentioning Mallināyaka, son of Maṅgināyaka. [The king came to the throne in 1166 and he has not been identified.]

315. 409 *of* 1893.—(Sanskrit and Telugu.) In the same tier. Records in his twenty-ninth year of Rājādhirājadēva and Ś. 1117, the gift of lamps. See the above epigraph.

316. 410 *of* 1893.—(Telugu.) In the same tier. A record of Rājādhirājadēva recording, in his twenty-eighth year and Ś. 1116, the gift of lamps. See No. 314.

317. 411 *of* 1893.—(Telugu.) In the same place, second tier. A record of the Kākatīya king, Gaṇapatidēva, dated in Ś. 1159, mentioning a minister of Kulōttuṅgarāya-Rājēndra-Chōḍa-Goṅka. [The latter was evidently a later chief of the Velanāṇṭi line.]

318. 412 *of* 1893.—(Telugu.) In the same tier. A record of the Chāḷukya-Chōḷa king Saptama-Vishṇuvardhana *alias* Kulōttuṅga-Chōḍadēva (I, 1070--1118) in his thirty-seventh year, relating the gift of a lamp.

319. 413 *of* 1893.—(Sanskrit and Telugu.) In the same tier. Dated in the reign of Velanāṇṭi-Kulōttuṅga Rājēndra-Chōḍayarāja (i.e., Vīrarājēndrachōḍa, son of Goṅka II). Records in Ś. 1102, the gift of a lamp by the wife of a Nāyaka.

320. 414 *of* 1893.—(Telugu.) In the same tier. A record of Vishṇuvardhana Mahārāja (Kulōttunga I ?) in Ś. 1037.

321. 415 *of* 1893.—(Telugu.) In the same tier. A record of the Chālukya-Chōḷa king Rājakēsarivarman, *alias* Saptama-Vishṇuvardhana, *alias* Kulōttuṅga-Chōḍadēva (I, 1070—1118) recording a gift in his forty-fifth year and Ś. 1037.

322. 416 *of* 1893.—(Tamil.) In the same tier. A record mentioning a Vatsa king.

323. 417 *of* 1893.—(Telugu.) In the same tier. A record in Ś. 1027, mentioning a Vatsa king.

324. 418 *of* 1893.—(Sanskrit.) In the same tier. A record in Ś. 1008, mentioning a minister of Rājarāja. [Was he Chōḍagaṅga, the eldest son of Kulōttuṅga I ?].

325. 419 *of* 1893.—(Sanskrit.) On the south wall of the same temple. A record of Sakalabhuvanachakravartin Mahārājasimha *alias* Avanyavanōdbhava in Ś. 1184. Refers to the lord of Karnāṭa and Gaṇapati Mahārāja (Kākatīya). Dr. Hultzsch believes that the donor was Kō-Peruñjiṅgadēva who came to the throne in Ś. 1165-6.

326. 420 *of* 1893.—(Telugu.) In the Navagraha-Maṇṭapa in the same temple. The Pallava king, Saubhāgyadēvarāja of Vīragōtta records in Krōdhin, the gift of fields.

327. 421 *of* 1893. –(Telugu.) In the Kalyāṇa Maṇṭapa in the same temple. Records that Anadēva-Mahārāja gave in Ś. ?, Tāraṇa, some golden bulls and constructed a golden pinnacle.

328. 422 *of* 1893.—(Sanskrit and Telugu.) In the Navagraha Maṇṭapa in the same temple. A record of the Reḍḍi king, Vēma-Reḍḍi, son of Kāṭama-Reḍḍi, in Ś. 1336, *Jaya*, relating the building of a maṇṭapa for the merit of his father. The exact date, as ascertained by Kielhorn, is Sunday, 28th October A.D. 1414. See *Ep. Ind.*, IV, pp. 328–9. Vēma was the son-in-law of Anavōta, the elder brother of Ana-Vēma and the founder of the Rajahmundry Reḍḍi line. See Gd. 17.

329. 423 *of* 1893.—(Sanskrit.) In the Navagraha Maṇṭapa in the same temple. A record dated in Ś. 1355, Paridhāvin, mentioning Allaya-Vēma, Vīrēśvara. Doḍḍaya and Annaya of Rājahmundry.

330. 424 *of* 1893.—(Telugu.) In the Navagraha Maṇṭapa in the same temple. A record in Ś. 1359, Piṅgaḷa, mentioning Allāḍa-Reḍḍi and Vēmareḍḍi. See No. 359 below.

331. 425 *of* 1893.—(Sanskrit.) In the Navagraha Maṇṭapa in the same temple. Records in Ś. 1349, Plavaṅga, the building of a maṇṭapa by Kuñcha-Nāyaka.

332. 426 *of* 1893.—(Telugu.) In the Navagraha Maṇṭapa in the same temple. A record in Piṅgaḷa, mentioning Allāḍareḍḍi-Vēmāreḍḍi. See No. 359 below.

333. 427 *of* 1893.—(Telugu.) At the east entrance to the same temple. A record of the Western Chāḷukya king Tribhuvana-malladēva (Vikramāditya VI) in Chālukya-Vikrama year 47.

334. 428 *of* 1893.—(Telugu.) At the east entrance to the same temple. A record of the Western Chāḷukya king Tribhuvana-malladēva (Vikramāditya VI) in Chāḷukya-Vikrama year 47 and Ś. 1044.

335. 429 *of* 1893.—(Telugu.) At the east entrance to the same temple. A record of Kulōttuṅga Chōḍadēva (I ?) in his thirteenth year.

336. 430 *of* 1893.--(Sanskrit.) At the east entrance to the same temple. A record mentioning Aniyaṅka-Bhīma. See No. 350.

337. 431 *of* 1893.--(Telugu.) At the east entrance to the same temple. Records in the eleventh year Kulōttuṅga-Chōḷa and Ś. 1065, the gift of land.

338. 432 *of* 1893.—(Telugu.) At the east entrance to the same temple. A record of Purushōttamadēva-Mahārāja.

339. 433 *of* 1893.—(Sanskrit and Telugu.) At the east entrance to the same temple. A record of Vishṇuvardhana Mahārāja (Kulōttuṅga I?) recording in Ś. 1030, the gift of a lamp.

340. 434 *of* 1893.—(Telugu.) At the east entrance to the same temple. A record of the Western Chāḷukya king Tribhuvanamalladēva Vikramāditya VI in Chāḷukya-Vikrama year 46 and Ś. 1043.

341. 435 *of* 1893.—(Sanskrit and Telugu.) At the south entrance to the same temple. An inscription of Kulōttuṅga-Rājēndra-Chōḍayarāja dated in Ś. 1192. [See No. 317. It is impossible to identify the two chiefs.]

342. 436 *of* 1893.—(Telugu.) At the south entrance to the same temple. Dated in the reign of Kulōttuṅga-Rājēndra-Chōḍayarāja. Records in Ś. 1161, the gift of a lamp by the son of an officer named Nunkaṇa. See the above epigraph.

343. 437 *of* 1893.—(Sanskrit and Telugu.) At the south entrance to the same temple. Records in Ś. 1102, the gift of a lamp by a goldsmith in the time of Vīrapa-Nāyaka.

344. 438 *of* 1893.—(Telugu.) At the south entrance to the same temple. Records in the reign of Rājādhirājadēva, in Ś. 1175, the gift by Vishṇuvardhana *alias* Rājēndradēva for the merit of his father Mallapadēva. [These chiefs have not been identified.]

345. 439 *of* 1893.—(Telugu.) At the south entrance to the same temple. A record of Vishṇuvardhana-Mahārāja in his fourth year and Ś. 1151. [So the king came to the throne in 1225.]

346. 440 *of* 1893.—(Sanskrit and Telugu.) At the south entrance to the same temple. A record of Rājadhirājadēva in his fifty-ninth year and Ś. 1197. See No. 341 which refers to the same chief.

347. 441 *of* 1893.—(Sanskrit.) At the entrance to the inner prākāra of the same temple. Records in Ś. 1352, Sādhāraṇa, the setting up of an image of Gaṇapati by a physician.

348. 442 *of* 1893.—(Telugu.) On a pillar near a Nāga shrine in the inner prākāra on the same temple. Dated in the reign of the Vijayanagara king Vīra-Pratāpa-Prauḍhadēvarāja. Records in Ś. 1366, Raktākshi, a gift by a minister.

349. 443 *of* 1893.—(Sanskrit and Telugu.) On a pillar in the Kalyāṇa-Maṇṭapa in front of the Māṇikyāmba shrine in the same temple. Records that Kaḍiyamu Māchinēm, a servant of the Rājahmundry Reḍḍi king Vēmā-reḍḍi, son of Kāṭama-reḍḍi, built for the merit of his master, his queen, etc., a maṇṭapa in Ś. 1328 ?, Durmukhi. [See No. 328 above and *Ep. Ind.*, IV, pp. 328-9. The actual date (Monday, eleventh tithi of the bright fortnight of Chaittra) corresponds to 9th March A.D. 1416. See also Kielhorn's *Southern List*, No. 598.]

350. 444 *of* 1893.—(Sanskrit.) On a pillar at the entrance to the inner prākāra of the same temple. A record of the Gaṅga king Rājarāja II, son of Aniyaṅka-Bhīma, son of Chōḷa-Gaṅga (i.e., Anantavarman, 1075—1146). Mentions a general Monkaṇa. Rājarāja II seems to have ascended the throne about A.D. 1167.

351. 445 *of* 1893.—(Sanskrit and Telugu.) On other pillar in the same place. A record of the Rājahmundry Reḍḍi king Allāḍa-reḍḍi in Ś. 1339, relating to the gift of a lamp held by a female figure.

352. 446 *of* 1893.—(Telugu.) At the same entrance. A record of the Koṇḍavīḍu Reḍḍi king Ana-Vēma in Ś. 1303, relating to the erection of some buildings. See Gd. 5 and Gd. 18.

353. 447 *of* 1893.—(Sanskrit.) On a pillar in the maṇṭapa near the tank in the same temple. A record of the Reḍḍi king Allaya-Vēma of Rājamahēndrapuri. See No. 329.

354. 448 *of* 1893.—(Sanskrit.) On the north wall of the outer prākāra of the same temple. A record of the Reḍḍi king Allaya-Vēma. See No. 329 above.

355. 449 *of* 1893.—(Telugu and Sanskrit.) On the outside of the west wall of the inner prākāra of the same temple. A record of the Chāḷukya-Chōḷa king Rājakēsarivarman *alias* Saptama-Vishṇuvardhana *alias* Kulōttuṅga-Chōḍadēva (I) recording in his forty-seventh year a gift apparently.

356. 450 *of* 1893.—(Telugu.) In the same place. A record of Vishṇuvardhana-Mahārāja (Kulōttuṅga I ?) in his forty-ninth year.

357. 451 *of* 1893.—(Kanarese.) At the western gōpura of the same temple. Mentions Anantapāla. See Fleet's *Dynas., Kanar. Dts.*, p. 51.

Bikkavōlu.

358. On the north side of the door of the Gōvindēśvarasvāmi shrine. A grant dated Ś. 1045 in the twenty-fifth year of the reign of Vijaya Rāja. [*Antiquities*, I, 25.]

Koṇḍukūru.

359. C.P. grant of Allaya Doḍḍa or Allāreḍḍi Doḍḍa or Doḍḍa II of the Rājahmundry Reḍḍi dynasty, dated in Ardhōdaya, in the month of Pausha, Ś. 1352, Sādhāraṇa, which, according to Prof. Kielhorn, corresponded to Sunday, 14th January A.D. 1431.

The object of the grant was the village of Gumpini or Allāḍa Reḍḍi Doḍḍāvaram (near Dēvarapalli, Palivēla, etc.). Mr. G. V. Ramamūrti edits the plates in *Ep. Ind.*, Vol. V, pp. 53—70. He compares the genealogy of the Rājahmundry Reḍḍis as given here with those of the *Kāśikhaṇḍam* and *Bhimakhaṇḍam* of Poet Śrīnātha who was the contemporary of the last three Reḍḍis. He also compares it with that of the Tottaramuḍi plates. The epigraph is thus of interest in throwing light on the history of an interesting line of chiefs whose services to literature were very great.

Kōṭiphalam.

360—363. Mr. Sewell gives (1) an undated record regarding the erection of the Mukhamaṇṭapam; (2) three slokas from the *Brahmāṇḍapurāṇa*, in praise of Kōṭiphalam and two records dated Ś. 1345 and Ś. 1348 regarding the erection of a maṇṭapam and a pillar by private persons. See *Antiquities*, I, p. 32.

Ṭēki.

364. A C.P. grant (Sanskrit and Telugu) of Vishṇuvardhana Rājarāja Chōḍagaṅga, the son of Kulōttuṅga Chōḍa I, who ascended the throne of Veṅgi in Ś. 1006. The details of the date (Thursday, the fullmoon *tithi* of Jyēshṭa, in the nakshatra Jyēshṭa, simhalagna), says Dr. Hultzsch, correspond to 22nd May, A.D. 1084. The grant confirms certain honorary privileges to the descendants of the Teliki family, who were divided into 1,000 families (10 of which are mentioned by name) and who were the hereditary servants of the Eastern Chāḷukyan family. See *Ep. Ind.*, Vol. VI, p. 334 ff. Dr. Hultzsch draws attention to the fact that the composer of the Ṭēki plates was the same as Vidyābhaṭṭa, the composer of the Chellūr and Piṭhāpuram plates of Vīrachōḍa, the predecessor of Vikrama Chōḷa as the Veṅgi Viceroy. The epigraph is of value for the light it throws on the different prince-viceroys of Veṅgi in the time of Kulōttuṅga I. See *Madr. Ep. Rep.*, 1903, p. 5; also Kielhorn's *Southern List*, No. 571.

TUNI DIVISION.

Chikkulla.

365. A C.P. grant of the Vishṇukuṇḍin king Vikramēndravarman II, the son of Indrabhaṭṭāraka, grandson of Vikramēndra I and great-grandson of Mādhava-varman, on the fifth day of the eighth fortnight of the summer of the tenth year of his reign. The object of the grant was a village on the Kistṇa to a Sōmagirīśvara temple. The record has been attributed to the eighth century. The dynasty evidently ruled at Vinukoṇḍa and Daṇḍatūru in Ellore taluk. See *Ep. Ind.*, Vol. IV, p. 193 ff.

GUNTŪR DISTRICT.

BĀPATLA TALUK.

Appikaṭla.

1. 164 *of* 1897.—(Sanskrit and Telugu.) On a black granite slab in front of the Viśvēśvara temple, west and south faces. A record of Kulōttuṅga-Rājēndra-Chōḍa (1163—80), son of Velanāṇṭi-Goṅka (II) and Sabbāmbika, in Ś. 1094, in the twenty-sixth year of Rājarāja (II ?). Records gifts of land to Viśvēśvara on the southern bank of the Tuṅgabhadra. See also *Antiquities*, p. 81. [Goṅka II, the son of Chōḍa who was Viceroy of Veṅgi under Kulōttuṅga-Chōḷa I (1070—1118), raised the power of his dynasty to its greatest height and ruled from Kaḷahasti (North Arcot) to Gañjām. It is doubtful whether Rājarāja was the Chōḷa who ruled from 1146 to 1178 or the son and successor of Anantavarman Chōḍagaṅga. See Gd. 350.]

2. 165 *of* 1897.—(Sanskrit and Telugu.) On a black granite slab in front of the Viśvēśvara temple, east face. A record of Rājēndra Chōḍa, son of Velanāṇṭi Goṅka (II) and Sabbāmbika, in Ś. 1094. Records gift of gold (*Birudu-gadyana*) for a lamp and gift of land for a garden to Viśvēśvara on the Tuṅgabhadra by Navaya-Nāyaka. Also a gift of land by a merchant and a gift of land by the king. See *Antiquities*, p. 81.

Bāpaṭla.

Mr. Sewell gives sixteen inscriptions in this place from Elliot's collection and is not confident as to their accuracy. The departmental list being complete and accurate, I have not thought it necessary to compare them.

3. 166 *of* 1897.—(Sanskrit and Telugu.) On the west wall of the Bhāvanārāyaṇa temple. A record of Tribhuvanachakravartin Rājarājadēva in Ś. 1073, in his sixth year. Records gift of a lamp by the Paṇḍit Ananta, who wrote a commentary on the Nārāyaṇīya, to the Bhāvanārāyaṇa temple at Prēmpaḷḷi in Kammanāṇḍu [Who is this Ananta ? There was one Anantabhaṭṭa, the author of the *Bhārata champu* ; and another Ananta Paṇḍita, the author of the *Vyaṅgyārthakaumudi*, a commentary on the Alaṅkāra work *Rasamañjari*. We have no evidence to show whether they are the same. See No. 1 above for the identity of the king.]

4. 167 *of* 1897.—(Telugu.) On the west wall of the Bhāvanārāyaṇa temple. Records in Ś. 1071 gift of a lamp by Kavaliya-Aṇṇaya, a subordinate of the Mahāmaṇḍalēśvara Tribhuvanamalladēva Pottappi-Chōḍamahārāja. [The latter was apparently

the Tribhuvanamalla who was at Konedena and who was the feudatory of Kulōttuṅgachōḷa II and whose dates range from 1137 to 1148. See the genealogy of the Telugu-Chōḷa chiefs.]

5. 168 *of* 1897.—(Sanskrit and Telugu.) On the west wall of the Bhāvanārāyaṇa temple. A record of the Chōḷa king Tribhuvanachakravartin Kulōttuṅga-Chōḍadēva (II) in Ś. 1067. Records gift of a lamp to the temple at Prēmpaḷḷi or Brahmapaḷḷi.

6. 169 *of* 1897.—(Telugu.) On the west wall of the Bhāvanārāyaṇa temple. Records in Ś. 1207, Pārthiva, gift of cows for a lamp.

7. 170 *of* 1897.—(Telugu prose and verse.) On the west wall of the Bhāvanārāyaṇa temple. Records in Ś. 1071 gift of a lamp by a servant of the Mahāmaṇḍalēśvara Tribhuvanamalladēva-Chōdamahārāja of the family of Karikāla. See No. 4 above.

8. 171 *of* 1897.—(Telugu prose and verse.) On the west wall of the Bhāvanārāyaṇa temple. Records in Ś. 1073 gift of gold *(Birudumāḍa)* for a lamp by a minister of Tribhuvanamalladēva Pottappi-Chōḍamahārāja. See No. 4 above.

9. 172 *of* 1897.—(Telugu prose and verse.) On the west wall of the Bhāvanārāyaṇa temple. A record in Ś. 1069, fifteenth year of the Chōḷa king Tribhuvanachakravartin Kulōttuṅga-Chōḍadēva (II). Records gift to various temples by the *Sandhivigrahin* of the Mahāmaṇḍalīka Bhīma-Nāyaka who had the surname Veṅgidēśa-Chālukyan-aṅkakāra.

10. 173 *of* 1897.—(Telugu.) On the west wall of the Bhāvanārāyaṇa temple. A record in Ś. 1071, sixteenth year of the Chōḷa king Tribhuvanachakravartin Kulōttuṅga-Chōḍadēva (II, 1123—46). Records gift of sheep for a lamp. [See *Ep. Ind.*, Vol. X, p. 136, where Mr. Sewell discusses the details of the date and says that it corresponds to Friday, March 25, A.D. 1149.]

11. 174 *of* 1897.—(Telugu.) On the west wall of the Bhāvanārāyaṇa temple. A record in Ś. 1066, twelfth year of the Chōḷa king Tribhuvanachakravartin Kulōttuṅga-Chōḍadēva (II, 1123—46). Records gift of cows for a lamp to the Bhāvanārāyaṇa temple at Prēmpaḷḷi in Kammanāṇḍu, a subdivision of Uttama-Chōḍa-vaḷanāṇḍu, by Sōmāṇḍi-amma, queen of the Mahāmaṇḍalēśvara Kulōttuṅga-Chōḍa-Goṅkarāja (i.e., Goṅka II). [See *Ep. Ind.*, Vol. X, p. 136, where Mr. Sewell gives the English equivalent of the date to be Monday, February 12, A.D. 1145.]

12. 175 *of* 1897.—(Telugu.) On the west wall of the Bhāvanārāyaṇa temple. A record in Ś. 1071, fourth year. Records gift of gold *(Birudu-maḍa)* for a lamp by Kanniśeṭṭi, the Sēnādhipati of Kulōttuṅgā-Chōḍa-Gāṅgēyarāya (i.e., Goṅka II ?).

13. 176 *of* 1897.—(Sanskrit and Telugu.) On the west wall of the Bhāvanārāyaṇa temple. A record in Ś. 1069, fifteenth year of the Chōḷa king Tribhuvanachakravartin Kulōttuṅga-Chōḍadēva (II). Records gift of gold *(Birudu-māḍa)* for a lamp by Nāgalādēvi, the queen of Paṇḍa, the son of Velanāṇṭi-Chōḍa and Guṇḍāmba. [Paṇḍa was evidently Goṅka II of the Velanāḍu line.]

14. 177 *of* 1897.—(Sanskrit.) On the west wall of the same temple. A record the date of which is lost. Records gift of a lamp by the queen of a Velanāṇḍu chief ; incomplete.

15. 178 *of* 1897.—(Telugu.) On the west wall of the same temple. Records in Ś. 945, Tāraṇa (wrong), gift of the village of Chaṅgallu to the Bhāvanārāyaṇa temple at Prēmpaḷḷi by Pina-Mallidēva-Chōḍamahārāja, who was a descendant of Karikāla. [This chief has not been identified.]

16. 179 *of* 1897.—(Telugu.) On the west wall of the same temple. Records in Ś. 1065, eleventh year, gift of a lamp by a servant of Kulōttuṅga-Chōḍa-Goṅkarāja (i.e., Velanāṇṭi Goṅka II, feudatory of Kulōttuṅga-Chōḷa II).

17. 180 *of* 1897.—(Telugu.) On the west wall of the same temple. A record in Ś. 1065, eleventh year of the Chōḷa king Tribhuvanachakravartin Kulōttuṅga-Chōḍadēva (II). Records gift of sheep for a lamp by a merchant. [See *Ep. Ind.*, Vol. X, p. 137, for the details of the date which corresponded to Wednesday, July 14, A.D. 1143.]

18. 181 *of* 1897.—(Telugu.) On the west wall of the same temple. A damaged record, the date of which is lost. Mentions Chōḍa-Goṅkamahārāja, the son of Akkamāmahādēvi. Records gift of a lamp. [The king should be Goṅka III as his mother's name was Akkamāmbikā. She was the queen of Vijaya Rājēndra Chōḍa, 1163—80.]

19. 182 *of* 1897.—(Sanskrit and Telugu.) On the west wall of the same temple. A record in Ś. 1058 of the Chōḷa king Tribhuvanachakravartin Kulōttuṅga Chōḍadēva (II). Records gift of a lamp by Guṇḍāmbika, the wife of Velanāṇṭi Goṅka (Chōḍa ?), the son of Goṅka (I ?).

20. 183 *of* 1897.—(Telugu.) On the west wall of the same temple. A record in Ś. 1058, fourth year of the Chōḷa king Tribhuvanachakravartin Kulōttuṅga-Chōḍadēva (II). Records gift of sheep for a lamp by Nīliśeṭṭi, a merchant from Penugoṇḍa, to the Bhāvanārāyaṇa temple at Bhāvapaṭṭaṇa. [Vide *Ep. Ind.*, Vol. X, p. 137, where Mr. Sewell concludes from the details of the date that it should be August 4, A.D. 1136.]

21. 184 *of* 1897.—(Telugu.) On the west wall of the same temple. A damaged record in Ś. 1132. Mentions Niḍumbrōlu.

22. 185 *of* 1897.—(Telugu.) On the west wall of the same temple. Records in Ś. 1214, Vijaya, gift of cows for a lamp.

23. 186 *of* 1897.—(Sanskrit.) On the south wall of the same temple. A record of the Vijayanagara king Kṛishṇarāya in

Ś. 1440, Bahudhānya. Records gift of land by Sōmarasa, the son of Mēlama of Chandragiri and an assistant of the minister Śāḷuva Timmaya, to the Bhāvanārāyaṇa temple at Bāpaṭla in the Koṇḍavīḍuvishaya.

24. 187 *of* 1897.—(Telugu.) On the north wall of the same temple. A record in Ś. 1078, tenth year of Tribhuvanachakravartin Rājarājadēva. Records gift of gold *(Birudu-māḍa)* for a lamp. See No. 1 above.

25. 188 *of* 1897.—(Sanskrit and Telugu.) On the north wall of the same temple. A record in Ś. 1076, ninth year of Tribhuvanachakravartin Rājarājadēva. Records gift of gold *(Birudu-māḍa)* for a lamp. Prēmpaḷḷi is surnamed Rājamāṇikkāvūra. See No. 1 above.

26. 189 *of* 1897.—(Telugu.) On the north wall of the same temple. A record in Ś. 1075, eighth year of Tribhuvanachakravartin Rājarājadēva. Records gift of gold *(Birudu-māḍa)* for a lamp by *a member of the guild of the Teliki thousand of Bejavāḍa.* See No. 1 above and Gd. 364.

27. 190 *of* 1897.—(Telugu verse and prose.) On the north wall of the same temple. A record in Ś. 1077 of Tribhuvanachakravartin Rājarājadēva. Records gift of gold *(Birudu-māḍa)* for a lamp by Kāmasāni, the wife of Īśāna-Peggaḍa, a minister of Goṅka (II). See No. 58 and No. 1 above.

28. 191 *of* 1897.—(Sanskrit and Telugu.) On the north wall of the same temple. A record in Ś. 1076, ninth year of Tribhuvanachakravartin Rājarājadēva. Records gift of gold *(Birudu-māḍa)* for a lamp by Nāmana-Peggaḍa, the minister of Paṇḍa-Nāyaka, who was the maternal uncle of Goṅkarāja (II). See No. 1 above.

29. 192 *of* 1897.—(Telugu.) On the north wall of the same temple. A record in Ś. 1076, eighth year of Tribhuvanachakravartin Rājarājadēva. Records gift of gold *(Birudu-māḍa)* for a lamp by *a member of the guild of the Teliki thousand of Bejavāḍa.* See No. 26 above and Gd. 364.

30. 193 *of* 1897.—(Telugu.) On the north wall of the same temple. A record in Ś. 1078 of Tribhuvanachakravartin Rājarājadēva. Records gift of sheep for a lamp by the Mahāmaṇḍalēśvara Jikkidēva-Chōḍa, the son of Pōtaṇa-Chōḍa of the family of Karikāla. See No. 1 above.

31. 194 *of* 1897.—(Telugu.) On the north wall of the same temple. A record in Ś. 1074 of Tribhuvanachakravartin Rājarājadēva. Records gift of gold *(Birudu-māḍa)* for a lamp by Damana-Peggaḍa of Prēmpaḷḷi, the son-in-law of Nallaśūraya-Peggaḍa, the minister of the Mahāmaṇḍalēśvara Kulōttuṅga-Chōḍa-Goṅkarāja [Goṅka II ?]

32. 195 *of* 1897.—(Telugu.) On the north wall of the same temple. Records in Ś. 1038, Manmatha, gift of Madhukambaḷḷi in

Kammanāṇḍu by the Mahāmaṇḍalēśvara Kōsūradēva Chōḍa of the Karikāla family.

33. 196 *of* 1897.—(Sanskrit and Telugu.) On the north wall of the same temple. A record in Ś. 1076, Śrīmukha; ninth year of Tribhuvanachakravartin Rājarājadēva. Records gift of gold *(Birudu-māḍa)* for a lamp by the Paṇḍit Ananta. See No. 3 above.

34. 197 *of* 1897.—(Telugu.) On the east wall of the same temple. A record of Tribhuvanachakravartin Rājarājadēva, the date of which is lost. Records gift of a lamp. Mentions the Mahāmaṇḍalēśvara Kulōttuṅga-Rājēndra-Chōḍa-Goṅka (II?). Damaged.

35. 198 *of* 1897.—(Telugu.) On the east wall of the same temple. An incomplete record in Ś. 1240, Kāḷayukti.

36. 199 *of* 1897.—(Telugu.) On the east wall of the same temple. A record in Ś. 1063, ninth year of the Chōḷa king Kulōttuṅga-Chōḍadēva (Goṅka II). Records gift of sheep for a lamp.

37. 200 *of* 1897.—(Sanskrit and Telugu.) On the east wall of the same temple. Records in Ś. 1052 gift of cows for two lamps by the Mahāmaṇḍalīka Bhīma-Nāyaka.

38. 201 *of* 1897.—(Telugu.) On the east wall of the same temple. Records in Ś. 1213, Khara, gift of cows for a lamp.

39. 202 *of* 1897.—(Telugu.) On the east wall of the same temple. Records in Ś. 1209, Sarvajit, gift of cows for a lamp to the Bhāvanārāyaṇa temple at Bhāvapaṭṭaṇa.

40. 203 *of* 1897.—(Telugu.) On the east wall of the same temple. A record in Ś. 1073, fourth year of Tribhuvanachakravartin Rājarājadēva. Records gift of sheep for a lamp by a servant of the Mahāmaṇḍalēśvara Tribhuvanamalladēva Chōḍamahārāja of the Karikāla family. See No. 1 above and also No. 7.

41. 204 *of* 1897.—(Telugu.) On the east wall of the same temple. Records in Ś. 1213, Khara, gift of cows for a lamp.

42. 205 *of* 1897.—(Telugu.) On the east wall of the same temple. Records in Chitrabhānu gift of cows for a lamp by a merchant to the Bhāvanārāyaṇa temple at Bhāvapaṭṭaṇa.

43. 206 *of* 1897.—(Telugu.) On the east wall of the same temple. Records gift of a lamp by the Mahāmaṇḍalēśvara Ballaya. A much damaged record. See No. 47 below.

44. 207 *of* 1897.—(Tamil.) On the east wall of the same temple. A damaged record in the forty-second year of the Chōḷa king Rājakēsarivarman *alias* Kulōttuṅga-Chōḷadēva (I, 1070—1118). The usual historical introduction.

45. 208 *of* 1897.—(Telugu.) On the east wall of the same temple. A record in Ś. 1034, Nandana, of Tribhuvanachakravartin. Records gift of gold *(Uttamagaṇḍa-māḍa)* for a lamp.

46. 209 *of* 1897.—(Telugu.) On the east wall of the same temple. A record in Ś. 1089 of Tribhuvanachakravartin Rājarājadēva. Records gift of gold *(Birudu-māḍa)* for a lamp. See No. 1 above.

47. 210 *of* 1897.—(Telugu.) On the east wall of the same temple. A record of the Chōḷa king Tribhuvanachakravartin Kulōttuṅga-Chōḍadēva (II, 1133—46) in Ś. 1057, Rākshasa. Records gift of gold *(Chāmara-māḍa)* for a lamp by the queen of the Mahāmaṇḍalēśvara Ballaya Chōḍamahārāja. See No. 43 above.

48. 211 *of* 1897.—(Sanskrit and Telugu.) On the east wall of the same temple. A record in Ś. 1073, sixth year of Tribhuvanachakravartin Rājarājadēva. Records gift of gold *(Birudu-māḍa)* for a lamp by Sūrāmba, the wife of Kulōttuṅga-Chōḍa-Goṅkarāja (Goṅka II, evidently).

49. 212 *of* 1897.—(Telugu.) On the east wall of the same temple. Records in Ś. 1042, Vikārin, gift of gold *(Gandhavāraṇa-māḍa)* for a lamp by a Reḍḍi.

50. 213 *of* 1897.—(Sanskrit and Telugu.) On the east wall of the same temple. A record in Ś. 1072 of Tribhuvanachakravartin Rājarājadēva. Records gift of gold *(Birudu-māḍa)* for a lamp by Rājēndra-Kōna-Lōkarāja, the son of the Chāḷukya Princess Rājāmbika and Mummaḍi-Bhīma, who was the son of Rājāditya of the family of Kārtavīrya. [Rājēndra was apparently that Lōkamahīpāla who was the joint ruler with Bhīma III. See the genealogy of the Kōna chiefs of Piṭhāpuram.]

51. 214 *of* 1897.—(Sanskrit and Telugu.) On the east wall of the same temple. A record in Ś. 1073, sixth year of Tribhuvanachakravartin Rājarājadēva. Records gift of gold *(Birudu-māḍa)* for a lamp by the wife of a merchant. See No. 1 above.

52. 215 *of* 1897.—(Telugu.) On the east wall of the same temple. A record in Ś. 1089, twenty-first year of Tribhuvanachakravartin Rājarājadēva. Records gift of cows. See No. 1 above.

53. 216 *of* 1897.—(Sanskrit and Telugu.) On the east wall of the same temple. A record in Ś. 1073, sixth year of Tribhuvanachakravartin Rājarājadēva. Records gift of gold *(Birudu-māḍa)* for a lamp by Prōḷāmbika, the daughter of Śūrāmbika, the wife of Kulōttuṅga-Chōḍa Goṅkarāja (II).

54. 217 *of* 1897.—(Telugu.) On the east wall of the same temple. A damaged record of the Chōḷa king Tribhuvanachakravartin Kulōttuṅga-Chōḍadēva, the date of which is doubtful.

55. 218 *of* 1897.—(Telugu.) On the east wall of the same temple. Records gift of a mango garden by a servant of Kulōttuṅga-Rājēndra-Chōḍarāja (C. 1163—80). [This is the same as the Kōna chief Vīra Rājēndra-Chōḍa who made valuable presents to the Drāksharāma temple.]

56. 219 *of* 1897.—(Telugu verse and prose.) On the east wall of same temple. Records in Ś. 1082 gift of a lamp by Kommaṇa-Peggaḍa, the Sandhivigrahin of Kulōttuṅga-Chōḍa-Goṅkarāja [Goṅka II ?].

57. 220 *of* 1897.—(Tamil.) On the east wall of the same temple. Records in Ś. 1040 gift of gold for a lamp. An incomplete record.

58. 221 *of* 1897.—(Sanskrit and Telugu.) On the east wall of the same temple. A record in Ś. 1078, eleventh year of Tribhuvanachakravartin Rājarājadēva. Records gift of gold *(Birudu-māḍa)* for a lamp by Jakkaṇa, the son-in-law of Iśāna Peggaḍa. See Nos. 27 and 83.

59. 222 *of* 1897.—(Telugu verse.) An incomplete record. On the east wall of the same temple. Mentions Komma, the *Sandhi-vigrahin* of Goṅka, whose capital was Dhanadapura (i.e., Tsandavōlu).

60. 223 *of* 1897.—(Telugu.) On the east wall of the same temple. A damaged record in Ś. 1064, Dundubhi, ninth year of the Chōḷa king Tribhuvanachakravartin Kulōttuṅga-Chōḍadēva (II, 1133—46). See *Ep. Ind.*, Vol. X, p. 137. [The details of the date of this epigraph are irregular.]

61. 224 *of* 1897.—(Sanskrit.) On the east wall of the same temple. A record in Ś. 1079 of Kulōttuṅga-Chōḍadēva (?). Records gift of a lamp by Vennāmbika.

62. 225 *of* 1897.—(Telugu.) In a room to the left of the entrance to the same temple. A record in the ninth year of the Chōḷa king. Records gift of sheep for a lamp by a Nāyaka, from Chilukūru in Pennātavāḍi.

63. 226 *of* 1897.—(Sanskrit.) In a room to the left of the entrance to the same temple. Mentions in Ś. 1057 Velanāṇṭi Goṅka (II, apparently) and Brahmapaḷḷi. A damaged and incomplete record.

64. 227 *of* 1897.—(Telugu.) In a room to the left of the entrance to the same temple. A record in Ś. 1060 of Tribhuvanachakravartin. Records gift of gold *(Chāmara-māḍa)* for a lamp by a Reḍḍi. Partially built in.

65. 228 *of* 1897.—(Telugu.) In a room to the left of the entrance to the same temple. A record of Vishṇuvardhana in Ś. 1050, Chāḷukya-Vikrama 3 (wrong), Kīlaka. Records gift of a lamp by the Mahāmaṇḍalēśvara Kaḍiyarāja, surnamed "the destroyer of Kīraṇapura."

66. 229 *of* 1897.—(Sanskrit and Telugu.) In a room to the left of the entrance to the same temple. Records gift of a coconut garden by Errama-Nāyaka, the store-keeper of Kulōttuṅga-Rājēndra-Chōḍarāja (1163—80).

67. 230 *of* 1897.—(Sanskrit and Telugu.) In a room to the left of the entrance to the same temple. Records in Ś. 1052, Chāḷukya-Vikrama 5 (wrong), gift of gold *(Chāmara-māḍa)* for lamp by Śūrāmba, the queen of Chōḍaya, the son of Goṅka and Sabbāmbika.

68. 231 *of* 1897.—(Sanskrit and Telugu.) In a room to the left of the entrance to the same temple. A record in Ś. 1089, twenty-second year of Tribhuvanachakravartin Rājarājadēva. Records gift of a lamp by Eriyama Nāyaka of Nidumbrōlu. See No. 1.

69. 232 *of* 1897.—(Telugu.) In a room to the left of the entrance to the same temple. Records in Ś. 1039, Hēvilambi, gift of gold *(Gandhavāraṇa-māḍa)* for a lamp by a Reḍḍi of Koṇḍapadumati Mavundala.

70. 233 *of* 1897.—(Kanarese and Telugu.) In a room to the right of the entrance to the same temple. Records gift of gold *(Gandhavāraṇa-māḍa)* by Chāvuṇḍamayya.

71. 234 *of* 1897.—(Kanarese and Telugu.) In a room to the right of the entrance to the same temple. Records gift of gold *(Gandhahasti māḍa)* by the Daṇḍanāyaka Kēśirāja.

72. 235 *of* 1897.—(Telugu.) In a room to the right of the entrance to the same temple. A record in Ś. 1058 of Velanāṇṭi Goṅkarāja (II ?). Records gift of gold for a lamp.

73. 236 *of* 1897.—(Telugu.) On the west wall of the garbhagriha of the same temple. A record in Ś. 1064, third year of the Chōḷa king Tribhuvanachakravartin Kulōttuṅga-Chōḍadēva (II, 1133—46). Records gift of gold *(Uttamagaṇḍa-māḍa)* for a lamp by a merchant.

74. 237 *of* 1897.—(Telugu.) On the west wall of the garbhagriha of the same temple. A record in the thirty-seventh year of the Chōḷa king Rājakēsarivarman *alias* Kulōttuṅga-Chōḍadēva (I, 1070—1118). Records gift of gold *(Rājarāja-māḍa)*. Compare *Ind. Antq.*, Vol. XXV, p. 321.

75. 238 *of* 1897.—(Tamil.) On the west wall of the *garbhagriha* of the same temple. A much damaged record of the Chōḷa king Rājakēsarivarman *alias* Kulōttuṅga-Chōḍadēva (I ?).

76. A C.P. in the place. Records that in Vikāri, Aśvija, Śuddha 15, in F. 1199, some land was given to Veṅka . . . at Amudālapaḷḷi in Bāpaṭla by the Mirasdars. *Mack. MSS.*, Bk. XVIII, pp. 155–6, and *Loc. Records*, LVII, 311 ff.

77. In the same place. An order to the local Karṇams to note the grant of Kaiṭēpalli as mānyam to Kollūr Bhāghavata Annāvadhāni. *Ibid.*

78. A grant of Nallūr Vēdamūrti Narasimhāchārya in F. 1149, by Rāja Śūrasāni Veṅkaṇṇa Gāru. *Ibid.*, pp. 157–8.

79. A grant in Ś. 1670, Śukla, Māgha Bahuḷa 15, by Śūrasāni Veṅkaṇṇa of some land near Nizampaṭam to a Mādhva teacher Ārādhya Tīrthāchārya. *Mack. MSS.*, Bk. XVIII, pp. 157–8.

80. In the hands of Bāpaṭḷa Varadānanda Narasimha Sōmayāji. Records in Ś. 1684, Chitrabhānu, Āshāḍha Śuddha 15, gift of land near Nizampatam to Dēvarakoṇḍa Śivarāma Avadhānilu. *Ibid.*, p. 159.

81. A grant in Ś. 1686, Śvabhānu, Kārttika Bahuḷa 5, by Puligaḍḍa Viraṇṇa. *Ibid.*, p. 160.

82. In the hands of Svayampāka Sūryanārāyaṇa. Records in Ś. 1648, Raktākshi, Kārttika Bahuḷa 10, gift of land by Śūrasāni Veṅkaṭapati. *Ibid.*

Chebrōlu.

[For an interesting account of the importance of the place see *Antiquities*, p. 82, and *Local Records*, XIX, 454 ff. See also *Ibid.* XXXVIII, p. 97. All the vaguely mentioned inscriptions of Mr. Sewell are found in the following departmental list.]

83. 144 *of* 1897.—(Telugu.) On a slab leaning against the east wall of the Nāgēśvara temple, left of the entrance. A record of Kulōttuṅga-Chōḍa-Goṅkarāja in Ś. 1075 (Goṅka II?) Records gift of gold (*Birudu-māḍa*) for a lamp by Jakkaṇarāja, the son-in-law of a Peggaḍa, to the Kumarāsvāmin temple at Chembrōlu. See No. 58.

84. 145 *of* 1897.—(Telugu.) On another slab in the same place; right of the entrance. A record of the Western Chāḷukya king Āhavamalladēva-Sattiga in Ś. 928, Parābhava. Records gift to Kumārasvāmin of Chembrōlu. [The king referred to was Satyāśraya II, 997—1008.]

85. 146 *of* 1897.—(Telugu verse and prose.) On a pillar on the left of the dvajastambha in the same temple. Records in Ś. 1067, gift of a lamp by Paṇḍa of the family of Buddhavarman.

86. 147 *of* 1897.—(Sanskrit and Telugu.) On a pillar in front of the gōpura of the same temple; right of entrance. A record of the Kākatīya king Gaṇapati in Ś. 1135, Śrīmukha. Records that Tāmrapuri (i.e., Chembrōlu) was granted by the Kākatīya king Gaṇapati to Jaya-Sēnāpati, and enumerates the villages belonging to Kumārasvāmin and to other temples at Chembrōlu. See the Gaṇapēśvaram inscription (*Ep. Ind.*, III, p. 95) for the genealogy of Jaya. For the edition of this epigraph itself see *Ep. Ind.*, Vol. V, pp. 142–51. Gaṇapati was the immediate predecessor of Rudrāmbā and ruled till about 1258. Kielhorn's *Southern List* No. 585.

87. 148 *of* 1897.—(Sanskrit and Telugu.) On the south face of the same pillar. Records in Ś. 1475, Paridhāvin (Phālguna, Suddha 11, Friday) the setting up of an image of Kumārasvāmin. See *Antiquities*, p. 82 (No. 2 in the local list) and *Mack. MSS.*, Bk. XX (15-3-63), pp. 118–9.

88. 149 *of* 1897.—(Sanskrit and Telugu.) On another pillar on the left of the entrance. A record of the Kākatīya king Gaṇapati in Ś. 1157 (गिरिशरण्या चन्द्र.) Records that Jaya-Sēnāpati built the temple of Chōḍēśvara, which was named after his father, and gave to it the village of Mrontukūru in Velanāṇḍu. Kielhorn who edits the inscription in *Ep. Ind.*, Vol. VI, pp. 38—40, says that the exact English date (of the *tithi* of Girijā in the bright half of Viśākha, Saturday) was Saturday, the 21st April, A.D. 1235. The inscription is referred to in *Antiquities*, p. 82, No. 4, in the local list. See *Mack. MSS.*, Bk. XX, pp. 111—8.

89. 150 *of* 1897.—(Sanskrit and Telugu.) On a slab in front of a large Nandi near the same temple; east face. Records in Ś. 1037 gift of a lamp by Guṇḍāmbika, the wife of Velanāṇṭi-Chōḍa, the son of Goṇka I. [Elsewhere this Chōḍa is said to have received the Veṅgi 16,000 country from Kulōttuṅga Chōḷa I, 1070—1118.]

90. 151 *of* 1897.—(Sanskrit and Telugu.) On a slab in front of a large Nandi near the same temple; west face. A record of the seventh-year Vishṇuvardhana-Mahārāja (VII) in Ś. 998, Naḷa, on Friday, Māgha Śu 15, lunar eclipse. Records gift of sheep for three lamps by the General Velanāṇṭi-Goṅka, the son of Guṇḍāmbika, to Mūlasthāna-Mahādēva and to Kumārasvāmidēva, and of five gold coins (*Jaya-māḍa*) for a garland to the latter. [The king referred to is Kulōttuṅga I and the General is apparently Goṅka II who came to the throne later on. See *Ep. Ind.*, Vol. VI, p. 278, where Dr. Kielhorn corrects Māgha into Phalguna and then gives the English date to be Friday, 10th February, A.D. 1077.]

91. 152 *of* 1897.—(Telugu prose and verse.) On a pillar of the gōpura of the same temple. A record in Ś. 1135. Mentions a concubine of Goṅka of Veṅgi; a damaged record.

92. 153 *of* 1897.—(Telugu.) On a slab in the Kēśavasvāmin temple. A record of the time of the Chōḷa king Rājakēsarivarman *alias* Vikrama-Chōḍadēva in Ś. 1049, Plavaṅga; in his ninth year. Records gift of sheep for a lamp by the Mahāmaṇḍalēśvara Nambaya, of the Durjaya family, lord of the city of Kollipāka and of the Shaḍsahasra country. *Ep. Ind.*, VI, 223—27. [Nambaya was a title borne by the later chiefs of Amarāvati. See Gd. 171 and 172 for further facts about the donor. The inscription shows that after 1124 Vikrama Chōḷa succeeded in recovering his northern dominions from Vikramāditya VI. See Gt. 112 below. The title Rājakēsarivarman is inconsistent.]

93. 154 *of* 1897.—(Kanarese verse and prose.) On a slab used as a mortar in the house of the pūjāri of the same temple. A record of the Western Chāḷukya king Tribhuvanamalladēva (Vikramāditya VI). Seems to record the repairing of temples and the building of a tank called Anantasarōvara by the Daṇḍanāyaka Anantapāla; incomplete. [Vikramāditya VI was in possession of Veṅgi from about 1118 to 1124, when the territory was recovered by Vikrama Chōḷa. This epigraph is in *Mack. MSS.*, Bk. XX, pp. 99—104. It is dated C.V. 40, Mārgaśira, Śuddha, 13, Thursday, Uttarāyaṇa, Saṅkrānti, solar eclipse.]

94. 155 *of* 1897.—(Telugu in archaic characters.) On a slab fixed into the bridge which leads to the Brahmēśvara temple in the middle of a square tank. A damaged record in Ś. 912.

95. 156 *of* 1897.—(Sanskrit and Telugu.) On a pillar of the doorway of the shrine of a goddess behind the Nāgēśvara temple. A record of Velanāṇṭi Goṅka in Ś. 1089 (i.e., Vīra Rājēndra Chōḍa ?). Records gift of a ḷamp by the daughter of the Daṇḍādīpa Paṇḍa; partly built in.

96. 157 *of* 1897.—(Telugu verse and prose.) On a pillar lying in the Mussalman street. Records in Ś. 1040 gift of a lamp by Śūra of the Viśvakarma-kula, an officer of Eṟṟa Maṇḍa.

97. In the Īśvara temple. Records the gift of a lamp to Chōḍēśvara in Ś. 1172, Āśvija, Bahuḷa 8, Thursday. *Mack. MSS.*, Bk. XX (15-3-63), p. 118.

98. A similar record in Ś. 1178, Pushya bahuḷa 3. *Ibid.*

Iḍupalapāḍu.

The following epigraphs have been taken from Brown's *Loc. Rec.*, Vol. 48, pp. 47—53.

98-A. In the Garuḍastambha of the Chenna Kēśavasvāmi. A Sanskrit record of Pratāparudradēva, dated in Ś. 1422, Śarad-Bhuja, lunar eclipse. [The latter part of the inscription is in Telugu padya.] Records grant of village Iḍupalapāḍu, to Mādhava-Budha of the Bhāradvāja gōtra. The praises of the latter are given. The king referred to was evidently the king of Orissa who, according to one version, ruled from 1504 to 1532, and according to another from 1503 to 1524.]

Jagarlamuḍi.

98-B. 611 *of* 1909.—(Telugu.) On a pillar set up in the grave-yard (now removed to the bund of the tank). A record of Mahāmaṇḍalēśvara Paṇḍiḍlapalli Kaṇṇaradēvarāju in Ś. 1195, Śrīmukha. Perhaps a gift of land to the temple of Sēturāmēśvara. Two of the faces are used for a modern epigraph. The other which is much damaged appears to be dated in Ś. 1686, Chitrabhānu, and mentions Guḍipāṭi Subbarāju-Nārāyaṇappamgāru. Kaṇṇara was evidently a feudatory of Queen Rudrammā (1257—1295).

Kommūru:

In his antiquities Mr. Sewell gives fourteen inscriptions in this place as inferred from Elliot collection, and feels diffident in regard to their accuracy. They are as follows.

99. (*a*) An undated grant by a private person in the reign of Pratāparudra.

(*b*) A private grant in Ś. 1041.

(*c*) Do.

(*d*) Do.

(*e*) A private grant in Ś. 1051.

(*f*) A record in Ś. 1438, in the reign of Kṛishṇadēva, regarding the erection of the Vīrabhadra temple by a private person.

(*g*) An undated private grant.

(*h*) Grant of some villages by "Rama Rāzu Nīlandīma Rājayyadēva Mahārāja" in Ś. 1470.

(*j*) A private grant in Ś. 1166.

(*k*) A damaged grant of Mahamaṇḍalēśvara Goṅka (II) in Ś. 1056.

(*l*) A private grant in Ś. 1056.

(*m*) An undated private grant.

(*n*) Another private grant in Ś. 1056.

The accuracy of these must be tested after a departmental survey of the place is made.

Koṇḍapāṭūru.

100. In a granite slab in the temple. Records in Ś. 1189 the building of the temple by a private person. (*Antiquities*, p. 83.) For traditional account of the place see *Loc. Rec.*, III, 506 and LX, 117 f.

*Mōṭupalle.**

This place is famous as the one visited by Marco Polo who describes in glowing terms the administration of Queen Rudrammā and the local trade in diamonds and fine cloths. See Yule II, 295, 272 and 357, *Antiquities*, I, 83. Inscriptions prove the greatness of the place.

101. 600 *of* 1909.—(Sanskrit in Telugu.) On a pillar of the maṇṭapa in front of the Vīrabhadrasvāmin temple. A record of the Kākatīya king Gaṇapatidēva-Mahārāja in Ś. 1166, Krōdhin. [The epigraph is of great value as it shows the extent of Kākatīya power in the Telugu land and as it refers to taxes on articles of export and import at the harbour of Mōṭṭuppalli *alias* Dēśyūyyak-koṇḍapaṭṭaṇa. The record is an *abhayaśāsana* to foreign traders whose vessels might be wrecked on the coast. While formerly the whole cargo of such ships became forfeited to the state, the edict

* See Brown's *Loc. Rec.*, Vol. 42, pp. 412—25, Vol. 48, pp. 151—61. I have added the details of date from these Manuscript records. A traditional account of the place is given in *Loc. Rec.*, Vol. V, 511 f. and LVI, 522 f.

now assured that nothing but the usual customs duties would be levied on it. See *Ep. Ind.*, XII, 188 ff., where Dr. Hultzsch edits the inscription. He draws attention to Marco Polo's reference to Mutfili and its trade.]

102. 601 *of* 1909.—(Tamil.) On another pillar of the same maṇṭapa. A record of the Reḍḍi king Annapōtta Reḍḍi in Ś. 1280, Viḷambi, Śravaṇa Śuddha 8, Tuesday. Refers to a concession given to the merchants on sea. [The edict in No. 101 is renewed by the Reḍḍi king a century later. See *Ep. Rep.*, 1910, p. 118, for details. Also Amarāvati inscription 258 of 1897. See also *Loc. Rec.*, Vol. 42, pp. 423—5.]

103. 602 *of* 1909.—(Sanskrit and Telugu.) On the same pillar. A record of the Reḍḍi king Annapōtta Reḍḍi in Ś. 1280 (A.D. 1358). Refers to a concession given to the merchants on sea. See No. 101. The charter was signed by the minister Sōmayamātya in the town of Mukūla (Mōṭupalli).

104. 603 *of* 1909.—(Tamil.) On the east wall of the same temple. A much damaged record in Ś. 1221, Vikāri. Records gifts by private persons of sheep or cows to the temple of Pāṭēśvaramuḍaiya-Nāyanār.

105. 604 *of* 1909.—(Telugu.) Round the base of the central shrine of the Kōdaṇḍarāmasvāmin temple in the same village. A record of the Kākatīya king Mahāmaṇḍalēśvara Pratāparudradēva Mahārāja (II) in Ś. 1244, Dundubhi. Records gift of a lamp to the temple of Gōpinātha consecrated in the year Durmati by the merchant Dharmarāma-śeṭṭi.

106. 605 *of* 1909.—(Telugu.) On a pillar lying in front of the same temple. Records in Ś. 1160, Viḷambi, gift of sheep for a lamp to the temple of Prasannakēśava at Mōṭṭupalli *alias* Dēśi-yuyyagoṇḍavaṭṭaṇa, by a native of Echchuvāka in Toṇḍamaṇḍa-lam. See No. 101 above.

107. 606 *of* 1909.—(Telugu.) On the same pillar. A record of Mahāmaṇḍalēśvara Siddayadēva Mahārāja in Ś. 1153, Khara, Jyēshṭhabahuḷa 30, solar eclipse. Records gift of the village Āḍūru to the temple of Gaṇapati Prasannakēśavadēva at Mōṭṭu-palli *alias* śrīmad-Vēlanagara for the merit of the Kākatīya king Gaṇapadēva Mahārāja. [See No. 101 above. Siddaya was evidently a co-vassal with Gaṅgayya Sāhiṇi. See *Loc. Rec.*, Vol. 42, p. 420.]

108. 607 *of* 1909.—(Telugu.) On the same pillar. A record of Mahāmaṇḍalēśvara Bāyya-Chōḍa-Mahārāja in Ś. 1164, Śubhakrit, Pushyaśuddha 3, Uttarāyaṇa, Saṅkrānti. Records gift of land, for the sake of his parents' merit, to Prasannakēśava Perumaḷ. *Ibid.*

109. 608 *of* 1909.—(Telugu.) On the same pillar. Records in Ś. 1188, Akshaya, Kārttikabahuḷa 13, Thursday, gift of cows for a lamp by a cowherd of Mōṭṭupalli, to the temple of Prasanna-Chennakēśavadēva. *Loc. Rec.*, Vol. 42, p. 421.

110. 609 *of* 1909.—(Telugu.) On the same pillar. Records in Ś. 1199, Īśvara, Bhādrapada-bahuḷa 11, Thursday, gift of cows for the merit of king Rudradēva-Mahārāja, i.e., Rudrāmbā who, as the *Pratāparudrīyam* says, was given a male title and elevated to the throne. *Ibid.*, p. 422.

111. 610 *of* 1909.—(Telugu.) On the same pillar. Records in Ś. 1215, Jaya, gift of money (30 māḍas) for a stone maṇṭapa in the temple of Prasannakēśava-Perumāḷ, by Sāniprēma Bommi Reḍḍi. The details of date as given in *Loc. Rec.*, are Akshaya, Chaittra-śuddha 1, Thursday. See *Loc. Rec.*, Vol. 42, p. 422.

111-A. In the same temple. A record of Dēvarāya Uḍaiyār, son of Harihara Rāya in Ś. 1312, Durmukhi, Māghaśuddha (I), Friday. Enumerates the taxes on imports at Muṭṭupalli to be paid to the king, e.g., 5½ Rūkas on 50 corals; 2 kāsus on sealed goods, etc. *Ibid.*, pp. 422–3.

Murukoṇḍa in Vinukoṇḍa Pargana.

(evidently Murukoṇḍapāḍu of this taluk).

111-B. A C.P. in the hands of the people. A record of Ś. 1322, Pramādhi, relating a gift by Dēvarāya to Mallānvaya of the Kauṇḍinya gōtra in the village of Maṇikoṇḍa in Pushya Paurṇami. *Mack. MSS.* Bk., XVIII (15—6—21), pp. 139—42.

Niḍubrōlu.

112. 163 *of* 1897.—(Sanskrit and Telugu.) On a pillar in front of the Chōḷēśvara temple. A record of the Chōḷa king Tribhuvana-chakravartin Vikrama Chōḍadēva (1118—35), in Ś. 1054, in his seventeenth year. Records gifts of land and lamps to the temple of Goṅkēśvara at Chērakumbaḷḷi or Ikshupaḷḷi by Mārāya Paṇḍa, the general and maternal uncle of Velanāṇṭi-Goṅka (II), son of Mallāmbika, and brother-in-law of king Chōḍa. [The inscription confirms Gt. 92 in showing that Vikrama Chōḷa deprived eventually Vikramāditya VI of the province of Veṅgi. See *Ep. Ind.*, VI, p. 281, where Kielhorn calculates the date to be 18th April, A.D. 1135. *Antiquities*, p. 80, and Brown's *Loc. Rec.*, Vol. XII, pp. 102–5.]

Parachūr.

113. C.P. No. 1 of 1906–7 and Nellore inscriptions of Messrs. Butterworth and Venugopal Chetti. A Sanskrit grant in Telugu character made by Rāmachandra, the son of Dēva Rāya (I) and Lord of Udayagiri of the Vijayanagara dynasty, in Ś. 1312 (A.D. 1390) to Chenna Bhaṭṭa, of the Bhāradvāja gōtra and Rig Vēda, who was a reputed Pauraṇic scholar. The village granted was 15 *maṇḍyas* in extent and lay on either side of the river Andala near Parachūr village in the kingdom of Addaṅki. The composer of the grant was Dēvarājamiśra, the court-poet of Rāmachandra. [This plate is the same as C.P. No. 94 in Mr. Sewell's list. The latter was unable to see the proper meaning of it as the verses were misplaced. The grant is important for its information about Rāmachandra and his relation to Dēva Rāya I.]

*Peddacherukūru.**

114. 239 *of* 1897.—(Sanskrit.) On the Garuḍastambha in the Trivikramasvāmin temple. A record of the Chāḷukya king Vishṇuvardhanamahāraja of Rājamahēndravara in Kali 4628. Records gift of many villages to the Trivikrama temple at Ikshupuri.

115. 240 *of* 1897.—(Telugu.) On a slab built into the prākāra of the same temple. A record in Ś. 1490, Vibhava, of the Vijayanagara king Sadāśivarāya. Records gift by the Mahāmaṇḍalēśvara Veṅkaṭarāja. An incomplete record.

116. 241 *of* 1897.—(Telugu.) On a slab in the Agastyēśvara temple. A record in Ś. 1145 of the Kākatīya king Gaṇapatidēva. Records gift of Tamalla *alias* Gaṇapavaram to a Brāhmaṇa.

117. 242 *of* 1897.—(Telugu.) On the same slab. Records in Ś. 1150, gift of Tamalla to the temple of Agastyēśvara.

118. 243 *of* 1897.—(Sanskrit.) On a slab in a street. Records gift of a village to the Bhīmēśvara temple at Ikshugrāma for the merit of Kākatīya Gaṇapati by Mallidēva-Chōḍa of Kaṇḍukūru in Pākanāṇḍu, of the family of Karikāla. See No. 101 above for another epigraph of Gaṇapati. [Was Mallidēva the same as the fourth of the name of the Pākanāḍu line ?]

119. 244 of 1897.—(Telugu.) On the same slab. Records in Ś. 1131, reconsecration of the Bhīmēśvara temple by Kōṭa-Kēṭamahārāja, and grant of land to it.

120. The Peddacherukūru forged plates of Vishṇuvardhana. See *Antiquities*, I, p. 84, where Mr. Sewell refers to this. The grant is " a recent forgery in Nāgari characters, though it professes to be an edict of a Chāḷukya king Vishṇuvardhana, grandson of another Vishṇuvardhana. The forger has been inconsiderate enough to date the inscription long before the time of the Nāgarī alphabet and of Indian inscriptions in general, viz., in the year 2625 of the

---

* Mr. Sewell mentions some epigraphs not noted by the department. Four of these are on the edge of a tank recording grants to the temple in Ś 1066. He also notes, besides the copper-plate grants of Vishṇuvardhana, two other plates dated Ś. 1221 and Ś. 1296, recording grants by Mallidēva and Vēmabhūmēśvara (of Koṇḍavīḍu). For a traditional history of the place see *Loc. Rec.*, *XIV*, 90 f.

Kali-yuga, which would correspond to 477 B.C. The object of the spurious grant is Ikshupuri, a Sanskrit translation of Cherukūru. See *Ep. Rep.*, Oct. 1890, p. 2.

Pērali * *(Peravali).*

121. *C.P. No.* 2 *of* 1915.—A C.P. grant (not dated) of the Eastern Chāḷukyan king Sarvalōkāśraya Vishṇuvardhana V (who ascended the throne in A.D. 843). Records the grant of the village of Reṇḍubaḷḷi in Guḍrahāra Vishaya to a certain Bhāvaśarman of the Kauśika gōtra and Taittirīya Śākhā.

122. *C.P. No.* 3 *of* 1915.—A record of the Eastern Chāḷukyan king Vishṇuvardhana III. Records in corrupt Sanskrit, the gift of the village of Māvindipaḷḷi in Veṅginā̄ṇḍu Vishaya to a certain Sōmayāji Bīraśarman of the Kauśika gōtra, a resident of Peravali.

Ponnūru.†

123. 158 *of* 1897.—(Sanskrit and Telugu.) On a slab fixed into the wall of a tank opposite the Bhāvanārāyaṇa temple. Records in Ś. 1338, Durmukhin, gift of land by Anavōtanāyaka for a garden to the temple of Bhāvanārāyaṇa or Gōshṭhīvananatha at Poranūru.

124. 159 *of* 1897.—(Telugu.) On the Garuḍastambha east of the same temple; east face. Records in Ś. 1315, Śrīmukha, gift of land to Bhāvanārāyaṇa of Poranūru. (*Antiquities*, p. 84.)

125. 160 *of* 1897.—(Sanskrit and Telugu.) On the Garuḍa-stambha, east of the same temple; west and south faces. Records in Ś. 1197, Yuvan, gift of land by Balañja-Goḍḷa Gōpāladāsa of Enumaḍala; other gifts of land by the Mahāmaṇḍalēśvara Parich-chhēda-Beṭarāja and others. (*Antiquities*, p. 84. See also Brown's *Loc. Rec.*, Vol. XII, pp. 94—6.)

---

* See *Loc. Rec.*, Vol. 48, pp. 7—14, for some local stone epigraphs. One of these dated in Ś. . . . (इमाद्रिवितारकम) records grant to Mādhavadēva by Gomma-māmba's son Chōḍa; (2) Another dated S. 1333 (भुवनेशगुणरामभूमि), Hēviḷambi, Māgha, Śuddha 13, Thursday, records that Kolani Rāsanna, son of Bhimaṇārya, established a garden and gave some land; (3) A record dated in Ś. 1443, Jaya, Pushyaśuddha 5, Tuesday, relating grant of land to Guruvappaṅgār, son of Chamuḍaiyangâr; (4) A grant of some land by Krishṇaḍēva Rāja to Tryambakarūpaiyangâr at Pēravali in Velanāṭi in Koṇḍavīḍu; (5) A record dated in S. 311 . . . (गुणचन्द्र धरणि), Vaisākha, Śuklapaksha, *Giriduhitatithi*, Monday, relating grant of a cow for lamp to God Gōpinātha, by Prōlabhūpa; and (6) A record dated in Ś. 1311, Jaya, Pushyaśuddha 8, Sunday, Makara, Saṅkrānti, relating gift of jewels to Gaṇapēśvara of Enumuḍala.

† Mr. Sewell mentions, in his *Antiquities* (p. 84) an epigraph not mentioned in the departmental list—namely a private grant in Ś. 1535 with the permission of "Guṇṭupalle Muthu Rāja." See also *Loc. Rec.*, Vol. 42, pp. 296—302, for epigraphs, dated A.D. 1231, 1577, etc. The former records a grant of land to the people of Ponnūru-Niḍupalapāḍu by Kēśavadēva Chōḍa Mahārāja. The other which is dated in Ś. 1500, Īśvara, Āshāḍha Śuddha 11, in the reign of Śrī Raṅga Rāya, records grant of land, by Śēshādri Nāyaḍu, of Koṇḍavīḍu, to God Raghunātha. This is followed by a grant of Tirumala Rāya.

126. 161 *of* 1897.—(Sanskrit and Telugu.) On the Garuḍastambha, east of the same temple; north face. Records in Ś. 1041, gift of villages by the Mahāmaṇḍalēśvara Kulōttuṅga-Chōḍayadēva of the Karikāla family in his second year. Noted in *Antiquities*, p. 84, and Brown's *Loc. Rec.*, Vol. XII, pp. 96—8.

127. 162 *of* 1897.—(Telugu.) On a slab in the Āḷvār shrine in the same temple. A record of the Vijayanagara king Sadāśivadēva in Ś. 1473, Virōdhikrit. Mentions the Mahāmaṇḍalēśvara Rāmarājayya, the son of Mūrtirāja and grandson of Rāmarāja. See *Loc. Rec.*, Vol. XII, pp. 98—100. See No. 133 below.

Santarāvūru.

128. In a local stone. A grant in Ś. 1350, by Kaṭhāri, Śāḷuva Teliṅgarāyadēva. *Antiquities*, p. 84.

129. A private grant in Ś. 1014. *Ibid.*

130. A grant in Ś. 1575. *Ibid.*

Sriraṅgarāyapuram.

130-A. In the western pillar of Gōpīnātha temple. A record of Ś. 1499, Īśvara, Kārttikaśuddha 10, in the reign of Śrīraṅgarāya; relating gift of land to Jātakarṇa Virūpāksha. *Loc. Rec.*, Vol. 48, pp. 64-5.

130-B. In the same temple. A record of Ś. 1494, Āṅgirasa, Vaiśākhaśuddha 12, relating gift of land to Gaṅgādhara Rāmēśvara for worship by Prince Śrīraṅga (II), son of Tirumaladēva of Apastamba sūtra and Yajus Śākhā. *Ibid.*

130-C. In the same temple. Grant of the village of Morampūḍi to the same by the same chief.

Vallūru.

131. On a pillar in the Gōpālasvāmi temple. A record of Ś. 1495, relating the erection of a maṇṭapam by a private person. *Ibid.* [In *Loc. Rec.*, Vol. XII, pp. 106--8, there are two epigraphs, dated A.D. 1774 and 1758.]

Vaṅgipuram. *

132. On the Garuḍastambha of the Vallabharāya temple. A record of Ś. 1487, in the reign of Sadāśivarāya. *Antiquities*, Vol. I, p. 84.

---

* See *Loc. Rec.*, Vol. 42, pp. 303—9 and Vol. 48, pp. 56—62, for epigraphs, dated A.D. 1464 and 1557. The former (in Táraṇa, Vaiśākhabahuḷa 6, Friday) records the building of the temple by Elliśeṭṭi, son of Aḍidam Malliśeṭṭi. The latter is of the same date as No. 133 above. A gift by the same chief to Ōbalaiyaṅgār of the Kāśyapa gōtra and Kātyāyana sūtra is also given.

133. On a pillar in the Agastyēśvara temple. A grant by Mūrti Rājayyadēva Chōḍamahārāja in Ś. 1478, Piṅgaḷa, Bhādrapada Śuddha 11, Thursday, in the reign of Sadāśivarāya, to Vīrayyadēva. *Antiquities,* p. 85 and *Loc. Rec.*, Vol. 48, p. 56. See No. 127.

GUNṬŪR TALUK.

*Gunṭūr.**

134. 139 *of* 1913.—(Telugu.) On a slab from Dharaṇikōṭa, preserved in the Collector's office. A mutilated record of the Kōṭa king Mahāmaṇḍalēśvara Gaṇapatidēvarāja in Ś. . . . Śrāvaṇa, *ba. di.* 6, Thursday. Seems to record a grant of land to the pūjāris and dancing women attached to some temple. (Date not calculable at present as neither the Śaka year nor the first regnal year is known.)

135. 140 *of* 1913.—(Telugu.) On a second slab preserved in the same office. A mutilated record in Ś. 1059, Piṅgaḷa, Chaitra. Records gift of sheep for a lamp to the god Buddhadēva, by a lady.

136. 141 *of* 1913.—(Telugu.) On the same slab. A record of the Velanāṇḍu king Kulōttuṅga-Chōḍa Goṅkarāja. This may be a grant made in continuation of the above inscription. States that a certain merchant of Penuṅgoṇḍa gave for the merit of his parents and of his elder brother, 55 sheep for a perpetual lamp to the temple of Buddhadēva.

137. 142 *of* 1913.—(Sanskrit and Telugu.) On a slab brought from Yenamaḍala and preserved in the same office. A damaged record of the Kōṭa king Bēta in Ś. 1173, Vaiśākha, *śu. di.* 8 *(Giri-duhitrā-tithi)*, Monday, corresponding, according to Mr. Swamikannu Pillai, to April 11, A.D. 1250. Records that the king ruling at Mahishāsuramarddhanagari (i.e., Yenamaḍala) founded the temple of Kṛishṇa in that village and granted the required land for its upkeep. Queen Gaṇapamādevi also gave land in the village of Garagapaḍa, an oil mill and a flower garden. The merchants of the village assigned some tolls. The marriage fees granted by Gaṇapamādēvi to the mahājanās of the village were also transferred by them to the temple of Gōpinātha (i.e., Kṛishṇa).

138. 211 *of* 1892.—(Telugu.) On a pillar in the Lakshmī-Narasimha temple. Records in Ś. 1407, expired, Viśvāvasu, private grant of cows to the temple of Mallikārjunadēva.

139. 212 *of* 1892.—(Telugu.) On a pillar in the Agastyēśvara temple. Records in Ś. 1310, expired, Vibhava, the erection of the pillar.

---

* Mr. Sewell notes in his *Antiquities* an epigraph, dated Ś. 1140, which is evidently not included in the above list. For a traditional account of the place and inscriptions in the district see *Loc. Rec.*, XIV, 171 ff. ; XLI, 471 ff. ; XLVII, 64—161 and LVII, 220 ff.

140. *C.P. No.* 5 *of* 1912.—(In ornate Sanskrit prose.) An unfinished copper plate grant which gives the Eastern Chāḷukyan genealogy as far as Vijayāditya III (Guṇaka). The real king and object of grant are missing.

141. *C.P. No.* 3 *of* 1914.—A Pallava C.P. grant of Vijaya Vishṇugōpavarman in Sanskrit (Telugu). Registers the grant of the village of Churā in Karmarāshṭra to a Brāhmaṇa (Chasmiśarman) while the king was encamped at Vijaya Palōtkaṭa. The king is called the son of Simhavarman, grandson of Mahārāja Vishṇugōpavarman, and great grandson of Skandavarman. The last three names are the last three names of the Maṅgaḷūr and the Pikīra grants of Simhavarman II. But on account of the facts that Vishṇugōpavarman is styled here a *Mahārāja* (and not *yuvarāja* as in other grants, and of the more modern character of the alphabet, Mr. Krishna Sastri is of opinion that the king was one of the missing line of kings between the line of Simhavaraman II and that of Simhavishṇu. See *Ep. Rep.*, 1914, p. 82.

Kaza.

In his *Antiquities* Mr. Sewell gives two epigraphs, dated Ś. 1066 and Ś. 1171, which, I believe, are mistakes for the first two inscriptions in the following list.

142. 253 *of* 1892.—(Telugu.) On the south face of a pillar in front of the Kōdaṇḍarāma temple. A record of Kulōttuṅga-Rājēndra-Chōḍa-Manma-Chōḍarāju in Ś. 1086. Records grant to the temple of Kēśava. [Mr. Sewell mistakes the king for Kulōttuṅga II.]

143. 254 *of* 1892.—(Telugu.) On the east and north faces of the same pillar. A record of the Kākatīya ruler Rudradēva (i.e., Rudrāmba), in Ś. 1191. Records grant by a Nāyaka. [Mr. Sewell mistakes Rudradēva for Pratāparudra I.]

144. 255 *of* 1892.—(Sanskrit.) On four faces of another pillar in the same temple. A record of the Vijayanagara king Kṛishṇarāya in Ś. 1443, expired, Vrisha. See *Ep. Ind.*, Vol. VI, p. 131. The major portion of the inscription is identical with Nos. 148 and 208 below.

145. 256 *of* 1892.—(Telugu.) On two faces of a pillar near the Agastyēśvara temple. A record of the Kākatīya sovereign Rudradēva (i.e., Rudrāmbā) in Ś. 1191. Records grant by a Nāyaka to the temple of Mallīśvara. See *Ind. Antq.*, Vol. XXI, p. 199.

Malkāpuram (Mārkāpuram).

146. In front of the Vīrēśvarasvāmi temple. An undated inscription of Kākatīya Rudradēva.

147. In the same temple. Records in Ś. 1204, a private grant to the temple. *Antiquities*, p. 75.

*Maṅgaḷagiri.**

For the natural cave and other antiquities, see Mr. Sewell's *Antiquities*, p. 75. He also refers to the first two epigraphs in the following list. I have traced them to the *Mack. MSS.* and given the references therein.

148. 257 *of* 1892.—(Sanskrit.) On four faces of a pillar near the steps leading to the temple on the hill. A record of Śāḷuva Timma, the minister of the Vijayanagara king Kṛishṇarāya in Ś. 1443, expired, Vrisha. See *Ep. Ind.*, VI, 108 f., where Dr. Luders edits it. The epigraph mentions the king's pillar of victory shining in Kaliṅgā. It gives the genealogy and achievements of Timma, the conquest of Koṇḍavīḍu on the 23rd June, A.D. 1515 and the appointment of Nādindla Appā, nephew of Śāḷuva Timma, as the governor under the former's control. A list of Nādinḍḷa's gifts to the shrines of Koṇḍavīḍu, etc., is then given. See *Loc. Rec.*, Vol. 48, pp. 108–119, and Kn. 230-D.

149. 258 *of* 1892.—(Telugu.) On four faces of a pillar in front of the Lakshmī-Narasimha temple. A record of the Vijayanagara king Sadāśivamahārāya in Ś. 1480, expired, Kāḷayukti. Records grant by Timmarājayya. [See *Mack. MSS.*, Bk. No. 18 (15–6–21), pp. 3—5, which gives the chronological details as Phālguna Śuddha 15, Sunday. A Vaishṇava grant.]

150. 259 *of* 1892.—(Telugu.) On three sides of an octagonal pillar in the bazaar street. A record in Ś. 1515, expired, Vijaya, Kārttika Śuddha 2. [See *Mack. MSS.*, Bk. 18 (15–6–21), pp. 5–6. Refers to the reign of Mahomed Quli of Golcondah, and his agent at Maṅgaḷagiri and Nizampatam and his assessment of tax on various communities. See also *Loc. Rec.*, Vol. 48, pp. 125—30, where Brown calculates the date (wrongly, I believe) to be A.D. 1668.

Nambūr.

151. 252 *of* 1892.—(Telugu.) On a pillar in the Mallēśvara temple. A fragment of record.

Niḍumukkala.

152. In a street of the village, on a slab. A record dated in Ś. 1431, in the reign of Kṛishṇadēvarāya. *Antiquities*, p. 75.

153. Near a tank to the south of the village, built by the Reḍḍis.

154. Near the Mukha maṇṭapam of the Sōmēśvarasvāmi temple east of the village. A record, dated Ś. 1571. *Ibid.*

---

* The other references to *Mack. MSS.*, besides those mentioned in the text are :— *Loc. Rec.*, Vol. 48, pp. 108—30 and Vol. 42, pp. 359—87.

*Pedda-kākāni.**

155-155-A. 249 *and* 250 *of* 1892.—(Telugu.) On a pillar in front of the Gōpāla temple. A record in Ś. 1184, expired, Dundubhi, Māgha Śuddha 10, Thursday. [Mr. Sewell gives in his *Antiquities*, p. 75, an inscription in Ś. 1192. This is given also in *Mack. MSS.*]

156. 251 *of* 1892.—(Sanskrit and Telugu.) On a pillar in front of the Vīrabhadra temple. A record of the Vijayanagara king Kṛishṇadēva in Ś. 1440, expired, Bahudhānya. Records the foundation of the temple by the minister Chitta of Reṇṭūru. [See *Antiquities*, p. 75, and *Loc. Rec.*, Vol. 57, p. 222. The details of the date are Śravaṇa Bahuḷa 5, Monday.]

Penumaka.

157. In the temple of Śiva. A record of Ś. 1710. *Antiquities*, p. 76.

Prattipāḍu.

158-A—F. At the Daṇḍēśvara temple:—A grant of lands in Ś. 1156; (*b*) a private grant of Ś. 1435, recording the erection of a maṇṭapam; (*c*) a private grant in Ś. 1144; (*d*) gift of a bell by a private party in Ś. 1560; (*e*) gift of a Chakra by a private party in Ś. 1450; (*f*) a private donation to the temple in Ś. 1476. For local accounts and epigraphs collected by Mackenzie, see *Loc. Rec.*, XIV, 65 f.; LVI, 291 f. and XV, 488 f.

Reḍḍipāḷem.

159. Near a tank on a slab. A record of Ś. 1172. *Antiquities.*

Śekūru.

The inscriptions of this place have been taken from *Mack. MSS.*, Bk. 18, p. 123 ff. and *Loc. Rec.*, Vol. 57, pp. 273–8.

160. Ten yards east of the village. Records gift of land to God Tiruvēṅkaṭēśvara in Ś. 1482, Raudri, Māgha Śukla 11, by Veṅgalappagāru in the time of Sadāśivarāya. Mentions Siddharāja Timmarāja.

161. A record of the same chief in the same date.

162. A record in Ś. 1180, Mēsha Saṅkrānti, recording gift of land to God Chōḷēśvara by Mallani Mallayya.

163. A record dated Ś. 1171, Makara Saṅkrānti. Gift of two *māḍas* to Bhōgēśvara by Bhīmarāju.

164. Grant of fields by Appa Kamma to God Sōmēśvara in Ś. 1187, Krōdhana, Makara Saṅkrānti.

165. A record of Ś. 1496, Māgha Śukla 11, Thursday, in the reign of Śrī-Raṅgarāya. Records gift to Tiruvēṅkaṭēśvara by

---

* See *Mack. MSS.*, Bk. 18, pp. 78—80; Brown's *Loc. Rec.*, Vol. 57, p. 222 ff.

Veṅkaṭayya, the son of Tirumalayyaṅgār, and grandson of Kollapaḷḷi Ōbalayyaṅgār of the Bhāradvāja gōtra for a festival.

166. A record dated in Ś. 1454, Nandana, Mārghaśira Śuddha 12, Thursday, in the reign of Achyutarāya. Gift of land to Tiruvēṅkaṭa by Śūrappanāyaḍu.

Vuṇḍavilli.

167. 46 *of* 1909.—In the rock-cut Anantaśayana temple. A grant by Māchama-Reḍḍi in Ś. 1265.

168. 47 *of* 1909.—In the temple of Bhāskarēśvarasvāmi, south of the village. A Telugu-Sanskrit record of Ś. 1448, relating the erection of the temple by some merchants.

169-A. 47-*A of* 1909.—On the same pillar. A record of Gajapati Vīrarudra Pratāpa in Ś. 1448, Pārthiva, mentioning the building of a temple at Maṅgaḷagiri.

169-B. In the same place. An undated epigraph evidencing the digging of a well in the reign of Kṛishṇadēvarāya. *(Antiquities.)*

Enamadala.

170 to 172. 115 *to* 117 *of* 1893.—(Telugu.) On a pillar in front of the Vīrabhadra temple. Records dated in Ś. 1163 to 1196. The epigraph of Ś. 1163 (Śārvari) records the *pratishṭha* of Rudrēśvara and gift of land for the merit of Kōṭa Bēṭa Rāja. See No. 180.

173. 118 *of* 1893.—(Telugu.) On a stone built into the eastern enclosure of the same temple. A record in Ś. 1191, expired, Śukla. See *Loc. Rec.*, Vol. 57, p. 257. It gives the details of date as Kārttikaśuddha, 5, Thursday.

174. 119 *of* 1893.—(Sanskrit, Telugu and Tamil.) On a stone built into the southern enclosure of the same temple. A record in Ś. 1453, Nandana. Mentions Mallayya Chinna-Bommu Nāyaka. [*Mack. MSS.*, Bk. XVIII, p. 104 and *Loc. Rec.*, Vol. 57, pp. 255–6. This says that Bommaya was a servant of Rāyasam Ayyappayya, Governor of Koṇḍavīḍu, and gives the details of date as Bhādrapadaśuddha 10, Monday.]

175 to 177. 120 *to* 122 *of* 1893.—(Telugu.) In the Vēṇugōpāla temple.* The first of these is said to be a record in Ś. 1190, Vibhava. The second continues the record of Gaṇapāmbā and describes her as the ruler of the 6,000 villages on the south bank of the Krishṇa. It is dated in Ś. 1172. The third records the grant of the village of Chintapalli for her father's merit.

178. 123 *of* 1893.—(Telugu.) On a pillar in front of the Rāmāsvāmin temple. A record dated in Ś. 1310, expired, Vibhava.

179. 124 *of* 1893.—(Telugu.) On a stone in the Āñjanēya temple. A record in Ś. 1217, Jaya. [The *Mack. MSS.* say that

---

* *Ep. Ind.*, Vol. III, pp. 95–96 and *Loc. Rec.*, Vols. XIV, XLII and XLVII.

the details of date are Pushyaśuddha 8, Sunday, and that the people gave various paraphernalia, etc., to the deity.]

180. 125 *of* 1893.—(Sanskrit and Telugu.) On a stone in the Vēṇugōpāla temple. A record of the daughter of the Kākatīya king Gaṇapati, named Gaṇapāmba who was married to Bēṭa, the son of Rudra and grandson of Kēṭa, a chief of Dhānyakapura (i.e., Amarāvati). The record says that after the death of her husband she performed a number of pious works, e.g., placing golden pinnacles on the shrine of Amarēśvara at Amarāvati, building two other Śiva temples, named Bēṭēśvara and Gaṇapēśvara in the same village. See *Kistna Manual*, p. 13 and *Ep. Ind.*, Vol. III, pp. 94—103. Dr. Hultzsch edits it here. He also refers to the other Telugu inscriptions on the pillar. See 175 to 177 above. The *Mack. MSS.* seem to attribute this to Ś. 1113, Vaiśākhaśukla, Monday, Giriduhitātithi.

181 to 183. An undated grant of 25 cows for a lamp to Bēṭēśvara; (2) Grant of a herd of sheep by a brother of Nārapa Rāja Mallayya to the same in Ś. 1192, Pramōda, *Pushya Śuddha* 13, Friday, Makara-Saṅkrānti; (3) A grant of twenty-five buffalo-cows by Bemma Nāyuḍu in Ś. 1196, *Bhava*, Aśvayuja, Śukla 1, Sunday; and (4) exemption of taxes on the temples and Brāhmaṇas in sixty villages connected with Yenumaṇḍalasthala (i.e., Enumaṇḍala). See *Ep. Ind.*, Vol. III, p. 96. Also *Loc. Rec.*, Vol. 57, p. 252 ff., where these are given.

NARASARAOPET TALUK.

*Boppuḍi.**

184. 205 *of* 1899.—(Sanskrit.) On three faces of a pillar set up in the street, near the Śiva temple. A damaged record of Nanni Chōḍa and his two younger brothers in Ś. 1079. Contains a long genealogy of the king. See No. 196.

185. 206 *of* 1899.—(Telugu.) On the fourth face of the same pillar. Records a gift of tolls to the temple of Chennakēśavadēva at Cherakūru by Dōchirāju-Gaṇapaya for the merit of the Kākatīya king Gaṇapati.

Challaguṇḍlā.

186. On a pillar in one of the temples of the village. A record in Ś. 1740 (A.D. 1818). *Antiquities*, p. 68.

Chēzarla.

With regard to the legend of the Kapōtēśvara temple and the chief antiquities of the place see Mr. Sewell's *Antiquities*, I, 68–69.

* See *Loc. Rec.*, Vol. I, p. 484 and Vol. 57, p. 194.

He also gives four definite epigraphs of which one is the same as No. 190 in the list and the others are given under Nos. 193—195.

187. 154 *of* 1899.—(Telugu.) On a pillar in the maṇṭapa in front of the Kapōtēśvara temple. A record in archaic characters; damaged at the beginning; mentions Vishamasiddhi (a surname of Vishṇuvardhana, the founder of the East Chāḷukyan dynasty).

188. 155 *of* 1899.—(Sanskrit.) On a slab set up in front of the central shrine in the same temple. A record in archaic characters; much worn; mentions the daughter of king Kaṇdara of the Ānanda gōtra.

189. 156 *of* 1899.—(Telugu.) On another slab in the same place. A record in Ś. 1169 mentions Cheñjērla and the god Kapōtēśvara who is surrounded by 4,444 liṅgas.

190. 157 *of* 1899.—(Telugu.) On a slab set up near the east wall of the same temple. Records in Ś. 1085, Svabhānu, gift of a lamp by Kēṭireḍḍi of the Manumakula.

191. 158 *of* 1899.—(Telugu.) On a slab close to the dvajastambha in the same temple. A damaged record in Ś. 1062, Raudri. Records the gift of a lamp.

192. 159 *of* 1899.—(Telugu.) On a slab near the Mādhavasvāmin shrine in the same temple. A record in Ś. 1087.

193. On a stone near the dvajastambha of Kapōtēśvara. A record of Ś. 1440. *Antiquities*, p. 68.

194. On a stone close to the Mādhavasvāmi temple. A private grant in Ś. 1551. *Ibid.*

195. In the same temple. Another grant in Ś. 1168. *Ibid.*

Degaramuḍi.

196. Inside the courtyard of the Mallikārjuna temple, on a Nāga stone. A grant in Ś. 1002 by "Sri Nanni Chōḍa Mahārāja," son of "Tribhuvana Mallidēva Chōḍa." [Nanni Chōḍa belonged to the Konidena branch of the Telugu Chōḍas and lived about Ś. 1070, 1073, etc.] *Antiquities*, p. 69. See No. 184 above.

Gōvindapuram.

Mr. Sewell notes two inscriptions in this place, one dated in Ś. 1092 and the other in Ś. 1082, recording a private grant. The first of these is probably the same as No. 197 in the list, but it is impossible to say whether the second is a mistake for the next epigraph or a different one.

197. 112 *of* 1893.—(Telugu.) On a stone in front of the Bhīmēśvara temple. A record of Kulōttuṅga-Rājēndra-Chōḍa in Ś. 1091. Was Rājēndra the Velanāṇṭi chief who ruled from 1163 to 1180?

198. 113 *of* 1893.—(Telugu.) On a stone in front of the Bhīmēśvara temple. A record of Kulōttuṅga-Rājēndra-Chōḍa in Ś. 1087. See the above epigraph.

199. 114 *of* 1893.—(Telugu.) On a stone in front of the Bhīmēśvara temple. Kulōttuṅga-Rājēndra-Chōḍa mentioned.

Ikkūṟṟu.

200. Close to the south-east wall of the temple on a stone. A private grant in Ś. 1038 in honour of Kulōttuṅga (I ?) Rājēndra Chōḷa.

201. In the same place. An epigraph of the same year relating grants to temple and Brahmans by the same sovereign.

202. In the Mallikārjuna temple. Records that in Ś. 1048, Āśvija, Suddha, Thursday, Mallināyaka gave a lamp for the merit of Mahāmaṇḍalēśvara Kulōttuṅga Rājēndra. *Mack. MSS.*, Bk. XVIII, p. 21.

Irlapāḍu.

203–204. 109 *and* 110 *of* 1893.—(Sanskrit and Telugu.) On a pillar in front of Sōmēśvara temple. A record in Ś. 1057, relating the building of the temple at Iṟṟalūru and the construction of a tank north of the village by Maṇḍalīka Maṇḍa who belonged to the Durjaya family. See *Ep. Ind.*, Vol. VI, p. 276, and Gt. 276.

205. 111 *of* 1893.—(Sanskrit and Telugu.) On a pillar in front of the Sōmēśvara temple. A record of Chōḍarāju in Ś. 1057. Records gift of land and of a lamp to the Sōmēśvara temple at Iṟṟalūru. [Chōḍa is said to have belonged to the Durjaya family and to be a bee at the divine lotus-feet of Kulōttuṅga Chōḍa dēva. Chōḍa's titles are enumerated. See *Ep. Ind.*, Vol. VI, p. 276.]

Jonnalagaḍḍa.

206. 545 *of* 1909.—(Telugu.) On a slab set up in front of the Vēṇugōpālasvāmin temple. A damaged record of the Kākatīya king Mahāmaṇḍalēśvara Pratāparudradēva-Mahārāja (1295—1323) in Ś. 1215, Nandana. Records gift of land to the temple of Gōpinātha at Jonnalagaḍḍa. The slab also bears a record, dated in S. 1241, Siddārthin, which appears to record a gift of land to the same temple. [For a local account see *Loc. Rec.*, Vol. 56, p. 419 f.]

Koṇḍakāvūru.

207. Near a figure of Hanūman west of the village. Records an act of worship done by Timmarasa, Pradhāni of Kṛishṇadēva Rāya in Ś. 1313 (wrong), Bahudhānya. *Antiquities*, p. 70. [This epigraph is in *Mack. MSS.*, Bk. 18, pp. 27–8, and curiously enough it gives the same wrong date.]

Koṇḍaviḍu.

The celebrated capital of the Reḍḍis who ruled from 1328 to 1427 (when they were overthrown by the Muhammadans. For the Mackenzie collections of the local inscriptions see *Loc. Rec.*, Vol. 23, pp. 281—441. See also Vols. 18, 49 and 57. I have not had time to examine these in detail and compare them with the departmental list.

208. 242 *of* 1892.—(Sanskrit and Telugu.) On a pillar. A record of Nādiṇḍla Gōpa, the governor of Koṇḍavīḍu, in the reign of the Vijayanagara king Kṛishṇarāya in Ś. 1442, expired, Vikrama. See *Ep. Ind.*, Vol. VI, pp. 230—39, where Dr. Luders edits it. The inscription has much in common with Nos. 144 and 148 above and grants, for the benefit of Sāḷuva Timma, ornaments, etc., to the Rāma temple at Koṇḍavīḍu. The inscription is of fiscal interest as it enumerates the taxes which were assigned to the temple for its expenses. These are said to be the *mūlavisas* in all parts of Koṇḍavīḍu country, where tolls were paid, viz., at *vasanta garuvas*, water-sheds, salt-beds, market-towns, roads to towns of pilgrimage, at the rate of half *padikamu* on every bag of certain articles, one *padikamu* on every bag of certain other articles, one *damma* on every bag of some goods, two *dammas*, three, four, six, etc., on still others. A double-bullock-load of women's garments had to pay a *chāvela*. Prof. Kielhorn calculates the date of the inscription to be Wednesday, the 2nd May, A.D. 1520. Gōpa was the brother of Nādeṇḍḷa Appā and author of the *Chandrikā*, a commentary on the *Prabōdhachandrōdaya*.

209—212. 243 *to* 246 *of* 1892.—(Telugu.) On four pillars in the mosque. A record in Ś. 1337, expired, Manmatha. Records private grants to the temple of Mailāradēva. [Mr. Se ll says that these were made in the reign of Kōmaṭi Veṅka Reḍḍi (1395—1423).]

213. 247 *of* 1892.—(Telugu.) Left of entrance to the north wall of a deserted temple in the front. A record of the Vijayanagara king Rāmarāju Tirumalarājayya, vassal of Sadāśivadēva in Ś. 1486, expired, Raktākshin.

214. 248 *of* 1892.—(Telugu.) Right of entrance to the same wall. A record of the Vijayanagara king Sadāśivadēva in Ś. 1468, expired, Parābhava.

215. The Koṇḍavīḍu plates of Rauta Rāya or Gaṇadēva, the son of Guhidēva and the grandson of Chandradēva, a descendant of Kapila Gajapati of Caṭaka (Cuttack) in Ś. 1377, Yuva (A.D. 1455), giving the village of Chāvali (Rēpalli taluk) to a number of Brahmans. Kapilēndra ruled, according to Hunter, from 1452—79. See *Ep. Rep.*, Oct. 1890, p. 2.

216. 537 *of* 1909.—(Uriya.) On a pillar of a ruined temple on the top of the hill. Two short Telugu inscriptions on other pillars in the same temple refer to the building of a maṇṭapa, and to the god Narasimhadēva and Lakshmīpati.

217. 538 *of* 1909.—(Sanskrit.) On a pillar of a ruined maṇṭapa called Varāhalakoṭṭu on the same hill. A mutilated record of the Reḍḍi king Peda-Kōmaṭi-Vēma in Ś. 1330. Records that the king's treasurer *(bhaṇḍari)* Dāmaṇa set up a pillar in the temple of Viśvapati, for the merit of his maternal uncle Raṇasāhi surnamed Ripurāyabandi-Chōḍa. [Pedda Kōmaṭi was the author of *Śriṅgāradipikā*, commentary on the *Amaruśataka*.]

218. 539 *of* 1909.—(Telugu.) On a beam of the same maṇṭapa. Records in Ś. 1327, Pārthiva, that a certain Damaḷapati Chennamanēniṁgāru presented the stone beam in the gōpura of the Viśvēśvara temple, for the merit of his spiritual teacher Śrīgiriayyaṁgāru who was the grandson of Paṇḍita Ārādhyadēva.

219. 540 *of* 1909.—(Telugu.) On another beam of the same maṇṭapa. A much damaged record in Ś. 1331, Sarvadhāri. Twelve other short Telugu epigraphs not dated, on pillars and beams of the same ruined maṇṭapa, record that these latter were presented to the temple of Viśvēśvara by certain merchants and Reḍḍis.

220. On a stone west of Vēmalamma temple. A record of Ś. 1447, in the reign of Kṛishṇadēva Rāya. *Ep. Rep.*, Oct. 1890, p. 2.

221. On a pillar of a maṇṭapam in the Rāmaliṅga temple. A record of Ś. 1588, relating to its erection. *Ibid.*

222. Near a blackstone 500 yards north of the village. A record of Ś. 1460. *Antiquities*, p. 70.

Koniḍena.

223. 163 *of* 1899.—(Telugu.) On a pillar built into the platform in front of the Saṁkarasvāmin temple, left of entrance, east face. Records in Ś. 1072, that a subordinate of Kulōttuṅga-Chōḍa-Goṅka (II, 1133—57) built the temple of Ballīśvara at Koṭyadōna.

224. 164 *of* 1899.—(Telugu.) On a pillar built into the platform in front of the Śaṁkarasvāmin temple, left of entrance, west face. A record of Kāma-Chōḍamahārāja (of the Konidena branch of the Telugu-Chōḷa line) in Ś. 1059. Records gift of land to the same temple.

225. 165 *of* 1899.—(Telugu.) On a pillar built into the platform in front of the Śaṁkarasvāmin temple, left of entrance, west face. Records in Ś. 1085, gift of land to the Kāmīśvara temple by Śrīyādēvi, queen of Kāma-Chōḍa. For Kāma-Chōḍa, see No. 224.

226. 166 *of* 1899.—(Telugu.) On a pillar built into the platform in front of the Saṁkarasvāmin temple, left of entrance, south face. A record of Tribhuvanamalladēva-Chōḍamahārāja, in Ś. 1069. Records gift of the village of Guṇḍiyapūṇḍi to the Ballīśvara temple. [Tribhuvanamalla was the son of Kāma-Chōḍa mentioned in the previous epigraph.]

227. 167 *of* 1899.—(Telugu.) On a pillar built into the platform in front of the Saṁkarasvāmin temple, left of entrance, south face. Records in Ś. 1085, gift of land to the same temple by

Śrīyādēvi, the daughter-in-law of Chōḍaballaya-Chōḍamahārāja, father of Kāma.

228. 168 *of* 1899.—(Telugu.) On another pillar in the same place, right of entrance, south face. A record of Tribhuvanamalla-dēva-Chōḍamahārāja in Ś. 1070, Vibhava. Records gift of land to the temple of Bhīmēśvara at Koṭyadōṇa for the merit of the king's father Pottapi-Kāma-Chōḍamahārāja and his mother Śrīyādēvi. See No. 225.

229. 169 *of* 1899.—(Telugu.) On another pillar in the same place, right of entrance, east face. Records in Ś. 1070, that the Bhīmēśvara temple was built by a servant of Tribhuvanamalla-dēva-Chōḍamahārāja. See No. 226 above.

230. 170 *of* 1899.—(Telugu.) On another pillar in the same place, right of entrance, east face. Records in Ś. 1070, gift of two lamps to the same temple.

231. 171 *of* 1899.—(Telugu.) On another pillar in the same place, right of entrance, north face. A record of Tribhuvana-malladēva-Chōḍamahārāja in Ś. 1073. Records the building of a tank. See No. 226.

232. 172 *of* 1899.—(Telugu.) On a pillar set up in the north prākāra of the same temple, east face. Mentions Hēmādridāna-chakravartin Annāreḍḍi and Śrīgirireḍḍi.

233. 173 *of* 1899.—(Telugu.) On a pillar set up in the north prākāra of the same temple, east face. Records in Ś. 1067, gift of a lamp to the temple of Saṁkara-Mahādēva.

234. 174 *of* 1899.—(Telugu.) On a pillar set up in the north prākāra of the same temple, east face. Records in Ś. 1143, gift of a lamp to the same temple for the merit of Gaṇapatidēvamahārāja.

235. 175 *of* 1899.—(Sanskrit.) On a pillar set up in the north prākāra of the same temple, north, west and south faces. The record gives an account of the ancestors of a certain Annā who was the minister of Nanni-Chōḍa (son of Tribhuvanamalla of No. 226).

236. 176 *of* 1899.—(Telugu.) On a pillar set up in the north prākāra of the Saṁkarasvāmin temple at Koniḍena, south face. Records in Ś. 1185, Rudhirōdgārin, gift of a lamp.

237. 177 *of* 1899.—(Telugu.) On another pillar in the same prākāra, east face. Records in Ś. 1170, gift of land by the Gajasāhaṇi Bhāskaradēva.

238. 178 *of* 1899.—(Telugu.) On another pillar in the same prākāra, west face. Records in Ś. 1184, gift of a lamp by relative of Bhāskaradēva, the Gajasāhaṇi of the Kākatīya king Gaṇapati-dēva.

239. 179 *of* 1899.—(Telugu.) On a third pillar set up in the same prākāra. A record of Tribhuvanamalladēva-Pottapi-Chōḍa-mahārāja in Ś. 1064, Dundubhi. Records gift of land to the temple of Saṁkara-Mahādēva ; mentions the king's father Pottapi-Kāma and mother Śrīyādēvi.

240. 180 *of* 1899.—(Telugu.) On a broken pillar lying in the east prākāra of the same temple. Records in Ś. 1080, Bahudhānya, gift of a lamp.

241. 181 *of* 1899.—(Telugu.) On a slab built into the south wall of the central shrine of the same temple. A damaged record in the twenty-eighth year and Ś. 1095 of Tribhuvanachakravartin Rājarājadēva. Records gift of a lamp for the merit of Kulōttuṅga Rājēndra-Chōḍa (apparently the Velanāṇṭi chief). For Rājarāja, see No. 1.

242. 182 *of* 1899.—(Telugu.) On a slab set up in the south-east corner of the prākāra of the same temple. Records in Ś. 1067, gift of a lamp.

243. 183 *of* 1899.—(Telugu.) On a pillar set up in the east prākāra of the same temple. A record of Opilisiddanadēva-Chōḍa-mahārāja (II) in Ś. 1156, Tāraṇa. The inscription contains a long genealogy of the Telugu-Chōḍas and records the gift of a village to the temple of Śaṁkarēśvara for the merit of king Gaṇapati (the Kākatīya to whom the Telugu-Chōḍas were evidently subordinate).

244. 184 *of* 1899.—(Telugu.) On a slab in the street near the Vishṇu temple at the same village. Records gift of land by Manumagaṇḍagōpāla to a certain Baṭṭu-Tikkaya. See No. 308 below.

245. 185 *of* 1899.—(Telugu.) On a stone near the ruined dvajastambha of the Kēśavasvāmin temple on the hill in the same village. A record in the fifteenth year and Ś. 1059 of the Chōḷa king Tribhuvanachakravartin Kulōttuṅga-Chōḍadēva. Records gift by Tribhuvanamalladēva-Chōḍamahārāja to the temple of Tribhuvanamalla-śrī-Kēśavadēva at Koṭyadōna.

246. 186 *of* 1899.—(Telugu.) On a stone near the ruined dvajastambha of the Kēśavasvāmin temple on the hill in the same village. Records in Ś. 1208, Vyaya, gift of a lamp to the god Chennakēśavadēva.

247. 187 *of* 1899.—(Telugu.) On another stone in the same place. Records in Ś. 1184, gift of a lamp to the temple of Prasanna-kēśava at Koṭyadōna by a relative of Bhāskara, the Gajasāhaṇi of the Kākatīya king Gaṇapati.

248. 188 *of* 1899.—(Telugu.) On the south wall of the same temple, first tier. A record in the eighth year (of ?) and S. 1075. Built in at the beginning. Mentions the temple of Kēśavadēva and refers to Śrīyāmahādēvi, the mother of Tribhuvanamalladēva-Chōḍamahārāja, and several other royal personages. See No. 227 above.

249. 189 *of* 1899.—(Telugu.) On the south wall of the Kēśava-svāmin temple on the hill at Koniḍena, first tier. A record in the fifteenth year of the Chōḷa king Tribhuvanachakravartin Kulōttuṅga-Chōḍadēva. Records a joint gift by Tribhuvanamalladēva-Chōḍamahārāja and Kulōttuṅga-Chōḍa-Goṅkarāja (Goṅka II, 1133—57).

250. 190 *of* 1899.—(Telugu.) On the south wall of the Kēśavasvāmin temple, first tier. Records in Ś. 1073 gift of a lamp by a Nāyaka.

251. 191 *of* 1899.—(Telugu.) On the south wall of the Kēśavasvāmin temple on the hill, second tier. A record of Tribhuvanamalladēva-Chōḍamahārāja in Ś. 1069. Mentions some fiscal terms.

252. 192 *of* 1899.—(Telugu.) On the south wall of the Kēśavasvāmin temple on the hill, second tier. A mutilated record in the fifteenth year of the Chōḷa king Kulōttuṅga-Chōḍadēva. Mentions the temple of Tribhuvanamalla-Kēśavadēva at Koṭyadōna in Kammanāṇḍu, the capital of Tribhuvanamalladēva-Chōḍamahārāja.

253. 193 *of* 1899.—(Telugu.) On the south wall of the Kēśavasvāmin temple on the hill, second tier. A record of Tribhuvanamalladēva-Pottapi-Chōḍamahārāja in Ś. 1069. Kammanāṇḍu is mentioned as the country ruled over by the king. Records a gift of money.

254. 194 *of* 1899.—(Telugu.) On the east wall of the same temple, first tier. A record of Chūraballirāja in Ś. 1073, Pramōda. Records gift of land. The king has a string of *birudas* similar to those of Bāṇa kings.

255. 195 *of* 1899.—(Telugu.) On the east wall of the same temple, first tier. Records in Ś. 1075, gift of a lamp.

256. 196 *of* 1899.—(Sanskrit and Telugu.) On the east wall of the same temple, second tier. A mutilated record. Records gift of a lamp by the minister Annā mentioned in No. 235 above.

257. 197 *of* 1899.—(Telugu.) On the east wall of the same temple, second tier. A damaged record. Mentions an officer of Tribhuvanamalladēva-Pottapi-Chōḍamahārāja. See No. 228 above.

258. 198 *of* 1899.—(Telugu.) On the north wall of the same temple, first tier. A record of Tribhuvanamalla (of the solar race) in Ś. 1072. Records gift of a lamp. The king is said to have been ruling over Kammanāṇḍu, Guṇḍikaṟṟu and Moṭṭavāḍi.

259. 199 *of* 1899.—(Telugu.) On the north wall of the same temple, first tier. A record of Nanni-Chōḍamahārāja in Ś. 1070. Records gift of land for the merit of the king's father Tribhuvanamalladēva-Chōḍamahārāja and mother Mābalamahādēvi.

260. 200 *of* 1899.—(Telugu.) On the north wall of the Kēśavasvāmin temple on the hill, second tier. Gift of land by Nanni-Chōḍamahārāja in Ś. 1073, Pramōda. [Was he the author of the recently discovered *Kumārasambhava ?*]

261. 201 *of* 1899.—(Telugu.) On the north wall of the Kēśavasvāmin temple on the hill, second tier. Records in Ś. 1079, Vibhava, gift of a lamp by the queen of Tribhuvanamalladēva-Chōḍamahārāja.

262. 202 *of* 1899.—(Telugu.) On the north wall of the Kēśavasvāmin temple on the hill, second tier. A record of Tribhuvanamalladēva-Chōḍamahārāja in Ś. 1069. Records gift of a lamp by Kētanapeggaḍa. Built in.

Kotapakoṇḍa.

263—269. 102 *to* 108 *of* 1893.—Trikōṭīśvara temple. A record in Telugu.

*Kuṅkalaguṇṭa.**

270. 151 *of* 1899.—(Telugu.) On a slab lying near the ruins of the Bhōgīśvara temple. A record in Ś. 1269, Sarvajit, of Koṇḍavīḍu Vēmayareḍḍi (1339—69). Records gift of land to the Vallabhēśvara temple at Krunkalakuṇṭa. [Is this the epigraph given by Mr. Sewell under date Ś. 1261 ?]

271. 152 *of* 1899.—(Telugu.) On a slab in the Vēṇugōpalasvāmin temple in the same village. A record in Ś. 1197 of Kēṭa-Rudrayarāja. Records gift of land to the temple of Mēṭṭu Viśvanātha by a servant of the king. [Is this the same as the epigraph given by Mr. Sewell in his *Antiquities*, p. 71, under date Ś. 1119 (A.D. 1197) ?]

272. 153 *of* 1899.—(Telugu.) On a slab set up in front of the Vīrabhadra temple at the same village. Records in Ś. 1243, Durmati, gift of land for the merit of the Kākatīya king Pratāparudradēva (1295—1323).

Liṅgamguṇṭa.

272-A.-B. A record relating the building of Sōmēśvara by Sōmana Preggaḍa in Ś. 1094, Uttarāyaṇa Saṅkrānti, gift of land by Maṇḍaṅa, son of Daṇḍanāyaka Sōmaṇa. *Loc. Rec.*, Vol. 48, pp. 165—67.

Maiḍavōlu.

273. A C.P. grant of Yuvarāja Śivaskandhavarman, the heir-apparent of a Pallava king (whose name is not given). It was issued from Conjeeveram and records the grant to two Brahmans of a village named Viripura which belonged to the Āndhrapatha or Telugu country. The order was issued by the king to his representative at Dhannakaḍa (i.e., Amarāvati). It is "in Prākrit dialect" and dated on the fifth tithi of the sixth fortnight of summer in the tenth year of the king (i.e., Śivaśkanda's predecessor). See *Ep.*

* For a traditional account of the place see *Loc. Rec.*, Vol. 56, p. 43 f.

Ind., Vol. VI, 84—89, where Dr. Hultzsch edits it. Dr. Hultzsch believes that as the prākrit of this epigraph is like that of the Hirahaḍagalli plates of Śivaskandavarman, the donor in both is the same. The date is of course prior to the seventh century and to the Simhavishṇu line. See also *Madr. Ep. Rep.*, 1900, pp. 4-5.

Murikipūḍi.

For a local account see *Loc. Rec.*, Vol. 60, p. 98 f.

274. 203 *of* 1899.—(Telugu.) On a slab in the Śiva temple. A record in Ś. 1082. Mentions a certain Mallanāyaka with a string of *birudas*, and records the gift of a tank.

275. 204 *of* 1899.—(Telugu.) On another slab in the same temple, A mutilated record of the Kākatīya king Pratāparudra-dēva in Ś. 1213. Mentions Manumagaṇḍagōpāladēva.

Nādenḍla.

276. 214 *of* 1892.—(Sanskrit.) On a pillar in the Mūlasthānēśvara temple. A record of Chōḍanripati in Ś. 1054, giving a lamp, ornaments, conch, bell, trumpet, etc., to the shrine. The donor was a descendant of Buddhavarman, an officer of Kubja Vishṇu and was the son of Buddhavarman, who was the son of Maṇḍa II, whose father and grandfather were Buddhavarman and Maṇḍa I. For the genealogy of the family see *Ep. Ind.*, VI, p. 274. See also Tsandavōlu (Kṛishṇa District and Gt. Nos. 203—5 above.

277. 215 *of* 1892.—(Telugu.) On the same pillar. A record of Chōḍarāju. The donor was Chōḍarāja, a vassal of Kulōttuṅga Chōḷa (II ?). Gift of lamp for the merit of Chōḍarāja's mother Bāda-madēvi. See *Ibid.*, p. 276.

278. 216 *of* 1892.—(Sanskrit and Telugu.) On the same pillar. A record of Velanāṇṭi-Goṅka (II), son of Rājēndra Chōḷa (Chōḍa ?), in Ś. 1060. Records gift by a certain Kanta.

279. 217 *of* 1892.—(Telugu.) On the same pillar. A gift of taxes at Noñchinapāḍu, for two lamps by Manma-Maṇḍaya in Ś. 1060. *Ep. Ind.*, Vol. VI, p. 275. [Manma-Maṇḍa or Maṇḍa II was the son of Buddhavarman II. See *Ibid.*, p. 274, for his place in the genealogy.]

280. 218 *of* 1892.—(Telugu.) On the same pillar. A record in Ś. 1061.

281. 219 *of* 1892.—(Telugu.) On the same pillar. A gift of land at Nādendla, to some Mahājanas by Chōḍarāju in Ś. 1054. *Ep. Ind.*, Vol. VI, p. 276.

282. 220 *of* 1892.—(Telugu.) On the same pillar. A record of Chōḍarāja.

283. 221 *of* 1892.—(Telugu.) On the same pillar. A record of Manma-Chōḍarāju.

284. 222 *of* 1892.—(Telugu.) On another pillar in the same temple. A record of Manma-Maṇḍa (Maṇḍa II ?) in Ś. 1061. The chief was the son of Maṇḍalīka, Buddha (II) and Gaḍiyamādēvi and he built the Śiva temple at Nādiṇḍla and gave it to the village Nonchedlapūṇḍi. For details see *Ep. Ind.*, Vol. VI, p. 275.

285. 223 *of* 1892.—(Sanskrit and Telugu.) On the same pillar. A record of Kulōttuṅga-Chōḍa-Goṅka (II), in Ś. 1063.

286. 224 *of* 1892.—(Telugu.) On the same pillar. A record of Velanāṇṭi-Kulōttuṅga-Chōḍa-Goṅka (II), in Ś. 1072.

287. 225 *of* 1892.—(Sanskrit and Telugu.) On the same pillar. A record of Goṅka (II), in Ś. 1062.

288. 226 *of* 1892.—(Sanskrit and Telugu.) On the same pillar. A record in Ś. 1073.

289. 227 *of* 1892.—(Telugu.) On the same pillar. A record of Manma Maṇḍa in Ś. 1052, recording gift of lamps and land to temple. The donor was a vassal of Kulōttuṅga-Chōḍa. The details of the date (Ś. 1052, Mēsha-Sitipañchami, Thursday) corresponded, according to Dr. Kielhorn, to 11th April, A.D. 1129. The genealogy of the family as shown by the inscription is given in *Ep. Ind.*, Vol. VI, p. 274.

290. 228 *of* 1892.—(Telugu.) On a third pillar of the same temple. A record of Buddharāju (son of Manma Maṇḍa of the above epigraph) in Ś. 1070. The donor was a vassal of Kulōttuṅga-Chōḍa (II), and made a gift of two lamps to the temple of Mūlasthānamahādēva at Nādenḍḷa. See *Ep. Ind.*, Vol. VI, p. 278.

291. 229 *of* 1892.—(Telugu.) On the same pillar. A record in Ś. 1192.

292. 230 *of* 1892.—(Sanskrit and Telugu.) On the same pillar. A record of Guṇḍāmbika, chief queen of Mahāmaṇḍalēśvara Buddha in Ś. 1093. The Buddha of this inscription was the son of Manma Maṇḍa (Maṇḍa II). The record is the gift of a land to the temple. *Ibid.*

293. 231 *of* 1892.—(Sanskrit and Telugu.) On the same pillar. A record of Velanāṇṭi-Kulōttuṅga-Chōḍa-Goṅka (II or III ?), son of Rājēndra-Chōḍa in Ś. 1065.

294. 232 *of* 1892.—(Sanskrit and Telugu.) On the same pillar. A record in Ś. 1068.

295. 233 *of* 1892.—(Sanskrit and Telugu.) On the same pillar. A record of Buddharāja (son of Maṇḍa II) in Ś. 1065. Records that his wife Guṇḍamādēvi gave to the temple of Mūlasthāna Mahādēva a tank constructed by her south of Nāḍendḷa. *Ibid.*, p. 277.

296. 234 *of* 1892.—(Telugu.) On a pillar in the deserted temple of Govardhanasvāmin. A record of Maṇḍarāju, son of Mallarāju (elder brother of Buddharāja of the above epigraph) in Ś. 1095. Records grant of lamp and land to the temple of Kēśavadēva. *Ep. Ind.*,Vol. VI, p. 277.

297. 235 *of* 1892.—(Telugu.) On the same pillar. A record of the Vijayanagara king Vīra-Śrīraṅgarāya (1578—86) in Ś. 1502, Pramādhin.

298. 236 *of* 1892.—(Telugu.) On the same pillar. A record in Ś. 1077.

299. 237 *of* 1892.—(Telugu.) On the same pillar. Gift of lamp by an officer of Maṇḍarāju in Ś. 1094. See No. 296 above and *Ep. Ind.*, Vol. VI, p. 277.

300. 238 *of* 1892.—(Telugu.) On the same pillar. A record in Ś. 1088.

301. 239 *of* 1892.—(Sanskrit.) On the same pillar. A fragment of record. Opens with the same genealogy as No. 233. *Ep. Ind.*, Vol. VI, p. 277.

302. 240 *of* 1892.—(Sanskrit.) On the same pillar. A record of Malla in Ś. 1061. See No. 296 above and *Ep. Ind.*, Vol. VI, p. 277.

303. 241 *of* 1892.—(Sanskrit and Telugu.) On the same pillar. A record of Mallarāju in Ś. 1069. The donor was an officer of Kulōttuṅga-Chōḍa. See No. 296 above and *Ep. Ind.*, Vol. VI, p. 277.

304. 350 *of* 1892.—(Telugu.) On a stone lying near the tank. A record of Timmarāja in Ś. 1481, Kāḷayukti.

305. 351 of 1892.—(Telugu and Kanarese.) On a stone built into a maṇṭapa of the Mūlasthānēśvara temple. A record in Chāḷukya Vikramavarsha 2 (for 52 ?), Plavaṅga. Mentions the Daṇḍanāyaka Anantapāla; see Dr. Fleet's Kanarese dynasties, p. 51.

306. 352 *of* 1892.—(Telugu.) On a second stone at the same place. A fragment of record.

307. In the Vēṇugōpāla temple. A record in Ś. 1215, Nandana, Māgha Bahuḷa 11, Thursday, relating gift of Pratāparudra during Vrishabha Saṅkrānti. *Mack. MSS.*, Bk. XVIII, p. 20.

Narasarāvupēṭa.

308. 213 *of* 1892.—(Sanskrit and Telugu.) On a pillar in front of the Paṭṭābhirāma temple. A fragment of record of Manma-Gaṇḍagōpāla, son of Nallasiddhi, Ś. 1219, Hēvilambin. The chief was the great-grandson of Tikka I and the contemporary of Pratāparudra II (1295—1323).

309. *C.P. No.* 3 *of* 1913-14.—A grant of king Vijaya Vishṇugōpavarman, son of Simhavarman, grandson of Vishṇugōpa mahārājavarman and great-grandson of Kandavarman while encamped at Vijaya Palōṭkaṭa, regarding a grant of land, to a certain Chasa(mi) śarman of the Kāśyapa gōtra who was a native of Kuṇḍūr. The grant is not dated, but from the reference to Vijaya Palōṭkaṭa the Government Epigraphist infers that it belonged to the period of Sanskrit charters. He says that the first three kings of the present grant may be the same as the last three of the Maṅgaḷūr or Pikire grants, in which case the last king of this grant should be considered to be the son of the last king of those grants; but from the difference in title which the Vishṇugōpavarman of this grant bears from that of his namesake in the other grants and from the comparatively modern nature of the character, the epigraphist concludes that the present grant should be attributed to a king named Vishṇugōpavarman in the intermediate group between the kings of the Sanskrit charters and the Simhavishṇu line.]

Rompicharla.

310. On a stone near the dvajastambha in the Śaṅkarēśvarasvāmi temple. A record of Ś. 1479. See *Ep. Ind.*, Vol. VI, p. 72, and *Mack. MSS.*, Bk. XVIII, p. 18. The lattergives the further details of date as Piṅgaḷa, Māgha, Bahuḷa 18, Monday, and says that Kumāra Koṇḍarāju gave to Kāryakartā Liṅgappa a grant of land during Mahā Śivarātri.

311. Near the above. Records in Ś. 1442, that Kumāra "Mikkili Nāyaḍu made a gift of two fields to God Śaṅkara." *Mack. MSS.*, Bk. XVIII, p. 18. For a local account of a traditional nature see Vol. LVI, p. 447 f.

Vipparla.

312. 147 *of* 1899.—(Telugu.) On a slab standing on the bund of the tank. A record in the eighth year of the Eastern Chāḷukya king Sakalalōkāśraya Jayaśiṁghavallabha (Jayasimha I). In archaic characters; mentions Viparta and records a gift of land.

313. 148 *of* 1899.—(Telugu.) On a slab near the ruined temple of Mallēśvara in the same village. A record in Ś. 995 which appears to mention Vishṇuvardhana-Vijayāditya (probably the uncle of Kulōttuṅga I and Viceroy of Veṅgi) and records the building of the temple by a merchant.

314. 149 *of* 1899.—(Telugu.) On another slab in the same place. A damaged record of Kīrtirāja-Mallidēva-Chōḍamahārāja in Ś. 1117. [Was he Malli IV of the Opilisiddhi line ?].

315. 150 *of* 1899.—(Telugu.) On a third slab in the same place. A record in Ś. 1186, Raktākshin. Mentions the Mahāmaṇḍalēśvara Allāḍapemmaya, who belonged to the family of a chief named Mukkanti Kāḍuveṭṭi, and records a grant of land.

*Yellamanda.**

316. In the Trikoṭīśvara temple, on the hill south of the village. A gift by Gundammādevi, the queen of Velanāṭi Goṅkarāja, of 55 sheep for a lamp. See *Mack. MSS.*, Bk. XVIII, p. 256.

317. At the southern entrance of the same temple. A gift in Ś. 1672, Akshaya, Kārttika Bahuḷa 13, Friday, recording a gift by Siddhamalla for the merit of his parents and for the increase of his family. *Ibid.*, pp. 26–7.

318. In the Rāmaliṅgasvāmi temple. A record dated in Ś. 1477, Rākshasa, Śravaṇa Śuddha 11, Thursday, during Sadāśiva's reign, recording a grant by Siddharāja Timmarājayyagāru. *Ibid.*, pp. 28–9, and *Antiquities*, p. 74.

319. In the same temple. A private grant in the reign of Vikrama-Chōḷa (1118—35) in Ś. 1053. *Antiquities*, p. 74.

320. In the same temple. A private grant of Ś. 1055. *Ibid.*

321. In the same temple. A record in Ś. 1053, of Nalla Nāgareḍḍi in the reign of Rājēndrachōḍa. *Ibid.*

322. In the same place. A private grant of Ś. 1155. *Ibid.*

Ongole Taluk.

Addaṅki.

323. From roof of Nānchāramma temple. (Telugu.) A record of a servant of one Bāṇa Siddhuru during the dark fortnight of Chaitra. O. 1, *N.I.*, p. 895 (i.e., Ongole 1 in *Nellore Inscriptions*).

324. From eastern wall of Rāmasvāmi temple. (Telugu.) Records that on the twelfth of the bright fortnight of Kārttika in Ś. 1326, Chinni Dontama Śeṭṭi plastered the wall of the temple for the religious merit of his father, of his mother Bāyyasāni and of himself. O. 2, *N.I.*, pp. 895–96.

325. In a backyard. (Telugu in Chāḷukyan character.) Records that in the first year after the coronation of a certain king, one Paṇḍuraṅgu Parama Māhēśvara granted land sowable with eight *puṭṭis* of seed in Dhammapuram (Dharmapuram) as charity to Āditya-Bhaṭāra. O. 4, *N.I.*, pp. 896–97.

Allūru.

326. Opposite Vīrabhadra temple. (Telugu.) Records that on Monday, the twelfth of the dark fortnight of Mārgaśira of the year Bahudhānya, Ś. 1500, the leading people of Pārvatīpuram and the residents of the fifty-six countries founded *mēras* as *Mūlavisam* in the village of Ayyapaḷḷi, the abode of the best of Brahmans, for providing worship to Śrī Vīrabhadra. *Ibid.* 4, pp. 897–98.

---

* I find the portion dealing with the epigraphs of this place missing in the *Mack. MSS.* (pp. 29—53). The latter part of the list is therefore taken from the *Antiquities*.

327. On stone in front of Aḍivi Rāmaliṅgasvāmi temple. (Telugu.) Records that Immānēni Kōṭiliṅgam, the son of Bāpayya, gave to Mallēśvara Svāmi for offerings and worship eight *kuchalas* of dry land and one *goṛṛu* of wet land, where three-fourths of a *puṭṭi* of seed could be sown. Besides this mānyam, the ryots, according to the deed of gift executed by them, should give at the rate of one anna for every *kuṇṭa* of land of high assessment and at four pies for every *kuṇṭa* of land of low assessment. It was the duty of the Karaṇams to collect and give this amount, to be utilized for the deity. O. 5, *N.I.*, pp. 898–99.

328. In Amarēśvara temple. (Telugu.) Records that on the occasion of Uttarāyaṇa Saṅkrānti, Ś. 1190, 240 guṇṭas of land were given for the religious merit of Śrīman Mahāmaṇḍalēśvara Kaḷārāyanāṇṭa Śiṅgadēva Mahārājulu, to Koṇḍavīḍu Kumārasvāmidēva for providing worship, enjoyment and *naivēdya*. *Ibid*. 6, p. 900.

329. On a big stone in the temple of Ishṭa-Kāmēśvara. (Telugu.) Records that on Wednesday, the tenth of the bright fortnight of Chaiṭra of the year Ānanda, Ś. 1236, on the day of Vishṇu Saṅkrānti, Rudranāyaka made a gift of land to Ishṭa-Kāmēśvaramahādēvara of Aralūru. The gift was made for the religious merit of Pratāparudra Mahārāja (1295—1323). *Ibid*. 7, pp. 901–2.

330. Inside the Ishṭa-Kāmēśvara temple. (Telugu.) Records that on Wednesday, the tenth of the dark fortnight of Śravaṇa, Piṅgaḷa, Ś. 1239, Gāla Muddana Bōyuṇḍu and Dāna Mādhava gave, in the presence of Pinnaya Veṅkaṅgāru, the Reḍḍis of Aralūru the Karaṇams and all other people, fifty *kuṇṭas* and one *kuncha* of ghee per month for a lamp, for the religious merit of Śrīman Mahāmaṇḍalēśvara Pratāpa Rudradēva Mahārājuluvāru (1295—1323). *Ibid*. 8, pp. 902–3.

331. On stone by the Ishṭa-Kāmēśvara temple. (Telugu.) Records that in the month of Āshāḍa of the year Raudri, Ś. 1242, Śrīman Bamma Nāyaniṅgāru gave (as vṛitti) 400 *kuṇṭās* of dry land to the deity Śrī Ishṭa Kamēśvara Mahādēva of Aralūr, etc., for the religious merit of Śrīman Mahāmaṇḍalēśvara Pratāpa Rudra dēva Mahārājulu. (1295—1323). *Ibid*. 9, pp. 903–4.

332. On the same stone by the temple of Ishṭa-Kāmēśvara-dēva. (Telugu.) Records that on the eleventh of the bright fortnight of Āshāḍha, Raudri, Ś. 1242, one Śrīmat Bammaya Nāyaḍu gave to Ishṭa-Kāmēśvaradēva of Aralūru 500 *kuṇṭas* of land, for the religious merit of Śrīman Mahāmaṇḍalēśvara Pratāpa Rudra dēva Mahārājulu. Records also a gift for a lamp. *Ibid*. 10, pp. 905—7.

333. On east side of enclosure of Ishṭa-Kāmēśvara temple. (Telugu.) Records a gift by Śrīmat Rudramma Nāyaniṅgāru, on

Sunday, the ninth of the bright fortnight of Āshaḍha of the year Ānanda. O. 11, *N.I.*, pp. 907-8.

Ammanabrōlu.

334. From eastern pillar of maṇṭapam of Chenna Kēśava temple. (Telugu.) Records that on the tenth of the dark fortnight of Jyēshṭa of the year Yuva, the Kāpus of Ammanabrōlu, the Karaṇams, and others issued an edict to the effect that additional lands under the tank were to be given by the Kāpus and that they should give *mēras* at three *tūms* on every *puṭṭi* of produce, to the Kēśava temple. *Ibid.* 12, pp. 908—911.

335. Opposite to Śiva temple. (Telugu.) Records the genealogy of a local chief Śīṅgarāya and his descendants down to the two brothers China Timma and Bhāskara Chāmunātha, "possessing the splendour of Rāma-Lakshmaṇa, praiseworthy like Rāma and Kṛishṇa, possessed of glory," who flourished as if "they were the sole fortresses to the garden which is the excellent town Koṇḍavīḍu." *Ibid.* 13, pp. 912—21.

Bollapalli.

336. On a boundary stone. (Telugu.) Records that the pillar was planted, after walking round the boundaries of the villages of Yasali, otherwise called Bollapaḷḷi, and Koṇḍa Muñjalūru. *Ibid.* 14, p. 921.

337. In front of Āñjanēya temple. (Telugu.) Records that on Thursday, the twelfth day of the dark fortnight of Āshāḍha Viśvāvasu, Ś. 1467, while Sadāśivadēva Mahārāya was seated on the diamond throne at Vijayanagar, he granted the village named Bollapaḷḷi in Addaṅki śīma, attached to Koṇḍavīḍu rājyam, as an agrahāra to Kōṭi Tiruvēṅgalanāthayya, the son of Srīmat Taḷapāka Tirumalayyagāru, "the establisher of the two schools of the Vēdānta." *Ibid.* 15, pp. 921-2. [The inscription begins with the salutation to Rāmānuja. The same scholar is referred to in No. 343].

338. Fallen stone opposite Agastyēśvara temple. (Telugu.) Records that on Saturday, the fullmoon day, under the Krittikā nakshatra in the month of Kārttika, Ś. 1193, Śrīmat Svayapa Nāyaka dedicated (this) to Agastyēśvara Mahādēva. *Ibid.* 16, p. 923.

Ballavarapāḍu (hamlet of Daivalarāvūru).

339. In front of Chenna Kēśava temple. (Telugu.) Records that in the reign of Kākatīya Gaṇapatidēva, in Ś. 1149, Śrīman Mahāmaṇḍalēśvara Mallidēva Chōḍa Mahārājulu, "who shines like a gem in the family of Karikāla, who built the dam across the Kaveri," gave Takkellapāḍu and old Dayyalarēvūru in Kammanāḍu to Brahmans. *Ibid.* 17, pp. 924-25. For Mallidēva see No. 228 above.

340. (Telugu.) Under the tank-bund to west of village. Records that in Ś. 1077, Vishama Saṅkrānti, the elders (mahājanas) of Dayyalarāvūru gave ten *puṭṭis* of land in the fields of the deity Rāmēśvara to Māḍāji-ayya, the sthānapati (temple servant) of the temple of Śiva, for providing worship, offering lighting, enjoyments and decorations for Rāmēśvaradēva. O. 18, *N.I.*, pp. 926–27.

341. (Telugu.) Under the tank bund. Records that on Vishṇu Saṅkrānti, Ś. 1075, in the reign of Śrīman Mahāmaṇḍalēśvara Tribhuvanadēva Chōḍa Mahārāja, the mahājanās of Dayyalarāvūru in Kammanāḍu presented some land to Ramēśvaradēva. *Ibid.* 19, pp. 928–29.

342. (Telugu.) Opposite Chintalamma temple. Records that all the elders (mahājanās) of the illustrious Dayyalarāvūru gave a field of one *puṭṭi* to Pattel Kētana for conducting the worship and offerings of the goddess. *Ibid.* 20, pp. 929–30.

Budavāda.

343. (Telugu.) In front of Gōpālasvāmi temple. Records that on Thursday, the twelfth of the bright fortnight of Āshāḍha of the year Viśvāvasu, Ś. 1467, while Sadāśivadēva Mahārāya was ruling at Vijayanagar, he granted the village of Mallāvaram situated in Addaṅki śīma, attached to Koṇḍavīḍu śīma, as an agrahāra to Tiruvēṅgalanātha, the son of Śrīmat Tāḷapāka Tirumalayaṅgāru, "the establisher of the path of the vēdas." *Ibid.* 21, pp. 930—32. See No. 337 above.

344. (Telugu.) From a fallen stone in an inam land. Records that the field was given as vritti to Śrī Paṅgalūri Bhīmēśvara. *Ibid.* 22, p. 932.

Chenḍalūru.

345. A copper plate grant discovered at this place (No. I of Appendix A in *Ep. Rep.*, 1906), is edited by Dr. Hultzsch in *Ep. Ind.*, Vol. VIII, pp. 233—36. It consists of four Sanskrit verses and a portion in prose. It is an edict issued from Conjeeveram in the second year of the Pallava king Kumāravishṇu (II), the son of Buddhavarman, the grandson of Kumāravishṇu (I) and great-grandson of Skandhavarman. It records that the king granted to a Brahman a field in the village of Chendalūru in Kavachakāra-bhōga, a subdivision of the district of Karmāṅkarāshṭra or Kammāṅkarāshṭra which is the same as the Karmarāshṭra of the Eastern Chālukyan grants. See *Ind. Antq.*, Vol. VII, p. 187 and Vol. XX, p. 105. A summary of the grant is also given in *Ep. Rep.*, 1906, p. 61, para. I. [It may be noted that at the time when Hultzsch wrote the village was in Nellore district, but now in Guṇṭūr. Dr. Hultzsch believes that on account of the close verbal resemblance between this grant and the Pikira, Mangalore and Uruvapalli grants and its archaic character when compared with the later Kūram and Kāśakuḍi plates, the four kings mentioned here must have ruled in the interval between Simhavarman (II) and Simhavishṇu line.

346. No. II in Appendix A of *Ep. Rep.*, 1906. This copper plate grant is by Mahārāja Vijayasiddhi Sarvalōkāśraya, son of Vishṇuvardhana (II), grandson of Indrabhaṭṭārakavarman (Simhavikrama), and great-grandson of Vishṇuvardhana (I), " who adorned the family of the Chāḷukyas." [In later inscriptions Vijayasiddhi has been named Maṅgiyuvarāja. The date of the grant—the lunar eclipse in Vaiśākha of the second year of the king—corresponds to 6th May, A.D. 673. The charter is to the effect that the king informed the villagers and the Naiyōgikas (officers) of Chendarūr that he granted the village to six Brāhmaṇas who were Chhāṇḍōgyas, i.e., students of the Sāmavēda, each of whom received two shares. The names of the donees are not given, but they are declared to be the *bizas* or residents of six other villages. See *Ep. Rep.*, Vol. VIII, pp. 236—41.]

347. (Telugu.) On a stone against a wall of Chennakēśava temple. Records that on Thursday, the eleventh of the bright fortnight of Kārttika of the year Vijaya, Ś. 1456, while Achyutadēva Mahārāja was seated on the diamond throne at Vijayanagar, Mallaraśayyavāru, the son of Chennekaṇṭi Viśvanāthayya, of the Srīvatsa gōtra, of the Apastambha sūtra and of the Yajus śākha performed the marriage of Kēśavanātha of Chandalūru village in Koṇḍavīḍu-durgam. Records that the prime minister (mahāpradhāni) Bācharaśayyavāru, to whom the village had been given, now gave some lands in it to Kāśivīrabhakta, who performed the above ceremonies, and to certain dancing girls of the Tiruvīdhi (sacred street) who did service to the deity. O. 23, *N.I.*, pp. 933—35.

348. (Telugu.) From "garbha wall" of Chennakēśava temple. Records gift of lands for providing worship and enjoyments to the deity, e.g., 400 *kuṇṭas* (measured with a pole of 12 *bārlu* (fathoms); 600 *kuṇṭas* to the *Tirupaṇi dāsi*, etc. *Ibid.* 24, pp. 935-36.

349. (Telugu.) From "wall of *garbha*" of Chennakēśava temple. A record of Śrī Śayaṇamdēvarulu, the lord of the town of Anumakoṇḍa. *Ibid.* 25, pp. 936-37.

350. (Telugu.) In front of Chennakēśava temple. Records the devotion of a Pēraḍlāla Jīyyamgāru to the deity, on Thursday, the fifteenth of the bright fortnight of Kārttika of the year Vikrit. *Ibid.* 26, pp. 937-38.

351. (Telugu.) From two sides of the stone before Rāmaliṅgēśvara temple from which the next inscription is taken. Records that, on the seventh day of *Vaiśākha*, Ś. 1175, Māyidēva Peggaḍa, the beloved of Vidēya (learning), the prime minister *(mahāpradāni)* and the principal authority *(sarvādhikāri)*, presented a *vritti* to Chenamallināthadēva of Chandalūru for the prosperity of Addaṅki Śiṅgaḷadēva who was his liege lord and of himself. Of this *vritti*, Māyidēva Preggaḍa presented 50 *kuṇṭas* to the same deity and 50 for one Brahmayya. O. 27, *N.I.*, pp. 938—40.

352. (Telugu.) From two sides of a stone opposite Rāmaliṅga temple. Records that on Sunday, the seventh of the bright fortnight of Vaiśākha, Ś. 1175, while Śrīman Mahāmaṇḍalēśvara Kākatīya Gaṇapatidēva Mahārāzulu was ruling the earth, his feudatory Śrī Maṇḍalēśvara Chakra Nārāyaṇa Śrī Śiṅgadēva Mahārājulu made a gift of lands for the priest, for decorations and enjoyments to the deity. *Ibid.* 28, pp. 940—44.

Chandrapāḍu.

353. In front of the Śiva temple. (Telugu.) Records that on Tuesday, the fifteenth of the dark half of Mārgaśira of the year *Vyaya*, Ś. 1089, on account of a solar eclipse, Koṇḍapa Nāyakuṇḍu, owner of Chandrūru on the bank of the Guṇḍi river, who was the son of Erramanāyaka, gave 55 she-goats to Śrī Nāgēśvaramahādēva of Chandrūru for a perpetual light. Rabbena Śeṭṭi, son of Naṅgarēku Naḍvi Śeṭṭi, should receive these and maintain the grant. He, his sons and grandsons should give for the lamp every day one *mānika* of ghee. *Ibid.* 28-A, pp. 944--46.

Cheḍalavāḍa.

354. In the Kalyāṇamaṇṭapam. (Telugu.) Records on Thursday, the eleventh of the bright fortnight of Āshāḍha of the year Krōdhana, Ś. 1488, while Mahārājādhirāja Śrī Vīra Pratāpa Sadāśivadēva Mahārāyalu was ruling the kingdom, in the kingdom of Koṇḍavīḍu which he granted to Srīman Mahāmaṇḍalēśvara Rāma Rājayyan Tirumala Rājayya Dēva Mahārajulugāru, Raṅgapa Rājayyadēva, the great-grandson of Siddhirājuṅgāru, the grandson of Vōbaḷarājuṅgāru, and the son of Timmarāju, presented on the holy occasion of the first *ēkādaśi* (eleventh day of the lunar fortnight) some gold to Śrī Raghunāyakulu of Chaḍaluvāḍa, besides the income derived from the Addagaḍa *śuṅkam,* from the *kaṭṇalu* (presents) in Chaḍalavāda, Mallāvaram, Alavalapāḍu and other villages, the *śuṅkam* from the *bharitas* (residents?) of the *sthala,* taxes like the *mulaviśālubaḍi*, etc. *Ibid.* 29, pp. 946—50.

355. 211 *of* 1894.—(Telugu.) In front of Śrī Raghunātha temple. Records that an agrahāra formerly granted, through Prauḍha Dēva Rāya Mahārāya, by Paṇṭa Maila Reḍḍi, to God Raghunātha of Chaḍaluvāḍa was, on the eleventh day of the bright fortnight of Māgha of the year Śubhakrit, Ś. 1404, revived by Timmareḍḍi, the son of Hindurāvu Suradhāni Sariyapati Timmareḍḍi. *Ibid.* 30, pp. 950–51. [Paṇṭa Maila was probably the chief referred to by Śrīnātha in one of his *chāṭu* verses.]

356. 212 *of* 1894.—(Telugu.) In front of Raghunāyaka temple. Records that an inscribed pillar was planted, for the religious merit of Siddhirāju Timmarājayya, the ruler of Koṇḍavīdu, by Maṇḍapaṭi Appaḷa Rāju, on the fifteenth of the bright fortnight of *phalguna* of the year Kāḷayukti, Ś. 1481, in the reign of Sadāśiva Rāya of Vijayanagar. The inscription records that the taxes levied on articles sold in Chaḍalavāḍa village, the *sthala* of the God, and on grain, the *aḍagaḍa śuṅkam*, the *mula-viśālu* collected in Addaṅki and Ammaṇabrōlu śīmas, and the *śuṅkam* and the old *kaṭṇam* collected in Śrī Raghunāyaka's *sthala* were given away to the deity. The temple authorities were therefore to collect them and give receipts to the merchants and other payers in the two *śimās*. Further remissions of the taxes on purchase and sale during festivals are recorded. O. 31, *N.I.*, pp. 952—55.

357. (Telugu.) Opposite Raghunāyaka temple. Records that on Thursday, the seventh of the dark fortnight of Jyēshṭa of the year Śrīmukha, Ś. 1565, while Śrī Raṅgadēva Mahārāya (1638—46) was ruling, a certain Polayareḍḍi of Cheḍaluvāḍa village in Ammaṇabrōlu śīma gave lands for the religious merit of his ancestor and his mothers Kṛishṇamma, Gaṅgamma and Śiṅgamma, at the junction of Chaḍaluvāḍa, Chiravana and Uppalapāḍu, for providing all enjoyments to Śrī Raghunāyaka of Cheḍalavāḍa. *Ibid.* 32, pp. 956—58.

Chezerla.

358. To south of the Chennakēśava temple. (Telugu.) Records that on the tenth of the bright fortnight of Āshāḍha of the year Paridhāvi, some land under the tank was granted by Rāmanāyaniṅgāru, for the daily offerings, lights and enjoyments to the deity. Records also the gift of the grazing fee levied on this field. *Ibid.* 33, pp. 959-60.

359. To north of Chennakēśava temple. (Telugu.) Records that in Ś. 1570, on the occasion of Uttarāyaṇa Śaṅkrānti, Śrīman Sōmarāju, the prime minister, gave 200 *kuṇṭas* of land to Mūlasthānadēva, for the religious merit of his master Chakra Nārāyaṇa Śiṅgaḷadēva Mahārāja. *Ibid.* 34, pp. 961-62.

Dēnuvakoṇḍa.

360. Opposite Vēṇugōpālasvāmi temple. (Telugu.) Records that on Thursday, the eleventh of the bright fortnight of Āshāḍha of the year Bahudhānya, Ś. 1260, a piece of land was granted to Dhēnuvakoṇḍa Gōpālakṛishṇa by Poddilapaḷḷi Śiṅgamanāyanimgāru, for providing offerings. *Ibid.* 35, pp. 962-63.

Dharmavaram.

361. In the threshold of the Sītārāmasvāmi temple. (Telugu.) Records that "the famous Epiran (or Pirān), commander of the elephants, with the permission of the emperor Ekalāśakhān founded that Punnuru." O. 36, *N.I.*, pp. 963–64. [Ekalāśakhān has been surmised to be a Golkoṇḍa prince.]

362. Stone in enclosure of Sītārāmasvāmi temple. (Telugu.) Seems to record that on Thursday, the twelfth of the bright fortnight of Aśvija of the year Pramōdūta, when the cavalry of the *Hivala* (area subordinate to a havaldar?) and the infantry were come, the people of the suburbs Yēkalāśapuram and Bālupuram gave, for the religious merit of Khan Ajyam Khaja Abul Saheb (a local officer?), certain contributions to the temple. These were 1 *dhā* (?) on every bag of vegetables and grain; 2 *dhā* on every *ratam* (spinning wheel); 1 *vam* on *śella* (muslin); and 1 *va* (?) on sundries. *Ibid.* 37, pp. 964–65.

363. On a rock in Urubōḍu hill. (Telugu.) Records that the pond was constructed by Nāparāvutu, son of Kōṭivusarāvutu. *Ibid.*, 38, p. 965.

364. East of village in Survey No. 381. (Telugu.) The first part is unintelligible. An incomplete record of the reign of Vijayāditya III, Guṇatēnamalla. Refers to Pāṇḍuraṅgapura and the burning of Kiraṇapura. *Ibid.* 39, pp. 966–67.

365. South wall of Mallikārjuna temple. (Telugu.) Records that Preggaḍa Pāṇḍuraṅga, the minister of a Māya Bajevarāju (Vijayarāju) who is said to have been a great statesman, well versed in the politics of all the neighbouring kingdoms, and to have constructed the niches for lamps, the *prākāra*, the enclosure wall, the portico, etc., gave certain gifts (to the temple?) in the village of Pāṇḍuraṅgapuram on the fullmoon day of *Pushya* of *Prabhava*. *Ibid.* 40, pp. 967–8.

Doḍḍavaram.

366. By a path to the east. (Telugu.) Records that on Thursday, the thirtieth of the dark fortnight of Kārttika of the year *Sarvadhāri*, Ś. 1350, on the holy occasion of solar eclipse, a certain Pāṅgula Chumpiri presented to Mallikārjunadēva of Vrudoḍḍaram (Doḍḍāvaram village) in Ammanabrōlu śīma, some *tūms* of land. *Ibid.* 44, p. 969.

367. To the east in a tope, from three sides of a stone. (Telugu.) Records a gift on Monday, the third of the bright fortnight of Bhādrapada of the year Sarvadhāri, by Poṅgula Mitinēnigāru to Vināyaka of Doḍḍāvaram. *Ibid.* 42, pp. 970–1.

368. To the east in a field. (Telugu.) A fragmentary record relating gift to a deity for offerings. *Ibid.* 43, p. 971.

Gonasapūḍi.

369. From dvajastambham of Vishṇu temple. (Telugu.) An unintelligible record. *Ibid.* 44, p. 972.

370. To the west of Kāśiviśvēśvara temple. (Telugu.) Records that on Wednesday, the eleventh of the bright fortnight of Kārttika of the year Bahudhānya, Ś. 1140, Śrīmat Sūryagiri Daṇḍanāyaka Chandra set up the image of Śrī Chandēśvara Mahādēva, naming it after himself, in Mānōpalli otherwise called Baṭṭirrappaṭṭam, which is said to have been on the coast of the eastern sea in Kammanāḍu, for the religious merit of Śrīmat Gaṇapatidēva Mahārāja (Kākatīya king, 1215—48). He also constructed a temple and a maṇṭapa. O. 45, *N.I.*, pp. 972-3.

Gōnuguṇṭa.

371. In front of Vīrabhadrasvāmi temple. (Telugu.) Records that on Tuesday, the eleventh of the bright half of Kārttika of the year Pramōdūta, Ś. 1433, while Śrīman Mahāmaṇḍalēśvara Rājādhirāja Rājaparamēśvara Rāja Tējōnidhi (Treasury of splendour) Srī Kṛishṇadēva Mahārāyulu was ruling the kingdom, Sūrnāyan, Abbānāyanivāru gave Goṇuguṇṭa in Kācharlakōṭa-Kaṭaka in Ami maṇabrōlu Śīma in Koṇḍavīḍu Rājya, for the religious merit of Timmarasuvāru (who was his immediate suzerain at Koṇḍavīḍu) for providing *amritapaḍi* to Amarēśvara of Gōnuguṇṭa. *Ibid.* 46, pp. 974-6. Timmarasu was evidently the celebrated minister.

Guḍimallapāḍu (or Vankāyapāḍu and Guṇḍimalla).

372. *C.P.* 22 *of Nel. Ins.*—A charter of Vira Śrī Gajapati Kākatīya Rudra Veṅkaṭarāya Śrī Pratāparudra dēva Mahārājaluṅgāru, ruler of Kalubarga, capital of the Karnāṭaka yielding a revenue of nine crores, on Monday, the thirtieth of the dark fortnight of Makara, in the ninteenth year of his reign on the holy occasion of *Ardhōdaya* in the *kaṭaka* of Velupukoṇḍa, recording the gift of two villages (Vankāyapāḍu in the Daṇḍampāḍu subdivision of Addaṅki and Guṇḍimalli in Ammanabrōlu) free of taxes to Kākolli Timma Paṇḍit.

Guṇḍlapalli.

373. Near Polameramma temple. (Telugu.) Records that on Sunday, the fifteenth of the bright fortnight of Kārttika of the year Pramādi, Ś. 1441, on the holy occasion of a solar eclipse, one Jīyarāju, gave 200 *kuṇṭas* of dry land on the boundary line of Koṭṭakōṭa and Nattipāḍu as a *sarvamānya* for the Gōpāla tank. *Ibid* 47, pp. 976-7.

374. Opposite Śiva temple. (Telugu.) A record of Tribhuvanāṅkuśa (the Chāḷukyan king Vijayāditya III). *Ibid.* 48, pp. 977-8.

Iḍamuḍi.

375. Inside shrine of Śiva temple. (Telugu.) Records that on Sunday, the second of the bright fortnight of Śravaṇa of the year

Viḷambi., Ś. 1221, Kāma Boppaniṅgāru, the minister of Kākatīya Pratāpa Rudradēva presented (lands ?) to Kandamūḍi Rāmajōsyalu for the religious merit of his father (Dēvaya) and his mother (Punnavalakshmi). O. 49, *N.I.*, pp. 978–9.

Ponguḷūru (Janakāpuram).

376. Stone in enclosure of Bhīmēśvara temple. (Telugu.) Records that in the year *Bhava*, Ś. 1076, on the occasion of a solar eclipse, Śrīman Mahāsāmanta (Provincial chief) Viyavelaru gave ten *maṭṭas* of land in the village Paṅgalūru, situated in Kammanāḍu, for providing oblation, sacrifice and worship to the great deity Tiruvēṅgala. *Ibid.* 50, pp. 979–80.

377. In the enclosure of Bhīmēśvara temple. (Telugu.) Records that in the tenth year of Rājarājadēva, on Sunday, the first of the dark fortnight of *Āśvija* of the year *Yuva*, Ś. 1077, Mahāsāmanta Jīyyaru, the servant of the divine feet of Śrīmad Rājarājadēva, gave on Vēṭiparva day (from the fields of *Guḍimaṇiyam*) one *Kuchela* of land to Mūlasthāna Bhīmēśvaradēva of Paṅgulūru. Setajiyya, son of Vīrajiyya, the temple servant of the Mūlasthāna (chief deity), should perform daily offerings and worship with lights. *Ibid.* 51, pp. 980–1.

378. On a stone to the east of Bhīmēśvara temple. (Telugu.) Records that on Monday, the fourteenth of the dark fortnight of Māgha of the year Āṅgirasa, Ś. 1554, some land was granted by Mudupaḷi Tirumalayya, the agent of Śrī Veligōṭi Komāra Timmanāyanivāru, to the God Bhīmēśvara of Paṅguḷūru. *Ibid.* 42, pp. 982–3.

Kandlaguṇṭa.

379. From four sides of a stone opposite Gōkarṇēśvara temple. (Telugu.) Records that on Monday, the first of the bright fortnight of *Chaitra* of the year *Vijaya*, Ś. 1215, while Śrīman Mahāmaṇḍalēśvara Kākatīya Pratāpa Rudradēva Mahārāja was ruling, *mānyams* were given by one Bahata Dēvarāja to Brahmans, etc., besides a village to Bhīmēśvara whose image was set up at Ravinūtula. *Ibid.* 53, pp. 983–6.

Kanuparti.

This village gave its name to Poet Abbāmātya, the author of *Purūravacharitra*.

380. On a small stone by the Vishṇu temple. (Telugu and Sanskrit.) Records that on Friday, the day of Śatabhisha, the first day of Kārttika in the year Bhava (or Parābhava), Ś. 12 ... Kāmaya Bōyāṇḍu of Alinanāṇḍu gave to Malamanḍala (Alamandala) Perumāḷ of Mōṭṭupaḷḷi 200 *māḍas* of wet land in Chaḍalavāḍa *sthala* under the Kāmasamudram tank at Kanuparti, for providing worship, *amritapaḍi*, vessels and the singing of *tirupadiyam*. *Ibid.* 54, pp. 987–8.

381. From stone removed from above the gate of the Vishṇu temple. (Sanskrit verse in Telugu character.) Records that in Ś. 1348, on the eleventh tithi of the bright fortnight of Māgha in the year *Parābhava* in the holy city called Kōśāmbika, which was situated at the junction of Brahmakuṇḍi (Guṇḍḷakamma) with the sea, and which was the abode of 1,000 liṅgas, king Vīra Amala (Abala), son of king Nuṅka, gave lands and wealth consisting of the eight species of property and the eight species of enjoyment to some Brahmans. O. 55, *N.I.*, pp. 988—90. [Kōśāmbika or city of gold is Kānuparti. The ancient grandeur of the place is seen even now in the existence of a large number of carved stones and liṅgams.]

382. From the stone by the Vishṇu temple referred to in the preceding inscription. (Sanskrit in Telugu character and Telugu.) Records that on Thursday, the eleventh of the bright fortnight of Māgha in the year Parābhava, Ś. 1348, Vīra Avu Bhudēva Chōḍa Mahāraja, the son of Ālamaṇḍala Nūkayadēva Chōḍa Mahārāja, gave Kānuparti to Brahmans as a sarvamānya for the religious merit of Vijaya Bukka Rāya Mahārāja, son of Śrīman Mahāmaṇḍalēśvara Rājādhirāja Rājaparamēśvara Śrī Vīra Dēvarāya Mahārāya (II) and his queen Dēmamma. *Ibid.* 56, pp. 990—93 [*Vīra Avu Bhudēva* is Vīra Aubaladēva. *Dēmaamma* has been surmised to be a misreading for Hemāmbika.]

383. From threshold of the gate of the Śiva temple. (Telugu.) A fragmentary record of king Vijayāditya Mahārāja. *Ibid.* 57, pp. 993–94.

Karavāḍi.

384. From a boulder in enclosure of Rāmaliṅgasvāmi temple. (Telugu.) Records that on Thursday, the tenth of the dark fortnight of Śravaṇa of the year Sādhāraṇa, Ś. 1232, in the reign of Pratāpa Rudradēva some land was presented to the deity Rāmanātha of Karavāḍi, by Kāmaya Boppaṇḍu-Dēvaya Reḍḍigāru. It is also recorded that the vendors and purchasers should give half a *kāśu* on all their goods and grain, and that the *Bēhris* (hawkers) who sold goods for thousands (on a large scale) should also pay. *Ibid.* 58, p. 994—96.

Koṇḍamūnjalūru.

385. On one side of Nāga stone to west of village. (Telugu.) Records that on Tuesday, the second of the dark fortnight of Kārttika, Ś. 1089, in the twenty-first year of the reign of Śrīmat Rājarājadēva, Yerrama Nāyaka, son of Nimbrōlu Sabbanāyaka, the superintendent of the treasury of Śrīman Mahāmaṇḍalēśvara Kulōttuṅga Rājendra Chōḍa Rāja (1163—80), son of Goṅka II of Velanāḍu and Subbamāmba, set up a liṅga in the name of his father in Koṇḍamūñjalūru in Kammanāḍu, erected a temple, and presented eight *kuṅchams* for offerings at the three sandhyas to Sabbēśvara

Mahādēva. (The details are then given.) Mallajīyalu, the son of Vēmajīyalu, received these, and he, his sons and grandsons should maintain the worship. O. 59, *N.I.*, p. 996—99.

386. On a Nāga stone to the west of village. (Sanskrit in Telugu character.) Records that in Ś. 1089, on the second tithi of the dark fortnight of the month named Kārttika, Kumbha nakshatra, he placed a *kalaśā* (dome) on the top of the temple of Sabhēśvara, in Kammarāshṭra. *Ibid.* 60, pp. 1000—4.

Konijēdu.

387. On stone in Janārdanasvāmi temple. (Telugu.) Records that Śrī Gōpinātha of Kodiñjēlu, Naraśingi Śeṭṭi, son of Balasāyani Śingama Śeṭṭi, of the Viṇḍila gōtra, of the Kōmaṭi sect of Kaṇḍukūru, caused the enclosure wall of the eastern side of the temple to be polished by Santanūtalapāḍu Punnayya for the religious merit of his mother Yalasāni and father Śingama Śeṭṭi. *Ibid.* 61, pp. 1004—5.

388. On a stone near the well of Chakradhara. (Telugu.) Records that the well was caused to be constructed on the fifteenth day of the bright fortnight, Āshāḍha, Ś. 1455, by Śrī Chakradhara for the religious merit of his father and mother. *Ibid.* 62, p. 1005.

Koṇiki.

389. On a fallen stone by the Bhīmēśvara temple. (Telugu.) Records a *vriṭṭi* of 4 *puṭṭis* given by Śrīman Mahāmaṇḍalēśvara Pratāpa Rudradēva Mahārāyulu. *Ibid.* 63, pp. 1005–6.

390. On the same stone. (Telugu.) Records a *vriṭṭi* given by Kōḍinka Laḍḍa Varma (?) of Kammanāḍu for the religious merit of Śaṅkama Mahārāja Siddhaṇa. *Ibid.* 64, pp. 1006–7.

391. Three inscriptions from Garuḍa stone opposite Raghunā yaka temple. (Telugu.) Records the devotion of Addēpalli Śiṅgarāju to Śrī Raghunāyaka of Koṇiki. A fragmentary record, dated on the fifth of the bright fortnight of Māgha of the year Krōdhi the bright fortnight of Kārttika of the year Raktākshi, is also given. *Ibid.* 65, pp. 1007–8.

Kopparapāḍu.

392. Opposite Mallēśvarasvāmi temple. (Telugu.) Records a gift by Betrumanāyakuḍu, prime minister of Mahāmaṇḍalēśvara Mallidēva Chōḍa Mahārājulu, to the deity for the religious merit of his parents. *Ibid.* 66, p. 1008.

Koppolu.

393. Opposite Bhīmēsvara temple. (Telugu.) Records that on the occasion of the Uttarāyaṇa Saṅkrānti, Ś. 1176, a certain chief gave for the religious merit of his father and his mother

(Mādamma) some land as vritti to Bhīmēśvaradēva of Kroppolu. O. 67, *N.I.*, pp. 1009—11.

394. To the north in the Shroff-mānyam. (Telugu.) Records that on Thursday, the fifteenth of the bright fortnight of Vaiśākha of the year Jaya, Ś. 1456, a certain Polavīra . . . Nāgani Nāyuḍu of the Rāvoli gōtra granted 5 *tūms* of land for providing oil for the anointing of the deity. *Ibid.* 68, pp. 1011–12.

Korisapāḍu.

395. On a wall of the Vēṇugōpālasvāmi temple. (Telugu.) Records a gift of the Rāja's share of the crop on certain land for the repair of the bund of the tank. *Ibid.* 69, p. 1012.

Maddipāḍu.

396. On a stone by the Narasimha temple. (Telugu.) Records that on Thursday, the tenth of the dark fortnight of Māgha of the year Yuva, Ś. 1197, Mañchirāju Gaṇapaya and Kāmayapreggaḍa, the younger brother of Pōchirāju, presented to Śrī Rāmanāthadēva of Mōṭupalli the village of Maddipāḍu for providing oblation, offering, worship and enjoyments. *Ibid.* 70, pp. 1013–14.

Malliyapūṇḍi.

397. *C.P. No.* 19 *of Nel. Ins.*—A grant of the Eastern Chāḷukyan king Ammarāja (II) issuing an order to the residents of the *vishaya* of Kommanāṇḍu and recording the gift of the village of Malliyapūṇḍi to the Jain temple *Kaṭakābharaṇa*, constructed by Duggarāja (south of Dharmāpuram), the son of Vijayāditya, grandson of Kaṭakādhipati and great-grandson of Kṛishṇarāja. It is said that this temple was presided over by a Jain saint named Dhiradēva, disciple of Divākara, first disciple of Jīnanandi who was of the Śrī Yāpunīya Saṅgha and of the Nandigachcha. The date of the grant was a certain Uttarāyaṇa which should have been after Ś. 867, the year of the grantor's coronation to which it refers. [See *Ind. Antq.*, VII, p. 16, for a similar grant. For the present epigraph see also *Ep. Ind.*, Vol. IX, p. 47 ff., where Dr. Hultzsch edits it.]

Mādanūru.

398. On a stone in the temple of Rāmaliṅgēśvara. (Telugu and Sanskrit in Telugu character.) Records that on Thursday, the fifteenth of the bright half of Māgha of the year Īśvara, Ś. 1421, on the holy occasion of a lunar eclipse, Śāḷuva Timmaraśu gave Mādanūru to Kātta Malaya for providing *amritapaḍi* (sacred food) and all enjoyments to the deity, for the religious merit of Śrī Kṛishṇadēva Mahārāya. *Ibid.* 71, pp. 1015—18.

Mainampāḍu.

399. From stone on tank bund. (Sanskrit except the last line which is in Telugu.) Records that in Ś. 1363, in the year Durmati, on Monday, Kārttika, Śrī Mallanārya or Mallaya Mantri, the son of Timmaya Mantri (who was the son of Narahari of Uḍayagiri) presented to Purarati (Śiva) land in the town named Maindanapāḍ, and a flower garden for the perpetual performance of daily worship. He also presented a village of great prosperity for a perpetual lamp and sacred food, and a spotless bronze vessel for daily offering. O. 72, *N.I.*, pp. 1091. "There is an exact copy of this inscription" in the temple at Tripurāntakam.

Mallāvaram.

400. To north in Survey No. 247. (Sanskrit in Telugu character.) Records that in Ś. 1277, on the day at the setting of Aśvin, on the lunar eclipse day, on Thursday, king Kōmaṭi Vēma apparently gave the city of Addaṅki to one Doḍḍamalla. . . . *Ibid.* 73, pp. 1022—29. The inscription gives the genealogy of Kōmaṭi Vēma and compares the donee apparently to Rāma. [Kōmaṭi was the son Śrīgiri and brother of Malla.]

Manikēśvaram.

401. On a stone bearing inscriptions on four sides, opposite Māṇḍūkēśvara temple. (Telugu.) Records that in the sixth year of the reign of Śrīman Mahāmaṇḍalēśvara Chōḍamādeva Mahārāja a gift of lands was made to Maṇḍūkēśvara Śrī Mahādēva of Buddapūṇḍi on the banks of the river Guṇḍi, in Kammanāḍu. *Ibid.* 74, pp. 1030—32.

402. On a stone inscribed opposite Māṇḍūkēśvara temple. (Telugu.) Records that on Monday, the first of the bright fortnight of Mārgaśira in Vikrama, Ś. 1202, Makara Saṅkrānti, Mahāmaṇḍaleśvara Nāgadēva gave a mango tope, a flower garden, and a field of 9 *puṭṭis* in Buddepūṇḍi to Maṇḍūkēśvarādēva for the religious merit of Rudradēva Mahārāja (evidently Rudrammā). *Ibid.* 75, pp. 1032—4. [It was to this chief that Tikkaṇa's son Māraṇa dedicated his *Mārkaṇḍēyapurāṇa*.]

403. From a stone inscribed on four sides opposite Maṇḍūkēśvara temple. (Telugu.) Records that on Monday, the tenth of the bright fortnight of Bhādrapāda of the year Vibhava, Ś. 1130, Śrīman Mahāmaṇḍalēśvara Śrī Mādhava Mahārāja gave a field of 40 *puṭṭis* in the land of Koṭikalapūṇḍi to the west of the Guṇḍlakamma to Maṇḍūkēśvara Śrī Mahādēva. *Ibid.* 76, pp. 1034-5.

404. In a street to the west. (Telugu.) Records that on the fifteenth of the bright fortnight of Phalguna of the year Jaya, Ś. 1455, Bāba Kāśayyavāru (or Bācharuśayya ?) presented a field to one Mallinātha. *Ibid.* 77, pp. 1036-7. The donor is said to have ruled at Koṇḍavīḍu and been skilled in bearing the burden of the kingdom of Achyuta Rāya. The dates are inconsistent.

405. In enclosure of Maṇḍūkēśvara temple. (Sanskrit in Telugu character and Telugu.) Records that in Ś. 1275, on the bright fortnight of Jyēshṭa, a Mañchirāja, son of Rāmaya Mantri, grandson of Mañchana and great-grandson of Rāmarāja Prēggaḍa (the minister of king Vēma), performed the consecration of a Siddhaliṅga to the south of the famous temple of Maṇḍūkēśa Śambhu, set up another liṅga named Sōma Śrigiri Siddhaliṅga (both of which had been brought from Śrīśailam), endowed a golden vessel resembling Kubera's car and brilliant as the reflection of the shining sun, constructed steps to the Kuṇḍika (Gunḍḷakamma), a new maṇṭapa at the gate and a new prākāra (enclosure), made also with plaster a circular hall to represent Sōma, constructed a beautiful kitchen room for the glorious lord Maṇḍūkēśa, and around the temple of Maṇḍukēśa Śambhu planted cocoanut trees. Rāmaya Mantri Mañchirāja also gave a golden lotus containing the nine kinds of gems. O. 78, pp. 1037—45. All this was done when his elder brother Anna Parvata Mallinātha, Minister of Anna Vōta, died. [Annāvōta was the son of Vēma, the builder of the flights of steps at Ahōbilam and Śriśailam. He was the father of Kumāragiri and Mallāmbikā who was the queen of Kaṭaya Vēma, the founder of the Rajahmundry line.]

Mannūru.

406. By the dvajasthambham in Rāmaliṅga temple. (Sanskrit in Telugu character and Telugu.) Records that on Sunday, the second of the dark fortnight of the month of Phalguna, Ś. 1033, Hasta nakshattra, a certain Gōsanayya, the son of Vīrareḍḍi, presented five *gadyānas* for a perpetual lamp in the temple of Rāmēśvaradēva of Īṭamukkala. Records also that in Ś. 1033, on Sunday, the second of the dark fortnight of Phalguna, Kōsanayya gave a lamp and five *gadyānas*. *Ibid.* 79, pp. 1045–6.

407. On boundary to the south. (Telugu.) Records that at Mādanūru there was half *khanḍrika* of land to Rāmēśvara. *Ibid.* 80, pp. 1046–47.

Muktinūtalapāḍu.

408. By the steps of the Śiva temple. (Telugu.) Records the construction of the temple on the occasion of Vishuva Saṅkrānti. *Ibid.* 81, p. 1047.

409. On the Nandi stone in front of the Śiva temple. (Telugu.) Records that on Tuesday, the second of the dark fortnight of Aśvayuja of the year Yuva, Ś. 1197, Vishuva Saṅkrānti—10,000 *kuṇṭās* of dry land were given to the deity Mallināthadēva of Murkinūtipāḍu by Keḷachapiḷa Cheṭṭi for the religious merit of his sons and grandsons. There was no tax on this vṛiṭṭi. One hundred *kuṇṭas* of land were also given to Bhairavadēva. O. 82, *N.I.*, pp. 1047—50.

410. On a stone in front of Śiva temple. (Telugu.) Records that on Monday, the fifteenth day of the bright fortnight of Chaitra of the year Manmatha, Ś. 1327, the Nāyak of Addaṅki, Bāṇāla Liṅgaṇa, the son of Akkaṇa and the grandson of Vīrappa, executed a charitable deed of land to the deity Muktinūtalapāṭi Chenna Mallikārjunadēva. He constructed the temple and at the time of consecrating the deity and gave one *kuchchala* of land at Kēsaripāḍu. *Ibid.* 83, pp. 1050–51.

411. On floor of Śiva temple. (Telugu.) Records a gift for the religious merit of one Vidyārāju. *Ibid.* 84, p. 1052.

Nāgaluppalapāḍu.

412. By west wall of Śiva temple. (Telugu.) Records that on Tuesday, eleventh day of the dark fortnight of Jyēshṭa, Kīlaka Ś. 1350, Gaṅgayadēva Chōḍa Mahārājulu, son of Anavōta Dēva Chōḍa and grandsòn of Tirumalarāju Gāru, granted vṛittis to the God, to Brahmans, to the Jāṅgam sect and Bamalas of Nāguluppalapāḍu. *Ibid.* 85, pp. 1053—55.

413. From stone lying to east of Śiva temple. (Telugu.) Records in the year Vikāri, Ś. 1161, Vishu Saṅkrānti, Mādēva Nāyakuḍu set up the image of Mallēśvara at Nāvuluppalapāḍu and presented land for providing oblation, offering and worship to that deity, for the religious merit of Śrīman Mahāmaṇḍalēśvara Gaṇapatidēva Mahārājulu (1213—59) and for the religious merit of his father and mother. *Ibid.* 86, pp. 1055—57.

414. From a stone near the Śiva temple. (Telugu.) Records that on Thursday, the first day of the bright fortnight of Jyēshṭa, Hēviḷambi, Ś. 1219, for the religious merit of Kākatīya Pratāparudradēva Mahārājulu, Muppaḍināyaniṅgāru gave 2,300 kuṇṭas of land to Mūlasthāna Mallinātha of Nāguluppalapāḍu. *Ibid.* 87, pp. 1057–58.

415. From a stone opposite the Śiva temple. (Telugu.) Records that in Vikāri, Ś. 1161, Vishuva Saṅkrānti, Mādhava Nāyaka consecrated the temple of Mallēśvara of Nāguluppalapāḍu and gave lands for providing oblation, offering and worship to that deity, for the religious merit of Śrīman Mahāmaṇḍalēśvara Gaṇapatidēva Mahārāja. *Ibid.* 88, pp. 1058—64.

416. From four sides of a stone opposite Gōpālasvāmi temple. (Telugu.) Records that in Ānanda, Ś. 1175, Vishuma Saṅkrānti, Śrīmat Sāraṅgapāṇi Dēvarasu consecrated Śrīgōpāladēva, naming him Chakranārāyaṇa Mādhava Gōpinātha of Nāgaluppalapāḍu, and gave land to the Nambi (priest) for providing oblation, offering and worship to the deity, for the religious merit of Śrīman Mahāmaṇḍalēśvara Gaṇapatidēva Mahārāja and of his father Mādhava Nāyakuḍu. O. 89, *N.I.*, pp. 1064—69.

Nannūrū.

417. On a stone bearing inscriptions on four sides opposite the Amma temple. (Telugu.) Records that in Ś. 1109, Vishuva-Saṅkrānti, Śrīman Mahāmaṇḍalēśvara Kāmaṇa Chōḍa Mahārāja (of the race of Karikāla), gave Nannūru, exempt from all taxes, to Hōṅkāradēvi of Nannūru in perpetuity. *Ibid.* 90, pp. 1069—71.

418. On the same stone opposite the Amma temple. (Telugu.) Records a gift to Hōṅkāradēvi (goddess) of the very sacred Nannūru by Śrīmat Ujvala Chōḍa Balaya (Ballaya) Chōḍa Mahārājulu. *Ibid.* 91, pp. 1071-72.

419. On the same stone. (Telugu.) Records that Rājamahēndra-Pottappi Chōḍa * gave land, exempt from all taxes, to Hōṅkāradēvi at Nannūru in the first day of the month of Mēsha, Ś. 1010. *Ibid.* 92, pp. 1072-73.

420. On the same stone opposite the Amma temple. (Telugu.) Records that a "king Kima (Timma) of Nannūru" who had the lord of the monkey tribe (Hanumān) as the emblem on his flag reigned with power. *Ibid.* 93, pp. 1073-74. "It is not clear what dynasty is alluded to."

Niḍamanūru.

421. Opposite the temple of Bhīmēśvarasvāmi. (Telugu.) Records that Pedda Pinna gave the village of Gaṇapapuram to the deity. *Ibid.* 94, pp. 1074—77.

422. In front of Bhīmēśvara temple. (Telugu.) Records the gift of the village, with all its income,—two-thirds to Śrī Paramēśa and one-third to Śrī Viśva Vanēśvara Dēva—to provide for decorations and enjoyments of the deities. *Ibid.* 95, pp. 1077-78.

423. In front of Bhīmēśvara temple. (Telugu.) A record in Ś. 1237 of Śrīman Mahāmaṇḍalēśvara Mūrurāyalagaṇḍa Kākatīya Pratāpa Rudra Dēva Mahārāja. *Ibid.* 96, p. 1079.

423-A. In front of Bhīmēśvarasvāmi temple. (Telugu.) Records that on Thursday, the fifteenth of the bright half of

---

* His genealogy is given as—

Chāgi Veṅkaṇa of the solar race
|
Ballerāju
|
Kanṭruvaṅkya Rāju
|
Nanni Chōḍa
|
Śūrapa Rāju
|
Rājamahēndra Pottapi Rāju.

Vaiśakha of the year Vyaya (Kshaya), Ś. 1368, one Birodi Gaṅga Bhairava Nāyaṅkaragaṇḍa Śrīmat Patalampula Nāyaniṁgāru issued a charitable edict to the people of the Śīma of Daiyalarayuru). O. 97, *N.I.*, pp. 1080–81.

423-B. In front of Bhīmēśvara temple. (Telugu.) Records that on Monday, the thirtieth of the dark fortnight of Pushya of the year Sādhāraṇa, Ś. 1232, a certain Vipapāṭi Mallayyaṁgāru presented a gift for the religious merit of his father Bhairinēniṅgāru, and settled that the *mēras* should be given at the rate of one *kuṅcha* per *puṭṭi*. *Ibid.* 98, pp. 1081–82.

Ongole.

424. In the Śiva temple. (Telugu.) Records that on the Uttarāyaṇa Saṅkrānti, Ś. 1212, Gajasāhiṇi Rudranāyakulu gave 100 *kuṇṭas* of dry land to Chōḍa Gōpinātha of Ongole on behalf of his parents. *Ibid.* 99, pp. 1082–83. See No. 248. [Was Rudra the son of Sāhiṇi Māra, who rendered the *Yuddhakāṇḍa* of the *Rāmāyaṇa* into Telugu ?]

425. On a stone by the side of the great northern road to the east of M.R.Ry. D. Markandayya Sastri's garden. (Telugu.) Records that on the occasion of Makara Saṅkrānti, the Karṇam Baicharāju Nāgarāju gave 100 *kuṇṭas* of dry land for providing daily offerings, worship and enjoyments to Vaijēśvara Dēvara of Ongole for the religious merit of his liege lord Śrīman Mahāmaṇḍalēśvara Chakra Nārāyaṇa Śrī Vaijēga Dēva Mahārāja. This charity was given by Dēvi Śeṭṭi's sons. *Ibid.* 100, pp. 1083–84.

426. On stone now removed to Sub-Collector's bungalow. (Telugu.) Records that on the Uttarāyaṇa Saṅkrānti, in the year Śrīmukha, Ś. 1194, while Śrī Mādhava Dēva Mahārāyalu (Chakranārāyaṇa) was ruling, he presented a *vṛitti* of 200 *kuṇṭas* to certain Reḍḍis. Records also grant of twelve *kuṇṭas* of land as *vṛiṭṭi* to Bhairava (deity) on the hill. *Ibid.* 101, pp. 1084—86. The cyclic and Śaka years differ by one year.

427. A paper grant in the possession of M.R.Ry. D. Markandayya Sastri Gāru. (Telugu.) Records a grant of lands by Maṇḍapāṭi Kumāra Rāmabhadrarāja, Rāja of Endlūr in Ongole, in Ś. 1684, Chitrābhānu, on the fifteenth of the bright fortnight of Śrāvaṇa. *Ibid.* 102, pp. 1086—88. The donee was a Mrityuñjaya Śastri of the Kaviṇḍinya gōtra, Yajus Śākhā and Āpastamba Sūtra.

428. From stone in supply channel of a tank. Now at Sub-Collector's bungalow, Ongole. (Telugu.) Records that this gift was made by Śrī Sōmarāja, the prime minister of Chakra Nārāyaṇa Śiṅgaladēva Mahārāja, on the occasion of Uttarāyaṇa Saṅkrānti, Ś. 1172, for the religious merit of his liege lord to the deity of Ongole. *Ibid.* 103, pp. 1088–89.

Paiḍipāḍu.

429. In the Mallēśvara temple. (Telugu.) Records that on Saturday, the tenth of the bright fortnight of Śrāvaṇa of the year Krōdhi, Ś. 1346, in the time of Paṇṭa Mayilāra Reḍḍigāru, a certain Mummaḍi Vēmayya Reḍḍi gave for the gods and Brahmans of Payindipāḍu certain *vṛiṭṭis*. O. 104, *N.I.*, pp. 1089–90. See No. 355 above.

Pallamalli.

430. Opposite to the Śiva temple. (Telugu.) Records a gift by a "Pallamalli Kantamamantapamadya Nāyinēndu of Kammanāḍu" in Ś. 1289. *Ibid.* 105, pp. 1092–93.

431. South of village under tank bund. (Telugu.) Records that on the tenth of the bright fortnight of Śrāvaṇa of the year Siddhārthi, Ś. 1660, Rāmasvāmi Gurvupādyāyaṅgāru caused this tank to be constructed for dedication to the God. *Ibid.* 106, pp. 1093–94. The cyclic and Śaka years do not agree.

432. Below a hill to the west. (Telugu.) Records that on the tenth of the bright fortnight of Mārgaśira, Raktākshi, two persons (Rāmasāmi and Guruvappa) caused this pond to be constructed for dedication to Paramēśvara. *Ibid.* 107, pp. 1094–95.

433. West of Gaṅgamma temple. (Telugu.) Records a gift. *Ibid.* 108, p. 1095.

Perayapāḷem (hamlet Modepalli).

434. On a hill opposite to the Āñjanēya temple. (Telugu.) Records on the thirteenth of the dark fortnight of Kārttika in the year Īśvara, Ś. 1259, gift to Lakshmīnarasimhadēva of Viruṇapāḍu. *Ibid.* 109, p. 1096.

Pernameṭṭu.

435. On a stone by the Rāmaliṅgaswāmi temple. (Telugu.) Records that in the year Vrisha, Ś. 1143, a certain Mainapalli Ma . . . granted 400 *kuṇṭās* to hūnāthadēva of Perṇamiṭṭa for the religious merit of his parents. *Ibid.* 110, p. 1097.

436. (Telugu.) On a pillar in the Vishṇu temple. Records on the fifteenth of the bright fortnight of Phalguna of the year Prabhava, Ś. 1548, the names of six persons who were karaṇams of this and five other villages. *Ibid.* 111, pp. 1098–99.

437. On a rock known as Goḍug-ubanda, on the hill. (Telugu in Chāḷukyan character.) Mentions a member of the Gaṅga dynasty and a descendant of the Haihaya race, who was the lord of the city of Māhishmati (i.e., Mandla). *Ibid.* 112, p. 1099.

Pondūru.

438. (Telugu.) Records that on Thursday, the fifteenth of the bright fortnight of Kārttika of the year Krōdhi, Koṇḍama Nāyaniṅgāru, son of Raviparvata Nāyanimgāru, and Rāmināyanimgāru gave the village of Pondūru to Tāḷḷapāka Tirumalayyaṅgāru for the religious merit of Sadāśivarāya. O. 113, *N.I.*, pp. 1100–1. See Nos. 337 and 343 above and 466 below.

Pōtavaram.

439. In a street. (Telugu.) Records that as it was represented to Timmarasayya that the tank at Pōtavaram dug by Poledayya for the religious merit of his parents, on the fourteenth day of the bright fortnight of Pushya of the year Bahudhānya, had no water, Mallayarayya made a gift of a field of 2 *goṟṟus* to the east of the village. *Ibid.* 114, pp. 1101–2.

Rāchapūḍi.

440. In a field to south of the village. (Telugu.) A record dated on Thursday, the eleventh of the bright fortnight of Āshaḍha of the year Ānanda, Ś. 1356. *Ibid.* 115, pp. 1102–3.

Rāmakūru.

441. On a rock opposite Rāmaliṅgēśvara temple. (Telugu.) Invokes the grace of Gaṇapēśvara that the residents of Amarapura should prosper. *Ibid.* 116, pp. 1103–4.

442. On a rock opposite Rāmaliṅgēśvara temple. (Telugu.) Records gift of field by Śrīman Mahāmaṇḍalēśvara Nanni Chōḍa Mahārāya to Rāmēśvara Dēva. [Naṇṇi Chōḍa might be the son of Tribhuvanamalladēva of the Konedena branch of the Telugu Chōḍas.] *Ibid.* 117, pp. 1104–5. See No. 260 above.

443. On rock opposite Rāmaliṅgēśvara temple. (Telugu.) A record of "Mallavarapu Timmayya by the grace of Śrī Rāmēśvara." *Ibid.* 118, p. 1105.

444. On a rock opposite Rāmaliṅgēśvara temple. (Telugu.) Records that on the second of the bright fortnight of Māgha of the year Paridhāvi, Chēvula Dattayavāru planted this flower garden for the worship of Rāmēśvara. *Ibid.* 119, pp. 1105–6.

445. From rock near dvajasthambham of Rāmaliṅgēśvara temple. (Telugu.) Records a gift of Chōḍa Dēva Chōḍa Mahārāyalu, son of Kāmaya, Jagadobbagaṇḍa, etc., of Kāśyapa gōtra and Lord of Oraiyūru, on Friday, the fifteenth day of the dark fortnight of Śrāvaṇa of the year Īśvara, Ś. 1134, on the occasion of the solar eclipse, for the religious merit of his parents and the prosperity of his kingdom. *Ibid.* 120, pp. 1106–7. [Was this prince the brother of Nanni Chōḍa of No. 442 ?]

446. On a rock opposite Rāmaliṅgēśvara temple. (Telugu.) Records that a Śrī Rāghavēśvaruṇḍu set up the image of Rāma, and presented some paddy field, for the daily service of the deity. *Ibid.* 121, pp. 1107–8.

447. On a rock opposite to the Vishṇu temple. (Telugu.) Records "the plastering work done for Lakshmaṇadēva" and the gift of a field of four kuṇṭas given as *vṛiṭṭi* to Lakshmīpati. O 122, *N.I.*, p. 1108.

448. On the same stone to east of Āñjanēya temple. (Telugu.) Records that on the occasion of Vishuva Saṅkrānti in the year Vishu, Ś. 1203, for the religious merit of Śrīman Mahāmaṇḍalēśvara Manumādripati Rājulu and Dēvabāgiya Mahārājulu, some vṛiṭṭis of land were presented to Gaṇapēśvara and Bhīmēśvara of Rāmakūru in Pārvativārikuṇṭa. *Ibid.* 123, pp. 1108–9.

449. On a stone to the east of Āñjanēya temple. (Telugu.) Records a mere list of the property in land and the *mēras* possessed by the temple. *Ibid.* 124, pp. 1109–10.

450. On a stone east of Āñjanēya temple. (Telugu.) Records a gift by Śrīman Mahāmaṇḍalēśvara . . . Nīlakaṇṭha Chōḍa Dēva Mahārāzulu in the year Īśvara, Ś. 1220, for his own religious merit. *Ibid.* 125, pp. 1110–12.

451. On a boundary stone east of the village. (Telugu.) Records the boundary of the village. *Ibid.* 126, p. 1113.

452. On a rock opposite to the Rāmaliṅga temple. (Telugu.) . . . *Ibid.* 127, p. 1113.

Rāparla.

453. On a fallen stone by Vishṇu temple. (Telugu.) A record on the eleventh of the bright fortnight of Jyēshṭa on the occasion of Uttarāyaṇa Saṅkrānti, Ś. 1040, in the reign of Chōḍa Dēva Mahārāyalu of the race of Karikāla over the kingdom in Kammanāḍu. [This chief might be the same as Chōḍaballaya Chōḍa, the father of Kāma of the Konedena branch of the Telugu Chōḍas.] *Ibid.* 128, pp. 1113–15.

Ravinūtala.

454. Opposite to the Mallēśvara temple. (Telugu.) Records that on Monday, the first of the bright fortnight of Chaitra of the year Vijaya, Ś. 1215, while Mahāmaṇḍalēśvara Kākatīya Pratāparudra Mahārājulu was ruling the kingdom, Bahada Dēva Rājulu gave lands to Bhīmeśvara Mahādēva, whose image he had set up at Ravinūtula for the religious merit of Rudra Dēva Mahārāja. *Ibid.* 129, pp. 1115–18.

455. Opposite to the Vishṇu temple. (Sanskrit in Telugu character.) Records that in Ś. 1205, on the first of Chaitra, a Brahman Śrī Padmaya, the minister of a certain king Kṛishṇadhara, planted a pillar bearing a garuḍa. *Ibid.* 130, pp. 1118–19.

Santanūtalapāḍu.

456. On a stone in the Chennakēśava temple. (Telugu.) Records gift of fields in Ammanabrōlu śīma, for the performance of daily worship, lighting and all enjoyments to the deity on the holy occasion of lunar eclipse, and gift of gold. O. 131, *N.I.*, pp. 1119–21.

Śiṅgarikoṇḍa.

457. On a fallen stone below the hill. (Telugu.) Records on Thursday, the tenth of the bright half of Phalguna of the year Rudhirōdgāri, Ś. 1365, on the occasion of a solar eclipse, Mānūri Devala granted, under the order of Daḷavāi Dēvarājayya, certain taxes for performing divine service to Narasimhadēva, for the religious merit of Vīra Pratāpa Dēva Rāya Mahārāya (II). The taxes were levied on articles of merchandise carried for sale on the road leading to Tirupati during the seven days' festival in Paṅguni aṇd on marriages, carts, slaves, horses, bullocks, cows, buffaloes and other live-stock; on all kinds of grain, oils, women's cloths, etc. The eighteen sects of people of the different countries and the Bhaktas of "the fifty-six countries" are referred to. [*Ibid.* 132, pp. 1121–4.]

Taṅgaṭūru.

458. In a street to the east—a fragment. (Telugu.) Records a gift. *Ibid.* 133, p. 1124.

459. On the threshold of Kēśavasvāmi temple. (Telugu.) An illegible record. *Ibid.* 134, p. 1124.

Trōvaguṇṭa.

460. On a stone in the Śiva temple. (Telugu.) Records that Śrīman Mahāmaṇḍalēśvara Bāyyaṇadēva Mahārāja and China Bāyyaṇadēva Mahārāja gave 1,000 kuṇṭas of land to the Mahādēva of the temple (mulasthana) of Toguṇṭa,—ten (kuṇṭas) to Kaṇṇēśvara Mahādēva, ten to Śrī Mahādēva of Yerraguḍipāḍu, ten to Veṭṭipaḷi Gaṇapēśvara Śrī Mahādēva, five to Vīrēśvara Śrī Mahādēva of Pādūru and ten to Śrī Koṇḍūrudēva. *Ibid.* 135, pp. 1125–26.

461. On a stone in the temple of Chennakēśava. (Telugu.) Records that Tōguṇṭa Nārāyaṇappa of the gōtra of Gautama constructed a temple, and maṇṭapams to Chennakēśavasvāmi in the month of Chaitra in the year Śārvari, Ś. 1224, and set up the image. He further gave lands to the temple. *Ibid.* 136, pp. 1126–27.

462. On a stone in the Kōdaṇḍa-Rāmasvāmi temple. (Telugu.) Records that Rāmaṇṇa, son of Tōvaguṇṭa Veṅkaṭappa, rebuilt the temple and consecrated the idol of Śrī Rāma in it, on the fifteenth day of the bright fortnight of Jyēshṭa of Viḷambi, Ś. 1700. *Ibid.* 137, pp. 1127–28.

Uppugundūru.

463. On a stone near the gate of the Gaurēśvara temple. (Telugu.) Records that on Sunday, the fifteenth of the bright fortnight of Adhika Jyēshṭa of the year Kīlaka in Ś. 1170, a gift of land was made for the religious merit of Śrīmat Gaga (Gaja) Sāhiṇi Jamulu to the deity. O. 138, *N.I.*, pp. 1128–29.

464. Near the Gaurēśvara temple. (Telugu.) Records that Vaitama Śeṭṭi, the son of Śrīmat Minda Guddali Cheṇḍi Śeṭṭi, constructed the big tank of Uppugoṇḍūrupalli, put up *achchukaṭṭuṣ* (bunds) to the paddy fields all round the village, and gave for the religious merit of his lord Gaṇapatidēva Mahārāja and of his parents and of himself, on Sunday, the fifteenth of the bright fortnight of Kārttika in Ś. 1140, to Gaurīśvara Mahādēva of Uppugoṇḍūru, 200 *kuṇṭas* of wet land under the Tada tank, besides some *puṭṭis* of dry land. *Ibid.* 139, pp. 1129–31. "The donor's father was apparently governor or headman of Nellore town."

Valaparla.

465. On a rock near the Yerraguṇṭa. (Telugu.) Mentions the tank of Kārempūḍi Peddanāyaṁgāru. *Ibid.* 140, p. 1131.

466. On a stone near the wall of Aravapalli Vīrabramham's yard. (Telugu.) Records that on Thursday, the twelfth of the bright fortnight of Āśvija of the year Krōdhi, Ś. 1466, Śrī Vīra Sadāśivadēva Mahārāyulu of Vijayanagar granted the village of Valaparli in Addaṅki Sīma together with gold to Kōnēṭi Tiruvēṅgalanāthayyagāru, son of Taḷḷapāka Tirumalaiyaṅgāru. *Ibid.* 141, pp. 1131–2. See Nos. 337, 343 and 438 above.

467. In front of Vēṇugōpālasvāmi temple. (Telugu and Sanskrit.) Records that in the sixteenth year of the reign of Śrīmat Tribhuvana Chakravarti Śrī Kulōttuṅga Chōḍadēvara(II), Ś. 1070, on the occasion of Vishuma Saṅkrānti, Śrīman Mahāmaṇḍalēśvara Tribhuvanamalladēva Chōḍa Mahārāyulu gave the village of Valaparla in Kammanāḍu, to Śrī Kēśavadēvara of Kontridona for oblations, offerings, worship, dancing girls and furniture, and for maintenance of the worshippers. Tribhuvanamalla was a Chōḍa of the Konedena branch whose records are available from Ś. 1059 to Ś. 1070. *Ibid.* 142, pp. 1133—5.

468. On a stone bearing a garuḍa opposite Vēṇugōpāla temple. (Telugu.) Records that on the occasion of Ardhōdaya, Ś. 1189, Śrīman Mahāmaṇḍalēśvara Kākatīya Rudradēva Mahārāyalu, being given to understand that Śrīmat Konidōna Tribhuvana Mallaprahāri Kēśava Dēvara was in possession of an ancient edict for the grant of the village named Volupara (Valaparla) in Kammanāḍu, presented it to him, for the religious merit of Gaṇapadēva Mahārāja (1213—58). *Ibid.* 143, pp. 1135–6.

Vallūru.

469. South of the Vēṇugōpālasvāmi temple. (Telugu.) An illegible record. O. 144, *N.I.*, p. 1136.

470. Opposite to the Vēṇugōpālasvāmi temple. (Telugu.) Records the gift of wet and dry fields as vṛitti by Kāmaya Boppaṇḍu to the descendants of Mattugāru. . . . *Ibid.* 145, p. 1137.

471. North of Sōmēśvara temple. (Telugu.) A record dated on Thursday, the fullmoon day of the bright fortnight of Śrāvaṇa of the year Vibhava. Fragmentary. *Ibid.* 146, pp. 1137–38.

Vulichi.

472. On the steps of the Vēṇugōpālasvāmi temple. (Telugu.) Records a charitable edict granted by Rudrapanāyaniṅgāru, son of Hiṇḍira Bhūnāri Sōbhamgāru of Hiragalūru on Thursday, the thirtieth of the dark fortnight of Māgha of the year Īśvara. *Ibid.* 147, pp. 1138–39.

473. East of village. (Sanskrit in Telugu character and Telugu.) Records that on Wednesday, the seventh of the bright fortnight of Kārttika of the year Durmukhi, Ś. 1340, Śrī Rāmaṇaṅgāru granted to Chandrēśvara and Sōmēśvara some land. The earlier part of the inscription refers to a Mādayya Narasimha of the race of Karikāl Chōḷa. *Ibid.* 148, pp. 1139–41.

Yendlūru.

474. Opposite to the Śiva temple. (Telugu.) Records a gift in the month of Māgha of the year Sādhāraṇa, Ś. 1232, on the holy occasion of lunar eclipse, for the religious merit of Śrīman Mahāmaṇḍalēśvara Śrī Vīra Pratāpa Rudradēva Mahārājulu, to Mallināthadēva. *Ibid.* 149, pp. 1142–43.

475. On three sides of a stone in enclosure of Mādhavasvāmi temple. (Telugu.) Records that on Wednesday, the fifth of the bright fortnight of Vaiśākha of the year Naḷa, Ś. 1174, Śrīman Gōvinda Nāyakulu, Mahāpradhāni of Gaṇapatidēva, founded this endowment to Śrī Mādhava Perumāḷ for providing all enjoyments, daily offering, lighting, etc. *Ibid.* 150, pp. 1143—47.

476. On three sides of a stone near Mādhavasvāmi temple. (Telugu.) Records that, during the year Ś. 1170, on the occasion of Uttarāyaṇa Saṅkrānti, Śrīman Mahāmaṇḍalēśvara Chakra-Nārāyaṇa Śiṅgaladēva Mahārājulu's minister gave to Śrimallināthadēva of Ongole for worship, enjoyment and daily offering three hundred *kuṇṭas* of dry land in the west of the village. *Ibid.* 151, pp. 1148—50. Records also that Nāganabōyuṇḍu, son of Dēvanabōya, granted to the deity Mallinātha ewes and cows for the maintenance of a lamp, for the religious merit of Jagadēva Mahārāju.

PALNĀD TALUK.

Readers of Mr. Sewell's ***Antiquities*** should be acquainted with the famous Palnāḍ heroes and the widespread cult which exists in the taluk in connection with them. The origin of this strange cult is obscure, but there are a number of epigraphs which show that it came to be in vogue in the time of the later Kākatīyas. See Karempūḍi, Māchērla and Gurizala inscriptions. None of these, however, show "when and on what particular occasion these heroes of Palnāḍ so gloriously distinguished themselves as to justify the existence even today of a number of śūdras of their following who almost deify them."

Adigoppula.

477. 587 *of* 1909.—On a slab fixed into the wall of the Āñjanēya temple. (Telugu.) Records in Ś. 1532, Saumya, the building of the temple by a private person and a gift of land to it.

478. 588 *of* 1909.—On an image of Gaṇapati in the same temple. (Telugu.) A record in Ś. 1033, Khara. The image was caused to be made by Komāra-Dōchaya, son of Divākara Peggaḍa, while he was ruling Adigoppula.

479. 589 *of* 1909.—On a slab built into the wall of the Tripurāntakēśvara temple in the same village. (Telugu.) Mentions in Ś. 1607, Raktākshi, that the temple was built by Āśankana-Vīraṇṇa.

Cherlaguḍipāḍu.

480. 591 *of* 1909.—(Telugu.) On a pillar by the road-side. Records in Ś. 1403, Plava, that a certain Minugu Malla-Nāyinigāru (with a long list of titles) ratified grants to gods and Brahmans in Cherlaguḍipāḍu *in Gurindala-śima.*

481. 592 *of* 1909.—(Telugu.) On a slab built into the platform of the flagstaff, in the Vēṇugōpālasvāmin temple in the same village. A damaged record in Ś. 1526. Records the building of the platform and the setting up of the flagstaff. Mentions a certain China-Yallamarāju of the Ātrēya-gōtra.

482. 593 *of* 1909.—(Telugu.) On the west wall of the central shrine in the same temple. Mentions in Ś. 1216, Jaya, the "learned men" of Guḍipāḍu and two other individuals.

483. 594 *of* 1909.—(Telugu.) On a slab set up near a wall outside the same village. Records in Ś. 1457, Pārthiva (wrong), the digging of the well in front of the temple of Kaḷēśvara.

Chintapalli.

484. 559 *of* 1909.—(Telugu.) On a slab set up in front of the Āñjanēya temple. A record in Ś. 1674, Prajōtpatti. Refers to the building of the temple and to a gift of land. [*Antiquities*, p. 56.]

485. 560 *of* 1909.—(Telugu.) On a pillar set up in front of the Doḍḍa Mallēśvara temple in the same village. Records in

Ś. 1224, Śōbhakrit, that a certain Paindi Mārareḍḍi erected the shrine of Muktēśvara in the temple of Doḍḍamallināthadēva at Chintapalli, for the merit of his father Bīra Muttireḍḍi. [See *Antiquities*, p. 56.]

486. 561 *of* 1909.—(Telugu.) On the same pillar. A record of the Kākatīya king Mahāmaṇḍalēśvara Pratāparudradēva Mahārāja (II) in Ś. 1226, Krōdhi. Records gift of land to the same shrine by Māchayanāyaniṅgāru for the merit of the king. [See *Antiquities*, p. 56 and No. 519 below for reference to Māchayanāyaniṅgāru.]

487. 562 *of* 1909.—(Tamil.) On a slab forming the wall of a small shrine in the courtyard of the same temple. A damaged record in Ś. 1163, Plava. Records gift of land to the Mūlasthāna Mallināthadēva temple at Chintapalli.

488. 563 *of* 1909.—(Telugu.) On a stone built into the trough which receives the sacred tīrtha of the same temple. Records in Āṅgirasa that a certain Mantraya built (i.e., renovated ?) the temple of Doḍḍa-Mallikārjuna.

Dāchēpalle.

Mr. Sewell gives a short though vague account of the local temples and antiquities of the place. He gives the following epigraphs.

489. (Place not given.) A record dated in Ś. 1117.

490. On a stone close to the Kalyāṇa-maṇṭapam of "one of the temples." Records in Ś. 1135, a grant by the sons of the prime minister of Śrī Tripurāntakadēva. See Ct. 320.

491. On a stone at the Śambuni temple. A private grant in Ś. 1371.

492. On another stone in the same temple. A record of Ś. 1292.

493. Near the Vishṇu temple in the hamlet of Gāmālapāḍu, on a stone bearing Nāga figures. Records a private grant in Ś. 1599.

Dārivēmula.

494. Near a ruined temple. A record of Ś. 1241 in the reign of Pratāparudra II. [*Antiquities*, I, p. 57.]

*Durgi.**

495. 568 *of* 1909.—(Telugu.) On a slab lying in the Vaṅkēśvarasvāmin temple. Records in Plava gift of a water-shed for the merit of Durga-Vīrēśvara and Rājaśrī Jagapatirāyaniṅgāru.

---

* In his *Antiquities* Mr. Sewell gives eight definite inscriptions in this place. Of these five are noted in the departmental list. The other three I have given under Nos. 502—4.

496. 569 *of* 1909.—(Telugu.) On a slab set up near a platform in the same temple. A record of the Vijayanagara king Kṛishṇarāyadēva Mahārāya in Ś. 1440, Bahudhānya. Records gift of the village of Guṇḍāla in Duggi-pālamu, in Nāgārjunikoṇḍa-śīma, by Pedaśingama-Nāyaniṅgāru, to the temples of Vīrēśvara and Vaṅkēśvara at Durgi. [This epigraph is also given in *Antiquities*, I, p. 57, No. 6.]

497. 570 *of* 1909.—(Telugu.) On another slab set up in the courtyard in the same temple. Records in Ś. 1219, Hēvilambi, gift of land to the temple of Vaṅkēśvara at Dugya by Goṅgūla Pōchi-Nāyuṇḍu, while Rudradēva, General of Pratāparudra (II), was ruling the country. [See *Antiquities*, I, p. 57, No. 7.] See No. 514.

498. 571 *of* 1909.—(Sanskrit and Telugu.) On a pillar set up in the same place. A record of the Kākatīya king Mahāmaṇḍalēśvara Gaṇapatidēva-Mahārāja (1213—58), ruling from his capital Orumgallu in Ś. 1173, Virōdhikrit. Records the building of the temple of Vaṅkēśvara by Nāmadēva-Paṇḍita and the gift to it, of the village of Neyyūru, by the king. [Nāmadēva was the minister of the celebrated Gaṇḍapeṇḍēra Gaṅgaya Sāhiṇi, the Kāyastha general of Gaṇapati, who was in charge of the country from Pānungallu to Mārājavāḍi. See also *Antiquities*, I, No. 8.]

499. 572 *of* 1909.—(Telugu.) On slab set up in the Gōpālasvāmin temple in the same village. Records in Ś. 1219, Hēvilambi, gift of land by Goṅgūla Pōchi-Nāiṇḍu to the temple of Gōpināthadēva at Duggya, while Rudradēva, Minister of Pratāparudra II (1295—1323) was ruling the country. [See *Antiquities*, I, p. 57 and No. 424 above.]

500. 573 *of* 1909.—(Telugu.) On a pillar set up in the same place. A record of the Kākatīya queen Rudra-Mahādēvi, ruling from her capital Orumgallu in Ś. 1111, Śukla. Records the consecration of the temple of Gōpināthadēva at the town of Dugya in Palli-nāṇḍu, by Karaṇamu Nāmaya and a gift of land to it. Rudrammā has been called Gaṇapati Dēva's *Paṭṭōddhati*, i.e., "one who was elevated to the crown." The inscription also mentions Gaṇḍapēraṇḍa Jannigadēva, the minister of Rudrammā, who, like his predecessor Gaṅgaya Sāhini, ruled the region from Panuṅgal to Mārājavāḍi. *Antiquities*, I, 57. See No. 520.

501. 574 *of* 1909.—(Telugu.) On a pillar set up in front of the Oṭiguḷḷu near Bugga, 1½ miles north of the same village. A record of the Kākatīya king Mahāmaṇḍalēśvara Pratāparudradēva-Mahārāja II (1295—1323), ruling from his capital Orumgallu in Ś. 1241, Siddhārthin. Records gift of lands to the temples of Rudrēśvara and Chōḷēśvara at Daravēmula by Dēvara-Nāyiniṅgāru.

502. On a pillar in the temple of Vaṅkēśvarasvāmi. Records in Ś. 1180, grant in the reign of Kākatīya Gaṇapati and the governorship of Jannigadēva. *Antiquities*, p. 57, No. 5. See Nos. 500 and 520.

503. On another pillar of the same temple. Records in Ś. 1177, in the reign of Pratāparudra II, that his minister Māchirāja granted for temple purposes the taxes of a village. *Ibid.*, No. 5. See No. 486 above.

504. On a stone outside the mukhamaṇṭapam of the same temple. " A long and valuable inscription giving a genealogy of the Gaṇapatis from Prōlarāja, father of Pratāparudra I, and apparently evidencing the building of the temple by the governor Gaṅgayya. But my copy is defective." *Ibid.*, No. 9. See No. 498 above.

Goli.

505. On a pillar near the Hanūmān temple. A record dated in Ś. 1547. *Antiquities*, p. 57.

506. Near the above. A record dated in Ś. 1577. *Ibid.*

Guṇḍḷapāḍu.

507. On a stone west of the village near the temple of Śiva-Kēśava. Said to date from A.D. 1175 or 1115. *Ibid.*, p. 58.

508. On a slab east of the Śiva and Vishṇu temples. A private grant to the temple in Ś. 1243, Durmati. *Ibid.*

Gurizāla.

This place was the capital of the king who figures in the story of the Palnāḍ heroes (see *Antiquities*, Appendix A). Mr. Sewell mentions the existence of an epigraph of Rājarāja Narēndra in Vīrabhadra temple, but as he himself says, it is doubtful.

509. 596 *of* 1909.—(Sanskrit and Telugu.) On the Nāgapillar (which invokes the presence of the 8 Nāgas). In the Vīrabhadrēśvara temple. A record of the Western Chāḷukya king Bhūlōkamalla (Sōmēśvara III, 1126—38) in Ś. 1051, Saumya. Mentions Mādhavi-paṭṭaṇa and records a gift of land by a Haihaya feudatory chief named Bēṭa Birudaṅkarudra to a temple of the Hindu trinity, founded at Mādhavīpaṭṭaṇa (*Gurindasthala* or Gurizāla) by a Brahman of Kāmanūru who had studied the *padapāṭha* of the Rig Vēda. For similar *Nāga* pillar see Māchērla. [Sōmēśvara known, on account of his erudition, as Sarvagña was the suzerain of Hoysaḷa Vishṇuvardhana.]

510. 597 *of* 1909.—(Telugu.) On a slab set up near the platform of the flagstaff, in the courtyard of the same temple. A record in Ś. 1430, Vibhava. Śrīnatharāju Rāmayadēva-Mahārāja ratified grants to gods and Brāhmaṇas in the Gurindāla-śīma. [Referred to in *Antiquities*, I, 58.]

511. 598 *of* 1909.—(Telugu.) On three *virakals* in front of the Gurizālamma temple, ½ mile south of the same village. A damaged record.

Jūlakallu.

512. 546 *of* 1909.—(Telugu.) On a slab set up in front of the Āñjanēya temple. Records in Ś. 1699, Hēviḷambi, the reconsecration of the Āñjanēya temple at Juvvulakallu in Bellamkoṇḍa-śīma during the rule of Mallarāju Guṇḍarāyaniṅgāru and a gift of land to it for offerings. Another slab in the same place records that twelve years later the temples of Gōpālasvāmin and Bhīmēśvara at Juvvulakallu were repaired and reconsecrated.

513. 547 *of* 1909.—(Telugu.) On a slab set up in front of the Bhīmaliṅgēśvarasvāmin temple in the same village. Records in Ś. 1635, Nandana, gift of land by a certain Ambarāju to the temple of Mūlasthānam Bhīmanāthaśvāmin at Jūlakallu.

514. 548 *of* 1909.—(Telugu.) On another slab set up in the same place. A record of the Kākatīya king Mahāmaṇḍalēśvara Kumāra-Rudradēva Mahārāja (Pratāparudra II, 1291—1323) in Ś. 1213, Khara. Records gift of land by the general Sōmayalula Rudradēva to the temple of Mūlasthanam-Bhīmanāthadēva at Juvvulakallu. For reference to General Rudra Dēva see Nos. 497, 499 and 424 above.

Kambampāḍu.

515. North of the path leading to Mācharla. A gift of lands by a private person in Ś. 1549. *Antiquities*, p. 58.

Kāmepalle.

516. In a maṇṭapam east of the village. A record of Ś. 1598. *Ibid.*

517. North of a well west of the village. A private record of Ś. 1564. *Ibid.*

Kāraḷapāḍu.

518. In the ruined Vaishṇava temple. A private grant in Ś. 1544. *Ibid.*

Kārempūḍi.

This place figures largely in the chronicle of the Palnāḍ heroes. Even now it is the seat of a Brahman Guru who presides over the Śūdra community which professes the hero-cult and the epigraphs which follow, though not informing as to the origin of the cult, yet concern it. The place is also architecturally very interesting. See Fergusson's *Ind.* and *E. Arch.*, p. 274. Mr. Sewell mentions fourteen inscriptions here. Of these twelve alone are definite. Of these twelve, six are noted by the department also. The other six I have given under Nos. 529 to 534.

519. 549 *of* 1909.—(Telugu.) On a pillar of the maṇṭapa in front of the Śūrēśvara temple. A record of the Kākatīya king Mahāmaṇḍalēśvara Pratāparudradēva Mahāraja (II) in Ś. 1225, Śōbhakrit. Records that a servant of Mañchaya-Nāyaniṅgāru (a prominent officer of Pratāparudra II) repaired the temples of Śurēśvaradēva and Kēśava-Perumāḷ at Kārempūṇḍi for the merit of his master who bore the title Immadi-Niśśankavīra. Māchaya was evidently connected with Guṇḍa Nāyaka referred to in Vappichērla inscriptions, and ruled till Ś. 1233 (A.D. 1311). See also No. 486.

520. 550 *of* 1909.—(Telugu.) On another pillar of the same maṇṭapa. A record of Jannigadēva-Mahārāja (Rudrammā's minister) in Ś. 1186, Raktākshi. Records gift of land to the temple of Śūrēśvaradēva by the king's subordinate Gaṇḍapeṇḍara Mēidēvarāja. Also records the building of the gōpura and the prākāra wall by a private individual. See No. 500 above. [The Kākatīya feudatories Gaṅgaya and Janniga had a territory which extended from Paṅgal (Nalgondo district, Hyderabad) to Marjavāḍa or Kaivara in the Chintamaṇi taluk of Kolar district, and which thus comprised the large area covered by Cuddapah, Kurnool, Bellary, Anantapur, Nellore and Guṇṭūr districts. See also *Antiquities*, I, 59, No. 11.] See No. 500 above.

521. 551 *of* 1909.—(Telugu.) On the third pillar in the same place. A record of the Kākatīya king Mahāmaṇḍalēśvara Pratāparudradēva-Mahārāja (II) in Ś. 1239, Anala. Records gift of land to the same temple by Ālavaṭṭam Peddaya. [See also *Antiquities*, I, p. 59, No. 12.]

522. 552 *of* 1909.—(Telugu.) On a slab set up in the courtyard of the Aṅkālamma temple in the same village. A record of the Vēlanāṇḍu king Mahāmaṇḍalēśvara Kulōttuṅga-Chōḍa-Goṅkarāja (II, 1133—57) in Ś. 1076, Bhava. Records the building of the temple of Śūrēśvara by Īśana-Peggaḍa, a minister (pradhāni) of the king, at Kārempūṇḍi and a grant to it of 50 goats for a lamp. Īśanaśakti and Kalyaṇaśakti are mentioned as the sthānapatis of the temple. [See *Antiquities*, I, p. 57, No. 9.] See No. 564 below.

523. 553 *of* 1909.—(Telugu.) On another slab set up in the same place. A mutilated record of the Haihaya king in Ś. 1086, Taraṇa, the king's name in which is last. Mentions the goddess Vindhyavāsi and the sthānapati Kalyāṇaśakti, referred to in No. 552.

524. 554 *of* 1909.—(Telugu.) On a slab set up in the courtyard of the Chennakēśavasvāmin temple in the same village. Records in Ś. 1547, Raktākshin, that the temple of Chennakēśavasvāmin which was formerly built by the heroes *(viruḷavāru)* in the town of Kārempūṇḍi *alias* Uddaṇḍavīra-Tirupati in Vilāyati-kasuba ? had become dilapidated and the image of the god mutilated. A servant of Aḍsumballi Rāmanāyaniṅgāru renovated the temple and the images, together with those of the Āḷvārs and made grants of land for offerings. [The inscription is given in Mr. Sewell's *Antiquities*, I, p. 59, local list No. 8, but the date as 1549.]

525. 555 *of* 1909.—(Telugu.) On a beam of the tower called Nāyuḍu-maṇṭapa in the middle of the same village. Records in Ś. 1367, Raktākshi, the erection of the tower *(mēḍa)* by Jīvaraksha Timaṇa, son of Māchērla Chennuḍu at the spot where Chīlama Nāyuḍu, planted his spear. Pinamallidēvarāju, Chilama Nāyuḍu, Jīvaraksha Timaṇa, Pedamallidēvarāju, Vōbinēni and his wife, his brother Māchērla Timaṇa and the latter's son, are all figured on the beam, some holding spears and others standing in a worshipping posture. ["These chiefs may have been later members of the family to which Brahmā Nāyuḍu and his colleagues mentioned in Mr. Sewell's *Chronicle of the heroes* belonged." See also *Antiquities*, local list, No. 7.]

526. 556 *of* 1909.—(Sanskrit and Telugu.) On a slab set up in the courtyard of the "temple of Heroes" *(virulaguḍi)* in the same village. Records in Ś. 1318, Yuva, a decision of the Śri-Vaishṇava teacher Nallān Gōvindachakravarti Ayyaṅgāru, regarding certain sectarian rights and privileges bestowed on Baḍagulavāru of Palināḍu. [The Baḍagulavāru represented themselves as natives of Pali-nāḍu and secured from the Achārya the right to observe the *kuṅkuma-vasanta* like other classes, and on the protest of the natives of Pali-nāḍu, the teacher inquired into the dispute, withdrew the privileges granted on the ground that it was an innovation, and communicated the fact to the Śrī-Vaishṇavas of the eighteen countries. The Government Epigraphist suggests that the *Baḍagalavāru* were probably northerners, who immigrated in the time of the Kākatīya Viceroys, to the dislike of the orthodox Vaishṇavas of Palnāḍ.]

527. 557 *of* 1909.—(Telugu.) On a pillar of the same temple. Mentions in Ś. 1346, Krōdhin, Anuṅgumaṇḍalēśvara, the lord of Ayōdhya, and appears to record that a merchant built the temple for *Virakōṭi* and set up the garuḍastambha.

528. 558 *of* 1909.—(Telugu.) On a slab set up in the field adjoining the same temple. Records in Ś. 1237, Ānanda, that the slab was set up by a merchant for the merit of his teacher who was an Ārādhya.

529. On a stone fixed south of the maṇṭapam of the temple of the Heroes. Records the erection of a pillar in Ś. 1536 (A.D. 1614) by a private person. *Antiquities*, p. 59.

530. On a stone east of a small maṇṭapam behind the dvajastambha of the temple. A record in Ś. 1246 (A.D. 1324). *Ibid.*

531. On a pillar of the mukhamaṇṭapam of the same temple. Records the erection of the said maṇṭapam in Ś. 1255 (A.D. 1333). *Antiquities*, p. 59.

532. On a stone fixed north-east of the north gate of the same temple. A record dated in the Naḷa year, mentioning Allu Rāja and others. *Ibid.*

533. On a pillar of the north gate. Records a visit to the temple by the son of some Rājā whose name is not decipherable, dated in Paridhāvi. *Ibid.*

534. On a pillar of the mukhamaṇṭapam in Śūrēśvarasvāmi temple. A record of Pratāparudra II in Ś. 1227. *Ibid.*

Kavelapalle.

535. Near a local well. Records a grant in Ś. 1564. *Ibid.*

Māchērla.

This is the capital city of the Palnāḍ heroes. Besides the departmental list of epigraphs in this, I have given two more stone inscriptions and one C.P. which have been taken from Mr. Sewell's *Antiquities.*

536. 575 *of* 1909.—(Sanskrit and Telugu.) On the Nāga-pillar in the courtyard of the Chennakēśavasvāmin temple. A record of the chief Bēṭa, son of Vīrakāma, the second of the four sons of Chāgi Bēṭa of the lunar race of Kārtavīryārjuna, in Ś. 1033, Khara. Records a gift of land to the temple of Ādityēśvara built at the capital town Mahādēvi-taṭāka, by a certain Āditya. [These were probably feudatories of the Western Chāḷukyas. From the fact that the engravers of the record are Kanarese and the record of their names in the inscription in Kanarese, the Government Epigraphist surmises that they show the Western Chāḷukya influence in this part of the country. The inscription is very interesting for the architectural technique it gives. See *Ep. Rep.*, 1910, pp. 117–8, for details.]

537. 576 *of* 1909.—(Sanskrit and Telugu.) On the same pillar. A damaged record in Ś. 1035, Vijaya. Records the setting up of the Nāga-pillar by Āditya.

538. 577 *of* 1909.—(Telugu.) On a pillar of the maṇṭapa in front of the same temple. Records in Ś. 1443, Vrisha, gift of the pillar by a certain Gōvindarāju Mahāpātra.

539. 578 *of* 1909.—(Telugu.) On another pillar of the same maṇṭapa. Records in Ś. 1351, Saumya, repairs made to the maṇṭapa in front of the Chennakēśava-Perumāḷ temple at Mahādēvichērla.

540. 579 *of* 1909.—(Telugu.) On the third pillar of the same maṇṭapa. Records in Ś. 1541, Siddhārthin, gift of land for a lamp.

541. 580 *of* 1909.—(Telugu.) On the same pillar. Records in Ś. 1319, Īśvara, repairs made to the central shrine *(garbhagriha)* of the temple of Chennakēśavadēva at Mahādēvichērla by a certain Pērūri Muktirāju.

542. 581 *of* 1909.—(Telugu.) On the fourth pillar in the same maṇṭapa. Records in Ś. 1450, Sarvadhāri, gift of land.

543. 582 *of* 1909.—(Telugu.) On the fifth pillar in the same manṭapa. Records in Ś. 1336, Jaya, repairs made to the maṇṭapa.

544. 583 *of* 1909.—(Telugu.) On the east face of the Garuḍa-stambha in front of the same temple. Records in Ś. 1566, Tāraṇa, the setting up of the garuḍastambha by a certain Paluṭḷa Vōban-naṁgāru.

545. 584 *of* 1909.—(Sanskrit and Telugu.) On a slab set up in the courtyard of the Vīrabhadrēśvara temple in the same village. A mutilated record of the Vijayanagara king Vīrapratāpa Sadā-śivadēvarāya-Mahārāya in Ś. 1476, Ānanda. Records gift of the village Liṅgapura to the temples of Vīrēśvara and Ishṭakāmēśvara at Māchērla, by the queen of Komāra Timma-Nāyaniṅgāru of the Rēcharlagōtra and Vēḷugōṭi family, represented today by the Zamindars of Veṅkaṭagiri. See Podili 27 of Nellore inscriptions which shows that this chief was the feudatory of Śrīraṅgadēva (1578—86) in Ś. 1497. He is not mentioned in the genealogy published in *Antiquities*, II, pp. 240—3.

546. 585 *of* 1909.—(Telugu.) On a slab set up in front of the Pōlēramma temple in the same village. A damaged record of the Kākatīya king Mahāmaṇḍalēśvara Pratāparudradēva-Mahārāja (II) in Ś. 1235, Pramādi. Provides for offerings to the temple of Gaṅgā-Paramēśvari. [Mr. Sewell notes this epigraph, but gives the wrong date of Ś. 1215.]

547. 586 *of* 1909.—(Telugu.) On a slab set up in front of the ruined "temple of heroes" on the bank of the Chandravaṅka stream in the same village. A record of the Kākatīya king Mahā-maṇḍalēśvara Pratāparudradēva Mahārāja (II) in Ś. 1237, Ānanda. Records gift of land for the benefit of the heroes *(Virapurshulu)*, while Dēvari-Nāyiniṅgāru was ruling Mahādēvichērla. [This man was the feudatory of Pratāparudra (II) in the last years of his rule and the title "Rescuer of the Kākatīya family" he had shows that he perhaps took a prominent part in the repulsion of Mussalmān invasions.]

548. On a stone near a stream called the "Chandravaṅka." Records the erection of a temple in Ś. 1710. *Antiquities*, p. 60, No. 6.

549. In a palmyra tope between Māchērla and Mutukūru. A grant dated in Ś. 1171. *Ibid.*

550. In the possession of "Vattem" Sītārāmayya. A C.P. dated Ś. 1549, apparently of local interest. *Ibid.*

Miriyāla.

551. 590 *of* 1909.—(Telugu.) On a slab near the platform of the flagstaff, in front of the Channarāyasvāmin temple. Records in Ś. 1530, Plavanga, the building of the platform and the setting up of the pillar on it by a certain Pōtinēṇḍu, while he was ruling Miriyāla. [In his *Antiquities* Mr. Sewell notes a pillar inscription dated in Ś. 1570. Is this a mistake for the above ?]

Morasampāḍu.

552. A private grant dated S. 1562. *Antiquities*, p. 60.

Mutukūru.

553. In the Sītārāma temple on a slab. Records a private grant to the temple in Ś. 1576. *Ibid.*

554. In the yard of a private house. A record dated in Ś. 1190, in the reign of Rudradēva (Rudramma ?) *Ibid.*

555. In the same place. Records another grant in the same date, but the sovereign's name is given as Gaṇapatidēva (1213—59). *Ibid.*

Nadikūdi.

556. In one of the local temples. A private grant in Ś. 1134. *Ibid.*

Naramalapāḍu.

557. In one of the ruined temples. A private grant in Ś. 1609. *Ibid.*

Paḷḷiguṇṭa.

558. 595 *of* 1909.—(Sanskrit.) On a mutilated pillar of white stone in the Śiva temple. A record mentioning Pulikallu.

Passarlapāḍu.

559. North of the Hanūmān temple. A private record dated in Ś. 1547. *Ibid.*

Pasvēmula.

560. In one of the three deserted temples. A record of Ś. 1556, recording a gift by a Nāyuḍu. *Ibid.*

Paṭḷaviḍu.

561. On a stone half a mile south of the village. Records a grant to the Mācharla temple by Kṛishṇadēvarāya in Ś. 1440. *Ibid.*

Peddagarlapāḍu.

562. In the local temple. A record dated Ś. 1695, saying that the temple was then built. *Ibid.*

Peddakoḍamaguṇḍla.

563. 143 *of* 1913.—(Sanskrit and Telugu.) On a slab set up in the courtyard of the Uttarēśvara temple. A record in Ś. 1435, Śrīmukha, Śrāvaṇa, ba. di. 12, Friday, the Sun being in Kīta (i.e., scorpion), combined with Karshaṇa (Yoga) and Bava (Karana), corresponding to July 29, A.D. 1513. [The date is not quite regular. See *Ep. Rep.*, 1914, p. 72.] States that a certain Mahēśvarāchārya (also called Mahēśvarayati) founded the temple of Uttarēśvara with the shrine (Śaṅkaraprasāda), bull, flagstaff, minor deities, Vīrēśvara (i.e., Vīrabhadra) and Kāḷika. He is further stated to have built the compound wall, the pond, the garden and the well attached to the temple and to have provided for the worship of the liṅga and distribution of food in charity. He was the successor in Pāśupata Sambhavadīksha of Śaṁkaraguru who attained Śivahood on the given date and had become a liṅga through the great penance of his teacher Mantramūrtiguru.

564. 144 *of* 1913.—(Telugu.) On a second slab set up in the same place. A record of the Velanāṇḍu king Kulōttuṅga Chōḍa Goṅkarāja (II) in Ś. 1069, Prabhava . . . śu. di. 5, Thursday, Vishnuva-Saṁkrānti. Registers that the taxes *Peruśuṇka*, *Vaddarāvula* and others, due in and around the agrahāra of Godamagūḍa to Īśāna-Peggaḍa, an officer of the king, was endowed by him and by others, one of whom was a member of the Haihaya family, for the maintenance of worship in the temples at that agrahāra for lamps and offerings and for supporting ascetics and students. Mr. Swamikannu Pillai says that in Ś. 1069 (A.D. 1147–8) there were two *Śuklapañchamis* associated with Thursday, viz., June 5 and February 26, A.D. 1148; but neither was a Saṅkrānti. See No. 522 above for the same officer.

565. 145 *of* 1913.—(Telugu.) On a third slab set up in the same place. A mutilated record in . . . Utthānadvādaśi. Mentions the Mahāmaṇḍalēśvara Rāmarāja Tirumalarāja and the village Kārempūṇḍi.

566. 146 *of* 1913.—(Telugu.) On a fourth slab in the same place. A record in Ś. 1810, Sarvadhāri, Mārgaśira, ba. di. 3, Friday (= April 13, 1888). Quotes inscription No. 563 noted above and records that Laṅka Sankhayya, one of the descendants of Laṅka Mantramūrtiguru, who was represented by a Liṅga in the temple of Uttarēśvarasvāmin, granted lands the income from which was to be devoted for worship and offerings to the said Mantramūrtiguru. The English dates on which the gifts were made and the extent of lands in acres and cents are also given.

567. 147 *of* 1913.—(Telugu.) On a slab set up at the entrance into the Rāmasvāmin temple in the same village. Records in Ś. 1809, Sarvajit, Phalguna, śu. di. 5, Friday (May 6, 1886), that the same individual renovated the temple of Sītārāmasvāmi at

Pedakoḍamaguṇḍla, built by his father about sixty years prior to the date of the inscription and set apart some of his own lands at Miriyāla and Paluvaya for the exclusive use of the temple. These lands had to be cultivated by his descendants and the income therefrom was to be utilized for the worship of the god.

Piḍugurāla.

568. 599 *of* 1909.—(Telugu.) On a mutilated slab set up in the village. A record of the Kākatīya king, lord of Anumakoṇḍa, in Ś. 1... Kāḷayuktī. Appears to record the consecration of a temple for Rāma and Lakshmaṇa.

569. In one of the ruined temples. Records repair to the temple in Ś. 1472. *Antiquities*, p. 61.

Pondugala.

570. In ruins of the old Mussalmān city. A record dated in Ś. 1672, mentioning some unusually high freshes in the Kistna river. *Ibid.*, p. 62.

Rentala.

571. In the Hanūmān temple. A private inscription of Ś. 1595. *Ibid.*

572. In the remains of the Reḍḍi Fort. A record of Ś. 1596. *Ibid.*

Śrigiripāḍu.

573. In one of the abandoned temples. A record of Ś. 1220, of Manivadi Gōpināyaḍu who describes himself as the grandson of Kākatīya Pratāparudra. *Ibid.*

Tangeda.

574. In the Gōpālasvāmi temple. Records in Ś. 1294, a grant by Aḷia-Vēma Reḍḍi. *Ibid.*

575. West of the Durgā temple. A private grant in Ś. 1474, in the reign of Sadāśivarāya of Vijayanagar. Mentions the names of Rāmarāja, Rāmadēva and Tirumaladēva. *Ibid.*

Terala.

576. On a stone before the Siddhēśvara temple. Records a private grant in Ś. 1165. *Ibid.*

577. In the same place. A record of Pratāparudra (I or II ?).

578. On a third slab. A private grant in Ś. 1366. *Ibid.*

Tummalachcheruvu.

579. In a local temple. A record of Ś. 1575. *Ibid.*

580. In another deserted temple. A partly legible record of Ś. 1575. *Antiquities*, p. 62.

Tumrikōṭa (Tumurkōṭa).

581-A.—D. Mr. Sewell mentions here four tombs of English officers in which mention is made of the Nawab Mahommed Ali and the death of officers in 1766, 1733, 1774 and 1778.

Voppichērla.

582. 564 *of* 1909.—(Telugu.) On a slab set up near the well called Dēvatulabhāvi. A damaged record of the Kākatīya king Mahāmaṇḍalēśvara Pratāparudradēva (II) Mahārāja in Ś. 1233, Virōdhikrit. Appears to record a gift of land for the merit of Guṇḍaya Nāyaka and Māraya Sāhiṇi. See *Antiquities*, p. 61. For Guṇḍa Nāyaka see No. 583 "Māraya Sāhiṇiṅgāru reminds us strongly of the Chief Sāhini mara to whom was dedicated a portion at least of the *Bhāskara Rāmāyaṇamu*."

583. 565 *of* 1909.—(Telugu.) On another slab set up near the same well. A record of the Kākatīya king Mahāmaṇḍalēśvara Pratāparudradēva Mahārāja (II) in Ś. 1221, Vikāri. Records a gift of land while the chief Guṇḍanāyaka was ruling Gurimdāla-sthala, Piṅgaḷi-sthala, and other provinces. See *Antiquities*, p. 61. [Guṇḍa was probably the patron of Mañchana, the author of *Kēyūra bāhucharitra*.]

584. 566 *of* 1909.—(Telugu.) On a slab set up in the Āñjanēya temple in the same village. Records in Ś. 1541, Siddhārthin, the construction of the maṇṭapa of Hanumanta at Vappicharla by a certain Sāgi Raghunāthayya. [See *Antiquities*, I, p. 61.]

585. 567 *of* 1909.—(Telugu.) On a slab set up near the well known as Channappabāvi in the same village. An unfinished record in Ś. 1560, Bahudhānya. Records a grant bestowed on all the learned mahājanas residing at Vappicharla, by Rāmarāju Vīramārāju Chakrappaṁgāru. [See *Antiquities*, I, p. 61.]

RĒPALLE TALUK.

Allaparru.

586. A grant in Ś. 1663, Durmati, Śravana Śuddha 2, to Koṇḍūr Veṅkaṭāchārya by Śūrasáni Veṅkaṭapati. *Mack. MSS.*, Bk. XVIII, pp. 170-1.

Bhaṭṭiprōlu.

For a short account of the Buddhistic antiquities discovered in this place and the bibliography on the same, see *Antiquities*, I, pp. 77-8. The following inscriptions have been taken from

Mack. MSS., Vol. 48, p. 95, and Vol. 42, p. 346, from *Antiquities* * and Kielhorn's *List of Brāhmi Inscriptions.*

In the Viṭṭalēśvara and Mallēśvara temples :—

586-A. A record dated in Ś. 1065, Śubhakrit, Āśvija Śuddha 12, Saturday, Kanyāsaṅkrānti, and relating grant of 55 sheep, by Kulōttuṅga Chōḍa (Goṅka ?) to God Bhōgēśvara. *Loc. Rec.*, Vol. 48, p. 95.

586-B. A record dated in 1066, Vishu, Māghabahuḷa 14, Tuesday, relating grant of land to Viṭṭhalēśvaradēva originally given by Vishṇuvardhana by Kulōttuṅga-chōḍa Goṅka. [Mr. Sewell's Local List No. 2.]

586-C. A record dated in Ś. 1074, Paritāpi, Āśvija bahuḷa 8, Friday, Tulāsaṅkrānti, by Paramahamsa Śivamahāmuni, son of Viśvēśvara Mahāmuni, the priest of the Kākatīya Gaṇapati. *Ibid.*, p. 96.

586-D. A record of Ś. 1083 (year not given), Chaitra Śuddha 6, Monday, Mēsha Saṅkrānti, relating grant of land in the time of Kulōttuṅga Mahārāja to Gaṇṇama Nāyuḍu, etc. *Ibid.*, p. 97.

586-E. A record of Ś. 1160, Viḷambi, Āśvijaśuddha 3, Tuesday, Tulāsaṅkrānti, relating gift of lamp by Kākatīya Gaṇapati to Koṇḍaya Preggaḍa, son of Chōḍama Preggaḍa for Bhōgēśvara.

586-F. A record in Ś. 1165, Śubhakrit, Āśvijaśuddha 12, Saturday, Kanyāsaṅkrānti, gift of lamp, 8 buffaloes and 150 sheep by Kākatīya Rudradēva to Bhōgeśvara. Viśvēśvara mentioned. See 586 C.

586-G. A record in Ś. 1174, Paritāpi, Chaitraśuddha 8, Monday, gift of land by Kākatīya Gaṇapati to Paripūrna Mahāmuni. son of Guru Viśvēśvara Mahāmuni mentioned in No. 586 C. [Mr. Sewell's Local List Nos. 4 and 6.]

586-H. A record in Ś. 1180, Saumya, Makarasaṅkrānti, grant of five salt pans to Bhōgēśvara by Kākatīya Gaṇapati.

586-I. A record in Ś. 1182, Virōdhikrit, Pushya bahuḷa 2, Sunday, Makarasaṅkrānti, relating that Amarēśvara Preggaḍa gave 55 sheep for his parents' merit to Bhōgēśvara. [Mr. Sewell's Local List No. 5.]

586-J. A record of Ś. 1193, Kārttika Paurṇami relating gift of 100 sheep to the same deity in Kākatīya Mahārāja's reign.

586-K. A record of Ś. 1460, Hēviḷambi, Phalguna Śuddha, 10 Sunday, relating grant of lands to Viṭṭhaḷēśvara. There is reference to Vishṇuvardhana.

The Buddhistic casket inscriptions of the place have been edited by Buhler, Fleet and others in various journals. They have been given by Doctor Kielhorn in his *List of Brāhmi Inscriptions*

---

* Two inscriptions which Mr. Sewell gives under dates Ś. 1450 and 1465 are not found in the *Mack. MSS.*

with full bibliographical references. They are Nos. 1329—1339. I give the texts of the inscriptions alone here.

586-L. *Kielhorn's List, No.* 1329.—(Prākrit.) "The casket *(majusā)* of Kura, the son of Banava, together with his parents."

586-M. *Ibid., No.* 1330.—(Prākrit.) Records gift of a quartz-casket *(majusā)* and a crystal box *(shamuga)* for relics of Buddha by the father of Kura, the mother of Kura, and Kura.

586-N. *Ibid., No.* 1331.—(Prākrit.) Records that "Utara (Uttara), the son of Pigaha *(Vigraha)*, was the Kānīṭha (?)."

586-O. *Ibid., No.* 1332.—Mentions a committee of 36 persons named.

586-P. *Ibid., No.* 1333.—(Prākrit.) Says that the ascetic of the committee *(goṭhisamaṇa)* was Kuba (Kumbha). The treasurer *(hiranakāra)* was Buba, the son of the village-headman (gāmaṇi).

586-Q. *Ibid., No.* 1334.—(Prākrit.) Mentions Samaṇadāsha (Śramaṇadāsa) and relics of the Budha (Buddha). The rest is uncertain.

586-R. *Ibid., No.* 1335.—(Prākrit.) Records that the committee (gōṭhi) of the inhabitants of the hamlet *(nigamaputa)*, i.e., the committee mentioned in No. 1332 was headed by the king (rājan) who was Khubiraka *(Kubēraka)*, the son of Shā . . . ; their gift was the casket *(majusā)*, the crystal box *(shamuga)* and the stone box *(shamuga)*.

586-S. *Ibid., No.* 1336.—(Prākrit.) Records that the ascetic *(Samaṇa)* Utara (Uttara), the son of Ghakha (or Chāghakhā ?) presented the park *(ārāma)*.

586-T. *Ibid., No.* 1337.—(Prākrit.) Names 21 inhabitants of the hamlet *(negama)*.

586-U. *Ibid., No.* 1338.—(Prākrit.) Records that this was the casket *(majusā)* and the box *(shamugā)* of the committee *(gōṭhi)* of the Arahadinas *(Arhadattas)*. At that time Kubiraka (Kubēraka) was king (rājan).

586-V. *Ibid., No.* 1339.—(Prākrit.) Gift by the women from Namdapura (?) and the novices (śamaṇudēśa) from Suvaṇamāha (?) in the Aya-Sakasaṭhi (Ārya-Śakasaṭhi ?) committee *(gōṭhi)* of Gilānakēra (? Glānakārya ?).

Kuchinapūḍi.

587. Grants in Ś. 1684 and Ś. 1685 to Śivarāma Dīkshita by Puligaḍḍa Vīranna. See *Mack. MSS.*, Bk. 18 (15-6-21), p. 175, for details.

Nadimpalle.

588. A grant to Buchireḍḍipāḷem Daṇḍarāma svāmi in Ś. 1725, Dundubhi, Vaiśākha Śuddha 10. See *Mack. MSS.*, Bk. 18 (15-6-21), pp. 171-2, for details.

*Nizampatam.**

589. A C.P. discovered by a local karaṇam. A record of Vishṇuvardhana granting a village to Kuppanayya, the son of Kariyarāja and grandson of Kavivarma of the Pallava-malla family. See *Mack. MSS.*, Bk. XVIII (15-6-21), pp. 136—38.

590. In the hands of Duggarāḷa Timmaṇa. A record of Ś. 1684, Chitrabhānu, Śravaṇa Śuddha 15, relating gift of some land at Tsandavole and other villages by Śūrasāni Veṅkaṇṇa Jamadār to Timmaṇa. *Ibid.*, pp. 153-4. See No. 586 above.

591. In the hands of Niḍuguṇḍi Narasimhāchārya. A record of Ś. 1685, Svabhānu, Śravaṇa Bahuḷa 15, relating gift to Narasimhāchārya by Puligaḍḍa Vīraṇṇa, of some land. *Ibid.*, p. 155.

592. In the hands of Appasāni Koṇḍasāni. A record of F. 1189, Vikāri, Āśvija Śuddha 15, relating a grant to the festival at Amudanapalle. *Ibid.*, pp. 172-3.

Pallapatta.

593. In the hands of Pōpūr Guru Rāmamūrti. A record dated in Ś. . . , Raktākshi, Vaiśākha bahuḷa 10, relating a grant at Kāvūr to Pōpūr Śītārama Gāru by Śūrasāni Veṅkaṭapati. *Mack. MSS.*, Bk. 18 (15-6-21), p. 164. See Nos. 590 and 586 above.

594. A similar gift in Ś. 1667, Krōdhana, Vaiśākha Śuddha 15, by the same person. *Ibid.*, p. 165.

595. In the hands of Popūr Gurubhaṭṭa. A grant by Veṅkaṇṇa in Ś. 1683, Vikrama, Nijaśravaṇa Śuddha 7. *Ibid.*, p. 166.

596. In the hands of Guḍimalla Rāmānujāchārya. A grant dated in Ś. 1683, Vikrama, Nijaśravaṇa Śuddha 10, to Rāmānujāchārya of the Bhāradvāja gōtra, grandson of Tiruvēṅkaṭāchārya and son of Veṅkaṭāchārya, by Jamadar Veṅkaṇṇa. *Ibid.*, p. 169.

Peddapulivarru.

597. In a pillar of the Narēndrēśvara temple. A record of Ś. 1512. *Antiquities*, p. 80.

598. In the Varadarāja temple. A grant of the same date.

Peddāvaram.

599. A C.P. in the hands of Allūr Tiruvēṅkaṭāchārya living at Peddāvaram in Rēpalli-Rāchur taluk. Records that in Vaiśākha Śuddha 2, Jaṅgaṇṇa Māṇikka Rao of Puṇyapalli gōtra, gave to Vēdala Tiruvēṅkaṭāchārya, the son of Tātāchārya and grandson of Tiruvēṅkaṭāchārya, of the Kauṇḍinya gōtra and Āpastambha

* See also *Loc. Rec.*, Vol. XII, pp. 190—211.

Śūtra, the village of Peddāvaram. See *Mack. MSS.*, Bk. XVIII, p. 143.

600. With the same. A record of Ś. 1721, Siddhārti, Phalguna Śuddha 1, recording a gift by Māṇikkarāo Bhāvanarāyaṇarāo (son of the above Jaṅgaṇṇa) to the same person, the village of Peddāvaram as srōtriyam. *Mack. MSS.*, Bk. XVIII, p. 143.

601. With the same person. Records that in Ś. 1707, Māgha Śuddha 7, Māṇikka Rāo gave the village of Śivaṅgulapāḷem as śrōtriyam to Vēdala Narasimhāchārya. *Ibid.*, pp. 145—7.

602. With the same person. A record in Ś. 1731, Siddhārti, Phalguna Śuddha 1, renewing the above śrōtriyam to Narasimhāchārya. *Ibid.*, p. 147.

603. With the same person. Records that in Ś. 1680, Tāraṇa, Kārttika Bahuḷa 10, Raja Māṇikka Rāo Raghupati Rāja Jaṅgaṇṇa Rāo gave some land at Mattiguṇṭa to Jañjāla Lakshmaṇamūrti Sāstri. *Ibid.*

Ponnapaḷḷi.

604. A C.P. in the village. Recording a grant by Vēmareḍḍi in Ś. 1330 to Siṅgarāya, the grandson of Bhaṭṭa Bhāskara, a scholar in all the 18 sciences, Ayurvedic doctor, of Kāśyapa gōtra, of the village of Ponnapaḷḷi on the Kṛishṇavēṇi in Triliṅga. *Mack. MSS.*, Bk. XX, pp. 120—22. [See next epigraph for the identity of the chief.]

604-A. Another C.P. in the same place. (Sanskrit and Telugu.) A record of Pedda Kōmati Vema Bhūpati in Ś. 1326, Tāraṇa, Pushya, solar eclipse, making gift of land to the same. *Loc. Rec.*, Vol. 42, pp. 269—74 and Vol. 48, pp. 24—8. [The king referred to was Kōmaṭi Vēmā, the author of the *Śringāradipikā*, a commentary on *Amaruśataka*.]

*Rēpalli.**

605. A C.P. in the hands of Jañjāla Purushōttama Sāstri. Records that in Ś. 1685, Chitrabhānu, Chaitra Śuddha 1, Rāja Jaṅgaṇṇa Māṇikka Rāo gave some land to Jañjāla Lakshminārāyaṇa Śāstri, son of Peru Śāstri and grandson of Rāmaśāstri. See *Mack. MSS.*, Bk. XVIII, p. 148.

606. A C.P. in the hands of the same. Records an order to the karaṇams in Fasli 1208 to fix the boundaries of land given to Jañjāla Vīrabhadra Dīkshitar. *Ibid.*, p. 150.

606-A.* A title-deed in the hands of Piśipāṭi Veṅkaṭayya. Gift of land by Māṇikka Rao Rāja Bhāvanārāyaṇa Rao in Fasli 1311 to him (i.e., A.D. 1802).

* See also *Loc. Rec.*, Vol. XII, pp. 69—71.

606-B.* In the hands of the same. A gift of land by Jagaṇna Māṇikka Rao to the same in A.D. 1778.

606-C.* Undated grant to Veṅkaṭa Bhāgavata at Majukūru.

Śiripūdi.

607. A C.P. in the hands of the agrahāra people in five plates. (Sanskrit.) A record of the Chāḷukyan king Vishṇuvarddhana (V or VI?) who issued an edict to the chief Sawrashtra families of Veluguntịgōshṭi, saying that he gave Śrīvūru to Kuppanayya (whose Panegyrics are given). Kavidharmadharmāchārya wrote this. A little incomplete. No date. *Mack. MSS.*, Bk. XX, pp. 41–3.

Tsandavōlu † *(Ancient Dhanadaprōlu or Dhanadapura).*

608. 245 *of* 1897.—(Sanskrit.) On a pillar lying in the prākāra of the Liṅgōdbhavasvāmin temple. Records gift of a lamp to Chaṇḍika by Gaṅgamā.

609. 246 *of* 1897.—(Sanskrit.) On the same pillar. A record in Ś. 1090. Mentions a concubine of Rājēndra-Chōḍa (Velanāṇḍu chief?) and the city of Dhanadapura.

610. 247 *of* 1897.—(Sanskrit and Telugu.)* On a pillar in the same temple. Records in Ś. 1092 gift of sheep for a lamp by a Nāyaka to the temple of Goṅkēśvara at Dhanadaprōlu. Mentions Kulōttuṅga-Goṅka. [Was he Gonka III of the Velanāṇḍu chiefs of Piṭhāpuram?]

611. 248 *of* 1897.—(Telugu.) On the same pillar. An incomplete record in Ś. ... , Dhātri, of the Kākatīya king Rudradēva (1295—1323).

612. 249 *of* 1897.—(Sanskrit and Telugu.) On a pillar opposite the same temple. Records in Ś. 1063 gift of land in Nādiṇḍla and of sheep for a lamp to the Pāṇāīśvara temple at Dhanadaprōlu in Velanāṇḍu by Koṇḍapaḍumaṭi-Buddharāja of the Durjaya family. This Buddharāja was the brother of Akkamā, the queen of Rājēndra-Chōḍa, the son of Goṇka (II) of Velanāṇḍu. See *Ep. Ind.*, Vol. VI, pp. 268—78. Koṇḍapaḍumaṭi is the eastern portion of the Sattenapalli taluk.

613. 250 *of* 1897.—(Sanskrit and Telugu.) On a pillar which forms a beam of the same temple. A record of the Kākatīya king Gaṇapati (1213—59). Records that Jāya-Sēnāpati repaired the temple of Pāṇḍīśvara, which Kulōttuṅga-Rājēndra-Goṅka had built and named after his younger brother, and that king Gaṇapati granted a village to this temple. [Gaṇapati married the two sisters of his general Jāya.]

---

* See also *Loc. Rec.*, Vol. XII, pp. 69—71.

† In his Antiquities Mr. Sewell gives two other inscriptions, viz., (*a*) a private grant in S. 1076 and (*b*) a grant in Ś. 1098 by Velanāṭi Goṅka, commander of the forces of "Vijaya Rāja."

614. In the hands of the Inamdar Kuchibhaṭṭa Jañjāla Rāmavadhāni. Records in Ś. 1670, Vibhava, Chaitra Śuddha 10, gift of land by Puligaḍḍa Nandirāju Dēśāyi. *Mack. MSS.*, Bk. XVIII, p. 162.

615. A record in the hands of Padmanābhaiyaṅgār. Records in Ś. 1671, Śukla, Kārttika Śuddha 15, gift of land to Śishṭāla Śūraṇṇagāru by Veṅkaṇṇa. *Ibid.*, p. 167.

Vōlēru.

616. On the left side of the entrance to the Madanagōpāla temple. A grant to the temple by a private person in Ś. 1460 in honour or Achyuta Rāya of Vijayanagar. *Antiquities*, p. 81. See also *Loc. Rec.*, Vol. 42, pp. 310—19. The details of the date are Viḷambi, Mārgaśira Śuddha 11, Thursday. A history of the donor's family is given. Dates 1792, 1793, etc., mentioned.

SATTENAPALLI TALUK.

Amarāvati.

For an excellent account of the importance and antiquities of this place and a bibliography of the same see Mr. Sewell's *Antiquities*, pp. 63-4.

617. 251 *of* 1897.—(Telugu verse and prose.) On a slab outside the prākāra to the east of the Amarēśvara temple. Records in Ś. 1100 gift of a lamp to the Amarēśvara temple by Appaṇa Reḍḍi, who was a servant of Kēṭa (II) and was governing the country east of Rāyūru.

618. 252 *of* 1897.—(Telugu.) On another slab in the same place. Records in Ś. 1051, Thursday, Uttarāyaṇa Sankrānti, Saumya Paushya Śuddha 13, gift of sheep for a lamp to Ishṭakāmīśvara by Kāmaṇa-Pregaḍa of Rāyūru in Kammanāṇḍu, who had built the shrine. [See *Mack. MSS.*, Bk. XX (15-3-63), p. 1. Also *Antiquities*, p. 64, for a defective note.]

619. 253 *of* 1897.—(Sanskrit and Telugu.) On a pillar in the same place. Records in Ś. 1079, Īśvara, gift of sheep for a lamp by Kavaliya-Siṇgaṇa-Peggaḍa, the minister of the Mahāmaṇḍalēśvara Pōtarāja, the son of Chāgi-Dora of the Durjaya family.

620. 254 *of* 1897.—(Telugu.) On another pillar in the same place. Records in Ś. 1416, Ānanda, gift of taxes by the goldsmith Mallaya-Mahāpatra to the Kamaṭhēśvara temple at Dharaṇakōṭa.

621. 255 *of* 1897.—(Sanskrit and Telugu.) On another pillar in the same place. Records in Ś. 1148 gift of the village Dāmalūru to the Amalēśvara temple by Chāgi-Gaṇapayamahārāja.

622. 256 *of* 1897.—(Prākrit.) At the entrance to the Chaṇḍi shrine outside the prākāra of the same temple. Records gift of a pillar by the nun Nandā.

623. 257 *of* 1897.—(Sanskrit and Telugu.) On a pillar in the main gōpura of the same temple. Records in Ś. 1104 (Māgha Śukḷa 10), gift of lamps by Kōṭa-Ketā (II) of Dhānyakaṭaka, the son of Bhīma, for the merit of his mother Sabbamā, his father Bhīma, his elder brother Kōṭa-Chōḍa, and himself. The mother of Kēṭa was the sister of Goṅka (III of Velanāṇḍu). This epigraph (like 630 and 635 below) refers, as Luders says, to the very day of the accession of Kēṭa II. See *Ep. Ind.*, Vol. VI, p. 148, *Mack. MSS.*, Bk. XX (15-3-63), pp. 9-10 and *Antiquities*, p. 64.

624. 258 *of* 1897.—(Sanskrit and Telugu.) On another pillar in the same place. Records in Ś. 1283, Plava, Śrāvaṇa, Śuklapañchami, Thursday, the reconsecration of the Amarēśvara temple at Dhānyavāṭi by Vēma, the son of Mallinātha, grandson of Kēṭa and minister of Anavōta-Reḍḍi, the son of Vēma (the builder of the flights of steps at Ahōbilam and Śrīśailam). See *Mack. MSS.*, Bk. XX (15-3-63), pp. 23—29. Also *Antiquities*, p. 64, No. 1.

625. 259 *of* 1897.—(Sanskrit and Telugu.) On another pillar in the same place. Records in Ś. 1308, Kshaya, Āshāḍha Śukla 2, Wednesday, of a flower garden by Peddi, the son of Appaya and minister of Vēmā Reḍḍi, the son of Kāṭama-Reḍḍi. [The latter was the founder of the Rājahmundry line and the husband of Mallāmbikā, the sister of Kumāragiri, the author of the *Vasantarājāiyam*.] See *Mack. MSS.*, Bk. XX (15-3-63), pp. 31-2. *Antiquities*, Local List, No. 2.

626. 260 *of* 1897.—(Sanskrit and Telugu.) On a slab leaning against the eastern entrance to the central shrine of the same temple. Records in Ś. 1548, Akshaya, Śravana Bahuḷa Daśami 10, Sunday, the third consecration of the Amarēśvara temple at Dhāraṇakōṭa or Dhānyavāṭi by Handrikē-Pedda of Juvvūru, and refers to the second consecration by Anna-Vēma of the Paṇṭakula. Anna Vēma was the brother of Annavōta referred to in No. 624 above. [This epigraph is given in *Mack. MSS.*, Bk. XX (15-3-63), pp. 39-40. See also *Antiquities* I, p. 64.]

627. 261 *of* 1897.—(Sanskrit and Telugu.) At the eastern entrance to the same shrine; pillar to the right. Records in Ś. 1119, Āśvija, Śuddha 15, Padmāvāram, gift of villages to Brāhmaṇas by Kōṭa-Kēṭarāja (II) and gift of lamps by five queens of his. [Padmāvāram = Thursday. See *Mack. MSS.*, Bk. XX (15-3-63), pp. 15-18, for the full inscriptions. There is another inscription of the same date in *ibid.*, p. 20.]

628. 262 *of* 1897.—(Sanskrit and Telugu.) At the eastern entrance to the same shrine, pillar to the left. Records gifts by relatives of Kōṭa-Kēṭarāja of Dhānyakaṭaka. *Ibid.*, p. 18.

629. 263 *of* 1897.—(Telugu verse.) On a pillar at the northern entrance to the same shrine. Mentions a poet named Tippaṇa.

630. 264 *of* 1897.—(Sanskrit and Telugu.) On a pillar within the same shrine. Records in Ś. 1104 (युगवेन्दुरूप) gift of villages to Buddha dēva by (Kāṭa) Kēṭarāja (II). A damaged record. See No. 623 above and *Mack. MSS.*, Bk. XX (15-3-63), pp. 3—8. The latter gives the further date Māgha Daśami.

631. 265 *of* 1897.—(Sanskrit and Telugu.) On a pillar built into the wall of the Sanyāsi's room adjoining the same shrine. Records in Ś. 1077 gift of a lamp by an officer of Kulōttuṅga-Chōḍa-Goṅka, 1133—58. [This inscription is in *Mack. MSS.*, Bk. XX (15-3-63), pp. 1—3. The officer referred to is Kamma Nāyaka whose praises are given in the usual magniloquent terms.]

632. 266 *of* 1897.—(Sanskrit.) On a slab in the same room. A record in Ś. 1437, Yuva, in the reign of the Vijayanagara king Kṛishṇarāya. Records that the king performed the *tulāpurusha* in the Amarēśvara temple and granted agrahāras. [See *Ep. Ind.*, VII, 17—22, where Dr. Luders edits the inscription and draws attention to the important clue it gives to the king's conquests of Śivasamudra, Vinukoṇḍa, Koṇḍavīdu and Vīrabhadra (the son of Gajapati king). Luders compares the inscription with Maṅgaḷagiri, Kaza and Koṇḍavīḍu inscriptions and with Albuquerque's *commentaries*, Paes, Nuniz, etc.] See *Mack. MSS.*, Bk. XX (15-3-63), pp. 35-6.

633. 267 *of* 1897.—(Telugu.) On a pillar leaning against the wall of the same room. Records in Ś. 1349, Kīlaka, gift of land. This inscription is given in *Mack. MSS.*, Bk. XX, but the date is Ś. 1347, Kīlaka, Śrāvaṇaśuddha 2, Thursday. Chiṭṭipātinēniṅgāru gave land for the merit of his parents to God Amarēśvara.

634. 268 *of* 1897.—(Sanskrit and Telugu.) On the same pillar. A record of the Reḍḍi king Vēmaya Reḍḍi in Ś. 1267, Pārthiva (A.D. 1345), Kārttika Śuddha 4, Thursday. Records that the king set up five golden pinnacles on the temple for the merit of his younger brother Mallaya-Reḍḍi. [Vēmaya was the son of Prōla and the third of his dynasty. See Kn. 11, Cd. 880, and Cd. 699, and *Ep. Ind.*, Vol. III, p. 10. See also *Mack. MSS.*, Bk. XX (15-3-63), pp. 29-30.]

635. 269 *of* 1897.—(Sanskrit and Telugu.) On a pillar at the southern entrance to the same shrine. Records in Ś. 1104, gift of villages and lamps by Kōṭa-Kēṭarāja (Kāṭa II), the son of Bhīma (II) and Sabbama and by two of his concubines to the Buddha at Dhānyakaṭaka. The "high chaitya" (i.e., Amarāvati stūpa) is referred to. Also gift of villages to Brāhmaṇas by Kēṭa. The chiefs are said to be the lords of the 6,000 country, south of the Kṛishṇa, obtained, it is said, through the favour of Śrināṛāyaṇa Pallava. See Enamadala inscription of Gaṇapāmba which carries the genealogy two generations further. See *Ep. Ind.*, Vol. VI, pp. 146—57. See also *Mack. MSS.*, Bk. XX (15-3-63), p. 5, for the present epigraph.

636. 270 *of* 1897.—(Sanskrit and Telugu.) On the same pillar. Records in Ś. 1156, Jaya, gift of a lamp to God Buddha by Kōta-Bayyalamahādēvi, the daughter of Rudradēva of Nathavāṭi. Bayyamāmba was evidently the queen of Bēṭa II. The date of the grant (Thursday, eleventh *tithi* of the bright fortnight of Jyēṣṭha in Ś. 1156) corresponded according to Kielhorn, to the 11th May A.D. 1234. See *Ep. Ind.*, Vol. VI, pp. 157—9. *Vide* also *Mack. MSS.*, Bk. XX (15-3-63), pp. 34-5.

637. 271 *of* 1897.—(Sanskrit and Telugu.) On a pillar lying in the prākāra of the same temple. Records in Ś. 1082 gift of two lamps by Kallaya-Nāyaka, the younger brother of Pōta, the son of Chāgi-Dora of the Durjaya family, and by his wife, who was the daughter of Muchchaya-Nāyaka of Rāchchūru, of the same family.

638. 272 *of* 1897.—(Telugu.) On another pillar in the same place. A record of the Vijayanagara king Kṛishṇarāya in Ś. 1437, Yuva, Āshāḍha Bahuḷa 12, Sunday. Records some of his conquests in the east and mentions his two queens Chinnādēvi and Tirumalādēvi. Records gift of villages. [*Mack. MSS.*, Bk. XX (15-3-63), pp. 37-8.]

639. On an octagonal pillar excavated at Amarāvati by Mr. Sewell and sent to the Madras Museum by Burgess. A record (Sanskrit) of the Pallava king Simhavarman (II) making a gift, on his return from an expedition to the north, at the sacred place of the Buddha Dhānyāghaṭa. See *S.I.I.*, Vol. I, pp. 24—8. In *Ep. Ind.*, Vol. X, pp. 43-4. Dr. Hultzsch compares the palæography of this epigraph with that of others and concludes that it should be assigned to about A.D. 1100, between the times of the Tēki plates of Chōḍagaṅga (*Ep. Ind.*, VI, A.D. 1086-87) and Piṭhāpuram plates of Vīrachōḍa. (See *S. Ind. Palæ.*, A.D. 1092-93.) The epigraph was originally printed in *Madras Journal* for 1886-87.

640. On a pillar south-west of the mukhamaṇṭapam. Records a grant by the wife of Prōli Nāyuḍu, a dependent of "Kulōttuṅga Chōḍa Goṅga Rāja," in Ś. 1030 (A.D. 1108). *Antiquities*, p. 64, No. 6.

641. On the wall south of the east doorway of the garbhālayam. Records the erection of a Śiva temple at Dharaṇikōṭa in Ś. 1548 (A.D. 1626). *Ibid.*, No. 7.

642. On the dhvajastambha of a Śiva temple south of the town. Records the erection of the pillar by Vāsi Reḍḍi Veṅkaṭādri Nāyaḍu, the Rāja of Chintapaḷḷi, in Ś. 1735. *Ibid.*, No. 9.

643. *Kielhorn's List, No.* 1206.—On a Buddhist rail (now in the British Museum). Records in Prākrit gift by a female lay worshipper, her brothers and sisters.

644. *Kielhorn's List, No.* 1207.—(Prākrit.) On a Buddhist rail. Records gift of tablets of homage *(yaghapata ?)* to the great Chaitya *(mahāchetiya)* of Bhagavat by two persons.

645. *Ibid., No.* 1208.—(Prākrit.) On a pillar. Records the gift of a pillar *(thabha)* by Halika and others.

646. *Ibid., No.* 1209.—(Prākrit.) On a pillar (now in the British Museum). Gift of two foot-prints by Śivaka. The members of his family named.

647. *Ibid., No.* 1210.—(Prākrit.) On a pillar in the same place. Gift of the Chatiya pillar by a perfumer *(gādhika)*, Hamgha (Saṁha), together with his sons and daughters.

648. *Ibid., No.* 1211.—(Prākrit.) A fragmentary record.

649. *Ibid., No.* 1212.—(Prākrit.) Illegible.

650. *Ibid., No.* 1213.—(Prākrit.) Records the gift of the slab *(paṭa)* of (Mūlaśiri), the son of a merchant (Vāṇiya) named Bōdhiśarman.

651. *Ibid., No.* 1214.—(Prākrit.) On a sculpture work. Records gift of a pillar for lamps *(divathabha)* at the southern entrance *(āyaka)* to the great Chaitya by a merchant (Vāṇiya) and family.

652. *Ibid., No.* 1215.—Gift of slab by some person and his family.

653. *Ibid., No.* 1216.—Gift of a Chaitya a *vēṭika* (rail) and a *paṭa* (slab) by a *gahapati (hagha)*.

654. *Ibid., No.* 1217.—(Prākrit.) Gift of slab with foot-prints *(pādukapaṭa)*.

655. *Ibid., No.* 1218.—On a pillar. Records a gift by Saghā, Saghadāsi (i.e., Saṁghadāsi), etc.

656. *Ibid., No.* 1219.—On a pillar (now in the British Museum). Gift of two foot-prints *(pāduka)* by the mother of Ānada (Ānanda).

657. *Ibid., No.* 1220.—Records a gift by the son of a gahapati (grihapati) Kanhati with his people.

658. *Ibid., No.* 1221.—Gift of a coping stone *(unisā)* by the grandson of the gahapati Mariti, the Akhasavādicha (inhabitant of Akhasavāda).

659. *Ibid., No.* 1222.—On a pillar (now in the British Museum). (Prākrit.) Gift of the grandson of the *gahapati* Pāpin, the Valikachaka (inhabitant of Valikacha), and his wife Kaṇhā (Kṛishṇā).

660. *Ibid., No.* 1223.—On a sculpture work. (Prākrit.) Gift of a lion seat (sihaṭhāna) by the two, the elder *(thēra)*, the Chaitya worshipper *(Chēṭiyavamdaka) bhayamta (bhadanta)* Budhi *(Buddhi)* and his sister, the nun *(bhikuni)* Budha (Buddhā).

661. *Ibid., No.* 1224.—On a sculpture work (now in the British Museum). (Prākrit.) Records that it was made by . . . the son of Dhamadēva (Dharmadēva), the Vīrapuraka (inhabitant of Vīrapura); also the gift of . . . female pupil (atēvāsini) of Budharakhita (Buddharakshitā).

662. *Ibid., No.* 1225.—On a rail (now in the British Museum) (Prākrit.) A fragmentary record. Gift of two Chaitya slabs (chēṭiyapaṭa), three foot-prints *(pāuka)*, a coping stone *(umnisā)*, a slab with a flower vase *(? puphaganiyapaṭa ?)* and other objects to the great Chaitya *(mahachēṭiya)* at Dhamnakata (Dhānyakaṭa), and erection of some object at (?) the great Chaitya *(mahāchētiya)* at Rājagiri at the northern door *(dāra)* by some person together with his relatives.

663. *Kielhorn's List, No.* 1226.—(Prākrit.) On a sculpture work. A fragmentary record. Gift of a slab *(paṭa)* by some person.

664. *Ibid., No.* 1227.—(Prākrit.) On a sculpture work. Not read except in the beginning which contains an invocation of Bhagavat.

665. *Ibid., No.* 1228.—(Prākrit.) On a sculpture work. Illegible.

666. *Ibid., No.* 1229.—(Prākrit.) On a pillar. Gift of a Chaitya pillar *(chētiyakhabha)* with a relic, at the southern entrance *(āyaka)* by the merchant (Vāṇiya) Kuṭa together with his relatives.

667. *Ibid., No.* 1230.—(Prākrit.) On a pillar. A fragmentary record. Records after an invocation of Bhagavat, the gift of a chief pavilion *(? padhānamaḍava)* to the order (saghā) by the perfumer *(gādhika)*, the merchant *(Vāniya)* Siridata (Śrīdatta), son of the merchant *(Vāṇiya)* Dhammila (Dharmila). . . of the pupil *(? sisiha)* of the teacher (achariya) Sariputa *(Sāriputra)*, the Mahāvanasaliya (who lives in Mahāvanasāla ?).

668. *Ibid., No.* 1231.—(Prākrit.) On a coping stone. A fragmentary record. Gift of a coping stone *(unisā)* by some woman together with her relatives.

669. *Ibid., No.* 1232.—(Prākrit.) On a sculpture work. A fragmentary record. Gift of . . . of the son of Mugudasama (Mukundaśarman) . . . with relatives.

670. *Ibid., No.* 1233.—(Prākrit.) On a sculpture work. A fragmentary record. Mentions the *bhāyaṁta (bhadanta)*, pupil of Nādhasiri (Nāthaśrī), the Mahemkhānājaka (inhabitant of Mahemkhānāja), disciple *(aṁtēvāsika)* of . . .

671. *Ibid., No.* 1234.—(Prākrit.) On a sculpture work. A fragmentary record. Mentions, after an invocation of Bhagavat Buda (Buddhā), the sister of the monk *(pavaita)* Sidamta (Siddhārtha), who lived at Maṁdara.

672. *Ibid., No.* 1235.—(Prākrit.) On a stone slab. A fragmentary record. Gift of an upright slab *(udhapaṭa)* by . . . Bhagommu (?), the wife of Sidhatha (Siddhārtha), . . . and Bōdhi.

673. *Ibid., No.* 1236.—(Prākrit.) On a sculpture work. A fragmentary record. Illegible.

674. *Ibid., No.* 1237.—(Prākrit.) On a sculpture work. Gift of the two female pupils *(atēvāsini)* of Aya-Kāmaya (Ārya Kāmaya).

675. *Kielhorn's List, No.* 1238.—(Prākrit.) On a pillar. A fragmentary record. No name has been preserved.

676 *Ibid., No.* 1239.—(Prākrit.) On a sculpture work. A fragmentary record. Records after an invocation of the enlightened one, the gift of Nākhā, the wife of the lay worshipper (upāsaka), the Narasala (inhabitant of Narasala ?), the merchant (Vāniya) Nāgatisa (Nāgatishya), together with her sons, the treasurer *(hēraṇika)* Budhi (Buddhi), Mūla . . .

677. *Ibid., No.* 1240.—(Prākrit.) On a sculpture work. A fragmentary record. Records the erection of a slab *(? pemḍaka)* by Hamgi (Samghi), the daughter of bhāyaṁtī *(bhadanti)* Bōdhi. . . of the nun *(pavajitikā)* Vasa (Vāśyā) resident in Kevurura.

678. *Ibid., No.* 1241.—(Prākrit.) On a sculpture work. A fragmentary record. Gift of a rail bar *(suji)* by Budharakhita (Buddharakshitā).

679. *Ibid., No.* 1242.—(Prākrit.) On a sculpture work. A fragmentary record. Gift of the female ascetic *(samaṇikā)* Sidhaṁthi (Siddhārthi).

680. *Ibid., No.* 1243.—(Prākrit.) On a sculpture work. Gift of an upright slab *(udhaṁpaṭa)* at the foot of the great Chaitya *(mahāchētiya)* by Damilakanha (Draviḍakṛishṇa) and his brother Chulakanha (Kshudrakṛishṇa) and his sister Nākhā.

681. *Ibid., No.* 1244.—(Prākrit.) On a pillar. Erection of a pillar for lamps (divakhaṁbha) at the foot of the great Chaitya *(mahāchētiya)* of Bhagavat by Khada (Skanda), wife of the householder (gahapati) Sidhatha (Siddhārtha) of the Jadikyas, together with her relatives.

682. *Ibid., No.* 1245.—(Sanskrit.) On a pillar. By the glorious Viprajātapriya (?).

683. *Ibid., No.* 1246.—(Prākrit.) On a pillar. Gift of Aya-Dhamā (Ārya-Dharmā), female pupil *(atēvāsini)* of Aya Rēti (Ārya-Rēti).

684. *Ibid., No.* 1247.—(Prākrit.) On a sculpture work. Gift of a rail bar *(suyi)* by the treasurer (hēraṇika) Sidhātha (Siddhārtha), the son of the householder (gahapati) Budhila (Buddhila), together with his relatives.

685. *Ibid., No.* 1248.—(Prākrit.) On a stone. A fragmentary record. Gift of a wheel of the Law (*dhamachaka*) at the western gate *(dāra)* to the great Chaitya *(mahāchētiya)* of Bhagavat by the householder *(gahapati)* Kahutara and Isila (Rishīla), the son of the householder *(gahapati)* Puri, of the Piṁdasutariyas, together with Isila's wife Nākānika (Nāgā) and other relatives, as the special property of the school *(nikāya)* of the Chētikiyas (Chaityakīyas).

686. *Kielhorn's List, No.* 1249.—(Prākrit.) On a sculpture work. A fragmentary record. Gift of an *abadamala* (?) by some man together with his relatives.

687. *Ibid., No.* 1250.—(Prākrit.) On a sculpture work. A fragmentary record. Gift of the nun *(bhikhuni)* Budharakhitā (Buddharakshita) . . . female pupil *(atēvāsini)* of the elder *(thēra)* bhayata *(bhadanta)* Budharakhita (Buddharaskhitā), the overseer of works (navakamaka) of the Chētikas (Chaityakas) who lived at Rājagiri, together with her daughter, and of Dhamadina (Dharmadattā) and of Sagharakhita (Saṁgharakshitā).

688. *Ibid., No.* 1251.—(Prākrit.) On a sculpture work. A fragmentary record. Gift of a coping stone *(unisā)* at the northern entrance *(āyāka)* to the Great Chaitya (mahāchētiya) by some female person together with her family.

689. *Ibid., No.* 1252.—(Prākrit.) On a coping stone. A fragmentary record. Gift of the lay-worshipper *(upāśika)* Kāmā (Kāmyā), daughter of the housewife Kanha (Kṛishṇa), daughter of the householder *(gahapati)* Ida (Indra), together with her relatives, and of the nun *(bhikhuni)* Nāgamitā (Nāgamitrā).

690. *Ibid., No.* 1253.—(Prākrit.) On a pillar. Gift of a slab with a wheel *(chakapaṭa)* by Koja (Kubja).

691. *Ibid., No.* 1254.—(Prākrit.) On a sculpture work. Gift of two rail bars *(suchi)* with circular panels *(parichaka)* by Makabudhi (Mṛigabuddhi), son of the householder *(gahapati)* Budhi (Buddhi), together with his relatives.

692. *Ibid., No.* 1255.—(Prākrit.) On a coping stone. A fragmentary record. Erection of a gate *(dāra)* at the southern side by the householder *(gahapati)* . . . son of the householder *(gahapati)* Sulasa, together with . . . Nāgatā (Nāgatta) and his son Sulasa, with his daughter.

693. *Ibid., No.* 1256.—(Prākrit.) On a stone. A fragmentary record. Gift of a coping stone *(unisā)* by Ajaka together with his father.

694. *Ibid., No.* 1257.—(Prākrit.) On a sculpture work. A fragmentary record. Gift of some nun *(bhikhuni)*.

695. *Ibid., No.* 1258.—(Prākrit.) On a sculpture work. A fragmentary record. Gift of some female ascetic *(samaniki)* together with her sister.

696. *Ibid., No.* 1259.—On a coping stone. Illegible.

697. *Ibid., No.* 1260.—(Prākrit.) On a pillar. Gift of a pillar (khaṁbha) by the grandsons of Kaṁmā (Kāmyā), daughter of Bhagi, wife of the householder *(gahapati)* Rāhula in Hiralūra.

698. *Ibid., No.* 1261.—(Prākrit.) On a sculpture work. Gift of a rail bar *(suchi)* by the righteous hamlet *(bhadanigama)* the Chhadakicha (of Chhadaka), headed by the bankers (sethin).

699. *Kielhorn's List, No.* 1262.—(Prākrit.) On a sculpture work. Gift of upright slabs *(upaṭa)* by the nun *(pavajitikā)* Sagharakhita (Saṁgharakshitā) living in Dēvaparavana (?), and by her daughter, the nun *(pavajitikā)* Haṁghā (Saṁghā), and by (the latter's ?) daughter Jiyavā.

700. *Ibid., No.* 1263.—(Prākrit.) On a sculpture work. Gift of a rail bar *(suchi)* by Papin (Pāpin), brother of bhayaṁta (bhadanta) Budhi (Buddhi), the Chaitya worshipper (Chētivadaka). Compare No. 1223.

701. *Ibid., No.* 1264.—(Prākrit.) On a coping stone. A fragmentary record. Gift of the nun *(bhikhuni)* Rōhā, daughter of Sujātā.

702. *Ibid., No.* 1265.—(Prākrit.) On a pillar. A fragmentary record. Records some gift.

703. *Ibid., No.* 1266.—(Prākrit.) On a sculpture work. The pillar *(thabha)* of the general *(sēnagōpa)* Mudukutala (Mṛidukuntala).

704. *Ibid., No.* 1267.—(Prākrit.) On a sculpture work. A fragmentary record. Gift of the preacher *(dhamakathika)* Budhi (Buddhi) dwelling in Oḍiparivenena ?).

705. *Ibid., No.* 1268.—(Prākrit.) On a sculpture work. A fragmentary record. Gift of the female lay-worshipper *(uvāsika)* Sivala (Sivalā) with her sons and daughters.

706. *Ibid., No.* 1269.—(Prākrit.) On a coping stone. A fragmentary record. Gift of a rail *(vētikā)* by several persons together with their relatives and friends.

707. *Ibid., No.* 1270.—(Prākrit.) On a pillar. A fragmentary record. Mentions a monk *(pavachita)* the pupil *(atēvāsika)* of the great Vinaya teacher *(mahāvinayaṁdhara)* Aya-Budhi (Ārya-Buddhi) of the . . . liyas.

708. *Ibid., No.* 1271.—(Prākrit.) On a sculpture work. A fragmentary record. Records the gift of upright slabs *(udhapata)* by the lay-worshipper *(upāsaka)* Budharakhitā (Buddharakshitā), the son of Gomdi, the Dhaṁnakaṭaka (inhabitant of Dhānyakaṭa), and by his wife Paduma (Padmā), his son Haṁgha (Saṁgha), Budhi (Buddhi), Bōdhi . . . Budharakhita (Buddharakshitā).

709. *Ibid., No.* 1272.—(Prākrit.) On a sculpture work. Gift of an upright slab *(udhapaṭa)* by the mendicant monk *(peṁdapāṭika)* Paśama (Praśama) residing in Mahāvanasala (Mahavanaśāla), the pupil *(atēvāsika)* of the great elder *(mahāthēra)* Paravanuta who dwells in Pusakavana ? (Pushyakavana), the brother of Saṁyutaka (? Saṁyuktaka), and by Hamgha (Saṁghā).

710. *Ibid., No.* 1273.—(Prākrit.) On a sculpture work. Gift of a slab with a filled vase *(punaghaḍa kapaṭa)* by the leather worker *(chammakāra)* Vidhika, the son of the teacher *(upajhaya)* Nāga, and by his son Nāga, together with their relatives.

711. *Kielhorn's List, No.* 1274.—(Prākrit.) On a sculpture work. A fragmentary record. Mentions Dusaka (? Dūshaka ?), the son of the householder *(gahapati)* Hamghi (Samghin).

712. *Ibid., No.* 1275.—On a pillar. Not read.

713. *Ibid., No.* 1276.—(Prākrit.) In the Buddhist chhattra. Gift of a parasol *(chhata)* to the Chaitya *(chētiya)* of the venerable *(aira)* Utayipabhāhis by the female lay-worshipper *(guvāsika)* Chadā (Chandrā), the mother of Budhi (Buddhi).

714. *Ibid., No.* 1277.—(Prākrit.) On a pillar. Gift of pillars *(thabha)* by Himala, the son of the householder *(gahapati)* Vasumitā (Vasumitra) together with his relatives.

715. *Ibid., No.* 1278.—(Prākrit.) On a sculpture work. A fragmentary record. Records the gift of some merchant (vāniya) together with his relatives.

716. *Ibid., No.* 1279.—(Prākrit.) On a sculpture work in the time of rājan Siri-Sivamaka-Sada. A fragmentary record. Mentions the superintendent of the water-houses *(? pāniyagharika)* of rājan Siri-Sivamaka-Sada.

717. *Ibid., No.* 1280.—(Prākrit.) On a stone. Gift of a pillar *(thambha)* by Chula-Ayira (Kshudra-Ārya), the pupil *(atēvāsika)* of the great elder *(mahāthēra)* Ayira-Bhūtarakhita (Ārya-Bhūtarakshitā) who lives at Rāyasēla (Rājaśaila), and by the nun *(bhikuni)* Nadā Nandā, the pupil *(atēvāsini)* of the Arhat *(arahata)* Ayira-Budharakhita (Arya-Buddharakshitā).

718. *Ibid., No.* 1281.—On a sculpture work (now in Bezwada). (Prākrit.) A fragmentary record. Gift of a coping stone *(unisā)* to the Great Chaitya (mahāchētiya) of Bhagavat by the wife of the merchant (vāniya) Samuda (Samudra) the son of the householder *(gahapati)* Hamgha (Samgha).

719. *Ibid., No.* 1282.—(Prākrit.) On a stone. A fragmentary record. Gift of four pillars *(khabha)* saphaṭha (?) and with slabs *(sapaṭa)*, by Mahānāga (Mahānāga).

720. *Ibid., No.* 1283.—(Prākrit.) On a sculpture work. A fragmentary record. Erection of a coping stone *(umnisā)* by . . . Hayaḍā, Kamdaḍā, Samghaḍā.

721. *Ibid., No.* 1284.—(Prākrit.) On a stone. Erected by the reverend *(? bhavāta)* Dhammasiria (Dharmaśrīka) and (?) Paśamā (Praśamā), with (?) (Hagisiri Agniśrī ?), Chapā (Chamba) and the lay-worshipper *(uvasaka)* Ravisiri (Raviśrī).

722. *Ibid., No.* 1285.—(Prākrit.) On a stone. Records the erection of a coping stone *(unisā)* by the merchant's wife (vaṇiyinī) Sidhi (Siddhi), daughter of Chada (Chandra), who lived at Vijayapura.

723. *Kielhorn's List, No.* 1286.—(Prākrit.) On a stone (now in the Madras Museum). Gift of foot-prints *(pāduka)* by Malā (Mālā), pupil *(atēvāsini)* of the female teacher *(uvajhāyini)* Samudiyā (Samudrikā), pupilatēvāsinī of the Vinaya teacher (vinayaṁdhara) Aya Punavasu (Ārya-Punarvasu).

724. *Ibid., No.* 1287.—(Prākrit.) On a stone. A fragmentary record. Gift of slabs with a svastika *(sothikapaṭa)* and of an abātamālā by Kanha (Kṛishṇa), wife of . . . ka together with her father . . . and her relātives and friends.

725. *Ibid., No.* 1288.—On a sculpture work. Not read.

726. *Ibid., No.* 1289.—(Prākrit.) On a coping stone. A fragmentary record. Mentions the elder *(thēra)* Mahādhammaka (Mahādharmaka).

727. *Ibid., No.* 1290.—On a sculpture work. Not read.

728. *Ibid., No.* 1291.—(Prākrit.) On a sculpture work. A fragmentary record. Gift of a slab *(paṭa)* by . . . and the scribe *(lēghaka)* Kanha (Kṛishṇa).

729. *Ibid., No.* 1292.—(Prākrit.) On a sculpture work. A fragmentary record. Mentions the merchant's wife *(vaṇiyiṇi)* Nākachampaka (Nāgachampakā), Chadasiri (Chandraśrī) and Budhila (Buddhila).

730. *Ibid., No.* 1293.—On a sculpture work. Not read.

731. *Ibid., No.* 1294.—On a sculpture work. Not read.

732. *Ibid., No.* 1295.—(Prākrit.) On a sculpture work. Gift of a slab *(paṭa)* at the northern entrance *(āyāka)* by the young monk *(daharabhikhu)* Vidhika, pupil *(atēvāsika)* of bhayata (bhadanta) Nāga, who resides at Kudūra, and by his female pupil *(atēvāsini)* Budharakhita (Buddharakshitā) and by her granddaughter Chūlabudharakhitā (Kshudrabuddharakshitā).

733. *Ibid., No.* 1296.—On a sculpture work. Not read.

734. *Ibid., No.* 1297.—(Prākrit.) On a Buddhist image. Mentions some treasurer *(hēraṇika)*.

735. *Ibid., No.* 1298.—(Prākrit.) On a stone. Gift of a pillar *(thabha)* by Nada (Nanda), daughter (?) of the artisan *(āvēsani)* Nadabhuti (Nandabhūti).

736. *Ibid., No.* 1299.—(Prākrit.) On a stone. Not read.

737. *Ibid., No.* 1300.—(Prākrit.) On a stone. A fragmentary record. Records the gift of some man together with his daughter.

738. *Ibid., No.* 1301.—(Prākrit.) On a stone. A fragmentary record. Records the gift of some man with his relatives.

739. *Ibid., No.* 1302.—(Prākrit.) On a stone. A fragmentary record. Gift of a pillar *(thaṁbha)* by some householder *(gahapati)*, together with his wife.

740. *Kielhorn's List No.* 1303.—(Prākrit.) On a stone. A fragmentary record. Gift of the lay-worshipper *(upāsaka)* Utara (Uttara), the Kaṭakasōlaka (inhabitant of Kaṭakasōla), together with his relatives.

741. *Ibid., No.* 1304.—On a sculpture work. A fragmentary record. Not read.

742. *Ibid., No.* 1305.—On a sculpture work. A fragmentary record. Not read.

743. *Ibid., No.* 1306.—On a sculpture work. Not read.

744. *Ibid., No.* 1307.—On a sculpture work. A fragmentary record. Not read.

745. *Ibid., No.* 1308.—(Prākrit.) On a sculpture work. A fragmentary record. No sense has been made out.

746. *Ibid., No.* 1309.—On a coping stone. A fragmentary record. Not read.

747. *Ibid., No.* 1310.—(Prākrit.) On a sculpture work. A fragmentary record. No sense has been made out.

748. *Ibid., No.* 1311.—On a sculpture work. A fragmentary record. Not read.

749. *Ibid., No.* 1312.—On a Buddhist rail. Not read.

750. *Ibid., No.* 1313.—On a sculpture work. Not read.

751. *Ibid., No.* 1314.—On a sculpture work. Not read.

752. *Ibid., No.* 1315.—(Prākrit.) On sculpture work. A fragmentary record. Records some gift and mentions the nun *(samaṇikā)* Saghamita (Saṁghamitrā).

753. *Ibid., No.* 1316.—(Prākrit.) On a sculpture work. A fragmentary record. No name has been preserved.

754. *Ibid., No.* 1317.—(Prākrit.) On a sculpture work. A fragmentary record. Records some gift.

755. *Ibid., No.* 1318.—On a Buddhist image. Not read.

756. *Ibid., No.* 1319.—On a coping stone. A fragmentary record. Not read.

757. *Ibid., No.* 1320.—On a sculpture work. Not read.

758. *Ibid., No.* 1321.—(Prākrit.) On a coping stone. A fragmentary record. Gift of some object by some man together with his son.

759. *Ibid., No.* 1322.—On a sculpture work. Not read.

760. *Ibid., No.* 1323.—On a stone. A fragmentary record. Not read.

761. *Ibid., No.* 1324.—On a stone. Not read.

762. *Ibid., No.* 1325.—On a sculpture work. A fragmentary record. Not read.

763. *Ibid., No.* 1326.—On a stone. A fragmentary record. Not read.

Aminabad. *

764. 541 *of* 1909.—(Telugu.) On a slab near the Durgi temple on the top of the hillock. A record in Ś. 1514, Nandana (A.D. 1582), of Mahammadu Kulli Pādaśaha Voḍeyalu, sọn of Yibhurāhimu Pāduseha Voḍeyalu. Records the conquests of the king's father in Ś. 1502 and the suppression of certain rebellious chiefs in Koṇḍavīḍu-śīma in the reign of Muhammad Kuḷi in 1591. [The inscription is of importance for the light it throws on the relation between Golcoṇḍa and Koṇḍavīḍu chiefs. See *Ep. Rep.*, 1910, pp. 119–20, for details. Muhammad Kuli's possessions extended as far as Chicacole. See Gj. 694 and Cg. 1175 for some of his feudatories.]

765. 542 *of* 1909.—(Telugu.) On the wall, right of entrance into the central shrine of the same temple. A record in Ś. 1496, Bhava, of the Vijayanagara king Vīrapratāpa Śrīraṅgarāyadēva-Mahārāya. Records gift of a village to the temple of Durgā-Paramēśvari or Mullaguri-Śakti by a certain Nāgapanāyaniṅgāru. Śrīraṅga came to the throne in 1578 and ruled till 1586.

766. 543 *of* 1909.—(Telugu verse in the *Sīsa* metre.) On a boulder called Pullaribōḍu in the same village. A record in Ś. 1337, Manmatha, of the Reḍḍi king Vēmaya-Rāchavēmana (son of Vēmaya). Refers to the tank Santāna-vāridhi constructed by his mother and the channel called Jagadobbagaṇḍakāluva, which he himself excavated as its feeder. The verse was composed by Śrīnātha. [Mr. Krishna Sastri points out, on the basis of this inscription, that the Koṇḍavīḍu dynasty continued after Kōmaṭi Vēma under a son of his named Rāchaya. The Vēmāpuram plates, on the contrary, seem to show that Kōmaṭi Vēma's family was uprooted by Allāḍa of the Rājahmundry branch. The inscription is also of interest in throwing light on the age of Kavisārvabhauma Śrīnātha, the author of the *Kāśikaṇḍam*, *Vidhināṭakam* and the *Śriṅgāranaishadha*. Viresalingam Pantulu points out that he was court poet of the Rājahmundry Reḍḍis Vēma and Vīrabhadra, the sons of Allāḍa. He was also the contemporary of a Diṇḍima Kavi and Sarvagña Śiṅgama of the Veṅkaṭagiri family. See No. 803.]

Bellamkoṇḍa.

767. In the Narasimhasvāmi temple. A record of Ś. 1476, Pramādīcha, Māgha Bahuḷa 7, relating a grant to Lakshmīnarasimhadēva by Veṅgalayyadēva Mahārāja in Sadāśivarāya's time. Mentions Rāmarāja. *Mack. MSS.*, Bk. XVIII, p. 1.

768. A record in Śrīmukha Vaiśākha Śuddha, Pañchami, Sunday, making a grant to Nagarikuṇṭa Santa Narasimha by Śiṅgabhūpa. *Ibid.*

* Mr. Sewell in his *Antiquities* refers to two inscriptions, dated Ś. 1114 and Ś. 1502. He gives no details.

769. A record in Ś. 1241, Viśvāvasu, Vaiśākha Bahuḷa 10 Saturday, relating the erection of a Garuḍa pillar by Tadi Sōmaṇa for the merit of his parents. *Mack. MSS.*, Bk. XVIII, p. 1.

770. In the temple of Tripurāntaka on a pillar. Records that in Sarvajit, Āshāḍabahuḷa 2, Karakaṇṭi Śrī Māchadēva Chillēla Ayyappanēni's son gave chatra, chāmara, etc., to the deity. *Ibid.*, p. 2.

Chintapalli.

771. On a fallen stone outside the village. Records a private grant in Ś. 1161 to the temple at Guḍimeṭla. *Antiquities*, p. 64.

Dharaṇikōṭa.

[For the bibliography of this place see *Antiquities*, I, p. 64.]

772. 273 *of* 1897.—(Telugu.) On a boulder in a field south of Dharaṇikōṭa. A record in the thirtieth year of Vishṇuvardhana-mahārāja. Records gift of land by three Maṇḍalīkas.

Madala.

773. East of the village. A record dated in Ś. 1447, saying that Maṇḍanāyak built a maṇṭapa in the Sakalēśvara temple and gave some land. *Loc. Rec.*, Vol. 57, p. 238.

774. A record dated in Ś. 1051, Phalguna, Bahuḷa 10, Thursday, to the effect that Vrittikaṇḍarāya's wife gave a lamp for Mahāmaṇḍalēśvara Kōṭa Nāyaka's merit to the God. *Ibid.*, p. 239.

775. A record in Ś. 1094, granting 55 sheep to Sakalēśvara by Kōṭama Nāyaḍu. *Ibid.*

776. A similar gift by Polanāyaḍu. No date. *Ibid.*

777. A record in Ś. 1073, Vishama Saṅkrānti, to the effect that Bhōgiśeṭṭi's son Māchaṇaśeṭṭi gave 55 sheep to Sakalēśvara for lamp. *Ibid.*

778. A record of Ś. 1071, recording gift of lamp by Maṇḍaya Nāyaka. *Ibid.*

779. A record in Ś. 1071, Vishama Saṅkrānti, regarding gift of lamp by Pola's son Kuchama Nāyak. *Ibid.*

780. An epigraph dated Ś. 1072, Uttama Saṅkrānti, recording gift of lamp by Polanāyaḍu's daughter for the merit of her parents. *Ibid.*

781. Gift of sheep in Ś. 1074, Uttarāyaṇa Saṅkrānti. *Ibid.*

782. Gift of land to various Bhaṭṭas by Maṇḍanāyak. *Ibid.*

Garikapāḍu-Agrahāra.

The *Mack. MSS.* reproduced in *Loc. Rec.*, Vol. XII, pp. 237—53, give the epigraphs of this place.

783. 4 *of* 1908.—(Brāhmi.) On a circular cup of white marble in a private house. Records the gift of a rail-pot by a merchant named Dabha.

Guḍipūḍi.

The inscriptions of this place have been taken from *Antiquities*, Vol. I, p. 65, and *Loc. Rec.*, Vol. 42, pp. 426—33 and *Loc. Rec.*, Vol. 48, pp. 161—65.

784. In the temple of Bhīmēśvara Liṅga. A grant in Ś. 1082 by Prolasāni, wife of Śrī Kōṭappanāyaka. *Antiquities*, p. 65.

785. A grant of the same person in the same year. *Ibid.*

786. In the same temple. A private grant in Ś. 1085. *Ibid.*

787. In the same temple. A private grant in Ś. 1165. *Ibid.*

788. In the same temple. A private grant in Ś. 1169. *Ibid.*

Kēṭāvaram.

789. In the local old fort, on a slab. Records that "Śrīnādha Rāja Rāmayyadēva Mahārāja, son of Lakshmīpatirāja and grandson of Śrī Nādha Rāja Rāmayya Sāmanta Śiṅgara Mahāpātra, granted to a private person the produce of certain taxes in the reign of Sadāśiva of Vijayanagar." *Ibid.*

790. An epigraph of Ś. 1075, Uttarāyaṇa Saṅkrānti, recording that the daughter of Pōlanāyak, servant of Velanāṭi Kulōttuṅga Chōḍa Goṅka (II), gave 55 sheep. *Ibid.*

791. A record of Ś. 1073, Māgha Bahuḷa, Pañchadaśi, Thursday, solar eclipse, records that a lady gave in the same reign a lamp for the God. *Ibid.*

792. A record of Ś. 1072, Vishama Saṅkrānti. A grant of Pōtana Reḍḍi. *Ibid.*

793. An epigraph of Ś. 1074, Paushya Uttama Saṅkrānti. Gift of a lamp. See *Loc. Rec.*, Vol. 57, p. 246, and original *Mack. MSS.*, p. 97.

794. An epigraph in Ś. 1169, Uttarāyaṇa Saṅkrānti, recording gift of lamp by a Rāmayyarāsu for the merit of his parents. *Ibid.*

Mōḍūpuru.

Brown's *Loc. Rec.*, Vol. 42, pp. 353—4 and Vol. 48, pp. 101—03 contain the following inscription :—

795. A record of the reign of Kulōttuṅga Rājadēva Chōḷa relating to the building of the Chenni Chōḍēśvara by Śūrapa Nāyuḍu in Ś. 1093, and also gift of lands. Pātakoṇḍa Bala śura Rāja Manmasūlaḍu is mentioned as the donor in the latter.

Munugōḍu.

796. On a stone in the street. Records the erection of a temple by Goṅka, undated. *Antiquities*, p. 65.

797. In the same place. A grant by Śrī Mahāmaṇḍalēśvara Goṅkayya in the thirty-seventh year of Sarvalōkāśraya Vishṇuvardhana. *Antiquities*, p. 65.

Panidem.

798. On a pillar east of the village. Records a grant in Ś. 1153, by Prōladēvi, wife of Mahāmaṇḍalēśvara Kōṭa Doḍḍa Kēṭa Rāja. *Ibid.* See No. 635.

799. On a pillar in the Viśvanātha temple. A private grant in Ś. 1204. *Ibid.*

800. On the same pillar. Another private grant of the same date, besides one without date. *Ibid.*

Peddamakkena.

The local inscriptions have been taken from *Antiquities*, I, 65, and *Loc. Rec.*, Vol. 42, p. 433 ff.

801. On a pillar east of the village. Records in Sanskrit a grant in Ś. 1097, by Mallabhūpati, son of Prōlana Nāyaka. *Ibid.*

802. In the same place. Records in Ś. 1082, a gift to the temple by Bhūtamādēvi, wife of Mahāmaṇḍalēśvara Kōṭa Gaṇḍapa Rāja. *Ibid.*

Phirangipuram.

803. 162 *of* 1899.—(Telugu and Sanskrit.) On a pillar in front of the Vīrabhadrēśvara temple. A record of the Reḍḍi king Kōmaṭi-Vēma in Ś. 1331, Virōdhin (A.D. 1409), *Phālguna, bahuḷa.* Records the building of a tank (called *santānavāridhi*) by Vēma's wife Suramāmbika. [The inscription is of great literary interest as it was composed by the Telugu poet Śrīnātha who held the office of *Vidyādhikāri* under this king. See No. 766 above. The present record is referred to in *Antiquities*, p. 65, and Brown's *Local Records*, Vol. 57, p. 234, which gives the further chronological detail Phalguna bahuḷa 2. See also *Loc. Rec.*, Vol. 42, pp. 331—41 and Vol. 48, pp. 81—90.

Rāzupālem.

804. On a stone in the middle of a small jungle. Records a grant to a temple in Ś. 1167, by "Śrīmat Muchhe Nāyakar," son of "Sonte Nāyakar." *Antiquities*, I, p. 65.

*Sattenapalle.**

805. 5 *of* 1908.—(Telugu.) On a slab lying on a mound in the Sahebu-bazaar. A damaged record in Ś. 1055.

---

* I find the inscriptions of this place in Brown's *Loc. Rec.*, Vol. 57, pp. 228—32. The original in *Mack. MSS.* (Bk. XVIII) is missing. The MSS. give eight inscriptions most of which are in the list given above. The only epigraph which it does not contain is a record of Ś. 1096, Uttarāyaṇa Saṅkrānti, relating to a gift of lamp.

806. 6 *of* 1908.—(Telugu.) On another slab lying in the same place. Records in Ś. 1049 a gift of land by Maṭṭa-Nāyaka to the Trikōṭīśvara temple at Vellantūru. Mentions Īśānaśiva-Paṇḍita as the sthānapati. See *Loc. Rec.*, Vol. 57, p. 232.

807. 7 *of* 1908.—(Sanskrit and Telugu.) On four faces of a pillar in the same place. Records in Ś. 1060 gift of land to the Trikōṭīśvara temple at Velantūru in Koṇḍapaḍumati by Maṇḍāḍi-Maṭṭa-Nāyaka for the merit of his elder brother Prōla-Nāyaka. Mentions Īśānaśivi-Paṇḍita among the donees and gives a list of lands endowed, the tanks built by the members of the donor's family. [I have found this inscription in *Mack. MSS.*, Bk. XX (15-3-63), pp. 45—49.]

808. 8 *of* 1908.—(Telugu.) On four faces of a pillar in the same place. Records in Ś. 1075 gift of 55 sheep for a lamp by a native of Tanarumbarti. [The *Mack. MSS.* give the details of the date as Uttarāyaṇa Saṅkrānti and refer to Matta Nāyaka, Kēṭa and Goṅka.]

809. 9 *of* 1908.—(Telugu.) On four faces of a pillar in the same place. Records in Ś. 1055 (Uttarāyaṇa Saṅkrānti) gift of sheep for a lamp by Vāsi-Nāyaka, son of Prōli-Nāyaka.

810. 10 *of* 1908.—(Telugu.) On four faces of a pillar in the same place. Records in Ś. 1060 gift of sheep for a lamp by Koṇḍapa-Nāyaka, son of Matte-Nāyaka.

811. 11 *of* 1908.—(Telugu.) On four faces of a pillar in the same place. Records in Ś. 1060 gift of sheep for a lamp by Pedda-Koṇḍapa-Nāyaka, son of Navi-Nāyaka of Tanarumbariti.

812. 12 *of* 1908.—(Telugu.) On four faces of a pillar in the same place. Records in Ś. 1091 gift of sheep for a lamp by Sāni-Prōlema. See No. 801 above.

813. *C.P. No.* 11 *of* 1915.—A record of the Eastern Chāḷukyan king Ammarāja II in Ś. 880, Mārgaśīrsha, ba. di. 13, Friday, Anurādha. Registers the grant of the villages of Taṇḍikoṇḍa and two others for repairs, offerings, etc., in Umāmahēśvara temple at Vijayavāṭa (Bezwada) built by Vijayāditya Narēndramrigarāja. A list of teachers of the Kāḷāmukha sect is given. See *Ep. Rep.*, 1915, p. 11, for details.

Śiripuram.

814. 48 *of* 1909.—(Sanskrit and Telugu.) On a pillar in front of the temple of Rāmaliṅgēśvara. Records in Ś. 1094 gift of 55 sheep for a lamp to the temple of Mūlasthāna Rāmēśvara-Mahādēva at Śiripuram by a Brāhmaṇa.

815. 49 *of* 1909.—(Sanskrit and Telugu.) On the second pillar in the same place. A record of the Velanāṇḍu king Rājendra Chōḍa-Kumāra, son of Kulōttuṅga-Chōḍa Goṅkaya-Mahārāja (II) in Ś. 1097. Records gift of a tank and a palmyra grove to the same temple. [Mr. Sewell mentions this inscription in his *Antiquities*, p. 65, but he gives the wrong date of Ś. 1087.]

Vadhavalli.

816. East of the village. Records that Koṇḍappa Nāyaḍu's wife Madhusāni gave in Ś. 1055, Uttara Saṅkarānti, ninety-five sheep for a lamp to God Mallikārjuna. *Mack. MSS.* in *Loc. Rec.*, Vol. 57, p. 233.

Vēmūr.

817. 50 *of* 1909.—(Sanskrit and Telugu.) On a broken pillar lying in front of the Rāmaliṅgēśvarasvāmin temple. Records in Ś. 1050 gift of a lamp to the temple of Rāmēśvara-Mahādēva at Vēmūru.

818. 51 *of* 1909.—(Sanskrit and Telugu.) On the same pillar. A record of the Velanāṇḍu king Kulōttuṅga-Chōḍa-Goṅkarāju, the date of which is doubtful. Records gift of a lamp to the temple of Rāmēśvara-mahādēva by a servant of the king.

Vēmalūrpāḍu.

819. *C.P. No.* 4 *of* 1909–10.—Here was found in 1909–10 a copper-plate grant in five plates "strung together on a copper ring bearing the usual *Tribhuvanāmkuśa* seal of the Eastern Chāḷukya kings and belonging to the time of Amma II." "The historical portion of the record is almost identical with that of the Malaiyapūṇḍi grant published by Prof. Hultzsch in *Ep. Ind.*, Vol. IX, pp. 47–56." The grant refers to the political troubles which preceded the accession of Amma II (945—70) and records on the occasion of an *Uttarāyaṇa* (summer solstice) a piece of land in the two villages of Ammaṇaṅgāru and Aṇḍeki, to a Brāhmaṇa of Karemchēḍu, called Musiyana, at the instance of the general Duggarāja, the great-grandson of the famous Pāṇḍaraṅga. (Exact year not given.) The plate has been purchased for the Madras Museum.

820. 544 *of* 1909.—(Telugu.) On a pillar lying near the Śiva temple. An unfinished record of the Vijayanagara king Vīrapratāpa Achyutadēva Mahārāya in Ś. 1452, Vikriti. Records that Peda Tirumalayyadēva Mahārājulugāru of the Sāḷaka family, built a tank and planted a garden both of which he presented to the temple of Gōpinātha at Vēlupāḷem, in Koṇḍavīḍu.

TENALI TALUK.

Chilumūru.

821. On a stone in the temple (?) A record dated in Ś. 1075, Uttarāyaṇa Saṅkrānti, relating gift of land to a choultry by Sunuvūru Reḍḍi Rāmappa Nara Nāyaka for his parents' merit. *Loc. Rec.*, Vol. 42, p. 440.

822. A record of the same chief in the same date. Besides gift of land to choultry there is one of lamp.

Dāvalūru.

823. In the Gōkēśvara temple, on a Nāga pillar. Records in Ś. 1054 a grant of land by Kōmaya Nāyaka for the merit of Velanaṭi Goṅka (II ?). *Loc. Rec.*, Vol. 57, pp. 205—8.

Duggirāla.

824. In the temple of Kēśavasvāmi. A record dated in Ś. 1056.

Gōvāda.

The following inscription has been taken from *Loc. Rec.*, Vol. 48, pp. 29—37 and Vol. 42, p. 274 ff.

825. A C.P. in the village (Sanskrit), dated in Ś. 1466 (रसाङ्गार्णवशीतांशु), Krōdhi, Pushya, Sunday, Paurṇami, in the reign of Sadāśiva Rāya, relating gift of the village to Vallabhāchārya, whose panegyrics as a Vaishṇava teacher are eloquently described.

826. A grant of land in Ś. 1616, Virōdhi, Vaiśākhaśuddha 10, Monday, to Chilukumarri Veṅkaṭāchārya by Dabir Veṅkaṇṇa.

Kolakalūru.

See *Antiquities*, I, p. 79 and *Loc. Rec.*, Vol. 42, pp. 438–9 and Vol. 148, pp. 172–3.

827. On a slab east of the south gateway of the Kēśavasvāmi temple. A grant in Ś. 1240, Kāḷayukti, Āśvija Śuddha 14, Monday, by Pōsu Veṅkan, the son of Sōmayya Veṅkan, Commander-in-chief of the armies of the Kākatīya king Pratāparudra II (1295—1323).

828. Close by the above. Grant by a private party in Ś. 1163.

829. In another pillar. A Chōḷa record of Ś. 1124.

830. On a slab south of the east gateway. A record in Ś. 1240 by the same person as in the first of the local inscriptions given above.

Kollūru.

The local inscriptions have been taken from *Antiquities*, I, p. 79, and *Loc. Rec.*, Vol. 42, p. 439 ff.

831. In the hands of the temple manager. A record dated in Ś. 1286, Śubhakrit, Māgha Śuddha 15, relating a grant to Rāmēśvara. See *Mack. MSS.*, Bk. (15–6–21) and Brown's *Loc. Rec.*, Vol. 57, p. 209 ff. [This is evidently the plate which the possessor refused to show to Mr. Sewell.]

832. In the Bhōgēśvarasvāmi temple. A record dated in Ś. 1071, Āshāḍha Bahuḷa 13, Sunday, relating a grant by Mallasāni to God Anantēśvara. *Ibid.*

833. A grant dated in Ś. 1074, Jyēshṭa Śuddha, 5, Monday, Uttarāyaṇa Saṅkrānti, recording gift of a lamp in the time of Velanāṭi Kulōttuṅga Chōḷa (II, 1133—57). *Loc. Rec.*, Vol. 57, p. 209 ff

834. A grant dated in Ś. 1094, Chaitra Bahuḷa Śuddha, 13 Friday, Vishama Saṅkrānti, in the twenty-sixth year of Rāja Rāja Dēva recording a grant of lamp to Narēndrēśvara by Kāṭaya Manma for the merit of his parents. See No. I above and *Loc. Rec.*, Vol. 57, p. 217.

835. A grant in Ś. 1095, Jyēshṭa Śukla 11, Friday, in the twenty-seventh year of Rājarāja-dēva, recording a gift of lamp. *Ibid.* See the above epigraph.

836. A grant dated in Ś. 1099, Paushya Śuddha 1, Sunday, Uttarāyaṇa, in the twenty-first year of Rājarāja (?). Grant of a lamp by Bōya Nāyaḍu, grandson of Bhaṭṭiprōlu Nāyaḍu, for the merit of his parents.

837. In the Gōpālasvāmi temple. Records that in Ś. 1465, Śubhakrit, Kārttika Śuddha 11, Thursday, Timmarasuvāru's Kārya-kartā "Polumāmulla-vāraiyangar" made a grant of land. *Ibid.*, p. 218.

Koṇḍamuḍi.

838. C.P. Grant of Jayavarman (Sanskrit and Prākrit) closely resembling that of Maiḍavōlu plates of Śivaskandavarman. Records that Mahārāja Jayavarman of the Brihatphalāyana gōtra, from his camp at Kūḍūra in District of Kūdūrapāra, informs his minister that he granted the village Pāṇṭūra to eight Brāhmans. Mr. Rāmayya believes that Kūḍūrapāra may be a more ancient form of Guḍrahāra. Dr. Hultzsch says that the language and phraseology of the inscription are so similar to the Karle and Nasik inscriptions of Gautamīputra and Vasishṭhiputra that Jayavarman's date cannot be very distant from that of the two Āndhra kings. See *Ep. Ind.*, Vol. VI, pp. 315—9.

Nandivēlugu.

839. In the Agastyēśvara temple. A record dated in Ś. 1154 (?). There is in the same place a private grant.

Peddapūḍi.

840. A C.P. in the possession of a Karaṇam. A record dated Ś. 1326 (?). *Antiquities*, p. 80.

Peravāli.

841. In the local temple. A private record in Ś. 1361. *Ibid.*

Tenali.

The following inscriptions have been taken from *Mack. MSS.*, Bk. 18, and Brown's *Loc. Rec.*, Vol. 57, pp. 278—87, and Vol.

48, pp. 103—8. They seem however to be not at Tenali proper. Guṇṭūr is mentioned with it.

842. An epigraph dated in Ś. 1411, Saumya, Vaiśākha Śuklapaksha, Saturday (Haridina), in the time of Kṛishṇadēvarāya. Mentions Śāḷuva Timma, and records gift to God Gōvardhana.

843. A grant of Appayya Mantri of Koṇḍavīḍu in Ś. 1439, Īśvara, to Aṅgaḍi Gōpinātha.

844. A record dated in Ś. 1438, Dhātu, relating the construction of maṇṭapa, prākāra, etc., by Nādaṇḍḷa Appaprabhu to the God of Maṅgaḷagiri.

845. A record of Ś. 1439, Īśvara, relating gift to Brāhmans by the same.

846. An incomplete record of the same chief in Ś. 1438.

VINUKONDA TALUK.

Bommarāsupaḷḷi.

847. In the hands of the local people. Records in Ś. 1662, Siddhārti, Chaitra Śuddha 15, grant by Vāsireḍḍi Rāmaliṅgaṇṇa, in F. 1148. *Mack. MSS.*, Bk. XVIII, p. 9.

848. With the same. Records in Ś. 1668, Pārthiva, Vaiśākha Śuddha 15, a gift by the same person. *Ibid.*

849. A similar grant in Ś. 1681, Bahudhānya, Aśvija 10. *Ibid.*

850. A record in Paritāpi, Kārttika Śuddha 15, relating gift to Erramśeṭṭi by Vāsireḍḍi Veṅkaṭādri Nāyuḍu. *Ibid.*, p. 10.

851. A gift to the same man by Vēṅkaṭādri Nāyaḍu in Ś. 1709, Parābhava, Māgha Bahuḷa 1, in F. 1196. *Ibid.*, p. 10.

852. A similar gift in Ś. 1688, Pārthiva, Māgha Śuddha 12, by Vāsireḍḍi Rāmaṇṇa. *Ibid.*

Chintalacheruvu.

853. In the temple of Chennakēśavasvāmi. Records that it was built and endowed by Ellappa Nāyaḍu in Ś. 1472. *Antiquities*, p. 66.

Inumella.

854. 160 *of* 1899.—(Telugu.) On a slab near the Sōmēśvara temple. Records in Ś. 1176 a gift of land for the merit of the Kākatīya king Gaṇapati (1213—59) by a chief who bore the titles Jaṭāchōḍarājya-samuddharaṇa, Manmakulābharaṇa, and Velanāṇṭi-Kulōttuṅga-Rājēndra-Chōḍanistāraka. *Ibid.*

855. 161 *of* 1899.—(Telugu.) On other slab near the Sōmēśvara temple. A damaged record. Records gift of land by a chief who belonged to the same family as the donor in above inscription.

Ipūru.

856. 532 *of* 1913.—(Telugu.) On a pillar lying in front of the Gōpālasvāmin temple. A record of the Kākatīya king Mahāmaṇḍalēśvara Rudradēva-Mahārāja (Rudrāmba?) in Ś. 1200, Bahudhānya, Āshāḍha, śu. ḍi. 11, Thursday. Records gift of land by the sons of Bolanāyuḍu, a body-guard *(aṅga-raksha)* of the king. [Mr. Swamikannu Piḷḷai says that the English equivalent of the date is 2nd July A.D. 1278, but the week day should be Friday or Saturday. See *Antiquities*, p. 66. See *Mack. MSS.*, Bk. 18 (15-6-21), p. 15. Where the date is wrongly given as Ś. 1220.]

857. 533 *of* 1913.—(Telugu.) On the same pillar. A record of the Kākatīya king Mahāmaṇḍalēśvara Rudradēva-Mahārāja in Ś. 1200, Bahudhānya, Āshāḍa, śu. di. 11, Thursday. Records gift of money by a merchant for offerings to the temple of Āllāḍanātha at Ipūru. See note to above inscription.

858. 534 *of* 1913.—(Telugu.) On the same pillar. Records in Ś. 1496, Śrīmukha, Āshāḍha, śu. di. 11, gift of land to the same temple by Chennapa, son of Rāvūri Timma-Nāyuḍu, for conducting special worship on the tenth *tithi* (daśami) of each fortnight. "Date can be calculated but not verified." See *Mack. MSS.*, Bk. 18, p. 16.

859. 535 *of* 1913.—(Telugu.) On the same pillar. Registers in Ś. 1179, Naḷa, Phalguna, ba. di. 6, Monday, the foundation of the temple of Allāḍanātha at Ipūru and of a gift of land to it, for the merit of the Mahāmaṇḍalēśvara Kōṭa-Gaṇapamādēvayammaṅgāru. The equivalent date is 7th March A.D. 1257, but Monday is an error for Wednesday, according to Mr. Swamikannu Piḷḷai. [The *Mack. MSS.* contain this inscription. See Bk. 18, p. 17. But it gives the wrong date Ś. 1130. Regarding the week day it contains the first letter गु, hinting thereby Thursday.]

860. 536 *of* 1913.—(Telugu.) On the same pillar. A record of the Kākatīya king Mahāmaṇḍalēśvara Rudradēva-Mahārāja in Ś. 1211, Virōdhin, Mārgaśira, śu. di. 15, Monday, corresponding to November 28, A.D. 1289. Records gift of land to the dancing girls of the same temple for the merit of Balanāyuḍu. [See *Mack. MSS.*, Bk. 18 (15-9-21), p. 15.]

861. 537 *of* 1913.—(Telugu.) On the same pillar. A record of the Kākatīya king Mahāmaṇḍalēśvara Rudradēva-Mahārāja in Ś. 1185, Raktākshi, Chaitra, śu. di. 13, Wednesday, corresponding to the 12th March, A.D. 1624. Records gift of 55 goats for a lamp to the same temple by Goṅkayya, son of Śūrapeggaḍa. [I have found this record in *Mack. MSS.*, Bk. 18 (15-6-21), p. 17.]

862. 538 *of* 1913.—(Telugu.) On a slab set up in the Vīrabhadrasvāmin temple in the same village. Registers in Ś. 1574, Khara, Vaiśākha, śu. di. Trētāyugādi-Akshayatritīya, Saturday,

Karkaṭakalagna corresponding to the 12th April, A.D. 1651, that Nandikēśvara, the sacred bull in the temple of Vīrēśvara at Yipūru, was renewed by Śūrērayini Timmājipantulu, the old one having become mutilated. A gift of land was also made for offerings. [See *Antiquities*, Vol. I, p. 66 and *Mack. MSS.*, Bk. 18, pp. 17–18.]

863. 539 *of* 1913.—(Telugu.) On a slab set up outside the prākāra of the same temple. A record of the Kākatīya king Mahāmaṇḍalēśvara Rudradēva Mahārāja in Ś. 1200, Bahudhānya, Āshāḍha, śu. 11, Tuesday. Records gift of money by the merchant Bāchchu Nārapa-śeṭṭi for offering to the temple of Kāḷēśvara Mahādēva for the merit of the king. Same date as that of 507 above and the week day should be Friday or Saturday.

Kanamarlapūḍi.

864. On a stone pillar in the village. Two grants dated A.D. 1080 and 1150. See *Antiquities*, p. 66.

Peddakāñchērla.

865. Near the Bhīmēśvara temple. Records in Ś. 1071, a grant, the details of which are not known. *Antiquities*, p. 67.

Remidichērla.

866. Near a well east of the village. A record of Ś. 1557. *Ibid.*

Tangirāla.

867. A record in the hands of Taṅgirāla Rāmabhaṭḷu, Records in Ś. 1685, Svabhānu, Śravaṇa Śuddha 5, a grant to Kāśipati Sōmayājulugāru by Puligaḍḍa Vīraṇṇa. See *Mack. MSS.*, Bk. 18, pp. 168–69.

Velpūru.

The inscriptions of this place have been taken from *Mack. MSS.*, Bk. 18, p. 106 ff. and *Loc. Rec.*, Vol. 57, pp. 257—73.

868. In a pillar of the Rāmaliṅgēśvara temple. A record in Ś. 1104, Māgha, Daśami, Śukla, Thursday, relating grant of land by Kēṭa to God Rāmēśvara.

869. Below the above. A grant of a village by the same chief to Rāmēśvara Mahādēva in Ś. 1104, Māgha Śuddha 1, Thursday.

870. North of the above pillar. Gift of lamp by the same chief in the same date.

871. Below the above. A gift of the same chief in Ś. 1104 in the same date.

872. East of the above. A record of the same chief in the same date for the merit of Sabbamā. The object granted was land to Brāhmans.

873. South of the above in the fourth pillar. Records in Ś. 1131, Chaitya Kṛishṇapaksha, Lunar eclipse, gift of lamp.

874. In the same temple. Records in Ś. 1122, Phalguna, Śuddha 9, Monday, gift of lamp by Golla Mattaya for Kōṭakēṭa's merit.

875. In the same temple. Records that in Ś. 1161, Vikāri, Bhādrapada Śukla 13, Sunday, Ibhasāni, gave a lamp for the merit of Kākatīya Gaṇapati (1213—59).

876. A record of Ś. 1170, Kīlaka, Māgha Bahuḷa 14, Friday, granting 25 māḍas for a lamp by Śūrappa for his parents' merit.

877. A record of Ś. 1131, Pushya Śuddha 11, Sunday, Uttarāyaṇa Saṅkrānti, relating gift of lamp by Guṇḍā, the wife of Kōṭakēṭa.

878. A record dated in Ś. 1162, Māgha Bahuḷa 15, Monday, recording gift of 55 buffaloes for lamp by Gaṇapaya, the son of Kōṭa Doḍḍakēṭa.

879. A record of Rāyasa Amātya in Ś. 1171, Śuchi (Jyēshṭa) Śukla, Pañchami.

[शाखाब्दे शशि शैलरुद्र गणिते मासे शुचौ निर्मले, मघे भूतदिने . . .]

See *Mack. MSS.*, Bk. 18, p. 123, and *Loc. Rec.*, Vol. 57, p. 273.

Vinukoṇḍa.

[For a short but excellent description of the antiquities of the place see Mr. Sewell's *Antiquities*, pp. 67–8.]

880. 527 *of* 1913.—(Telugu Sanskrit.) In the ruined temple of Narasimhasvāmin at the foot of the hill, right of entrance. Registers in Ś. 1399, Hēmalambi, Kārttika, śu. di. 10, Thursday, corresponding to 16th of October 1477, that the Sagi chief Gaṇṇa or Gaṇṇama Nāyaka, son of Gāda, grandson of Peda-Gaṇṇa and great-grandson of Annama Nāyaka of the fourth (i.e., Śūdra) caste, founded the temple of Narasimha or Lakshmi Nrisimha at Vīnikoṇda. [See *Antiquities*, p. 67 and *Mack. MSS.*, Bk. 18 (15-6-21), p. 14.]

881. 528 *of* 1913.—(Telugu.) In the same place, left of entrance. A record in Ś. 1399, Hēmalambi, Kārttika, śu. di. 10, Thursday, a translation of No. 527. The chief Gaṇṇama Nāyaka receives the titles Karavāḷa-Bhairava, Puliyamarkoḷugaṇḍa and Gaṇḍabhēruṇda. Below the inscription is a fine figure of the fabulous man-bird Gaṇḍabhēruṇḍa, lifting up two elephants with his two hands. [See *Mack. MSS.*, Bk. 18, pp. 14-5.]

882. 529 *of* 1913.—(Telugu, archaic.) On a stone placed in the verandah of the Sub-Registrar's office in the same village. This stone was set up by Padavalu Kaṭṭirāju entitled Immaḍigaṇḍa, Biruddaṅga-Rudra, Kalliga-Nārāyaṇa and Ghaṇḍaśārdūla.

883. 530 *of* 1913.—(Telugu.) In the same place. A record of the Vijayanagara king Vīrapratāpa Sadāśivadēva-Mahārāya, ruling at Vidyānagara, in Ś. 1484, Dundubhi, Āshāḍha, śu. di. 11, Thursday (mistake for Friday), corresponding to June 12, A.D. 1562. Registers a gift of land for maintaining a flower-garden of the temple of Raghunāyaka at Vinukoṇḍa-śīma which was the fief given to Koṇḍarājayyadēva Mahārāja by the Mahāmaṇḍalēśvara Rāmarāja-Tirumalarājayyadēva-Mahārāja. [See *Antiquities*, Vol. I, pp. 67–8, where this is referred to under date Ś. 1483.]

884. 531 *of* 1913.—(Arabic and Persian.) On a slab built into the wall of the big mosque in the same village. A record of Qutb Shahi Nawab Abdullah Qutb Shah in A.H. 1050 (=1640–41 A.D.). Records the erection of the mosque by 'Ali Riza Khan. Begins with quotations from the Quran as well as praises of the Prophet and the twelve Imāms of the Shia ! (Dr. Horovitz.) [Mr. Sewell refers to this epigraph. *Antiquities*, p. 68.]

885. Records that in Ś. 1642, Durmukhi, Kārttika Śuddha 15, a grant by Koṇḍalarāju to Dharvēmula Rāmabhadrappa. *Mack. MSS.*, Bk. XVIII, p. 7.

886. Records in Ś. 1694, Nandana, Māgha Bahuḷa 15, to Jakkapaṭṇam Tirumala Śrīnivāsa Tātachārya, son of Kumāra Tātachārya, a gift of land by Miriyala Mallarāju Guṇḍarāju. *Mack. MSS.*, Bk. XVIII, p. 8.

887. A record dated in Ś. 1078 (?), Ānanda, Vaiśakha Śuddha 15, relating the gift by the same donor to the same donee of the village of Koṇḍa Timma Piṭhāpuram as a śrōtriyam. *Ibid.*

KANARA (SOUTH) DISTRICT.

General Copper Plates.

These copper plate grants are given in Mr. Sewell's *Antiquities*, Vol. II, and they are given here as it is impossible to distribute them according to the geographical units.

1. *C.P. No.* 88 *of Mr. Sewell's List.*—(Kanarese.) Records grant of land by Chennammā Dēvi, Rāṇi of Chātḷur, to one Viṭṭala Kamti of Kumbḷa. The grant is in *Yuva*, no Śaka year being given. It confers on the grantee certain lands near Bahujatra beṭṭa. "Chantar is a small chieftainship at Mudabidri, 21 miles from Mangalore."

2. *C.P. No.* 91 *of Mr. Sewell's List.*—(Kanarese.) Records a grant of land by a prince named Kinniga Bhūpāla for the purpose of maintaining the worship in a Jain temple, Ś. 1513 (A.D. 1591), *Khara*.

3. *C.P. No.* 102 *of Mr. Sewell's List.*—(Kanarese.) Records grant of certain lands to a temple by Dēva Rāja, acting under the orders of the Vijayanagar sovereign Dēva Rāya (II, 1422–49), in Ś. 1352 (A.D. 1430), Sādhāraṇa.

4. *C.P. No.* 103 *of Mr. Sewell's List.*—(Kanarese.) Records grant of certain lands to Dasaṇṇa Nāyaka, son Baṇḍi Yellappa Nāyaka, by Śaṅkara Dēvi, sister of "Vīra Narsimha Lakshmapparasa Baṅgār," in Ś. 1565 (A.D. 1643), Subhānu.

5. *C.P. No.* 104 *of Mr. Sewell's List.*—(Kanarese.) Records grant of certain lands to one Veṅkaṭapatidēva by the same Śaṅkaradēvi in Ś. 1566 (A.D. 1644), Tāraṇa.

6. *C.P. No.* 105 *of Mr. Sewell's List.*—(Kanarese.) Records grant of certain lands to the *maṭham* of Dharmapuram by Chennamāji, wife of Sōmaśēkhara Nāyaka, in Ś. 1497 (A.D. 1675), Ānanda. [Is this identical with Dharmasthala in Mudabidri Taluk?] See No. 51 below.

Coondapoor Taluk.

Basrūr.

This is the ancient Barcelore, the Barace of Pliny and an important seat of trade according to Arabian geographers. See *South Kanara Manu.*, II, p. 242, for its history. The following epigraphs have been taken from the *Mack. MSS.* See Taylor's List of Mackenzie's *Inscriptions in Mysore, Kanara,* etc., bound in the same volume as *Ins., S. Dts.*

7. In the pagoda of Mahāliṅgasvāmi at Basrūr. (Kanarese.) Records in Ś. 1336, Raktākshi, in the reign of Dēvarāya Mahārāya (II), that Timmaṇa Uḍaiyār granted to the God the customs on the houses, merchants, etc. *Ins., Mys. Kan.*, p. 61, No. 403.

8. In the pagoda of Nagarēśvara. Records that in Ś. 1354, Pramōdūta, in the same reign, Chaṇḍapparasa Uḍaiyār granted lands for the maintenance of Brahmans. *Ins., Mys. Kan.*, p. 61, No. 405. See No. 137 below.

9. In the Kōṭēśvara temple. A record of Narasimha Rāya in Ś. 1432, Śukla, relating the gift of the village of "Bellatoor" to God Mahāliṅgēśvara for worship by Mallappa Rāya. *Ibid.*, p. 62, No. 406. [Was Narasimha the son of Tuḷuva Narasa and the predecessor of Kṛishṇadēva Rāya ?]

10. In the same. A gift of land by Chandapparasa Uḍaiyār in Ś. 1363 in the reign of Dēvarāya (II) to God Kōṭēśvara. *Ibid.*, No. 407.

11. In the same temple. A grant of Mallikārjuna Rāya (1449—65), in Ś. 1377, Bhava, to God Mahāliṅga. *Ibid.*, No. 408.

12. In the same temple. Records the grant of a tax on jungles to God Mahāliṅgēśvara, in Ś. 1384, Pārthiva, by Chaṇḍra "Danaik" in the reign of Dēvarāya Mahārāya (II). *Ibid.*, No. 409. See No. 137 below.

13. In the same place. Records that in Ś. 1384, Pārthiva, in the reign of Dēvarāya Mahārāya (II), Chandra-Daṇāika Daṇḍanāyaka, granted a tax on jungles. *Ibid.*, No. 409. See No. 137 below.

14. In the same place. Records gift of land to Brahmans in Ś. 1322, Vikrama, in the reign of Harihara Rāya (II, 1377—1402). *Ibid.*, No. 410.

15. In the same place. Records grant of land to God Mahāliṅgēśvara by Nārāyaṇaśeṭṭi in Ś. 1366, Raktākshi, in the reign of Dēvarāya (II, 1422—49). *Ibid.*, No. 411.

16. In the same place. Records that in Ś. 1374, a servant of Mallikārjunarāya (1442—65), gave a garden to the same deity. *Ibid.*, No. 412.

17. In the same place. Records that in the reign of the Pāṇḍya Chakravarti the people of Basrūr gave some land to the God in Ś. 1377. *Ibid.*, No. 413.

18. In the same place. Records grant of 45 *mudies* of rice in land to local deity in Ś. 1465, Śubhakrit, by Basroor Nārāyaṇa and others. *Ibid.*, No. 414. [The *moody* is a land measure in South Kanara even now. It is land requiring 60 seers of seed to sow it and is roughly equal to an acre. *S. Kan. Manu.*, p. 215.]

19. In the same temple. Records grant of 80 *gadyānas* for repairing a maṭha in Ś. 1470, Kīlaka, in the reign of Sadāśiva Rāya. *Ibid.*, No. 416.

20. In the same temple. A record of Kṛishṇadēvarāya dated Ś. 1446, Tāraṇa, relating gift of a village to God Lakshmīnārāyaṇa of Bārkūr. *Ibid.*, No. 417.

21. In the same temple. A record of Śadāśivarāya in Ś. 1476, Ānanda, relating purchase of land from Brahmans by Sadāśiva Nāik. *Ins., Mys. Kan.*, p. 62, No. 415. Sadāśiva was the eldest son of Basavappa Gauḍa, the founder of the Keḷaḍi or Ikkēri dynasty. See *Mys. Gazr.*

22. A record of Dēvarāya II in Ś. 1358, Naḷa, relating grant of land to a choultry by Aṇṇappa Uḍaiyār. *Ibid.*, No. 418.

23. A record of Kṛishṇadēvarāya in Ś. 1450, Sarvadhāri, relating gift of 57 *muḍies* of land for the same by Timmaṇa Uḍaiyār. *Ibid.*, No. 419.

24. Records in Ś. 1526, Krōdhi, grant of 50 *gadyānas* of land by the people to the herdsmen for grazing their cattle. *Ibid.*, No. 420.

25. A record of Dēvarāya (Mallikārjuna, ? 1449—65), in Ś. 1377, Bhava, relating purchase of land from the people of Coondapoor and gift of it to a choultry by the Cheṭṭis of Bāsrūr. *Ibid.*, No. 421.

26. A record of Dēvarāya (II, 1422—49) in Ś. 1353, making grant of land for the same. *Ibid.*, No. 422.

27. A record of the same ruler in the same year relating gift of one *Koḷaga* of paddy on every bullock load coming from other places to Basrūr for the benefit of the Jain Basti, by the Cheṭṭis of Basrūr, etc. *Ibid.*, No. 423.

28. In the pagoda of Sāntarāyasvāmi. A record of Achyutarāya in Ś. 1456 relating gift of the village of "Coodera" to God Tirumaladēva by "Sunkuna Nāik" (Śaṅkaṇṇa Nāyaka). *Ibid.*, p. 64, No. 424.

29. In the same temple. A record of Naraśiṅgarāya in Ś. 1492, Pramōdūta, granting 65 *muḍies* of land to the same deity by Koṇḍappa Nāik. *Ibid.*, No. 425.

30. A record of Sadāśivarāya in Ś. 1486, Prabhava, granting 35 *muḍies* for a choultry by Tirumalacheṭṭi and others. *Ibid.*, No. 426.

31. A record of Virūpāksha (II, 1465—86), in Ś. 1394, Khara, relating a gift to the same by some merchants. *Ibid.*, No. 427.

32. A grant of land to ten Brahmans by Vijaya Uḍaiyār in the reign of Kṛishṇarāya in Ś. 1440, Pramādhi. *Ibid.*, No. 428.

33. A record of Achyutarāya, in Ś. 1456, Jaya, relating gift of land and houses to a Bhaṭṭa by Koṇḍēśvaradēva Bhaṭṭa. *Ibid.*, No. 429.

34. A record of Dēvarāya (II, 1422—49) in Ś. 1358, Piṅgaḷa, relating grant of 24 *gadyānas* of land to God Chandranātha of "Auty Angady." *Ibid.*, No. 430.

35. A record of Kṛishṇarāya in Ś. 1441, Pramādhi, recording grant of lands bought from a Gōvinda Hebbār for a choultry *Ibid.*, No. 431.

36. A record of Kṛishṇarāya in Ś. 1431, Śukla, relating a similar grant by Śaṅkarachetti of Basrūr. *Ins., Mys. Kan.*, p. 64. No. 432.

37. A record of Dēvarāya (I, 1406—18) in Ś. 1332, Virōdhikrit, relating grant of 36 *mudies* of land to the same choultry by Dēvachetti. *Ibid.*, No. 433.

Coondapoor.

38. On a stone in the Narasimhasvāmi pagoda. Records that in the reign of Pāṇḍyadēva, in Ś. 1184, Dundubhi, Narasimha Heggaḍi granted 140 *gadyānas* of land to the deity. *Ibid.*, p. 61, No. 399. [The *Heggadis* or Hegades, also called Ballals, were Brahman chiefs over groups of villages. Many of their descendants exist today. See *S. Kana. Manu.*, Vol. I, p. 607.

39. In the same place. A record of Mallikārjuna Dēvarāya in Ś. 1374, Āṅgirasa, relating gift of the office of Jyōtisha and the customs on salt works to the amount of 648 pagodas to " Humada Josee Hareyapa " by his pradhāni Dēvadāna Nāik. *Ibid.*, No. 400.

40. In the same place. Records that Narasimha Heggaḍi settled a dispute between the purōhita and the Jōsya above mentioned in Ś. 1347, Viśvāvasu, in the reign of Dēvarāya (II, 1422—49). *Ibid.*, No. 401.

Gangolli.

41. A C.P. in the hands of the local pūjāri. Records in Pramādīcha, grant of 90 pagodas and 2½ *paṇams* of land to God Veṅkaṭēśvara by Chennamāji. *Ibid.*, No. 462. See No. 51 below.

Hattiyanguḍi.

42. At the temple of Lōkanāthēśvara, in the courtyard east of the Valaga-maṇṭapam. Grant by an Uḍaiyār, dated Ś. 1499 (A.D. 1577).

43. In the same place. Grant by an Uḍaiyār in Ś. 1498.

44. In the same place. Grant by an Uḍaiyār in Ś. 1492.

45. In the same place. As in No. 42.

46. Dated only in cyclic year. Grant by a lady.

47. Dated only in cyclic year. Grant by an Uḍaiyār.

Hebbige (Haberee).

48. In the local pagoda of Hanumantēśvara. Records that Kṛishṇadēvarāya gave some land to the God in Ś. 1444, Chitrabhānu. *Ibid.*, No. 401, p. 61.

Kollūru.

49. A C.P. in the Heera Maṭha. A Kanarese record, dated in Ś. 1597, Ānanda, recording gift of 37 *gadyānas* of land to the Jaṅgamaguru. See *Ibid.*, p. 66, No. 443.

50. A C.P. in the same place. A record of the Keladi chief Veṅkaṭappa Nāik (1604-26) in Ś. 1538, Rākshasa, relating 25 *gadyānas* of land, 1,300 Areca-nut trees, and 70 cocoanut trees to the same guru. *Ins., Mys. Kan.*, p. 66, No. 444.

51. A paper grant in the same. A grant by Sōmaśēkhara Nāyaka in Śubhakrit, of a garden of 200 areca-nut trees to the same. *Ibid.*, No. 445. [Sōmaśēkhara was the Keladi chief who ruled from 1681 to 1686. He was succeeded by his widow Dodda Chinnamāji, 1686—98.]

52. In the same place. A grant of 48 *gadyānas* and 3 paṇams of land by the same to the same donee. *Ibid.*, No. 446.

53. In the pagoda of "Moocambeca." Gift of 207 *muḍies* of "Guddeh" to the Goddess in Ś. 1444, Plava, by "Hona Cumbaly Pundharee Dēva" Uḍaiyār. *Ibid.*, No. 477. The Kumblas were one of the numerous lines of local chiefs.

54. In the same place. A record of Ś. 1215, Akshaya, relating to the repair of the pagoda. *Ibid.*, No. 448.

55. In the hands of the local Brahmans. A record, dated in Ś. 1563, Vishu, relating gift of 102 *gadyānas* and ¾ paṇams of land by Vīrabhadrappa Nāik. *Ibid.*, No. 449. This chief ruled till 1649 evidently.

56. In the hands of the same. Grant of 40 *muḍies* of paddy fields in Ś. 1482, Siddhārti, by "Hona Cumbaly Baukee Arasaree." *Ibid.*, No. 450.

57. In the hands of the same. Grant of 607 pagodas and 9 paṇams of land in Ś. 1565, by Veṅkaṭappa Nāik. *Ibid.*, No. 451.

58. In the hands of the same. Grant of 21 pagodas and 5¼ paṇams of land by Vīrabhadrappa Nāik in Ś. 1564, Chitrabhānu. *Ibid.*, No. 452. See No. 55.

59. In the hands of the same. Grant of 33 pagodas of land in Ś. 1550, Prabhava, to the Goddess by Heera Veṅkaṭappa Nāik. *Ibid.*, No. 453. [He is evidently the chief who is supposed to have ruled from 1604 to 1626.]

60. In the hands of the same. Records in Ś. 1485, Dundubhi, grant of 88/16 *muḍies* of land to the Goddess by Rāma Bhaṭṭa. *Ibid.*, No. 454.

Kōṭēśvara.

61. In the local pagoda of Kōṭēśvara. A record dated in Ś. 1415, Parītāpi, relating gift of 300 *gadyānas* of land to God Kōṭēśvara. *Ibid.*, p. 65, No. 434.

62. In the same temple. Records that Echappa Uḍaiyār gave in Ś. 1468, Prabhava, in the reign of Sadāśivarāya 50 *gadyānas* of land to the same deity. *Ibid.*, No. 435. [Echappa was evidently the same as the Jain chief of Gairsappa who married a daughter of the last Karkal king Bhairasu Uḍaiyār about 1560.]

63. A record of Bukkaṇa Uḍaiyār in Ś. 1347, Krōdhi, recording grant of 120 *gadyānas* of land for a lamp by "Auchapa Uḍaiyār." *Ins., Mys. Kan.*, p. 65, No. 436.

64. A record of Sadāśivarāyain Ś. 1484, Dundubhi, recording grant of land by a cheṭṭi to God Kōṭēśvara. *Ibid.*, No. 437.

65. A record of Virūpākshi Rāya in Ś. 1444, Plavaṅga, recording grant of 40 *gadyānas* of land for the vasanta festival. *Ibid.*, No. 438.

66. A record of Bukkaṇa Uḍaiyār (I, 1350—79), in Ś. 1295, Parītāpi, recording grant of land by Vīrabhadra- dēva. *Ibid.*, No. 439.

67. A record of Bukkaṇa Uḍaiyār (I, 1350—79), in Ś. 1279, Viḷambi, recording grant of ten *gadyānas* of land for a lamp to God Kōṭēśvar. *Ibid.*, p. 66, No. 440.

68. A record of Pāṇḍya Chakravarti in Ś. 1183, Vishu. *Ibid.*, No. 441. See No. 97 below.

69. A gift of land by Bommarasa in Ś. 1300, Piṅgaḷa, in the reign of Bukka Rāya (I, 1350—79). *Ibid.*, No. 442.

Sēnapūr.

70. A copper plate in the place. Records in Ś. 1596, Ānanda, gift of ninety pagodas and two and a half paṇams of land in the village by "Chenmanjee" to God Vishṇu. *Ibid.*, p. 80, No. 588. [Chennamaji was the queen of Sōmaśēkhara Nāyaka. See No. 51 above.]

Shankaranārāyan.

71. A C.P. in the place. Records in Ś. 1424, Dundubhi, grant of eighty-four and a half "*cantees*" of land, thirty-seven *muḍies* of rice-ground and thirty-two and a half *pagodas* and four *paṇams* of land to God Śaṅkaranārāyaṇa by Basavappa Nāyaka. *Ibid.*, p. 67, No. 455. [Are the *cantees* the same as *goontas* or fortieths, a term generally used for measuring land by revenue authorities? *S. Kan. Manu.*, I, p. 215.]

72. Another C.P. in the same place. Records in Ś. 1504, Svabhānu, grant of one hundred and one *muḍies* of land to the same deity. *Ibid.*, No. 456.

Ullūru.

73. A C.P. in the place. Records in Ś. 1352, Sādhāraṇa, grant of one hundred and forty-two *canties* of land in the village to the local *maṭha* by Dēva Uḍaiyār (II, 1422—49). *Ibid.*, No. 589. See No. 71 above.

Villupuṇḍa.

Mr. Sewell gives the following three inscriptions in the temple of durgā.

74. Grant by one Paramēśvara Vīrapratāpa Uḍaiyār of Bārkūr and Rāmanātha Rāja of Villupuṇḍa, in Ś. 1338 (A.D. 1416). (Mr. Sewell surmises that as the latter part is a Vijayanagara title, Bukka II might be the person intended.)

75. Grant by Vīra Dēva Rāya (II, 1422—49) of Vijayanagar and an Uḍaiyār of Bārkūr in Ś. 1367.

76. Grant by the same in Ś. 1369 (A.D. 1447).

KASARAGOD TALUK.

Āḍūr.

76-A. A Sanskrit and Kanarese damaged inscription of the reign of the Western Chāḷukyan king Kīrttivarman II (747—57). *Ind. Antq.*, Vol. IX, p. 69, and Kielhorn's *Southern List*, No. 50.

Tenka Kumbla.

77. At the gate of the fort. (Kanarese.) Records the erection of the fort by a Nāyaka (of Ikkeri).

Viṭṭhala.

78. At the foot of the *dvajasthambha.* A copper plate inscription in Kanarese recording the execution of certain temple works in Ś. 1666.

79. A C.P. (Kanarese) fixed at the foot of the dvajasthambha, recording the execution of certain temple works in Ś. 1666 (A.D. 1744).

80. Near the Anantēśvara temple, in "illegible Malayāḷam."

MAṄGALORE TALUK.

Bōlūru (suburb of Maṅgalore).

81. 24 *of* 1901.—On a slab set up in warg No. 2. A record of the Vijayanagara king Harihara, in Kanarese. (Date doubtful.)

82. 25 *of* 1901.—On a slab set up in warg No. 6 in the same village. A record of the Vijayanagara king Dēvarāya (II, 1422—49), in Ś. 1347, Krōdhin, in Kanarese, mentioning Nāgaṇṇa Oḍeya.

Kadri (3 miles north-east of Maṅgalore).

83. 26 *of* 1901.—On a slab set up in the courtyard of the Mañjunātha temple. A record of the Ālupa king Baṅkidēv-Āḷupēndra, in Kanarese. (Date doubtful.) Baṅki dēva lived about the close of the thirteenth century. See No. 175.

84. 27 *of* 1901.—On another slab in the same place, right of entrance. The Vijayanagara king Harihara (II) records in Ś. 1308, Kshaya, in Kanarese, a gift of land. Mentions Mañjunātha.

Kodiyal-Bail (near Maṅgalōre).

85. 22 *of* 1901.—(Kanarese.) On a slab set up in warg No. 26. A record of the Vijayanagara king Dēvarāya (II), in Ś. 1341, Viḷambi, mentioning Timmaṇṇa-Oḍeya.

86. 23 *of* 1901.—(Kanarese.) On a slab set up in warg No. 7. The Vijayanagara king Harihara (II) records in Ś. 1318, Dhātri, a gift of land.

Maṅgalōre.

87. 17 *of* 1901.—(Kanarese.) On a pillar in front of the deserted temple of Gollara-Gaṇapati. The Ālupa king Baṅkidēv-Ālupēndra records in Ś. 1225, Śubhakrit, a gift of land. See No. 83 above.

88. 18 *of* 1901.—(Kanarese.) On a slab set up to the left of the entrance into the Chakrapāṇi temple at Attavara, a quarter of the same place. Records in Ś. 1289, Parābhava, a gift of land. (A damaged record.)

89. 19 *of* 1901.—(Kanarese.) On a slab set up to the right of the entrance into the same temple. A record of the Vijayanagara king Vīra-Bukkaṇṇa-Oḍeya (I) in Ś. ? Mentions Śaṁkaraḍēva-Oḍeya. (A damaged record.)

90. 20 *of* 1901.—(Kanarese.) On a slab set up to the right of the entrance into the central shrine of the Pāṇḍyēśvara temple. A record dated in Ś. ? (Damaged.)

91. 21 *of* 1901.—(Kanarese.) On a slab set up in the courtyard of the same temple. A much damaged record.

Mulki.

92. 81 *of* 1901.—(Kanarese.) On a slab set up in the Durgā temple at Bappanāḍ, a hamlet of the place. A damaged record of the Vijayanagara king Vīrapratāpa-Dēvarāya (I) in Ś. 1333, Vikrita.

93. 82 *of* 1901.—(Kanarese.) On the south face of the mānastambha in front of the Jaina basti. Records five verses, arranged in 25 squares and praising the Tīrthamkaras.

Pāḍuvapanambūr.

94. 84 *of* 1901.—(Kanarese.) On a slab set up at the entrance into the Bayilaṅgaḍi-Melebasti. Records in Ś. 1464, Śubhakrit, a gift of land. (Referred to by Mr. Sewell.)

95. 85 *of* 1901.—(Kanarese). On a slab set up in the Śiva temple at the same village. Records in the reign of the Vijayanagara king Vīra-Immaḍi Dēvarāya (II) in Piṅgaḷa, a gift of land. (A damaged record.)

Pavañja.

96. 83 *of* 1901.—(Kanarese.) On a slab lying in front of the Mahāliṅgēśvara temple. Records in the reign of the Vijayanagara king Vīra-Immaḍi-Dēvarāya (II) in Ś. 1340, Hēviḷambin, a gift of land. Mentions Aṇṇapa-Oḍeya as governing the Maṅgaḷūru and Bārakūra-rājya. Belugula in the Hoyisaṇa-rājya is also referred to.

MUDABIDRI TALUK.

Beluvāyi.

97. 61 *of* 1901.—(Kanarese.) In a field near the house of Lōkayyaśeṭṭi. Records gift of paddy to the temple of Kaṇṭēśvara in the time of Pāṇḍyachakravartin Pāṇḍyadēva. See No. 68 where a Pāṇḍyachakravarti's date is given as Ś. 1183.

Kantavāra.

98. 56 *of* 1901.—(Kanarese.) On a pillar set up in the Phalmāru-*maṭha*. Records in the reign of the Vijayanagara king Vīrapratāpa-Dēvarāya (II) in Ś. 1355, Pramādin, gift of land to Rājarājēśvaratīrtha of the *Baḍagaṇa-maṭha* at Kantāra.

99. 57 *of* 1901.—(Kanarese.) On a slab set up behind the kitchen in the Kaṇṭēśvara temple at the same village. Records in the reign of the Vijayanagara king Vīra-Hariyappa-Oḍeya (I) in Sarvadhārin, a gift of money.

100. 58 *of* 1901.—(Kanarese.) On another slab set up in the same place. A record of the Vijayanagara king Vīrapratāpa-Kṛishṇarāya. (A damaged record ; the date is lost.)

101. 59 *of* 1901.—(Kanarese.) On a broken slab lying in the same place. A fragment of a record of the Vījayanagara king Vīra-Hariyappa-Oḍeya (II) in Ś. 1301, Siddārtin.

102. 60 *of* 1901.—(Kanarese.) On a slab set up to the right of the entrance into the Kaṇṭēśvara temple. Records in Ś. 1731, Vibhava, repairs to the temple made by a private person under orders from the " company " (Kampini).

Mudabidre (Mudabidri).

An excellent account of this highly important Jain centre is given by Dr. Hultzsch in his *Ep. Rep.*, 1901, p. 3. It was called formerly *Bidire* or Vēṇupura or Vaṁśapura and belonged to the province of Tuḷudēśa. The earliest inscription in it belongs to the Āḷupa king Kulaśēkhara, dated in A.D. 1205. The remaining belong to the Hoysaḷa and the Vijayanagara dynasties. Dr. Hultzsch points out that it is the seat of the Jain priest Chārukīrti Paṇḍitāchārya and his maṭha, of sixteen Jaina shrines or *bastis* dedicated to Tirthaṁkaras, Yakshis, etc., the latest of which is dated A.D. 1429. For descriptions of these see *Ep. Rep.*, 1901, p. 30. Ferguson's *Hist.*, *Ind.*, *E. Arch.*, pp. 270--8, and *Buchanan*, Vol. II, p. 254. The members of the local Jain dynasty called the Chautars even now receive pension, and have got a ruined palace.

103. 28 *of* 1901.—(Kanarese.) On the north wall of the Gaḍḍigēmaṇṭapa in the Hōsabasti, right of entrance. A record of the Vijayanagara king Vīra-Dēvarāya (II) in Ś. 1351, Saumya. Refers to Perumāḷdēva-Daṇṇāyaka and to Dēvarāja-Oḍeya of Nāgamaṅgala, who was ruling the Maṅgaḷūra-rājya, and to the building of the *basti.* (This is the largest and finest in the place.) [Perumāḷdēva was a famous General of Dēvarāya II. For reference to him and his two sons as well as Dēvarāja Uḍaiyār see *Mys. Arch. Rep.*, 1908, p. 17.]

104. 29 *of* 1901.—(Kanarese.) On the same wall. A record of the Vijayanagara king Prauḍha-Dēvarāya (II) in Ś. 1373. Prajāpati. Mentions Gaṇappaṇṇa-Oḍeya and refers to the building of a mukhamaṇṭapa of the basti, called Bhaira dēvi maṇṭapa. Dr. Hultzsch draws attention to sculptures round its base amongst which is a *giraffe.*

105. 30 *of* 1901.—(Kanarese.) On the same wall. Records in the reign of the Vijayanagara king Virūpāksha in Ś. 1394, Khara, a gift of land in the time of Viṭṭharaśa.

106. 31 *of* 1901.—(Kanarese.) On the same wall. Records in Ś. 1409, Parābhava, a gift of land.

107. 32 *of* 1901.—(Kanarese.) On the same wall. Records in Ś. 1383, Vikrama, gift of money for offerings.

108. 33 *of* 1901.—(Kanarese.) In the same place, left of entrance. A record of the Vijayanagara king Dēvarāya (II) in Ś. 1351, Saumya. Mentions the building of the *basti* and contains a long genealogy of a chief named Bhairava.

109. 34 *of* 1901.—(Kanarese.) In the same place, left of entrance. Records in Ś. 1384, Vishu, gift of paddy in the time of Hiriya-Bhairavadēva-Oḍeya or Nāgararājya.

110. 35 *of* 1901.—(Kanarese.) In the same place, left of entrance. Records a list of merchants who built the second storey of the *basti.*

111. 36 *of* 1901.—(Kanarese.) In the same place, left of entrance. Records the names of merchants who built the third storey of the *basti.*

112. 37 *of* 1901.—(Kanarese verses.) On the east, north and west faces of a pillar in the Bhairadēvimaṇṭapa of the same basti. A record in praise of the Mahāmaṇḍalēśvara Sāḷva-Malla. Incomplete.

113. 38 *of* 1901.—(Kanarese.) On another pillar in the same maṇṭapa. Records five verses in praise of the Tīrthaṁkaras, arranged in 25 octagons ; see *Ind. Antq.*, Vol. V, p. 44 f.

114. 39 *of* 1901.—(Kanarese.) On a slab built into the wall of the Kshētrapāla shrine in the Hōsabasti. An inscription of the Vijayanagara king Virūpāksharāya (II, 1465—86) in Ś. 1398,

Durmukhin. Mentions Śiṅgappa Daṇṇāyaka and Viṭṭharāsa-Oḍeya. A damaged record.

115. 40 *of* 1901.—(Kanarese.) On a slab leaning against the south wall of the inner enclosure of the same basti. Records in Ś. 1493, Prajōtpatti, a gift of land, and mentions the Chauta family which had its seat at Mudabidri.

116. 41 *of* 1901.—(Kanarese.) On a slab set up in the Gurugalabasti at the same village. An epigraph of the Vijayanagara king Vīra-Bukkarāya (II, 1399—1406), son of Hariharāya (II, 1377—1402), in Ś. 1329, Vyaya. Mentions Bāchappa-Oḍeya and a gift of land.

117. 42 *of* 1901.—(Kanarese.) On another slab set up in the same place. Records in the reign of the Vijayanagara king Vīra-Kṛishṇarāya in Ś. 1437, Yuva, the gift of paddy, and mentions Ratnappa-Oḍeya who belonged to the family of Vaicha-Daṇḍādhipa.

118. 43 *of* 1901.—(Kanarese.) On the third slab set up in the same place. Records in the reign of the Hoysaḷa king Vīra-Ballāḷa (III), son of Vīra-Narasimha (III), in Vishu, a gift. Mentions Dēvappa-Daṇṇāyaka.

119. 44 *of* 1901.—(Kanarese.) On a pillar in the Gaḍḍigēmaṇṭapa of the Gurugalabasti. A record of Ś. 1460, Bahudhānya (wrong), mentioning the building of the maṇṭapa.

120. 45 *of* 1901.—(Kanarese.) On a broken slab in front of the Nāyibasti at the same village. Records the death of a Jaina teacher named Chandrakīrti and the building of the maṇṭapa (i.e., the Nāyibasti) in his memory. See No. 128 below. [A Chandrakīrti under date A.D. 1605 is mentioned as one of the teachers of the Sarasvati gachcha and Balātkāragaṇa in the *Jaina-Siddhānta Bhāskara*. See *Epitome of Jainism*, p. LXXIII.]

121-A—D. 46 to 49 *of* 1901.—(Kanarese.) On stones built into Jaina tombs at the same village. No details given.

122. 50 *of* 1901.—(Kanarese.) On a slab lying in the courtyard of the Gauri temple at Prāntya, a quarter of the same place. A damaged record in Ś. 1318, mentioning Vīra-Pāṇḍyadēvaraśa.

123. 51 *of* 1901.—(Kanarese.) On another slab lying in the same place. A damaged record of the Āḷupa king Kulaśēkhara-Āḷupēndra in Yuva. See the next epigraph.

124. 52 *of* 1901.—(Kanarese.) On the third slab lying in the same place. Records in the reign of the Āḷupa king Kulaśēkhara Āḷupēndra in Ś. 1127, Krōdhana, a gift of land.

125. 53 *of* 1901.—(Kanarese.) On the fourth slab lying in the same place. Records in the reign of the Āḷupa king Kulaśēkhara Āḷupēndra in Raktākshin a gift of land.

126. 55 *of* 1901.—(Kanarese.) In a field one mile south-east from the travellers' bungalow. Records in the reign of the Vijayanagara king Vīra-Hariharāya (II) in Ś. 1312, Śukla, a gift of land to the Gurugalabasti at Bidire. Mentions Maṅgarasa-Oḍeya as governor of Maṅgaḷūra-rājya.

Puttige.

127. 54 *of* 1901.—(Kanarese.) On a slab set up in front of the Sōmanātha temple. A record of the Vijayanagara king Kṛishṇarāya in Ś. 1434, Āṅgirasa, mentioning the minister Śāḷva-Timmayya, Ratnappa-Oḍeya and the Chauta chief Tirumalarāya.

Vēṇur.

128. 72 *of* 1901.—(Sanskrit.) On the right side of the colossal statue of Gummaṭa on the hill. Records in Ś. 1525, Śōbhakrit, the setting up of the image of Bhujabalin (i.e., Gommaṭēśvara) by Timmarāja of the family of Chāmuṇḍa, at the instance of the family teacher Chārukīrti of Belgola. [The inscription has been published by Rice in his *Śravaṇa Belgola inscriptions* and by Dr. Hultzsch in *Ep. Ind.*, Vol. VII, pp. 112-13. According to Prof. Kielhorn the date corresponds to Thursday, 1st March, A.D. 1604. Dr. Hultzsch points out that this inscription mentions Timma Rājā's mother (Queen Pāṇḍyaka) and uncle Rāyakuvara (i.e., Rāyakumāra) and not his father, and that it can be inferred from this that the family practised the *aḷiyasantāna* system. Chārukīrti was, like Laḷitakīrti, the Pontiff of Belgola and Mūḍabidri, just as Dēvēndrakīrti was the Pontiff of Humcha. From a list in the *Jaina Siddhānta bhāskara* I find no Chārukīrti under this date, but one in A.D. 1207. See Nahar and Ghosh's *Epitome of Jainism*, p. LXXII, in the appendix and *Ind. Antq.*, Vols. XX and XXI. Chāmuṇḍarāja was probably the great minister Chāmuṇḍarāja who set up the colossal statue at Belgola.]

129. 73 *of* 1901.—(Kanarese verse.) On the left side of the same statue. Records in Ś. 1526, Śōbhakrit, the same act. [See *Ep. Ind.*, VII, pp. 112-13. The date is the same as in the previous inscription, but the *current* and not the expired year is given. See *S. Kanara Manual*, Vol. II, p. 259, for an account of the statue.

130. 74 *of* 1901.—(Kanarese.) On a slab set up in front of the Akkaṅgaḷabasti within the Gummaṭabasti. Records in Ś. 1526, Śōbhakrit, that Pāṇḍyakadēvi *alias* Vardhamānakkagaḷu and Mallidēvi, two queens of Vīra-Timmarāja-Oḍeya, built a Chaityālaya of Chandranātha and granted land to it. See No. 128.

131. 75 *of* 1901.—(Kanarese.) On a slab set up in front of the Binnāṇabasti within the Gummaṭabasti. Records in Ś. 1526, Śōbhakrit, that Binnani, a queen of Vīra-Timmarāja-Oḍeya, built a

Chaityālaya of Śāntīśvara and granted land to it. [An inaccurate translation of this is given in *Ind. Antq.*, Vol. V, p. 38.]

132. 76 *of* 1901.—(Kanarese.) On a slab built into the floor of the Mahāliṅgēśvara temple at the same village. A record in Ś. 8[90], Prabhava, in archaic characters.

133. 77 *of* 1901.—(Kanarese.) On the Nandi-pillar in front of the same temple. Records that a merchant set up the *mānastambha*, a big monolithic column set up in front of the *bastis*. From the fact that almost all of them are known as *Śeṭṭārabastis* it is inferred that the Jain merchants constructed them. See *Ind. Antq.*, Vol. V, pp. 38–9.

134. 78 *of* 1901.—(Kanarese.) On a slab set up close to the east wall of the Tīrthaṅkarabasti within the Śāntīśvarabasti at the same village. Records in Ś. 1544, Durmati, the gift of land to the basti by Rāmanātha araśa, while Madhurakadēvi was ruling over the Puñjaḷikēyarājya. [This is also mentioned in 2 and 9 in the list.]

135. 79 *of* 1901.—(Kanarese.) On a slab set up in the south-east corner of the maṇṭapa in front of the Śāntīśvarabasti. Records in Ś. 1459, Hēmalambin, the consecration of the 24 Tīrthaṁkaras in the basti. See *S. Kanara Manual*, Vol. II, p. 260.

136. 80 *of* 1901.—(Kanarese.) On a slab set up to the right of the entrance into the same maṇṭapa. A record dated in Ś. 1411, Saumya, mentioning a chief of Puñjaḷiyarājya. [This is the earliest inscription in the Śāntiśvarabasti.]

UDIPI TALUK.

Bārkūr (nine miles north of Udipi).

This is the traditional capital of Tuḷuva, known formerly as Bārahakanyāpura. Formerly a seaport, now an inland town, tradition represents it as one of the seats of Brahman governors, when Brahmans were introduced into Malabar, and later on as scene of a mosque erected by the royal convert Chēramān Perumāḷ. Epigraphy furnishes us with a list of the early Ālupa kings, the Hoysaḷas and then of the Vijayanagar rulers who had it as their provincial capital. Amongst the Āluva kings may be mentioned Kavi about A.D. 1150 (Nos. 189 and 194); Sōyidēva about 1315 (No. 175). For the Hoysala inscription see No. 4. The rest are Vijayanagara ones.

137. 119 *of* 1901.—(Kanarese.) On the first slab set up close to the west wall of the Sōmēśvara temple at Mūḍakēri near the same place. The Vijayanagara king Vīrapratāpa-Dēvarāya (II) records in Ś. 1353, Sādhāraṇa, the settlement of dispute among certain merchants of Bārakūru, while Chandarāsa-Oḍeya was ruling the Bārakūra-Tūlu-rājya. For a previous Vijayanagar feudatory in the time of Dēvarāya I see next epigraph; for another in the reign of Harihara II see No. 144; and for still another in the time of Bukka I, No. 148.

138. 120 *of* 1901.—(Kanarese.) On the third slab set up in the same place. A record of the Vijayanagara king Vīra-Dēvarāya-Oḍeya (I), dated in Ś. 1335, Nandana. Mentions Śaṁkharadēva Oḍeya as governing the Bārakūra-rājya and a gift of paddy. See No. 161.

139. 121 *of* 1901.—(Kanarese.) On the fourth slab set in the same place. A record of the Vijayanagara king Vīrapratāpa-Dēvarāya (II), dated in Ś. 1353, Virōdhikrit, making gift of paddy. Mentions Chandra-Oḍeya as governor of the Bārakūra-Tūlu-rājya. See No. 137.

140. 122 *of* 1901.—(Kanarese.) On the seventh slab set up in the same place. Records in the reign of Hoysaḷa king Vīra-Ballāḷa (III) in Ś. 1258, Dhātri, gift of paddy. Mentions Vayichappa Daṇṇāyaka and the pradhāni Ajjaṇa-Sāhaṇi. [The record shows that the Āḷupas were overthrown by the Hoysaḷas in the Government of the district.]

141. 123 *of* 1901.—(Kanarese.) On the eighth slab set up in the same place. Records in the reign of the Vijayanagara king Gajabēṭegāra-Dēvarāya (II) in Ś. 1362, Siddhārthin, gift of paddy. (A damaged record.)

142. 124 *of* 1901.—(Kanarese.) On the ninth slab set up in the same place. A damaged record mentioning Gagana-śivāchārya who belonged to the spiritual lineage of Durvāsas and an Āḷva king. [Durvāsa is generally supposed to be the founder of the earliest of the Śaivite maṭhas, called the Āṁartaka.]

143. 125 *of* 1901.—(Kanarese.) On the tenth slab set up in the same place. Records in the reign of the Vijayanagara king Vīrapratāpa-Mallikārjuna (1449—65), in Ś. 1380, Bahudhānya, gift of money. Mentions Sidappa-Daṇṇāyaka. The record shows that the Vijayanagar hold over the west was strong even in the weak reigns following Dēva-Rāya II. See also Nos. 148 and 162.

144. 126 *of* 1901.—(Kanarese.) On the eleventh slab set up in the same place. An epigraph of the Vijayanagara king Vīra-Hariyappa-Oḍeya (II) recording in Ś. 1301, Kāḷayukta, gift of paddy. Mentions Bommarasa-Oḍeya as the governor of the Bārakūrarājya. See No. 153.

145. 127 *of* 1901.—(Kanarese.) On the twelfth slab set up in the same place. Records a gift in the reign of the Vijayanagara king Vīra-Harihara-Mahārāya (II) in Ś. 1308, Kshaya. (Damaged.) See No. 151.

146. 128 *of* 1901.—(Kanarese.) On the thirteenth slab set up in the same place. A record of the Vijayanagara king Gaja-bēṭekāra-Dēvarāya II recording in Ś. 1362, Siddhārthin, gift of gold to a Brāhmaṇa. Mentions Lakhanna-Daṇṇāyaka. [Was this the same as the chief governor of the south, the Lord of the southern ocean and the brother of Madaṇṇa Nāyaka ?] See No. 181.

147. 129 *of* 1901.—(Kanarese.) On the fourteenth slab set up in the same place. Records in the reign of the Vijayanagara king Vīra-Bukaṇṇa-Oḍeya (I) in Ś. 1293, Virōdhikrit, gift of land. Mentions Gōparasa-Oḍeya who was governing the Bārakūra-rājya. See No. 150.

148. 130 *of* 1901.—(Kanarese.) On the fifteenth slab set up in the same place. Records in the reign of the Vijayanagara king Vīrapratāpa-Virūpāksha-Mahārāya-Oḍeya (II, 1465—86), in Ś. 1387, Vyaya, a gift of paddy. See No. 143.

149. 131 *of* 1901.—(Kanarese.) On a slab set up in the outside close to the west wall of the same temple. Records in the reign of the Vijayanagara king Vīrapratāpa-Sadāśivarāya in Ś. 1507, Pārthiva, gift of land. Mentions Rāmarājanāyaka, grandson of Sadāśivarāya Nāyaką of Kēḷaḍi.

150. 132 *of* 1901.—(Kanarese.) On a slab lying near the tank at Mūḍakēri near the same temple. Records in the reign of the Vijayanagara king Vīra-Bukaṇṇa-Oḍeya (I) in Ś. 1282, Śārvarin, the gift of paddy. Mentions Malleya-Daṇṇāyaka who was governing the Bārakūra-rājya. Malleya was evidently a predecessor of Goparasa mentioned in No. 147. The inscription shows that the Vijayanagar arms reached South Kanara as early as A.D. 1360. See No. 157 below.

151. 133 *of* 1901.—(Kanarese.) On a slab lying in the house of Subbanna aḍigaḷ in the same village. A record of the Vijayanagara king Vīrapratāpa-Harihara-Mahārāya (II), dated in Ś. 1324, Chitrabhānu, mentioning Basavaṇṇa-Oḍeya who was governing the Bārakūra-rājya. (Damaged.) See No. 145 for another feudatory of Harihara II.

152. 134 *of* 1901.—(Kanarese.) On another slab lying the same house. Records in the reign of the Vijayanagara king Vīrapratāpa-Harihara-Mahārāya (II) in Ś. 1324, Chitrabhānu, gift of paddy. Mentions Basavaṇṇa-Oḍeya who was governing the Bārakūra-rājya. See the previous epigraph.

153. 135 *of* 1901.—(Kanarese.) On a slab lying near the well in the Gōpālakṛishṇa temple at Mūḍakēri. Records in the reign of the Vijayanagara king Vīra-Harihara-Mahārāya (II) in Ś. 1302, Raudra, gift of gold. Mentions Bommarsa-Oḍeya who was governing the Bārakūra-rājya, and states that Kumāra Mādhavasvāmin set up the image of Gōpinātha in the Bārakūra-maṭha. See No. 144 above.

154. 136 *of* 1901.—(Kanarese.) On a *viragal* set up to the left of the entrance into the Sōmēśvara temple at the same village. A record of the Āḷupa king Baṅkiy-Āḷupēndra. See No. 83 above.

155. 137 *of* 1901.—(Kanarese.) On a *viragal* set up to the left of the same entrance. A fragment of record of the Āḷupa king Baṅkiy-Āḷupēndra. See No. 83 above.

156. 138 *of* 1901.—(Kanarese.) On a slab lying in Paramēś-varabhaṭṭa's house in the same village. Records in the reign of the Vijayanagara king Vīra-Bukaṇṇa-Oḍeya (I), in Ś. 1282, Śārvarin, gift of paddy. Mentions Mallēya-Daṇṇāyaka who was governing the Bārakūra-rājya. See No. 150 above.

157. 139 *of* 1901.—(Kanarese.) On a slab built into the wall of Padmanābhabhaṭṭa's house in the same village. The Vijaya-nagara king Vīra-Bukaṇṇa-Oḍeya (I) records in Ś. 1281, Vikārin, gift of paddy. Mentions Malleya-Daṇṇāyaka who was governing the Bārakūra-rājya. See No. 150 above.

158. 140 *of* 1901.—(Kanarese.) On a slab lying in Śrīdhara-śāstri's house in the same village. Records in the reign of the Vijayanagara king Vīrapratāpa-Sadāśivarāya in Ś. 1508, Sarvajit, gift of paddy.

159. 141 *of* 1901.—(Kanarese.) On a slab lying in Sōma-śāstri's house in the same village. The Vijayanagara king Vīra-Bukaṇṇa-Oḍeya (I) records in Ś. 1287, Viśvāvasu, gift of paddy. Mentions Malleya-Daṇṇāyaka who was governing the Bārakūra-rājya. See No. 150 above.

160. 142 *of* 1901.—(Kanarese.) On a slab set up close to Śiva-rāma-Kāraṇika's house in the same village. Records in Ś. 1470, Kīlaka, a gift of land.

161. 143 *of* 1901.—(Kanarese.) On a slab set up in the Gaṇa-pati temple at Chaulikēre near the place. Dated in the reign of the Vijayanagara king Vīrapratāpa-Dēvarāya (I). Records in Ś. 1338, Manmatha, gift of paddy for feeding Brāhmaṇas on the occasion of the anniversary *(samārādhana)* of Ānanda-Sarasvati. Mentions Śaṁkaradēva Oḍeya who was governing the Bārakūra-rājya. Mentions also Amritēndratīrtha, pupil of Ānanda-Saras-vati, Amritaprajña and Nārāyaṇagiri. See No. 138 for the same feudatory and No. 165 for the same teachers.

162. 144 *of* 1901.—(Kanarese.) On another slab set up in the same temple. Records in the reign of the Vijayanagara king Vīrapratāpa-Immaḍi-Dēvarāya in Ś. 1380, Bahudhānya, gift of gold. Mentions Guruvappa-Oḍeya who was the governor of the Bārakūra-rājya. Immaḍi Dēva was the same as Mallikārjuna, 1422—65. See No. 143 above.

163. 145 *of* 1901.—(Kanarese.) On the third slab set up in the same temple. Dated in the reign of the Vijayanagara king Immaḍi-Dēvarāya. Records in Ś. 1372, Śukla, gift of money, and mentions Rāyarasa-Oḍeya, as the governor of Bārakūra-rājya.

164. 146 *of* 1901.—(Kanarese.) On the fourth slab set up in the same temple. Records in the reign of the Vijayanagara king Vīrapratāpa-Mallikārjuna in Ś. 1383, Vishu, a gift of land.

165. 147 *of* 1901.—(Kanarese.) On the fifth slab set up in the same temple. Records in the reign of the Vijayanagara king Vīrapratāpa-Dēvarāya (II) in Ś. 1338, Manmatha, gift of paddy. Mentions Ānanda-Sarasvati and his pupils Amritaprajña and Nārāyaṇagiri. See No. 161.

166. 148 *of* 1901.—(Kanarese.) On a slab lying in the same temple. A damaged record of the Vijayanagara king Vīrapratāpa-Dēvarāya (II), dated Ś. 1353, Sādhāraṇa. Mentions Chaṇḍarasa-Oḍeya as the governor of Bārakūra-Tuḷu-rājya. See No. 137.

167. 149 *of* 1901.—(Kanarese.) On a slab set up near the same temple. Records in the reign of the Vijayanagara king Vīra-Harihararāya (II) in Ś. 1318, Yuva, gift of a coconut garden.

168. 150 *of* 1901.—(Kanarese.) On another slab set up in the same place. Dated in the reign of the Vijayanagara king Vīrapratāpa-Kṛishṇarāya. Records in Ś. 1447, Tāraṇa, a gift of land. Mentions Viṭharaśa-Oḍeya, son of Lakshminārāyaṇa-Karaṇīka, as governor of Bārakūrarājya.

169. 151 *of* 1901.—(Kanarese.) On the third slab set up in the same place. Dated in the reign of the Vijayanagara king Vīra-Harihara-Mahārāya (II). Records in Ś. 1314, Aṅgirasa, the building of a feeding-house. Dhorasamudra is mentioned as the capital *(nelebidu)* of the king. Śingaṇṇa-Oḍeya was ruling Tuḷu and Malaha-rājya from the capital (rājadhāni) of Bārakūru. The record shows that Sīṅgaṇṇa Uḍaiyār should have ruled between Bommarasa and Basavaṇṇa, the two other feudatories of Harihara II.

170. 152 *of* 1901.—(Kanarese.) On the fourth slab set up in the same place. Records in the reign of the Vijayanagara king Vīrapratāpa-Vīra-Naraśiṅgarāya in Ś. 1424, Durmati, the building of a feeding house. Mentions Basavarāsa-Oḍeya as the governor of Bārakūra-rājya.

171. 153 *of* 1901.—(Kanarese.) On the fifth slab set up near the Gaṇapati temple at Chaulikere. Records in the reign of the Vijayanagara king Vīrapratāpa-Virūpāksha (II, 1465—86), in Ś. 1387, Manmatha (wrong), a gift of land. Mentions Viṭharasa-Oḍeya as governor of Bārakūra-rājya and Śiṅgaṇa-Daṇṇāyaka. See No. 148 above.

172. 154 *of* 1901.—(Kanarese.) On a slab lying near the house of Subbarāyabhaṭṭa in the same village. Records in the reign of the Vijayanagara king Vīra-Harihara-Mahārāya (II) in Ś. 1309, Prabhava, the building of a feeding house. Dhorasamudra is mentioned as the capital *(nelebidu)* of the king. Mallappa-Oḍeya was ruling the Tuḷu-Haive, and Koṅkaṇa-rājya from the capital (rājādhani) of Bārakūru. See No. 174.

173. 155 *of* 1901.—(Kanarese.) On a slab set up in the Sōmanāthēśvara temple at Maṅgarakēri near Bārakūru. An inscription of the Vijayanagara king Vīra-Hariyappa-Oḍeya (II), son of Vīra-Bukkaṇṇa-Oḍeya (I), recording in Ś. 1301, Kālayuktakshin, gift of money. Mentions Bommarasa-Oḍeya as governor of Bārakūra-rājya. See No. .

174. 156 *of* 1901.—(Kanarese.) On another slab set up in the same place. Records in the reign of the Vijayanagara king Vīra-Harihara-Mahārāya (II) in Ś. 1312, Śukla, a gift of land. Mentions Mallappa-Oḍeya as governor of Bārakūra-rājya. See No. 172.

175. 157 *of* 1901.—(Kanarese.) On the third slab set up in the same place. The Āḷupa king Sōyidēv-Āḷupēndra records in Ś. 1238, Rākshasa, a gift of gold. Mentions Baṅkidēvarasa.

176. 158 *of* 1901.—(Kanarese.) On the fourth slab set up in the same place. Records in the reign of the Vijayanagara king Vīrapratāpa-Prauḍhadēvarāya in Ś. 1393, Khara, a gift of land. Mentions Viṭṭharaśa as governing the Bārakūra-Tuḷu-rājya.

177. 159 *of* 1901.—(Kanarese.) On the fifth slab set up in the same place. Records in the reign of the Vijayanagara king Vīrapratāpa-Harihara (II) in Ś. 1316, Śrīmukha, gift of land. Mentions Śaṁkaradēva-Oḍeya as governor of Bārakūra-rājya.

178. 160 *of* 1901.—(Kanarese.) On the sixth slab set up in the same place. Records in the reign of the Vijayanagara king Vīrapratāpa-dēvarāya (I) in Ś. 1343, Śārvarin, gift of oil for lamps. Mentions Śaṃkaradēva-Oḍeya as governor of Bārakūra-rājya.

179. 161 *of* 1901.—(Kanarese.) On the seventh slab set up in the same place. Dated in the reign of the Vijayanagara king Vīra-Bukkaṇṇa-Oḍeya (I). Records in Ś. 1295, Pramādīcha, gift of paddy.

180. 162 *of* 1901.—(Kanarese.) On the eighth slab set up in the same place. Dated in the reign of the Vijayanagara king Vīrapratāpa-Prauḍha-Virūpāksha (II, 1465—86). Records in Ś. 1398, Dhurmukhin, gift of land. Mentions Viṭṭharaśa as governor of Bārakūra-rājya.

181. 163 *of* 1901.—(Kanarese.) On the ninth slab set up in the same place. Dated in the reign of the Vijayanagara king Vīra-Mallikārjunarāya. Records in Ś. 1385, Svabānu, gift of land. Mentions Lakkhaṇa-Oḍeya as governor of Bārakūra-rājya. See No. 146.

182. 164 *of* 1901.—(Kanarese.) On the tenth slab set up in the same place. An incomplete record of the Vijayanagara king Vīra-Harihara-Mahārāya (II), dated 1311, Vibhava. Mentions Mallappa-Oḍeya as governor of Bārakūra-rājya, and gift of land.

183. 165 *of* 1901.—(Kanarese.) On a slab set up in the house of Paramēśvarabhaṭṭa at Manigarakēri. A damaged record of a gift of land by the Vijayanagara king Vīra-Harihara-Mahārāya (II), dated Ś. 1317, Bhava.

184. 166 *of* 1901.—(Kanarese.) On a slab lying at the entrance into the Sōmanāthēśvara temple at the same village. A record of the Vijayanagara king Immaḍi-Naraśiṅgarāya recording in Ś. 1421, Siddhārthin, gift of land. The king was the son of the celebrated Śāḷuva usurper, afterwards overthrown by the Tuḷuva Narasa Nāyaka.

185. 167 *of* 1901.—(Kanarese.) On a slab lying near a well close to the same temple. Records in the reign of the Vijayanagara king Vīrapratāpa-Dēvarāya gift of paddy. Date doubtful.

186. 168 *of* 1901.—(Kanarese.) On another slab lying in the same place. A record of the Vijayanagara king Vīrapratāpa-Sadāśivarāya recording in Ś. 1486, Dundubhi, a gift of land. Mentions the Mahāmaṇḍalēśvara Veṅkaṭādrirāja Mahā-araśa and Sadāśivarāya-nāyaka of Keḷaḍi. Was Veṅkaṭādri the brother of Aḷiya Rāma Rāyā? For Sadāśiva see No. 71 above.

187. 169 *of* 1901.—(Kanarese.) On a slab set up near the Sōmanāthēśvara temple at Maṇigarakēri. Records in the reign of the Vijayanagara king Pratāpa Achyuta in Sarvajit, gift of paddy.

188. 170 *of* 1901.—(Kanarese.) On another slab set up in the same place. Dated in the reign of the Vijayanagara king Vīra-pratāpa-Śrīraṅga (II, 1578—86) in Ś. 1502, Vikrama. Records a gift of land to a feeding house by Achchappa-Oḍeya, the governor of Bārakūra-rājya, and mentions Saṅkaṇa-nāyaka. See No. 62 above. Saṅkaṇa was probably the Ikkēri chief who retired after ruling from 1585 to 1596.

189. 171 *of* 1901.—(Kanarese.) On a slab set up in the Pañcha-liṅgeśvara temple at Kōṭakēri near Bārakūr. A record of the Āḷupa king Bhujabala-Kaviy-Āḷupēndra. Mentions in Ś. 1077, Yuva, Bārakanyāpura.

190. 172 *of* 1901.—(Kanarese.) On another slab set up in the same place. Dated in the reign of the Vijayanagara king Vīra-dēvaraya (II). Records in Ś. 1338, Durmukhin, gift of paddy. Mentions Śamkaradēva-Oḍeya as governor of Bārakūra-rājya.

191. 173 *of* 1901.—(Kanarese.) On the third slab set up in the same place. A record of the Vijayanagara king Virapratāpa-Dēvarāya (II) recording in Ś. 1354, Virōdhikrit, gift of paddy. Mentions Chaṇḍarasa-Oḍeya as governor of Bārakūra-rājya.

192. 174 *of* 1901.—(Kanarese.) On the fourth slab set up in the same place. A record of the Vijayanagara king Vīra-Hari-yappa-Oḍeya (II) recording in Ś. 1304, Dundubhi, gift of land. Mentions Jakkaṇṇa-Oḍeya as governor of Bārakūra-rājya.

193. 175 *of* 1901.—(Kanarese.) On the fifth slab set up in the same place. Mentions Vīra-Jagadēvaraśa, his queen and Pāṇḍya-dēvaraśa of Paṭṭipombucha as joint rulers; refers to Barahakanyāpura and records a gift of land.

194. 176 *of* 1901.—(Kanarese.) On the sixth slab set up in the same place. A record of the Āḷupa king Bhujabala-Kaviy-Āḷupēndra, recording in Ś. 1062, Siddhārthin, gift of money by a certain Śivānandayōgin. See No. 189.

195. 177 *of* 1901.—(Kanarese.) On a pillar set up in the outer enclosure of the Pañchaliṅgēśvara temple at Kōṭakēri. A record of the Vijayanagara king Vīrapratāpa-Immaḍi-Mahādēvarāya (II) recording in Ś. 1356, Pramādin, gift of land. Mentions Perumāḷ-Daṇṇāyaka.

196. 178 *of* 1901.—(Kanarese.) On a slab set up near the same temple. Records in Ś. 1336, Jaya, the building of a *maṭha.*

197. 179 *of* 1901.—(Kanarese.) A record of the Vijayanagara king Vīrapratāpa-Dēvarāya (II) recording in Ś. 1347, Krōdhin, gift of paddy. Mentions Narasimhadēva-Oḍeya as governor of Bārakūra-rājya.

198. 180 *of* 1901.—(Kanarese.) On a slab lying near the tank in front of the same temple. A record of the Vijayanagara king Vīrapratāpa-Dēvarāya (II) recording in Ś. 1347, Krōdhin, gift of paḍdy. Mentions the Mahāmantrin Narasimhadēva-Oḍeya as governor of Bārakūra-rājya.

199. 181 *of* 1901.—(Kanarese.) On another slab set up in the same place. Records in the reign of the Vijayanagara king Vīrapratāpa-Sadāśivarāya gift of paddy. Date doubtful.

Ellūru (Yellūru).

200. In the pagoda of Viśvanātha. Records that "Coonda Hagada" gave in Ś. 1408, Viśvāvasu, 140 pagodas of land to the God. *Ins., Mys. Kan.*, p. 70, No. 482.

201. In the same place. An illegible record in Ś. 1407, Krōdhi. *Ibid.*, No. 483.

202. In the same place. An illegible record dated in Ś. 1421, Siddhārti. *Ibid.*, No. 484.

203. In the same place. An illegible record in Ś. 1410, Kīlaka. *Ibid.*, No. 485.

Kāp.

204. 91 *of* 1901.—(Kanarese.) On a slab set up in the Janārdana temple. A record dated in Ś. 1421, Siddhārtin, mentioning Tirumale-araśa.

205. 92 *of* 1901.—(Kanarese.) On a slab near a peepul-tree in the bazaar street at the same village. A record of the Āḷupa king Sōyidev-Āḷupēndra in Ś. 1247, Raktākshi, mentioning Bārahakanyāpura. See No. 175 above.

206. 93 *of* 1901.—(Kanarese.) On a *viragal* set up north of the same village on the road side. A record mentioning Tirumala-araśa and Bāyiraraśa of Bidire.

Karkala.

207. 62 *of* 1901.—(Sanskrit and Kanarese.) On a slab set up close to the west wall of the Chaturmukhabasti. Records in Ś. 1508, Vyaya, the building of the basti and gifts of land and money by Immaḍi-Bhairaraśa-Oḍeya of Paṭṭipom-buchcha (modern Humcha in Mysore). [See *Ind. Antq.*, Vol. V, page 40 ff., for a tentative transcript and translation of this record by Mr. Walhouse and *Ep. Ind.*, VIII, pp. 122—38, for a more accurate edition by Mr. Krishna Sastri. The date of the inscription, according to Kielhorn, is Wednesday, 16th March, A.D. 1586.]

208. 63 *of* 1901.—(Sanskrit.) On the right side of the colossal statue of Gummaṭa at the same village. Records in Ś. 1353, Virōdhikrit, the setting up of the image of Bāhubalin (Gummaṭēśvara) by Vīra-Pāṇḍya, the son of Bhairava of the lunar race at the instance of the teacher Laḷitakīrti of Panaśōka (Hanasoge in Mysore) and of the Dēśigaṇa who was also evidently the *guru* of the Karkāla chiefs. The inscription was first edited tentatively by Burnell in *Ind. Antq.*, II, p. 353, then by Mr. Rice in his *Sravaṇa Belgōla Inscriptions* (Introd. p. 31), and by Dr. Hultzsch in *Ep. Ind.*, VII, p. 109 ff. Kielhorn calculates the date to be Wednesday the 13th February, A.D. 1432. See *Ind. Antq.*, XXIII, p. 119.] See also No. 210 for the same chief. The *Jaina Siddhānta Bhāskara* gives two Laḷitakīrtis in A.D. 1204 and 1565, but not in 1461. Laḷitakīrti was apparently a general title of the Hanasoge Pontiffs.

209. 64 *of* 1901.—(Kanarese.) On the left side of the same statue. Records in verse the same fact, but gives the name of the image as Gummaṭa-Jinapati. See *Ep. Ind.*, VII, p. 111. See No. 210.

210. 65 *of* 1901.—(Kanarese.) On the Brahmadēvastambha in front of the same statue. A record dated in Ś. 1358, Rākshasa (on the twelfth *tithi* of the bright fortnight of Phalguṅa). Invokes the blessing of Brahman and mentions Vīra-Pāṇḍya, the son of Bhairava of the family of Jīnadatta, the chief referred to in the previous two inscriptions. See *Ep. Ind.*, VII, pp. 111-2.

211. 66 *of* 1901.—(Kanarese.) On a pillar in the verandah in front of the Ammanavarabasti at Hiriyaṅgaḍi (big bazaar) near the same village left of entrance. Records in Ś. 1397, Manmatha, the building of the mukhamaṇṭapa in front of the Tīrthakarabasti by several merchants. The teacher Laḷitakīrti Bhaṭṭārakadēva Maladhāri is mentioned. See No. 208 above for the same teacher.

212. 67 *of* 1901.—(Kanarese.) On a slab set up in the north-east corner of the same *basti.* Records in Ś. 1501, Pramādin, gift of money by Śrāvakas for the study of the Śastras. Laḷitakīrti is to be the *vichārakartā* (supervisor) of the charities. See No. 208 above.

213. 68 *of* 1901.—(Kanarese.) On a slab built into the north wall of the Gururāyabasti at Hiriyaṅgaḍi near the same place. Records in Ś. 1514, Vijaya, gift of gold by a merchant in the time of Pāṇḍyappa-Oḍeya, son of Vīra-Bhairaraśa-Oḍeya.

214. 69 *of* 1901.—(Kanarese.) On a slab set up to the left of the entrance into the Hirēnēmīśvarabasti at the same village. A record in Viḷambi, mentioning Bhairarasa-Oḍeya. (A damaged record.)

215. 70 *of* 1901.—(Kanarese.) On another slab set up in the same place. A record dated in Ś. 1379, Īśvara, mentioning Abhinava-Pāṇḍyadēva-Oḍeya of Paṭṭipombucha, who belonged to the family of Jīnadatta, and the gift of paddy by a merchant. Laḷitakīrti is said to have belonged to the Kundakunda division and the Kālōgragaṇa. Mr. Krishna Sastri surmises that this was probably a local branch of the Dēśigaṇa. See Nos. 218, 211 and 212.

216. 71 *of* 1901.—(Kanarese.) On a slab set up close to the west wall of the Gurugalabasti near the same village. A record dated in Ś. 1256, Bhava. The inscription begins with a long list of *birudas* of Lōkanāthadēvaraśa (son of Bommidēvaraśa and Siddaladēvi) and a gift of land to the Śāntināthabasti, which was built in that year.

Kote (Cotah).

217. In the local Mahāliṅgēśvara temple. Records that in Ś. 1166, Ānanda, king "Veboodhavasoo of the Bhoota Paundiah race" gave a village valued 1,000 pagodas. *Ins., Mys. Kan.*, p. 69, No. 464.

218. In the same place. A gift of 14 (*canties*) of land by Chaṇḍarasu in Ś. 1362, Raudri. *Ibid.*, No. 465.

219. In the same place. Records gift of 75 (*canties*) of land by "Aubunah Yagada" in Ś. 1382, Vikrama. *Ibid.*, No. 466.

220. A record in Vikrama relating gift of 3 pagodas of land to God Vināyaka by "Siddapa Nāik Neeroopah." *Ibid.*, p. 69, No. 476.

Mulūru (Mooroor).

221. On a local slab. Records that in Ś. 1530, Kīlaka, Sōmaśēkhara Nāik gave 120 pagodas of land to the Jaṅgama Maṭhā. *Ibid.*, p. 80, No. 591. [He is evidently an earlier chief than he who ruled from 1681 to 1686.]

Padur.

222. *C.P. No.* 90 *of Mr. Sewell's List.*—(Kanarese.) Records grant of land in Ś. 1569 (A.D. 1647), Ānanda, by a prince named Mullūru to a Brāhman for the maintenance of worship in a Śiva temple. The land is in the village. [The *Mack. MSS.* give this epigraph. As summarized by Taylor, it is dated Ś. 1596 (Ānanda) and records a grant of 60 *muḍis* of land in the village to "Mulla Veera Jungum" by "Shankar Arasoo Moolapoo". (Saṅkara Arasu Mallappa ?)

Pāṇḍēshvara.

223. In the pagoda of Śaṅkaranārāyaṇa. Records that Kampaṇa Uḍaiyār (II ?) gave in Ś. 1330, Jaya, 251 *canties* of land, 11 *gadyāna*, and 6 *haṇas* to the God. *Ins., Mys. Kan.*, p. 69, No. 475.

Paraṁpalli (Paurumhally).

224. In the Vishṇu pagoda. Records that Vīra Araśa Uḍaiyār gave to the God 18 *canties* of land in Ś. 1389, Sarvajit. *Ibid.*, No. 474.

Perduru (Paradoor).

225. In the pagoda of Anantadēva. Records a gift in Ś. 1441, Pramādhi, to the God Anantēśvara by Ratnappa Uḍaiyār. *Ins., Mys. Kan.*, p. 70, No. 486.

226. In the pagoda of Durgā Paramēśvari. Records in Manmatha, the gift of all kinds of allowances of the pagoda to the Sanyāsis of "Poolegah" by the people of the Śīma. *Ibid.*, No. 487.

Pasarala.

227. 86 *of* 1901.—(Kanarese.) On a slab set up in a field. Records in the reign of the Vijayanagara king Pratāpa-Dēvarāya (II) in Ś. 1348, Parābhava, a gift of land.

Phalmāru.

228. 87 *of* 1901.—(Kanarese.) On a slab set up in the Vishṇu temple. A much damaged record of the Vijayanagara king Vīra-Hariyapp-Oḍeya. (Date doubtful.)

229. 88 *of* 1901.—(Kanarese.) On a slab set up in the Śiva temple. A much damaged record mentioning Vīra-Bukaṇṇa-Oḍeya.

*Uḍipi.**

230. 109 *of* 1901.—On a slab built into the north wall of the Krishṇamaṭha. Records in the reign of the Vijayanagara king Vīrapratāpa-Dēvarāya (II) in Ś. 1358, Naḷa, a gift of land. Mentions Śiṅgaṇa-Daṇḍanāyaka and Aṇṇapa-Oḍeya who was ruling the Bārkūra-rājya.

231. 110 *of* 1901.—(Kanarese.) On another slab built into the same wall. A record of the Vijayanagara king Vīra-Veṅkaṭapati

---

* Taylor's List of *Mack. Ins.* in this place contains 40 inscriptions, all of which are unknown to the Department and I have included them here.

(I) recording in Ś. 1536, Pramādin, the grant of the village of Huvinakēre by Veṅkaṭappa-Nāyaka of Keḷaḍi, while Vēdavēdyatīrtha, pupil of Vādirājatīrtha, was the priest of the temple. See Nos. 234 and 235 below. Vādirāja was a man of great erudition and wrote several works.

232. 111 *of* 1901.—(Kanarese.) On the third slab built into the same wall. Fragment of record mentioning a grant by Vīra-Hariharayya (II ?).

233. 112 *of* 1901.—(Kanarese.) On the fourth slab built into the same wall. Records in the reign of the Vijayanagara king Vīra Harihara (II) a gift in Ś. 1317, Bhava. Mentions Heggaḍe-Samkaraśa who was ruling the Bārakūra-rājya, and registers the lands owned by the temple.

234. 113 *of* 1901.—(Kanarese.) On a slab built into the west wall of the same *maṭha.* A record in Ś. 1536, Ānanda, mentioning Vidyādhīśatīrtha, and Vibudhēśatīrtha and providing for offerings. [The seventeenth of the Madhvāchārya line of teachers was known as Vidyādhīśatīrtha. He was the third from the celebrated Vēdavyāsatīrtha, the contemporary of Kṛishṇadēva Rāya.]

235. 114 *of* 1901.—(Kanarese.) On another slab built into the same wall. A record in Ś. 1535, Pramādin, mentioning Vādirājatīrtha and his pupil and providing for offerings.

236. 115 *of* 1901.—(Kanarese.) On a slab built into the south wall of the same *maṭha.* A damaged record registering gift made by Hariharārāya at the instance of Vidyādhirājatīrtha.

237. 116 *of* 1901.—(Kanarese.) On a slab built into the wall surrounding the tank near the same *maṭha.* A damaged record in Ś. 1397, Manmatha, mentioning Viṭharaśa-Oḍeya of Bārakūru.

238. 117 *of* 1901.—(Kanarese.) On a slab set up to the left of the entrance into the Anantēśvara temple. A record of the Vijayanagara king Vīra-Bukaṇṇa-Oḍeya (I), dated in Ś. 1288, Parābhava, mentioning the Mahāpradhāna Gōparaśa-Oḍeya who was ruling the Bārakūra-rājya, and recording a gift of land.

239. 118 *of* 1901.—(Kanarese.) On a slab set up to the east of the same temple. A record in archaic characters.

240. In a local copper plate. Records that in Ś. 1667, Raktākshi, Kīlaḍi Basavappa Nāik (1740—53) gave 467 pagodas and five gold paṇams to the Pāṇḍuraṅgasvāmi Maṭha. *Mack. Ins., Mys. Kan.*, p. 71, No. 488.

241. In the local Kṛishṇapūr Maṭha. Records gift of 200 *canties* of land to Vidyādhirājatīrta in Ś. 1331, Sarvadhāri, by Dēvarāya-Mahāraya. *Ibid.*, No. 489. [This teacher might be the same as the "seventh of the Madhva line of teachers from Ānandatīrtha, the founder of Madhvaism.]

242. In the same place. A gift of nine " Cunchana Moode " of land by Śaṅkaradēva Araśu. *Mack, Ins., Mys. Kan.*, p. 71, No. 490.

243. In possession of the people of the Kṛishṇapūr Maṭha. Records that Bhadrappa Nāik "Neerupah" (1671—81 ?) granted some lands in Śubhakrit, to build the maṭha. *Ibid.*, No. 491.

244. In possession of the same people. Records that Chennamāji Rāṇi (1686—98) of Bednore gave 15 pagodas and some land to the same. *Ibid.*, No. 492.

245. With the same persons. Records that Bhadrappa Nāik (1671—81 ?) Narapa granted 50 pagodas of land in Śubhakrit to the same. *Ibid.*, No. 493.

246. With the same. Records that " Chennamāji Narapa " granted 18 pagodas of land in Naḷa to the same. *Ibid.*, No. 494.

247. With the same. Records that Chinna Basavappa (1753—55) gave 130 pagodas and 4 paṇams to the same. *Ibid.*, No. 495.

248. With the same. Records grant of a village to Vīrabhadrasvāmi of the Kṛishṇapuram Maṭha by Śrī-Nārāyaṇarāo. *Ibid.*, No. 496.

249. On a stone in the " Seeroo " maṭha. Records in Ś. 1440, Bahudhānya, gift of 40 pagodas of land to the maṭha by Ratnappa Uḍaiyār. *Ibid.*, No. 497.

250. In the same. Gift of 10 pagodas of land to the same in the same date by Vijayappa Nāik. *Ibid.*, No. 498.

251. In the same. Records gift of 8 pagodas of land to the same in Ś. 1444, Chitrabhānu, by Viṭṭharaśa Uḍaiyār. *Ibid.*, No. 499.

252. On a stone in the same maṭha. Records in Ś. 1394, Sādhāraṇa, gift of 11 pagodas and 5 paṇams to the maṭha by Ratnappa Uḍaiyār. *Ibid.*, p. 72, No. 500.

253. In the same. Records gift of 40 pagodas by the same chief in Ś. 1439, Dhātu. *Ibid.*, No. 501.

254. In the same place. Records gift of 8 pagodas and ¼ paṇam in Bahudhānya by Sōmaśēkhara Nāik. [Was he the chief who ruled from 1714 to 1740 ?] *Ibid.*, No. 502.

255. In the same place. Records in Yuva, gift of money by Chinna Basavappa Nāik (1753—35). *Ibid.*, No. 503.

256. In the same place. Gift of a village to the same maṭha by Chennamāji Nārappa (1686—98) in Vikrama. *Ibid.*, No. 504.

257. In the same place. A gift in Pārthiva of 24 pagodas and 5¼ paṇams by Nawab Hyder. *Ibid.*, No. 505. Hyder captured Bednose in December 1760.

258. In the " Pootega " maṭha. Records in Ś. 1440, Bahudhānya, the gift of 140 *canties* of land to the sanyāsins of the maṭha by Vaiyappa Uḍaiyār. *Ibid.*, No. 506.

259. A gift of land by the same chief in the same year. *Ibid.*, No. 507.

260. In the " Aundmaura " maṭha. Records that Puṇḍarīka-dēvarasa gave some land to the maṭha in Ś. 1365, Dundubhi. *Ins., Mys. Kan.*, p. 72, No. 508.

261. A gift of land by the same in the same year. *Ibid.*, No. 509.

262. A paper grant at Uḍipi. Records that Sōmaśēkhara Nāik gave some land to the same in Pramādi. *Ibid.*, No. 510.

263. A record of Vīra-Narasimha Lakshmiapparasu in Ś. 1631, Virōdhi, relating grant of six pagodas of land to the same maṭha. *Ibid.*, No. 511.

264. On a copper plate in the same place. Gift of gold to the same maṭha by Dēvarasa Narappa in Pramādhi. *Ibid.*, p. 73, No. 512.

265. On a stone in the same place. A record of Ś. 1666, Krōdhana, relating gift of a village to the same maṭha by " Yaloor Coonda Hagada." *Ibid.*, No. 513.

266. In the same place. Records grant of nine *muḍis* of land in Īśvara, to the maṭha by " Keneka Hagada." *Ibid.*, No. 514.

267. On a copper plate in the same place. Records that in Ś. 1612, Virōdhi, Chinnamā Dēvi (1686—98) gave to the maṭha some land. *Ibid.*, No. 515.

268. A paper grant in the same. Gift of land in the same year by Vīra-Narasimha Lakshmappayya Narappa. *Ibid.*, No. 516.

269. A P.G. in the place. Records that in Śubhakrit, Ambikā-dēvi-Chauṭarasa Narappa gave some land to the maṭha. *Ibid.*, No. 517.

270. A P.G. in the same place. Records gift of land to God Veṅkaṭēśvara in Īśvara by Koṇḍa Heggaḍi. *Ibid.*, No. 518.

271. Another P.G. grant in the same place. Gift of land by Ambikādēvi to the maṭha in Śubhakrit. *Ibid.*, No. 519.

272. A copper plate in the same place. Records gift of 101 pagodas to the Kṛishṇadēva maṭha in Ś. 1588, Viśvāvasu, by Sōmaśēkhara Nāik. *Ibid.*, No. 520. [Sōmaśēkhara was ruler from 1681 to 1686. This grant should have been made while his father Śivappa (1649—71) was ruling.

273. Another C.P. in the same place. Records in Ś. 1561, Bahudhānya, gift of twelve pagodas by Vīrabhadra Nāik. *Ibid.*, No. 521.

274. Gift of 282 pagodas by Chennamāji in Ś. 1606, Rudhirōd-kāri. *Ibid.*, No. 522.

275. On a stone in the Uḍipi maṭha. Records that Chinna Baṇḍāra Rāmakṛishṇa gave a village to Kṛishṇadēva in Ś. 1536, Pramādhi, in the reign of Veṅkaṭapati Nāik. *Ibid.*, No. 523.

276. Records gift of land to Kṛishṇadēva in Ś. 1359, Naḷa, by Aṇṇapa Uḍaiyār. *Ibid.*, No. 524.

277. Records gift of 7½ pagodas of land in Ś. 1441, Bahudhānya, to Kṛishṇadēva by Ratnappa Uḍaiyār. *Mack. Ins., Mys. Kan.*, p. 73, No. 525.

278. A P.G. in the same place. Records gift of 180 pagodas of land to Kṛishṇadēva by Sōmaśēkhara Nāik Narappa in Virōdhikrit. *Ibid.*, p. 74, No. 526.

279. Another P.G. in the same place. Gift of 49 pagodas by the same chief to the same in Kāḷayukti. *Ibid.*, No. 527.

280. A P.G. in the same place. Gift of 120 pagodas of land to Kṛishṇadēva by Bhadrappa Nāik in Plava. *Ibid.*, No. 528. [It is not known which of the Bhadrappa Nāiks is referred to.]

Udiyāvara.

This is the ancient Udayāpura (near Uḍipi) and historically interesting as the site of the earliest monuments found in the South Kanara district. These are the pillars referred to in 281, 287 and 295 in the following list, which contain the names of the Āḷupa kings Raṇasāgara, Prithivīsāgara and Vijayāditya. The local inscriptions also refer to the later Āḷuva king Kavi (see No. 293) and then to the Vijayanagara dynasty. [For the other Āḷuva kings who ruled in the district and who are referred to in previous inscriptions see *Ep. Rep.*, 1901, p. 5, and references given therein.]

281. 94 *of* 1901.—(Kanarese.) On an octagonal pillar in front of the Śambhukallu-Bhairava (Chamkal) temple. Records in the reign of the Āḷupa king Raṇasāgara the death of a hero and mentions Chitravāhana. See No. 287.

282. 95 *of* 1901.—(Kanarese.) On a slab close to the balipīṭa in the same temple. A damaged record in Ś. 980, Viḷambin.

283. 96 *of* 1901.—(Kanarese.) On an octagonal pillar built into the platform at the entrance into the inner enclosure of the same temple. A record mentioning Āḷuvaraśar (i.e., the Āḷupēndra). See *Ep. Ind.*, Vol. IX, pp. 15—24.

284. 97 *of* 1901.—(Kanarese.) On an octagonal pillar in the courtyard of the same temple. A record of the Āḷupa king Vijayāditya *alias* Uttamapāṇḍya, mentioning Udayāpura.

285. 98 *of* 1901.—(Kanarese.) On the same pillar. An epigraph of the Āḷupa king Vijayāditya *alias* Uttamapāṇḍya (also called Māramma) mentioning the same and Pombuccha.

286. 99 *of* 1901.—(Kanarese.) On another pillar in the same place. Records a gift in the reign of the Āḷupa king Māramma. See the above epigraph.

287. 100 *of* 1901.—(Kanarese.) On the third pillar in the same place. A record of the Āḷupa king Raṇasāgara, mentioning Chembukallu and Śivalli. See No. 281.

288. 101 *of* 1901.—(Kanarese.) On the fourth pillar in the same place. Records in the reign of the Āḷupa king Prithvīsāgara the death of a hero who was a servant of the king.

289. 102 *of* 1901.—(Kanarese.) On the fifth pillar in the same place. A record of the Āḷupa king Prithvīsāgara *alias* Udayāditya Uttama-Pāṇḍya mentioning Erega and Raṇavikrama.

290. 103 *of* 1901.—(Kanarese.) On an octagonal pillar in the south-west corner of the courtyard of the same temple. A record of the Āḷupa king Prithvīsāgara.

291. 104 *of* 1901.—(Kanarese.) On a slab set up in the courtyard of the same temple. A damaged record of the Vijayanagara king Vīrapratāpa-Dēvarāya (II), in Ś. 1351, Kīlaka.

292. 105 *of* 1901.—(Kanarese.) On an octagonal pillar in front of Rāghavēndrabhaṭṭa's house. Records the death of Śvētavāhana, the son of Pāṇḍyavillaraśa.

293. 106 *of* 1901.—(Kanarese.) On a slab built into the platform at the entrance of the same house. A record of the Āḷupa king Kavy Āḷupēndra in Ś. 1036, Vijaya, mentioning Udayādityaraśa. (A damaged record.) See Nos. 53 and 58 of Bārakūr.

294. 107 *of* 1901.—(Kanarese.) On an octagonal pillar lying in the backyard of the same house. Records the death of a hero.

295. 108 *of* 1901.—(Kanarese.) On another octagonal pillar lying near a well in the same place. Records in the reign of the Āḷupa king Raṇasāgara the death of Śvētavāhana. See No. 292.

296. In the Vīrabhadra temple. A record of Dēvappa Uḍaiyār in Ś. 1052, Sādhāraṇa, recording gift of 160 *canties* of land to God Vīrabhadra. Taylor's summary of Mack.'s *Mysore and Kanara Ins.*, p. 70, No. 481.

Uppargeri (Uppūru?).

297. *C.P.* 106 *of Mr. Sewell's List.*—(Kanarese.) Records grant of certain lands to a maṭham at Uppargēri by Keḷaḍi Vīrabhadra Nāyaka in Ś. 1554 (A.D. 1632), Prajōtpatti. [The chief referred to was one of the two Bhadrappa Nāyakas who followed Vēṅkaṭappa in 1626.]

Varangana (Varaṅga Śivapuram?).

298. *C.P.* 89 *of Mr. Sewell's List.*—(Sanskrit and Kanarese.) By this document the village is made over to endow the temple of Varaṅganēminātha (Śiva). The grantor is King Dēva Rāya (II, 1422—49) of Vijayanagar, the date Ś. 1346 (A.D. 1424), Krōdhi.

Yermal.

299. 89 *of* 1901.—(Kanarese.) On a pillar in the Janārdana temple. Records in Pingaḷa, gift of paddy. Mentions a certain Tirumalaraśa.

300. 90 *of* 1901.—(Kanarese.) On a slab set up in the same temple. Records in the reign of the Vijayanagara king Vīra-Harihar̄aya (II) in Ś. 1324, Chitrabhānu, a gift of land. Mentions Basavaṇṇa-Oḍeya as governor of Bārakūru-rājya.

Uppinangādi Taluk.

Kadaba.

300-A. A C.P. grant of the Rāshṭrakūṭa king Prabhūtavarsha (Gōvinda III) made at the request of a Gaṅga chief Chāgirāja to a Jain sage Arkakīrti, disciple of Vijayakīrti (who was a disciple of Kūliāchārya) for having removed the evil influence of Saturn from the Chāgirāja's sister's son Vimalāditya. Issued from Mayūrakhaṇḍi. The details of date corresponded to Monday, 24th May, A.D. 812. See *Ind. Antq.*, Vol. XII, p. 13. *Ep. Ind.*, Vol. IV, p. 340, and Kielhorn's *Ins.*, *S. Ind.*, No. 66. Also *Ind. Antq.*, Vol. XXIV, p. 9, No. 61. [" Kadaba is said to have been the seat of one of the four Brahman governors appointed for Tuḷuva in the eighth century." *S. Kan. Manu.*, II, p. 271.

Kukke.

301. In the local temple. An "old Kanarese inscription recording a grant of land to the temple by Mādhava Rāya of Goa in Ś. 1309 (A.D. 1387)."

Subrahmaṇya.

Mr. Sewell mentions seven copper plate grants in possession of the Muktēśvara temple. These are—

302. A Nāgari grant, dated in *Prabhava*, of Mahādēva, sovereign of Goa.

303. A Nāgari grant by an Uḍaiyār of Goa who is said to have ruled in the province of Mangalore.

304. A Kaṇarese grant, dated Ś. 1587 (A.D. 1665), by the son of the ruler of Śrīraṅgapaṭṭana.

305. A Kanarese grant of Śrīraṅga Rāya, " son of the ruler of Vēlāpuram," dated in Ś. 1581. [Was he the son of the last of the Chandragiri chiefs who was deprived of his dominions by the Muhammadans in 1646? For a grant of his to the Vyāsarāya maṭha at Sosale in 1662, see *Mys. Arch. Rep.*, 1911–2, p. 53.]

306. A grant by the same (who in this calls himself a ruler of Vēlāpuram) in Ś. 1588. See note to the above.

307. (Kanarese.) Grant by the same in Ś. 1588.

308. (Kanarese.) Grant by Vēṅkaṭādri Nāik and Tippayya of Bēlūr in Ś. 1603.

KISTNA DISTRICT.

BANDAR TALUK.

Akulamannāḍu.

1. On a pillar in the mukhamaṇṭapa of the local Lakshmī Narasimha temple. Records a gift in Vikriti, Phālguna Śuddha 10, Monday, by Annapāla Śūryuḍu (whose birudas are given) to Ainampūshi (?) Śiṅgarayya. See *Mack. MSS.*, Bk. XVI, pp. 5–6, in the second part.

2. On the other side of the above. Records that in the reign of Vīrapratāpa Rudradēva Mahārājāṅka a certain Śri "Śāraṅgabhanapāyilla Rāya Mahāpātra" paid homage to Narasimhanātha of Karlimalla and with the consent of Pratāparudra, gave him "*amritamaṇi.*" *Ibid.*, p. 6.

*Masulipatam Bandar.**

3. *C.P.* 1 *of Mr. Sewell's List.*—(Sanskrit and Telugu.) The Masulipatam plates of Amma II (Vijayāditya V, 945—70). Records that the king granted some land in the village of Pambaṟṟu in the Guḍravāra vishaya to the Yuvarāja Baitāladēva Vēlābhaṭa or Boḍḍiya, son of Lady Pammavā of the Paṭṭavardhini family. See *Ind. Antq.*, Vol. VIII, p. 74, ff.; *Ibid.*, Vol. XX, p. 271; Kielhorn's *Southern List*, No. 564, and *Ep. Ind.*, Vol. V, pp. 139—42. The coronation of Amma II took place on Friday, 5th December, A.D. 945.

4. (Sanskrit.) The Masulipatam Plates of Amma I (918—25). No. 2 of Mr. Sewell's List, now in the Madras Museum. Records grant of the village of Drujjūru in Pennātavāḍi-vishaya to Mahākāla, a general and son of a foster-sister of the king's grandfather Chāḷukya Bhīma I. See *Ind. Antq.*, Vol. VIII, p. 77 f., *Ibid.*, Vol. XX, p. 266-K, Kielhorn's *Southern List*, No. 558, and *Ep. Ind.*, Vol. V. pp. 131—34.

5. *C.P.* 81 *of Mr. Sewell's List.*—Records grant by Sadāśiva Rāya in Ś. 1482, Siddhārthi. The name of the village seems to be Gonnamgaripadra. (Was it at Sattenapalle Taluk, formerly in the Kistṇa District, now in Guṇṭūr ?). The grant was made to a Brahman.

5-A. *C.P.* 84 *of Mr. Sewell's List.*—A record of Amma II (945—70) or Vijayāditya. This is No. 8 of 1908–09. It records a gift by the king to two Jaina temples at Vijayavāṭika (Bezwāḍa). He is said to have had for his enemy Rājamārtāṇḍa and Mallapa

* The local inscriptions of Mackenzie are given in Brown's *Loc. Rec.*, Vol. XII, pp. 291—300.

(probably Yuddhamalla II). See *Ind. Antq.*, Vol. XX, p. 104, and *Madras Ep. Rep.*, 1909, p. 109, paragraph 60. For other references to Ammarāja's patronage of Jain religion see Kaḷachamburru and Malayapūṇdi grants in *Ep. Ind.*, Vol. VII, pp. 177–92 and *Ibid.*, Vol. IX, pp. 47–56.

6. *C.P.* 85 *of Mr. Sewell's List.*—(In Nandināgarī.) In the District Court, Masulipatam. Records grant of the village of Pallavāḷ to a Brahman by Śrīraṅga Rāya, son of Bukka, in Ś. 1447, Yuva (wrong). [It has been suggested that Śrīraṅga was the father of Sadāśiva Rāya.]

7. (Sanskrit.) The Masulipatam plates of Vijayāditya III. Records that the Eastern Chaḷukya Vijayāditya III (Guṇaka), the son of Vishnuvardhana V, and grandson of Vijayāditya II, gave, on the occasion of a lunar eclipse, the village of Traṇḍapāru in the Guḍravāra-vishaya to a Brahman named Vinayadiśarman of Urpuṭūru for advice given in the defeat of an enemy named Maṅgi. Undated. See *Ind. Antq.*, Vol. XX, p. 103, and *Ep. Ind.*, Vol. V, pp. 122—26. [The king is also said to have frightened the Rāshṭrakūṭa Kṛishṇa II and Saṅkila and burnt their city, Kiraṇapura.]

8. The Masulipatam plates of Chāḷukya Bhīma II (934–35). Now in the British Museum. Records that the king, during the sun's progress to the north, granted a field in the village of Akulamannāḍu in the Guḍravāra-vishaya to a scholar of the Kramapāṭha named Viddamayya, a son of Mādhava Sōmayāji of Vaṅgiparru. Not dated. See *Ind. Antq.*, Vol. XX, p. 270 and *Ep. Ind.*, Vol. V, pp. 135–9, and Kielhorn's *Southern List*, No. 561.

9. The Masulipatam plates of Chāḷukya Bhīma I (888—918). Records that the king defeated the armies of Kṛishṇavallabha and his allies and the vile kings of Lāṭa and Karnāṭa; that his son, a prince of sixteen years, died in the battle of Niravadyapura and Peruvaṅgūr grāma, killing in the latter from the back of his elephant the general of the Vallabha king Daṇḍēśa Guṇḍaya; that after the performance of the obsequies to the deceased prince (Inimartigaṇḍa) the king granted to 45 learned Brahmans the village of Vedatalūru in Uttarakaṇḍeruvāṭi-vishaya. [The Government Epigraphist points out that Niravadyapura should have been named after Vijayāditya II (699—729) who had that surname and that the Vallabha king is the Rāshtra-kūṭa Kṛishṇa II. See *Ep. Rep.*, 1914, pp. 84–85.

9-A. On a stone in the temple of Ekāmbaranāthasvāmi. A private grant in Ś. 1319. *Antiquities*, p. 53. The details of date are Īśvara, Pushyaśuddha I, Thursday, Makarasāṅkrānti. See *Loc. Rec.*, Vol. XII, p. 291.

9-B—D. On a pillar in the maṇṭapam of Rāmaliṅga in Robertson-peṭṭah. Three records dated in Ś. 1070, 1051 and 1071. *Ibid.*

9-E-F. Two C.P. grants with the family of Erṛama Cheṭṭi Vīraṇṇa, dated in Ś. 1428, referring to a settlement of caste customs and disputes. *Loc. Rec.*, Vol. XII, p. 291.

10-A. In the hands of a Janjāla Jayakṛishṇa Dāsa. A record dated in Ś. 171(?), Kīlaka, Vaiśākha, Śuddha 11 (F. 1198), relating gift of land by Rāja Māṇikka Rāo Tirupati Rāo. See *Mack. MSS.*, Bk. 18 (15-6-21), p. 152.

10-B. In the hands of the same. A record in Ś. 171(?), Paritāpi, Vaiśākha bahuḷa 5, of the same person, for building a maṭha, etc. *Ibid.*

10-C—F. Records dated Ś. 1617, 1628 (Vyaya, Āshāḍhaśuddha 5), and Ś. 1610 (Prabhava, Vaiśākha śuddha 15) and Ś. 1644 (Śubhakrit, Mārgaśira Śuddha 15), which record gift of land to Ōbalayya of Āśvalāyanasūtra and Rik Śākhā.

Pedana.

Mr. Sewell mentions four inscriptions in the local temple of Agastyēśvarasvāmi. These are—

10-G. A grant of the general of "Vuttuṅga Jaggan Mahādēva Rāja" in Ś. 1225 (A.D. 1303).

10-H. A grant by a certain Santāna Mahārāja in the same year.

10-I. A grant by Mahāsēna Peggaḍa. Ś. 1220.

10-J. A grant by Kāma Reḍḍi, a servant of Eravattu Gaṇḍa Pedda dēva Rāja in Ś. 1225.

BEZWĀDA TALUK.

Āṭukūru.

11. The Madras Museum Plates of Vēma, the son of Kōmati Prōla (by Annamāmba) one of five brothers, and grandson of Vēmaya, the founder of the family of the Koṇḍavīḍu Reḍḍis. Records that Vēma gave to several Brahmans as an agrahāra the village of Aṭakūr. Vēmā's capital is said to be Addaṅki (now in Ongole Taluk) in Puṅgi which extended from Śrī Śailam to the sea on both sides of the river Kuṇḍi (i.e., Guṇḍalakamma). The date of the grant was Ś. 1267, lunar eclipse, chaittra, corresponding, according to Kielhorn, to Friday, 18th March, A.D. 1345. See *Ep. Ind.*, Vol. VIII, p. 9—15, where Mr. J. Ramayya edits the plates and gives additional information from the *Harivamśām*, the *Koṇḍaviti-Daṇḍakāvili* and the *Vēḷugōṭivārivamśāvaḷi* incidentally.

Bezwāḍa.

A town of great historical interest, Bezwāḍa is full of antiquarian remains, Hindu and Buddhistic, as it was the religious capital of

Veṅgi and the Eastern Chāḷukyans. For its connection with Hiouen Thsang, its Buddhistic and Hindu antiquities see *Antiquities*, Vol. I, p. 47, and references given therein. Mr. Sewell gives 28 inscriptions in this place while the department has got epigraphs of nearly 75. Some of them I have identified. For Mackenzie's List see *Loc. Rec.*, Vol. XII, p. 178 ff. and pp. 225—34.

12—17. 260 *to* 265 *of* 1892.—(Sanskrit and Telugu.) On the first pillar of the ruined Kanakadurga maṇṭapa at the foot of the Indrakīla hill. Records in Ś. 1138 to 1177 gifts to the temple of Mallēśvara.

18—20. 266 *to* 268 *of* 1892.—(Telugu.) On the second pillar of the same maṇṭapa. Records in Ś. 1065 and 1141, private gifts.

21. 269 *of* 1892.—(Telugu.) On the same pillar. A record of Tribhuvanachakravartin Kulōttuṅga-Chōḍadēva in his sixteenth year and Ś. 1062.

22—30. 270 *to* 278 *of* 1892.—(Telugu.) On the same pillar. Records in Ś. 1072 to 1155, private gifts.

31. 279 *of* 1892.—(Telugu.) On the third pillar of the same maṇṭapa. A record of Mahāmaṇḍalēśvara Rudradēva, son of Buddarāju of Māḍapalli, in Nāthavāḍi, in Ś. 1123, Durmukhin (mistake for Durmati). The donor was the brother-in-law of the Kākatīya king Gaṇapati, and the father of Bayyamāmba, for whose inscriptions see Amarāvati. Māḍapalli is identified with a village near Madhira, a station in Nizam's Railway. Luders thinks it might be near Ellore. The date of the grant is, according to Kielhorn, Thursday, 19th April, A.D. 1201. See *Ep. Ind.*, VI, pp. 159–60.

32. 280 *of* 1892.—(Telugu.) On the same pillar. A record of Veṅgi-Mahādēva.

33. 281 *of* 1892.—(Sanskrit.) On the same pillar. A record of Mahādēva, son of Goṅka and grandson of Malla, in Ś. 1152.

34. 282 *of* 1892.—(Telugu.) On the same pillar. A record of Vishṇuvardhana *alias* Parāntakadēva in his fifth year and Ś. 1037, expired, Manmatha.

35. 283 *of* 1892.—(Telugu.) On the same pillar. Records in Ś. 1169, gift by a Reḍḍi.

36. 284 *of* 1892.—(Telugu.) On the same pillar. A record of the Chāḷukya-Chōḷa king (Kulōttuṅga I?) in his forty-sixth year, the king's name of which is obliterated.

37. 285 *of* 1892.—(Telugu.) On the same pillar. Records in Ś. 1022, private grant.

38. 286 *of* 1892.—(Telugu.) On the same pillar. A record of Manumarāju in Ś. 1175. [This king was probably the same as Manmakshmā Vallabha, the contemporary of Kākatīya Gaṇapati and the patron of Tikkaṇa Sōmayāji.]

39 to **44**. 287 *to* 292 *of* 1892.—(Telugu.) On the same pillar. Records in Ś. 1056 to 1183 private grants.

45. 293 *of* 1892.—(Telugu.) On the fourth pillar of the same maṇṭapa. A record of Trinayana Pallava Siddhaya in Ś. 1150. [Was he Manma Siddha, the grandfather of the king referred to in No. 38?]

46 to **54**. 294 *to* 302 *of* 1892.—(Sanskrit and Telugu.) On the same pillar. Records in Ś. 1069 to 1165 private grants.

55. 303 *of* 1892.—(Telugu.) On a stone in the Executive Engineer's office. A record in Ś. 1204, expired, Chitrabhānu.

56. 304 *of* 1892.—(Prākrit.) On a pillar from Amarāvati in the same office. A fragmentary record.

57. 305 *of* 1892.—(Telugu.) On four sides of a stone in the same office.

58. 306 *of* 1892.—(Telugu.) On two faces of a broken pillar in the same office. A record of the Kākatīya king Pratāpa-Rudradēva (1295—1323) in Ś. 1220, expired, Viḷambin. In 1316 Conjeeveram was taken by one of his generals.

59. 307 *of* 1892.—(Tamil.) On a stone in the same office. A fragmentary record of the Chōḷa king.

60. 308 *of* 1892.—(Sanskrit.) On a broken pillar in the same office. A record of the Gajapati king Kapilēśvara in Ś. 1387. See *Ind. Antq.*, XX, p. 390. This inscription is given in *Mack. MSS.*, Bk. XVI (15-3-4), pp. 17-8, where the date given is अश्विवसु अमिशशि (1387). It records that Kapilēśvara gave to Gods Pāpavināśa and Rudrapadēva a village near Koṇḍapalli.]

61 to **67**. 309 *to* 315 *of* 1892.—(Telugu and Sanskrit.) On a pillar in the Mallēśvara temple. Records in Ś. 1053 to 1193 private grants.

68 to **70**. 316 *to* 318 *of* 1892.—(Telugu.) On another pillar in the same temple. Records in Ś. 1177 private grants.

71. 319 *of* 1892. *(No. 6 of Mr. Sewell's local list.)*—(Telugu.) On three faces of a pillar* in front of the Mallēśvara shrine in the same temple. A record in Ś. 1359, expired, Piṅgaḷa. A grant to the temple by a dancing girl. [See *Mack. MSS.*, Bk. XVI (15-3-4), p. 13, which however gives the date Ś. 1357, Piṅgaḷa, Śrāvaṇa-Bahuḷa 5, Monday.]

72. 320 *of* 1892. *(No. 1 in Mr. Sewell's local list.)*—(Telugu.) On a pillar in the maṇṭapa in front of the same shrine. Records in Ś. 1331, expired, Virōdhin, the building of the maṇṭapa.

---

* The *Mack. MSS.* (Book XVI, p. 14) say that on the other face of this pillar there is another inscription regarding the contribution of two taṅkas to Mallēśvara and Rudrapāda for marriage festival; one puṭṭi of land in several villages (*Ibid.*, p. 15) to the deity.

73. 321 *of* 1892. (*No. 12 of Mr. Sewell's list.*)—(Telugu.) On a pillar in front of the Vighnēśvara shrine in the same temple. A record in Śrīmukha.

74. 322 *of* 1892.—(Telugu.) On another pillar in front of the same shrine. A record in Ś. 1381, Bahudhānya. [This seems to be No. 10 of Mr. Sewell's local list, but date misread as Ś. 1341. See also *Mack. MSS.*, Bk. XVI (15-3-4), pp. 10-11, which gives the details of date as Mārgasira bahuḷa 7, Monday. Records building of a Gaṇēśa temple.]

75. 323 *of* 1892.—(Telugu.) On a pillar built into the verandah of the same temple. A record of the Eastern Chāḷukyan Yuddhamalla. In very archaic characters. Mentions the king's grandfather Mallaparāju. The king intended is evidently Yuddhamalla II, son of Tāḍa or Tāḍapa and grandson of Yuddhamalla I.]

76. 324 *of* 1892.—(Telugu.) On the same pillar. A record in Ś. 1087.

77. 325 *of* 1892.—(Tamil.) On the same pillar. A record in the forty-first year of the Chōḷa king Kulōttuṅga-Chōḷadēva (I). Gives Rājēndra-Chōḷapuram as another name of Bezwāḍa.

78. 326 *of* 1892. (*No. 11 of Mr. Sewell's local list.*)—(Sanskrit and Telugu.) On a stone built into the roof of the Vighnēśvara shrine in the same temple. An incomplete record of the son of Chōḍabhūpa, a descendant of Buddhavarman.

79. 327 *of* 1892.—(Telugu.) On a pillar in the maṇṭapa in front of the Mallēśvara shrine in the same temple. A record in Khara.

80. 328 *of* 1892.—(Telugu.) On a stone built into the roof of the same maṇṭapa. A record in Ś. 1199.

81. 329 *of* 1892. (*No. 18 of Mr. Sewell's list?*)—(Sanskrit and Telugu.) On a broken pillar in front of the Kanakadurga shrine on the Indrakīla hill in the same place. A record of the Vijayanagara king Kṛishṇadēva in Ś. 1440, expired, Bahudhānya (Vaiśākaśuddha 15). Mentions the minister Sāḷuva Timmaraśa. [This inscription is fully given in *Mack. MSS.*, Bk. XVI (Oppert's No. 15-3-4) pp. 1—3. The grant is made by Śiṅgayya Dēva Mahārāya, the son of Pāparāja by Vākamā Dēvi, for the merit of his parents and of his elder brother Basavarāja. The building of temples, prākāras, etc., is enumerated. The genealogy of the chief as well as the Sanskrit verses on the back side of the pillar are given.]

81-A. On the back of the above. (Sanskrit.) Records that Śiṅgarāja built in the same date maṇṭapams, etc., the tank Guṇḍamasamudram, shrines to Vishṇu and Brahma. *Ibid.*, pp. 3—7. Further details of village constructions, festivals, etc., by the same chief are given in pp. 7–8.

82—83. 330 *and* 331 *of* 1892.—(Telugu.) Right of the east entrance to the Mallēśvara temple in the same place. Records dated in Ś. 1112. See *Ibid.*, pp. 8–9.

84. 332 *of* 1892.—(Telugu.) Left of the same entrance. A record in Ś. 1196.

85–86. 333 *and* 334 *of* 1892.—(Telugu.) On a stone built in a small shrine in the Mallikārjuna street. A record in Ś. 1511, expired, Virōdhin, Nijabhādrapāda Śuddha 11, Wednesday. Records that Akshatala Tirumala Bhaṭṭa of the Bhāradvāja gōtra built a "*Vasupatham*." See *Mack. MSS.*, Bk. XVI, (15–3–4), p. 16.

87. 335 *of* 1892.—(Sanskrit.) On a stone built into the roof of the maṇṭapa in front of the Mallēśvara shrine. An incomplete record in Ś. 1119.

88–89. 336 *and* 337 *of* 1892.—(Telugu.) On a pillar in the maṇṭapa in front of the east entrance of the Mallēśvara temple in the same place. Records dated in Ś. 1348 and 1475. Former is No. 2 of Mr. Sewell's local list and latter No. 3 of *ibid.* The latter of these is given in *Mack. MSS.*, Bk. XVI (15–3–4) in p. 12. It gives the details of the date as Ś. 1475, Paritāpi, Phalguna Śuddha 3, Wednesday, and records that the people of all lands from Koṇḍapalli to Rājahmahēndrapuram decided that the ōli (?) maryāda in a first marriage should be 21 chinnam of gold, that the bridegroom's party should give 12½ of silver and the bride's party 20½ of gold. The former record is also given in the *Mack. MSS.* and the details are to the effect that in Ś. 1348, Parābhava, Māgha Śuddha 2, Monday, Śrāvaṇa puṇyakāla, the people of several villages repaired the gōpuram and mukhamaṇṭapam. *Ibid.*, p. 13.

90. 536 *of* 1909.—(Sanskrit and Telugu.) On a mutilated slab dug up in the courtyard of the Mallēśvarasvāmin temple. A record of the Pallava king Mahāmaṇḍalēśvara Pallaketa. Registers some legends (See *Ep. Ind.*, 1910, for details) in connexion with the Mallēśvara temple and refers to the chief as being born in the family of king Kāḍuveṭṭi and being subordinate to the Chāḷukya king of Veṅgidēśa. The inscription refers to a certain Paṇḍitārādhya who came to this place, and proclaimed the superiority of Śivabhaktas to Brahmaṇs by holding live coal in China muslin with the tender twig of a Śami tree.]

91. The C.P. grant of Chāḷukya Bhīma I. (Sanskrit.) Records that the king gave at the time of his coronation *(paṭṭabandha)* the village of Kūkipaṟṟu in Uttarakaṇḍeruvāḍi-Vishaya to a student of the *krampāṭha* named Pōtamayya. See *Ep. Ind.*, Vol. V, pp. 127–31.

92. On a pillar. Records the building of a temple at Bezwāda for the God Kumārasvāmi by a certain Nripadhāmuṇḍu while king Rājasalki Rājāśraya Satyatrinētra Yuddhamalla was ruling. Another part records the king's building, for the merit of his grandfather Mallappa Rāju, a mansion for the God. A third part says that, at the king's coronation, a certain Mallaṇḍu, son of Trinayana, came to Bezwāda, saw a manifestation of Kārtikēya and raised a temple for Him. [Mr. Krishna Sastri believes that the

Kārtikēya temple here referred to was the same as the Śiva temple that the transformation of it into the latter was perhaps the work of the Paṇḍitārādhya mentioned in 79 above. If so, the real builder of the Mallēśvara temple was Mallaṇḍu. The epigraph has been attributed to the ninth century, and it is of great literary interest as it shows that Telugu literature flourished even before the time of Rājarāja I, the patron of Nannaya Bhaṭṭa, at such a high stage of culture as to cause public records to be written in poetry.]

92-A. On a pillar in the Kalyāṇamaṇṭapa of Mallēśvara. (Telugu.) Dated in Ś. 1123, Durmukhi, Vaiśakha Śuddha 15, Thursday. Records that Mahāmaṇḍalēśvara Bīruda Dēva Rāja, the brother-in-law of Kākatīya Gaṇapati, gave God Mallēśvara for the merit of his father Buddharāju, 55 rūkas for a lamp. [*Mack. MSS.*, Bk. XVI, p. 9.]

92-B. On another pillar of the same. (Sanskrit.) A record of Mahāmaṇḍalīka Goṇṭūru . . . rāja's Samastānādhipati Rāyanapreggaḍa gave to god Mallēśvara in Ś. 1139, Uttarāyaṇa Saṅkrānti, an *akhaṇḍa* lamp. *Ibid.*, pp. 9–10.

92-C. On another pillar of the same. Near the ruined Śālā. (Telugu.) Records that in Khara, Āshāḍha Śuddha 10, Thursday, Pinna Kōnammā gave 1,200 *taṅkas* to Kumāra Telugu Rāya besides other charities. *Ibid.*, p. 11.

92-D. On a pillar in a neighbouring maṇṭapa. (Telugu.) Records that Bhōgam Nambūri Annasami's daughter-in-law built the east gōpura of the Mallikārjuna temple in Ś. 1313, Prajōtpatti, Śravaṇa Śuddha 13, Tuesday. *Ibid.*, pp. 11–12.

Bōdapāḍu.

92-E—J. *Mack. MSS.* (*Loc. Rec.*, Vol. XII, p. 108).—Records dated in A.D. 1742, 1793, 1811, 1755 and 1788.

Dāmalūr.

92-K. A record of Velanāṭi Goṅka, son of Chētana, son of Rājēndra Goṅka. Records that he gave to the God Goṅkēśvara at Dāmalūr in Ś. 1054, (वारिवाणां नरशारि) 3 puṭṭis of land and 55 buffaloes. *Mack. MSS.*, Vol. XX, pp. 73—6.

Kāvulūru.

Mr. Sewell gives five inscriptions in this place of which three alone, identified with the following, are definite.

93. 154 *of* 1913. (*No. 1 of Mr. Sewell's local list.*)—(Telugu.) On a slab set up on the bund of a tank. Registers in Ś. 1648, Parābhava, Mārgaśira, śu. di. 15, Sunday, corresponding to November 27, A.D. 1726, that this is one of the Akkadēvadulu pillars fixed by a certain Śēshādri Ramaṇappa and his elder brother, in the tank constructed by them near Kāvulūru.

94. 155 *of* 1913. (*No. 4 of Mr. Sewell's list.*)—(Telugu.) On a stone lying in a palmyra tope, in the same village. Records in Ś. 1305 (a mistake for 1310), Vibhava, Pushya, ba. di. 14, Sunday, corresponding to December 27, A.D. 1388, that a certain Pōti-Nāyuṇḍu of Intamukkula gōtra, granted to the gods Chenna-Mallinātha and Varadagōpinātha of Kaurūru, a flower garden with fruit trees, for the merit of his parents.

95. 156 *of* 1913. (*No. 2 of Mr. Sewell's list.*)—(Telugu.) On a slab set up in a field to the north of the road leading to Koṇḍapalli from the same village. A damaged record of the Gajapati king Pratāpa Purushōttamadēva, the date of which is doubtful. Mentions Mogalrāju-Mahāpātra who was governing the country.

96. On the boundary between Kāvalūru, Koṇḍapalle and Ilaprōlu. An undated epigraph evidencing a grant to a temple by a Rāja named Jagannātha Prasāda, "acting under the orders of Malla Māra Rāja."

97. East of the village. A record dated in Ś. 1106 (A.D. 1184), and recording the digging of a well, etc., by "Poli Kōśa Birarāja." *Antiquities*, I, 50.

Kōlavennu.

98. A C.P. Grant of Chāḷukya Bhīma II (now in the Madras Museum). Consists of an order addressed by him to the inhabitants of Kaṇḍeruvāṭi-vishaya and issued at the request of a vassal king Vājjaya, giving the village of Koḍhatalli to Kommaṇa, the son of Deṇiya and a *kramavid.* See *S.I.I.*, I, No. 37, pp. 43—6.

Koṇḍapalli.

See *Antiquities*, I, 49-50, for a description of the place.

99. 207 *of* 1899.—(Telugu.) On a boulder near the fort on the hill. A mutilated record in Īśvara-samvatsara. Mentions the temple (nagaru) of Hanumanta-Perumāḷ.

100. 208 *of* 1899.—(Uriya.) On a boulder near the fort on the hill. No details given.

101. On an inscribed slab let into the wall of the first gateway of the lower fort. Records in Ś. 1358 the erection of a temple on the banks of the Kistna by private person. *Antiquities*, I, 49.

102. A C.P. grant in the village which "is dated in the reign of Ana Vēma Reḍḍi of Koṇḍavīḍu, Ś. 1272 (A.D. 1350). It records a grant of a village to a Brahman."

Kōṭṭūru.

102-A. On a slab north of the village. An epigraph dated in S. 1498, Dhātu, Chaitra, Śuddha 2. See *Loc. Rec.*, Vol. XII, p. 236.

Malkāpuram.

103. 152 *of* 1913.—(Telugu.) On a pillar lying near the Mussalman chāvaḍi. A record of Qutb Shahi king Mahamandu Sahu Sulutanu (Muhammad Shah Sultan) in Ś. 1452, Khara, Chaitra, śu. di. 2, Monday, corresponding to March 20, A.D. 1531. States that Masanada Eli Kutumana-Malka-Oḍaya, a friend of the Sultan, reduced by his prowess Koṇḍapalli and other hill fortresses and established a feeding-house *(langara)* at Kēdārabāda which he had founded near Peyyalagallu, south of Koṇḍapalli, for the helpless, blind and cripple and for dervishes. For the maintenance of this *(langara)*, he gave the two villages Kāvurūru and Kēdārabāda. See *Antiquities*, I, p. 50.

104. 153 *of* 1913.—(Persian.) On another face of the same pillar. Records in 931 A.H. (= 1524-5 A.D.) that "Malik Qutb-ul-Mulk set aside the income derived from certain villages for the maintenance of a *langar*, in memory of Khwaja Khizr." (Dr. J. Horovitz.)

Mōgalrājapuram.

105. 151 *of* 1913.—(Telugu archaic.) Near a rock-cut cell. Refers to a certain Chōḷa-Chāki Vilvirāḍu. See *Antiquities*, I, p. 50, and the memorandum referred to there.

Pōtavaram.

106. On a stone in the Fakir Takya Mound. Records in Ś. 1079 (A.D. 1157) a grant by Prōlammādēvi, daughter of Mahāmaṇḍalēśvara Pōta Rāja. *Antiquities*, I, p. 50. See No. 114 above.

Tāḍepalle.

107. On a stone near the deserted temple in the Vasantarāyalagaṭṭu hill. A private grant dated in Ś. 1312 (A.D. 1390).

Velagalēru.

108. 149 *of* 1913.—(Telugu.) On a slab bearing the figure of Āñjanēya, near a well. Refers to the god Anumanta (Hanūmanta) near the well Veṅkaṭādri-kōnēru and to the gift of a lamp-stand by a certain Siṅgadāsiri of Reḍḍipalle.

109. 150 *of* 1913.—(Telugu.) On a slab near a tank in the same village. Records that this is the charity-well of the son of Garigipāṭi Veṅkaṇṇa.

Yenikepāḍu.

In his *Antiquities* Mr. Sewell refers to all the following inscriptions. With regard to the second he gives the wrong date of Ś. 1096.

110. 157 *of* 1913.—(Telugu.) On a slab set up in the village. A record of Velanāṇḍu king Kulōttuṅga-Chōḍayadēva-Mahārāja.

Registers that the village Yenikepāḍu was granted to the temple of Rājanārāyaṇa at Bezwāḍa. The Gajapati prince Kumāra Hambiradēva-Mahāpātra apparently ratified the grant and distributed Yenikepāḍa among the servants of that temple. The latter included the worshippers, accountants, purōhits, goldsmiths, dancing girls, painters, men who rang the bell, makers of garlands, watchmen, the blowers of the conch and torch-bearers.

111. 158 *of* 1913.—(Telugu.) On a pillar set up in the same place. A record of the Vēlanāṇḍu king Kulōttuṅga-Rājēndra-Chōḍayarāja, in Ś. 1093, Uttarāyaṇa-Saṅkrānti. Registers that the king granted lands in the neighbourhood of Yenikepāḍu to the temple of Kēśavadēva at Bezwāḍa. The grant was intended for providing oblations, offerings, perpetual lamps, dancing girls and other servants.

112. 159 *of* 1913.—(Telugu.) On a pillar in a field of the same village. A mutilated record, the date of which is lost. Mentions the Mahāmaṇḍalēśvara Chāgi-Dorayarāja.

*Zakkampūḍi.**

113. On a stone west of a small tank. An undated grant by Ambadēva, son of Vīra Gajapati Gaurēśvara Pratāpa Kapilēśvaradēva Mahāraja.

114. On a slab in the village street. A grant dated Ś. 1079 (A.D. 1157) by "the son of Prōlāmba." (*Antiquities.*) See No. 106 above.

Zūpuḍi.

115. 160 *of* 1913.—(Telugu.) On the cross beam at the entrance into Veṅkaṭēśvarasvāmin temple. Records that the beam was the gift of the two *paṭṇasvāmi* (merchant) brothers, Śarabharāju and Appayya.

BHIMAVARAM TALUK.

Dumpagaḍapa Agrahāram.

116. On a pillar in the Varadarājasvāmi temple. Records the building of a Durgā shrine and its endowment in Ś. 1075 (A.D. 1153) by a private person.

Gaṇapavaram.

Mr. Sewell mentions eleven inscriptions in this place, most of which are on three pillars in the mukhamaṇṭapa of the ruined temple. These are—

117. A grant by Mahāmaṇḍalēśvara Kōna Maṇḍalīka Sōmayarāja in Ś. 1117.

---

* See *Loc. Rec.*, Vol. XII, p. 235.

118. A private grant in Ś. 1165.

119. A private grant in the seventh year of Rājarāja in Ś. 1077 (A.D. 1155).

120. A grant by Gōka, son of Veṅgi Mallidēva Rāja in Ś. 1096.

121. A grant by Mahāmaṇḍalēśvara Kolanisāmi (?) Nāyaka in Ś. 1073.

122. A grant dated Ś. 1109 (A.D. 1187).

123-A.—D. Private grants dated in Ś. 1195, Ś. 1117, Ś. 1187 and Ś. 1086.

Mōgallu.

124. On pillars in front of the Bhīmēśvara temple. Five inscriptions, dated Ś. 1237 (A.D. 1315), recording grants to temple by private persons.

125. On another pillar. A private grant, dated Ś. 1243.

Pāṇḍuva.

126. A C.P. grant in the local temple, dated Ś. 1056 (A.D. 1134), recording the grant of the village of Pāṇḍuva to Brahmans by Kolani Kōṭappa Nāyaka, "lord of Sanasipuram" in the reign of Kulōttuṅga Chōḷa II.

Vāṇḍram.

127. A C.P. grant of Ammarāja II of the Eastern Chāḷukyan dynasty (former part of which is identical with the Elavaṟṟu grant of the same king—see *Ind. Antq.*, Vol. XII, p. 91 ff.). Addresses the ryots, rāshtrakūṭas of the twelve villages of the Pāvunavāra district (of which Prāṇḍoru, i.e., Vāṇḍram? was one) that he gave certain lands and villages to Kuppaṇāmatya, grandson of Tūrki Yajvan or Tūrkayya referred to in the inscriptions of the period. See *Ep. Ind.*, Vol. IX, pp. 131—135, where Dr. Hultzsch edits the plates.

Vēṅkaṭapuram.

128. A C.P. grant in the possession of Kandāḷa Raṅgāchārya, recording a grant by a zamindar.

DIVI TALUK.

Avanigaḍḍa.

In his *Antiquities* Mr. Sewell mentions four definite inscriptions in this place. These are dated in Ś. 1090, Ś. 1075, Ś. 1074 and Ś. 1074. The first is said to be a grant of a Chōḷa, the second of a private person in the time of a Danadaprōli Chōḍa Nārāyaṇa Dēva; the third by Chaṇḍa Chōḍa Nārāyaṇa Dēva and the fourth in the same chief's time. These are evidently the undated records given in the departmental list.

129. 126 *of* 1893.—(Telugu.) On the east face of a pillar in the Lakshmī-Nārāyaṇa temple. A record of Vēlanāṇṭi Goṅka.

130. 127 *of* 1893.—(Telugu.) On the north face of the same pillar. A record in Ś. 1050.

131. 128 *of* 1893.—(Telugu.) On another pillar in the same temple. No details given.

132. 129 *of* 1893.—(Telugu.) A record on another pillar in the same temple. No details given.

133. 130 *of* 1893.—(Sanskrit.) A record at the entrance to the shrine in the same temple. No details given.

Ayyaṅki.

134. On a slab in the centre of the village. Records a grant by Balla Bhūpati in Ś. 1077 (A.D. 1155) to the Śiva temple at Śrīkākuḷam. *Antiquities*, Vol. I, p. 54.

135. Between this village and Pāmarru. An undated epigraph recording a grant to the Śiva temple at Bezwāḍa. *Ibid.*

Gaṇapēśvaram (near Talagoḍadēvi).

136. 131 *of* 1893.—(Sanskrit and Telugu.) On the west, south and east faces of a pillar in front of the Durgāmbā temple. A record of the time of the Kākatīya king Gaṇapati in Ś. 1153, expired, Khara, tithi of Gauri, bright fortnight, Vaiśākha, saying that his general Jaya built a Śiva temple at Dirpa (Divi) dedicated to Gaṇapēśvara named after his patron. The date corresponded, according to Dīkshit, to Monday, the 7th April, A.D. 1231. The inscription gives the Kākatīya genealogy from Prōla down to Gaṇapati and that of his general Jaya from his great-grandfather Bhīma downward. In the Telugu portion it is recorded that every boat touching at Nanēgaḍḍa should pay certain dues to the temple and that Jaya assigned the revenue of a number of villages to it. See Mr. Sewell's *Antiquities*, Vol. I, p. 54 (which is inaccurate), Mackenzie's *Kistna Manual*, p. 214 and *Ep. Ind.*, Vol. III, pp. 82—93, where Dr. Hultzsch edits it. It is an inscription of fiscal and economic interest and says that the inhabitants of the eighteen districts on both sides of the Kistna gave at Nanjēgaḍḍa a revenue of a *faṇam (chinna)* on every boat.

137. 132 *of* 1893.—(Telugu.) On the east face of the same pillar. A record in Ś. 1693, expired, Khara.

138—40. 133 *to* 135 *of* 1893.—(Telugu.) On the north face of the same pillar. Records dated in Ś. 1235, 1268 (*Vyaya*), and Ś. 1605. The first of these records the grant of a lamp to God Gaṇapatīśvara in Peda-Divipura at the junction of the Kistna and the sea, and the third to the Liṅga called after Gaṇapati and "set up by Chōḍa Rāja at the junction of the Vēṇi and the sea." [Mr. Sewell notes all these inscriptions, but his dates are different.]

Kaza.

141-A-B. Mr. Sewell mentions two inscriptions here, one dated Ś. 1146 and incomplete and the other undated and evidencing a private charity. *Antiquities*, Vol. I, p. 54.

Niḍumolu.

142. A grant to the Kēśava temple by Gōkarṇa Indumauḷi in "the fourteenth year of Rājarāja," Ś. 1148 (A.D. 1226) (doubtful reading).

143. A private grant in the reign of Kulōttuṅga Rājēndrachōḍa, dated Ś. 1100.

144. A private grant dated Ś. 1095.

*Peḍdakallepalli.**

145. 125 *of* 1897.—(Sanskrit and Telugu.) On a slab to the left of the entrance to the Nāgēśvara temple. Records in Ś. 1718, Rākshasa, the building of the gōpura by Yerlagaḍḍa Nāgēśvara Nāyaka. [I have traced the inscription to *Mack. MSS.*, Bk. XVI, pp. 2—4, in section 2 under Dēvarakōṭa.]

146. 126 *of* 1897.—(Telugu.) On the south wall of the same temple. A record of the Kākatīya king Kumārarudradēva in Ś. 1214, Nandana. Records the building of a stone temple over the liṅga of Nāgēśvara at Kaḍalupuri by Sōmaśivāchārya of the Pushpagiri *maṭha.* Noticed by Mr. Sewell. See *Mack. MSS.*, Bk. XVI, p. 2, and Bk. XX (15-3-63), p. 71.

147. 127 *of* 1897.—(Sanskrit and Telugu.) On the south wall of the same temple. Records in Kali 4883, Ś. 1704, Śubhakrit, repairs made by Yarlagaḍḍa Dēśāyi Kōdaṇḍarāma. See *Mack. MSS.*, Vol. XVI, p. 2.

148. 128 *of* 1897.—(Telugu.) On a pillar at the southern entrance to the shrine in the same temple. Records in Ś. 1210, gift of two lamps by Errapa to the Nāgēśvara temple at Kaḍalupaḷḷi. No. 6 in Mr. Sewell's local list.

149. 129 *of* 1897.—(Telugu.) On another pillar at the same place. Records in Vrisha gift of a lamp by a merchant.

150. 130 *of* 1897.—(Telugu). On the Nandi pillar in the same temple, north face. Records in Ś. 1158 gift of cows for a lamp by Jñanōttamaśivadēva to the Nāgēśvara temple at Kaḍalupaḷḷi.

---

* In his *Kistna Manual* Mackenzie observes that this place has "fifteen inscriptions of which three are of the twelfth and three of the eleventh century, and one is by Kulōttuṅgachōḍa Goṅkayya in the thirteenth year of the reign of Vishṇuvardhana" (p. 215). See also *Antiquities*, Vol. I, pp. 54-55, where twelve inscriptions are given.

151. 131 *of* 1897.—(Telugu.) On the Nandi-pillar in the same temple; south face. Records in Ś. 1076 gift of gold *(Kulōttunga-māḍa)* for a lamp by the queen of Ballanarēndra. No. 3 of Mr. Sewell's local list.

152. 132 *of* 1897.—(Telugu.) On the Nandi-pillar in the same temple; east face. Records in Ś. 1076 gift of gold *(Kulōttunga-māḍa)* for a lamp by Sōmaḷādēvi, the queen of Balladhinātha, the son of Chaḷukya-Bhīma and Abbalādēvi and grandson of Balla of the lunar race. No. 4 of Mr. Sewell's local list.

153—160. Besides the above Mr. Sewell mentions epigraphs dated Ś. 1118, Ś. 1108, Ś. 1213, Ś. 1225, Ś. 1262, and two undated grants. Of these I am able to obtain the particulars of the following from the *Mack. MSS.*, Bk. XVI (15-3-4):—

(*a*) In the Vīrabhadra maṇṭapam on a pillar. Records that in Ś. 1213, Khara, Uttarāyaṇa Saṅkrānti, one Taṇḍi Śeṭṭi gave, for the merit of his parents, 25 *māḍas* for a lamp.

(*b*) On the back of the above. A gift of 25 *māḍas* by Uyyasāni for a lamp in Ś. 1210.

(*c*) On another side of the above. Records that in Ś. 1225, Pramādi, Uttarāyaṇa Saṅkrānti, Śūrapa Reḍḍi and another gave 25 *māḍas* to the God for the merit of their parents.

(*d*) Below the above, on the Sōmaśivachāryapīṭa. The name of the Āchārya alone in Telugu.

(*e*) In the first pillar of the mukhamaṇṭapa in the Nāgēśvara temple. (Telugu.) Records that in Sādhāraṇa, Kārttika Śuddha 10, Thursday, the Bālījas and Panchānanam-vāru made a settlement in regard to marriage processions and took an oath to observe it before Nāgēśvara temple.

Śrikākuḷam.

Traditionally this place is important as the Brahmans are said to have been first settled here by Trilōchana Pallava, "perhaps as early as the third century A.D.," but no inscription earlier than the eleventh century has been found. It may be noted that this was the native place of Anantāmātya, the author of the *Rasābharaṇa* or *Bhōjarājiyam*, who lived about Ś. 1356. See Vīrēśalingam Pantulu's *Lives of the Telugu poets*, p. 151. In his *Antiquities* Mr. Sewell gives 29 inscriptions in this place, some of which are not evidently included in the list below. The survey of the place is yet to be completed.

161—174. 136 *to* 148 *of* 1893.—(Telugu.) On stones built into the shrine of Śrīkākuḷēśvara. Records dated in Ś. 1177 to 1214. No. 147 (undated) mentions the Kākatīya king Gaṇapati.

175–178. 149 *to* 52 *of* 1893.—(Telugu.) On stones built into the maṇṭapa in front of the same shrine. Records dated in Ś. 1054 and Ś. 1275.

179. 153 *of* 1893.—(Telugu.) On a stone built into the same. Mentions a chief of Dhānyakaṭaka (Amarāvati) and the temple of Amarēśvara (at Amarāvati).

180. 154 *of* 1893.—(Telugu.) On a stone built into the same. Appears to mention the Kākatīya king Gaṇapati.

181. 155 *of* 1893.—(Telugu.) On a stone built into the same. Resembles the above epigraph.

182. 156 *of* 1893.—(Sanskrit.) On a stone built into the same. A list of *birudas*.

183 to 185. 157 *to* 159 *of* 1893.—(Telugu.) On stones built into the same. Records dated in Ś. 1178 and Ś. 1220.

186 to 188. 160 *to* 162 *of* 1893.—(Telugu.) On walls connecting the different shrines in the same temple. Records dated in Ś. 1205, expired, Svabhānu.

189. 163 *of* 1893.—(Telugu.) A record on the east gōpura of the same temple.

190. 164 *of* 1893.—(Telugu.) On a pillar in the maṇṭapa near the same gōpura. A record in Ś. 1085 of Kulōttuṅga-Rājēndra-Chōḍarāju of the Velanānti line (1163—80).

191. 165 *of* 1893.—(Telugu.) On the same pillar. A record in Ś. 1080.

192. 166 *of* 1893.—(Telugu.) On a pillar lying in the same temple. A record in Ś. 1094. Mentions the Narēndrēśvara temple.

193. 167 *of* 1893.—(Telugu.) On a pillar lying at the entrance to the same temple. A record in Ś. 1078. Mentions the Narēndrēśvara temple.

194 to 196. 168 *to* 170 *of* 1893.—(Telugu.) On the same pillar. A record of Rājēndra-Chōḍarāju (1163—80 A.D.) in Ś. 1079. Records gifts to the same temple.

197. 171 *of* 1893.—(Telugu.) On the same pillar. A record of Rājarājadēva in Ś. 1077 and in his fifth year. Mentions Kulōttuṅga Ghōḍa-Goṇka (II) as a vassal. So Rājarāja should have come to the throne in Ś. 1150. He has not been identified.

198. 172 *of* 1893.—(Telugu.) On a pillar in the Kalyāṇa maṇṭapa of the same temple. A record in Īśvara.

199. 173 *of* 1893.—(Telugu.) A record on a pillar in the maṇṭapa of the Mallēśvara temple.

200 to 203. 174 *to* 177 *of* 1893.—(Telugu.) On stones built into the floor of the same maṇṭapa. A record of the Kākatīya king Pratāpa-Rudradēva (II ?) in Śōbhakrit.

204 to 206. 178 *to* 180 *of* 1893.—(Telugu.) Records on the north gōpura of the same temple. No details given.

ELLORE TALUK.

Ambarupēta.

206-A. A record dated in A.D. 1765, relating gift of land by Apparao Bahadūr to Pūjāri Lakshmi Narasu. Brown's *Loc. Rec.*, Vol. XII, p. 74.

Chōdi Malla.

206-B. In the hands of an inamdār. An epigraph dated in Pārthiva Māghabahuḷa 8, and recording a gift by Appā Rao Bahadūr. *Ibid.*, p. 89.

Dendulūru.

Considered to be the ancient capital of Veṅgi, this place is epigraphically disappointing. See *Antiquities*, I, 34, *Loc. Rec.*, Vol. XII, p. 93 also.

207. 112 *of* 1902.—(Telugu.) On a pillar lying under a pipal tree. A gift of land to Vīramahēśvara temple in Ś. 1213, *Khara*.

208. 113 *of* 1902.—(Telugu.) On the dhvajastambha of the Śōmēśvara temple. Records the setting up of the pillar.

Doṇḍapāḍu.

209. On a granite slab in a local tope. A record of Ś. 1477.

Duggirāla,

209-A. Records that in the reign of Kākatīya Gaṇapatidēva, his brother Bhaṭṭa Bhāskara gave in Ś. 1056 the village of Duggīrāla in Khaṇḍavāṭi in 22 parts to Brahmans of 12 gōtras, and similarly 43 other villages. *Mack. MSS.*, Bk. XX, pp. 67—70.

Ellore.

In his *Antiquities* Mr. Sewell gives thirty-one inscriptions in this place, which have been identified with the corresponding ones below. It was evidently known formerly as Kamalākarapura or Kolamu.

210. 527 *of* 1893.—(Telugu.) On a pillar in the masjid. Records in Ś. 1122 the gift of a lamp to Kolani-Mūlasthāna Sōmēśvara Mahādēva by a *vēśya* of the king Kēśava dēvarāja of Kamalākarapura or Kolanāḍu. Dr. Hultzsch points out that as no other trace of this temple remains, it must have been destroyed by the Mussalmāns. No. 7 of Mr. Sewell's local list.

211. 528 *of* 1893.—On the same pillar. Records in Ś. 1116, the gift of a lamp by the wife of king Sōmayarāja of Kolanu.

[These chiefs formed, like the Velanāṇṭu Goṅkas, the Bēṭa Vijayāditya, branch, and others one set of local rulers in the period of the Chōḷa decline.]

212. 529 *of* 1893.—(Sanskrit and Telugu.) On the same pillar. A record of Kēśavadēvarāja of Kolanu in Ś. 1134, No. 17 of Mr. Sewell's local list.

213. 530 *of* 1893.—(Telugu.) On the same pillar. Kēśavadēvarāja of Kolanu records the gift of a lamp. (Date indistinct.)

214. 531 *of* 1893.—(Telugu.) On the same pillar. Kēśavadēvarāja of Kolanu records in Ś. 1118, the gift of a lamp. No. 2 of Mr. Sewell's local list.

215. 532 *of* 1893.—(Telugu.) On the same pillar. Kēśavadēva of Kolanu records in Ś. 1114, the gift of a lamp. No. 13 of Mr. Sewell's local list.

216. 533 *of* 1893.—(Telugu.) On the same pillar. Records in Ś. 1118, the gift of a lamp by Kēśavadēvarāja's wife Sōmāmbikā. No. 2 of Mr. Sewell's local list.

217. 534 *of* 1893.—On a pillar at the Kazi's house. Records in Ś. 1155, the building of a maṇṭapa in the Sōmēśvara temple by a minister. No. 27 of Mr. Sewell's local list.

218. A C.P. grant (Sānskrit and Prākrit) of Vijayadēvavarman of the Sālaṇkāyana Mahārājās of Veṅgipura (Pedā-Veṅgi in Ellore Taluk), addressed to the villagers of Elūra (Ellore), making a grant of 20 *nivarattnas* of land to Gaṇaśarman. See *Ep. Ind.*, Vol. IX, pp. 56—59, where Dr. Hultzsch edits it. This is Kielhorn's *List of Brāhmi Inscrns.*, No. 1194.

218-A. In the hands of the Śrōtriyamdār Pōtukūchi Kāśipati. Records that in Āṅgirasa, Nija-Ashāḍhabahuḷa 7, Appa Rao gave Veṅkaṭēśa Śāmbaśiva and Mallēśa the agrahāra of Etur. *Loc. Rec.*, Vol. XII, pp. 9–10.

218-B. In the hands of Tātāchārya, grandson of Prativādibhayaṅkara Tātāchārya. Records that in Śrīmukha, Jyēshṭaśuddha 13, Thursday, Appā Rāya gave an agrahāra to Tātāchārya. *Ibid.*, pp. 10–11.

218-C—U. The other inscriptions given by Mr. Sewell are dated Ś. 1223, 1221, 1123, 1150, 1123, 1124, 1152, 1111, 1119, 1223, 1121, 1219, 1131, 1145, 1134, 1283, etc., and are mostly private grants. One is dated in Ś. 1150 and records a grant by Indradēva, son of Mahāmaṇḍalēśvara Chōḍa Mahārazu Narapati Razu ; another on a stone in the bazaar, dated Ś. 1545, recording a grant by Śrī Raṅga Rāya of Vijayanagar, son of Gōpāla. Lastly Mr. Sewell gives a copper plate inscription in the hands of a Karaṇam which gives the order of precedence in which betel-leaves were served to various chiefs by Ibrahim Kutb Shah after his conquest of this country, about A.D. 1566. See *Antiquities*, I, pp. 34–5.

Koniki.

219-A. In the hands of inamdārs. A record dated in Ś. 1708 (A.D. 1786), Prabhava, Śravaṇa bahuḷa 4, Sunday, relating gift of land. See Brown's *Loc. Rec.*, Vol. XII, pp. 86–7.

Kovvali.

219-B. A sanad in the hands of Rāmaliṅgambhaṭḷa. An epigraph dated in Khara, Mārgaśirsha Śuddha 10, Friday, gift of land by Appā Rao to Kuṇḍa Rāmaliṅgambhaṭḷa. *Ibid.*, p. 88.

Koppāka.

220-A. On the dhvajastambha of the Gōpālasvāmi temple. Records a grant to the temple by a zamindar. No date is given.

Mupparru.

220-B. In the hands of the inamdār Garimalla Jaggayya. A record dated in A.D. 1763, Svabhānu, Māgha Śuddha 15, Thursday, gift of land by Appayagāru. *Ibid.*, pp. 90 and 92.

Peddapāḍu.

221. On a pillar of the kalyāṇa maṇṭapa in the Sōmēśvara temple. Records the erection of the maṇṭapam by private parties in Ś. 1140. (*Antiquities*, I, 36. See also Brown's *Loc. Rec.*, pp. 81—5, for a late epigraph, dated A.D. 1778, 1763, etc.).

*Peddavēgi.**

222-A. 114 *of* 1902.—(Telugu.) On two faces of a pillar set up on the *bund* of the Ratnam tank. Records the construction of the tank by the Kastūri Veṅkaṭaratnam in a *Vikrama*.

Piṅnakaḍimi.

222-B. In the hands of the inamdār Eḍavalli Śēshayya. A record dated in A.D. 1792. See *Loc. Rec.*, Vol. XII, p. 91, for details.

Poṅnangi.

222-C. *C.P.* 3 *of* 1908–9.—A grant of Guṇaka Vijayāditya III (844—88).

Satyavōlu.

222-D. A record dated in A.D. 1764. See *Loc. Rec.*, Vol. XII, p. 85, for details.

---

* This is supposed to be the site of the former capital of the Veṅgi country, but nothing ancient is found there except a mound which, Dr. Hultzsch was informed, represented the temple of Chitranāthasvāmi, referred to in a set of copper plates discovered at Kollēru (K.N. 237). (See *Ep. Ind.*, IV, p. 143, also *Antiquities*, I, 36.)

Taḍikalpūḍi.

223. 535 *of* 1893.—(Telugu.) On the enclosure of Gaṅgēyēś-vara temple. A record in Ś. 1126. Mentions the Ayyanēśvara temple at Taḍikalpūḍi, which was the capital *(rājadhāni)* of Veṅgi.

224. 536 *of* 1893.—(Telugu.) On a pillar. A record of the time of Veṅgi-Mahādēvarāja in Ś. 1130. The gift of a lamp to the Aruṇiśvara temple by a Nāyaka.

225. 537 *of* 1893.—(Telugu.) On the same pillar. Records in Ś. 1182, the gift of a lamp by a Sēnāpati to the Araṇīśvara temple.

226. 538 *of* 1893.—(Telugu.) On the same pillar. Records in Ś. 1165, the gift of a lamp by Anugrahaśivāchārya to the Haradēva temple.

Taṅgellamuḍi.

226-A-B. In the hands of one Rāchakoṇḍa Rāmachandra. A record dated in Vibhava, Phālguṇa Śuddha 2, Friday. The *Mack. MSS.* (see *Loc. Rec.*, Vol. XII, p. 80) give an epigraph in this place, dated A.D. 1748. It records a gift by Appā Rao.

GUDIVĀDA TALUK.

Guḍivāḍa.

For the Buddhistic and Jain antiquities of this place and for numismatic finds therein see *Antiquities*, I, 92, and bibliography given therein.

227. 539 *of* 1893.—(Sanskrit and Telugu.) On the right door pillar of the Bhīmēśvara temple. A record of the Kākatīya king in Ś. 1158. (The right of each line is built in.) Mentions the Kākatīya Gaṇapati and his ancestor Prōla. Guḍivāḍa belonged to the district of Guḍrāra "which is another form of Gudrahāra, Guḍravāra or Guḍḍavāḍi district of the Eastern Chāḷukya inscriptions."

228. 540 *of* 1893.—(Telugu.) On the same pillar. Records in Ś. 1159, a private gift to the Kuṇḍēśvara temple, which, Dr. Hultzsch points out, was the ancient Bhīmēśvara temple.

229. 541 *of* 1893.—(Telugu). On the left door pillar of the same temple. Records the gift of a lamp by a merchant.

230. 542 *of* 1893.—(Sanskrit and Telugu.) On the same pillar. Records in Ś. 1165, the gift of a lamp by Guṇḍa, nephew of the builder of the temple.

Kudaravalli.

231. 161 *of* 1913.—(Telugu.) On a slab lying in the Gōkulammā cheruvu. Records in Saumya, Āshāḍha śu. di. 3, Thursday, that a certain Abudalu Husēnu, servant of Abudulākhānu, who was again the servant of Sēkhajākhānu, built the sluice of the tank at Kudūrapalli.

Mandapādu.

Both these inscriptions are given by Mr. Sewell in his *Antiquities.*

232. 543 *of* 1893.—(Telugu.) On the slab near the Karaṇam's house. The Kākatīya king Gaṇapatidēva-Mahārāja records in Ś. 1176 the gift of a lamp to the Vishṇu temple of Rājarāja-Viṇṇahara.

233. 544 *of* 1893.—(Telugu.) On the same slab. Records in the 37th year of Vishṇuvardhana-Mahārāja the gift of a lamp to the same temple, which was situated in the district of Guḍravāra, by Nārāyaṇa Preggaḍa.

Viṅnakōṭa.

234. On a stone in a field north of the village. An inscription, dated Ś. 1360, recording an act of piety by a private person.

Pērūr.

234-A. In the Sōmēśvara temple. In Ś. 450, Saumya, Jyēshṭa bahuḷa 2, Friday, "Kārakulli Dēvachōḍa Mahārāja" gave to the deity some land at Mākuchalle Pērūru in Koṇḍavīḍu. *Mack. MSS.*, XX, p. 50.

234-B. In Ś. 925, Uttarāyaṇa Saṅkrānti, Chikka Bhīma gave to the same deity 2 *bharanas* of land. *Ibid.*

234-C. In the Vīrabhadra temple. In Ś. 1148, Solar eclipse, Kusumarāja, son of Bhīmarāja, gave some gift to Brahmans who are enumerated. *Ibid.*, pp. 50—2.

234-D. In the same temple. Dated in Ś. 1437. Records in the reign of Kṛishṇadēva Rāya that Appaya and Goppaya, Śāluva Timma's nephews, distinguished themselves. Nādenḍla Appaprabhu is said to have obtained power from Śāḷuva Timma. *Ibid.*, pp. 52—4. [It is to this Appa that Mādayyagiri Mallaṇa dedicated his poem *Rājaśēkharacharitramu.* Appa was also the son-in-law of Śāḷuva Timma and in charge of Koṇḍavīḍu after its conquest by Kṛishṇadēvarāya. Gōpa was the Governor of Gutti, a good Saṇskrit scholar and the author of the *Chandrikā*, a commentary on Kṛishṇamiśra's *Prabōdhachandrōdayam.*]

234-E. In the same temple. A record of Kṛishṇadēvarāya dated in Ś. 1442, Vishu, Kārttika Śuddha 5, Monday. Records a grant to God Sōmēśvara Kēśavarāya by Ayyaṇa and Gōppayya, the sons of Nādeṇḍḷa Timmaya. *Ibid.*, pp. 54-5.

234-F. Near the Chennakēśava temple. Records in Ś. 1443, Chitrabhānu, Śravaṇa Śuddha 15, Monday, the building of the bhōgamaṇṭapa by Veṅkaṭayōgi. *Ibid.*, No. 55.

Ilapaṟṟu.

235. 162 *of* 1913.—(Telugu.) On a slab set up near a tank. In old Telugu characters. The inscription is partly mutilated at the beginning and seems to register a gift of land by Kaḍaladēva, son of Bandayāri, to a certain Ba[śa]riya of Barugālpariti in the villages of Jakipōḍi, Illupāḍu, Penurōḍi and Karivrinda. The second of the village is probably identical with Ilaparru.

Kaikalūru.

236. In the Veṅkaṭēśvara temple. A record dated Ś. 1550 recording a private donation to the temple. *Antiquities*, Vol. I, p. 52.

Kollēru lake.

237. Near this lake was found the C.P. grant of the Sālaṅkāyana dynasty of Veṅgi, published by Elliot in *M.J.L.S.*, XI (304), by Fleet in *Ind. Antq.*, Vol. V, p. 177, and referred to by Burnell in his *S. Ind. Pal.*, p. 14 and plates 20 and 21. It records that Mahārāja Vijaya Nandivarma, the son of Chandravarma, gave a village in Guḍrahāra vishaya to Brahmans in his seventh year, Paushya, Kṛishṇapaksha Ashṭami.

NANDIGĀMA TALUK.

Aḍavi Rāvulapāḍu.

238. On a stone close to a stream east of the village. An inscription of Ś. 1164 (A.D. 1242), recording a grant by a local chieftain to a temple. *Antiquities*, I, p. 43.

Anumañchipalle.

239—243. Mr. Sewell gives five inscriptions in this place, four in front of the garbhālaya of the Śiva temple and one on another slab close by. The first three are incomplete. Two of them are dated Ś. 1182. The fourth is dated Ś. 1182 and records a private grant in the time of Manma Bhūpati. The last is dated in Ś. 1134 and mentions the name Pōta Bhūpati. *Antiquities*, Vol. I, p. 43. [Manma was the patron of Tikkaṇa Sōmayāji, the translator of the *Mahābhārata*.]

Babbellapāḍu.

244. North of the Śiva temple. The settlement of a boundary dispute in Ś. 1470.

245. On a stone in front of the small shrine north of the village. A private grant in Ś. 1442.

Bhimāvaram.

246. On the side of a tank east of Koṅgaramalayagaṭṭu hill. A grant to a temple in Ś. 1068.

Budavāḍa.

247. In the yard of a house west of the temple of Mutyal amma, on a slab. Records a grant to the temple in Ś. 1367.

Ēṭūr.

247-A. In the hands of Gaṅgādhara Avadhāni. Records that in Svabhānu Āśvija Śuddha 3, Rājanārāyana Rāo Gāru gave to Subbāvadhāni (in 1173 fasli) some lands. *Loc. Rec.*, Vol. XII, pp. 5—7.

Guḍimeṭla.

248. On a stone east of the mosque. Grant of lands in Ś. 1190 by Rudradēva and Gaṇama Nāyuḍu to a temple. [Rudradēva was apparently Rudrammā who assumed that title.]

249. On the same. An inscription (incomplete) of Pōta Nripa, son of Rājēndrachōḍa.

250. On the same. A private grant.

251. On the same. A private grant dated Ś. 1236.

252. On another slab close by. A grant dated Ś. 1217 by a General of Rudradēva (i.e., Pratāparudra II, 1295—1323).

253. On the same. Grant to the temple in Ś. 1086 by "the son of Vāsta Nripa" (doubtful reading).

Jaggayyapēṭa.

See Mr. Sewell's *Antiquities*, Vol. I, p. 44; Bhagavan Lal Indraji's *Notes on Amar. Stupa*, p. 55 ff.; *Ind. Antq.*, Vol. XI, p. 258 ff. and *Arch. Surv., S. Ind.*, Vol. I, pp. 110-11, for an account of the Buddhistic antiquities and inscriptions of the place. They are reproduced in Dr. Kielhorn's *List of Brahmi Inscriptions*, Nos. 1202—4. The texts of the inscriptions are—

253-A. *Kielhorn's List No.* 1202.—On a Buddhistic pillar. (Prākrit.) Records in the time of Rāja Madhariputa Sirivara Purisadata of the Ihākus, gift of five entrance pillars (*āyakakambha*) at the eastern door of the great *chaitya* at Vēlagiri by an artisan named Sidhatha (Siddhārtha), son of Nākamchanda (Nāgachandra) of Naḍatura in the district of Kammaka.

253-B. On a pillar. (Prākrit.) A gift of the same kind as the above.

253-C. A similar gift in the time of the same king.

Jayantipuram.

254. On the dhvajastambha of the Āñjanēya temple. Records the erection of it by a private person in Ś. 1528 (A.D. 1606).

Kanchāla.

255. On a stone in the local fort. Ś. 1187 (A.D. 1185). A private grant.

256. In the same place. Two other undated private grants.

Kavutāvari agrahāram.

257. Near the temple on the Pālēru. Endowment of the temple by Śrī Nrisimha Nripati in Ś. 1670 (A.D. 1748).

Kōṇakāñchi.

258. A private grant in the reign of Mahāmaṇḍalēśvara Pōtarāja at Guḍimeṭḷa. See No. 249 above.

259. A grant by Rājēndrachōḷa in Ś. 1068.

260. A record of Ś. 1699, fixing a boundary stone.

261. An undated private charity.

Mukhtiyāla.

Mr. Sewell gives five inscriptions here, two in the Vishṇu temple and three in the Śiva. These are—

262. An incomplete epigraph, undated, containing a portion of a genealogical table giving the names Durjaya, Pōta, Dorabhūpa, Tyāgi Pōta Rāja.

263. Undated. Grant by Tyāgi Pōta Rāja.

264. Undated. A genealogy given, in which the names Paṇḍa Bhīmēśvaran, Kaṇṭa Bhūpa, Kēśava Dharaṇīśa, Goṅka Dharādhinātha, Kēśava Nripa occur.

265. Undated grant by Kēśava Nripa.

266. Grant by the same in Ś. 1129 (A.D. 1207).

Munagālapalle.

* **267.** On stones west of the tamarind tope east of the village. Grant in Ś. 1180 (A.D. 1258) by Manma Chāgi Rāja, son of Bhīma Rāja and grandson of Peda Chāgi Rāja.

268. Undated private grant.

269. Undated. Records the erection of some stone figures by a private party.

Muppālla.

270. Near the prākāra wall of the Mallēśvara temple. Grant by the general of Chāgi Manma Rāja in Ś. 1168.

Navāb-pēṭa.

271. At the temple of Sōmanāthasvāmi. Grant by Chāgi Pōta Rāja in Ś. 1152.

272. In the same place. Undated. Grant by Chāgi Gaṇapati dēva.

273. Grant by Chāgi Pōta Rāja in Ś. 1152.

274. Grant by the same king in the same year.

---

* See *Loc. Rec.*, Vol. XII, p. 157, for copies of sanads in the hands of the Zamindar.

275. A private grant in Ś. 1216.

276. An undated and private grant.

Peddavaram.

For some local *sanads* see *Loc. Rec.*, Vol. 57, p. 297.

277. At the Āñjanēya temple. A private grant in Ś. 1236 (A.D. 1314).

278. On a stone south of the village. Grant by a private person in Ś. 1190 with the consent of the Sāhiṇi Gannama Nāyuḍu, General of Kākatīya Rudradēva (Rudrammā).

279. In the temple of Nīlakaṇṭha. Undated and private.

Penugañchiprōlu.

280. In Karla Narasimha's garden. Records in Ś. 1542 the setting up of an image in the garden by a private person. See *Loc. Rec.*, Vol. XII, 188 f.

Pokkunūru.

281. East of the Garbhālaya of the Rāmaliṅgasvāmi temple. A private grant in Ś. 1115.

Rāvulapāḍu.

282—286. Mr. Sewell mentions five inscriptions here of which one is dated Ś. 1164, another (undated) a grant of Mahāmaṇḍalēśvara Kōṭa Guṇḍa Rāja, and a third dated in Ś. 1275 and recording a grant by a private party. The other two are very incomplete as the inscribed stones are broken.

Tāḍavāyi (Munagala Zemindari).

286-A-B. In the local temple of Mallīkārjuna. Records dated in Ś. 1228 in the time of "Annayya Reḍḍi," and in Ś. 1222 in the time of Prātāparudra of Warangal. Both are private grants. [*Antiquities*, I, p. 46. See also Brown's *Loc. Rec.*, Vol. XII, p. 124.]

Tsāvuṭapalle.

287. On a pillar in front of the Āñjanēya temple. Records its erection in Ś. 1144.

Vedādri.

288. A private grant dated Ś. 1548.

289. Another private grant dated Ś. 1395.

290. A grant of Tyāgi Manma Gaṇapatidēva in Ś. 1181.

NARASAPŪR TALUK.

Āchanṭa.

291. On the north wall of the Vishṇu temple. A record of Ś. 1177 (A.D. 1255). Rāja Mahārāja, Lakshmī Rāja, Veṅgīśvara, Pina Lakshmī Rāja mentioned.

292. In the same place. Grant by Pina Lakshmī Rāja in Ś 1181 (A.D. 1259) of land which had been given to his family by Vijayādityadēva (Vishṇuvardhana).

293. In the same place. A private grant of Ś. 1181 (A.D. 1259).

294. Above the southern doorway of the mukhamaṇṭapa. Illegible.

295. In the same place. Gōkarṇa Chakravarti mentioned.

296. Above the doorway of the Ammavāru shrine. A grant in Ś. 1074 (A.D. 1152) by Mallaṇṇa Sāmi Nāyuḍu, son of Mahāmaṇḍalēśvara Mummuḍi Bhīma Rāja.

Koḍamañchali.

297. On the north wall of the Gōpālasvāmi temple. A private grant to temple in Ś. 1074 (A.D. 1152).

Narasapūr.

297-A. *C.P. No.* 1 *of* 1904.—A record in Sanskrit and Telugu of the Eastern Chāḷukyan king Chāḷukya Bhīma (I). Records gift of the village of Vedatalūru in Uttarakaṇḍeruvāṭi Vishaya by the king to forty-six Brāhmaṇas on the occasion of the *nityaśrāddha* of his son who died on the battle-field.

297-B. A Kanarese inscription of the seventh year of the Kaḷachūri Bhujabalachakravarti Sōvidēva (son of Bijjala, 1168—1174) in Vijaya, Ś. 1095, an irregular date. See Kielhorn's *Southern List*, No. 287.

Palakol.

This early Dutch possession which came into the hands of the English in 1781 has, according to Elliot, 21 inscriptions which Mr. Sewell has given in his *Antiquities*.

298. 508 *of* 1893.—(Telugu.) On the Āñjanēya shrine in the Kshīrarāmēśvara temple. Records in Ś. 1562, Vikrama, the building of the shrine by a merchant.

299. 509 *of* 1893.—(Sanskrit.) On a Nandistambha in the same temple. Records in the time of Vīrabhadra, son of Induśēkhara, son of Vishṇuvardhana, in Ś. 1188, the gift of a lamp by the king's mother. [Nothing is known about this chief. He apparently belonged to line Kōṇa.]

300. 510 *of* 1893.—(Telugu.) On a pillar in the maṇṭapa at the entrance to the same temple. A record of Vishṇuvardhana-Mahārāja *alias* Niḍudaprōli- Mahādēva in Ś. 1220. The gift of a lamp by the king's daughter.

301. 511 *of* 1893.—(Telugu.) On the same pillar. A record of Vishṇuvardhana Mahārāja *alias* Mahādēva in Ś. 1218, Durmukhi. Mentions the king's daughter and her husband, the Mahāmaṇḍalēśvara Kōṇa-Gaṇapadēvarāja. See Nos. 310 and 313 below.

302. 512 *of* 1893.—(Telugu.) On the same pillar. A record of Vishṇuvardhana-Mahārāja *alias* Mahādēva recording in Ś. 1222, Śārvari, the gift of a lamp by the same queen.

303. 513 *of* 1893.—(Telugu.) On another pillar in the maṇṭapa. A record of Ś. 1240. Mentions the son of the Mahāmaṇḍalēśvara Kōṇa-Bhīmavallabharāja, evidently a later chief of the Haihaya Kōṇas like Gaṇapa. See 312.

304. 514 *of* 1893.—(Telugu.) On the same pillar. A record of the Reḍḍi king Anavōta-Reḍḍi in Ś. 1344, Śubhakrit. A gift by Poṇḍūri-Nāgarāja. Anavōta was the Koṇḍavīḍu Reḍḍi who was the father of Kumāragiri (the author of *Vasantarājiyam*) and father-in-law of Kāṭaya Vēmā, the founder of the Rājahmundry branch of the Reḍḍis.]

305. 515 *of* 1893.—(Sanskrit and Telugu.) On another pillar in the same maṇṭapa. A record of the Reḍḍi king Doḍḍaya-Allāḍa (of Rājahmundry). Records in Ś. 1338, Durmukhi, a gift by Narahari, an officer of the king. See Gd. 14.

306. 516 *of* 1893.—(Sanskrit and Telugu.) On the same pillar. A record of the time of the Reḍḍi king Doḍḍaya Allāḍa in Ś. 1337, Manmatha. The gift of a golden car by the same officer. See Gd. 14.

307. 517 *of* 1893.—(Telugu.) On another pillar in the same maṇṭapa. Records in Ś. 1129 the gift of a lamp by an officer of the Kōna (Haihaya) king Satyarāja (i.e., Manma Satya II).

308. 518 *of* 1893.—(Telugu.) On another pillar in the same maṇṭapa. Annadēva, son of Atirāja, records in Ś. 1325, Jaya, a gift. The Śaka and cyclic years do not correspond.

309. 519 *of* 1893.—(Telugu.) On another pillar in the same maṇṭapa. Records in Ś. 1222, the gift of a lamp by Vishṇuvardhana *alias* Induśēkhara, son of Vishṇuvardhana.

310. 520 *of* 1893.—(Sanskrit and Telugu.) On another pillar in the same maṇṭapa. Records in Ś. 1184, the gift of a lamp by Malli-Nāyaka, a servant of Kōṇa-Gaṇapatidēva-Mahārāja (who seems to have been a later chief of the Haihaya Kōṇa line).

311. 521 *of* 1893.—(Telugu.) On another pillar in the same maṇṭapa. Records in Ś. 1307, Krōdhana, a gift by the Reḍḍi king Vēma Reḍḍi, son of Kāṭama Reḍḍi.

312. 522 *of* 1893.—(Telugu.) On the same pillar. Records in Ś. 1286, the gift of gold. Mentions Kōṇa-Bhīmavallabharāja. See 303 above.

313. 523 *of* 1893.—(Telugu.) On the same pillar. Records in Ś. 1198, a gift by Kōṇa-Gaṇapatidēva-Mahārāja. See No. 310.

314. 524 *of* 1893.—(Sanskrit.) On a pillar of the enclosure of the same temple. Records in the reign of Velanaṇṭi-Chōḍa,

(1163—80), son of Gonka (II, 1133—57, *circa*) and Subbāmbika, in Ś. 1058, the gift of a lamp.

315. 525 *of* 1893.—(Sanskrit.) On the same pillar. Records grant by Guṇḍāmbika, wife of Velanāṇṭi king Chōḍa, son of Gonka I and Sabbāmbika.

316. 526 *of* 1893.—(Telugu.) On a pillar near the Śayānagara in the same temple. A record of Vishṇuvardhana-Mahārāja in Ś. 1518, Durmukhi. A late example of the occurrence of the name Vishṇuvardhana.

NUZVID TALUK.

Āgiripalli.

317. Two C.P. grants dated Ś. 1550 and recording private grants to the fine temple on the hill. *Antiquities*, p. 51.

Aiyutūru.

318. On a stone near the Rāmaliṅgēśvara temple. An epigraph dated Ś. 1563.

(*Eḍēru*) *Īdara.*

This village is said to be in Nuzvid Zamindari, but not found in the alphabetical list of inscriptions.

319. *C.P.* 180 *of Mr. Sewell's list.*—The C.P. grant of Vijayāditya II (794—842 A.D.). (Sanskrit.) Records that this Eastern Chāḷukyan king granted, on the occasion of a solar eclipse, part of the village of Vaṇḍrupiṭēyu in Kaṇḍeruvāḍi-vishaya to a Brahman. Undated. See *Ind. Antq.*, Vol. XIII, p. 55 f., *Tam. and Sans. Inscrns.*, pp. 179—81, *Ep. Ind.*, Vol. V, pp. 118—22,

320. *C.P.* 179 *of Mr. Sewell's list* (now in the Madras Museum). A C.P. grant of Rājamahēndra Amma I (Vishṇuvardhana VI) of the Eastern Chāḷukyan dynasty. Records the donation of a village named Gomṭūru (with 12 hamlets) to Kuṇḍāditya, son of Prithirāja, who was a military officer and the son of Sōmāditya of the family of Paṭṭavardhana, in the presence of the Kuṭumbis of the district of Kaṇṭeruvāṭi. See *S.I.I.*, I, No. 36, pp. 36—43; *Antiquities*, Vol. II, pp. 25–6, and *Tam. and Sans. Inscrns.*, pp. 176—9. Kielhorn's *Southern List*, No. 559.

Enamalakuḍūru.

In his *Antiquities* (I, 55–6) Mr. Sewell gives eleven inscriptions and the department has copied an equal number.

320-A. 133 *of* 1897.—(Telugu.) On an octangular pillar lying in front of the Kēśavasvāmin temple. Records in Ś. 1163, Śarvarin, gift of cows for a lamp by a merchant to the Mallēśvara temple at Bezwāḍa.

320-B. 134 *of* 1897.—(Telugu.) On an octangular pillar lying in front of the Kēśavasvāmin temple. Records in Ś. 1163 gift of cows for a lamp to the Mallēśvara temple.

321. 135 *of* 1897.—(Sanskrit.) On an octangular pillar lying in front of the Kēśavasvāmin temple. Records in Ś. 1054 (or 1052) gift of the town Vijayavāṭa (i.e., Bezwāḍa) to the Mallēśvara temple by Bhīma, the son of Boddana and Lōkāmbika. Bōddaṇa had acquired this town from the Chōḍa king Tripurāntaka of Veṅgi and from the Karnāṭa king. See No. 329 below.

322. 136 *of* 1897.—(Telugu.) On an octangular pillar lying in front of the Kēśavasvāmin temple. Records in Ś. 1163 gift of cows for a lamp by a Reḍḍi to the Mallēśvara temple at Vijayavāḍa.

323. 137 *of* 1897.—(Telugu.) On an octangular pillar lying in front of the Kēśavasvāmin temple. Records in Ś. 1163 gift of cows for a lamp by a Reḍḍi to the Mallēśvara temple.

324. 138 *of* 1897.—(Telugu.) On an octangular pillar lying in front of the Kēśavasvāmin temple. Records in Ś. 1137 gift of sheep for the merit of Chāgi Pōtarāja.

325. 139 *of* 1897.—(Sanskrit.) On an octangular pillar lying in front of the Kēśavasvāmin temple. Records in Ś. 1167 gift of a lamp.

326. 140 *of* 1897.—(Sanskrit and Telugu.) On an octangular pillar lying in front of the Kēśavasvāmin temple. Records in Ś. 1172 gift of cows for a lamp for the merit of Chāgi Gaṇapayarāja. Begins with Goṅka, who was the lord of the Veṅgi one thousand country; his son was Ayyapadēva who married Muppalamahādēvi, and their son was Gaṇapati. This Gaṇapati Rāya was different from his namesake referred to in Nos. 310 and 313.

327. 141 *of* 1897.—(Telugu.) On an octangular pillar lying in front of the Kēśavasvāmin temple. Records in Ś. 1053 gift of twenty lamps to the Mallēśvara temple at Bezwāḍa; a damaged record.

328. 142 *of* 1897.—(Sanskrit and Telugu.) On an octangular pillar lying in front of the Kēśavasvāmin temple. Records in Ś. 1152 gift of cows for a lamp to the Mallēśvara temple by Nīliśeṭṭi, a merchant from Penuṅgoṇḍa.

329. 143 *of* 1897.—(Telugu prose and verse.) On an octangular pillar lying in front of the Kēśavasvāmin temple. Records gifts by Bhīmaṇa, the son of Boddaṇa, to the Mallēśvara temple at Bezwāḍa. See No. 321 above.

Koṇḍanāyanavaram.

330. On a stone near the temple. Grant by Manma Rāja in Ś. 1179 (A.D. 1257).

331. On the same place. Ś. 1173. Mentions the name Vīranārāyaṇa Buddiga Dēvarāja.

332. In the same place. A record dated in Ś. 1358.

333. On a stone in the inner chamber. Records gift by a merchant in Ś. 1165 (A.D. 1243).

Mēḍūru.

334. On a copper plate attached to the dhvajastambha in ancient characters. No details given.

335. In a sheet, on a stone. A record of Ś. 1438 (1516) describing apparently the military operations of Kṛishṇadēva Rāya. See *Gōdāvari Manu.*, pp. 214–5.

Mustābāda.

336. An epigraph dated Ś. 1482 (A.D. 1560) by a Mussalman chief.

Pedda Maddāli.

337. *C.P. No.* 3 *of Mr. Sewell's List.*—An Ẹastern Chāḷukyan grant of Jayasimha (I) in his eighteenth year, at the time of the equinox. The order is issued from the city of Udayapura and records the grant of village near Mardavalli (Pedda madali) in the district of Guḍrahāra (Guḍivāḍa). Edited in *Tamil and Sanskrit Inscriptions*, pp. 166–7. Also *Ind. Antq.*, XIII, 137 f., and *Ibid.*, X, 243, No. 7.

Purushōttamapaṭṇam.

338. On a stone east of the village. Records an act of piety by Śrīman Mahāmaṇḍalīka Bhīmayya in Ś. 1105. *Antiquities*, p. 51.

Tanuku Taluk.

Chēbrōlu.

339. On a fallen stone in the mound Bhāvāyakara gaṭṭu. Records the construction of a tank by a private person in Ś. 1475 (A.D. 1553).

Duvva.

340. On a pillar in the temple. Records in Ś. 1570 (A.D. 1648) the erection of a maṇṭapam by a private party.

Iragāvaram.

341. On a slab fixed east of the temple Garbhālayam. A private grant dated Ś. 1150.

342. An undated private grant in honour of "Pōta Nripa."

343. A private grant dated Ś. 1156 (A.D. 1234).

344. A grant by the minister of Sarvalōkāśraya Vishṇuvardhana Mahārāja in Ś. 1169 (A.D. 1247).

Juttiga.

345. In the local temple. A grant in Ś. 1000 by "the eldest daughter of Veṅgīśvara."

346. Grant by Malli Rāja, son of Vijayāditya, in Ś. 1074.

347. Grant by Vīrappa Naiḍu in Ś. 1111.

348. A private grant in Ś. 1082.

Kaḷachumbarru.

349. A C.P. grant of Amma II, called also Vijayāditya VI. It is undated and records the grant of the village Kaḷachumbarru in the Attiliṅāṇḍu province to a Jain teacher named Arhanandin of the Valahāri-Gaṇa and Aḍḍakali Gachcha for repairing the dining hall of a Jain temple called Sarvalōkāśraya Jīnabhavana. The grant was made at the instance of Chāmekāmbā of the Paṭṭavardhīka lineage, a pupil of Arhanandin. See *Ep. Ind.*, VII, 177—92.]

Kānūru.

350. In the temple of Śōmēśvara. Records in Ś. 1595 (A.D. 1673) the erection of the temple by a private person.

351. In the temple of Vallabhasvāmi. Records in Ś. 1555 (A.D. 1633) the erection of the temple by a private person.

Maṇḍapāka.

352. On a stone east of the Ellaramma temple. Gift to the temple by a private person.

353. A C.P. document by Chāḷukya Bhīma (887—917 A.D.). *Antiquities*, p. 37.

Pandulaparru.

354. On a fallen stone in front of the garbhālayam of the Mallēśvara temple, two inscriptions dated Ś. 1228 (A.D. 1306), recording the erection of two pillars by private persons.

Tanuku.

355. On pillars of the Kēśavasvāmi temple. Mr. Sewell mentions three inscriptions, two of which are dated Ś. 1443, and record private grants and one is an undated and private one.

Vēlpūru.

356. In the temple of Rudrēśvarasvāmi. Records the erection of the temple by a private person in Ś. 1557 (A.D. 1635).

357. In the same place. Records the erection of a pillar by a private person in Ś. 1198.

KURNOOL DISTRICT.

The *Mack. MSS.* are singularly rich in regard to this district. They are in the following books :—

(A) No. 538 (*No.* 27, *C.M.* 996).—Two hundred and twenty-two inscriptions from Kōilkuṇṭḷa and Kaṇḍanavōli [divisions. The Library number is 15-4-30.

(B) No. 540 (*No.* 48, *C.M.* 1017).—Two hundred and five inscriptions in Kaṇḍanavōli and Chittavōli (Sirvel) districts. Transcribed in *Loc. Rec.*, Vol. 20. The Library number is 15-3-8.

(C) No. 546 (*No.* 35, *C.M.* 1004).—Two hundred and eighty-nine inscriptions in Kaṇḍanavōli and Chittaguṇṭa (Chintaguṇṭa) divisions. The Library number of this book is 15-3-6.

(D) No. 579 (*No.* 37, *C.M.* 1006).—Two hundred and sixty-six inscriptions in Kanavōli district. The Library number of this book is 15-3-5.

(E) No. 615 (*No.* 34, *C.M.* 1003).—Hundred and forty inscriptions from Chittavōli taluk (Sirvel taluk). The Library number of this book is 15-4-18. It has been transcribed in *Loc. Rec.*, Vols. 48 and 56, p. 582 f.

I have not examined the originals, but have given references to their summary as given by Taylor in *Ins., Ced. Dts.* How far the summary is accurate and how many of the originals are not included therein are yet to be discovered by a comparison of them, which will take much time. My belief is that the originals contain too many repetitions of the same epigraphs and that the summary as given in *Ins., Ced. Dts.*, is a fairly full one. I have to state that some of the records are not inscriptions in the strict sense of the term but *grants* in paper ; but as in the case of Ganjām, having once made the list, I have thought it better to retain them.

General Copper Plates.

1. *C.P. No.* 95 *of Mr. Sewell's List.*—In the Collector's office, Kurnool. Records grant of certain lands in the villages of Muṇḍakaḷḷu and Palgire to two Brahmans in the first year of the reign of Vikramāditya I of the Western Chaḷukya dynasty (655—80), the conqueror of the Pallavas and the captor of Conjeeveram. See *Mys. Gazr.*, I, p. 323. *Ind. Antq.*, Vol. XI, p. 67 ; *Jour., Bo. As. Soc.*, XVI, p. 238 ; and Kielhorn's *Southern List*, No. 25.

2. *C.P. No.* 97-*A of Mr. Sewell's List.*—In the Collector's office, Kurnool. Records the gift of certain land to one Vīradēvamulu by the village officers of Bijanēmulu, in Ś. 1702 (A.D. 1780), Śārvari. (Bijanēmulu seems to be Bijinavēmula in Kōilkuṇṭḷa taluk.)

3. *C.P. No.* 97-*B of Mr. Sewell's List.*—Records a grant by Kōlukoṇḍa Appanāyuḍu and Rāmanāyaniṁgāru, described as

chiefs of the "Mahā Nāyakas," of lands, to a Brahman in Ś. 1688 (A.D. 1766), Vyaya. (Is Kōlukoṇḍa a mistake for Koilkuṇṭḷa ?)

4. *C.P. No.* 98 *of Mr. Sewell's List.*—In the same office. It professes to be issued by Vikramāditya I (655—80) of the Western Chāḷukyas, bestowing the village of Agundi on a Brahman. It bears no date and is considered to be spurious. *Jour., Bo. As. Soc.*, Vol. XVI, p. 240, and Kielhorn's *Ins., S. Ind.*, No. 22.

5. *C.P. No.* 99 *of Mr. Sewell's List.*—In the same office. Records grant of 15 acres (120 *nivártanas*) of land, at the village of Ratnagiri in the district of Nāḷavāḍi, to a Bráhman by Vikramāditya I (655—80) of the Western Chāḷukyas, in the third year of his reign (C. 658). *Jour., Bo. As. Soc.*, Vol. XVI, p. 235, and Kielhorn's *Southern List*, No. 18.

6. *C.P. No.* 100 *of Mr. Sewell's List.*—In the same office. Records grant of 63¾ acres (510 *nivartanas*) of land in the village of Raṭṭagiri on the west bank of the river Andirika to a Brahman, in the tenth year of the reign of Vikramāditya I of the Western Chāḷukyas, i.e., A.D. 662-63. The grant was made at the request of king Dēvaśakti of the Śendraka family. See *Jour., Bo. As. Soc.*, Vol. XVI, p. 238, and Kielhorn's *Ins., S. Ind.*, No. 19.

7. *C.P. No.* 222 *of Mr. Sewell's List.*—At first in the Collector's office and now in the Museum. Records grant by the Vijayanagar king Achyuta, who, in Ś. 1455 (A.D. 1533), Vijaya, presented to fifty Brahmans, the village of Narasēndrapuram *alias* Kallavāya.

8. *C.P. No.* 223 *of Mr. Sewell's List.*—In the same place. Records that the Vijayanagara king Achyuta granted in Ś. 1461 (A.D. 1539), Vikāri, the village of Upyalapalle (Uppalapalle) in the Kaṇḍukūru country to some Brahmans.

9. *C.P. No.* 224 *of Mr. Sewell's List.*—In the same place. Records that Rāmarāja Tịrumala Rāja, during the reign of Sadāśiva of Vijayanagar, in Ś. 1479 (A.D. 1557), Piṅgaḷa, presented to one Yeṟṟama Nāyuḍu, the seven villages of Gauti (Gooti ?), Yadari (Vedurūru ?), Tāḍparti, Vellatūru, Śiṅganamalai, Yeduchēru and Koṇḍḷakarūru.

10. *C.P. No.* 226 *of Mr. Sewell's List.*—In the same place. Records a grant by the Vijayanagara king Tirumala Rāja (1568—77) to the Vishṇu temple of the village of Guṇḍāla in Ś. 1490 (A.D. 1568), Prabhava. Also the village of Zonnagiri in the Drōṇāchalam Paragaṇa is referred to.

11. *C.P. No.* 227 *of Mr. Sewell's List.*—In the same place. Records that Timmarāja confirmed the grants made by former sovereigns in the village of Peddahuḷiki, north of Gooty, Ś. 1470 (A.D. 1548), Śrīmukha. (The dates do not correspond, nor does the inscription belong to the time of Harihara whom it mentions. Mr. Sewell therefore considers it to be of doubtful authenticity.)

12. *C.P. No.* 228 *of Mr. Sewell's List.*—In the same place. Records that the same Timma Rāja did, in Ś. 1293, or 1296 (A.D. 1371 or 1374), during the reign of Bukkadēva Rāya, confirm the grants of earlier sovereigns in the villages of Gaḍikalu and Molakalapāḍu, in the Puravakoṇḍa country of the district of Gautti (Gooty). (The discrepancies of the inscription throw doubts as to its authenticity.)

12-A. The Kurnool District plates of the eleventh year of the reign of the Western Chaḷukya Vinayāditya Satyāśraya, recording a grant made at the request of the Yuvarāja Vijayāditya and issued from Eḷumpundale. See *Ind. Antq.*, Vol. VI, p. 88, and Kielhorn's *Southern List*, No. 28.

CUMBUM TALUK.

Ākaviḍu.

13. On a stone in the centre of the village. Records that in Prabhava Harihara Rāya Yādava Mahārāya came to this village with his retinue and employed the inhabitants to dig a canal to the tank at Guṇḍlakamma. See *Ins., Ced. Dts.*, p. 146, No. 5.

14. On a stone in a field. Records that Śiṅga Rāju, son of "Duva" Rāju, gave the ruined village of Marlamarakapāḍ to Mylār Mudda, a disciple of Mallikārjuna, in Ś. 1154, Vijaya. *Ibid.*, No. 6. See No. 19 below.

Bādinēpalle.

15. At the south gate of the Rāmasvāmi temple. A private grant dated in Ś. 1477 (A.D. 1555). *Antiquities*, I, p. 97.

Basinēpalle.

16. Near the deserted temple of Ōbalēśvara Svāmi. An epigraph dated Ś. 1423, Durmati, recording a private grant in the reign of Vīra Narasimha Rāya of Vijayanagar (evidently the son of the Tuḷuva usurper Narasa Nāyaka). *Antiquities*, p. 97.

17. On another side of the same stone. An inscription dated in Ś. 1510 (A.D. 1588). *Ibid.*

Bōllupalle.

18. On a stone in the village. Records that Jaṅgamalli, son of Vamula Kandaśeṭṭi, dug a well in Ś. 1470, Plavaṅga, on the way to the local forest. *Ins., Ced. Dts.*, p. 146, No. 4.

Chinagānipalle.

19. On a stone in the road. Records that "Katamali Naidu" and Kuṅkuma Nāyaḍu gave some land in Ś. 1157, Manmatha, to Mylār Mudda, disciple of Mallikārjuna. *Ibid.*, p. 146, No. 7. See No. 14 above for the same individual.

Cumbum.

20. 1 *of* 1908.—(Telugu verse.) On a stone lying on the bund of the tank. Records a brief history of the tank which was built by Gōpaṇa-Oḍiyalu (Gōpaṇa Uḍaiyār?).

21. 2 *of* 1908.—(Telugu.) On a stone in the choultry in the same village. A damaged record in the middle. Mentions Udayagiri-rājya.

22. 3 *of* 1908.—(Telugu.) On a slab in the same choultry. Records an agreement among merchants to contribute for the requirements of the Vīrabhadra temple at Mattipeṇṭa. Mentions Panimayyaṅgāru, son of the Mahāmaṇḍalēśvara-antyembaragaṇḍa Vallabhayyadēva-Mahārāju.

Dadivāḍa.

23. In a deserted Vishṇu temple in the village. Records a grant by Kākatīya Pratāpa Rudradēva II in Ś. 1234 (A.D. 1312). *Antiquities,* Vol. I, p. 97.

24. In the same place. A record in Ś. 1353 (A.D. 1431), of the erection of an image of Hanumān by "Urumaya Vīra Mahārāja." *Ibid.*

Giḍḍalūru (Griḍḍalūru).

25. In the temple of Pātāḷa Nāgēśvarasvāmi. An undated record of a private grant to the temple. *Antiquities,* Vol. I, p. 97.

26. On a stone situated in Pātāḷa Nāgēśvara pagoda. Records that "Rangasi" Veṅkaṭa Ramaṇa, etc., inhabitants of Giḍḍalūru, granted one *tūm* of dry field in the village for the divine service of God Pātāḷa Nāgēśvara, in Plava. *Ins., Ced. Dts.,* p. 145, No. 1.

Guḍimeṭṭa.

27. East of the dhvajastambha of the deserted temple of Chennakēśava. A record of a private grant in Ś. 1356 (A.D. 1434). *Ibid.*

Iḍamakaḷḷu.

28. Near a Vishṇu temple. Records a grant by "Chinna Avubalayya Rāja" in Ś. 1466 (A.D. 1544). *Ibid.* [The chief was evidently the Nandyāla chief of that name, who was the ruler of Uḍayagiri.]

Komarōlu.

29. On a stone in the hamlet of Hanumantarāyinipalle, near a deserted temple of Āñjanēya. An undated record of a grant of lands to the temple by a private person. *Ibid.*

30. Under the bund of a tank in the village. Records a charity by Reḍḍicharḷa Chinna Basava Rāja in Ś. 1511 (A.D. 1589). *Ibid.* See No. 40 below.

Kommanūru.

31. On a stone in a field in the village. Records a grant by "Pāṇḍarugaṅgu Bhūpati Rāja" to a poet in Ś. 1162 (A.D. 1240). *Antiquities*, Vol. I, pp. 97-98.

32. On a stone close to a wall east of the village. Records the sinking of a well in Ś. 1643 (A.D. 1721). *Ibid.*

Kishtamśeṭṭipaḷḷi.

33. On a stone near a weḷl, a mile west of the village. Records the construction of a tank by a private person in Ś. 1644. *Ibid.*

Muṇḍlapāḍu.

34. In a deserted temple of Bhairava. An illegible record, dated in Ś. 1042 (A.D. 1120).

35. In the same place. An undated and unintelligible record.

Poḍilekoṇḍapaḷḷi.

36. Near a well south of the village on the road to Rājapāḷem. An undated record of a private grant. *Ibid.*

37. In the same place. Records a private grant, dated Ś. 1500 (A.D. 1578). *Ibid.*

Pōtavaram.

38. West of a tank in the village. Records a private grant in Ś. 1472 (A.D. 1550). *Ibid.*

Rācharla.

39. Near a deserted temple of Bhīmēśvara. A record of Ś. 1310. *Ibid.*

Reḍḍicharla.

40. In the temple of Ballamarāya. Records that in Ś. 1509, Ahōbalarāja, son of Rājapparāja, and Chinna Basavarāja, son of Śūrama Rāja, made a grant. *Ibid.*, p. 99. See No. 30 above.

41. Close to the above. An undated and private. *Ibid.*

Salakalaviḍu.

42. In a pillar of the Āñjanēya temple. Records that it was erected in Ś. 1340, by a private person. *Ibid.*

Śūravaripalli (Śūravarampalle).

43. In the hamlet of Boddavānipalle, on a stone. A private grant in Ś. 1499. *Ibid.*

Tāṭicherla.

44. In the deserted temple of Śaṅkara Bhairava and Rāmēśvara. A record of Śrīraṅgarāja Bhūpāla, elder brother of Kṛishṇadēvarāya, said to be dated in Ś. 1102. (Evidently a mistake.) *Antiquities*, Vol. I, p. 99.

Turimella (Turumilla).

45. In the temple of Surabhēśvaramma. A record in Ś. 1462, recording a grant in the reign of Achyutarāya of Vijayanagar. *Ibid.*

Uyyālavāḍa.

46. In a stone in the hamlet of Jamullapalle, south-west of the village. Records a grant by Vīra Dēvarāya (I) in Ś. 1307. *Ibid.*

DHONE TALUK.

Guṇḍāla.

47. *C.P. No. 225 of Mr. Sewell's C.P. List.*—Records a grant by the Vijayanagara king Tirumala Rāja (the founder of the Chandragiri dynasty, 1568—77) of some lands in the village during a solar eclipse, to a Brahman in Ś. 1490, Prabhava.

48. 137 *of* 1913.—(Telugu.) On a slab set up near the entrance into the Chennakēśavasvāmin temple. Records in Ś. 1490, Prabhava, Vaiśākha, śu. di. 10, that the Mahāmaṇḍalēśvara Rāmarāja Tirumalarājadēva Mahārāja, granted the two villages of Pedavēpaḍinne in the district of Drōṇāchala and Jonnagiri in the district of Gutti, to the god Channarāyalu of Guṇḍāla durga, for worship and festivals. "Dates not enough for calculation." The donor was Tirumala I of the last Vijayanagar dynasty. See the above epigraph.

49. 138 *of* 1913.—(Telugu.) On a slab set up in a field in the same village. A damaged record of the Vijayanagara king Vīrapratāpa Sadāśivadēva-Mahārāya, dated Ś. 1491, Śukla, Chaitra, śu. di. 10. Registers that Doḍḷa Veṅkaṭanāyaniṅgāru having died, his son appointed an agent to supervise the Doḍḷa charities, viz., the construction of the prākāra wall, pavilions, flower-gardens, ponds and other works, in the temple of Chennakēśava-Perumāḷ at Guṇḍāḷa in Dhōṇiśīma, and gave him some land in Tīḍūru with the consent of the Reḍḍi, Karaṇam and the Talāri of that village. "Date can be calculated, but not verified."

Pyāpali.

50. 136 *of* 1913.—On a slab set up in the Basavēśvara temple. A damaged record, dated in Ś. 1667, Raktākshi, Māgha, śu. di. 5

mentioning a certain Veṅkaṭapatināyaniṅgāru. Details of date not enough for calculation.

KŌILKUNTLA TALUK.

Akumalla.

51. On a stone in a pial. Records the grant of the village by Chinna Timmarāja to Brahmans in Ś. 1466, Krōdhi, in the reign of Sadāśivarāya. *Ins., Ced. Dts.*, p. 147, No. 3. See Cg. 717 for details about China Timma.

52. On a stone in front of the Chennakēśava temple. Records that the same chief gave two *kaṇḍrikas* of land to God Lakshmi-nārāyaṇa in Ś. 1475, Pramādi. *Ibid.*, No. 4.

53. A record to the effect that the wife of Madirani (?) Bhyraṇṇa ascended the funeral pile with her husband in Ś. 1329, Sarvajit. *Ibid.*, No. 5.

54. A C.P. in the hands of the local Brahmans. Records that Kṛishṇadēvarāya granted the village of Suṅgapaṭṇam in the district of Gutti, in Ś. 1430, Prabhava, to Nāgabhaṭṭa, son of Mādhavabhaṭṭa. *Ibid.*, No. 6.

55. On a stone in the village. Records that Āravīti Chinna Timmayyadēva made a grant of the village to learned Brahmans in Ś. 1466, Krōdhi, in the reign of Sadāśivarāya. *Ibid.*, No. 7.

56. On a stone near the Pāpavināśēśvara temple. Records that Vīra Bukkarāya gave the village of Viñjanampāḍu to one Papavēna (Pāpavināśa?) Sōmaḍēva in Ś. 1274, Paritāpi. The village is said to be in Vinukoṇḍa district. *Ibid.*, No. 9.

57. On a stone in the same place. Records that Nāgappa, son of Paṇḍari Kāmabhaṭṭu, granted Pōtāvaram in the district of "Yarusa," to God Pāpavināśēśvara in Ś. 1462, Śārvari, in the reign of Achyutarāya. *Ibid.*, No. 10.

58. On a stone in the same place. Records that Chikka Uḍaiyār, the minister of Vīra Bukkarāya (I), granted the village of Chaṅgalavāḍa in the same district to the same deity in Ś. 1274, Paritāpi. *Ibid.*, p. 148, No. 11. [In Ap. 144 and 145 Chikka Uḍaiyār has been identified with Bukka I himself.]

Allūru.

59. On a stone in the town gate. Records that Nandyāla Chinna Aubaladēva remitted the tax on local barbers in Ś. 1469, in the reign of Sadāśivarāya. *Ibid.*, p. 452, No. 23. Chinna Avubaḷa has been elsewhere called ruler of Chandragiri.

60. A damaged record dated Ś. 1315, Āṅgirasa, recording a grant by Kumarēśa Liṅgappa in the reign of Kṛishṇadēvarāya. *Ibid.*, No. 24.

Āluvakoṇḍa (Alavakoṇḍa).

61. In front of the Vīrabhadra temple. Records grant by a local chief in Ś. 1466, in the reign of Sadāśivarāya of Vijayanagar. *Antiquities*, p. 99.

62. In the same place a private grant in Ś. 1454. *Ibid.*

Annāvaram.

63. On a stone in the village. Records that Chinna Timmayyadēva gave the village in Ś. 1466, Krōdhi, to poet Anantarāja, in the reign of Sadāśivarāya. *Ins., Ced. Dts.*, p. 155, No. 48. [Was Anantarāja identical with Maṭla Ananta? See Cg. 762.]

Bhimunipāḍu.

64. On a stone in front of the Hanumanta temple. Records that a Reḍḍi erected a stone hall in Śubhakrit. *Ibid.*, p. 151, No. 18.

65. On a stone in front of the same. Records that Sadāśivarāya exempted God Gōpālakṛishṇa from tax in Ś. 1476, Ānanda. *Ibid.*, No. 19.

66. On a stone in front of the same. Records that Nandyāla Ahōbalayya granted the village to some learned Brahmans in Ś. 1469, Plavaṅga, in the reign of Sadāśivarāya. *Ibid.*, No. 20 and No. 59 above.

Bōdimannūru (Bondamanore).

67. On a stone in the Chennakēśava pagoda. Records that Āravīṭi Chinna Timmayyadēva granted twelve puṭṭis of land in Tirumalapuram village to its learned Brahmans, in Ś. 1466, Krōdhi, in the reign of Sadāśivarāya. [*Ibid.*, p. 152, No. 25. Chinna Timma was the brother of Viṭṭhala, the conqueror of the Tiruvāḍi Rājya, the Governor of Trichinopoly and the patron of Dōsūri Kōnērukavi, the author of the *Bālabhāgavatamu*.]

68. On a stone at the gate of the village. Records the exemption of the tax on the *vrittis* of Karaṇams by the same chief in Makam? *Ibid.*, No. 26.

69. A record of Tirumaladēva, exempting the taxes on jugglers and barbers in Ś. 1418, Kaḷayukti, in the reign of Sadāśivarāya. *Ibid.*, No. 27. The date is inconsistent.

70. A damaged grant of Aravīṭi Chinna Timmayyadēva Mahārāja in Ś. 1472, Sādhāraṇa, in the reign of Sadāśivarāya. *Ibid.*, p. 153, No. 28. See No. 67 above.

71. A record of the same chief in Ś. 1476, Ānanda, granting one puṭṭi of land in Guḍḍalūrpāḍu to Ahōbalayya. *Ibid.*, No. 29.

72. A damaged grant of Tippayyadēva, dated Ś. 1439, Īśvara, in the reign of Kṛishṇadēvarāya. *Ibid.*, No. 30.

73. A damaged grant of Kṛishṇadēvarāya, dated Ś. 1435, Yuva. *Ins., Ced. Dts.;* p. 153, No. 31.

Chintakuṇṭa.

74. On a stone in Viṭṭhalēśvara pagoda. Records that Naraśiṅgarāja gave the village to Pāṇḍuraṅga Viṭṭhalēśvara Perumāḷ in Ś. 1493, Prajōtpatti, in the reign of Tirumaladēva Mahārāya (of the Penukoṇḍa-Chandragiri dynasty). *Ibid.*, p. 150, No. 8.

Hanumantaguṇḍam.

75. In the local Raghunātha temple. Grant of land for the Gōd by Jillēla Raṅgapati Rāya in Ś. 1550, Kīlaka. *Ibid.*, p. 154, No. 38. See Cd. 168.

76. In the Vīrabhadra pagoda. A record of Bukkarāju Timmayya granting the Mittalappāḍu village to the deity in Ś. 1433, Prajōtpatti. *Ibid.*, No. 39. [Was Timmayya the chief of that name who was the grandson of Āravīṭi Bukka ?]

77. In charge of "Carnasamullubhutt" in the village. Records that one Narasakēśava gave the village of Nāgareḍḍippaḷḷi to Kṛishṇasvāmijilu for a śrōtriyam rent of 80 pagodas in Bhava. *Ibid.*, p. 179, No. 116.

78. With the same person. A record in Śrīmuka, reducing the above rent, by Raṅga-Raghunāth to 70 pagodas. *Ibid.*, No. 117.

79. With the same person. A grant to the Reḍḍis and Karaṇams to continue the village cultivation. *Ibid.*, No. 118.

80. A Telugu record granting a licence to the farmers to cultivate some lands in the neighbourhood by Śrīnivāsa Timmarasa. *Ibid.*, p. 180, No. 119.

81. A grant of Nawab Saheb in H. 1195, to the Reḍḍis and Karaṇams of Nāgareḍḍippaḷḷi in the subdivision of Jammalamuḍugu. *Ibid.*, No. 120.

82. A record of Mādhavamānōji Śrīrāya Prakāśarāo, Zamindar, dated F. 1195, ordering the Reḍḍis to continue the cultivation as usual. *Ibid.*, No. 121.

83. An order of Kṛishṇareḍḍi to another Reḍḍi to pay 10 pagodas to Umāmahēśvara Śastri. *Ibid.*, p. 181, No. 122.

84. A record of Toglak Nawab "Naknamkhan" in F. 1172, Virōdhikrit, giving two *tūms* of land to Kṛishṇa Śastrulu. *Ibid.*, No. 123.

85. A record of Hazarat "Lavari," asking the Reḍḍis and Karaṇams to continue the śrōtriyam tenure of Kṛishṇa Sōmayājulu. *Ibid.*, No. 124.

86. A record of Hariyappa Reḍḍi and Kṛishṇama Reḍḍi of Hanumatguṇṭa-Samastānam, ordering payment of 10 pagodas to

an individual for his salary in Krōdhi. The order is addressed to Kṛishṇasōmayājulu. *Ins., Ced. Dts.*, p. 180, No. 125.

87. An order of the same chief to continue the village of Vinuturāla to one Tursalanāyaḍu. *Ibid.*, No. 126.

88. A record of the same chief, ordering a payment of three *tūms* of land in Banutūrla to an individual in Pramādhi. *Ibid.*, No. 127.

89. A record of Nawab Bahadur in H. 1190, granting a cowl to Kṛishṇamareḍḍi for Hanumatguṇḍam, Narasapuram and another village for Rs. 24,000. *Ibid.*, p. 183, No. 128.

90. Records that Hariyappareḍḍi gave some land in the village of Hanumatguṇḍam in Ś. 1583, Plava, to Śiṅgarāchārya. *Ibid.*, No. 129.

91. Records that Hariyappa Reḍḍi Gōpālayya gave some land in Eṛṛagūḍam and Vanutūrla in Ś. 1635, Viḷambi, to Bukkapaṭṇam Narasimma Tātāchārya. *Ibid.*, No. 130.

92. In charge of Veṅkaṭarāo. Records that Hariyappa Reḍḍi Kṛishṇa Reḍḍi gave some lands in " Cocuṇṭi " and " Condore ", in Ś. 1649, Plavaṅga, to " Yāgonu " Ayyappa. *Ibid.*, No. 131.

Dornipāḍu (Donnepāḍu).

93. In the local fort. A private grant in Ś. 1460, in the reign of Achyuta Rāya. *Antiquities*, p. 99.

94. In a maṇṭapam near the above. A record dated in Ś. 1489 " in the reign of Narasimhadēva", probably a local chieftain. [In commenting on this Mr. Sewell says that the then ruler was Achyuta Rāya. As a matter of fact it was Sadāśiva Rāya.]

95. Near a wall. Records that in Ś. 1121 a private person constructed it. *Ibid.*, p. 100.

Guḷḷadurti.

96. In the Āñjanēya temple. An undated epigraph, recording the erection of the temple by a private person. *Antiquities*, p. 100.

97. In the shrine of Aṅkālamma. Records a grant by Timma Rājadēva in Ś. 1500 (A.D. 1578) in the reign of Sadāśivarāya. *Ibid.* [The inscription is perhaps the last in Sadāśiva's reign. Tirumala usurped the throne shortly after.]

Injēḍu.

98. West of the village in the Vishṇu temple. A grant in Ś. 1455. *Ibid.*

99. In the same place. A private record of a gift in Ś. 1461.

100. A record of Ś. 1480, in the reign of Sadāśivarāya. *Ibid.*

101. A record of Ś. 1476, in the same reign. *Ibid.*

Kampamalla (Cupmullo).

102. On a stone in the Īśvara pagoda. Records that Erramaśeṭṭi erected the temple in Ś. 1726, Rudhirōdgāri. *Ins., Ced. Dts.*, p. 152, No. 22.

Kōilkuṇṭla.

103. On a stone in the place. Records that Siddarāmappanāyaḍu gave some land in the village to Rāmēśvarasvāmi in Ś. 1505, Chitrabhānu, in the reign of Śrī-Vīra-Raṅgarāya (1578—86). *Ibid.*, p. 150, No. 7.

104. On a stone in front of the temple. Records that Veṅkaṭādri Mahārāja (afterwards Veṅkaṭa I ?) granted the taxes of different villages to Viṭṭhalēśvara of Kōilkuṇṭla in Ś. 1509, Tāraṇa, in the reign of Vīra-Raṅga-Rāya (1578—86). *Ibid.*, No. 9.

105. On a stone in the Pāṇḍuraṅga-Viṭṭhalēśvāra temple. A damaged grant of Nandyāla Naraśiṅgarāya in Ś. 1495. *Ibid.*, No. 10. [This chief was evidently the father of Krishṇarāja to whom Pingali Sūraṇa dedicated his *Kaḷāpūrṇōdayamu*.]

106. On a stone in front of the Aṅkālamma Goddess. Records that Nandyāla Ahōbalarāya gave the duties of the district in Ś. 1465, Śōbhakrit, to the Goddess. *Ibid.*, No. 11.

107. On a stone in front of the Āñjanēya pagoda. Records that "Bolanamantri Parvadayya" granted the taxes of the Vipravinōdins in the village to God Pāṇḍuraṅga Viṭṭhala in Ś. 1476, Ānanda, in the reign of Sadāśivarāya. *Ibid.*, No. 12.

108. Records that Nāgappa Reḍḍi gave some grant to God Siddhēśvara in Ś. 1450, Sarvadhāri, in the reign of Krishṇadēvarāya. Damaged. *Ibid.*, No. 13.

109. On a stone near the Gōpāladēva pagoda. Records that one Tirumalappa gave some land in Kaspa Kōilkuṇṭla to Gōpāladēva in Ś. 1509, Sarvajit, in the reign of Śrī-Vīra-Veṅkaṭapati Rāya (i.e., Veṅkaṭa I, 1586—1616). *Ibid.*, No. 14.

110. On a stone near the Chennakēśava pagoda. Records that Gobbūri-Koṇḍarāja gave some land for a reservoir of water for cattle in Ś. 1473, Ānanda, in the reign of Sadāśivarāya. *Ibid.*, p. 151, No. 15.

111. On a stone in the village. Records that Pōlusāni dug a well in the village of "Sowdaridinne" in Ś. 1525, Śubhakrit, in the reign of Vīra-Veṅkaṭapatirāya (i.e., Veṅkaṭa I, 1586—1614). *Ibid.*, No. 16.

112. In the Gaṇapti "Tsāvaḍi." A record dated in Ś. 1565, mentioning Śrī Raṅga Rāya (VI) of Vijayanagar (1638—46). *Antiquities*, I, 100.

113. A record of Mahommed Wali in 113, Sun, ordering the Reḍḍis and Karaṇams of Kōilkuṇṭla to allow to an individual ½ *kāśu* per head-load and Re. 1 per each bag. *Ins., Ced. Dts.*, p. 157, No. 52.

114. Records that Mahommed Khan "Badadaja" gave in F. 1171, an order to Padsha Saheb to continue certain allowances to Gōvindappa-Veṅkaṭapati Mustajir of Kōilkuṇṭḷa. *Ibid.*, No. 53.

115. The same chief orders Nāgaśeṭṭi, the contractor of the custom house, to allow Fakir "Gafur Shah" a paṇam per each bag in F. 1171. *Ibid.*, No. 54.

116. Bāburāo orders the Reḍḍis and Karaṇams to continue the allowances to one Khādar Shah of Liṅgāla in F. 1171. *Ibid.*, No. 55.

117. Bāburāo (Amil) orders the grant of two *tūms* to the same person in F. 1171. *Ibid.*, p. 158, No. 56.

118. A record of Abdul Mahommed allowing Khadar Shah to get from the Tānedārs, Reḍḍis and Karaṇams of Rāvanūr, Dudyāla and five other villages one *kāśu* per each bag of grain, etc. *Ibid.*, No. 57.

119. An order of Mahommed Wali to the contractor of the duties at Kōilkuṇṭḷa to allow one *kāśu* per each bag and ½ *kāśu* per each head-load to Fakir Khādar in F. 1173. *Ibid.*, No. 58.

120. Records that the Reḍḍis and Karaṇams of Kōilkuṇṭḷa granted two *tūms* in the capital of Cuddapah in Ś. 1683, Vishu, to the same Fakir. *Ibid.*, p. 159, No. 59.

121. A gift by the same donors of some land to build a mosque. *Ibid.*, No. 60.

122. A record of Alumghir in 35 Z. ordering the Dēśmuks and Dēśa-Pāṇḍyas to give four *tūms* of land in Rāvanore to Abu Mahomed Hāji. *Ibid.*, No. 61.

123. Records that Mahommed Fariki ordered the Dēśmuks and Dēśa-Pāṇḍyas in 47 Z. to give to Sayud Ali, two *tūms* of land in Kōilkuṇṭḷa and allowance of ½ *rukah (kāśu)* and ¼ seer of oil daily. *Ibid.*, No. 62.

124. Records that Zasi Khan ordered the Dēśmuks, etc., to grant to "Enayadd" Fakir five *tūms* of land in Kanugaṭḷa in H. 1196. *Ibid.*, p. 160, No. 63.

125. A similar order of Nawab Asud Khan in favour of Sayud Dervish in 40 Z. *Ibid.*, No. 64.

126. A record of Alumghir Abdul Agim in F. 1163, granting 3½ *tūms* of land to "Shahawasaruff Pirjada" in F. 1163. *Ibid.*, No. 65.

127. An order of Mahommed Hussain Khan in F. 1217, to continue the above gift. *Ibid.*, No. 66.

128. An order of the same chief to continue the same in F. 1197. *Ibid.*, No. 67.

129. Records that "Sahebga" Mahommed ordered in F. 1174. the customs agent Veṅkaṭarāo to allow some rights in a village to an astronomer named Sītārāma. *Ibid.*, No. 68.

130. An order of " Amanud Khan Mahommed Jai " in H. 1184 to pay Rs. 8 daily to the same donee as in the above. *Ins., Ced. Dts.*, p. 160, No. 69.

131. An order of Asim Khan to Mahommed Ali to allow daily eight pieces to Sītārām Jōsyalu in F. 1187. *Ibid.*, p. 162, No. 70.

132. An order of " Mīr Rāja Ali Khan " in H. 1179, to Siddāji Murēśwar to allow daily half gold paṇam from the duties of Kōilkuṇṭḷa to Sītārāma Jōsya. *Ibid.*, No. 71.

133. An order of the same chief to the same effect in H. 1193, to " Sobāji ", Mustaghir of Dinnipāḍu. *Ibid.*, No. 72.

134. A record of Nawab Mir Kumaruḍīn Khan in H. 1198, ordering Hassan Mahommed to allow half gold paṇam daily to Rāmajōsya. *Ibid.*, p. 163, No. 73.

135. A similar order in H. 1198 to Badamalla Rāju. *Ibid.*, No. 74.

136. A record of Nawab Muzaffar Mulk or " Asaulli Khan " to the Amīl of Kōilkuṇṭla to allow eight pieces daily to Sītārām Jōsya. *Ibid.*, No. 75.

137. A record of Muzaffar Mulk ordering Gōpālarāo to do the same to Rāmajōsyalu in H. 1206. *Ibid.*, No. 76.

138. A record of " Chunoolall " ordering Gōvindarāo to allow Rāmajōsyalu to get one paṇam from duties at Kōilkuṇṭḷa, in H. 1210. *Ibid.*, p. 164, No. 77.

139. A similar order in the same date. *Ibid.*, No. 78.

140. An order of Alumghir Pādsha's agent Kutub Khan to the Amīl to give four *tūms*, half seer of oil, etc., to Hāji Mahommed, etc., in H. 1114. *Ibid.*, No. 79.

141. A record of Nandyāla Rāghavadēva Mahārāja in Tāraṇa, ordering Kṛishṇamarāju to continue the above. *Ibid.*, p. 165, No. 80.

142. Records that " Jahāgur Padusha " Amin Khan issued an order to Amil to grant four *tūms* of land and half seer of oil in the village of Vajerabad to " Sakeabeer " in 1159, Sun. *Ibid.*, No. 81.

143. Records that Abdul Azim Khan issued a precept to Piṅgaḷa Reḍḍis and Karaṇams to pay the arrears of three years to Sītārām Jōsyalu, in H. 1167. *Ibid.*, No. 82.

144. An order by the same chief to the Reḍḍis and Karaṇams of Chintaguṇṭa to continue the above as customary to Sītārām Jōsyalu, in F. 1168. *Ibid.*, No. 83.

145. An order by Abdul Azim Khan to the Reḍḍis and Karaṇams of Dinnipāḍu to continue two puṭṭies to Sītārām Jōsyalu, in F. 1168. *Ibid.*, p. 166, No. 84.

146. An order by Abdul Azim Khan to Gulam Hassan to allow eight pieces daily to Sītārām Jōsyalu, in F. 1186. *Ins., Ced. Dts.*, p. 166, No. 85.

147. An order by Mahommed Ali to "Mukkumulla Chalm" to continue the customary gifts of Sītārām in H. 1191. *Ibid.*, No. 86.

148. An order by the same chief to the same person to allow eight pieces daily to Sītārām Jōsyalu from the duties of capital, in H. 1191. *Ibid.*, No. 87.

149. Records that Sivāji "Aloharaswar, Amil of Kōilkuṇṭḷa," issued an order to the Reḍḍis and Karaṇams of Kōilkuṇṭḷa, to continue the mānyam lands of Sītārām Jōsyalu, in F. 1189. *Ibid.*, No. 88.

150. Records that Mahommed Rasul issued an order to the Reḍḍis and Karaṇams of the same place to continue the same, in H. 1197. *Ibid.*, No. 89.

151. Records that Subbarāo, Amil of Kōilkuṇṭḷa, issued an order to the Reḍḍis and Karaṇams of Kōilkuṇṭḷa to continue the lands in four villages, in F. 1183. *Ibid.*, No. 90.

152. Records that Nawab Hanumantarāo of Koilkuṇṭḷa issued an order to the Reḍḍis and Karaṇams of Kōilkuṇṭḷa in F. 1190. *Ibid.*, p. 168, No. 91.

153. Records that Abdul "Shukow" issued an order to "Lulip Khan" to continue ten *tūms* of land (five in Sadara Dinne and five in Amadāla villages) to Chennakēśvara in H. 1088. *Ibid.*, No. 92.

154. Records that Durgam Tumnaji Pantulu, Tānedār of Kōilkuṇṭḷa, issued an order to "Alodamala Gōpāl, Havaldar", to grant five *tūms* of land in the village of Kōilkuṇṭḷa to Muttina Pāṇḍudēva. *Ibid.*, No. 93.

155. Records that the Reḍḍis and Karaṇams of Mudavāla granted five *tūms* of land in the village of Amaḍāla to Chinna Basavayya. *Ibid.*, No. 94.

156. Records that "Asevadha" Nāraṇappa, Amīl of Kōilkuṇṭḷa, issued an order to the Reḍḍis and Karaṇams of Sadurdinne to continue the above to a Jaṅgam priest in F. 1172. *Ibid.*, No. 95.

157. Records that Nawab Azim Khan issued an order to the Amil to grant five *tūms* in Sadurdinne to Basavayya in H. 1176. *Ibid.*, p. 169, No. 96.

158. Records that Mallikārjuna Appanāyaka issued an order to the Reḍḍis and Karaṇams of Bijenamala to grant six *tūms* of land in the village to Muttinadēva. *Ibid.*, No. 97.

159. Records that Nandyāla Kṛishṇamarāju Dēva Mahārājulu granted six *tūms* of wet field and fifteen *tūms* of dry field and two mustas of gardeṇ land in the subdivision of Tummayanipeṭṭa and allowed one pagoda from the duties to Toliparti Tipparāju in

Ś. 1658, Naḷa. *Ins., Ced. Dts.*, p. 169, No. 98. Kṛishṇamarāju must be a later chief of the line.

160. An order by Nandyāla Kṛishṇamadēva Mahārājulu to the Reḍḍis and Karaṇams of Tanparti, Bāginapēṭṭa, etc., to grant two *tūms* of wet field and ten *tūms* of dry field. *Ibid.*, p. 170, No. 99. See the above epigraph.

161. An order by the same chief to the Reḍḍis and Karaṇams of Timmanāyaḍupēṭṭa to sow the land for the Karaṇam and act agreeably to his directions. *Ibid.*, No. 100.

162. An order by the same chief to the merchants of Timmanāyaḍupēṭṭa to follow the directions of the Karaṇam. *Ibid.*, p. 171, No. 101.

163. An order by the same chief to the Reḍḍis and Karaṇams of the subdivision of the Pēṭṭa to continue the cultivation of the lands of the Pēṭṭa. *Ibid.*, No. 102.

164. Records that the inhabitants of Timmanāyaḍupēṭṭa granted in Ś. 1652, Sādhāraṇa, one *tūm* wet field in Anantapuram, allowed three *paṇams* for the lamp, in Kārttikai month, and ten seers of rice and two and a half seers of dall for the offering and four pieces on every Monday. *Ibid.*, No. 103.

165. Records that the Reḍḍis and Karaṇams of the subdivision of Timmanāyaḍupēṭṭa granted in Ś. 1658, Piṅgaḷa, two *tūms* of dry land, one and two *puṭṭis* and ten *tūms* of garden fields in Timmanāyaḍupēṭṭa ; two pagodas in cash, two *tūms* of wet land, two *puṭṭis*, ten *tūms* of garden field, and three *tūms* of dry field in Bayana Talipurti besides other grants at Uppalūr, Ittikālapaḷḷe in Kanakādripuram, in Chinn ālayapaḷḷe, Mādantapuram, etc. *Ibid.*, pp. 172–73, No. 104.

166. Records that Fyz Mahommed Khan issued an order in F. 1161, to the Reḍḍis and Karaṇams of "Calcutta" (Kalugoṭla ?) to continue the gift of some lands to Shummukha (Shaṇmukha) Śastrilu. *Ibid.*, p. 173, No. 105.

167. An order by the same chief in F. 1161, to the Reḍḍis and Karaṇams of "Jolada Rase" to continue the above gift to the same person. *Ibid.*, No. 106.

168. An order by the same chief in F. 1161, to the Reḍḍis and Karaṇams of Gōvindadinne to continue the gift of land of Shummukha (Shaṇmukha ?) Sāstrilu for the last two years. *Ibid.*, p. 174, No. 107.

169. An order by the same chief in the same year to the Reḍḍis and Karaṇams of Chinna Pāperla, Liṅgāla, Guṇḍipāpala, Kalugoṭla, etc., to continue the mānyams of the same person in his village. *Ibid.*, No. 108.

170. An order in F. 1161, by Nawab Ahmad Khan to the Reḍḍis and Karaṇams of Liṅgāla, Gōvindadinne, Chinna Pāparla,

Guṇḍipāpala, Kalugoṭla and Gobbinūtuḷa to continue the above gift. *Ins., Ced. Dts.*, p. 173, No. 109.

171. An order of Fyz Mahommed Khan to the Karaṇam of Kaluguṭla to continue the above gift. *Ibid.*, p. 175, No. 110.

172. An order by the same chief in F. 1161, to Pōtareḍḍi of Jaladarasi to continue the mānyam of the above gift. *Ibid.*, No. 111.

173. An order by Syud Yusuf Subēdhar, in Kīlaka, to the Reḍḍis and Karaṇams of Uppalapuram, to continue the gift. *Ibid.*, p. 176, No. 112.

174. An order by the same chief in Plavaṅga, to the Reḍḍis and Karaṇams of the same village to continue the customary gift. *Ibid.*, No. 113.

175. An order by "Khyr Mahommed Amil" of Kōilkuṇṭḷa to continue the *Bhaṭṭa-vritti* mānyams of Shaṇmukha Śāstrilu in five villages of Kaluguṭḷa. *Ibid.*, No. 114.

176. An order of Tippu Sultan to Chennayya of Hanumuntguṇḍam to restore the Karaṇamship of Pāpayya and Pārayyā in Peddavanatūrla. *Ibid.*, No. 115.

Kolimiguṇḍla.

177. On a stone in the Hanumanta pagoda. Records that Chinna Timmayya granted the village as a *śrōtriyam* to learned people in Ś. 1466, Krōdhi, in the reign of Vīra-Sadāśivarāya. See *Ins., Ced. Dts.*, p. 155, No. 42, and *Antiquities*, I, p. 100. For Chinna Timmayya see No. 67 above.

178. On a stone at the gate of the village. Records that a Reḍḍi built a well in Ś. 1630, Sarvadhāri. *Ibid.*, p. 105, No. 43.

179. On a stone west of the village. Records that Chōḷarāja erected the local Īśvara temple and granted some land in Nandana, Chāḷukya Vikrama (actual date is not given), in the reign of Trailōkyamallarāja at Kalyāṇi. *Ibid.*, No. 44. [Two sovereigns of the Kalyāṇa-Chāḷukyan line had the title of Trailōkyamalla, viz., Sōmēśvara I (1042—68) and Nūrmaḍi Taila III (1150—82). As the C.V. era is mentioned, the latter is evidently intended.]

Koṇḍapuram.

180. In the eastern Tsāvaḍi. Dated Ś. 1703. A private charity. *Antiquities*, p. 100.

181. Place? A private grant in Ś. 1614. *Ibid.*

Nichenameṭḷa (Nichanametla).

182. Near the temple east of the village. Records a grant in Ś. 1470, in the reign of Sadāśiva of Vijayanagar. *Antiquities*, p. 100.

Owk (Avuku or Auku).

This was the seat of a powerful line of chiefs in the mediæval period. Mr. Sewell gives the following definite inscription in the place.

183. In the local temple. A private grant in Ś. 1629.

Peddavenuturla.

184. On a stone near a local water cistern. Records that Ahōbalarāya repaired the cistern for cattle and gave two *tūms* of land for that use in Ś. 1328, Vyaya, in the reign of Vīra-Bukkarāya (II). See *Ins., Ced. Dts.*, p. 154, No. 34.

Perusōmula.

185. On a stone in the Vishṇu temple. Records in Ś. 1249, execution of certain works by a private person. *Antiquities*, p. 101.

186. On a stone west of the village. Records that Vīra-Araśu . . . (?) erected the pagoda of Vīrabhadra and granted land in Ś. 991, Viśvāvasu, in the reign of Trailōkyamalla. See *Ins., Ced. Dts.*, p. 149, No. 2. See No. 179 above.

187. In charge of one Śiṅgarācharya. Records the grant of a cowl to two men (Pedda and Chinna Veṅkaṭa) for the local Karaṇamship in Yuva. *Ibid.*, p. 184, No. 132.

Savudaradinne.

188. In front of the Janārdanasvāmi temple. Records execution of some works by a private person in Ś. 1525, in the reign of Veṅkaṭa I (1586—1614). *Antiquities*, p. 101.

189. Grant of a local chief in Ś. 1477. *Ibid.*

Tummalapenṭa.

190. On a stone in the Āñjanēya pagoda. Records that Rāmarāja Tirumalrājayya gave the village and the dues to jugglers to Timmabōyulu in Ś. 1476, Piṅgaḷa, in the reign of Vīra-Sadāśivarāya. *Ins., Ced. Dts.*, p. 154, No. 40.

191. A record of Anantarāja Narasayyadēva Mahārāja in Ś. 1459, Hēmalambi. *Ibid.*, No. 41.

192. A record of Vīra-Sadāśivarāya in Ś. 1481, granting the taxes on the barbers to Koṇḍaji. *Ibid.*, No. 41. The *Mack. MSS.* (as given in *Ins., Ced. Dts.*) give the same number to this and the preceding inscription.

Uppalūru.

193. On a stone north of the village. Records that Kṛishṇadēvarāya granted the village to Brahmans in Ś. 1449, Sarvadhāri. *Ins., Ced. Dts.*, p. 483, No. 213.

Uyyalavāḍa (Voyalwar).

194. In charge of "Yalaradoo," Zamindar of "Voyalwar." Records that in H. 1084, Sayud Amir Sadalla appointed one Pāpareḍḍi for his father's situation and granted a cowl for payment of 4,000 pagodas. *Ins., Ced. Dts.*, p. 184, No. 133. [This is the Karnatik Nawab Sa'ādatullāh Khan who was also known as Muhammad Sayid and who was in power from 1710 to 1732.]

195. A record of Nizam Ali Khan Bahadur in H. 1206, appointing Alāuḍin to manage his affairs. *Ibid.*, No. 134.

196. A record of Abdul Nabi Khan Bahadur Padsha in F. 1137, ordering Malla Reḍḍi to prevent disturbance in his districts. *Ibid.*, p. 185, No. 135.

197. A record of Alamghir "Tajadavud" (in Persian and Marathi) in F. 1110, granting some allowances and Foujdari to Malla Reḍḍi of Śiṅgapaṭṇam. *Ibid.*, No. 136.

198. Records that Alamghir Mayani Gaffi Khan rented three villages for 655 pagodas in F. 1129. *Ibid.*, No. 137.

199. Records that Nawab Daud Khan in F. 1114, presented an elephant and a turban to Mallareḍḍi. *Ibid.*, No. 138.

200. Records that Abdul Alim Khan ordered Malla Reḍḍi in F. 1182 to manage the district so as to prevent disturbances from thieves. *Ibid.*, p. 186, No. 139.

201. Records that "Jujetul Amasil Yacarah" ordered Malla Reḍḍi in H. 1196 to save the country from the disturbances of Hyder Ali's troops for the regard of the Honourable Company. *Ibid.*, p. 186, No. 140.

202. Records that Nandyāla Kumāra Rāghavarāja granted the village of Chinnaguṇḍa in Ś. 1662, Raudri, to one Mud . . . *Ibid.*, No. 141.

203. Records that Rāja Tajopunt in H. 1205 ordered Muttu Mallareḍḍi to pay Rs. 10,800 by instalments. *Ibid.*, p. 187, No. 142.

204. Records that Sayud Alāudin ordered in H. 1206 the payment of the balance of the revenue. *Ibid.*, No. 143.

205. Records that Muzuffur Malik issued an order to Muttumalla Reḍḍi in H. 1211 to pay the balance of Rs. 16,000 through Mahommed Khan Siddhi. *Ibid.*, No. 144.

206. The same chief ordered the same man to pay the amount according to "the rule fixed in H. 1212." *Ibid.*, No. 145.

207. A record of the same chief in H. 1213, granting a cowl to Malla Reḍḍi for paying Rs. 16,000 by instalments. *Ibid.*, No. 146.

208. Records that the Reḍḍis and Karaṇams of "Vuppalapali" granted two *tūms* of land in the village in Ś. 1677, Yuva (to some person). *Ibid.*, No. 147.

209. A record of "Shahanevess" in Ś. 1008, continuing five *tūms* of lands which had been sequestered. No more details given. *Ins., Ced. Dts.*, p. 187, No. 148.

210. Records that "Naknamakhan Mahummed Tukki Beg" granted two *tūms* of land below the tank in the village of "Vuppulor" in 1172, Sun, Virōdhikrit, to Kṛishṇa Śāstrilu. *Ibid.*, p. 188, No. 149.

Vallampāḍ.

211. On a stone in the south side of Gōpālasvāmi temple in the fort. Records that Nandyāla Chinna Aubalarāja exempted the tax of the local Brahmins in Ś. 1469, Plavaṅga. *Ibid.*, p. 482, No. 210. See also *Antiquities*, p. 101.

212. On a stone near the temple. Records that the Vipravinōdins gave their local allowance to the Brahmans in Ś. 1477, Rākshasa, in the reign of Sadāśivarāya. The village was also called Vīra Narasimhapuram. *Ibid.*, No. 211.

213. On a stone north of the above. Records that the same chief exempted the rent of the local barbers in the same date. *Ibid.*, No. 212.

Yarraguḍi.

214. On a stone in the village. Records that Nandyāla Pedda Vīrayya granted the local allowance of the Vīramushṭi people to the God Bhōgēśvara in Ś. 1477, Ānanda. *Ibid.*, p. 154, No. 35.

215. On a stone near the Gōpinātha pagoda. Records that Nāgarāja and Viṭṭhalarāja gave one *puṭṭi* of land to one Basavayya, son of Tirumalabhaṭṭa, in Ś. 1474, Virōdhikrit, in the reign of Tirumaladēva Mahārāya (1568—77). *Ibid.*, No. 36.

216. On a stone in the temple of Gōpinātha. Records that the Vipravinōdinș granted their local allowance to the deity in Ś. 1475, Paritāpi, in the reign of Sadāśiva. *Ibid.*, No. 37.

Kurnool Taluk.

Dēvanapāḍu (Devunepod).

217. On a stone near the ruined Hanumanta pagoda. Records that Koṇḍappa, minister of Mukuntirāya Uḍaiyār, granted in Ś. 1484, Rudhirōdgāri, an agreement to the merchants of the village. *Ins., Ced. Dts.*, p. 425, No. 14.

Dupāḍ.

218. A record of Kōṭanāyaka in Ś. 1054, Kārttika, Śuddha 13, *Ādivāram*, relating that he gave 100 kuṇṭas of land to God Bhīmēśvaradēva. *Mack. MSS.*, Bk. XX, pp. 61–2.

Gādidenadugu.

219. In the Chenna-Kēśava temple. A grant by a local chief in the reign of Sadāśiva Rāya in Ś. 1469. *Antiquities*, p. 88.

220. In the Śiva temple. A record dated Ś. 1473.

Gopputi (?).

220-A. A record of Bappabhūpati, whose panegyrics is given. Records that Channachōḷa Naradēva Chōḷadēva Mahāchōḍa, Bhīma Mahīpāla called the Rāshṭrakūṭas, families, mantris, etc., and issued the edict that Bhīma Nāyaka gave in Ś. 1009 (दिविन्योमक्ष्मा), Kārttika, to Kēśava some land in "Gannachōḍa Śuddhi" grāma in Sudhanapati daśaka (?). *Mack. MSS.*, Bk. XX, pp. 57—60.

Gōranṭla.

221. On a stone in the ruined Śiva temple. Records that Pāpanāyak, the son of a prime minister of Śiṅgaḷadēvarāya "of the race of Yādhavanārāyaṇa Pratāpachakravarti," set up the image of Lakshmīśvara in Ś. 1127, Yuva, and granted 10 *māḍas* of land. *Ins., Ced. Dts.*, p. 424, No. 10.

222. On stone near the Mādhavasvāmi pagoda. Records that Śrī-Raṅgarāja (1578—86), descendant of Rāmarāja, gave Gōranṭḷa in the district of Velladūrti, to Mādhavasvāmi in Ś. 1507, Pārthiva. *Ibid.*, p. 425, No. 11. See also *Antiquities*, I, p. 92.

223. On a stone near the Aḷvār pagoda north of the above. Records that Rāmappa and Timmappanāyuḍu gave thirteen *tūms* of land to the deity in Ś. 1457, Manmatha, in the reign of Achyuta-dēva Mahārāya. *Ibid.*, No. 12.

224. On a stone near the Vīrabhadra pagoda. Records that the Vīramushṭi jugglers granted their allowance from the village to God Vīrabhadra in Ś. 1474, Paritāpi. *Ibid.*, No. 13.

Kallūru.

225. On a stone in the place. Records a private charity in Ś. 1686 (A.D. 1764). *Antiquities*, p. 92.

226. An undated grant by a Mussalman.

Karanamadakala (Cunnamudakala).

(Originally in Nandikōtkūr taluk.)

227. On a stone near the local Hanumantarāya pagoda. Records that Tipparāju "Panamarāju" exempted the rent of this agrahāram to Ēṭṭūr Anantāchārya and Veṅkaṭāchārya in Ś. 1482, Raudri, in the reign of Sadāśivarāya. *Ins., Ced. Dts.*, p. 481, No. 208. Also *Antiquities*, I, 88.

228. On a stone south of the same pagoda. Records that Rāmarāja Veṅkaṭādrirāja exempted the village rent in Ś. 1469,

Plavaṅga, in the reign of Sadāśivarāya to the same two Brahmans mentioned above. *Ins., Ced. Dts.*, p. 481, No. 209.

229. A private grant (mentioned by Mr. Sewell), dated in Ś. 1473. *Antiquities*, I, 88.

Kontalapāḍu.

230. On a stone in the pagoda of Īśvara. Records that one Dude-Reḍḍi established the image of Amṛtēśvara in Ś. 1679, Īśvara, and fixed a contribution from the produce of the village for worship. See *Ins., Ced. Dts.*, p. 423, No. 4.

231. On a stone in the Chennakēśava temple. Records that the chief inhabitant of the village gave some land and fixed a contribution from the village, in the same date, to Chennakēśava. See *Ibid.*, No. 5.

Kurnool.

232. On a stone near the darogah. Records in Ś. 1201, a grant to a temple by a merchant, of property which had been conferred on him by Pratāparudra I of Waraṅgal. *Antiquities*, p. 92.

Mallāpuram.

233. West of the village. A private grant in Ś. 1559. *Ibid.*, p. 98.

Nārṇūru (Nannūru).

234. In front of the local Vīrabhadra temple. A record dated in Ś. 1467. *Ibid.*, p. 92.

Nāyakallu.

235. On a stone in the Mādhavaśvāmi pagoda. Records that in Ś. 1470, Kīlaka, Koṇḍarāju, son of Annamarāju, gave some land at Nāyakallu or Tippasamudram for the daily festival of God. *Ins., Ced. Dts.*, p. 424, No. 9.

Uppalapāḍu (Wuapullapad).

236. On a stone in the village near Hanumantarāya pagoda. Records that Rāya Rāyuḍu, grandson of Haṇḍe Hanumappanāyaḍu, granted the village to Rāmēśvara in Ś. 1520, Viḷambi, in the reign of Veṅkaṭapatirāya (I, 1586—1614). *Ibiḍ.*, p. 425, No. 51.

Uyyalavāḍa.

237. On a stone near the local Vīrabhadra pagoda. Records that Basavappaṇāyaḍu gave two *tūms* of land to the God for the marriage festival, in Ś. 1457, Manmatha, in the reign of Achyutarāya. *Ibid.*, p. 423, No. 6.

Vōravakallu (Vōruvakaḷḷu).

238. A grant in the reign of Sadāśiva Rāya in Ś. 1476 (A.D. 1554). See *Antiquities*, I, p. 96.

MĀRKĀPUR TALUK.

*Mārkāpur.**

239. 156 *of* 1905.—(Sanskrit and Telugu.) On the south wall of the antarāḷa-maṇṭapa in the Chennakēśavasvāmin temple. Records, in Ś. 1474, Paridhāvin, in the reign of the Vijayanagara king Vīrapratāpa Sadāśivadēva-Mahārāya, gift of ten villages in the Kochcharlakōṭa-śīma (district) to the temple of Chennakēśava-rāya of Mārakāpura by Tirumalayyadēva-Mahārāju, son of the Mahāmaṇḍalēśvara Rāmarāju-Peda Śrīraṅgayyadēva Mahārāju. [See *Ins., Ced. Dts.*, p. 222, No. 27, for a copy of this epigraph.]

240. 157 *of* 1905.—(Telugu.) On the west wall of the same maṇṭapa. Records in the reign of the Vijayanagara king Vīra-pratāpa Sadāśivadēva-Mahārāya, in Ś. 1476, Ānanda, the gift of the village of Nāgulavaraṁ (situated) on the bank of the Gumḍakamma river and belonging to the Dūpaṭi-śīma (district), to the same temple by Timmarāju, son of the Mahāmaṇḍalēśvara Rāmarāju Kōnēṭayya. [*Ins., Ced. Dts.*, p. 223, No. 29.] See By. 347 and 348.

241. 158 *of* 1905.—(Telugu.) On the north wall of the same maṇṭapa. A record of the Vijayanagara king Vīrapratāpa Sadā-śivadēva-Mahārāya, dated in Ś. 1481, Raudri. Mentions a Vaishṇava sanyāsin named Emberumānāru-Jīyyaṅgāru and the Mahāmaṇḍalēśvara Siddhirāju Timmarājayya. [The *Mack. MSS.* (*Ins., Ced. Dts.*, p. 224, No. 31) give Ś. 1482.]

242. 159 *of* 1905.—(Telugu.) On the east wall of the same maṇṭapa, right of entrance. A record of the Vijayanagara king Vīrapratāpa Achyutadēva-Mahārāya, dated in Ś. 1458, Durmukhi. Records gift of two villages (Bodichērla and Boṇḍalapāḍ) in the Toṇḍamaregulla-śīma (district) to the same temple on the occasion of a lunar eclipse. Mentions Bhūtanātha Rāmabhaṭḷu, ruler of Udayagiri. [See *Ins., Ced. Dts.*, p. 221, No. 25 ; Cb. 325.]

243. 160 *of* 1905.—(Sanskrit and Telugu.) In the same place. A record of the Vijayanagara king Vīrapratāpa Sadāśivadēva-Mahārāya, in Ś. 1466, Śōbhakrit. Records gift of a village in the Kōchcherlakōṭa-śīma (district) to the same temple by Aubalayya-dēva-Mahārāju, son of the Mahāmaṇḍalēśvara Śiṅgarayyadēva-Mahārāju I of Nandyāla. See *Ins., Ced. Dts.*, p. 222, No. 26.

---

* Mr. Sewell notes six inscriptions in this place. Of these three are the same as 241, 245 and 246 above. Of the other three, one is attributed to Telugu Rāya and the second to Tirumaladēva and the third is a private record of Ś. 1567. The *Ins., Ced. Dts.*, gives fourteen inscriptions under this heading. Of these nine have been identified. The remaining five have been included above.

244. 161 *of* 1905.—(Sanskrit and Telugu.) On the same wall left of entrance. A record of the Vijayanagara king Vīrapratāpa Sadāśiva-dēva-Mahārāya, dated in Ś. 1476, Ānanda. Mentions the Mahāmaṇḍalēśvara Madrāju-Nāgappadēva-Mahārāju, son of Avubalayya-dēva-Mahārāju, grandson of Mahāmaṇḍalēśvara Madrāju-Śiṅgarayyadēva-Mahārāju of the solar race and of the Kāśyapa-gōtra, and nephew of the Mahāmaṇḍalēśvara Rāmarāju-Tirumalayyadēva-Mahārāju (the Āravīḍu chief) of the lunar race and of the Ātrēyagōtra. *Ins., Ced. Dts.*, p. 223, No. 30. [See the genealogy of the Āravīḍu chiefs.]

245. 162 *of* 1905.—(Telugu.) In the same place. A record of the Vijayanagara king Vīrapratāpa Achyutadēva-Mahārāya in Ś. 1455, Vijaya. Records gift of two villages by the Mahāmaṇḍalēśvara Sāḷakarāju-Pina-Tirumalayyadēva-Mahārāju for the God's festival. The king is styled "the establisher of the Yavana-rājya." [See *Ins., Ced. Dts.*, p. 221, No. 23.] See the genealogy of the Sāḷakas.

246. 163 *of* 1905.—(Telugu.) On the east wall of the Lakshmīdēvi shrine in the Chennakēśavasvāmin temple. A record of the Vijayanagara king Vīrapratāpa Sadāśivadēva-Mahārāya. Records in Ś. 1489, Prabhava, a grant by Veṅkaṭayyadēva-Mahārāju (Veṅkaṭa I ?), son of Tirumalarājayya-dēva-Mahārāju and grandson of Āravīti-Rāmarāju-Śrīraṅgarājayyadēva-Mahārāju of the Ātrēya-gōtra and Āpastamba-sūtra. *Ins., Ced. Dts.*, p. 220, No. 22. It says that the donee was the Paurāṇist Parāṅkuśan Lakshmaṇaiya.

247. 164 *of* 1905.—(Sanskrit and Telugu.) On the east wall of the Garuḍa-maṇṭapa in the same temple. A damaged record containing a genealogy of the Karnāṭa dynasty of Vijayanagara.

248. 165 *of* 1905.—(Telugu.) On a pillar of the same maṇṭapa. Mentions the Mahāmaṇḍalēśvara Siddhirāju-Timmarājayya and refers to the building of a maṇṭapa. See No. 241 above.

249. 166 *of* 1905.—(Telugu.) On another pillar of the same maṇṭapa. A record of the Vijayanagara king Vīrapratāpa Sadāśivadēva-Mahārāya in Ś. 1491, Śukla. Records a gift by Chinnapanāyaniṅgāru, son of Komāra-Timmanāyaniṅgāru and grandson of Veligōṭi-Peda-Timmanāyaniṅgāru of the Rācherla-gōtra, a subordinate of the Mahāmaṇḍalēśvara Rāmarāja-Tirumalarājayyadēva-Mahārāju. [See *Ins., S. Dts.*, p. 224, No. 32.]

250. 167 *of* 1905.—(Telugu.) On a slab set up near the platform in front of the same temple. A damaged record of the Vijayanagara king Vīrapratāpa Sadāśivadēva-Mahārāya, dated Ś. 1475, Pramādin.

251. A C.P., dated in Ś. 1464, recording the grant of a village, for temple purposes, by Sadāśiva Rāya of Vijayanagar. [See Mr. Sewell's *Antiquities*, I, p. 86.]

252. On a stone at Mārkāpuram. Records that Vīrapratāpa Dēvarāya Mahārāyalu granted some land to Daṇḍamahāśiva at the time of his installation at Vijayanagar, in Ś. 1329, Sarvajit. See *Ins., Ced. Dts.*, p. 213, No. 2.

253. On the wall of the kalyāṇa maṇṭapam in the pagoda. Records that Sāḷaka Rāja Pina Tirumalayya granted the villages of "Carvepulla and Achyutarāyapuram" as free gift for the annual festival of the God in Ś. 1455, Vijaya, in the reign of Achyutadēva Mahārāya. *Ibid.*, p. 221, No. 24. See No. 245 above.

254. On a stone west of the Garuḍastambham in the temple. Records that in Ś. 1474, Parītāpi, in the reign of Sadāśivarāya. Padmanābha, Mallappa and other villagers granted to Chennakēśava, the tax on betel-gardens. *Ibid.*, p. 222, No. 28.

255. On a stone pillar opposite to the kalyāṇa maṇṭapam. Records that Kamalanābhuḍu granted some land to the deity in Ś. 1567, Tāraṇa. *Ibid.*, p. 224, No. 33 and *Antiquities*, p.

256. On a stone south of Mārkāpuram. Records that one "Aulumpanah" gave three *kuchalas* of land to Tripurabhaṭṭa Mahājōsya. *Ibid.*, No. 47, p. 229.

Millampalle.

257. 284 *of* 1905.—(Telugu.) On a slab set up in the courtyard of the Vēṇugōpālasvāmin temple. Records in Ś. 1440, Bahudhānya, gift of the village of Kunebōyinipalle *alias* Avubaḷapuramu in the Kolaṅkula-sīma (district), to the temple of Gōpināthadēva at Milempaḷḷi by a certain Varadarāju. [Mr. Sewell says that there are "two inscriptions" in this place, dated in Ś. 1440 and recording private grants. The above epigraph is evidently one of the two. The present inscription is also given in *Ins., Ced. Dts.*, p. 226, No. 40.]

Narasamāpāḷem.

258. On a stone in the village. Records that Kāmarāya Śrī-Raṅgarāya built the villages of Śrī-Raṅgarājapuram in the district of Dupoda (Dupad) in Ś. 1485, Rudhirōdgāri, and gave it to Kāñcherla Narasayya. *Ibid.*, p. 220, No. 21.

Timmaṇapāḷem.

259. On a stone in the Chennakēśava pagoda. Records that Kambaḷa Vallabayya gave some land to the deity in Ś. 1499, Dhātu, in the reign of Velugōṭi Chinna Timmanāyaḍu. *Ibid.*, p. 228, No. 46.

260. On a stone in a field of a Reḍḍi. Records grant of two *kuchalas* in the village to Māchareḍḍi, a native of the place. *Ibid.*, p. 229, No. 48.

Tripurāntakam.

The *Mack. MSS.* (*Ins., Ced. Dts.*, pp. 214—20, Nos. 4—20 and Nos. 41 and 49) mention nineteen inscriptions in this place, while the departmental list contains 116. I have therefore not thought it desirable to compare the two lists. I have however given a C.P. found in the *Mack. MSS.*

261. 168 *of* 1905.—(Telugu.) On the south wall of the central shrine in the Tripurāntakēśvara temple. Ambadēva-Mahārāja * records in Ś. 1194, Śrīmukha (A.D. 1272), gift of land to the priests who offer mantrapushpa (i.e., consecrated flowers) to the god Tripurāntakadēva. Ambadēva who defeated several Telugu chiefs including a certain Śrīpati Gaṇapati Dēva and practically for a time usurped the Kākatīya dominion between Rudrāmba and her grandson Pratāparudra, was the greatest of the Turaga Sāhiṇikas who bore the titles *maṇḍalikas, Brahmarākshas* and *Geṇḍapeṇḍera* and were later on feudatories of Kākatīyas. He is said to have defeated Eruva Mallidēva, Kēśava with Sōmi dēva and Allugaṅga, Maḷlikārjuna (who is called an enemy of Brahmans and Gods), Dāmōdara, Kāḍavarāya, and established Manmagaṇḍagōpāla at Vikramasimhapura (Nellore) of which he had been deprived. He was also a friend of the king of Dēvagiri. See No. 266 below.

262. 169 *of* 1905.—(Sanskrit and Telugu.) On the same wall. A record of the Kākatīya king Gaṇapati (1199—1260) in Ānanda (i.e., Ś. 1177). Records that the central shrine (*vimāna*) was built of stone, under the orders of the king by Śāntaśambhu, son of Viśvēśācharya. See N.A. 155, 166, 190, 191 and 194 for a Śaivite teacher of this name.

263. 170 *of* 1905.—(Telugu and Sanskrit.) On the same wall. Vikramōttuṅga Rājēndra records in Ś. 1214 (A.D. 1292), Nandana, gift of a golden trumpet to the temple of Tripurāntaka. [He was evidently another feudatory chief who took advantage of the Kākatīya weakness to establish his power.]

264. 171 *of* 1905.—(Sanskrit and Grantha.) On the same wall. A record of the Kākatīya king Gaṇapati. Records in Ānanda (i.e., Ś. 1177) that the central shrine (*vimāna*) was built of stone, under the orders of the king, by Śāntaśambhu, son of Viśvēśācharya. See No. 262 above.

265. 172 *of* 1905.—(Telugu.) On the same wall. A partly damaged record in Ś. 1215, Vijaya, mentioning the construction of two tanks.

266. 173 *of* 1905.—(Telugu.) On the same wall. An incomplete record of Ambadēva-Mahārāja, dated Ś. 1213, Khara. He is

---

* It is advisable to give in the form of a genealogical tree the various members of the Kāyastha family.

Gaṅgaya Sāhiṇi (A.D. 1255).
(Feudatory of Gaṇapati)
| ?
Janniga dēva Mahārāja
|
Tripurāri dēva Mahārāja. | Ambadēva Mahārāja A.D. 1274—92.

said to have taken the head of Eruva-Mallidēva, to have captured the forces of Mallikārjuna, to have worsted Kāḍavarāya and to have been on friendly terms with the Pāṇḍya and Dēvagiri kings. For Kāḍavarāya see S.A. 124 and 223.

267. 174 *of* 1905.—(Telugu.) On the same wall. A record of Ambadēva-Mahārāja, dated in Ś. 1212, Vikrita (A.D. 1290). Records that the king, who bore the titles Gaṇḍapeṇḍara and Maṇḍalīka-Brahmarākshasa, belonged to the Kāyastha family. On the same stone is another damaged inscription—apparently of the same king. See Nos. 261 and 266.

268. 175 *of* 1905.—(Telugu.) On the same wall. A record of the Telugu Chōḍa king Siddhayadēva-Chōḍa Mahārāja, dated in Ś. 1189, Prabhava. Records gift of fifty cows for a lamp by the king for the merit of his father, the Mahāmaṇḍalēśvara Perumāḍidēva-Chōḍa-Mahārāja, and his mother Dāmaḷādēvi. [It will be seen that he does not recognize the sovereignty of Queen Rudrammā.]

269. 176 *of* 1905.—(Telugu.) On the same wall. Belongs to the reign of the Kākatīya king Gaṇapatidēva-Mahārāja in Ś. 1177, Rākshasa. Records that Gaṅgayya-Sāhiṇi, who belonged to the Kāyastha family, bore the titles Gaṇḍapeṇḍara and Maṇḍalīka-Brahmarākshasa, and who claims to have defeated a certain Dāmōdara of the west, granted, for the prosperity of the king and of himself, the village of Pulachervu in the district of Moṭṭavāḍi on the day of a lunar eclipse.

270. 177 *of* 1905.—(Telugu.) On the west wall of the same shrine. Records in Ś. 1190, Vibhava, gift of fifty cows for a lamp by a private individual on the day of a lunar eclipse.

271. 178 *of* 1905.—(Telugu.) On the same wall. Records in Ś. 1242, *Raudri,* in the reign of the Kākatīya king Pratāpa-Rudradēva-Mahārāja (II) gift of taxes from a garden of areca palms.

272. 179 *of* 1905.—(Telugu.) On the same wall. A record of the time of the Kākatīya king Pratāpa-Rudradēva Mahārāja (II, grandson and successor of Rudrammā), in Ś. 1216, *Jaya.* Records a gift by the general Aḍidamma, who bore the title *misaragaṇḍa* and who claims to have "cut off the head of Manma-Gaṇḍagōpāla." [Ambadēva of the Gaṅgaya Sāhini line claims to have established Manma Gaṇḍa at Nellore or Vikramasimhapura.]

273. 180 *of* 1905.—(Telugu.) On the north wall of the same shrine. A record, dated Ś. 1244, Nandana, in which the Vīra-Baḷañjya (merchants) are mentioned with a long string of titles. They claim to belong to the Manumakula and to have immigrated from Ahichchatra. See No. 367 below.

274. 181 *of* 1905.—(Telugu.) On the south wall of the maṇṭapa in front of the same shrine. A record of the Kākatīya king Gaṇapatidēva Mahārāja in Ś. 1181, Siddhārthin, sixty-first year. Records gift of fifty cows for a lamp by Kumāra-Gaṇapatidēva-

Mahārāju of Nātavāḍi. [The inscription shows that the king ascended the throne in 1199–1200 and that he ruled till 1260. See Nos. 289, 306 and 313.

275. 182 *of* 1905.—(Telugu.) On the same wall. Records in Ś. 1214, Nandana, a gift by Ravinuṇṭu-Timmapparāju.

276. 183 *of* 1905.—(Telugu.) On the south wall of the maṇṭapa in front of the central shrine in the Tripurāntakēśvara temple near Tripurāntakam. Records in Ś. 1213, Khara, gift of fifty cows and a metallic lampstand by Mummaḍi-Nāyunḍu, who is called "lord of the Ammanagallu city." Mentions at the end the gift of two umbrellas called Vīrarājēndra-Chōḷagoḍagulu. At the end of the inscription the syllable *śri* is engraved in Telugu, Nāgari and Grantha characters.

277. 184 *of* 1905.—(Telugu.) On the same wall. Records in Ś. 1275, Vijaya, a gift for the merit of Rāma-Nāyaka by another Nāyaka, who was the lord of the town of Ālakuṇṭala, and who claims to have captured the forts belonging to king Karikāla-Chōḷa and cut off the head of Manuma-Mallidēva.

278. 185 *of* 1905.—(Telugu.) On the same wall. A record of the time of the Reḍḍi king Anavōta-Reḍḍi (the father of Kumāragiri), in Ś. 1278, Durmukhi. Records gift of a lamp by Aḍapa-Vēmaṇa.

279. 186 *of* 1905.—(Telugu.) On the same wall. A damaged record, dated Ś. 1192, Pramōda.

280. 187 *of* 1905.—(Telugu.) On the same wall. A much damaged record, the date of which is doubtful. Records gift of twenty-five cows for a lamp. Traces exist of some *birudas* like Gaṇḍapeṇḍara, which may connect the inscription with the Kāyastha family to which Ambadēva Mahārāja belonged.

281. 188 *of* 1905.—(Telugu and Sanskrit.) On the west wall of the same maṇṭapa, right of entrance. A record of Ś. 1193, Prajāpati. Mentions a Brāhmaṇa resident of Madhurāntaka (perhaps Madhurāntakam in the Chingleput district), who bore the title Chōḍamaṇḍala-pratishṭhāchārya, and a certain Śrīkaṇṭhaśiva, probably a Śaiva ascetic. Was he the author of the *Brahmamīmāmsābhāshya*? See Hultzsch's *Sans. MSS.*, 1896, p. 46, No. 1229.]

282. 189 *of* 1905.—(Telugu.) On the same wall, left of entrance. A damaged record, the date of which is doubtful. The king's *birudas* are nearly the same as in the next epigraph.

283. 190 *of* 1905.—(Telugu.) In the same place. A record of a certain Eruva-Manumilidēvarāja, in Ś. 1189, Prabhava. The king's name is preceded by a list of *birudas* from which it appears that he belonged to the Kāśyapa gōtra and to the family of Karikāla. He was also the lord of Orayūr (Uraiyūr near Trichinopoly). [He does not recognize the sovereignty of Rudrammā.]

284. 191 *of* 1905.—(Telugu.) On the east wall of the same maṇṭapa close to the blocked up doorway. An inscription of the Reḍḍi king Vēmaya Reḍḍi. Mentions in Ś. 1268, Vyaya, Anavōta-Reḍḍi (Vēma's son and father of Kumāragiri).

285. 192 *of* 1905.—(Telugu.) In the same place. Records in Ś. 1192, Pramōda, a private agreement among merchants.

286. 193 *of* 1905.—(Telugu.) In the same place. A record of Parichchhēda-Allāḍanāthadēvarāja and his younger brother Bhīmarāja, in Pramādin. Allāḍa was a local chief called "the lord of Vijayavāṭika (Bezwada)" and "the lord of the (district) called Shaḍsahasra (i.e., six thousand), situated to the south of the Krishṇaveṇi (Krishṇa) river."

287. 194 *of* 1905.—(Telugu.) On the same wall, right of entrance. A record of the Kākatīya sovereign Rudradēva-Mahārāja (Rudrāmbā), dated Ś. 1183, Durmati, second year. The temple at Tripurāntakam is called the eastern gate of Śrīparvata (i.e., Śriśailam). The donor was a Kākatīya general who served under king Gaṇapati and claimed to belong to the Chāḷukya family. He also fought battles on the banks of the Gōdāvari and took the head of Goṇṭūri-Nāgadēva.

288. 195 *of* 1905.—(Telugu.) On the base of the south wall of the kitchen (called) *vantamidde* in front of the same maṇṭapa. An unfinished record of the Kākatīya king Gaṇapatidēva-Mahārāja, dated Ś. 1174, Paridhāvin, fifty-fourth year. The existing portion of the inscription mentions the *birudas* of a Śaiva teacher in charge of the Gōḷagi-maṭha, whose influence extended over three lakhs of villages. See N.A. 201.

289. 196 *of* 1905.—(Telugu and Sanskrit.) On the east wall of the same kitchen. A record of the Kākatīya king Gaṇapatidēva-Mahārāja (1199—1260), dated in Ś. 1182, Raudri, sixty-second year. Records gift of two villages, viz., Cheṭalapāḍu on the north bank of the river Guṇḍēru (Guṇḍlakamma) in the district of Kammanāṇḍu and Rēḍumaḷḷapalli on the bank of the Muśi in Pūṅgināṇḍu.

290. 197 *of* 1905.—(Sanskrit and Telugu.) On the same wall. A record of the Pallava king Sarvajñakhaḍgamalla, Niśśaṅkamalla Mahārājasimha. Venkayya identifies this king with Kōpperuñjīṅgadēva.

291. 198 *of* 1905.—(Sanskrit and Grantha.) On the same wall. The record of the Pallava king Mahārājasimha. Is almost identical with No. 290. The king is said to be the son of Jīyamahīpati by his wife Śīlavati. Jīya is Tamil Śiya or Aḷagia Śiya, and it is found prefixed to Kōpperuñjiṅgadēva in inscriptions.

292. 199 *of* 1905.—(Sanskrit and Grantha.) On the base of the same wall. Partially damaged record. Seems to register the names of the god Śiva.

293. 200 *of* 1905.—(Tamil.) On the north wall of the same kitchen. A damaged record.

294. 201 *of* 1905.—(Tamil.) On the same wall. A record of Mahārājādhirāja Narapati Rājēndra-Chōḷa (III). Refers in fifteenth year, Raudri (i.e., A.D. 1260–61) to a tank at Tripurāntakam. The king claims to have taken the heads of two Pāṇḍyan kings. His power in the Kurnool district shows that he perhaps extended his arms there about the time of the death of the Kākatīya Gaṇapati which took place in 1260.

295. 202 *of* 1905.—(Sanskrit and Nāgari.) On the same wall. A record of the Pallava king Mahārājasimha. [The king claims to have destroyed the Hoysaḷa king's pride, been like a sun to the lotus-tank of the Chōḷa line and to be the established Pāṇḍyan. His gifts to various shrines from Drākshārāma to Madura are then enumerated.] See No. 290 above and N.A. 444.

296. 203 *of* 1905.—(Telugu.) On the top of the doorway in the same wall. Records in Ś. 1179, Piṅgaḷa, gift of a village on the bank of the Muśi (river) by the Mahāmaṇḍalēśvara Vishṇuvardhana (Bhīma)-rāju-Siddhhayadēva-Mahārāja who was a worshipper of the god Bhīmēśvara of Drākshārāma and was the lord of the city of Veṅgi.

297. 204 *of* 1905.—(Sanskrit and Telugu.) On four faces of a pillar set up in front of the liṅga on the north side of the kitchen (called *vantamidde*) in the Tripurāntakēśvara temple near Tripurāntakam. A record of the Kākatīya king Gaṇapati, dated in Ś. 1131, Śukla. Records that the king's sister Mēlāmbika, who had married Vakkaḍimalla Rudra, second son of Nātavāḍi Buddha, built and consecrated the temple called Mēlāmbikēśvara near that of Tripurāntaka. She granted some land below the tank of the village called Tīrtalu and also gave 25 goats for a lamp. [The marriages of the Nātavāḍi chiefs with the princesses of the Kākatīya line explain the presence of their epigraphs at Tripurāntakam. See Nos. 318, 320 and 321 below.

298. 205 *of* 1905.—(Sanskrit and Telugu.) On the south wall of the dark room (called *chikatimidde*) in the same temple. An unfinished record giving an account of the Koṇḍavīḍu Reḍḍis. The first was Kōmaṭi-Prōḷa. His wife was Anyamāmbā, daughter of Doḍḍaya. Their sons were Mācha, Vēma, Doḍḍa, Aṇṇa. The epigraphist believes that Doḍḍaya might be the same as Doḍḍa Sainya-nāyaka mentioned in the Telugu poem *Harivaṁśam.*

299. 206 *of* 1905.—(Telugu.) On the west wall of the same room. Records in Ś. 1205, Chitrabhānu, gift of land by a private individual.

300. 207 *of* 1905.—(Telugu.) On the same wall. Records in Ś. 1188, Kshaya, gift of 25 cows for a lamp by a servant of the minister of Gaṇapatidēva-Mahārāja.

301. 208 *of* 1905.—(Telugu and Sanskrit.) On the same wall. A record of the Kākatīya king Gaṇapatidēva in Ś. 1181, Siddhārthin. Records a gift by the Mahāmaṇḍalēśvara Gaṇḍapeṇḍēra Jannigadēva-Mahārāju. [He belonged to the Kāyastha family of Gaṅgaya Sāhiṇi.]

302. 209 *of* 1905.—(Telugu.) On the base of the same wall. Records in Ś. 1172, Sādhāraṇa, gift of cows.

303. 210 *of* 1905.—(Telugu.) On the same base. Records in S. 1177, Rākshasa, gift of cows for a lamp.

304. 211 *of* 1905.—(Telugu.) On the same base. A damaged record dated Ś. 1177, Rākshasa. Records gift of two lamps.

305. 212 *of* 1905.—(Telugu.) On the same base. Records gift of cows for a lamp.

306. 213 *of* 1905.—(Telugu.) On the same base. The Kākatīya king Gaṇapatidēva-Mahārāja (1199—1260) records in Ś. 1181, Siddhārthin, sixty-first year, gift of twenty-five cows for a lamp.

307. 214 *of* 1905.—(Telugu.) On the same base. Records in Ś. 1183, Durmukhi (for Durmati), gift of twenty-five cows for a lamp.

308. 215 *of* 1905.—(Telugu.) On the same base. Records in Ś. 1180, Kāḷayukti, gift of twenty-five cows for a lamp.

309. 216 *of* 1905.—(Telugu.) On the same base. Records in Ś. 1175, Pramādin, gift of cows for a lamp.

310. 217 *of* 1905.—(Telugu.) On the same base. Records that the Pallava king Immaḍi-Basavaśaṁkara Allāḍa-Pemmayadēva-Mahārāja gave in Ś. 1181, Siddhārtin, twenty-five cows for a lamp. He was one of the numerous local chiefs of the period and called "the lord of Kānchīpura" and a devotee of Kāmakōṭyāmbika (i.e., Kāmakshi temple).

311. 218 *of* 1905.—(Telugu, verse and prose.) On the north wall of the same room. A record of the Kōṭa king Kōṭa-Gaṇapatidēva-Mahārāja (son of Keṭa III), dated in Ś. 1185, Rudhirōdgārin. Records gift of 25 cows for a lamp by Māchi-Nāyuḍu, brother of queen Komārāmbika. The king is said to have been the son of Bayyamāmbikā. [The close relationship of the Kōṭa chiefs to Kākatīya Gaṇapati explains the existence of their epigraphs at Tripurāntakam.]

312. 219 *of* 1905.—(Telugu.) On the same wall. Records in Ś. 1175, Pramādin, gift of fifty cows for a lamp by the brother-in-law of the Mahāpradhānin Bhāskaradēva of Mōṭupalli. [Was this minister the author of the Bhāskara Rāmāyaṇa ?]

313. 220 *of* 1905.—(Telugu.) On the same wall. The Kākatīya king Gaṇapatidēva-Mahārāja (1199—1260) records in Ś. 1181, Siddhārtin, sixty-first year, gift of twenty-five cows for a lamp.

314. 221 *of* 1905.—(Telugu.) On the same wall. The Kākatīya king Gaṇapatidēva-Mahārāja records in Ś. 1172, Saumya, gift of tax on salt payable by ryots manufacturing it in the village of Tripurāntakam.

315. 222 *of* 1905.—(Telugu.) On the same wall. An incomplete record dated Ś. 1192, Pramōda. Records gift of a lamp by the Mahāmaṇḍalēśvara Raṇaraṅgabhairava Parichchhēda Vaḍamāni (?) Kōṭadēvarāju. [Did he belong to the Kōṭa or Parichchēda lines ?]

316. 223 *of* 1905.—(Sanskrit and Telugu.) On the same wall. Records in Ś. 1174, Paridhāvin, in the reign of the Kākatīya king Gaṇapatidēva-Mahārāja, gift of gold by Viśvēśvaraśiva-dēśika, the pupil of Dhārmaśivāchārya of the Gōḷagi-maṭha. The inscription gives the names of eleven Śiva shrines around the main temple. See N.A. 166, 190 and 194, etc., for a teacher of the same name in the Bhikshāmaṭha.]

317. 224 *of* 1905.—(Telugu.) On the base of the same wall, first tier. A fragment of record of the Kākatīya king Gaṇapatidēva-Mahārāja, dated in Ś. 1175, Pramādin. Refers to the village of Viśvanāthapuram and to a tank, both of which were founded after clearing the forest.

318. 225 *of* 1905.—(Telugu.) On the same base, second tier. Records in Ś. 1170, Kīlaka, gift of twenty-five cows for a lamp by Rudradēva, son of Rudradēva-Mahārāja of Natavāḍi and of the Kākēta princess Mailāḷa-Mahādēvi (i.e., Mēlambika, Gaṇapati's sister). See Nos. 297 and 329.

319. 226 *of* 1905.—(Telugu.) On the same tier. Records in Ś. 1172, Sādhāraṇa, gift of cows for a lamp by the Mahāmaṇḍalēśvara Murāri-Gaṇapadēva-Mahārāja of the Koṇḍapaḍumati (family).

320. 227 *of* 1905.—(Telugu.) On the same tier. Records in Ś. 1170, Kīlaka, gift of twenty-five cows for a lamp by Mahādēvarāju, son of Rudradēva-Mahārāju of Natavāḍi and of the Kākēta princess Mailāḷa-Mahādēvi. See No. 318 above.

321. 228 *of* 1905.—(Telugu.) On the same tier. Records in Ś. 1170, Kīlaka, a gift by Mummaḍi-Gaṇapadēva, another son of the same chief and queen. See No. 318 above.

322. 229 *of* 1905.—(Telugu.) On the base of the north wall of the dark room (*chikaṭimidde*) in the Tripurāntakēśvara temple near Tripurāntakam, first tier. Records in Ś. 1174, Parīdhāvin, gift of twenty-five cows for a lamp.

323. 230 *of* 1905.—(Telugu, verse and prose.) On the east wall of the same room. An incomplete and damaged record, dated Ś. 1264, Chitrabhānu. Mentions some Telugu-Chōḍa chiefs. The hill on which the temple is built is called Kumārādri. Records the putting up of a golden flagstaff.

324. 231 *of* 1905.—(Telugu.) On the same wall. A record of the Kākatīya king Gaṇapatidēva-Mahārāja (1199—1260), ruling at Orugallu (Warangal), dated in Ś. 1176, Ānanda. Records a gift by Nāmadēvapaṇḍita, the minister of the Mahāmaṇḍalīka

Gaṅgayya-Sāhiṇi, who had the title Gaṇḍapeṇḍēra and who claims to have defeated Dāmōdara of the west and Rākkasa-Gaṅgarasa. He was the first of the influential Kāyastha dynasty. See No. 373.

325. 232 *of* 1905.—(Telugu.) On the same wall. Records in Ś. 1170, Kīlaka, gift of a lamp.

326. 233 *of* 1905.—(Telugu.) On the same wall. An epigraph of the Kākatīya king Pratāpa-Rudradēva-Mahārāja, dated in Parīdāvin (i.e., Ś. 1235). Mentions the Śaiva teacher Chandrabhūshaṇaśivāchārya.

327. 234 *of* 1905.—(Telugu.) On the same wall. Records in Ś. 1168, Parābhava, gift of twenty-five cows for a lamp by the Mahāmaṇḍalēśvara Chāgi-Gaṇapayarāju, who bore the title Narasimhavardhana.

328. 235 *of* 1905.—(Telugu.) On the same wall. Records in Ś. 1168, Parābhava, gift of twenty-five cows for a lamp by the Mahāmaṇḍalēśvara Chāgi-Muppaladēvi-Ammaṅgāru, whose titles are the same as those of Gaṇapa in the above epigraph.

329. 236 *of* 1905.—(Telugu.) On the same wall. Records in Ś. 1164, Śubhakrit, gift of cows for a lamp by the same queen whose titles, however, are not mentioned here. Below this is the beginning of an incomplete record, which mentions Vakkaḍimalla-Rudradēva-Mahārāja of Natavāḍi and his queen Mailāla-Mahādēvi. See No. 318 above.

330. 237 *of* 1905.—(Telugu.) On the same wall. Records in Vyaya gift of cows for a lamp.

331. 238 *of* 1905.—(Telugu.) On the same wall. Records in Ś. 1213, Khara, gift of fifty cows for a lamp by Annaladēva, son of the Mahāpradhānin Gaṇṇayapregaḍa of Iṁdalūru.

332. 239 *of* 1905.—(Telugu.) On the same wall. Records in Khara gift of one hundred and sixty-five cows for lamps by Manuma-Gaṇaya.

333. 240 *of* 1905.—(Sanskrit and Telugu.) On the same wall. Records in Ś. 1170, Kīlaka, gift of twenty-five cows for a lamp by Daṇḍenapeggaḍa, a subordinate ? of Ponuṅgōṭi Gaṇapaya. The Sanskrit portion is left unfinished.

334. 241 *of* 1905.—(Telugu.) On the same wall. Records in Ś. 1168, Parābhava, gift of fifty cows for a lamp.

335. 242 *of* 1905.—(Telugu.) On the same wall. A record of Mahāmaṇḍalēśvara Gaṇḍapeṇḍara Ambadēva-Mahārāja in Ś. 1210, Sarvadhārin, relating gift of fifty cows for a lamp by Ambaya-Reḍḍi.

336. 243 *of* 1905.—(Telugu.) On the same wall. A record of the Kōṭa king Kōṭa-Mummaḍi-Pōtarāja, dated in Ś. 1168, Parābhava. Records gift of twenty-five cows for a lamp by the king for the merit of his father Chōḍarāju, his mother Vimjamādēvi, and his younger brother Rājaya. He has almost all the titles of the

Kōṭa chiefs of Amarāvati (*Ep. Ind.*, Vol. VI, p. 152), who had intermarriages with the Kākatīya line. See No. 311 above.

337. 244 *of* 1905.—(Telugu.) On the same wall. A record in Ś. 1168, Parābhava, of a subordinate of Chāgi Dhōrayarāju.

338. 245 *of* 1905.—(Telugu.) On the same wall. Dated in the reign of the Kākatīya king Gaṇapatidēva-Mahārāja, in Ś. 1167, Viśvāvasu. Records remission of tolls for the merit of the king, on the three hundred pack bullocks used for importing articles into the village of Tripurāntakam, by Dāchena-Preggaḍa-Gaṇapaya.

339. 246 *of* 1905.—(Telugu.) On the base of the same wall. A damaged record of the Kākatīya sovereign Mahāmaṇḍalēśvara-Rudrayyadēva-Mahārāja, dated Ś. 1192 (1270 A.D.), Pramōda. Mentions Śrīkaṇṭhaśiva. The sovereign is the celebrated queen Rudrammā who was given a male name by her father. See No. 281 above.

340. 247 *of* 1905.—(Telugu.) On the same wall, left of entrance. Records in Ś. 1189, Prabhava, gift of cows for a lamp by Nārapa, son of Siddhamarāju and pupil of Sōmāchārya.

341. 248 *of* 1905.—(Sanskrit and Telugu.) On the door-post of the same room. Records in the reign of Gaṇḍapeṇḍara Tripurāridēva-Mahārāja (of the Gaṅgaya Sāhiṇi family) in Ś. 1194, Āṅgirasa, gift of gold ornaments and vessels to the temple of Tripurāntaka by the king. Ambadēva was Tripurāri's younger brother.

342. 249 *of* 1905.—(Sanskrit and Telugu.) On a pillar at the entrance into the same room, right side. Records in Ś. 1171, Saumya, gift of fifty goats for a lamp by Jayasāni, the wife of Chōḍa-Bōya, who was a servant of the Velanāṇḍu chief Rājēndra-Chōḍa (Prithvīśvara ?)

343. 250 *of* 1905.—(Telugu.) On the same pillar. Records in Ś. 1269, Sarvajit, in the time of the Reḍḍi king Annama-Reḍḍi gift of one hundred cows for lamps in the temple of Tripurāntakadēva and fifty cows for lamps in the temple of Tripura-Paramēśvari. The king bore the titles Jaganobbagaṇḍa and Kōlādirāya.

344. 251 *of* 1905.—(Telugu.) On the same pillar. Records in Ś. 1173, Virōdhikrit, gift of twenty-five cows for a lamp by a merchant.

345. 252 *of* 1905.—(Telugu.) On another pillar in the same place, left side. Records in Ś. 1173, Virōdhikrit, gift of twenty-five cows for a lamp by a merchant.

346. 253 *of* 1905.—(Telugu.) On a pillar at the entrance into the dark room *(chikaṭimidde)* in the Tripurāntakēśvara temple near Tripurāntakam, left side. Records in Ś. 1169, Plavaṅga, that Dharmaśivāchārya, pupil of Bhīmaḷaśivāchārya of Gōḷagiri in Navalaksha-Dāhaḷa-Tripuri, built a *maṭha* for the temple treasury. This is probably the *chikaṭimidde*, where the temple treasury is said to have been located.

347. 254 *of* 1905.—(Sanskrit and Telugu.) On a slab set up to the east of the same dark room. Annadēva records in Ś. 1310, Vibhava, gift of the village of Kāñchanapalli. The King's father is called Bhaktēśa, which seems to be a Sanskrit translation of some Telugu name like Annadēva or Annarāja.

348. 255 *of* 1905.—(Sanskrit and Telugu.) On another slab set up in the same place. An epigraph of the time of the Vijayanagara king Vīra-Bukka (III). Records in Ś. 1345, Śōbhakrit (A.D. 1423), gift of rice fields on the bank of the Gandhavati tank by Nāgayamantrin, son of Chauṇḍapāmātya of the Hārīta-gōtra (who had been patronized by Vīra Bhūpati, son of Bukka II). Chauṇḍapa was apparently.

349. 256 *of* 1905.—(Telugu verse.) On the third slab set up in the same place. Records in Ś. 1761, Vikārin, the setting up of a flagstaff by a chief named Śēshanripa who belonged to the family of Śāyapanēni.

350. 257 *of* 1905.—(Telugu.) On the fourth slab set up in the same place. Records in the reign of the Vijayanagara king Vīra-Harihararāya in Ś. 1308, Kshaya, gift of land by the Mahāpradhānin-Bhavadūra-Oḍeya, who purchased it for 200 *Śiṅgaya-māḍa*, at Kēsaripāḍu from Bhikshāvritti-Siddhayadēva.

351. 258 *of* 1905.—(Kanarese, prose and verse.) On the fifth slab set up in the same place. Belongs to the reign of the Western Chāḷukya king Tribhuvanamalladēva Vikramāditya VI, in Chāḷukya-Vikrama year 51 (A.D. 1126–27), Parābhava. Records that Govindaraśa-Daṇḍanāyaka, who was ruling over the Koṇḍapalli three hundred district and who was the nephew of the famous chief Anantapāla, was the donor. Mentions the village of Chāpalamaḍuge. Gōvindaraśa claims to have burnt Beṅgipura, defeated a prince at Janañāthapura and conquered Goṅka (perhaps the Velanāṇḍu feudatory of the Eastern Chāḷukyas). For a reference to Gōvindaraśa see *Ep. Ind.*, Vol. V, p. 215. [Evidently Gōvindaraśa re-established the Western Chāḷukyan power in 1126 after the temporary mastery of Vikramachōḷa between 1123 and 1126.]

352. 259 *of* 1905.—(Kanarese.) On three faces of a pillar set up in the same place. Dated in the reign of the Western Chāḷukya king Tribhuvanamalladēva (Vikramāditya VI). Records in Chāḷukya Vikrama year 47 (A.D. 1122–23), Śubhakrit, gift of 44 villages in the Moṭṭavāḍināḍu for the requirements of the temple of Tripurāntakadēva, for feeding and clothing Vēdic students, religious teachers and ascetics, and 54 visitors; for repairs and for oblations to be offered during the day in the Svayambhu-temples of the sacred place (*tirtha*).

353. 260 *of* 1905.—(Telugu.) On the fourth face of the same pillar. A record of the Kākatīya king Pratāpa-Rudradēva-Mahārāja, dated in Ś. 1230, Kīlaka. Mentions Vollaya-Reḍḍi, elder brother of the Sarvādhikārin Ellaya-Reḍḍi, and refers to import of articles on pack bullocks.

354. 261 *of* 1905.—(Telugu.) On a Nandi-pillar set up in front of the same room. Records in Ś. 1257, Yuvan, a gift by two Reḍḍis for the merit of Ambadēvarāju and Lōkanāyaniṅgāru, sons of Chelināyuni-Komma-Nāyuḍu. The latter was the champion of Rudra, the right arm of Tenuṅgu-bhūpāla, lord of the town of Rēvanūru and worshipper of the feet of Kaḷēśvara.

355. 262 *of* 1905.—(Telugu.) On another Nandi-pillar set up in the same place, east face. Dated in the time of the Chōḷa king Tribhuvanachakravartin Kulōttuṅga-Chōḷadēva (I). Records in Ś. 1033, Khara, forty-third year, gift of fifty buffalo-cows for a lamp by Bhīmaya, the Peggaḍa of Pottapi-Kāmachōḍa-Mahārāja (of the konidēna section?). The priest of the temple was a Nanni-Dīkshita.

356. 263 *of* 1905.—(Telugu.) On the same face. A record of the Chōḷa king Tribhuvanachakravartin Kulōttuṅga-Chōḍadēva (I) dated in Ś. 1033, Khara, forty-third year. Records gift of fifty buffalo-cows by Rāmaṇa, the daṇḍanāyaka of Kāmadēva-Chōḍa-Mahāraja. Rāmaṇa was the son of the daṇḍanāyaka Guṇḍaya.

357. 264 *of* 1905.—(Sanskrit and Telugu.) On the same pillar, west face. The Vēlanāṇḍu king Rājēndra-Chōḍa records in Ś. 1095, gift of cows for a lamp. Rājēndra-Chōḍa was the son of Vēlanāṇti-Goṅka and Sabbāmbikā.

357-A. 265 *of* 1905.—(Telugu.) On the same face. A record of the Chōḷa king Tribhuvanachakravartin Kulōttuṅga-Chōḍadēva (I). Mentions in thirty-seventh year, Vyaya, the Mahāmaṇḍalēśvara Karikāla-Chōḷa-Mahārāju and the Moṭṭavāḍa district.

358. 266 *of* 1905.—(Tamil.) On the same pillar, north face. Mentions a certain Kīrtinārāyaṇa-Vēḷān.

359. 267 *of* 1905.—(Telugu.) On the same face. Records in Ś. 1028, that the pillar was set up by Śrīdhara-Bhaṭṭa, the priest of Pottapi-Kāmadēva-Chōḍa-Mahārāju (of konidēna ?).

360. 268 *of* 1905.—(Sanskrit and Telugu.) On a slab set up to the north of the same room. Records that Gaṇḍapeṇḍara Ambadēva-Mahārāja, in Ś. 1212, Vikrita (A.D. 1290), remitted all taxes in the villages owned by the temple on a representation made by a certain Nandaśiva. For this service Nandaśiva, in return, got from Tryambakaśivāchārya and other temple servants the village of Gaṅgavaramu, east of Penukoṇḍa. [Ambadēva, the younger brother of Tripurāri Mahādēva, was the greatest of the Gaṅgaya Sāhiṇi line.

361. 269 *of* 1905.—(Sanskrit.) On another slab set up to the north of the dark room *(chikatimidde)* in the Tripurāntakēśvara temple near Tripurāntakam. A record of the Vijayanagara king Dēvarāya (II). Records in Ś. 1363, Durmati, that Mallaṇārya, a

Brāhmaṇa from Uḍayagiri, built a tank at the village of Maṇḍanapāṭi, and gave some land for a flower garden.

362. 270 *of* 1905.—(Sanskrit and Telugu.) On the third slab set up in the same place. A damaged record of the Vijayanagara king Vīra-Harihararāya (II), dated Ś. 1307, Krōdhana. Mentions Bhikshāvritti-Siddhaya, the tank Gandhāvatī and the king's son Vīra-Dēvarāya (I), for whose merit the gift was made.

363. 271 *of* 1905.—(Telugu.) On four faces of a pillar set up in the same place. Records in Ś. 1134, Āṅgirasa, gift of several villages by the Mahāmaṇḍalēśvara Manma-Rāmachandra, son of Goṅka and grandson of Rāmadēvarāja. This chief calls himself "Lord of Orayūru, the best of towns."

364. 272 *of* 1905.—(Telugu.) On a slab built into the south wall of the Rāmadēva shrine in the prākāra of the same temple. A record of Vijaya-Gaṇḍagōpāla in Ś. 1185, Rudhirōdgarin (A.D. 1263). Records gift of land below the tank called Gaṇapasamudram built at Abhinava-Gaṇapavaramu by Śāntaśiva, a disciple of the *Rājaguru* presiding over the famous Gōḷaki-maṭha whose spiritual influence extended over three lakhs of villages. The donor was a chief named Karumāṇikka-Perumāḍi-Nāyaka. See No. 262.

365. 273 *of* 1905.—(Telugu.) On a slab lying on the roof of a small maṇṭapa in front of the same shrine. A record of the Kākatīya king Rudradēva-Mahārāja (I), dated in Ś. 1107, Viśvāvasu, gift of a village on the bank of the river Kṛishṇavēṇa in the district of Koṇḍapalli-nāṇḍu for the temple of Tripurāntakadēva at Kumāragiri, which was the head jewel of Śrīparvata.

366. 274 *of* 1905.—(Telugu.) On a pillar in front of the Śiva shrine north of the same shrine. Records in Ś. 1099, a gift by Vyāsarāśipaṇḍita, the manager *(sthānādhipati)* of the temple of Tripurāntaka.

367. 275 *of* 1905.—(Telugu.) On a slab set up close to the prākāra on the right side of the blocked up western entrance into the same temple. Records in Ś. 1309, Prabhava, gift of *ūramāḍa* and *mūla-visa* by the guild of merchants, who followed the Vīra-Baḷañjya doctrine and who claimed to have immigrated from Ahichchhatra. See No. 273 above.

368. 276 *of* 1905.—(Kanarese.) On another slab set up in the same place. A record of the reign of the Western Chāḷukya king Tribhuvanamalladēva (Vikramāditya VI), dated in Chaḷukya Vikrama year 51 (A.D. 1126–27), Parābhava. Records gift of the village of Chāpalamaḍuge in the Moṭṭavāḍi-nāḍu by the Mahāpradhāna Anantapāla-Daṇḍarasa.

369. 277 *of* 1905.—(Telugu.) On the third slab set up in the same place. The Velanāḍu king Goṅkarāja records in Ś. 1028, Sarvajit, gift of the village of Cheṭalapāḍu in Kamma-nāṇḍu, on the bank of the Guṇḍēru. Goṅka is called the chief supporter of the Chāḷukya kingdom and was ruling over the thousand-three-hundred (district).

370. 278 *of* 1905.—(Telugu.) On the fourth slab set up in the same place. Records in Ś. 1157, Manmatha, in the reign of Anuṅgudēva-Mahārāju (unidentified) that a cavalier gave twenty-five cows for a lamp on his success in a combat at Chintalapūṇḍi.

371. 279 *of* 1905.—(Telugu.) On the fifth slab set up in the same place. Records in Ś. 1138, Dhātri, gift of twenty-five cows for a lamp.

372. 280 *of* 1905.—(Telugu.) On the Nandi pillar set up at the main entrance into the same temple from the south. Records in Ś. 1371, Śukla, the setting up of the pillar.

373. 281 *of* 1905.—(Sanskrit and Telugu.) On the Nandi pillar set up by the side of the steps on the hill, leading to the same temple. A damaged record dated Ś. 1353, Virōdhikrit. Records the building of the steps.

374. 282 *of* 1905.—(Sanskrit and Telugu.) On another Nandi pillar lying by the side of the same steps. A much damaged record, the date of which is doubtful. Seems to be a Kākatīya inscription recording the establishment of a Śaiva *maṭha* near the temple of Tripurāntaka.

375. 283 *of* 1905.—(Telugu.) On a slab set up in the courtyard of the Mūlabrahmēśvara temple at the foot of the Tripurāntakam hill. A record of the time of the Kākatīya king Gaṇapatidēva-Mahārāja in Ś. 1172, Sādhāraṇa. Records gift of a village in the Dupali-Kampaṇa (district) to the temple of Mūlasthānadēva of Tripurāntakam by Mahāmaṇḍalēśvara Gaṇḍapeṇḍara-Gaṅgaya Sāhiṇi (who conquered the army of Dāmōdara of the west) for the merit of the king.

376. 45 *of* 1909.—On a slab in the courtyard of the Tripurāmbā temple in the bed of the tank. Records that in Kākatīya-Pratāparudra's reign, in Ś. 1218, Durmukhi, the local merchants gave the tolls for the merit of the king, of Rudradēva, the commander of all forces, and Pōchirāju Piṭṭirāju, the prime minister.

A C.P. in charge of Tumbala Guruvappa in the place. Records that the Śaivites paid 100 *māḍas* for God Gaurēśvara. *Ins., Ced. Dts.*, p. 229, No. 49.

Vēmulakōṭa.

377. At the sluice of the local tank. A record of "a local chief" dated Ś. 1578 (A.D. 1656), concerning repairs made to it. [See *Antiquities*, Vol. I.] See also *Ins., Ced. Dts.*, p. 228, No. 45, where the donor is named Tiruvēṅgalayya, son of Kaṇṭamarāju.

378. Near the above. Records that in Ś. 1525, Śubhakrit, Vatapartikoṇḍa, son of Basavanāyuḍu, restored certain land to the Brahmans in the pagoda. *Ibid.*, No. 44.

Venkatarēḍḍipāḷayam.

379. 285 *of* 1905.—(Sanskrit and Telugu.) On a huge pillar lying at the entrance into the Chennakēśavasvāmin temple. Records in Ś. 1544, Dundubhi, gift of the two villages Śiṅgarikoṇḍa and Battapaṭṭi, both in the district of Kōchcharlakōṭa, to the Chennakēśava temple at Veṅkaṭādrinagara, by Malla, son of Vīrappa and grandson of Malla of the Rāvela family, in the reign of the Vijayanagara king Rāmadēva (1620—30). [See *Antiquities*, Vol. I, p. 87, and also *Ins., Ced. Dts.*, p. 227, No. 43.]

380. 286 *of* 1905.—(Sanskrit and Telugu.) On a huge pillar lying at the entrance into the Chennakēśavasvāmin temple. Records in the reign of the Vijayanagara king Veṅkaṭadēvarāya (I, 1586—1616), in Ś. 1536, Ānanda, gift of four villages in the Dupaṭiśīma (district), east of Śrīśaila, to the Chennakēśava temple by a certain Gaṅgapa-Nāyaka, the governor of the Śrīgiri-maṇḍala, the son of Veṅkaṭādri and grandson of Gaṅga. [*Antiquities*, Vol. I, p. 87, and also *Ins., Ced. Dts.*, p. 227, No. 42, which however gives Ś. 1537.]

NANDIKŌTKŪR TALUK.

Ātmakūr.

381. 54 *of* 1915.—(Telugu.) On a slab set up in front of the Siddhēśvarasvāmin temple. Dated in the reign of the Vijayanagara king Immaḍi-Narasa-Nāyaniṅgāru (i.e., Vīra Narasimha Bhujabalarāya), son of Narasa-Nāyaniṅgāru, the son of Īśvara-Nāyaniṅgāru. Records in Ś. 1428, Krōdhana, Kārttika, ba. di. 3, Thursday, Kanyā-Brihaspati, corresponding to 16th October, A.D. 1505, gift of the village of Āṭukūru to the temple of Mallikārjuna on Śrīparvata, for offerings.

382. A "private inscription," dated in Ś. 1474 (A.D. 1552), in the same temple, referred to by Mr. Sewell in his *Antiquities*, Vol. I, p. 87. [See also *Ins., Ced. Dts.*, p. 456, No. 125. It records gift of 5 *tūms* of land by a Vīraśaiva Siddha Bhikshāvritti aiyavāru to one "Curreveerana" Uḍayalu.]

383. A C.P. grant, evidently a forgery, in the name of Chāḷukya Chakravarti, in the hands of a pūjāri. "The particulars of its contents sent to me are entirely untrustworthy, and the copy in my possession is not much better. It bears date Ś. 1275 (A.D. 1353) and professes to testify to the grant of a village by a king of the lunar race, Chāḷukya Chakravarti." [*Ibid.*]

384. On a stone on the bank of a well. Records that Besta Saddebōyaḍu dug up the well and built a *goḍḍu* on its banks for watering the cattle in Ś. 1216, Nandana. *Ibid.*, p. 457, No. 130.

Bannūru.

385. On a stone close to the Hanumanta pagoda. Records that Rāmarāja Veṅkaṭarāja exempted the tax of the Brahmans in this village (called also Koṇḍamasamudram) in Ś. 1693, Plavaṅga, in the reign of Sadāśivarāya. *Ins., Ced. Dts.,* p. 480, No. 203. [Vēnkaṭarāja is the celebrated Veṅkaṭādri, one of the three Āravīḍu brothers who distinguished themselves in this reign. The date is wrong.]

Bollavaram.

386. On a wall in the Prasannēśvara temple. Records that the Karaṇams of the place dug a well near the temple and granted some land to a Brahman Musalayya in Ś. 1619, Īśvara, in the reign of Aurangazeb Padshah. *Ibid.,* p. 448, No. 97 ; *Antiquities,* p. 87.

387. South of the above. A grant by the same Karaṇams in the same year to the Karaṇam of Pālakoṇṭa named Kṛishṇayya. *Ins., Ced. Dts.,* p. 448, No. 98.

388. Grant in the reign of Raṅgarāja (II, 1578—86) of Vijayanagar in Ś. 1503 (A.D. 1581). See *Antiquities* (which also mentions an undated private grant).

Brāhmaṇakōṭkūr.

389. On a broken stone near the Bhōgēśvara pagoda. A damaged record of Kākatīya Pratāparudra II in Ś. 1233, Śubhakrit. *Ins., Ced. Dts.,* p. 449, No. 103, and Mr. Sewell's *Antiquities,* p. 87.

Chantukūru.

390. Near the Kēśavasvāmi pagoda. Records that Rāmarāja Veṅkaṭādri Rājayya exempted the śrōtriyam rent of one Cunala (Kandāḷa ?) Śrīraṅgāchāryalu in Ś. 1469, Pḷavaṅga, in the reign of Sadāśiva Rāya. *Ins., Ced. Dts.,* p. 480, No. 204. Kandāḷas were one of the important Vaishṇava families who propagated the cult of Vishṇu in the Telugu country in the middle ages ; Most of them were the followers of the Prabandhic cult. See No. 395.

Cherukuchērla.

391. In front of the Vishṇu temple. A grant of Sadāśiva Rāya in Ś. 1469. *Antiquities,* p. 87.

Chintalapaḷḷe.

392. In the temple of Āñjanēya. A record of Sadāśiva Rāya, dated in Ś. 1469. *Ibid.*

393. In the temple of Vīrabhadra. An undated private grant.

Dāmagaṭḷa (Damagutla).

394. On a maṇṭapam in front of the Bhōgēśvara temple. Records that Śeshāchala, son of Basavarāja, erected the temple in Ś. 1658, Rākshasa. *Ins., Ced. Dts.,* p. 448, No. 99.

395. In the Vighnēśvara temple opposite the above. Records that Rāmarāja Veṅkaṭādrirāja (the brother of Aḷiya Rāma Rāya) exempted the tax of the local Brahmans in Ś. 1469, Pḷavaṅga, in the reign of Sadāśivarāya. *Ins., Ced. Dts.*, p. 448, No. 100.

396. In the Vighnēśvara temple near the fort. Records that the Vipravinōdins and jugglers of the place gave their local allowance from the Brahmans to God Chennakēśava in Ś. 1476, Ānanda, in the reign of Sadāśivarāya. *Ibid.*, No. 101.

397. On a stone near the Bhōgēśvara temple. Records that Mahārāja Upparamalla "Sammuma" presented an iron lamp with a chain and a cow (for oil) to God Bhōgēśvara in Ś. 1233, Virōdhi, in the reign of Kākatīya Pratāparudra (II, 1295—1323). *Ibid.*, No. 102 and *Antiquities*, I, p. 88.

398. Near the Garbhālaya of the Kēśavasvāmi temple. A private inscription dated Ś. 1650. *Antiquities*, I, p. 88.

Dēvanūru.

399. On a stone near a local well. Records that Peddarāja Lōkappagāru dug the well in Tiruvēṅgalanātha temple at Dēvanūr or Raṅgamāmbāpuram, and gave 20 *tūms* of land for its occasional repair, in Ś. 1512, Vikriti. *Ins., Ced. Dts.*, p. 479, No. 202.

Dudyāla.

400. On a stone in the village. Records that Basantarāyaḍu, son of "Yatagar" Vasantarāyaḍu, populated the deserted village of Dudyāla and gave some land to one Veṅgalareḍḍi in Ś. 1489, Prabhava, in the reign of Sadāśivarāya. *Ibid.*, p. 473, No. 180.

401. On a stone north of the above, in a pillar of the tank sluice. Records that Śrīraṅgamma, consort of Gobbūri Giriapparāju, repaired the sluice and its canal in Ś. 1529, Prabhava. *Ibid.*, No. 181.

Gaṇapuram.

402. In the Ellamma shrine. An epigraph dated in Ś. 1207. *Antiquities*, I, p. 88.

Iskala.

403. On a stone in front of the Vighnēśvara temple. Records that the local people set up the image of Kēśavapperumāḷ and granted 10 *tūms* of land to certain goldsmiths in Ś. 1486, Raktākshi, *Ins., Ced. Dts.*, p. 473, No. 182. [This is evidently the inscription of Ś. 1484, which Mr. Sewell refers to in his notice of the place in *Antiquities*, I, p. 88.]

404. On a stone near the Nāgēśvara pagoda. Records that Brahma Śivachārlu Bhagavanta granted to the temple the villages of Kambaḷapaḷḷi and Āṭukūru, in Ś. 1224, Śubhakrit. *Ins., Ced. Dts.*, p. 744, No. 183.

Jūtūrū.

405. On a stone east of the village in the hamlet of Liṅgāla. Records that Dēvaśeṭṭi and Nāgaśeṭṭi gave two *tūms* of land to God Nāgēśvara in Ś. 1178, in the reign of Gaṇapatidēva Mahārāja (1199—1260). *Ins., Ced. Dts.*, p. 474, No. 184.

Kaḍamūru.

406. On a carved stone lamp pillar near the local pagoda. Records that Aubalayya Tirumalayya, son of Bhōjanappaḷḷi Annayaṅgār, raised the pillar in front of the Hanumantarāya temple in Ś. 1457, Vyaya. *Ibid.*, p. 475, No. 191.

407. In the Vishṇu temple. An epigraph dated in Ś. 1470. *Antiquities*, I, p. 88.

408. On the dhvajastambha in the Āñjanēya temple. A private record dated in Ś. 1467. *Ibid.*

Maddigala (Madigaṭla ?).

408-A. Near the temple. A Telugu record in Ś. 1437, Yuva, Āshāḍha bahuḷa 13, Thursday. Records that Mahāpradhāna Śāḷuva Timma, minister of Kṛishṇadēvarāya, made certain gifts to Goddess Mādhavadēvi and temple servants, lands, etc. *Mack. MSS.*, Bk. XX (15-3-63), pp. 55-56.

408-B. In the same place. A Telugu record in Ś. 1482, Raudri, Māgha Śuddha 15, Thursday, in the reign of Sadāśivarāya. Records that Koṇḍarāju, grandson of Rāmarāju Koṇḍarāju and son of Veṅkaṭeśvara Rāju of Ātrēya gōtra, Apastambasūtra and Yajus Śākha, gave Mattagela (Maddigala) village to Mādhavadēvi. *Ibid.*, pp. 56-57.

Mallyala (Mullala).

409. On a stone in the Sarvēśvara temple. Records that Rudradēva, son of Sāmanta Beraku, and Bollayareḍḍi gave ten "*kuṇṭas*" of land and garden to God Sarvēśvara in Ś. 1212, Vikriti, in the reign of Kākatīya Rudrakumāruḍu. See *Ins., Ced. Dts.*, p. 450, No. 105.

410. On the other side of the above. Records that Mummaladēva Sarvēśvara Rāya gave to Gods Ballēśvara and Sarvēśvara whose liṅgams they established, some lands in Ś. 1208, Vyaya. *Ibid.*, No. 106.

411. On a stone south of the above. A gift of cows and oxen by Sarvēśvarayya in Ś. 1213, Khara. *Ibid.*, No. 107.

412. On a stone close to the Hanumanta pagoda. Records that a certain Liṅgayya dug a tank and gave some land to a person named Narasayya in Prajōtpatti. *Ibid.*, No. 108.

413. On the other side of the above. A gift of land by one "Chambole Sunta Dēvarāju" to the same person, *Ibid.*, p. 450, No. 109.

Miḍutūru.

414. In the temple of Kēśavasvāmi. A grant by "one of the Vijayanagar family called Kōnayya dēva," in Ś. 1469, in the reign of Sadāśiva Rāya. *Antiquities*, I, p. 89. Was Kōnayya the elder brother of Aḷiya Rāma Rāya?

415. In the same temple. A grant in the same reign in Ś. 1475. *Ibid.*

416. In the same. A grant of Raṅgappa Rājayya Mahārāja in Ś. 1503, in the reign of Śrī Raṅga (I, 1578—86).

417. In the same temple. A private grant in the reign of Sadāśiva in Ś. 1483.

418. In the same temple. Grant by the same as the above in the same date.

419. In the Vīrabhadra temple. Grant to a temple by Kōnayya dēva in Ś. 1469, in the reign of Sadāśiva Rāya. See No. 414 above.

Mittakandāla.

420. In the southern gate of the deserted temple of Siddhēśvara. A private record dated in Ś. 1621.

Mosalimaḍugu.

421. On a stone lying on the fort gate. Records that "Nundala Vekarecha Bālaya Dēva Rājalu" exempted the barbers from taxes in the village, in Ś. 1469, Pḷavaṅga, in the reign of Sadāśiva-Rāya. *Ins., Ced. Dts.*, p. 453, No. 113.

422. Mr. Sewell mentions an inscription on a stone at the entrance of the village dated in Ś. 1461, recording a private grant in the reign of Achyuta-Rāya of Vijayanagar. *Antiquities*, I, 89. [He mentions two other undated private grants.]

Nāgalūṭi.

423. 53 *of* 1915.—(Telugu.) On a pillar set up in front of the Vīrabhadra temple. Dated in the reign of the Vijayanagara king Vīrapratāpa Vīra Rāmadēva-Mahārāya, "ruling at Penugoṇḍa-paṭṭaṇa." Records in Ś. 1546, Raktākshi, Jyēshṭa, *śu. di.* 5, that Bontala Nāgi-Śeṭṭi, a Vaiśya of Vichchupākala-gōtra, built the eastern gōpura of the Vīrabhadra temple at Laṅgalūṇṭi in Siddhapura, set up the images of Kāśi-Viśvēśvara and Kalyāṇa-Basavēśvara, gave a piece of wet land below the tank called *Māḷacheruvu* with the permission of Timma Nāyuḍu, son of Sāyapa Nāyuḍu, who was then ruling over that country, and gave some copper and bronze vessels, a bell and a plate for waving incense. "The date can be calculated but not verified." [The inscription is given in *Ins., Ced. Dts.*, p. 456, No. 126.]

424. On a stone in front of the Āñjanēya temple. Dated Ś. 1469 in the reign of Sadāśiva Rāya and recording a grant by him. *Antiquities*, I, 89.

425. On a stone in the pagoda of Aṅkāḷamma. Records that Siddha Bhikshāvritti Ayyavāru gave some land and allowances in the village to Guḍivāḍa Eṛṛachinnappa, manager of the temple, in Ś. 1515, Vyaya. *Ins., Ced. Dts.*, p. 457, No. 127.

426. On a stone in the Śrīśaila road. Records that Mutina Mayiśeṭṭi, son of Yēkadēvanāyaka, built a village in his name in Ś. 1329, Sarvajit, and an inn for pilgrims. *Ibid.*, No. 128.

427. On a stone near Chennakēśava pagoda. Records that Kṛishṇadēva-Rāya re-established Carevana (Karivēna) agrahāra and granted it to Brahmans. *Ibid.*, No. 129.

Nandikōṭkūr.

428. On a stone near the Āñjanēya temple in the fort. Records that "Cullepāparāju," son of "Rauvechate Bhyrava Rāju", set up the image of Vishṇu in Ś. 1571, Sarvajit. *Ibid.*, p. 447, No. 94.

429. South of the above. Records that Appaḷarāju, son of Tipparāju, gave a grant to the Brahmans and temples of the village in Ś. 1469, Pḷavaṅga, in the reign of Sadāśivarāya. *Ibid.*, No. 95.

430. On a broken stone on the tank bank. Records that Ūttukūr Yōga-Raṅgappa Bhairavarāju made a grant. Damaged. *Ibid.*, p. 448, No. 96.

Pagidyāḷa (Pagidēḷa).

431. In the Añjanēya temple. A private grant dated in Ś. 1439. *Antiquities*, I, 89.

432. In the same temple. Ś. 1705. *Ibid.*

433. In the same place. A private grant in the reign of Sadāśiva of Vijayanagar in Ś.1477. *Ibid.*

434. In the Vīrabhadra temple. Same date and reign. *Ibid.*

435. In the same temple. A record of Ś. 1698. Copy incomplete. *Ibid.*

Parumañchala.

436. On a pillar in the Raṅgamaṇṭapam of the Kēśavasvāmi pagoda. Records that the Reḍḍis and Karaṇams of the village erected the temple in Ś. 1436, Bhava. *Ins., Ced. Dts.*, p. 477, No. 194. [This is apparently the inscription which Mr. Sewell assigns to Ś. 1446. Besides this Mr. Sewell notes an "illegible" inscription in the Nandi figures in the Vīrabhadra temple and a modern record of A.D. 1868. See *Antiquities*, I, 89.]

Prātakōṭa (Pātakōta).

437. On a stone near Chennakēśava pagoda. Records that the Reḍḍis and Karaṇams of the village granted 3¼ *tūms* of dry field to God Chennakēśava, for the lamp ceremony, in Ś. 1590, Pḷavaṅga. *Ins., Ced. Dts.,* p. 453, No. 114. [Referred to by Mr. Sewell also in his *Antiquities,* I, 90.]

438. On a stone near Vīrabhadra pagoda at the market. Records that the merchants fixed a contribution at one-quarter pagoda for the lamp festival of Vīrabhadra, in Ānanda. *Ibid.,* No. 115.

439. On a stone on the west side of Nāgēśvara pagoda. Records that Penukoṇḍa Nārāyaṇayya, son of Purāṇam Bāpayya, remitted the taxes of the lands of the temple in Ś. 1523, in the reign of Veṅkaṭapatirāya (I, 1586—1616). *Ibid.,* No. 116. [Referred to by Mr. Sewell, but under date Ś. 1522.]

Siddēpalli.

440. West of the village, on a stone in the field. A private grant in Ś. 1370. See *Antiquities,* I, p. 90.

Śivapuram (Sevapuram).

441. On a stone situated in the pagoda of Siddhēśvar. Records that Bhuvanēkamalla (Sōmēśvara II, 1068—75) granted a portion of land in the village, in Ś. 991, Saumya, at the request of his queen for the alms of Śivapuram and o* the school of the Mallikārjuna pagoda, during his reign. *Ins., Ced. Dts.,* p. 455, No. 120.

442. On the fourth side of the above inscription. Records that Padita Dēvaru granted twelve *muttas* of land for the repair of the pagoda in the thirty-third year of the reign of Chāḷukya Vikrama. *Ibid.,* No. 121.

443. On a stone on the north of the above inscription. Records that "Trylōkyā Malla Dēva and his consort" granted Jamatūr and Kallugoṭḷa in free gift to Bhairavadēva in Ś. 990, Viḷambi. *Ibid.,* No. 122. Trailōkyamalla was Sōmēśvara I, 1042—68.

444. On a stone north of above inscription. A record in the reign of Tribhuvanamalladēva (Vikramāditya VI). *Ibid.,* No. 123.

445. On the west side of the above. Records that Tribhuvanamalladēva granted seventeen *muttas* of land for the daily worship of God Mallikārjunadēva. *Ibid.,* No. 124.

Śriśailam.

For detailed descriptions of this important place, its religious and architectural features, etc., see *Asiatic Researches,* Vol. V, (1798); *Madr. Journ.,* Vol. XXIII, Pt. II, p. 132; Sewell's *Antiquities,* Vol. I, pp. 90–1.

446. 10 *of* 1915.—(Kanarese.) On a stone built into the floor of the central shrine of the Mallikārjuna temple. Records that the Vijayanagara king Vīrapratāpa Vīra-Naraśiṅgarāya-Mahārāya visited the temple of Mallikārjunadēva and paid homage to the god.

447. 11 *of* 1915.—(Sanskrit and Telugu.) On two pillars in the southern porch of the mukha-maṇṭapa of the same ṭemple; right and left of entrance. Records that Vijayanagara king Vīrapratāpa Harihara-Mahārāya (II) presented in Kali 4505 and Ś. 1326, Tāraṇa, Magha., ba. ḍi. 14, Monday, Śivarātri, the *mukhamaṇṭapa* to the temple of Mallikārjuna. The inscription includes a long praśasti of the king. [Mr. Swamikannu Pillai calculates the English equivalent of the date to be January 29, A.D. 1405, but Monday is an error for Thursday. Harihara is called Rājavyāsa and Raja-Vālmīki either because of his own learning or because of his patronage of learning. He also caused the *Vēdabhāshya* to be written and re-established the orthodox creeds of both Śiva and Vishṇu.]

448. 12 *of* 1915.—(Telugu.) On a slab buiḷt into the floor of the platform in the same porch; right of entrance. Records in Ś. 1440, Iśvara, Chaitra, śu. di. 15, Monday, corresponding to April 6, A.D. 1517, that a certain Parvatayya and his wife, who were adherents of Siddhabhikshāvritti-Ayyaṅgāru paid homage to Mallikārjuna, constructed tank near Bhīmunikoḷamu and planted a flower garden at Siddhapura. Records also the grant of a paddy field below the tank at Siddhapura for the daily offerings in the temple by Jaṅgam Basavayya, on Jyēshṭa, ba. di. 30, Friday, of the same year.

449. 13 *of* 1915.—(Sanskrit and Telugu.) On a slab built into the floor of the platform in the northern porch of the same maṇṭapa; right of entrance. States in Ś. 1451, Virōdhin, Mārgaśira, śu. di. Paurṇami (full moon), a date which can be calculated, but not verified, that the great minister Chandraśēkharāmātya, the son-in-law of Dēma and a devoted servant of Kṛishṇarāya, built the kalyāṇamaṇṭapa on the northern side of the Mallikārjuna shrine, set up a golden pinnacle on it and also built a shrine for the liṅga called Dēmēśa. A Telugu record in continuation of this gives the date Ś. 1451, Vikriti, Śravaṇa, ba. di. 30, and registers the grant by the same minister of the village Kōragoṭṭa in Chāgalamaṛṛi śīma to a servant (?) of the same temple. [This inscription is given in *Mack. MSS.* also. See *Ins., Ced. Dts.*, p. 464, No. 153.]

450. 14 *of* 1915.—(Telugu.) In the same place; left of entrance. A record of the Vijayanagara king Kṛishṇadēvarāya in Ś. 1452, Vikriti, Chaitra, ba. di. 3, Monday, corresponding to Monday, 6th March 1530. Records that Chandraśēkharayya ruling the Śrīśaila-rājya as the king's representative *(avasaram)*, built a maṇṭapa in front of the bed-room of the god Mallikārjuna, presented golden images of Nandīśvara and Bhriṅgīśvara, set up standing stone figures of his master Kṛishṇarāya, his father-in-law Dēmarasa and of himself in that maṇṭapa, and for meeting the expenses of worshipping the god in that maṇṭapa, gave the village of Śivapura in Mosalimaḍuguśīma which was included within his jurisdiction. He also gave a golden cup and a silver pedestal *(panivaṭṭam)* for the god, set up to the north of Mallikārjuna the liṅga called after Dēmaya and set up in front of it a golden pillar. At Nāgalūṭi which is at the foot of the hill he erected a temple for Vīraṇa (i.e., Vīrabhadra), consecrated a liṅga called Dēmaya within it and presented the village Dēmasamudra to Brahmans. [See *Ins., Ced. Dts.*, p. 460, No. 140, for a defective version of this epigraph.]

451. 15 *of* 1915.—(Telugu.) In the same place; left of entrance. A record of the Vijayanagara king Kṛishṇadēvarāya, dated in Ś. 1451, Virōdhin, Kārttika, śu. di. 15, Sunday, corresponding to October 27, A.D. 1529, recording gift of the village Gatirājupeṇṭa to Rāchūṭi-Vīraṇṇōḍaya of *Basava-maṭha*, by the same Chandra-śēkharayya, for the merit of the king Dēmarasayya and himself. [*Ins., Ced. Dts.*, p. 464, No. 152.]

452. 16 *of* 1915.—(Sanskrit.) On the right and left pillars of the eastern porch of the same maṇṭapa. Records in Kali 4611 and Ś. 1433, Prajōtpatti, Māgha, ba. di. 14, Monday (corresponding to 6th February, 1512), a lengthy account of the gifts made to the temple of Śrīśailam by a certain chief Liṅga, the son of Śānta, who was evidently a Vīraśaiva, one of his pious acts being the beheading of the Śvētambara Jainas.

453. 17 *of* 1915.—(Kanarese.) On the west face of the right pillar in the same place. Records that Mādaya and Mallarasa in the service *(ūliga)* of king Kṛishṇarāya worshipped the god.

454. 18 *of* 1915.—(Telugu.) On stones built into the floor of the platform in the same porch; right of entrance. A record of the Vijayanagara king Vīrapratāpa Kṛishṇadēva-Mahāraya, dated in Ś. 1438, Yuva, Śravaṇa, śu. di. 15, Wednesday, lunar eclipse, stating that after his conquests Kṛishṇarāya made gifts at Amarēśvara, came to Śrīparvatam and had maṇṭapas constructed in the car street. Prior to this in the year Śrīmukha (Vaiśākha, śu. di. 11, Thursday) he had made a gift of the villages of Porumañchāla and Āṭukūru to the temple of Mallikārjuna. He also remitted tolls on *kāvaḍis*, pack-horses, bullocks, asses and head-loads. For the date see next inscription. [See *Mack. MSS., Ins., Ced. Dts.*, p. 462, No. 145, for this record.]

455. 19 *of* 1915.—(Kanarese.) In the same place; left of entrance. A record of the Vijayanagara king Vīrapratāpa Kṛishṇadēva Mahārāya, dated in Ś. 1438, Yuva, Śravaṇa, śu. di. 15, Wednesday, lunar eclipse. An exact translation of the above. The date corresponds to Wednesday, July 25, A.D. 1515. [*Ins., Ced. Dts.*, p. 462, No. 146.]

456. 20 *of* 1915.—(Sanskrit and Telugu.) On the right and left pillars of the maṇṭapa adjoining the Nandi-maṇṭapa in the same temple. Records in the reign of the Reḍḍi king Jaganobbagaṇḍa Anna-Vēma in Ś. 1299, Piṅgala, Māgha, śu. di. 7, Wednesday (corresponding to January 6, A.D. 1378), the building of the Vīramaṇṭapa for the merit of his father Annaya-Reḍḍi. Supplies a genealogy of the Reḍḍis of whom the first was Pōla. It is stated that in this maṇṭapa many heroes voluntarily cut off their heads and tongues. The two faces of the right pillar which contain a long list of the *birudas* of Anna-Vēma give the date Ś. 1298, Piṅgaḷa, Māgha, śu. di. 7, Wednesday. Annaya was not the father but the uncle of Anna Vēma. He calls him father because of the affection he bore him. Amongst Anna Vēma's titles are mentioned "the Lord of the eastern ocean"; the destroyer of Rājamahēndra, Niravadyapura and other *sthaladurgas*. He belonged to the Vellachēri gōtra.

457. 21 *of* 1915.—(Kanarese.) On the west face of the third pillar in the same maṇṭapa. Mentions in Ś. 1448, Sarvadhāri, Māgha, ba. di. 10 (a date which "can be calculated but not verified)" Mallapaṇṇa of Alabaragi, a household servant of Kṛishṇarāya.

458. 22 *of* 1915.—(Kanarese.) On the south face of the same pillar. A record of the Vijayanagara king Vīrapratāpa Prauḍhadēvarāya Mahārāya recording in Ś. 1379, Īśvara, Magha, ba. di. 5, Thursday, that Demarasayya, a servant of the palace, purchased some land and presented it to the temple for providing one plateful of oblation to the god and feeding five *jaṅgams* every day. [The date corresponds to Saturday (not Thursday), 4th February, A.D. 1458. The inscription is also given in *Ins., Ced. Dts.*, p. 462, No. 147.]

459. 23 *of* 1915.—(Telugu.) On the fourth pillar in the same maṇṭapa. A record of Vijayanagara king Vīrapratāpa Achyutarāya recording in Ś. 1452, Vikriti, Pushya, ba. di. 11, Friday, corresponding to 19th August, A.D. 1530, that a certain Mallappa-Nāyaṇḍu presented a bell to the temple of Mallikārjuna and a lace cloth to the goddess Bhramarāmba, for the merit of the king and his brother (Kṛishṇarājadēva-Mahārāya).

460. 24 *of* 1915.—(Kanarese.) On the west face of the fifth pillar in the same maṇṭapa. Records in Ś. 1381, Pramāthin, Phalguṇa, śu. di. 3, Monday, corresponding to February 25, A.D. 1460, a gift of land by purchase to the same temple by Lakhumāji-Āyi, wife of Pāṇḍya-Perumāḷdēva and daughter of Vīrapratāpa Vijayarāya-Mahārāya for feeding five jaṅgams every day with one plateful of oblation. [The epigraph is given in *Ins., Ced. Dts.*, p. 463, No. 149.]

461. 25 *of* 1915.—(Kanarese.) On the north face of the same pillar. A record of the Vijayanagara king Vīrapratāpa Prauḍhadēvarāya Mahārāya (1449—65), dated in Ś. 1379. Records gift of land for the same purpose by a female servant of the palace. [This is evidently the same as *Ins.*, *Ced. Dts.*, p. 463, No. 148.]

462. 26 *of* 1915.—(Telugu.) On a broken slab set up in the eastern courtyard of the same temple. A record of the Sāḷuva king Peda-Mallapparāju, son of Yaram-Kampayadēva-Mahārāja in Ś. 1407, Viśvāvasu, Bhādrapāda, śu. di. 15, Thursday, lunar eclipse, corresponding to August 25, A.D. 1485, recording the gift of a tank (with lands below it) for providing offerings, to the same temple. [See Ct. 9-H. and Ct. 13, the Śirumallayyadēva of which was perhaps Peda Malla's younger brother.]

463. 27 *of* 1915.—(Telugu.) On a pillar set up in the same courtyard. Records that in the reign of the Kākatīya king Pratāparudradēva-Mahārāja (1295—1323), in Ś. 1234, Paridhāvin, Phalguna, śu. di. 5, Thursday, corresponding to February 1, A.D. 1313, a gift of land, in Kam-nāḍu for providing midday offerings to the same temple was made by the chief minister (mahāpradhāni) Vēpēṭi Kommayya.

464. 28 *of* 1915.—(Telugu.) On a broken image lying in the same courtyard. Records that this image of Bhairava was set up on the Śrīgiri hill by the *gavare* (merchant) Muddama-Śeṭṭi Gaṅga-Malli-Śeṭṭi of Rājamahēndravaramu.

465. 29 *of* 1915.—(Telugu.) On the image of Bhriṅgi in the same courtyard. Records that this image of Bhriṅgināthа was set up by the same merchant, here stated to be the son of Gavare-Muddama-Śeṭṭi Malli-Śeṭṭi.

466. 30 *of* 1915.—(Telugu.) On a slab set up in the same courtyard. Records in Ś. 1382, Vikrama, Āshāḍha, śu. ḍi. 15, Thursday, lunar eclipse, corresponding to July 3, A.D. 1460, a long but incomplete eulogistic account evidently of certain kings. One-half of the slab from top to bottom is occupied by a Uriya record.

467. 31 *of* 1915.—(Telugu.) On a pillar set up in the southern courtyard of the same temple. Records in Virōdhin, Śravaṇa, ba. di. 30, that a certain Mallasāni Aṇṇapa Ayapa provided for daily oblations in the shrines of Mallikārjuna and Bhramārāmba, built the mukhamaṇṭapa in front of Siddhēśvara, repaired the southern prākāra wall, set up the iron pillars, and inscribed stones in their proper places and repaired the maṇṭapa of the southern gōpura. The east face of the pillar contains the usual long *praśasti* of Kṛishṇarāya which breaks off with the verse *Kirtyā yasya sāmantāh*, etc. [*Ins.*, *Ced. Dts.*, p. 465, No. 154?]

468. 32 *of* 1915.—(Kanarese.) On the iron lamp-pillar set up in the same courtyard. Records in the reign of the Vijayanagara king Veṅkaṭapatirāya (1586—1616), in Ś. 1524, Śubhakrit, Māgha, ba. di. 5 (?), Śivarātri, the setting up of this iron lamp-pillar (with chains) for the merit of Mudiyapa-Nāyaka by a certain Chikaiya, son of Doḍa-Halagaiya, a carpenter of Henjēra in the Miḍugalla-śīme where a golden shower is said to have fallen for the merit of the Chōḷa king. "The date can be calculated but not verified." See *Ins., Ced. Dts.*, p. 461, No. 141.

469. 33 *of* 1915.—(Sanskrit and Telugu.) On another pillar in the same courtyard. Records that the Sāḷuva king Mahāmaṇḍalēśvara Sāḷuva Parvatayyadēva Mahārāja provided, in Ś. 1389, Sarvajit, Māgha ba. di. 14, Monday, Śivarātri, corresponding to February 22, A.D. 1468, for daily offerings in the temple by granting wet lands below the tank called Gaṅgasamudra which he had built at Siddhapura. He also gave a garden near the Siddhasamudram tank on the Śrīparvata hill, milch-cows and two buildings for feeding 30 Brāhmaṇas and 30 Jaṅgamayyas. See Ct. 12.

470. 34 *of* 1915.—(Telugu.) On the fourth pillar in the same courtyard. Records in Ś. 1426, Raktākshi, Māgha, ba. di. 14, Monday, corresponding to 3rd February 1505, the gilding, with gold plate, of the southern entrance into the mukha maṇṭapa of the Mallikārjuna temple by a certain Vīrayya, son of Nāgiśeṭṭi and Lakkammā.

471. 35 *of* 1915.—(Telugu.) On the fifth pillar in the same courtyard. Records in Ś. 1452, Virōdhin, Śravaṇa, śu. di. 15, Monday (which is wrong for Wednesday), corresponding to 21st July 1529, that the sons of Yalikaṇṭi Kāmarāju, the *sthalakaraṇam* of Śrīparvata, set up an image of Annapūrṇa-Bhavāni within the kitchen of the temple and a Nandi-pillar in the place intended for chaṇḍi.

472. 36 *of* 1915.—(Telugu.) On the sixth pillar in the same courtyard. Records that in the reign of the Kākatīya king Pratāparudradēva-Mahārāja (II) in Ś. 1235, Pramādīcha, Chaitra, śu. di. 1, Monday, corresponding to February 26, A.D. 1313, that Iśvaraśivāchārya of Arasa-maṭha and Ārādhya-Preggaḍa gave a deed of declaration in the presence of all the great Mahēśvaras of Śrī-Kailāsa (i.e., Śrīśaila) who had met together in the mukha-maṇṭapa of the Vīrabhadra temple attached to the Gaṇa-maṭha, for the purpose of managing the affairs in the temple of Mallikārjunadēva. Mentions seventy villages granted to the temple by emperors, Mahāmaṇḍalēśvaras and others, in former times, for worship and for feeding lay devotees and ascetics. Noticed vaguely by Mr. Sewell in his *Antiquities*, Vol. I, p. 91. See also *Ins., Ced. Dts.*, p. 465, No. 157.

473. 37 *of* 1915.—(Telugu.) On the bali-pīṭa in the northern courtyard of the same temple. Records that this balipīṭa in the north-eastern corner of the temple was erected by Gaṅga-Malli Seṭṭi of Rājamahēndravaramu.

474. 38 *of* 1915.—(Telugu.) On a hero stone in the same courtyard. Records that this figure represents the killing (in fight) of a tiger by Nāgarāju-Timmaṇa, a servant of Baṇḍāru Vīramarāju.

475. 39 *of* 1915.—(Telugu.) On a stone set up in the plantain garden of the same temple. Records in Ś. 1384, Svabhānu, Bhādrapada, śu. di. 15, Monday, gift of a flower garden to the temple by Vairāgi Śāntayya for the merit of his wife Siddhamā. An irregular date. See *Ep. Rep.*, 1915, p. 84.

476. 40 *of* 1915.—(Telugu.) On a slab set up near the eastern gōpura of the same temple. Records in Ś. 1370, Vibhava, Āshāḍha, śu. di. 15, Monday, gift of voluntary fees by the guild of merchants for conducting the Śivarātri festival in the temple of Mallikārjuna. [An irregular date as Monday is a mistake for Sunday. The date would then correspond to 16th June, A.D. 1448. See also *Ins., Ced. Dts.*, p. 466, No. 159.]

477. 41 *of* 1915.—(Telugu.) On a slab set up in front of the Vīrabhadrasvāmin temple on the same hill. Records in Ś. 1237 Rākshasa, Śravaṇa, ba. di. 10, Tuesday (?), that the Mahēśvaras residing on the Śrī-Kailāsa (i.e., Śrīśaila) having met together in the mukha maṇṭapa of the Vīrabhadra temple attached to Gaṇamaṭha, the presiding priests and the preggaḍas of Arasa-maṭha and Kalu-maṭha made a declaration (before them) that they would conduct worship and festivals in the temple of Mallikārjuna regularly. Mr. Swamikannu Pillai says that the week day ought to be Sunday.

478. 42 *of* 1915.—(Sanskrit, Nāgari.) On the lintel of the entrance into a small shrine in the Vīrabhadrasvāmi-maṭha on the same hill. Records that this shrine of Ghaṇṭa-Siddhēśvara (was constructed) by the pupil of Mallikārjunāchārya.

479. 43 *of* 1915.—(Telugu.) On a slab set up near a tank west of the Mallikārjuna temple on the same hill. Records that in the reign of the Vijayanagara king Vīrapratāpa Rāmarājayyadēva-Mahārāja, son of Vīra-Tirumalayyadēva-Mahārāya, in Ś. 1499, Bhava, Vaiśākha, ba. di. 30, Friday (an irregular date) that the bund across the stream Bhōgavati on the west side of the temple, which was out of repair, was repaired by the king's agent Dantikaṇṭi Liṅgappaṇa. He caused the bund to be reconstructed and made a gift of it together with the tank for raising a flower garden to the temple of Mallikārjuna. Rāmarāja is generally known as Rāma III. The repair is said to have been made at the instance of the Vīraśaiva teacher Śāntabhikshā vritti Ayyavāru.

480. 44 *of* 1915.—(Telugu.) On a pillar set up in front of the Sāraṅga-maṭha on the same hill. Records in Ś. 1507, Pārthiva, Āśvija, ba. di. 2, Thursday, corresponding to September 30, A.D. 1585, an agreement *(samākhyā)* made among themselves, by the presiding priests of the five *maṭhas* including Bāla-Siddaya of the

Sāraṅga-maṭha, the five houses and temples (on the Srisailam hill), such as those of Nandinātha, Bhriṅginātha, Vīrabhadra and others. The agreement evidently consisted in not allowing the successive priests of the Sāraṅga-maṭha to have any attendants *(añcha-pañcha-parivāra ?)*.

481. 45 *of* 1915.—(Telugu.) On a sandal-stone in the verandah of the same *maṭha*. Records in Ānanda, Ashāḍa, śu. di. 2, Sunday, that this is the sandal-stone *(sāna)* presented by Śiṅgayya, son of Puli Annama-Nāyuḍu, to the temple of Mallikārjuna.

482. 46 *of* 1915.—(Telugu.) On a slab set up on the way leading to Pātāḷa-Gaṅga from the Mallikārjuna temple. Records in Ś. 1567, Svabhānu, Phalguna, ba. di. 10, that the chief Veṅkaṭa-pati-Nāyaniṅgāru of the Mādala-gōtra remitted all taxes and tolls payable by metal-dealers *(kañchara)* who sold their wares in Śrīgiri during festivals or other days.

483. 47 *of* 1915.—(Sanskrit, Nāgari.) On three sides of a pillar set up in front of a ruined shrine on the same way. Records in Ś. 1315, Śrīmukha, the construction of steps to the Pātāḷa-Gaṅga by the Kadamba princess Viṭṭhalāmba, wife of Harihara (II ?), under orders given by god Mallikārjuna in a dream. [*Ins., Ced. Dts.*, p. 467, No. 161.] See No. 487.

484. 48 *of* 1915.—(Telugu.) On two faces of another stone set up on the same way. Records in Sarvajit, Phalguna, śu. di. 11, Thursday, that a certain Dāvāla Dāramā Sāhibu and Timāji-Pantulu remitted, for the merit of Hajarāti-Navābu, the fee *(gaṇāchāra)* on beggars who begged on the Śriśaila hill, as originally it had been remitted by Veṅkaṭapati-Nāyuḍu, son of Sāyapa-Nāyuḍu.

485. 49 *of* 1915.—(Sanskrit and Telugu.) On four faces of a pillar set up on the same way. Records in Ś. 1318, Śrīmukha, a copy of No. 483 above.

486. 50 *of* 1915.—(Sanskrit, Grantha.) On four faces of another pillar set up on the same way. Records in Ś. 1315, Śrīmukha, a copy of No. 483 above.

487. 51 *of* 1915.—(Sanskrit, Nāgari.) On a boulder by the side of the steps on the same way. Records in Ś. 1318 that Viṭṭhalāmba, the princess, consecrated an image of Viṭṭhalēśvara near the flight of steps. See No. 483 above.

488. 52 *of* 1915.—(Telugu.) On a pillar set up on the way to Peddacheruvu on the same hill. Records in Ś. 1344, Śubhakrit Kārttika, śu. di. 5, Thursday, that a certain Uḍayagiri Appaṇayyaṁ-gāru, son of Dēvanayyaṁgāru, built the steps from the Nandi-pillar at the southern main entrance *(gavani)* right up to the shrine of Durgidēvi. The week day should be Tuesday, and the date corresponds to October 20, A.D. 1422.

489. *C.P. No.* 96 *of Mr. Sewell's list.*—Records the settlement of a dispute between the Vaiśyas and the two upper classes of the

Dvijas (i.e., the Brahmans and Kshattriyas) in the local temple, whereby the former were granted certain religious privileges. Dated in Ś. 1387 (A.D. 1465), *Pārthiva*.

489-A. On the gilt wall of the inner pagoda. Records that Chandraśēkhara, the minister of Kṛishṇadēvarāya, re-established the pagoda with the *kalaśams* and set up the Garuḍastambham. No date. *Ins., Ced. Dts.*, p. 458, No. 132.

489-B. North of the above. A gift by the same chief. *Ibid.*, No. 133.

489-C. Near the above. (Telugu.) Records that the same chief built the Vīrabhadra pagoda at Nāgalūṭi. *Ibid.*, No. 134.

489-D. On the south gilt wall at the bottom of the Chaturmukha Brahma in Śriśailam. Records that Śiṅgayya, son of Śāntaliṅgayya, built the maṇṭapam in Ś. 1435, Śrīmukha, in the reign of Kṛishṇadēvarāya. *Ibid.*, No. 135.

489-E. On the eastern gilt gate of the same pagoda. Records that Mallanāyaḍu, son of Tippanāyaḍu, had the gate and doors gilt and granted the village of Pallivōli to God Mallikārjuna. *Ibid.*, No. 136.

489-F. Near the above. Records that Koṇḍabhaṭṭa, son of Nandikuṇṭa Kāśī Nāgabhaṭṭuḍu, the architect, made the gilt work in the temple. *Ibid.*, No. 137.

489-G. On the gold pillar of dhvajastambham. Records that Sāḷakarāja Pinna Tirumalarāja erected in Ś. 1458, Manmatha, a sacrificial hearth and raised the gold pillar on the east side of the temple. *Ibid.*, No. 138. See No. 245 above.

489-H. On another dhvajastambham south of the temple. (Sanskrit, Tamil and Telugu.) Records that Sāḷuva Tirumalarāja, son of Goppa, raised the stambham in Ś. 1378, Dhātu. *Ibid.*, No. 139. [He made great donations to Śrīraṅgam, Jambukēśvaram and Rāmēśvara shrines and was the contemporary of the Tamil poet Kāḷamēgha.]

489-I. On a dhvajastamba of the temple. Records that Annamarāja, son of Sūryarāja, made a copper pillar and had it gilt in Ś. 1556, Śrīmukha. *Ibid.*, No. 142.

489-J. On a copper dhvajastambham. Records that Māchala "Chitapa", and another who were the watchers of the temple placed a copper pillar in Ś. 1516, Vijaya. *Ibid.*, No. 143.

489-K. On a bell opposite the God in the Basavaṇṇa maṇṭapam. Records that Vīrayyarāja, son of Srīkaṇṭharayya, prince of the city of Nañjarājapaṭṇam, granted the bell in Ś. 1712, Vikriti. The record is in Kanarese. *Ibid.*, p. 461, No. 144.

489-L. On the north pillar of the mahāmaṇṭapam. Records that Anavēma Reḍḍi (1339—69), prince of Koṇḍavīḍu, erected the steps to the Śriśailam hill. *Ibid.*, No. 150.

489-M. On a pillar of the maṇṭapam in front of the eastern gate of the pagoda. Records that Liṅgayya and Kōṭachinnaśeṭṭi built a temple on the north-east of the mukhamaṇṭapam of the God and suspended a gilded bell in the pagoda in Ś. 1434, Prajōtpatti, in the reign of Kṛishṇadēva Mahārāya. *Ins., Ced. Dts.*, p. 464, No. 151.

489-N. On the southern gate pillar of the pagoda. Records that Nāyanigāru built a mukhamaṇṭapam opposite the pagoda of the God Mallikārjuna in Ś. 1225. *Ibid.*, No. 155.

489-O. Round the stone pillar of the maṇṭapam on the south of the pagoda. Records that Harihara Rāyalu (II) erected the mukhamaṇṭapam south of the pagoda with gold works during his reign in K. 4505, Tāraṇa. *Ibid.*, p. 465, No. 156.

489-P. On the gate pillar of the Sàlumaṇṭapam, west of the temple. Records that Haṇḍe Dēvapa Nāyaḍu built a number of the shrines and a maṇṭapam of stone around the Garbhaguḍi pagoda of the God in Ś. 1525, Śubhakrit. *Ibid.*, p. 466, No. 158.

Tarigōpula.

490. In the temple of Kēśavasvāmi. An "unimportant" record of Ś. 1679 (A.D. 1757). *Antiquities*, I, p. 91.

491. In the temple of Vīrabhadrasvāmi. A private grant dated in Ś. 1571. *Ibid.*

492. Near a well in the Siddhēśvara temple. A private record of Ś. 1567. *Ibid.*

Tartūr (Taratur).

493. On a stone north of the local Kēśavasvāmi temple. Records that Mallipēṭa Annamarāju granted one *puṭṭi* of land for two pipers in Ānanda. *Ins., Ced. Dts.*, p. 475, No. 187. [The village Mallipēṭa is not improbably the Mallapēṭa of Mārkāpūr taluk as given in the alphabetical list of villages.]

Vaḍḍamānu.

494. On a stone near a local well. Records that Veṅkaṭarāju, son of Koṇḍarāju, gave eleven *tūms* of land for digging a tank to a person named Muddū Eṛṛakoṇḍayya in Ś. 1466 in the reign of Sadāśiva-Rāya. *Ibid.*, p. 450, No. 104.

495. In the local Yellammā temple. A grant in Ś. 1485 (A.D. 1563). *Antiquities*, p. 91. [The *Antiquities* places this inscription on the stone near the well and the other in the Yellammā temple. But the *Mack. MSS.* which mention only the former locate it near the well.]

Velapanūru (Velpunure).

496. On a stone north of the local Siddhēśvara pagoda. Records that four Reḍḍis of the village built in Ś. 1646, Śōbhakrit, the twenty-pillared and four-pillared maṇṭapams. See *Ins., Ced. Dts.*, p. 468, No. 164.

497. On a stone east of the temple. Records that Rāmarāja Nalla Timmarāja re-established the temple and granted four *tūms* of land in Ś. 1476, Ānanda. *Ins., Ced. Dts.*, No. 165.

498. South of the above. Records that "Baraku" Mahēśvara Reḍḍi gave two puṭṭis of land to the temple in Ś. 1240, Kāḷayukti, in the reign of Kākatīya Pratāparudra (1295—1323). *Ibid.*, No. 166.

Velugōḍu (Yellagōdu).

499. In the Kēśavasvāmi pagoda. Records that Rāmarāja Nalla Timmarāja remitted the tax of the local barbers in Ś. 1476, Ānanda, in the reign of Sadāśivarāya. See *Ibid.*, p. 467, No. 163. See No. 497.

Veepanagaṇḍla.

500. On a stone near a local well. Records that Madagani Basavareḍḍi Kumāruḍu exempted the tax of the lands of the Gods Mallikārjuna and Vīrabhadra in Ś. 1511, Sarvadhāri, in the reign of Veṅkaṭapati Rāya (I, 1586—1616). *Ibid.*, p. 475, No. 188.

501. On a stone east of the village. Records that Śivayōgadēvarāja, son of "Dravaladēva," granted the village which he re-named Dravalapuram after his father to the Brahmans in Ś. 1174, Paritāpi, in the reign of Kākatīya Gaṇapatidēva Mahārāya (1200—60). *Ibid.*, No. 189.

502. On a stone near the above. Records that Aubala Bommareḍḍi dug the well and gave some land to some watermen for distributing water to the cattle in Ś. 1632, Virōdhi, in the reign of Sultan Paḍshah at Bijapur (Vijapuram). *Ibid.*, p. 476, No. 190.

Vempeṇṭa (Vempēṭa).

503. On a stone near the Umāmahēśvara temple. Records that Chinnama-Rāju and other local people built the Īśvara pagoda and gave some land in Ś. 1560, Saumya. See *Ibid.*, p. 467, No. 162.

Yerramaṭham (Yedumutta).

504. On a stone near the local Bhairavēśvara pagoda. Records that "Sutersu Timmayem Bhekursanum," the prime minister of Bhuvanēkamalla (i.e., Sōmēśvara II, 1068—75) of the city of Tēkapuram, set up the image of the God and granted the village in Ś. 997, Śubhakrit. See *Ibid.*, p. 452, No. 12.

NANDYĀL TALUK.

Ayyalūru.

505. On a stone in front of the Nīlakaṇṭha pagoda. Records that "Āṇḍigaṇāchāri" Nandyāla Basavayya gave the allowances of his people in the village to God Nīlakaṇṭha in 1453, Khara, with the permission Vibhūti Bhīmayya. See *Ins., Ced. Dts.*, p. 477, No. 196. See also *Antiquities*, p. 93.

506. In the Kēśavasvāmi pagoda in the local fort. Records that jugglers granted the allowance they had been receiving from the agrahāra to the Gods Kēśava and Nīlakaṇṭha in Ś. 1450, Sarvadhāri, in the reign of Kṛishṇadēvarāya. *Ibid.*, No. 197. See also *Antiquities*, p. 93.

Ayyavāru-Kōḍūru.

507. A private record dated in Ś. 1450, mentioning repairs to the local temples of Chennakēśava by private party. See *Antiquities*, p. 94.

Baṇḍiyātmakūr.

508. On a stone near the Janārdana pagoda. Records that "Hasa" Nāyaniṅgāru granted sixteen *tūms* of dry field to the deity in Ś. 1468, Manmatha, in the reign of Achyutarāya. See *Ins., Ced. Dts.*, p. 471, No. 176. See also Mr. Sewell's *Antiquities*, p. 95.

509. On a stone in the Chowḍasvāmi pagoda in the local market. Records that the local people built the pagoda of Vīramātā and made a grant for her worship in 1647, Viśvāvasu. *Ins., Ced. Dts.*, p. 472, No. 178.

510. On the iron lamp pillar in the Nandi pagoda. Records that Mutyāla Ammagāru, mother of Nandyāla Tipparāja, set up the pillar in the Mahānandīśvara temple in Ś. 1332, Vikriti. *Ibid.*, No. 179.

Beṭamcheruvu.

511. Mr. Sewell gives two definite inscriptions in this place, of which one is dated in Ś. 1470, in the reign of Sadāśivarāya and the other in Ś. 1467, in the same reign recording a private grant. See *Antiquities*, p. 94.

Bilakalaguḍūru.

512. A record in the time of Kōmayya, minister of Pratāparudra II (1295—1323) in Ś. 1229. *Antiquities*, Vol. I, p. 94.

513. A private inscription, dated Ś. 1642. *Ibid.*

Brāhmaṇappaḷḷi.

514. On a stone south of the temple of Hanūmān. Records that the temple was erected in Ś. 1479. *Ibid.*

Būjanūru.

515. In the temple of Mahādēva. An epigraph dated in Ś. 1182. *Ibid.*

Chābōlu.

516. On a stone near the Gōpāla temple. Records that Immaḍi-Narasimharāya (son of the usurper Śāḷuva Naraśiṅga) granted the village to the temple in Ś. 1415, Paritāpi. See *Ins., Ced. Dts.*, p. 478, No. 198.

Chilakala.

517. A copper-plate grant (three plates) of this place was received from the Collector by the Department in 1904. It records the grant by Mallikārjuna or Immaḍi Dēvarāya or Immaḍi Prauḍha-dēva Rāya of the village of Oḍḍugaṇḍḷa in the Paṇeyadēśa of the Guttirājya in Ś. 1381. The village of Chilakala figures among the boundaries of Oḍḍugaṇḍḷa. [See *Madras Ep. Rep.*, 1905, p. 59. Venkayya points out that Padea Rao of Nuniz should be "Mallikārjuna or Immaḍi Prauḍha-dēva Rāya, the latter part of whose second name was apparently corrupted into Padea Rao."]

Chiṇḍukūru.

518. At the temple of Vīrabhadrasvāmi. A private grant in Ś. 1676 (A.D. 1754). *Antiquities*, p. 94.

Gaḍigarēlu (Gaḍigarēvula).

519. *C.P. No. 220 of Mr. Sewell's List.*—In the taluk cutcherry at Nandyal? In Ś. 1285 (A.D. 1363), Plava, Bukka (I) residing on the banks of the Tuṅgabhadra, and worshipping the god Virūpāksha, granted, for the support of a temple of Bhairava, and for the maintenance of a priest, the village of Gaḍigarēlu *alias* Bukkarāyapuram, in the Peḍakal District of the Province of Ghanādri. The bulk of the inscription is in Sanskrit, only the description of the village boundaries being given in Kanarese.

520. On a stone north of the Āñjanēya temple. Records that Aḷiya Rāmarāja granted the village to Gods Siddhēśvara and Bhōjēśvara in Ś. 1464, Śubhakrit, in the reign of Sadāśivarāya. *Ins., Ced. Dts.*, p. 469, No. 167. See also *Antiquities*, I, p. 94.

521. Close to the above. A gift by the same chief in Ś. 1469, Plavaṅga, to God Śēshēśvara. *Ibid.*, No. 168.

Gaḍivēmula.

522. On a stone at the bottom of dhvajastambha in the local temple. Records that Kaṇṇayyarāja (?), son of Koṇḍarāja, set up the image of Lakshmi in the Kēśava temple and granted some land for food and flower garden besides three pagodas from the market tax in Ś. 1475, Pramādīcha. *Ibid.*, No. 169.

Gōrakaḷḷu (Gōrukaḷḷu).

523. On a stone near the local Vishṇu temple. Records that local people fixed some allowance to the Vipravinōdins in Ś. 1509, Sarvajit. *Ibid.*, p. 429, No. 30.

524. On a stone which stands in front of the village choultry. A record dated Ś. 1061. *Antiquities*, Vol. I, p. 94.

Guṇṭanāla.

525. A record making a grant by Rāmarāja Veṅkaṭādridēva in Ś. 1469 in the reign of Sadāśivarāya. *Ibid*., p. 95.

Kadamalakālva.

526. In the Hanūmān temple. A private record dated in Ś. 1444. *Ibid.*

527. In the same place. A private grant dated S. 1431. *Ibid.*

Kālva.

528. In the ruined Raṅganāyaka temple. A record of Sadāśivarāya in Ś. 1482. *Ibid.*

529. In the Buggaramēśvara temple, A grant in the reign of Achyutarāya in Ś. 1452. *Ibid.*

530. In the same place. A private grant dated Ś. 1222. *Ibid.*

Kānāla (Pedda).

531. On a stone in the Chennakēśava pagoda in the fort. Records that Kṛishṇamarājayya gave ten pagodas on the rent of the village Kānāla or Kṛishṇarāya-Samudram to God Chennakēśava for a lamp in Ś. 1480. Siddhārti, in the reign of Sadāśivarāya. See *Ins., Ced. Dts.*, p. 478, No. 199, and *Antiquities*, p. 96.

532. On a stone south of the above. Records that Rāmarāja Veṅkaṭādri Rāja exempted the tax of the local Brahmaṇs in Ś. 1469, Plavaṅga, in the reign of Sadāśivarāya. *Ins., Ced. Dts.*, p. 478, No. 200. [Veṅkaṭādri was evidently the brother of Aḷiya Rāma Rāya.]

533. On a stone east of the village. Records that Kommanāyaḍu Muḷikināyaḍu granted some land to God Mūlasthānadēva in Ś. 1230, Kīlaka, in the reign of the Kākatīya Pratāparudra (II). *Ibid.*, No. 201.

Karimaddala.

534. On a stone near the Yellamma pagoda. Records that Naṇḍyāla Timmarājayya gave one *tūm* and nine *muttās* of land to the Goddess in Ś. 1490 in the reign of Sadāśivarāya. *Ibid.*, p. 470, No. 172. [He was apparently the same as the ruler of Ghaṇḍikōṭa and the brother of Kṛishṇarāja to whom Piṅgaḷi Sūrana dedicated his *Kaḷāpūrṇōdayamu.*]

535. On a stone close to the same. A similar gift by the same chief in the same date. *Ibid.*, No. 173.

536. South of the above. A gift of the same chief similar to the above in the same date. *Ibid.*, No. 174.

537. South-west of the above. A similar record of the same chief in the same date. *Ins., Ced. Dts.*, p. 470, No. 175.

538. On a stone at the foot of a local tree. Records that Gutti Singaṇṇa, manager of Rāmarājagōpāla temple, exempted the tax of the local barbers in Saumya. *Ibid.*, p. 472, No. 177.

Kāvalūru.

539. On a stone in the Chennakēśava temple. Records in Ś. 1051, the construction of the temple. *Antiquities*, Vol. I, p. 95.

Maddūru.

540. On a stone near the Gaṇapati pagoda. Records that Basavayyadēva Mahārāja granted some land to some gardeners for cultivating a flower garden for God Gaṇapatidēva in Ś. 1420, Kālayukti. *Ins., Ced. Dts.*, p. 434, No. 47.

Mahānandi.

See *Antiquities*, I, 95, *Madras Journal*, Vol. XXIII (ii), 74.

541. 172 *of* 1913.—(Telugu.) On the dhvajastambha in the Mahānandīśvarasvāmin temple. Records in Ś. 1446, Tāraṇa, Māgha, ba. di. 14, Monday, Śivarātri, corresponding to February 20, A.D. 1525, that a merchant built the maṇṭapa called *mukhabhadram* at the southern entrance into the tank (*guṇḍamu*) and the pillar surmounted by a bull, in the temple of Mānandīśvara.

541-A. 173 *of* 1913.—(Telugu.) On an iron pillar near the western gate of the same temple. Records in Ś. 1332, Vikriti, Māgha, ba. di. 13, Friday, corresponding to February 20, A.D. 1410, that the great-grandmother (?) of Tipparāju, son of Pina-Tipparāju, son of Velugōṭi-Gaṅgalrāju-Chenrājuṅgāru, the hero of Krottachērlakōṭa, set up this lamp-pillar before the shrine of Mahānandiśvara. See *Antiquities*, I, 95. [The record is important for the information it gives of three generations of Velugōṭi rulers not found elsewhere. They had the titles of "Born of the matchless Chōḍa race"; Lords of the city of Naṇḍyāla, worshippers of Mahānandīśvara and the hero on the battle field of Krottachērlakōṭa (i.e., Kōchchērlakōṭa in Palnāḍ).]

542. 174 *of* 1913.—(Kanarese, Telugu and Nāgari.) On seven detached stones in the same temple. Records in ancient characters of the eighth and ninth centuries of the Christian era. Four in Telugu-Kanarese record the names Śarigēśampunna-mahāmuni; Ayōgavā(ñji)tan; Utpātipiḍugu-kāḷāmukkān Mēru-pritivi; Śri-Vyāḷasiṃhaguravar and Tellapūṇḍi-Apparāju. One in Nāgari, reads Śrī-Lallamkagōva [Ī]harāja.

543. 175 *of* 1913.—(Telugu.) On six other detached stones. Contains the signatures of devotees, three of which seem to be rather old. Among these are Jayaravi and Dōrāchārya, a mine of architect-intelligence *(chitratējōnidhi)*.

Nandyāl.

544. A C.P. (in whose possession it is not mentioned) grant, dated in Ś. 1569 (A.D. 1647), recording a gift by Śrī Raṅga Rāya of Vijayanagar. *Antiquities*, I, p. 95.

545. In the Veṅkaṭēśvara ṭemple. A private grant in the same reign and the same date. *Ibid.*

546. *C.P. No.* 192 *of Mr. Sewell's List.*—Records a grant by Vinayāditya I, called "Vinayāditya Yuddhamalla" or "Vinayāditya Satyāśraya" (A.D. 680—695), in Ś. 612 (A.D. 690), in the tenth year of the king's reign. This is the same as C.P. No. 10 of 1915 and No. 564-A below. It has been published by Dr. Fleet in the *Ind. Antq.*, VI, 85 ff.

547. On a stone east of the place near the lake. A damaged record of Eṛṛa Timmayyarāja, son of Jagatapa Śrīgiri Rāja, in the reign of Achyutarāya. *Ins., Ced. Dts.*, p. 429, No. 26.

Pānem.

548. 163 *of* 1913.—(Telugu.) On a slab set up in the courtyard of the Vīranārāyaṇasvāmin temple. Dated in the reign of the Kākatīya king Pratāparudradēva-Mahārāya, ruling at Orungallu (i.e., Warangal), in Ś. 1241, Siddhārthi, Māgha, śu. di. 15, Monday, lunar eclipse. Records that the chief minister Mummaḍi Maṭṭaya, ruling the southern country including Peḍakallu, made a grant of some land on the south side of Pānya. Certain fees *(mēra)* to be paid by the residents of Pānem and a *tūm* of grain from the markets held in specified villages were also granted for the expenses of worship in the temple of Śrī Vīranārāyaṇadēva of that village. The week day should be Saturday (not Monday) and the date corresponds to 26th January, A.D. 1320. See *Ibid.*, p. 428, No. 25.

549. 164 *of* 1913.—(Telugu.) On a slab set up in the courtyard of the Paṇikēśvarasvāmin temple, in the same village. A record of the Vijayanagara king Vīrapratāpa Kṛishṇadēvarāya-Mahārāya, dated in Ś. 1451, Virōdhi, Vaiśākha, śu. di. 15, lunar eclipse, corresponding to Friday, 23rd April 1529. Records that Vākīta Pedapa-Nāyuḍu, son of Bokkasam Pedapa Nāyuḍu, a servant of Kṛishṇadēvarāya, granted the *Kāvalikaṭṇam* (police fee), for the enjoyment of the god Paṇikēśvara of Pāṇemu, a village included in Kandanavōlu (i.e., Kurnool) on all the lands held by the temple in that village and in the agrahāra villages of Būpālunipāḍu and Liṅgapuram. See *Ibid.*, p. 427, No. 22, and *Antiquities*, I, p. 96.

550. 165 *of* 1913.—(Telugu.) On a second slab set up in the same place. Records that in the reign of the Vijayanagara king Vīrapratāpa Kṛishṇarāya-Mahārāya, in Ś. 1431, Pramōda, Chaitra, śu. di. 15 (a date which "can be calculated but not verified"), that Honnapa-Nāyuḍu, son of Bokkasam Dēvapa-Nāyuḍu, granted the village of Būḍidepāḍu in Pānem-śīma to the worshippers (*tammaḍa*) of the god Paṇikēśvara of Paṇēya for conducting oblations and other services in the temple. *Ins., Ced. Dts.*, p. 428, No. 23.

551. 166 *of* 1913.—(Telugu.) On a third slab set up in the same place. Dated in the reign of the Sāḷuva king Immaḍi-Naraśiṅga-rāya-Mahārāya. Records in Ś. 1425, Rudhirōdgāri, Śravaṇa, śu. di. 15, Monday, corresponding to August 7, A.D. 1503, a grant of land for the merit of himself and Narasa-Nāyaniṅgāru, in the village of Pāṇem, included in Penugoṇḍachāvaḍi, to four sthānikas of the Paṇikēśvara temple for building a village and conducting the services in the temple. [See *Ibid.*, p. 428, No. 24, which gives the date Ś. 1424 but the year correctly and *Antiquities*, p. 96.]

552. 167 *of* 1913.—(Telugu.) On a fourth slab set up in the same place. Records in the reign of the Sāḷuva king Nara-śiṅgarāya Mahārāya in Ś. 1425. Rudhirōdgāri, Śravana, śu. di. 15, Monday, the grant registered in the above epigraph (with a few changes in the wording). Same date as that of the above inscription.

553. 168 *of* 1913.—(Kanarese, Telugu, Tamil and Nāgari.) On a pillar in the courtyard of the same temple. The oldest, which is in Kanarese, records that a certain Paḷḷapaḍiyāran obeyed the orders *(bāyinvēḷirdōn)* of the god and the remaining three state that Vibhūti Gauraya visited the temple.

554. 169 *of* 1913.—(Telugu, Sanskrit, Grantha and Nāgari.) On a pillar in the mukha maṇṭapa of the same temple. Records the visit of the same Vibhūti Gauraya. It is stated that he was born at Māchirājupalli near Oruṅgallu, settled on the top of Śrīgiri and was the servant of Panditārādhya. Another record in Telugu on the same pillar states that a certain Ākana paved with stone the *Āppāḷike* (?) of the maṇṭapa.

555. 170 *of* 1913.—(Telugu.) On a slab lying in the Āñjanēya temple in the same village. Records in Ś. 1623, Vikrama Āśvija, śu. di. 15, that Komāra-Timma-Nāyuḍu, son of Narasimha-Nāyuḍu and grandson of the Nāyaṅkāchārya China-Veṅkaṭappa-Nāyuḍu granted land (12 *tūms*) to a certain Anumabōyi. The date "can be calculated but not verified." See *Ibid.*, p. 427, No. 21.

556. 171 *of* 1913.—(Telugu.) On a slab set up in the same temple. A record of the Vijayanagara king Vīra-Narasimharāya recording in Ś. 1428, Krōdhana, śu. di. 3, Thursday, Kanyā-Brihaspati, gift of land in Pāṇem village of Pedakaṇṭi-śīma to Mallikārjuna, one of the three self-born liṅgas, for the merit of his father Narasa Nāyaniṅgāru. The date corresponded to July 23, A.D. 1506, but the solar month was Karkaṭaka, not Kanyā. Vīra Narasimha was the immediate predecessor of Kṛishṇadēva Rāya.

Pesaruvāyi.

557. On a stone north of the Kēśavasvāmi pagoda. A Telugu record of Narasappa Nāyaḍu in Ś. 1475, Vijaya. *Ins., Ced. Dts.*, p. 470, No. 170.

558. On a stone in front of the Vīrabhadra temple in the fort. Records that in Ś. 1466, Krōdhi, Veṅkaṭādri Rājayya exempted the barbers from tax. *Ibid.*, No. 171.

559. On the boundary between this village and an adjoining one. A record dated in Ś. 1698. *Antiquities*, p. 96.

560. In the temple of Vīrēśvarasvāmi. Grant of land in Ś. 1366. *Ibid.*

Pōlūr.

Besides three inscriptions taken from the *Mack. MSS.* this place had an epigraph dated in Ś. 1452 and recording a private grant, according to Mr. Sewell.

561. On a stone situated at Pōlūr. Records that Chintamarāja gave some land for repairing a well in Ś. 1457, Jaya, in the reign of Achyutarāya, to a private person. *Ins., Ced. Dts.*, p. 429, No. 27.

562. On a stone north of the local fort. Records that Bukkarāju Timmarāju, Siddhaguru and other people fixed an allowance of five *māḍas* for the daily worship of God Mūlasthānēśvara in Ś. 1467, Śubhakrit. *Ibid.*, No. 28.

563. On a stone near the Narasimha temple in the local market. Records that Rāmarāja Tirumalarājayya exempted the local barbers from tax in Ś. 1480, Kāḷayukti, in the reign of Sadāśivarāya. *Ibid.*, No. 29.

Pulimaddi (" Pulimadala ").

564. On a stone near the local Nāgēśvara pagoda. Records that Sāhiṇi Timmayya gave an allowance of three pagodas to the deity in Ś. 1455, Vijaya, in the reign of Achyutarāya. *Ibid.*, p. 477, No. 195. The inscription is also given in *Antiquities*, Vol. I, p. 96.

Togarchēḍu.

564-A. A C.P. grant of the tenth year of the Western Chāḷukya king Vinayāditya Satyāśraya issued from Pampātīrtha. See *Ind. Antq.*, Vol. VI, p. 86; *J. Bo. R.A.S.*, XVI, p. 242, and Kielhorn's *Southern List*, No. 27. See also No. 546 above.

Yerraguṇṭa (Yerraguṇṭḷa).

565. On a stone near the Chennakēśava temple in the fort. Records that Aubaḷarāja gave the various allowances from the village to God Chennakēśava in Ś. 1469, Plavaṅga, in the reign of Sadāśivarāya. *Ins., Ced. Dts.*, p. 431, No. 36.

566. In the temple of Aṅkālamma. A "doubtful" record dated in Ś. 1373 "in the reign of Vīra Narasimha Rāya of Vijayanagar." *Antiquities*, p. 96.

PATTIKONDA TALUK.

Khairuvvala.

567. In the temple of Vishṇu. Two inscriptions dated in S 1490 (A.D. 1568) recording grants in the reign of Tirumala, the founder of the Penukoṇḍa dynasty. *Antiquities*, p. 93.

568. In "another" temple. Records a grant by a private person in Ś. 1308. *Ibid.*

SIRVEL TALUK.

*Lower Ahōbalam.**

For accounts of Ahōbalam see *Antiquities*, Vol. I, pp. 101-2, Ferguson's *Ind. and E. Arch.*, p. 378, and *Ep. Rep.*, 1915, pp. 94-5.

569. 55 *of* 1915.—(Telugu.) Round the base of the central shrine of the Narasimhasvāmi temple. A much damaged record of the Vijayanagara king Vīrapratāpa Achyutaḍēva-Mahārāya, dated Ś. 1458, Manmatha. Mentions a Purushōttama-Jīyyaṅgāru and the chief China-Tirumalarājayya.

570. 56 *of* 1915.—(Telugu.) On the same base. Records a grant in the reign of the Vijayanagara king Vīrapratāpa Achyutadēva Mahārāya, in Ś. 1453, Khara, Māgha, śu. di. 15, a grant of land by purchase at Diguva Tirupati to the temple of Ahōbalēśvara by Abbarāju, son of Abbarāju Tipparāju of Pōrumāmilla.

571. 57 *of* 1915.—(Telugu.) On the south wall of the shrine of the goddess in the Narasimhasvāmin temple. Records that in Siddhārthin, Āśvija, śu. di. 10, that a certain Sarvadēva Sōmayājulu of Pērūr built the maṇṭapa called Kshīrābdhi-Navanarasimha-maṇṭapa, for the god Ahōbalēśvara. [According to tradition there were nine Narasimhas in this place.]

572. 58 *of* 1915.—(Telugu.) On the north wall of the same shrine. Records that in the reign of the Vijayanagara king Vīrapratāpa Vīra-Sadāśivadēva-Mahārāya, in Ś. 1469, Plavaṅga, Āśvija, ba. di. 7, that Dēvarasayyaṅgāru of Guḍiya-Chillūru, of Kāśyapa-gōtra granted money for providing eight offerings to the god Ahōbalēśvara during the festival held on the fifteenth day of the bright half Kārttika, when the image was taken round in procession in a paḷanquin. "Date can be calculated but not verified."

---

* In his *Antiquities* Mr. Sewell mentions fourteen inscriptions in Upper and Lower Ahobalams. All of them are evidently included in the more complete departmental list. The *Mack. MSS.* are summarized in *Ins.*, *Ced. Dts.*, pp. 437—43. They contain twenty-four inscriptions of which seventeen are traceable in the departmental list. The rest are given under No. 600-A—600-G. For originals see *Loc. Rec.*, XV, 431; XVI, 431 f. and XL, 147 f.

573. 59 *of* 1915.—(Telugu.) On the west wall of the Narasimhasvāmin shrine in the same temple. A damaged record of the Vijayanagara king Vīrapratāpa Sadāśivadēva-Mahārāya, dated Ś. 1478, Rākshasa, Śravaṇa, ba. di. 7, Monday (mistake for Friday), corresponding to 9th August 1555. Mentions a chief of the solar race who was the grandson of Kṛishṇamarāju and son of Nandirāju.

574. 60 *of* 1915.—(Telugu.) On the same wall. A damaged record of the Vijayanagara king Vīrapratāpa Vīra-Sadāśivadēva-Mahārāya, dated 1468, Viśvāvasu. One slab missing in the middle. Seems to mention Rāmabhaṭḷayya, the son of Bhūtanātha Brahma-Jyōyisalu, who was a minister of the king. Provision was evidently made for oblations in the temple.

575. 61 *of* 1915.—(Telugu.) On the same wall. A record of the Vijayanagara king Vīrapratāpa Vīra-Sadāśivadēva-Mahārāya recording in Ś. 1474, Virōdhikrit, Pushya, śu. di. 7, Sunday, corresponding to January 3, A.D. 1552, gift of the village Gurijepalli in Dupaṭi-śīma for maintaining a *Rāmānujakūṭa* in the shrine of Bhāshyakāra within the temple of Ahōbalēśvara at Diguva Tirupati, by Koṇḍayadēva-Mahārāja, son of the Mahāmaṇḍalēśvara Rāmarāja Kōnēṭirāja of the lunar race. Stones out of order. [Koṇḍaya dēva was not improbably the Koṇḍarāja of the British Museum Plates of Śadāsiva Rāya.]

576. 62 *of* 1915.—(Telugu.) On the same wall. A fragmentary record of the Vijayanagara king Sadāśivadēva-Mahārāya, the date of which is lost. Mentions the grant of the village Nālūru in Poḍile-śīma for providing offerings to the god Ahōbalēśvara, in a certain maṇṭapa.

577. 63 *of* 1915.—(Telugu.) On the same wall. Records in the reign of the Vijayanagara king Vīrapratāpa Sadāśivadēva-Mahārāya, in Ś. 1469, Kīlaka, Āshāḍha, śu. di. 11, the gift of 120 *varāhas* by Narasammaṅgāru, wife of the Mahāmaṇḍalēśvara Gobūri Obayadēva-Mahārāja of the Kāśyapa-gōtra for providing offerings to the god Ahōbalēśvara during festivals when he was installed in the vasanta-maṇṭapa which she had constructed on the north side of the temple at Diguva-Tirupati. Date "can be calculated but not verified."

578. 64 *of* 1915.—(Telugu.) On a slab set up at the entrance into the Narasimhasvāmin shrine in the same temple. A record of the Vijayanagara king Vīrapratāpa Vīra-Kṛishṇadēva-Mahārāya, dated in Ś. 1438, Yuva, Pushya, śu. di. 15, Friday, corresponding to December 21, A.D. 1515. Refers to conquests of Kṛishṇarāya in the east and states that on his second campaign against Kaliṅga he visited Ahōbala and presented to the god a necklace, a pendant set with diamonds and an emerald, wristlets set with rubies, a golden plate and 1,000 *varāhas*. His queen also gave one pendant to the god. The village Madūru in Chaṅgalamari-śīma was also granted for providing offerings to the god. See *Ins.*, *Ced. Dts.*, p. 439, No. 66.

579. 65 *of* 1915.—(Telugu.) On a slab set up in the courtyard of the same temple. Dated in the reign of the Vijayanagara king Vīrapratāpa Vīra-Sadāśivādēva-Mahārāya. Records in Ś. 1477, Ānanda, Mārgaśira, ba. di. 5 (a date which "can be calculated but not verified"), that the Vaishṇava teacher Parāṅkuśa Vaṇ-Śaṭhagōpa-Jīyamgāru, the trustee of the Ahōbala temple and the agent of Aḷiya-Rāmappayyadēva Mahārāja, granted a *daśa-vanda-mānya* to Avubaḷarāja, son of Kōnēṭi-rājayya and grandson of Rāmarāja-Peda-Koṇḍayyadēva-Mahārāja of the Ātrēya-gōtra and the lunar race, for having built at Alamūru, which was a village of the temple *(tiruvaḷayāṭu)*, the tank Kōnasamudram, otherwise called Nārāyaṇasamudram. *Ibid.*, p. 438, No. 65. See *Ep. Ind.*, IV, p. 4, for reference to Pedda Koṇḍarāja. Parāṅkuśa was the sixth of the apostolic line of the Ahōbala *maṭha* founded by Ādivaṇ-Śaṭhakōpa who lived from A.D. 1379 to 1459. Shashṭa Parāṅkuśa is said in the *Satsampradāyamuktāvaḷi* to be the contemporary of Sadāśiva Rāya but under the wrong date of 1498—1511 for his spiritual headship. It further says that he healed the Rāya's daughter who had become possessed and that he received from Sadāśiva the village of Bhāshyapuram on the Pinākini. Parāṅkuśa was the uncle of Pañchamata-bhañjanam Tātāchārya and the author of a number of works including *Siddhāntamaṇidipam*, *Pañchakāladipikā*, *Prapattiprayōga*, and *Nrisimha-stava*. The tradition is that he disappeared in the great cave of Ahōbalam shrine.

580. 66 *of* 1915.—(Telugu.) On a second slab set up in the same place. Records in the reign of the Vijayanagara king Vīrapratāpa Vīra-Sadāśivadēva Mahārāya, in Ś. 1477, Ānanda, Mārgasira, ba. di. 5, that the same Aubaḷarāja purchased from the same temple authorities one *puṭṭi* of land at Alamūru for raising on it a sacred grove and flower garden for the benefit of the temple, himself enjoying two-thirds of the produce. See *Ins.*, *Ced. Dts.*, p. 439, No. 67.

581. 67 *of* 1915.—(Telugu.) On a slab set up to the right of the entrance into the *Kañchugumba-gōpura* of the same temple. Records that in the reign of the Vijayanagara king Vīra-Veṅkaṭa patirāyadēva-Mahārāya (1586–1616), "ruling at Penugoṇḍa," in Ś. 1531, Saumya, Jyēshṭa, ba. di. 10, Friday, corresponding to June 16, A.D. 1609, a gift of seven gold gilt pinnacles *(kalaśa)* for the big gōpura of the Vīra-Narasimha temple at Diguva-Tirupati, and of two fly whisks and an umbrella of white silk with a gilt *kalaśa* over it, was made by some merchants of Āravīḍu, for the merit of 150 headmen *(nagarasvāmins)* of their community. Gives some details about the guild of merchants who are called devotees of Vāsavakanyakā, the followers of Bhāskarāchārya and the progeny of the celestial cow born from its ears.

582. 68 *of* 1915.—(Telugu.) On a second slab set up in the same place. A damaged record of the Vijayanagara king Vīrapratāpa Veṅkaṭapatirāyadēva-Mahārāya, "ruling at Penugoṇḍa," dated Ś. 1512, Virōdhin, Phalguṇa, ba. di. 30. Records a gift of land for offerings by a certain Raṅgappa of the Maudgalya-gōtra to the god Vīra-Narasimha of Ahōbala at Diguva-Tirupati. The date "can be calculated but not verified." [*Ins.*, *Ced. Dts.*, p. 443, No. 81.]

583. 69 *of* 1915.—(Telugu.) On the third slab set up in the same place. A record of the Vijayanagara king Vīrapratāpa Vīra-Sadāśiva dēva-Mahārāya, in Ś. 1479, Dundubhi (wrong), Māgha, ba. di. 5, Wednesday. Records that Rāmānuja-Jīyyamgāru, the agent *(mudrakartā)* of Vaṇ-Śaṭhagōpa-Jīyyamgāru, the trustee of the Ahōbala temple and the agent of the Mahāmaṇḍalēśvara Rāmarāja Tirumalarājayyadēva-Mahārāja sold five *marutus* of land to Ōbalrāju, son of Ōbalrāju and grandson of the Mahāmaṇḍalēśvara Pōchirāju Rāmarājumgāru of the solar race and the Viśvāmitragōtra. This chief gave it back to the temple and stipulated that the thirty *puṭlu* of paddy realized from the land each year was to be utilized for daily offerings in the shrine of Nammāḷvār situated in the Bhārgava street near the shrine of Prahlāda-Varada in the Ahōbalēśvara temple at Diguva-Tirupati and that the offerings were to be distributed among twelve Śrī-Vaishṇavas. The date is an irregular one. [Mr. Swamikannu Pillai says that the right year is Ś. 1477, and the date Wednesday, January 1, A.D. 1556. See *Ep. Rep.*, 1915, p. 81. Also *Ins.*, *Ced. Dts.*, p. 441, No. 76. Prahlāda Varada is one of the nine forms of God Narasimha in this place. For Vaṇ Śaṭhakōpa see No. 579 above.]

584. 70 *of* 1915.—(Telugu.) On the south slab set in the same place. Records that in the reign of the Vijayanagara king Vīrapratāpa Vīra-Raṅgarāyadēva-Mahārāya (1578—87) "ruling at Penugoṇḍa," in Ś. 1506, Tāraṇa, Vaiśākha, śu. di. 14, Veṅkaṭrājadēva Chōḍa-mahārāja, son of Timmaṇa of the solar race and the Kāśyapagōtra, came to receive certain privileges in the temple. The inscription says that, under orders of the king and at the request of Vaṇ Śaṭhagōpa-Jīyyamgāru, his grandfather Koṇḍarāja-Veṇkaṭrāja-Timmarāja had expelled the Muhammadan chief Vibhurāmu (Ibrahim II of Golcoṇḍa), who had occupied the temple of Ahōbalam for seven years in alliance with the Haṇḍēvāru (chiefs). It was for thus restoring the temple to its original state that the family was granted the privileges mentioned above. Date "can be calculated but not verified." *Ibid.*, No. 75. [Veṅkaṭrāya has the titles *mūrurāyara Basava-Śaṅkara*, *Gutti-hannibbaragaṇḍa* and *Oraiyūri-purivarādhiśvara* and these, together with the title Dēva-chōḍa Mahārāja, have made the Government Epigraphist surmise that he belonged to the Maṭḷa family. The Haṇḍe chiefs of Anantapūr were ardent Śaivites and so co-operated with Ibrahim Qutb Shah in the spoiling of Ahōbalam, and Veṅkaṭrāja defeated the vandals and restored the prosperity of the place. See *Kurnool Manual* for details. The Vaṇ-Saṭhakōpa of this epigraph is the seventh of the Ahōbalam Śvāmis. He belonged to Iḷaṅgāḍu Vaṅgipuram, wrote the *Vāsantikāpariṇaya* and had the titles of कविसार्वभौमशतलेखिनिलेखानुगुण कवितधुरन्धर कवितार्किक कण्ठीरवत्रण शठकोपस्वामि.

585. 71 *of* 1915.—(Telugu.) On the fifth slab set up in the same place. A record of the Vijayanagara king Vīrapratāpa Vīra-Veṇkaṭa-patirāyadēva-Mahārāya (I, 1586–1616), "ruling at Penukoṇḍa," recording in Ś. 1507, Pārthiva, Phalguna, śu. di. 1, that the chief mentioned above granted to the temple 80 *varāhās* which were due to him year after year from the temple villages as the fee for protection (kāvali). The money was to be utilized for maintaining certain services in the temple. Date "can be calculated but not verified." *Ins., Ced. Dts.*, p. 442, No. 77.

586. 72 *of* 1915.—(Telugu.) On a slab set up to the left of the entrance into the same gōpura. An incomplete record of the Vijayanagara king Vīrapratāpa Vīra-Sadāśivadēva-Mahārāya dated Ś. 1486, Rudhirōdgārin, Śravaṇa, ba. di. 3, Friday, corresponding to 6th August, A.D. 1563. Records that the chief Mahāmaṇḍalēśvara Kōnēṭi Ōbalrāja, son of Kōnēṭayyadēva-Mahārāja and grandson of Rāmarāja Peda-Koṇḍarājayyadēva-Mahārāja of the Ātrēya-gōtra granted the income from certain villages for offerings and services. [*Ibid.*, p. 422, No. 80.] See No. 579.

587. 73 *of* 1915.—(Telugu.) On a second slab set up in the same place. A record of the Vijayanagara king Vīrapratāpa Vīra-Sadāśivadēva-Mahārāya in Ś. 1486, Rudhirōdgārin, Māgha, śu. di. 15. Says that Parāṅkuśa Vaṇ-Saṭhakōpa Jīyyamgāru assigned a piece of land in the village of Liṅgamdiva in Ghaṇḍikōṭa śīma, which had been presented to him by a certain Narasayya, for providing offerings at the garden festival of Ahōbalēśvara conducted near the square tank *(kōnēru)* constructed by himself on the way to the tank Bhārgava *(tirtham)*. "The date can be calculated but cannot be verified." The inscription is also given in *Mack. MSS.* [See *Ibid.*, No. 79.] See No. 579 above.

588. 74 *of* 1915.—(Telugu.) On a round water trough preserved in the goddess's shrine in the same temple. Records a gift by Basavayya, son of the goldsmith *(agasāli)* Hanumanta of Ahōbalam.

589. 75 *of* 1915.—(Telugu.) Round the platform of the huge pillar jayastambha, in the same temple. Records in the reign of the Vijayanagara king Vīrapratāpa Vīra-Sadāśivadēva-Mahārāya in Ś. 1472, Saumya, Phalguna, śu. di. 3, gift of land to the temple for a flower and fruit garden, by Aubaḷarājumgāru who had purchased it from Vaṇ-Saṭhagōpa-Jīyyamgāru, the trustee of the Ahōbala (temple) and Uggaraśa, agent of the Mahāmaṇḍalēsvara Koṇḍrāju China-Timmayyadēva-Mahārāja, by paying the sale-money into the temple treasury. The date "can be calculated but cannot be verified."

590. 76 *of* 1915.—(Telugu.) On the same platform. Records in Ś. . . . , Pramādīcha, Māgha, śu. di. 5, that the Mahāmaṇḍalēśvara Śūrappa Ōbalayyadēva-Mahārāja, set up the Garuḍa-stambha in the street opposite to the temple and deposited money in the temple treasury for providing offerings on 220 festival days in the year on which the God was brought in procession and seated on the platform of this pillar. The management of the charity was placed in the hands of Purushōttama Jīyyamgāru, the trustees of Ahōbalam temple and the chief Harihara-nātha-Pedirāja, the representative of the Mahāmaṇḍalēśvara Aḷiya Rāmarājadēva-Mahārāja.

591. 77 *of* 1915.—(Telugu.) On a slab set up in the bazaar street outside the same temple. The record refers in Ś. 1739, Īśvara, Phalguna, ba. di. 10, to a grove planted near the temple and a tank repaired by some private persons. [This is No. 11 in Mr. Sewell's local list.]

Upper Ahōbalam.

592. 78 *of* 1915.—(Telugu.) On a slab set up on way. Dated in the reign of the Vijayanagara king Vīrapratāpa Vīra-Sadāśiva-dēva-Mahārāya. Records in Ś. 1482, Raudri, Pushya, śu. di. 12, gift of land by purchase, for providing an offering of cakes during festivals when the god Ahōbalēśvara was brought in procession and seated in the four-pillared maṇṭapa in the south-east corner of the street *(tiruvidhi)*. This maṇṭapa was built and the provision made by the chief Gōpinātharāju, son of Gōparāju and grandson of the Mahāmaṇḍalēśvara Bhatrāju of Juṭūru of the lunar race and the Ātrēya-gōtra. [Date "can be calculated but cannot be verified." *Ins., Ced. Dts.*, p. 440, No. 69.]

593. 79 *of* 1915.—(Telugu.) On a slab set up near the sixteen-pillared maṇṭapa on the same way. A much damaged record of the Vijayanagara king Vīrapratāpa Vīra-Sadāśiva-Mahārāya, dated Ś. 1480, Kāḷayukta, Māgaśira, śu. di. 3. Seems to record a lease (?) granted to a chief of the solar race by Parāṅkuśa Vaṇ-Saṭhagōpa-Jīyyaṁgāru, by the trustees of the temple, and the representative of the king. See No. 579 above.

594. 80 *of* 1915.—(Telugu.) On a slab set up near the Dūruḍu-maṇṭapa on the same way. Records in the reign of the Vijayanagara king Vīrapratāpa Vīra-Sadāśivadēva-Mahārāya, in Ś. 1476, Pramādīcha, Śravaṇa, ba. di. 10, Thursday (August 26, A.D. 1553), a gift of money by Veṅkaṭādridēva-Mahārāja, son of Ōbalrāja, and grandson of the Mahāmaṇḍalēśvara Timmarājadēva-Mahārāja of Kurujēḍu, who was of the solar race and the Kāśyapa-gōtra, for providing offerings in the maṇṭapa, to the god on the *nidhi* (i.e., Upper Ahōbalam) on his way to and back from Diguva Tirupati during festivals held on sixteen different days in the year. See *Ins., Ced. Dts.*, p. 438, No. 64.

595. 81 *of* 1915.—(Telugu.) On a slab set up in the courtyard of the Narasimhasvāmin temple. Records in the reign of the Vijayanagara king Vīrapratāpa-Sadāśivadēva-Mahārāya in Ś. 1470, Kīlaka, Chaitra, śu. di. 10, Śrī-Rāmanavami, gift of the village Jambuladinne in Kōyilakuṇṭa-śīma, by China-Avubaḷayyadēva-Mahārāja, son of Naraśiṅgayyadēva-Mahārāja and grandson of the Mahāmaṇḍalēśvara Naṇḍyāḷa Śiṁgarāyadeva-Mahārāja of the lunar race and the Ātreya-gōtra, in order to provide six plates of food (called *śriṅgārataḷiga*) to the God Ahōbalēśvara for the merit of Havali Pedda-Avubaḷarāja. The date "can be calculated but cannot be verified." See *Ibid.*, p. 437, No. 59.

596. 82 *of* 1915.—(Telugu.) On another slab set up in the same place. A mutilated record of the Vijayanagara king Vīrapratāpa Sadāśivadēva-Mahārāya, dated Ś. 1486, Rudhirōdgārin. Records gift of land in the village China-Komerḷa in the Ghaṇḍi-kōṭa-śīma, by Vaṇ-Śaṭhagōpa-Jīyyaṁgāru, to Ahōbalēśvara for providing offerings of rice cakes on specified festivals in the maṇṭapa in front of the *maṭha* which he had constructed on the nagari (i.e., Upper Ahōbalam). The village China-Komerḷa was a gift made to the Jīyyaṃgāru by the chief Kṛishṇamarāja, son of Nandēla China-Ōbaṇṇamgāru. [This epigraph is in *Mack. MSS.* See *Ibid.*, p. 437, No. 58.]

597. 83 *of* 1915.—(Telugu.) On a slab built in the courtyard of the same temple. Records that the upper portion of the slab is missing. Gives a long list of the various things required for preparing dishes to be offered to Śrī-Bhāshyakāra (i.e., Rāmānuja) on the twelve days of his *tirunakshatram* in each year.

598. 84 *of* 1915.—(Telugu.) On a slab set up on way to the temple of Pāmuleṭi-Narasimha on the same hill. Records in Ś. 1332, Vikriti, Mārgaśira, śu. di. 15, Thursday, gift of the village Kaluvachēru surnamed Komāragiripuram by Kāṭama-Reḍḍi Vēma-Reḍḍi, to provide daily offerings in the temple of Ahōbaladēva for the merit of Komāragiri-Reḍḍi. The record also gives a list of all the villages named Komāragiri-maṇḍalam, granted to temples and Brahmans by the same chief for the merit of his master (and brother-in-law) Komāragiri-Reḍḍi and his wife Ammaṅgāru. Gifts made by Tallasānammaṅgāru and Mallasānammaṅgāru, wives of Kāṭama-Reḍḍi-Vēma-Reḍḍi are also registered. Kāṭama Vēma was the brother-in-law of Kumāragiri, the founder of the Rājahmundry Reḍḍi line and the author of *Kumāragiri rājiyamu*. See Gd. 19. The present record says that Kāṭama had also a son named Kumāragiri, who is called a re-incarnation of the earlier Kumāra-giri. This chief is also mentioned in Gd. 328.

599. 85 *of* 1915.—(Telugu.) On a detached slab on way to the shrine of Jvālā-Narasimha on the same hill. Records that Bhīra-Ravutu, son of Kanōji Ravutu Mukunda-Ravutu, a servant of Aḷiya-Rāmarāja, paid his homage to the god. A figure of this man with his characteristic head-dress and sword is also pictured.

600. 86 *of* 1915.—(Telugu.) On a slab in the roof of the same shrine. Records that this was the maṇṭapa built by Narasimha-Jīyyaṁgāru who was fully devoted to the feet of Jvālā-Narasimha.

Chāgalamarri.

601. On a stone in the Chennakēśava pagoda. Records that Śiṅgabhūpāla, descendant of Mādhavavarma of Bezwāḍa, built a compound wall, spire, etc., in the temple and gave some land and garden to God Chennakēśava in Ś. 1373, Prajōtpatti, in the time of Mallikārjuna Rāya of Vijayanagar. *Ins., Ced. Dts.*, p. 434, No. 48.

602. On a stone near the above. Records that Śāḷuva Immāḍi Naraśiṅgarāya's Pradhāni Timmarasa granted land to the God in Ś. 1413, Virōdhikrit *Ibid.*, No. 49. [Immaḍi Naraśiṅga was the son of Naraśiṅga, the usurper. Was Timmarasa the same as the Timmarasa who, according to Nuniz, killed the elder and the unnamed son of Naraśiṅga I?]

603. On a stone south-east of the village. Records that Koṇḍa, dēva Rāya gave some land to God Ahōbaḷēśvara in Ś. 1480 Piṅgaḷa, in the reign of Sadāśivarāya. *Ibid.*, No. 50.

Chinna Bōdanam.

604. In the temple of Veṅkaṭēśvara. A record of Ś. 1646 (A.D. 1724), regarding the erection of the *garbhagriha* by a private person. *Antiquities*, I, p. 101.

Chintakommaḍinne.

605. In the Chennakēśava pagoda. Records that Chinna Reḍḍi, the chief of the place, repaired the temple and set up the idol in Ś. 1655, Ānanda. *Ibid.*, p. 433, No. 44.

606. On a stone of the stairs of the tank near the local Īśvara pagoda. Records that Chinna Timmareḍḍi planted a garden and dug the tank in Ś. 1628, Sarvajit. *Ibid.*, No. 45.

607. On a stone in the Hanumantarāya pagoda. Records that Pōlapalli Bukkarāju Timmayyadēva Mahārāja gave to God Tiru-vēṅgalanātha this village in Ś. 1455, Durmukhi, in the reign of Achyutadēva. *Ibid.*, No. 46.

Chintakuṇṭa.

608. On a stone in the Hanūmaṅta temple, west of the fort. Records that Āravīṭi Chinna Timmarāja exempted the rent of the local Karaṇams in Ś. 1470, Kīlaka, in the reign of Sadāśivarāya. See *Ins., Ced. Dts.*, p. 484, No. 219.

609. In the Rāmēśvara temple. Records that Kaṭhāri Śāḷuva Kamparāja exempted the tax of the temple in Ś. 1364, Durmati. *Ibid.*, No. 220.

610. In the temple of Pāṇḍuraṅgasvāmi. A record of Ś. 1493. In the same place. A grant by a Nandyāl chief in Ś. 1495. In the same place. A grant by another Nandyāl chief in Ś. 1506.

610-A. On a stone near the western gate wall. Records that "Cāraṇika Bumurusu" granted two and a half *mattas* of paddy field for the daily offerings of the God in Ś. 1466, Krōdhi, in the reign of Sadāśivadēva Mahārāja. *Ibid.*, p. 437, No. 61.

610-B. North side of Raṅgamaṇṭapam. Records that Kōnēṭi Ōbaḷa Rāju, son of Kōnayya, granted a village in free gift for the daily worship in Ś. 1466, Krōdhi. *Ibid.*, p. 438, No. 62.

610-C. On the top of above Raṅgamaṇṭapam. Records that Harihara Rāyalu (II) erected the Raṅgamaṇṭapam on the hill in Ś. 1317, Bhava. *Ibid.*, No. 63.

610-D. On the second divisions of the stone compound wall of the pagoda. Records that Timmarāju, son of Kōnēṭi Raju, granted the village Muktibhōjanam in free gift for the worship of the God in Ś. 1483, Raudri, in the reign of Kṛishṇadēva Mahārāya. *Ibid.*, p. 439, No. 68. For Timmarāja see *Nellore Ins.*, pp. 1472–3.

610-E. On a stone in front of the compound wall of the above pagoda. Records that Achchamma purchased 250 pagodas of land at Bommi-Reḍḍi-Cheruvu and granted in free gift to the flower garden of the God in Ś. 1480, Kāḷayukti, in the reign of Sadāśivadēva Mahārāju. *Ibid.*, p. 440, No. 70.

610-F. On the south side of the above. Records that Rāmānuja Jīyaṅgāru and "Vuggursu" and others exempted the barbers' tax of Bommi-Reḍḍi-Cheruvu in Ś. 1481, Sādhāraṇa. *Ibid.*, No. 71.

610-G. On a stone pillar in the same place. Records that Ramani Rāma-Nāyaḍu set up a Garuḍastambham (with steel) on the hill, in Krōdhana. *Ibid.*, p. 441, No. 73.

610-H. On the two poles east of the above stambham. Records that "Chencha", son of Ōbaḷayya, set up two pillars of steel on the hill. *Ibid.*, No. 74.

Dēvalapuram.

611. On a stone in the Hanumantarāya temple. Records that Nandyāla Chinna Aubaḷarāja remitted the tax on the Brahmans of the Dēvarāyapura Agrahāram in Ś. 1469, Plavaṅga, in the reign of Sadāśivarāya. *Ibid.*, p. 484, No. 221.

Gōṭlūru.

612. On a stone south of the Gōpālasvāmi temple. Records that Chinna Timmarāja remitted the land tax of the local Karaṇams in Ś. 1417, Kīlaka, in the reign of Sadāśivarāya. *Ins., Ced. Dts.*, p. 436, No. 55.

613. On a stone near the same. Records that Rāmarāja Timmarāja exempted the local barbers from tax in Ś. 1480, Kāḷayukti, in the reign of Sadāśivarāya. *Ibid.*, No. 56.

Gubaguṇḍam.

614. On a stone in the village. Records that Chinna Timmarāja, great-grandson of Āravīṭi Bukkarāja, exempted the local Brahmans from tax in Ś. 1466, Krōdhi. *Ibid.*, p. 485, No. 222.

Jillela.

615. On a stone near the Hanumantarāya pagoda, north of the village. Records that Veligōṭi Kṛishṇamanāyaniṅgāru remitted the tax of the village in Sarvajit, for the lamp expense of Paramēśvara. *Ibid.*, p. 430, No. 31.

616. East of the above. A similar record of the same chief in the same year in favour of God Chennakēśava, *Ibid.*, No. 32.

617. East of the above. Records that the Vipravinōdins granted their allowance from this village to God Chennakēśava in Ś. 1477, Rākshasa. *Ibid.*, No. 33.

Kalugoṭla (palli).

618. On a stone near a local channel. Records that in the reign of Achyutadēvarāya, in Ś. 1456, Vijaya, some land was granted for digging a well to two tank diggers Mummaya and Basavayya. See *Ibid.*, p. 436, No. 57.

Kōṭakaṇḍukūru.

619. On a stone near the Chennakēśava temple. Records that Nandyāla Kumāra Ōbaḷa Rājayya exempted the tax of this village and of another in favour of God Chennakēśava in Ś. 1496, Bhava, in the reign of Śrīraṅgarāya (II). *Ibid.*, p. 432, No. 42.

620. On the door frame of the above temple. Records that Valamakāri Veṅkaṭēśvara, a native of the place, set up a pillar in the temple in Ś. 1690, Sarvadhāri. *Ibid.*, No. 43.

Liṅgamdinnē.

621. On a stone standing near a well outside the village is an inscription, dated Ś. 1429 (A.D. 1507), "recording a gift of land by a private person in the reign of Narasiṁhadēva of Vijayanagar".

(*Antiquities*, Vol. I, p. 102.) Narasiṁha was the son of Narasa Nāyaka and the predecessor of Kṛishṇadēva Rāya.

Nallagaṭla.

622. On a stone near the Chennakēśava temple, east of the village. Records that Bukkarāja Timmarāja erected a maṇṭapam in front of the temple and granted one *puṭṭi* of dry field for its repair, in Ś. 1440, Bahudhānya. *Ins., Ced. Dts.*, p. 484, No. 217.

623. On a stone near the same. Records that Timmarāja, the Karaṇam, erected a temple of the Āḷvārs and granted 2½ *tūms* of land in Ś. 1460, Viḷambi, in the reign of Achyutarāya. *Ibid.*, No. 218.

Rāchavēli.

624. On a stone near the Mosafar Khana. Records that Rāmarāja Tirumalarājayya exempted the local barbers from tax in Ś. 1479, Piṅgaḷa, in the reign of Sadāśivarāya. *Ibid.*, p. 435, No. 52. Tirumala was afterwards the founder of the Chandragiri dynasty.

625. On the east of the above. Records that the same chief exempted the tax on the local Karṇams from Ś. 1470, Kīlaka. *Ibid.*, No. 53.

626. On a stone near the Gōpālasvāmi temple. Records that the same chief gave in Ś. 1466, Krōdhi, to a Brahman Māmillapilla-Narasiṁhabhaṭṭu, one *puṭṭi* of land at Goṭḷūru. See *Ibid.*, p. 436, No. 54.

Sirvel.

627. On a stone near the Narasiṁha pagoda. Records that Aubaḷarāja, grandson of Nandyāla Śiṅgarāja (I), remitted the tax of the district of "Servole" in favour of the temples in Ś. 1469, Plavaṅga, in the reign of Sadāśivarāya. *Ibid.*, p. 430, No. 34.

628. Near the above. Records that Sayud Khan "Turun" exempted the tax of the village in Ś. 1587, Krōdhi, in reign of "Khandvijumkharum"? *Ibid.*, No. 35.

Yadavāḍa (Yadade).

629. On a stone in the village near a well. Records that Nandyāla Chinna Aubaḷarāja granted the village to Brahmans in free gift in Ś. 1469, Plavaṅga, in the reign of Sadāśivarāya. See *Ibid.*, p. 432, No. 40.

630. West of the above. Records that Ōbaḷa, the Daḷavāy of Śrī-Raṅgarāya (II), dug a tank at Almūr in Ś. 1494, Āṅgirasa. *Ibid.*, No. 41.

Yerraguḍidinne.

631. On a stone near the local Īśvara pagoda. Records that Guṇḍarāja erected the temple of Malamuṇḍidēva and granted lands for daily worship in Ś. 1293, Sādhāraṇa, in the reign of Bukkarāya. *Ins., Ced. Dts.*, p. 431, No. 37. [Guṇḍa was evidently the Śāḷuva chief Guṇḍa II.]

632. On a stone in the Raṅgamaṇṭapam in front of the above. Records that Tippa Reḍḍi and another repaired the temple and built a maṇṭapam in Ś. 1590, Kīlaka. *Ibid.*, No. 38.

633. On a stone near the Veṅkaṭēśvara pagoda. Records that Chinna Aubaḷarāja gave the village to Brahmans in Ś. 1469, Plavaṅga, in the reign of Sadāśivarāya. *Ibid.*, p. 432, No. 39.

MADRAS DISTRICT

The following copper-plate grants are now in the Madras Museum:—

1—175. Ap. 169.

NA. A, B, E, 150, 212, 325A.

SA. 194, 335, 538, 539.

By. 22, 23, 24, 25, 45, 46, 47, 48B, 50, 51, 51A, 52, 53, 54, 56, 57, 59, 163A, 461, 470.

Cg. 1, 2, 3, 4, 4A, 5, 6, 7, 8, 9, 10, 11, 12, 13, 14, 15, 367, 368, 370, 400, 510, 856, 1146.

Ct. 370.

Cb. 433.

Cd. 455, 674.

Gj. 1, 2, 3, 4, 5, 6, 7, 9, 10, 11, 12, 13, 143A, 265, 290, 422.

Gd. 3, 7, 8, 17, 18, 67, 68, 81, 143, 359, 365.

Gt. 113, 120, 121, 122, 140, 273, 397, 813, 819.

S.K. 3, 4, 5, 6, 297.

Kt. 3, 4, 5A, 11, 91, 98, 127, 218, 297A, 319, 320.

Kl. 1, 2, 3, 4, 5, 6, 7, 8, 9, 10, 11, 12, 47, 489, 546, 517, 519, 564A.

Md. 3, 4, 15, 82, 85, 94, 95, 224, 226, 227, 274, 275, 313.

Nl. 27, 23A, 73A, 189, 384, 565.

Rḍ. 34, 35, 66, 103, 104, 105, 106, 107, 108, 109, 110.

Tj. 549A–E.

Tn. 280, 462.

Tp. 784A, 785, 786, 787 and 909.

Vg. 35A, 35B, 51, 212, 213.

F.T. 21.

The following plates have not been assigned to particular districts. They are therefore given here with summaries of their contents :—

176. *C.P. No.* 31 *of Mr. Sewell's List.*—This is " an unimportant but rather curious document, drawn up by one of ' three dismissed chieftains of Kāñchīvaram Kāmākshi Ammāḷ, Rāṇi of the Akhaṇḍa Kāvēri,' who had settled down in Vaḍamāttūr. Their names as given in the Tamil are ' Vannikkan, Manitakkān, and Puḷukkan '. The terminations appear to be the common Mussalman title Khan. The document states that one of the three chiefs (name not mentioned) decided a dispute between some thieves and some people who had settled at the village, and received some land for his services," in Ś. 1525 (A.D. 1603), in the year *Jaya.* The boundaries of the land were scrutinized by the Kavuṇḍars, Ambalakāras, Kaḷḷas and Śērvaikkāras of the surrounding villages, and the whole

was then engraved in a copper-plate. [The inscription is interesting for the insight it gives into the movements and organization of the Kaḷḷas and other criminal castes. See *Tam. and Sans. Ins.*, pp. 62—5. Vaḍamāttūr is believed by some to be a village six miles north of the road leading to Kumbakōṇam, but it is evidently in South Arcot and the birth-place of Mādai Tiruveṅgaḍa Aiya of Tamil literature.]

177. *C.P. No.* 174 *of Mr. Sewell's List.*—A grant by a certain Śrīkaṇṭha who does not bear royal titles, but who claims descent from Brahmā and Karikāla. Resembles Eastern Chāḷukyan grants of the tenth or eleventh century and later. After Karikāla the names mentioned are Sundarānanda, Navarāma, Eṟeyammā, Vijaya Kāma, Vīrārjuna, Agaṇipiḍugu, Kokili Mahēndravarma, Eḷajōḷa, Nṛipakāma, Divākara and Śrīkaṇṭha. See *Ep. Ind.*, Vol. V, p. 123; *Ep. Rep.*, 1900, p. 21 and Kielhorn's *Southern List*, No. 888.

178. *C.P. No.* 175 *of Mr. Sewell's List.*—A grant in Sanskrit and Tamil (Vaṭṭeḷuttu of the eleventh century) of the Pāṇḍya king Jaṭilavarman, son of Māravarman, in his seventeenth year. No details of date. The record gives an account of the king Neḍuñjaḍayan's achievements. The agñāpti or Dūtaka of the grant was Mahāsāmanta Dhīrataran Mūrti Eyiṇan of the Vaidya community, chief of Vīramaṅgalam. See *Ind. Antq.*, Vol. XXII, p. 57 ff. and Kielhorn's *Southern List*, No. 937.

179. *C.P. No.* 176 *of Mr. Sewell's List.*—An Eastern Chāḷukyan grant in three plates. Records the grant of Kūtalapaṟṟu in the Karmarāshṭra country by a donor whose name cannot be ascertained, but who appears to be Śaktivarman Vijayāditya Bhaṭṭāraka. *S. Ind. Palæ.*, p. 21.

180. *C.P. No.* 181 *of Mr. Sewell's List.*—A grant of Bhaktirāja, a descendant of Karikāla and son of Gaṅganṛivara (Gaṅgādhara ?), who bore the titles Gaṇḍabēṇḍara and Rāyavēśyābhujaṅga. Sent by the Nuzvid Zamindar.

181. *C.P. No.* 221 *of Mr. Sewell's List.*—Originally in the hands of the Collector and now in the museum. A Vijayanagar plate, modern in character, but professing to date from A.D. 1410 and recording grant of the town of Ādavāni (Adōni) as an agrahāram to a number of priests of the Vīrabhadra temple there by the Vijayanagar king Dēvarāya II.

182. *C.P. No.* 111 *of June* 1891, *pp.* 5–6.—Originally with the Sub-Collector of Cuddapah and now in the museum. It is in very faulty Sanskrit and Nandināgari character. It gives a confused genealogy of the Vijayanagar dynasty and records a grant by Achyuta in Ś. 1203, which is absurd and which indicates the record to be a forged one.

183. *C.P. No.* 1 *of* 1905.—From the Collector of Nellore and now in the museum. It is an ancient Pallava record, recording that Siṁhavarman (II), the son of Yuvarāja Vishṇugōpa, gave from his victorious camp at Mēnmatura, in the fifth year of his reign, the village of Pikira in the Muṇḍarāshṭra, to a Brahman named Vilāsaśarman. See *Ep. Ind.*, Vol. VIII, pp. 159—63, and p. 989 below.

184. *C.P. No.* 10 *of* 1905-06.—(Sanskrit in Nāgari.) A record of the Vijayanagara king Achyuta in Ś. 1459, Hēmalamba. Records gift of a village in Kuṇḍravardhanakōṭaka, a district of Tuṇḍiramaṇḍala, which was a subdivision of the Chandragirirājya, to the Vishṇu temple at Veṅkaṭādripura, which was founded near Vēdāraṇyam on the bank of the Vēdanadi river by a chief named Vāraṇāśi Varadappa.

185. *C.P. No.* 11 *of* 1905-06.—(Sanskrit in Nāgari.) A record of the Vijayanagara king Achyuta in Ś. 1456, Jaya. Records gift of the villages of Teṅgūru and Vallāguḷam in the same district by the king at the request of his minister Pedda Timma of the Sāḷaka family. No. 11 of 1905-06.

186. *C.P. No.* 12 *of* 1905-06.—(Sanskrit in Nāgari.) A record of the Western Chāḷukyan king Vinayāditya Satyāśraya Ś. 520, Kāḷayukti (wrong).

187. *C.P. No.* 13 *of* 1905-06.—(Sanskrit in Nāgari.) A record of the Vijayanagara king Achyuta in Ś. , Vikāri. Records gift of a village in Chandragirirājya to a Vishṇu temple.

188. *C.P. No.* 15 *of* 1905-06.—(Sanskrit.) Records the grant of the village of Tāmara cheru in Varāhavartini by the Eastern Gaṅga king Anantavarma-Vajrahasta (III), in Ś. 984 (20th June, A.D. 1061) to 500 Brāhmans. See *Ibid.*, Vol. IX, p. 94 ff. Also Gj. 143-A.

189. *C.P. No.* 16 *of* 1905-06.—(Sanskrit in Grantha.) A record of the Vijayanagara king Dēvarāya (II) in Ś. 1346, Krōdhin, Utthānadvādaśi. Records gift of a village (called Nīpataṭāka) by the king's brother Śrīgiri, who was governing Maratakanagara (Viriñchiparam), to a learned doctor named Sampatkumāra Paṇḍita. The date corresponded to Friday Nov. 3, A.D. 1424. See *Ibid.*, Vol. VIII, p. 306 ff.

190. In possession of M.R.Ry. Seshāchāri, Madras. A record of the Vijayanagara king Veṅkaṭapatidēvarāya in Ś. 1527, Viśvāvasu. Records gift of the village of Vlāṅgāḍu surnamed Kastūriraṅgapuram.

191. *C.P. No.* 2 *of* 1907-08.—This is the same as No. 66 in Mr. Sewell's List. It is a Telugu grant of the village of Tiruvīḍu in Ś. 1357 by Dēvarāya Voḍeya of Kāśyapa Gōtra to the local temple of Ahōbaḷēśvara, for the merit of his father Parvata Rāya, his mother Pārvati Dēvi, etc. It was received by the priest Purushōttamayya of Parāśara gōtra. The chief was an ardent devotee of Śrī Rāmānuja.

192. *C.P. No.* 5 *of* 1907-08.—A Sanskrit grant of Mallikārjuna Immaḍi Prauḍhabhūpa in Ś. 1383, Vrisha.

193. *C.P. No.* 6 *of* 1907–08.—A grant of Sadāśiva Rāya in Ś. 1470, Plavaṅga.

194. *C.P. No.* 4 *of* 1908–09.—A Ganjām plate. No details given.

195. *C.P. No.* 5 *of* 1908–09.—A C.P. grant of Tāḷa II in Sanskrit. This is very interesting as it refers to a king of the Eastern Chāḷukyan family who does not belong to the regular line of accession. It gives the usual genealogy from Kubja Vishṇuvardhana to Amma I and then, after some unusual accessions, comes to Tāḷa I, a younger brother of Chāḷukya Bhīma I. Tāḷa's son was Yuddhamalla II and his sons were Bāḍaba and Vishṇuvardhana Tāḷa II, the donor of the present grant. He made a grant of a village in Velanāṇḍu vishaya to a certain Kuppanayya of the Pallavamalla family who was a grandson of Kalivarma. [Tāḷa II was perhaps the Velanāṇḍu viceroy in Eastern Chāḷukyan times. For Kuppanayya see also Vandram plates of Amma II (Kt. 127). *Ep. Rep.*, 1908–09, pp. 109–10.

196. *C.P. No.* 6 *of* 1908–09.—A grant of the village of Ālapāḍi in Velanāṇḍu to a certain Viśvēśvara by Pedda Kōmaṭi Vēma in Ś. 1334, Nandana. The record is in Sanskrit.

197. *C.P. No.* 7 *of* 1908–09.—An incomplete Vijayanagara grant in Sanskrit, received from the Kistna Collector in 1902. No details given.

198. The Madras Museum Plates of Maṅgi Yuvarāja, the Eastern Chāḷukyan king, the son of Vishṇu Vardhana II. Records a grant in his twentieth year. See *Ind. Antq.*, Vol. XX, p. 105, and Kielhorn's *Southern List*, No. 552.

199—226. There are about twenty-seven other copper-plates in the museum (of which five belong to 1917–18). The summaries of these I have not been able to get. They are, however, I understand, about to be published by Mr. Srinivasaraghava Ayyangar of the Madras Museum, to whom I am indebted for the knowledge that there are 226 inscriptions on the whole in the museum.

227. 290 *of* 1895.—(Tamil.) On a stone in the Government Central Museum, Madras. A record in the ninetieth year of the Chōḷa king Kō-Rājarāja-Rājakēsarivarman *alias* Rāja-Rājadēva (I). Records gift of ninety sheep for a lamp.

228. 291 *of* 1895.—(Tamil.) On the same stone. A record in the nineteenth year of the Chōḷa king Kō-Rājarāja-Rājakēsarivarman *alias* Rājarāja (I). Records gift of ninety sheep for a lamp.

229. 292 *of* 1895.—(Kanarese.) On another stone in the same place. A damaged record of the Kaḷachūrya king Āhavamalla in Śārvarin (A.D. 1180–81). Vijaya Pāṇḍya is mentioned. Records a grant of land by a Nāyaka on the day of a solar eclipse.

230. 294 *of* 1895.—(Tamil.) On a stone in the same place from Chingleput. A damaged record of the Vijayanagara king

Vīra-Veṅkaṭapatirāya (I, 1586—1616), dated in Ś. 1530, expired, Saumya.

231. 295 *of* 1895.—(Tamil.) On a stone in the same place. Records a grant of land to a Vaishṇava temple in the time of Nīlagaṅgaraiyan. See No. 312 below.

232. 296 *of* 1895.—(Vaṭṭeḷuttu.) On a stone in the same place. A mutilated record. The king's name is lost.

233. 297 *of* 1895.—(Tamil.) On a stone in the same place from Chingleput. Records in the fifth year of the Chōḷa king Tribhuvanachakravartin Vīrarājēndra-Chōḷadēva (i.e., Kulōttuṅga III), gift of land by Nīla-Gaṅgaraiyan. See No. 312 below.

234. 298 *of* 1895.—(Persian.) On a stone in the same place. A record dated A.H. 1104.

235. 299 *of* 1895.—(Tamil.) On a stone in the same place from Chingleput. A much damaged record of the Vijayanagara king Achyutadēvamahārāya.

236—269. 536—569 *of* 1907.—On slabs recently removed from Amarāvati to the Madras Museum. These have been noticed already under Amarāvati.

270. 35 *of* 1912.—On a slab lying near a godown in the Museum. A Greek and Latin inscription, dated in A.D. 1727, forming an epitaph on the tombstone of a certain John Constantine, a native of Greece, born in Transylvania, who died on May 17th, A.D. 1727. It was erected by his brother. According to Mr. Cotton "it is the only Greek tombstone found in South India and the most ancient Greek tombstone anywhere in India."

271—282. 473–483 *of* 1913.—(Pāli.) On inscribed slabs from Amarāvati preserved in an underground room of the Central Museum. One of these mentions the Āndhra king Gōtamiputa Araka Arhat Siri-yana-Śātakaṇi and another, the Upāsaka Ura. For the last see *Ep. Rep.*, July 1888, p. 3.

283. 484 *of* 1913.—(Telugu.) On another slab in the same room. A record of the Kōṭa king Mahāmaṇḍalēśvara Manma-Kēṭarāja in Ś. 1157, Thursday. Records gift of a lamp to the temple of Buddha. The king was evidently a grandson of Kēta II, for whose inscription see Gt. 635.

284. 485 *of* 1913.—(Telugu.) On another slab in the same room. Records the *niśidhi* (tomb) of Chōchi Śeṭṭi, son of Honniśeṭṭi, a merchant of Penugoṇḍa.

285—302. 486—503 *of* 1913.—(Pāli.) On another slab in the same room. One of the slabs mentions a Vākāṭaka gahapati and another a certain Mahā-Chaḍamukha. A third registers the gift of a rail bar (*sūchi*) by Tuka.

303. 504 *of* 1913.—(Telugu and Sanskrit). On another slab in the same room. Records that the temple Chāḷukya-Vishṇugriha was built for a certain Nandaputra, native of Bōrikāpura, by the learned artisan Jayakīrti, son of Ādūrāchārya.

304. 505 *of* 1913.—(Nāgari and Sanskrit.) On another slab in the same room. Records that the image of Kīrtinārāyaṇa was made for the same person, perhaps also by the same artisan, here mentioned to be a brother-in-law *(sāḷuka)* of the former.

305. 506 *of* 1913.—(Nāgari and Sanskrit.) On another slab in the same room. Appears to record the visit of a pilgrim named Padmavārichandra Kuśalakārin.

306. 507 *of* 1913.—(Telugu.) On a slab in the grounds outside the Museum building. A damaged record in Akshaya, Śivarātri. Mentions the temple of Viśvēśvara at Viśvanāthapura.

307. 508 *of* 1913.—(Kanarese.) On a slab in the grounds outside the Museum building. A damaged record in . . . Śārvari, Āshāḍha, Amāvāsya, Monday, Solar eclipse. Seems to record grant of lands on this occasion to the temple of Gōpāladēva with the permission of the great men of Hosavaḍaṅgilu which was an ancient agrahāra of the time of Janamējaya. The temple is stated to have been founded by the Ēkadaṇḍi-vrati Gōpālapriyasvāmi. Refers at the beginning to Vijaya Pāṇḍyadēva who was ruling the Noṇambavāḍi 32,000 country. Details of date "not enough for calculation."

308. 509 *of* 1913.—(Kanarese.) On a slab in the grounds outside the Museum building. A record of the Western Chāḷukyan king Tribhuvanamalladēva Vikramāditya VI, in Chāḷukya Vikrama year 18, Śrīmukha, Āshāḍha, Amāvāsya, Vaḍḍavāra, Wednesday (wrong for Sunday), Dakshiṇāyana Saṁkrānti (= June 26, A.D. 1093). Records that 1,000 men of Kukkanūr met together to make a grant of land to Vāsudēva-Ghaiśāsa.

309. 510 *of* 1913.—(Tamil.) On a slab in the grounds outside the Museum building. A mutilated record in the twenty-third year of the Chōḷa king Rājakēsarivarman Rājarājadēva I. Mentions Kōvūr in Māṅgāḍu-nāḍu and seems to record gift of a lamp.

310. 511 *of* 1913.—(Tamil.) On a slab in the grounds outside the Museum building. A mutilated record of the Vijayanagara king Vīra-Kampaṇa Uḍaiyār (II) in Kali 4472, Ś. 1293, Virōdhikrit, Mithuna, ba. di. 5, Wednesday, Dhanishṭha, corresponding to 4th May, A.D. 1371. Seems to register the gift of the village Tiḷaikkārāṇai to Brāhmaṇas, by a certain Timmaiya-Nāyaka.

311. 512 *of* 1913.—(Tamil.) On a slab in the grounds outside the Museum buildings. A record in the nineteenth year of the Chōḷa king Rājarāja-Rājakēsarivarman *alias* Rājarājadēva I. Records gift of ninety sheep for a lamp to the temple of . . . at Taṇṇiyālattūr in Śurattūr-nāḍu, a subdivision of Puliyūrkōṭṭam, by a member of the *Gaṇattār* who were administering that village. Another record in continuation, of the same king and of the same date, provides also for a lamp, and a garden.

312. 513 *of* 1913.—(Tamil.) On a stone set up at the entrance into the Museum. A record of the Chōḷa king Tribhuvanachakravartin Vīrarājēndrachōḷadēva (i.e., Kulōttuṅga-Chōḷa III) in his fifth year, Rishabha, su. di. 3, Sunday, Punarvasu. Records gift of the village of Taṇṇiyālattūr in Śurattūr-nāḍu, a district of Puliyūr-kōṭṭam *alias* Kulōttuṅga-Śōḷavaḷanāḍu in Jayaṅgoṇḍaśōḷa-maṇḍalam, to the *Ariyaviratam-koṇḍān-maṭha* of Tiruvaṇṇāmalai. The order was issued by Pañchanadivāṇan Nīlagaṅgaraiyan. Diwan Bahadur Swamikannu Pillai says that *Rishabha* is a mistake for *Mithuna* and *Sunday* for *Thursday*, and then calculates the date to be 26th May, A.D. 1183.

313. 514 *of* 1913.—(Tamil.) On another stone in the same place. A much damaged record of the Vijayanagara king Achyutadēva-Mahārāya in Ś. 1452, Virōdhin, Vrischika (mistake for Kumbha), śu. di. 13, Monday, Pushya. Refers to the village Poḷichchalur of Taṇṇiyālattūr-śīrmaī in Śurattūr-kōṭṭam, a district of Puliyūr in Jayaṅgoṇḍaśōḷa-maṇḍalam.

314. 515 *of* 1913.—(Tamil.) On a third stone in the same place. A much damaged record in the second year, Mārgaḷi. Mentions the temple of Nirvaṇṇa Perumāḷ at Tirunīrmalai.

315. 516 *of* 1913.—(Tamil.) On a fourth stone in the same place. A record of the Vijayanagara king Vīra-Veṅkaṭapatirāya-dēva Mahārāya, in Ś. 1535, Saumya (wrong), Rishabha, Rēvati, 11, Friday, presumably 19th May, A.D. 1609. Registers that a certain Kāḷa Vaiyyappar having built a temple for Agarēśvara-Uḍaiyār at Poḷichchalūr in Śurattūr-nāḍu, a subdivision of Puliyūr-kōṭṭam in Jayaṅgoṇḍa-Toṇḍamaṇḍalam, Katti-Yellappa-Nāyaka made a grant of land to the temple for the merit of king Veṅkaṭapatirāya (I, 1586—1616).

316—323. 517—524 *of* 1913.—(Pāli.) On slabs in the Archæological show room of the Madras Museum. (Will be forwarded to Dr. Luders for publication in the *Epigrāphia Indica*.) One of these mentions the thēra Mahādhamakaṭhaka.

324. 525 *of* 1913.—(Kanarese.) On the base of a Jaina image in the same place. This is the image of Śāntināthadēva of the temple Yeṛaga Jinālaya, founded by the Mahāpradhāna Brahadēvaṇa, a lay disciple of Sakaḷabhadra Bhaṭṭāraka entitled Mahāmaṇḍalāchārya and belonging to Mūlaśaṅgha, Kuṇḍakundānvaya, Kāṇūrgaṇa and Tintriṇi-gachcha.

325. 526 *of* 1913.—(Kanarese and Sanskrit.) On the base of another Jaina image in the same place. Records that king Sālvadēva, a great lover of Sāhitya, got an image of Śānti-Jina made according to rule and set it up.

TRIPLICANE.

An ancient temple. Its Chōḷa and Pāṇḍya inscriptions were later on misplaced and scattered in the course of renovation in Vijayanagar times. There are fragments of tombstones in Roman characters near the *garbhagriham*, the presence of which is unaccountable.

326. 234 *of* 1903.—(Tamil.) On a stone built into the floor at the entrance into the *garbhagriha* of the Pārthasārathisvāmin temple. A record in the twelfth year of the Pallava king Dantivarma-Mahārāja. Records that the temple priests mortgaged one of the fields of the temple, that the offerings to the God in consequence fell short and that a certain Puguḷttuṇai-Viśaiyaraiyan redeemed the field and arranged for the usual quantity of rice offerings every day. [The inscription corroborates the testimony of Tirumaṅgai Āḷvār's *Periatirumoḷi* which attributed the foundation of the temple to the Toṇḍa king (i.e., Pallava).] See *Ep. Ind.*, Vol. VIII, pp. 290—6, where Venkayya edits it.

327. 235 *of* 1903.—(Tamil.) On the north wall of the central shrine in the same temple. A record of the Vijayanagara king Vīra-Veṅkaṭapatidēva-Mahārāja (Veṅkaṭa I) in Ś. 1527, Vikārin. Refers to the king as seated on a jewelled throne at the city of Peruṅgoṇḍai.

328. 236 *of* 1913.—(Tamil.) On the south base of the same shrine. A record of the Vijayanagara king Vīra-Veṅkaṭapatidēva-Mahārāya (I, 1586—1616), in Ś. 1525, Śōbhakrit. Refers to the king as seated on a jewelled throne at the city of Peruṅgoṇḍai and to the consecration of an image of Tirumaḷiśai-Āḷvār and a gift of twenty varāhas to this shrine.

329. 237 *of* 1903.—(Telugu.) On the same base. A record of the Vijayanagara king Raṅgarāyadēva-Mahārāya (I, 1578—86) in Ś. 1507, Tāraṇa. Records the gift of the villages of Śembiyam and Niḍāmbaram (Nadumbarai), besides a garden by Tirumala-Nāyaniṅgāru, the general of Rāmarāja Veṅkaṭapatirāju (Veṅkaṭa I?). The revenue from these two villages was 180 *rēkha chakra gadyāṇa* and from the garden 20 *chakra gadyāṇa*.

330. 238 *of* 1903.—(Tamil.) On the north base of the same shrine. A mutilated record in the forty-ninth year of the Pāṇḍya king Māravarman *alias* Tribhuvanachakravartin Kula-śēkharadēva. Records a sale of land. Mentions God Teḷḷiyaśiṅga Nāyanār.

331. 239 *of* 1903.—(Tamil.) On the same base. A record of the Vijayanagara king Mahāmaṇḍalēśvara Vīrapratāpa Sadāśiva-dēva-Mahārāya in Ś. 1486, Raktākshin. Records that a private individual built certain portions of the temple (e.g., shrines of Poḷḷikoṇḍaperumāḷ, Kṛishṇa, Vēdavalli Nāchchiyār, the Tiruvāy-moḷi maṇṭapa, the kitchen and enclosure wall and set up a number of images and granted three villages, Puduppākkam, Vēppēri and Veshārupāḍi (Vyāsarpāḍi).

332. 240 *of* 1903.—(Tamil.) On the east and north bases of the maṇṭapa in front of the same shrine. A record of the Vijayanagara king Vīrapratāpa Vīra-Vēṅkaṭapatidēva-Mahārāya (I, 1586—1616), in Krōdhin (i.e., Ś. 1527). Built in.

333. 241 *of* 1903.—(Tamil.) On a stone built into the floor of the same maṇṭapa. A fragmentary record of the Chōḷa king Tribhuvanavīradēva (Kulōttuṅga III), the date of which is lost. Mentions Tiruvāmiyūr (i.e., Tiruvāmūr near Mylapore) in Koṭṭūr-nāḍu.

334. 242 *of* 1903.—(Tamil.) On another stone built into the same place. A fragmentary record in the twenty-third year of the Chōḷa king Rājarājadēva. Four other similar fragments are built into this maṇṭapa and a number of others in other portions of the temple.

335. 243 *of* 1913.—(Tamil.) On the south and east walls of the Aḷagiyaśiṅga-Perumāḷ shrine in the same temple. Records certain arrangements referring to temple servants made while Etirāja-nāyakar was the manager.

Supplementary note to No. 183 *above.*

The Uruvapalli and Māṅgaḷūr grants.

It may be pointed out that Yuvarāja Vishṇugōpa and his son Siṁhavarman II are the respective sovereigns of the Uruvapalli and Māṅgaḷūr plates. The former says that Yuvarāja Vishṇugōpa was the son of Skandavarman II, grandson of Vīravarma and great-grandson of Skandavarman I. It records that Vishṇugōpa granted in the eleventh year of Siṁhavarman I (evidently his elder brother and the then actual ruler) 200 *nivarttanas* of land to the temple of Kaṇḍukūr founded by Sēnāpati Vishṇuśarma. It was issued from Palakkāḍa. See Kielhorn's *Southern List*, No. 619, and *Ind. Antq.*, Vol. V, pp. 50—3. The Māṅgaḷūr plates belong to the eighth year of Dharma Mahārāja Siṁhavarman II, and record the grant of the village of Māṅgaḷūr in Veṅgirāshṭra to certain Brahmans. The grant was issued from Daśanapura. See *Southern List*, No. 620, and *Ind. Antq.*, Vol. V, pp. 154—7. The exact places where these plates were discovered are not known.

MADURA DISTRICT.

DINDIGUL TALUK.

Agaram.

1. 4 *of* 1894.—(Tamil.) On a stone. Dated in the reign of the Vijayanagara king Kṛishṇadēva-Mahārāya, in Ś. 1444, expired, Chitrabhānu. Records gift of two villages near Dāḍikkombu.

Ānaipaṭṭi.

2. *C.P. No.* 160 *of Mr. Sewell's List.*—Records a grant by Śinna Kadirappa Nāyakka, a chief of the *Kaṇṇivāḍi* estate near Diṇḍigul, of some lands to some priests of the temple at Ānaipaṭṭi, in A.D. 1729. The grant was made to a Brahman for temple service. The genealogy of Śinna Kadir for nine generations is given. [Compare No. 33, the genealogy of which corresponds for five generations with that of the present one. Ānaipaṭṭi is a village in Diṇḍigul taluk.]

Āttūr.

3. Mr. Sewell gives a C.P. grant in the possession of one Śiva Rāma Avadhāni, recording gifts of lands to the Diṇḍigul choultry.

Bhūpālasamudra near Diṇḍigul.

3-A. *C.P. No.* 33 *of Mr. Sewell's List.*—Records grant and sale, made in Ś. 1651 (A.D. 1729), Kaliyuga 4830, Saumya, by Śinna Kadirappa Nāyakkan, a chief residing near Diṇḍigul, of the village to a number of paṇḍits in Saundararājapuram, otherwise called Ānaipaṭṭi. The grant was made during the reign of Vijaya Raṅga Chokkanātha (1705—31) at Madura, and it states that he was governing the country as viceroy for the Vijayanagar sovereign Śrī Raṅga Rāya. The grant gives lists of the ancestors of Śrī Raṅga Rāya, Vijaya Raṅga Chokkanātha, and the grantor. Edited by Burgess and Natesa Śastri in *Tam. and Sans. Ins.*, No. 27, pp. 117—121. The inscription enumerates the Vijayanagar kings and the Madura Nāiks and the Polygars of Kaṇṇivāḍi. The Polygar, in return for 300 Madura *kuḷipaṇams*, gave the village in proprietorship. The purchasers and donees were to enjoy the wet fields and had to pay, in case of new fields, one-fourth of the proceeds, one-third of the proceeds in the next crop, two-fifths of the third crop and one-fourth of the proceeds of sesamum, pulses and *pūvaraśa* trees. On the dry lands they had to pay eight *pons* for lands sowing one *kalam* of seeds. They were, however, to enjoy free the public paths and cowstalls. The palace had the right to collect the tax with interest in case of failure. Otherwise they had all the eight characteristics of property.

Bālakṛishṇa Mahādānapuram.

(Bālakṛishṇapuram of Diṇḍigul taluk?)

4. *C.P. No.* 19 *of Mr. Sewell's List.*—(Telugu.) Records a grant of the village as an agrahāram to certain Brāhmans in Ś. 1622 (A.D. 1700), in Vrisha, by "śrī Maṅgamma, wife of Chokkanātha Nāyuḍu, who was son of Muttu Vīrappa Nāyuḍu, and grandson of Viśvanātha Nāyani Tirumala Nāyuḍu of Madura."

Dāḍikkombu.

The departmental list gives one inscription in this place, and the *Mack. MSS. (Ins., S. Dts.,* p. 70*)* give four more. I have given the latter under Nos. 5-A to 5-D.

5. 3 *of* 1894.—(Tamil.) On the south wall of the Garuḍa shrine in the Sundararāja-Perumāḷ temple. An incomplete record of Rāmadēva-Mahārāya, dated Ś. 1551, expired, Śukla. See *Ins., S. Dts.,* p. 70, No. 1. Rāma IV ruled from 1620 to 1630. He came to the throne as a result of the victory over his opponents in the succession war which followed the death of Veṅkaṭapati I (1586—1616). The full details of these struggles, as based upon all available authorities, are given by me in *Ind. Antq.,* 1916.

5-A. On a stone in the Sundara Pāṇḍya maṇṭapam. Records the performance of the marriage festival of God Aḷagar by one Rāmānujāchāriar and a worshipper. *Ibid.,* No. 2.

5-B. On a stone in the west of the sixteen-pillared maṇṭapam in the Mutyālamma temple. Records that Rāyasam Koṇḍamarasāyya granted twenty-four shares in a village and erected twenty-four houses in it and gave it to the people, in Ś. 1444, Chitrabhānu, in the reign of Kṛishṇadēvarāya. *Ibid.,* No. 3. See Ap. 47.

5-C. On the eastern wall of the inner temple of Sundararāja Perumāḷ. Records that one Sundarēśvara appointed the priests and granted lands to them. *Ibid.,* No. 4.

5-D. A C.P. in the hands of "Paryan mteedauyangar." (Tamil.) Records that in Ś. 1502, Vikrama, in the reign of Prauḍhadēva-Mahārāya, his prime minister Chakrarāyan granted to a Brahman Timmaiyangār? thirty-three *mās* of land in Puduppuram village, two *mās* in Aḷagar-Samudram, and an allowance of a pagoda. *Ibid.,* No. 5. [The record seems suspicious.]

Diṇḍigul.

6. 1 *of* 1894.—(Tamil.) On the wall of a shrine in the fort. An incomplete record of the Vijayanagara king Achyutadēva-Mahārāya, dated Ś. 1460, expired. See *Antiquities,* Vol. I, p. 289.

7. 2 *of* 1894.—(Tamil.) On the wall of another shrine in the same place. A damaged record of Kōnērimaikoṇḍān.

7-A. In the possession of a resident Gaṅgādhara Sāstri. A C.P. grant relating to the hamlet of Rāmayyanpaṭṭi.

7-B. A C.P. in the hands of Gurumūrti Gurukkaḷ in the temple of Padmagirīśvara. Records that Baruki Veṅkaṭarāya gave seven villages to the God and Goddess in Ś. 1665, Rudhirōdgāri. See *Ins., S. Dts.*, p. 72, No. 8.

7-C. A C.P. in the hands of Rāmakṛishṇa Gurukkaḷ. Records that Daḷavāy Nārayaṇappayya re-established certain temple villages in Ś. 1672, in the reign of Vijaya Raṅgachokkanātha Nāyakar. *Ibid.*, p. 72, No. 9. [The date is inconsistent, as Vijayaraṇga was the Nāik king of Madura from 1705 to 1731.]

Rāmanāthapuram.

8. 690 *of* 1905.—(Tamil.) On a rock near Diṇḍigul. Belongs to the reign of the Pāṇḍya king Mārañjaḍaiyan. Records the building of a tank by Parāntakapaḷḷi-Vēḷān *alias* Nakkambuḷḷan, who accompanied the Pāṇḍya king in his expedition against Iḍavai in the Chōḷa country. [Venkayya identifies Iḍavai with the village of the same name in Maṇṇi-nāḍu, a subdivision of Rājēndra-Simhavaḷanāḍu on the northern bank of the Kāvēri. See *S.I.I.*, Vol. II, p. 53. Māraňjaḍaiyan was the Varaguṇa Mahārāja who ascended the throne in A.D. 862. See *Ep. Ind.*, Vol. IX, p. 84; *Ibid.*, Vol. XI, p. 253; also the inscriptions at Ambāsamudram, Trichinopoly, Tiruveḷḷarai and Tillaisthānam.]

MADURA TALUK.

Ānaimalai.

9. 63 *of* 1905.—(Vaṭṭeḻuttu.) On a rock to the left of the entrance into the central shrine of the rock-cut temple of Naraśiṅga-Perumāḷ. Records in the thirty-third year of the Chōḷa king Madiraikoṇḍa Parakēsarivarman (i.e., Parāntaka I (906—47) the digging of a tank called Kaliyanēri, the donor being Aruṇidi Kaliyaṇ, an officer of the king. Refers to Kīḻ-Iraṇiyamuṭṭam and the village of Naraśiṅgamaṅgalam included in it; also to the temple of Naraśiṅga-Permānaḍigaḷ on the Tiruvānaimalai hill. [Iraṇiyamuṭṭam is known in Tamil literature and included Peṛuṇguṇṛūr, the native place of Poet Perunkauśikanār, the author of the *Malaipaḍukaḍām*.]

10. 64 *of* 1905.—(Tamil.) In the same place. Records in the twenty-first year of the Chōḷa-Pāṇḍya king Jaṭāvarman *alias* Uḍaiyār Sundara-Pāṇḍya-Śōḷadēva, Viceroy of Madura under Rājēndra Chōḷa I, gift of sheep for a lamp. Mentions Kīḻ-Iraṇiyamuṭṭam and Tiruvānaimalai.

11. 65 *of* 1905.—(Tamil.) On the rock to the right of the entrance into the central shrine of the same temple. A damaged record of the Chōḷa-Pāṇḍya Jaṭāvarman *alias* Uḍaiyār Sundara-Śōḷa-Pāṇḍyadēva (the Viceroy under Rājēndra Chōḷa I), dated twenty-first year. Records gift of a lamp. The shrine is called after Narasiṁha Āḷvār on the Tiruvānaimalai in Kīḷ-Iraṇiya-muṭṭam in Rājēndrachōḷa-Vaḷanāḍu (a subdivision) of Rājarāja-Paṇḍināḍu.

12. 66 *of* 1905.—(Vaṭṭeḷuttu.) At the entrance into the maṇṭapa of the cave near the same temple. A partly mutilated record. Mentions Sōmāsiparivirājakar.

13—20. 67 *to* 74 *of* 1905.—(Vaṭṭeḷuttu and Tamil.) On a rock with sculptures overhanging a natural cave in the same village. Mentions Naraśiṅgamaṅgalam, Ajjaṇandi, Ten-kaḷavaḷināḍu Porkōḍu, Tiṇaikaḷattār, Veṇbaikuḍi-nāḍu. [For mention of Ajjaṇandin see N.A. 710-D.]

21. 454 *of* 1906.—On the left side of the entrance into the central shrine. (Grantha.) Records that Madhurakavi, the son of Māra, resident of Karavandapura, and minister of the Pāṇḍya king Parāntaka made this stone temple, gave away this rich agrahāra to Brahmans and set up the image of the God in K. 3871, on the day of the sun in the month of Kārttika. Madhurakavi is called a *Vaidya*. [See *Ep. Ind.*, Vol. VIII, pp. 317—20, where Mr. Venkoba Rao edits the inscription.]

22. 453 *of* 1906.—On the right side of the entrance. (Archaic, Vaṭṭeḷuttu and Grantha.) Records that Māran-Kāri, the minister of the Pāṇḍyan king Śaḍaiyan (son of Māran), excavated the cave at Ānamalai, but ascended heaven before consecrating it, and his younger brother Māran Eyinan Pāṇḍimaṅgalaviśaiyaraiyan, who became prime minister made the mukha-maṇṭapa and consecrated the image. [*Ibid.*, Mr. Venkoba Rao identifies Māran-Śaḍayan with a predecessor or probably grandfather of that Mārañjaḍayan who was known as Varaguṇa and who, according to the Trichinopoly cave inscription (414 of 1904), ascended the throne in A.D. 862. Mr. Venkoba Rao further surmises that Nammāḷvār, the teacher of Madhurakavi, who was known as Kāri-Māran, was probably the son of the minister Māran-Kāri. This is however inconsistent with the Vaishṇava *Guruparampara* which says that Kāri-Māran, the Āḷvār, was a man of the fourth caste, while his elderly contemporary and disciple Madhurakavi was a Brahman. The names Māran, Kāri and Madhurakavi seem however to show that by about A.D. 770 the Āḷvārs Nammāḷvār and Madhurakavi were well known.]

23. 455 *of* 1906.—(Grantha.) On the west wall of the maṇṭapa in front of the same shrine. A record of Kṛishṇadēva Rāya of Vijayanagar, dated Ś. 1441, Pramāthin. Mentions Timmabhūpa as the king's door-keeper and a certain Māḍhura-Rāmaṇātha as his agent.

24. 456 *of* 1906.—On a stone built into the platform in front of the shrine of the goddess in the same temple. A record of the sixth year of Śrī-Vallabha Pāṇḍya. Mentions Kandāḍai Kāḷamēghabhaṭṭan of Āpastamba sūtra. See No. 160 below.

25. 457 *of* 1906.—(Paḷi.) At the entrance into the natural cave known as *Pañchapāṇḍavarpaḍukkai* in the same village. In the Brāhmi character. The cave and beds have been described in *Ep. Rep.*, 1907, pp. 60–61.

Gōripāḷaiyam.

26. 77 *of* 1905.—(Tamil.) On a pillar set up within the Muhammadan masjid. Records in the reign of the Nāyaka king Kṛishṇappa-Nāyaka Vīrappa-Nāyaka in Ś. 1495, expired, *Bhava*, gift of land. Mentions a number of names of Vijayanagara kings and refers to Kūṇa-Pāṇḍya. [The inscription records that a considerable area of land was presented by Kūṇa Pāṇḍya to Muhammadans and that it was confirmed by Vīrappa Nāik in A.D. 1573. Nelson translates it in his *Madura Manual*, p. 67.]

Kaḷugumalai Hill (Māṅgulam).

27—32. 460 *to* 465 *of* 1906.—(Pāḷi.) On four boulders. In the Brāhmi characters. See for description of this place and similar antiquities in the neighbouring village of Ariṭṭāpaṭṭi, *Ep. Rep.*, 1907, p. 61. The Epigraphist assigns the inscription which resembles the alphabets of the Aśōka edicts to the end of the third and the beginning of the second century B.C. These are amongst the earliest lithic records of the Tamil country and the presence of Pāḷi shows that it was understood in the Pāṇḍya country even in that early period. Its connection with the origin and development of the Tamil Vaṭṭeḷuttu is still to be ascertained.

Kiḷaḍi.

33. 447 *of* 1906.—(Tamil.) On the south wall of the central shrine in the Arjunēśvara temple. Records in the twenty-third year of the Pāṇḍya king Māravarman *alias* Tribhuvanachakravartin Kulaśēkharadēva (I, 1268—1308), "who was pleased to take every country," that Kūpakarāya, the son of Maḷavarāya, rebuilt the temple and gave different names to the God and his consort in order to secure merit for his parents. The temple is called Muchukunda Tiruvirāmīśvaramuḍaiya-Nāyanār at Śrī-Kuntidēvi-chaturvēdimaṅgalam, a brahmadēya to the east of the tank *(kuḷakkiḷ)* at Vēlūr in Madhurōdaya-vaḷanāḍu. See *Ep. Ind.*, Vol. IX, pp. 223.

34. 448 *of* 1906.—(Tamil.) On the north, west and south walls of the same shrine. A mutilated record. Seems to register a sale of land.

35. 449 *of* 1906.—(Tamil.) On the same wall. Records in the thirty-first year of the Pāṇḍya king Māravarman *alias* Tribhuvanachakravartin Kulaśēkharadēva (I, 1268—1308), "who was pleased to take every country," sale of land to Kūttan Tennāḍan *alias* Tribhuvanaśiṅgadēva of Kaṇṇanūr in Malaimaṇḍalam by the sabhā of Śrī-Kuntidēvi-chaturvēdimaṅgalam, a brahmadēya to the east of the tank at Vēlūr in Madhurōdaya Vaḷanāḍu which was a dēvadāna of (the temple of) Muḍivaḷaṅgu-Pāṇḍya-Īśvaramuḍaiya-Nāyanār; refers to the executive committee *(nirvāha sabhai)* of the village and to the twenty-fourth year of the king's reign. See *Ep. Ind.*, Vol. IX, pp. 224, where it is pointed out that the date (Karkaṭaka 8, Aparapaksha, Ekādaśi, Rōhiṇi) corresponded to Saturday, 5th July, A.D. 1298.

36. 450 *of* 1906.—(Grantha and Tamil.) On a stone set up near a channel in the same village. Records in the twenty-second year of the Pāṇḍya king Kulaśēkhara the construction of the channel. This is the " unreadable " inscription referred to by Mr. Sewell.

37. 451 *of* 1906.—(Tamil.)- On another stone set up in the same place. A much damaged and mutilated record, the date and the king's name of which are lost.

38. 452 *of* 1906.—(Tamil.) On a stone set up in a field, near the same village. In modern characters. [Referred to by Mr. Sewell.]

Kīḻakkuḍi.

In the natural cave called *Śettippoḍavu* near this village are Jain images and beds described in detail in *Ep. Rep.*, 1910, pp. 77-8. The sculptures are of great iconographical interest and Mr. Krishna Sastri believes that they are different from those sketched by Dr. Burgess in his article on Digambara Jain iconography in *Ind. Antq.*, Vol. XXXII, p. 459 ff. The following Vaṭṭeḻuttu inscriptions have been copied.

39. 330 *of* 1908.—On the pedestal of one of the Jaina images. Records that the image was cut at the instance of Guṇasēnapperiyaḍigaḷ, the pupil of Varttamānava Paṇḍitar who was the pupil of Guṇaśēnadēva presiding over Kuraṇḍi-Tirikkāṭṭambaḷḷi Veṇbunāḍu. [No information is available about the teachers mentioned here. See N.A. 385 and 744 for teachers with similar names. The *Jainasiddhāntabhāskara* gives two Guṇasēnas in the apostolic line of the Sēna Gaṇa, founded by Jiṇasēna I about 16 B.C. These are the fifteenth and forty-fifth of the list. The same treatise gives a Guṇasēna as the fifty-fifth from Mahāvīra in the Kashtha Saṅgha line of teachers.]

40. 331 *of* 1908.—On the pedestal of another Jaina image on the hill. Records that the image was cut at the instance of a pupil of Guṇasēnadēva who was in charge of this *paḷḷi*. See the above epigraph.

41. 332 *of* 1908.—On the pedestal of a third Jaina image in the same place. A damaged record. Mentions Guṇasēnadēva who presided over this paḷḷi. See No. 39 above.

42. 63 *of* 1910.—Below the Jaina figure cut on the boulder outside the cavern. Damaged in the beginning. Records that Abinandan Bhaṭāra, a pupil of Arimaṇḍala Bhaṭāra, who was the pupil of Abinandan Bhaṭāra, who in turn was the pupil of Kanakanandi Bhaṭāra, caused this image to be cut. It also refers to Kuraṇḍi Tirukkāṭṭambaḷḷi. [I have not been able to get information about these in any of the Jain Paṭṭāvalis. Kanakanandi Bhaṭāra is, I suppose, different from Kanakavīra mentioned in N.A. 744.]

Kiramāttūr.

43. 16 *of* 1894.—(Vaṭṭeḻuttu.) On the north wall of the Śiva temple. An incomplete record of the Pāṇḍya king "who took the head of the Chōḷa," dated ninth year.

Koḍimaṅgalam.

44. On the front of the first pillar, left side, of the mahāmaṇṭapa in the local Kārttikasvāmi temple, over a figure. States that it is Aṇṇāvipperumāḷ Piḷḷai. *Tam. and Sans. Inscrns.*, p. 2.

45—49. On similar pillars, over their respective figures. The names Śevandiyappa Piḷḷai, Aḻagiri Nāik, Piratāni (Pradhāni) Nāiken, Aṇṇāvipperumāḷ Piḷḷai and Kuppayāṇḍi (son of Aḻagappa Piḷḷai) are recorded. *Ibid.*, pp. 2-3.

50. On a stone to the north of the village in front of the Kumārasvāmi temple. A record of K. 4774, Pramādīcha, Puraṭṭāśi, making gifts of lands and revenues to God Kumāra by the *Karttās*. *Ibid.*, pp. 3-4.

Madura.

For a full notice of Madura see *Antiquities*, I, pp. 291-2, and the bibliography given there. Mr. Sewell gives two lists of inscriptions in this place, one of which numbers 49 and the other 13. These overlap each other and it is unnecessary to compare them with the list given below.

51. 46 *of* 1890.—In the north wall of the second prākāra of the Sundarēśvara temple. A record of Kōnērinmaikoṇḍān Sundara Pāṇḍya.

52. 47 *of* 1890.—In the same place. An inscription of the twenty-first year of Kō-Jaṭāvarman Tribhuvanachakravartin Vīra Pāṇḍya dēva. [Was he the same as the king who came to the throne in 1253 and who, after conquering Īḻam, Koṅgu and Śōḻamaṇḍalam, anointed himself at Perumbaṟṟappuliyūr ?]

53. 48 *of* 1890.—Similar to 52.

54. 50 *of* 1890.—On the north wall of the second prākāra of the Sundarēśvara temple. A record of Tribhuvanachakravartin Kōnērinmaikoṇḍān. (No other details.)

55. 58 *of* 1905.—On the north wall of the west gōpura. Tamil verse. Refers to Parākrama Pāṇḍya.

56. 59 *of* 1905.—(Tamil.) On four pillars in the second storey of the east gōpura. A record of the second year of Jaṭāvarman Tribhuvanachakravartin Kulaśēkhara (1190—1217). [Beginning lost. Incomplete.]

57. 60 *of* 1905.—(Tamil.) On the same pillars. A record of the fifteenth year of Māravarman Tribhuvanachakravartin Sundara Pāṇḍya dēva I "who took the Chōḷa country and was pleased to perform the anointment of heroes and anointment of victors at Muḍikoṇḍachōḷapuram." [He ruled from 1216 to 1235. The date corresponds to Tuesday, 3rd December 1230. See *Ep. Ind.*, Vol. VIII, p. 276.]

58. 60 *of* 1905.—(Tamil.) On the same pillars. An incomplete and mutilated record of the tenth year of Māravarman Tribhuvanachakravartin Sundara Pāṇḍya dēva "who was pleased to re-present the Chōḷa country" (1216—35).

59. 62 *of* 1905.—On the fifth pillar in the same place. A record of the second year of Jaṭāvarman Tribhuvanachakravartin Kulaśēkharadēva (1190—1217) making a gift of land.

60-A. In the east gōpuram. First inscription at the southern wall at the entrance. A record dated Ś. 1501, Pramāthi (Purattāśi), granting exemption of tax to the Śēdars of the province of Rāmanāthapuram who brought the first betel-leaf and nut to the palace. *Tamil and Sanskrit Inscrns.*, No. 22, p. 109.

60-B. In the east gōpura, a little before the south door-jamb. Records that in Ś. 1532, Saumya (Āni, pūśam) Viśvanātha-Vīrappa Nāiker exempted the Mudaliyār servants of the Chokkanātha temple at Anakkuḍi and other villages from the levying of brokerage. *Ibid.*, No. 23, pp. 109-10. Vīrappa was the predecessor of Tirumal Nāik and reigned from 1609 to 1623. See *Ind. Antq.*, 1916, p. 132 f.

60-C. On the east gōpura on the north door-jamb. An interesting record dated in Ś. 1632, *Khara*, Paṅguni 20, Saturday, in the time of Vijaya Raṅga Chokkanātha Nāik (1705—31). Refers to a temple servant's falling down from the temple tower as a protest against undue collection of tax from some tax-free villages and the yielding of the State officials. See *Tamil and Sanskrit Inscrns.*, No. 24, pp. 110-11.

60-D. 502 *of* 1907.—(Vaṭṭeḻuttu.) On a detached stone lying in the Madanagōpālasvāmin temple. A fragment of record, dated thirty-eighth year. The king's name is lost. Mentions Tirutturutti-Mahādēvar and Perumūr in Aṇḍa-nāḍu; seems to record the gift of a lamp.

61. 503 *of* 1907.—(Vaṭṭeḻuttu.) On another stone in the same place. A fragmentary record of Kōchcha, the date of which is lost. Seems to record the gift of a lamp.

62. 504 *of* 1907.—(Vaṭṭeḻuttu.) On a third stone in the same place. Records gift of a lamp by Kunṛañjundari of Koṟṟavāyir chēri in Vaḍa-Madirai to the temple at Tirutturutti, a dēvadāna in Aṇḍa-nāḍu. King's name and date lost.

63. 505 *of* 1907.—(Vaṭṭeḻuttu.) On a fourth stone lying in the Madanagōpālasvāmin temple. A fragment. Seems to register gift of cows.

64. 506 *of* 1907.—(Tamil.) On eight other stones in the same place. Fragment of a record of the Pāṇḍya king Māravarman *alias* Tribhuvanachakravartin, dated twelfth year. Mentions Parākrama-Pāṇḍyadēva and the Śaivāchārya Śivagōchari-Mahādēva of the Bhāradvāja-gōtra.

65. 507 *of* 1907.—(Tamil.) On the thirteenth stone in the same place. A record of the Pāṇḍya king Tribhuvanachakravartin Śrī-Vallabhadēva in his second year. Records a gift by the queen Ulagamuḻuduḍaiyāḷ. [Was he Māravarman Śrī Vallabha who was apparently a predecessor of Jaṭāvarman Kulaśēkhara I (1190—1217) or the Jaṭāvarman Śrīvallabha who is mentioned in the third year of Māravarman Sundara Pāṇḍya I (1216—35) ?]

66. 508 *of* 1907.—(Tamil.) On the fourteenth stone in the same place. The stone bears at the top the Pāṇḍya crest, i.e., two fish with a *triśūla* between them. Records the gift of a flower garden by the queen Ēḻulagumuḻudumuḍaiyāḷ.

67. 509 *of* 1907.—(Tamil.) On the fourteenth and sixteenth stones in the same place. A fragment of record.

68. 510 *of* 1907.—(Grantha and Sanskrit.) On thirteen other stones in the same place. Purports to be the genealogy of the Mahāmaṇḍalēśvara Rāmarāja-Tirumalarāya-Mahārāja, dated Kaliyuga (mistake for 4647), Ś. 1468, Parābhava.

69. 500 *of* 1907.—(Tamil and Grantha.) On the west wall of same temple. An unfinished record dated Ś. 1520, expired, Hēviḷambi.

70. 35 *of* 1908.—(Telugu.) On one of the pillars in the Kambattaḍi-maṇṭapa in the Sundarēśvara temple. Records in the reign of the Nāyaka king Vīrappa-Nāyaka (1572—95), son of Viśvanātha-Nāyaka-Kṛishṇappa-Nāyaka, in Ś. 1505, expired, Subhānu, the construction of the maṇṭapa. A Tamil copy of the document is added below the inscription. [See *Ind. Antq.*, 1916, pp. 90—2, for an account of Vīrappa's reign.]

71. 36 *of* 1908.—(Tamil.) On a stone set up in front of the Perumāḷ temple in the same town. A record of the Vijayanagara king Vīra-Veṅkaṭa-Mahārāya (I, 1586—1616). Mentions in Ś. 1523, expired, Śubhakrit, the temple of Madanagōpāla at Madura and Bhāshyakāra, i.e., Śrī-Rāmānujāchārya. Veṅkaṭa was, it is well known, a disciple of Kōṭikanyādānam Tātāchārya and an ardent Vaishṇaviṭe.

72. 557 *of* 1911.—On the south wall of the maṇṭapa in front of the Kūḍal-Aḷagar temple. Records that stones were supplied for the building of the Ardha-maṇṭapa and the garbhagriha of the Kūḍal-Aḷagiya-Perumāḷ temple, by Kandāḍai Kōnamman for the merit of Kandāḍai-Aṇṇan and states that the work was finished during the administration of Yellappa-Nāyakkar. Mentions Rāmarāja Viṭṭhaladēva-Mahārāja and his subordinate Timmappa-Nāyakar, son of Vasavaṇa-Nāyakkar. Kandāḍai Aṇṇan was a descendant of Mudaliyāṇḍān, the uncle and contemporary of Rāmānuja. It was this family that first broke the Āchāryic tradition and embraced the creed of the Prabandhic teacher Varavaramuni. The present Aṇṇan was probably the son or grandson of the disciple of Maṇavāla-Mahāmuni or a member of the same family.

73. 558 *of* 1911.—(Tamil.) On the north, west and south walls of the central shrine in the same temple. A damaged and unfinished record. Records gift of money and a house for offerings to the same temple by Vasavaṇa-Nāyakkar-Timmappa Nāyakkar.

74. 559 *of* 1911.—(Tamil.) On the same walls. Dated in the reign of the Vijayanagara king Vīrapratāpa Sadāśivadēva-Mahārāya in Ś. 1473, Virōdhikrit. Records gift of three villages for offerings and festivals to the temple of Kūḍal-Aḷagiya-Perumāḷ by Timmappa-Nāyakkar, son of Vasavaṇa-Nāyakkar for the merit of Rāmarāja-Viṭṭhaladēva-Mahārāja. [He was the Viceroy of the south which he reconquered for Vijayanagar in 1545.]

75. 560 *of* 1911.—(Tamil.) On a pillar set up in the Collector's bungalow in the village. A record of Tribhuvanachakravartin Kōnērimēlkoṇḍān in his fourteenth year. Records that a certain Jñānamūrtī dēva of the Nandikēśvaradēvar-santāna in the Āmuṇḍa-maṭha, built in the name of Aṇṇan Viḷuppādarājar of Vaḍagarai Vāraṇavāśi-paṭṭinam in Malaikkuḍināḍu, a *maṭha* called *Mānamperiyān-maḍam* and endowed it with 10 *mā* of land, which the king made tax-free *(iraiyili)*.

76. 4 *of* 1915.—(Tamil.) On the east wall of the third gōpura in the Sundarēśvara temple. A record of Tribhuvanachakravartin Konerinmaikoṇḍān in his thirteenth year, three hundred and sixth day, describing gift of land for the maintenance of a flower garden and for feeding Mahēśvaras in the Naralōkasūryan-tirumaḍam. The land was situated in Pāganūr-kūṟṟam. Built in at the beginning.

77. 5 *of* 1915.—(Tamil.) On the south wall of the first gōpura in the same temple. A damaged record dated Ś. 1469, Kīlaka, Dakshiṇāyana, 12, Friday, Pūrva-Phalguni. Seems to record a gift of land for the *maṭha* presided over by Jñānakūttar *alias* Śattijñānaderiśanaigaḷ.

78. 6 *of* 1915.—(Tamil.) On a pillar in the same gōpura. Dated in the reign of the Nāyaka king Vijayaranga-Chokkanātha Nāyaka (1705—31), son of Muttu-Vīrappa-Nāyaka (1680—89). Records in Ś. 1633, Khara, Panguni, tenth day, śu. di. 11, Āślēsha, Sukarma-yōge, Bhadravākaraṇa, Saturday, corresponding to March 8, A.D. 1712, remission of taxes on four villages granted to the bearers of the image of the god Śokkanāthasvāmin. Mentions the commander-in-chief Kumāra Daḷavāy Kastūri Rangayyan and the pradhāni Venkaṭakṛishnayyan. See my *Hist., Nāik king. Madura in Ind. Antq.*, 1917, pp. 186—90.

79. *7 of* 1915.—(Tamil verse.) On the east wall of the third prākāra of the Mīnākshi-Amman temple in the same village; right of entrance. A much damaged record. Two verses in praise of a Pāṇḍya king (vaḷudi) who had the surname *vāḷāl vaḷi tiṛandān.* A second set of two verses evidently in praise of the same king who is here called Kūḍalar-kōmān, mentions the damming of the sea with his sword.

80. The Daḷavāi agrahāram plates of Venkaṭapati I (so called because it was obtained from one Anantāchārya of the Daḷavāi Agrahāram, Madura). A record of Venkaṭapati I of Penukoṇḍa, dated Ś. 1508, *Vyaya, Utthāndvādaśi* of the bright half of Kārttika, recording the gift of the village of Gangavārāppaṭṭi or Vīrabhūpasamudram to a number of Brāhmans at the request of Vīrabhūpa (Vīrappa Nāik) of Madura (1572—95), the son of Kṛishṇappa (1563—73), and grandson of Viśvanātha (1559—63). See *Ep. Ind.*, Vol. XII, pp. 159—87, where Mr. Gopinatha Rao edits the inscription. The inscription mentions Tātāchārya, the preceptor of Venkaṭa I and Mr. Gopinatha Rao traces his connexion with the Vijayanagara dynasty on the basis of the *Prapannāmruta.* He also enumerates from the *Tiruppaṇimālai* of the Madura temple, the holy works of Vīrappa Nāik.

80-A. Daḷavāi agrahāram plates of Varatunga Rāma Pāṇḍya. Records that on Wednesday, Māgha Kṛishnapaksha chaturdaśi, in Chitrabhānu, Ś. 1504, Varatunga granted the village of Muruganēri to Chandraśēkhara, son of Chokkappa Paṇḍita, a doctor. *Trav. Arch. Ser.*, Vol. I, pp. 117—25.

80-B. Another C.P. from the same place. Records on Āshāḍha 30 of Ś. 1510, Sarvadhārin, that king Varatunga Rāma Vīra Pāṇḍya granted the village of Śilārippaṭṭi to Gōvindabhaṭṭa, son of Udayambhaṭṭa. *Ibid.*, pp. 126—33.

81. *C.P. No. 22 of Mr. Sewell's List.*—(Tamil.) In the District Court of Madura. Records a grant of property in some lands to a Śiva temple dedicated to the god Viśvēśvara and the goddess Akhilāṇḍēśvari, in Ś. 1691 (A.D. 1769) = Kaliyuga 4780, Virōdhi, by Hiraṇyagarbha Ragunātha Sētupati Kāttar Avargaḷ, lord of Tēvainagara. The grant is said to have been made when "the

Aśvapati, Narapati, Gajapati and Sētupati kings were reigning over the countries of Chōḷamaṇḍalam, Toṇḍamaṇḍalam, Yāpāṇapaṭṭaṇam (Jaffna) and Yeṟumaṇḍalam (Ceylon)."

82. *C.P. No.* 23 *of Mr. Sewell's List.*—(Tamil.) Records a grant of some lands by Muttu Kumāra Vijaya Raghunātha Sētupati, son of Kumāra Muttu Vijaya Raghunātha Sētupati, and son-in-law of Hiraṇyagarbhayāji Raghunātha Sētupati Kāttar, to a Brahman in Ś. 1658 (A.D. 1736), *Naḷa*.

83. *C.P. No.* 27 *of Mr. Sewell's List.*—(Modern Tamil.) This is the same as No. 20 in *Tam. and Sans. Inscrns.*, pp. 107-8. Records a private document drawn up between two brothers, after a dispute as to which was the elder. The younger, Śinna Vaḍāvada Nāyakkar Tummiśi, having been declared in an assembly consisting of 18 Kōḍaṅgi Naiks and Polygars, that he was junior, the elder, Rāma Rāya Tummiśi Nāyakkar, granted him some lands. Rāma Rāya Tummiśi calls himself head of Śillavārs and assumes great titles. The document is dated in Ś. 1455 (A.D. 1533), Śōbhakrit (wrong) in Makara, new moon day. [The record is of singular value as illustrating the nature of caste decisions and methods of decision.]

84. *C.P. No.* 59 *of Mr. Sewell's List.*—Records grant of lands for a charitable purpose, viz., for an Annadāna *maṭham*, or place where food is cooked and distributed gratis, by the chief of Punnalpālaināḍu, Muttu Vaḍuganātha Periya Uḍayā Tēvar, son of Vijaya Raghunātha Sēvaran Periya Uḍayā Tēvar, in Ś. 1681 (A.D. 1759), Pramādi.

85. *C.P. No.* 63 *of Mr. Sewell's List.*—In the Collector's office. (Tamil.) Records in K.A. 775, Śārvari (A.D. 1599), that the Śūdra priests of a certain "Toḍukuḷai Mūtta Rāja," created one Kuppayāṇḍi Piḷḷai Karaṇam of seven villages, and endowed, besides some lands for his and his descendants' maintenance, the right to collect two *paṇams* from each large family and one *paṇam* from each small family. See *Tam. and Sans. Inscrns.*, No. 25, pp. 111-2.

86. *C.P. No.* 197 *of Mr. Sewell's List.*—Records grant by Tirumala Nāyakka (1623—59) of Madura to Śrī Raṅga Nāyakka, lord of Veḷḷikurchi *(Veḷḷikurichiśimāikku Kartar)*, as a reward for his services in slaying tigers, in Jaya, which must have been A.D. 1654.

87. *C.P. No.* 198 *of Mr. Sewell's List.*—Records an order signed by Kōḍi Nāgama Nāyakka, commanding Muttumūvaraittēvan, lord of Kōḍi Kuḷattukkōṭṭai and Araśirippu in the province of Muduku, to pay tribute to the Karṇāṭa Samasthānam (the Carnatic). The date of the grant was in the reign of Tirumala Nāyakka of Madura. The date is K.A. 821, Pārthiva (A.D. 1645). A succession of Naiks is given, but these do not correspond to the Naiks of Madura.

88. *C.P. No.* 199 *of Mr. Sewell's List.*—Records a grant by Tirumala Nāyakka of Madura to a private individual in the year

Khara. "No other date is given, but the document must have been executed in A.D. 1651."

89. *C.P. No.* 62 *of Mr. Sewell's List.*—(Modern Tamil.) Records a document drawn up by two people of the Kauṇḍar caste conferring certain privileges on the watchmen of the village of Amandūr in Krōdhana, Vaikāśi 12 (but without any other guide to the period). One Pichchan of the Nāṭṭukkaḷḷar community was appointed by them as village watchman and he was entitled to the gift of a woman's *sāḍi* (śēlai), a *duppaṭṭi*, a turban, and handful of gruel and of alms. See *Tam. and Sans. Inscrns.*, No. 33, p. 136. Mr. Sewell calls the village Amatur.

89-A. A C.P. grant of Vijaya Raṅga Chokkanātha (1705—31) of the Nāik dynasty of Madura, in Ś. 1639, Kārttika 21, recording gift of a *maṭha* at Tirukkaḷukkunṛam in Chingleput district. The plate has been deposited in the Madras Museum.

90. *C.P. No.* 108 *of Mr. Sewell's List.*—Records grant of some lands, by a private person in Ś. 1638, Kaliyuga 4827, Plavaṅga (A.D. 1716), to the Rāmagiri temple in the "Taṭṭaināḍu." No sovereign is mentioned. [The dates are not consistent.]

91. *C.P. No.* 136 *of Mr. Sewell's List.*—(Nāndināgari.) Records a grant of two villages in the Madura district, Marudaṅguḍi and Kārupuram, otherwise called Madanagōpālapuram, to several Vaishṇava Brāhmaṇs in Ś. 1519 (A.D. 1597), Hēviḷambi. The grant was issued by Veṅkaṭapati (I) of Chandragiri at the request of Kṛishṇappa Nāik of Madura who is styled *Pāṇḍya Pārthiva Kṛishṇa Nripati.*

92. *C.P. No.* 211 *of Mr. Sewell's List.*—(Grantha and Sanskrit.) Records that, at the request of Rāmakṛishṇappa, "sitting on the lion throne of Vallabha Narēndra after 33 years have passed, and after Ś. 1517," King Ativīra Rāma Pāṇḍya granted the village of Nadikkuḍi or Ativīrarāmapuram to a number of Brahmans. The figure of a boar with a dagger standing on its nose is engraved at the end. See *Trav. Arch. Ser.*, Vol. I, pp. 133—146. This is the same as the third Daḷavāi agrahāram plates.

93. *C.P. No.* 1 *of* 1911.—A record of Vijaya Raṅga Chokkanātha of Madura, dated in Ś. 1643, Śubhakrit, recording gift of land to a certain Narasapantulu, probably a physician, who "was to enjoy lands rent free, by offering prayer to Dhanvantri."

94. *C.P. No.* 3 *of* 1911.—A record of Rāṇi Maṅgammāḷ, dated S. 1623, Vrisha, while "Vīra Veṅkaṭadēva Mahārāya was ruling at Ghānagiri (Penukoṇḍa). Records gift of land for a feeding institute to a certain Subbayya Bhāgavata. The inscription gives an instance of the formal acceptance of Vijayanagara suzerainty long after it ceased to exist.

94-A. *C.P. No.* 4 *of* 1910-11.—Originally in the hands of the District Judge of Madura and now in the museum. A Tamil record dated in Ś. 1105, Āṅgirasa (wrong), but in modern characters thereby showing that it is a forgery. Records gift of a maṭha, a flower garden and a well to a certain Nīlakaṇṭha Paṇḍārakkuṭṭi of Toṇḍipaṭṭaṇam by the Mudaliyāṇḍi Paṇṇāṭṭār of Iravuśari.

95. *C.P. No.* 9 *of Appendix A, Mad. Ep. Rep.*, 1906.—Now preserved in the Madras Museum. This is a grant of the reign of Veṅkaṭapati Dēva Rāya in Ś. 1531, *Saumya*, recording the gift of the village of Nāganallūru surnamed Muttuvīramahīpālasamudram to Brāhmaṇas by the king at the request of the Nāik of Madura, Muttu Vīrappa. [The record shows that in 1609 the Nāik kingdom acknowledged the supremacy of Chandragiri. See my *Hist. Nāik. king., Madura*, in *Ind. Antq.*, 1916, p. 104.

Muttuppaṭṭi (hamlet of Vaḍapalaṅgy).

96–98. 58—60 *of* 1910.—(Brāhmi.) On the pillow side of a stone-bed on the hill and on a boulder of the same hill. Unread. [For the description of the Jain images and beds see *Madr. Ep. Rep.*, 1910, p. 77.]

99. 61 *of* 1910.—(Vaṭṭeḷuttu.) On the same boulder below a Jain figure. Records that Kanakavīra Periaḍigaḷ, a disciple of Guṇasēnadēva who was a disciple of Kuraṇḍi Aṭṭa-upavāsi-Bhaṭāra of Veṇbu-nāḍu, caused this image to be cut in the name of the inhabitants of Kuyiṛkuḍi. (Modern Kīḷakkuḍi.) See No. 42 above.

100. 62 *of* 1910.—(Vaṭṭeḷuttu.) In the same place. Records that Māganandi, a disciple of Kuraṇḍi Ashṭa-upavāsi, caused this image to be cut in the name of the inhabitants of the district.

Paśumalai.

100-A. With Rev. Mr. Jones of this place. A Tamil C.P. grant of the fifteenth year of Kōnērinmaikoṇḍān. Records gift of land to a Vaishṇavamaṭha at Tirumāliruñjōlai (Aḷagarmalai), and to Vikrama Pāṇḍya Viṇṇahar Āḷvar at Kiḷaikoḍumaḷūr.

Pēchchi-paḷḷam.

The findings in this place are akin to those at Koṅgar-Puḷiyaṅguḷam, Kīḷakkuḍi, etc. Foundations of ruined buildings and Jain relics are still to be seen here. The Government Epigraphist points out in his *Mad. Ep. Rep.*, 1910, p. 78, that there is a large courtyard in front of a rock which "bears a row of Jaina sculptures all facing east. Five of these are standing naked figures with a canopy of five serpent-hoods spreading overhead and attendant deities on the sides. They are undoubtedly representations of the seventh Tīrthaṅkara Supārśva." The following inscriptions have been copied:—

101. 64 *of* 1910.—(Vaṭṭeḷuttu.) Below a Jaina figure. Records that Guṇamatiyār, mother of Ajjaṇandi, caused this image to be cut. See N.A. 710-D.

102. 65 *of* 1910.—(Vaṭṭeḻuttu.) In the same place. Records that the image was caused to be cut on behalf of a certain Āchchān Śrīpālan, nephew of Anattavaṉ Māśēṉaṉ, a disciple of Guṇasēnadēva who was in charge of this *Paḷḷi*. See No. 39 above.

103. 66 *of* 1910.—(Vaṭṭeḻuttu.) In the same place. Records that the image was cut by Kaṇḍan Porpaṭṭan of Śirukaḍaippuram, a pupil of Guṇasēnadēva who was in charge of this *Paḷḷi*. See No. 39 above.

104. 67 *of* 1910.—(Vaṭṭeḻuttu.) In the same place. Records that the image was cut on behalf of Vēḷāṉ Śaḍaiyan, a shepherd of Pārūr in Miḻalai-kūṟṟam, by his wife.

105. 68 *of* 1910.—(Vaṭṭeḻuttu.) In the same place. Records that the image was caused to be cut by Kanakanandi, a servant of Tirukkuṟaṇḍi of Veṇbunāḍu. See No. 42 above.

106. 69 *of* 1910.—Records that this image was caused to be made on behalf of his younger brother by Araiyaṅgāvidi, pupil of Guṇasēnadēva, who was in charge of this *Paḷḷi*.

*Tirumogūr.**

107. 75 *of* 1905.—(Tamil.) On the south wall of the maṇṭapa of the Kaḷamēgha-Perumāḷ temple. Records in Ś. 1473, expired, Virōdhikrit, gift of land by Basavaṇa-Nāyaka Timmappa-Nāyaka. See No. 72 above.

108. 76 *of* 1905.—(Tamil.) On the same wall. A record connected with the above epigraph and dated in Ś. 1473, expired, Virōdhikrit.

Tiruparaṅkuṉṟam.

In his *Antiquities* Mr. Sewell gives a list of eleven inscriptions in this place, but with no details.

109. *C.P. No.* 61 *of Mr. Sewell's List.*—(Tamil.) Records that Vīrasimha Taittu, a descendant of Maṅgammāḷ (presented something ?) in Ś. 1765 (A.D. 1843), Bahudhānya, to the Subrahmaṇya temple, four miles south of Madura. The dates are inconsistent and the first part of the inscription is in old Tamil while the latter part is in quite modern Tamil.

110. 49 *of* 1890.—On the east wall of the rock-cut cave, now called Umaiyāṇḍān kōyil, on the south side of the local rock. A record of the seventh year of the Pāṇḍya king Kō-Māravarman *alias* Tribhuvanachakravartin Sundara Pāṇḍya dēva (I, 1216—35),

* In his *Antiquities* Mr. Sewell says : "An ancient Śiva temple with many inscriptions, copies of two of which have been sent me. One is dated Ś. 1473 (A.D. 1551) and records a private gift of lands to the temple. The other records repairs carried out by Daḷavāi Sētupati in Ś. 1622 (A.D. 1700)." The first of these is evidently the same as No. 107 in the above list.

who boasts of having burnt Tanjore and Uraiyūr and presented the Chōḷa country to a favourite of his (evidently Rājarāja III). [Edited by S. M. Natesa Sastri in *Tam. and Sans. Ins., Arch. Sur., S. Ind.*, Vol. IV, pp. 43—55. The inscription refers to Māḍakkuḷakkīḷ Madurai of the Madhurōdaya vaḷanāḍu and says that the king gave, at the instance of Maḷavarāyar, the village of Sundara Pāṇḍyapuram or Puḷinkunṟūru, situated to the east of the tank of Vīranārāyaṇakkuḷam, for temple worship, service, etc., to the Sthānapatis, Śiva-Brāhmaṇas, etc., of the temple of Śrī Sundara Pāṇḍya Īśvaramuḍaiyār. Nelson gives a summary of the inscription in his *Madura Manual.* See also *Antiquities*, Vol. I, p. 295, for Mr. Sewell's remarks which are of course antiquated.

111. On the inner gōpuram of the Subrahmaṇya temple. A record of Ś. 1714, Paritāpi, Paṅguni 4, Wednesday, Śuklapaksha dvitīya, Rēvati, saying that when "Asāta Kēpila Napāpu" was ruling and "Amīr Kātar Sāyapu" was local Governor, and Rājagōpāl Rāyar was diwān, a regiment of Europeans came to Madura, destroyed the temple, seized the town and were advancing further, when at the instance of the temple managers and local people, a certain Kuṭṭi, son of Vairāvi Muttukkaruppan, threw himself down, in order to stop the enemy from further progress, from the tower and that the grateful people gave his descendants some lands and shares in temple food offerings as a reward, themselves undertaking to pay the tax on the endowed lands. See No. 60-C above. *Tam. and Sans. Ins.*, No. 28, pp. 41—43.

111-A. On the north side of the tower. A record dated Ś. 1593 (A.D. 1671). (*Antiquities*, Vol. I, p. 295.)

111-B. 37 *of* 1908.—(Vaṭṭeḷuttu.) On one of the pillars in the rock-cut cave. A record of the Pāṇḍya king Māraňjaḍaiyan, dated sixth year. See *Ind. Antq.*, Vol. XXII, p. 67 ff. The king has not been identified. He might be the same as the sovereign who figures in Md. 21 and 22 above.

112. 333 *of* 1908.—On the pillow side of the Pañchapaṇḍava beds on the eastern slope of the hill. Records in Brāhmi characters. Unread.

Varichchiyūr.

113. 38 *of* 1908.—(Brāhmi.) On a rock overhanging the Pañchapāṇḍavar-paḍukkai. See *Ep. Rep.*, 1908, p. 58.

114. 39 *of* 1908.—(Tamil.) Near the same rock. Records in the reign of the Sāḷuva king Immaḍi-Naraśiṅga-Mahārāya a gift for the merit of Narasaṇa-Nāyaka by the governor of Madurai-maṇḍalam, to the temple of Vīrabhadra-Nāyinār at Varuchchiyūr. Immaḍi Narasimha was the son of the usurper Sāḷuva Naraśiṅga, to be ultimately overthrown by the Tuḷuva Narasana Nāyaka.

Viḷāchēri.

114-A. On the ardhamaṇṭapa of the Śiva temple. A private gift of lands to the temple in Ś. 1400 (A.D. 1478). *Antiquities,* Vol. I, p. 295.

MĒLŪR TALUK.

Aḻagarkōvil.

115. *C.P. No.* 164 *of Mr. Sewell's List.*—Records a document belonging to the Aḻagarkōvil temple, professing to be executed in Ś. 1311 (A.D. 1389), *Saumya.* [The inconsistency of the dates and the nature of the inscription have made Mr. Sewell think that it is a modern forgery.]

116. *C.P. No.* 165 *of Mr. Sewell's List.*—Records another grant belonging to the same temple, and the same remarks as No. 164 apply to it. As it stands, it professes to have been executed in Ś. 1135 (A.D. 1213), *Ānanda.*

117. *C.P. No.* 166 *of Mr. Sewell's List.*—Another document, precisely similar in its rough, clumsy execution to the above. It comes from the same temple. It professes to have been executed in Ś. 1394 (A.D. 1472), *Virōdhi,* during the (imaginary) reign of "Mallikai Rāyar, Arjuna Rāyar, Virūpākshi Rāyar, Śrīraṅga Rāyar, Śivaśaṅku Rāyar, Śapāśiva (? Sadāśiva) Rāyar, Gōpāla Rāyar and Rāmadēva Rāyar."

117-A. *Tamil and Sanskrit Inscriptions, No.* 26.—A C.P. grant, dated K. 4707, Ānanda, Tai 15, saying that an assembly of the Nāiks, Ambalakāras, Kavuṇḍas, etc., met, inquired into a suit between two cousins who were employed as watchmen in the Aḻagar temple, and divided the income incumbent upon their offices equally. The inscription is very interesting for the method of administering justice in those days. It refers to a father's killing his son for suspicion of theft. See pp. 112—117. The inscription is said to be in the Collector's office, Madura.

118. 334 *of* 1908.—On the pillow-side of one of the beds in the huge cavern known as Pañchapāṇḍava-beds on the hill. A record in Brāhmi characters.

119. 80 *of* 1910.—(Tamil.) On a pillar of a maṇṭapa in the temple of Sundararāja-Perumāḷ. A damaged record of the Chōḷa king Rājarājakēśarivarman *alias* Śrī-Rājarājadēva I, dated twenty-second year. Seems to register a gift of land.

120—129. *70—79 of* 1910.—(Brāhmi.) On the roof of the cavern called Pañchapāṇḍavar-paḍukkai. "The inscriptions," says Mr. Krishna Sastri, "are difficult of interpretation, being neither Pāḷi nor Dravidian." The numerous Jaina figures and beds and the Brāhmi records "existing in one and the same cavern, raise the suspicion that these caverns, once occupied by the Buddhists, were in a subsequent period appropriated by the Jaina ascetics." (*Mad. Ep. Rep.*, 1910, p. 80.)

Karuṅgālakkuḍi.

130. 561 *of* 1911.—(Brāhmi.) On a rock of the cavern in the Pañchapāṇḍavarkuṭṭu hill. Not read.

131. 562 *of* 1911.—(Vaṭṭeḻuttu.) Below the pedestal of a Jaina image on a rock to the left of the same cavern. Records that "this image *(tirumēni)* was caused to be made by the glorious Ajjanandi." See Nos. 13—20 above.

132. 563 *of* 1911.—(Vaṭṭeḻuttu verse.) On one of the stone beds in a second cavern on the same hill. Registers the several acts performed by a certain Paḷḷidaraiyan, while he was in the service of the Pāṇḍya king (Vaḻudi, Mīnavan). Amongst his services were the building of a bright *vimāna,* stopping the sea, protecting sacrifices at Tiruppodiyil by the powers of his scholarship, asceticism and saintliness. [The Government Epigraphist says that there is an apparent reference here to Agastya and the Podiya mountain, but no information about the age of the Pāṇḍya and Paḷḷidaraiyan mentioned here is available. "The Vaṭṭeḻuttu characters however suggest a period approximating to the ninth century. A.D."

133. In a Muhammadan tomb ("the tomb of Chandasa"), on another part of the same hill. A much damaged Tamil record of Ś. 1704, *Śōbhakrit.*

Kiḻavaḷavu.

134. 395 *of* 1907.—(Vaṭṭeḻuttu.) On a boulder of the Pañchapāṇḍavamalai near Mēlūr. Records that a certain Śaṅgaran Śirivallavan caused an image to be cut on the rock and gave thirty sheep for a lamp and an endowment for daily offerings. [A description of the Jain images of the place is given in *Ep. Rep.*, 1910, p. 78. They are, in the Government Epigraphist's opinion, remnants of a Jain temple or hermitage as at Seṭṭippoḍavu and Pēchchippaḷḷam.]

135. 135 *of* 1903.—A Brāhmi inscription. Unread.

Kottampaṭṭi.

136. *C.P. No.* 162 *of Mr. Sewell's List.*—In the local choultry. Records grant of lands for the erection and maintenance of two choultries, in Ś. 1703, Kaliyuga 4882, *Plava* (A.D. 1781) in the village.

Kōvilpaṭṭi.

137. *C.P. No.* 210 *of Mr. Sewell's List.*—In the local Śiva temple. A record authorizing the local temple authorities to collect tax from visitors. Dated in Ś. 1663, Durmati, A.D. 1741.

138. On a stone in front of a large choultry. Records gift of lands in Ś. 1713. (Sewell's *Antiquities.*)

Mēlūr.

139. 133 *of* 1903.—Very much damaged. On a rock in the Pañchapāṇḍavamalai near Mēlūr.

140. 134 *of* 1903.—On another rock in the same place. (Tamil.) A private record, dated Virōdhikrit, in modern characters.

141. 135 *of* 1903.—On a boulder in the same place. In archaic characters.

Pūdakkuḍi.

141-A. In front of one of the two local choultries. Records that it was erected in Ś. 1703 (A.D. 1781).

141-B. A C.P. grant in the "Appar choultry" recording gift of lands.

Pulippaṭṭi.

142. 564 *of* 1911.—(Tamil.) On a rock near the Ayyanār temple. An unfinished and damaged record of the Pāṇḍya king Māravarman *alias* Tribhuvanachakravartin Kulaśēkharadēva (I, 1268—1308), "who was pleased to take every country," dated thirty-eighth year. Seems to record the gift of the village Śiṅgaṅkuḷam to Puliyūr-uḍaiya-Nāyanār by the residents of Pādirikkuḍi, in Tenparappunāḍu.

Tiruchchunai.

Ancient Śulivaragaṇḍa. Besides the inscriptions given below Mr. Sewell gives two modern inscriptions, dated A.D. 1782, in the temple.

143. 122 *of* 1903.—(Tamil.) On the south wall of the central shrine in the local Agastyēśvāra temple. A record of the sixth year of Tribhuvanachakravartin Sundara Pāṇḍya who conquered the Chōḷa country. (Was it Māravarman, who ruled from 1216 to 1234 ?)

144. 123 *of* 1903.—(Tamil.) On the same wall. A record of the eleventh year of Sundara Pāṇḍya, making a gift of land.

145. 124 *of* 1903.—(Tamil.) In the same place. A record of the ninth year of Tribhuvanachakravartin Kulaśēkharadēva recording gift of land.

146. 125 *of* 1903.—(Tamil.) On the north wall of the same shrine. An incomplete epigraph of the fourteenth year of Jaṭāvarman Tribhuvanachakravartin Sundara Pāṇḍya "who conquered every country," regarding a gift of land. [Mentions a certain Vaidyādhirāja. This king ruled from 1251 to 1264.]

147. 126 *of* 1903.—(Tamil.) On the same wall. A record of the second year of Māravarman Tribhuvanachakravartin Sundara Pāṇḍya (I, 1216—35), making a gift of land.

148. 127 *of* 1903.—(Tamil.) At the entrance into the *garbhagriha* of the same shrine. An incomplete inscription of the seventh year of Parākrama Pāṇḍya recording gift of paddy for offerings to a shrine of Gaṇapati.

149. 128 *of* 1903.—(Tamil.) On the south wall of the maṇṭapa in front of the same shrine. An epigraph of the eleventh year of Sundara Pāṇḍyadēva about a gift of land. Mentions a Sāmanta named Vīraśiṅgadēva, and a village called Śuḷivaragaṇḍa in Śuravi nāḍu.

150. 129 *of* 1903.—(Tamil.) On the same wall. A similar record as the above.

151. 130 *of* 1903.—(Tamil.) On the north wall of the same maṇṭapa. A record of the fourth year of Tribhuvanachakravartin Sundara Pāṇḍyadēva. Mentions the thirteenth year of Kulaśēkharadēva.

152. 131 *of* 1903.—On the same wall. Dated in the twenty-seventh year of Tribhuvanachakravartin Kulaśēkharadēva (Jaṭāvarman, 1190—1217). A gift of land mentions Tiruvarapāti nāḍu. Date corresponds to Wednesday, 29th March 1217. See *Ep. Ind.*, Vol. VIII, p. 275.

153. 132 *of* 1903.—On the front of the same temple. A record of the thirteenth year of Tribhuvanachakravartin Kulaśēkharadēva (Jaṭāvarman, 1190—1217), corresponding to Thursday, 6th October 1216. Gift of land. *Ibid.*

Tiruvādavūr.

154. 136 *of* 1903.—(Tamil.) On a slab set up at Tiruvādavūr. A damaged record of the sixteenth year of Māravarman Tribhuvanachakravartin Sundara Pāṇḍya (I, 1216—35), who took the Chōḷa country and performed the anointment of heroes and victors at Muḍikoṇḍaśōḷapuram.

155. 137 *of* 1903.—(Tamil.) On a slab lying in the big tank in the same place. A damaged record of Viśvanātha Nāik, recording gift for the merit of Muttu Vīrappa Nāiker Aiyan.

Vēlampaṭṭi.

156-A. *C.P. No.* 163 *of Mr. Sewell's List.*—Records grant of a choultry in the village in Ś. 1571, K. 4750, Virōdhi (A.D. 1649). Mr. Sewell doubts its genuineness.

156-B. On a stone in front of the choultry. Records grant of lands in Ś. 1571 by Muttuliṅga, son of Toṇḍiliṅga Nāyaka.

NILAKKŌTTAI TALUK.

Kṛishṇāpuram.

157. *C.P. No.* 20 *of Mr. Sewell's List.*—(Telugu.) Records a grant of the village to a Brahman in Ś. 1600, Kāḷayukti, by Muttu Āḷakādri, younger brother of the Madura Nāyaka Chokkanātha, who reigned from A.D. 1660 to 1682. The grant was made in the year in which Āḷakādri was in power in the place of his brother. [For the circumstances under which this happened see *Madura Manual*, Taylor's *O.H. MSS.* and my *Hist.*, *Nāik King, Madura*, in *Ind. Antq.*] Āḷakādri recognizes the nominal suzerainty of Śrī Vīrapratāpa Śrī Raṅga Rāya Mahārāja.

Kuruvitturai.

158. 318 *of* 1908.—(Tamil.) On the north wall of the central shrine in the Chitrarathavallabha-Perumāḷ temple. Records in the eleventh year of the Pāṇḍya king Jaṭāvarman *alias* Tribhuvana-chakravartin Śrīvallabhadēva that a native of Māṅgāḍu, a village in Māṅgāḍu-nāḍu in Puliyūr-kōṭṭam, a district of Toṇḍai-maṇḍalam, made a gift of a number of lands collectively named Kulaśēkhara-maṅgalam to the temple of Tiruchchakkarattāḷvār at Śōḷāntaka-chaturvēdimaṅgalam in Pāganūr-kūṟṟam and registers an order of the king regarding certain changes to be made in these lands. Mentions *Parākkiramapāṇḍiyan-kullaṇai.*

159. 319 *of* 1908.—(Tamil.) On the same wall. Records in the twenty-second year the confirmation of a previous grant made to the Śrī-Vaishṇavās of the temple, by order of Kāḷiṅgarāyan. [The throne of Māravarman Kulaśēkhara I was named after Kāḷiṅgarāyan.]

160. 320 *of* 1908.—(Tamil.) On the same wall. Records in the twenty-second year (of ?) confirms a previous grant made to the Śrī-Vaishṇavās of the temple, by order of Kāḷiṅgarāyan.

161. 321 *of* 1908.—(Tamil.) On the same wall. Dated in the seventh year of the Pāṇḍya king Jaṭāvarman *alias* Tribhuvana-chakravartin Śrīvallabhadēva. Records gift of gold by a merchant of Kēraḷāntakapuram in Nerkkuppai-nāḍu, for offerings to the image of Uyyakkoṇḍāḷvār set up by him in the temple of "Paramasvāmin who was pleased to stand" at Tiruchchakkara-tīrtham in Pāganūr-kūṟṟam. [Śrīvallabha was a contemporary of Māravarman Sundara Pāṇḍya I, 1216—35.]

162. 322 *of* 1908.—(Tamil.) On the same wall. Dated in the reign of the Pāṇḍya king Jaṭāvarman *alias* Tribhuvanachakra-vartin Śrīvallabhadēva. Records in his twenty-second year that the grant mentioned in No. 159 above was issued while the king was seated on his throne in his palace at Madura on the eastern side of Māḍakkuḷam.

163. 323 *of* 1908.—(Tamil.) On the west wall of the same shrine. Records in the second year of the Pāṇḍya king Jaṭā-varman *alias* Tribhuvanachakravartin Śrīvallabhadēva gift of money for a lamp to the temple of the god *(emberumān)* at Tiruchchakkaratīrtha. [This inscription apparently is the one referred to in Burgess and Natesa Sastri's *Tam. and Sans. Inscrns.*, No. 16, pp. 8–9.]

164. 324 *of* 1908.—(Tamil.) On the west and south walls of the same shrine. Records in the sixteenth year of the Pāṇḍya king Jaṭāvarman *alias* Tribhuvanachakravartin Śrīvallabhadēva that further changes were made in the lands granted under the name Kulaśēkharamaṅgalam by a native of Maṅgāḍu (see No. 158 above), on account of a mistake committed by the ryots, which was reported by the assembly of Śōḷāntaka-chaturvēdimaṅgalam.

165. 325 *of* 1908.—(Tamil and Grantha.) On the south wall of the same shrine. Registers the lease to a Brāhmaṇa of a specified temple land in Parākkiramapāṇḍiyan-kaṭṭaḷai, situated to the east of *Parākkiramapāṇḍiyan kallaṇai.* [No. 17 of Burgess and Natesa Sastri's *Tam. and Sans. Inscrns.*, p. 9.] See No. 158.

166. 326 of 1908.—(Tamil and Grantha.) On the same wall. Dated in the reign of the Pāṇḍya king Jaṭāvarman *alias* Tribhuvanachakravartin Śrīvallabhadēva. Refers in his ninth year to the same lease which is here stated to have been made at the instance of Kaḷiṅgarāya. See No. 161 above.

167. 327 *of* 1908.—(Tamil and Grantha.) On the south and east walls of the maṇṭapa in front of the same shrine. A damaged record of the Pāṇḍya king Jaṭāvarman *alias* Tribhuvanachakravartin Kulaśēkharadēva (I, ? 1190—1217), dated fifteenth year. Refers to the construction of a maṇṭapa and a *māḷigai* named after the king. The work is said to have been undertaken at the instance of a native of Tirunelvēli *alias* Kulaśēkharachaturvēdimaṅgalam in Kīḻvēmbanāḍu. See *Tam. and Sans. Inscrns.*, No. 13, pp. 6–7.

168. 328 *of* 1908.—(Tamil, verse.) At the entrance into the kitchen of the same temple. A record of the Pāṇḍya king Parākrama-Pāṇḍya in his ninth year. Mentions Śrīvallava-Viṇṇagar. Below the inscription is engraved an incomplete introduction beginning with the words *tirumagaḷ jayamagaḷ*, etc.

169. 329 *of* 1908.—(Tamil, verse.) On a pillar lying in the courtyard of the same temple. Records that the pillar was the gift of Śiṟṟambalamuḍaiyān Pāṇḍaraṅgi-Vāṇan.

169-A. On the south side door-jamb of the mani-maṇṭapam. A record of Sundara Pāṇḍya Brahmādhi *alias* Sōmayāji Śrīvallabha of Tirunilaikāl-Punnamaṅgalam. *Tam. and Sans. Inscrns.*, No. 14, pp. 7–8.

169-B. On the door-jamb of the kitchen. A fragmentary record of the ninth year of Tennava Parākrama Pāṇḍya, Śirivana-vañjivallava, etc. *Ibid.*, No. 15, p. 8.

Mēṭṭuppaṭṭi.

170. 44 *of* 1908.—(Tamil.) On the north, south and east walls of the temple, on the hill. Records in Ś. 1410, expired, Kīlaka, a gift by Timmachchi-Nāyakar Tirumalaiyan of Toṇḍai-maṇḍalam, a feudatory of Mahābali-Vāṇādhirāja. The hill is called Siddhamalai. Mahābali Vānādhirāja was not improbably the son of that Mahābali Vāṇa who embraced the creed of Prabandhic Vaishṇavism as taught by Śrī Maṇavāḷa Mahāmuni.]

171. 45 *of* 1908.—(Brāhmi.) On the beds in the Pañchapāṇḍavar-paḍukkai in a cavern on the same hill. Unread.

172. 46 *of* 1908.—(Tamil.) In the same cavern. Contains the name Tripurādēviyār with the syllable *Śri* prefixed to it. [The name might have been cut at the instance of the Tantric Teacher referred to in the next epigraph.]

173. 47 *of* 1908.—(Tamil.) On the rock near the sandals engraved close to the same cavern. Records that a native of Vikramachōḷapuram named Śelvagñanasambandar got the sandals engraved of Sahajānandanātha. The latter was "author of the *Manōramā*, a commentary on the *Ānandalahari*." In the colophon of this work he is described as the pupil of the ascetic Sachchidānandanātha, who, according to the *Catalogus Catalagorum*, was also the teacher of Vidyānandanātha, author of the Tantric work *Saubhāgya-ratnākara*. As Vidyānandanātha is said to have been a native of the Tamil country *(Drāviḍavishaya)* at the end of the *Saubhāgya-ratnākara* (Dr. Hultzsch's *Rep., Sans. MSS.*, III, p. 59) it is not unlikely that his fellow-disciple Sahajānandanātha also belonged to Southern India." *Ep. Rep.*, 1908, p. 91, para. 99. See also Tn. 304-M.

Sōḻavandān.

174. 118 *of* 1910.—(Vatteḻuttu.) On a slab set up on the platform of the railway station. An epigraph of the fourteenth year of the Pāṇḍya king Śaḍaiyamāran. Records gift of 25 cows for a lamp, to the "big temple" at Tirumaygñānam which was a brahmadēya in Pāganūr-kūṟṟam, by the wife of Tennavan Aṇukkappēraraiyan *alias* Panaiyan Māṇikkan who was a native of Perum-Pāganūr. [He was an early chief, but the materials are not sufficient to identify him with any in the Vēḷvikuḍi list. He might be either Jaṭilavarman who was the donor of the Vēḷvikuḍi grant or his grandfather.]

175. 78 *of* 1905.—On the west wall of the central shrine in the Janakanārāyaṇa temple. Dated in Ś. 1530, expired. Gift of land.

176. 79 *of* 1905.—(Tamil.) On the north wall of the same shrine. A damaged inscription of Tribhuvanachakravartin Kōnērinmaikoṇḍān.

177. 80 *of* 1905.—(Tamil.) On the same wall. A record of the second year of Māravarman *alias* Tribhuvanachakravartin Sundara Pāṇḍyadēva (I or II ?) remitting certain taxes on the occasion of his coronation.

178. 81 *of* 1905.—(Tamil.) In the same place. Records in the second year of Jaṭāvarman Tribhuvanachakravartin Kulaśēkharadēva (I ?, 1190—1217) a fresh settlement of the assessment in certain lands.

179. 82 *of* 1905.—(Grantha and Tamil.) In the same place. A record of the second year of Māravarman Tribhuvanachakravartin Sundara Pāṇḍya. Registers a grant similar to the above epigraph and refers to the twenty-seventh year (apparently of the king's predecessor).

Teṅkarai (near Sōḻavandān).

180. 5 *of* 1894.—(Tamil.) On the north wall of the Mūlanātha shrine. Records gift of land in the reign of the Pāṇḍya king Kō-Jaṭāvarman *alias* Kulaśēkharadēva to the mūlasthāna temple. The date of the record is doubtful.

181. 6 *of* 1894.—(Tamil.) On the same wall. Dated in the reign of the Pāṇḍya king Kō-Jaṭāvarman *alias* Śrī-Vallabhadēva. Records in the third year gift of land. Edited in *Tam. and Sans. Inscrns.*, pp. 4-5. The king might be the same as the contemporary of Māravarman Sundara Pāṇḍya I, 1216—35.]

182. 7 *of* 1894.—(Sanskrit and Tamil.) On the west wall of the same shrine. A record of the Pāṇḍya king Parākrama Pāṇḍya recording in his third year gift of land.

183. 8 *of* 1894.—(Tamil.) On the south wall of the same shrine. Dated in the second year of the Pāṇḍya king Kō-Jaṭāvarman *alias* Kulaśēkharadēva. Records gift of gold by a chief from southern Koṅgu. [Was the king the sovereign who ruled from 1190 to 1217 ?]

184. 9 *of* 1894.—(Tamil.) On the same wall. An incomplete record of the Pāṇḍya king Kō-Māravarman *alias* Parākrama-Pāṇḍya-dēva. [Is this identical with the inscription of nine lines beginning with Parākrama Vikrama Pāṇḍya which Burgess and Natesa Sastri refer to ?]

185. 10 *of* 1894.—(Tamil.) On the same wall. Records in the fourth year of the Pāṇḍya king Kō-Jaṭāvarman *alias* Śrī-Vallabhadēva gift of a lamp. See No. 181 above.

186. 11 *of* 1894.—(Tamil.) On the inside of the north wall of the second prākāra of the same temple. An incomplete record of the Pāṇḍya king Kō-Jaṭāvarman *alias* Vikrama-Pāṇḍyadēva, dated fourth year. [There was a king of this name who was the contemporary of Vīrachampa and who lived about A.D. 1315.]

187. 12 *of* 1894.—(Tamil.) On the same side of the same wall. A damaged record of the Pāṇḍya king Kō-Māravarman *alias* Sundara-Pāṇḍyadēva (I, 1216—35), "who distributed the Chōḻa country (among Brāhmaṇas)," dated ninth year.

188. 13 *of* 1894.—(Tamil.) On the inside of the south wall of the same prākāra. Records in the second year the Pāṇḍya king

Kō-Jaṭāvarman *alias* Kulaśēkharadēva gift of land. See No. 183 above.

189. 14 *of* 1894.--(Tamil.) On the same side of the same wall. Records in the third year of the Pāṇḍya Kō-Jaṭāvarman *alias* Kulaśēkharadēva gift of land. See No. 183 above.

190. On a stone on the western side of the *garbhagriham*. Burgess and Natesa Sastri give the beginning alone of an inscription of 46 lines and this shows that it is dated in Ś. 1551, Paritāpi (date is inconsistent). See *Tam. and Sans. Inscrns.*, p. 5, No. 11.

191. On the south side wall of the *garbhagriham.* A fragment at the end of an inscription written by Tiruvīṭipiḷḷai *alias* Vīdiviḍaṅgan Mānināyakan and testified to by "Śendappirān, the barber attached to this temple." *Ibid.*, p. 5, No. 10. [This may be the end of one of the inscriptions above.]

192. 121 *of* 1910.—(Tamil.) On the south wall of the first prākāra in the Mūlasthānēśvara temple. Tribhuvanachakravartin Kōnērmaikoṇḍān records in his fourth year gift of land to the ascetics in the Vāṇanāyakan-*maṭha* situated south of the temple of Mūlasthānam Uḍaiyār in Ten-Kaḷḷaga-nāḍu, by certain residents of Śōḷakulāntaka-chaturvēdimaṅgalam in Pāganūrkūṟṟam.

193. 122 *of* 1910.—(Tamil.) On the same wall. A record of the Pāṇḍya king Māravarman *alias* Tribhuvanachakravartin Sundara-Pāṇḍyadēva (I, 1216—35), "who was pleased to take the Chōḷa country" recording in his fourth year a gift of land to the same *maṭha.*

194. 123 *of* 1910.—(Tamil.) On the west wall of the same prākāra. A damaged and incomplete record of the Pāṇḍya king Māravarman *alias* Tribhuvanachakravartin Kulaśēkharadēva (1268–1308) "who was pleased to take all countries," dated twenty-third year. Mentions Ten-Kaḷḷaganāḍu. *Ep. Ind.*, Vol. X, p. 262.

195. 124 *of* 1910.—(Tamil.) On the same wall. A damaged record of the Pāṇḍya king Māravarman *alias* Tribhuvanachakravartin Kulaśēkharadēva (I), "who was pleased to take all countries," dated twenty-eighth year. Quotes the tenth year of Sundara-Pāṇḍyadēva and mentions the Ālālasundaran-tirumaḍam in the same temple. *Ibid.*, p. 263. Mr. Sewell calculates the date to be Sunday, 27th November A.D. 1295.

196. 125 *of* 1910.—(Tamil.) On the same wall. A fragment of record of the Pāṇḍya Kulaśēkharadēva, "who was pleased . . . dated twenty-seventh year. Mentions Teṅ-Kaḷḷaganāḍu. [Most probably the same king as in the above epigraph is referred to.]

197. 126 *of* 1910.—(Tamil.) On the same wall. An incomplete record of the Pāṇḍya king Māravarman *alias* Tribhuvanachakravartin Kulaśēkharadēva (I), "who was pleased to take all countries," dated fourteenth year. Mentions the Tirujñānasambandan-tirumadam in the same temple. See *Ep. Ind.*, Vol. XI, p. 263, where Mr. Sewell fixes the date to be Sunday, September 21st, A.D. 1281. The *maṭha* was presided over by the Mudaliyārs of the Paṇḍaraṅgavāṇar Santāna, one of whom was Umayōrupāgar of Kulaśēkharapuram or Āṭkoṇḍān.

197-A. 127 *of* 1910.—(Tamil.) On the north wall of the same prākāra. Dated in the eighth year of the Pāṇḍya king Māravarman *alias* Tribhuvanachakravartin Parākrama-Pāṇḍyadēva. Mentions a resident of Tirupputtūr, the twelfth hamlet of Śōḷakulāntaka-chaturvēdimaṅgalam, which was a *brahmadēya* in Pāganūr-kūṟṟam; also refers to the temple of Mūlasthānam Uḍaiyār at Kaṭṭikkaḷḷūr in Ten-Kaḷḷaga-nāḍu, a subdivision of Mahurōdayavaḷanāḍu. The king has not been identified.

198. 128 *of* 1910.—(Tamil.) On the same wall. A record of the Pāṇḍya king Jaṭāvarman *alias* Tribhuvanachakravartin Kulaśēkharadēva, (I, 1190—1217). Contains only the historical introduction, the date of which is lost.

199. 129 *of* 1910.—(Tamil.) On the same wall. An incomplete record. Records the building of the shrine of the goddess and a gift to it under orders of Naraśiṅgadēva.

200. 130 *of* 1910.—(Tamil.) On the same wall. Records in the eleventh year of the Pāṇḍya king Māravarman *alias* Tribhuvanachakravartin Parākrama Pāṇḍya gift of the village of Śeṅguḷam *alias* Vīraiyaviṭaṅkanallūr to the temple of Mūlasthānam-uḍaiya-Mahādēva in Kaṭṭikkaḷḷūr at the request of Śēramān Tōḷan. Refers to the king's palace at Madura and the royal seat *Iśaiyaḷavugaṇḍān* in the hall *Mānābharaṇan*. See No. 197-A.

201. 131 *of* 1910.—(Tamil.) On a pillar of the maṇṭapa in front of the central shrine in the same temple. An unfinished record, dated fifteenth year. Records a gift of land for offerings to the temple of Śrī-vallava-Viṇṇagar-Āḻvār on the western bank (of the Vaigai river), at Śōḷa-Kulāntaka-chaturvēdimaṅgalam in Pāganūr-kūṟṟam. The remainder of the record is stated to have been continued on a pillar (to the west of this). This pillar, however, does not now exist.

202. 132 *of* 1910.—(Grantha.) On another pillar in the same maṇṭapa. Dated in the reign of the Chōḷa king Rājāśraya (Rājarāja I). Records in his seventeenth year that a certain Jananātha Pallavaraiyan *alias* Kōdaṇḍa-Chōḷa made a gift of land to the temple of Madhubid (i.e., Vishṇu) in the village of Tēnūr *alias* Jananātha-chaturvēdimaṅgalam.

203. 133 *of* 1910.—(Tamil.) On the third pillar in the same place. Tribhuvanachakravartin Kōnērinmaikoṇḍān records in his fifteenth year gift of land to the temple of Śrīvallava-Viṇṇagar-Āḻvār, at the request of Maḻavarāyan.

204. 134 *of* 1910.—(Tamil.) On the fourth pillar in the same place. A damaged record of the Chōḷa king Rājarājakēsarivarman, dated seventeenth year. Records gift of land situated at Perundēnur by Jananātha-Pallavaraiyan *alias* Kōdaṇḍan-Śōlai to the god Naḍuvil Śrīkōil Śrī-Vīrakēraḷa-Viṇṇagardēvar at Jananātha-chaturvēdimaṅgalam in Pāganūr-kūṟṟam.

205. 135 *of* 1910.—(Tamil.) On the fifth pillar in the same place. Dated in the second year of the Pāṇḍya king Jaṭāvarman *alias* Tribhuvanachakravartin Kulaśēkharadēva. Records gift of land by the assembly of Śōḷāntaka-chaturvēdimaṅgalam to the servants of the yōgasthāna of Kaṟṟavar-dāsar situated in the ninth hamlet of the village. See *Ep. Ind.*, Vol. XI, p. 261, where Mr. Sewell discusses the details of the date (Mithuna 20, Pūrvapaksha, Wednesday, Anurādha). He says that it is regular; that it suits neither Jaṭāvarman Kulaśēkhara I nor Māravarman Kuḷaśēkhara II; that two days are possible, namely, 15th June A.D. 1239 or 15th June 1334. If the latter is taken we have a new king between Māravarman Kulaśēkhara II and Māravarman Parākrama Pāṇḍya, and if the former is accepted, we have to suppose a new king between Māravarman Sundara Pāṇḍya I and Māravarman Sundara Pāṇḍya II.

206. 136 *of* 1910.—(Tamil.) On the sixth and seventh pillars in the same maṇṭapa. Records that the pillars were the gift of a certain Kandan Uḍaiyān of Vallanagara, a village in Malaimaṇḍalam.

207. 137 *of* 1910.—(Tamil.) On a slab lying in the same maṇṭapa. A mutilated record dated Ś. 1595, Paridhāvi.

208. 138 *of* 1910.—(Tamil.) On a stone set up in the courtyard of the same temple. Dated in the twenty-first year of the Pāṇḍya king Jaṭāvarman *alias* Tribhuvanachakravartin Śrīvallabhadēva. Mentions in his twenty-first year the merchants of Ayyapoḷil. [Mr. Krishna Sastri believes that the reference is to the guild called "500 of Ayyapoḷil" (i.e., Aiyavole or Aihole in Bijapur District) "who are known from a large number of epigraphical records, to have run a flourishing trade in the early centuries of the Christian era both in land and on sea." *Ep. Rep.*, 1910, p. 97. See No. 181 above and By. 176.

209. 139 *of* 1910.—(Tamil.) On a pillar in the gōpura of the same temple. A mutilated record of the Pāṇḍya king Māravarman *alias* Tribhuvanachakravartin Sundara-Pāṇḍyadēva (I ?), date of which is lost. Contains portions of the historical introduction of the king.

Tiruvēḍagam.

210. 667 *of* 1905.—(Tamil.) On the south wall of the central shrine in the Patrikāparamēśvara temple. Dated in the reign of the Vijayanagara king Kṛishṇadēva Mahārāya. Records in Ś. 1448,

Vyaya, gift of land by Pachchai-Perumāḷ Pachchai Kaṇḍiyadēvar with the approval of Chinnappa-Nāyaka.

211. 678 *of* 1905.—(Tamil.) On the south wall of the central shrine in the Patrikāparamēśvara temple. A record of the Pāṇḍya king Māravarman *alias* Tribhuvanachakravartin Sundara-Pāṇḍya-dēva (II, ? 1238—51 ?), dated sixth year. Built in at the beginning. Introduction resembles that of the next number.

212. 679 *of* 1905.—(Tamil.) On the west wall of the same shrine. Dated in the reign of the Pāṇḍya king Māravarman *alias* Tribhuvanachakravartin Sundara-Pāṇḍyadēva (II ?). Seems to record a gift of land in the seventh year. Built in in the middle.

213. 680 *of* 1905.—(Tamil.) On the east wall of the maṇṭapa in front of the same shrine, left of entrance. A damaged record of the Pāṇḍya king Jaṭāvarman *alias* Tribhuvanachakravartin Kula-śēkharadēva (I, 1190—1217), dated second year. Introduction resembles that of the Tiruppuvanam plates (Rd. 170.) Appears to record a gift of land.

214. 681 *of* 1905.—(Tamil.) On the same wall right of entrance. A damaged record of Tribhuvanachakravartin Kōnēri-maikoṇḍān. Records gift of land for feeding twenty ascetics *(tapasyar)* in the Tirujñanāsambandan-maḍam.

215. 682 *of* 1905.—(Tamil.) On the east wall of the first prākāra of the same temple, right of entrance. A partly damaged record of the Pāṇḍya king Māravarman *alias* Tribhuvanachakra-vartin Sundara-Pāṇḍya (I, 1216—35) "who took the Chōḷa country and was pleased to perform the anointment of heroes and the anointment of victors at Muḍigoṇḍachōḷapuram," dated fourteenth year. Records gift of land.

216. 683 *of* 1905.—(Tamil.) In the same place. A record of the Pāṇḍya king Māravarman *alias* Tribhuvanachakravartin Vīra-Sundara-Pāṇḍya (I, 1216—35) "who was pleased to present the Chōḷa country," recording in his ninth year a copy of a grant of land made in the third year of Jaṭāvarman *alias* Tribhuvanachakra-vartin Śrīvallabhadēva to the temple of Tiruvēḍagamuḍaiya-Nāyanār at Tiruvēḍagam in Pāganūr-kūṟṟam.

217. 684 *of* 1905.—(Tamil.) On the same wall left of entrance. The Pāṇḍya king Tribhuvanachakravartin Kōnērinmaikoṇḍān Māravarman *alias* Sundara-Pāṇḍya (I, 1216—35), "who was pleased to present the Chōḷa country," records in his eighth year gift of land.

218. 685 *of* 1905.—(Tamil.) On a stone built into the east wall of the second prākāra of the same temple. A fragment of record of the Pāṇḍya king Sundara-Pāṇḍyadēva, dated second year.

219. 686 *of* 1905.—(Tamil.) On a stone built into the south wall of the same prākāra. A fragment of record of the Pāṇḍya king Tribhuvanachakravartin Parākrama-Pāṇḍyadēva (unidentified), the date of which is lost.

220. 687 *of* 1905.—(Tamil.) On a stone built into the north wall of the same prākāra. A fragment of record of Pāṇḍya king Jaṭāvarman *alias* Tribhuvanachakravartin Vikrama-Pāṇḍyadēva, the date of which is lost. Appears to refer to a Vishṇu temple. See No. 186 above.

221. 688 *of* 1905.—(Tamil.) On another stone built into the same wall. A mutilated record. Seems to record the gift of the stone.

222. 688 (*a*) *of* 1905.—(Tamil.) On a pillar near the same prākāra. A partially damaged record of the Pāṇḍya king Jaṭāvarman *alias* Tribhuvanachakravartin Kulaśēkharadēva (I, ? 1190—1217), dated thirteenth year.

223. 689 *of* 1905.—(Tamil.) On a slab used as a seat by garland makers. The Pāṇḍya king Tribhuvanachakravartin Parākrama-Pāṇḍyadēva appears to record in his fourteenth year the gift of the slab.

Vaittilaikuṇḍu Vairivanāyakkanēri alias *Vira Bhūpāla-samudram.*

224. *C.P. No. 60 of Mr. Sewell's List.*—Records a deed executed in the name of all the inhabitants of a village called Vīra Bhūpālasamudram, jointly with Raghunātha Ayya, agent of one Vēṅkaṭa Rāya, in Ś. 1665 (A.D. 1743), Rudhirōdgāri, Wednesday, Āvaṇi 18, Trayōdaśi, establishing a band of *trumpeters* and drummers in the Śiva temple of their village. The inscription has been edited in *Tam. and Sans. Inscrns.*, No. 30, pp. 124-25. The band consisted of six men, and these were to be paid six *pons* and seven *paṇams* each month. This sum was to be collected in this manner:—one *pon* from the palace endowments, three *pons* from the wages of the inhabitants, and two *paṇams* from the temple endowments. The payment was to be made by the responsible men, in kind, " at the rate at which paddy is then sold in the village."

Vaittilaikuṇḍu Vairivanūr.

225. *C.P. No. 64 of Mr. Sewell's List.*—(Tamil.) Records a deed drawn up by the villagers and temple authorities of the village, authorizing their karaṇam to collect a tax from various people for temple purposes, in Ś. 1653 (A.D. 1731), Virōdhikrit. The rates are: 2 *paṇams* on bazaars, ⅜ *paṇam* on temple Sampratis, ½ *paṇam* on accountants, ¼ *paṇam* on different classes of temple servants, ½ *paṇam* on the tax collector, ½ *paṇam* on the Nīrāṇikkam people, 1 *paṇam* on Śeṭṭis, ½ *paṇam* on silk-weavers, ⅜ *paṇam* on goldsmiths, ¾ *paṇam* on oil sellers, etc. Total 1 *pon* and 2¼ *paṇams* (12¼ *paṇams*). Two *paṇams* on village shroff added. Edited in *Tam. and Sans. Inscrns.*, No. 29, pp. 122–4.]

226. *C.P. No.* 65-*A of Mr. Sewell's List.*—(Tamil.) Records an agreement drawn up by eight men who represented the eight communities of banker, Naṭṭāmai, Kōmaṭis, Muhammadans, Kavuṇḍas, Weavers, Nāḍārs, Vāṇiyars of the village near Madura in Ś. 1641 (expired) (A.D. 1719), Vikāri (Tai 13, Wednesday, pūśa, Daśami) promising to give a share of their gains annually to support the ritual of their village temple. The shares are enumerated and of an interesting kind. The grant is stated to have been executed with the consent of the Sabhā, the "Palace agent" Kūḷappa Nāik, Kāval Ettilappa Nāik, etc. Vijaya Raṅga Chokkanātha (1705—31) was then in power at Madura. See *Tam. and Sans. Inscrns.*, No. 12, pp. 89–90.

227. *C.P. No.* 65-*B of Mr. Sewell's List.*—(Tamil.) Records a deed drawn up in Ś. 1650, Ānanda (A.D. 1735), by the village authorities, permitting a Kailāsa Mudaliyār to take, for certain temple purposes, one *paṇam* a day from the toll income due to the palace. No king is mentioned. The *maṇiya* of the five villages, whether he is a Brahman officer or Sūdra, is authorized to pay one *paṇam* every day to the Mudaliyār and descendants. [Mīnākshi, the last of the Nāyakkas, was then ruling at Madura, which finally fell under sway of the Muhammadans in the ensuing year.] See *Ibid.* No. 28, pp. 121–2.

PALNI TALUK.

Aivarmalai.

228—235. 691 *to* 698 *of* 1905.—(Vaṭṭeḷuttu and Tamil.) Below the images cut out near Aiyambāḷaiyam. Mention Ajjaṇandi (No. 692), Indrasēna (No. 694) and Mallisēnappēriyar (No. 697). See *Antiquities*, I, pp. 285–6, where Mr. Sewell gives a popular but wrong version of the images of this place. See Nos. 13—20, 39, etc., above.

236—239. 699 *to* 702 *of* 1905.—(Vaṭṭeḷuttu.) Above the natural cave in the same place. Mention Pārśvapaḍāra (No. 700) Puvvaṇandikkuratti, the female pupil of Paṭṭinikurattiyār of Perumbattiyūr (No. 701) and Ayiraimalai (No. 702).

240. 703 *of* 1905.—(Tamil.) In the same place. A mutilated record.

241. 704 *of* 1905.—(Tamil.) In the same place. A record in modern characters.

242. 705 *of* 1905.—(Vaṭṭeḷuttu.) In the same place. Records in Ś. 792 and eighth year of the Pāṇḍya king Varaguṇa that Śāntivīraguravar, pupil of Kuṇavīrakkuravaḍigaḷ, renewed the images of Pārśvapaḍārar at Tiruvāyirai and the yakshis. [The inscription is important for the fact that it settles the date of the accession of this eminent king, the conqueror of Trichinopoly, Ceylon, Toṇḍaināḍu, of Iḍavai and Veṇbil, etc., till he received a check and was defeated at Tiruppirāmbiyam.]

Ambilikkai.

242-A. On a stone below the Aśvattha tree in the village. Records that Tirumalai Chinnappa Nāyaka granted in Ś. 1651, Pramōdūta, to God Viśvanāthasvāmi at Kanakagiri, some land west of Śaḍaiyaṅkuḷam and east of "Coopalapuram." *Ins., S. Dts.*, p. 82, No. 42.

Ayakkuḍi.

242-B. An epigraph in the hands of Venkatarāma Aiyar of the village. Records that in Ś. 1718, Naḷa, Obala Koṇḍama Nāyaka gave 8 *mās* of land to a Brahman Raṅgayya in the village of Pudukkuḍi. *Ibid.*, p. 85, No. 49.

Bālasamudram.

242-C. On the north wall of the Amman temple in the Ahōbala perumāḷ temple. Records that Kṛishṇammāḷ, wife of Kumāra Chinnappa Nāyakar, erected the shrine of Śūḍikkoḍutta Nāchchiyār. *Ibid.*, p. 84, No. 47.

Kallimandayam.

242-D. Near the Garuḍastambha of the Vishṇu temple. A record recording its erection by a private party. *Ibid.*

Kavuñji.

242-E. On a stone in the street. "Believed to be dated in Ś. 1013 (A.D. 1091)." *Antiquities*, I, p. 285.

*Kiranūr.**

It belonged to Poṅgaḷakkanāḍu, a division of Koṅgu. Mr. Sewell gives a list of thirty-one inscriptions in this place, some of which are perhaps repetitions and almost all of which are easily identified with the following list. Mr. Sewell takes Vīra Rājēndra to be Kulōttuṅga I and so attributes almost all the inscriptions to the period between 1070 and 1095. See *Ibid.*, pp. 286–7. [The *Mack. MSS.* (*Ins., S. Dts.*, p. 726, Nos. 23—41) give nineteen inscriptions. Twelve of these have been identified with the corresponding ones in the departmental list, the others are given under Nos. 265-A—265-F.]

243. 586 *of* 1893.—(Tamil.) On the north wall of the shrine in the Vāgīśvara temple. A record in the thirteenth year of the

* There is a Tamil literary tradition that a certain Naṭarāja of Kīranūr was the author of the *Jātakālaṅkāra*.

Chōḷa king Vīra-Rājēndradēva. Records gift of a lamp (5 *paṇams*) by Kalikulōttaman (?). See *Ins.*, *S. Dts.*, p. 80, No. 33.

244. 587 *of* 1893.—(Tamil.) On the same wall. A record in the eleventh year of the Chōḷa king Vīra-Rājēndradēva. Records gift of a lamp.

245. 588 *of* 1893.—(Tamil.) On the same wall. A record in the eleventh year of the Chōḷa king Vīra-Rājēndradēva. Records gift of a lamp.

246. 589 *of* 1893.—(Tamil.) On the same wall. A record in the twelfth year of the Chōḷa king Vīra-Rājēndradēva. Records gift of 5 gold *paṇams* for a lamp (by Uttama Kōnan ?). See *Ibid.*, p. 79, No. 29.

247. 590 *of* 1893.—(Tamil.) On the same wall. A record in the eleventh year of the Chōḷa king Vīra-Rājēndradēva. Records gift of gold ornaments.

248. 591 *of* 1893.—(Tamil.) On the same wall. A record in the tenth year of the Chōḷa king Vīra-Rājēndradēva. Records gift of a lamp.

249. 592 *of* 1893.—(Tamil.) On the same wall. A record in the thirteenth year of the Chōḷa king Vīra-Rājēndradēva Records gift of a lamp (5 *paṇams*). See *Ibid.*, No. 30.

250. 593 *of* 1893.—(Tamil.) On the same wall. A record in the fifteenth year of the Chōḷa king Vīra-Rājēndradēva. Records gift of a lamp. [Is this the same as *Ibid.*, p. 78, No. 26 ? The latter says however that it was a grant of land in the fifth year.]

251. 594 *of* 1893.—(Tamil.) On the same wall. A record in the twelfth year of the Chōḷa king Vīra-Rājēndradēva. Records gift of a lamp by a merchant. [*Ibid.*, p. 81, No. 39 ?]

252. 595 *of* 1893.—(Tamil.) On the base of the same wall. A record in the twentieth year of the Chōḷa king Vīra-Chōḷadēva. Records gift of land by Ananta (?) Pallavaraiyan. See *Ibid.*, p. 79, No. 31.

253. 596 *of* 1893.—(Tamil.) On the west wall of the same shrine. A record in the twentieth year of the Chōḷa king Vīra-Rājēndradēva. Records gift of a lamp.

254. 597 *of* 1893.—(Tamil.) On the same wall. A record in the seventh year of the Chōḷa king Kō-Rājakēsarivarman *alias* Vīra-Rājēndradēva. Records gift of land by "Auroovacootandiyem." *Ibid.*, p. 78, No. 25.

255. 598 *of* 1893.—On the south wall of the same shrine. A record in the twelfth year of the Chōḷa king Vīra-Rājakēsarivarman *alias* Kulōttuṅga-Chōḷadēva (I ?). Records gift of land (1 *mā*). See *Ibid.*, p. 77, No. 23.

256. 599 *of* 1893.—(Tamil.) On the same wall. A record in the sixteenth year of the Chōḷa king Vīra-Rājēndradēva. Records gift of a lamp by Iruṅgōḷ Pallavarāyan. *Ins., S. Dts.*, p. 81, No. 38.

257. 600 *of* 1893.—(Tamil.) On the same wall. A record in the eighth year of the Chōḷa king Kō-Rājakēsarivarman *alias* Vīra-Rājēndradēva. Records gift of land. See *Ibid.*, No. 24.

258. 601 *of* 1893.—(Tamil.) On the same wall. A record in the eighth year of the Chōḷa king Kō-Rājakēsarivarman *alias* Vīra-Rājēndradēva. Records gift of gold.

259. 602 *of* 1893.—(Tamil.) On the same wall. A record in the tenth year of the Chōḷa king Vīra-Rājēndradēva. Records gift of land.

260. 603 *of* 1893.—(Tamil.) On the same wall. A record in the tenth year of the Chōḷa king Vīra-Rājēndradēva. Records gift of a lamp.

261. 604 *of* 1893.—(Tamil.) On the base of the same wall. A record in the eighth year of the Chōḷa king Kō-Rājakēsarivarman *alias* Vīra-Rājēndradēva. Records gift of a lamp.

262. 605 *of* 1893.—(Tamil.) In the same place. A record in the eleventh year of the Chōḷa king Kō-Parakēsarivarman *alias* Vīranārāṇadēva (Parāntaka I?). Records gift of land (13 *mās*). *Ibid.*, p. 80, No. 35.

263. 606 *of* 1893.—(Tamil.) In the same place. A record in the seventh year of the Chōḷa king Kulōttuṅga-Chōḷadēva. Records gift of land. [This is probably *Ibid.*, p. 78, No. 27, but it gives the regnal year as 9.]

264. 607 *of* 1893.—(Tamil.) On the south wall of the maṇṭapa in front of the same shrine. A damaged record in the twenty-third year of the Chōḷa king Vikrama-Chōḷadēva (1118—35). See *Ins., S. Dts.*, p. 80, No. 34, which however gives the regnal year as twenty-second. [As Vikrama ruled only for seventeen years after his formal accession we have to suppose from the present epigraph that he was joint ruler with his father during the last five years of the latter.]

265. 608 *of* 1893.—(Tamil.) On a stone near the police station. A record in the fourteenth year of the Chōḷa king Vīra-Rājēndra-dēva.

265-A. On the north side of the Vimānam in the temple. Records that Kulōttuṅgachōḷa Iruṅgōḷan presented 16 golden *kaḻañju* and some *paṇams* for a lamp to the God Tirupiḷḷaiyār Nāchchiyār, in the reign of Vīrā-Rājēndradēva. *Ibid.*, p. 78, No. 28.

265-B. Below the above. Records that Kulōttuṅgachōḷa Iruṅ-gōḷan granted ½ *mā* of land west of Vīranvadi and one *mā* of land in Śirukuḷam to the Gods Tiruvāgīśvara Uḍaiyār, Tiruppiḷḷaiyār,

Nāchchiyār, Sundarapperumāḷ, Paravanamalayar and Tirunāyakar, in the seventh year of reign of Vīra-Rājēndradēva. *Ins., S. Dts.*, p. 79, No. 32.

265-C. Below the above. Records that "Anuthinapallavarayan" granted ½ *mā* of land in Kāḷikottu village to Peruvāyīśvara, in the twentieth year of the reign of Vīra-Chōḷadēva. *Ibid.*, p. 80, No. 36.

265-D. Below the above. A damaged record in the twentieth year of the reign of Vikramachōḷadēva (1118—35). *Ibid.*, p. 81, No. 37.

265-E. On a stone in the west of the Basava pagoda in the garden of Periyakoppachi Kavuṇḍan. Records that Kāḷahastiyappa Mudaliār, Prime Minister of Viśvanātha Naik, and the Kavuṇḍas of 24 Nāḍs granted the village Koṇḍarinji Karanūr as free gift to the Brahmans, in the reign of Viśvanātha Nāyakar. *Ibid.*, No. 40. Viśvanātha was apparently the founder of the Naik dynasty of Madura (1559—63).

265-F. On a stone below the "Asoda" tree to the north of the above inscription. Records that the Nāṭṭār granted a portion of land to the God for worship and for repairing the temple of Kuḷandamala Nāyanār of Kōsalarāya, Nellore village, in the seventeenth year of the reign of Vīra Pāṇḍyadēva. *Ibid.*, p. 82, No. 41.

Mandavāḍi.

265-G. On a stone north of the village Śāvaḍi. A record dated Ś. 1601 (A.D. 1679) recording gifts of land by Kadiri Tirumalai Śinnappa Nāyakkar.

Mānūr.

266. 150 *of* 1908.—(Tamil.) On the south wall of the Chōḷēśvara temple. An unfinished record of the Hoysaḷa king Vīra Ballāḷadēva.

267. 151 *of* 1908.—(Tamil.) On the same wall. Belongs to the reign of Tribhuvanachakravartin Kōnērinmaikoṇḍān. Records in his fifteenth year gift of land to the temple of Vīrarājēndrachōḷīśvaram-Uḍaiyār.

268. 152 *of* 1908.—(Tamil.) On the west wall of the same temple. Records in the second year of Tribhuvanachakravartin Kōnērimaikoṇḍān gift of land for offerings to the temple of Vīrarājēndrachōḷīśvaram-Uḍaiyār at Mānūr *alias* Vīrarājēndraśōḷanallūr in Vaigāvūr-nāḍu.

269. 153 *of* 1908.—(Tamil.) On the north wall of the Chōḷēśvara temple. An incomplete record of the fourth year of the Pāṇḍya king Tribhuvanachakravartin Kōnērimēlkoṇḍān Sundara-Pāṇḍyadēva, dated fourth year. Records gift of land by private persons for offerings to the same temple. [Noticed by Mr. Sewell in *Antiquities*, I, p. 287.]

Paḷani (*Paḷni*).

Mr. Sewell notices eight inscriptions in this place of which only four are definite and these have been identified.

270. 609 *of* 1893.—(Tamil.) On the north wall of the shrine in the Subrahmaṇya temple. A record in Rudhirōdgārin of Vīra-Nañjana-Uḍaiyār. Noticed by Mr. Sewell. See also *Ins., S. Dts.*, p. 75, No. 17. Records grant of land belonging to the village of Kalayamuttūr.

271. 610 *of* 1893.—(Tamil.) On the same wall. A record in Viḷambin of the Vijayanagara king Devarāya-Mallikārjunarāya (1422—65). Records gift of land. Noticed by Mr. Sewell in his *Antiquities*. See *Ibid.*, No. 16. Gift of Eravamaṅgalam village to the God Yellaya Tamburānār for worship.

272. 611 *of* 1893.—(Tamil.) On the south wall of the same shrine. A record in the twenty-second year of the Pāṇḍya king Kō-Jaṭāvarman *alias* Vīra-Pāṇḍyadēva. Records gift of land. Apparently inscription 4 in Mr. Sewell's list. See *Ibid.*, p. 73, No. 11. It gives the date of the grant as fifteenth year of the king. Was he the king who came to the throne in 1253?

273. 612 *of* 1893.--(Tamil.) On the same wall. A record of the Vijayanagara king Kṛishṇadēva-Mahārāya in Ś. 1442, expired, Vikrama. Records a gift by a tributary, Koṇḍayadēva Mahārāja, son of Śennarājayya. Noticed by Mr. Sewell also. See also *Ibid.*, p. 74, No. 13. It says that Koṇḍayadēva Mahārāja granted the village Kalayamuttūr as free gift to the God Vēlāyudhaperumāḷ.

273-A. On the Vimānam in the temple of Daṇḍāyudhasvāmi on the Śivagirimalai. Records that Kōnērinmaikoṇḍān granted the village Avanivēndanellūr for the offering of food and worship to the God Piḷḷaiyār Avanivandār and Sthānattār. *Ibid.*, p. 73, No. 10.

273-B. Below the above. Records that Vīra-Pāṇḍyadēva granted some land in the village of Paḷani during the eighth year of his reign to the God Piḷḷayār. *Ibid.*, No. 12.

273-C. In the Daṇḍāyudhapāṇi temple. Records that Rāmarāyar and Navakumbavandān granted 612 *mās* of land in the village of Sundara Pāṇḍyanellūr to the God Daṇḍāyudhasvāmi in the reign of Kōnērinmaikoṇḍān. *Ibid.*, No. 14.

273-D. On the east of vimānam in the temple. Records that the inhabitants of Amarapāṇḍyanellūr granted the village of Sundara-Paṇḍyanellūr to the God Nayanār in the twenty-sixth year of the reign of Vīrapāṇḍyadēva. *Ibid.*, No. 15.

273-E. On the west of the inner temple of Lakshmīnārāyaṇapperumāḷ at Paḷani village. Records a grant of the land of Nallamkoḷam tank belonging to the village of Āyakkuḍi to the God, and three Vaishṇava Brahmans. *Ibid.*, No. 18.

273-F. On the north of inner temple of Lakshmīnārāyaṇapperumāḷ. Records the grant of a garden by an Ayyaṅgār in the fifteenth year of Sundarapāṇḍyadēva. *Ins., S. Dts.*, p. 23, No. 19.

273-G. On the north side of the mahāmaṇṭapam in the Periya Āvaḍaiyār temple. Records that the people of Śrīmaṅgalam village gave in the reign of Śiviledēva half a *ma* and one *kāṇi* of land to the God. *Ibid.*, No. 20.

273-H. West of the above. Records that Kōnērinmaikoṇḍān granted five *mās* of land to God Subrahmaṇya. *Ibid.*, No. 21.

273-I. North of the inner temple. A damaged record of the fourth year of Rājarājadēva. *Ibid.*, No. 22.

273-J. On a stone at the foot of the Paḷani mountain near a canal. A damaged grant of Kumārachinnappanāyaka to God Vēlāyudhasvāmi in Ānanda. *Ibid.*, p. 85, No. 48.

274. *C.P.* 24 *of Mr. Sewell's List.*—(Tamil.) Records the erection of a chattram by a pilgrim named Vēma Reḍḍi, on the Paḷani hills. The epigraph is engraved by his descendant Raṅga Reḍḍi in Ś. 1728 (A.D. 1806), *Akshaya,* "in the reign of Maṅgammāḷ and under the management of Immaḍi, Kumāra Chinnōba Nāik of Paḷani." The Reḍḍis give an agreement that for the maintenance of the charity and for worship they will pay a tax of two *paṇams* by the bridegroom and two by the bride in every marriage, etc. The first portion of the grant contains a great eulogy of Subrahmaṇya. See *Tam. and Sans. Ins.*, No. 32, pp. 131—36. [Maṅgammāḷ as a matter of fact ruled only from 1689 to 1704.]

275. *C.P.* 15 *of* 1911.—(Tamil.) A record of K. 4765, Ś. 1438 (the dates do not agree), Plavaṅga, registering the construction of a *maṭha* called *Tirunilakaṇḍarmaḍam* at Paḷaṇi-nagaram and sanctioning certain specified fees for its maintenance.

276. A C.P. grant belonging to the Paḷani temple (No. 31 of Burgess and Natesa Sastri's *Tam. and Sans. Ins.*, pp. 125—31). Records that in the reign of Chinnōba Nāik (whose genealogy is given) of the Vaikāpuri province (who was a polygar under the Madura Nāiks who are enumerated down to Tirumal Nāik), the Vīramuḍivāḷars of the four countries of Chēra, Chōḷa, Pāṇḍya and Toṇḍa, undertook to maintain the charity of feeding six persons every new moon and twelve persons every Monday in the Maṭham of the Śiva temple. One Chidambaramuḍaiyār Śivan was ordered in K. 4584 (A.D. 1483), Tai. 15, Monday *(pūśa)* to conduct the charity. The charity was to be maintained by contributions of the Vīramuḍivāḷars throughout the country at the rate of two *paṇams* for every family, one *paṇam* for every bridegroom, one for the bride and half *paṇam* for every Piḷḷayār pūjai feast. The inscription is full of fulsome praises of the polygar and gives an imaginary list of Vijayanagar and Madura rulers.

277. 706 *of* 1905.—(Vaṭṭeḻuttu.) On the north wall of the Periya Uḍaiyār temple near Paḻani. A record of the Kēraḷa king Vīranāraṇa Vīrakēraḷa. Mentions in his eleventh year the village of Iravimaṅgalam. This and the following epigraphs show that the Kēraḷa dynasty owned possessions which extended as far as Paḻani. The identification of this chief is for the present impossible. See Cb. 106.

278. 707 *of* 1905.—(Vaṭṭeḻuttu.) On the same wall. A partly damaged record of the Kēraḷa king Vīrānāraṇar Vīrākēraḷa, dated in his eighth year. Mentions Kōdaimaṅgalam and Amarabhujaṁga. See Cb. 106. Vīra Kēraḷa was a title assumed by various kings, and it is impossible to exactly identify the present king. [Was he a contemporary of Vīranārāyaṇa Parāntaka Chōḷa (906—47) ?]

279. 708 *of* 1905.—(Vaṭṭeḻuttu.) On the same wall. A mutilated record of the Kēraḷa king Vīranāraṇa Atiśayaśōḷadēva, dated thirty-first year. In the fourth line the inscription runs into Tamil.

280. 709 *of* 1905.—(Vaṭṭeḻuttu.) On the same wall. A mutilated record of the Kēraḷa king Vīrakēraḷa Amarabhujaṁgavarman dated twenty-third year. Mentions Naraiyanūr-nāḍu.

281. 710 *of* 1905.—(Tamil.) On the same wall. The Kēraḷa king Kēraḷa Adhirājarāja Rājarājadēva records in his fourth year a gift by the queen of Atiśayachōḷa *alias* Adhirājarājadēva. See Tinnevelly 83.

282. 711 *of* 1905.—(Tamil.) On the same wall. A mutilated record of the Kēraḷa king Vīrakēraḷa Adhirājarājadēva, dated fortieth year. Refers to the building of a hall and mentions Kōdaimaṅgalam.

283. 712 *of* 1905.—(Tamil.) On the same wall. A mutilated record of the Pāṇḍya king Jaṭāvarman *alias* Tribhuvanachakravartin Śrīvallabhadēva, the date of which is lost. [Was he the contemporary of Māravarman Sundara Pāṇḍya I (1216—35) ?]

284. 713 *of* 1905.—(Vaṭṭeḻuttu.) On the south wall of the same temple. A mutilated record of the Kēraḷa king Vīrakēraḷa Amarabhujaṁgavarman, dated twenty-eighth year. Records a sale of land and mentions a native of Puraṅgarambai-nāḍu. See No. 278.

285. 714 *of* 1905.—(Vaṭṭeḻuttu.) On the same wall. Records in the twenty-ninth year the Kēraḷa king Vīranāraṇa Vīrakēraḷa gift of a gold ornament. See No. 278.

286. 715 *of* 1905.—(Vaṭṭeḻuttu.) On the same wall. A mutilated record of the Kēraḷa king Vīrakēraḷa Vīranāraṇa, dated sixth year. Mentions Veśālippādi. See No. 277 above.

287. 716 *of* 1905.—(Vaṭṭeḻuttu.) On the same wall. A much damaged record of the Kēraḷa king Vīrakēraḷa Amarabhujaṁgavarman, the date of which is lost. See Cb. Nos. 121 and 120 where Ravīvarma and Amarabhūjaṅga are implied to be the same. [Were Vīrakēraḷa and Kōkkandan Ravi the same ?]

288. 717 *of* 1905.—(Tamil.) On the same wall. A mutilated record of the Chōḷa (?) king Parakēsarivarman *alias* Tribhuvanachakravartin Perumāḷ Vīrachōḷadēva, "who reigned over the two Koṅgus together," the date of which is lost. Mentions the temple of Paramēśuramuḍaiyār of Iravārūr in Vaigāvi-nāḍu.

289. 718 *of* 1905.—(Vaṭṭeḷuttu.) On the same wall. A mutilated record of Vīranārana Atiśayaśōḷadēva, the date of which is lost.

290. 719 *of* 1905.—(Vaṭṭeḷuttu.) On the same wall. A much-damaged record of Vīranārana Atiśayaśōḷadēva, the date of which is lost. See No. 279.

291. 720 *of* 1905.—(Vaṭṭeḷuttu.) On the same wall. A much damaged record of Vīranārana Atiśayaśōḷadēva, the date of which is lost. Next to this is a much-damaged Chōḷa inscription in Tamil characters. See No. 279.

292. 721 *of* 1905.—(Tamil.) On the west wall of the Periyavuḍaiyār temple. Records in the twenty-eighth year of Tribhuvanachakravartin Kōnērinmaikoṇḍān gift of land. Mentions Kōdaimaṇgalam *alias* Ellaśōḷa-chaturvēdimaṅgalam in Vaigāvūr-nāḍu. The temple is called Iruvirāl-Paramēśvaram-Uḍaiya-Nāyanār. Refers to the goddesses set up by Vikrama-Pāṇḍya-Gaṅganārāyaṇa-Chakravartin.

Periyakōṭṭai.

293. 455 *of* 1907.—(Tamil.) On the door post of the central shrine in the Chōḷēśvara temple; left side. Dated in the reign of the Chōḷa (?) king Vikrama-Chōḷadēva (1118—35). Records in his twentieth year the gift of the door-post by a native of Pulariyūr in Aṇḍanāḍu. [It seems that the king might be the Koṅgu chief who ruled from 1004 to 1045.]

294. 456 *of* 1907.—(Tamil.) In the same place; right side. Dated in the eighteenth year of Chōḷa (?) king Vīrarājēndradēva. Records the gift of the door-post by a native of Pulariyūr in Poṅgaḷūr Kānanāḍu (Poṅgalūkkā-nāḍu).

295. 457 *of* 1907.—(Tamil.) (Noticed by Mr. Sewell in his *Antiquities*, I, p. 288.) On the north wall of the same shrine. A fragment of record of the Chōḷa king Vikrama-Chōḷadēva, dated twenty-second year. Close to this is another fragment belonging to the ninth year of the reign of a Pāṇḍya king whose name is lost.

296. 458 *of* 1907.—(Tamil.) On the south wall of the same shrine. A fragment of record of Rājakēsarivarman *alias* Tribhuvanachakravartin, the date of which is lost. Records the gift of a lamp to the shrine of Nachchinārkiniyar. Another fragment refers itself to the reign of a Pāṇḍya king whose name is lost. A third one is dated in the eleventh year of some king. Nachchinārkiniyar reminds us of the Tamil commentator. See Cb. No. 23.

297. 459 *of* 1907.—(Tamil.) On the rock north of the shrine in the same temple. Records in the fourth year of the Pāṇḍya king Jaṭāvarman *alias* Tribhuvanachakravartin Sundara-Pāṇḍyadēva gift of money for offerings to the temple of Ariyapirāṭṭīchchura-muḍaiyār (at Tiruppākkiyam in Aṇḍa-nāḍu?). [It is difficult to say whether the king was he who ascended the throne in 1251 or 1270 or 1276.]

298. 460 *of* 1907.—(Tamil.) On the south wall of the Brihadāmbā shrine in the same temple. An incomplete record of Tribhuvanachakravartin Kōnērkoṇḍān. Refers to a disturbance in the ninth year of the king's reign.

299. 461 *of* 1907.—(Tamil.) On the south wall of the Brihadāmbā shrine in the Chōḷiśvara temple. Records in the reign of Rājakēsarivarman *alias* Tribhuvanachakravartin śrī-Vīrarājēndradēva gift of money for a lamp to the shrine of Chaṇḍēśvara-Piḷḷaiyār. The date of the record is lost. The king referred to was apparently not the Chōḷa but the Koṅgu one. See No. 302.

300. 462 *of* 1907.—(Tamil.) On the same wall. Records in the eighth year of Tribhuvanachakravartin Vikrama-Chōḷadēva gift of money for a lamp to the shrine of Tiruppāṇḍiśvaramuḍaiyār. [It is doubtful whether the king was a Chōḷa or Koṅgu Chōḷa. See No. 293 above.]

301. 463 *of* 1907.—(Tamil.) On the same wall. An incomplete record of Tribhuvanachakravartin Kōnērimaikoṇḍān, dated thirteenth year. Seems to record the grant of certain privileges.

302. 464 *of* 1907.—(Tamil.) On the same wall. A fragment of record of Rājakēsarivarman *alias* Tribhuvanachakravartin Vīrarājēndradēva, date of which is lost. The temple pūjaris who were entrusted with the endowment seem to be the same as in No. 300 above. [Vīrarājēndra was not improbably the Koṅgu ruler who ruled from 1207 to 1252.]

303. 465 *of* 1907.—(Tamil.) On the same wall. A damaged record of Tribhuvanachakravartin.

304. 466 *of* 1907.—(Tamil.) On the west wall of the same shrine. A much damaged record, dated eighth year. The name of the king is lost.

305. 467 *of* 1907.—(Tamil.) On the same wall. A much damaged record of Tribhuvanachakravartin Tribhuvanavīradēva (unidentified), dated third year.

306. 468 *of* 1907.—(Tamil.) On the north wall of the same shrine. Records in the fifth year of the Pāṇḍya king Tribhuvanachakravartin Vīra-Pāṇḍyadēva gift of money for a lamp to the temple of Uḍaiyār Tiruppāṇḍīśvaramuḍaiyār at Āḷvānkōil *alias* Vīraśōḷadēvanallūr. [Was he the Koṅgu Pāṇḍya who ruled from 1265 to 1281?]

307. 469 *of* 1907.—(Tamil.) On the same wall. Records in the twenty-ninth year of the Pāṇḍya king Jaṭāvarman *alias* Tribhuvanachakravartin Sundara-Pāṇḍyadēva gift for offerings to the temple of Pāṇḍīśuramuḍaiya-Nāyanār at Āḷvānkōil in Aṇḍa-nāḍu. See No. 297 above.

308. 470 *of* 1907.—(Tamil.) On the north, west and south walls of the Kadalī-Narasimha-Perumāḷ temple in the same village. Records in Jaya the building of the temple of Kadirināga-nātha-Perumāḷ and of a tank by an agent of Vīrappa-Nāyakkar Aiyan, " who levied tribute from every country."

309. 471 *of* 1907.—(Vaṭṭeḷuttu.) On a boulder north of the same temple. A damaged record of Kaṇḍakūttāḷan, dated fourth year. Registers provision for offerings and lamps by a certain Pāradayan Brahmāśrīrājan.

310. 472 *of* 1907.—(Tamil.) On a rock in a field to the west of the same village. Records in modern characters, in Jaya, a private gift. Mentions Tirumalai Śinnappa-Nāyakkar. See the next epigraph.

Poduvārpaṭṭi.

310-A—C. This place is noticed by Mr. Sewell. On a stone near the tank is an undated epigraph recording a private grant to the local temple. There is another on a stone near it, carved with five female figures, recording a grant of land to the same. In the local mosque is an inscription stating that Tirumala Chinnappa Nāik gave in Raktākshi, some lands to a Muhammadan. [*Antiquities*, I, p. 288.] Tirumala Chinnappa Nāik was the family title of the Virūpakshi Polygars. For their history see *Mack. MSS.*, Vol. VI (17-5-52), pp. 30—85.

Poruḷūr.

311. 145 *of* 1908.—(Tamil.) On a broken slab lying in the compound of the Perumāḷ temple. Refers in the ninth year of the Pāṇḍya king Vīra-Pāṇḍyadēva to the setting up of an image of Piḷḷaiyār (Gaṇapati) and to a gift of money for a lamp.

Tēvattūr.

312. 155 *of* 1908.—(Tamil.) On a rock west of the village. A much damaged record of Tribhuvanachakravartin Kōnērimai-koṇḍān, dated thirteenth year. Refers to Dēviyarturai in Aṇḍa-nāḍu.

PERIYAKULAM TALUK.

Bōdhināyakanūr.

313. *C.P. No.* 13 *of* 1911.—A record of Fasli 1213 (*Krōdhana*, 1805-6), recording the construction of a *māl* (palace ?) for Rāsayya Pāṇḍyanār, the then Zemindar, and the gift of a copper-plate charter by him to four *Manrāḍis* of the village of Agamalai. [For the history of the Bōdhināyakanūr chiefs see Taylor's *Restored Mack. MSS.*, Vol. II, pp. 228—35.]

Dēvadānappaṭṭi.

313-A. A C.P. grant in the possession of the temple priest, said to have been executed by Tirumaḷ Nāik of Madura (A.D. 1623—59). *Antiquities,* I, p. 290.

Gūḍalūr.

314. 420 *of* 1907.—(Tamil.) (Noticed by Mr. Sewell.) On a slab set up in the Aḷagiri-Perumāḷ temple. Records in the reign of Kulaśēkhara-Perumāḷ, in Ś. 1591, expired and K.A. 844, Kīlaka, gift of land in Gūḍalūr by the king to Neḍumākkal-Paṇikkar in order to provide for worship at the following temples. Maṅgalādēvi-Amman, Aḷagar, Vānmīkanāthasvāmin, Periyāṟṟu-Śāstā, Punaiyāṟṟu-Śāstā and Naḍaikkal Bhagavati.

Kambam.

315. 421 *of* 1907.—(Tamil.) On the south wall of the Subrahmaṇya temple. Records in the tenth year of the Pāṇḍya king Jaṭāvarman *alias* Tribhuvana-chakravartin Vīra-Pāṇḍyadēva, "who took Īḷam (Ceylon), Koṅgu and Śōḷa-maṇḍalam", gift of land to the shrine of Śēvagattēvar *alias* Tiruchcheṇḍapiḍittapiḷḷai. [He was evidently the sovereign who came to the throne in A.D. 1253.]

Kottaguḍi.

316. 389 *of* 1914.—(Tamil.) On a pillar set up near the Gaṇēśa temple. A mutilated record of the Pāṇḍya king Tribhuvanachakravartin, dated sixth year. Mentions Tuṟaiyūr-nāḍu. Two sides of the pillar bear no inscription.

317. 390 *of* 1914.—(Tamil.) On the pillar set up near the *dhvaja stambha* of the same temple. A damaged record.

318. 391 *of* 1914.—(Tamil.) On a pillar set up in a street of the same village. An incomplete record of the Pāṇḍya king Jaṭāvarman *alias* Tribhuvanachakravartin Vīra-Pāṇḍyadēva, dated eighth year Arpaśi 13, Monday. Mentions Tuṟaiyūr nāḍāḷvān. See No. 315 above.

Kullapuram.

319. 141 *of* 1908.—(Tamil.) On the west wall of the central shrine in the Sundararāja-Perumāḷ temple. The historical introduction begins *pūmalar-tiruvum,* dated second year. End built in.

320. 142 *of* 1908.—(Tamil.) On the same wall. A record of the Pāṇḍya king Māravarman seeming to record the gift of a flower garden. The historical introduction begins *pūmaruviya tirumaḍandai.* End built in.

321. 143 *of* 1908.—(Tamil.) On the north wall of the same shrine. Records in the nineteenth year of the Pāṇḍya king Māravarman *alias* Tribhuvanachakravartin Sundara-Pāṇḍyadēva, "who took the Chōḷa country and was pleased to perform the anointment of heroes at Muḍigoṇḍachōḷapuram" gift of lands for the maintenance of two flower gardens belonging to the temple of Aḷagiyamaṇavāḷapperumāḷ; one of the two donees was a native of Iḍavai. The king was the first of this name and ruled from 1216 to 1235.

322. 144 *of* 1908.—(Tamil.) On the same wall. A damaged and mutilated record of the Pāṇḍya king Māravarman *alias* Tribhuvanachakravartin Sundara-Pāṇḍyadēva, "who took the Chōḷa country and was pleased to perform the anointment of heroes at Muḍigoṇḍachōḷapuram, dated nineteenth year. Seems to record a gift of land. See the above epigraph.

323. 145 *of* 1908.—(Tamil.) On the south wall of the maṇṭapa in front of the same shrine. Built in at the beginning. Mentions Kāḍūr in Malai-maṇḍalam.

324. 146 *of* 1908.—(Tamil.) On the north wall of the maṇṭapa in front of the central shrine in the Nīlakaṇṭhēśvara temple in the same village. Records in the nineteenth year of the Pāṇḍya king Sundara-Pāṇḍyadēva gift of land for conducting festivals, etc., in the temples of Tirumarudanduṟaiyuḍaiya Nāyanār, and Rājarāja-Īśvaramuḍaiya Nāyanār at Kūḍalūr *alias* Rājachūḍāmaṇi-chaturvēdimaṅgalam in Aḷa-nāḍu.

325. 147 *of* 1908.—(Tamil.) On the same wall. Records in the nineteenth year (of a certain king) gift of land to the same two temples by the donor of the above epigraph.

326. 148 *of* 1908.—(Tamil.) On the north wall of the Vināyaka shrine in the same temple. A damaged record of the Pāṇḍya king Māravarman *alias* Tribhuvanachakravartin Sundara-Pāṇḍyadēva (I, 1216—35), "who was pleased to take the Chōḷa country," dated fifth year. Mentions Rājarāja-Īśvaram-Uḍaiyār at Rājachūḍāmaṇi-chaturvēdi-maṅgalam in Aḷanāḍu.

327. 149 *of* 1908.—(Tamil.) On a slab set up on the bund of the tank in the same village. Records in the ninth year of the Pāṇḍya king Vīra-Pāṇḍyadēva the remission of fishing taxes *(pāśippāṭṭam)* to those who remove silt from the tank at Rājachūḍāmaṇi-chaturvēdimaṅgalam.

Periyakuḷam.

328. 409 *of* 1907.—(Tamil.) On the west wall of the central shrine in the Rājēndrachōḷēśvara temple. Records in the twenty-sixth year of the Pāṇḍya king Māravarman *alias* Tribhuvanachakravartin Kulaśēkharadēva "who was pleased to take every country" gift of lamps. Built in at the end. The temple is called Rājēndra-Chōḷīśvaramuḍaiya-Nāyanār. Mentions Ālaṅguḷam in Mēneḍuṅgaḷa-nāḍu and the *muppaduvaṭṭam* of the temple. [The king ruled from 1268 to 1308.]

329. 410 *of* 1907.—(Tamil.) On the same wall. The temple is called Rājēndra-Chōḷīśvaramuḍaiya-Nāyinār at Periyakuḷam in Neḍuṅguḷa-nāḍu. Built in Virōdhikrit at the end.

330. 411 *of* 1907.—(Tamil.) On the south wall of the Subrahmaṇya shrine in the same temple. A fragment of record of the Pāṇḍya king Māravarman *alias* Tribhuvanachakravartin Sundara Pāṇḍyadēva (I or II ?), dated fifteenth year.

331. 412 *of* 1907.—(Tamil.) On the west wall of the same shrine. A fragment of record of the Pāṇḍya king Māravarman *alias* Tribhuvanachakravartin Sundara-Pāṇḍyadēva, dated fifteenth year. [It is difficult to say, whether the king is identical with the one who came to the throne in 1216 or 1239—probably the former.]

332. 413 *of* 1907.—(Tamil.) On a stone built into the floor of the ardha-maṇṭapa of the same shrine. A fragment of record of the Pāṇḍya king Māravarman *alias* Tribhuvanachakravartin "who was pleased to perform the anointment of heroes," dated ninth year. [The king, it is certain, was the first of the name and ruled from 1216 to 1235.]

333. 414 *of* 1907.—(Tamil.) On stones built into the floor of the courtyard of the same temple. A fragment of record of the Pāṇḍya king Māravarman *alias* Tribhuvanachakravartin Sundara-Pāṇḍyadēva (I, 1216—35), "who was pleased to perform the anointment of heroes." Date uncertain.

334. 415 *of* 1907.—(Tamil.) On a stone built into the west wall of the Kailāsanātha temple on the hill near the same village. Records the gift of the stone.

335. 416 *of* 1907.—(Tamil.) On the west, south and north bases of the same temple. Records in the nineteenth year of the Pāṇḍya king Māravarman *alias* Tribhuvanachakravartin Sundara-Pāṇḍyadēva (I, 1216—35), "who took the Chōḷa country and was pleased to perform the anointment of heroes at Muḍigoṇḍachōḷapuram," gift of land to the temple of Tirumalaiyil-Nāyanār at Vēḷakularāma-nallūr in Mēneduṅgaḷanāḍu.

336. 417 *of* 1907.—(Grantha.) On the rock to the west of the same temple. Mentions Sundararāja Aḷagiya-Perumāḷ in Tamil.

337. 418 *of* 1907.—(Grantha.) On the same rock. Mentions Sundararāja Aḷagiya-Perumāḷ in Tamil. A damaged record.

338. 419 *of* 1907.—(Tamil.) On a slab set up in a field near the same village. Dated in Śarvarin. On the same slab is another Tamil record, dated in the Pārthiva year.

Śinnamanūr.

339. 428 *of* 1907.—(Tamil.) On the south wall of the central shrine in the Rājasimhēśvara temple. Records in the third or thirtieth year of the Pāṇḍya king Māravarman *alias* Tribhuvanachakravartin Kulaśēkharadēva (I, 1268—1308) "who was pleased to take every country" a sale of land. Mentions the temple of Rājasiṁhēśvaramuḍaiya-Nāyanār in Śrī Arikēsari-nallūr, a *brahmadēya* in Aḷa-nāḍu. [See *Ep. Ind.*, Vol. X, p. 140, where it is pointed out that the date (Rishabha, Pūrvapaksha, Chaturthi, Thursday, Punarvasu) corresponded either to May 14th, A.D. 1271 or May 15th, A.D. 1298.]

340. 429 *of* 1907.—(Tamil.) On the same wall. A mutilated record of the Pāṇḍya king Māravarman *alias* Tribhuvanachakravartin Kulaśēkharadēva (I, 1268—1308) "who was pleased to take every country," dated forty-first year. Refers to the tenth year of Śrī-Sundara-Pāṇḍyadēva.

341. 430 *of* 1907.—(Tamil.) On the same wall. Records in the twenty-sixth year of the Pāṇḍya king Jaṭāvarman *alias* Tribhuvanachakravartin Vīra-Pāṇḍyadēva gift of the proceeds of contributions on the sale of certain articles of merchandise. Mentions Piḷḷai-Kulaśēkhara-Mahābali Vāṇarāyar, also the temple of Vikrama-Pāṇḍīśvaramuḍaiya-Nāyanār at Śivallavanpaḍaivīḍu. The Government Epigraphist points out that the name Kulaśēkhara Vāṇarāyar was perhaps taken from either the son or father of Vīra Pāṇḍya and that as Māravarman Kulaśēkhara I was preceded by a Jaṭāvarman Vīra Pāṇḍya, we have to identify the ruling king of this epigraph with him.

342. 431 *of* 1907.—(Tamil.) On the north wall of the same shrine. An unfinished record of the Pāṇḍya king Māravarman *alias* Tribhuvanachakravartin Kulaśēkharadēva (I, 1268—1308), "who was pleased to take every country," dated forty-first year. The temple is called Uḍaiyār Tiruppūlānduṟai Uraiuḍaiyār *alias* Rājasiṁha-Chōḷīśvaramuḍaiyār at Arikēsari-nallūr. See *Ep. Ind.*, Vol. X, p. 141, where it is pointed out that the details of the date (Āni, 14, Pūrvapaksha 1, Monday, Punarvasu) corresponded to Monday, 9th June, A.D. 1309. Mr. R. Sewell remarks that this is the latest date of the king thus far available; and that the present epigraph further proves "that the king's reign could not have begun before the 10th June 1268, and gives us as the limit of possible accession the period June 10th to 27th, 1268 A.D."

343. 432 *of* 1907.—(Tamil.) On the same wall. A record of the Pāṇḍya king Māravarman *alias* Tribhuvanachakravartin Kulaśēkharadēva "who was pleased to take every country," in his twenty-sixth year. Records gift of land by the mahāsabhā, the *paṇṇaiśeyvārgaḷ* and the *vēliśeyvārgaḷ* of Śrī-Arikēsari-nallūr, a *brahmadēya* in Aḷa-nāḍu. Mentions the Śūruḷi-āṟu.

344. 433 *of* 1907.—(Tamil.) On the north wall of the central shrine in the Rājasiṁhēśvara temple. Records in the sixth year of the Pāṇḍya king Jaṭāvarman *alias* Tribhuvanachakravartin

Sundara-Pāṇḍyadēva gift of the proceeds of tolls levied on certain articles of merchandise.

345. 434 *of* 1907.—(Tamil.) On the same wall. Records in the seventh year of the Pāṇḍya king Jaṭāvarman *alias* Tribhuvanachakravartin Sundara-Pāṇḍyadēva gift of certain contributions on exports for maintaining a flower garden. Mentions the temple referred to in No. 341. See *Ep. Ind.*, Vol. X, p. 144, where Mr. Sewell points out that the details of the date (Makara, Pūrva 3, Friday, Mrigaśīrsha) correspond to no regular date either in the reign of Jaṭāvarman I (1251—64) or Jaṭāvarman (1276—90), called the second by Mr. Sewell and third by Mr. Swamikannu Pillai.

346. 435 *of* 1907.—(Tamil.) On the south wall of the shrine of the goddess Śivakāmi in the same temple. A damaged record of the Pāṇḍya king Māravarman *alias* Tribhuvanachakravartin Kulaśēkharadēva (I, 1268—1309), "who was pleased to take every country," dated third year. Seems to record a gift of land.

347. 436 *of* 1907.—(Tamil.) On stones built into the maṇṭapa in front of the same temple. A record of the Pāṇḍya king Māravarman *alias* Tribhuvanachakravartin Sundara-Pāṇḍyadēva (I? 1216—35), "who was pleased to present the Chōḷa country," in his tenth year. The stones are out of order.

348. 437 *of* 1907.—(Tamil.) On the south wall of the Lakshminārāyaṇa-Perumāḷ temple in the same village. Records in the fifteenth year of the Pāṇḍya king Tribhuvanachakravartin Parākrama-Pāṇḍyadēva gift of money for a lamp.

349. 438 *of* 1907.—(Vaṭṭeḻuttu.) On the same wall. Records gift of lamp to the temple of Tirunaḍuvūr-Paṭṭaḷagar in Arikēsarinallūr. Mentions Vādavūr in Ten-Parappu-nāḍu.

350. 439 *of* 1907.—(Tamil.) On the west wall of the same temple. A record of the Chōḷa king Parakēsarivarman *alias* śrī-Rājēndra-Chōḷa dēva (I, 1012—43) in his fifth year. Sale of land for a lamp to the shrine of Durgā-Paramēśvariyār by the assemblies of three villages, viz., Arikēsarinallūr, Arapadaśēkharamaṅgalam and Mandaragauravamaṅgalam. It seems that the price of one *mākāṇi* of land was fifteen *kāśus*.

351. 440 *of* 1907.—(Tamil.) On the same wall. Records in the forty-sixth year of the Pāṇḍya king Śaḍaiyamāran an agreement referring to a channel called Śrīkaṇḍavāykkāl. [It is not improbable that the king was the same as the donor of the Vēḷvikuḍi grant who lived about A.D. 770.] See also Md. 22.

352. 441 *of* 1907.—(Vaṭṭeḻuttu.) On the same wall. Records in the tenth year of the Pāṇḍya king Śaḍaiyamāran gift of gold for a lamp to the temple of Tirunaḍuvu-Paṭṭaḷagar in Arikēsarinallūr, a *brahmadēya* in Aḷa-nāḍu. [Was he the son of the king of the above epigraph and the father of Varaguṇavarman who ascended the throne in A.D. 862 ?]

353. 442 *of* 1907.—(Tamil.) On the same wall. Records in the ninth year of the Pāṇḍya king Tribhuvanachakravartin Kulaśēkharadēva gift of fifty sheep for a lamp to the Naḍuvilkōyil at Tirupputtūr (a hamlet of) Arikēsarinallūr, a *brahmadēya* in Aḷa-nāḍu.

354. 443 *of* 1907.—(Vaṭṭeḷuttu.) On the north wall of the same temple. An incomplete record of the Chōḷa king Parakēsarivarman, dated thirty-sixth year. Records gift of a lamp. Mentions Arikēsarinallūr.

355. 444 *of* 1907.—(Tamil.) On the same wall. A fragment of record, dated second year (of a certain king).

356. 445 *of* 1907.—(Tamil.) On the same wall. A fragment of record of the Pāṇḍya king Jaṭāvarman *alias* Tribhuvanachakravartin Kulaśēkharadēva (I ?), dated thirty-first year.

357. 446 *of* 1907.—(Tamil.) On the same wall. Records in the eleventh year of the Pāṇḍya king Tribhuvanachakravartin Kulaśēkharadēva gift of a lamp. A few Vaṭṭeḷuttu letters are engraved on the right side of this inscription.

358. 447 *of* 1907.—(Vaṭṭeḷuttu.) On the north wall of the Lakshmīnārāyaṇa-Perumāḷ temple. Records in the ninth year of the Pāṇḍya king Śaḍaiyamāran gift of fifty sheep for a lamp by a certain Nāgan Vikkiramādichchan. See No. 352 above.

359. 448 *of* 1907.—(Tamil.) On the same wall. A record of the Pāṇḍya king Tribhuvanachakravartin Kulaśēkharadēva recording in his ninth year gift of fifty sheep for a lamp.

360. 449 *of* 1907.—(Tamil.) On the same wall. A damaged record of the Pāṇḍya king Māravarman *alias* Tribhuvanachakravartin Sundara-Pāṇḍyadēva (I, 1216—35), 'who was pleased to present the Chōḷa country,' dated eleventh year.

361. 450 *of* 1907.—(Tamil.) On the same wall. Records in the second year of the Pāṇḍya king Jaṭāvaram *alias* Tribhuvanachakravartin Kulaśēkharadēva (I or II ?) a grant of land.

362. 451 *of* 1907.—(Tamil.) On the north, west and south walls of the same temple. A record of the Pāṇḍya king Jaṭāvarman *alias* Tribhuvanachakravartin Kulaśēkharadēva (I or II ?) in his thirteenth year. The stones are out of order. One of them mentions the twenty-first year of some king.

363. 452 *of* 1907.—(Tamil.) On a stone built into the wall of the kitchen in the same temple. A damaged record of the Chōḷa king Rājēndra-Chōḷadēva, dated fourth year. Mentions the assemblies of Arikēsarinallūr, Mandiragauravamaṅgalam and Tirupputtūr, which was apparently a hamlet of the other three. See No. 350 above.

364. 453 *of* 1907.—(Vaṭṭeḻuttu.) On a stone lying in front of the same temple. A fragmentary record.

365. 454 *of* 1907.—(Vaṭṭeḻuttu.) On a pillar lying in the same place. A fragment of record. Seems to mention Tirupputtūr.

366. *C.P. No.* 13 *of* 1907.—A record of the Pāṇḍya king (whose name is lost) in his eighteenth year. It is in Sanskrit and Tamil. Opens with two verses in Sanskrit, of which the first contains an invocation to Vishṇu and the second a prayer for the prosperity of the Pāṇḍya kings. Then follows a Tamil passage in the Vaṭṭeḻuttu alphabet describing in general terms the achievements of Pāṇḍyan kings. The first historical person is Jayanta Varman. His son was Arikēsarin Māravarman, a friend of the Brahmans, performer of *tulābhāra*, etc. His son (name missing), who is called the remover of the Kali. age, fought a battle at Marudūr. The last plate shows that the object granted was land and the executor was, one Tāyan Śiṅgan, the Uttaramantrin of Kuṇḍūr in Kuṇḍūr Kūṟṟam in Aṇḍanāḍu.

367. *C.P. No.* 14 *of* 1907.—"The larger Chinnamanūr plates." Four plates in Sanskrit and three in Tamil. The historical part gives the genealogy of the early Pāṇḍyan dynasty from Arikēsarin to Rājasimha II, Abhimānamēru Māravarman. In his eighteenth year he gave, while encamped in the village of Chūḷal in Rājasimhakuḷakīḻ, the village of Narcheygai Puttūr in Aḷanāḍu to a Brahman of the Kauśikagōtra. The Tamil portion gives more details of the same line of kings. See *Ep. Rep.*, 1907, pp. 64—69, for a detailed discussion of the value and importance of this and the previous epigraph. See the Pāṇḍyan genealogy.

Uttamāpāḷaiyam.

368. 722 *of* 1905.—(Vaṭṭeḻuttu.) Above the first three images first row, on the Karuppaṇṇasāmi rock. A damaged record of the Pāṇḍya king Śaḍaiyamāran, dated twentieth year. The Government Epigraphist points out that there is no clue as to the time in which he lived, whether he was earlier or later than Varguṇa Pāṇḍya. See No. 352 and Śuchīndram, Cape Comorin, Tiruppaḍaimarudūr and Kuḍumiyāmalai inscriptions.

369—377. 723 *to* 731 *of* 1905.—(Vaṭṭeḻuttu.) Below the same images. Mention Veṇbaikuḍi-nāḍu (No. 723), Arattanēmipperiyār, pupil of Attopavāsigaḷ (No. 725), Śeṅguḍi-nāḍu (Nos. 728 and 731) and Ajjaṇandi (No. 729).

378. 732 *of* 1905.—(Vaṭṭeḻuttu.) On a boulder near the same rock. Records a gift of money by Anantavīra-Aḍigaḷ for a lamp to the shrine of Tirukkuṇagiridēva.

379. 733 *of* 1905.—(Tamil.) On a slab set up at the main entrance into the Kāḷahastīśvara temple in the same village. The

Nāyaka queen Maṅgammāḷ (1689—1705) records in Kaliyuga 4794, Ś. 1615, Śrīmukha, gift of land. [Mr. Sewell evidently misreads the date as Ś. 1415 or A.D. 1493.]

Virapāṇḍi.

380. 422 *of* 1907.—(Tamil.) On a stone lying near the Kaṇṇīśvara temple. A record of the Pāṇḍya king Tribhuvanachakravartin Sundara-Pāṇḍyadēva. Mentions in his thirteenth year one of the sons or disciples of Aghōradēva of the Nandikēśvara santāna and the Āmuṇḍamaḍam. See Cd. 72.

381. 423 *of* 1907.—(Tamil.) On a second stone in the same place. A record of the Pāṇḍya king Vikkira-Pāṇḍyadēva in his fifth year. Mentions the temple of Kaṇṇuḍai-Īchcharamuḍaiya-Nāyanār.

382. 424 *of* 1907.—(Tamil.) On a third stone in the same place. A record of the Vijayanagara king Kṛishṇadēva-Mahārāya in Ś. 1451, Sarvadhārin. The temple is called Uḍaiyār Kaṇṇīśura-muḍaiya-Nāyanār at Pullai-nallūr *alias* Vīra-Pāṇḍya-nallūr.

383. 425 *of* 1907.—(Tamil.) On a fourth stone in the same place. A fragment of record of the Pāṇḍya king Tribhuvana-chakravartin Vikrama-Pāṇḍyaḍēva, dated sixth year. Mentions Pullinallūr in Aḷa-nāḍu.

384. 426 *of* 1907.—(Tamil.) On a fifth stone in the same place. A record of the Pāṇḍya king Vikrama-Pāṇḍyadēva in his seventh year. Mentions the temple of Uḍaiyār Kaṇṇuḍai-Īchcharamu-ḍaiya-Nayanār at Pullainallūr in Aḷa-nāḍu.

385. 427 *of* 1907.—(Tamil.) On a sixth stone in the same place. Records in the thirteenth year of the Pāṇḍya king Sundara-Pāṇḍyādēva "who was pleased to present the Chōḷa country", the construction of the doorway of the ardhamaṇṭapa in the temple of Kaṇṇuḍai-Īchcharamuḍaiya-Nāyanār at Pullainallūr in Aḷa-nāḍu, a subdivision of Pāṇḍi-maṇḍalam.

TIRUMANGALAM TALUK.

Kōḍikuḷam.

386. On the north wall of the garbhagriham in the local Śiva temple. A record of the year Viḷambi, Puraṭṭāśi 22, mentioning certain agents of the Chokkanātha temple. See *Antiquities,* I, p. 296, for an interesting notice of the place.

Kallāttuppaṭṭi.

386-A. A C.P. grant in the Śiva temple (Tamil) recording gift of lands by a private party in the reign of Achyuta Rāya of Vijayanagar.

387. 458 *of* 1906.-(Tamil.) On the Ānaimalai hill close to the Vēdanārāyaṇa-Perumāḷ temple. Records in the thirty-fifth year of the Pāṇḍya king Māravarman *alias* Tribhuvanachakravartin Kulaśēkharadēva (I, 1268—1309), "who was pleased to take every country," sale of land to the God Sēnāpati-Āḷvār in the Kāḷamēghan (temple).

388. 459 *of* 1906.—(Tamil.) On a stone set up in a field near the same temple. Records that the temple is called Nāyanār Añjāda-Perumāḷ *alias* Vēdanāthar on the bank of the tank called Brahmatīrtha in the middle of the Tuṅgavanam forest. The forest belonged to the district of Vēlaṅgāl paṟṟu on the eastern side of the Tiruvānaimalai hill to the north of Tirumōgūr in Ten-Paṟappu-nādu.

Koṅgar-Puḷiyanguḷam.

The Epigraphical Department at first wrongly included under this village the inscriptions 39—42 above. They as a matter of fact belonged to Kīḷakkudi. The following inscriptions are found in this place :—

389. 54 *of* 1910.—(Vaṭṭeḷuttu.) Below a Jaina figure on the hill. The record contains the syllables Śrī-Ajjaṇandi. See *Ep. Rep.*, 1909, p. 70.

390—392. 55 *to* 57 *of* 1910.—(Brāhmi.) In the cavern facing south on the same hill. [The characters have been attributed to the second or third century before the Christian era. (See *Ep. Rep.*, 1910, p. 76). The cavern contains six so-called Pañchapāṇḍava beds used formerly by Buddhistic ascetics for keeping the *vassa*. For the description of these beds see *ibid.*

Kuppālnattam.

393. 105 *of* 1909.—(Vaṭṭeḷuttu.) On rock near the Jaina images on the hill. A much damaged record, referring to the cutting of the images.

Nallamaram.

394. *C.P. No.* 92 *of Mr. Sewell's List.*—Records that in Ānanda (A.D. 1656) Tirumala Nāyakka of Madura proceeded on a tour round his territories, and, being hospitably entertained by a man of the Kauṇḍan caste in the village, made him a grant of lands as a reward for his loyalty.

Pudūr.

395. 395 *of* 1914.—(Tamil.) On a stone set up near the Śiva temple. Records in Ś. 1565, Pramādi, Āni, sixteenth day, gift of the village of Tirumalasamudram to the temple of Śokkanāthasvāmin for conducting certain festivals in the months of Tai, Vaiyāśi and Āni for the merit of Tirumalai-Nāyakkar (1623—59), son of Viśvanātha-Nāyakkar.

Śinduppaṭṭi.

396. On a stone in front of the Veṅkaṭāchalapati temple. (Tamil.) Records that, in Tai 2 of year Bhava, the inhabitants of the country of Tiḍiyan gave to God Tiruvēṅkaṭanātha of Sinduppaṭṭi all the lands fit for ploughing in the village of Eṛa-pāppanapaṭṭi, a part of Tummakkuṇḍu (a village in the Tirumaṅgalam taluk). This is No. 27 of Burgess and Natesa Sastri's *Tamil and Sanskrit Inscrns.*, p. 40.

Tiḍiyan.

397. On the south wall of the Kailāsanāthasvāmi temple. (Tamil.) A donation, for the purpose of conducting the "Rudrapārāyaṇa," by two Naiks in Ś. 651 (mistake for 1568), Vyaya, Tai, Trayōdaśi, Śravaṇa, Śivarātri. *Tamil and Sanskrit Inscrns.*, No. 26, p. 39.

Vikkiramaṅgalam.

398. 15 *of* 1894.—(Tamil.) On the inside of the north wall of the enclosure of the temple. A record of the Pāṇḍya king Kō-Jaṭāvarman *alias* Sundara-Pāṇḍyadēva (I or II?), dated in his ninth year. [See *Ibid.*, p. 10, where a description of the temple is given.]

399. On the back wall of the prākāram of the temple. (Old Tamil.) A record of the twenty-third year of Jaṭāvarman Tribhuvanachakravartin Kulaśēkharadēva (I, ? 1190—1217), in which the citizens of Vikramaśōḷapuram in Tenkaḷḷaka country gave lands for temple service, worship, etc. *Ibid.*, pp. 10—13.

400. In the same place. (Tamil.) A record of the twenty-third year of Tribhuvanachakravartin Parākrama Pāṇḍya dēva. Records a gift of lands (ten *mās*) to God Madhurōdaya by Aḷakiri Pāṇḍya Anantapālan *alias* Jayaṅkoṇḍanāthan of Śaraḷanallūr, himself and his descendants undertaking to pay the taxes. The citizens have this inscribed. [*Ibid.*, pp. 13—15.]

401. On the north wall towards the west end. A record of Kō-Jaṭāvarman *alias* Kulaśēkharadēva (I?, 1190—1217), in his twenty-first year. Records grant of certain taxes by the citizens of Vikramaśoḷapuram for the holy vestment, etc., of God Madhurodayēśvara. *Ibid.*, No. 20, pp. 15—17.

402. On the north wall. (Tamil.) A record of the fifth year of Jaṭāvarman Kulaśēkharadēva (I?, 1190—1217), similar to 399 but incomplete. *Ibid.*, No. 21, pp. 15—17.

403. In the same place. (Tamil.) A record of the first year of Ko-Jaṭāvarman Tribhuvanachakravartin Sundara Pāṇḍya (Saturday, seventh lunar day of the dark fortnight of Tulā, Pushya asterism). Records that the citizens of Vikramaśōḷapuram sold for one thousand *paṇams*, certain lands to Aḷagia Tiruchchiṟṟambalam-uḍayār, one of the disciples of Kīḷai *maṭha*, which belonged to the *santati* of Gōḷakimaṭha of Tirupparaṅkunṟam. [The document furnishes an excellent example of the privileges of landlordship.] *Sanskrit and Tamil Inscrns.*, No. 22, pp. 18—21. For Gōḷakimaṭha see N.A. 201 and Cd. 30.

MALABAR DISTRICT.

GENERAL.

(A) C.P. No. 6 *of* 1911-12.—In the hands of the Collector. A Vaṭṭeḷuttu record, registering a hypothecation deed in which the parties were a certain Śuvaram Dēvan, King Karumbattu Rāman Ravivarman Kōlattu Tiruvaḍi and the *Iraṇḍutaḍai* of Peruñchellūr.

CALICUT TALUK.

Calicut.

For a history of the place see *Antiquities*, I, p. 246; J.A.S.B., XV, p. 224; Oppert's *Historical Tables, Madras Journal*, 1879, p. 107; *Buchanan*, Vol. II, p. 139, and *Malabar Gazr.*, pp. 382—9.

1. 219 *of* 1895.—(Vaṭṭeḷuttu.) On a slab from Tirupparaṅgōḍu in the Collector's house. Records in the twenty-seventh year of Kō-Kōdai·Ravi gift of land. See No. 4 below.

2. 220 *of* 1895.—(Vaṭṭeḷuttu.) On a slab from Tiruvannūr in the same house. Records in the eighth year of the Kēraḷa king Rāma gift of lamp to the god of Tirumannūr, and certain privileges to "the 600". Translated by Guṇdert.

3. In the Mach-chinda mosque in the hamlet of Nagaram. (Arabic and Kanarese.) No details given.

Chōkūr.

4. 13 *of* 1901.—(Vaṭṭeḷuttu.) On a slab in front of the Chokūr temple in Puttūr amśam. A record of king Kōdai Ravi in his fifteenth year, making a gift of land. [It is difficult to say who this Kōdai Ravi was. A chief of this name figures in the Cochin Jews' Deed attributed by Burnell to the eighth century A.D.]

Maṇapuram.

5. 12 *of* 1901.—(Vaṭṭeḷuttu.) On a slab in the courtyard. Records grant of land.

Pāypalasēri.

6. 10 *of* 1901.—(Vaṭṭeḷuttu.) On a slab set up in the courtyard of the Karipūra temple. A damaged record.

Talakoḷattūr.

7. 2 *of* 1901.—(Vaṭṭeḷuttu.) On a stone set up in the Madilagat-tambalam. Appears to record a grant of land. King's name illegible.

CHIRAKKAL TALUK.

Chūraḷi.

8. In the Neḍiyaṅgu temple. A record regarding the erection of a stone in K.A. 801 (A.D. 1625).

Eramara.

9. In the ruined temple at Chālappuratu. A Vaṭṭeḻuttu record.

Erone.

10. On a granite slab at a tank attached to the temple. A Vaṭṭeḻuttu record.

11. On a granite rock in the hamlet of Nerambil. A Vaṭṭeḻuttu and Malayāḷam record. The latter gives the word *adiyōdi.*

Kaṇṇapuram.

12. In the village of Çhuṇḍa, on the south side of the Kuruvu Kāru temple. No details given.

Kayarāla.

13. In the local temple, on a slab. A Dēvanāgari epigraph.

Kuṭṭiyattūr.

14. In the gate of the temple, on a stone. In "unknown" characters.

Māḍāi (Māḍāyi).

This place is supposed to be the ancient Mazare. For the description of the fort constructed by Eli Perumāḷ, the Jews' Tank (which suggests an early Jewish colony), the mosque and other antiquities see *Malabar Gazr.*, pp. 397-8.

15. In the local mosque. An Arabic inscription commemorating its foundation in H. 518 (A.D. 1124).

16. In the same village. A record stating that a tank was constructed by a Hindu.

Taḷiparamba.

17. On a slab in the building on the temple tank. A record dated K.A. 700 (A.D. 1524), saying that the bathing-house was finished in that year. For the purāṇic story of the Lakshmīpuram temple see *Ibid.*, p. 399.

18. At the foot of a banyan tree in front of the temple. An epigraph, dated in K.A. 954 (A.D. 1778). *Ibid.*, p. 399.

ERNĀD TALUK.

Iruveṭṭi.

19. At the entrance of the *mēleḍat.* (Tamil.) A record of K.A. 825 (A.D. 1649).

Mānjēri.

20. In the east wall of the Muttrukunna (Durgā) temple. A record dated K.A. 827 (A.D. 1651) stating that a certain Māna Vikrama built it. *Antiquities*, I, 248, and *Malabar Gazr.*, p. 418.

21. Near a well to the north. A record dated K.A. 833 (A.D. 1657) recording its excavation by the same person, the victorious Vikrama Tirumalpād.

Mannūr-Ambalam.

22. 217 *of* 1895.—(Malayāḷam.) On the base of the north wall of the kitchen of the same temple. Mentions in K.A. 734 the Śiva temple of Mannūr.

23. 218 *of* 1895.—(Vaṭṭeḻuttu.) To the right of the entrance into the Śiva shrine in the same temple. Records gift to the god of Tirumannūr.

Nilambūr.

24. A C.P. grant (Sanskrit) of the fifth year of the reign of the Dharma-mahārāja Ravivarman of the Kadamba family. While at Vaijayanti (Banavāsi), on the full moon *tithi* of Kārttika, he gave the two *paḷḷis* (hamlets) of Muḷṭāgi and Maḷkāvu to a Brahman named Gōvindasvāmin of Kāśyapa gōtra and Yajur vēda. [See *Ep. Ind.*, Vol. VIII, pp. 146—9, where Messrs. T. A. Gopinatha Rao and G. Venkoba Rao edit the plates. They identify the villages granted with hamlets near Talakkāḍ. They further point out the palæographical resemblance of the epigraph to the Kūḍgere plates of Vijaya Śiva Māndhatrivarman (*Ep. Ind.*, Vol. VI, p. 12), to the plates of Vijaya Śrī Mrigēśavarman (*Ind. Antq.*, Vol. VII, p. 37) and Halsi plates of Harivarman and Ravivarman (*Ibid.*, Vol. VI, pp. 25—32).]

25. On a block of gneiss rock in the Cherupuṟa river. An epigraph (visible only in dry weather) consisting "of only about five letters, each a foot high." *Antiquities*, I, 248, and *Malabar Gazr.*, p. 418.

Paḷañjannūr.

26. In the mosque in the hamlet of Chāliyam, on a marble slab in the south wall. Arabic inscription to the memory of one 'Ali Abdu'lla who died in H. 720, K.A. 478, A.D. 1302. [*Antiquities*, Vol. I, p. 246. The place was the scene of a fight between the Portuguese who built a fort here in 1531 and the Zamorin (who was assisted by the Moors). See *Malabar Gazr.*, p. 414, for details.]

Tirukkaḷangōd.

27. On a granite slab at the edge of a wall. A Vaṭṭeḷuttu record. See *Antiquities*, Vol. I, p. 224, for a short history of the place.

Kōttayam Taluk.

Tellicherry.

28. On a slab in the Tiruveṅgāḍar or Tirukaṇyūr shrine. A record in an "unknown character." This is the well-known "Brass Pagoda," so called because of the copper sheeting of its roof. See *Malabar Gazr.*, p. 429.

29. 9 *of* 1901.—(Vaṭṭeḷuttu.) On the base of the *balipiṭha* in front of the Tiruvaṅgāṭṭ-ambalam. Records the construction of the *balipiṭha* by a Brāhmaṇa woman.

Kurumbranād Taluk.

Kaliyamballi-Ambalam.

30. 8 *of* 1901.—(Vaṭṭeḷuttu.) On a stone near the *balipiṭha*. Records gift of a lamp.

Kiṇalūr.

31. 14 *of* 1901.—On a slab in front of the Kiṇalūr temple. Gift of two lamps.

Kollam.

32. 3 *of* 1901.—(Vaṭṭeḷuttu.) On three stones built into the floor near the washing tank of the Jamātpaḷḷi. Three fragments. This is evidently the inscription dated K.A. 684, referred to by Mr. Sewell in his *Antiquities*, Vol. I, p. 245. For an account of the mosque which was founded by Malik Ibn Dinar, see *Malabar Gazr.*, I, p. 436.

33. 4 *of* 1901.—(Vaṭṭeḷuttu.) On two stones built into the platform in front of the Taḷiyil-ambalam (Talayil). A damaged record.

34. 5 *of* 1901.—(Vaṭṭeḷuttu.) On a stone built into the floor of the courtyard of the Maraḷūr-ambalam. A mutilated record. Mentions Maraḷūr and four illams.

35. 6 *of* 1901.—(Vaṭṭeḷuttu.) On a stone set up in the courtyard of the Pandalāyini-ambalam at Kōyilāṇḍi. The record mentions Pandalāyini. The name of the king is doubtful.

Tiruveṅgayūr (Tiruvāṅgūr).

36. 15 *of* 1901.—(Vaṭṭeḷuttu.) On a rock south of the temple. A damaged record. Name of the king illegible.

Veḷḷikuḷaṅgara-Ambalam.

37. 7 *of* 1901.—(Sanskrit in Malayāḷam characters.) On a stone lying close to the *balipīṭha* in front. Records under the auspices of Udayavarma, the sea of courage and the gem of the royal line, descended from Ghaṭōt-kacha (Bhīma's son), in Kollam 905 (A.D. 1730), the setting up of a pinnacle by a Brāhmaṇa. *Malabar Gazr.*, p. 4378.

PALGHĀT TALUK.

Kalpāti.

38. 205 *of* 1895.—(Vaṭṭeḻuttu.) On a stone set up in front of the Viśvanātha temple. Mr. Sewell says that it was dated in K.A. 640 (A.D. 1464), and records an endowment to the temple. *Antiquities*, I, p. 253. But the *Malabar Gazetteer* says that it is dated in K.A. 600 (A.D. 1425) and records that it was built by Itti Kombi Rāja of Palghāt who endowed it with land sowing over 4,000 *paras* of paddy. See *Malabar Gazr.*, p. 445.

Kāvaśēri.

39. 561 *of* 1908.—(Vaṭṭeḻuttu.) On a slab from the Kāvu temple (now in the Deputy Tahsildar's office at Ālattūr).

Poraṅgātri-deśam.

40. 11 *of* 1901.—(Vaṭṭeḻuttu.) On a slab in the Subramaṇya-svāmi temple. A damaged record. Records an agreement. Name of the king is lost.

PONNĀNI TALUK.

Āṇṇakarai.

41. 212 *of* 1895.—(Malayāḷam). On the base of a lamp pillar in front of the Śiva temple. Records the erection of the lamp pillar.

42. 213 *of* 1895.—(Vaṭṭeḻuttu.) On the south wall of the central shrine of the same. Records in K.A. 858 that the temple was covered with copper.

Chāvakkāḍ.

43. 734 *of* 1905.—(Vaṭṭeḻuttu.) On a slab placed under a tree in the Deputy Tahsildar's office. A damaged record in the middle. Mentions Vaḷḷuva-nāḍu in line 5 and Pālaiyūr in line 14. [This is evidently the inscription in "Roman characters" referred to by Mr. Sewell in his *Antiquities*, I, 250.] For an excellent account of the tradition concerning the arrival and exploits of St. Thomas in this place and Pālaiyūr, see *Malabar Gazr.*, I, pp. 450–1.

Guruvāyūr.

The following inscriptions are in *Malabar Gazr.*, I, 453.

43-A. On one of the slabs in the porch of the local two-storeyed gōpuram. (Sanskrit, in modern Malayāḷam characters.) Records that "the temple within is heaven," that the gateway was built by "the Lord of the Seas and the Hills" and that it had been trodden by the feet of many kings. The editor of the *Malabar Gazetteer* believes that the Zamorin is apparently referred to.

43-B. On the *dipastambha* in front of the gateway. Records the erection of it by a native of Travancore in K.A. 1011 (A.D. 1836).

43-C. On a broken slab of granite in the house of Mallissēri Nambūdri. "Unknown tongue."

43-D. On the granite door-post of the *ārāt-kuḷam.* Records that the gateway was erected by Paṇikka Vīttil Ittirāricha Menon in K.A. 922 (A.D. 1747).

Panniyūr.

44. 214 *of* 1895.—(Vaṭṭeḷuttu.) On a stone lying to the right of the north entrance into the Vishṇu (Varāhamūrti) temple. Records gift by the villagers of Panṟiyūr. [This place figures in the Syrian deed but still formed an important Brahman centre. For an account of the local Vishṇu temple see *Malabar Gazr.*, p. 454.

45. 215 *of* 1895.—(Vaṭṭeḷuttu.) On the base of the Kuṇḍil-Varāhasvāmin shrine in the same temple. Seems to record in K.A. 669 the building of the shrine.

46. 216 *of* 1895.—(Malayāḷam.) On a stone lying near the well in the Śiva temple.

Śembaravaṭṭam.

47. 206 *of* 1895.—(Malayāḷam.) On the base of a lamp pillar in front of the Aiyappan temple. Records in K.A. 10'8 the erection of the lamp pillar.

Śukapuram.

48. 208 *of* 1895.—(Vaṭṭeḷuttu.) On a stone lying in the north verandah of the Dakshiṇāmūrti temple. Records a gift of a lamp to the temple at Śōgiram.

49. 209 *of* 1895.—(Vaṭṭeḷuttu.) On the base of the second pillar of the platform in front of the same temple.

50. 210 *of* 1895.—(Vaṭṭeḷuttu.) On the base of the first pillar of the same.

51. 211 *of* 1895.—(Vaṭṭeḷuttu.) On a stone built into the pavement of the courtyard of the same temple. Records gift of land and of a lamp.

Verūr.

52. 207 *of* 1895.—(Tamil.) On a pillar in the maṇṭapa in front of the Subramaṇya temple. Modern.

WALAVANĀD TALUK.

Aṅgāḍippuram.

53-A. On a beam in the copper-roofed shrine of Tirumānthan kunnu. Records that it was built in A.D. 1732. *Malabar Gazr.*, p. 466.

Killikkuruchchimaṅgalam alias *Zēkkamaṅgalam.*

53-B. On the west and south sides of the maṇṭapam in the Śiva temple. A Vaṭṭeḻuttu record.

Mangaḍa (Mankada).

54. On a granite slab. On the Maniyoṭi Vishṇu temple. A vaṭṭeḻuttu record.

Ottapālam.

54-A. On a granite slab in the local temple, sacred to both Siva and Vishṇu. An epigraph in "an unknown tongue."

Pāṅga.

55. On a rock. A record of K.A. 934 (A.D. 1758).

WYNAAD TALUK.

*Gaṇapativaṭṭam (*see *Sultan's Battery).*

56. On the Nālapāt-Chāla Kunnu hill. (Old Tamil.) Not read.

57. On the *dipastambha* of the Gaṇapati temple. No details given.

58. On a stone in the northern court of the Māriyamma temple. No details given.

Pūtāti.

59. On the east wall of the maṇṭapa in the Arimula Ayyappan temple. An inscription, dated K.A. 922 (A.D. 1746) in "a mixture of four languages."

60. In the Pātiri temple formerly and "now in the possession of Pātiri Nanjaya Gauṇḍan." A Kanarese record.

Sultan's Battery.

This place is the same as Gaṇapati-vaṭṭam, but came to be so-called as Tippu had a fort here (on the site of the present police station). See *Malabar Gazr.*, p. 477.

61—64. 120 *to* 123 *of* 1897.—(Cave characters.) In a cave near the same place. The first of these refers to the propagator of the family of a householder named Śrī Vishṇuvarman. Dr. Hultzsch translates it as "the writing of the glorious Vishṇu Varma, the propagator of the kuṭumbiya family." He is said to be the earliest king known by epigraphic research in Malabar. It has been suggested that he might be a Kadamba king, but it is doubtful. "The inscription is in Sanskrit and therefore probably not earlier than the fifth century A.D." See *Malabar Gazr.*, p. 34. The rest are unintelligible.

65. 124 *of* 1897.—(Kanarese.) In the same place. Begins with *Śride.*

Tirunelli.

66. C.P. grant of king Bhāskara Ravivarman, "a sovereign whose name appears also in the deed of the Cochin Jews, which has engaged the attention of most Dravidian scholars and is considered by them as the oldest historical record of Malabar." The present epigraph which is in Tamil and Vaṭṭeḻuttu contains an order regulating the management of the temple of Tirunelli and issued by Śaṅkara Kōdavarman of Puraikiḻa-nāḍu, who was apparently a vassal of the king. See *Ep. Rep.*, 1890, October, p. 1.

NELLORE DISTRICT.

Ātmakūr Taluk.

Amānicheruvalla.

1. Near the local tank bund. (Telugu.) A record of Mārakampi Nāyaningāru, feudatory of Vīra Veṅkaṭapati Rāya (I, 1586—1616) of Vijayanagar, stating that on the twelfth of the bright fortnight of Kārttika of the year Naḷa, Ś. 1538, he gave the hereditary privilege of worship in the temple of Kōna Vallabhārya, to one Kandagaḍa Guruvayya. This is Ātmakūr No. 1 in Messrs. Butterworth and Venugopal Chetty's *Nellore Inscrns.*

2. South of the village. (Telugu.) An incomplete record beginning with salutation to Śrī Rāmānuja. *Ibid.* No. 2.

Anantasāgaram.

3. (Telugu and Sanskrit.) On a stone near the sluice of the tank between Manchalapalli and Mustafapuram. Dated in Ś. 1550, Vaiśākha Śukla-Tritīya (the day of Akshayatritīya), year Vibhava, on Wednesday, in the reign of Śrī Vīrapratāpa Śrī Vīra dēva Mahārāja. Records that when Vēṅkaṭapati Nāyaniṅgāru of the race of Padmanāyaka and of the Rēcharla gōtra, the son of Kumāra Timmanāyaniṅgāru and the grandson of Veligōṭi Peda Toṇḍamanāyanigāru, was ruling over the Śīmās of Rāpūr, Nellūru, Pōrūr, Kāḷahasti, Veṅkaṭagiri, etc., which had been granted as *amaram* by Rāmadēva Rāya, his mother (Raghupati Ammagāru, daughter of Muchintala Raṅgappa Nāyanivāru) strengthened the tank bund of the Muddala tank in the Anantarāgara agrahāra which had fallen into disrepair. *Ibid.* No. 3. See No. 36 below.

4. On a boundary stone in the tank bed to the north. *Ibid.* No. 4. The name Koṇḍamarasayya carved in Telugu.

5. In the tank bed. To the same effect as No. 2 above. *Ibid.* No. 5.

6. On the tank bund above the Gollabhāma temple. (Telugu.) A record of Kṛishṇa Dēva Rāya of Vijayanagar, dated in Ś. 1444, Vikrama, Jyēshṭa, Śukla 15, Thursday, saying that Mahārāja Śrī Rāyasam Koṇḍamarasayya, the *Kāryakarta* (agent) of the Rāya, constructed a tank at Anantasāgaram for the religious merit of his mother Saṅkāyamma and his father Timmarasayya Gāru, a temple in their name, and an agrahāra to Brahmans. *Ibid.* No. 6.

Annamāsamudram.

7. On a stone in the tank bed of the village. (Telugu.) A record of Śrīman Mahāmaṇḍalēśvara Allu Tirukāḷatidēva Mahārāja,

dated on Friday, Śukla 11, of Bhādrapada in *Pārthiva* corresponding to Ś. 1168. It says that while he was ruling at Kāñchi he consecrated Dānava Murāri Perumānanda Dēva at Śrī Ātukūru (Ātmakur) for the religious merit of his father-in-law Tirukāḷadēva Mahārāja and a temple for the increase of his own life, health and wealth. He further made a gift of four *paṭṭus* of land out of *prabhumānyam*, measured by the twenty-span-rod of this village; twenty *paṭṭus* of dry Government land, measured by the twenty-six span pole. At the rate of a *māḍa* for two *paṭṭus* of *koru* land and a *māḍa* per *paṭṭu* on dry land, one Rāma Reḍḍi undertook to pay every year in the month of Vaiśākha one hundred and thirty *māḍas* to the temple. [*Nellore Inscrns.*, Ātmakur No. 7, pp. 206—10.]

8. In a mosque. (Persian.) A small epigraph, comparing this mosque with "the famous mosque of the Prophet of Medina" and invoking the praise of God on him and his descendants. *Ibid.* No. 8, p. 210.

9. In a mosque. (Persian.) Dated in A.D. 1762–63. The four Kalifs referred to, Haidar's name representing that of 'Ali. *Ibid.* No. 9, pp. 211–2.

10. On a stone near the mosque. (Arabic.) Four lines addressed to one Āyēsha, to the effect that death is preferable to long illness.

Ātmakūr.

11. In the Aḷagaṇāthasvāmi temple. (Telugu.) Records that in Ś. 1201, Kārttika Kr. 13, Friday, one Bahava (?) Mahārāja constructed a temple to Aḷahapurapatidēva of Aṭukūr (Ātmakūr). The kāpus and (karaṇams ?) of Jillēri are also referred to. *Ibid.* No. 11, pp. 213–4.]

12. From the same temple. (Telugu.) Records the worship of Aḷaganāthasvāmi by a karaṇam of the Ātmakūr village, the son of Tirumalayya, on Śukla 2 of āshāḍha in Bhava. *Ibid.* No. 12, p. 214.

13. From the same temple. (Telugu.) Dated in Ś. 1199, Īśvara, Phalguna, Śukla 13, Sunday. Records that one Āṭukūri Vāmana Prichudēvaḍu gave to Nambi Upureḍi Sūraya, the temple servant, certain gifts. *Ibid.* No. 13, pp. 214–5.

14. From the same temple. (Tamil.) Dated in Ś. 1198, Bhava. One Kāraikkiḷān Bhaṭṭan gave (some lands) free of tax to God Aḷagapperumāḷ. *Ibid.* No. 14, p. 215.

15. From the tank bund. (Telugu.) The name of Velidaṇḍu Kōnēru Mānapati Timmarasu given. He is called the worshipper of Śrī Veṅkaṭēśvarasvāmi.

16. From the same place. (Telugu.) Says that the tank was constructed by Kōnēti Timmarājayya in Ś. 1471, Naḷa (?), *Pushya*, Ś. 13, Thursday. *Ibid.* No. 16.

Bhaṭṭepāḍu.

17. On a well to the south of the village. (Telugu.) Dated in Ś. 1471, Kīlaka, Bhādrapada, su. 5, Wednesday; records that on the orders of Vīrapratāpa Śrī Sadāśiva Mahārāyar of Vijayanagar, Śrīman Mahāmaṇḍalēśvara Rāmarāja Timmayyadēva Mahārāja, issued an edict exempting the barbers of Baṭṭepāḍu in Uḍayagiri Rājya from the *Kulasiddhāyalu* (?), marriage fees, presents, and *veṭṭi* tax. [The editors of *Nellore Inscrns.* translated *kulasiddhāyalu* as fines levied for breaking rules of caste.]

18. On a stone opposite to the Śiva temple. (Tamil.) Dated in the thirty-fifth year of Tribhuvanachakravartin Kulōttuṅga Chōḷa (I). Seems to record a gift of Madhurāntaka Pottappichōḷa *alias* Nallaśittiyaraśan of Nellūr. *Ibid.*, Ātmakūr No. 18, pp. 219–20.

Bhimāvaram.

19. North of the village. (Telugu.) A fragmentary record, mentioning the gift of some fields by a certain Gontappa Nāyaḍu to a deity. [*Ibid.* 19, pp. 220–1.]

Bommavaram.

20. "To the west of the village." (Telugu.) A fragmentary inscription referring to the tank of Bommavaram in Uḍayagiri Śīma which is said to have been granted as an *amaram* by "Srīraṅgarājayyavāru" to . . . [*Ibid.* No. 20, pp. 221—23.]

21. On three sides of a stone, in the road to the west of the village. A record similar to the above and giving the same information. [*Ibid.* No. 21, pp. 223—5.]

Cheruvapalli.

22. On two stones opposite Rāmaliṅgam temple. (Telugu.) Fragmentary. [*Ibid.* No. 22, pp. 225—8.]

Chēzerla.

23. In the Chennakēśavasvāmi temple. (Telugu.) "On Friday, the thirtieth of the dark fortnight" of Īśvara, Ś. 1609 (which does not correspond), on a solar eclipse, Śrīmat (Dāvu Suratrāna ?) Māradattam Gāru gave to God Chennakēśava of Chēzerla and to Nāganātham Timmavōjihalu of the Yajus Śākha and Kauṇḍinyagōtra, a village with its eight species of enjoyment and eight species of ownership. [*Ibid.* No. 23, pp. 228—30.]

23-A. *C.P. No.* 87 *of Mr. Sewell's List and C.P. No.* 18 *of Nellore Inscrns.*—(Sanskrit in Nandināgari script.) A record of Pratāpa Dēva Rāya (II), dated on the Śivarātri day of the month of *Māgha* in the year *Kīlaka* in Ś. 1351 (A.D. 1429). The grant was made in the temple of Virūpāksha, at the request of Panta Mailāra, great-grandson of Sūra, grandson of Pōta and the son of

Mumbāmba and Mummaḍīndra, a valiant lieutenant of Dēva Rāya in battle, who had the *birudas* of Dharaṇīvarāha, Ghaṇṭānada and Chauhatimalla. The object of the grant was Chēzerla in Pūṅgināḍu on the Kuṇḍi (Guṇḍlakamma) river in 80 shares to 54 Brahmans. See Gt. 355.

Chiramana.

24. Near a well to the north of the village. (Sanskrit and Telugu.) Records that in Ś. 1109 one Dāmanēndu consecrated Kēśavadēva of Cherumana and that four other Nāiks of Gollapūṇḍi made certain gifts of land. [Ātmakūr No. 24, pp. 230–1.]

25. On the west wall of the Chandramauḷīśvara temple.—(Telugu.) On Thursday, the thirteenth of the bright fortnight of Bhādrapada, Ś. 1207, in the kingdom of Śrīman Mahāmaṇḍalēśvara Vijayagaṇḍa-Gōpāla Mahārāja, two Nāik chiefs of Gollapūṇḍi, gave four *puṭṭis* of paddy field to dancing girls for dancing in the temple of Chirumana Mallikārjuna. The deed says that in case the donees leased out the lands, the kāpus of the village should treat them as *sarvamānya*. The inscription records certain gifts to the temple itself and enjoins on the kāpus to cultivate the lands and pay each year 155 *puṭṭis* of paddy and a half share in the second crop, besides three-fourths *māḍa* on every female cloth. [*Ibid.* No. 25, pp. 231—6.] See N.A. 441, Cg. 49 and 342.

26. On the south wall of the Chandramauḷīśvara temple.—(Tamil.) Records that in the eighteenth year of Tribhuvana-chakravartin Kulōttuṅga Chōḷadēva, Gollapūṇḍi Nāyakkar left as free of taxes (இருலிகைடயாட்டம்) certain lands to God Kēśavapperumāḷ of Śerudinai. [*Ibid.* No. 26, pp. 237—7.]

Yādavalli.

27. *C.P. No.* 80 *of Mr. Sewell's List and C.P. No.* 13 *of Nellore Inscrns.*—(Sanskrit in Nandināgari script.) King Achyuta Rāya grants, on a Śukladvādaśi of Kārttika, in *Plava*, Ś. 1463, the village of Yādavalli in Paṅganāḍu *Śima* of Uḍayagiri, to Tirumala Bhaṭṭa, son of Bhairava Bhaṭṭa (of the Kauṇḍinya gōtra). [The plate is identical in part, with the Pōlepalli grant and was issued under similar circumstances.]

Jammavaram.

28. East of the tank. (Telugu.) On Sunday, the fifth of the bright fortnight of Māgha, year Viḷambi, Maparusayya, son of Śrīmat Śāḷuva Narasappayya, granted *mēras* at one *kuñcha* for the tanks constructed by him at the village of Jammalamaḍugu. [*Ibid.* No. 27.]

Kaluvāyi.

29. On a bank of the tank west of the village. (Telugu.) On Thursday, the fifteenth day of the bright fortnight of Vaiśākha, year Pramādi, Ś. 1441, in the reign of Kṛishṇa Dēva Rāya, Rāyasam Koṇḍamarasayya constructed, for the religious merit of his father Timmaraśa Gāru and his mother Saṅkāyamma Gāru, the Kaluvāyi tank and built temples dedicated to Malalamma and Bīrapa. [Ātmakūr No. 28, pp. 238-9.]

Kāmareḍḍipāḍu.

30. Near the Durgamma temple. (Telugu.) While Mahāmaṇḍalēśvara Nāne Dēva was ruling at Nellore, his servant Hadapamunu Lunkkarāja provided offerings to Durga on the festival day of Mahā Lakshmi, on Sunday, the tenth day of the bright fortnight of Aśvayuja, year *Yuva*, Ś. 1197. [*Ibid.* No. 29, pp. 239-40.]

Kōlagoṭla.

31. In a field west of the village. (Telugu.) In Kārttika of year Vikriti, one Kamana (the son of Basavarāyapati) and Annam Gāru of the Kārumañchi family granted to Basavayya Dēva of Kōlagoṭla a field north of the village well as *mānyam*. [*Ibid.* No. 30, p. 241.]

32. On a stone in front of Nāgavaruppu temple. (Telugu.) Records that Vidayanchami Jaṅgamayya, the *mahāpātra* (minister) of Śrīman Mahāmaṇḍalēśvara Vīrapratāpa Virūpāksharāya, presented the village of Kāmpu Kīmasi to Jagadīśa of Śaṅgam in Pākanāḍu *sthala* in Uḍayagiri Rājya. (The king was evidently Virūpāksha, son of Dēva Rāya II.) *Ibid.* No. 31, pp. 242-3.]

33. In a field to the north of the village. (Telugu.) Illegible. [*Ibid.* No. 32, p. 244.]

Korimerla.

34. Opposite to Nāgavarappamma temple. (Telugu.) Fragmentary. [*Ibid.* No. 33.]

Kōṭitirṭham.

35. Koṭīśvarasvāmi temple. (Telugu.) Records that one Niḍugaṇḍi who abandoned enjoyment and desire and went in quest of Brahma, came at His instance to Kōṭīśvara temple, performed penance and saw God revealed. *Ibid.* No. 34.

Kullūru.

36. Near the Śiva temple. (Sanskrit in Telugu character and Telugu.) Records that on Monday, the twelfth of the dark fortnight of Kārttika, in Paritāpi, Ś. 1534, when Śri Vēṅkaṭapati Rāya (I, 1586--1616) was ruling the earth, his feudatory Veṅkaṭapati Nāyaniṅgāru of the race of Padmanāyaka and Rēcherla gōtra, the grandson of Velugōṭi Pedda Koṇḍama Nāyaḍu, and son of Kumāra Timma Nāyaḍu, sent for Rudrappa of the Paisāla gōtra, the ruler of Kullūru, the grandson of Chintapaṭla Śiṅgāma Nāyaḍu and the son of Cheñchama Nāyaḍu, and asked him to construct the eastern weir of Kullūr tank, which he did. Ātmakūr No. 35, pp. 245—9. See also No. 3 above.

37. On the sluice of the tank. (Telugu.) Mentions that the weir work was done by Marāra Duggarajā Vīrappa. *Ibid.* No. 36.

Lakkirāzupalli.

38. In Muppu Śeṭṭi's tope to the north. (Telugu.) An incomplete record of Nārāyaṇarāju, dated on the twelfth Mārgaśira, regarding a hamlet of Minagallu. *Ibid.* No. 41, pp. 258–9.

Mahimalūru.

39. On a fallen stone by a small tank north of the village. Records that on the fifteenth of the bright fortnight of Mārgaśira, year Vyaya, Madhura Perumāḷḷa Rāju, the emperor of the three worlds, and Kāḷati Rāju, son of Kulaśēkhara Kāvēri, gave 100 *kuṇṭas* of land in Mahimalūru in Giribhāvivēlibōyaviḷa "which is attached to our chiefdom," to the Gods Mūlasthāna Tśayadēva and Nāgēśvaradēva of Mahimalūru. *Ibid.* No. 37.

40. In the Vishṇu temple. (Telugu.) Records that, on Wednesday, the eighth of the bright fortnight of Jyēshṭa, Ś. 1139, Bommi Nāyaka, younger brother of Gollapūṇḍi Bijapa Nāyaka, the protector of the kingdom of Erra Siddhanadēva Chōḍa Mahārāja, the ornament of the race of Manma, the establisher of the kingdom of Chōḍa Mahārāja, gave lands to Chenna Kēśava of Mahimalūru, the capital of Toṅkakūḍūrunāḍu in Tiruvaḍi Kāvalillu in Paṅkanāḍu. *Ibid.* No. 38, pp. 251—5.

Maṅgampaḷḷi.

41. South of Chenna Kēśavasvāmi temple. (Telugu.) Records that on Thursday, the tenth of the bright fortnight of Śravaṇa in Ś. 1331, Virōdhi, while Vīrapratāpa Dēva Rāya (II), son of Harihara Rāya, was ruling at Vijayanagar, Appaḷayya of the yajus Śākha and Bharadvāja gōtra, son of Mādhava Jōsyulu (who was the son of Yēputtila Appaya Jōsyulu), constructed a Raṅgamaṇṭapa in the Chennakēśāva temple at Bahadūrpuram or Guḍakuṇṭu (hamlet of Maṅgampaḷḷi).

Minagalu (hamlet of Veṅkaṭareḍḍipaḷḷi).

42. Near Liṅgarāzu Guṇṭa. (Telugu.) Records that on the thirtieth of *Mārgaśira* of Ś. 1532, *Sādhāraṇa*, Veligōṭi Timmanāyaniṅgāru issued this charitable edict to Liṅgarāju, Karaṇam of Minnakallu . . . The grant was 100 *kuṇṭaṣ* of wet land within the four boundaries in Minnakallu as a *sarvamānya*. *Ibid.* No. 40, pp. 257–8.

Minagallu (Minakallu).

43. On the boundary of Nallarāzupāḷem. (Telugu.) Records a grant as an *amaram* by Raṅganātharājuṅgāru to Raṅganātha of Mahimalūru. Ātmakūr No. 42, p. 259.

Nāvūru.

44. To the east of Nāgēśvara temple. (Tamil.) A record in the thirty-ninth year of the king Kulōttuṅga-Chōḷadēva, in the temple of Tirunāgēśvara at Nāvalūr. *Ibid.* No. 43, pp. 259-60.

45. On the defaced stone to south of Pōlēramma temple. (Telugu.) Records grant of two *paṭṭus* of paddy field to him . . . and states that whoever obstructs this charity will be considered to have killed a tawny cow near the Ganges. *Ibid.* No. 44, p. 260.

46. To the east of Pañchaliṅgāla temple. (Telugu.) Records that Śrīman Mahāmaṇḍalēśvara Rājādhirāja Paramakuśalava Prōshi Eṟṟasiddhi Rāja, Hari Bairapa Nāyaka, Ammanāyaka and Pahiṇḍināyaka, all of Gaṇḍavāraṇamupāḍu, having consecrated Siddha nāthadēva in the name of their fathers, gave a number of *paṭṭis* of land as *vriṭṭis* for enjoyments and decorations to that deity. *Ibid.* 45, pp. 261—3. [This Eṟṟasiddhi might be Eṟṟa Siddhaṇadēva Chōḍa. See No. 39 above.]

Pedda Annalūru.

47. Near tank sluice. A record under water and so not copied. *Ibid.* No. 46, p. 263.

Pellēru.

48. Opposite Chennakēśavasvāmi temple. (Telugu.) A partially defaced record of Śrīmat Kō . . . . nāyaniṅgāru on the fifteenth of *Vaiśākha* of the year *Prabhava*, in Ś. 1409. Records the construction of something at Prātapāḍu. *Ibid.* No. 47, pp. 263-4.

49. In front of the Sīta temple. (Telugu.) Records that on the fifteenth day of the bright half of Śravaṇa in Ś. 1544, Durmati, in the kingdom granted by Śrīmat Rājādhirāja Rāja Paramēśvara śrī Vīra Pratāpa Śrī Vīra Veṅkaṭapatidēva Mahārāya, to Veligōṭi Komāra Timmanāyaningāru, in Nellūru śīma, Veṅkaṭapatināyaniṅgāru gave the village Pellērlu as an *amaram* to Chintagumpalli Basappa Nāyaniṅgāru. The produce raised on dry fields should be divided into four shares, of which three should go to the ryot and one to the estate every year; and the grain raised under the tanks should be divided into three shares of which two should go to the ryot, and one to the estate every year. "In this manner whoever is the ruler should cause to be done." *Ibid.* No. 43, pp. 264-5. [The inscription is interesting as a record which fixes the obligations of landlord and tenant.]

Peramana.

50. Near Tummalamma temple. (Telugu.) Records the erection of the temple for the goddess Tummalamma by Bāchāmu Akkayya and Inagureḍḍi Kṛishṇamma on the second day of *Māgha*, Śubhakrit. Ātmakūr No. 49, pp. 265–6.

51. Near Āñjanēya temple. (Telugu.) Records gift of the village Yoḍalrupāḍu on the fifth day of the dark fortnight of Chaitra in Ś. 1196, the Dāmirapu Rāmināyaḍu and Mallināyaḍu for the religious merit of Nāgadēva Mahārāja. *Ibid.* No. 51, pp. 267–8.

52. Near Tummalamma temple. (Telugu.) Records that on the thirtieth day of Aśvija of the year Khara, in Ś. 1693, certain Dommaras gave a charitable edict to the great śakti (goddess) Tummalamma of Permana who is otherwise called Mahākāḷi and Mahādurgi. Signatures of Dommaras who roam over the earth carrying a drum named *Gangaḍōlu?* *Ibid.* No. 50, pp. 266–7. [The inscription is of interest for its mention of a dramatic company.]

Poṅgūru.

53. On western boundary. (Telugu.) Records grant (details gone) with libation of water, on the fifteenth of the bright fortnight, during a lunar eclipse (while a certain Oḍayalu was ruling the earth), by the son of Pōlināyaka, son of Mallimpāḍu. *Ibid.* No. 52, pp. 268–9.

Prabhāgiripaṭṇam.

54. On a stone in front of Perumāḷsvāmi temple. (Telugu.) Records gift of the village Nandirāyi in Prabhākarapaṭṇam on the eleventh day of the bright fortnight of Kārttika, Śubhakrit, Ś. 1524, by Śrīman-Mahāmaṇḍalēśvara Muddayadēva Mahārāja, son of Koṇḍa . . . dēva Mahārāja to Śrī Chennakēśavarāya of Paṭṇam, for providing light, refreshments, incense, etc. The donor acknowledges the suzerainty of Śrī Veṅkaṭarāya Mahārāyalu (I, 1586—1616) of Vijayanagar.

Punugōḍu.

55. Near Nallūruvāri well west of the village. (Telugu.) Records gift of land in the village for providing incense, lamps and the sixteen services to the deity of Nīlakaṇṭhēśvara, by Chintanūri Kēśanāyuḍu, while ruling the village of Ponuṅgōḍu, on Monday, the thirtieth day of the dark fortnight of *Vaiśākha*, Vishu, Ś. 1503. *Ibid.* No. 54, pp. 271—3.

Rājavōlu.

56. Near the *calingulah* (sluice) of the tank. (Telugu.) Records that on Monday, the tenth of the bright fortnight of Āshāḍha, Vikriti, in Ś. 1212, while Śrīman Maṇḍalēśvara Mallidēva Mahārāja, son of Śrīman Mahāmaṇḍalēśvara Vijayādityadēvamahārāja, was the king, Pinnama Nāyakuḍu, son of Maṇḍi Sunki Nāpakuni Kēśavanāyaka, the supreme lord of Orayūru, the best of cities, gave with libation of water, the village of Bayiṇḍipāḍu as an *ēkabhōgam* to the deity Aṇḍama of Koḍumana which was situated in Aṅgaḍamantanāḍu. *Nel.: Ins., Ātmakūr*, No. 55, pp. 273—6.

Śrikolanu.

57. Near a well east of the village. (Sanskrit in Telugu characters and Telugu.) Records gift of gold on Monday, the fourteenth of the dark fortnight of Māgha of the year . . . Ś. 1200, after setting up the deity. Mentions Śrī Muppaḍēndra, the prime minister of Pratāpa Rudra Dēva (Rudrammā ?).

Vasili.

58. From the outside of Varadarājasvāmi temple. (Telugu.) Records on Wednesday, the tenth of the bright fortnight of Pushya, Vyaya, in Ś. 1208, a gift by Śrīman Mahāmaṇḍalēśvara ma . . . Dēva Mahārāja for the religious merit of his father and his mother. *Ibid.*, No. 57, pp. 280–1.

59. In the Varadarājasvāmi temple. (Telugu.) Records a gift of something by the Dommaras who play on drums and perform on poles to the deity for the religious merit (of some person). *Ibid.*, No. 58, p. 281.

60. On a stone west of the mud-fort, with a Bhairava figure. Unread.

DARSI TALUK.

Alavalapāḍu.

61. North of the Āñjanēya temple. (Telugu.) Records that on Wednesday, the fifteenth of the bright fortnight of *Śravaṇa* of *Āṅgirasa*, Ś. 1194, Śrīman Mahāmaṇḍalēśvara Tripurāri Dēva Mahārāja, who was the director of 72 offices, gave for providing enjoyments to Śrī Tripurāntaka Dēva, the village of Alavalapāḍu in Pōligoṇḍa sthala with its four boundaries and with its income, after pouring water into the hand of Śrīmat Triyambaka Śivāchārya, the worshipper of the illustrious lotus feet of Śrī Tripurāntaka Dēva, for the increase of his life, health and wealth. *Nel. Ins., Darsi*, No. 1, pp. 282—6. Tripurāri is called the worshipper of the lotus feet of Rudra Dēva Mahārāja, whose *birudas* are enumerated. Rudradēva was not improbably queen Rudrammā of Warangal who assumed a man's name on her accession.

Annavaram Agrahāram.

62. At the twenty-sixth mile on the road. (Telugu in Chāḷukyan characters.) A record of Śrī Vikramāditya Mahārāja, descendant of the Śrī Chāḷukya dynasty. Records some gift. The whole is unintelligible. *Ibid.*, No. 2, p. 287.

Baḍugulēru.

63. On a stone near a well. (Telugu.) A record on the tenth of the bright fortnight of Āśvija in Ś. 1649, Virōdhi. Mentions Māchavarapu Mūrti Rāju, the karaṇam of the village of Baḍugulēru, Gaṇṭa Yarrā Reḍḍi, descendant of the Kūnapaiḍipaḷḷa gōtra, Gauta Timma Reḍḍi, etc. [The years do not correspond.]

Baṭlapaḷḷi.

64. In a field to the north. (Telugu.) A mere record of the name Bhīma Mallaparāju, son of Nandipāṭi Akkirāju. *Nel. Ins., Darsi*, No. 4, p. 288.

65. In a garden to west. (Telugu.) Records on the fifth of the bright fortnight of Māgha of Vikriti, that a well was the charity of a resident of Bhaṭlapaḷḷi *agrahāra.* Records also the construction of a Śiva temple to Mallēśvara by the same person. *Ibid.*, No. 5, p. 289.

Bhimavaram.

66. Opposite the Bhīmēśvara temple. (Telugu.) Records on the fifth day of the bright fortnight of Mārgaśira of Khara, Ś. 1212, that a certain Chōḍa-Mallidēva Mahārāja consecrated the image of Gōpālanātha in Bhīmavaram and presented to the deity a field where four *puṭṭis* and ten *tūms* can be sown for providing *amritapaḍi* (food for the God), worship, etc., . . . and a wet field for maintaining a light for the religious merit of Pratāpa Rudradēva Mahārāja. Records also gift of another *mānyam* for the religious merit of Mōpu Veṅkaṁgāru. *Ibid.*, No. 6, pp. 289—91. [The years do not correspond.]

Bōdanampāḍu.

67. On tank bund north of village. (Telugu.) The character of the record is Chāḷukyan, and the sense could not be made out. *Ibid.*, No. 7, pp. 291–2.

Boddikurapāḍu.

68. Opposite Vishṇu temple. (Telugu.) Records that a certain karaṇam should maintain a charity details of which are not legible. *Ibid.*, No. 8, pp. 292–3.

Chandalūru.

69. On a stone in the bed of the tank. (Telugu.) Records on Thursday, the fifteenth of the bright fortnight of Kārttika of Ānanda, in Ś. 1416, Kasvānēnigāru, son of Bāllimalli Abbanēni, caused to be dug two channels, one at the southern end of the tank bund and the other at the northern end, and strengthened the tank for the religious merit of his son Dhadhipati Rao who was ruling Chandalūru. *Ibid.*, No. 9, p. 293.

Darsi.

70. On stone in front of Śiva temple. (Telugu.) Records in the reign of Kākatīya Pratāpa Rudradēva Mahārāja on the day of Vishu Saṅkrānti, in *Rudhirōdgāri*, that Tattinūri Nāndēvarājulu gave for providing enjoyment to Svayambhudēva of Darsi, ten *puṭṭis* of land in different villages, as a *sarvamānya*, for the religious merit of the Mahārāja and of his own father Jayadēvaniṅgāru. *Nel. Ins., Darsi*, No. 10, pp. 294-5. [The cyclic and Śaka years do not correspond.]

71. In the Śiva temple. (Telugu.) Records that on the fifth of the dark fortnight of Māgha of Śrīmukha, Chennam Śeṭṭi of the Kummara (potter) caste caused to be built a temple to Chenamalaya (Śiva) at Pōlavaram for the religious merit of his parents. *Ibid.*, No. 11, p. 295.

72. In front of stone bearing a Hanūmān. (Telugu.) Records that on the fifteenth day of the bright fortnight of Kārttika in *Pramādicha* in Ś. 1235, under the orders of Pōtaya Śāhiṇaṁgāru, the servant of Śrīman Maṇḍalēśvara Kākatīya Pratāpa Rudradēva Mahārāja Mallinandavanaṁgāru, planted a garden for Śrīman Tripurāntaka Mahādēva in Tripurāntaka village, and gave for the site of that garden ten *puṭṭis* of land as a *vriṭṭi* and *sarvamānya*. *Ibid.*, No. 19, pp. 296-7.

73. On a stone near the Achannacheruvu. (Telugu.) Records that on Thursday, the fifteenth of the bright fortnight of Māgha of Rākshasa, in Ś. 1317, Śrīman Maṇḍalēśvara Āsnadēva Mahārāja constructed a tank in the name of his mother Aryamādēvi, a temple to Pratāpa Gōpinātha of Darsi, etc., and made various gifts including twenty *puṭṭis* of land north of Darsi to Bōjūri Vaju, the *Vojulu* (artisan) who constructed this temple. *Ibid.*, No. 13, pp. 297—303.

73-A. C.P. grant of a great-grandson of Śrīvīra Kūrchavarman (the portion dealing with the real donor being lost) whose epithets are those of Skandavarman I and Skandavarman II (see *Ind. Antq.*, V, p. 51 and VIII, p. 168). The grant was issued from Daśanapura. Venkayya believes that the donor of this grant was the Simhavarman II who issued the Pikire grant. See *Ep. Ind.*, I, pp. 397-8 and *Mad. Ep. Rep.*, 1906, pp. 46-7.

Dēkanakoṇḍa.

74. To the west. On a stone standing on a rock. (Telugu.) A record of Siddhirāju Timmarāju who constructed a bhōga maṇṭapa (pleasure hall) to Śrī Chennarāya. *Nel. Ins., Darsi*, No. 14, p. 304.

Dēvavaram.

75. Near the well. On four sides of a stone. (Telugu.) Records on Thursday, the first of the dark fortnight of Jyēshṭa of the year Plava, Ś. 1464, that Veṅkaṭapati of the Parakutla gōtra, grandson of Śēsham Raṅgappagāru, and son of Chennappagāru, constructed this well, for the religious merit of Gādi Lakshmīnarasiṁha. Records also that Śēsham Veṅkaṭapati constructed a well in the village of Divvaram (Dēvavaram) which belonged to Rāja Śrī Gummaḍappa Rāghavappa Nāyaniṅgāru. *Nel. Ins., Darsi*, No. 15, pp. 304—7.

Dōnakoṇḍa.

76. In the temple of Gaṅgamma. A record in Telugu. *Ibid.*, No. 16, p. 308.

77. On a stone in the temple of Madiyaladēvata. (Telugu.) Records on the fifteenth of the bright half on Nija Āśvija of the year *Naḷa*, the perpetual devotion of Pōtaya Jayaliḍu, son of Veṅgala, the ***pūjāri*** (priest) of Śrī-Dōnakoṇḍa Gaṅgādēvi. *Ibid.*, No. 17, p. 308.

78. (Telugu.) On a stone in Gaṅgammā temple. Records a gift by Vīra Pratāpa Śrī-Kṛishṇarāya to Gaṅga Paramēśvari of Dōnakoṇḍa. *Ibid.*, No. 18, p. 309.

79. (Telugu.) On a stone in the temple of Gaṅgamma. Records that on the fifth day of the dark fortnight of Kārttika of Vyaya, Ś. 1328, while the son of Dēvarāya Mahārāyulu (II) was ruling the kingdom, Kapratidēva *alias* Chāma Voḍayalu, who was ruling the village, constructed maṇṭapas and a stone temple to Māṅkalamma (goddess), besides a temple to the *viralu* (heroes) and a fortified enclosure. *Ibid.*, No. 19, pp. 310—2.

80. (Telugu.) On a stone in the temple of Gaṅgamma. Records that on the eleventh of the bright fortnight of Kārttika of Paridhāvi, in Ś. 1354, in the reign of Vīra Pratāpa Dēvarāya (II), Dēvamahārāju, son of Gummaḍūri Koṇḍurāju Chinnirāju, gave a village to Gaṅga Paramēśvari, the goddess of all the sciences, besides some gold.

81. (Telugu.) On a stone in front of Gaṅgamma temple. An incomplete record in the month of Vaiśākha of the year *Naḷa*. . . . *Ibid.*, No. 21, p. 315.

82. (Telugu.) In front of the Gaṅgamma temple. Records, on Monday, the fifteenth of the bright fortnight of Pushya in year Pārthiva, Ś. 1447, lunar eclipse, a gift by Kṛishṇarāya Mahārāya to Gaṅga Paramēśvari of the village of Dēvara Dōnakoṇḍa, which was the principal seat of the Nandagōpa and the Baḍugula castes. *Ibid.*, No. 22, pp. 315—8.

83. In the Gaṅgamma temple. (Telugu.) Records that on Thursday, the fifteenth of the bright fortnight of Māgha of the year Plavaṅga, Ś. 1349, Rāmayadēva Mahārāja, son of Śrīman Mahāmaṇḍalēśvara Antyambaragaṇḍa Gummuḍūri Kāmayadēva

Mahārāja, made a gift to Kalā-Paramēśvari of Dōnakoṇḍa for the merit of Śrī-Vīra Pratāpa Dēvarāya Mahārāya (II). *Nel. Ins., Darsi*, No. 23, pp. 319—21.

Edururallapāḍu.

84. (Telugu.) Records that on Thursday, the fifteenth of the bright fortnight of Kārttika of the year Prabhava, Ś. 1189, Śrīmat Komminayuḍu, the governor (Rakshadhīśvara) of Taḍlūru, gave lands to lord Mallināthadēva of Pratishṭapura for the merit of Mahāmaṇḍalēśvara Śiṅgayadēva Gaḍidēva of the race of Karikāla of Rudramahārāja, the ruler of Koṇḍavīḍu, of his parents and of himself. *Ibid.*, No. 24, pp. 321—3.

Gaṅgāvaram.

85. In the tank bed. (Telugu.) Records that on Thursday, the thirteenth of the bright fortnight of Māgha of the year Ānanda, Ś. 1176, Gaṇapatidēva Mahārāja gave to Śrīmaṭ Śānta Śivagurudēva, the worshipper of the divine and illustrious lotus feet of Tripurāntakadēvara, whose head was adorned with the excellent lotus feet of Śrīmat Rāja Gurudēva, the village named Chalamatti Gaṇḍapuram, for the setting up of the image of Śrī-Gaṅgēśvara in the holy place of Tripurāntaka. *Ibid.*, No. 25, pp. 323—5.

86. In the Āñjanēya temple. (Telugu.) Records gift in the reign of Pratāpa Rudradēva Mahārāja.

87. In the tank bed. (Telugu.) Records that Śrīman Mahāmaṇḍalēśvara Kākatīya Gaṇapatidēva Mahārāja presented Chalamatti Gaṇḍapuram with all its income to Śrī Tripurāntaka Mahādēvēśvara. *Ibid.*, No. 27, p. 326.

88. In the tank bed. (Telugu.) Records that on Thursday, the thirteenth of the bright fortnight of Māgha of the year Ānanda, Ś. 1176, Śrīman Mahāmaṇḍalēśvara Haridēva Chōḍa Mahārāju gave the village named Chalamatti Gaṇḍapuram, for the setting up of the image of Śrī-Paru (Parama) Mahēśvaradēva at the holy place of Śrī-Tripurāntaka, to Śrīmat Śānta Śiva Gurudēva, the worshipper of Tripurāntakadēva. *Ibid.*, No. 28, pp. 327-8.

Guḍipāḍu.

89. Opposite the Vēṇugōpālasvāmi temple. (Telugu.) Records the gift of a Bṛindāvanam by . . . Kumāra Mallaṇa. *Ibid.*, No. 29, p. 328.

Kallūru.

90. On the tank bund near the Gaṅgādhara temple. (Telugu and Sanskrit.) Records that on the first of the bright half of Bhādrapada of the year Paridhāvi, Ś. 1594, the Pedda-Samudram tank was constructed by Mēdarameṭla Peddammaṅgāru of the gōtra of Tammanūru, the great-granddaughter of Rāyavināyani

Gōpāla Nāyanivāru of the gōtra of Madali, the granddaughter of Raṅgappa Nāyanivāru, and the daughter of Veṅkaṭādri Nāyanivāru. *Nel. Ins., Darsi*, No. 31, pp. 329–30.

91. On the tank bund near Gaṅgādhara temple. (Telugu.) Records a gift on the first of the dark half of Pushya of the year Sādhāraṇa, Ś. 1292, to Gaṅgēśvaradēva. *Ibid.*, No. 32, pp. 330–1.

92. On four pieces of a stone on the tank bund near Gaṅgādhara temple. (Telugu.) Records that on Saturday, the tenth of the dark fortnight of Pushya of the year Sādhāraṇa, Ś. 1292, Anapōti Nāyuṇḍu presented an oil mill to Gaṅgēśvaradēva for providing an oil-bath for the God, for the religious merit of his uncle Bāri Nāyuḍu and his aunt Nūṅkasāni. *Ibid.*, No. 33, pp. 331–2.

Kambhampāḍu.

93. To the south of the Āñjanēya temple. (Telugu.) Records that on Wednesday, the fifth of the bright fortnight of Śravaṇa in year Paridhāvi, Ś. 1534, the temple for Sōmēśvara was erected by Bhāva Śiripurapu Yatni Maṇirāju for the religious merit of his guru Śrī-Parvatārādhya, his grandfather Vīramarāju, his grandmother Vīramā, his father Lakna, his mother Vīrama and his elder brother Jaggarāju. *Ibid.*, No. 34, pp. 332–3.

Kōcherlakōṭa.

94. Near Vīraṇṇabāvi. (Sanskrit and Telugu.) Records that on Monday, the tenth of the bright fortnight of Jyēshṭa of the year Sādhāraṇa, Ś. 1232, in the reign of Pratāpa Rudradēva Mahārāja, Śrīmat Dēvari Nāyaniṅgāru, son of Śrīman Māchaya Nāyaka, set up the images of Gaurīśvara, Sōmēśvara and Mahādēva by constructing temples at Koṭṭacherla and Mācherla ; appointed Dalamu Varadanna and Tammalla-Peddini as priests ; granted *vriṭṭi* fields as *sarvamānya* for providing decorations to the deities, besides a *pullāri mānyam* (a grant of pasture land free of tax for cattle belonging to the deity), the *śuṅkam*, etc. *Ibid.*, No. 35, pp. 333—41, where the local *sthalapurāṇa* is also summarized.

95. At the gate of the temple of Śrī Varadarāja Svāmi. (Telugu.) An unintelligible record.

96. On a stone in the temple of Varadarājasvāmi. (Telugu.) Records that, on the eleventh of the bright fortnight of Mārgaśira of the year Vijaya, Ś. 1455, Chintaguṇṭa Chennamarāju, constructed a temple at Kōcherlakōṭa for the merit of Mannārappa Nāyaniṅgāru, set up the image of Janārdanadēva and gave some land in Muddapāḍu village for the performance of the marriage festival and for providing food. *Ibid.*, No. 37, pp. 342—4.

97. In the temple of Varadarājasvāmi. (Telugu.) Records that on Sunday, the first of the dark fortnight of Māgha, Ś. 1089, Malli Peddidēvulu gave a *paṭṭu* of land for providing worship and daily offering to Śrī Varadarājasvāmi for the merit of Srīman Mahāmaṇḍaleśvara Paṇṭadēva Chōḷa Mahārājulu. *Nel. Ins., Darsi,* No. 38, pp. 344-5.

98. In the Varadarājasvāmi temple. (Telugu.) Records that on Wednesday, the fourteenth of the dark fortnight of Durmukhi, Ś. 1064, some wet land in rear of Jamasamudram of Krottacheruvu was granted to Śrī Mallaṇadēva. *Ibid.*, No. 39, p. 345.

99. In the Varadarājasvāmi temple. (Telugu.) Records on Thursday, the eleventh of the dark fortnight of Vaiśākha, in Ś. 1066, the gift of land under Vēmacheruvu of Krottacheruvu to Śrīdēva, and to Kēśava for providing daily offerings and food. *Ibid.*, No. 40, pp. 345-6.

100. On a pillar in the temple of Varadarājasvāmi. (Telugu.) Records on Monday, the fifteenth of the dark fortnight of Mārgaśira in year Ānanda, Ś. 1057, that Tulliḷla Pemmarāju constructed a *mukhamaṇṭapa* in the temple of Śrī Varadarājasvāmi. *Ibid.*, No. 41, pp. 346-7.

Korlamaḍugu.

101. *C.P. No.* 12 *of Nel. Ins.*—A Telugu grant, dated on the fifteenth of the bright half of Māgha, year Vijaya, Ś. 1360, by Rāja Śrī Vēḷugōṭi Kastūri Raṅgapaṭi Nāyaniṅgāru, of 8 *kuchchalas* of dry land and wet land sowable with 18 *tūms* of paddy to Varadarājasvāmi of Kōcharlakōṭa during a lunar eclipse.

102. In a street. (Telugu.) An illegible record. *Ibid.*, No. 42, p. 347.

Kottapaḷḷi.

103. On a stone in front of the Sōmēśvara temple. (Telugu.) Records that, in the year Pramōdūta, Ś. 1079, Śrīman Mahāmaṇḍaleśvara Vijayādityadēva Mahārāja, who was descended from the family of Mukkanti Kāḍuveṭṭi, gave to Śrī Sōmēśvaradēva of Korraḍlamaḍugu a field of ten *tūms* of paddy on the northern side of the village. This *vriṭṭi* was given with libation of water to Muppaṇa Paṇḍita. *Ibid.*, No. 43, pp. 347-8.

Kurichēḍu.

104. In the temple. (Telugu.) Records that Tammala Vīrajiyyalu and his wife Dāda Sāni daily make one thousand salutations together to Śrī Kāḷahasti Īśvara of Kurichēḍu. *Ibid.*, No. 44, p. 349.

105. In the Śiva temple. (Telugu.) Records that on Monday, the eleventh of the dark fortnight of Śravaṇa, Ś. 1092, a certain person gave a *paṭṭu* of wet field for providing a perpetual lamp to Divyakīrti Vara Mahādēva of Kurichēḍu, for the religious merit of Śrīmat Kulōttuṅga Rājendra Chōḍa Mahārāja. *Ibid.*, No. 45, pp. 349-50.

Mangyanapūḍi.

106. Near a well. (Telugu.) Records that on Thursday, the fifth of the bright half of Vaiśākha in *Manmatha*, Ś. 1337, in the reign of Dēvarāya Mahārāyulu (II) Jannappa Murārinēni Chennammanēṇḍu, son of Jēdēvarāṇa Jannapanēni Bamminâyuḍu, gave 4 *puṭṭis* of land to Vallaki Peddi Avubala Reḍḍi, and Pina Siganti Reḍḍi, for some charitable purpose. *Nel. Ins.*, *Darsi*, No. 46, pp. 350–1.

107. On the tank bund to the east of the village. (Telugu.) Records that on Wednesday, the fifth of bright half of Śravaṇa in Śaumya year, Ś. 1351, in the reign of Dēvarāya Mahārāyulu (II), Maṅginapūṇḍi was made over, at the request of Chilalasālu Vissanu Oḍayaṁgāru, to be ruled by Kāḍiruchirāju Liṅgarāju. Records that the tank in front of the village which was in ruins, ordered to be maintained, at the instance of the local officer Bommarāju Śiṅgarāju, out of 10 *marutu* of land given for its maintenance by Nāgarāju, the chief officer of the village. *Ibid.*, No. 47, pp. 352—4.

Mannēpaḷḷi.

108. On two fragments of a stone opposite Chennakēśava temple. (Sanskrit and Telugu.) Records that Śrīman Mahāmaṇḍalēśvara Ballichōḍa Mahārāja, the son of Kāma, grandson of Veṅka and great-grandson of Nanni Chōḍa, gave, on the occasion of Uttarāyaṇa Saṅkrānti, Ś. 1067, the village of Dēvarampaḷḷi to Śrīmat Mallēśvara Mahādēvaru of Mānyapaḷḷi for sacrifices, worship, offerings, lighting and decoration to his person. The priest of the temple took possession of it and he, his sons and grandsons should enjoy it and maintain the charity. *Ibid.*, No. 48, pp. 354—6.

109. On the road to Viṭhalapuram. (Sanskrit and Telugu.) Records that on the occasion of Uttarāyaṇa Saṅkrānti, Ś. 1088, Śrīman Mahāmaṇḍalēśvara Balli Chōḍa Mahārājulu granted three *puṭṭis* for providing daily offering to Śrī Chōḍēśvara Mahādēvaru of Mānyapalli in Guṇḍakāḍu. *Ibid.*, No. 49, pp. 356—9.

Mārella.

110. Opposite the Vēṇugōpalasvāmi temple. (Telugu.) Records that on Saturday, the seventh of the bright fortnight of Śravaṇa of the year Hēviḷambi, Ś. 1459, Koṇḍamarāju of the Kaṇva Śākha, of the Bhāradvāja gōtra, grandson of Mārella Nāgarāju and son of Abbaḷarāju, constructed a temple and set up the image of Madanagōpinātha. *Ibid.*, No. 50, pp. 359–60.

Mullamūru.

111. On the Āñjanēya stone near the Vēṇugōpālasvāmi temple. (Telugu.) Records that on the tenth day of the bright fortnight of

Māgha in year Ananda, Rampa Anantabhaṭlu caused this edict to be inscribed. *Nel. Ins., Darsi,* No. 51, pp. 360–1.

Nāyuḍupāḷem.

112. On Bollikoṇḍa in front of the temple. (Telugu.) Records that on Thursday, the tenth of the bright fortnight of Kārttika of the year Vyaya, Ś. 1519, Śiṅgaṛāju, *karaṇam* of Māchchapuram, Gaṅgarāju's son Koṇḍamarāju, Veṅgarāju, son of Koṇḍamarāju, and Vobulurāju, son of Veṅgarāju, who set up the image of Anumanta (Hanūmān) Perumāḷ of Māchchapuram Bollikoṇḍa, presented for *Amritapaḍi* (sacred food) to Hanumanta, 1/16 field to the east of the Banri sluice for the religious merit of their ancestors. Records also grant at ⅛ *tūm* on every *puṭṭi* (measured) at the threshing floor of all kinds of grain raised in their *karaṇam mānyam* land. *Ibid.,* No. 52, pp. 361–2.

Pōlavaram.

113. In the garden of K. Kōṭi Reḍḍi. (Telugu.) Records that on the holy occasion of Kṛishṇashṭami (birth of Kṛishṇa), the eighth of the dark fortnight of Śravaṇa in Ś. 1451, Virōdhi, Rāyasam Ayyappa made a gift of land to Śrī Tiruvēṅkaṭādri. Records also that while Śrī Kṛishṇadēva Mahārāyulu was ruling, Ayyapparasayya, the son of Vēmarasayya and the subordinate of Rāyasam Timmarasayya, who was of the Āśvalāyana sūtra of the Bhāradvāja gōtra, and student of the Rik Śākha, gave the village of Pōlavaram in Addaṅki Sīma in Koṇḍavīḍu Rājya for providing *amritapaḍi* (sacred food) to Śrī Tiruvēṅkaṭādri Nātha. *Ibid.,* No. 53, pp. 362—5.

Pōlēpalli.

114. In the Śiva temple. (Telugu.) Records that on Sunday, the fifth of the dark half of Māgha of the year Śrīmukha, Kummara Channam Śeṭṭi constructed a temple to Channamalaya of Pōlavaram for the religious merit of his mother Dadema and his father Gōpi Śeṭṭi. *Ibid.,* No. 54, pp. 365–6.

114-A. *C.P. No.* 10 *of Nel. Ins.*—(Nandināgari alphabet and Sanskrit language.) A grant of king Achyuta Rāya of Vijayanagar in Ś. 1458, Durmukhi (Kārttika, Śukladvādaśi), during his stay on the bank of the river Tuṅgabhadra, in the presence of the deity Viṭṭhalēśvara. The object of the grant was the village of Pōlēpalli, in the Mahārājya of Koṇḍavīdu in the *Sīma* of Kōcharla Kōṭa *alias* Yeruvanāḍu. The donee was Annama, son of Chintapalli Siṅganārya, of the Viśvāmitra gōtra, Āśvalāyana Sūtra and Rik Śākha. [A large part of the grant is identical with the Unamañjēri plate of Achyuta and also of the Hampi inscription of Kṛishṇarāya. The incomplete grant of Penubarti (C.P. No. 11 of *Nel. Ins.*) is identical in its available portio with the present one.]

Potakamūru.

115. Below the dhvajastambham of the Vēṇugōpālasvāmi temple. (Telugu.) An unintelligible record.

Pōtavaram.

116. To the west of the Rāmaliṅgasvāmi temple. (Telugu.) Records that, on Monday, the twelfth of the bright fortnight of Vaiśākha of the year Vibhava, Ś. 1370, Paṇṭa Burrēla Chinama Reḍḍiṅgāru set up the images of Achchaḍa Pōtavara, Rāma Dēva, and Śrī Kēśava Perumāḷ and founded an endowment, for providing daily offerings to those deities, consisting of 10 *tūms* of dry land and 10 *kuṇṭās* of wet land at Reḍḍipāḍu. *Nel. Ins., Darsi*, No. 56, pp. 366–7.

Poṭlapāḍu.

117. Opposite the Vīrabhadra temple. (Telugu.) Records a gift on Thursday, the fifteenth of the bright fortnight of Āśvija, in Ś. 1151, Pramādi, on the occasion of a lunar eclipse, for providing decorations, daily worship, sandal, musk, camphor, saffron, milk, etc., to Śrī Tripurāntaka Mahādēva and to the dancing girls of the temple. *Ibid.*, No. 57, pp. 367—71.

118. In front of the Vīrabhadrasvāmi temple. (Sanskrit and Telugu.) Records gift of cows, jewels and land. An incomplete record.

119. In front of the Vīrabhadrasvāmi temple. (Telugu.) Records a gift by Śrī Tripurāridēva Mahārāja, feudatory of Rudradēva Mahārāja of the Kākatīya line.

120. Opposite the Vīrabhadrasvāmi temple. (Telugu.) Records gift on Tuesday, the fifteenth of the bright half of Āśvija in Ś. 1157, Pramādi, on the holy occasion of a lunar eclipse to Śrīman Mahādēva of Śrī Tripurāntaka for providing decorations to the deity. *Ibid.*, No. 60, pp. 375–6.

Rājampaḷḷi.

121. In front of the Gōpālasvāmi temple. (Telugu.) Records that on the eleventh of the bright half of Kārttika in Ś. 1651, Viḷambi, Gōpanaṅgāru, of the Damarti gōtra, grandson of Dhūḷipaḷḷa Akkanaṅgāru and son of Gurvanaṅgāru, had the consecration performed in the temple of Gōpālasvāmi of Rājampaḷḷi. A grant also to the three artizans who carved this temple. *Ibid.*, No. 61, pp. 376–7.

122. Opposite the Janārdanasvāmi temple. (Telugu.) Records that on the tenth of Śravaṇa in Ś. 1597, Rākshasa, some fields were presented to Gōpāla of Rājampaḷḷi for food *(amritapaḍi)*. *Ibid.*, No. 62, p. 378.

123. Opposite the Janārdanasvāmi temple. (Telugu.) Records that on Thursday, the tenth of the bright fortnight of

Kārttika of the year Chitrabhānu, Ś. 1324, Tātireḍḍi and Sandramalapaḷḷi Śiṅgama Śeṭṭi consecrated Śrī Gōpināthadēva of Rājyapaḷḷi. At the time of consecration Rājannaṁgāru and others dedicated lands in Rājyampaḷḷi and elsewhere. *Tūms, puṭṭis, maruta, kuṇṭa, na* are the technical terms used. *Nel. Ins., Darsi,* No. 63, pp. 379—82.

Rudrasamudram.

124. On the tank bund. (Telugu.) Records a *mānyam* granted to *Upparas* (diggers) on the fifteenth of Nija Bhādrapāda in year Virōdhi for their having constructed the tank at Vāviḷḷapaḷḷi. *Ibid.* No. 64, pp. 382–3.

Sāmantapūḍi.

125. On a wall of the Āñjanēya temple. (Telugu.) Records that on Sunday, the fifteenth of the bright fortnight of Jyēshṭa in Ś. 1460, Viḷambi, Bhāskarayyaṅgāru, who was of the Arṭāri gōtra, who was the grandson of Sāminēni and son of Mummaṇi, constructed a temple in the village of Sāmantapūṇḍi and set up the image of Śrī Hanumaṅta for the religious merit of his son Yellaya and of his daughter-in-law Yellamā. *Ibid.*, No. 65, p. 383.

126. Opposite Chennakēśava temple. (Telugu.) Records that on Thursday, the fifteenth of the bright fortnight of Chaitra of the year Manmatha, Ś. 1458, for the religious merit of Appaḷayya, the son of Palleḷa Basuvanāyaniṅgāru of the illustrious Veruṭla gōtra, made a temple, a tope and a tank to Kēśavanātha of Sāmantapūṇḍi. *Ibid.*, No, 66, p. 384.

Śivarāmpuram.

127. To the west in a tamarind tope. (Telugu.) Records that on Friday, the fifth of the bright fortnight of Kārttika of the year Jayavibhava, Ś. 1250, a wet field of four *kuṇṭās* under the tank of Pollabōyaniyūru was presented to Agastyaliṅga for the merit of Bayyaparāju and Mārasāniamma. *Ibid.*, No. 67, pp. 385–6.

128. To the north of the Agastyēśvara temple. (Telugu.) Records that in Ś. 1069, Prabhava, Śrīmān Mahāmaṇḍalēśvara Bālaya-chōḍadēva gave a *paṭṭi* field to the deity Agastya of Sthānamāpāliṭidāna (?) for a perpetual lamp. *Ibid.*, No. 68, pp. 386—8.

Sōmavarapāḍu.

129. *C.P. No.* 21 *of Nel. Ins.*—A record of Śrī Vīrabhadra Rāya Mahārāya, evidently a scion of the Gaṇapatis of Warangal, dated in the twenty-third year of his reign, on Thursday, the fifteenth of the bright fortnight of Kumbha, making the gift of the village of Sōmavaram in the Addaṅki *Śima* to Kākolli Nārāyaṇa Paṇḍit of Koṇḍavīḍu. The king had the titles of Paramabhaṭṭāraka, Lord of the Drāviḷa country and of Kalubarga, the capital of the Karnāṭaka yielding a revenue of nine crores.

130. On a big rock near Gaṅgamma temple. (Telugu.) Records that Śrīman Mahāmaṇḍalēśvara Paramēśvara Abhidēva Malidēva Mahārāja of the Pallava line, Lord of Kāñchi, etc., built a temple and set up the image of Mallikārjunadēva in Viddarakāntārapuram in Vishu Saṅkrānti, Ś. 1140. *Nel. Ins., Darsi*, No. 69, p. 388--90.

Taḷḷūru.

131. Near the Vēṇugōpālasvāmi temple. (Telugu.) Records that on Monday, the second of the bright fortnight of Vaiśākha in Ś. 1227, Viśvāvasu, Chennakēśava Perumāḷ of Taḷḷūru was consecrated, and that Koṇḍapi, Vāyapōti Nāyuḍu bought and gave ten *tūms* of paddy field in Chiṇtaguṇṭa swamp as a *mānyam* for the religious merit of his parents. In the same locality Mummaḍi, the son of Padmākshaḍu, and Śrīraṅganāthuḍu, son of Kanchikuḍu, bought and gave ten *tūms* of land for the religious merit of their parents. Śrīmān Mahāmaṇḍalēśvara Pratāpa Rudradēva Mahārāja (1295—1323) is mentioned. *Ibid.*, No. 70, pp. 391-2.

132. Near the Āñjanēya temple. (Telugu.) Records gift of gold for the deity Gōpinātha. *Ibid.*, 71, pp. 392-3.

Tammalūru.

133. West of the village. (Telugu.) Records on Thursday, the fifth of the bright fortnight of Phalguna in Āṅgirasa, Ś. 1194, in the reign of Kākatīya Rudrayyadēva Mahārāja, Mallanadēvilammaṅgāru, daughter of Śrī Gōpāladēva, the paternal uncle of Śrīman Mahāmaṇḍalēśvara Chakra Nārāyana Śrī Mādhavadēvarāja, the Governor of Addaṅki sthala, set up the image of Gōpīśvaradēva in the name of her father at Tammalūr, and gave lands and a flower garden. *Ibid.*, No. 72, pp. 393-4.

Tsalivēndra.

134. Below the hill near a figure of Gaṅgamma. (Telugu.) Records that, on the fifteenth of the bright fortnight of Pushya in Ś. 1509, Vyaya, Timmanāyaniṅgāru, of the gōtra of Inigela, son of Dāmera Kēśamanāyaḍu of the lineage of Padmanāyaka, excavated Tellamgaḍḍa tank, set up an image of Gaṅgādēvi, and issued a deed giving a *kuchchala* of land to that deity. *Ibid.*, No. 73, pp. 395-6.

Tummerlapāḍu.

135. (Telugu.) Records the gift of the village named Pōtalapāḍu and gold to Śrī Gaṅgēśvaradēvaru of the holy place of Śrī Tripurāntaka for providing the eight enjoyments for the deity. *Ibid.*, No. 74, pp. 397-8.

Vēmparāla.

136. On the road to Kambhampāḍu. (Telugu.) Records a boundary line.

GUDUR TALUK.

Akkampēṭa.

137. On the Nandi miṭṭa. (Telugu.) Records gift of land, on the occasion of Vishama Saṅkrānti in Ś. 1505, for the religious merit of Śrīman Mahāmaṇḍalēśvara Bhujabala Nalla Siddhana Dēva Chōḍa Mahārājulu, for performing daily offerings to Śrī Yajñēśvara of Khāḍipūṇḍi. *Nel. Ins., Gudur* No. 1, pp. 399–400.

138. In Paddapāṭi field. (Telugu.) Records that the inscription was planted by Rāmachandra Sūrapa on Monday, the thirtieth of the dark fortnight of Chaitra in the year Raudri. "Whoever covets the *mēra* grain of the tank and does not give it will be considered to have been born to a donkey."

Brahmadēvam.

139. In a street to the south. (Telugu.) A fragment relating to work done to a tank and a tope. *Ibid.*, No. 3, p. 401.

Chennūru.

140. On the wall of Chennakēśava temple. (Tamil.) Records that in the thirteenth year of the reign of the emperor Vīrarājēndrachōḷadēva, in the month of Āni, "we three, Mēḍabhaṭṭan, Sāmibhaṭṭan and Śaṅkarabhaṭṭan (having assembled) at the temple of Nīlakaṇṭha at Cheruvanūr, sold our shares at Kumbakkappūṇḍi to Puḍōlabhaṭṭa, the son of Anniṭṭa (Agnishṭa), so that he may enjoy the share just as we enjoyed (i.e., with all our rights) it before, in order to marry Perumāḷ, the son of Mēḍabhaṭṭan." *Ibid.*, No. 4, pp. 401–2.

141. In the Chennakēśava temple at Chennūru. (Tamil.) A record in the eighteenth year of Rājarājadēva (III), relating to gift of a lamp by Namaśivayya. *Ibid.*, No. 5 pp. 402–3.

142. A record in the nineteenth year of Rājarājadēva (III), relating to gift of a lamp by Namaśivayya. *Ibid.*, No. 6.

143. A record of a list of persons who presented a lamp. *Ibid.*, No. 7.

144. A record in the twenty-seventh year of Rājarājadēva (III), Ś. 1164 (A.D. 1242–43), gift of a lamp by Piminā yakkan. *Ibid.*, No. 8, pp. 402–3.

145. In the Somēśvara temple. (Tamil.) Records apparently the gift of a pillar in Ś. 1191 (A.D. 1209—70). *Ibid.*, No. 9.

146. Records in the thirtieth year of Rājarājadēva (III), gift of 1½ *māḍai* for a lamp by Eraman. *Ibid.*, No. 10.

147. Records gift of a pillar and a drum in Ś. 1190 (A.D. 1268–69). *Nel Ins., Gudur,* No. 11.

148. A record in the twenty-eighth year of Rājarājadēva, gift of 1½ *māḍai* for a lamp by Īśan Kōśan. *Ibid.,* No. 12.

149. A record in the twenty-sixth year of Rājarājadēva, gift of 1½ *māḍai* for a lamp by Bhayiri Cheṭṭi. *Ibid.,* No. 13.

150. A record in the fifteenth year of Rājarājadēva, gift of 1 *māḍai* for a lamp. *Ibid.,* No. 14.

151. Records gift of a lamp in the reign of Kulōttuṅga Chōḷa (III ?). *Ibid.,* No. 15.

152. An unintelligible fragment of record. *Ibid.,* No. 16.

152-A. Records the names of a number of people who presented lamps, in Ś. 1171 (A.D. 1249–50). *Ibid.,* No. 17.

153. Records the names of persons who gave lamps. *Ibid.*. No. 18, p. 403.

Chitēḍu.

154. East of village. (Sanskrit and Telugu.) Records that on the second of the dark fortnight of Nija Jyēshṭa in Bahudhānya, Ś. 1619, Lakshamma Gāru, the elder sister of Kṛishṇappa Gāru, the son of Chiṭṭeṭi Jaṅganna Gāru, built a temple, tank and maṇṭapa, and granted this charitable edict. *Ibid.,* No. 19, pp. 404–5.

Gūdūru.

This place is described as Kumulūr in Mēlaipaṭṭayanāḍu, a subdivision of Jayaṅkoṇḍa-chōḷamaṇḍaḷam. (Tamil.) The following inscriptions have been noted in the local Aḷaganātha temple and are the same as 542—553 of 1908 :—

155. Records in the twenty-ninth year of . . . Chōḷadēva, gift of a *māḍai* for lamp by Āchchamallināyakkan. *Ibid.,* No. 20.

156. A fragment of record relating to a lamp. *Ibid.,* No. 21.

157. Records in the twenty-fifth year of Rājarājadēva, a gift by Tiru . . . nar Kāṇiyāḷan *alias* Vikramachōḷa Mūvēndai. *Ibid.,* No. 22.

158. Records a gift by Jakkama Reḍḍi, son of Kāviri Muppi Reḍḍi of Vilakkaṇḍai. *Ibid.,* No. 23.

159. Records in the twenty-fifth year of Rājarājadēva the gift of a lamp by Kāppan. *Ibid.,* No. 24.

160. Records in the twenty-sixth year of Rājarājadēva, the gift of 1¼ *māḍai* for a lamp by Chōḍi Śeṭṭi. *Ibid.,* No. 25.

161. Records in the thirty-sixth year of Rājarājadēva, gift of 1½ *māḍai* for a lamp by Nāgan. *Ibid.,* No. 26.

162. Records gift of 1½ *māḍai* for a lamp by Mādanimāri Śeṭṭi, in Ś. 1169 (A.D. 1247–48). *Ibid.,* No. 27.

163. Records in the eighteenth year of Rājarājadēva, gift of 1½ *māḍai* by Kāmayan. *Ibid.,* No. 28.

164. Records gift of 1½ *mādai* for a lamp by Irāsāni, wife of Pālama Reḍḍi, in Ś. 1198 (A.D. 1276–77). *Nel. Ins., Gudur*, No. 29.

165. Records in the twenty-fifth year of Rājarājadēva, gift of 51 *mādai* for a lamp by Kāppan *alias* Lakshmaṇadāsan. *Ibid.*, No. 30.

166. Records in the nineteenth year of Rājarājadēva gift of 1¼ *maḍai* for a lamp by Eṛama Reḍḍi. *Ibid.*, No. 31.

167. Records gift of two *mādai* for a lamp by Pāchchaperumāḷ Cheṭṭi. *Ibid.*, No. 32.

168. Records in the thirty-fifth year of Kulōttuṅga Chōḷa gift of lands. *Ibid.*, No. 33.

169. *No.* 554 *of* 1908.—On the south wall of the same temple. (Tamil.) Damaged. Gift of money for a lamp by a native of Śīṛṛāṛkkāḍu in Puliyūr-kōṭṭam, a district of Jayaṅkoṇḍa-chōḷa-maṇḍalam. The donor had the surname Tirukkāḷatti Uḍaiyān.

170—181. 542 *to* 553 *of* 1908.—(Tamil.) In the Aḷaganātha Perumāḷ temple. Fresh copies of Nos. 155—169 above.

182. 554 *of* 1908.—(Tamil.) On the south wall of the same temple. A damaged record of the Chōḷa king Kulōttuṅga-Chōḷa-dēva, dated seventeenth year. Records gift of money for a lamp by a native of Śiṛṛāṛkkāḍu in Puliyūr-kōṭṭam, a district of Jayaṅ-goṇḍachōḷa-maṇḍalam. The donor had the surname Tirukkāḷatti-Uḍaiyān.

183. 555 *of* 1908.—(Tamil.) On the same wall. A mutilated record of the Chōḷa king Rājarāja-Chōḷadēva, dated nineteenth year. Mentions Pottappi-Nāḍu.

Gunupāḍu.

184. In a pillar of the maṇṭapa of Puttanāthasvāmi temple. (Tamil.) Records in the twenty-seventh year of the reign of the emperor Kulōttuṅgachōḷadēva, that Madhurāntakapottapichōḷa *alias* Nallasiddharasa gave to the God at Tiruvēṅgaḍam in the month of Chitrai, the village of Vēlūr in Melaip-paṭṭayanāḍu with all kinds of taxes, small and big *(chilvari* and *peruvari). Ibid.*, No. 34, pp. 406–7.

185. In the ceiling of Puttanāthasvāmi temple. (Sanskrit and Grantha characters.) Records that one Bhīmarāja constructed a palace as pleasing as the Kailāsa to Mahādēva, "The first few words of the record evidently refer to some date." *Ibid.*, No. 35, p. 408. The expression is ഖസ്രദ്ദിശ്വചഢലവെഗ്രഃ |

Īpūru.

186. In the north gate of Chennakēśava temple. (Tamil.) Records that in the year Śōbhakrit, Uśaka Muhamad, the son of Ā. Silaimān, erected this tomb and paḷḷi (mosque). *Ibid.*, No. 36, p. 408.

187. On the lintel of the south gate of the Chennakēśava temple. (Tamil.) Records that two rooms were built in the mosque and that wages were given by one Mulla Mohidin Shah. *Nel. Ins., Gudur*, No. 37, p. 409.

Bandepaḷḷi.

188. In the field No. 138. (Telugu.) Records on the thirteenth of the dark fortnight of Kārttika in year Virōdhi, that one Rāja Śrī . . . Ayyavāru granted a *mānyam* to Hussain Muhammad. *Ibid.*, No. 38, pp. 409–10.

Kapalūr.

189. *C.P. No.* 15 *of Nel. Ins.*—A Nandināgari grant consisting of 50 Sanskrit verses and a portion in Telugu, dated in Ś. 1258, and purporting to record the grant of the village of Hariharapuram as an agrahāra to a Brahman named Anantasūrayya, son of Śaṅkukēśava Bhaṭṭa of the Viśvāmitra gōtra. (He divided the village into sixty shares, kept thirty for himself and gave the rest to Brahmans.) The donor was king Harihara Rāya of Vijayanagar and he made the grant after his coronation. [This is the same as C.P. No. 79 of Mr. Sewell's List.]

Kistnapatam.

190-A. In the north wall of the Siddhēśvarasvāmi temple. (Tamil.) Records that, in the thirteenth year (Ś. 1178, expired) of the reign of the emperor Vīrarājēndrachōḷadēva (III ?), on Makara Śukla 13, Rōhiṇi, Saturday, all the men of the town of Kollatturai *alias* Gaṇḍagōpālapaṭṭaṇa and the foreigners of the eighteen countries, assembled together at the sacred flower garden of Dēśanāyakan attached to the temple of Chandirattiraipiḷḷaiyār, and gave to the god Manumasiddhēśvara a sum of money. The deity was apparently named after the Telugu-chōḷa Manmasiddha, father of Tikka I.

190-B. Records that, in the thirteenth year of the reign of Vīrarājēndrachōḷadēva, Ūruḍaiyān Maḍapaḷisvāmi gave for sacred food to Tiruppaḷḷiyaraināchchiyār (the goddess of the sacred bedroom), 300 *kuḻis* of arable land, free of tax, at Iruvuḷavāṇigi in Munaiyūr.

190-C. Records in the fifteenth year of the reign of the abovementioned king that under the orders of Manumasiddharaśar, Āṇḍa . . . kiḻān *alias* Tiruvaraṅgamuḍaiyār gave, free of tax, to the abovementioned goddess, a certain area of arable land.

190-D. Records in the sixteenth year of the reign of the abovementioned king that a certain Dhanmapālan gave, to the abovementioned goddess, some *kuḻis* of arable land for service on the great night of Śivarātri. *Ibid*, No. 39, pp. 410—3.

191. In a stone in a street. (Telugu and Tamil.) A fragmentary and unintelligible record of a grant by certain *kāpus*. *Nel. Ins., Gudur*, No. 40, p. 413.

192. To the east in the dhōby's inam. (Tamil.) An illegible record. *Ibid.*, No. 41, p. 414.

193. In a house in Ayyavārappa Khaṇḍriga. (Tamil.) Records in Ś. 1330, expired, Sarvadhāri, Paṅguni Śukla 10, Monday, Punarpūśa, in the reign of Mahāmaṇḍalēśvara, Vīradēvarāya (I), the son of Harihararāya (II), a certain charity apparently made originally by Manusiddharaśa. Mentions Rājavibhāṭapaṭṭiṇam in Nellūrnāḍu. *Ibid.*, No. 42, p. 414.

194. In a stone bearing a Telugu inscription. Two fragments which are unintelligible. *Ibid.*, No. 43, p. 415.

195. On the steps of shrine of Siddhēśvara temple. (Tamil.) Records in the twenty-sixth year of the reign of some king (name not clear) the erection of a gōpuram and a maṇṭapam for some Vaishṇava god (Perumāḷ), and the gift of 300 *pon*, the sale-proceeds of certain lands, for oblations of rice and a lamp. *Ibid.*, No. 44, p. 416.

196. In the south wall of Siddhēśvara temple. (Tamil.) Records that in the second year, Ś. 1201, expired, Mīna Śukla 10, Rōhiṇi, Saturday, in the reign of Irumuḍi Tirukkāḷattidēva, the merchants of the *nāḍus*, towns, hills and the five *maṇḍalams* and the foreigners from Kōḷḷituṛai *alias* Gaṇḍagōpālapaṭṭaṇam assembled at Tirukkāvaṇam gave for expenses connected with building, sacred food and ornaments for the god Manumasiddhēśvara of this village, one-fourth per cent on the cost of all the bags exported and imported at this port. *Ibid.*, No. 45, pp. 417–8.

197. To the south of the Salt Cotaurs. (Telugu.) Records on Wednesday, the fourth of the bright fortnight of Bhādrapada in Ś. 1470, Kīlaka, that the son of Achchinēni Rāmanāyuḍu, the agent of Śrīman Mahāmaṇḍalēśvara-mārāju Timmayadēva Mahārājulu Gāru granted lands as a *sarvamānya*. *Ibid.*, No. 46, pp. 418—20.

198. In a field to the west. (Telugu.) A record mostly illegible. *Ibid.*, No. 47, p. 420.

Kōṭa.

199. Opposite to the Sōmēśvara temple. (Telugu.) Records on the second of the bright fortnight of Māgha in year Kāḷayukti, that Śrīman Mahāmaṇḍalēśvara Aḷiya (Rāma) Dēvamahārājulum Gāru, the agent of Śrī Sadāśiva Dēva of Vijayanagar, issued a grant to barber Koṇḍōji. *Ibid.*, N. 48, pp. 420—2.

Kuruchērlapāḍu.

200. East of the village on a tank bund. (Telugu.) Records the gift of a Surabhivāru on a certain day of the bright fortnight of Āshāḍha of the year Raudri, for the religious merit of Veṅkaṭapati Rāyuḍu. *Ibid.* 49, pp. 422–3.

201. To the west of the village in a yard. (Tamil.) Records in the sixteenth year of the reign of Kulōttuṅgachōḷadēva (III), in Ś. 1114, Pramādi, on Saturday, Anusha, of the bright half of the month of Makara, that Madhurāntakapottapichōḷan *alias* Rājagaṇḍagōpālan *alias* Raṅganāthan gave to the god Gōpālaperumāḷ at Nellūr *alias* Vikramaśiṅgapuram in Pākanāḍu in Chēdikulamāṇikkavaḷanāḍu, a subdivision of Jayaṅkoṇḍachōḷamaṇḍalam, a piece of land in Śiṅgaṭṭaināḍu (?) as exclusive and *sarvamānya* property. *Nel. Ins.*, *Gudur*, No. 50, pp. 423–4.

Maḍamannūru.

202. On the tank bed. (Tamil.) An incomplete record in the thirty-second year of the reign of Tribhuvanavīradēva (i.e., Kulōttuṅga III). Records that Irāyan Koḷaraivachchiyān Akkan of Muriṇōttamaṅgalam, situated in Vaḷḷuvanāḍu, a subdivision of Malaimaṇḍalam, dug a tank in the village of Maḍuvanūr in Śingaṭṭaināḍu, a subdivision of Jayaṅkoṇḍachōḷamaṇḍalam. He further gave, for the protection of this tank and this village, two *paṭṭis* of land, besides one *paṭṭitarai* to Śrīkāri Māśidāsar for a sacred flower garden and one *paṭṭitarai* to Tirumanōjñadāsardāsar. *Ibid.*, No. 51, pp. 424–5.

203. In a street. (Telugu.) Records that on the tenth of the bright fortnight of Kārttika of S. 1634, Nandana, Gurappallita Bhāsandāru, the secretary *(mudrakarta)* of Rāvela Muddu-Kṛishṇappa Nāyani Vāru ordered the payment of one *tūm* for each *puṭṭi* of all grain and produce raised in this village for the tank. *Ibid.*, No. 52, pp. 426–7.

Mallam.

[For other epigraphs of this village wrongly included here see No. 624 f. below.]

204. On the east wall of Subramaṇyēśvara temple. (Tamil.) Records in the twenty-sixth year of the reign of the emperor Kulōttuṅgachōḷadēva (III), who was pleased to take Madurai and the crowned head of the Pāṇḍyans, that Peddaraśar, the son of Rājarājapaṭṭaivattiyaraśar, the lord of the best of the cities Ahichatra, the lord of the Phaṇamaṇḍala, Śivapādaśēkhara, who belonged to the pure Ātrēya gōtra, gave to the god Subrahmaṇyapiḷḷaiyār at Tiruvānbūr situated in Kīḷa-paṭṭaiyanāḍu in Paiyūriḷaṅgōṭṭam, a subdivision of Jayaṅkoṇḍachōḷamaṇḍalam, some lands in the village of Īndaiyūr. *Ibid.*, No. 53, pp. 427—9.

205 and 206. On the floor of the Subramaṇyēśvara temple. (Tamil.) Records in the fifteenth year of the reign of Nandipōttaraśar, that the men of the district, the villagers and the heads of assemblies, gave, at the order of Chaḷukkiaraśar, on the petition of Āḷuva-araśar, 35 *kaḷanji* of gold for maintaining lamps to the god Subrahmaṇya at Tiruvānbūr, situated in Paiyyūriḷaṅgōṭṭam, *Ibid.*, No. 54, pp. 429–30. [We infer that the ancient name of this village was Tiruvānbūr, and that it was situated in Okkāṭṭunāḍu in Kīḻaippaṭṭaiyanāḍu in Paiyuriḷaṅgōṭṭam, a subdivision of Jayaṅkoṇḍachōḷamaṇḍalam.]

207. A record in the twenty-sixth year of Kulōttuṅga Chōḷa by Uḍaiyappa Nāyakkan. *Nel. Ins., Gudur*, No. 55, p. 430.

208. A record in the twenty-seventh year of Rājarājadēva (III ?) by Chēmiyāṇḍan, son of Sāmi Ruttan *alias* Nānādēśi Malaimaṇḍala Nāḍāḷvān. *Ibid.*, No. 56.

209. A record in the twenty-fourth year of Vijayagaṇḍagōpāladēva by Sataya Vaḷittuṇai Apparaśa. *Ibid.*, No. 57.

210. A record in the eleventh year of Rājarājadēva by Siddharaśa, brother-in-law of Madhurāntaka Pottapi Chōḷa *alias* Eṛasiddaraśa. *Ibid.*, No. 58.

211. A record in the tenth year of Rājarājadēva (III) by Madhurāntaka Pottapichōḷa *alias* Eṛasiddaraśa. *Ibid.*, No. 59.

212. A record in the thirteenth year of Rājarājadēva (III) by Madhurāntaka Pottapichōḷa *alias* Tirukkāḷattidēva *alias* Gaṇḍagōpāla. *Ibid.*, No. 60.

213. A record in the ninth year of Rājarājadēva (III) by Tamasiddhi Bhuvanēkānikadhīran *alias* Pāṇḍya Gaja Kēsari *alias* Rāja Brahma Chōḷa Vaiṭumbana *alias* Vāṇan Mahārājan *alias* Madanudēvan *alias* Dāsaiyaraśan. *Ibid.*, No. 61.

214. A record in the fourth year of Rājarājadēva by Chīramāṇḍai. *Ibid.*, No. 62.

215. A record in the twentieth year of Vikramavarmadēva. *Ibid.*, No. 63.

216. A record in A.D. 1314–15. *Ibid.*, No. 64.

217. A record in the fifth year of Rājarājadēva (III) by Vikramachōḷa Mūvēndavēḷān *alias* Eriyamireḍḍi Muppi Reḍḍi. *Ibid.*, No. 65.

218. A record in A.D. 1289–90 by Sāmināyakkar, Sandamanāyakkar and another. *Ibid.*, No. 66.

219. A record in the ninth year of Vīragaṇḍa-Gōpāḷadēva by Tyāgasamudrapaṭṭai Mallidēvaraśan. *Ibid.*, No. 67.

220. A record by Nāvan Pōyāṇḍān. *Ibid.*, No. 68.

221. A record in the twenty-first year of Vijayagaṇḍagōpāladēva by the Cheṭṭis of Vikramaśiṅgapuram *alias* Nellūr. *Ibid.*, No. 69.

222. A record in the thirty-sixth year of Kulōttuṅgachōḷa (III ?) *Ibid.*, No. 70.

223. A record in the twelfth year of Rājarājadēva (III) by Chenavaṇi *alias* Iḍaikkamināṭṭuvēḷān *alias* Pichchan *alias* Tiruvēkambamuḍaiyān *alias* Rājanārāyaṇavēḷān. *Ibid.*, No. 71.

224. A record in the seventeenth year of Kulōttuṅgachōḷa (III ?) by Śivaputan *alias* Vānavanāyakan *alias* Baladēvan. *Ibid.*, No. 72.

225. A record in the twenty-second year of Rājarājadēva (III ?) by donor Marudulān, the commander-in-chief (sēnāpati) of Ulagāludaiyān (the ruler of the world). *Nel. Ins., Gudur*, No. 73.

226. A record in the twenty-first year of Vijayagaṇḍagōpaladēva by Ālikkonṟaikiḷān *alias* Irājamallan *alias* Karumbāṇḍai and his brother Pēṟṟu Piḷḷai. *Ibid.*, No. 74.

227. A record in the eleventh year of Vijayagaṇḍa Gōpaladēva by Chakkama Reḍḍi, son of Vilakkandai Kaviriyār *alias* Vikramachōḷa Mūvvēḷār *alias* Muppi Reḍḍiyār. *Ibid.*, No. 75. See No. 217 above.

228. A record in the twenty-seventh year of Kulōttuṅgachōḷa by Mayilamādēvi Paṭṭaraśa, son of Madhurāntaka Pottapichōḷa *alias* Nallasiddharaśa. *Ibid.*, No. 76. [Was Nallasiddha the elder brother of Eṟa Siddha ? See Telugu Chōḷa genealogy.]

229. A record in the third year of Alluntirukkāḷattidēva *alias* Gaṇḍagōpāla Mahārāja by Tiruchchiṟṟambalamuḍaiyān *alias* Vāḷavandān. *Ibid.*, No. 77. See S.A. 146, Cg. 300, 328 and 747.

230. A record in the eighteenth year of Rājarājadēva (III) who took Madura and the crowned head of the Pāṇḍyan, by Siddharaśa, son of Kulōttuṅgachōḷa paṭṭai Śēkharadēva, the lord of the best of towns Ahischatrapuṟa, the lord of the middle country, the lord of the Phaṇamaṇḍala, having the *biruda* Śivapādaśēkhara and belonging to the Ātrēya gōtra. *Ibid.*, No. 78.

231. A record in the twenty-first year of Rājarājadēva (III) by Tirukkāḷattivēḷān, son of Vilakkandai Kāviri *alias* Vikramachōḷa Mūvēndavēḷān *alias* Muppi Reḍḍi. *Ibid.*, No. 79. See 217 above.

232-A. A record in the twenty-seventh year of Vijayagaṇḍagōpāladēva (1250—83) by donor Dēśavēḷān *alias* Tennaviḷupparaiyan *alias* Varantarumperumāḷ. *Ibid.*, No. 80. See Cg. 139.

(The above list of records merely relate to grants of land, money, lamps and so on.)

Muṭṭumbāka.

232-B. To the west of No. 136. (Tamil.) An illegible record. *Ibid.*, No. 81.

Muṭṭukkūr.

233. South of the village. (Telugu.) Records that on the thirtieth of the dark fortnight of Vaiśākha, Vijaya, Ś. 1456, Timmanāyaniṅgāru, the agent of *(kāryakarta)* Śrīman Mahāmaṇḍalēśvara Sālaka Rāju Tirumala Dēva Mahārāyalu, gave to Nāgēśvara Dēva of Muttukūru, the village of Muttukkūru in Sariyapalli *Śima*, for providing worship, daily offerings, enjoyments and marriage festivities, for the merit of Tirumalarāya. *Ibid.*, No. 82, pp. 432—6.

Mutyālapāḍu.

234. Near the hamlet of Writer-satram. (Telugu.) Records on the fifteenth of the bright fortnight of Jyēshṭa in Ś. 1713, Virōdhikrit, that Kaligiri Veṅkaṭāchalam Gāru caused a reservoir to be dug in the fields of Mutyālpāḍu on the road leading to Kāśī and Rāmēśvaram, constructed a rest-house in the village and continued the charity. His second brother Kaligiri Rāmayya Gāru, then his third brother Kaligiri Śēshayya and after him the above-said Veṅkatāchalayya Gāru's grandson, Kaligiri Sundarayya, maintained the charity. On the fifth of the bright fortnight of Māgha of the year Durmukhi he constructed a rest-house and entered it on Thursday, the second of the dark fortnight of Āshāḍha of the year Śārvari. *Nel. Ins., Gudur*, No. 83, pp. 436-7.

Nārikēḷḷapaḷḷi.

235. In a street. (Telugu.) Records on (?) of the bright fortnight of Pushya in Ś. 1610, Vibhava, under the orders of Rāvela Muddu Kṛishṇappa Nāyanivāru, Yirāvarapu Timmanna Gāru ordered that *kuñchams* should be collected for the tank in the village of Nārikēḷḷapaḷḷi which was an *amaram* of his in Sariyapalli *sīma*. The *mērādār* or *amaradār* or the *sandhāta*, whoever ruled the village, should do work and not covet the tank *mēras*. *Ibid.*, No. 84, pp. 437—9.

Punjulūrupāḍu.

236. To the north of village. (Tamil.) Records in Ś. 1185, expired, the twentieth year of the reign of Vīra Rājēndrachōḷadēva (III), on Tulā, Śukla 10, Friday, Māgha, the grant of some land to the lord Śāntīśvara at Vikramaśiṅgapuram *alias* Nellūr. *Ibid.*, No. 85, pp. 439—41.

Reḍḍipālem Pāntraṅgam.

237. In the Pāṇḍuraṅga temple. (Tamil.) Records in the thirty-sixth year of the reign of Tribhuvanavīradēva, that Sittaraśan, the son of *Mattimadēsam* Rājarājapaṭṭaipettaraśan, presented one sacred lamp in the temple of the lord Pāṇḍuraṅga, situated in Perūrnāḍu in Pavvattirikōṭṭam, a subdivision of Rājēndrachōḷamaṇḍalam, on behalf of his elder sister Pāchchaldēvi, the consort of Madhurāntakapottapichōḷa *alias* Manumasittaraśan. Records that (for this lamp) Rājarājapaṭṭaisittaraśa gave the tax on *Vēmugar*, the tax on house front (doors), the tax on looms, the tax on goldsmiths, and the temple dues on the garden lands. Records also that three Śiva Brāhmans of the temple, bound themselves to pay the interest on this gold and maintain a sacred lamp. *Ibid.*, No. 86, pp. 441—3.

238. In the Pāṇḍuraṅga temple. (Tamil.) Records in the thirty-second year of the reign of Kulōttuṅgachōḷadēva (I) who abolished tolls, gift of some land to the gods Pāvanavināyakadēva and Pāṇḍaraṅgēśvara of Kākaṇḍi in Kaḍalkoṇḍa Pavvattirikōṭṭam, a subdivision of Rājēndrachōḷamaṇḍalam called after the emperor. *Nel. Ins., Gudur,* No. 87, pp. 443-4.

239. Records in the eighth year of Rājarājadēva, gift of a lamp by Mummuḍivaiṭumba Mahārājan *alias* Vishṇudēvan *alias* Durai Araśan. *Ibid.*, No. 88.

240. Records in the twenty-ninth year of Kulōttuṅgachōḷa, gift of 13 *māḍai* for a lamp by Tāttān Tanapālapanmamuḍaiyān, a merchant of Conjeeveram. *Ibid.*, No. 89.

241. Records in Ś. 1185 (expired) A.D. 1263-64 and twentieth year of Vīrarājēndrachōḷadēva (III) gift of 1 *māḍai* for a lamp by Tikkaṇai Āṇḍān. *Ibid.*, No. 90.

242. Records in the seventh year of Vijayagaṇḍagōpāla (1250—83) gift of an image of the goddess of Tirukkāmakkōṭṭam. *Ibid.*, No. 91. See Cg. 139.

243. Records in the thirty-sixth year of Tribhuvanavīradēva (i.e., Kulōttuṅga III) gift of 98 "full grown, undying and unaging" sheep for a lamp by Irumaḍiśrīyādēvi, wife of Rājarājapaṭṭai Siddaraśa and daughter of Uraiyūr Chōḷan *alias* Śūraḷvār Kaṭṭidēvar. *Ibid.*, No. 92.

244. Records in the third year of Rājarājadēva (III ?) gift of five lamps by Vaṇiyan Nalluḷān *alias* Chēramān Tōḷan *alias* Pāvāṇḍān. *Ibid.*, No. 93.

245. Records in the eighth year of Vikramachōḷadēva (1118—35) gift of land in several villages. *Ibid.*, No. 94.

246. Two fragments of record. *Ibid.*, No. 95.

247. Records in the sixth year of Kulōttuṅgachōḷa *alias* Chokkanāyanār grant of land. *Ibid.*, No. 96.

248. A fragment of record relating to a grant of land. *Ibid.*, No. 97.

249. Records in the fifth year of Vijayadēva grant of a lamp. *Ibid.*, No. 98.

250. Records in the fourteenth year of Rājarājadēva (III ?) grant of a lamp. *Ibid.*, No. 99.

251. Records a grant of land. *Ibid.*, No. 100.

252—256. Record in the thirty-second year of Kulōttuṅgachōḷa (III ?) grant of cattle for the maintenance of a lamp. *Ibid.*, No. 101. *Ibid.*, Nos. 102, 103, 104 and 105. Illegible records.

Raṭṭamala.

257. To the east of the Prasanna Kāḷahasti Īśvara. (Tamil.) Records that on the fourteenth of the month of Tai in the year . . . Pottappichembar built the temple and gave to Ādirājattidēva Tribhuvananāyaka all his rights in the lands, tank, backwater and wells. Salutation to the Buddha. *Ibid.*, No. 106, pp. 446-7.

Sarvēpaḷḷi.

258. On the gate of the Śiva temple. (Telugu.) An illegible record. *Nel. Ins., Gudur*, No. 107, p. 447.

Vākāḍu.

259. In the enclosure of the Vishṇu temple. (Telugu.) Records that on Thursday, the tenth of the bright fortnight of Pushya in Ś. 1452, Vikriti, while Śrīman Mahārājādhirāja Rājaparamēśvara, Śrī Vīra Pratāpa Achyutarāya Mahārāyulu was ruling the earth, Śrīman Mahāmaṇḍalēśvara Sālaka Rāju Tirumalayya Dēva Mahārājulu, who was on the banks of the Svarṇamukhi on the holy occasion of Makara Saṅkaramaṇa, gave gold and the village of Nēlaṭūru, otherwise known as Achyutarāyapuram and Chirumaṇampūṇḍi, in eastern Paḍanāḍu *sima* in the Rājya of Chandragiri, for performing the sixteen ceremonies to Onkāḍa Aḷaganātha Dēva, for the merit of Achyutarāyulu. *Ibid.*, No. 108, pp. 447—9.

Vallūru.

260. In the street to the west. (Telugu.) Records a gift on the first of the dark fortnight of Kārttika in Ś. 1502, Pramādi, by Veṅkaṭādri for a tank in the village of Vallūru. *Ibid.*, No. 109, pp. 449—51.

Vanjivāka.

261. In the enclosure of Chennakēśava temple. (Telugu.) Records on the tenth of the bright fortnight of Pushya of Ś. 1536, Krōdhi, that Veṅkaṭapati Rājum Gāru, son of Śrī Veligōṭi Rājayyapātūru, granted eighty *kuṇṭas* to the dancers, drummers, pipers and dancing girls, after worshipping Chennarāya of Vanjivāṅka, besides the lease fees and the pound fees in the town for providing lamps to the deity. *Ibid.*, No. 110, pp. 451—3.

Vindūru.

262. In a field. (Telugu.) Records that in the reign of Achyutarāya Mahārāyalu on the third of the bright fortnight of Vaiśākha in Ś. 1456, Jaya, on the holy occasion of Akshatadiya, Bōḍi Reḍḍi, son of Dinadēvi Reḍḍi, planted a tope and presented lands for the religious merit of Achyutarāya, and of his own parents. *Ibid.*, No. 111, pp. 453-4.

Vīrānna Kanupūr.

263. Near the Śiva temple. (Telugu.) Records in the reign of Śrī Veṅkaṭapati Rāja, on the thirtieth of the dark fortnight of Śravaṇa of the year Piṅgaḷa, Ś. 1538, Rāvula Veṅgalappa, of the gōtra of Lōkapāla, grandson of Śrī Veṅgalappa, and son of Rāvula Veṅkaṭappa, presented the tax due from the village of Vīranna

Kanupūr (which was his *amaram*) for the merit of Veṇkaṭappa Nāyaniṅgāru. *Nel. Ins., Gudur*, No. 112, pp. 454—6.

264. Near the Vīrabhadra temple. (Telugu.) Records that on Wednesday, the fourteenth of the dark fortnight of Māgha of the year Siddhārthi, Ś. 1475, Allūri Aṇṇā Reḍḍi, the agent of Śrīman Mahāmaṇḍalēśvara Rāma Rāju Tirumalarājayyavāru made a grant for the religious merit of Tirumala Rājayyavāru. *Ibid.*, No. 113, pp. 456—8.

265. Near Vīrabhadra temple. (Telugu.) Records that on Monday, the third (or seventh) of the dark fortnight of Māgha of the year Rākshasa, Ś. 1476, Koṇḍapalli Yallaparāju, the agent, of Śrīman Mahāmaṇḍalēśvara Rāma Rāju Tirumala Rājayyavāru, gave the village of Yadimalu in the *śima* of Saryapalli for the religious merit of Tirumala Rājayya. *Ibid.*, No. 114, pp 458—60.

266. On a stone removed from above the gate of the Vīrabhadra temple. (Tamil.) Records that in Ś. 1222, Vikāri, the ninth year of Rājagaṇḍagōpāladēva, on the third day of the bright half of the month of Tai, Aviṭṭa, Madurāntakapottapichōḷan *alias* Rājagaṇḍagōpāladēvan gave to the god Piḷḷaiyuḍaiya Nārāyaṇaperumāḷ for worship, on behalf of Tirukkachchinambi, residing in the merchant street at Nellūr *alias* Vikramaśiṅgapura in Paḍaināḍu in Jayakulamāṇikkavaḷanāḍu, a subdivision of Jayaṅgoṇḍachōḷamaṇḍalam. *Ibid.*, No. 115, pp. 460—2.

Yērigaṭipalli.

267. In a street to the east. (Tamil.) Records in the nineteenth year of the reign of Vijayagaṇḍagōpāladēva, thirteenth day of the bright half of the month of Kaṭaka, nakshatra Pūśa, the grant of a Chitramēḷa "perhaps a surname of Śrī Vijayagaṇḍagōpāladēva." *Ibid.*, No. 116, pp. 462–3.

Yērūru.

268. Near the ruined Vīrabhadra temple. (Telugu.) Records grant of grain which should be utilized for keeping the tank in order. *Ibid.*, No. 117, pp. 463–4.

269. Over the door of the Chennakēśava temple. (Tamil.) Records that the paḷḷi (mosque) was founded by Mālikāḍuru (Málik Kádr), the son of Śilaiyamānār (Sūlaiman) on the first of Āvaṇi of the year Hēviḷambi. *Ibid.*, No. 118, p. 464.

KANDUKŪR TALUK.

Bhimavaram.

270. On a stone at the gate of the temple of Chennakēśava. (Telugu.) Records on the holy occasion of Makara Saṅkrānti of the year Rākshasa, Ś. 1237, that Śrīmān Muppaḍi Nāyanka Puraharu, the prime minister (Mahāpradhāni), of Śrīmān Mahāmaṇḍalēśvara Kākatīya Pratāpa Rudra Dēva Mahārāja, gave a field as a *sarvamānya* (free grant) to the deity Prasanna Chennakēśavadēva of Bhīmavaram agrahāra, in Pūṅgināḍu, for the religious merit of his master Pratāpa Rudradēva and of himself. *Nel. Ins., Kanḍukūr*, No. 1, pp. 465–6.

271. On a small stone in front of the temple of Rāma. (Telugu.) Records the gift of the village Bhīmavaram to Parṇaśāla-Narasiṁha (Narasiṁha of Śiṅgarāyakoṇḍa) by Ayyapparusayya. *Ibid.*, No. 2, p. 466.

272. Opposite the Rāmasvāmi temple. (Telugu.) Records on Thursday, the seventh of the dark fortnight of Vaiśākha of the year Virōdhikrit, Ś. 1475, gift of dry and wet lands in the village of Iruvapaḷḷi to Vānduya and Jāmu Gāru. Records also that the choultry shall acquire all the crops raised in the village under the tank. *Ibid.*, No. 3, pp. 467–8.

Bitraguṇṭa.

It is doubtful whether the following grant refers to this place or its namesake in Kāvali Taluk. I have, therefore, given it in both Taluks.

273-274. *C.P. No.* 20 *of Nel. Ins.*—(Sanskrit in Telugu character.) A record of Saṅgama II, son of Kampa (one of the five sons of Saṅgama I of Vijayanagar), dated in the third month of Durmukhi, Ś. 1278. It records the gift of the village of Bitraguṇṭa to 28 Brahmans at the request of the king's preceptor Śrīkaṇṭhanātha, in consequence of which the agrahāram itself came to be called Śrīkaṇṭhapuram. The occasion was the anniversary of the king's father's death. [See *Ep. Ind.*, Vol. III, pp. 21—35, for the edition of the plates.] See No. 404-A. It is the same as C.P. No. 58 of Mr. Sewell's List.

Boganampāḍu.

275. On the tank bund. (Telugu.) Records on the fifteenth of Śravaṇa of the year Tāraṇa, Ś. 1566, grant of lands by Parachūru Yangana Gāru, the grandson of Timmaṇa Gāru and the son of Vōbhanēśuḍu, of the Chivikāpākala gōtra to one Ayyappa. (The record is fragmentary.) *Ibid.*, No. 4, pp. 469–70.

Chalamachala.

276. In a street. (Telugu.) Records in Virōdhi gift of land in the village of Chalamachala to the Upparas (diggers) by the son of Bālabhadrayya. *Ibid.*, No. 5, pp. 471–2.

Chēmeḍadapāḍu.

277. On an image to the south. (Telugu.) Records that on Tuesday, the thirteenth of the bright fortnight of Māgha of the year

Khara, Mallu Bhīma Tammi, son of Dammi pūvula Śiṅgaya, made gifts for the merit of his parents, for the *mēra* of the local tank. *Kanḍukūr*, No. 6, p. 472.

278. On two sides of a stone to the east. (Telugu.) Records that Śrīmān Mahāmaṇḍalēśvara Gōpāla Mahā Rājulu founded a Charity for the merit of his mother. *Ibid*., No. 7, p. 473.

Chennipāḍu.

279. On a stone standing in temple of Saṅgamēśvara. (Sanskrit and Telugu.) Records in Ś. 1309, Prabhava, eleventh of the bright fortnight of Āśvayuja, the construction of the temple of Śiva. Records also the repairing of the ruined temple of Saṅgamēśvara on the holy junction of the rivers Kshīra Nadi *(Pālāru)* and Mākēru, 15 *yōjanas* to the north-east of the peak of Śrīśaila. *Ibid*., No. 8, pp. 474–5.

280. On a stone in the temple of Saṅgamēśvara. (Telugu.) An unintelligible record which is broken on the left side. *Ibid*., No. 9, pp. 475–6.

281. On a stone in the temple of Saṅgamēśvara. (Telugu.) Records gift of two villages (Oḍḍumgaṇṭu and Chennunipāḍu), situated at the sacred confluence of the Kshīra Nadi (*Pālāru*) and the Mākēru, for providing *amritapaḍi*, and enjoyments to Śrī Kūḍali Saṅgamēśvara. *Ibid*., No. 10, pp. 476–7.

282. On a stone by the field of Managavāru to the north of the pond of Baḍe Sahib. (Telugu.) Records a grant by Jōvipallikha Naraśiṅgamanāyaniṅgāru to Jaṅgam Pāpaya, the priest of Saṅgamēśvara, on Thursday, the eleventh of the bright fortnight of Chaitra of the year Vyaya. Records grant of 1,000 *kuṇṭās* of dry waste land south of Chenupaḷḷi in Chuṇḍi śīma by Koṇḍamarusayya as an *amaram*, for providing *amritapaḍi* to Saṅgamēśvara. *Ibid*., No. 11, pp. 478—80.

Chēvūru.

283. In field No. 233-A to the east of village; from four sides of a stone. (Telugu.) A record of Sunday, the fifteenth of the bright fortnight of Māgha of the year Svabhānu, Ś. 1566, mentioning a man of the Śrīvatsa gōtra, Āpastambas sūtra and the Yajuśśākha, grandson of Kāṭamrāju, son of Ayyapparāju. Concerns grant of *mēras* in the village. *Ibid*., No. 12, pp. 480—3.

Chouṭapāḷem.

284. Opposite the Gōgulamma temple. (Telugu.) Records that on the twelfth of the dark fortnight of Āshāḍha of the year Īśvara gift of the village Chavuṭāripāḷem. *Ibid*., No. 13, p. 483.

Chuṇḍi.

285. On four sides of a stone to the west of Liṅganapāḷem hamlet. (Telugu.) Records on Sunday, the tenth day of the dark fortnight of Chaitra of the year *Pramādicha*, Ś. 1535, certain acts of piety performed by Ayyar piyandu Balinendu Virappaṅgāri Rapamādharuṇḍu . . . Nāyaṅiṅgāru, grandsons of Kāminēni Dādi Nāyaniṅgāru, and sons of Vīrarāghava Nāyaniṅgāru and Koṇḍamāmbā, while he was ruling the town of Chuṇḍi granted to him as an *amaram* by Mahimandu Khulikuḍupullamgāru. He gave *mēras* and *mānyams* in the villages under his jurisdiction to Brahmarēśvara of Ārumūru for daily offerings and worship with a lamp. He further founded a village and a tank in the name of his father Vīrālaya, another in the name of his mother, sank a well, constructed a tank in the name of his brother Ayyana and gave *mānyams* under it to deities and Brahmans. Other gifts recorded. The temple of Chuṇḍi Janārdanasvāmi had been in ruins since the days of the Reḍḍis; he had the temple plastered with chunam, set up the deity in the temple, and founded an endowment for daily offering and worship. *Nel. Ins.*, *Kanḍukūr*, No. 14, pp. 484—9.

286. On a stone outside Rāmaliṅgasvāmi temple. (Sanskrit and Telugu.) Records the construction of a two-roomed mansion of Umēśvara by Kōna Śiṅgaya Śrēshṭhi (Kōmaṭi), the minister of Mallabhūpa, one of the eleven sons of Vēma, the son of Alla Bhūpati. Records a gift in the year Ratākshi, in the month of Chaitra, for the merit of Malla's father. *Ibid.*, No. 15, pp. 489—94.

287. On three sides of a stone in front of Kāmākshamma temple. (Telugu.) Records on Thursday, the eleventh of the bright fortnight of Phalguna of the year Sādhāraṇa, under the Vrishabha lagna, Ś. 1352, Kommana Sōmayājulu, the prime minister of Kōmaṭi Reḍḍi, the son of Śrīgiri Reḍḍi of the Maitrāvaruṇa gōtra, and Āpastamba sūtra, brought a Svayambhu Liṅga from the Pātāḷagaṅga at Śrīśaila to the sacred place where he had performed the two sacrifices "Agnishṭōma" and "Atirātri" in the town of Chuṇḍi, and set it up as Yajñēśvaradēva. This Kommaṇa Sōmayājulu built a stone temple and a *manṭapa* for this deity, set up shrines for the images of Vighnēśvara, Durga, Gōpāladēva and Bhairavadēva, planted two sacrificial stone pillars and a grove all round the prākāra, built a sacrificial fire-place on the north-west of it, and founded an endowment for providing all enjoyments to the deity. Records also gift of lands to the deity by his sons, the sinking of a fresh water well by himself in the path to the north of Chuṇḍi fort for the religious merit of his son Hariharanātha (probably deceased) and the construction of a tank and the planting of fig trees around it by his son Rāmachandra. *Ibid.*, No. 16, pp. 495—9.

288. On the fourth side of the same stone. (Sanskrit verses in Telugu.) Records that in Ś. 1352, Sādhāraṇa, on the eighth *tithi* of Śiva in the bright fortnight in the month of Phalguna, on Wednesday, Rishabha lagna, Kommanārya, the son of the minister Rāma, performed here the sacrifices Agnishṭōma and Atirātri according to scripture, and permanently set up the image of Yajñēśvara. *Nel. Ins., Kaṇḍukūr*, No. 17, pp. 501–2. See the above epigraph.

289. On one side of a stone near the Janārdanasvāmi's temple. (Telugu.) Records that on Saturday the thirteenth of the bright fortnight of Śravaṇa of the year Sarvadhāri, Ś. 1330, Malla Reḍḍi, the younger brother of Kōmaṭi Reḍḍi, the son of Śrīgiri Reḍḍi, grandson of Pina Kōmaṭi and great-grandson of Malla Reḍḍi, the younger brother of Vēma who built the flight of steps at Śrīparvata, and who made unlimited gifts as described by Hēmādri, for the purpose of securing the four kinds of human objects, set up an image of Śrī Janārdanadēva in the town of Chuṇḍi, constructed a temple and a *maṇṭapa* and bestowed, besides dry and wet lands at Chuṇḍi and Prōlasamudram, a tax of two pies on each of his soldiers, to provide for the great festivals of that deity. *Ibid.*, No. 18, pp. 502—5.

290. On three sides of the same stone. (Sanskrit verse in Telugu.) Records that king Mallaya, descendant of Vēma Reḍḍi who rendered Śrī Parvata accessible to men by building a flight of steps, consecrated in Ś. 1330, in the bright fortnight of Śravaṇa, on the day of Kāma (thirteenth), the temple of Vishṇu, of glorious splendour, in the town of Chuṇḍi, which he constructed along with its maṇṭapa, its gōpura, prākāra, etc. He also gave to Janārdana a collection of jewels. *Ibid.*, No. 19, pp. 505—12. [The genealogy given here is more detailed than that in the previous inscription.]

291. In a *maṇṭapa* opposite Janārdanasvāmi's temple. (Telugu.) Records on the second day of the bright fortnight of Phalguna of the year Vikrama, Ś. 1563, Kāminēni Muttarāju of the race of Vālmīki, of the gōtra of Ammasāni, who was the grandson of Vīra Rāghava Nāyaniṅgāru and the son of Polinēniṅgāru, gave to one Vīra Bhaṭṭu, some lands in the village of Chuṇḍi in Kaṇḍukūr śīma. Refers to the grant of the country as an *amaram*, by Rājā Śri Sultan Abdul-Padushah, in order to keep in good repair the temples in this Śīma. *Ibid.*, No. 20, pp. 513—15.

292. In the same *maṇṭapa*. (Telugu.) Records that Mallaya Reḍḍi, the son of Śrīgiri Reḍḍi, set up, on Saturday the thirteenth of Śravaṇa in the year Sarvadhāri, Ś. 1330, an image of Śrī Janārdanadēva in the town of Chuṇḍi and constructed a temple, a maṇṭapa, a gōpura and an enclosure wall, for the purpose of securing the four kinds of human desires. *Ibid.*, No. 21, pp. 515–6. See Nos. 289 and 290 above.

*Guḍlūr.**

293. On a fallen stone in the Nīlakaṇṭhēśvarasvāmi temple. (Telugu.) Records that on the day of Vishama Saṅkrānti in Ś. 1159, Chōḍadēva Chōḍa Mahārāja, Mallidēvarāja, and Chikkarāja constructed a front hall, a kitchen and a garden well, and gave one *paṭṭu* of dry land for them and four *paṭṭus* of dry land to "Padi Mokati Sim Baṭṭi Sānu." The *Monkatisanulu* (?) should lease out the low land in the lands attached to the treasury of Nīlakaṇṭhadēva for a half share of the produce to their friends. *Nel. Ins., Kaṇḍukūr*, No. 22, pp. 516–7.

294. On a fallen stone near the temple of Nīlakaṇṭhasvāmi. (Telugu.) Records on Tuesday, the fourteenth of the bright fortnight of Śravaṇa, that Muppuri (Muppaḍi) Nāyakaḍu, the prime minister of Rudradēva and the worshipper of the divine and illustrious lotus feet of Sōmanāthadēva, gave (lands) for providing all enjoyments to Śrī Nīlakaṇṭhadēva of Gūḍḷur in Pūṅgināḍu, for the religious merit of his lord, Śrīman Mahāmaṇḍalēśvara Kākatīya Pratāpa Rudradēva Mahārāja, and that of his own mother Gaṅgasānamma and of his father Nāgināyaniṅgāru. *Ibid.*, No. 23, pp. 517–8.

295. On a fallen stone in the same locality. (Telugu.) Records that on Sunday, the fifteenth of . . . in the year Īśvara Pedda Śināyakuṇḍu made a gift to Śri Nīlakaṇṭhadēva of Guḍḷūr. *Ibid.*, No. 24, pp. 518–9.

296. On a pillar in front of Chennakēśavasvāmi temple. (Telugu.) Records that on Thursday, the twelfth of the bright fortnight of Śravaṇa of the year Krōdhi, Ś. 1466, Tallayya, the son of Kiḷari Koṇḍamanāyuḍu, granted, for providing *amritapaḍi* to Chennakēśvaradēva of Guḍḷūr, a field of four *gor̤r̤us* in Rāvulaguṇṭa, a field of five *gor̤r̤us* in Pakkela guṇṭa, etc. *Ibid.*, No. 25, pp. 519–20.

Guṇḍlapāḷem.

297. On a fallen stone in Brahmarēśvara temple. (Telugu.) Records that on Thursday, the fifth day of the bright fortnight of the month of Kārttika of the year Kāḷayukti, Ś. 1170, when Nallasiddhi Rāja of Nellore advanced with an army, Vallu Rāja who was of the Ātrēya gōtra and who was a Yādava Kshatriya, descended from the divine feet of Śrī Vishṇuyōgamāya, the lord of Madhurāpura and Gōpikāvallabha of Dvāraka of the lineage of the famous Puru, and his son Pōlu Rāja and Peddi Rāja and their sons and other Yādavas met Siddhi Rāja in battle at the junction of Liṅgalakoṇḍa and Yaragaḍḍapāḍu in the presence of Sōmēśvara

* This place was the birth place of Errā Pregaḍa, the court poet of Ana Vēma Reḍḍi (1340—1369) of Koṇḍavīḍu, who was the author of the *Harivamśa*, the translator of the *Mahābhārata* and the composer of the *Ahōbalamāhātmya*. See p. 1087, No. 305.

and perished. *Nel. Ins., Kaṇḍukūr*, No. 26, pp. 520—35. The cause of the battle was the refusal of the chiefs to pay *pulvari*, grazing tax to Nalla Siddhi. See Mr. Sewell's *Antiquities*, Vol. I, for an account of these shepherd chiefs.

298. On a stone by the Brahmarēśvara temple. (Sanskrit and Telugu.) Records that on Thursday, the thirteenth of the bright fortnight of Bhādrapada of the year Bhava, Ś. 1436, Rāyasam Koṇḍamarusayya—who holds authority to carry out the orders of Kṛishṇarāya in Udayagiri—presented the village Ārumūruguḍḷu in Pūṅgināḍu which formerly belonged to Brahmarēśvara Śrīman Mahādēva for restoration of the temple (*punarōddhārana*) and for providing all enjoyments to the deity. *Ibid.*, No. 27, pp. 536—8.

299. On a stone in the same temple. (Sanskrit and Telugu.) Records that in Ś. 1251, in the year Śukla, in the bright fortnight of Māgha on Thursday, on full-moon day and lunar eclipse, the village of Ārumūru was presented to Brahmans. Records also that Śrī Vīra Pratāpa Rudradēvapatirāja Mahārāya, lord of the Karnāṭaka country, presented to Brahmāramēśvara Liṅga of Ārumūruguḍḷu in Pūṅgināḍu that village for the restoration of the temple, besides dry land, wet land, and *mēras* in the villages of Kaṇḍukūr śīma. *Ibid.*, No. 28, pp. 538—40.

300. (Telugu.) On a stone in same temple. Records that on Vaddavāram (Saturday), the seventh of the bright fortnight of Bhādrapada of the year Śukla, Ś. 1132, during Kanyā Saṅkrānti, one Śenāṅgulam, who was the son of Śrīman Dēva of Nellūrikōṭa, the head servant of Śrīman Mahāmaṇḍalēśvara Tirukāḷatidēva Chōḍa Mahārāja, granted some wet fields in Ārumūru in Pūṅgināḍu, to Brahmans. *Ibid.*, No. 29, pp. 540—2.

Jillelamuḍi.

301. (Telugu.) In the shrine of the Āñjanēya temple. Records that on Wednesday, the fifteenth of the bright fortnight of Vaiśākha of the year Vikrama, Ś. 1442, while Rāyasam Koṇḍamarusayyavāru of the Bharadvāja gōtra and of the Āśvalāyana sūtra was the ruler of Udayagiri, Śrī-Vīra-Pratāpa Śrī-Kṛishṇa Dēvarāya gave the deity Janārdana of Skandasthāna (Kaṇḍukūr) in the north-eastern quarter of Śrīśaila the village of Dāvi on the Pālēru in Kaṇḍukūru śīma, in Udayagiri Rājya as a *sarvamānya*. *Ibid.*, No. 30, pp. 542-3.

Kaṇḍukūr.

302-303. (Telugu.) These were found on a stone built into the Rāmasvāmi Mēḍa in Kaṇḍukūr town. They are about some Chāḷukya king. *Ibid.*, Nos. 31 and 32, pp. 544-5.

304. (Sanskrit and Telugu.) On a demarcation stone to the west of fort. Records the merit of one who keeps the grant of a village (granted as a gift). *Ibid.*, No. 33, pp. 545-6.

305. (Sanskrit and Telugu.) On the south front pillar of the mosque in the fort. Records that in Ś. 1320, in the month of Kārttika, on the day of solar eclipse, the younger brother of Śrīgiri the lord Rācha Vēma, presented an "incomparable tank" in Baddepūṇḍi to God Janārdana of Skandapura (Kaṇḍukūr), for the religious merit of his elder brother. *Nel. Ins., Kaṇḍukūr*, No. 35. pp. 549—56. [The inscription is very important as it gives an excellent account of the Reḍḍis. It refers to Vēma's patronage of poet Śambudāśa or Errāpragaḍa, the composer of the *Rāmāyaṇa* and *Harivamśa* in Telugu. See p. 1085, footnote.]

306. (Sanskrit and Telugu.) On the front side, north pillar in the mosque in the fort. An incomplete record of the Reḍḍi dynasty coming as far as Malla, younger brother of Vēma and son of Prōlaya. *Ibid.*, No. 34, pp. 546—9.

307. (Telugu.) On the western pillars of the mosque in fort. Records that the polished pillar was erected by Liṅgaśeṭṭi and Mādhavaśeṭṭi, sons of Bhaṇḍāru Mādhavōttamaśeṭṭi of Rāvūr. *Ibid.*, No. 36, p. 557.

308. (Telugu.) On the eastern pillars of the mosque in front. Records that the polished pillar was erected by Bāpirāju, son of Gullapaḷḷi Goṅkarāju for the religious merit of his parents. Records also that the pillar was erected by Chennu Rāju, son of Gullapaḷḷi Goṅkarāju. *Ibid.*, No. 37, p. 558.

309. (Telugu.) On the middle pillars of the mosque in the fort. Records that the polished pillar was erected by Naraśiṅgu, son of Bālāśaya Śiṅgama, and Bandariśeṭṭi, son of Bhandari Kāmiśeṭṭi, etc. *Ibid.*, No. 38, p. 559.

310. (Telugu.) On a stone built into the northern wall of the mosque. Records gift to Kalikēśvaradēva (deity) of Kaṇḍukūr on the holy occasion of Makara Saṅkrānti by Rāyasam Koṇḍamarusayyaṅgāru, servant of Kṛishṇadēvarāya of Vijayanagar. *Ibid.*, No. 39, pp. 560–1. See No. 301 above.

311. (Telugu.) On a stone built into the steps of the Pīrla Bhāvi. Records on Monday, the fifth of the bright fortnight of Chaitra in Ś. 1244, in the reign of Śrīman Mahāmaṇḍalēśvara Kākatīya Pratāpa Rudradēva Mahārāja that a chief gave lands at Guḍipāḍu (on the auspicious occasion of Śivarātri) for the performance of daily worship of Kalikēśvaradēva of Kaṇḍukūr, for the religious merit of Rāja Rudradēva (1295–1323). *Ibid.*, No. 40, pp. 561—3.

312. (Telugu.) On a stone near the temple of Iṭamukkalammā near Taluk Cutcherry. Records that on Tuesday, the thirtieth day of the dark fortnight in the month of Māgha of the year Rudhirōdgāri, Ś. 1606, the two acrobatic companies of Mannekmāri Annareḍḍi and Mannekmāri Pāpayya performed various feats on poles and ropes. Then Aṇṇāreḍḍi fell down from the rope and died in the midst of the assembly. The members of this assembly therefore requested the Muhammadan ruler to make some provision for the future for the children of the deceased by giving them some land by the tank of this village and to grant them an hereditary *inām* with full ownership. Therefore they gave one *goṟṟu* of cultivable dry land in the eastern fields of the kasba village and as much cultivable wet land as could be sown with four *tūms* of paddy under the Nallangaṭṭa tank. *Nel. Ins.*, *Kaṇḍukūr*, No. 41, pp. 563—6. [The inscription is interesting for its reference to twenty-four other classes of Dommaras.]

Karēḍu.

313. On the tank bund. (Telugu.) Records on Wednesday, the thirteenth of the bright fortnight of Śravaṇa of the year Dundubhi, Ś. 1725, on August 11 of the year 1802, that Pakala Rāmaṇṇa, the Brahman Karaṇam of Banginapalle, having trodden the boundary between Karēḍu and Banginapalle, won a victory under the orders of M.R.Ry. John Pinnvarat (Benward) Travers, Collector of Ongole and Nellore. Therefore this stone inscription was set up under the orders of that lord. *Ibid.*, No. 42, pp. 566–7.

Koṇḍamudusupāḷem.

314. On a stone over the Mōpād tank sluice. (Telugu.) Records that on Monday, the fifteenth of the bright fortnight of Āshaḍha of the year Vikrama, Ś. 1222, in the reign of Śrīgirīśvara Reḍḍi, the excellent son of Kōmaṭireḍḍi, Kōmaṭi Rāja ordered that the soldiers stationed in the town of Kaṇḍukūr, which was ruled by him, should contribute one *duggāṇi* (about six pies) on each house from their pay, and presented this as an endowment to God Kanda Sōmēśvaradēva at Kaṇḍukūr. *Ibid.*, No. 43, pp. 568–9.

315. On the sluice of the tank. (Telugu.) Records on Friday, the second of the dark fortnight of Mārgaśira of the year Vikriti, Ś. 1573, that Antōji, the agent of Śrī Rāmōji Mambāji Narōji Raghōji Pantulu gave a *goṟṟu* of wet land for maintaining the tank. It was settled that one *kuñchadu* of grain for every *puṭṭi* of paddy and of all other produce raised under the tanks belonging to them in Kaṇḍukūr, which had been given to them by Haji Koti (Kutb ?) Sultan Abdulla Padushah as *mokhāsa*, should be collected as tank *kuñchas (mēras)*; and that the grain thus realized should be given to *Upparas* (diggers), so that they might keep the tanks in good condition. It should be maintained in this manner for the merit of Haji Koti Padushah. *Ibid.*, No 44, pp. 569—72.

Kovūru.

316. In a backyard. (Telugu.) Records the construction of a *manṭapa* to Kovūru Viśvanātha and an endowment of land. *Ibid.*, No. 45, p. 572.

Māchavaram.

317. On a fallen stone by the roadside. (Telugu.) Records on Thursday, the fifteenth of Māgha of the year *Dundubhi*, Ś. 1604, the founding of certain charities in the villages of Māchavaram and Mōpāḍ. *Nel. Ins., Kandukūr*, No. 46, pp. 572—4.

318. On a stone near the temple of Perantalu, below the tank bund. (Telugu.) Records that on Friday, the third of the bright fortnight of Mārgaśira of the year Vikriti, Ś. 1573, Antoji Pantulu, Havildar, the agent of Śrī Rāmōji Māmbāji Narōji Śrī Raghōji Pantulu, granted *mēras* at the rate of one *kuñchaḍu* on every *puṭṭi* of paddy and other produce raised under the tanks in the *śima* of Kaṇḍukūr (which was bestowed on him as a *mokhasa* by Hazarat Sultan Abdulla Padushahi of Hyderabad Sarkar. The grain collected should be given to Upparas (diggers) in order that they might keep the tanks in good condition. *Ibid.*, No. 47, pp. 574--7. See No. 315 above.

319. On a stone near the same temple. (Telugu.) Records on Friday, the third of the bright half of Mārgaśira of the year Vikriti, Ś. 1573, a grant by Challa Timmareḍḍi, Mummaḍi Timmareḍḍi and the *dharmakartas* (trustees) who constructed the tanks. It was to the effect that on all kinds of produce raised from the wet fields irrigated by the tanks of the four villages of Kaṇḍukūr, Koṇḍamudusupāḷem, Mōpāḍu and Māchavaram, a contribution of one *kuñcha* on every *puṭṭi* was to be given to certain Voḍḍars and Peddabōyas. These persons also received lands on which twelve *tūms* of seed could be sown as an entire *inām*. They had also the privilege of grazing their cattle and sheep without paying *pullari* (grazing fees). Moreover the other Voḍḍars of these four villages who do *amji (amañji)* work (customary labour) to the tanks along with these were exempted from *pullari*. Further, only these persons should perform the duties of *nirukaṭṭu* (distributor of water) for all the wet fields under these tanks, for which special lands were given. *Ibid.*, No. 48, pp. 577--83. The inscription throws light on the important position occupied by this community in those days.

Malakoṇḍa Hill.

320. On a pillar of the Narasiṁhasvāmi temple. (Telugu.) Records on the twelfth of the bright fortnight of Kārttika in the year Plava the construction of a maṇṭapa to Narasiṁha of Śrī Malakoṇḍa. *Ibid.*, No. 49, p. 583.

321. *C.P. No.* 5 *of Nel. Inscns.*—A Telugu grant, dated on the fifteenth of the bright fortnight of Vaiśākha in Ś. 1328, Vyaya, and recording the gift of the hereditary right of priesthood to Malakoṇḍa Kēśava Dīkshit, the son of Raṅgachārya and grandson of Peddayya, of the Parāśara gōtra, Āpastamba sūtra and Yajuśākhā, in certain villages (enumerated). The donor was Mallaya

Reḍḍi, son of Śrīgiri Reḍḍi, grandson of Pina Kōmaṭi Reḍḍi and great-grandson of Mallaya, the brother of Vēmaya Reḍḍi. See the genealogy of the Koṇḍavīḍu and Rājahmundry Reḍḍis.

Pakāla.

322. On a stone in front of the Śiva temple. (Telugu.) Records on the day of Vishuma Saṅkrānti, on the tenth day of the bright half of Chaitra of the year Vibhava, Ś. 1190, that Rudra-pregaḍa, the prime minister of the illustrious Rudradēva, gave about 13,000 *kuṇṭas* of land for the religious merit of Rudradēva (Kākatīya Rudrammā ?) and his own parents. *Nel. Ins., Kandukūr*, No. 50, pp. 584–5.

323. On the bell in the Śiva temple. (Telugu.) Records on the seventh of the bright fortnight of Pushya in the year Khara, that two Reḍḍis (Battula Śarabha Reḍḍi and Chinna Liṅga Reḍḍi) caused this bell to be made for a certain Himaḍaka Pēranṭāla. *Ibid.*, No. 51, p. 586.

324. On a stone pillar in the Śiva temple. (Telugu.) Records on Thursday, the first of the bright fortnight of Mārgaśira in the year Śubhakṛit, Ś. 1224, gift (for the performance of occasional festivals to Śrīman Mahā Rāmanāthadēva of Pakāla) of certain *vṛittis* (shares of land) for Brahmans near Vailumulaguṇṭa, Bitra-guṇṭa, etc. *Ibid.*, No. 52, pp. 586–7.

325. On a stone pillar in the Śiva temple. (Telugu.) Records on a day of Uttarāyaṇa Saṅkrānti in the year Śrīmukha, Ś. 1195, that Sītaya, the younger brother of Periya Reḍḍi Nāyani, the karaṇam of the village, presented a lamp to the religious merit of his parents and of himself. *Ibid.*, No. 53, pp. 587–8.

326. On a stone pillar in the Śiva temple. (Telugu.) Records that on Sunday, the sixth of the bright fortnight of Chaitra of the year Raudri, Ś. 1242, in the reign of Śrīman Mahāmaṇḍalēśvara Kākatīya Pratāpa Rudradēva Mahārāja, the Kōmaṭis *(Nagaramlōni-vāru)* of Nellore who were ruling the illustrious village of Pakāla gave a field on which five *tūms* of seed can be sown for a lamp. *Ibid.*, No. 54, pp. 589–90.

327. On a stone pillar in the Śiva temple. (Telugu.) Records on Sunday, the sixth of the bright fortnight of Chaitra of the year Raudri, Ś. 1242, in the reign of Śrīman Mahāmaṇḍaḷēśvara Kākatīya Pratāpa Rudradēva Mahārāja, the Kōmaṭis of Nellore gave a wet field on which five *tūms* of seed can be sown to Śrī Rāmayadēva of Pākāla. Records also the gift of lamp by Nitya Dipila, the son of Pērla Śeṭṭi. *Ibid.*, No. 55, pp. 590–1.

328. In the Rāmaliṅgasvāmi temple. (Tamil.) Records that four persons of this place received one *Gaṇḍagōpālamāḍai* for one evening lamp to the God Ilaṅgaśenukuḷiya. *Ibid.*, No. 56, pp. 592–3.

329. In the Rāmalingasvāmi temple. (Tamil.) Records in Ś. 1194, in the month of Āvaṇi, that a man of Uttaramēlūr presented 500 *kuḷis* of land for maintaining a sacred flower garden to the deity. *Nel. Ins., Kandukūr*, No. 57, pp. 593-4.

330. In the image of Vighnēśvara. (Tamil.) An incomplete record, dated in Ś. 1199, expired, on Monday, the fifth day of the first bright half of the month of Karkaṭaka. *Ibid.*, No. 58, p. 594.

Peddakanḍlaguṇṭa.

331. To the east of village. (Telugu.) Records a gift by an unknown person on the fifteenth day of the bright fortnight of Kārttika of the year Promōdūta, for the religious merit of his father and mother. *Ibid.*, No. 59, p. 595.

Penṭrāla.

332. On one side of a fallen stone near the river. (Telugu.) Records that on Thursday, the fifteenth of the bright fortnight of Āshāḍha of the year Kāḷayukti, Ś. 1179, Śrīman Mahāmaṇḍalēśvara Bhujabala Vīra Manma Siddhaya Dēva Mahārājulu gave an agrahāra for enjoyment to the *purōhit* (priest) of the deity Mārgamu Pahindimukkala Mārga Nārāyaṇa Perumāḷ, through the agency of the son of Mārgamu Pahindimukkala Vīra Tiruvēngala, the illustrious establisher of the path of the Vēdās. The Nambi Tiruvēngaḍayya and Padmanābha have 1,000 *kuṇṭas* of land for the marriage festivals of the deity. *Ibid.*, No. 60, pp. 595-7.

333. On another side of the same stone. (Telugu.) Records that on Thursday, the tenth of the bright fortnight of Vaiśakha of the year Siddhārthi, Ś. 1180, Śrīman Mahāmaṇḍalēśvara Allāḍu Sudha Dēva Mahā Rāju, grandson of Podakanūrisiddi Rāju, who was a descendant of the race of Mukkanti Kāḍuveṭṭu, made certain gifts to Mārga Nārāyaṇa Perumāḷ, through the agency of the son of Mārgamu Pahindimukkala Vīra Tiruvēngala, for the prosperity of the kingdom of Śrīman Mahāmaṇḍalēśvara Bhujabala Vīra Manma Sidhhaya Dēva Chōḍa Mahārājulu. *Ibid.*, No. 61, p. 598-9. [Manma Siddha was the patron of the Telugu poet Tikkaṇa Sōmayāji.]

334. On the same side of the same stone. (Telugu.) Records that on Thursday, the fifth of the bright fortnight of Chaitra of the year Raudri, Ś. 1181, Madhusūdana Dēva Mahārāju, the grandson of the Śrīman Mahāmaṇḍalēśvara Andulūri Vijayāditta Dēchini, who was descended from the race of Mukkanti Kāḍuveṭṭi, granted the village of Vēligaṇḍla Mārga Nārāyaṇapuram as an agrahāra to the purohit (priest) of Mārga Nārāyaṇa Perumāḷ, through the agency of the son of Mārgamu Pahindimukkala Vīra Tiruvēngala, for the prosperity of the kingdom of Śrīman Mahāmaṇḍalēśvara Immaḍi Gaṇḍa Gōpāla Vijayāditta

Dēva Mahārājulu. *Nel. Ins., Kandukūr,* No. 62, pp. 599-600. See N.A., No. 441, for reference to Madhusūdana Dēva.

335. On another side of the same stone. (Telugu.) Records on Thursday, the . . . of the bright fortnight of Phalguna of the year Durmukhi, Ś. 1183, that Siddhama Dēvulu Vijaya Dēvaṇḍu, son of Śrīman Mahāmaṇḍalēśvara Ka . . . rāya Bhīma Dēva Mahārāju, of the race of Mukkanti Kāḍuveṭṭi, granted the villages of Marripalli and Ālāpālapaḷḷi to Śrī Mārga Nārāyaṇa Perumāḷ, through the agency of the son of Śrīmad Mārgamu Pahindimukkala Vīra Tiruveṅgala, the illustrious establisher of the path of the Vēdās, for the prosperity of the kingdom of Śrīman Mahāmaṇḍa-lēśvara Bhujabala Vīra Manma Siddhaya Dēva Chōḍa Mahārājulu. *Ibid.*, pp. 600—3. See No. 333 above.

336. On the fourth side of the same stone. (Three separate inscriptions.) (Telugu.) Records that on Thursday, the tenth of the bright fortnight of Āshāḍha of the year Prabhava, Ś. 1189, Śrīman Mahāmaṇḍalēśvara Bijji Rāju Siddhaya Dēva Chōḍa Mahārājulu gave certain land to Mārganārāyaṇa Perumāḷ, through the agency of the son of Śrīmad Mārgamu Pahindimukkala Vīra Tiruveṅgala, the illustrious establisher of the path of the Vēdās. *Ibid.*, No. 64, pp. 603-4. See No. 333 above.

337. On the same side of the stone. (Telugu.) Records on Thursday, the fifteenth of the bright fortnight of Chaitra of the year Vibhava, Ś. 1190, that Gaḍi Dēva Rāju, son of Śrīman Mahāmaṇḍalēśvara Sāhattumalla Perumāṇḍi Dēva Chōḍa Mahārājulu gave a flower garden and a cow to Mārganārāyaṇa Perumāḷ through the agency of the son of Śrīmad Mārga Pahindimukkala Vīra Tiruveṅgaḍa, the illustrious establisher of the path of the Vēdās. *Ibid.*, No. 65, pp. 604-5. See No. 333 above.

338. On the same side of the stone. (Telugu.) Records that on Thursday, the first of the bright fortnight of Śravaṇa of the year Śukla, Ś. 1191, Śrīman Mahāmaṇḍalēśvara Bhīma Rāju Siddhaya Dēva Mahārājulu gave the village of Kūchipūṇḍi to Mārga Nārāyaṇa Perumāḷ, through the agency of the son of Śrīmad Mārgamu Pahindimukkala Vīra Tiruveṅgaḍa, the illustrious establisher of the path of the Vēdās. *Ibid.*, No. 66, pp. 605-6. See No. 333 above.

Petlūru.

339. On a wall of the Vīrabhadrasvāmi temple. (Telugu of ancient type.) Records that a certain Koṇḍivillu, son of Duggirāju, granted land, sowable with ten *tūms* of seed, to Rachchayirru. *Ibid.*, No. 67, pp. 606-7.

340. Opposite the Bhīmēśvara temple. (Telugu.) Records that on Monday, the fifteenth of the bright fortnight of Vaiśākha of the year Vyaya, Ś. 1328, the temple of Bamayadēvaru of Peṭlūru which was in ruins was repaired by Ama-Reḍḍi Sigi-Reḍḍi of the Kāṇḍrabōla gōtra, at the request of all classes of devotees of Pēṭlūru. *Nel. Ins., Kandukūr*, No. 68, pp. 608–9.

341. Opposite the Bhīmēśvarasvāmi temple. (Telugu.) An incomplete record. *Ibid.*, No. 69, p. 609.

Polinēnipāḷem.

342. Near an image of Hanūmān. (Telugu.) An illegible record.

Rāmayyāpaṭṇam.

343. *C.P. No. 4 of Messrs. Butterworth and Venugopaul Chetty.*—Records the agreement in Telugu of certain Lambādi, Brinjari and other Salt traders of the ports (enumerated) to pay Re. 1 per *puṭṭi* of salt bought by them to Bāva Mōgandas Rāghavadās and his heirs for maintaining a Bhairāgi *maṭham* at Bandar Rāmayapaṭnam, in Ś. 1668 (A.D. 1746).

Śākāvaram.

344. To the east in a field. (Telugu.). Records that on Wednesday, the eleventh of the bright fortnight of Kārttika of the year Īśvara; Koṇḍamarasayyagāru gave to Skandha Sōmēśvaradēva of Kaṇḍukūru, 120 *kuṇṭās* of wet land under the tank of Chāvatlampūḍi, and 2 *gorṛus* of dry land, for providing *amritapaḍi* to the deity. *Ibid.*, No. 71, p. 611.

Śiṅgarāyakoṇḍa.

345-A—D. (Telugu.) On different slabs within the temple. (A) On the floor of the southern gate: "The constant and daily service of Kaṇḍukūr Sītāpati." (B) In the same place: The service of Kaṇḍukūr Śēshāchāri." (C) On the floor of the eastern gate: "The service of Kāñchirāju Vēṅkaṭēśa." (D) On the same: "The service of Chakravarti Śinayya." *Ibid.*, No. 72, p. 612.

346. On a stone in the eastern *gōpuram*. (Telugu.) Records on the tenth *tithi* (lunar day) of the month of Bhādrapada in the year Bhava that the famous Liṅga Paṇḍit, a resident of Ponnampaḷḷi, a village in Koṇḍavīḍu Mahāmaṇḍala (kingdom), who was accomplished in doing good to others and who was a man of righteous conduct, constructed the pond named Bhavanāśi for the glory of Śrī Narasiṁha. *Ibid.*, No. 73, pp. 612–3.

347. On the southern pillar in the mukha-maṇṭapam. (Telugu.) Records that Kāñchirāju, son of Vallūr Śarabharāju, who was the karaṇam of Sōmarājapaḷḷi, presented an image of Garuḍa on Monday, the twelfth of the dark half of Vaiśākha, in the year Prabhava, Ś. 1489.

348. On the same pillar. (Telugu.) Records the service of plastering dedicated to Śrī Narasiṁha of Parṇaśāla, by Baṇḍāri

Śeṭṭi, son of Baṇḍāni Kāmiśeṭṭi, and by Kuniśeṭṭi, the excellent son of Kommasāni, who were both of the Gōpāla gōtra, on Monday, the thirteenth of the dark half of Māgha of the year Khara, Ś. 1371. *Nel. Ins., Kandukūr*, No. 75, p. 614.

349. On the northern pillar in the mukhamaṇṭapa. (Telugu.) Records that Dontayya, son of Koṇḍavīḍu Nallambaṭṭi Vissābhadra, presented an image of Hanūmān on the twelfth of the dark half of Phalguna of Sarvadhāri, Ś. 1450. *Ibid.*, No. 76, pp. 614-5.

350. On a stone in front of the temple. (Sanskrit and Telugu.) Records that on Thursday, the fifteenth of the bright half of Śravaṇa of the year Sarvajit, Ś. 1449, Rāyasam Ayyapparaśu gave the village of Jillēlamuḍi, situated on the southern bank of the Pālēru, in the *sīmu* of Kaṇḍukūr, in the rājya of Udayagiri, as a *sarvamānya*, to Śrī Narasiṁhadēva, for the religious merit of Kṛishṇadēvamahārāya. Records also the construction of the Narasiṁha temple by Rāmachandra between the river Manikā (Mannēru) and the three hills, known as Parṇaśāla. *Ibid.*, No. 77, pp. 615—8. [This is the same as No. 209 of 1894. The figure 1449 is misread for 1447. Mr. Krishna Sastri points out, on the basis of this inscription, that after the conquest of Udayagiri by Kṛishṇadēva Rāya it was made the seat of a provincial Government.]

351. On another slab in front of the temple. (Same as No. 210 of 1894.) (Telugu and Sanskrit.) Records that on Thursday, the tenth of the bright half of Phalguṇa of the year Manmatha, Ś. 1458, while Bhūtanātha Rāmabhaṭlu, of Gautāma gōtra and Aśvalāyana sūtra, was ruling the Udayagiri durgam, Vēṅkaṭādri, who had been appointed by him to the office of Governor of Udayāchala, gave the village of Cheṅgollu on the bank of the river Mushika (Yelikēru), as a *sarvamānya* to Śrī Narasiṁhadēva for the religious merit of Achyutadēvarāya and Rāmabhaṭlu. *Ibid.*, No. 78, pp. 618-21.

Somarāzupaḷḷi.

352. On a big stone in front of Śiva temple. (Telugu.) Records the gift of certain lands to a temple and its staff. *Ibid.*, No. 79, pp. 622-3.

353. On a stone in front of the Sun temple. (Telugu.) Records on the thirtieth of the dark fortnight of the month Āśvija of the year Vrishu, Ś. 1564, gift of the grain produced in the fields of Sōmarājapalli by Kutb Shah to Peda-Narasarāju, Pina Narasarāju, Kṛishṇamarāju, of the gōtra of Śrī Vasishṭha, grandsons of Ayyaparāju, for tank repairs. *Ibid.*, No. 80, pp. 624—6.

354. In the Narasiṁhasvāmi temple. (Telugu.) Records that Vālicherla Raṅgamma, a lady of the Vāsavāri family, constructed a maṇṭapa to Śrī Nṛisiṁhasvāmi. *Ibid.*, No. 81, p. 626.

Tangeḷḷa.

355. On a stone in front of Vēṇugōpāḷasvāmi temple. (Telugu.) Records a gift on the third of the bright fortnight of Chaitra of the year Durmukhi, Ś. 1458, by Mallūru Chintama Reḍḍi Gaṅgi Reḍḍi, to God Janārdana of the village of Taṅgeḷḷa which is said to be subject to the rule of the illustrious Āḍaya Rudra. *Nel. Ins., Kandukūr,* No. 81, p. 627.

356. On a stone in front of the temple of Janārdanasvāmi. (Telugu.) Records on Thursday, the tenth of the bright half of Chaitra of the year Vyaya, Ś. 1448, that the grandson of Jūpalli Rāma Nāyaniṅgāru ordered that the Brahman ināmdars and every one else should contribute one *nā*, that is, one *ṭūm* on every *puṭṭi* of the total produce for repairing the tank every year. *Ibid.,* No. 83, pp. 628—30.

Vēmpāḍu.

357. (Telugu.) Near Pōlēramma temple. A record, dated on Wednesday, the fifteenth of Nija Jyēshṭa of the year Jaya, Ś. 1216, on the occasion of a lunar eclipse, in the reign of Śrīman Mahāmaṇḍalēśvara Rudra Dēva Mahārāya, the (gem) of the Kākatīya family. Mentions Śrīmat Muppaḍi Nāyani Gāru and Śrī Tripurāntakadēvā. *Ibid.,* No. 84, pp. 630—2.

Virapaḷḷi.

358. In a field to the east. (Telugu.) Records on Monday, the fourteenth of the bright fortnight of Māgha of the year Dhātu, Ś. 1441, on the holy occasion of the Śivarātri, that Maradhavi Pōṭi Dējatayamgāru gave for the religious merit of his father Pallā Reḍḍi, 100 *kunṭas* of land for the daily offerings and enjoyments of Nāgēśvara of Vīrapalli. *Ibid.,* No. 85, pp. 632–3.

359. In the supply channel of the tank. (Telugu.) Records that on Wednesday, the fourteenth of the dark fortnight of Māgha of the year Dhātri, Ś. 1498, on the auspicious occasion of Śivarātri, Mallidēvi Donti Liṅgappagāru gave certain lands to the deity for the religious merit of his father Pallari Tamvōji. *Ibid.,* No. 86, p. 634.

KĀNIGIRI TALUK.

Arivēmula.

360. On a stone in the temple of Chennakēśava. (Telugu.) Records the act of devotion performed by a Jaṅgamarāju of the Ātrēya gōtra, who was the son of Hingi Rāmarāju, in planting the *dhvajasthamba* (flagstaff) and celebrating the sacred kalyāṇamahōtsava (the marriage festival) of God Chennakēśava, on the fifteenth of the bright half of the month Chaitra of the year Khara, Ś. 1575. *Nel. Ins., Kānigiri,* No. 1, p. 635.

361. In the tank to the west of village. (Telugu.) Records that two *goṟṟus* of *mānyam* were owned by a Dēva Gurayya in the hamlet of Arivēmula. *Nel. Ins.*, *Kānigiri*, No. 2, pp. 635-6.

Chākirēla.

362. On a pillar of the Rāmaliṅgaśvāmi temple. (Telugu.) An illegible record. *Ibid.*, No. 3, p. 636.

Dādireḍḍipaḷḷi.

363. On a stone close to the tank bund. (Sanskrit and Telugu.) Records that in Ś. 1338, in the year Durmukhi, in the bright fortnight of Śravaṇa, on the fifth *tithi*, under Pushya, on Thursday, Kaṇṭaya Bhāvi Nāyaka constructed a tank named after his brother Gaṅgaya. Records also that on Thursday, the fifth of the bright fortnight of Śravaṇa of the year Durmukhi, Ś. 1338, in the reign of Śrīman Mahārājādhirāja, Rājaparamēśvara, Chatussamudrādhīśvara, Śrī Vīra Pratāpa Dēvarāya Mahārāya of Vijayanagar I, and in the viceroyalty of Śrī Rāmachandra Rāja Oḍayalu, son of Dēvarāya at Uḍayagiri Bhāvināyanigāru, son of Kaṭṭiga Kaṇṭināyanigāru, constructed a tank named Gaṅgasamudram in the name of Gaṅgi Nāyaniṁgāru, his younger brother. *Ibid.*, No. 4, pp. 636—9.

Dāsalapaḷḷi (Dāsāḍipaḷḷi).

364. South of the Aṅkālamma temple. (Telugu.) Records on Sunday, the eleventh of Āshāḍha of the year Sarvadhāri, Ś. 1450, that a Rāvuri Rāghava Reḍḍi and Timmanāyanigāru, son of Veligōṭi Raṅganāyaḍu, the servants (devotees) of Śrī Tiruvēṅgalanātha of Veligoṇḍa, presented to the deity the village of Dāsaḍipaḷḷi attached to the *sīma* of Kanakagiri, in the Uḍayagiri rājya. The tax and other fees raised in this village were to be paid for the enjoyments and sacred food of the deity. The gift was made for the merit of Koṇḍaṁarusayyavāru, Rāvūri Basuva Reḍḍi Gāru, and Veligōṭi Raṅganāyaniṁgāru. *Ibid.*, No. 5, pp. 640—2.

Gōgulapaḷḷi.

365. On a stone called Dhanaṁguṇḍu (because it is believed to mark a hidden treasure). (Telugu.) A fragmentary record. *Ibid.*, No. 6, p. 642.

Gōzalaviḍu alias *Vāgupalli.*

366. In a garden in the east. (Telugu.) Records that on Thursday, the fifth of the bright fortnight of Vaiśākha of the year Ānanda, Ś. 1236, a certain Iḍumakaṇṭi Gaṅgi Reḍḍi Gāru, the servant of Bukkarāya Oḍāyalu, gave for the religious merit of his (Gaṅgi Reḍḍi's) father Peddi Reḍḍi and his mother Chānasāni, certain lands to God Mallikārjuna of Gonuvīḍu. *Nel. Ins., Kānigiri*, No. 7, pp. 642—5.

Guruvājipēṭa.

367. In a field called Mudām Tōṭa. (Sanskrit in old Telugu letters.) Records that this field of 12 *nivartanas* was given by king Kuḍubi Prāvēśa to the temple of Śīlādēvi at Kaṇḍa Sōmēśvara. *Ibid.*, No. 8, p. 645.

368. From a stone near the Chennakēśavasvāmi temple. (Telugu.) Records that on Friday, the seventh of the bright half of Nija Śravaṇa of the year Vyaya, Ś. 1688, one Gaja . . . nēmi Nāyanimgāru gave to Nāgaṇḍi Yallayya some gift (daśabandha rights). *Ibid.*, No. 9, pp. 646-47. The donor was the feudatory of Veligōṭi Kumāra Timma Nāyaningāru.

369. On a stone in front of the Chennakēśavasvāmi temple. (Telugu.) Records that on Sunday, the fifteenth of the bright fortnight of Āshāḍha in the year Piṅgaḷa, Ś. 1299, while Śrīman Mahāmaṇḍalēśvara Śrī Vīra Hari-Hara Mahārāyalu was ruling the kingdom of Vijayanagar, a Dērṇāvūri Koladula Bālināyanim-gāru who was ruling over Bōyaviṇḍlu in Udayagiri sthala, bestowed lands on Mallikārjunadēva, for the religious merit of his parents. *Ibid.*, No. 10, pp. 647—50.

Kambhampāḍu.

370. On a fallen stone to the south of village. (Telugu.) Records that on Wednesday, the fifth of the bright fortnight of Chaitra of the year Ānanda, Ś. 1176, while Śrīman Mahāmaṇḍalēśvara Gaṇḍa . . . yadēva Chōḍa Mahārājulu was reigning over Nellūru in Pākanāḍu a certain Śrīman Mahāmaṇḍaleśvara Pōtaya-dēva Chōḍa Mahārājulu presented gifts on the occasion of Vishuma Saṅkrānti. *Ibid.*, No. 11, pp. 651—53.

Kāñchipuram alias *Kāmañchipuram.*

371. On four sides of a stone in a field. (Telugu.) Records a gift of land on Thursday, the fifteenth of the bright fortnight of year Rakshasa, on the occasion of Vyatipāta for the religious merit of Maṅgiyuvarāju. *Ibid.*, No. 12, pp. 653—55.

Kānigiri.

372. On a rock near the pool. (Telugu.) Records that Ānanda Śīladāyinēnni Reḍḍi, son of Dāḍim Reḍḍi, worshipped Hanūmaṅ-tadēva of Dōsapāḍu who took compassion on him and saved him from peril. *Ibid.*, No. 13, pp. 655-56.

Kaṭṭakindipaḷḷi.

373. On a stone in front of the Mahālakshmi temple. Records gift of lands on Monday, the fifth of the bright fortnight of

Kārttika of the year Yuva to Kēśavanātha of Pōlichela. *Nel. Ins., Kānigiri*, No. 14, pp. 656–57.

374. On a stone in front of the Hanūmān's temple. (Telugu.) Records that on the eleventh of the dark fortnight of Āshāḍha of the year Pramādi, Ś. 1501, while Śrīmad Rājādhirāja Rājaparamēśvara Śrī Vīra Pratāpa Śrī Raṅgarāyadēva Mahārāyulu (1578—86) was ruling at the town of Penugoṇḍa, Chennappa Nāyaniṁgāru, of the Iniyāla gōtra, son of Varada Nāyaniṁgāru, granted to Śrīmat Akhilāṇḍakōṭi Brahmāṇḍa Nāyaka Vēda Vēdānta Vēdya Purāṇa Purushōttama, Chennarāya (deity) of Pōlicherla, some land in the village of Pōlicherla and the hamlet attached to it, in the *śima* of Kānigiri-Pōlicherla, for service to the deity and worship on the five *parvas*. *Ibid.*, No. 15, pp. 657—9.

Kūṭaguṇḍḷa.

375. Opposite Niruvagōpālasvāmi temple. (Telugu.) Records that on the fifth day of the bright fortnight of Ashāḍha of the year Hēmalambi (Hēviḷambi), Ś. 1579, Pērareḍḍi, Jaṅgam Reḍḍi, Koṇḍa Reḍḍi, Peda Veṅgaṇa, Timma Reḍḍi and China Veṅgaṇa Gāru, of the Yipparla gōtra, sons of Lakshmi Reḍḍi, and grandsons of Yērva Koṇḍa Reḍḍi, got the ruined temple of Niruva Gōpālasvāmi built in stone. *Ibid.*, No. 16, pp. 660–1.

Mārel̤la.

376. In front of the Vēṇugōpālasvāmi temple. (Telugu.) Records that on Sunday, the fourteenth of the dark fortnight of Māgha of the year Manmatha, Ś. 1457, on the holy occasion of Mahā Śivarātri, Śrīmat Vēṅkaṭādri Ayyavāru granted as a Bhaṭa (personal) Agrahāra the village of Cheruvupaḷḷi in the *śima* of Kānagiri which was attached to Udayagiri, to Jīvaraksha Bhaṭṭu Nandi Rāju, for the religious merit of Rāmabhaṭḷayyavāru. *Ibid.*, No. 17, pp. 661–2. See No. 351 above.

377. In a field to the east of the village. (Telugu.) A record dated on the tenth of the bright fortnight of Kārttika of the year Śukla. *Ibid.*, No. 18, p. 662.

378. On the southern boundary. (Telugu.) An illegible record. *Ibid.*, No. 19, p. 664.

379. In front of the Vēṇugōpālasvāmi temple. (Telugu.) Records that while Śrīman Mahārājādhirāja Rājaparamēśvara Śrī-Sadāśivarāyadēva Mahārāja was ruling on Thursday, the thirteenth of the bright fortnight of Māgha in the year Ānanda, Ś. 1476, Mangaḷa Timmōju Koṇḍōjugāru, feudatory of Śrīman Mahāmaṇḍalēśvara Rāmarāju Rāmayya Dēvā Mahārāju, obtained a royal decree exempting the barbers from the payment of the taxes *kaṭṭamēras, kōru, kāṇike, khaḍḍāyam, veṭṭi, etc.*, throughout the kingdom. Accordingly the kings who rule over the Kānagiri-Pōlacherla śīma should remit taxes on the barbers. *Nel. Ins.*, *Kānigiri*, No. 20, pp. 664—6. [*Kaṭṭamēras* is suggested to mean *fixed mēras*, and *kōru* the share of the produce paid to the State. *Kāṇike* is a benevolence and *khaḍḍāyam*, compulsory purchase of goods.]

Māsāyapēṭa.

380. On fallen stone south of village. (Telugu.) Records that on the fifteenth of the bright fortnight of Mārgaśira, Ś. 1476, on the holy occasion of a lunar eclipse, a certain Kaṇṭibōyina Peda Koṇḍama nēṇḍu gave lands to Nambi Rāmaṇṇa, for the religious merit of Veligōṭi Kumāra Timmanāyaḍu and Liṅgamakka-Gāru. *Ibid.*, No. 21, pp. 666–7.

381. On a wall of the Ādinārāyaṇa temple. (Telugu.) Records that on Monday, the fifteenth of the bright fortnight of Mārgaśira of the year Vyaya, Ś. 1508, Lālu-Khānuniṅgāru (Lal Khan) presented the village of Uppunūtula as a tax-free agrahāram to Podila Mārkaṇḍa Sōmayājulu, Sadāśiva Sōmayājulu, and Yajñēśvarachayana Pañchāgni Dīkshitulu, for the religious merit of Muhammad Kulipātaśāniṅgāru. The act of piety of Sēku Issā (Sheikh Isa). *Ibid.*, No. 22, pp. 667-8.

Mogilicherla.

382. On north boundary. (Telugu.) Records that on Monday, the seventh of the dark fortnight of Kārttika of the year Śrīmukha, Ś. 1396, Śrī Vīra Dēva Oḍayalu, the son of Śrīman Mahāmaṇḍalēśvara Harirāyarahita Mūrurāyaragaṇḍa, constructed the tank Dēvarāyasamudram, for the religious merit of his father Harihara Rāya. *Ibid.*, No. 23, pp. 668—70. [The date is inconsistent.]

Nāgalāvaram.

383. Taken from three sides of a standing stone and from three fragments in a field. (Telugu.) Records that on Thursday, the fifth of the bright fortnight of Vaiśākha of the year Vibhava, Ś. 1190, Śrīman Mahāmaṇḍalēśvara Immaḍidēva Mahārāja set up the image of Chennakēśava Perumāl, for the religious merit of his father Bhīmarāju and his mother Sriyādēvi. He appointed Perumāḍi Nambi, grandson of Śrī Raṅgabhaṭlu, of the Kāśyapa gōtra, resident of the village Śrī Suka, and worshipper of Tiruvēṅgaḍanātha, to perform the worship, and gave to the deity 13 *tūms* of land as measured with a pole of 22 cubits. Various gifts: For *amritapaḍi* (sacred food) 14 *tūms*: for all kinds of decorations in Kākanampāḍu, 1 *puṭṭi* and 10 *tūms;* In Guḍipāḍu 3 *tūms*; In Rāvulakola 3 *tūms*; for *Kariyamadu* (food with vegetables) and flowers two gardens; for the rice (to be distributed among the travellers of different countries) and for sandal to the God, a piece of land given by Masikāṭṭu Toḍuvu prolē: for (keeping) the light, a big plate given by Namana Appana; a gong given by Malluka

Kāmaṇa; a bell used at the time of offering incense and horns *(ēka śaṅkalu)* and for the *abhishēkam* (anointing of the God) with milk—13 cows, given by the royal family *(rāchavāru)*. *Nel. Ins., Kānigiri*, No. 24, pp. 670—6.

384. *C.P. No.* 16 *of Nel. Ins.*—(Sanskrit and Nandināgari.) A record of Kṛishṇa Dēva Rāya, dated in Ś. 1437 (A.D. 1515) evidently after the capture of Koṇḍavīḍu, making the gift of Nāgalāvaram to a Brahman astronomer Śūra Bhaṭṭa, son of Rāmabhaṭṭa. A field named Timmayapāḷem and measuring 2,250 *kuṇṭas* was also granted for the maintenance of the village. The gift was made at the request of Gaṅga Reḍḍi, son of Viṭṭa, evidently "a chief who accepted Kṛishṇa Rāya's lordship at the very commencement of his exploits on the east coast".

385. *C.P. No.* 86 *of Mr. Sewell's List.*—Records grant, in Nandināgari characters, by Kṛishṇadēva Rāya of the Vijayanagar dynasty in Ś. 1437 (A.D. 1515), Yuva, of the village of Nāgalāvaram to the temple of Mallikārjuna at Śrīśailam, during a lunar eclipse that occurred in that year in the month Śravaṇa.

Nalajanampāḍu.

386. To the north-east of the village. (Sanskrit and Telugu.) Records that Bōdirāju, son of Paḷeyaru, gave land sowable with three *puṭṭis* of seed to Paḷayāri. *Ibid.*, No. 25, pp. 676–7.

Nallagaṇḍḷa.

387. On a figure of Vināyaka under the tank bund. (Telugu.) An illegible record. *Ibid.*, No. 26, p. 678.

Nandanavanam.

388. On an image in the Mallikārjuna temple, Velagoṇḍa hills. (Telugu.) Records that in the place where Rāmasvāmi released Gautama's wife from her curse while he marched against Laṅka, the deities Malēśvara (Amarēśvara) and Umāraṅga (or Mahāliṅga) were set up. *Ibid.*, No. 27, p. 678.

389. On the doorway of the Āñjanēya temple. (Telugu.) Records some gift on the tenth of the bright fortnight of Māgha of the year Viśvāvasu, Ś. 1708, by a certain Sarasi . . . Pantulu to the temple of Hanumantarāyalu. *Ibid.*, No. 28, p. 679.

390. On a stone inside Mallikārjunasvāmi temple in Velagoṇḍa hills. (Telugu.) "Nothing can be made of the inscription as it contains letters of a peculiar type unknown to us." The only words that can be made out are "*Gautama Mahāmuni*" and "*Avadhūtasvāmi*". *Ibid.*, No. 29, p. 680.

391. In a small tank near the Mallikārjunasvāmi temple, Velagoṇḍa hills. (Telugu.) "The first and last lines contain letters of a type unknown to us." The inscription is incomplete and unintelligible in parts. Records that while the great sage Gautama was living here, Avadhūtasvāmi came from Ayōdhya, and induced him to go to Śalaya Parvata (Śrī Śailam), bring a liṅga, and establish it here, as a Rudrābhishēkam performed here in the months of Śravaṇa (Aśvija), Kārttika, Mārgaśira and Māgha would bring one the merit of having made a *pradakshiṇam* from Benares to Laṅka. *Nel. Ins., Kānigiri,* No. 30, pp. 681-2.

Naramārella.

392. A hero-stone at the Collector's bungalow at Nellore. (Telugu.) It bears an armed god or hero and smaller figures. The inscription is not fully legible. It is dated in Ś. 1106. *Ibid.*, No. 31, pp. 682-3.

Pāṇḍavanāgalavaram.

393. On tank bund. (Telugu.) A record on Wednesday, the tenth of Jyēshṭa of the year Sarvadhāri, about the devotion of Kōṭiśeṭṭi, son of Vākicherla Vīriśeṭṭi. *Ibid.*, No. 32, p. 684.

Pedda Alavalapāḍ.

394. On a rock in the bed of the river. (Telugu.) Records that on Thursday, the fifteenth of the bright fortnight of Pushya of Ś. 1448, Rāpūr Rāghava Reḍḍigāru presented the village of Gaṅgapaṭṇam, situated in Kānagiri-Pōlacherla-Musumdūru śīma, to Sōmēśvara and Bagādi Gaṅga for service, for the religious merit of his father Basava Reḍḍi and his mother Amalāmbikā. *Ibid.*, No. 33, pp. 684-5.

Perugupaḷḷi.

395. In front of the temple on Raṅganāyakulu hill. (Telugu.) Records on Thursday, the tenth of the dark fortnight of Vaiśākha of the year Virōdhi, Ś. 1331, a gift to Śrī Kāṇṭha Rāmēśvaradēva of Śrī Palēṭikoṇḍa. Records also that Murāri Nāyani Chennama Nāyaniṅgāru set up this deity and presented three *goṟṟus* of land. *Ibid.*, No. 34, p. 686.

Pōlavaram.

396. In a field to the south. (Telugu.) Records that on Thursday, the fifteenth of the bright fortnight of Māgha, lunar eclipse, a certain person excavated, for the religious merit of his father Gōpināyaniṅgāru, a well, provided for a water-shed, constructed a temple and planted a mango tope, and a tope of trees yielding all kinds of fruits. *Ibid.*, No. 35, pp. 687—9.

Punugōḍu.

397. On a stone front of the Siddhēśvarasvāmi temple. (Telugu.) Records that on Friday, the first of the bright fortnight of Śravaṇa of the year Raudri, Ś. 1755834581,* Vipaḷam Vēja Annapagāru of the family of Malipūṇḍi Aubuḷayyaṅgāru made a thousand liṅgas, consecrated them, and built a temple. He performed the marriage of Vīrajiyya, son of Tammaḷḷu Mādaśivalu; and purchased and presented a field of 10 *Śiṅgamṭūms* to the deity. *Nel. Ins., Kānigiri*, No. 36, pp. 689–90.

Rāllapaḷḷi.

398. On a rock to the south-east of the village. (Telugu.) Records that on the full-moon day of Māgha of the year Vijaya, Channamanēḍu, son of Bījam Channamanēḍu, gave as a *mānyam* to Kāśa Koṇḍa Baṭṭuḍu a field of one *ṭūm* at the southern extremity of Gollakuṇṭa in the village of Dūku Nāgacheruvupaḷḷi for the goddess Gaṅgā. *Ibid.*, No. 37, p. 691.

Śākhavaram.

399. On a stone in a field. (Telugu.) Records that on the eleventh day of the dark fortnight of Kārttika of the year Īśvara, Koṇḍamarasayya presented to the deity Harimskandasōmēśvara of Chuṇḍi, a piece of wet land measuring 120 *goṟṟus*, etc. *Ibid.*, No. 38, pp. 691–2.

Tāllūru.

400. Opposite the Chennakēśava temple. (Telugu.) Records that on Thursday, the first of the bright fortnight of Chaitra of the year Vikrama, on the auspicious occasion of the consecration of Śrī Kēśavanātha of Tālūru, the following lands were given by Akāchi Maldēva Rājuṅgāru, two *puṭṭis* of dry land, half a *chatu paḍi* (?) of wet land, and three *kuṇṭas* of garden land. *Ibid.*, No. 39, pp. 692–3.

Uppalapāḍu.

401. On a fallen stone near the ruined fort to the south. (Kanarese.) Records an edict under the order of Dēvarāya Mahārāyaru. *Ibid.*, No. 40, pp. 693—5.

Vālicherla.

402. On steps of temple of Īśvara in the fort. (Telugu.) "The stone being broken and rough, the record is illegible." *Ibid.*, No. 41, pp. 695–6.

KĀVALI TALUK.

Ānēmaḍugu.

403. This inscription was conveyed a few years ago from Anēmaḍugu to the Collector's Cutcherry, Nellore, where it now lies (Telugu.) Records on Wednesday, the second day of the bright

* "The meaning of the date figures is not understood." *Śingam-ṭūms* have been interpreted to be *ṭūms* of a standard named after the village of Śiṅgampāḍu.

fortnight of Phalguṇa in the year Chitrabhānu, Ś. 1564, the grant of *mēras* (grain fees) attached to the tank of Ānēmaḍugu (as *amaram*) in the śīma of Kaṇḍukūru, by Vējarla Narasarāju Gāru, son of Ayyaparāju Gāru and grandson of Kēśava Rāju Gāru, of the Gōtra of Vasiṣṭha, Āpastamba sūtra, and Yajuśśākha. *Nel. Ins., Kāvali*, No. 1, pp. 697–8.

404. In tank bed. (Telugu.) An illegible record. *Ibid.*, No. 2, p. 699.

Bitraguṇṭa.

404-A. A C.P. grant of the Vijayanagara king Saṅgama II in Ś. 1278. Engraved by Bhōganātha, the *Narmasachiva* of the king. See Nos. 273–4 above.

Boḍaguḍipāḍu.

405. West of the village. (Telugu.) A fragmentary record dated Ś. 1046. Gift to Mallikārjunadēva. *Ibid.*, No. 3, pp. 699–700.

Brāhmaṇakrāka.

406. On a pillar of a temple. (Telugu.) This is an incomplete record and is partly illegible. It seems to record a gift to Chennakēśava. *Ibid.*, No. 4, pp. 700–1.

407. On a pillar of the same temple. (Telugu.) This is also partly illegible. Records the construction of a temple in Brāhmaṇakrāka attached to Jaladaṅki. *Ibid.*, No. 5, p. 701.

408. On a pillar in the same temple. (Telugu.) An assurance of belief in Śrī Rāmaliṅgasvāmi. *Ibid.*, No. 6, pp. 701–2.

Chinna Aṇṇalūru.

409. In a maṇṭapam of Kālabhairavaḍu temple. (Telugu.) A fragmentary record of a Vijayanagara king, dated on the second of . . . fortnight of Āshāḍha of the year Sādhāraṇa. *Ibid.*, No. 7, pp. 702–3.

Chinnakrāka.

410. On a large stone opposite the small Śiva temple. (Telugu.) Records on the occasion of Uttarāyaṇa Saṅkrānti, in Kīlaka, Ś. 1110, that Prōl Dēsāhi, son of Nalagarula Kāpa Dēśāhi, who belonged to the Dēśaṅgulu sect of Vinuradaka (town ?) of Pākināḍu, constructed a temple to Śrī Mallikārjunadēva, for the religious merit of Talāru Prōli Nāyaka, and gave one *paṭṭu* of wet land to the east of the village in rear of the tank, for offerings and worship to the deity. Records the gift to this temple of a large censer, a small censer, a plate for burning camphor, two perpetual lamps, a bell, and a conch; and dry fields in the west of the village for the performance of worship at the three *sandhyās* (morning, noon and evening). Tripurāntaka Paṇḍit should receive these; he, his sons, and grandsons should maintain the charity. *Ibid.*, No. 8, pp. 703–4.

411. On rough stone gate-posts of the temple of Gōpālasvāmi. (Telugu.) Records that one *paṭṭu* of dry land and hundred *paṭṭu* of wet land (for maintenance of a lamp and for daily offering), and hundred *paṭṭus* of wet paddy fields were given to Śrī Gōpāladēva by Pōtana Bōya. *Nel. Ins., Kāvali*, No. 9, p. 705.

412. In the same place. (Telugu.) Records that on Monday, the eleventh of the bright half of Śravaṇa, Ś. 1109, as the idol of Vēṇugōpāladēva was being consecrated, one Apāpi Reḍḍi gave to the Nambi Vaishṇavite priest one *puṭṭi* of wet land, and fourteen *paṭṭus* of dry land for providing oblation, offering and worship to Vēṇugōpāladēva, so that religious merit might accrue to Dalāri Dāmi Nāyukuḍu. *Ibid.*, No. 10, p. 706.

413. In the same place. (Telugu.) Records that on Thursday, the eleventh of the bright half of Āshāḍha, Ś. 1244, a certain Nallamdērvula Peda Kōṭi Reḍḍi Gāru constructed a temple to Śrī Gōpāladēva, for the religious merit of Śrī Mahāmaṇḍalēś-vara Daśavarma Dēva Mahārāja, his brothers, and his father Tim-madēva Mahārāja . . . *Ibid.*, No. 11, p. 707.

414. In the same place. (Telugu.) Records that Chāmaya, son of Dāsarāju, gave one *paṭṭu* of paddy field as a gift, so that religious merit might accrue to his grandfather. *Ibid.*, No. 12, pp. 707–8.

Dūbaguṇṭa.

415. To the south of the village near the Polimēra stream. (Telugu.) Records a gift on the day of Uttarāyaṇa Saṅkrānti, Ś. 1136, for the religious merit of Śrīman Mahāmaṇḍalēśvara Manma Siddhanadēva Chōḍa Mahārājulu, son of Rājēndradēva Chōḍa Mahārājulu, "on whose lotus feet are set the eyes of Trilōchana and all other kings of the earth, who is the jewelled lamp of the race of Karikāla, by whom the dam of the Kāveri was built, who is an elephant goad to wicked princes, who is of the Kāśyapa gōtra, who is sprung from the solar race, who is the lord of the best of cities Orayūr, who is Kīrti Nārāyaṇa, and who took tribute from Kāñchi". *Ibid.*, No. 13, pp. 708—10.

Gaṭṭupaḷḷi.

416. From stone in bed of tank. (Telugu.) Records a gift on Monday, the first of the bright fortnight of Phalguṇa of the year Iva (?), Ś. 1363, by Śrī Vīra Dēva, the son of Śrī Hari-Hara-Rāya, to Rāmachandra Perumāḷ, the excellent son of Aṅkula Kōṭēśvara-dēvara of Jaladaṅki in Pākināḍu, for the increase of life and health of Rāmachandra Bhaṭḷu. *Ibid.*, No. 14, pp. 710–11.

Gouravaram.

417. On two sides of a stone by the Chennakēśvarasvāmi temple. (Telugu.) Records that on the twelfth of the bright fortnight of Śravaṇa, Ś. 1..., the daughter of a certain Śrīmat Chelvarāju, gave one *māḍa* for a twilight lamp to Manma Kēśavadēva. Perumā Bhaṭṭu should receive this *māḍa* and keep up the lamp. *Nel. Ins., Kāvali*, No. 15, pp. 711-2.

418. On a pillar to the south of the Chennakēśavasvāmi temple. (Telugu.) An illegible record. *Ibid.*, No. 16, p. 713.

419. On a pillar to the north of the Chennakēśavasvāmi temple. (Telugu.) Records the construction of a pillar by Śrī Ādūri Mummaḍi Śeṭṭi. *Ibid.*, No. 17, p. 713.

420. Over the door of the Pārvati temple. (Telugu.) A record on the fifteenth of the bright fortnight of Chaitra of the year Śubhakrit, Ś. 1344, . . . *Ibid.*, No. 18, p. 713.

Jaladaṅki.

421. On the south front pillar of the Chennakēśavasvāmi's temple. (Telugu.) The inscription is illegible in various places. Records a gift of lamp on the thirtieth of the dark fortnight of Kārttika, Ś. 1196, to the illustrious Chennakēśava of Jaladaṅki. *Ibid.*, No. 19, p. 714.

422. In the same place. Records on the twelfth of the dark fortnight of Pushya of the year Sādhāraṇa, Ś. 1712, two *guṇṭas* of land were given for the purpose of an evening lamp to Chennakēśavadēva of Jaladaṅki. *Ibid.*, No. 20, pp. 714-5.

423. In the same place. (Telugu.) Records that on Saturday, the third of the dark fortnight of Vaiśākha, Ś. 1196, Purushōttamadēvara, son of Perumāreḍḍidēva, gave 66 ewes for the purpose of lighting lamps every evening to Chennakēśavadēva, of Jaladaṅki, so that religious merit might accrue to his mother and father. *Ibid.*, No. 21, pp. 715-6.

424. In the same place. (Telugu.) Records that on Monday, the eleventh of the bright half of Āśva (yuja), Ś. 1197, Reḍḍi Dāmi Reḍḍi, Pandru Prōḷi Reḍḍi, Pinnama Reḍḍi, Kāmi Reḍḍi, Prōlama Reḍḍi, and Annama Reḍḍi, son of Vāmmi Reḍḍi, gave certain gifts to Chennakēśavadēva for lamps and festivals on the Ēkādaśi day. *Ibid.*, No. 22, pp. 716-7.

425. In the same place. (Telugu.) Records on Saturday, the first of the bright half of Māgha, Ś. 1198, Bamayāṇḍi Cheṭṭi, son of Chendāmara-Kaṇṇan, gave eighteen ewes for two evening lamps to Chennakēśavadēva of Jalandaṅki, so that religious merit might accrue to his parents. Records also the gift of a *śiṛasu rūkā* ("the value of this coin is not known") and a cow. *Ibid.*, No. 23, pp. 717-8.

426. On the north front pillar of the same temple. (Telugu.) This is mostly illegible. Records a gift to Chennakēśavadēva of Jaladaṅki in Ś. 1173. *Ibid.*, No. 24, p. 718.

427. On the south back pillar of the same temple. [Same as inscription 208 of 1894.] (Telugu.) Records that on Thursday, eleventh day of the bright fortnight of Kārttika under the Uttara Phalguni Nakshatra, Ś. 1166, in the reign of Śrīman Mahāmaṇḍalēśvara Alluntirukāḷatti Dēva Chōḍa Mahārājulu, the servant of Peddināyaka, who was the director of seventy-two offices, gave for the religious merit of Nāganabōyuṇḍu and of his father and mother, a "*māḍa*" for evening lamps to the temple of Chennakēśavadēva of Jaladaṅki. From the interest derived therefrom the Nambis should maintain the evening lamp. *Nel. Ins., Kāvali*, No. 25, pp. 719–20.

428. In the north back pillar of the same place. [Same as inscription 207 of 1894.] (Telugu.) Records that on Wednesday, the seventh of the bright fortnight of Āshāḍha of the year Raktākshi, Ś. 1186, Pemmaya, son of Kampanu Bōyuḍu, gave a "*Gadya*" (a gold coin) to the Nambi on condition that he should light the evening lamps in a row in half the temple of Chennakēśavadēva, for the religious merit of his parents. *Ibid.*, 26, pp. 720–1.

429. In the same place. (Telugu.) Records that on Thursday, the tenth day of the dark fortnight of Māgha, Ś. 1200, Orula Siddhaya and Perumāṇḍi Nambigāru, Chennakēśava's son Nāraparāzu, Śiṅgaya, and Pemmaya bought a fourth part in Jaladaṅki village, gave it to Kēśava Nambi and registered it in his name. *Ibid.*, No. 27, pp. 721–2.

430. In the south back pillar of same temple. (Telugu.) Records that on Friday, the third of the bright fortnight of Phalguna, Ś. 1198, Vallama Prōlu Cheṭṭi presented 66 ewes for lighting a lamp to Śrī Chennakēśavadēva of Jaladaṅki for the religious merit of his parents. *Ibid.*, No. 28, p. 722.

431. In the north back pillar. (Telugu.) Records that on Sunday, the eleventh day of the bright fortnight of the month of Mārgaśira, Ś. 1196, Bumaya gave nineteen ewes as chārity, on behalf of his parents, for lighting two evening lamps in the temple of Chennakēśavadēva of Jaladaṅki. *Ibid.*, No. 29, p. 723.

432. In the same place. (Telugu.) Records that on Friday, the third of the dark fortnight of Māgha, Ś. 1199, Chendāmara-Dēvanalla Gōpāla Śeṭṭi gave nine ewes for an evening lamp in the temple of Chennakēśavadēva of Jaladaṅki, so that religious merit might accrue to his father and mother. *Ibid.*, No. 30, pp. 723–4.

Kadanūtala.

433. In the enclosure of the Mallēśvarasvāmi temple. (Telugu and Sanskrit.) Records that on Thursday, the tenth of the bright fortnight of Chaitra, on the day under Pushya, Ś. 1139, Śrīmat Kāmi Reḍḍi, son of Aitama Reḍḍi, and his wife Prōlasāni, gave a perpetual lamp to Śrī Mallikārjunadēva of Kaḍavanūnṭi, situated in Poritināḍu, for the religious merit of Śūrapa Reḍḍi and Vennasāni, and presented 50 ewes. The *pūjāri* (worshipper) Prōlamrāju should receive this property and keep up two lamps. Records also that Śrīmat Kāmasāni, daughter of Śrīmat Aitama Reḍḍi and Prōlasāni, gave a perpetual lamp to Śrī Mallikārjunadēva, for the religious merit of Mādi Reḍḍi Mārasāni, Prōli Reḍḍi, Vēmasāni, Prōli Reḍḍi and Gaṅgasāni, and presented 50 ewes. Prōlamrāju should receive these and keep up the lamp. *Nel. Ins.*, *Kāvali*, No. 31, pp. 724–5.

Kākuṭūru.

434. To the north of the village near Guṟṟapurāllaguṇṭa. (Telugu.) Records apparently a gift to a tank. *Ibid.*, No. 32, p. 726.

435. To the south. (Telugu.) Records that on Monday, the day of Vishama Saṅkrānti, Ś. 1304, Bairapa Nāyuṇḍu, constructed a temple for the increase of wealth to Dānam-Guraya, his sons and grandsons, and constructed a tank. *Ibid.*, No. 33, p. 727.

Kaligiri.

436. On the tank bund. (Telugu.) An illegible record.

Kāṭrāyapāḍu.

437. To the west of village, on cattle stand. (Telugu.) Records that on Thursday, the fifteenth of the bright fortnight of Bhādrapada of the year Saumya, Ś. 1231, on the occasion of a lunar eclipse, under the Pūrvabhadra star, Śrīmat Tiruvēṅgaḍanātha Mahīpāla (king) gave Tiruvēṅgaḍanātha Chaturvēdimaṅgalam *alias* the Kāṭravāvi (Kāṭravāpi) to Śrīmat Tyāgasamudra Dharma . . . māditya Dēvaniṇḍu, Kāṭravāpi Aṅgarēni Tiruvēṅgaḍa Bhaṭṭu of the Kauśika gōtra who evidently gave it to those who were versed in Vēdās. "Kings should protect this *vriṭṭi*." *Ibid.*, No. 35, pp. 728–9.

438. On a big stone north of the village. (Telugu.) Records that on Friday, the eleventh of the bright fortnight of Phalguna of the year Paridhāvi, Ś. 1233, Sādamabo Arupāliśeṭṭi presented a *mānyam* to Chennakēśava Perumāḷ of Kāṭrāvipāḍu for the religious merit of Śrīmat Maṇḍa . . . Nāyaṅkaruvāru, while Kākatīya Pratāpa Rudradēva Mahārājulu was ruling. *Ibid.*, No. 36, pp. 730–3.

439. On the cattle stand to the south of the village. (Sanskrit and Telugu.) Records the presentation of the agrahāra of Kāṭravāyapāḍu in Ś. 1231, in the year Saumya, on the day of a holy lunar eclipse, while king Raṅganātha was ruling the earth, to Bhīmarāmēśvara. *Ibid.*, No. 37, pp. 733–4. The editors of *Nellore Inscriptions* point out that the king might be Madhurāntaka Pottappi Chōḷa Rāja Gaṇḍa Gōpāla Dēva.]

440. On the caliṅgulah of the tank, north of the village. (Telugu.) Records that on the first Ēkādaśi, Ś. 1150, in the reign of Śrīman Mahāmaṇḍalēśvara Gaṇḍagōpāla Tirukāladēva Chōḍa

Mahārājulu, a certain Śrīmat Patināyakuṇḍu constructed a temple, for the treasury of Kēśavadēva of Kaṭravāvi, for the religious merit of his parents and himself and further gave a piece of land, to the east of the tank. *Nel. Ins., Kāvali,* No. 38, pp. 734-5.

Kāvali.

441. On a stone near a tank bund. (Mainly Sanskrit in Telugu character.) This stone appears to be within the boundaries of Maddurpāḍ village. Records that in Ś. 1129, Prabhava, on a holy day, at equinox, Śri Tammu Siddīśvara, son of Yeṛrasiddha, grandson of Bēṭa, and younger brother of Nallasiddha, presented in perpetuity large gifts and an agrahāra called Śrīpura after his own mother (Śrī Dēvi), in the illustrious Vishaya (territory) of Duddūra to Baṇḍari Tripura Rāya and other Brahmans. *Ibid.*, No. 39, pp. 735—40.

442. In the gateway of a detached shrine in enclosure of Āñjanēśvara Svāmi's temple. [Inscription 206 of 1894. Telugu.] Records the gift of the village Jeldapāḍu to the deity of Jeldapāḍu for the religious merit of Śrīman Mahāmaṇḍalēśvara Manma Siddhi Dēva Chōḍa Mahārāja, son of Śrīman Mahāmaṇḍalēśvara Jagadobba-Gaṇḍa Kāmaya Dēva Mahārāja. *Ibid.*, No. 40, pp. 740-1.

Kottapaḷḷi.

443. To the north of village. (Telugu.) Records the gift of 55 *kuṇṭas* of field. *Ibid.*, No. 41, p. 741.

Mungamūru.

444. On south wall of Ganēśa temple. (Telugu.) Records the gift of 1,100 *kuṇṭas* of wet land under the tank as a *mānyam* to Kāśi Pāpa Bhaṭṭuḍu, who constructed these temples. *Ibid.*, No. 42, p. 742.

445. On a stone to east of the Nīlakaṇṭhēśvara temple. (Telugu.) Records that on Thursday, the fifth of the bright fortnight of Chaitra, of Ś. 1185 . . . of the Śrīvatsa gōtra, who is the prime minister (Mahāpradhāni) of Śrīman Mahāmaṇḍalēśvara Manma Siddhi dēva Chōḍa Mahārājulu, gave 50 ewes for two twilight lamps to Gaurīśvaradēva of . . . varam in Poritināḍu (a subdivision of) Pākanāḍu. The *kāpus* of the village received these ewes and maintained the lights. *Ibid.*, No. 43, pp. 742-3.

446. On the south wall of the Gaṇēśa temple. (Telugu.) Records that on Thursday, the eleventh of the bright fortnight of Māgha of the year Manmatha, Ś. 1660, as the temple of Gaṇādhipati (Gaṇēśa) of Muṅgamūr was in ruins, Kēśima Reḍḍi Liṅga Reḍḍi, son of Perumā Reḍḍi, constructed a maṇṭapa in front of the temple of Nīlakaṇṭhēśvara of Muṅgamūru, a temple to Mātaṅgidēvi, a sluice to the tank of Muṅgamūr, and a temple to Vināyakasvāmi, for the religious merit of his parents. *Ibid.*, No. 44, pp. 741—5.

Mūsanūr.

447. On a tank between Mūsanūr and Kāvali. (Telugu.) The inscription is not clearly legible. Records that in Ś. 1152, on Monday under the Uttara Phalguni Nakshatra, in the reign of Gaṇḍa Gōpāla Dīpakāḷtidēva (Kaḷatti ?) Karāru Manmarāmuṇḍu, the ruler of Muraṇapura (lit. the beloved of the lady Muraṇapura), the protector of all virtuous people, presented with libation of water, free of encumbrance, two parts under the Taṭicheruvu in the village of Musuṇḍu (Mūsanūr), while his minister Kētana presented one part to Gaṇḍa-Gōpāla. *Nel. Ins., Kāvali,* No. 45, pp. 745–6.

448. On a stone in the garden of Rēvūr Lakshmayya. (Telugu.) Records the edict relating to Mūsanūr taluk granted by Velugōṭi Veṅkaṭapati Nāyanivāru, in Ś. 1560, Bahudhānya, on the second of the dark fortnight of the month of Chaitra. The *sandhāta* (village official), lessee, amaradār, or ruler of the village, should do work to the tank and channel for the *mēras* attached thereto. *Ibid.*, No. 46, pp. 747–8.

449. On a stone opposite the old temple of Vēnugōpālasvāmi at Chentasugānipālem (hamlet of Mūsanūr). (Sanskrit in Telugu character.) Records that in Ś. 1152, on Monday, the twelfth of the bright half of Kārttika, the ruler of Muraṇapura named Kōdarāma, gave an endowment for lamps to Gōpāla in Mūsanūr village. *Ibid.*, No. 47, pp. 748—50.

Peddakoṇḍūru.

450. To the east of the hamlet Vīrareḍḍipāḷem. (Telugu.) Records that on Saturday, the day of Vishuma Saṅkrānti, in the year Śrīmukha, Ś. 1195, Śrīman Mahāmaṇḍalēśvara Nāgadēvarājulu, gave (lands ?) to Mehāyini Tikkināyuḍu of Prapa Koṇḍūru, for the religious merit of Rudradēva Mahārājulu for worship, sacred food, light, and dancing. *Ibid.*, No. 48, pp. 750–1.

Tāllapāḷem.

451. On a stone in front of the old temple. (Telugu.) Records that in Ś. 1558, Bahudhānya, on the fifth day of the month Phalguna, while Vīra Pratāpa Śrī Vīra Veṅkaṭapatirāya was seated on the throne of Penugoṇḍa, it was settled that the *mēras* were to be at one *kuñcha* per *puṭṭi* for the tank of Juṭūr village, situated in Udayagiri śīma, which was given to Velugōṭi Veṅkaṭapati Nāyanivāru by the Rāja as an *amaram*. *Ibid.*, No. 49, pp. 751–2. Date inconsistent.

452. On a stone by a pond near the temple. (Telugu.) Records that in Ś. 1558, Dhātu, on the seventh day of the dark fortnight of Chaitra, while Vīra Veṅkaṭapatirāya was seated on the throne of Penugoṇḍa, Kuñchala Veṅgaṇṇa, the agent of Veṅkaṭapati Nāyanivāru, fixed the *mēras*, under the orders of Veṅkaṭapati Nāyanivāru, at one *kuñcha* per *puṭṭi*, for the tank attached to the village of Kāvali in the *śima* of Udayagiri which had been given to Velugōṭi Veṅkaṭapati Nāyanivāru as *amaram* (service-tenure) by the Rāja Śrī Vīra Veṅkaṭapati. *Nel. Ins.*, *Kāvali*, No. 50, pp. 753–4.

Timmasamudram.

453. On a stone in the field bearing survey number 170. (Telugu.) Records that on Sunday, the eleventh of the bright half of Vaiśākha, under the Uttara Nakshatra, in the year Kāḷayukta, Ś. 1120, Śrī-Pati Nāyuḍu set up the image of Prasannakēśavadēva at Chintaguṇṭa for the religious merit of his father, and gave four *paṭṭus* of dry land at Kāḷavarmaguṇṭa, and 200 kuṇṭas of dry land behind Chintacheruvu, to Kēśava Bhaṭṭa Nambi, to provide offerings and worship to the deity. Records some other gifts. *Ibid.*, No. 51, pp. 754—6.

KŌVŪR TALUK.

Allūru.

454. On the Nandi maṇṭapam opposite Śiva temple. (Telugu.) Records that on the second of the bright half of Chaitra of the year Bahudhānya, Ś. 1560, Śrīmat Velugōṭi Veṅkaṭapati Nāyaniṅgāru ordered that the tank *mēras* of the various villages should be spent for the maintenance of the tanks of the respective villages. *Nel. Ins.*, *Nellore*, No. 1, pp. 757—9.

455. In the Vishṇu temple. (Telugu.) Records a gift to the deity Kēśavanātha on the dark fortnight of Āśvija of the year Vijaya, Ś. 1455. *Ibid.*, No. 2, p. 760.

Batrakāgollu.

456. On fallen stone in a street in the south of the village. (Telugu.) Records that on the second of the bright half of Chaitra of the year Bahudhānya, Ś. 1560, Velugōṭi Veṅkaṭapati Nāyanivāru ordered the village *sandhātāgar*, the lessee, the *amaradār* or whoever was the ruler, to keep the tank and channel in order with the *mēras* of the tank at Kāmgollu. *Ibid.*, No. 4, p. 762.

457. On same stone. (Telugu.) Records that on the tenth day of the bright fortnight of Āśvija of the year Vijaya, Ś. 1575, Boligadacha Vrajagoruvinḍla ordered that the *residents* of the village of Kāgallu which had been a *mānyam* of Pākanala Kṛishṇappa Nāyanivāru were exempted from fees for the marriage of their daughters. *Ibid.*, No. 5, pp. 762–3.

Chennūru.

458. In the bed of tank. (Telugu.) Records that on the second of the bright half of Chaitra of the year Bahudhānya,

Ś. 1560, Velugōṭi Veṅkaṭapati Nāyaniṅgāru issued a similar edict for the tank at Chennūru. *Nel. Ins., Nellore*, No. 7, pp. 765—7.

459. On a stone in the enclosure of Mūlasthānēśvara temple. (Telugu.) Records that one Peddanaṁgāru presented to the deities a number of villages for the religious merit of his father Basavanāyaniṁgāru, and his mother Mummammāgāru. *Ibid.*, No. 8, pp. 767–8.

Daggadarti.

460. On boundary between Chennūru and Daggadarti. (Telugu.) Records that on Tuesday, the seventh of the dark half of Phalguna of the year Manmatha, Ś. 1458, the Governor of Udayagiri durgam had the boundary between this village and Chennūru settled in the manner that the people of the four villages of Jaidaṇka, Allūru, Gaṅgāram and Vavveru did (desire ?). *Ibid.*, No. 10, p. 770.

Dāmavaram.

461. South of the village. (Telugu.) Records that on the second day of the bright fortnight of Chaitra of the year Bahudhānya, Ś. 1560, a *mēra* grant was issued for the tank of Dāmavaram by Velugōṭi Veṅkaṭapati Nāyuḍu. *Ibid.*, No. 11, p. 771.

Duvvūru.

462. On the gōpuram of Dūrvāsula Kōṭēśvara temple. (Sanskrit in Grantha character and Tamil.) This is a fragmentary record. The beginning is Sanskrit and mentions Rājagaṇḍagōpāla. *Ibid.*, No. 12, p. 772.

Gaṇḍavaram.

463. On the southern wall of the enclosure of the Vēṇugōpālasvāmi temple. (Telugu.) Records that on Sunday, the seventh of the dark half of Jyēshṭa of the year Pramādīcha, Ś. 1535, Vōbanāyaniṁgāru of the Rācharla gōtra, who was the grandson of Choṇḍakunāyaniṅgāru and the son of Pullanāyaniṅgāru, constructed a stone prākāra to Gōpāladēva of Gaṇḍavaram, for the religious merit of his preceptor Tirumala Tātāchārlu Ayyavāru, Velugōṭi Veṅkaṭapati Nāyaniṅgāru, who is the ruler of the *śima*, his father Pullanāyaniṅgāru, and his mother Dharmayammagāru. *Ibid.*, No. 13, pp. 772–3.

464. On the eastern wall of the enclosure of Vēṇugōpālasvāmi temple. (Telugu.) Records that Timmaṇa, son of Jannā Jējam Śeṭṭi, caused this well to be constructed and presented it to Gōpālasvāmi of Gaṇḍavaram. *Ibid.*, No. 14, p. 774.

465. On a stone bearing also a Tamil inscription to the north of gate of Udayakālēśvara temple. (Telugu.) Records that a certain man who had obtained the village of Boṇḍavāḍa by the grace of Allun Tirukālti, who is called the ornament of kings, and the crest jewel of the Pallava family, excavated a tank in that village, constructed a village which he named Dāmavaram after his father and gave it to Udayakālavatīśvaradēva in perpetuity. *Nel. Ins., Nellore*, No. 15, pp. 774–5.

466. On the same stone. (Sanskrit in Grantha.) Records that Prōli Reḍḍi of Prabhugaṇḍavara obtained from the king Alluntikka, "a blossom among Pallavas," a village to the god Vaḷḷīśvara in the month of Mārgaḷi, in Ś. 1104. *Ibid.*, No. 16, pp. 776–7.

467. By the Śiva temple. (Telugu.) Records that Śrīman Mahāmaṇḍalēśvara Chitrakaṇva Tribhuvana Chakravarti Kulōttuṅga Chōḍadēvara gave to the deity Mahādēva and his wife Udaya Kalavati twenty *paṭṭis* of wet land at Bōdemaram. This was given to Nambi Vasamuradēvalēṇḍu, who was to receive and enjoy it in peace. Nine cows were also given. *Ibid.*, No. 17, pp. 778–9.

468, (Telugu.) On a stone to the south of Udayakālēśvara temple, bearing also a Tamil inscription. An illegible record. *Ibid.*, No. 18, p. 779.

469. On the same stone. (Tamil.) Records the grant of five *vēḷis* of demarcated dry land in the village to the *pujāri* and to the Śrī Mahēśvaraṣ of the temple of god Vallēśvara at Kanṭhanārāyaṇapuram *alias* Kulōttuṅga-chōḷapuram, situated in Muṇḍaināḍu in . . . Kulamāṇikkavaḷanāḍu (a subdivision of) . . . Chōḷamaṇḍala for three rice offerings, and five other *vēḷis* of land in the village of Tunamaśiridūr, for festival and other expenses. *Ibid.*, No. 19, pp. 779—81.

Koḍavalūru.

470. Near the western gate of the Nāgēśvara temple. (Telugu.) Records on Sunday, the seventh of the bright half of Kārttika of the year Vyaya, Ś. 1268, Mudra Chiddi Sāyanna Oḍayālu, the prime minister of Kampaṇati Uḍayār, presented a lamp to Śrīdhara Perumāḷ at Koḍavalūr for the expiation of the sins of his parents. *Ibid.*, No. 28, pp. 789—91.

Kovūru.

471. Opposite the Vishṇu temple. (Tamil and Sanskrit in Grantha character.) Records that in Ś. 1112, the king Siddhi gave to the god Gōvinda the village of Kōvūr. *Ibid.*, No. 40, pp. 807—9.

Marripāḍu.

472. On a stone near the choultry. (Telugu.) Records that in Ś. 1513, Veṅkaṭādri Nāyaniṅgāru, the servant of Veṅgappa Nāyaniṅgāru, who was the grandson of Pọli Nāyaniṅgāru, and the son of Veṅgappa Nāyaniṅgāru, granted the village of Marripāḍu in Rāpūr śīma and Udayagiri rājya in ratification of a former gift. *Nel. Ins., Nellore*, No. 49, pp. 811—14.

Mōḍeguṇṭa.

473. Near a choultry to the west of the village. (Telugu.) Records that on the second of the bright half of Chaitra of the year Bahudhānya, Ś. 1560, Velugōṭi Veṅkaṭapati Nāyanivāru made a gift for the tank. *Ibid.*, No. 47, pp. 814-15.

Nāyuḍupāḷem.

474. On a fallen stone in a field to the north of the village. (Telugu.) Records the gift of a field to Prakāḷa Dēvata. *Ibid.*, No. 48, pp. 815-16.

Śaṅgam.

475. In northern wall of temple. (Telugu.) Records that on Thursday, the seventh of the bright half of Chaitra, Ś. 1149, on the day of Vishu Saṅkrānti, Kandamūri Baichana Api Reḍḍi Prolisāni presented an evening lamp tō Saṅgamēśvara for the religious merit of her husband. *Ibid.*, No. 102, p. 866.

476. On the northern wall of the temple. (Telugu.) Records that on Tuesday, the third of the dark fortnight of Phalguna, Ś. 1140, Pāti Reḍḍi, Śūrapa Reḍḍi, and another person gave three slaves to Saṅgamēśvara Mahādēva, so that religious merit might accrue to their parents. *Ibid.*, No. 103, pp. 866-7.

477. On the western wall of the temple. (Telugu.) Records that on Sunday, the seventh of Chaitra of the year Virōdhikrit, Ś. 1473, while Śrīmad Rājādhirāja Rājaparamēśvara Vīrapratāpa Śrī Sadāśivadēva Mahārāya was seated on the diamond throne of Vijayanagar, Rāmi Reḍḍi, son of Duvvūri Koṇḍāvara Nandi Reḍḍi, granted the proceeds realized from the sale of the produce of the tope planted in the sthala of Śaṅgam in Udayagiri rājyam for providing worship to Saṅgamēśvara, for the religious merit of Chivvakkalūri Bayacha Rājayya, the Governor of Udayagiri rājya. *Ibid.*, No. 104, pp. 867-8.

478. On a stone in front of the temple. (Telugu.) Records that on Monday, the seventh of the dark fortnight of Chaitra of the year Pramōdūta, Ś. 1492, in the reign of Sadāśiva Mahārāya, Velugōṭi Timmappa Nāyaniṅgaru, the agent of Śrīman Mahāmaṇḍalēśvara Rāmarāja Śrī Raṅgarājayyadēva, made provisions on the holy occasion of Mēsha Saṅkrānti for enjoyments and worship to Saṅgamēśvara and remitted the taxes on cattle and sundry articles of merchandise and service for the river channel. *Ibid.*, No. 105, pp. 868—70.

479. In survey number 253 to the east of the village. (Telugu and Tamil.) Records that on Thursday, the fifth of the bright fortnight of Chaitra, Ś. 1105, a certain Kollapūḍi Nīlama Nāyakuḍu presented the tank of Koṇḍakarrikili to the east of the temple of Saṅgamēśvarādēva. *Nel. Ins., Nellore*, No. 106, pp. 871–2.

480. In the northern wall of the temple. (Tamil.) Records the gift of some money for a sacred lamp by one Nāyakkayakka. *Ibid.*, No. 107, p. 873.

481. On two sides of a stone which also bears two Telugu inscriptions. (Tamil.) Records that in the fifth year of the reign of Rājarājadēva, Nīlamanāyakkar, Keṭṭamanāyakkar and Mummaḍi Nīlamanāyakkar who governed Viriyūr and Kollappūṇḍi, made gifts for incense, lights, sacred food and other expenses, to Maridēva known as Kadikkili in the temple of Saṅgamēśvara on the north bank of the Peṇṇār at Viriyūr in Pākkaināḍu in Jayaṅkoṇḍa-chōḷamaṇḍala. *Ibid.*, No. 108, pp. 873—75.

Talamañchi.

482. On the gate of the Rāmaliṅgasvāmi temple. (Tamil.) Records a gift in Ś. 1143 of money in previous years by various persons for the gods Sēnāpatipiḷḷayār (Subrahmaṇya) and Uḍutomuḍaiyār in the temple of the lord of Āḍūr (situated) in Rājēndrachōḷamaṇḍala for a lamp. *Ibid.*, No. 109, pp. 875–76.

483. *C.P. No. 24 of Nellore Ins.*—A grant of Vikramāditya I of the Western Chāḷukyan dynasty. The object of the grant was the village of Edusanti, north of Kovorukoṇṭa. The donee was the spiritual preceptor of the king Mēghāchārya of Vasishṭa gōtra. The actual date was the sixth year of the king's rule in the month of Śravaṇa at a solar eclipse. The epigraph has also been edited by Dr. Hultzsch in *Ep. Ind.*, Vol. IX, pp. 98—102.

Vāṅgallu.

484. On the tank bund. (Telugu.) Records that on the eighth of the bright half of Māgha of the year Kāḷayukti, Ś. 1480, the lease of the tank in Duvvūru sthalam in the sīma of Udayagiri was granted by Śrīman Mahāmaṇḍalēśvara Rāmarāja Timmaya Dēvara Mahārājulugāru to Śrīman Mahāmaṇḍalēśvara Chāḷukya-Nārāyaṇa, Chauhattamalla, Raṇa Vijaya, Velamapāṭi Veragalayya (Veṅgalayya) Dēva Mahārājulu Ayyavāru. *Ibid.*, No. 112, pp. 880–1.

Vāviḷla.

485. Opposite the Vishṇu temple. (Telugu.) Records that on the second of the bright fortnight of Chaitra of the year

Bahudhānya, Ś. 1560, Velugōṭi Kumāra Timmanāyanivāru gave grain for maintaining the tank of Vāvilla. *Nel. Ins.*, *Nellore*, No. 116, pp. 884–5.

Vavvēru.

486. In a garden to the east of the village. (Telugu.) Records that on the eleventh of the bright half of Śravaṇa of the year Āṅgirasa, Ś. 1494, this "Raṅga" fountain was constructed by Māmaṇḍu (Muhammad) Miyā for the religious merit of the illustrious Rājādhirāja Rāja Mahārāja Rājaśrī Kōvaṭi (Kōnēṭi ?) Raṅga Rao Gāru. *Ibid.*, No. 117, p. 885.

487. In purōhit's *mānyam* to south of village. (Telugu.) A record in Ś. 115. *Ibid.*, No. 118, p. 886.

488. In Chennakēśava temple. (Telugu.) Records the service to the goddess of the perpetual devotion of Gummarāju-Guravayya. *Ibid.*, No. 119, p. 886.

Vēgūru.

489. In an enclosure of the Kailāśanātha temple. (Tamil.) Records that in the twenty-first year of the reign of the emperor of the three worlds, the glorious Kulōttuṅgachōḷadēva, Ṡevvan Pōyiṇḍan gave to the God of Śrīkailāśa at Veṅgūr for Amāvāsipaḍi 330 *kuḷis* of land measured with twenty-śāṇ-rod settled by Tantipōyiṇḍan. *Ibid.*, No. 120, pp. 887–8. *Amāvāsipaḍi* is an "endowment to the temple in memory of a certain disease having been cured."

490. In an enclosure of the Kailāśanātha temple. (Tamil.) Records that in Ś. 1165, Chittirai, the ryot Pūśali Reḍḍi, the son of Piḍammi Reḍḍi of Kottappūṇḍi, gave for a sacred lamp to the god of Śrīkailāśa at Vēlūr in Muṇḍaināḍu in Nellūrnāḍu in Paiyyūriḷaṅkōṭṭam, a subdivision of Jayaṅkoṇḍachōḷamaṇḍala, fifty full-grown, undying and unaging sheep. *Ibid.*, No. 121, pp. 888–9.

Viḍavalūru.

491. On a rock on Pōlērammamiṭṭa. (Telugu.) Records that on the fifth of the bright half of Chaitra of the year Chitrabhānu, Ś. 1504, while Śrīmad Rājādhi Rāja Rāja Paramēśvara Śrī Vīra Pratāpa Śrī Vīra Raṅgarāyadēva Mahārājulugāru (1578—86) was seated on the diamond throne at the city of Penugoṇḍa, a certain Kōnēṭi China Timma Nāyaniṁgāru of the Vellaṭlagōtra, grandson of Rāvēla Kaṇṭi Nāyaniṁgāru, and son of Tirumalayyagāru, revived certain *mēras* for the tank. The rate was at one *kuñcha* per *puṭṭi* on all kinds of grain raised in the village, including fields leased by the estate, garden lands, and *bhaṭṭa vriṭṭi mānyams* (personal *ināms*). Records also the gift of hundred *kuṇṭas* under the tank to the south of the *bāḍava* (marshy land) as a *mānyam*. *Ibid.*, No. 124, pp. 892—4.

NELLORE TALUK.

South Āmalūru.

492. From a stone to east of village. (Telugu.) Records a gift of *mēra* on the fifteenth of the dark half of Āshāḍha of the year Dhātu, Ś. 1678, for the upkeep of tanks. *Nel. Ins., Nellore*, No. 3, pp. 760–1.

Bhujabhujanellūru.

493. On a stone near the village. (Telugu.) Records that on the third of the bright half of Jyēshṭha of the year Krōdhana, Ś. 1547, Velugōṭi Veṅkaṭapati Nāyanivāru ordered that hereafter one *kuñchaḍu* more on every *puṭṭi* should be collected, so that the tank of Bhujabujanallūr was kept in repair. *Ibid.*, No. 6, pp. 763—5.

Chinna Cherukūru.

494. Near the Vināyakuḍu temple. (Telugu.) Records that on a certain day of Bhādrapada of the year Yuva, under the orders of Ākula Raṅganāthayya, agent of Śrīmat Velugōṭi Veṅkaṭapati Nāyanimvāru, Bōyinapalli Bāpanamgāru issued a grant for the tank at Cherukūru. *Ibid.*, No. 9, pp. 768-9.

Guḍipaḷḷipāḍu.

495. On a stone opposite the Śiva temple. (Telugu.) A record of Śrimat Velugōṭi Timmanāyaniṅgāru, on the tenth day of the bright half of Bhādrapada of the year Yuva. *Ibid.*, No. 20, pp. 781–2.

Idūru.

496. On the west wall of the Chokkanāthasvāmi temple. (Sanskrit in Grantha and Tamil.) Records that in Ś. 1193, expired, Āṅgirasa, Monday, Pūśa, the tenth day of Māgha, one Nāgadēvan of Nellūr *alias* Vikramaśiṅgapura gave to the lord Bhīmanadēva *alias* the god of Veṭṭuvan Paṭṭaivīḍu, for offerings, some lands in Aṅgapaḷandanāḍu free of tax. *Ibid.*, No. 21, pp. 782–3.

Indukūrpēṭa.

497. In the gōpuram of Narasiṁhasvāmi temple. (Tamil.) Records that one Kāvanūrkiḷavan Malaikiḷiyaninrān Pichchan Uḍaiyār of Māḷigaikāvanūr situated in Pōḷigaināḍu in Maṇavīrkōṭṭam, a subdivision of Jayaṅkoṇḍachōḷamaṇḍalam, gave a sacred flower garden and mango tope of 750 *kuḷis*. *Ibid.*, No. 22, p. 783.

498. On the threshold of the gōpuram of the Vīrabhadrasvāmi temple. (Telugu.) Records that the grain realized from the *kuñchas* of the tank should be spent by these in repairing the channel and the tank. If there should be any balance, it should be given for the repairs of these temples. *Ibid.*, No. 23, p. 784.

Kākaṭūru (Hamlet Patachennudu Gunṭa).

499. On the bed of the tank. (Telugu.) Records that on the fifteenth of the bright half of Kārttika, Ś. 156..., on the holy occasion of a lunar eclipse, somebody granted the village as an *amaram*. Therefore the different kinds of grain received from this village as *mēras* should be spent on doing earthwork to the tank. *Nel. Ins., Nellore,* No. 24, pp. 785—7.

Kandamūru.

500. To the north of the village, survey No. 61. (Telugu.) Records that, on the thirtieth of the dark fortnight of Āshāḍha of the year *Sarvadhāri*, on the holy occasion of a solar eclipse, Bairapa Reḍḍi Annayya of Pāṇḍēru gave 200 *kunṭas* of dry land to Chennakēśavanātha of Kandamūru for the religious merit of Basavaruśayya Ayyavāru. *Ibid.*, No. 25, p. 787.

Kanupartipāḍu.

501. In field No. 30 to the north of village. (Telugu.) Records that on the second of the bright half of Chaitra of the year Bahudhānya, Ś. 1560, Velugōṭi Veṅkaṭapati Nāyanivāru issued a charitable edict for the *mēras* of the tank of Kanuparti. The village *sandhātā,* lessee, *amaradār*, or ruler should see the tank and channel in order. *Ibid.*, No. 26, p. 788.

502. In field No. 383 to the east of village. (Tamil.) Records that in the thirty-seventh year of the reign of the emperor, Rājarājadēva, one Pramaladēvi had the steps leading to the shrine *(paḷḷichchandam)* of the Jain temple (called after) Karikālachōḷa, built on behalf of Matisāgaradēva. *Ibid.*, No. 27, p. 789.

503. In the gateway on the southern side of Śrīdharasvāmi temple. (Telugu.) A record of Sāyaṇṇa Oḍayalu. *Ibid.*, No. 29, pp. 791-2.

504. In the eastern gateway of Śrīdharasvāmi temple. (Telugu.) Records that in Ś. 1190, the children of Naraparāju and Appaḷarāju made a partition of their *vriṭṭis* in Rāmapuram; that the sons of Naraparāju of Guḍlūr divided their property into seven parts; and that Tikkaṇa, etc., sons of Gutto Appaḷarāju, divided their property into seven. The witnesses for this were the elders of the village *(mahājanalu)*. *Ibid.*, No. 30, pp. 793-4.

505. On a fallen stone in the tank bed. (Sanskrit in Grantha character and Tamil.) Records that in Ś. 1206, in the month Māgha, a certain image of a god was set up. Records also that in the third year of the reign of Manumagaṇḍagōpāladēva, Tāraṇa, Saṅkrānti, on Monday, the first day of the bright half of the month of Pushya, the sons of the ryots Kāmireḍḍi and Chōḷappireḍḍi, gave on behalf of their parents, for the God Tirunāgēśvara, at Koḍavalūr in Muṇḍaināḍu, the money collected at the rate of *half a chinnam per month on every loom.* *Ibid.*, No. 31, pp. 794—7.

Kōḍūr.

506. On stone bearing figure of Āñjanēśvara at Chennakēśava temple. (Telugu.) Records gift of land on Sunday, the fifteenth of the bright half of Aśviyuja of the year Jaya, Ś. 1236, on the holy occasion of Tulā Saṅkramaṇa to Koṭēśvaradēva and Kēśava-perumāḷ of Kōḍūr. *Nel. Ins., Nellore*, No. 32, pp. 797-8.

507. In a street of the village. (Telugu.) Records that on the second of the bright half of Chaitra of the year Pārthiva, Ś. 1567, while Śrīmat Rājādhirāja Rāja Paramēśvara Śrī Vīra Pratāpa Veṅkaṭādri Ayyavāru was seated on the diamond throne at the city of Peṇugoṇḍa, Kṛishṇappa Nāyaṅiṅgāru gave as an *amaram* to Rāvulu Veṅkaṭādrigāru, the village of Kōḍūru, attached to the śīma of Sarvempaḷḷi, and that he made a grant relating to the *mēras* of the tank. It is ordered that one *kuñcha* should be given as *mēras* on all sorts of grain raised in and all income of this village, which was to be spent on the tank. *Ibid.*, No. 33, pp. 798—801.

508. In the Koṭēśvarasvāmi temple. On the ceiling near the door. (Telugu.) Records that Rājayya, son of Śrīmat Śītayya, constructed a temple to the goddess Śrī Naṭarājēśvari of Śikralapāḍu. . . . *Ibid.*, No. 34, p. 802.

Kommarapūḍi.

509. On a step in the temple on Narasiṁhakoṇḍa. (Telugu.) Records that on Wednesday, the fifteenth day of the bright half of Phalguna of the year Pārthiva, Ś. 1448, while Śrīman Mahāmaṇḍa-lēśvara Achyutadēva Mahārāyulu was seated on the diamond throne at Vijayanagar, Timmarāju Nandayyagāru, the agent of Śrīman Mahāmaṇḍalēśvara Śrī Rāju China Tirumala Rāju Mahārājulu, gave away to Vēdādri Śrī Narasiṁhadēva, on the holy occasion of Utthāna (the day of the awaking of Vishṇu) the village of Komārapūḍi, situated to the south of the hill Vēdādri in the *śima* of Prabhākarapaṭṇam, in Pākanāḍu, in Udayagiri Rājya. *Ibid.*, No. 34-A, pp. 802—4.

510. On the outside wall of the temple on Narasiṁhakoṇḍa. (Telugu.) Records that on the fifteenth of the bright half of Kārttika of the year Piṅgaḷa, Śrīman Mahāmaṇḍalēśvara Chāḷukya Nārāyaṇa Chauhattamalla Raṇavijaya Velamapāṭi Tīrumala Rāja-yadēva Mahārājulavāru performed service to Vēdādri Śrī Nara-siṁhadēva and the shrine of that deity. *Ibid.*, No. 35, pp. 804-5.

Koruṭūru.

511. On the east wall of Puttanāthēśvara temple. (Telugu.) Records that on the ninth day of the dark fortnight of Phalguna of the year Hēviḷambi, Chaṅgappa, son of Barhari Kōnēri Śeṭṭi, founded endowment for providing a daily offering of three measures of rice to Puttanātha and Pārvatidēvi of Koruṭūru, for the religious merit of his father and mother. *Ibid.*, No. 36, pp. 805-6.

512. On the west wall of Puttanāthēśvara temple. (Telugu.) Records that Bāsudēva gave golden ornaments to Śrī Puttanātha deity. *Nel. Ins., Nellore*, No. 37, p. 806.

513. On a wall of the enclosure of the temple. (Tamil.) Records gift of land free of tax for sacred food and garland. *Ibid.*, No. 38, pp. 806–7.

514. On the east wall of the temple. (Tamil.) An unintelligible record. *Ibid.*, No. 39, p. 807.

Lēbūru.

515. On the pillars of the gōpuram of the Chennakēśava temple. (Persian.) Records that this building was constructed by Muhammad Husain Beg Khan. "If in the present building, the descendants of Husain Beg Khan live, they must look after the condition of the fakirs. Should they hesitate, his younger brother Hamza Husain Khan will be invested with full powers." *Ibid.*, No. 41, p. 809.

516. On a pillar of the gōpuram of Chennakēśava temple. (Persian.) Records that this building was presented to Imām Husain for the purpose of an Ashur Khan (a temporary house erected in the Muharram for the purpose of prayer). *Ibid.*, No. 42, pp. 809–10.

517. In the Vālēśvara temple. (Telugu.) Records that they should spend on the tank the *kuñchams* of grain set apart for it in the village of Vēmūru. They should give the balance to the temple. *Ibid.*, No. 43, p. 810.

518. In the Vālēśvara temple. (Telugu.) Records the gift of a field to the temple. The gift was made so that it might be maintained as a *sarvamānya* (tax free). *Ibid.*, No. 44, p. 811.

519. In the interior of Kuntakalamma temple. (Tamil.) An illegible record. *Ibid.*, No. 45.

Māmiḍipunḍi.

520. *C.P. No.* 14 *of Nellore Ins.*—A Sanskrit grant of Ś. 1471 (part in Telugu), similar to and identical in early parts with the British Museum plates, by Sadāśiva Rāya of Vijayanagar (1542—68), recording the grant of the village of Māmiḍipūṇḍi in Pākanāḍu, Sarvapaḷḷi *sīma* in Uḍayagiri Rājya (surnamed Śrīraṅgarājapuram to a learned Śrīvaishṇava Brahman Achārayya, son of Anantayārya. The gift was made at the request of Tirumala (I) of the last Vijayanagar dynasty.

Nellore.

The epigraphical department has copied fourteen inscriptions in this place. Of these ten have been identified with ten of the "Nellore Inscriptions". The remaining four (201—204 of 1894) are evidently the same as 15, 16, 17 and 20 in the list.

521. In a Muhammadan tomb at Dargamiṭṭa. (Telugu.) An unintelligible fragment of record. *Nel. Ins., Nellore*, No. 49, p. 817. See *Nellore Ins.*, p. 817, footnote, for the legendary account of Dargamiṭṭa.

522. Built into the big Muhammadan tomb at Dargamiṭṭa. (Tamil.) Records that Kitti Āḷvān, goldsmith of Kūvam and son of Māveḍuttān, presented one evening lamp, and Perumāḷ, the goldsmith, son of Toṇḍāravēn, the son of Oṟṟikoṇḍār of Paḷantaṇḍāla, presented one evening lamp. (For these lamps they gave a *māḍai*. This *māḍai* was to be lent out on interest. On the second side is an epigraph of the reign of Kulōttuṅga Chōḷadēva which seems to record the grant of some land to the god Akkasālīśvara.) *Ibid.*, No. 50, pp. 818-9.

523. Built into the big Muhammadan tomb at Dargamiṭṭa. (Tamil.) Two fragmentary records. One of these records the gift of gardens by Pottapichōḷa *alias* Gaṇḍagōpāla to the deity Akkasāli, and prays that it may be kept under the protection of the Mahēśvaras. The second appears to be a gift to the god Tirunāgēśvara. It was received by a Dēva Piḷḷai, and Kāḷatti Uḍayār who bound themselves to maintain the charity. *Ibid.*, No. 51, pp. 819—20.

524. From the bund of the big Nellore tank. (Telugu.) Records that on the fifteenth day of the bright half of Śravaṇa Yuva, Ś. 1557, Arula Rāghayamgāru issued a charitable edict for the *mēras* of the tank of Nellore under the orders of Śrīmat Velugōṭi Veṅkaṭapati Nāyanayyamvāru. It was to the effect that the *mēras* collected from all the fields under this tank should be spent on the tank by the residents of the town. "Therefore those who walk by those places, the cultivators, the *kāpus*, and the karaṇams, should give the grain derived from the *mēras* of this tank to Upparas and get the tank put in order by them." *Ibid.*, No. 52, pp. 820-21.

525. Alongside the Madras road. (Telugu.) A record of the *maṭham* of the illustrious Paramahamsa Dattātrēya Svāmi, the excellent guru. *Ibid.*, No. 53, pp. 821-2.

526. In the northern wall of Raṅganāyakalusvāmi temple. (Telugu.) Records that on the fifteenth of the bright half of Vaiśākha, Śrīmukha, Ś. 1495, Veṅkaṭapa Nāiḍu, the Secretary of Veligōṭi Timmapa Nāyaniṅgāru, the agent of Srī Raṅgarāyadēva Mahārāya (1578—86), made certain arrangements for showing respect to the Pañchahānas during the festival days of Paḷḷikoṇḍanātha of Nellore. "We shall show respect to all the Pañchahānas who come in the car as at Tirupati (?), the *sthala* karaṇams, *kāpus*, Śeṭṭis and Paka Reḍḍis having been made to agree to the observance of this etiquette." *Ibid.*, No. 54, pp. 822-3.

527. 197 *of* 1894.—On the north wall of Raṅganāyakalusvāmi temple. (Tamil.) Records that in Ś. 1119, the nineteenth year of Kulōttuṅga Chōḷadēva (III), the inhabitants of a number of *nāḍus*

(Pēdainādu, Pērāttinādu, Mungalārattainādu, Kaḍaiyaśinganāḍu, Pūngainādu, Tongaipūnūlnādu, Chakalanādu, Pottappinādu) of Jayankoṇḍa-chōḷamaṇḍalam assembled at Chittiramēḷimaṇṭapa in Tiruppārkaḍarchittiramēḷiviṇṇagar, gave to the god at Chittiramēḷiviṇṇagar, free of tax, lands to the extent of 2,200 *kuḷis*. *Nel. Ins.*, *Nellore*, No. 55, pp. 824–5. The inscription is of special chronological interest as it gives a Śaka date for the Chōḷa king.

528. 198 *of* 1894.—In northern wall of the Ranganāyakalusvāmi temple. (Tamil.) Records grant of land in various villages. *Ibid.*, No. 56, p. 56.

529. In the north wall of Ranganāyakalusvāmi temple. (Tamil.) Records in Pingaḷa, second year of Kulōttungachōḷadēva (III) "who was pleased to take Madurai, Īḷam (Ceylon) and the crowned head of the Pāṇḍya king", and the fifteenth year of the reign of Kulōttungachōḷadēva "who was pleased to take the crowned head of Vīrapāṇḍya", on Friday, Rēvati, the fourteenth day of the month of Vrischika, grant of 250 *kuḷis* of land. *Ibid.*, No. 57, pp. 826—8. [The king referred to is Kulōttunga III, 1178—1216.]

530. On the northern wall. of the Ranganāyakalusvāmi temple. (Tamil.) Records list of lands granted to the temple. *Ibid.*, No. 58, p. 828.

531. On the western wall of the Ranganāyakalusvāmi temple. (Telugu.) Records that on the fifth of the dark fortnight of Chaitra in the year Śrīmukha, the dancing girl of Śrī Talpagiri Ranganāthasvāmi gave a *paṭṭi* of dry land in Pāta Chintapalli for providing services with sandal and basil (ocymum sanctum). *Ibid.*, No. 59, pp. 828–9.

532. On the western wall of the Ranganāyakalusvāmi temple. (Tamil.) Records that in Ś. 1224, Plavanga, twelfth year of the reign of Rājagaṇḍagōpāladēva, on Monday, Rōhiṇi, the tenth day of the bright half of the month of Makara, Madurāntakapottapichōḷa *alias* Ranganāthan *alias* Rājagaṇḍagōpāladēva, gave to the god of Chitramēḷiviṇṇagar, namely, Paḷḷikoṇḍa Perumāḷ at Tiruppārkaḍal in Nellore *alias* Vikramaśingapura in Paḍainādu in Chēdikulamāṇikkavaḷanādu, a subdivision of Jayankoṇḍachōḷamaṇḍala, for ceremonies, sacred food, ornaments, daily offerings and temple repairs, free of tax and as exclusive property, the dry and wet lands included within the four boundaries of the village. *Ibid.*, No. 60, pp. 829–30.

533. 196 *of* 1894.—On the western wall of the Ranganāyaka temple. (Tamil.) Records that in the reign of the emperor Sundara Pāṇḍyadēva, he gave at the recommendation of Kāḷingarāyar the village of Māvaḍikuṇḍai in Muṇḍanāḍu, all the lands in the village, wet, dry, house-sites, gardens, etc., besides the rights of ryots, *inevari*, *śittāya* (toll ?) and all kinds of taxes accruing from the village, from the month of Āvaṇi of the same year, for offerings to the deity in the hall constructed in his name and called Sundarapāṇḍyaśandi. *Nel. Ins., Nellore*, No. 61, pp. 830—2. [This Sundara Pāṇḍya was evidently the same as the one referred to in the Jambukēśvaram and Tirukkaḷukkunram inscriptions as the hero anointed in the town of Nellore.]

534. In the western wall of the Raṅganāyaka temple. (Tamil.) Records that in Ś. 1221, ninth year of the reign of the emperor Gaṇḍa Gōpāladēva, on Monday, Anusha, in the bright half of the month of Makara, Madhurāntakapottapichōḷa, the glorious Raṅganātha *alias* Rājagaṇḍa Gōpāladēvan gave to the god of Chitramēḷiviṇṇagar, namely, Paḷḷikoṇḍaperumāḷ at Tiruppārkaḍal in Nellore *alias* Vikramaśiṅgapura in Chēdikulamāṇikkavaḷanāḍu, a subdivision of Jayaṅgoṇḍachōḷamaṇḍala, the dry and wet lands included within the four boundaries of the village for daily offerings and temple repairs, free of tax. *Ibid.*, No. 62, pp. 832-3.

535. On the southern wall of the Raṅganāyakalu temple. (Tamil.) Records that the emperor of the three worlds, who was pleased to take Madurai and the crowned head of the Pāṇḍya, the glorious Kulōttuṅgachōḷadēva, gave to Chittiramēḷiviṇṇagar *alias* Paḷḷikoṇḍaperumāḷ certain villages, free of tax. *Ibid.*, No. 63, pp. 833-4.

536. On the southern wall of the Raṅganāyakasvāmi temple. (Tamil.) A fragment of record, dated in the reign of Kulōttuṅgachōḷadēva who was pleased to take Madurai and the crowned head of the Pāṇḍya, and appears to grant the village Peṭṭiḍakuṇḍai . . . at Nellore *alias* Vikramaśiṅgapura, situated in Paṭṭaināḍu. *Ibid.*, No. 64, pp. 834-5.

537. On the southern wall of the Raṅganāyakasvāmi temple. (Tamil.) Records the list of evening lamps given up to the month of Chittirai of the thirty-fifth year of the reign of the emperor Kulōttuṅgachōḷadēva (III), who was pleased to take Madurai and the crowned head of the Pāṇḍya. *Ibid.*, No. 65, p. 835.

538. 200 *of* 1894.—On the south wall of the Raṅganāyaka temple. (Tamil.) Records that in the twenty-eighth year of the reign of the emperor Rājarājadēva, in the month of Āni, one *māḍai* was presented for an evening lamp to be burnt before Tirukkēḷi Uḍaiya Viyalāḷvār by Vaiṭumban Pitusuramuḍaiyān. *Ibid.*, No. 66, p. 836.

539. 205 *of* 1894.—On the south wall of the Raṅganāyakasvāmi temple. (Tamil.) Records in the thirty-first year of the reign of the emperor Kulōttuṅgachōḷadēva (III) who was pleased to take Madurai and the crowned head of the Pāṇḍya king, in the month of Mēsha, Periyasiddhappanāyaka, a follower of Madhurāntakapottapichōḷa *alias* Nallasiddharasa, gave to the god Chittaramēḷiviṇṇagar *alias* Paḷḷikoṇḍaperumāḷ at Tiruppārkaḍal in Nellūr the village of Virkāḍu free of tax. *Ibid.*, No. 67, pp. 836—8.

540. On the southern wall of Raṅganāyakasvāmi temple. (Tamil.) Records that Dēvaṇḍai, son of Śivapūtan Śēnda Piḷḷai, presented one *māḍai*, for one evening lamp; similar gifts by two men. *Nel. Ins., Nellore*, No. 68, p. 838.

541. 193 *of* 1894.—On the eastern wall of the Raṅganāyakasvāmi temple. (Tamil.) Records that in the tenth year of the reign of the emperor Kulōttuṅgachōḷadēva (III), who was pleased to take the crowned head of the Pāṇḍya and Madurai, the Mudalis belonging to the army and the citizens of the three streets of Nellore *alias* Vikramaśiṅgapuram in Paḍaināḍu in Chēdikulamāṇikkavaḷanāḍu, a subdivision of Jayaṅkoṇḍachōḷamaṇḍala, gave the sum of ten *chinnams*, accruing from certain dues to Tiruppārkaḍal Paḷḷikoṇḍaperumāḷ of this city of Nellore. *Ibid.*, No. 69, p. 839.

542. 192 *of* 1894.—On the eastern wall of the Raṅganāyakasvāmi temple. (Tamil.) Records in the thirty-first year of the reign of the emperor Kulōttuṅgachōḷadēva (III), who was pleased to take Madurai and the crowned head of the Pāṇḍya, a certain Vēmayāḷvān, the son of Veṭṭandandainambiyāṇḍi of the city of Pūndamalli in Puliyurkōṭṭam *alias* Kulōttuṅgachōḷavaḷanāḍu, a subdivision of Jayaṅkoṇḍachōḷamaṇḍala, gave two shares of land to Śrīvarāha Emberumān (whose image was set up by his father Nambiyāṇḍi or Uraṅgā viḷḷidāsar in the inner sacred enclosure of the temple of Chittiramēḷiviṇṇagar). *Ibid.*, No. 70, pp. 840–1.

543. 194 *of* 1894.—On the shrine of Raṅganāyakasvāmi temple. (Tamil.) Records that in Ś. 1218, expired, sixth year of the reign of Vijayagaṇḍagōpāladēva, on Wednesday, Uttirāḍa and Saṅkrama, the first day of the bright half of the month of Makara, Madhurāntakapottapichōḷan *alias* Raṅganāthan *alias* Rājagaṇḍagōpāladēvan gave for the daily offerings and for building purposes, to the god Chittiramēḷiviṇṇagar, the dry and wet lands of the village of Ālaṅgāḍu in Muṇḍaināḍu. *Ibid.*, No. 71, pp. 841–2.

544. 195 *of* 1894.—On the Raṅganāyakasvāmi temple. (Tamil.) Records that in the twenty-sixth year of Kulōttuṅgachōḷadēva (III), who was pleased to take Madurai and the crowned head of the Pāṇḍya, Madhurāntakapottapichōḷa *alias* Tammusiddharasa gave to Paḷḷikoṇḍaperumāḷ at Tiruppārkaḍal (Nellore), the village of Tāmarai maḍuvu (the lotus tank) *alias* Chitramēḷinallūr, in Muṇḍaināḍu, free of tax. *Ibid.*, No. 72, pp. 843–4. See 35 of 1893 at Conjeeveram, 104 of 1892 at Tiruvoṟṟiyūr, etc.

545. 199 *of* 1894.—In the shrine of Raṅganāyakasvāmi temple. (Tamil.) Records that in Ś. 1202 a certain Vaiṭumāpperumāppiḷama and Pāmaṇḍai gave an evening lamp to Paḷḷikoṇḍaperumāḷ. *Ibid.*, No. 73, p. 844.

546. In the shrine of Raṅganāyakasvāmi temple. (Tamil.) Records that in Ś. 1237, expired, the twenty-fifth year of the reign of Rājagaṇḍagōpāladēva, on Wednesday, Punarpūśa, the tenth day of the bright half of the month of Mīna, Madhurāntakapottapichōḷa *alias* Rājagaṇḍagōpāladēvan provided for a lamp to the god at Chittramēḷiviṇṇagar, Paḷḷikoṇḍaperumāḷ. *Nel. Ins., Nellre*, No. 74, pp. 844-5.

547. On the dhvajastambham of the Raṅganāyakasvāmi temple. (Tamil.) A fragment of record in Grantha, which mentions Tammusiddhi and his ancestors Kalikāla and Bēdabhānātha. (Beta). *Ibid.*, No. 75, pp. 845-6.

548. In the outer wall of the Raṅganāyakasvāmi temple facing river. (Tamil.) Records that in Ś. 1322, twenty-fifth year of the reign of Rājaparamēśvara Harihararāya (II), on Sunday, Pūśa, during the bright half, the fifteenth of Vaikāśi, the big maṇṭapa in the temple of Śayyanārāyaṇaperumāḷ at Vikramaśiṅgapuram *alias* Nellore was the charity of Puḷavadalvār *alias* Chamayattār. Records also the gift of five sacred lamps, and mentions the emperor Sundarapāṇḍya. *Ibid.*, No. 76, pp. 846-7.

549. On the threshold of the Āñjanēya temple in Santhapet. (Telugu.) Records the perpetual devotion of Gādam Śeṭṭi Śēshayya and two others. *Ibid.*, No. 77, p. 847.

550. On the gate jambs of Irukalāmmā temple. (Telugu.) Records that on Friday, the fifth of the dark fortnight of Mārgaśira of the year Krōdhi, Ś. 1286, while Śrīman Mahāmaṇḍalēśvara Vīra Śrī Savaṇṇa Oḍayalu was ruling the earth, the people of all countries came to agreement in connexion with the Friday market established by Kāñchaṇṇaṁgāru in Nellore. They arranged to devote the fees raised in the market for the provision of all sorts of enjoyment for Irukalā Paramēśvari, for the religious merit of Kāñchaṇṇaṁgāru, the best of officials *(adhikāri)*. *Ibid.*, No. 78, pp. 847—9.

551. On a pillar of the shrine of Irukalāmmā. (In Dēvanāgari character.) Records the name Irukalāparamēśvari. *Ibid.*, No. 79, p. 849.

552. In the shrine of Irukalāmmā temple. (Telugu.) Records that on Monday, the fifteenth of the dark fortnight of Bhādrapada of the year Ānanda, Ś. 1239, while Śrīman Mahamaṇḍalēśvaran Kākatīya Pratāparudradēva Mahārājulu was ruling the earth, two persons named Nāgayanulōka Bōyuḍu and Brammana Bōyuḍu, the sons of Hari Dēva, the servant of Nāganāgana, caused a maṇṭapa to be constructed, for the merit of the agent and Viceroy of Pratāparudradēva, Śrī Muppaḍi Nāyani Gāru, and for the prosperity of the kingdom.

553. In the Irukalāmmā temple. (Tamil.) Records the gift of a pillar by Ammanadēvanātha to the god Salīśvara. *Ibid.*, No. 81, pp. 851-2.

554. In a house in Kāpu street. (Tamil.) A fragmentary record. Appears to record grant of lands in Eṛṛayapaḷḷi in

Pūṅgaināḍu to the god Nāgarīśvara in Nellore *alias* Vikramaśiṅgapuram in Chēdikulavaḷanāḍu by Madhurāntakapottapichōḷa *alias* Manumasiddharasa. *Nel. Ins., Nellore,* No. 82, p. 852.

555. In a house in the Chinna bazaar. (Tamil.) Records that in the reign of Kulōttuṅgachōḷadēva (III), who was pleased to take Madura and the crowned head of the Pāṇḍya king, a native of Valuvanāḍu, presented a sacred lamp to Manumakēśavaperumāḷ of Nellore *alias* Vikramaśiṅgapuram. *Ibid.,* No. 83, pp. 852–3.

556. In the coping of a well by the Dharmarāja temple. (Tamil.) An illegible record. *Ibid.,* No. 84, p. 853.

557. Over a drain in the Big Mosque street. (Tamil.) Records in the ninth year of Kulōttuṅgachōḷadēva (III), who was pleased to take Madurai, Ceylon and the crowned head of the Pāṇḍya, gift to the god Manumasiddhīśvara at Nellore *alias* Vikramaśiṅgapura, by Madhurāntakapottapichōḷa *alias* Nallāsiddharasa. *Ibid.,* No. 85, pp. 853–4.

558. Built into the Collectors's cutcherry. (Tamil.) This is the imprecatory end of a record. *Ibid.,* No. 86, p. 854.

559. Built into the Collector's cutcherry. (Tamil.) Records in the thirty-sixth year of the reign of Kulōttuṅgadēva (III ?), that certain Śivabrāhmaṇas of the temple (Śrīmādēvabhaṭṭa, etc., of the Bharadhvāja gōtra, Madānugrahacharaṇabhaṭṭa, Āṭkoṇḍapiḷḷai and Śittāṇḍār) agreed to light one evening lamp without failure, from the month of Tai, in a niche in the temple of Āḷuḍaiyār Manumasiddhēśvara at Nellore *alias* Vikramaśiṅgapuram in Jayaṅkoṇḍachōḷamaṇḍalam. *Ibid.,* No. 87, pp. 854–5.

560. Built into the Collector's cutcherry. (Tamil.) A fragmentary record. Mentions the name of god Manumasittīśvara. *Ibid.,* No. 88, p. 855.

561. Built into the Collector's cutcherry. (Tamil.) A fragment of record dated in the twenty-fifth year of the reign of Vīrarājēndrachōḷadēva. *Ibid.,* No. 89, pp. 855—6.

562. Built into the Collector's cutcherry. (Tamil.) A fragment. Mentions Nellore. *Ibid.,* No. 90, p. 856.

563. Built into the Collector's cutcherry. (Tamil.) Records the grant of one *māḍai* for an evening lamp to Manumasiddhēśvara by one Vaḷḷuvāṇḍān, the son of Kumarandaiperumāḷ. The money was received from the month of Tai of the thirty-sixth year of some king's reign by Āṭkoṇḍapiḷḷai, Siddāṇḍār and Bharadvāja Mahādēva. *Ibid.,* No. 91, pp. 856–7.

564. Built into the Collector's cutcherry. (Tamil.) A record of the reign of Kulōttuṅgachōḷadēva. The object of the grant is not ascertainable. *Ibid.,* No. 92, p. 857.

565. Built into the Collector's cutcherry. (Tamil.) A record of the thirtieth year of the reign of Kulōttuṅgachōḷadēva (III), who was pleased to take Madurai and the crowned head of Pāṇḍya, at the time of the equinox during the month of Aippaśi. *Nel. Ins., Nellore*, No. 92, p. 858.

566. Built into the Collector's cutcherry. (Tamil.) Records that a certain Kaḍambāṇḍi presented one evening lamp to God Nāgēśvara. *Ibid.*, No. 94, pp. 858–9.

567. On a stone lying by the gate of the Collector's cutcherry. (Tamil.) A fragment. No meaning can be made out of it. *Ibid.*, No. 95, p. 859.

568. In the Nīlakaṇṭhēśvara temple. (Telugu.) Records that on the fourteenth of the dark fortnight of Māgha of the year Vyaya, Ś. 1628, this *vritti* was given to Nīlakaṇṭhasvāmi at Śrī Vīra-vikramasimhapura. *Ibid.*, No. 96, pp. 859–60.

569. On a stone in front ot Aḷaganāthasvāmi temple. (Tamil.) Records the gift of a perpetual lamp to Aḷagaperumāḷ by somebody (name not clear) in the month of Ādi of Ś. 1189, Bhava, "which should probably be Prabhava." *Ibid.*, No. 97, p. 861.

570. On a stone bearing another inscription in front of Aḷaganāthasvāmi temple. (Tamil.) Records that in the reign of Vijayagaṇḍagōpāladēva, on Monday, Rōhiṇi, the thirtieth day of the bright half of the month of Dhanus, a certain Veṅgaḍamuḍaiyān *alias* Ēṛan and his sons gave 85 ewes for a sacred lamp to the god Aḷagaperumāḷ at Vikramachōḷachaturvēdimaṅgalam. *Ibid.*, No. 98, pp. 861–2.

571. To the east of village. (Telugu.) Records that on the second of the bright half of Chaitra of the year Bahudhānya, Ś. 1560, Śrīmat Velugōṭi Veṅkaṭapati Nāyaniṅgāru granted the *mēras* of certain tanks. *Ibid.*, No. 99, pp. 862–3.

Rāmatīrtham.

571-A. *C.P. No.* 87 *of Mr. Sewell's List.*—Records grant in Nandināgari characters, made in Ś. 1351 (A.D. 1429), Kīlaka, by the Vijayanagar sovereign Dēva Rāya (II) of the village of Abhūri, to a number of Brahmans of different gōtras. The grant is said to have been made at the request of a dependent chief, a devoted adherent of the king's, by name Maulara, described as son of Mummaḍi and Mumbāmbā, grandson of Pōta Mahibhuja and cousin of Śūranṛipati.

572. Above the door of the temple. (Telugu.) A gift for the merit of Bhujabala Malla Siddhi Chōḍa Mahārāja, son of Chōḍēśvara at Rāmatīrtham. *Ibid.*, No. 100, pp. 864–5.

573. Over the shrine of the temple. (Tamil.) Records in the thirty-first year of the reign of Kulōttuṅgachōḷadēva (III), who was pleased to take Madura and the crowned head of the Pāṇḍya king that Madhurāntakapottapichōḷa *alias* Tirukkāḷattidēva gave to Manumakēśava Perumāḷ of Manumakēśavapura, a suburb of

Nellore *alias* Vikramaśiṅgapura, situated in Pērūrnāḍu in Chēdikulamāṇikkavaḷanāḍu, a subdivision of Jayaṅgoṇḍachōḷamaṇḍala, free of tax, the village of Iḍappūr, situated in Maṇḍaināḍu, also a subdivision of Chēdikulamāṇikkavaḷanāḍu. *Nel. Ins., Nellore*, No. 101, pp 864-5.

Tōṭapaḷḷiguḍūr.

574. In a street to the east. (Telugu.) Records that under the orders of Ākula Raṅganāthayyagāru, agent of Rāja Veṅkaṭapati Nāyaningāru, a certain Boyanipalli Bāpannagāru granted the collection of one *kuñchaḍu* for the maintenance of the tank of the village. *Ibid.*, No. 100, pp. 876-7.

575. Opposite Vināyaka temple. (Tamil.) Records that in Ś. 1126, on Wednesday, Rōhiṇi, the fourth day of the bright half of the month of Tulā, Malaikiḷiyaninrān Pichchan Uḍaiyān, the headman of Kāvanūr (part of the village of Māḷigaikkāvanūr) in Ponagaināḍu in Maṇavīrkōṭṭa gave to the temple of the lord of Siddhappa at Pōyiṇḍanpaḷḷi in Paḍaināḍu after having set up in the temple an image of Madhurāntakapottapichōḷa *alias* Peddarasa, 1,500 *kuḻi* of areca nut plantation. *Ibid.*, No. 111, pp. 877—9.

Varakavipūḍi?

576. To the south of the village. (Telugu.) Records that the village Varakalapāṇḍu was received as a gift by Tirumala Sōmayājulu. *Ibid.*, No. 113, pp. 881-2.

Varigoṇḍa.

577. On a stone bypath to the east of the village. (Telugu.) Records that on the third of the bright half of Chaitra of the year Bahudhānya, Ś. 1560, Velugōṭi Veṅkaṭapati Nāyaniṅgāru issued *mēras* for the tank at Varigoṇḍa. *Ibid.*, No. 114, pp. 882-3.

Vāvilētipād?

578. Now at Collector's bungalow. (Telugu.) Records that on the eighth day of the bright fortnight of Bhādrapada of the year Yuva, under the orders of Ākula Raṅganāthayya, the agent of Śrīmat Velugōṭi Veṅkaṭapatināyanivāru. One Bōyanapaḷḷi Bāpanaya Gāru granted the *kuñcha* grain of the tank. *Ibid.*, No. 115, pp. 883-4.

Vellaṇṭi.

579. Opposite to the Āñjanēya temple. (Telugu.) Records that on Sunday, the tenth of the bright half of Kārttika of the year Tāraṇa, Ś. 1447, Śrīman Mahāmaṇḍalēśvara Dantalūr Chāgaṇṭi Dēva Mahārājulu gave lands for providing offerings to the deity Hanūmān, etc., to the merit of his father Vōbularāju. *Ibid.*, No. 122, pp. 889-90.

580. In a street to the south. (Telugu.) Records the gift of *mēra* for a tank on the second of the bright half of Āshāḍha of the year (damaged) (by ?) Velugōṭi Veṅkaṭapati Nāyaniṁgāru. *Nel. Ins., Nellore*, No. 123, p. 891.

PODILI TALUK.

Budamanārayalapāḍu.

581. Near the Gaṅgamma temple. (Telugu.) Records in the twelfth year of the reign of Vishṇuvardhana Mahārāja the grant, in the northern part of Ballam Bhantarala, of a field requiring four *puṭṭis* of seed, to Ishṭa Sōmu. *Nel. Ins., Podili*, No. 1, pp. 1151–2.

582. Near the Gaṅgamma temple. (Telugu.) Records that in the first year of the reign of Vishṇuvardhana Mahārāja, Śivapparāja made a grant to Ubilīśvara Bhaṭṭar. Refers also to a well and a temple in Śrī Nittasōmula erected by Śrī Komorapolu Koṇḍayya, best of kings, and a temple built by Vallūri Atarla Mārayya, to which the Reḍḍis gave land. *Ibid.*, No. 2, pp. 1152—5.

583. Near the Gaṅgamma temple. (Telugu.) An unintelligible record on a stone close to No. 582. *Ibid.*, No. 3, p. 1155.

Chilamakūru.

584. To the south of village. (Telugu.) Records that on Thursday, the thirtieth of the dark fortnight of Śravaṇa of the year Bhava, Ś. 1437, on the holy occasion of solar eclipse, Rāyasam Koṇḍamarasayyaṅgāru granted to Bhīmēśvara Mahādēva and Kailāsanātha Mahādēva of Podela, the village of Chilumakūru in Podila śīma, for the religious merit of Śrīman Mahārājādhirāja Rājaparamēśvara Śrī Vīra Pratāpa Kṛishṇadēva Mahārāya, the lord of Śrīkarnāṭa Vijayanagar. *Ibid.*, No. 4, pp. 1155–6.

585. On the same stone. (Telugu.) Records that on Thursday, the fifteenth of bright fortnight of Māgha of the year Bahudhānya, Ś. 1140, the temple trustees *(samasthānakulu)* of Kailāsanātha and Bhīma granted one *kuchchala* of dry land and ten *kuṇṭas* of wet land as a *sarvamānya* to Mēdarameṭṭa Śrīgiri-nāyuḍu " who walked over the boundary line " of the village. *Ibid.*, No. 5, p. 1157.

Chimaṭa.

586. Opposite the Bhīmēśvara temple. (Telugu.) Records on Tuesday, day of *Saṅkrānti*, the thirteenth of the dark fortnight of Pushya of the year Paridhāvi, Ś. 1234, that Kākatīya Pratāparudra . . . Nāyaniṅgāru issued a charitable edict, for the enjoyments of the temple of Bhīmanāthadēva of Chimaṭa. *Ibid.*, No. 6, pp. 1158-9. [The king referred to is Pratāparudra II.]

Doṇḍalēru.

587. East of the Mādiga hamlet. (Telugu.) Records on Thursday, the fifteenth of the dark fortnight of Bhādrapada of the year Raudri, in the reign of the Kākatīya Gaṇapatidēva, a gift by a feudatory named Bhīmarāja Peddana, for the religious merit of Siddhirāya. *Nel. Ins., Podili,* No. 7, pp. 1160–1.

588. Near a well. (Telugu.) A record in Phalguṇa of the year Durmukhi, Ś. 1083. *Ibid.*, No. 8, pp. 1161–62.

589. Opposite the ruined Mallēśvara temple. (Telugu.) Records that on Thursday, the seventh of the bright fortnight of Mārgaśira of the year Piṅgaḷa, Ś. 1179, Śrīmat Madādidēvuṇḍu gave, for the religious merit of his lord Bhīmarāju Siddhaya Rudra Mahādēva, provision for worship and all kinds of enjoyment to Dontalēṭi Mallināthadēva. *Ibid.*, No. 9, pp. 1162—65. Kulōttuṅgachōḷadēva (Kulōttuṅga III?) was evidently the suzerain of this Bhīmarāju.

590. On a fallen stone near the ruined Mallēśvara temple. (Telugu.) Records a gift on Thursday the first of the bright fortnight of Chaitra of the year Raudri, Ś. 1182, by an agent of the Kākatīya Gaṇapatidēva (1200--60.) *Ibid.*, No. 10, pp. 1165–66.

591. On a fallen stone near the Mallēśvara temple. (Telugu.) A record of a feudatory of Śrīman Mahāmaṇḍalēśvara Kākatīya Gaṇapatidēva Mahārāja. *Ibid.*, No. 11, p. 1166.

Gārladinne.

592. On a stone in Hanumanta temple situated in the temple of Veligoṇḍarāyasvāmi. (Telugu.) Records on Saturday, the fifth day of the dark half of Kārttika of the year *Prabhava,* Ś. 1369, the consecration by one Nimmāju Hētimgāru of an image of Hanumanta Perumāḷ, for the religious merit of "the illustrious Nāradarājuṅgāru." *Ibid.*, No. 12, p. 1167.

593. In the Veligoṇḍa temple. (Telugu and Sanskrit.) Records that on Thursday, the eleventh of the dark fortnight of Jyēshṭha, on the holy occasion of the aforesaid *tithi* of the year Chitrabhānu, Ś. 1564, Barugugāru (son of Liṅgappa and grandson of Nāmubhanāyaniṅgāru) put up an image of Chakra Perumāḷ on the steps; arranged for the *kalyāṇa mahōtsava*; sent for all the Śrī Vaishṇava people by the four main gates; converted the temple servants to Śrī Vaishṇavism; brought the shrine to its former glory; made it another Tirupati; instituted the distribution of holy food and water; and willingly made an agreement with the people. *Ibid.*, No. 13, pp. 1167—69. [The inscription is one of the valuable documents proving the progress of Śrī Vaishṇavism in Telugu territory in the sixteenth century.]

594. In Veligoṇḍa temple. (Telugu and Sanskrit.) Records that on Thursday, the fifteenth of the bright half of Vaiśākha in the year Īśvara, Ś. 1443, on the holy occasion of the lunar eclipse, while Śrī Mahāmaṇḍalēśvara Rājādhirāja Rājaparamēśvara Vīra Pratāpa Krishṇadēva Mahārāja was ruling at Vijayanagar, Rāyasām Koṇḍamarasayya gave the villages Gārladinne and Kattirallagumpu in Podali śīma, to the deity. *Nel. Ins.*, *Podili*, No. 14, pp. 1170—72. See No. 584 above.

595. On a stone in the village. (Telugu and Sanskrit.) This seems to be an exact copy of the above one but it is illegible in part. *Ibid.*, No. 15, p. 1172.

Gōṭlāguṇṭapāḍu.

596. In the Vēṇugōpālasvāmi temple. Records a few letters only. *Ibid.*, No. 16, p. 1173.

Goṭlagaṭṭu.

597. Opposite the Śiva temple. (Telugu.) Mentions a Pallava, the lord of the city of Kāñchi, who "obtained an excellent boon from the goddess Kāmakōṭi." *Ibid.*, No. 17, pp. 1173-74. (The inscription is fragmentary.)

Gurralamaḍugu.

598. Opposite the Āñjanēya temple. (Telugu.) Records on Thursday, the thirtieth of the dark fortnight of Jyēshṭha of the year Saumya, Ś. 1291, a gift of land for maintenance to a certain Kōrumāmaḷḷa Raghupatīśvara Śāstrulu for the religious merit of one Śāyapanēni Veṅkaṭādri Nāyanivāru. The village of Guralamaḍugu was given as an *amaram*. *Ibid.*, No. 18, pp. 1174-75.

Igalapāḍu.

599. Near the Saṅgamēśvarasvāmi temple. (Telugu.) Records on the fifteenth of the bright fortnight of Āshāḍha of the year Rudhirōdgāri, Ś. 1497, in the reign of Śrīmad Rājādhirāja Rājaparamēśvara Śrī Vīra Pratāpa Śrī Sadāśivadēva Mahārāyulu of Vijayanagar, that Tirumalanāyaniṅgāru (grandson of Rāvela Tippanāyaḍuṅgāru) made a gift of land to the deity Saṅgamēśvara. *Ibid.*, No. 19, pp. 1175—78.

Kākarla.

600. On an image opposite the Vishṇu temple. (Telugu.) Records that Śīlam Timmareḍḍi made 10,000 salutations to Vēṅkaṭēśvaradēva. *Ibid.*, No. 20, p. 1178.

Kalujuvvalapāḍu.

601. (Telugu.) A record in the dark fortnight of Chaitra of the year Prabhava, Ś. 1347, in the time of Śrīman Mahāmaṇḍalēśvara Manma Anta Rājulu. The rest is fragmentary. *Ibid.*, No. 21, pp. 1178-79.

602. In the temple. (Telugu.) Records that a certain Toṇḍayyarāzu of the solar dynasty, Kāśyapagōtra and lineage of Karikāla, gave some land south of Tammalūru village to the temple constructed by Tammalūru Veṅkayya Raḍḍoḍiya. *Nel. Ins.*, *Podili*, No. 22, pp. 179-80.

603. In a field. (Telugu and Sanskrit.) This is a copy of No. 594, but dated in *Pramādi* corresponding to Ś. 1442. *Ibid.*, No. 23, p. 1181.

Kāśipuram.

604. On a stone by the Vēṇugōpālasvāmi temple. (Telugu.) Records that on Thursday, the tenth of the bright fortnight of Āshāḍha of the year *Virōdhikrit*, Ś. 1473, Rāchirājadēva Mahārāja of the lunar race, of the Ātrēya gōtra, son of Vallabharāja and grandson of Malakarāja, set up an image of Śrī Madanagōpāla, constructed a temple and performed the consecration ceremony and made certain gifts of land and gold for providing *amritapaḍi* (sacred food) and all means of enjoyments to the deity. *Ibid.*, No. 24, pp. 1181—83. The suzerainty of Sadāśiva Rāya is recognized.

Kātraguṇṭa.

605. Near the gate of the Veligoṇḍasvāmi temple. (Telugu.) Records that in Ś. 1468, a certain Gaṇaparapura Śrīman Nāginēnigāru gave a *puḷḷāri mānyam* for the religious merit of Śrīman Mahāmaṇḍalēśvara Veṅkāṭaraṅgapatidēva Mahārāja ruling " at Vidyānagar." *Ibid.*, No. 25, pp. 1183-84.

Kūchapūdi.

606. Opposite the Āndhrarāmaliṅgasvāmi temple. (Telugu.) Records that on Sunday, the first of the bright fortnight of Chaitra of the year Prabhava, Ś. 1348, Śrīman Mahāmaṇḍalēśvara Mēdinimisaragaṇḍa Kaṭhāri Śāḷuva Śamburāyadēva Mahārājulu constructed the temple for the religious merit of his father Rāya "Vibhaladēva Mahārāja". *Ibid.*, No. 26, pp. 1184-85.

607. *C.P. No.* 23 *of Nel. Ins.*—A forged grant in the name of Achyuta Rāya of Vijayanagar with the wrong date of Ś. 1270 (Sarvajit, Kārttika, Śukla Paurṇami), purporting to grant ten *kuchchalas* of land in the village of Kūchipūḍi, a wet field capable of being sown with ten *tūms* of seed in Marripūḍi and half a *kuchchala* of land in every village of the *śima* together with the *mēras* of two measures on every *puṭṭi* of produce and a fee of 2 per cent on the revenue, to the temple of Rāmaliṅgasvāmi in Poḍili sīma, for offerings and food to pilgrims.

Kuñchēpalli.

608. In front of the Añjanēya temple. (Telugu.) Records on the fifteenth of the bright half of Jyēshṭha in the year Yuva, Ś. 1407, that Śrīman Rājādhirāja Rājaparamēśvara Śrī Vīrapratāpa Śrī Raṅgadēva Mahārāyalayyavāru of Vijayanagar granted the village of Kuñchēpalli in Podilaśīma, to "Brityāri Timmamūṇḍuḷa Atnōga Chāryulayyavāru." *Nel. Ins., Podili*, No. 27, pp. 1185–86. [Podiliśīma was then under the rule of Veḷugōṭi Kumāra Timmanāyaniṅgāru.] The cyclic and śaka year do not agree.

Maṛṛipūḍi.

609. Below the dhvajastambham of the Vēṇugōpālasvāmi temple. (Telugu.) Records the dedication of a Garuḍa pillar by Punnam Śeṭṭi to Gōpinātha, on Wednesday, the second of the bright fortnight of Māgha of the year *Pramōdūta. Ibid.*, No. 28, p. 1187.

Pamulapāḍu.

610. In a garden. (Telugu.) Records on Monday, the fifteenth of the bright half of Māgha of the year, Yuva, Ś. 1437, in the reign of Śrīman Mahārāja Rājadhirāja Rājaparamēśvara Śrī Vīra Pratāpa Śrī Kṛishṇadēva Mahārāja of Vijayanagar, Rāyasam Koṇḍamarasayyaṁgāru granted the village of Kiraḷḷapalli to Dudala Mallikārjuna (deity). *Ibid.*, No. 29, pp. 1187–89.

Patagārḷapēṭa.

611. To the south in the purōhit's field. (Telugu.) Records the gift of land made to Koṇḍūri Obayēśvara by Chintagumpalli Pedda Nāyaniṅgāru on Monday, the fifteenth of the bright fortnight of Kārttika of the year Plavaṅga, Ś. 1469, in Gārlapēṭa village, on the holy occasion of lunar eclipse. *Ibid.*, No. 30, pp. 1189–90.

Pedarikaṭḷa.

612. In front of the Chennakēśavasvāmi temple. (Telugu.) Records a gift on Thursday, the eleventh of the bright fortnight of Śravaṇa of the year Sarvadhāri. Rest lost. *Ibid.*, No. 31, pp. 1190–91.

Podili (Podila, Podiyala).

613. On a stone outside the Vīrabhadra temple. (Telugu.) Records on Thursday, the first of the bright fortnight of Phalguṇa, Ś. 1211, that a certain Śrīman Mahāmaṇḍalēśvara Dharma Vijayādityadēva Mahārāja gave 100 *puṭṭis*, free from taxes, to Tirupurāntaka Kommanappa of the Vaṅgipura gōtra, for the merit of Manumagaṇḍagōpāladēva. *Ibid.*, No. 32, pp. 1191—93.

614. On a stone in the mosque. (Telugu.) The inscription is practically identical with No. 610. *Ibid.*, No. 33, p. 1193.

615. On a stone near the Muhammadan darga. (Telugu.) Records on the eleventh day of the bright fornight of Śravaṇa in the year Svabhānu, Ś. 1501, that Komāra China Timmanāyaniṅgāru (son of Kumāra Timma and grandson of Veḷugōṭi Pedda Timma of the Rācherla family) gave away to pious Brāhmans, agrahārams and *Bhaṭṭavirti mānyams* in Podilaśīma, for carrying on work connected with learning. *Nel. Ins., Podili,* No. 34, pp. 1193—95.

616. In the Āñjanēya temple. (Telugu.) Records on Sunday, the fifteenth of the bright half of Kārttika of the year Plavaṅga Ś. 1469, in the reign of Sadāśivadēva Mahārāyaluṅgāru of Vijayanagar Jillēlla Raṅgapatidēva Mahārājuluṅgāru exempted the taxes and *veṭṭi* fees on all the barbers in Podilaśīma under the orders of Śrīman Mahāmaṇḍalēśvara Aḷiya Rāma. *Ibid.*, No. 35, pp. 1195—97.

617. In front of the Nirmalēśvara temple. (Telugu.) Records on Thursday, the thirtieth of the dark half (i.e., new-moon day) Śravaṇa in the year Bhava, Ś. 1437, solar eclipse, Rāyasam Koṇḍapparasayya Gāru granted, for the religious merit of Śrī Vīrapratāpa Kṛishṇadēva Mahārāya, the village of Chirramakūru to the deities Bhīmēśvaradēva and Kailāsarāya of Podila. *Ibid.*, No. 36, pp. 1197—1200.

618. On a pillar in the Nirmalēśvara temple. (Telugu.) Records that Śrī Pōtaya Sāhiṇiṅgāru, son of Vīraya Sāhiṇi, made some gifts to the kāpus of Podiyala *sthalam*. . . . *Ibid.*, No. 37, pp. 1200-1.

619. Opposite the Rāmaliṅgēśvara temple. (Sanskrit in Telugu character and Telugu.) Records that on Friday, the full-moon day of Vaiśākha, Ś. 890, the illustrious Aggaparāju of the family of Mahābali, whose banner was a black buck, etc., granted to Annaguri Agastīśvara Bhaṭṭāra some land. Parivīpura is mentioned. *Ibid.*, No. 38, pp. 1201—3. [The king, it has been suggested, was a Bāṇa.]

Tippaldēvipalli.

620. To the west by a ruined tank. (Telugu.) Records on Sunday, the third of the bright fortnight of Vaiśākha of the year Kāḷayukti, Ś. 1360, that Tippaladēvi, the daughter of Pedda-rāya, granted a village to Tinta Tammaṇārya of the Bhāradvāja gōtra. [Pedda Rāya was the son of Pedda Śamburāya who was the son of Rāja Vibhāla. Tippaladēvi was the queen of king Jagatāba Śiṅga and had a son, king Timma. *Ibid.*, No. 39, pp. 1203—6. See No. 26, Podili, above.

Tuvvapādu.

621. By the Vaḍḷavāḍi pond. (Telugu.) Records on Monday, the tenth of the dark fortnight of Śravaṇa of the year Bahudhānya, that Śrīmat Śrī Velugōṭi Komāra China Timma Nāyaniṅgāru made a grant to the *Jaṅgama* (priest) who worships Kūdaḷi Saṅgamēśvara. *Ibid.*, No. 40, pp. 1206-7.

Uppalapādu.

622. On the floor of Rāmaliṅgasvāmi temple. (Sanskrit in Chaḷukyan character.) A record which makes no sense. *Nel. Ins., Podili,* No. 41, p. 1207.

Vāgimaḍugu.

623-A. Opposite the Vīrabhadrasvāmi temple. (Telugu.) A record on the fifteenth of the bright fortnight of Mārgaśira of the year *Naḷa,* Ś. 1297.

PŌLŪR TALUK.

Liṅgampāḍu.

623-B. *C.P. No.* 3 *of Nel. Ins.*—A C.P. grant (Sanskrit) of Dēva Rāya II in Ś. 1351, *Saumya* (Kārttika, Śu. 12) recording the gift of the village of Liṅgampāḍ, thenceforward known as Pratāpadēva Rāyapuram, to Anna Mārādhya *alias* Kompalli, the son of Mallikārjuna. Liṅgampāḍu is said to be in Paḍanāḍu, in the Chandragiri Rājya, in the Pōrūr śīma, and to the south of the river Svarṇamukhi. The donee "is said to have been the Governor of the northern gate of Śrī Śaila," a strong Śaiviṭe. [The inscription is said to closely resemble the Satyamaṅgalam grant of the same king, for which see *Ep. Ind.*, Vol. III, p. 35.]

Mallam.

Owing to a mistake this village was included in the Gudur taluk under Nos. 204 to 232. I find from the alphabetical list of villages that it belongs to Pōlūr taluk and that therefore its proper place is here. It may be noted that Nos. 204—232 above are apparently the same as inscriptions 488—515 of 1908. Besides these we have the following epigraphs from the same source :—

624-A. 516 *of* 1908.—(Tamil.) On the east wall of the prākāra of the same temple. Records in the twenty-third year of the Chōḷa king Tribhuvanachakravartin Kulōttuṅga-Chōḷadeva III "who was pleased to take Madura and the crowned head of the Paṇḍya," gift of twenty *māḍai* for twenty evening lamps *(śandi viḷakku.)*

624-B. 517 *of* 1908.—(Tamil.) On the same wall. An unfinished record of the Chōḷa king Tribhuvanachakravartin Rājarājadēva, dated seventh year. Mentions the temple of Subrahmaṇya-Piḷḷaiyār at Tiruvānbūr, a village in Kiḷaippaṭṭaya-nāḍu, in Okkadunāḍu, a subdivision of Paiyuriḷaṅgōṭṭam which was a district of Jayaṅgoṇḍachōḷamaṇḍalam.

624-C. 518 *of* 1908.—(Tamil.) On the south wall of the same prākāra. Tribhuvanachakravartin Rājagaṇḍagōpāladēva records in his eleventh year gift of two lamp-stands and a copper pot to the temple of Sēnāpati Piḷḷaiyār Nāyanār.

624-D. 519 *of* 1908.—(Tamil.) On the same wall. Records in the thirty-fifth year of the Chōḷa king Tribhuvanachakravartin Kulōttuṅgachōḷadēva gift of forty-eight sheep for a half lamp by a native of Śūralūr in Vēlūr-nāḍu.

624-E. 520 *of* 1908.—(Tamil.) On the same wall. Tribhuvanachakravartin Vijayagaṇḍagōpaladēva records gift of land for a lamp. Built in the middle. Mentions Puḷarkōṭṭam *alias* Vikramachōḷa-vaḷanāḍu in Jayaṅgoṇḍachōḷamaṇḍalam. Date of the record is lost.

624-F. 521 *of* 1908.—(Tamil.) On the same wall. A record of the Chōḷa king Tribhuvanachakravartin Kulōttuṅgachōḷadēva (III), "who was pleased to take Madura and the crowned head of the Pāṇḍya," recording in his thirtieth year gift of three lamps to be maintained with the thirty-six *māḍai* collected from *kuṟṟattaṇḍam* and *śiṟṟāyam*.

624-G. 522 *of* 1908.—(Tamil.) On a slab built into the floor in front of the entrance into the same temple. A fragment of record of the Chōḷa king Rājarājadēva, dated eleventh year.

624-H. 523 *of* 1908.—(Tamil.) On a slab set up in the bazaar street. Records gift of land apparently to the hero who is represented on the stone as cutting his head with a sword placed across his neck and held by both the hands.

624-I. 524 *of* 1908.—(Tamil.) At the entrance into the Mārkaṇḍēśvara temple in the same village. Records a gift of land to the temple of Mārkaṇḍīśuramuḍaiya-Nāyanār by Muppiḍi-Nāyaka on his return to Orangal after having entered Nellore.

Maṅgaḷampāḍ.

625. *C.P. No.* 5 *of Nel. Ins.*—This grant which is in Nandināgari alphabet and Sanskrit language, and which is dated in Ś. 1524 (A.D. 1602–3), *Śubhakrit*, on the twelfth day of the month of Āshāḍha, records a gift by Veṅkaṭa I to Śrī Raṅga Rāja, son of Jagannāthāchārya, grandson of Śrīraṅgarājārya, of the gōtra of Atri, Āpastamba śūtra and Yajus śākha. The donee was the descendant of Vēdāntōdayana, the cook of Śrī Rāmānuja and of Vādihamsāmbuvāha, the teacher of the celebrated Vēdānta Dēśika. [For the details of Vādihamsāmbuvāha's life and labours and his relations with Vēdānta Dēśika see my article on Vēdānta Dēśika in the *Journal of the Bombay Branch of the Royal Asiatic Society*, 1915–16.] The object of the grant was the village of Maṅgaḷampāḍ *alias* Parūr, surnamed Jagannāthapuram, situated in the division of Paḍanāḍu. [Composed by Chidambara kavi, sister's son of Śivasūrya.]

Mannar Pōlūru.

626. In the gōpuram of Aḷagumalāru Kṛishṇasvāmi temple. (Tamil.) Records that . . . Alluntikka Mahārājan presented a piece of land for providing sacred food during festivals. *Nel. Ins.*, *Śūlūrpet*, No. 1, p. 1307.

Mannemuttēri.

627. In a street to the west. (Tamil.) Records a charity of Nalla Sittarasa (Nalla Siddha) of the Pallava race . . . *Ibid.*, No. 2, p. 1308.

Śūḷūrpēṭa.

628. On a pillar in the Nāgēśvara temple. (Tamil.) Records that in the twenty-fourth year of the reign of Vijayagaṇḍagōpaladēva a gift was endowed to the god Tirunāgēśvara at Śiṅgaḷāntapuram *alias* Śūralūr, a village in Mēlnāḍu, for a procession on the new-moon day. *Ibid.*, No. 3, pp. 1308—10.

629. On the southern wall of the Nāgēśvara temple. (Tamil.) Records that in the reign of the emperor Vijaya dēva Tanikkūṭṭukkaṇḍāḷ, the consort of Taimmāḍidēvan presented one sacred perpetual lamp in the temple of the lord Tirunāgēśvara of Śūralūr *alias* Śiṅgaḷāntapura in Veṅganāḍu, a subdivision of Paiyyūriḷaṅkōṭṭam. For this lamp and for the Tirumārgaḷi festival he gave land (600 *kuḷis*) free from all kinds of taxes. *Ibid.*, No. 4, pp. 1310-11.

630. On the south wall of the Nāgēśvara temple. (Tamil.) Records that in the fifth year of the reign of Kulōttuṅgachōḷadēva a certain Uraiyūruḍaiyān *alias* Tiruppālaivanamuḍaiyān presented one evening lamp in the temple of the lord Tirunāgēśvara of Śūralūr. *Ibid.*, No. 5, p. 1311-12.

631. On the western wall of the Nāgēśvara temple. (Tamil.) Records that in the twelfth year of the reign of Rājarājadēva, a feudatory named Kulōttuṅgachōḷa Talaivarāya presented one evening lamp to the god Tirunāgēśvara of Śūralūr. The Śiva Brahmans of this temple received every day three good, old *kāśu* as interest on the donor's gift, and bound themselves to maintain the lamp. *Ibid.*, No. 6, pp. 1312-13.

632. On the western wall of the Nāgēśvarasvāmi temple. (Tamil.) A record in the thirteenth year of the reign of Rājarājadēva. One Āṇḍapiḷḷai Sōmadēvan is referred to. *Ibid.*, No. 7, pp. 1313-14.

633. On the western wall of the Nāgēśvarasvāmi temple. (Tamil.) Records that in the second year of the reign of Vijayagaṇḍagōpaladēva, Rājēndrachōḷa Mummuḍi Vaiḍumba Mahārājan presented 500 *kuḷis* of land for one lamp in Eṇṇāyiraparaiyūr Puttēri and for the performance of a festival during Tiruvādirai in the month of Mārgaḷi. *Ibid.*, No. 8, p. 1314.

634. On the south wall of the Nāgēśvarasvāmi temple. (Tamil.) A record in the thirty-eighth year of the reign of Kulōttuṅgachōḷadēva. Śūralūr is said to be in Vēlur nāḍu in Paiyūriḷaṅkōṭṭam in Jayankoṇḍa-chōḷamaṇḍalam. *Nel. Ins., Sulūrpet*, No. 9, p. 1315.

Tummūru.

635. On the roof of Nīlakaṇṭhasvāmi temple. (Telugu.) An illegible record. *Ibid.*, No. 10, pp. 1315–16.

636. On a pillar of the western porch of Kariyamāṇikkasvāmi temple. (Tamil.) Records that in Ś. 1435, Śrīmukha, on Monday, the eleventh day of the bright half of the month of Mithuna, a grant of several villages was agreed to by the glorious Kṛishṇarāya Mahārāya to the temple treasury of the God Tirukkāḷahastīśvara. The villages mentioned were: Puliyūr, Tonpākkam, Chennāḷi, Nitti, Kārumbēḍu, Śattambaiyūr and Tummūru. All the dues from these villages, including the dues appertaining to water, land, etc., were given by them for the maintenance of services and festivals. The king's birthday is said to be Jyēshṭha in the month of Vaikāśi. *Ibid.*, No. 10, pp. 1316—19.

637. On the east wall of Kariyamāṇikkarāya temple. (Tamil.) Records that in the thirteenth year of the reign of Rājarājadēva, the temple and the sacred place for Karumāṇikkaperumāḷ of Tumbaiyūr were performed by Tyāgasamudrapaṭṭai Vimarśan. Madhurāntaka Pottappichōḷa Gaṇḍagōpāla Tirukkāḷatti Dēva is also mentioned. *Ibid.*, No. 12, p. 1320.

638. On the east wall of Kariyamāṇikyarāya temple. (Tamil.) An illegible record. *Ibid.*, No. 13, p. 1321.

639. On the south wall of Kariyamāṇikyasvāmi temple. (Tamil.) A fragment recording the gift of a lamp. *Ibid.*, No. 14, p. 1321.

640. On the gate of Kariyamāṇikyarāya temple. (Tamil.) A record in the sixteenth year of the reign of Rājarājadēva. Tumbaiyūr or Jaynakondachōḷa chaturvēdimaṅgalam is said to be in Paṭṭaiyanāḍu in Paiyūriḷaṅkōṭṭam. See *Ibid.*, No. 15, pp. 1321-2.

641. On the gate of Kariyamāṇikyarāya temple. (Telugu.) Records that on Sunday, the twelfth of the bright fortnight of Mārgaśira of the year Vijaya, Ś. 1516, Velugōṭi Rāya Channāyani Liṅgam Gāru caused a mukhamaṇṭapa to be constructed to Karimāṇikya Nāyanār (deity) of Tummūru for his own religious merit. *Ibid.*, No. 16, p. 1322.

642. In the shrine of Kariyamāṇikyarāya temple. (Tamil.) Records that in the twenty-third year of the reign of Rājarājadēva, Eṛamireḍḍi, who possessed rights in Tiruvānbūr village, gave one *māḍai* to God Karumāṇikkaperumāḷ of Tumbaiyūr. *Ibid.*, No. 17, p. 1323.

643. On the tank bund. (Telugu.) Records that on the eleventh of the dark fortnight of Āshāḍha of the year Ānanda, Ś. 1716, Mahārāja Rāja Śrī Velugōṭi Kumāra Yāchama Nāyanivāru presented a *khaṇḍriga* on which ten *tūms* can be sown at Tumbūr to Nīlakaṇṭhēśvarasvāmi. *Nel. Ins., Sulūrpet*, No. 18, p. 1374.

Utsūru.

644. On the door of the Chennakēśava temple. (Tamil.) Records a gift in the twenty-third year of the reign of Vijayagaṇḍagōpāladēva . . . for the erection of the sacred doorway for the sacred maṇṭapam of Chennakēśavaperumāḷ of Uchchiyūr. *Ibid*, No. 19, p. 1325.

645. Opposite Bhīmēśvarasvāmi temple. (Telugu.) Records that on Tuesday, the thirteenth of the dark fortnight of Māgha of the year Vikrama, on the holy occasion of Śiva-Rātri Pina Kūpi Nāyuḍu (son of Rāvūru Pāpi Nāyuḍu) presented to Bhīmēśvaradēva a field situated in the fort and under the Ponnēri guṇṭa. *Ibid.*, No. 20, pp. 1325–26.

646. By the tank bund. (Telugu.) A record on the twelfth of the dark fortnight of Vaiśākha of the year Vikriti . . . *Ibid.*, No. 21, p. 1326.

647. *C.P. No. 7 of Nel. Ins.*—(Nandināgari alphabet and Sanskrit language.) A grant by Raṅga VI of Karnāṭa in Ś. 1569 (A.D. 1647), *Sarvajit*, in the month of Chaitra on Śrīrāmanavami making the gift of the village of Utsūr or Vilāsapuram in the Chandragiri Rājya and Pōrūr Śīma to Anantāchārya, son of Anantaśayanārya and grandson of Kḍāmbi Anantārya of the Ātrēya gōtra. The gift is said to have been made in the temple of Śrīraṅgam.

Rāpūr Taluk.

Ākilavalsa.

648. There is a defaced inscription on the tank bund. *Nel. Ins., Rāpūr*, No. 1, p. 1209.

Ākupalli.

649. Near the tank to the west of the village. (Telugu.) Records on the second of the bright half of Chaitra of the year Bahudhānya, Ś. 1560, a grant by Śrīmat Velugōṭi Veṅkaṭapati Nāyanimgāru for the tank at Ākupalli. He ordered that the tank-work should be done with the *mēra* grain in the same manner in which it had been formerly collected and utilized. *Ibid.*, No. 3, pp. 1209—11.

Āltūrti.

650. Opposite Chennakēśvarasvāmi temple. (Tamil.) An illegible record. *Ibid.*, No. 2, p. 1209.

Chāganam (Rāzupalem hamlet).

651. On a rock below the hill to the north of the village. (Tamil.) Records that in the twenty-third year of the reign of the emperor Kulōttuṅgachōḷadēva, Pichchāṇḍināyaka gave images to the temple of the lord Kaḷai Iṭṭa Kāḍuchcharudēva at Nellūr *alias* Vikiramaśiṅgapuram and dug a tank at the foot of Ūṭṭukkūkan hill. There seems to be reference to Nallasittarasar and the Veḷāḷas of Udukkūr, etc. *Nel. Ins., Rāpūr*, No. 4.

652. On a stone in the middle of the village. (Telugu.) Records on the thirtieth day of the dark fortnight of Pushya of the year Dhātri, Ś. 1558, while Śrī Vīra Vēṅkaṭapatidēva Mahārājulu (1630—40) was seated on the diamond throne at the town of Penugoṇḍa, Velugōṭi Veṅkaṭapati Nāyaniṁgāru gave Dāgdama agrahāra in Nellore śīma which was ruled and presided over by himself to Pūsala Veṅgaṇṇa Kaḍappa as an *amaram*. *Ibid.*, No. 5, pp. 1212—14.

653. North of the village on Tirragatrāla Bōdu. (Telugu.) An incomplete record, dated on the thirtieth day of the dark fortnight of Pushya of the year Dhātri, Ś. 1558, while Śrīmad Vīra Vēṅkaṭapatidēva Mahārājulu was on the diamond throne at Penugoṇḍa. *Ibid.*, No. 6, pp. 1214-15.

Chikavōlu.

654. On the tank bund. (Telugu.) Records on the second day of the bright half of Chaitra of the year Bahudhānya, Ś. 1560, that Śrīmat Velugōṭi Vēṅkaṭapati Nāyaniṁgāru ordered that the *mēras* collected for the tank of this village at one *kuñcha* for every *puṭṭi* should be spent on the tank. *Ibid.*, No. 7, pp. 1215-16.

655. To the north in Survey No. 510 in the hamlet of Yarraguṇṭapālem. (Sanskrit in Grantha and Tamil.) Records that in the thirty-sixth year of the reign of the emperor Kulōttuṅgachōḷadēva, Tukki Nāyaka gave, on behalf of Piḷḷaiyār Tirukkāḷattidēva (the son of Manumasiddharasa), a village including all taxes leviable within its four boundaries. *Ibid.*, No. 8, pp. 1216—19.

Chintalātmakūru.

656. Opposite the Āñjanēya temple. (Telugu.) Records that on the third day of the dark fortnight of Śravaṇa of the year Kīlaka, Anumantu, son of Chiru Māmilla Gōpanna, caused to be made an image of Sañjīva Rāya in Chintalātukkūru and consecrated it. He also caused five lamp-posts to be planted. *Ibid.*, No. 9, pp. 1219-20.

Chipināpi.

657. Near the Ōṭaguṇṭa to the south of the village. (Telugu.) Records that, on the third of the bright fortnight of Aśvija of the year Manmatha, Timma Rājugāru, the agent *(kārvakartā)* of

Śrīman Mahāmaṇḍalēśvara Tāḍigoṭḷa Timmarājuvāru made a gift to the goddess Ammagāru of Vāvilla. *Nel. Ins., Rāpūr*, No. 10, p. 1221.

Chittalūru.

658. In the tank bed in the hamlet of Ādūrupalle. (Telugu.) A charitable edict of Ś. 1492. Mostly illegible. *Ibid.*, No. 11, pp. 1222–23.

659. On the tank bund. (Telugu.) Records on the tenth of the bright fortnight of Śravaṇa of the year Śrīmukha that Dummarapu Vēṅkaṭādri Nāyanigāru gave a grant for the tanks of the villages of Chittallūru and Ādūrupalle. *Ibid.*, No. 12, p. 1223.

660. Near a well to the east of the village. (Telugu.) Records that a liṅga was carved out by Nāyiṇḍu for the flower garden to the west of the Nāgināyini well . . . *Ibid.*, No. 13, p. 1224.

661. Near the same well. (Telugu.) An incomplete record. *Ibid.*, No. 14, p. 1224.

Dātsūru.

662. On one side of a tall stone east of the village. (Telugu.) An incomplete record in Adhika Āshāḍha of the year Raktākshi, Ś. 1607. *Ibid.*, No. 15, p. 1225.

663. On the same stone. (Telugu.) This seems to record a *mantra* and prescription for cattle diseases. Some parts are unintelligible. *Ibid.*, No. 16, pp. 1225—27. [The record is of singular interest for the instructions it gives for the preparation of the mystic specific.]

664. On the same stone. (Telugu.) A record praising Hanūmān. *Ibid.*, No. 17, pp. 1227–28. Also evidently a *mantra* or spell.

665. On two sides of a stone near the police station. (Telugu.) Records that on the eleventh day of the bright fortnight of Phalguṅa of the year Dundhubhi, Ś. 1544, Veṅkaṭapati Nāyaniṅgāru, son of Velugōṭi and grandson of Koṇḍama Nāyaniṁgāru, ordered that one *kuñcha* should be given for every *puṭṭi* for the upkeep of the tank of Dātsūru. *Ibid.*, No. 18, pp. 1229–30.

666. On the same stone. (Telugu.) Mostly illegible. A record in Ś. 1463. *Ibid.*, No. 19, p. 1231.

Dēvaravēmūru.

667. East of the village in Survey No. 350. (Telugu.) Records that on Thursday, the eighth of the bright half of the month of Māgha of the year Plavaṅga, Ś. 1169, Śrīmat Chivapāṇi Śeṭṭi gave land for providing offering to the deity for the religious merit of king Vijayāditya Chōḍamahārāja. *Ibid.*, No. 20, pp. 1231–32.

668. Near the Vēṇugōpālasvāmi temple. (Telugu.) Records that the *mēra* grain settled at one *kuñcha* for every *puṭṭi* for the tank should be spent for the maintenance of the tank. *Nel. Ins., Rāpūr*, No. 21, p. 1233.

Duggunṭa.

669. On the tank bund to the south. (Telugu.) Records that on the fifth of the bright half of Jyēshṭa (Jyēshṭha) of the year Rudhirōdgāri, Śrīmat Velugōṭi Veṅkaṭapati Nāyaniṅgāru made a gift of the paddy-field under the tank Duguṇṭa, called Koṇangu and measuring four *goṟṟūs*. *Ibid.*, No. 22, pp. 1233–34.

Gilakapāḍu.

670. On Boyela tank bund. (Tamil.) Records that in the month of Māśi of Yuva, thirty-eighth year of the king Kulōttuṅga-chōḷadēva, Māsavipetti Nāyaka gave the tank named Peddasamudram to Sitthavaṭēśvara. He also gave ¾ *vēḷi* and three *mās* of land to the three Veḷḷāḷas who dug the tank. *Ibid.*, No. 23, pp. 1234—36.

Griḍḍalūru.

671. On a stone in the middle of village. (Telugu.) An incomplete record on Sunday, the thirtieth of the dark half of *Pushya* of the year Viḷambi, Ś. 1460, while Śrīman Mahāmaṇḍalēśvara, Śrī Achyutadēva Mahārāja was ruling the kingdom. *Ibid.*, No. 24, pp. 1236–37.

672. In the same locality. (Telugu.) Mostly illegible. A record on the fifth of the bright fortnight of Mārgaśira of the year *Bahudhānya*, Ś. 1560. *Ibid.*, No. 25, pp. 1237–38.

Guṇḍavōlu.

673. Below the tank bund to the south of the village. (Telugu.) A record of the grant of *mēra* grain for the repair of the tank. *Ibid.*, No. 26, pp. 1238–39.

674. On two stones near the calingula of the tank. (Telugu.) Incomplete and partly unintelligible. A record in the year Āṅgirasa, Ś. 1214. *Ibid.*, No. 27, pp. 1239–40.

Guruvāyapāḷem.

675. Near calingula of the tank. (Telugu.) Records that on the second of the bright half of Chaitra of the year Bahudhānya, Ś. 1560, Śrīmat Velugōṭi Veṅkaṭapati Nāyaniṅgāru ordered that the *mēras* should be given at one *kuñcha* for every *puṭṭi* of produce on all lands under the tank, for the repair of the same at Guruvāyapalli. *Ibid.*, No. 28, pp. 1240–41.

Inukūrti.

676. On the west bank of a ruined tank. (Telugu.) Records grant of *mēras* for the repair of the tank. An incomplete record. *Ibid.*. No. 29, pp. 1241–42.

Kalichēḍu.

677. On the eastern tank bund. (Telugu.) Records that on the second of the bright fortnight of Chaitra of the year Bahudhānya, Ś. 1560, Śrīmat Velugōṭi Veṅkaṭapati Nāyaniṅgāru caused to be planted this charitable edict for the tank of Kalichēḍu. *Nel. Ins., Rāpūr*, No. 30, pp. 1242–43.

678. On the north bund of the tank. (Telugu.) An incomplete record of a charitable gift. *Ibid.*, No. 31, pp. 1243–44.

Kanuparti.

679. Near the Śiva temple north of village. (Telugu.) Records that on the fifteenth of the full-moon day of the bright half of the month of Āshāḍha of the year Khara . . . the southern sluice was constructed. *Ibid.*, No. 32, pp. 1244–45.

680. East of the village in Survey No. 129. (Telugu.) Records on the third day of the bright fortnight of Kārttika in the year Śukla, Ś. 1558, Ākula Peda Veṅgaṇa, the minister of Velugōṭi Veṅkaṭapati Nāyanivāru, issued the edict in respect of the *mēra* due for the tank of Kanuparti. The grain payable at *kuñcha* per *puṭṭi* on the produce from the dry and wet lands of this village should be utilized for the improvement of the tank. *Ibid.*, No. 33, pp. 1245-46.

Kompēḍu.

681. On the bund of the tank to the west of the village. (Telugu.) Records that in Ś. 1560, Velugōṭi Veṅkaṭapati Nāyaniṅgāru ordered that the *mēras* should be collected on all the tank-fed lands, on *mānyas*, on *dēvadāya* and *brahmadāya mānyas* and on fields under the pond of Darabandapāḍu at one *kuñcha* on every *puṭṭi*, and on dry lands and *mānyas* at one *kuñcha* on every *puṭṭi*, and that the proceeds should be used for the upkeep of the tank. *Ibid.*, No. 34, pp. 1247–48.

682. To the south of the village. (Telugu.) Illegible in parts. A record of the fifteenth of the bright half of Māgha of the year Tāraṇa, Ś. 1556, while Śrīmat Rājādhirāja Paramēśvara Śrī Vīra Pratāpa Śrī Veṅkaṭapati Rāya Dēva Mahārāyalu (1630—40) was seated on the diamond throne in the city of Penugoṇḍa. Mentions Lakshmappa *Nāyanimgāru*, son of Sāri Lakshmi Śrī Nāyanimgāru of Udayagiri, the *karaṇam*, *kāpus* and *Voḍḍas*. *Ibid.*, No. 35, pp. 1248–49.

683. On a high stone near a ruined temple. (Telugu.) Records on Monday, the fifth of the bright half of Pushya, Ś. 1139, Uttarāyaṇa Saṅkrānti, that Kōnangi Siddhappa Nāyakan, feudatory of Vīra Nalla Siddhaṇadēva, set up the images of Ishṭa Kāmēśvaradēva, Nāgēśvaradēva and Mallikārjunadēva at Bommini in Śrī Pākināḍu, constructed temples for them so as to resemble a hill of three peaks, and maṇṭapas, and also a temple to Chennakēśava, for the religious merit of their parents and Bairava Nāyaka his brother-in-law. *Nel Ins., Rāpūr*, No. 36, pp. 1249—52.

Kōṭūrupalli Śrōtriyam.

684. On a stone two miles to the east of the village. (Telugu.) Records that Nārapa Sāhiṇi Bhīmanāyakuṇḍu, feudatory of Eṟṟa Siddhi Chōḍa, Lord of Uraiyūr and Kāñchi, etc., had for his preceptor Śrikarakaṇṭha Kēśayyaṅgāru, who is called a great yōgin. *Ibid.*, No. 37, pp. 1252—56.

Liṅgaṇapāḷem.

685. To the south. (Tamil.) Records that in the eighth year of the reign of the emperor Rājarājadēva (III), the servants of the minister of Madhurāntaka Pottapi Chōḷa *alias* Eṟṟa Sittaraśan of Vikramaṣiṅgapura *alias* Nellūr, Bayirappa Nāyaka and Tikka Nāyaka and their elder brother Kusani Nāyaka, presented a sacred lamp to the deity. *Ibid.*, No. 38, pp. 1256-57.

Marupūr.

686. By the little tank. (Tamil.) A record of the Ś. 1165 in the month of Vaiśākha, recording a gift by Śrīkaṇṭha Cheṭṭi residing in the great kingdom of Śrīman Mahāmaṇḍalēśvara Madhurāntaka Pottapi Chōḷa *alias* Tilakanārāyaṇa *alias* Manumasiddharaśa. *Ibid.*, No. 39, pp. 1257-58.

687. On the big tank bund. (Telugu.) Records that on the second of the bright fortnight of Chaitra of the year Bahudhānya, Ś. 1560, Velugōṭi Veṅkaṭapati Nāyanivāru issued a grant for the tank of Marupūr. The *sandhāta, lessee amaradār*, or the ruler of the village should get the tank and channel work done with the *mēras* settled on the tank. *Ibid.*, No. 40, pp. 1258-59.

Mogallūru.

688. In the middle of the village. (Telugu.) Records on Thursday, the tenth of the dark fortnight of Vaiśākha of the year Yuva, Ś. 1497, while Śrī Raṅgarāyadēva Mahārāya (1578—86) was ruling at Penugoṇḍa, the image of Chennakēśavarāya was set up in the village of Mogallūru (granted as an *amaram* by Paṭṭikoṇḍa Timmarāja) in the *sīma* of Udayagiri, and a paddy field of 10 *tūms* under the big *aṇaikaṭ*, two *tūms* of dry land, and two *goṟṟus* of saline land were presented. *Ibid.*, No. 41, pp. 1259—61.

689. In the same locality. (Telugu.) Records gift for the repair of the tank. *Ibid.*, No. 42, p. 1261.

690. On the tank bund to the east of the village. (Telugu.) Records on the second day of the bright half of Vaiśākha of the year Bahudhānya, Ś. 1560, that Śrīmat Velugōṭi Veṅkaṭapati

Nāyanimgāru issued this charitable edict for the tank of Mogallūru. The tank work should be done with the *mēra* grain collected at one *kuñcha* for every *puṭṭi* on all lands including *dēvadāya* and *brahmadāya* lands. *Nel. Ins., Rāpūr*, No. 43, pp. 1261–62.

Mudigōḍu.

691. Opposite the temple of the goddess. (Telugu.) A record of a charitable edict. *Ibid.*, No. 44, p. 1263.

Nandivāya.

692. There is said to be an inscription here which is entirely defaced. *Ibid.*, No. 45, p. 1263.

Nernūru.

693. Opposite to the Dēśamma temple, three miles from the village. (Telugu.) Records gift of land by one Ku . . . palli Naragayya to Śrīmat . . . Vurti Kēśavadēva in Rāpūr śīma in Udayagiri. *Ibid.*, No. 46, pp. 2263–64.

Pālicherlapāḍu.

694. On four sides of a stone on the tank bund in front of the Śiva temple. (Telugu.) Records on Monday, the day of Dhanishṭa nakshatra, the seventh of the dark fortnight of Mārgaśira, Ś. 1133, Dāmi Nāyakuḍu, son of Talāra Denimija Nāyakuḍu, and the wife of this Dāmi Nāyakuḍu Śrīmati Pōtasāni built a temple to Śrīmat Bhujabala Mallikārjuna Mahādēva in Pālachēlam, for the religious merit of Vīra Tikkakālatidēva Chōḍa Mahārāja (whose *birudas* are enumerated). They also presented lands for providing oblation, offering and worship to the deity. *Ibid.*, No. 47, pp. 1624—69.

Pallakoṇḍa.

695. Near the Aṅkamma temple. (Telugu.) Records a charitable gift by Hechu Savunaṭi of Rāpūr. *Ibid.*, No. 48, p. 1269.

Penubarti.

696. Opposite the Śiva temple. (Telugu) Records on Monday, the third of the dark fortnight of Adhika Śravaṇa of the year Bahudhānya, Ś. 1559, an endowment to Uḍumēśvara Svāmi in the *sarvamānya* agrahāra called Koḍḍavāsili Baṇḍāru Penubarte (or Kṛishṇarāyasamudram). A quit-rent of five *māḍas* was collected from this endowment and Veṅkatāchalam, grandson of Voḍḍe Arjinēni, remitted that for the religious merit of Arjinēni and Kōnētayya. *Ibid.*, No. 49, pp. 1270—72.

697. On the tank bund. (Telugu.) Records that on the eighth day of the bright fortnight of Chaitra of the year Bahudhānya, Ś. 1560, Śrīmat Velugōti Veṅkaṭapati Nāyanigāru granted *mēras* for the maintenance of the tanks of the villages of Rāpūr śīma. *Rāpūr*, No. 50, pp. 1272—74.

Perumāḷḷapāḍu.

698. On four sides of a stone on tank bund. (Telugu.) Records that on the second day of the bright half of the year Bahudhānya, Ś. 1560, Śrīmat Velugōṭi Veṅkaṭapati Nāyaniṁgāru ordered that the *mēra* grain levied on dry and wet fields including *dēvadāya* and *brahmadāya* lands should be utilized for the tank of this village. *Ibid.*, No. 51, pp. 1274-75.

699. In a tope. (Telugu.) Records that the village of Penumbala pāḍu was presented to the deity Mūlasthānēśvara of Udayagiri by Koṇḍamarusayya for the religious merit of Krishṇarāya. *Ibid.*, No. 52, pp. 1275-76.

Podalakūru.

700. Near a well by the Vināyakasvāmi temple. On two stones. (Telugu.) Records that on the second of the bright fortnight of Chaitra of the year Bahudhānya, Ś. 1560, Śrīmat Velugōṭi Veṅkaṭapati Nāyaniṅgāru ordered that the *mēra* grain should be utilized for tank work in the manner in which the tank *mēras* were formerly collected. *Ibid.*, No. 53, pp. 1276-77.

Pōteguṇṭa.

701. On the bund of the tank to the east of the village. (Telugu.) Records that in the year Bahudhānya, Ś. 1560, Śrīmat Velugōṭi Veṅkaṭapati Nāyaniṁgāru granted the *mēras* of the tank for the repair of the same at Pōteguṇṭa. *Ibid.*, No. 54, pp. 1278-79.

Pulikollu.

702. To the east of the village near Polimera stream. (Telugu.) An incomplete record. Records a gift. *Ibid.*, No. 55, pp. 1272—80.

Rāpūru.

703. In front of Rāpūramma's temple. (Telugu.) Legible only in parts. Records construction of a mukhamaṇṭapa for Ammagāru of Rāpūru. *Ibid.*, No. 56, pp. 1280-81.

Saidāpuram.

704. On a rock on Dēvara Tippa. (Telugu.) Records that on Wednesday, the seventh of the bright half of Pushya of the year Svabhānu, Vaddu Arināya Bhānuṇḍu of Gummaḍūru constructed maṇṭapas and consecrated Vināyaka. *Ibid.*, No. 57, p. 1281.

Tānamcherla.

705. On a stone on the tank bund. (Telugu.) Mostly illegible. Records a charitable edict. *Ibid.*, No. 58, p. 1282.

706. On the same stone. (Telugu.) Records gift of *mēras* for the repair of the tank. An incomplete record. *Nel. Ins., Rāpūr*, No. 59, pp. 1282—84.

Tegacherla.

707. To the south on tank bund. (Telugu.) Records that on the fifteenth day of the bright fortnight of the month of Śravaṇa of the year Paridhāvi, Ś. 1534, while Śrīmad Rājādhirāja-Rāja-paramēśvara Śrī Vīra Vēṅkaṭapatirāya Dēva was ruling at Penugoṇḍa, Kumāra Timma-Nāyanivāru and Rudrappanāyanivāru caused a low level sluice to be built for this tank. *Ibid.*, No. 60, pp. 1284—86.

708. On the boundary towards Gōnupalli. (Telugu.) Records that on Sunday, the fifth of the bright half of Pushya of the year Naḷa, the villagers of Yerrapalli, Nāgalavelli, etc., constructed a street. *Ibid.*, No. 61, pp. 1286–87.

Tsuṭṭupāḷem.

709. Near Komiṭi guṇṭa. (Telugu.) Records gift by Yanamadam Suddama of Matlapūṇḍi. *Ibid.*, No. 64, pp. 1289–90.

Tummalatalapūr.

710. On the tank bund to the north of the village. (Telugu.) Records that the *mēra* grain settled for the tank of Tummala talapūru was at 1/2 *kuñchas* per *puṭṭi*.[1] *Ibid.*, No. 62, pp. 1287–88.

Turimerla.

711. On the south bank of the tank. (Telugu.) Records that on the sixth of the bright half of Chaitra of the year Bahudhānya, Ś. 1560, Śrīmat Velugōṭi Veṅkaṭapati Nāyaniṅgāru ordered that the *mēra* grain collected in the manner in which it had been collected formerly for the tank of Tullimerla should be utilized for the tank work. *Ibid.*, No. 63, pp. 1288–89.

Ūṭukūru.

712. In the middle of the village. (Tamil.) A record of the sixteenth year of the reign of Kulōttuṅga Chōḷadēva (III), Ś. 1153. Madhurāntaka Pottapichōḷa *alias* Gaṇḍagōpāḷa *alias* Tirukkāḷatti-dēva is mentioned. *Ibid.*, No. 65, pp. 1290–91.

713. On stones dug up on the site of an old temple near the *chāvaḍi*. (Tamil.) Records that in the thirty-seventh year of the reign of Kulōttuṅgachōḷadēva, one Nallappa Reḍḍi built a Śiva temple named after Nallikādēva at Ūṭukūr in Śiṅgaṭṭaināḍu and gave to this temple fifty *kuḷi* of land under the Nāchchān well and fifty *kuḷi* of land under the big tank, constituting one *paṭṭi* of wet land and two *pon*. In addition to the above lands, Vīmarasanpōyan Tikkarasan of Āṇḍūr, Dēva Pōyiṇḍan, Nallappa Reḍḍi,

Puḍolam Reḍḍi and Muppiḍi Reḍḍi dug a tank in the north of the village Ūṭukūr and gave the land irrigated by the water of this tank and one *paṭṭi* of dry land. *Nel. Ins., Rāpūr*, No. 66, pp. 1291–92.

714. This is a defaced inscription in Telugu in the middle of the village. *Ibid.*, No. 67, p. 1293.

715. To the east of the drinking-water well. (Telugu.) Mostly illegible. A record in Dundubhi, Ś. 1605. *Ibid.*, No. 68, p. 1293.

716. On three sides of a stone in the middle of the village. (Telugu.) This record in unintelligible. *Ibid.*, No. 69, pp. 1294—96.

717. In the site of the old temple opposite the *chāvaḍi* (Tamil.) Records a gift to Rāmēśvaram Uḍaiyār at Ūṭukūr in Ś. 1158, on the new-moon day after Śivarātri in the month of Māśi, in the reign of Rājarājadēva (III) . . . *Ibid.*, No. 70, pp. 1296–97.

Vaḍlapūḍi.

718. Opposite Ponnūramma temple. (Telugu.) The impression of this rough record appears to have been lost. *Ibid.*, No. 71, p. 1297.

719. Half a mile south of the village. (Telugu.) Records that on the eleventh of the bright fortnight of Māgha of the year Pārthiva, Dāmi Nāyuṇḍu presented to Śrī Kāḷahastīśvara a wet field in Pina Vodlamūnḍi and 100 *kuṇṭas* of land in Dārabandampāḍu village of Nellūru. *Ibid.*, No. 72, pp. 1297–98.

720. On a stone in front of the temple of Ponnūramma. (Telugu.) Records gift of cows by Tanapusala Veṅkaṭa Reḍḍi of Vaḍlapūḍi for perpetual lamp. *Ibid.*, No. 73, p. 1298–99.

721. Near the sluice of the tank to the west. (Telugu.) Records on the second of the bright half of Chaitra of the year Bahudhānya, Ś. 1560, that Śrīmat Velugōṭi Veṅkaṭapati Nāyaniṁgāru granted the *mēras* for the tank at Voḍlapūḍi. *Ibid.*, No. 74, pp. 1299–1300.

722. On the Bainēṭi hill near the village. (Tamil.) An illegible record. *Ibid.*, No. 75, p. 1300.

Vēbinābi.

723. On a stone in a street to the west. (Telugu.) These are two spells to avert epidemics among men and cattle. *Ibid.*, No. 76, pp. 1300—2. [The record is of interest as showing a common superstition of the age.]

Yēpūru.

724. On a stone on the tank bund. (Telugu.) Records that the tank of Channamgāru was constructed by the daughter of Veligōṭi Timmanāyaḍu on Wednesday, the tenth of the dark fortnight of Phalguṇa of the year Vijaya. *Ibid.*, No. 7", p. 1303.

725. West of the village, in Survey No. 78. (Telugu.) Records that on Tuesday, the fourth of the bright half of Kārttika of the year Vrishu, Ś. 1323, one Vāṇḍadēva (?) Gaṇḍaragaṇḍa Mānyabhūmi Nāyanimgāru gave a wet paddy-field to Śrīgirinātha. *Nel. Ins., Rāpūr,* No. 78, pp. 1303—5.

Yerraguṇṭapāḷem (hamlet of Chikavōlu).

726. On the tank bund. (Telugu.) Records that on the fifth of the bright fortnight of Chaitra of the year Bahudhānya, Ś. 1560, Śrīmat Velugōṭi Veṅkaṭapati Nāyaniṅgāru issued this charitable edict for the tank at *Yerraguṇṭapāḷem.* He ordered that *mēra* grain for the tank should be levied at one *kuñcha* per *puṭṭi* even on *inām* lands. *Ibid.,* No. 79, p. 1306.

UDAYAGIRI TALUK.

Alamēlumaṅgāpuram.

727. On a stone near the Āñjanēya figure. (Telugu.) Records that on Thursday, the thirteenth day of the bright half of Śravaṇa of the year Vibhava, Ś. 1444, Śiṅgaḷa Akkalayya set up an image of Hanumanta Perumāḷ and built a temple at Bōyamaḍugu, for the religious merit of his father Koṇḍamanēni and his mother Raṅgammā. *Nel. Ins., Udayagiri,* No. 1, p. 1327.

728. On another stone near the image of Āñjanēya. (Telugu.) Records that on the thirteenth day of the bright fortnight of Śravaṇa of the year Vibhava, Ś. 1444, Śrīmat Rājādhirāja Rājaparamēśvara Śrī Vīra Pratāpa Śrī Vīra Bhujabala Tirumaladēva Mahārājulu Ayyavāru who was ruling at Vidyānagara, was pleased to grant an *amaram* to Kammarajangam Vaḍla Prasannaṁgāru of Udayagiri for doing his *amara* service . . . *Ibid.,* No. 2, pp. 1328-29.

Ayyavāripalli.

729. On the four sides of an upright stone. (Telugu.) Records the gift of Tende tank made to Siddhanāthadēva, on Thursday, the tenth of the bright half of Chaitra of the year Krōdhi, Ś. 1167, for the religious merit of Śrīman Mahāmaṇḍalēśvara Bhujabala Chōḍa Tirukāḷati Dēva Mahārāja and for the religious merit of Ālu Tikarājudēva (evidently Allun Tirukkāḷattidēva). *Ibid.,* No. 3, pp. 1330—33.

Dāsarapalli.

730. 210 *of* 1892.—On the steps in a cave. (Telugu.) A record of the reign Śrī Kṛishṇadēva Mahārāya, mentioning Rāyasam Koṇḍamarusayya Gāru, on the third day of the dark fortnight of Jyēshṭha of the year Bhava, Ś. 1436. *Ibid.,* No. 4, pp. 1333—34.

Guvvāḍi.

731. An incomplete record in Telugu. *Ibid.,* No. 5, pp. 1334-35.

Jaḍadēvi.

732. On two sides of a stone on the bank of Pilapperu, south of the village. (Telugu.) Records that Yamma Rāju, one of the five sons of Mahamaṇḍ Dorapu Rāja (Pallava family, Lord of Kāñchi, etc.), while he was ruling Pōnugōḍu and Māḍurēvi (?), on the occasion of a lunar eclipse in the month of Kanyā, presented some villages in Pūṅginādu, as agrahāras to Brahmans, and constructed two temples, maṇṭapas, gōpuras and prākāras to Dāorēśvara (?) and Irugēśvara of Pādaṭūru, dug a tank named Podarasamudram, excavated a channel named after himself, built a sluice for the tank, planted a flower garden, and gave lands to the deities Rishabhakēśvara and Baddidōrīśvara. *Nel. Ins., Udayagiri*, No. 6, pp. 1335—39.

Nallagoṇḍa.

733. In the Narasiṁha temple on the hill. (Telugu.) Records that the stone temple and sacred tank were dedicated to Śrī Raṅgarāju (God) of Nallagoṇḍa by Abba Paṇḍita, younger brother of Narasiṁha Paṇḍita, son of Gaṅgādhara Paṇḍita, and his wife Appasāni Amma, who belonged to the gōtra of Kauśika, on Friday the tenth of the bright half of Māgha of the year Krōdhana. *Ibid.*, No. 7, p. 1340.

734. In the same place. (Telugu.) Records the charity given by Vēṅkaṭādri Ayya, son of Rāmajōsyulu, for providing food to the god of Dūbaguṇḍāḷa village. *Ibid.*, No. 8, pp. 1340–41.

735. In the same place. (Telugu.) Records gift of a village by Śrī Vīrapati . . . Rājādhirāja Rājaparamēśvara. *Ibid.*, No. 9, p. 1341. Fragmentary. Śrī Rāmānuja is invoked.

736. In the same place. (Telugu.) Records that a grove was planted by Śrī Raṅgarāju Chāmarāja Voḍayār. *Ibid.*, No. 10, p. 1342.

737. In the Vināyaka maṇṭapam. (Telugu.) Records that on the thirteenth of the dark half of Māgha in the year Prabhava, Liṅgareḍḍi, son of Liṅgareḍḍi Timmareḍḍi, constructed at his own expense a temple to Vighnēśvara of Nallagoṇḍa. *Ibid.*, No. 11, p. 1342.

Nandavaram.

738. Opposite the Chennakēśava temple. (Telugu.) Records that the gift was for the increase of sons and grandsons of a certain . . . nāyakuṇḍu, son of Bramminājakuṇḍu . . . *Ibid.*, No. 12, pp. 1343–44.

739. On the sluice of the tank in the hamlet of Rāmanāiḍupalli. (Telugu.) Records the endowment made for the tank Kottacheruvu, constructed in the village of Nandavaram by Śauryanāyani Raghupati Nāthaya on the second of the bright fortnight of Māgha. The rulers of the village should collect *mēras* at 1 *kuñcha* per *kirai* (?) *puṭṭi* of all grain raised under that tank, give it to the *mēradār* of the tank and see that the repairs were done to the tank and the channel. *Ibid.*, No. 13, pp. 1344—46.

Nandipāḍ.

740. On a four-sided stone surmounted by a Nandi in a field about half a mile from the store shed. (Telugu.) Records that on Tuesday, the fifteenth of the bright half of Chaitra of the year Viśvāvasu, Ś. 1168, Aludiḍlayyadēva Mahārāya, Gaṇḍāvaram Prōli Reḍḍi, and two others agreed among themselves and obtained the consent of the king Chōḍadēva Tirukkāḷattidēva, to the gift of the village Nāgulavanam in the names of Kēdāradēva and Daṇḍapatidēva (two deities), for providing rest-houses to travellers. *Nel. Ins., Udayagiri*, No. 14, pp. 1346—51. The inscription is very interesting for the mention of eleven sciences and eleven experts in them. The sciences are *rasa, rasāyanā, pādāñjana, khaḍgayāga, ghuṭika* (magic), *kanyakāvāda* (love), *mantravāda* (spells), *dhātu-vāda* (metallurgy), *dhūmravāda* (" art of producing optical illusions in smoke"), *gāruḍavāda* (science of birds) and *rasavāda* (alchemy).

741. On a stone bearing a Nāga Kanyakā near the above stone. (Telugu in ancient characters.) Records that the service of fanning was done to Padāksha Lakshmayanātha (deity) of Śrī Murudupuri. There are two other inscriptions about a mile from the rest-house, but they are defaced; one records a gift of land.) *Ibid.*, No. 15, p. 1352.

Pallavōlu.

742. On two sides of a stone near Avulamma temple. (Telugu.) Records that on the tenth of the bright fortnight of Bhādrapada of the year Dundubhi, Saiyid Abdulla Sahib gave 10 *gorrus* in Raudulachēnu as *karaṇam mānyam*, and 1 *gorru* as Avulamma *mānyam* (grant for the goddess Avulamma). *Ibid.*, No. 16, pp. 1352-53. [The inscription is interesting as a Mussalman's gift to a Hindu deity.]

Pāṇḍraṅgam.

743—755. 525 *to* 537 *of* 1908.—(Tamil.) In the Pāṇḍaraṅgēśvara temple. Fresh copies of Nos. 86 to 94, 96, 98, 99 and 101 (Gudur) published in *Nellore Inscriptions.*

756. 538 *of* 1908.—(Tamil.) On the south wall of the central shrine in the same temple. A damaged record of the Chōḷa king Tribhuvanachakravartin Vīrarājēndra-Chōḷadēva, dated twenty-first year. Mentions the temple of Pāṇḍuraṅgamudaiya-Nāyanār.

757. 539 *of* 1908.—(Tamil.) On the same wall. A much damaged record of the Vijayanagara king Achyutadēva-Mahārāya, dated Ś. 1454.

758. 540 *of* 1908.—(Tamil.) On two slabs built into the floor in front of the same shrine. Fragments of record of the Chōḷa king Rājakēśarivarman *alias* Uḍaiyār Śrī-Kulottuṅga-Chōḷadēva with portions of the king's historical introduction beginning with the words *pūmādu punora.*

759. 541 *of* 1908.—(Tamil.) On a broken slab lying near the same temple. A damaged record of the Chōḷa king Chakravartin Kulōttuṅga-Chōḷadēva, dated thirty-ninth year. Records gift of land to the temple of Pāṇḍuraṅgamuḍaiya-Mahādēva at Pavittiri in Pērūr-nādu, a subdivision Pavittirikkōṭṭam which was a district in Rājēndra-Chōḷamaṇḍaḷam.

Pēriśeṭṭipalli.

760. On a rock on a hill known as Sāsanālabōḍu. (Telugu.) Records a gift on the fifteenth . . . fortnight of Chaitra of the year Prabhava, Ś. 1369, by Śrīman Mahāmaṇḍalēśvara. Bāsatappuvarāyaragaṇḍa, Mūrurāyaragaṇḍa, Ashṭadigrāya Mānōbhayaṅkara Śrī Vīra Dēvarāya Mahārāya, son of Vīra Harihararāya for the various enjoyments of the deity . . . *Nel. Ins., Udayagiri,* No. 17, p. 1354.

Śiṅgareḍḍipalli.

761. *C.P. No.* 8 *of Nel. Ins.*—A Telugu grant of Mahārāja Rāja Śrī Vāḍa Pedda Vēṅkaṭādri Nāyaniṅgāru, in Ś. 1573 (A.D. 1652–53), Nandana, Chaitra, Paurṇami, to Kandāḷa Doḍḍāyāchārlu Ayyavārlugāru. The village of Śiṅgareḍḍipalli was given as jaghir to the donee. [The record is of great religious importance as it gives us the date of the celebrated Doḍḍayāchārya or Mahāchārya of Sholinghūr.

762. *C.P. No.* 9 *of ibid.*—A Telugu grant of the same chief but under different date (Ś. 1608, Prabhava, Śravaṇa, Śukla-Pañchami) to Ādūri Govindāchārlu, Śēsham Rāghavāchāryulu, Garimalla Vōbulāchāryulu, Nāranapāṭi Bhāvanāchāryulu, Vinnapāla Veṅkaṭāchāryulu, Rāmāyaṇam Tirumalāchāryulu, Śālagrāmam Narasiṁhāchāryulu, Mahaṅkāḷi Varadāchāryulu, etc. The details of the different shares in the agrahāra are given, after provision for karaṇam, the *mēradārs,* etc. Land is measured in *tūms* and *gorrus* of seed. [The inscription is of interest in naming some of the Vaishṇava leaders of the period.]

Rāvimānidinne.

763. On fragments of a stone in the Siddhēśvara Kōna. (Sanskrit in Telugu character.) Only a few lines of the record are legible. *Ibid.,* No. (18*a*), p. 1355.

Tōtacheruvupalli.

764. (Telugu.) Records that in Ś. 1537, Śrīmat Rājādhirāja Rājaparamēśvara Veṅkaṭapati Rāyadēva gave the village Kumāraka Kōṭi situated in Kampināḍu to Kāmarti Mānikēdari. *Ibid.,* No. 19, pp. 1359–60.

Udayagiri.

765. Place not given. A record mentioning a son of Bukkarāja of Vijayanagar. *Ibid.,* No. (18*b*), pp. 1355–56.

766. Records that a certain king built a temple for Siddhēśvara. He also built a tank there for holy men to bathe which resembled the *mānas* lake, in Ś. 1308 when Harihara was ruling Vijayanagar. *Nel. Ins., Udayagiri,* No. (18*c*), pp. 1356–57.

767. An illegible record. Mentions Rājādhirāja Arirāyagravīryarāja Hindurāya. *Ibid.,* No. (18*d*), pp. 1357–58.

768—70. Nos. 18 (*e, f, g*) are illegible records, pp. 1358–59.

771. 204 *of* 1892.—In the Raṅganāyakasvāmi temple. (Telugu.) Records that Timmarāju, son of Śrīman Mahāmaṇḍalēśvara Rāma Rāja-Kōnētayya Dēva Mahārāja, built a gōpura, a maṇṭapa, a compound wall, and a reservoir and other pious services to Raghunāyakulu (deity). Records that when the car passed along the street when the naṭṭuvas and servants were in it a pañchahāṇa (artisan) member had the privilege of going in front of it. He was then to wear a head-cloth, a cloth tied loosely round the waist, with sandal-mark between the eyebrows and holding a chisel, a mallet, a nail and a sickle in his hands. He ought not to chew betel then. *Ibid.,* No. 20, pp. 1360–1.

772. In the same place. (Telugu.) Records some gifts on the twelfth day of the bright fortnight of Ashāḍha of the year *Parābhava,* to the treasury of Śrī Raghunāyakulu of Udayagiri by the pañchahāṇas of Udayagiri, Nellore, Koraṭūr, Gaṇḍavaram, Duvūr, Āṭukūr, Jaladaṅki, Koḍavalūr, Allūr, Kōvūr, Vovvēru, Prabhākarapaṭṇam, Krishṇarāyapaṭnam, Sariyapaḷḷi, Rāpūr, Kaṇḍukūr, Poḍile, Keṇagiri, Kegipa, and other villages in the kingdom of Udayagiri and the 54 countries of the earth. *Ibid.,* No. 21, p. 1362.

773. 205 *of* 1892.—In the same place. (Telugu.) Records that on Friday, the thirtieth of the dark fortnight of Pushya of the year Paridhāvi, Ś. 1475, Timmayadēva Mahārājulu, son of Śrīman Mahāmaṇḍalēśvara Rāmarāju Konēṭayyadēva Mahārājulu, gave to Vīragaṅgayya, the income derived from sundry articles in the villages situated in Udayagiri durgam which belonged to him and which were formerly attached to the temple of Raghunāyakulu, for providing daily offerings, worship with lights, and miscellaneous offerings in the temple. *Ibid.,* No. 22, pp. 1363—65.

774. 206 *of* 1892.—In the same place. (Telugu.) Records on the twelfth of the bright fortnight of Āshāḍha of the year Vyaya, Ś. 1508, while Śrīmad Rājādhirāja Rājaparamēśvara Śrī Vīra Pratāpa Śrī Vīra Veṅkaṭapati Rāyadēva Mahārājulu Ayyavāru was seated on the diamond throne at the city of Penugoṇḍa, that Kuñchi-Nāyaniṅgāru (son of *Chalamaiya* and grandson of Kampināyaniṅgaru) gave the village of Appanimādara in Udayagiri *sthala* for performing *vasanta mahōtsava* (spring festival) to the deity, for the merit of Vēṅkaṭapati Rāyulu and of his father, mother and others. *Ibid.,* No. 23, pp. 1365—67.

775. In the same place. (Telugu.) Records on the twelfth of the bright fortnight of Āshāḍha of the year Vyaya, Ś. 1508, while Śrī Vīra Vēṅkaṭapati Rāyadēva Mahā Rāyulu Ayyavāru was seated on the diamond throne at Penukoṇḍa, a tank was constructed in the village of Pranava Visikhara(?) in Udayagiri rājya. At the time of the consecration of the deity Veṅkaṭa Pinnaya Nāyaniṅgāru (son of Pinnama Nāyuḍu) presented that village for performing the great garden festivals of the deity for the religious merit of Srī Raṅgarāyalu Ayyavāru. *Nel. Ins., Udayagiri*, No. 24, pp. 1367—69.

776. In the Ahōbala Narasiṁhasvāmi temple. (Telugu.) An incomplete record. *Ibid.*, No. 25, pp. 1369–70.

777. On a stone near the forest bungalow. (Persian and Telugu.) Records that in the reign of Kutb Shah Abdullah, one of his courtiers, Saiyid Muzaffar, laid out in 1661–2 a beautiful garden of his own device in the fort of Udayagiri. *Ibid.*, No. 26, pp. 1370–71.

778. In the same stone. (Telugu.) Records that in Plava, Sultan Abdullah Padshah, Saiyid Muzaffar Zill ul lah u taala gave to Shaikh Hasan's garden the name of *Pārsmisāl* and erected an inscribed pillar. *Ibid.*, No. 27, pp. 1371–72.

779. 208 *of* 1892.—On a stone near Baptist Mission bungalow. (Telugu.) Records on Sunday, the eleventh of the bright fortnight of Śravaṇa of the year Vikriti, Ś. 1382, that Tamarāyaniṅgāru, son of Kaṇṭamarāju Valabhayya, built a temple to the deity Kāśi Viśvēśvara on the hill of Udayagiri and gave for daily offering and worship 1,000 *kuṇṭas* of land in the rear of the *amara* tank under the middle sluice. *Ibid.*, No. 28, pp. 1372—74. (Weights and measures and fraction signs are noteworthy.)

780. 209 *of* 1892.—On a stone near the Baptist Mission bungalow. (Telugu.) Records that on Sunday, the eleventh of the bright fortnight of Śravaṇa of the year Vikriti, Ś. 1382, that Tammarāyaniṅgāru, king of the race of Raghu, constructed a temple dedicated to Gōpālakṛishṇa on the hill of Udayagiri and presented free from all burdens 1,000 *kuṇṭas* of land in rear of the tank under the middle sluice for providing all enjoyments to this deity. *Ibid.*, No. 29, pp. 1374—76. See 255 of 1904 at Tirumala for a chief of this family.

781. 207 *of* 1892.—On a big rock near the Madaru gate. (Telugu.) A record on Wednesday, the eleventh day of the bright fortnight of Kārttika of the year Śōbhakrit, Ś. 1465, that Aḷiya Rāmayyadēva Mahārājulu Gāru (and ?) Rāmarāju Timmayyadēva Mahārājulu Gāru were ruling at Udayagiri durgam. Imperfect and obscure. *Ibid.*, No. 30, p. 1377.

782. In the same place. (Telugu.) Records gift for *amritapaḍi* to the deities. *Ibid.*, No. 31, p. 1378.

783. In the same place. (Telugu.) Records that Yatathi Veṅgayya and others granted some gift to Narasiṁhadēva. The term *irasam* (a measure) is mentioned. *Nel. Ins., Udayagiri,* No. 32, p. 1379.

784. In the same place. (Telugu.) Records that China Vallabhayya, son of Chinnanna, made endless obeisance to Narasiṁhadēva (deity). *Ibid.*, No. 33, p. 1380.

785. In the same place. (Telugu.) Records gift of grain by several persons to Narasiṁhadēva. *Ibid.*, No. 34, pp. 380–81.

786. On a rock near the western postern above the forest bungalow. (Telugu.) Records a particular fight took place on the durgam was on Monday, the third of the bright half of Pushya in the year Vikāri. *Ibid.*, No. 35, p. 1381.

787. In the little mosque. (Persian.) Records that Abdullah Kutb Shah, the pride of kings, destroyed a temple and constructed a mosque for the purpose of prayers in A.D. 1660–61. *Ibid.*, No. 36, pp. 1381–82.

788. 203 *of* 1892.—In the rock known as Vrata guṇḍu. It is written with an unusual slope. (Kanarese.) Records that Śrī Vīra Pratāpa Śrī Kṛishṇadēva Mahārāya on his return to Vijayanagar after his pursuit of Pratāparudra Gajapati up to Koṇḍavīḍu and the siege and capture of his nephew, Tirumala Rāghava Rāya at Udayagiri, gave the village of Kanupare (Kanuparti) to God Rāmachandradēva, the village of Śrikallu to the deity Kōnēvallabha Rāja, and the village of Batulapalli to Jalasiddhēśvara (deity). The worship of the deities should be carried on with the revenue and grain derived from these villages. *Ibid.*, No. 37, pp. 1382–83.

789. In the same place. (Telugu.) This is a mere copy of the above record in Telugu. *Ibid.*, No. 38, p. 1384.

790. In the big mosque. (Persian.) Mentions Ghazi Ali, a general of Abdullah Kutb Shah, who captured the fort of Udayagiri and burnt away the sweepings of idolatry and founded a mosque. *Ibid.*, No. 39, p. 1385. The date is 1642–43 A.D.

791. In a rock by the Lakshmamma temple. (Telugu.) Records that on the second day of the dark fortnight of Jyēshṭha of the year *Bhava*, Ś. 1436, Śrī Vīra Pratāpa-Śrī Kṛishṇa Rāya Mahārāyulu Gāru presented one village, namely, Śrikallu, situated in Nellore śīma, to the deity Kōnavallabha Rāya of Udayagiri. From the revenue and grain derived from the village daily offerings and all enjoyments to the deity should be performed. The king was then encamped at Udayagiri after capturing Tirumala Kanta Rāya, the Gajapati's nephew. See No. 788 above. *Ibid.*, No. 40, pp. 1386–87.

792. In the same place. (Kanarese.) This is a copy of No. 791. *Ibid.*, No. 41, pp. 1387–88.

793. In the same place. (Telugu.) Records that on Thursday, the fourteenth of the dark fortnight of Māgha of the year Vijaya,

S. 1455, Madinēṇḍu (son of Golavobenēḍu and doorkeeper of Sālarāja Pinna Tirumalayya Mahārāju), consecrated the twelve Āḻvārs (Vaishṇava saints) on the east of the temple of Kōnavallabharāya of Udayagiri, constructed a *kōnēru* (reservoir) for bathing for the removal of all sins for the devotees of Hari and for Vaishṇava disciples and constructed maṇṭapas on both sides of it. Madinēni presented to Kōnavallabharāya the *kōnēru* and a garden on the holy occasion of Mahāśivarātri. *Nel. Ins., Udayagiri*, No. 42, pp. 1388–89.

794. In the same place. (Telugu.) Records that on Thursday, the eleventh of the dark fortnight of Phalguna of the year Bahudhānya, Tirumalayya of the Vallabharāya family caused a Bhōga-maṇṭapa (a pleasure hall for cooking room for the deity) and a flight of steps to be constructed. *Ibid.*, No. 43, p. 1390.

795. In the Lakshmamma temple. (Telugu.) Records that all the acts of devotion projected by Timmarāju, son of Kōnēṭaya, were successfully brought to a close. *Ibid.*, No. 44, p. 1390.

796. In a rock below the Madāru gate. (Telugu.) Records that the son of the chief (Rāzulu) of the bearers of Udayagiri Durgam has suffered (or the son of Bōyarāzulu of Udayagiri durgam has suffered). *Ibid.*, No. 45, p. 1391.

Veṅkaṭapuram.

797. On a stone on tank bund. (Telugu.) Records that on Thursday, the fifteenth of the bright half of Śravaṇa of the year Parābhava, Ś. 1348, while Śrīman Mahāmaṇḍalēśvara Śrī Vīra Pratāpa Dēva Rāya Mahārāyulu (II) was ruling at Vijayanagar, Bayichana Bōyuḍu, the grandson of Mutta Rāju Śiṅgaṇarāju and Tudirula Dharmasāni gave a sale deed for the *daśabandham* tank constructed by them at Bōyavīḍu and Kudichalapāḍu in Udayagiri rājya. *Ibid.*, No. 46, pp. 1391–92.

Virūru.

798. East of the village on the south bank of Uppuṭēru. (Telugu.) Records that on the third of the bright fortnight of Phalguna of the year *Pramādi*, the paid servant of the ruler of Vīrūru granted the villages Aśavēmula, Vilaṭilaṅgam and Parlapalli as *agrahāra* to Bommalāṭa Vīrappa for the religious merit of Voda Komāra Vēṅkaṭādrināyanivāru. *Ibid.*, No. 47, pp. 1392–93. [The inscription is interesting for the mention of a puppet show organizer.]

Yēpilaguṇṭa (Chilakapāḍ).

799. On three sides of a stone. (Telugu.) Records that on Friday, the fifteenth of the dark fortnight of Phalguna in the year *Paridhāvi*, Ś. 1174, the ninth year of the reign of Śrī Vīra Rājēndra Chōḍachakravarti, on the occasion of the eclipse of the sun, Tikkayadēva, his minister, presented to Tripurāntakadēva, and his younger brother to Kēdāradēva, the village Bodapāḍu in Chilakapāṭi Kampanagalam. *Nel. Ins., Udayagiri*, No. 48, pp. 1393—96.

VENKATAGIRI TALUK.

Chāpalapalli.

800. In the Vishṇu temple. (Tamil.) Records a gift (to Brahmans) by Bejjadēvi, the consort of Yādavarāya Bhujabalasiddharaśa, in Ś. 1152, expired, fifteenth year of the reign of Rājarājadēva III, on a date in the month of Tai. *Nellore Ins., Veṅkaṭagiri*, No. 1, pp. 1397–98. Pākkināḍu in Jayaṅkoṇḍachōḷamaṇḍaḷam is referred to.

801. On the north wall of the Vishṇu temple. (Tamil.) Records that in the twenty-first year of the reign of Rājarājadēva, in the month of Āḍi, Savanar Āḷuḍaippiḷḷai gave one *māḍai* as interest for three evening lamps presented to the God Yādavanārāyaṇaperumāḷ in the city of Nāgapuḍōl *alias* the glorious Rājamallachaturvēdimaṅgala. *Ibid.*, No. 2, pp. 1398–99.

802. Round the Vishṇu temple. (Tamil.) Records that in the fifteenth year of the reign of Rājarājadēva III, on a date in the month of Tai, Bejjadēvi, the consort of Yādavarāya, gave to the God Emperumān Yādavanārāyaṇa lands in the city which they established at Nāgapuḍōl for the maintenance of a sacred perpetual lamp. *Ibid.*, No. 3, pp. 1399—1401. The priest Tiruvēṅgaḍa Bhaṭṭan was given 220 *kuḷis.*

803. In the Vishṇu temple. (Tamil.) Records that, in the nineteenth year of the reign of Rājarājadēva, in the month of Aippaśi, Kāśāṇmai, the son of Yādavarāyar, gave to Emberumān Yādavanārāyaṇaperumāḷ at Rājamallachaturvēdimaṅgaḷam for maintenance of one evening lamp endowed by him. *Ibid.*, No. 4, p. 1401.

804. In the Vishṇu temple. (Tamil.) A record of Attiyammai, the daughter of Iraṭṭāḍi Bhīmabhaṭṭan of Tumbaiyūr, in the thirteenth year of the reign of Rājarājadēva on the date of *Chittirai.* Tumbaiyur was in Paḍikāmanāḍu in Pākkaināḍu. *Ibid.*, No. 5, p. 1402.

805. In the Vishṇu temple. (Tamil.) Records that in the eleventh year of the reign of Rājarājadēva, on the date of the Uttarāyaṇasaṅkrānti, Toṇḍaimān Āṟṟūr Kāntarāyan, the prime minister of Yādavarāyan, gave to Emberumān Yādavanārāyaṇaperumāḷ four cows for the maintenance of four evening lamps. For these four cows were given four *māḍai* in the hands of Koṇḍuperumāḷ of Nāyarunāḍu. *Ibid.*, No. 6, pp. 1402–3.

806. In the Vishṇu temple. (Tamil.) Records that Yādavarājan gave lands as exclusive property to the deity. The Veḷḷāḷas of Kanumili and Madhurāntaka Pottappichōḷa Erasiddharaśa are mentioned. *Ibid.*, No. 7, pp. 1403–4.

807-808. In the Vishṇu temple. (Tamil.) Two fragmentary records, the first recording the grant of one *mādai* to Aṅgadabhaṭṭar by Yādavarāyar of the town of Nāgarpuḍōl (in Pākkaiṅāḍu), the second mentions Tēmāṇḍi Ammai, the wife of Bhujabalasiddharaśar. *Nel. Ins.*, *Venkatagiri*, Nos. 8 and 9, p. 1405.

809. In the Vishṇu temple. (Tamil.) Records that in the second year of Rājarājadēva, one Nārumidan Piṟṟaiyāṇḍān set up the image of Maḍhurāntaka Pottappichōḷa Siddharaśa and granted lands in Nāgapuḍōl set up by Kulōttuṅga in his thirty-ninth year. *Ibid.*, No. 10, pp. 1405—7.

810. In the Vishṇu temple. (Tamil.) Records that in the reign of Kuḷōttuṅgachōḷadēva Rājamalladēvan *alias* Bhujabalasiddharaśa (Lord of Conjeeveram and Veṅgi, Saśikulachāḷukki, etc.) created through Madhurāntakapottapichōḷa *alias* Erasiddharaśa, the town of Nāgapuḍōl, in Paganānāḍu in Pākkaināḍu in Jayaṅkoṇḍachōḷamaṇḍaḷam. *Ibid.*, No. 11, pp. 1407—9.

811. On the west wall of Vishṇu temple. (Tamil.) An illegible record. *Ibid.*, No. 12, p. 1409.

Pākkaināḍu.

812. Round the temple. (Tamil.) Records in the thirty-ninth year of the reign of Kulōttuṅgachōḷadēva that Rājamalladēvan *alias* Bhujabalasiddharaśan gave a flower garden called after Rājamallan, measuring hundred *kuḻi*, a mango tope measuring twenty *kuḻi*, and jack fruit tope measuring twenty *kuḻi*, etc. *Ibid.*, No. 13, pp. 1409-10.

813. East of the Vishṇu temple. (Tamil.) Records that in the twenty-fifth year of the reign of Kuḷōttuṅgachōḷadēva, in the month of Āḍi, Nīlamareḍḍi Kaṭṭaiyan made a gift for one evening lamp to Yādavanārāyaṇaperumāḷ and for reading the *Bhārata* on the sacred temple doorway. *Ibid.*, No. 14, pp. 1410-11.

814. On the east wall of Vishṇu temple. (Tamil.) Records that in the twelfth year of the reign of Rājarājadēva, on the date of Chittirai, he gave one *mādai* for one evening lamp to the god Yādavanārāyaṇaperumāḷ. *Ibid.*, No. 15, pp. 1410-11.

815. On the east wall of Vishṇu temple. (Tamil.) Records that Veṅgivallabhan granted the big channel named after Kamalamahādēvi, certain lands under Toṇḍaimān tank and also thirty-three cows for ten evening lamps to Yādavanārāyaṇaperumāḷ. *Ibid.*, No. 16, pp. 1411-12.

Mōpūr.

816. In the south wall of Chennākeśava temple. (Tamil.) A fragment of record, dated in the eighteenth year of Rājarājadēva and mentions Kēśavaperumāḷ of Muṇoyūr. *Ibid.*, No. 17, p. 1412.

817. In the south wall of the Chennakēśava temple. (Tamil.) Records gift of 2½ *māḍai* by a relation of Tikkamareḍḍi for an evening lamp. *Ibid.*, No. 18, pp. 1412-13.

818. On the south wall of the Chennakēśava temple. Records that in the eighteenth year of the reign of Rājarājadēva Chōḷadēvar, Chōḍappireḍḍi gave in the name of Chāḷukkinārāyana *alias* Manumasiddaraśar of Periyamuṇoppūr in Pāgamaināḍu, for interest, one *māḍai* for an evening lamp to the temple of Kēśavaperumāḷ. *Nel. Ins., Venkatagiri*, No. 19, pp. 1413–14.

819. On a stone to the north of the Śiva temple. (Tamil.) Records that in the twenty-second year of the reign of Rājarājadēva, Viṭṭami Reḍḍi, the son of Vayirappa Reḍḍi, a Reḍḍi resident in Muṇoppūr, gave one evening lamp to the god of Tiruvēṅgaḍam. Nārappa Reḍḍi, the son of Paṇḍāri Kēṭṭama Reḍḍi, gave one evening lamp and similar gifts. *Ibid.*, No. 20, pp. 1414–15.

Pāḷēmkōṭa.

820. On Venkaṭagiri-drug near the spring. (Telugu.) Records that on the tenth day of the dark fortnight of *Bhādrapada* of the year Tāraṇa, Bhujabala Boppayya Dēva Mahārājuḷu constructed a cistern on the Kalimili durgam. *Ibid.*, No. 21, p. 1415.

821. On Venkatagiri-drug near the spring. (Telugu.) Records that on the fifth day of the dark fortnight of Māgha of the year Prabhava, Mādirāju, son of Kalimili Bopparāju, repaired the fortress (dūrgam). *Ibid.*, No. 22, p. 1416.

Vazzavāripāḷem.

822. In a field north of the village. (Telugu.) Records that on the twelfth day of the dark fortnight of Jyēshṭha of the year *Vikāri*, Ś. 1580, while Hizarat Alam Ennasa was seated on the diamond throne, Raṅgapparāzugāru bestowed lands . . . in Udayagiri śīma. *Ibid.*, No. 23, pp. 1416—18.

823. In a street. (Telugu.) Records that on the fourteenth day of the bright fortnight of Jyēshṭha of the year *Śubhakrit*, Ś. 1584, while Śrīmad Rājādhirāja Rājaparamēśvara Śrī Vīrapratāpa Śrī Vīra Bhujabala Vīra Vēṅkaṭapatirāyadēva Mahārāyalayyavāru was seated on the diamond throne at Penugoṇḍa, Śrīman Mahāmaṇḍalēśvara Kochūri Jaggarājayyadēva Mahārājalayyavāru made a grant for the tank of Inuguṇṭa. *Ibid.*, No. 24, pp. 1418–19.

824. On the north wall of the Vēṇugōpālasvāmi temple. (Telugu.) An illegible record. *Ibid.*, No. 25, p. 1420.

825. On the north wall of the Bhīmēśvara temple in the hamlet of Inuguṇṭa. (Tamil.) Records in the thirty-ninth year of the reign of Kuḷōttuṅgachōḷadēva, Uṇḍiyappaḍavaḷavan placed an evening lamp in the temple of Kēśavaperumāḷ of Iluṅguṇḍai. *Ibid.*, No. 26, pp. 1420–21.

826. On the south wall of the Bhīmēśvara temple. (Tamil.) A fragment of record in the reign of Rājarājadēva which mentions the temple Vīmēśvara at Iruṅguṇḍai. *Ibid.*, No. 27, p. 1241.

RĀMNĀD DISTRICT.

ARUPPUKKŌTTAI TALUK.

Aruppukkōttai.

1. 402 *of* 1914.—(Tamil.) On the south wall of the central shrine in the Sundarēśvara temple. A record in the fifth year of the Pāṇḍya king Māravarman *alias* Tribhuvanachakravartin Sundara-Pāṇḍya dēva (I, 1216—35) "who was pleased to take the Chōḷa country." Records gift of oil for three lamps by the inhabitants of Iḍattuvaḷi to the temple of Kuraḷmāṇīśvaram Uḍaiyār at Śeṅgāṭṭirukkai Iḍattuvaḷi.

2. 403 *of* 1914.—(Tamil.) On the same wall. A record in the eighteenth year of the Pāṇḍya king Jaṭāvarman *alias* Tribhuvanachakravartin Kulaśēkharadēva. Records gift of a stone at the entrance into the ardhamaṇṭapa of the temple of Kuraḷmāṇīśvaramuḍaiya-Nāyanār at Śeṅgāṭṭirukkai Iḍattuvaḷi in Veṇbil-nāḍu.

3. 404 *of* 1914.—(Tamil.) On the same wall. An incomplete record in the third year of the Pāṇḍya king Tribhuvanachakravartin Sundara-Pāṇḍyadēva (I, 1216—35 ?). Records gift of offerings by the order of a certain Śokkāṇḍār on the day of Śatabhishaj in which he was born.

4. 405 *of* 1914.—(Tamil.) On the same wall. A damaged record of the Pāṇḍya king Sundara-Pāṇḍyadēva, the date of which is lost. Records gift of land for maintaining a flower garden and for supplying two flower garlands to the temple of Kuraḷmāṇīchchuraṁ-uḍaiya-Nāyanār.

5. 406 *of* 1914.—(Tamil.) On the same wall. A record in the eighth year of the Pāṇḍya king Sundara-Pāṇḍyadēva (I, 1216—35), "who was pleased to distribute the Chōḷa country." Records the setting up of the image of Arundavañjeida-Nāchchiyār (Pārvati) by Śēgal-Śēvagattēvan, one of the Vaḷañjiyars of South Ceylon (Tennilaṅgai). See *Ep. Rep.*, 1913, p. 101, for further references to the Vaḷañjiyars of Ceylon.

6. 407 *of* 1914.—(Tamil.) On the west wall of the same shrine. A record in the eighth year of the Pāṇḍya king Sundara-Pāṇḍya (I, 1216—35), "who was pleased to distribute the Chōḷa country." Records the setting up of the image of Liṅgapurāṇadēva (Lingōdbhava) by the same individual, who lived in a street called Vikrama Pāṇḍya perundēru named evidently after a king of that name previous to the time of Sundara Pāṇḍya I.

7. 408 *of* 1914.—(Tamil.) On the north wall of the same shrine. A damaged record in the fourteenth year, Dhanus, śu. di. 3,

Wednesday, Śravaṇa, of the Pāṇḍya king . . . varman *alias* Tribhuvanachakravartin Sundara-Pāṇḍyadēva (I, 1216—35) "who, having taken the Chōḷa country, was pleased to perform the anointment of heroes at Muḍigoṇḍachōḷapuram." Records gift of land for offerings by Aḷagan Aruḷāḷapperumāḷ *alias* Ulaganārāyaṇachakravartin at the service of Ulaganārāyaṇan-śandi called after the donor. [Mr. Swamikannu Pillai says that there is no date suiting the week day in the fourteenth year, but there is a regular one in the fourth year, viz., December 11, A.D. 1219.]

8. 409 *of* 1914.—(Tamil.) On the same wall. A record in the eleventh year, Mārgaḷi, fifth day of the Pāṇḍya king Sundara-Pāṇḍyadēva (unidentified). Quotes an order of Śōḷagaṅgadēvan. Records gift of land for offerings to the images of Inakkunalla perumāḷ (set up in the name of Śōḷagaṅgan), the (stone) goddess and the goddess which is taken out in procession through the streets. "It is stated that, while the right of cultivating these lands (*kārāṇmai*) belonged to certain persons who were donors, the taxes accruing on them were paid to the temple. The rate at which the taxes were paid was fixed at 3 *kalam* on each *mā* of land or one-half of what prevailed in other *dēvadāna* lands. In doing this, crops of full yield alone were taken into consideration," those who had sustained damages or failure being excluded.

9. 410 *of* 1914.—(Tamil.) On the same wall. Records gift of land to the temple of Eḍuttaduvaliya-Piḷḷaiyār in the same village. Quotes the eighteenth year of Kulaśēkharadēva "who was pleased to take every country," and an order of Śōḷagaṅgadēvan.

10. 411 *of* 1914.—(Tamil.) On the same wall. A record in the fifteenth year of the Pāṇḍya king Tribhuvanachakravartin Sundara-Pāṇḍyadēva (I, 1216--35) "who, having taken the Chōḷa country, was pleased to perform the anointment of heroes at Muḍigoṇḍachōḷapuram." Records the setting up of an image of Durgaiyār in the temple.

11. 412 *of* 1914.—(Tamil.) On the same wall. A record of the Pāṇḍya king Māravarman *alias* Tribhuvanachakravartin Sundara-Pāṇḍyadēva (I, 1216—35) "who distributed the Chōḷa country" in the fourteenth year, Mithuna, ba. di. 13, Monday, Rōhiṇi (corresponding to Monday, 10th June, A.D. 1230). Records a gift of land to the temple of Vināyaka-Piḷḷaiyār called Eḍuttaduvaliya-Piḷḷaiyār at Iḍattuvaḷi. Refers to sale of land by temple authorities to a person who was thereby entitled to receive payments in paddy and *tiramand* (i.e., *ḍramma*). See *Ep. Rep.*, 1909, p. 80, and *ibid.*, 1910, p. 97.

12. 413 *of* 1914.—(Tamil verse.) On the east wall of the central shrine in the Vāḷavanda-Amma temple in the same village. Records in Ś. 1090 the setting up of the God Aḷagiya-Āḷvār by Śōḷagaṅgan.

13. 414 *of* 1914.—(Tamil.) On the same wall. A damaged record in the fifteenth year of the Pāṇḍya king Tribhuvana-chakravartin Kulaśēkharadēva. Records gift of paddy to the temple of Aḷagiya-Āḷvār in Śeṅgāṭṭirukkai Iḍattuvaḷi in Veṇbuḷa-nāḍu, a subdivision of Madhurōdaya vaḷanāḍu which was a district of Pāṇḍi-maṇḍalam.

14. 415 *of* 1914.—(Tamil verse.) On a stone of the well opposite to the choultry in the same village. Records in Ś. 1154, the construction of the well.

15. 416 *of* 1914.—(Tamil.) On a slab set up in a field two miles east of the same village. Records in Dundubhi (A.D. 1664) gift of land in the village of Bommakōṭṭai for the daily worship of Vāḷavan-dāḷ-ammai at Aruppukkōṭṭai by an agent (Tambi Uḍaiyā Tēvar) of Tirumalai Sētupati Kātta Raghunāthadēva for the merit of the latter. The Government Epigraphist apparently thinks that the Tambi referred to in this epigraph was the opponent of Daḷavāi Sētupati, for whose sake Rāmappaiya, the General of Tirumal Nāik, led his celebrated campaign against Rāmēśvaram. But as a matter of fact the Tambi of the present epigraph was, it seems to me, a later man. See my *History of the Nāik Kingdom of Madura* in *Ind. Antq.*, Dec. 1916, p. 201.

Kōvilaṅguḷam.

16. 396 *of* 1914.—(Tamil verse.) On the south base of the Ambalappasvāmi temple (of which the basement alone now remains). A record in praise of a certain Śōḷakōn who was the lord of Kumbanūr, Kuraṇḍi, Kunṛattūr and Puttūr.

17. 397 *of* 1914.—(Tamil.) On the west and south bases of the same temple. A record in the forty-eighth year of the Chōḷa king Tribhuvanachakravartin Kulōttuṅga-Chōḷadēva (I ?). Records that a golden *vimāna* with a maṇṭapa to Mukkuḍaiyār was constructed by 25 Jains at Kumbanūr in Śeṅgāṭṭirukkai, a subdivision of Veṇbu-vaḷanāḍu. Two copper images of "the god of the three umbrellas" and Yakshi were also presented. It is also stated that land for a temple site and a watershed for the use of Jain devotees were given. The Government Epigraphist notes the unique literary style of the inscription and considers that some of the donors should have been well versed in the Tamil language.

18. 398 *of* 1914.—(Tamil.) On the south base of the Eṅgu-maḷagiya-Perumāḷ temple in the same village. A record in the eleventh year of the Pāṇḍya king Māravarman *alias* Tribhuvana-chakravartin . . . Pāṇḍyadēva. Records gift of land to the temple of Guṇagaṇābharaṇa-Viṇṇagar-Emberumān at Śeṅgāṭ-ṭirukkai Kumbanūr *alias* Guṇagaṇābharaṇanallūr in Veṇbuḷanāḍu.

19. 399 *of* 1914.—(Tamil.) On the north base of the same temple. A record in the seventeenth year of the Pāṇḍya king

Tribhuvanachakravartin Kulaśēkhara. Records gift of a cow for a lamp to the same temple.

20. 400 *of* 1914.—(Tamil.) On the same base. A record in the twenty-seventh year of the Pāṇḍya king Tribhuvanachakravartin Kulaśēkharadēva. Records gift of money for a lamp.

21. 401 *of* 1914.—(Tamil.) On the same base. A record in the thirteenth year of the Pāṇḍya king Tribhuvanachakravartin Kulaśēkharadēva. Records gift of a *paḻaṅgāśu* (old *kāśu*) and two *drammas* for a lamp. See No. 11 above for the mention of *drammas* and Cg. 217.

Paḷḷimaḍam.

This place, called in inscriptions Tiruchchuḻiyal Paḷḷimaḍai, was a *dēvadāna* village in Paruttikkuḍināḍu. The temple was named after a certain Sundara Pāṇḍya, apparently a close relation of the Vīra Pāṇḍya who is referred to in the inscriptions below.

22. 420 *of* 1914.—(Tamil, Vaṭṭeḻuttu.) On the south base of the Kalānāthasvāmin temple. A record in the seventh year of the Pāṇḍya king Vīra-Pāṇḍya, "who took the head of the Chōḷa." Records gift of 75 sheep for a lamp to the Bhaṭārar of the temple of Sundara-Pāṇḍya-Īśvaram at Tiruchchuḻiyal Paḷḷimaḍai, a *dēvadāna* in Parittikkuḍi-nāḍu, by Śōḻantakap-Pallavaraiyan *alias* Māran Ādichchan of Poḻiyūr. [The Government Epigraphist identifies this Vīra Pāṇḍya with the opponent of Sundara Chōḷa Parāntaka II and Ādiya Karikāla II. The latter is said to have beheaded him, but as Vīra-Pāṇḍya also boasts of having beheaded a Chōḷa we have to infer that "before he was beheaded by Āditya II he would probably have killed a Chōḷa."

23. 421 *of* 1914.—(Tamil, Vaṭṭeḻuttu.) On the same base. A record in the seventh year of the Pāṇḍya king Vīra-Pāṇḍya, "who took the head of the Chōḷa." Records gift of 25 sheep for a lamp to the same temple. Mentions Veṇbu-nāḍu. See No. 22.

24. 422 *of* 1914.—(Tamil, Vaṭṭeḻuttu.) On the north base of the same temple. An incomplete record in the twenty-sixth year of an unknown king.

25. 423 *of* 1914.—(Tamil, Vaṭṭeḻuttu.) On the same base. A record in the eleventh year of the Pāṇḍya king Vīra-Pāṇḍya "who took the head of the Chōḷa." Records gift of twenty sheep for a lamp to a *maṭha* of the Mahāvratins. Mentions the liquid measure called Śōḻantakan-nāḻi. See No. 22. The Government Epigraphist suggests that Sōḻantaka might have been a surname of Vīra-Pāṇḍya in consequence of his victory over the Chōḷas. For another reference to the *mahāvratins* or Kāpālikas see Cg. 965 and 1037.

26. 424 *of* 1914.—(Tamil, Vaṭṭeḻuttu.) On the same base. An incomplete record of the Pāṇḍya king Vīra-Pāṇḍya, "who took the head of the Chōḷa," in his ninth year. Records gift of sheep for a lamp. See note to 22 above.

27. 425 *of* 1914.—(Tamil, Vaṭṭeḻuttu). On the same base. A damaged and unfinished record of the Pāṇḍya king Śaḍaiyamāran in the second year. Seems to provide for a lamp. Mentions Vānavanmādēvi, a *brahmadēya* in Veṇbunāḍu, named evidently after the queen of king Vīra Nārāyaṇa Śaḍayan. [The king might be the father of Jaṭilavarman of the Vēḷvikuḍi grant.]

28. 426 *of* 1914.—(Tamil, Vaṭṭeḻuttu.) On the same base. A record in the thirteenth year of the Pāṇḍya king Vīra-Pāṇḍya, "who took the head of the Chōḷa." Records gift of 100 sheep for two lamps to the same temple by Poḷiyūr-nāṭṭu Mūvēndavēḷān *alias* Araṅgam Pūdi, a native of Śuḍuvūr in Poḷiyūr-nāḍu.

29. 427 *of* 1914.—(Tamil.) On the same base. A damaged fragmentary record of the Pāṇḍya king Māravarman *alias* Tribhuvanachakravartin Sundara-Pāṇḍyadēva in . . . śu. di. 11, Monday, Rōhiṇi.

30. 428 *of* 1914.—(Tamil, Vaṭṭeḻuttu.) On the same base. Records gift of fifty sheep by Śāttaṅgāri for a lamp to the temple of Tirukkāṭṭambaḷḷidēva at Kuṟaṇḍi in Veṇbunāḍu. Kuraṇḍi was evidently a very important Jain centre in the south of the peninsula. See Md. 99, 100 and 105.

31. 429 *of* 1914.—(Tamil, Vaṭṭeḻuttu.) On the same base. An incomplete record in the ninth year of the Pāṇḍya king Vīra Pāṇḍya, "who took the head of the Chōḷa." See No. 22 above.

32. 430 *of* 1914.—(Tamil, Vaṭṭeḻuttu.) On the parapet stone of the entrance into the same temple, right side. A record in the twenty-sixth year of the Pāṇḍya king Mārañjaḍaiyan. Built in at the right end. Records gift of 100 sheep for a lamp by a native of Kunnūr in Nilakkuḍi-nāḍu. Mentions Kuraṇḍi Tirukkāṭṭambaḷḷi in Veṇbunāḍu. [Was Mārañjaḍayan the donor of the Vēḷvikudi grant or his grandfather ?]

33. 431 *of* 1914.—(Tamil, Vaṭṭeḻuttu.) In the same place, left side. A record in the thirty-fifth year of the Pāṇḍya king Mārañjaḍaiyan. Built in ât the bottom. Mentions Kuraṇḍi Tirukkāṭṭambaḷḷi in Veṇbu-nāḍu. See the above epigraph.

34. *C.P. No.* 5 *of* 1911.—A record of the time of Tirumal Ṉāik of Madura, dated in *Vikriti* (A.D. 1650–51). Mentions that the king and Mutturāmaliṅgatorai met at Paḷḷimaḍam, when they gave a C.P. charter to Paḷuttāṇḍi Kuppāchchi Ambalakāṛan. See *Ind. Antq.*, December 1916, p. 201–2.

35. *C.P. No.* 6 *of* 1911.—(Tamil.) A record of the same king under the same circumstances, making a similar gift to the same person.

Tiruchchuḷi.

36. 417 *of* 1914.—(Tamil, Vaṭṭeḷuttu.) On the north wall of the prākāra of the Sahāyavalli shrine in the Tirumūlanāthasvāmin temple. A fragment of record in the tenth year of the Chōḷa king Rājakēsarivarman (Rājarāja I). Records gift of a lamp.

37. 418 *of* 1914.—(Tamil, Vaṭṭeḷuttu.) On the same wall. A fragment of record in the twelfth year of the Chōḷa king Rājakēsarivarman (985—1013), "who destroyed the ships at Kāndalūr."

38. 419 *of* 1914.—(Tamil.) On the door post of the Praḷayaviṭaṅkar shrine in the same temple. An unfinished record of Ś. 1152. Seems to refer to the defeat of a certain Jananātha.

MUDUKULATTŪR TALUK.

*Koḍumalūr.**

39. 399 *of* 1907.—(Tamil.) On the door post of the Kumiḷīśvara temple. A record the beginning of which is mutilated. Records in the fourth year gift of land to the temple of Uttama-Pāṇḍya-Īśvaramuḍaiyār at Mēlaikkoḍumalūr *alias* Uttama-Pāṇḍyanallūr in Vaḍatalai-Śembināḍu.

40. 400 *of* 1907.—(Tamil.) On the west wall of the same temple. A record of the Vijayanagara king Vīrapratāpa Immaḍi Achyutadēva Mahārāya, in Ś. 1456, expired, Jaya. Records the gift of the village of Mēlailkkoḍumalūr *alias* Uttama-Pāṇḍyanallūr in Vaḍatalai-Śembināḍu for worship in the temple of Sētumādhava-Perumāḷ and for repairs to the temple of Rāmanātha.

Kōyil-Māriyūr.

41. 96 *of* 1905.—(Tamil.) On the south wall of the central shrine in the Pushpavanēśvara temple. A record in the sixth year of the Pāṇḍya king Māravarman *alias* Tribhuvanachakravartin Sundara-Pāṇḍyadēva. Records gift of land.

42. 97 *of* 1905.—(Tamil.) On the east wall of the Pavaḷaniravalli Amman shrine in the same temple. Records in Dhātri gift of money.

Mēl-Kiḍāram.

43. 91 *of* 1905.—(Tamil.) On the north wall of the central shrine in the deserted Īśvara temple. A mutilated record. Seems to record a gift of land.

44. 92 *of* 1905.—(Tamil.) On the east wall of the same shrine. A mutilated record in the fifth year of the Pāṇḍya king . . . Sundara Pāṇḍyadēva.

---

* Mr. Sewell says that the Śiva temple here was built by Varaguṇa Pāṇḍyan. It needs confirmation.

45. 93 *of* 1905.—(Tamil.) On the same wall. A mutilated record of the Pāṇḍya king Māravarman *alias* Tribhuvanachakravartin, the date of which is lost.

46. 94 *of* 1905.—(Tamil.) On the same wall. A mutilated record of the Pāṇḍya king Māravarman *alias* Tribhuvanachakravartin Sundara-Pāṇḍya, "who was pleased to take the Chōḷa country," the date of which is lost. The king was evidently Sundara Pāṇḍya I (1216—35).

47. 95 *of* 1905.—(Tamil.) On the south wall of the central shrine in the same temple. A mutilated record in the sixth year of the Pāṇḍya king Māravarman *alias* Tribhuvanāchakravartin Sundara-Pāṇḍyadēva. Records gift of land. The temple is called Tiruvanandīśvaramuḍaiyār.

Peruṅgaruṇai.

48. 401 *of* 1907.—(Tamil.) On the door posts of the Īśvara temple. An incomplete record in the forty-fourth year of the Chōḷa king Rājakēsarivarman *alias* Chakravartin śrī-Kulōttuṅga-Chōḷadēva (I, 1070—1118). Seems to record a gift of land to the temple of Tiruvēḷaikkāra-mūnṛukai-Īśvaramuḍaiya-Mahādēvar. Mentions Madhurāntaka Vaḷanāḍu in Rājarāja-Pāṇḍināḍu.

49. 402 *of* 1907.—(Tamil.) On stones built into the base of the same temple. A fragment of record of the Pāṇḍya king Tribhuvanachakravartin Vīra-Pāṇḍyadēva, "who took Īḷam (Ceylon), Koṅgu and Śōḷa-maṇḍalam in his fourteenth year." [Was this king the same as Jaṭāvarman Vīra Pāṇḍya who came to the throne in 1253 and who was known as the conqueror of Īḷam, Koṅgu and Śōḷamaṇḍalam and anointer of victors at Perumbaṟṟappuliyūr ?]

50. 403 *of* 1907.—(Tamil.) On the west and south walls of the Paṭṭābhirāmasvāmin temple in the same village. Registers in Ś. 1480, expired, Siddhārthin, the gift of the village of Śiruguḍi *alias* Tiruvaḷanallūr in Peruṅgaruṇaippaṟṟu to the temple of Nāyinār Peruṅgaruṇai-Perumāl.

51. 404 *of* 1907.—(Grantha.) On the door post of the maṇṭapa in front of the Varadarāja-Perumāḷ temple in the same village, right of entrance. A fragment of record in Manmatha (Ś. 1513). Mentions Kṛishṇabhūpa, son of Vīrabhūpa (i.e., Kumāra Kṛishṇappa II, son of Peria Vīrappa, 1572—1595). See my article on the *Nāik kingdom of Madura* in *Ind. Antq.*, June 1916, p. 100.

52. 405 *of* 1907.—(Grantha.) In the same place, left of entrance. A record of Sundarēśa (Sundara-Pāṇḍya). Records gift of land in Kaliśēkhara-maṅgalam to Brāhmaṇas.

53. 406 *of* 1907.—(Tamil.) On a stone built into the base of the gōpura of the same temple, right of entrance. A fragmentary record in the second year of the Pāṇḍya king Tribhuvanachakravartin Kulaśēkharadēva (unidentifiable). Seems to record a gift of land.

54. 407 *of* 1907.—(Tamil.) On a second stone built into the same base, left of entrance. A fragmentary record in the third year of the Pāṇḍya king Tribhuvanachakravartin Sundara-Pāṇḍyadēva. To the right of this is another much worn fragment belonging apparently to Māravarman Sundara-Pāṇḍya I (1216—1235).

PARAMAKUDI TALUK.

Paramakuḍi.

55. 392 *of* 1914.—(Tamil.) On the west base of the Emanīśvara temple at Emanīśvaram hamlet. Records in Ś. 1489, Prabhava, Kanyā, Monday, Māgha, 12, Śubhayōga, Varāha karaṇa, gift of the village Māvilaṅgai Śembināḍu to the temple of Tirukkayilāyam *alias* Iyamanīśuram-uḍaiya-Nāyaṅār, by a member of the Śammaṭṭi family. According to Mr. Swamikannu Piḷḷai the date corresponded to Monday, September 29, A.D. 1567.

56. 393 *of* 1914.—(Tamil.) On the west wall of the Amman shrine in the same temple. A fragmentary record of the sixth year of the Pāṇḍya king Māravarman *alias* Tribhuvanachakravartin Sundara-Pāṇḍyadēva (I, 1216—39) "who was pleased to take the Chōḷa country."

57. 394 *of* 1914.—(Tamil.) On a stone lying near the same temple. A mutilated record of the Pāṇḍya king . . . *alias* Tribhuvanachakravartin Kulaśēkharadēva, "who was pleased to take every country," the date of which is lost. Mentions Maṭṭiyūr Śivapuri in Kēraḷaśiṅga-vaḷanāḍu.

RĀMNĀD TALUK.

Dēvipaṭṭaṇam.

This place is famous as the holy *navapāshāṇam*. See *Mad. Journ.*, Vol. V, p. 376; *Antiquities*, Vol. I, p. 298.

58. 117 *of* 1903.—(Tamil.) On the north wall of the central shrine in the Tilakēśvara temple. A record in the fourth year of the Pāṇḍya king Jaṭāvarman *alias* Tribhuvanachakravartin Vikrama-Pāṇḍyadēva. Records gift of taxes levied within the four boundaries of Śivallavapaṭṭaṇam.

59. 118 *of* 1903.—(Tamil.) On the south wall of the central shrine in the same temple. A record in the fourth year of the Pāṇḍya king Māravarman *alias* Tribhuvanachakravartin Sundara-Pāṇḍyadēva. Records gift of land.

60. 119 *of* 1903.—(Tamil.) On the east wall of the maṇṭapa in front of the same shrine. A mutilated record in the third year of the Pāṇḍya king . . . *alias* Tribhuvanachakravartin Kula-śēkharadēva, " who conquered every country."

61. 120 *of* 1903.—(Tamil.) On the north wall of the same maṇṭapa. A record in the thirteenth year of the Pāṇḍya king Māravarman *alias* Tribhuvanachakravartin Sundara-Pāṇḍyadēva. Appears to record an agreement among the pūjārins of the temple. Built in at the end.

62. 121 *of* 1903.—(Tamil.) On the south wall of the Kaḍala-ḍaitta-Perumāḷ temple in the same village. An incomplete record of Sundarattōḷuḍaiya Mahābali-Vāṇadarāyar, in Ś. 1455, Manmatha (wrong).

Kiḻakkarai.

63. 396 *of* 1907.—(Tamil.) On the door-post of the maṇṭapa in front of the Śokkanāthasvāmin temple. Registers in Ś. 1453, expired, Vikrita, an agreement by which half a *paṇam* was to be given on every 100 pearls sold in Kīḷakkarai and the proceeds to be utilized for worship and repairs to the temple of Ninaittadumu-ḍitta-Piḷḷaiyār.

64. 397 *of* 1907.—(Tamil.) On a slab set up in the same temple. A damaged record of the Sētupati king Tirumalai-Sētupati-Mahārāja. Mentions Kōdaimaṅgalam *alias* Ninait-tadumuḍitta-Vināyagar-paṭṭaṇam.

65. 398 *of* 1907.—(Tamil.) On a second slab in the Śokka-nāthasvāmin temple. Mentions in Ś. 146... Achyutarāya and Tummuśi-Nāyakkar.

66. A C.P. No. 1 of 1912. A Mūvaraivēndan grant of Abhi-rāma Ativīra Rāma (II), the son of Ativīra Rāma Pāṇḍya, who is said to have resembled his father both in character and in name. It is to the effect that, at the request of one of his officers Aiyaṅ-kārappa, son of Peddappa and grandson of Nāgama Nāyaka (who bore the titles of Mōkālipaṭṭavardhana and Kāñchimahāpurādhīśa). Abhirāma gave to 69 Brahmans the two villages of Mūvaraivēndan and Śattalēri, clubbing them together under the new name of Peddanāyakan-Samudram.

Periyapaṭṇam.

67—70. 565 *to* 568.—(Arabic.) On four slabs kept in the courtyard of a mosque. Examined by Dr. J. Horovitz, PH.D., Epigraphist for Moslem inscriptions, Aligarh. Two of these contain verse 26 of Sura 55 of the Qurān, and the third and fourth refer to a woman who died a martyr for some cause.

Rāmēśvaram.

A history of this important and historic temple has been given in Burgess and Natesa Sastri's *Tamil and Sanskrit Inscriptions*, pp. 56-7. See also Mr. Sewell's *Antiquities*, Vol. I, p. 300, Fergusson's *Ind. and East. Arch.*, pp. 355—358, *Asiatic Researches*, Vol. VI, p. 426.

71. *No.* 1 *of Tamil and Sanskrit Inscriptions*, p. 57.—Over a figure of a Rāmnād Zamindar between the third prākāram and the entrance to the Amman temple, left side. Records the name Hiraṇyagarbhayāji Vijaya Raghunātha Sētupati Kātta Tēvar.

72. *No.* 2 *ibid.*—In a pillar in the Amman temple outside porch, over a statue. The same name recorded.

73. *No.* 3 *ibid.*—In front of the same. The same name.

74. *No.* 4 *ibid.*—On the bracket of the same. The same name recorded.

75. *No.* 5 *ibid.*—On the right side of the same. The same name recorded.

76. *No.* 6 *ibid.*—A small inscription in the same place, over a cow. "The Kāmadhēnu and the Kalpaka tree."

77. *No.* 7 *ibid.*—On the west side of the door leading out of the Svāmi's first prākāra. Records that in Kaḷayukti the ruined prākāra was repaired by Rāmanātha, the prince of sages, who is versed in all the rites and *āgamas* of the Śaiva system.

78. *No.* 10 *ibid.*—On the west wall of the first prākāra to the south of the Vināyaka temple. A record of Ś. 1530 in the days of Vīśu Bhūpati, saying that the temple was repaired by sage Rāmanātha.

79. *No.* 13 *ibid.*—On the front of the silver swinging cot in the Paḷḷiyarai. Records that it was the gift of Vijaya Raghunātha Sētupati Kātta Tēvar, son of Hiraṇyagarbhayāji Raghunātha Sētupati Kātta Tēvar. The amount of silver and its cost given.

80. *No.* 14 *ibid.*—Over the figure of a zamindar on the left side of the passage from the third prākāra to the entrance of the Amman temple. The name of Hiraṇyagarbhayāji Raghunātha Sētupati Kātta Tēvar recorded.

81. *No.* 15 *ibid.*—On the west wall of the first prākāra. A record of Ś. 1545, Rudhirōdgāri, Māśi 21, Wednesday, uttiram, saying that the Naḍamālikai maṇṭapam and "Ārūḍhamaṇṭapam" were built by Kūttan Sētupati Kātta Tēvar, son of Uḍaiyān Sētupati Kātta Tēvar.

82—87. *Nos.* 16, 17, 18, 19, 20 *and* 23 *ibid.*—Records the names on their respective statues of Vaḍuganātha Tēvar, Peria Uḍaiyā Tēvar, Raghunātha Śērvaikāran, Pradhāni Muttu Tirumalappa Piḷḷai and Rājarājēśvari Amman and Śinnaṇa Tēvar.

88. 89 *of* 1905.—(Sanskrit and Nāgari.) On the dhvajastambha of the Parvatavardhani Amman temple. A record of Gōpa-Tippa in Ś. 1390. Records the setting up of the guilt dhvajastambha. A Grantha copy of it is engraved on another side of the same pillar. This is the same as Nos. 11 and 12 of *Tam. and Sans. Inscrns.*, p. 59. [Tippa or Tirumalayya dēva was Viceroy of the South from 1453 to 1468 and gave great donations to Śrīraṅgam,

Jambukēśvaram and Rāmēśvaram shrines. He was the contemporary of poet Kāḷamēgha.]

89. 90 *of* 1905.—(Vaṭṭeḻuttu.) On the *balipīṭha* close to the dhvajastambha of the Rāmanāthasvāmin temple in the same village. A much damaged record.

90. 97 *of* 1903.—(Tamil.) On the south wall of the central shrine in the Rāmaliṅgēśvara temple. Records in Chitrabhānu gift of land for the merit of Viśvanātha Nāyaka Vīrappa Nāyakkar Ayyan. See No. 95 below.

91. 98 *of* 1903.—(Tamil.) On the west and south walls of the same shrine. A mutilated record in Ś. 1500, Vikrama (wrong). Mentions the Nāyaka referred to in the above epigraph.

92. 99 *of* 1903.—(Tamil.) On the south wall of the maṇṭapa in front of the same shrine. Records in Ś. 1520 the building of the maṇṭapa (Āḍal-maṇṭapa) by the learned sage Rāmanātha. Referred to in Mr. Sewell's *Antiquities* (No. 1 of the Local List). Also No. 8 in *Tam. and Sans. Inscrns.*, pp. 58–9.

93. 100 *of* 1903.—(Tamil.) On the west wall of the Kōṭitīrtha maṇṭapa in the same temple. Records in Ś. 1530 the building of the maṇṭapa by the same Rāmanātha. See *Tam. and Sans. Inscrns.*, No. 9, p. 59 and *Antiquities*, Local List, No. 2.

94. 101 *of* 1903.—(Tamil.) On the south wall of the first prākāra of the same temple. Records in Ś. 1545, Rudhirōdgārin, the building of the first prākāra.

95. 102 *of* 1903.—(Tamil.) On the same wall. Records in Ś. 1530 the building of a shrine at Rāmēśvaram during the time of Vīrabhūpati [i.e., Vīrappa Nāik (1609—23) of the Madura dynasty. See *Ind. Antq.*, 1916, August, pp. 132—6.]

96. 103 *of* 1903.—(Grantha.) On the north wall of the Chidambaranārāśam in the same temple. Records in Kāḷayukta the building of the first prākāra.

97. 104 *of* 1903.—(Tamil.) On the west wall of the Chidambarēśvara shrine in the same temple. A record of the Pāṇḍya king Vīra-Pāṇḍyadēva. There is also another fragmentary Pāṇḍya inscription.

98. 105 *of* 1903.—(Tamil.) On a pillar near the Āñjanēya shrine at the eastern gōpura of the same temple. A damaged record in Ś. 1549, Prabhava.

99. *No.* 21 *of Tam. and Sans. Inscrns.*—On the west side of the "Chavukai" in the Amman temple. Records that it was built by Periyanāyakam Piḷḷai Avargal, the manager and *dharmakarta* in Ś. 1786, Raktākshi, Āḍi 30.

100. *No.* 22 *ibid.*—On the west step of the dhvajastambha of the Amman temple. Records that on Vaikāśi 15 of Ś. 1785, Periyanāyakam Piḷḷai planted the dhvajastambha.

101. 8 *of* 1915.—(Kanarese.) At the entrance into the central shrine of the Rāmanātha temple. A damaged record in Śōbhakrit, Bhādrapada, ba. di. 12. Records gift of a jewelled armour (*kavacha*) to the temple of Rāmanāthadēva. Mentions Savaṇṇa-Daṇṇāyaka. Details of date not enough for calculation.

102. 9 *of* 1915.—(Tamil.) In the same place, left side. A damaged record of the Pāṇḍya king Tribhuvanachakravartin Sundara-Pāṇḍyadēva in the eleventh year, Kanyā, fifteenth day, Saturday, 12, Māgha.

103. *C.P. No. 7 of* 1911.—(Tamil.) A record of Muttu Rāmaliṅga Vijaya Raghunātha Sētupati Kātta Tēvar, dated Ś. 1692, Vikriti, making gift of land for feeding people and providing a water-shed. [This Sētupati was the adopted son of Hiraṇyagarbhayāji Raghunātha Sētupati and an opponent of the Nawab of Trichinopoly and the English. He was defeated by the latter near Trichinopoly in 1773, made prisoner and deprived of his possessions. He was restored by the Nawab in 1780, but deposed in 1794 and sent as State prisoner to Madras. See *Antiquities*, Vol. I, p. 228.]

104. *C.P. No.* 9 *of* 1911.—(Tamil.) A record of Muttu Vijaya Raghunātha Sētupati Kātta Tēvar (A.D. 1709—23) who performed the *Hiraṇyagarbha* ceremony, dated Ś. 1635, *Vijaya*, making gift of houses and lands at Attiyūttu to 14 Brāhmaṇa families. [He was known as Tiruvuḍaiya Tēvar.]

105. *C.P. No.* 10 *of* 1911.—(Tamil.) A record of Tirumalai Raghunātha Sētupati Kātta Tēvar (1645—1670), dated Ś. 1579 (A.D. 1656), making a gift of land to Ahōbaḷaiya of the Kauṇḍinya gōtra.

106. *C.P. No.* 11 *of* 1911.—A record of Daḷavāi Sētupati Kātta Tēvar (A.D. 1604—21), dated Ś. 1529 (A.D. 1607), *Parābhava*, making gift of five villages to the temple of Rāmanāthasvāmin at Rāmēśvaram. [This is No. 30 of Mr. Sewell's C.P. list. He has however read the date wrongly as Ś. 1521. It has been edited in *Tam. and Sans. Inscrns.*, pp. 66—8.]

107. *C.P. No.* 12 *of* 1911.—A record of Daḷavāi Sētupati (A.D. 1604—21), dated Ś. 1530, Plavaṅga, registering gift of eight other villages to the same temple. This is No. 32 of Mr. Sewell's list and edited in *Tam. and Sans. Inscrns.*, pp. 68—70.

108. *C.P. No.* 14 *of* 1911.—(Tamil.) A record dated in the year Nandana registering an agreement between the *Dharmakarta* Rāmanātha Paṇḍāram and the 512 Ārya *mahājanas* of the Rāmēśvaram temple.

109. *C.P. No.* 16 *of* 1911.—(Tamil.) A badly engraved record of a . . . Vijayan Sētupati in the year *Prabhava*.

110. *Sētupati grant No.* 2 (*in Tam. and Sans. Inscrns., pp.* 65-6).—In the possession of Raghunātha Gurukkaḷ of Rāmēśvaram. Records in Ś. 1529, expired, Plavaṅga, fourth lunar day in

Âḍi, gift of lands by Tirumalai Uḍayān Sētupati, on the occasion of his pilgrimage to the people of "the five countries" who served as priests and cooks in the Rāmēśvaram temple.

111. *Sētupati grant No.* 5 (*in Tam. and Sans. Incrns., pp.* 70—72).—A grant of land by Raghunātha Sētupati in Ś. 1581 (A.D. 1659), to a "Mahratta Brahman Śaṅkara Gurukkaḷ and others." The donor is called the son of Hiraṇyagarbhayāji Raghunātha Sētupati. The object of the grant was to provide for the comfort of Mahratta and other pilgrims who had now a priest of their own.

112. *Sētupati grant No.* 6 (*Ibid., pp.* 72—4).—A record of Ś. 1580, expired, Hēviḷambi (Uttarāyaṇa, Hēmanta Ritu, Śuklapaksha, new moon, Monday) recording a grant by Raghunātha Tirumalai Sētupati Kātta Tēvar, son of Tirumalai Sētupati Kātta Tēvar, to Śaṅkara Gurukkaḷ and others for conduct of Navarātri festival.

113. *Sētupati grant No.* 7 (*Ibid., pp.* 75—8).—A grant, dated Ś. 1589, expired, Plavaṅga, Uttarāyaṇa, Vaikāśi, Śuklapaksha 3, Thursday, Punarvasu, by a Perumāḷ Sērvaikāran of Pāṇḍi to the Rāmēśvaram temple for the merit of Tirumalai Hiraṇyagarbhayāji Raghunātha Tēvar, son of Daḷavāi Sētupati Kātta Tēvar. The objects of grant were the two villages Ānāndūr and Pāpāṅkuḍi.

114. *Sētupati grant No.* 8 (*Ibid., pp.* 79-80).—A record of Ś. 1601, expired, year Chitra, Uttarāyaṇa, Pūrvapaksha, dvitīya in Makara Thursday and Śataya. Records the grant of villages by Raghunātha Sētupati Kātta Tēvar, son of Hiraṇyagarbhayāji Raghunātha Sētupati Kātta Tēvar, for festivals and offerings. These were placed under the *mirās* of Raghunātha Gurukkaḷ, son of Śaṅkara Gurukkaḷ. His functions, privileges and honours are enumerated. [The record is interesting for the insight it gives into the position and emoluments of the priesthood.]

115. *Sētupati grant No.* 9 (*Ibid., pp.* 81—6).—A grant of Ś. 1606, K. 4785, Raktākshi, Uttarāyaṇa, Vaikāśi, Śuklapaksha, new moon, Sunday, Vaiśākha, by Hiraṇyagarbhayāji Raghunātha Sētupati Kātta Tēvar, to God Viśvēśvara and Goddess of Eḷuvāpuri in Tennālainādu, in Kaḷayār kōil Śīmai. The objects of the grant were the three villages Pudukkōṭṭai, Kaḷḷikkuḍi and Eḍayanvayal.

116. *Sētupati grant No.* 10 (*Ibid., pp.* 83—7).—A record of Ś. 1636, expired, Jaya (Chitrai 12, Monday, Śravaṇa, Daśami) by Hiraṇyagarbhayāji Vijaya Raghunātha Sētupati Kātta Tēvar, son of Hiraṇyagarbhayāji Raghunātha Sētupati Kātta Tēvar. [This is a very interesting document which enumerates the various sources of revenue granted to the deities of Rāmēśvaram.]

117. *Sētupati grant No.* 11 (*Ibid., pp.* 87—9).—A record of Ś. 1637, *Manmatha*, Māśi 2, Monday, giving the details of an agreement between Rāmanātha Paṇḍāram and Viṭṭhala Nāyakar, son of

Ananta Nāyakar of Parakkādu, in regard to the measures of oil to be presented to the temple in interest for money borrowed. [The inscription is interesting for the rate of interest and price of oil, etc., given therein.]

118. *Sētupati grant No.* 13 (*Ibid., pp.* 90–92).—A record of Ś. 1655, expired, Saturday, full moon, Kārttikai 10, Rōhiṇi (year Pramādīcha), recording the grant of the village of Kuḷattūr to God Sabhāpati of Tēvai (Rāmnāḍ).

119. *Sētupati grant No.* 14 (*Ibid., pp.* 92—5).—A record of Ś. 1656, expired, Ānanda, Kārttigai, Aparapaksha Trayōdaśi, Monday, Svāti. Records a grant of villages by Hiraṇyagarbhayāji Kumāra Muttu Vijaya Raghunātha Sētupati, son of Hiranyagarbhayāji Raghunātha Sētupati Kātta Tēvar, to God Vēlāyudhasvāmi of Paḷni.

120. *Sētupati grant No.* 15 (*Ibid., pp.* 95—8).—A record, dated in Ś. 1659, Naḷa, Uttarāyaṇa, Hēmanta Ritu, Pushya Kṛishṇapaksha, Amāvāsya, Thursday, Śravaṇa nakshattra, made by Muttu Vijaya Raghnātha Sētupaṭi Ayyar Avargal, the son of Kumāramuttu Vijaya Raghunātha Sētupati Avargal who was the nephew of Hiraṇyagarbhayāji Raghunātha Sētupati Avargal. Records the gift of the village of Mudalūru or Gōvindarājasamudram to Ramaṇayya, the son of Kalānidhi Kōnayya of the Kāśypagōtra, Aśvalāyana Sūtra and Rig Śākha.

121. *Sētupati grant No.* 16 (*Ibid., pp.* 98—100).—A record, dated Ś. 1585, expired, Subhānu Pushya, Aparapaksha-Amāvāsya, Monday, Uttira nakshattra. Grants the hereditary priesthood *(purōhita-khāṇiyāksh)* of the Sētupati family by Hiraṇyagarbhayāji Ravikula Muttu Rāmaliṅga Vijaya Raghunātha Sētupati to Raghunātha Gurukkaḷ, the son of Tātta Sivarāma Bhaṭṭar of the Kāśyapagōtra, Āpastamba Sūtra and Yajus Śākha.

122. *Sētupati grant No.* 17 (*Ibid., pp.* 100—3).—A record, dated Ś. 1706, expired, Śōbhakrit, Chaitra Śuklapaksha, Guruvāsara-Ashṭami-Punarvasu. Records grant of the village of Seppoḍukoṇḍān or Mutturāmaliṅgapuram to Kṛishṇa Aiyaṅgar, son of Śēshādri Aiyaṅgar of the Hārītagōtra, Āpastamba śūtra and Yajus śākha, during Mēsha-Saṅkrānti, by Muttu Rāmaliṅga Vijaya Raghunātha Sētupati Kātta Tēvar, descendant of Ravikulaśēkhara Hiraṇyagarbhayāji Raghunātha Sētupati Kātta Tēvar. The village was in Kaiki nāḍu.

123. *Sētupati grant No.* 18 (*Ibid., pp.* 103—5).—A record, dated Ś. 1705, expired, K. 4884, Śōbhakrit, Mithuna, Śuklapaksha-Trayōdaśi, Anusha, Friday. Records grant of the village of Bhuvanēśvarapuri or Muḍindanāvayal in the Brahmadēśa of Varaguṇavaḷanāḍu to Śaṅkaraliṅga Gurukkaḷ, the son of Mantranātha Gurukkaḷ by Hiraṇyagarbhayāji Muttu Rāmaliṅga Vijaya Raghunātha Sētupati Kātta Tēvar.

Tiruppullāṇi (Darbhaśayanam).

This place which is one of the *Vishṇusthalas* of the Pāṇḍya country figures in the *Nālāyiraprabandha* as Tirumaṅgai Āḻvār sings about it.

124. 106 *of* 1903 (*No.* 1 *of Mr. Sewell's Local List*).—(Tamil.) On the second gōpura of the Jagannāthasvāmin temple, right of entrace. An incomplete record of the Vijayanagara king Vīra-Kampaṇa Uḍaiyār (II) in Ś. 1293, Virōdhin. Mentions the Deyvachchilai-Perumāḷ temple. [The inscription proves conclusively the conquest and occupation of the Pāṇḍyan kingdom by the general of Vijayanagar by Ś. 1293.]

125. 107 *of* 1903.—(Tamil.) In the same place. A record in the twenty-second year of the Pāṇḍya king Māravarman *alias* Tribhuvanachakravartin Kulaśēkharadēva (I, 1268—1308), "who conquered every country." Records gift of sheep for a lamp. The date corresponds to Monday, 27th June, A.D. 1289. See *Ep. Ind.*, Vol. VIII, p. 277.

126. 108 *of* 1903.—(Tamil.) In the same place. A damaged and incomplete record in the fifth year of the Pāṇḍya king Māravarman *alias* Tribhuvanachakravartin Sundara-Pāṇḍyadēva (I) ? 1216—35), "who conquered the Chōḷa country."

127. 109 *of* 1903.—(Tamil.) In the same place. A damaged record of Sundarattōḷudaiyār Mahāvali-Vāṇadarāyar * in Ś. 1450, Vijaya (A.D. 1528.) [This seems to be No. 3 of Mr. Sewell's Local List but date misread as Ś. 1400.]

128. 110 *of* 1903.—(Tamil.) On the same gōpura, left of entrance. A mutilated record in the thirty-seventh year of the Pāṇḍya king Māravarman *alias* Tribhuvanachakravartin Kulaśēkharadēva (I, 1268—1308), "who conquered every country." Records an order of a certain Āryachakravartin.

129. 111 *of* 1903.—(Tamil.) In the same place. A record of the Vijayanagara king Vīra-Kampaṇa-Uḍaiyār (II) in Ś. 1293, Virōdhin. Records gift of land. Built in. See No. 124.

130. 112 *of* 1903 (*No.* 2 *of Mr. Sewell's Local List.*)—(Tamil.) In the same place. A damaged record in the fifth year of Tribhuvanachakravartin Kōnērinmaikoṇḍān. Records gift of land.

131. 113 *of* 1903.—(Tamil.) In the same place. A damaged record of Mahābali-Vāṇadarāya-Nāyakar in Ś. 1440, Īśvara. [This seems to be No. 4 of Mr. Sewell's Local List.] See No. 127 above.

132. 114 *of* 1903 (*No.* 5 *of Mr. Sewell's Local List*).—(Tamil.) In the same place. A record of the Vijayanagara king

---

* It was just at this time, in 1524, that Virākavi Rāya of Nallūr published his monumental Arichchandirapurāṇa at Tiruppullāṇi.

Vīra-Kampaṇa-Uḍaiyār (II) in Ś. 1296, Ānanda. Records a private agreement. See note to 124.

133. 115 *of* 1903.—(Tamil.) At the entrance into the maṇṭapa in front of the central shrine in the same temple, left side. A damaged record in Ś. 1700, Hēviḷambin.

134. 116 *of* 1903.—(Tamil.) On a slab built into the floor at the entrance of the first gōpura of the same temple. A record in the eighth year of the Pāṇḍya king Māravarman *alias* Tribhuvanachakravartin Sundara Pāṇḍyadēva (I ?). Records gift of land.

Tiruttarakōśamaṅgai.

This important seat of Śaivite worship is traditionally famous as the place where Śiva appeared before Māṇikkavāśaga in the guise of his teacher.

135. 83 *of* 1905 (*No.* 4 *of Mr. Sewell's Local List*).—(Tamil.) On the south wall of the maṇṭapa of the Maṅgaḷēśvara temple. Records in Ś. 1393, expired, Khara, a private gift to the temple.

136. 84 *of* 1905 (*No.* 3 *of Mr. Sewell's Local List*).—(Tamil.) On the same wall. A record in Ś. 1505, expired, Chittrabhānu, of the Nāyaka king Śevvappa-Nāyaka-Achyutappa-Nāyaka. Records the gift at Rāmasētu by the king of a village in the Chōḷa country to the temple at Tiruvuttarakōśamaṅgai in Śrīdēśam, a subdivision of Śembi-nāḍu. See *Tanj. Gazr.*, pp. 38—9.

137. 85 *of* 1905 (*No.* 6 *of Mr. Sewell's Local List*).—(Tamil.) On the same wall. Records in Ś. 1425, expired, Dundubhi, gift of money. The village is described as in the above record.

138. 86 *of* 1905.—(Tamil.) (This is No. 5 of Mr. Sewell's Local List, but date misread as 1305.) On the same wall. A record in Ś. 1355 and twelfth year of the Pāṇḍya king Māravarman *alias* Tribhuvanachakravartin Vīra-Pāṇḍyadēva. Records gift of land. Mentions Muttūṟṟu-kūṟṟam. [So this king came to the throne in A.D. 1421.]

139. 87 *of* 1905 (*No.* 1 *of Mr. Sewell's Local List*).—(Tamil.) On the east wall of the kitchen of the same temple. Records in Ś. 1530, expired, Kīlaka, gift of money for celebrating certain festivals for the merit of Muttuvīrappa-Nāyaka (1609—23).

140. 88 *of* 1905 (*No.* 2 *of Mr. Sewell's Local List*).—(Tamil.) On the same wall. A record in the twenty-seventh year of the Pāṇḍya king Māravarman *alias* Tribhuvanachakravartin Kōnērimēlkoṇḍān Śrī-Kaliyugarāman Tirunelvēli-Perumāḷ Vīra-Pāṇḍyadēva. Records gift of land. Mr. Sewell misreads the date as the twenty-fifth year. [This king was the joint ruler with the celebrated Arikēsari Ponnum-Perumāḷ Parākrama Pāṇḍya Jaṭilavarman, the founder of the Teṅkāśi temple, who ruled from 1422 to 1464.]

SĀTTŪR TALUK.

Edirkōṭṭai.

141. 474 *of* 1909.—(Vaṭṭeḷuttu.) On a rock close to the Śunai-Kaṇṭhēśvara temple. A damaged record in the nineteenth year of the Pāṇḍya king Vīra-Pāṇḍya, "who took the head of the Chōḷa." Mentions Veṇbaikkuḍi-nāḍu and appears to record a gift of sheep for a lamp. [Mr. Krishna Sastri believes that Vīra Pāṇḍya's conquest of the Chōḷa should have earned for him the title Chōḷāntaka; for No. 65 of 1896 at Śuchīndram which refers to this Vīra Pāṇḍya refers to a signatory Śōḷāntaka Brahmamārāya. Later on the epithet was adopted by Jaṭāvarman Śrīvallabha.]

142. 475 *of* 1909.—(Vaṭṭeḷuttu.) On the same rock. A record in the thirteenth year of the Pāṇḍya king Śaḍaiyamāran. (Evidently one of the early kings referred to in the Vēlvikkuḍi grant.) Records a gift to the temple of Śunaikkuḍi-Paḍārar and mentions Kūttaṅkuḍi in Veṇbaikkuḍi-nāḍu.

143. 476 *of* 1909.—(Vaṭṭeḷuttu.) On the south wall of the Vēṇugōpālasvāmin temple in the same village. A much damaged record of the Pāṇḍya king Jaṭāvarman *alias* Sundara-Pāṇḍyadēva, the date of which is lost. In continuation of this slab, is a fragment in Vaṭṭeḷuttu characters which records a portion of the historical introduction of Rājarāja I and the twenty-second year of his reign. Sundara Pāṇḍya has not been identified.

144. 477 *of* 1909.—(Vaṭṭeḷuttu.) On the west wall of the same temple. A much damaged record of the Chōḷa king Rājarāja-kēsarivarman *alias* . . . In continuation of this is a fragment of a Pāṇḍya inscription in Tamil characters.

145. 478 *of* 1909.—(Vaṭṭeḷuttu.) On the north wall of the same temple. A damaged record of the Chōḷa king Rājakēsarivarman (i.e., Rājarāja I), the date of which is lost. Begins with the historical introduction *tirumagaḷ*, etc. Mentions Nārāyaṇa-Viṇṇagar-tēvar. [The existence of Vaṭṭeḷuttu in Rājarāja's inscriptions shows that it was not yet replaced by Tamil in the Pāṇḍyan country in this period.]

146. 479 *of* 1909.—(Tamil.) On a slab set up to the east of the same village. A damaged and unfinished record in the ninth year of the Pāṇḍya king Jaṭāvarman *alias* Tribhuvanachakravartin Sundara-Pāṇḍyadēva. Records gift of land to the temple of Kuḷanagaikkāvalīśvaramuḍaiya-Nāyanār at Pullaṇaikkuruchchi, a *dēvadāna* village of Vikramapāṇḍīśvaramuḍaiya-nāyanār at Veṇbaikkuḍi in Veṇbaikkuḍi-nāḍu. [It is not known which of the kings of this name is referred to.]

Kōlavārpaṭṭi.

147. On a copper plate fixed to the eastern wall of the temple. Records the British proclamation (like that at Eṭṭiyāpuram) in A.D. 1799 in the course of the great Pāñjālamkuruchchi war.

Māranēri.

148. 480 *of* 1909.—(Tamil.) On the west wall of the ruined Śiva temple. A damaged and incomplete record in the eighteenth year. Appears to record a gift of land to the shrine of the goddess in the temple of Sundarapāṇḍīśvaramuḍaiya-Nāyanār.

149. 481 *of* 1909.—(Tamil.) On the north wall of the same temple. A record in the twelfth year of the Pāṇḍya king Vīra-Pāṇḍyadēva. Records gift of land for offerings to the temple of Sundarapāṇḍīśvaramuḍaiya-Nāyanār at Māramaṅgalam *alias* Sundarapāṇḍyanallūr in Karunilakkuḍi-nāḍu.

Nenmēni.

150. On a stone in front of the temple of Anantarāja Svāmi. Records the grant of a tank to the temple in Ś. 1583 (A.D. 1661) in honour of Chokkaliṅga Nāyakkar of Madura and others. For an account of the reign of Chokkanātha Nāik see *Ind. Antq.*, 1917 (February—April).

151. On a stone north of the Perumāḷ temple. Records a grant in honour of Chokkaliṅga Nāyakka "and others" in Ś. 1587 (A.D. 1665).

SIVAGANGA TALUK.

Kāḷaiyarkōvil.

152. 575 *of* 1902.—(Tamil.) On the south wall of the Kāḷīśvara temple. A record in the twelfth year of the Pāṇḍya king Jaṭāvarman *alias* Tribhuvanachakravartin Sundara-Pāṇḍyadēva (II, 1276—90), corresponding to Wednesday, August 27, A.D. 1287. Records gift of land to the temple of Kānappēr by Aghōraśiva Mudaliyār *alias* Vaidyachakravartin. Mentions also a certain Pushpavanaśiva. *Ep. Ind.*, Vol. VIII, p. 279. [Śaivite legends say that Kānappēr or Kāḷaiyār Kōvil was one of the fifteen Śaivite holy places in the Pāṇḍyan land. It is associated with sage Kauṇḍilya and also with Sundaramūrti Nāyanār. The Sun-god is also said to have worshipped Śiva here.]

153. 576 *of* 1902.—(Tamil.) On the east wall of the same temple. A damaged record in the fourteenth year of Tribhuvanachakravartin Kōnērinmēlkoṇḍān.

154. 577 *of* 1902.—(Tamil.) On the east wall of the 100 pillared maṇṭapa in the same temple. An incomplete record in the fortieth year of the Pāṇḍya king Māravarman *alias* Tribhuvanachakravartin Kulaśēkharadēva (I, 1268—1308), "who conquered every country."

155. 578 *of* 1902.—(Tamil.) On the north wall of the kitchen in the same temple. A record in the fourteenth year of the Pāṇḍya king Māravarman *alias* Tribhuvanachakravartin Vīra-Pāṇḍyadēva, corresponding to Sunday, 16th January 1457. Records gift of land. See *Ep. Ind.*, Vol. VIII, p. 283.

156. 579 *of* 1902.—(Tamil.) On the west wall of the same kitchen. A much damaged record of the Pāṇḍya king Māravarman *alias* Tribhuvanachakravartin Kulaśēkharadēva "who conquered every country", the date of which is doubtful. See No. 140 above.

157. 580 *of* 1902.—(Tamil.) On the same wall. A record of the Pāṇḍya king Jaṭāvarman *alias* Tribhuvanachakravartin Sundara-Pāṇḍyadēva, the date of which is doubtful. Records gift of land. Mentions Aghōraśiva and Pushpavanaśiva. See No. 152 above.

158. 581 (*a*) *of* 1902.—(Tamil.) On the west wall of the Saundaryanāyaki shrine in the same temple. A record in the eleventh year of the Pāṇḍya king Tribhuvanachakravartin Sundara-Pāṇḍyadēva. Records gift of land.

159. 581 (*b*) *of* 1902.—(Tamil.) On the same wall. A record in the tenth year of the Pāṇḍya king Tribhuvanachakravartin Sundara-Pāṇḍyadēva. Records gift of land.

160. 582 *of* 1902.—(Tamil.) On the same wall. A record of the Pāṇḍya king Kulaśēkharadēva, the date of which is doubtful. Mentions gifts by Vikrama-Pāṇḍyadēva and Vīra-Pāṇḍyadēva.

161. 583 *of* 1902.—(Tamil.) On the same wall. A damaged record of the Pāṇḍya king Jaṭāvarman *alias* Tribhuvanachakravartin Sundara-Pāṇḍyadēva, the date of which is lost. [The king is not identifiable.]

162. 584 *of* 1902.—(Tamil.) On the same wall. A record in the tenth year of the Pāṇḍya king Jaṭāvarman *alias* Tribhuvanachakravartin Sundara-Pāṇḍyadēva. Records gift of land. [It is not known which of the kings of this name is referred to.]

163. 585 *of* 1902.—(Tamil.) On the east wall of the same shrine. A record of Sundarattōḷ-Uḍaiyār Māvali-Vāṇadarāyar in Ś. 1452, Manmatha (wrong). Records gift of land. See No. 127 above.

164. 586 *of* 1902.—(Tamil.) On the south wall of the same shrine, right of entrance. A record in the twenty-fourth year of the Pāṇḍya king Tribhuvanachakravartin Vīra-Pāṇḍyadēva. Records gift of land.

165. 587 *of* 1902.—(Tamil.) On the same wall, left of entrance. A record of Māvali-Vāṇadarāyar in Ś. 1454, Hēviḷambin (wrong). Records gift of land. See No. 127 above.

Koṇḍagai (Kuntipura).

166. *No.* 21 *of Sanskrit and Tam. Inscrns., pp.* 108-9.—An inscription of the time of Sadāśiva Rāya of Vijayanagar, dated on Thursday in the month of Dhanus in Viśvāvasu, Ś. 1467 (expired). Records that, in the presence of Viśvanātha Nāiker, Dimmappa Nāiker, the agent of Sadāśiva Rāya, settled some disputes between the two sections of the inhabitants of Koṇḍakai. [The great Prabandhic teacher Śrīśailēśa or Tiruvāymoḷipiḷḷai, the preceptor of the celebrated Maṇavāḷa Mahāmuni, was according to the *Guruparampara*, born at Kuntīnagara, and we can be sure that this is the place referred to. For Śrīśailēśa's career and teachings see my article on the *History of Śri Vaishṇavism from the death of Vēdānta Dēśika to the present day* in *Mythic Society Journal*, 1917.]

Śivagaṅga.

167. *C.P. No.* 28 *of Mr. Sewell's List.*—Dated in Ś. 1706 (A.D. 1784), K. 4885, *Śōbhakrit*, Chitrai 5. By this document the then Zamindar of Śivagaṅga makes over certain lands in *sarvamāṇyam* (freehold) to a Muhammadan named Moṭṭai Fakir Saheb of Śivagaṅga. The Zamindar's name is given as "Muttu Vaḍuganātha Tēvar, son of Vijaya Raghunātha Śivanna Periya Uḍaya Tēvar." [The dates are not quite consistent. This is the same as C.P. 19 in *Tam. and Sans. Inscrns.*, pp. 105—7.]

Śōḻapuram.

168. 88 *of* 1908.—(Tamil.) On the north, west and south bases of the ruined Gaṇēśa temple. Stones out of order. Seems to contain portions of the historical introduction of Māravarman Sundara Pāṇḍya (I, 1216—35), which begins *pū-maruviya*, etc.

168-A. On the steps of the south gate of the Vikrama Pāṇḍyēśvara temple. Records that Kōnērinmaikoṇḍān granted to the deity, in his fifth year, a village which he purchased for 1,000 *paṇams*. *Ins., S. Dts.*, p. 278, No. 49.

168-B. On a stone in the north side of the same temple. Records grant of one *mā* of land and the appointment of a superintendent of the temple by Kulaśēkhara dēva Ativīra Rāma, in his thirteenth year, in Ś. 1483, Durmati. *Ibid.*, No. 50. [This ruler should have been different from Śrī Vallabha Ativīra Rāma whose coronation was in 1562.]

168-C. In the same place. A damaged grant of Parākrama Pāṇḍya in Ś. 1409, Śrīmukha, in his second year. *Ibid.*, No. 5.

Tiruppūvaṇam.

[One of fifteen Śaivite holy places of the Pāṇḍyan kingdom.]

169. 17 *of* 1894.—(Tamil.) On the east wall of the manṭapa in front of the Pushpavanēśvara shrine. A record in the eighth year of Kōnērinmaikoṇḍān. Records gift of land.

170. A copper-plate grant (Sanskrit and Tamil) in the possession of the temple authorities, recording a gift of lands to 1,080 Brahmans well versed in Vēdās, etc., by Śrī Kōchchaḍaivarman Tribhuvanachakravartigaḷ Śrī Kulaśēkhara Dēva Rājagambhīradēva (I, 1190—1217) in the twenty-fifth year of his reign. The plate was first published by Caldwell in *Ind. Antq.*, Vol. VI, 142 ff., but only *facsimiles* of five out of the ten plates were given. Burgess and Natesa Sastri have published the whole together with the translation in their *Tamil and Sanskrit Inscrns.*, pp. 21—36 (No. 23). See also *Mad. Ep. Rep.*, 1899, pp. 14-15, where it is summarized; *Ind. Antq.*, XX, p. 288, and *Ep. Ind.*, VI, p. 301, where Dr. Kielhorn points out that the date (Svāti, Saturday, eleventh of the second fortnight and Dhanus fourth) was Saturday, 29th December, A.D. 1214.

171. Another copper-plate grant of the same temple (Tamil) recording an order issued by "Kōnōnaḷaikoṇḍān" to the assembly of Rājagambhīrachaturvēdimaṅgalam to the effect that the twenty-five *kāśus* which were the share of the temple from three villages were to be paid half in paddy and half in coin. Certain men bind themselves to carry out the order and give an agreement to that effect to the assembly. This plate was also published first by Caldwell in *Ind. Antq.*, VI, and then by Burgess and Natesa Sastri in *Tamil and Sanskrit Inscrns.*, No. 24, pp. 37-8; see also *Mad. Ep. Rep.*, 1899, p. 15. [The king's name Sundara Pāṇḍya "who presented the Chōḷa country" occurs incidentally in the inscription. He is said to have conquered the Chōḷa country and then given it back to the Chōḷa who prostrated himself at his feet.] Venkayya points out that both this and No. 170 are closely connected, and were evidently written during the reign of Sundara Pāṇḍya, the former being perhaps a little earlier in time. From the fact that a minister, Rāman Pallavarāyar by name, is simply referred to in the earlier grant but signs the later, Venkayya concludes that both were issued during the lifetime of the same man and that Māravarman Sundara Pāṇḍya I, 1216—35, was in all probability the successor of Kulaśēkhara. [See *Mad. Ep. Rep.*, 1899, p. 15.] His Chōḷa opponent should have been Rājarāja III who ruled from 1216 to 1248.

Vēmbaṅguḍi.

172. 120 *of* 1910.—(Tamil.) On a stone set up in the bed of the tank. Records in Ś. 1562, Vishu (Vrisha), a gift for the merit of Tirumalai-Nāyakkarayyan (A.D. 1623—59).

ŚRIVILLIPUTTŪR TALUK.

Pudukkōṭṭai.

173. *No. 7 of Appendix A, Ep. Rep.*, 1906.—This is a copper-plate grant (Sanskrit and Grantha) of Srī Vallabha and Varatuṅga Rāma Pāṇḍya in Ś. 1505, *Subhānu*, which "gives a short account of the later Pāṇḍyas and records the gift of the village of Pudukkōṭṭai by a certain Tirumala Nāyaka with the approval of Vīrapa Nāyaka" of Madura. The date Ś. 1505 is said to be the twenty-first year after the coronation of Śrī Vallabha Ativīra Rāma Pāṇḍya and thereby shows that his coronation took place in

1562—63. The whole grant is excellently summarized by Venkayya in *Ep. Rep.*, 1906, pp. 71-2. He refers to the various kings of the line as given in the grant, the previous epigraphical references to them, Dr. Caldwell's description of them, and above all to the literary works of Ativīra Râma and Varatuṅga Rāma. The inscription has also been edited by Mr. Gōpinātha Rāo in his *Travancore Archæological Series*, Vol. I, pp. 61—89, together with the plates. Mr. Gōpinātha Rāo differs from Mr. Venkayya in regard to the relation between Ativīra Rāma and Śrīvallabha and holds that the latter was the younger brother of the former. Mr. Venkayya, on the other hand, believes them to be identical. The whole is referred to in detail in my *History of the Nāik Kingdom of Madura, Ind. Antq.*, 1915. The inscription is thus of the greatest value in regard to the political and literary history of South India in the sixteenth century.

Puduppāḷaiyam.

174. 503 *of* 1909.—(Tamil.) On the south wall of the Parannaṅgāttaruḷiyasvāmin temple. A much damaged record of the Pāṇḍya king Śrīvalladēva, dated in his sixth year. Appears to record a gift of money for a lamp.

175. 504 *of* 1909.—(Tamil.) On the east wall of the same temple. Dated in the eleventh year of the Pāṇḍya king Māravarman *alias* Tribhuvanachakravartin Sundara-Pāṇḍyadēva whom the Government Epigraphist identifies with Māravarman Sundara Pāṇḍya I who ruled from 1216 to 1235. Refers to his palace at Māḍakkuḷakkīḷ-Madurai and to the seat called *Maḷavarāyan*, and seems to register a gift of land for feeding the ascetic Īśānadēva and his pupils who were residing at Nalla perumāḷ-maḍam at Karuṅgaḷam *alias* Sādavāchakanallūr and had emigrated from Kṛishṇa-Gōḷaki *matha* at Tiruvārūr. [See *Ep. Rep.*, 1909, p. 104, for another *matha* called the *Āchāramaḷagia* in the same place.]

176. 505 *of* 1909.—(Tamil.) On the lintel of the entrance into the same temple. Records that the door posts and the step stone were the gift of Śrīvala-Pāṇḍyadēva (Ativīra Rāma ?).

Śrivilliputtūr.

See Mr. Sewell's *Antiquities*, I, 305, for a short description of this important place. It is celebrated as the birth-place of Periāḷvār and Gōdā and is therefore one of the most sacred places of Vaishṇavism. For its religious structures and its figure in later history see my *Hist. Nāik Kingdom of Madura*, in *Ind. Antq.*, 1916 (September and October). Mr. Sewell gives three inscriptions here, but the *Mack. MSS.* contain as many as forty-six inscriptions. These are summarized in *Ins., S. Dts.*, pp. 268—78, and though they are very meagre I have included them here.

177. In the south side of the Nāchchiyār temple. Records a grant of lands in A.D. 1453 by "Vīra Valivānātha Rāya" of Madura.

177-A. In the same place. A record of Valivānāthi (Mahābali Vāṇanātha ?) Rāyar in 1476.

177-B. In "the principal temple" of the place. A record of Parākrama Pāṇḍya, dated Ś. 1546.

178-A. On the south of the ardhamaṇṭapam in the pagoda of Śūḍikkuḍutta Nāchchiyār. A damaged grant of Mahābali Bāṇa Rāja. *Ins., S. Dts.*, p. 268, No. 1.

178-B. East of the above. Records that Mahābali Bāṇa Rāya gave in Ś. 1355, Śrīmukha, the village of Tiruvāṅganallūr and some jewels to the God. *Ibid.*, No. 2.

178-C. West of the above. The same king gave in Ś. 1399, Hēviḷambi, the village of Māṅguḍi to the Goddess. *Ibid.*, No. 3.

178-D. Below the ardhamaṇṭapam. Records that Parākrama-dēva gave some land to Ulaġuḍayaperumāḷ in his second year, in Ś. 1408, Prabhava. *Ibid.*, No. 4.

178-E. Below the above. Records that Vīra-Pāṇḍyadēva gave in his second year the village of Vayur to the Goddess. *Ibid.*, No. 5.

178-F. On the altar near the temple. Records that Kula-śekharadēva granted in Nandana a village. *Ibid.*, No. 6.

178-G. On a stone near the Śēnamudaliār shrine. A damaged grant of Kōnērinmaikoṇḍān. *Ibid.*, No. 7.

178-H. In the same place. Kulaśekharadēva granted in Ś. 1456, Jaya, twenty-one *tūms* of rice and 100 *palams* of curry a month to the Goddess for food. *Ibid.*, No. 8.

178-I. On a stone near Śēnamudaliār shrine. Records that Kulaśekharadēva gave some grant in rice for the Goddess and worshippers in his second year. *Ibid.*, No. 9, p. 270.

178-J. In the same place. A damaged grant in the second year of Vīra-Pāṇḍya. *Ibid.*, No. 10.

178-K. In the same place. A grant dated in Ś. 1504. No details. *Ibid.*, No. 11.

178-L. In the same place. Records that Sadāśivarāya gave the village of Puḷiyaṅguḷam to the Goddess in Ś. 1472, Sādhāraṇa. *Ibid.*, No. 12.

178-M. On a stone north of the Nāchchiyār temple. Records that Sadāśiva-Rāya gave in the same year the village of "Pattar-ungull." *Ibid.*, No. 13.

178-N. In the same place. Records that Sundaraśōḷadēva gave in Ś. 1398, Durmukhi, the village of Sundaranallūr and a golden chair to the Goddess. *Ibid.*, No. 14.

178-O. In the same place. Records that one Tiruvēṅgaḍamuḍayān gave the village of "Culculloor" in Chōḷamaṇḍalam for the Goddess. *Ins., S. Dts.*, p. 268, No. 15.

178-P. In the same place. Records that Narasiṁharāja Uḍaiyār gave the Goddess in Ś. 1375, Śrīmukha, some land in Teṅkarai and Vaḍakarai villages. *Ibid.*, No. 16.

178-Q. On a stone in the Vaṭapatraśāyi temple. Records that in the reign of Kōnērinmaikoṇḍān, 377th day, Śaṅkaramuḍaiyān gave some land to the God. *Ibid.*, No. 17.

178-R. North of the maṇṭapam in the temple. A Tamil record of the second year of a certain king. No details. *Ibid.*, No. 18.

178-S. In the same place. A damaged grant of Bhuvanachakravarti. *Ibid.*, No. 19.

178-T. In the same place. A damaged grant of the second year of a Sundara Pāṇḍya. *Ibid.*, No. 20.

178-U. In the same place. A damaged grant of the twenty-eighth year of Kulōttuṅgachōḷa. *Ibid.*, No. 21.

178-V. In the same place. A damaged grant of the eleventh year of Vikrama-Pāṇḍyadēva. *Ibid.*, No. 22.

178-W. In the same place. A damaged grant of the thirty-seventh year of Rājarājadēva. *Ibid.*, No. 23.

178-X. In the same place. Records that Parākrama Pāṇḍya gave the village of Pāpāgni to Paḷḷikoṇḍaruḷiya Paramasvāmi and Sūḍikkuḍuttanāchchiyār in his second year, Vishu (?). *Ibid.*, No. 24.

179. On a stone on the inner temple. Records that Vīra Uḍaiya Mārttāṇḍavarma gave the village of Parāntakanallūr in his seventieth year to the God and Goddess. *Ibid.*, p. 273, No. 25.

179-A. In the same place. Records that Vīrapāṇḍyadēva granted some land to the Goddess in his second year. *Ibid.*, No. 26.

179-B. Place not given. Records that Sundara Pāṇḍya gave the village of "Cadarattore" in the second year of his reign to the Goddess. *Ibid.*, p. 274, No. 27.

179-C. North of the above. Records that Kulaśēkharadēva gave some land in Vīramākuḷam in his twentieth year to Paḷḷikoṇḍaperumāḷ. *Ibid.*, No. 28.

179-D. In the same place. A damaged record of Kulaśēkharadēva in Ś. 1465, Krōdhi. *Ibid.*, No. 29.

179-E. In the same place. A damaged grant of Abhirāma Parāntaka Pāṇḍya in Ś. 1483. (Parāntaka is evidently a mistake for Parākrama.) *Ibid.*, No. 30.

179-F. In the same place. A damaged grant of Tribhuvanachakravarti to ten Brahmans. *Ibid.*, No. 31.

179-G. On the foundation of the wall of the Vaṭapatraśāyi temple. Records that Kōnērinmaikoṇḍān gave 122 shares of dry and wet land and gardens in the village to the Chaturvēda Bhaṭṭārakaṣ. *Ins., S. Dts.*, p. 275, No. 32.

179-H. Place not given. Records that in the eleventh year of the reign of Sundara Pāṇḍya Gaṅgādhara and Trivikrama gave quarter *puṭṭi* of ghee for lighting in the temple. *Ibid.*, No. 33.

179-I. On the north wall of the inner pagoda. Records that Kōnērinmaikoṇḍān granted a village in his fifteenth year to the Sabhā. *Ibid.*, No. 34.

179-J. In the same place. A damaged grant of Sundara Pāṇḍya. *Ibid.*, No. 35.

179-K. The next three inscriptions are assigned to "Aumbala Rāja", Tribhuvana and Vīrachōḷa and no details are given about these. *Ibid.*, Nos. 36 to 38.

179-L. On a stone in the inner temple of Vaidyanātha in Maḍaviḷāham near Śrīvilliputtūr. Records that Vīra-Pāṇḍyadēva gave some dry field in Karuṅguḷam to the God, in his second year. *Ibid.*, No. 39.

179-M. In the same place. A grant of land in Rājaśiṅgapūr by Kulaśēkharadēva in Ś. 1456, Jaya, to the God. *Ibid.*, No. 40.

179-N. In the same place. Records that the minister of Vikrama Pāṇḍya gave fifteen *mās* of land in 3,675th day ?. *Ibid.*, p. 277, No. 41.

179-O. In the same place. An effaced grant of Vīra-Pāṇḍya, in his second year. *Ibid.*, No. 42.

179-P. In the same place. A damaged record of Kōnērinmaikoṇḍān, in his fifth year. *Ibid.*, No. 43.

179-Q. In the same place. Records that Rājēndra Vīra-Pāṇḍya gave sixty-eight lamps and ten *mās* of land for oil. *Ibid.*, No. 44.

179-R. In the same place. An effaced grant of the second year of Vīra-Pāṇḍya. *Ibid.*, No. 45.

179-S. In the same place. A damaged grant of Ativīrarāma in Ś. 1479, Yuva. *Ibid.*, No. 46.

179-T. In the same place. A damaged record of the second year of Kulaśēkharadēva. *Ibid.*, No. 47.

179-U. On a stone in the temple of Kṛishṇasvāmi, near the Tirumalaśayana maṇṭapam. Records that Viśvanātha Nāyakar, Vīrappa Nāyakar and Kṛishṇappa Nāyakar built the temple in Bhava, and set up the idols of Rukmaṇi, Satyabhāma and Kṛishṇa and granted a portion of land. *Ibid.*, p. 278, No. 48.

180. A C.P. grant in the possession of a local Brahman, edited by Mr. T. A. Gōpinātha Rao in his *Trav. Arch. Series*, I, pp. 106—14 (No. XI). Records that Abhirāma Pāṇḍya (i.e., Varatuṅga Rāma), the son and grandson respectively of Parākrama Pāṇḍya and Abhirāma Pāṇḍya, gave in Ś. 1474, Virōdhikrit (Uttarāyaṇa, Hēmantaritu, Makara, new moon, Śravaṇa Nakshattra), during a solar eclipse, the village of Kshīrārjunapura in Mallināḍu to a number of Brāhmaṇas.

TIRUPPATTŪR TALUK.

Kunnakkuḍi.

This village is noted for its cave temples adjoining the modern temple of Tēnāṟṟīśvara at the foot of the hill. The iconographical features of the place have been described by Mr. Krishna Sastri in *Ep. Rep.*, 1910, p. 79. Of the five inscriptions which Mr. Sewell mentions in this place, three have been identified, but not the two others which are attributed to the twentieth year of Tribhuvanachakravartin Vīra-Pāṇḍya and Ś. 1442 (A.D. 1550).

181. 24 *of* 1909.—(Tamil.) On a pillar of a rock-cut cave in the hill. An unfinished record in the forty-eighth year of the Chōḷa king Tribhuvanachakravartin Kulōttuṅga-Chōḷadēva. Mentions the temple of Tirumalai-uḍaiya-Mahādēva at Tirukkunṟakkuḍi, one of the villages irrigated by the river Tēnāru in Rājēndraśōḷa-vaḷanāḍu in Rājarāja-Pāṇḍināḍu.

182. 25 *of* 1909.—(Tamil.) On a second pillar in the same cave. A record in the sixth year of the Pāṇḍya king Tribhuvana-chakravartin Vikrama-Pāṇḍyadēva. Records gift of land for offerings to the temple of Tirumalai-uḍaiya Tenāṟṟu-Nāyakkar at Tirukkunṟakkuḍi in Aḍalaiyūr-nāḍu, a subdivision of Kēraḷaśiṅga-vaḷanāḍu. This is No. 3 of Mr. Sewell's list.

183. 26 *of* 1909.—(Tamil.) On the same pillar in the same place. A record in the sixth year of the Pāṇḍya king Tribhuvana-chakravartin Vikrama-Pāṇḍyadēva. Records gift of land to the same temple by Uyyavandān Gaṇḍan *alias* Gāṅgēyan *alias* Tyāga-mīgāman. This is No. 4 of Mr. Sewell's list.

184. 27 *of* 1909.—(Tamil.) On the third pillar in the same place. A damaged record in the fourth year of the Pāṇḍya king Jaṭāvarman *alias* Tribhuvanachakravartin Śrīvallabhadēva. Seems to record a gift of land to the temple of Mūlasthānamuḍaiya-Nāyanār on the hill in the same village.

185. 28 *of* 1909.—(Tamil.) On the fourth pillar in the same place. A record in the fortieth year of the Chōḷa king Tribhuvana-chakravartin Kulōttuṅga-Chōḷadēva. Records gift of land by a certain Aḍalaiyūr-nāḍāḷvān to the temple described as in No. 181.

186. 29 *of* 1909.—(Tamil.) On the same pillar in the same place. In modern characters. Records in Plavaṅga the sale of a sluice (*marugal*).

187. 30 *of* 1909.—(Tamil.) On the rock, left of entrance into the same cave. An unfinished record in the fourth year of the Pāṇḍya king Jaṭāvarman Tribhuvanachakravartin Śrīvallabhadēva. Registers a gift to the temple mentioned in No. 184 by Aḍalaiyūr-nāḍāḷvān Mummuḍi-śōḷan Vīraśēkharan. [Was the king the contemporary of Māravarman Sundara Pāṇḍya I?]

188. 31 *of* 1909.—(Tamil.) In the verandah of the same cave, north side. A much damaged record of the Pāṇḍya king Śrīvallabhadēva, the date of which is doubtful. Records gift of land for a lamp to the temple of Tirumalai-uḍaiya-Nāyanār.

189. 32 *of* 1909.—(Tamil.) In the same place. A record in the forty-ninth year of the Chōḷa king Tribhuvanachakravartin Kulōttuṅga-Chōḷadēva (I). Records gift of taxes for offerings to the temple of Tirumalai-uḍaiya-Nāyanār by Vīraśēkharan *alias* Aḍalaiyūr-Nāḍāḷvān.

190. 33 *of* 1909.—(Tamil.) In the same verandah, south side. An unfinished record of the Chōḷa king Chakravartin-Kulōttuṅga-Chōḷadēva (I), in his fortieth year. Refers to the residents of Iḍaikkuḍi *alias* Ravikulamāṇikkanallūr and other villages irrigated by the river Tēnāru, in Rājēndraśōḷa-vaḷanāḍu, a subdivision of Rājarāja-Pāṇḍināḍu. At the bottom is an inscription in modern characters dated in the cyclic year Āṅgirasa.

191. 34 *of* 1909.—(Tamil.) On a pillar of another rock-cut cave in the same hill. A record in the twenty-second year of the Chōḷa king Tribhuvanachakravartin Kulōttuṅga-Chōḷadēva. Records gift of land to the temple of Tirumalai-uḍaiya-Mahādēva by the villagers of Kunṟakkuḍi *alias* Tenpugallūr.

192. 35 *of* 1909.—(Tamil.) On the second pillar in the same cave. A record in the fortieth year of the Chōḷa king Tribhuvanachakravartin Kulōttuṅga-Chōḷadēva (I). Records that Vīraśēkharan *alias* Virudarājabhayaṁkara Aḍalaiyūr-Nāḍāḷvān granted a remission of taxes on all the *dēvadāna* lands belonging to the same temple.

193. 36 *of* 1909.—(Tamil.) On the second and third pillars in the same place. A damaged record of the Pāṇḍya king Māravarman *alias* Tribhuvanachakravartin Sundara-Pāṇḍyadēva (I, 1216—35), "who was pleased to distribute the Chōḷa country." The record gives a long historical introduction. [This may be No. 1 of Mr. Sewell's list, where it is attributed to the eighth year of the reign.

194. 37 *of* 1909.—(Vaṭṭeḷuttu.) On the third pillar in the same place. The record bears the single word Māśilīchchuram.

195. 38 *of* 1909.—(Tamil.) On the fourth pillar in the same place. A record in the eighth year of the Pāṇḍya king Jaṭāvarman *alias* Tribhuvanachakravartin Śrī-vallabhadēva. Records gift of land for the maintenance of a garden to the temple of Tēnāṟṟu Nāyakar by Kaṭṭi-araśa, a resident of Tirukkunṟakkuḍi. See No. 187 above.

196. 39 *of* 1909.—(Tamil.) In the verandah of the same cave, below two images. A much damaged record in the seventh year of the Pāṇḍya king Tribhuvanachakravartin Sundara-Pāṇḍyadēva, "who was pleased to distribute the Chōḷa Country." Seems to record a gift of land to Āḷuḍaiya-Piḷḷaiyār. The king was most probably Māravarman Sundara Pāṇḍya I, 1216—35.

197. 40 *of* 1909.—(Tamil.) On a wall in front of the same cave. A much damaged record in the sixteenth year of the Pāṇḍya king Māravarman *alias* Tribhuvanachakravartin Sundara-Pāṇḍyadēva (I, 1216—35), "who took the Chōḷa country and was pleased to perform the anointment of heroes and the anointment of victors at Muḍigoṇḍaśōḷapuram." Seems to record a gift of land for offerings to the temple of Tēnāṟṟu-Nāyakar.

198. 41 *of* 1909.—(Tamil.) On the north wall of the Agastyēśvara shrine at the foot of the hill in the same village. An incomplete record in the twenty-second year of the Pāṇḍya king Māravarman *alias* Tribhuvanachakravartin Kulaśēkharadēva (I, 1268—1308), "who has pleased to take every country." Mentions the temple of Tēnāṟṟu-Nāyakar.

199. 42 *of* 1909.—(Tamil.) On the same wall. A record of the Pāṇḍya king Jaṭāvarman *alias* Tribhuvanachakravartin Rājarājan Sundara-Pāṇḍyadēva. Built in at the end and damaged. [The king has not been identified.]

200. 43 *of* 1909.—(Tamil.) On the east wall of the Madhunadīśvara shrine at the foot of the hill. A damaged record in the seventeenth year of the Pāṇḍya king Māravarman *alias* Tribhuvanachakravartin Sundara-Pāṇḍyadēva (I, 1216—35), "who took the Chōḷa country and was pleased to perform the anointment of heroes at Muḍigoṇḍaśōḷapuram." Records gift of land to a private person. Mentions Niyamam "irrigated by the river Tēnāru" in Kēraḷaśiṅgavaḷanāḍu.

201. 44 *of* 1909.—On the roof of a natural cavern called Jñāniyārmaḍam on the same hill. In Brāhmi characters. [The huge boulder here is similar to that at Pañchapāṇḍavamalai near Kīḷavaḷavu and "must have contained below it a number of the usual stone beds. The whole space under the boulder is, however, now converted into a building with several compartments and is occupied by mendicant beggars who call it *Gñāniār-maḍam*. In the *maḍam* they have placed figures of a nāga, a Hanūmān and a seated image which they call Gñāniār." (*Mad. Ep. Rep.*, 1910, p. 80.)

Pirānmalai.

In his *Antiquities* Mr. Sewell gives ten inscriptions in this place of which Nos. 2, 3, 5 and 6 have been identified with 203, 204, 205 and 212 of the following list. The other inscriptions of

Mr. Sewell are not identifiable. Two of them are attributed to the thirteenth and tenth years of Tribhuvanachakravartin Kulaśēkhara and the other four are given under Nos. 220 to 223 below.

202. 138 *of* 1903.—(Tamil.) • On the rock in the central shrine of the Maṅgainātha temple. An incomplete record in the thirty-fifth year of the Chōḷa king Chakravartin Kulōttuṅga-Chōḷadēva (I ?).

203. 139 *of* 1903.—(Tamil.) On the south wall of the kitchen belonging to the Maṅgainātha temple. A mutilated record of the Śāḷuva king Immaḍi-Narasiṁharāya (son of Naraśiṅga), in Ś. 1422, Raudri. Appears to record a gift for the merit of Tipparasar Ayyan. Mentions Eppuli-Nāyakar and Kēraḷaśiṅga-vaḷanāḍu and the district of Piramalai-śīmai.

204. 140 *of* 1903.—(Tamil.) On the west wall of the same. A record in the thirty-eighth year of the Pāṇḍya king Māravarman *alias* Tribhuvanachakravartin Kulaśēkharadēva (I, 1268—1308), "who conquered every country.". Records gift of cows to the temple of Koḍunguṉṟamuḍaiya-Nāyanār.

205. 141 *of* 1903.—(Tamil.) On the west wall of the Sundara-Pāṇḍyan maṇṭapa in front of the central shrine of the same temple. A record of the Vijayanagara king Vīra-pratāpa Dēvarāya (II, 1422—49) in Ś. 1360, Kāḷayukta. Records gift for the merit of Madana Uḍaiyār, younger brother of the minister Lakshmaṇa Daṇṇāyaka, who calls himself "the lord of the southern ocean."

206. 142 (*a*) *of* 1903.—(Tamil.) On the north wall of the Lakshmi maṇṭapa close to the same shrine. A record in the third year of the Pāṇḍya king Māravarman *alias* Tribhuvanachakravartin Sundara-Pāṇḍyadēva (I, 1216—35), "who took the Chōḷa country." Records gift of sheep for a lamp.

207. 142 (*b*) *of* 1903.—(Tamil.) On the same wall. A record of the Pāṇḍya king Tribhuvanachakravartin Sundara-Pāṇḍyadēva (I, 1216—35), "who took the Chōḷa country," the date of which is doubtful. Records gift of sheep for a lamp.

208. 143 *of* 1903.—(Tamil.) On the same wall. A record in the twenty-seventh of the Pāṇḍya king Tribhuvanachakravartin Kulaśēkharadēva. Records gift of a lamp stand. Mentions Karavandapuram.

209. 144 *of* 1903.—(Tamil.) On the north wall of the six-pillared maṇṭapa in front of the same shrine. A record in the third year of the Pāṇḍya king Jaṭāvarman *alias* Tribhuvanachakravartin Vīra-Pāṇḍyadēva. Records gift of money for offerings. Tirukkoḍuṅguṉṟu was situated in Tirumalai-nāḍu. Mention is made of Aḷagapuri *alias* Śeliyanārāyaṇapuram in Kēraḷaśiṅgavaḷanāḍu. [According to Śaivite legends Tirukkoḍuṅguṉṟam or Pirānmalai was one of the fifteen Śaivite centres in the Pāṇḍyan kingdom and renowned as the place where Mahōdara Rishi performed worship.]

210. 145 *of* 1903.—(Tamil.) On the base of the same maṇṭapa. A record of Tribhuvanachakravartin Kōnērinmaikoṇḍān. Records gift of land. Mentions Tuvarāpati-Vēḷār and Bhūpāla-Puramdara. The latter was probably a title of the king. Contains also a fragment of an inscription of Sundara-Pāṇḍya "who performed the anointment of heroes at Nellūr," *i.e.*, Jaṭāvarman Sundara Pāṇḍya I who ruled from 1251 to 1264.]

211. 146 *of* 1903.—(Tamil.) On the west wall of the Viśvanātha shrine in the same temple. An incomplete record of the Vijayanagara king Vīrapratāpa Kṛishṇadēva Mahārāya "who conquered Īḻam and every country and witnessed the elephant hunt," in Ś. 1440, Chitrabhānu (wrong); Venkayya points out that this inscription is "a unique" record among the Tamil inscriptions of the Emperor in claiming the conquest of Īḻam for Kṛishṇarāya.

212. 147 *of* 1903.—(Tamil.) On the north wall of the same shrine. Mentions Tuvarāpatī-Vēḷār and Bhūpāla Puramdara. Records in the thirty-fourth year gift of land. [This is evidently inscription No. 2 in Mr. Sewell's list assigned to the thirty-fourth year of Tribhuvanachakravartin Kulaśēkhara.]

213. 148 *of* 1903.—(Tamil.) On the north and west walls of the same shrine. A record in the sixteenth year of the Pāṇḍya king Tribhuvanachakravartin Sundara-Pāṇḍyadēva. Built in at the end. Records gift of land. Contains the Sanskrit introduction beginning with *Samastu-jagadādhāra,* etc.

214. 149 *of* 1903.—(Tamil.) On the south wall of the steps leading to the Maṅgainātha shrine. An incomplete record. Records an order of Māḷavachakravartti.

215. 150 *of* 1903.—(Tamil.) On the east wall of the same. A record in the tenth year of the Pāṇḍya king Jaṭāvarman *alias* Tribhuvanachakravartin Parākrama-Pāṇḍyadēva. Records a sale of land. [Was he the king who came to the throne in 1334 ?]

216. 151 *of* 1903.—(Tamil.) On the west wall of the steps leading to the Maṅgainātha shrine in the same temple. A record of the Sāḷuva king Immaḍi Naraśiṅgarāya (son of Naraśiṅga, the usurper) in Ś. 1422, Raudra. Records gift of land for the merit of Tipparasa Ayyan by Eppuli Nāyakar.

217. 152 *of* 1903.—(Tamil.) Inside the Subrahmaṇya shrine in the same temple. A record in the sixteenth year of the Pāṇḍya king Māravarman *alias* Tribhuvanachakravartin Kulaśēkharadēva (I, 1268—1308), "who conquered every country." Records gift of money for offerings.

218. 153 *of* 1903.—(Tamil.) On the north wall of the same shrine. Records in fifteenth *Vibhava,* gift of land.

219. 154 *of* 1903.—(Grantha and Tamil.) On the south wall of the Śokkanātha temple in the same village. An incomplete record. Mentions a *corporation of merchants.*

220. A record dated in Ś. 1424 (A.D. 1502). No details given. *Antiquities*, I, p. 297, No. 7.

221. A record dated in Ś. 1452 (A.D. 1530). *Ibid.*, No. 8.

222. A record dated in S. 1610 (A.D. 1688). *Ibid.*, No. 9.

223. A record dated in Ś. 1510 (A.D. 1588), in the reign of Veṅkaṭapati I of Vijayanagar who ruled from 1586 to 1616. It shows that his suzerainty was acknowledged in the Nāik kingdom of Madura. *Ibid.*, No. 10.

Tirukkōlakkuḍi.

Spelt Tirukkalākkuḍi in the alphabetical list. In his *Antiquities* Mr. Sewell gives abstracts of three inscriptions in the local temple. These are :—

224. A record of Tribhuvanachakravartin Sundara Pāṇḍyadēva, in the eleventh year of his reign.

225. Another inscription of the same king in the twentieth year.

226. An inscription of the thirty-first year of Vīra Pāṇḍyadēva.

Tirukkōshṭiyūr.

226-A. In the Śiva temple. A record of Raghunātha Tirumalai Sētupati in Ś. 1601 (A.D. 1679) making a gift of lands. For an account of this Sētupati's administration see *Ind. Antq.*, 1917, pp. 45–6.

Tiruppattūr.

Mr. Sewell refers to two inscriptions only in this place and they can be identified with Nos. 236 and 249 in the following list :—

227. 89 *of* 1908.—(Tamil.) On the south wall of the central shrine in the Tiruttaḷiśvara temple. A record of the Sāḷuva king Immaḍi Narasiṁha-Mahārāya, son of Narasiṁharāya, in Ś. 1421, Siddhārthin. Records that the residents of the village of Tirupputtūr, a *brahmadēya* in Kēraḷaśiṅga-vaḷanāḍu, were allowed to enjoy their rent-free lands without imposition of any cess or service.

228. 90 *of* 1908.—(Grantha and Tamil.) On the north wall of the same shrine. A record in the fourth year, 593rd day of the Pāṇḍya king Māraṅjaḍaiyan. Records gift of 40 *kalchanju (Kṛishṇa-kācha)* for a lamp to Tirukkaṟṟalibhaṭṭārar at Tirupputtūr,*

---

* Also spelt Tirupputtūr and Tirupputūr. It is one of the centres of Śaiviṭism in the Pāṇḍyan country and is well known as the place where Umā (in the name of Śivakāmittāyammai) and others worshipped the Lord. It has formed the theme of a *padika* both of Gñānasambanda and Appar.

a *brahmadēya* of Mīguṇḍāru in Koḷuvūr-Kūṟṟam, by Tennavan Pallavaraiyan *alias* Māran Āchchan of Poḷiyūr.

229. 91 *of* 1908.—(Tamil.) On the same wall. A record of the Vijayanagara king Mahāmaṇḍalēśvara Kṛishṇarāya, in Ś. 1432, Pramōda. Records gift of land to a native of Tirupputtūr by Śiṅgama-Nāyaka for the merit of Vīra-Narasiṁharāya-Nāyaka *alias* "the lord and the prosperous Śellappa." This chief figured afterwards as a rebel. For details see my *History of the Nāik Kingdom* in *Ind. Antq.*, 1914.

230. 92 *of* 1908.—(Tamil.) On the same wall. An unfinished record of the Vijayanagara king Mahāmaṇḍalēśvara Vīrapratāpa Kṛishṇayadēva Mahārāya, in Ś. 1432, Pramōda. Records gift of the two villages Nāraṇamaṅgalam and Kāraiyūr in Kēraḷaśiṅga-vaḷanāḍu, a district of Pāṇḍimaṇḍalam for the merit of Vīra-Narasiṁharāya (Nāyakkar *alias*) Śellappar. These two villages were clubbed together under the name Śellappapuram.

231. 93 *of* 1908.—(Tamil.) On the east wall of the maṇṭapa in front of the central shrine. A record in the twenty-first year of the Pāṇḍya king Tribhuvanachakravartin Śrīvallabhadēva. Records gift of 50 sheep for a lamp by Rājēndraśōḷan Kēraḷan *alias* Nichuḷarāja to Śrītaḷipparamēśvara at Tirupputtūr, a *brahmadēya* in Kēraḷaśīṅga-vaḷanāḍu.

232. 94 *of* 1908.—(Tamil.) On the same wall. A record in the eleventh year of the Pāṇḍya king Tribhuvanachakravartin Parākrama-Pāṇḍyadēva. Records gift of paddy by Rājēndraśōḷan *alias* Nishadharāya of Ponnamarāpadi in Puramalaināḍu, for a festival in the temple of Tiruttaḷiyāṇḍār.

233. 95 *of* 1908.—(Tamil.) On the same wall. A record in the fifteenth year of the Pāṇḍya king Tribhuvanachakravartin Kulaśēkharadēva. Records gift of a lamp-stand and money for a lamp by a native of Niyamam, which was irrigated by (the river) Tēnāru *(Tēnāṟṟuppōkku)*.

234. 96 *of* 1908.—(Grantha.) On the same wall. Records an unfinished verse in the Ārya metre, which mentions Kuntalapati and Śrīsthali (i.e., Tiruttaḷi).

235. 97 *of* 1908.—(Tamil.) On the south wall of the same maṇṭapa. A record in the seventeenth year of the Pāṇḍya king Jaṭāvarman *alias* Tribhuvanachakravartin Śrīvallabhadēva. Records gift of paddy and gold by a merchant of Aruviyūr *alias* Dēśi Uyyavandapaṭṭaṇam.

236. 98 *of* 1908.—(Tamil.) On the same wall. A record in the third year of the Pāṇḍya king Māravarman *alias* Tribhuvanachakravartin Parākrama-Pāṇḍyadēva. Records that the assembly *(mūlaparishai)* of Tirupputtūr met together in the temple of Jayaṅgoṇḍaśōḷa Viṇṇagarāḷvār and decided to utilize the proceeds from the sale of certain lands for a festival in the Śrītaḷi-Paramēśvara temple, known as Naralōkavīran-śandi.

237. 99 *of* 1908.—(Tamil.) On the same wall. A record in the fourth year of the Pāṇḍya king Tribhuvanachakravartin Kulaśēkharadēva. Records assignment of certain taxes in Atiśayapāṇḍiyanallūr *alias* Kūttakkuḍi for the recitation of the *Tiruppadiyan* hymns, etc., in the temple of Tiruttaḷiyāṇḍa Nāyanār by Gaṇḍan Uyyavandān *alias* Gāṅgayan of Niyamam. The village was originally a gift to the temple of Naṭarāja (Kūttāḍudēvar) by Varaguṇapperumāḷ.

238. 100 *of* 1908.—(Tamil.) On the same wall. A damaged record in the ninth year of Tribhuvanachakravartin Kulaśēkharadēva. Records gift of taxes by Tiruvālanduṟaiyuḍaiyān Tirukkoḍuṅgunṟamuḍaiyān *alias* Nishadharājan of Ponnamarāpadi to a Śaiva *maṭha*, in the same temple.

239. 101 *of* 1908.—(Tamil.) On the same wall. A record in the fifth year of the Pāṇḍya king Tribhuvanachakravartin Kulaśēkharadēva. Records that the assembly *(mūlaparishai)* of Tirupputtūr wished to go to Madura to pay respects to king Kulaśēkhara, and accordingly made certain temple lands rent-free on receipt of a specified amount, for the expenses of the journey. *Ep. Ind.*, Vol. XI, p. 137.

240. 102 *of* 1908.—(Tamil.) On the same wall. A record in the fifteenth year of the Pāṇḍya king Tribhuvanachakravartin Kulaśēkharadēva. Records gift of money for a lamp by a native of Niyamam, irrigated by the river Tēnāru.

241. 103 *of* 1908.—(Tamil.) On the same wall. A record in the third year of the Pāṇḍya king Tribhuvanachakravartin Kulaśēkharadēva. Records that some lands belonging to the temple of Kailāsamuḍaiya-Nāyanār were made rent-free for money received by the sabhā of Tirupputtūr in order to provide for offerings on a festival in the same temple. Mentions *samvatsara-vāriyam*.

242. 104 *of* 1908.—(Tamil.) On the same wall. A record in the thirteenth year of the Pāṇḍya king Tribhuvanachakravartin Kulaśēkharadēva. Records a similar transaction by the sabhā which met together in the hall called *dayāpañjaram* within the temple. Mentions *Tiruttoṇḍattogaiyān-tirumaḍam*. See Cg. 1006.

243. 105 *of* 1908.—(Tamil.) On the north wall of the same maṇṭapa. A record in the twenty-eighth year of the Chōḷa king Rājarājakēsarivarman *alias* Rājarājadēva (I, 985—1013). Begins with the usual historical introduction. Mentions the meeting of the sabhā at the foot of *Urangāppuḷi*. An incomplete and damaged record.

244. 106 *of* 1908.—(Tamil.) On the same wall. A record in the fourteenth year of the Pāṇḍya king . . . ma Pāṇḍyadēva.

Built in at the beginning. Records gift of money for a lamp by a Brāhmaṇi.

245. 107 *of* 1908.—(Tamil.) On the same wall. A record in the twentieth year of the Pāṇḍya king Tribhuvanachakravartin Parākrama-Pāṇḍyadēva. Records gift of gold for offerings to the goddess Tiruppaḷḷiaṛai-Nāchchiyār by the same Brāhmaṇi.

246. 108 *of* 1908.—(Tamil.) On the same wall. A record in the twentieth year of the Pāṇḍya king Tribhuvanachakravartin Śrīvallabhadēva. Records gift of 25 cows and one bull for a lamp.

247. 109 *of* 1908.—(Tamil.) On the same wall. A record in the twentieth year of the Pāṇḍya king Tribhuvanachakravartin Śrīvallabhadēva. Records gift of 25 cows and one bull for a lamp. The donor was a native of Pūddanūr in Marugal-Nāḍu, a subdivision of Gēyamāṇīkkavaḷanāḍu in the Chōḷa country.

248. 110 *of* 1908.—(Grantha and Tamil.) On the same wall. A record of the Chōḷa king Rājakēsarivarman *alias* Uḍaiyār Śrī-Vīrarājēndradēva, the date of which is lost. Stones out of order. The Sanskrit portion mentions Kollāpura. In the Tamil portion a part of the historical introduction of the king is preserved, and a reference is made to ayyar (father) Rājēndra-Chōḷa "who took Gaṅgai, Pūrvadēśam and Kiḍāram. [Vīrarājēndra was evidently the king who ruled from 1063 to 1070.]

249. 111 *of* 1908.—(Tamil.) On the north wall of the maṇṭapa in front of the central shrine. A record in the tenth year of the Pāṇḍya king Jaṭāvarman *alias* Tribhuvanachakravartin Śrīvallabhadēva. Records gift of two villages by the king at the request of a certain Kāḷiṅgarāyan.

250. 112 *of* 1908.—(Tamil.) On the south wall of the Agastyēśvara shrine in the same temple. A record of the Vijayanagara king Vīrapratāpa Achyutadēva-Mahārāya in Ś. 1452, Vikrita. Records gift of two lamps by a native of Ariviyūr-nagaram *alias* Kulaśēkhara-paṭṭaṇam. Refers to a grant of land made by Veṅgala-Nāyakkar on the occasion of a solar eclipse.

251. 113 *of* 1908.—(Tamil.) On the west wall of the same shrine. A record of the Vijayanagara king Achyutadēva-Mahārāya in Ś. 1457, Jaya. Records gift of the village of Varaguṇaputtūr for the merit of Viśvanātha-Nāyakkar, son of Nāgama-Nāyakkar. Viśvanātha is the founder of the Naik dynasty of Madura. For his career see my *History of the Nāik kingdom* in *Ind. Antq.*, 1915.

252. 114 *of* 1908.—(Tamil.) On the north wall of the kitchen in the same temple. A record in the thirteenth year of the Pāṇḍya king Tribhuvanachakravartin Vikrama-Pāṇḍyadēva. Records gift of money for offerings to the shrine of Āḷuḍaiya-Piḷḷaiyār in the temple of Kailāsamuḍaiya-Nāyanār at Tirupputtūr. The money was deposited in the treasury of *Tiruttaḷiyāṇḍa-Nāyanār*.

253. 115 *of* 1908.—(Tamil.) On the same wall. A record in the twentieth year of the Pāṇḍya king Tribhuvanachakravartin Śrīvallabhadēva. Records that the kitchen was built by the queen Ulagamuḻududaiyār.

254. 116 *of* 1908.—(Tamil.) On the same wall. A record in the seventeenth year of the Pāṇḍya king Vīra-Pāṇḍyadēva. Records a remission of taxes by the sabhā of Tirupputtūr on lands belonging to *Tiruttoṇḍattogaitirumaḍam* and refers to the repairs made to the hall *dayāpañjaram*. See No. 242 above.

255. 117 *of* 1908.—(Tamil.) On the same wall. A record in the twelfth year of the Pāṇḍya king Tribhuvanachakravartin Vikrama-Pāṇḍyadēva. Records gift of money for offerings to the image of Tirunāvukkaraśudēva set up in the temple of Kailāsa-muḍaiya Nāyanār, by a dancing girl *(dēvar aḍiyāḷ)*.

256. 118 *of* 1908.—(Tamil.) On the same wall. A record in the twenty-third year of the Pāṇḍya king Kulaśēkharadēva. Records gift of money for three-fourth lamp by a Brāhmaṇi of Kulaśēkharachaturvēdimaṅgalam in Śōḻapāṇḍyavaḷanāḍu.

257. 119 *of* 1908.—(Tamil.) On the east wall of the first prākāra of the same temple. A record in the forty-sixth year of the Pāṇḍya king Jaṭāvarman *alias* Tribhuvanachakravartin Vīra-Pāṇḍyadēva. Records that in Karkāṭaka 14, Pūrvapaksha 5, Monday, Uttaraphalguni, Avaiyan Periya Nāyanār *alias* Viśālayadēva, a native of Kuṟaikkuḍi irrigated by (the river) Tēnāru, in Aḍalaiyūr-nāḍu, consecrated again the image in the temple of Tiruttaḷiyāṇḍa-Nāyanār which was polluted by the occupation of the Muhammadans. See *Ep. Ind.*, XI, p. 138, where the date is pointed out to be Monday, the 2nd August A.D. 1339.

258. 120 *of* 1908.—(Tamil.) On the same wall. A record in the forty-fourth year of the Pāṇḍya king Jaṭāvarman *alias* Tribhuvanachakravartin Vīra-Pāṇḍyadēva, in Mithuna 21, Pūrva 12, Sunday, Anurādha. Records the Muhammadan occupation of the temple and its consecration by Viśālayadēva mentioned in No. 257. He was on this account given certain special privileges in the temple by the temple priests. See *Ibid.*, where the date is pointed out to be 16th June, A.D. 1342.

259. 121 *of* 1908.—(Tamil.) On the same wall. A record of the Vijayanagara king Vīrapratāpa Achyutadēva-Mahārāya in Ś. 1460, expired, Viḷambi. Records gift of land for the merit of the king by Periya Rāmappa-Nāyakkar to a shrine of Bhairava in the same temple.

260. 122 *of* 1908.—(Tamil.) On the same wall. A record in the forty-fourth year of the Pāṇḍya king Jaṭāvarman *alias* Tribhuvanachakravartin Vīra-Pāṇḍyadēva in Dhanus 5, Pūrva I, Thursday, Mūla. Records sale of privileges pertaining to *Pādikkāval* by the sabhā of Tirupputtūr to Avaiyan *alias* Maḷavachakravartin of

Śuraikkuḍi. See *Ep. Ind.*, Vol. XI, p. 138, where the date is shown to be 2nd December, A.D. 1339.

261. 123 *of* 1908.—(Tamil.) On the same wall. A record in the twenty-fourth year of the Pāṇḍya king Jaṭāvarman *alias* Tribhuvanachakravartin Kulaśēkharadēva (I or II ?). Records sale of the right of *Kārāṇmai* by a temple tenant in favour of the goddess Tirukkāmakkōṭṭamuḍaiya-Nāchchiyār who was set up by Kaṇḍiyadēvar.

262. 124 *of* 1908.—(Tamil.) On the south wall of the same prākāra. A record of the Pāṇḍya king Jaṭāvarman *alias* Tribhuvanachakravartin Vikrama-Pāṇḍyadēva in the twenty-second year and Ś. 1344, Śubhakrit, Dhanus 19, Pūrva 3, Wednesday, Śravaṇa. Records grant of a lease of certain temple lands to three private individuals, viz., Śeṇbagaraiyar, Parākrama-Pāṇḍya Vijayālayadēvar and Ariyarāyar. [See *Ep. Ind.*, Vol. XI, p. 139, where it is shown that the date corresponded to Wednesday, 16th December, A.D. 1422, after changing the third *tithi* to the second.]

263. 125 *of* 1908.—(Tamil.) On the same wall. A record in the twenty-third year of the Pāṇḍya king Māravarman *alias* Tribhuvanachakravartin Kulaśēkharadēva (I, 1268—1308), "who was pleased to take every country." One of the stones is misplaced. Continuation not traceable. Seems to record a list of temple lands acquired by sale and refers to the misbehaviour of a temple servant.

264. 126 *of* 1908.—(Tamil.) On the same wall. Records in Ś 1309, Prabhava, sale of rights and privileges attached to the place of the temple accountant, by the priests.

265. 127 *of* 1908.—(Tamil.) On the same wall. A record in Ś. 1309, Prabhava. Similar to the above. But, here, the sabhā takes the place of the temple priests.

266. 128 *of* 1908.—(Tamil.) On the same wall. A record in the twentieth year of the Pāṇḍya king Jaṭāvarman *alias* Tribhuvanachakravartin Vīra-Pāṇḍyadēva. Records that certain temple lands were leased out by the priests. [Vide *Ep. Ind.*, Vol. XI, p. 137, where it is shown from the details of the date (Rishabha 4, Pūrva 2, Rōhiṇi) that it corresponded to Sunday, 3rd May, A.D. 1318. The solar day, however, was the eighth and not the fourth.]

267. 129 *of* 1908.—(Tamil.) On the west wall of the same prākāra. A damaged record in the twenty-first year of the Pāṇḍya king Māravarman *alias* Tribhuvanachakravartin Sundara-Pāṇḍyadēva (I, 1216—35), "who was pleased to distribute the Chōḷa country." Records a sale of land to Śrīkaṇṭhaśiva, one of the Āchāryas residing in *Tirujñānasambanda-maṭha* at Tirupputtūr, by Malayamāṇikkam Tirukkānaippēruḍaiyān *alias* Maḷavachakravartin of Śembonmāri in Talaiyūr-nāḍu.

268. 130 *of* 1908.—(Tamil.) On the north wall of the first prākāra of the Agastyēśvara shrine in the same temple. A record in the second year of the Pāṇḍya king Tribhuvanachakravartin Sundara-Pāṇḍyadēva, in Dhanus 11, Pūrva 10, Wednesday, Aśvini. Records sale of land for the maintenance of a flower-garden which was founded by Ponpaṟṟiyuḍaiyān Viḻuppadaraiyar of Puḷḷūrkuḍi in Naḍuvir-kūṟṟu in the district of Miḻalai-kūṟṟam. [See *Ep. Ind.*, Vol. XI, p. 135, where it is shown that the date corresponded to 7th December, A.D. 1239.]

269. 131 *of* 1908.—(Tamil.) On the west wall of the second prākāra of the same temple. A record in the twelfth year of the Pāṇḍya king Māravarman *alias* Tribhuvanachakravartin Parākrama-Pāṇḍyadēva. The record gives a list of the gifts made by Uyyavandān Kaṇḍidēva *alias* Gāṅgēya to the temple of Tiruttaḷiyāṇḍār at Tirupputtūr.

270. 132 *of* 1908.—(Tamil.) On the south wall of the same prākāra. A damaged record in the ninth year of the Pāṇḍya king Māravarman *alias* Tribhuvanachakravartin Kulaśēkharadēva (I, 1268—1308), "who was pleased to take every country."

271. 133 *of* 1908.—(Tamil.) On the same wall. A damaged record in the thirty-sixth year of the Pāṇḍya king Māravarman *alias* Tribbhuvanachakravartin Kulaśēkharadēva (I, 1268—1308), "who was pleased to take every country." Records gift of land to a certain Perumbaṟṟappuliyūr-nambi by the temple priests. Records that in the thirty-fourth year of the reign of the king a certain Vaḷḷuvanāḍāḷvān took possession of the village and dispossessed the donee of his lands.

272. 134 *of* 1908.—(Tamil.) On the west wall of the store room in the same temple. An incomplete record in the tenth year of the Pāṇḍya king Jaṭāvarman *alias* Tribhuvanachakravartin Vīra-Pāṇḍyadēva. Refers to the shrine of Sūryadēva in the temple of Tiruttaḷiyāṇḍa-Nāyanār and to the Kannaḍiya horsemen from a foreign country.

273. 135 *of* 1908.—(Tamil.) On the same wall. An incomplete record in the twenty-third year of the Pāṇḍya king Tribhuvanachakravartin Kulaśēkharadēva. Seems to record a gift of four water-pots for the sacred bath by Avanimuḻuduḍaiyār, wife of Dēvaragaṇḍan.

274. 136 *of* 1908.—(Grantha and Vaṭṭeḻuttu.) On a slab built into the floor of the first prākāra of the same temple. A record in the tenth year of the Pāṇḍya king Mārañjaḍaiyan. Records gift of ten *dīnāras* (*kāśu* in Tamil) for a lamp to the temple of Tiruttaḷipperumānaḍigaḷ by a Brāhmaṇi.

275. 137 *of* 1908.—(Grantha and Vaṭṭeḻuttu.) On a second slab built into the same floor. A damaged record in the fourth year and 4,535th day of the Pāṇḍya king Varaguṇa-Mahārāya. Records gift of money for one lamp and eleven flower garlands by Maravan-Aṇukkapperaraiyan *alias* Kaḍamban-Vēḷān to the temple of Tiruttaḷipaḍārar, at Tirupputtūr, a *brahmadēya* in Koḷuvūrkūṟṟam.

276. 138 *of* 1908.—(Vaṭṭeḻuttu.) On a slab lying in the Aṅgālamman temple in the same village. A record of the Pāṇḍya king Māraṅjaḍaiyan, the date of which is lost. Records gift of sheep for a lamp to the temple of Jalaśayanattuppaḍārar at Tirupputtūr, a *brahmadēya* in Koḷuvūr-kūṟṟam, by Manōmayan Māran of Veṇbaikkuḍi-nāḍu.

277. 139 *of* 1908.—(Tamil.) On the second slab set up in the same temple. A much damaged record in Ś. 1476, Ānanda. Mentions Aṅgālamman.

278. 140 *of* 1908.—(Tamil.) On the south wall of the Ninṟa-Nārāyaṇa Perumāḷ temple in the same village. A record in the twenty-first year of the Pāṇḍya king Sundara-Pāṇḍyadēva. Records gift of land to the temple of Kōlavarāhaviṇṇagar-Emberumān by the chief Gāṅgēyan.

Tiruvāḍānai Taluk.

Hanumantaguḍi.

279. 408 *of* 1907.—(Tamil.) On stones lying in front of the Maḷavanātha (Jaina) temple. A fragment of record in Ś. 1455, expired, of the Vijayanagara king whose name is lost. One of them mentions Jinēndramaṅgalam *alias* Kuruvaḍimidi . . . in Muttōoru-kūṟṟam and Añjukōṭṭai in the same kūṟṟam.

280. In the local masjid. A stone epigraph recording gift of lands to a Mussalmān in Ś. 1595 (A.D. 1673) by Tirumalai Sētupati Kātta Tēvar. [*Antiquities*, Vol. I, p. 298.]

281. A C.P. grant in the masjid. Records gift of lands to a Mussalmān in Ś. 1666 (A.D. 1744) by Muttukumāra Vijaya Raghunātha Sētupati, son of Muttu Vijaya Raghunātha Sētupati and grandson of Hiraṇyagarbhayāji Muttu Vijaya Raghunātha Sētupati. [*Ibid.*, p. 298.]

Rājāsiṅgamaṅgalam.

282. 119 *of* 1910.—(Tamil.) On the north, west and south walls of the central shrine in the Kailāsanāthasvāmin temple. A record of the Pāṇḍya king Jaṭāvarman *alias* Tribhuvanachakravartin, the date of which is lost. Stones out of order. Mentions Rājasiṁha-maṅgalam, a *brahmadēya* in Varaguṇa-vaḷanāḍu.

Tiruvāḍānai.

283. 433 *of* 1914.—(Tamil.) On the main gōpura of the Ādiratnēśvara temple, right of entrance. Registers in Ś. 1557, Yuva,

Tai, fourteenth day, śu. di. Paurṇami, Pushya, corresponding to January 12, A.D. 1636, an order of Tirumalaiyan that each village had to pay one *kāśu*, one *paṇam* and one *kalam* of paddy to the temple of Āḍānai Nāyakar for the merit of Sētupatidēvar. [The local god was so called because, it is said, Bhrigu got relief from God Śiva from the goat's head and elephant's body with which he had been cursed by sage Durvāsas.]

284. 434 *of* 1914.—(Tamil.) In the same place. A record in the seventeenth year of Tribhuvanachakravartin Kōnērinmaikoṇḍān. The stone is cut off at the right end. Seems to register gift of paddy.

285. 435 *of* 1914.—(Tamil.) On the same gōpura ; left of entrance. A record in the sixteenth year of the Pāṇḍya king Māravarman *alias* Sundara-Pāṇḍya "who having taken the Chōḷa country was pleased to perform the anointment of heroes and the anointment of victors at Muḍigoṇḍachōḷapuram." The stone is cut off at the right end. Seems to register a gift of land.

286. 436 *of* 1914.—(Tamil.) On a slab set up near the tank in the same temple. Records in Ś. 1642, Vikāri, the digging of the Sūryapuṭkaraṇi tank in front of the temples of Āḍānai Nāyakar and Anbirpiriyāda-Amman for the merit of Muttuvayiravanātha Sētupati Kāttadēvar.

287-288. Mr. Sewell mentions two C.P. grants in the temple, dated Ś. 1601 (A.D. 1679) recording gift of lands by Hiraṇyagarbha Sētupati. [*Antiquities*, Vol. I, p. 302.]

SALEM DISTRICT.

Āttūr Taluk.

Āragal (Āragaḷūr).

Āragaḷūr was in Aṛṛūṛkuṛṛam, a subdivision of Magadai Maṇḍalam in Malāḍu or Jananāthavaḷanāḍu (which extended into modern South Arcot district).

1. 408 *of* 1913.—(Tamil.) On the north wall of the central shrine in the Kāmēśvara temple. An incomplete record of the Vijayanagara king Kumāra Vīra-Narasiṁha Bhujabala Vasanta-rāya in Ś. 1430, *Vibhava, Kumbha, śu. di.* 7, Friday, *Śubhayōga*, corresponding to Friday, January 26, A.D. 1509. Registers that Eṛamāñchi Timmaya-Nāyaka's son Tulukkaṇa-Nāyaka, provided a car which had not existed since the time of the Pāṇḍya king to the temple of Tirukkāmīśvaram-uḍaiya-Tambirānār at Āragaḷūr in Aṛṛūr-kūṛṛam, a subdivision of Magada maṇḍalam in Malāḍu *alias* Jananātha-vaḷanāḍu. [Bhujabala was Nuniz's Busbal Rao and the elder brother of Kṛishṇadēva Rāya. His title *Viravasanta* is met for the first time in this epigraph. The *Kōyiloḷugu* refers to Eramāñchi Timma Nāyaka and says that Uttamanambi, the manager of the Śrīraṅgam shrine, received in Ś. 1409 as many as 20 villages from him. He is styled the inspirer of fear in the Chēra, Chōḷa, Pāṇḍya and Vallāla kings, the establisher of Yādavarāya and enemy of Śambuvarāya.]

2. 409 *of* 1913.—(Tamil.) On the same wall. A record of the Vijayanagara king Kṛishṇadēva-Mahārāya in Ś. 1435, *Bhāva, Simha, śu. di.* 11, Wednesday, Svāti. Registers that Eṛamāñchi Akki-Timmaya-Nāyaka rehabilitated the deserted village of Paṇattaḷai, a *dēvadāna* and *sarvamānya* of the same temple, under the name Immaḍi-Tulukkaṇa Nāyakkan pēṭṭai and fixed certain taxes which were evidently collected by the temple. [The date is irregular and inconsistent. The Kaikkōḷars and other classes who took the village as *Kaṭṭukkuttagai* had to pay 3 *paṇams* for each loom and 3 for each plough, but were free from obligations and assessments like *ecāchōru, variśōru, āḷamañji, etc.*]

3. 410 *of* 1913.—(Tamil.) On the same wall. A record in the fourth year of the Chōḷa king Tribhuvanachakravartin Rājarāja-dēva (III ?). Records gift of the village Naraittalai Nāvalūr to the temple of Tirukkāmīśvaram-uḍaiya-Nāyanār at Āragaḷūr in Aṛṛūr-kūṛṛam, a subdivision of Magada-maṇḍalam, for burning 150 lamps in the shrines of the god and goddess and the subsidiary shrines.

4. 411 *of* 1913.—(Tamil.) On the south base of the same shrine. Records in Ś. 1430, *Vibhava, Kumbha, śu. di.* 10, Sunday, Āślēsha, that Eramāñchi Tulukkaṇa-Nāyaka, seeing that the temple of Tirukkāmīśuram-Uḍaiya-Nāyanār at Āragaḷūr was not provided with festive processions since the time of the Pāṇḍya, constructed a car for it and fixed the days for the festivals. Also registers a grant of land by the temple authorities and a house to a certain *kaikkolan* called Parayan of Tāmadanallūr. The date is irregular. See *Ep. Rep.*, 1914, p. 73, for details.

5. 412 *of* 1913.—(Tamil.) On the west base of the same shrine. A record of the Sāḷuva king Dharmarāya (Immaḍi Narasiṁha), son of Sāḷuva Naraśiṅga Bhujabhala Dēva-Mahārāya (i.e., the celebrated usurper Naraśiṅga) in Ś. 1426, *Raktākshi, Simha, śu. di.* 13, Friday, Svāti. Registers that Pākkambāḍi, a village in Tenkarai Naraiyūr-kūṟṟam, a district of Magadai-maṇḍalam in Malāḍu *alias* Jananāthavaḷanāḍu, was for a long time a *dēvadāna* of the temple and that subsequently taxes *(rājāgaram kāṇikkai)* were collected from it; Eramāñchi Tulukkaṇa-Nāyaka restored the village to the temple with all its income for worship and repairs. [Mr. Swamikannu Pillai calculates the corresponding date to be Friday, April 26, A.D. 1504, but the solar month was not *Simha* but *Mēsha.*]

6. 413 *of* 1913.—(Tamil.) On the north base of the same shrine. Registers in Raktākshi, Kārttigai, twenty-seventh day, the decision of Tirumalli Nāyaka regarding the right of worship in the temple of Tirukkāmīśvaram-uḍaiya-Nāyanār.

7. 414 *of* 1913.—(Tamil.) On the same base. A record in the thirteenth year, Tai, of the Hoysaḷa king Rāmanāthadēva. Registers an order of Rāhuttarāyan that the village Nattamaṅgalam in Śēla-nāḍu which was given to him as a *jivita* by the king, was now granted with all its income as a rent-free *dēvadāna* to the temple of Tirukkāmīśvaram-uḍaiya-Nāyanār at Āragaḷūr, for maintaining worship and repairs.

8. 415 *of* 1913.—(Tamil.) On the south wall of the maṇṭapa in front of the same shrine. A record of the Chōḷa king Tribhuvanachakravartin Rājarājadēva (III) in his fourteenth year *Rishabha, ba. di.* 7, Monday, *Dhanishṭha* (corresponding, according to Mr. Swamikannu Pillai, to Monday, 6th May, A.D. 1230). Records grant of 15,000 *kāśu* by a certain Nāchchi for maintaining worship, sacred bath, garlands, cloths, lamps, oil, offerings and festivals in the shrine of Kāriyāṇa-Īśvaramuḍaiya-Nāyanār set up in the north-west corner of the first enclosure in the temple of Tirukkāmīśvaram-uḍaiya-Nāyanār. The donation was accepted by the servants of the temple.

9. 416 *of* 1913.—(Tamil.) On the same wall. A record in the fifteenth year of the Chōḷa king Tribhuvanachakravartin Kulōttuṅga-Chōḷadēva (III). Registers that the village of Ilattipāḍi which had been purchased from Malaiyanuḍai-Śambai by the trustees, was made tax-free in favour of the same temple, for maintaining worship, festivals and repairs by the trustees of that temple. The document is attested by the officers Vānakōvaraiyan and Villavarāyan.

10. 417 *of* 1913.—(Tamil.) On the same wall. A record in the thirteenth year of the Chōḷa king Tribhuvanachakravartin Kulōttuṅga-Chōḷadēva (III). Records sale of Ilattipāḍi to the trustees of the temple by Malaiyanuḍaiyān Śambaiyāḷvān, for 135 *pon.*

11. 418 *of* 1913.—(Tamil.) On the same wall. A record of the Chōḷa king Tribhuvanachakravartin Kulōttuṅga-Chōḷadēva (III) in his twenty-ninth year, *Kanyā, śu. di.* 2, Wednesday, *Hasta* (corresponding to September 6, A.D. 1206). Records gift of 5,000 *kāśu* for maintaining the sacred bath, twilight lamps, garlands, cloths and offerings to the three saints *(emberumakkaḷ)* (i.e., Appar, Sundarar and Sambandar) set up in the temple of Tirukkāmīśvaram-uḍaiya-Nāyanār at Āragaḷūr. [The date in reality refers to Tuesday, September 5 and not September 6. See *Ep. Rep.*, 1914, p. 64.]

12. 419 *of* 1913.—(Tamil.) On the south base of the same maṇṭapa. A record in the fifteenth year of the Pāṇḍya king Jaṭāvarman *alias* Tribhuvanachakravartin Sundara-Pāṇḍyadēva (I, ? 1251—64). Registers a gift of 1,000 *kuḻi* of land, made rent-free in the thirteenth year of the king, for the maintenance of two Brāhmaṇas who recited the Vēdas in the temple, by the chief Śēdirāyan. Also at the command of the king, the *nāṭṭār* inhabiting the districts included between the rivers Vēmbarāṟu and Peṇṇai were required to assign certain specified taxes to the temple for the health of the king. The *nāṭṭār*, having, however, collected the *kāṇikkai-paṇam* in the fifteenth year of the king, they were ordered to return the collections immediately to the temple.

13. 420 *of* 1913.—(Tamil.) On the same base. A record of the Sāḷuva king Tamarāya Immaḍi-Narasa Nāyaka (son of Narasiṅga) in Ś. 1427, *Krōdhana, Makara, śu. di.* 3, Sunday, *Dhanishṭha, Mahā-Saṁkrānti* day. Registers that Allāḷanātha Iḷaiya-Nāyaka and the inhabitants of Āṟṟur-nāḍu and Mulaippāṟu-nāḍu, having met together, provided for supplying oil to burn perpetual lamps and twilight lamps in the temple for the health of Eṛamāñchi-Tulukkaṇa-Nāyaka. [Mr. Swamikannu Pillai points out that in January 11, A.D. 1506, the intended date, the week day is correct, but not Kṛttikā or Dhanishṭha. Nor was it *Saṅkrānti* of any kind.]

14. 421 *of* 1913.—(Tamil.) On the same base. Registers in his seventh year that the chiefs Vānakōvaraiyan and Villavaraiyan granted annually ten of their bull-calves as *vrishabhas* to the temple and assigned the remainder for work in connexion with temple repairs including that of the enclosure wall called *Ponparappina Perumāḷ-tirumadil.*

15. 422 *of* 1913.—(Tamil.) On the same base. Registers in Plava, Māśi, tenth day, a pledge *(aḍai-ōlai)* granted by Tyāgaṇa-Nāyaka to the inhabitants of the districts *(nāṭṭār)* of Magadai-maṇḍalam who had left the country owing to much oppression. Mentions svāmi Īśvara-Nāyaka.

16. 423 *of* 1913.—(Tamil.) On the same base. Built in at the beginning. Fixes the details of *aḍandēṟṟam* to be observed by the inhabitants of Magadai-maṇḍalam.

17. 424 *of* 1913.—(Tamil.) On the same base. A record in the 13th year and 319th day of Tribhuvanachakravartin Kōnērin-mēlkoṇḍān. Registers the grant of the village Ālambaḷam in Magadai-maṇḍalam with all its income for instituting a service in the temple called Kōdaṇḍarāman śāndi, after the king, for celebrating a festival on his birthday every year and for repairs. Attested by Kaḷiṅgarāya.

18. 425 *of* 1913.—(Tamil.) On the north wall of the same maṇṭapa. A record of the Pāṇḍya king Jaṭāvarman *alias* Tribhuvanachakravartin Sundara-Pāṇḍyadēva in his tenth year Mīna, śu. di. 13, Thursday, Makha. Registers that the king granted ½ *vēli* of land at Ponparappi *alias* Rājanārāyaṇanallūr as a *dēvadāna* to the shrines of Kulaśēkhara Āvuḍaiyār and Vāḷvitta Maṅgaiyār which Kaṇḍiyadēva had founded in the same temple in the name of the king's elder brother *(annāḷvi).* Attested by Ādichchan Gaṇapati Āḷvān *alias* Kāḍuveṭṭi of Kappalūr in Muttūṟṟukūṟṟam, a subdivision of Pāṇḍi-maṇḍalam. Mr. Swamikannu Pillai points out that two dates are possible, viz., Thursday, February 26, A.D. 1260 or Thursday, February 27, 1287. The latter would be the eleventh year (not the tenth) of that Jaṭāvarman Sundara Pāṇḍya who ruled from 1276 to 1290 and the former would be in the ninth (but very near the tenth) year of his namesake who ruled from 1251 to 1264. Mr. Swamikannu Pillai considers the latter to be more probable as the king has the title *Samastajagadādhāra.*

19. 426 *of* 1913.—(Tamil.) On the same wall. A record of the Pāṇḍya king Jaṭāvarman *alias* Tribhuvanachakravartin Sundara-Pāṇḍyadēva (I, ? 1251—64) in his ninth year, Āḍi. Records gift of 3,000 *kuḷi* of wet land below the tank Kulaśēkharan-Periyēri at Āragaḷūr, to the shrine of Kulaśēkhara-Āvuḍaiyār mentioned above, for offerings. [The mention of a Kulaśēkhara as the elder brother of the king shows that he had a co-regent or predecessor in him. Mr. Swamikannu Pillai postulates from astronomical details the accession of a Kulaśēkhara in 1237 (see *Ind. Antq.*, Vol. 42) and this might be the person intended.]

20. 427 *of* 1913.—(Tamil.) On the same wall. A record of the Vijayanagara king Kṛishṇarāya (A.D. 1509—30) in Ś. 1430, Śukla,

Mīna, śu. di. 7, Thursday, Viśākha. The king receives Sāḷuva titles. Registers that Eṟamāñchi Tulukkaṇa-Nāyaka built a car for the temple which had not been in existence subsequent to the rule of the Pāṇḍya kings, instituted a festival called after Śivili-Nāyaka and appointed a private individual providing him with maintenance, for carrying the god in processions *(śri-pātam tāṅgi)*. [The date is an irregular one.]

21. 428 *of* 1913.—(Tamil.) On the same wall. An incomplete record of the Vijayanagara king Kṛishṇadēva-Mahārāya in Ś. 1436, Yuvan, Mithuna, śu. ḍi. 5, Monday, Aśvini. The king receives Śāḷuva titles. Records that Akki-Timmaya Nāyaka of Eṟamāñchi and the temple authorities together, granted to a private individual, 250 *kuḻi* of land as *uramai.* [This is also an irregular date. See *Ep. Rep.*, 1914, p. 68.]

22. 429 *of* 1913.—(Tamil.) On the same wall. A record in the ninth year, Māśi, nineteenth day of the Pāṇḍya king Jaṭāvarman *alias* Tribhuvanachakravartin Sundara-Pāṇḍyadēva (I, 1251—64), "who took every country." Records gift of 2,000 *kuḻi* of wet land below the tank Kulaśēkharan Periyēri for a garden, by the king. Attested by Āchchan Gaṇapati Āḷvān *alias* Kāḍuveṭṭi, native of Kappalūr, *alias* Ulagaḷandaśōḷanallūr in Muttūṟṟu-kūṟṟam, a subdivision of Pāṇḍi-maṇḍalam.

23. 430 *of* 1913.—(Tamil.) On the north base of the same maṇṭapa. A record of the Vijayanagara king Viruppaṇṇa Uḍaiyār (Virūpāksha I), son of Vīra-Ariyaṇa-Uḍaiyār (Harihara II), in Ś. 1306, Raktākshi, Mēsha, śu. di. (Paurṇami), Wednesday, Svāti, (corresponding to Wednesday, April 6, A.D. 1384). Registers the sale of the right *(kāṇi)* of worship by three priests of the temple of Tirukkāmīśvaramuḍaiya-Nāyanār at Āragaḷūr to a priest of the temple of Tiruvalañjiram Uḍaiya-Nāyanār at Valañjiram in Pānūr-kūṟṟam, a subdivision of Malāḍu *alias* Jananātha-Vaḷanāḍu, in Magadai-maṇḍalam.

24. 431 *of* 1913.—(Tamil.) On the same base. A record of the Vijayanagara king Vīra-Kampaṇṇa-Ūḍaiyār, son of Vīra-Bukkaṇṇa-Uḍaiyār II, in Ś. 1297, Rākshasa, Vrischika, śu. di. 11, Friday, Rōhiṇi. The servants of the temple, viz., the *śri-rudras, śri-mahēś-varas* and temple accountants having assembled together, gave to a certain Ennuḍaiya Nāyanār, son of Aghōraśiva-Mudaliyār, the work of supervising the different services in the temple and a house for his living. Mr. Swamikannu Pillai says that the week day and solar month are wrong, and Rākshasa, śu. 11, Rōhiṇi, fell on Thursday, 3rd January 1376.

25. 432 *of* 1913.—(Tamil.) On the same base. A record of the Pāṇḍya king Jaṭāvarman *alias* Tribhuvanachakravartin Sundara-Pāṇḍyadēva III (1276—90), in his thirteenth year, Mithuna, śu. di. 13, Friday, Anurādha, corresponding to Friday, June 3, A.D. 1289.

Refers to a dispute between the oil-merchants *(Vāṇiya-nagarattār)* and the *śeṭṭis* in which the latter permitted the former to manage the business of the temple. The management continued to be in the hands of the oil-merchants for sometime. This having failed, the district people *(nāṭṭavar)* granted the village of Talaivāy for conducting permanently the festivals in the temple. [The inscription is of social interest, and shows how caste disputes in regard to the management of temples existed in those days.]

26. 433 *of* 1913.—(Tamil.) On the same base. A damaged record of the Vijayanagara king Achyutadēva-Mahārāya (1530—42) in Ś. 1461, Vikarin, Kanyā, śu. di. 7, Friday, Mūla (corresponding to Friday, September 19, A.D. 1539). Seems to record a grant of land, and the *mathāpatya* to a private individual for doing the duties of the temple *(kōyil-ūḷiyam)*.

27. 434 *of* 1913.—(Tamil.) On the same base. Registers in the thirteenth year, Paṅguni, that the temples of Tirukkāmīśuram-uḍaiya-Nāyanār, Tāyilunalla-śōḷīśuram-uḍaiya-Nāyanār and Ponparappina-śōḷīśuram-uḍaiya-Nāyanār were granted as *kāṇi* to a certain Śēramānār. Also 200 *kuḷi* of wet land and 2,000 *kuḷi* of dry land were given to this same person in the villages of Kurukkaipāḍi, Pākkanpāḍi, Ilattipāḍi and Viśalūr.

28. 435 *of* 1913.—(Tamil.) On the west wall of the same maṇṭapa; right of entrance. A record in the thirty-fifth year of the Chōḷa king Tribhuvanachakravartin Kulōttuṅga-Chōḷadēva (III). Registers a political compact between Śeṅgēṇi Ammaiyappan Aḷagiyaśōḷan *alias* Ediriliśōḷachchambuvarāyan and the chiefs Ponparappina-Vānakōvaraiyar, Kulōttuṅgaśōḷa Vānakōvaraiyar, and brother-in-law *(maichchunānār)* Kāḍavarāyar. The latter three chiefs bind themselves not to be enemies of the first and give no shelter to offenders against him, and he in turn vows to do the same. If he acted against this he would be "the bearer of shoes and betel-bags both to his kinsmen and to his enemies" and not the son of his father! See No. 33 below.

29. 436 *of* 1913.—(Tamil.) On the wall behind the dvārapāla image in the same maṇṭapa; right of entrance. A record of the Chōḷa king Tribhuvanachakravartin Rājarājadēva (III) in (date is lost) Tulā, ba. di. 4, Monday. Built in at the end. Records gift of 2,000 *kāśu* for one lamp and of 49 cows for seven other lamps to be burnt in the temple of Tirukkāmīśvaram-uḍaiya-Nāyanār and subordinate shrines.

30. 437 *of* 1913.—(Tamil.) In the same place; left of entrance. A record in the twelfth year of the Chōḷa king Rājarājadēva. Built in at the beginning. Records gift of land for offerings by Āchchi who has been mentioned in No. 8 above.

31. 438 *of* 1913.—(Tamil.) On the south wall of the second prākāra of the same temple. Records in the tenth year an order from the king to the managers of the temple, stating that the weavers settled by them outside the northern gate of Āragaḷūr were to be cultivators *(kuḍimakkaḷ)* of the *dēvadāna* lands belonging to the shrine of Kulaśēkhara-Āḷuḍaiyār founded in this temple by the chief Kaṇḍiyadēvar. Attested by Ādittan Gaṇapati-Āḷvān *alias* Kāḍuveṭṭi of Kappalūr.

32. 439 *of* 1913.—(Tamil.) On the north wall of the same prākāra. A record of the Pāṇḍya king . . . *alias* Tribhuvana-chakravartin Sundara-Pāṇḍyadēva (I ?) in his twelfth year, Mēsha, śu. di. Pūrṇai, Thursday, Svāti. The right of worship for 3⅛ days of a month in the temple which had been owned by a certain lady was ordered to be sold evidently on account of the defalcation of temple jewels by her and her accomplices. The lady was arrested by the temple *mahēśvaras* and officers who then met in a maṇṭapa and decided that 250 *paṇam* (=25,000 *śōḷiya kāśu*) was to be paid by the other worshippers of the temple for distributing among themselves the privileges that were under sale. [The inscription is of value in illustrating the method of temple management. In discussing the date of the inscription Mr. Swamikannu Pillai says that it might be taken to be either Thursday, April 6, A.D. 1262, in the eleventh (very near the twelfth) year of Jaṭāvarman Sundara Pāṇḍya I (1251—1264), or Thursday, April 23, A.D. 1282 in the twelfth year of a king of the same name who, according to his own researches, ascended the throne in 1271. See *Ind. Antq.*, Vol. 42, June and Aug. 1913.]

33. 440 *of* 1913.—(Tamil.) On the east wall of the same prākāra ; right of entrance. A record in the thirteenth year (of an unknown king). Stones out of order. Refers to the terms of a political compact between the two chiefs Rājarājadēvan Ponparappinār *alias* Kulōttuṅgaśōḷa-Vānakōvaraiyar and Kiḷyūr Malaiyamān of Tirukkōvalūr. They fix the boundaries of their dominions, bind themselves not to oppose each other, combine in serving the king and defend each other against external enemies. [See No. 28. The Government Epigraphist sees in these political compacts the decline of the Chōḷa central government.]

34. 441 *of* 1913.—(Tamil.) On the same wall ; left of entrance. Records in the thirteenth year, Pūraṭṭādi, gift of 3,000 *kuḻi* of wet land reclaimed from forest in the village of Dēviyakuruchchi in Āṟṟūr-nāḍu for worship and repairs in the shrines of Kulaśēkhara-Āḷuḍaiyār and Vāḷvitta-Maṅgaiyār in the temple of Tirukkāmīś-varam-uḍaiya-Nāyanār at Āragaḷūr. Attested by Kāḍuveṭṭi, chief of Kappalūr.

35. 442 *of* 1913.—(Tamil.) On the same wall ; left of entrance. Records in the eleventh year, Āvaṇi, gift of land, tax free, for the maintenance of the gardeners of a flower-garden belonging to the temple of Tirukkāmīśvaram-uḍaiya-Nāyanār. Attested by the same person.

36. 443 *of* 1913.—(Tamil.) On the same wall; left of entrance. Registers an order of the king to the managers of the temple stating that the service Ulagamuḻuduḍaiyāḷ-śandi founded in his name was to be maintained from the 8,500 *kuḻi* of land granted at Ālambaḷam in Naraiyūr-kūṟṟam, a subdivision of Milāḍu *alias* Jananātha-vaḷanāḍu.

37. 444 *of* 1913.—(Tamil.) On the same wall; left of entrance. Records in the eleventh year, Āḍi, gift of four *vēlis* of wet land in Āṟṟūr for feeding ten persons in the temple. Attested by Kāḍuveṭṭi.

38. 445 *of* 1913.—(Tamil.) On the north base of the central shrine in the Karivaradarāja-Perumāḷ temple in the same village. A record of the Śāḷuva king Dharmarāya (i.e., Immaḍi Narasiṁha), son of Śāḷuva Naraśiṅgarāya in Ś. 1444, Durmati, Simha, śu. di. 10, Monday, Hasta. The third figure of the Śaka year must be two. Records that a certain Ammaṇa-Nāyakka gave to the temple of Karivarada-Perumāḷ at Āragaḷūr, the fee called *aḍimai-kāśu* collected from the Kaikkōḷas and a female servant *(aḍiyāḷ)* providing for her maintenance in order that svāmi Narasa-Nāyaka may be victorious in his *digvijaya*. See No. 43. [Shows that Tuḷuva Narasa was *de facto* king while Immaḍi Narasiṁha was ruling. The date is declared by Mr. Swamikannu Pillai to be irregular as Śukla 10 and Hasta can join in *Rishabha* and not Siṁha.]

39. 446 *of* 1913.—(Tamil.) On the north wall of the same shrine. Registers in the fourth year, Paṅguni, twelfth day, an order of Vānakōvaraiyan that wet and dry lands in different villages were to be purchased as *Viramāgadapperuvilai*, the former at 6 *kāśu* per *kuḻi* and the latter one at 2 *kāśu* per *kuḻi*, and granted as *tirunāmattukkāṇi* to the temple of Kariya-Perumāḷ at Āragaḷūr.

40. 447 *of* 1913.—(Tamil.) On the same wall. Records that the *Śrivimāna* (i.e., central shrine) of this Kariya-Perumāḷ temple called also Rājarāja-Viṇṇagār was built of stone by Puṇyavatiyār, wife of Rājarāja-Vānakōvaraiyan. She was the daughter of Iraṇan Kōvalarāyan.

41. 448 *of* 1913.—(Tamil.) On the east base of the same shrine. Records in the thirteenth year (of an unknown king), Pūraṭṭādi, an eclipse (not specified), gift of 1,000 *kuḻi* of wet land below the tank at Ponparappi *alias* Rājanārāyaṇanallūr for oblations and repairs to the shrine of Śiṅga (i.e., Nṛisiṁha) in the temple of Kariya-Perumāḷ in order to secure happiness to the king's elder brother *(annāḻvi)* Sundara-Pāṇḍya. Attested by Ādittan Gaṇapati-Āḻvān of Kappalūr who was surnamed Vāṇadarāyan.

42. 449 *of* 1913.—(Tamil.) On the same base. A record of the Vijayanagara king Kṛishṇadeva Mahārāya (1509—30) in Ś. 1441,

Pramāthin, Mithuna, śu. di. 13, Friday, Anurādha. Registers that three *sthānikas* of the temple of Perumāḷ-Kariyavar went on a deputation to the king, to Vijayanagara and complained of the injustice done by the authorities *(rājāgaram)* stationed at Dēviyakuruchchi, a village belonging to the temple. The chief *Amaram* Timmarasa introduced them to the king, got their grievance redressed, presented them each with a garland, a head dress, a horse and an umbrella, and granted 900 *kuḻi* of wet land at Ponparappi and at Dēviyakuruchchi, as *sarvamānya* gift. [The date has been verified to be Friday, June 10, A.D. 1519.]

43. 450 *of* 1913.—(Tamil.) On the south base of the same shrine. A record of the Śāḷuva king Tammayyarāya, son of Śāḷuva-Naraśiṅgarāya (the founder of the Śāḷuva dynasty) in Ś. 1424, Rudhirōdgārin (wrong), Siṁha, śu. di. 10, Friday, Svāti. A certain Tammayya-Nāyaka in the name of his master Kumārasvāmi-Ammaṇa-Nāyaka granted land at Śiṟṟēri, a hamlet of Āragaḷūr, to three worshippers in the temple of Perumāḷ-Kariyavar who were in the enjoyment of the privilege called *archanāvibhava-kāṇi* for the victory of Narasa Nāyaka. The Government Epigraphist points out that this as well as No. 38 refer to the latter part of the year in which Narasa Nāyaka died and was succeeded by his son Vīra Narasiṁha. [The date is irregular.]

44. 451 *of* 1913.—(Tamil.) On the south base of maṇṭapa in front of the same shrine. A record of the Vijayanagara king Kṛishṇadēva-Mahārāya (1509—30) in Ś. 1446, Tāraṇa, Makara 11, Rēvati, Friday, Saṁkramaṇa-puṇyakāla. The record gives a genealogy of the king from Tammayyarāya. Registers a grant of eight Emberumān-aḍiyār for service in the temple of Kariya-Perumāḷ and a provision of 1,000 *kuḻi* of land for their maintenance, by a certain Mrityuñjaya-Nāyaka for the merit of his master Tirumalai-Nāyaka. The date is declared by Mr. Swamikannu Pillai to be irregular as Śukla 11 and Rēvati can join in Vrischika, not in Makara.

45. 452 *of* 1913.—(Tamil.) On the north base of the same maṇṭapa. A record of the Vijayanagara king Achyutadēva-Mahārāya, "who levied tribute from all countries", in Ś. 1454, Nandana, Kumbha, śu. di. 3, Monday, Uttara-Bhādrapada, corresponding to Monday, January 27, A.D. 1533. (But *Uttara* Bhādrapāda is wrong for *purva* Bhādrapada.) The epigraph is to the effect that Kaṇṇan, a *kaikkōḷa* of Kuhaiyūr, having instituted a car festival in the temple, the managers met together in the Sōpāna-maṇṭapa and decided to grant him and his descendants, a house, a loom, a piece of land and some privileges in the temple.

46. 453 *of* 1913.—(Tamil.) On the south wall of the Kamalamaṅgai shrine in the same temple. A record in the eighteenth year of the Pāṇḍya king Jaṭāvarman *alias* Tribhuvanachakravartin

Sundara-Pāṇḍyadēva (I, ? 1251—64). Records gift of 1,000 *kuḻi* of land below the tank at Toḻuvūr for worship and repairs in the temple of Vairāvaṇa-Īśvaram-uḍaiya-Nāyanār at Āragaḷūr.

47. 454 *of* 1913.—(Tamil.) On the south base of the Chōḷēś-vara temple in the same village. Records in the ninth year (of ?), Paṅguni, eighth day, gift of the village Kurukkaipāḍi for worship and repairs in the temple of Tāyilumnalla-Chōḷēśvaram-uḍaiya-Nāyanār at Āragaḷūr. Attested by Vānakōvaraiyan and Viḻup-pādarāyan and order communicated to Vilāḍarāya, and the accountants (*puravariyār*).

48. 455 *of* 1913.—(Tamil.) On the north base of the same temple. Records in the seventh year (of an unknown king) gift of land at Kīḻ-Magaṟūr to the same temple. Attested and communicated as before.

Āttūr.

49. 403 *of* 1913.—(Tamil.) On the south base of the Kāya-nirmalēśvara temple. A record of the Vijayanagara king Kṛishṇa-rāya (1509—30) in Ś. 1435, Śrīmukha, Śittirai, thirteenth day, 3, Friday, Rōhini, Saubhāgyayōga (which corresponded, according to Mr. Swamikannu Pillai, to Friday, 8th April, A.D. 1513). Registers that the chief Akki-Timmayya-Nāyaka who was ruling Malāḍu *alias* Jananātha-vaḷanāḍu in Magadai-maṇḍalam, gave the village called Villavarāyanattam on the northern bank of the river Nīvā, in the district of Aṟṟūr-kūṟṟam in Āṟṟūr-nāḍu, to a certain Śrīraṅga-rāja-bhaṭṭa, son of Aruṇagiri-nātha, a native of Iṟaivānaṟaiyur. The granted village received the surname Akki-Timmaya-Nāyaka-chaturvēdimaṅgalam, after the donor. See No. 52 below.

50. 404 *of* 1913.—(Tamil.) On the west base of the same temple. An incomplete record of the Vijayanagara king Vīrapra-tāpa Kṛishṇarāya-Mahārāya in Ś. 1449, Virōdhi (wrong), Siṁha, śu. di. 11, Sunday, Pushya. Seems to record the grant of a village for the merit of the king. The date corresponded to March 1st, A.D. 1528.

51. 405 *of* 1913.—(Tamil.) On the same base. Registers in the thirty-second year the order of Vaṇṇeñja-Perumāḷ that the gift of 200 *kuḻi* of wet land granted to the temple of Tirmēltaḷi-uḍaiya-Nāyanār at Āṟṟūr for maintaining lamps, was to be demarcated by *tri-śūla* stones and the transaction engraved on stone.

52. 406 *of* 1913.—(Tamil.) On the north base of the same temple. A damaged record in Ś. 1431, Śukla, Aipaśi, twenty-second day. Seems to refer to the gift of Kallinattam near Āṟṟūr in Āṟṟūr-nāḍu, a subdivision of Magadai-maṇḍalam, under the name Māyittāy-agaram by a certain Tulukkaṇa-Nāyaka, to Parpa-nābha-Bhaṭṭa, son of Aruṇagirinātha of Iṟaivānaṟaiyūr. The document was engraved on the *kumuḍappaḍai* in the temple of

Tirumēnitteḷivuḍaiya-Tambirānār at Āṟṟūr. Aruṇagirinātha is referred to in No. 49 and ought not to be confounded with the great Tamil poet and devotee of that name who was the contemporary of Dēvarāya II.

53. 407 *of* 1913.—(Tamil.) On a slab set up in the same temple. A record in the fourteenth year of Chōḷa king Parakēsarivarman. Records gift of paddy to the temple of Tirumēṟṟaḷi-Nāyakkar (or Āḷvār) at Malaiyamānāru, a *brahmadēya* in Āṟṟūr-kūṟṟam, which was a subdivision of Milāḍu, by three servants of that temple.

Eṭappūr (Eṭṭappūr).

54. Mr. Sewell gives a copper-plate inscription "in the town, dated Ś. 1636 (A.D. 1714), recording a deed of sale in the reign of Doḍḍa Kṛishṇa Uḍaiyār of Maisur." [*Antiquities*, Vol. I, p. 201 and *Salem Manual*, p. 87.]

Kariyarāman Kōyil.

55. In front of the temple on the hill. Le Fanu in his *Salem Manual*, p. 80, gives a translation of this epigraph. See Supplement.

Taḍāvūr.

56. 456 *of* 1913.—(Tamil.) On the south wall of the Ekāmranāthasvāmin temple. Records in the ninth year (of a king not given) gift of land at Vīraśōḷanallūr, to the temple Tiruvēgambam-Uḍaiya-Nāyanār at Taḍāvūr. Attested by Tāyilunalla-Perumāḷ and Viḷuppādarāyan and communicated to Vilāḍarāya and the accountants *(puravariyār)*.

57. 457 *of* 1913.—(Tamil.) On the same wall. A record in the tenth year of the Chōḷa king Vijayarājēndradēva (Kulōttuṅga III). Records gift of land for worship and repairs to the temples of Tiruvēgambam-uḍaiya-Nāyanār and Kunṟameṟinda-Perumāḷ.

58. 458 *of* 1913.—(Tamil.) On the same wall. A record in the twenty-seventh year of the Chōḷa king Tirubhuvanachakravartin Kulōttuṅga-Chōḷadēva III, "who was pleased to take Madurai (Madura) and the crowned head of the Pāṇḍya." Registers that the temple of Tiruvēgambam-uḍaiya-Nāyanār at Mēlgaṅgapāḍi *alias* Taḍāvūr in Āṟṟūr-kūṟṟam a subdivision of Milāḍu *alias* Jananāthavaḷanāḍu, was built of stone, the cost being met from gold already in possession of the temple and from what was presented now by the king and the youngest of the queens.

59. 459 *of* 1913.—(Tamil.) On the north wall of the same temple. Records in the seventeenth year (of ?), Vaikāśi, gift of land which had been lying waste for many years as a *dēvadāna* to the same temple for worship, repairs and festivals. Attested by Adittan Gaṇapati-Āḷvan *alias* Vāṇādarāyan of Kappalūr.

60. 460 *of* 1913.—(Tamil.) On the same wall. Records in the twentieth year and fifty-seventh day, Āvaṇi, gift of 500 *kuḻi* of land at Taḍāvūr as *kāṇi* to a certain Perukkāḷaparaiyan Pakkamaḷagiyan by Magadēśan Ulaṁgakātta Vānakōvaraiyan.

61. 461 *of* 1913.—(Tamil.) On the same wall. A record in the fifth year of the Chōḷa king Kulōttuṅga-Chōḷadēva (III). Records gift of land to the temple of Tiruvēgambam Uḍaiya-Nāyanār at Taḍāvūr in Mēl-Gaṅgapāḍi-nāḍu, a subdivision of Āṟṟūr-kūṟṟam in Malāḍu *alias* Jananātha-vaḷanāḍu, for worship, repairs and festivals, by Kulōttuṅgaśōḷa Vānakōvaraiyan.

62. 462 *of* 1913.—(Tamil.) On the same wall. A record in the ninth year of the Chōḷa king Vijayarājēndra-Chōḷadēva (i.e., Kulōttuṅga-Chōḷa III). Records gift of land to the same temple by the same chief.

63. 463 *of* 1913.—(Tamil.) On the same wall. Records in the seventh year gift of the village of Puttūr *alias* Mēl-Gaṅgapāḍi-nāḍu. Attested by Tāyilunalla-Perumāḷ and Viḷuppādarāyan and communicated to Vilāḍarāyar and the accountants of the temple.

64. 464 *of* 1913.—(Tamil.) On the stone through for the sacred *tirtha* in the same temple. Registers that this *nirmālya* trough was the gift of a certain Vāṇiyan Kāvan Kūttāṇḍān.

DHARMAPURI TALUK.

Adhamankōṭṭai.

65. 200 *of* 1910.—(Kanarese.) On a slab set up in front of the Aṅkālamma temple. A record of the Vijayanagara king Immaḍi-Achyutadēva-Mahārāya in Ś. 1452, *Vikriti.* Records gift of taxes (*āḷu* and *aḍikāśu*) collected from the people and stalls in an old market revived at the place to the temple of Bhairavadēva by a certain Kāmiyappa-Nāyaka, son of Madde Bommaiyappa Nāyaka, son of Bappa Nāyaka.

66. 201 *of* 1910.—(Tamil.) On the north and west bases of the Bhairava temple in the same village. A record of the Hoysaḷa king Vīra-Narasiṁhadēva in Kaliyuga 4336, Ś. 1157, and in his seventeenth year (i.e., A.D. 1235). Records that Paramaya Sāhaṇi, the minister of the Mahāpradhāni Paramaviśvāsi Mādhava-Daṇṇakkar, built and consecrated the temple of Paramēśvaram Uḍaiyār at Mahēndramaṅgalam and granted lands to Viḍugādar, the priest of that temple who was residing at Nandimaṅgalam. [From the Dindagur plates Kielhorn fixes Vīra Narasiṁha's accession on Thursday, the 16th April, A.D. 1220. See *Ep. Ind.*, Vol. V, Appendix II, p. 14. The Government Epigraphist infers from the present epigraph that his accession—perhaps as a crown prince—should have been one or two years earlier. He further points out that Vīra Narasiṁha was the first to interfere in the south; that he

rescued the Chōḷa king from the Kāḍava king Kōpperuñjiṅgadēva (see S.A. 329) and that it was on his return perhaps from that campaign that these gifts were made by his general.]

67. 202 *of* 1910.—(Tamil.) On the west wall of the same temple. A record of the Hoysaḷa king Rāmanāthadēva in Ś. 1182, and in his sixth year. Records gift of money for a lamp by a native of Maṅgalam to the temple of Mayindīśuram-Uḍaiyār. [The inscription proves that Rāmanātha came to the throne in 1255, apparently at the lifetime of his father. (See *Ep. Ind.*, Vol. III, p. 10).]

68. 203 *of* 1910.—(Tamil.) On the same wall. An unfinished record. Records gift of land to the temple of Paramēśuram Uḍaiyār at the eastern entrance into the village of Mayīndiramaṅgalam for the merit of Vīra-Sōmēśvaradēva and Sōmaya-Daṇṇakkar. Mentions Śiṅgaya Daṇṇakkar who was, perhaps, a son of Sōmaya. For Sōmaya see next inscription and also those at Ratnagiri (103 of 1892) and Tirumalavāḍi (73 of 1895). A servant of Sōmēśvara for a long time, he was honoured with the title *Kumāragaṇḍarakōva.*

69. 204 *of* 1910.—(Tamil.) On the south wall of the maṇṭapa in front of the same temple. A record of the Hoysaḷa king Sōmēśvaradēva (A.D. 1233—54) in Ś. 1171, Sādhāraṅa, and in his seventeenth year. Records gift of land below the tank of Kuḷattūr to the temple of Mayindīśuramuḍaiya-Nāyanār by Sōmaya-Daṇḍanāyaka for the health of the king. [The inscription shows that the first years of Vīra Sōmēśvara overlapped the last years of his father Vīra Narasiṁha II. Nj. 36 shows that he was at Kaṇṇanūr (taken by his father about 1224) in 1228. He helped his father against Kāḍavarāya and the Pāṇḍya in Ś. 1156. See *Ep. Carna.*, V, Ak. 123. Later on, he was in cordial terms with Māravarman Sundara Pāṇḍya II (see Tirumayyam and Tinnevelly inscriptions). With Jaṭāvarman Sundara Pāṇḍya I (1251—64), on the contrary, he was not friendly. See Śrīraṅgam inscription in *Ep. Ind.*, Vol. III, p. 7 ff.]

70. 205 *of* 1910.—(Tamil.) On a slab lying in front of the Sōmēśvara temple in the same village. A damaged record in the fifteenth year of the Hoysaḷa king Sōmēśvaradēva. Records remission of certain taxes on temples in Tagaḍaināḍu and Puramalai-nāḍu by the residents of the seventy-nine districts, for the health of the king and of Sōmaya-Daṇṇakkar. See No. 68 above.

71. 206 *of* 1910.—(Tamil.) On the north base of the same temple. A much damaged record in the nineteenth year of the Chōḷa king Kulōttuṅga-Chōḷadēva.

72. 207 *of* 1910.—(Tamil.) On the same base. A much damaged record in the twenty-fifth year of the Chōḷa king Kulōttuṅga-Chōḷadēva. Seems to record gift of paddy by a native of Ariyambākkam to the temple of Mayindīśiram Uḍaiyār.

73. 208 *of* 1910.—(Tamil.) On the same base. A record of the Chōḷa king Tribhuvanachakravartin Rājarājadēva III in Ś. 1163, and in his twenty-sixth year. Records gift of gold for a lamp to the temple of Mayindīśvaram-Uḍaiyār by a Vāṇiyan of Arumbākkam. [The inscription is interesting for its mentioning a Śaka date for a Chōḷa king.]

Dharmapuri.

Known in the ninth century as Tagaḍūr this place played a prominent part in early South Indian history. It was a famous city with rich temples, "pleasure-gardens of kings and high enclosure walls," a centre of Jainism and Śaivitism. The still attractive temple of Mallikārjuna, the Jain sculptures in the Rāmakka tank and Adhamankōṭṭai (not far from it) and the archaic epigraphs show its importance in antiquity in the age of the Chēra kings. Subsequent to the Chēra epoch and till about A.D. 931 it was the capital of the Noḷambas. (See Nos. 82 and 83.)

74. 304 *of* 1901.—(Kanarese.) On the four faces of a pillar built into the floor of the maṇṭapa in front of the Mallikārjuna temple. A record of king Mahēndrādhirāja-Noḷamba in Ś. 815, Paridhāvin. Records a grant to a Jaina basadi by a certain Nidhiyaṇṇa and Chaṇḍiyaṇṇa. The former received from the king the village of Mūlappaḷḷi which he made over to Kanakasēna Siddhānta Bhaṭāra, pupil of Vinayasēna Siddhānta Bhaṭāra of the Pogarīyagaṇa with the *Sēnānvaya, Mūlasaṅga*, etc., for the repairs to the *basti*. The witnesses of the transaction were the four Samayins, the *Nāḍunagara-narasāsana* officers, etc. See *Ep. Ind.*, Vol. X, pp. 54—70.

75. 305 *of* 1901.—(Kanarese.) At the bottom of the four faces of the same pillar. A record of the Pallava king Ayyappadēva, son of Mahēndra-Noḷamba. Records a grant of the village of Budugūru perhaps to the same basadi (for Nidhiyaṇṇa is mentioned) by a certain Lōkayya. [See *Ep. Ind.*, X, where Mr. Krishna Sastri gives an excellent history of the Noḷamba-Pallavas. See also Fleet's *Dyn., Kan. Dts.*, p. 332 and *Ep. Carna.*, Vol. IV, p. 10 f.]

76. 306 *of* 1901.—(Kanarese.) On a broken piece of another pillar in the same temple. A fragment of record of a Pallava king, the date of which is lost. Begins with the same passage as No. 74 above.

77. 307 *of* 1901.—(Tamil.) On the south wall of the Kāmākshi shrine in the same temple. A record in the tenth year of Chōḷa king Tribhuvanachakravartin Kulōttuṅga-Chōḷadēva. Mentions two temples, viz., Tiruvēḷalīśvara and Irāyarāyīśvara.

78. 308 *of* 1901.—(Tamil.) On the east wall of the same shrine. A record in the twelfth year of the Chōḷa king Tribhuvanachakravartin Kulōttuṅga-Chōḷadēva. Records repairs made for the merit of Adiyamān (i.e., the king of Adigai).

79. 309 *of* 1901.—(Kanarese verse.) On a slab set up on the tank bund in the same village. Mentions the preceptor Viddērāśi (Vidyārāśi) of Tagaḍūru.

80. 347 *of* 1901.—(Tamil.) On a slab built into the floor of the maṇṭapa in front of the Mallikārjuna temple. A much damaged record of Kulōttuṅga Chōḷadēva.

81. 348 *of* 1901.—(Kanarese.) On four sides of a broken pillar lying in the Māriyamman temple in the fort. A record of the Pallava Mahēndra Noḷamba, dated in Ś. 800, *Viḷambin*, apparently making grant to a Jaina temple. [It was this Mahēndra who conquered Mahābali Bāṇa Rāya about A.D. 890 and gave his name Mahēndramaṅgalam to Adhamankōṭṭai.]

81-A. In a slab in the street of Virūpākshipuram. A record making the grant of a village by a local chief in the reign of Śrī Raṅga of Vijayanagar in Ś. 1541 (A.D. 1619) the king having his capital at Penukoṇḍa. [*Salem Manual*, p. 223.]

82. 198 *of* 1910.—(Kanarese.) On a granite pillar lying in the quarter known as Virūpākshipuram. A record of the Noḷambha king Iruḷa, son of Aṇṇiga, in Ś. 853, *Virōdhi.* The record gives a list of the Noḷamba kings and their queens. The last face which usually records the grant is damaged. This is an important inscription giving the Noḷamba-Pallava genealogy from Pallavādhirāja to Iruḷa and showing that the Tagaḍūr nāḍu was under the Noḷambas even after the conquest of the neighbouring Bāṇa territory by Parāntaka I.

83. 199 *of* 1910.—(Kanarese.) On the fragment of a pillar lying in the house of Īśvarayya in the same village. A record of a Noḷamba king, whose name and date are lost. Appears to have contained a genealogy of the Noḷambas. Mentions, among the boundaries, the roads to Puramale-nāḍu and Piribeḷḷōle. [The inscription gives the details of the actions of the individual kings of the line.]

84. Tagaḍūr spurious Sanskrit and Kanarese plates of the W. Gaṅga king Harivarma Mahārāja issued from Talavanapura. See *Ep. Carna.*, Vol. III, p. 202, No. 122 and Kielhorn's *Southern List*, p. 20, No. 109. The date of the grant (Ś. 188, Vibhava, daśami, Guruvāra, Punarvasu) is irregular.

Hanumantapuram.

85-86. 16 *and* 17 *of* 1900.—(Vaṭṭeḷuttu.) On a slab in a field. A record in the seventeenth year of "Gaṅga-Pallava king" Vijaya-Īśvaravarman. Record the death of two heroes in battle in the service of Kāṭṭirai. [Dr. Hultzsch believes the latter to be identical with Kaḍava or Pallava. He is not, however, the chief conquered by the Hoysaḷa Narasiṁha II but evidently Īśvaravarman himself. See *Ep. Ind.*, Vol. VII, pp. 23-4.]

Indūr (near Dharmapuri).

87. 13 *of* 1900.—(Kanarese.) On a slab in the Prasanna-Vēṅkaṭēśa-Perumāḷ temple. A much damaged record of the Vijayanagara king Kṛishṇarāya (1509—30).

Kaḍagattūr.

88. 193 *of* 1910.—(Tamil.) On the south wall of the Chōḷēśvara temple. An unfinished record of the Vijayanagara king Vīrapratāpa Dēvarāya-Mahārāya (1422—49) in Ś. 1352, Sādhāraṇa. Mentions Kaḍaikkōṭṭūr *alias* Dēśi-Uyyakoṇḍaśōḷapaṭṭaṇam in Tagaḍa-Nāḍu, a subdivision of Gaṅga-nāḍu, which was a district of Nigarilisōḷa-maṇḍalam.

89. 194 *of* 1910.—(Tamil.) On the same wall. Records gift of taxes on looms within the premises *(tirumaḍaiviḷāgam)* of Muḍigoṇḍa-Chōḷīśvaramuḍaiya-Nāyanār temple, by the *nagarattār* of the village, for maintaining a lamp in the temple.

90. 195 *of* 1910.—(Tamil.) On the north and west walls of the same temple. A record in Ś. 1398, Durmukhi, of the Vijayanagara king Mallikārjunarāya, son of Pratāpadēvarāya (II), "who received tribute from all countries and from Ceylon and witnessed the elephant hunt." Records gift of land in favour of the dancing women of the same temple.

91. 196 *of* 1910.—(Tamil.) On the west wall of the same temple. A record of the Vijayanagara king Vīrapratāpa Dēvarāya-Mahārāya (II) in Ś. 1362, *Durmati.* Records gift of the taxes *Nāḍutalavārikkai* (police rate?), *Śeṭṭiyārmagamai*, collected on either side *(ubhayamārga)* of the roads, the *aḷḷāyamānyam* and *aḍikāśu* on each shop opened in the village of Varagūr, a *dēvadāna* of the temple of Muḍigoṇḍa-Chōḷīśvaramuḍaiya-Nāyanār, by the Telugu chief Malla-Rāhutta, son of Viḍamiṭṭa-Rāhutta of Muḷa-vāychchāvaḍi, while the Pradhāni Mādaṇa-Daṇṇāyakkar of Muḷvāy was governing the country. [See inscription No. 141 of 1903 at Pirānmalai in Rāmnād district. In Ś. 1356 Mādaṇṇa gave, under the king's orders, charge of the Tekal country to Sāḷuva Gōparāja, nephew of Dēva Rāya II.]

Kārimaṅgalam.

91-A. 5 *of* 1900.—(Kanarese.) On a rock in front of the Vīrabhadrasvāmin temple. A record of the Vijayanagara king Sadāśivadēva (1542—65) in Ś. 1478. Mentions the Mahāmaṇḍalēśvara Aḷiya-Rāmarāja.

Koḷagattūr (near *Kaḍagattūr*).

92. 197 *of* 1910.—(Telugu.) On a slab lying on the tank bund. A record in Dundubhi. Stipulates that the cultivators of lands below the tanks in the Kaḍagattūr country must give *sarivāram*, i.e., equal share of the produce to the owner and pay a specified fee for strengthening the tank bunds with stone and earth. This was done for the merit of the chief Kumāra Jagadēva. This was evidently the chief of Channapaṭṭaṇa in Bangalore district conquered by the rising Mysore chiefs about 1635. [See *Mys. Gazr.*, II, p. 62.]

Mōdūr.

93. 209 *of* 1910.—(Tamil.) A damaged record in Sarvadhārin. Refers to an officer "who possessed the strength and powers of the Hoysaḷa king Vishṇuvardhana" and to the remission of the *marriage tax* in Tagaḍa-nāḍu.

94. 210 *of* 1910.—(Tamil.) On a boulder in front of the temple of Nelapperumāḷ in the same village. A record in the third year, Āṅgiras, of the Chōḷa king Rājakēsarivarman *alias* Tribhuvanachakravartin Tribhuvanavīra-Chōḷadēva. Records gift of the village of Mōdūr in Tagaḍa-nāḍu, a district of Nigarilichōḷamaṇḍalam (E. Gaṅga country), to the temple of Śiṅgapperumāḷ which was attached to the temple of Durgaiyār in Padi-nāḍu, a district of Mēl-maṇḍala. [Mr. Krishna Sastri identifies Padināḍu in Mēlmanḍala with Haḍināḍu in Mysore and Durgaiyār with the famous Chāmuṇḍi of that place, a proof of which he sees in the existence of a field named Chāmuṇḍi Ammanāṇḍu. As regards the identity of the king he believes that he might be the same as the king of the Tiruvaṇṇāmalai record whose accession Dr. Hultzsch attributes to A.D. 1341–2 and whose third year fell in Āṅgiras. See *Ep. Ind.*, Vol. VIII, p. 7 ff.]

Peṇṇāgaram.

95. 14 *of* 1900.—(Kanarese.) On a slab set up near the *dhvajastambha* in the Narasiṁhasvāmin temple at Haḷēpuram near Peṇṇāgaram. A damaged record in Vijaya.

96. 15 *of* 1900.—(Tamil.) On a slab set up at Kūttappāḍi near Peṇṇāgaram. A much damaged record.

97. 46 *of* 1898.—(Tamil.) On the south wall of the Brahmēśvara temple. Records the building of the temple and its maṇṭapa for the merit of the Pallava king Nandivarman.

98. 47 *of* 1898.—(Tamil.) On the north wall of the Brahmēśvara temple. Records in the fourth year of the Pāṇḍya king Ravivarman *alias* Vīra-Pāṇḍyadēva gift of money for six lamps.

99. 48 *of* 1898.—(Tamil.) On the same wall. Records in the twenty-fifth year of the Chōḷa king Tribhuvanachakravartin Rājarājadēva gift of gold for four lamps.

HŌSŪR TALUK.

Budimatlu.

100. 210 *of* 1911.—(Tamil.) On a slab set up in a field to the south of the village. Records in Krōdhin the gift of one big *kaṇḍaga* of land by Kannigāmiṇḍan Viḍukādan, chief of Eyi-nāḍu, to a certain Śrīramabhaṭṭa of Pūdamuṭṭal in Virivi-nāḍu, for the merit of the lord of the east (Pūrvādhirāya). Śrīrāmabhaṭṭa reminds us of the Vaishṇava sage, the brother of Parāśara Bhaṭṭa, the successor (according to the prabandhic school) of Rāmānuja; but the identity is impossible.

Dēvar-kundani.

The ruined fortifications, temples and residences of this place show its antiquity. Mr. Richards, I.C.S., suggested it might be the capital of the Hoysaḷas in this region. The inscriptions, however, point out Mr. Krishna Sastri do not call it a Rājadhāni but a village in Virivināḍu in Nigarilišōḷamaṇḍalam (the Chōḷa name to the district between Anantapur and Salem, i.e., Kolar and Bārama-hal.) Mr. Sewell attributes the local hill fort to a "Poḷegar."

101. 201 *of* 1911.—(Tamil.) On the south wall of the maṇṭapa in front of the central shrine in the Kuntīśvara temple. Records in Ś. 1200, Bahudhānya, gift of the village of Kalakkimuṭṭal *alias* Kākkunāyakkanallūr in Puduppaṟṟu, to the temple of Tiruvēgam-bamuḍaiya-Nāyanār, "lord of the east." Mentions a number of items under which the income from a village was generally calculated.

102. 202 *of* 1911.—(Tamil.) On the same wall. Records in Ś. 1190, Vibhava, gift of land below the tank Dēvasamudram in Māśandi-nāḍu, to the temple of Kailāsamuḍaiya-Nāyanār in Dēva-samudram-Kundāṇi, by a native of Marudūr in Malai-nāḍu.

103. 203 *of* 1911.—(Tamil.) On the north wall of the same maṇṭapa. An unfinished record of the Vijayanagara king Malli-kārjuna-Mahārāya, son of Prauḍhapratāpa-Dēvarāya (II) in Ś. 1385, Svabhānu. Seems to record the gift of two villages in Virivi-nāḍu to the temple of Kailāsamuḍaiya-Nāyinār at Kundāṇi, a village in the same nāḍu, by the Mahāsāmantādhipati Chikka-Vīrabhadra-Nāyaka, son of Peria Ṭimma Nāyaka, son of Varada Nāyaka, who was again the son of Śennaiya Nāyaka of Pūmali.

104. 204 *of* 1911.—(Tamil.) On two detached slabs built into the gōpura of the Kundāṇi-Amman temple in the same village, left side. A record of the Hoysaḷa king Vīra-Viśvanāthadēvarasa, (son of Vīra Rāmanātha), "the establisher of the Chōḷa kingdom," in Kali. 439. Refers to a temple which was located at the southern entrance into Kundāṇi in Virivi-nāḍu, a subdivision of Nigarilišōḷa-maṇḍalam.

105. 205 *of* 1911.—(Tamil.) On four other detached slabs in the same place. A record of the Hoysaḷa king in Ś. 1219, Hēviḷambi, and in his third year. Refers very probably to the temple mentioned in No. 104 and calls it Uḍaiyār Sōmanāthadēvar at Kundāṇi in Virivi-nāḍu, a subdivision of Nigarilišōḷa-maṇḍalam.

106. 206 *of* 1911.—(Tamil.) Left of entrance into the Bhairavēśvara temple on the hill near the same village. A much damaged record in Ś. 1252, Prajāpati. Mentions Kundāṇi in Virivi-nāḍu.

Doḍḍa Bēlūr.

107. On a local anicut. An inscription, dated Ś. 1595 (A.D. 1673), recording its construction by Kumāra Rāya Daḷavāi in the reign of Chikkadēva Rāja. *Antiquities*, Vol. I, p. 194.

Hōsūr.

108. *C.P. No. 9 of Mr. Sewell's List.*—Records a deed drawn up in Ś. 1683 (A.D. 1761), in the year Vrisha, by certain merchants of Hōsūr in the Salem district, promising to give to the priests a certain fixed proportion on every bale of cloths and thread bought in that town.

109. On a rock in the neighbourhood. Records that one Kēśava Nāyakan inscribed and dedicated the stone to Nārāyaṇa, the protector of the five classes of people in Aippiśi 1 of K. 4266, *Pramādhi*, in order that "Srī Vallan Dēvar may attain the throne." [The cyclic year is wrong by six years. The reigning Ballāḷa king was Vīra Narasiṁha, and he was succeeded by Vīra Ballāḷa in 1188, i.e., 22 years after the date of this epigraph. *Antiquities*, I, App. C, p. XXXIII.

Taḷi.

110. On the local tank bund. (Kanarese.) Records the construction of the tank in Ś. 1452 (A.D. 1530), during the reign of Achyuta Dēva Rāya by some merchants.

111. An epigraph of A.D. 1799, recording the fall of Śrīraṅgapaṭṭaṇam (Seringapatam).

112. An epigraph, dated A.D. 1802.

113. In the temple of Gōpāla. Records that it was built by Kṛishṇa Rāya Uḍaiyār of Maisūr in Ś. 1640 (A.D. 1718).

Tīrtham.

114. 207 *of* 1911.—(Tamil.) On the west wall of the central shrine in the Tīrthagirīśvara temple. Records in Ś. 1197, Vibha (mistake for Bhava) gift of gold for a lamp to the temple of Tītta-Nāyanār at Puśavūr in Viravi-nāḍu.

115. 208 *of* 1911.—(Tamil.) On the south, east and north walls of the maṇṭapa in front of the same shrine. An unfinished record of the Vijayanagara king Immaḍi-Bukkaṇa-Uḍaiyār (II, 1399–1406), son of Harriyaṇṇa-Uḍaiyār (Harihara II), in Ś. 1316, Bhava. Records gift of income from the parachchēri of Tītta-Puśavūr *alias* Tīttam to the temple of Śivanīśvaramuḍaiyār in that village which was situated in Viruvināḍu, a subdivision of Nigariliśōḷa-maṇḍalam.

116. 209 *of* 1911.—(Tamil.) On the south wall of the same maṇṭapa. A partly damaged record of the Vijayanagara king Vīra-Dēvarāya-Uḍaiyār (I), son of Hariyarāya (II), in Ś. 1339 and Kaliyuga 4518, Hēviḷambi. Records gift of tolls by merchants to the temple of Śivanīśvaramuḍaiya-Nāyanār at Tīttaga Puśavūr *alias* Tīttam in Virivu-nāḍu, a subdivision of Nigariliśōḷa-maṇḍalam, by the *mahā-odda-viyāpāri* Aṇṇāmalai-śeṭṭi for the health of Annadāta-Uḍaiyār.

KRISHNAGIRI TALUK.

Rāyakōṭa.

117. 1 *of* 1900.—(Tamil.) On the top of the Durvāsa hill at Rāyakōṭa. A damaged record.

118. 2 *of* 1900.—(Kanarese.) On a rock in the fort at the same village. A slightly damaged record in the fourth year of the Bāṇa king Mahāvali-Bāṇarasa.

119. 3 *of* 1900.—(Tamil.) On the south wall of the maṇṭapa in front of the Lakshmīnārāyaṇa temple at the same village. A mutilated record in Plava. Mentions Kulōttuṅga-Śōḷa Tagaḍādirāyar *alias* Māraśiṅgadēvan. [He evidently belonged to the family of Viḍugādaḷagiyaperumāḷ who is mentioned in 208 below who played a large part in the weak times of Kulōttuṅga III.]

120. 4 *of* 1888.—(Tamil.) On the south wall of the maṇṭapa in front of the Lakshmīnārāyaṇa temple at the same village. A fragmentary record of the Hoysaḷa king Vīra-Rāmanāthadēva (1257–71) in his sixth year. Rāmanātha was the brother of Vīra Narasiṁha III (1254—86) and was in charge of the southern parts of the Hoysaḷa Empire.

121. A C.P. grant of Skandaśishya. (Tamil and Sanskrit.) Records that a Skandaśishya (who calls himself a Pallava and the descendant of an older Skandaśishya, the son of Aśvatthāman by a Nāga woman) issued in his fourteenth year, at the request of Mahābali Vāṇarāja, an order to the inhabitants of Paḍavūrkōṭṭam and Mēl-Aḍaiyārnāḍu by which he granted the village of Śārugūr (near Udayēndiram in Guḍiyāttam taluk, North Arcot district) to a Brahman. [Dr. Hultzsch is disposed to believe that Skanda was a prince of the so-called "Gaṅga-Pallava" age and line, two proofs of which he sees in the palæography of the epigraph and in the reference to Mahābali Vāṇarāya, a title bestowed on the Gaṅga Prithvīpati II by Parāntaka Chōḷa I (906—47). See *Ep. Ind.*, Vol. V, pp. 49—53.]

Tukkōjinahalli ?

121-A. 6 *of* 1900.—(Tamil.) On a rock near the Lakshmīnarasiṁha temple. Records gift by a private individual to the temple of Śiṅgaperumāḷ on the hill at Tiṇḍal.

121-B. 7 *of* 1900.—(Tamil.) On another rock at the same place. Records in Śōbhakrit gift to the Brāhmaṇas of the village of Tiṇḍal *alias* Madhurāntaka Vīra-Nuḷamba-chaturvēdimaṇgalam by Madhurāntakan Vīra-Nuḷamban Rājanārāyaṇa Vayiravan Ponnambalakkūṭṭan.

Ōmalūr Taluk.

Tārāmaṅgalam.

In his *Antiquities* Mr. Sewell gives thirteen inscriptions in this place. Of these nine have been identified with those of the departmental list. The other four are not identifiable. Two of them are undated and record gifts or repairs by private parties. One records gift of land by the temple authorities to a Brahman for conducting the service; and the fourth records a grant of land to temple by the inhabitants of a village in the sixteenth year of Tribhuvanachakravartin Sundara Pāṇḍya.

122. 19 *of* 1900 (*No.* 1 *of Mr. Sewell's List*).—(Tamil.) On the north wall of the maṇṭapa in front of the Kailāśanātha temple. A record of Vīravasantarāyar in K. 4009 (mistake for Ś. 1490), expired, Vibhava, third year. Records the grant of the village of Iḷamasamudram to the Kailāśa and Iḷamīśvara temples at Tārāmaṅgalam.

123. 20 *of* 1900.—(Tamil.) On the north wall of the same maṇṭapa. A much damaged record in the fourteenth year of Rāmanāthadēva. Records gift of land. See No. 120 above.

124. 21 *of* 1900 (*No.* 3 *of Mr. Sewell's List*).—(Tamil.) On the south wall of the maṇṭapa in front of the Iḷamīśvara temple at the same village. A record of the Vijayanagara king Achyutarāya (1530—42) in Kaliyuga 4642, expired, Plava. Records the building of a *maṭha* at Chidambaram by a native of Tārāmaṅgalam and registers the grant of the proceeds of certain taxes for the maintenance of the *maṭha*.

125. 22 *of* 1900 (*No.* 7 *of Mr. Sewell's List*).—(Tamil.) On the south wall of the maṇṭapa in front of the Iḷamīśvara temple at the same village. A record in the sixth year of Tribhuvanachakravartin Kōnērinmēlkoṇḍān. Records gift of land.

126. 23 *of* 1900.—(Tamil.) On the south wall of the maṇṭapa in front of the Iḷamīśvara temple at the same village. A record in the fourteenth year of the Pāṇḍya king Jaṭāvarman *alias* Tribhuvanachakravartin Sundara-Pāṇḍyadēva III (1276—90). Records gift of a tank to the Brāhmaṇas of Lakshmaṇa-chaturvēdimaṅgalam. Dr. Kielhorn discusses the date in *Ep. Ind.*, Vol. VI, p. 312, and concludes that it should be Monday, 15th May, A.D. 1290.

127. 24 *of* 1900 (*No.* 10 *of Mr. Sewell's List*).—On the north wall of the same maṇṭapa. A record in the thirteenth year of the Pāṇḍya king Jaṭāvarman *alias* Tribhuvanachakravartin Sundara-Pāṇḍyadēva (III, 1276—90). Records gift of a tank to certain Brāhmaṇas by the Mudalis of Tāramaṅgalam, among whom is a person named Iḷamāṇḍai. See *Ep. Ind.*, Vol. VI, p. 310, where Dr. Kielhorn gives the most probable equivalent date to be Monday, 1st August, A.D. 1289.

128. 25 *of* 1900 (*No.* 11 *of Mr. Sewell's List*).—(Tamil.) On the north wall of the same maṇṭapa. A record in the sixth year of the Pāṇḍya king Jaṭāvarman *alias* Tribhuvanachakravartin Sundara-Pāṇḍyadēva III (1276—90). Registers a sale of land to the Brāhmaṇas of Lakshmaṇa-chaturvēdimaṅgalam founded by Iḷaiyan Nalla Uḍaiyappan, one of the Mudalis of Tāramaṅgalam, in the name of his father. Dr. Kielhorn fixes the date on Monday, 21st July, A.D. 1281. See *Ep. Ind.*, Vol. VI, p. 311.

129. 26 *of* 1900 (*No.* 12 *of Mr. Sewell's List*).—(Tamil.) On the north wall of the same maṇṭapa. A record in the twentieth year of the Hoysaḷa king Vīra-Rāmanāthadēva (1257—71). Records gift of land.

130. 27 *of* 1900 (*No.* 5 *of Mr. Sewell's List*).—(Tamil.) On the east wall of the same maṇṭapa. A record of the Vijayanagara king Sadāśivadēva in K. 4646, expired, Plavaṅga. Records gift of a village by one of the Mudalis of Tāramaṅgalam to a temple called Rāmakūḍal.

131. 28 *of* 1900.—(Tamil.) On the east wall of the same maṇṭapa. A record of the Vijayanagara king Achyutarāya in K. 4640, expired, Śārvarin. Records gift of a village by the same donor.

132. 29 *of* 1900 (*No.* 9 *of Mr. Sewell's List*).—(Tamil.) On the west wall of the central shrine in the same temple. A record in the twentieth year of the Hoysaḷa king Vīra-Rāmanāthadēva (1257—71). Records gift of land by several Mudalis, among whom was a certain Iḷaman.

133. 30 *of* 1900 (*Evidently No.* 8 *of Mr. Sewell's List*).—(Tamil.) On the west wall of the central shrine of the Iḷamīśvara temple. A record in the twenty-seventh year of the Pāṇḍya king Jaṭāvarman *alias* Tribhuvanachakravartin Sundara-Pāṇḍyadēva. (Mr. Sewell reads "Kanaka Pāṇḍya Dēva".) Records gift of a village by Kaṇḍiyadēvar, lord of Vaḍapūvāṇiya-nāḍu.

134. 31 *of* 1900.—(Tamil.) On the north wall of the same shrine. Mentions a certain Śrīkaṇṭhadēva, who bore the *birudas* Gauḍachūḍāmaṇi and Vidyāsamudra, and records a gift of land made to his father as *gurudakshina* by the six Veḷḷāḷas of Tāramaṅgalam, of whom Nalla Uḍaiyappar was one.

Vanavāsi.

135. *C.P. No.* 195 *of Mr. Sewell's List.*—Records in Ś. 1698 (A.D. 1776), K. 4876, Manmatha, the grant of a garden to the Śiva temple at Vanavāsi in the "Vanjināḍu" of Maisūr, by a private person, during the reign of Immaḍi Vīra Rāja Uḍaiyār at Maisūr. [There is a village of the name of Vanavāsi in Ōmalūr taluk and the present epigraph may refer to it.]

Veḷḷār.

136. 655 *of* 1905.—(Tamil.) On a slab set up at the foot of the hill. A damaged record in the seventh year of Rājarājadēva.

137. 656 *of* 1905.—(Grantha and Tamil.) On two faces of a broken slab in the same place. A fragmentary record. The preserved portion contains a few Hoysaḷa *birudas.*

138. 657 *of* 1905.—(Tamil.) On the top of the hill in the same village. An incomplete record in the seventeenth year of the Pāṇḍya king Rājakēsarivarman *alias* Tribhuvanachakravartin Vīra-Pāṇḍyadēva. Mentions Madaga-nāḍu *alias* Veḷḷārai-nāḍu and the temple Tirukkunṟīśvaramuḍaiyār. [The inscription is interesting for its reference to a Pāṇḍyan king with a Chōḷa title. It is difficult to identify him, but it seems to me that he might be the Koṅgu-Pāṇḍya of the same name who ruled from A.D. 1265 to 1281 at least. See Cb. 196 and Cb. 197.]

Yelavampaṭṭi.

139. On a local rock. Date not clear. A record stating that during the reign of Achyuta Dēva of Vijayanagar a man of the Mudali caste presented this village to the temple at Tāramaṅgalam. *Antiquities*, Vol. I, p. 201.

SALEM TALUK.

Rāśipuram.

140. *C.P. No.* 193 *of Mr. Sewell's List.*—Records a private agreement by the Śūdras of the place to pay a tax for the maintenance of service in the Vishṇu temple at Rāśipuram in Ś. 1726 (A.D. 1804), Kaḷiyuga 4905, Kaḷayukti.

141. *C.P. No.* 194 *of Mr. Sewell's List.*—Records another similar agreement for tax for the support of worship in the same temple in Ś. 1746 (A.D. 1824), K. 4925, Tāraṇa.

Salem.

In his *Antiquities*, Vol. II, Mr. Sewell gives six copper-plate grants in this district. Of these Nos. 193, 194, 195 and 9 have been allocated to the villages proper. Nos. 8 and 196 are vague and have therefore been given here. They are said to be in the District Court and Tahsildar's office, Salem.

142. *C.P. No.* 8 *of Mr. Sewell's List.*—Records grant " by a Rāja of Maisūr, part of whose name is 'Kṛishṇa Raja,' given in a year of the Kaliyuga, of which only the first three figures, 482, are visible, the last figure, the name of the cyclic year, and the Śaka date all having been tampered with. The grantor was probably Doḍḍa Kṛishṇa Rāja, who reigned over Maisūr from A.D. 1714—31. The grant, then, dates within the years A.D. 1719—1728."

143. *C.P. No.* 196 *of Mr. Sewell's List.*—(Kanarese and Telugu.) Records a private agreement between villagers to maintain worship in a temple in Ś. 1709 (A.D. 1787), Kaliyuga 4889, Plavaṅga.

144. 42 *of* 1888.—Right of entrance into the *garbhagriha* of Śukavanēśvara temple. Beginning lost.

145. 43 *of* 1888.—Left of entrance into *garbhagriha* of the same temple. A record in the fifth year of Kō-Parakēsarivarman.

146. 44 *of* 1888.—A record on a pillar in the Nrittamaṇṭapa.

147. 45 *of* 1888.—On a pillar in the Nrittamaṇṭapa. A record in the twenty-sixth year of Sundara-Pāṇḍyadēva.

148. 46 *of* 1888.—On the north wall. A record in the twenty-sixth year of Sundara-Pāṇḍyadēva.

149. 47 *of* 1888.—On a stone at the entrance of Svarṇāmbika shrine. A record of Kō-Rājakēsarivarman.

150. 48 *of* 1888.—On a stone at the entrance of Svarṇāmbika shrine. A record in the sixth year of Kō-Parakēsarivarman.

151. 49 *of* 1888.—Right of entrance of Svarṇāmbika shrine. A record in the fifth year of Kō-Rājakēsarivarman.

152. 50 *of* 1888.—Left of entrance of Svarṇāmbika shrine. A record of Kō-Parakēsarivaram.

153. 51 *of* 1888.—On a pillar to the right of Svarṇāmbika shrine. A record in the twenty-sixth year of Sundara-Pāṇḍya-dēva.

154. 52 *of* 1888.—On a pillar in mahāmaṇṭapa in the Saundara-rāja Perumāḷ Temple. A record in the twenty-fourth year of Sundara-Pāṇḍya-dēva.

155. 53 *of* 1888.—On a pillar in mahāmaṇṭapa in the same temple. A fragment of record.

156. 54 *of* 1888.—On a pillar in mahāmaṇṭapa in the same temple. A record in the twenty-fourth year of Sundara-Pāṇḍya-dēva.

157. 55 *of* 1888.—On a pillar at the mahāmaṇṭapa in the same temple. A record in the twenty-fourth year of Sundara-Pāṇḍyadēva.

158. 56 *of* 1888.—Right of entrance of *garbhagriha* of the same temple. A record in the twenty-fourth year of Chakravartin Sundara-Pāṇḍyadēva.

159. 57 *of* 1888.—North wall of the same temple. A record of Kō-Māravarman *alias* Tribhuvanachakravartin.

160. 58 *of* 1888.—Round Saundaravalli shrine in the same temple. The stones do not seem to be in their original order.

Uttamachōḷapuram.

161. 59 *of* 1888.—On the south wall of the Karabūranāthēśvara temple. A record in the twenty-seventh year of Kṛishṇarāya.

162. 60 *of* 1888.—On the west wall of the *garbhagriha* of the same temple. A defaced fragment of record.

163. 61 *of* 1888.—On a stone on the floor of mahāmaṇṭapa of the same temple. Name of king illegible.

TIRUCHENGŌDU TALUK.

Kokkarāyanpeṭ.

164. 465 *of* 1913.—(Tamil.) On the south wall of the Brahmapurīśvara temple. A record of the Vijayanagara king Vīrapratāpa Achyutadēva-Mahārāya (1530—42) in Ś. 1453, Vikriti, Aippaśi, twenty-fifth day, śu. di. 12, Punarvasu, Monday. Records gift of the village of Tagaḍappāḍipālaiyam *alias* Vaḍivuḍaiyamaṅgaipuram to the temple of Brahmīśvaram-uḍaiya-Tambirānār, by a certain Śāma-Nāyinār, agent of Kṛishṇarāya-Nāyaka. [The date is irregular; Monday, 25th *Aippaśi,* was October 24, A.D. 1530, but does not agree with the other data.]

165. 466 *of* 1913.—(Tamil.) On the east wall of the same temple; left of entrance. A record of the Vijayanagara king Vīrapratāpa Kṛishṇadēva Mahārāya (1509—30) in Ś. 1438, Iśvara (wrong), Tai, twenty-ninth day, Pūrva-Phalguni, 14, Āyushya-yōga, Monday (corresponding to Monday, 25th January 1518). The king receives, among others, the title *Rājākkaḷ-tambirān.* Registers the gift of the village Śaṅgamapura to the same temple.

166. 467 *of* 1913.—(Tamil.) On the same wall. An unfinished and damaged record in Sarvadhārin, Āḍi, first day. Seems to record a gift of two villages for the enjoyment and repairs of the temple of Brahmīśvara and for the maintenance of a dancing master, etc., in the temple.

167. 468 *of* 1913.—(Tamil.) On four slabs built into the floor of the same temple. A record in the fourth year of the Chōḷa king Rājakēsarivarman *alias* Chakravartin Kulōttuṅga-Chōḷadēva (I).

Registers the detailed provision made for offerings at the temple of Brahmīśvaram Uḍaiyar at Kīḷkarai . . . maṅgalam in Nāḍāḷva-nāḍu, a district of Koṅgu *alias* Vīraśōḷa-maṇḍalam, by Gaṅgai-koṇḍān Ammaiyappan *alias* Mādhavarāja, for the health of the emperor (chakravartin).

Tiruchcheṅgōḍu.

168. 622 *of* 1905.—(Grantha and Tamil.) On the rock just below the boulder known as Nagarguṇḍu, west of the steps leading to the Ardhanārīśvara temple on the hill. A record in the ninth year of the Pāṇḍya king Jaṭāvarman *alias* Tribhuvanachakravartin Sundara-Pāṇḍyadēva (I, ? 1251—64). Records gift of land by the people of Kīḷakarai-Pūndurai-nāḍu in Koṅgu *alias* Vīraśōḷa-maṇḍalam. Refers to the breach of a tank and states that the land irrigated by it was lying fallow for a long time. Koṅgu was later on called Chōḷakēraḷa-maṇḍalam.

169. 623 *of* 1900.—(Tamil.) On the rock to the west of the same boulder. A record in the fourteenth year of the Chōḷa king Rājakēsarivarman. Records gift of gold for a lamp.

170. 624 *of* 1905.—(Tamil.) On the same rock. A damaged record in the fourteenth year of Rājavarman.

171. 625 *of* 1905.—(Tamil.) On the same rock. A record in the sixteenth year of the Chōḷa king Rājakēsarivarman. Records gift of gold for Brāhmaṇas.

172. 626 *of* 1905.—(Tamil.) On the same rock. A damaged record in the tenth year of the Chōḷa king Parakēsarivarman *alias* Rājēndra-Chōḷadēva (I). Seems to record an agreement among the *uvachchar* to play on the drum.

173. 627 *of* 1905.—(Tamil.) On the same rock. A record in the fourteenth year of the Chōḷa king Rājakēsarivarman. Records gift of gold for feeding Brāhmaṇas. The village is called Tiruchcheṅgōḍu.

174. 628 *of* 1905.—(Tamil.) On the same rock. A record in the twelfth year of the Chōḷa king Parakēsarivarman. Records gift of gold for feeding Brāhmaṇas.

175. 629 *of* 1905.—(Tamil.) On the same rock. A record in the thirteenth year of the Chōḷa king Rājakēsarivarman. Records gift of gold for feeding twenty Brāhmaṇas on the day of *ēkādaśi.*

176. 630 *of* 1905.—(Tamil.) On a rock east of the steps known as Arubadāmpaḍi on the same hill. A record in the twenty-eighth year of the Chōḷa king Parakēsarivarman. Records gift of gold for a lamp.

177. 631 *of* 1905.—(Tamil.) On the same rock. A damaged record in the twenty-seventh year of the Chōḷa king Parakēsari-varman. Mentions Pugaḷiyūr. Records gift of gold for feeding

Brāhmaṇas. [This is perhaps the place where the king Adiyan (Adigaimān) is reported to have met the Pāṇḍyan Neḍuñjaḍayan. See *Ep. Rep.*, 1906, p. 75, paragraph 36.]

178. 632 *of* 1905.—(Tamil.) On the same rock. A damaged record in the thirty-seventh year of the Chōḷa king Madiraikoṇḍa Parakēsarivarman (Parāntaka I). Records gift of a lamp.

179. 633 *of* 1905.—(Tamil.) On the same rock. An incomplete record in the twentieth year of the Chōḷa king Madiraikoṇḍa Parakēsarivarman (Parāntaka I). Mentions Tiruppiḍavūr. A damaged record.

180. 634 *of* 1905.—(Tamil.) On the same rock. A damaged record. Records gift of gold. Pilgrims' scrawls have been freely engraved in modern characters over this inscription.

181. 635 *of* 1905.—(Tamil.) On the same rock. A record in the thirty-seventh year of the Chōḷa king Parakēsarivarman. The last remark made with reference to the previous number holds good here too.

182. 636 *of* 1905.—(Tamil.) On the same rock. A record in the ninth year of the Chōḷa king Parakēsarivarman. Records gift of gold for feeding Brāhmaṇas by a native of Īrōḍu (Erode).

183. 637 *of* 1905.—(Tamil.) On the same rock. A mutilated record in the twelfth year of the Chōḷa king Parakēsarivarman. Close to it is a modern record, dated Kaliyuga 4991 (= A.D. 1889–90).

184. 638 *of* 1905.—(Tamil.) On the same rock. A record in the twenty-eighth year of the Chōḷa king Parakēsarivarman. Records gift of gold for feeding Brāhmaṇas.

185. 639 *of* 1905.—(Tamil.) On the same rock. A record in the twenty-sixth year of the Chōḷa king Parakēsarivarman. Records gift of gold for feeding Brāhmaṇas.

186. 640 *of* 1905.—(Tamil.) On the same rock. A record in the twenty-seventh year of the Chōḷa king Madiraikoṇḍa Parakēsarivarman (Parāntaka I). Records gift of gold for a lamp by a native of Kiḷinallūr in Kiḷār-kūṟṟam. The money was entrusted to the assembly of Tiruchcheṅgōḍu, while the people of the "eighteen districts" were to protect the grant.

187. 641 *of* 1905.—(Tamil.) On a boulder to the west of the same steps. A damaged record in the tenth year of the Pāṇḍya king Jaṭāvarman *alias* Tribhuvanachakravartin Sundara-Pāṇḍyadēva (I, ? 1251—64). Seems to record a gift of land. Mentions the god Subrahmaṇya-Piḷḷaiyār standing on the hill.

188. 642 *of* 1905.—(Tamil.) On the same boulder. A mutilated record in the fourteenth year of the Chōḷa king Parakēsarivarman *alias* Uḍaiyār Rājēndra-Chōḷadēva (I). Records gift of gold.

189. 643 *of* 1905.—(Tamil.) On the rock close to the Pāpanāśa-tīrtha on the top of the same hill. A partially damaged record in the twenty-third year of the Chōḷa king Parakēsarivarman *alias* Uḍaiyār Rājēndra-Chōḷadēva (I). Seems to record a gift of land.

190. 644 *of* 1905.—(Tamil.) On the rock west of the Gaṇapati-tīrtha on the same hill. A damaged record in the seventh year of the Pāṇḍya king Jaṭāvarman *alias* Tribhuvanachakravartin Sundara-Pāṇḍyadēva (I.? 1251—64). Seems to record a gift of land.

191. 645 *of* 1905.—(Tamil.) On the south wall of the central shrine in the Ardhanārīśvara temple on the same hill. An incomplete record. Records a gift by Pemmarasa-Uḍaiyār, the agent of Narasiṁharāja-Uḍaiyār, to the temples of Ardhanārīśvara and Subrahmaṇya on the hill at Tiruchcheṅgōḍu in Kīḻkarai-Pūndurai-nāḍu, a district of Koṅgu *alias* Vīraśōḷa-maṇḍalam.

192. 646 *of* 1905.—(Tamil.) On the west wall of the maṇṭapa in front of the same shrine. Records in Ś. 1521, Śārvari, the building of the maṇṭapa. [This is perhaps the inscription No. 3 of Mr. Sewell's List which is dated Ś. 1522.]

193. 647 *of* 1905.—(Tamil.) On the south wall of the same maṇṭapa. Registers in Ś. 1549, Vibhava, the building operations of a native of Mōrūr in Kīḻkarai-Pūndurai-nāḍu. [This is perhaps the inscription No. 4 of Mr. Sewell's List, which is dated Ś. 1551.]

194. 648 *of* 1905 (*No.* 1 *of Mr. Sewell's List*).—(Tamil.) On the north wall of the maṇṭapa in front of the Subrahmaṇya shrine in the same temple. A record in Ś. 1541, Siddhārthin. Similar to the above.

195. 649 *of* 1905.—(Tamil.) On the same wall. A record in Ś. 1588, Kīlaka (wrong), of the Nāyaka king Chokkanātha-Nāyaka (1560—82). Records gift of land. The king was the son of Viśvanātha-Nāyaka Tirumala-Nāyaka Muttuvīrappa-Nāyaka (1559 A.D.). See *Ind. Antq.*, February-May 1917, where I have given a detailed account of his reign.

196. 650 *of* 1905 (*No.* 2 *of Mr. Sewell's List*).—(Tamil.) On the north wall of the maṇṭapa in front of the Subrahmaṇya shrine in the Ardhanārīśvara temple on the hill. A record in Ś. 1581 Viḷambi, of the Nāyaka king Viśvanātha-Tirumala-Nāyaka, (1623—59). Records gift of the village of Kōḷaṅgaṇḍai in Parittip-paḷḷi-nāḍu for the merit of Kumāra-Muttu-Tirumala-Nāyaka. For Kumāra Muttu's career see *Ind. Antq.*, 1917, pp. 37–8.

197. 651 *of* 1905.—(Tamil.) On the base of the same maṇṭapa. An incomplete record of the Vijayanagara king Vīrapratāpa Kṛishṇadēva-Mahārāya (1509—30) in Kaliyuga-Śaka 1444, Chitrabhānu. Records the gift of the market tolls for celebrating certain festivals. Mentions Kunṟattūr-durgam in Koṅgu *alias* Vīraśōḷa-maṇḍalam.

198. 652 *of* 1905.—(Tamil.) Above the east wall of the *Nṛitta maṇṭapa* in the Kailāśanāthasvāmin temple in the same village. Records in Rudhirōdgārin the building of the maṇṭapa. A Telugu version of this inscription in engraved close to it.

199. 653 *of* 1905.—(Tamil.) On the north wall of the Subrahmaṇya shrine in the same temple. Records in Kāḷayukti the building of the shrine by a native of Āṇḍiyūr in Vaḍagarai-nāḍu.

200. 654 *of* 1905.—(Mentioned by Mr. Sewell also.) (Tamil, prose and verse.) On the ceiling of the gōpura in the same temple. A record of the Nāyaka king Viśvanātha-Chokkaliṅga-Nāyaka (1660—1682) in Ś. 1585, Śōbhana. Records the building of the gōpura and of the temple of Kāśi-Viśvēśvara on the hill. See No. 195 above.

201. Above the goddess, on the ceiling of the *garbhagriha*. Undated. Records gift of lands to temple by the agent of Narasiṁha Uḍaiyār. *Antiquities*, Vol. I, p. 203.

202. A C.P. grant (" in the possession of Śivarāma Paṇḍitar "), dated in Ś. 1656 (A.D. 1734). Records grant of land to temple on the hill by Kṛishṇa Rāja Uḍaiyār of Maisūr. *Ibid.*

202-A. *C.P. No.* 10 *of* 1914-15.—(In the possession of one Muttusāmi Kōnār.) A record in Tamil of the Chōḷa king Rājarāja I in his tenth year. Records that a certain Maḷavarāyan *alias* Kollimaḷavan Piridigaṇḍan Sundaraśōḷan fixed the taxes and fines due from the merchants of Dūśiyūr and evidently granted these in favour of the local Paramēśvara temple, on the occasion when he constructed a stone well to appease the spirit of his father who died at Īḷam.

202-B. *C.P. No.* 11 *of* 1915.—A record of the fifth year of Rājarāja I. The same individual (here also called Oṟṟiyūrān) gave to the temple of Tirumūlasthāna Uḍaiyār at Dūśiyūr, some lands, a tank and the village of Gaṇapatinallūr *alias* Amaṇkuḍi. The temple transferred it to the drummers *(uvachchars)* who made the five great sounds in the temple.

UTTANGARAI TALUK.

Buḍḍireḍḍipaṭṭi.

203. 155 *of* 1905.—(Tamil.) On the central shrine of the ruined Amman temple. An incomplete record of Tammayadēva Mahārāya (i.e., Immaḍi Narasiṁha), son of Narasiṁhadēva-Mahāraśugaḷ in Raudra (i.e., Ś. 1423). The king's agent Narasana Nāyaka (the founder of the Tuḷuva dynasty) and his agent Tipparaśa-Uḍaiyār are mentioned; also Kundāṇichchīmai.

Kallāvi.

204. 213 *of* 1910.—(Kanarese.) On a boulder near the 157th mile stone on the railway line. Records that this is the *liṅga-*

mudre (stone) in the garden land of the (Liṅgāyat) *maṭha* built by Paravata-muḍeya for Karibasappadēva of *Hiratta-maṭha.*

Kambayanallūr.

205. 8 *of* 1900.—(Tamil verse.) On the south wall of the central shrine of the Dēśināthēśvara temple. A record in the twenty-second year of the Chōḷa king Tribhuvanachakravartin Kulōttuṅga-Chōḷadēva (III ?). Mentions Viḍukādaḷagiyaperumāḷ *(Vyāmuktaśravaṇōjvala)*, son of Rājarāja Adiga, the Lord of Tagaḍūr. See *Ep. Ind.*, Vol. VI, pp. 332-3. For the political activities of this chief in the weak times of Kulōttuṅga III see N.A. 393-4, 422 and 414.

206. 9 *of* 1900.—(Tamil.) On the same wall. A record in the second year of the Hoysaḷa king Vīra-Viśvanāthadēva. Records gift of the village of Kadambarpaḷḷi in Puramalaināḍu, a sub-division of Tagaḍāi-nāḍu, by Madhurāntaka Vīranuḷamban Rāja-nārāyaṇa-Bhairavan for the merit of the king and for his own merit.

207. 10 *of* 1900.—(Tamil.) On the north and west walls of the same shrine. A record in the second year of the Hoysaḷa king Vīra-Viśvanāthadēva. Records gift to the temple of Dēśināyakar at Nāgaiyanpaḷḷi *alias* Kāḷiṅgarāya-chaturvēdimaṅgalam by Uttama-Śōḷa-Gaṅgādirāyan.

208. 11 *of* 1900.—(Tamil.) On the west and south walls of the same shrine. A record of the Vijayanagara king Immaḍi-Bukka-rāya (i.e., Bukka II, 1399—1406), son of Harihararāya (II), in Kshaya. Mentions Bukkaṇa-Uḍaiyār, i.e., Bukka I.

209. 12 *of* 1900.—(Tamil.) On a slab at the sluice of the tank in the same village. A record in the thirteenth year of the Chōḷa king Vikrama-Chōḷadēva (1118—35).

Mallapuram.

210. 18 *of* 1900.—(Tamil.) On a slab at the sluice of the tank. A mutilated record in the fourteenth year of the Chōḷa king Rājarājadēva. Mentions Tagaḍūr-nāḍu in Gaṅga-nāḍu, a sub-division of Nigarili-Śōḷamaṇḍalam.

Oḍḍappaṭṭi.

211. 211 *of* 1910.—(Vaṭṭeḷuttu.) On a slab set up near a well. A record in the twenty-seventh year of the Western Gaṅga king Śrīpuruśaparumar (Śrīpurushavarman). Records that Erumaiya Nakkanār, a servant of Teḷiṇiyyār, fell while the latter captured Yeruvāyil. See note to No. 212.

212. 212 *of* 1910.—(Vaṭṭeḷuttu.) On another slab close to the same. A record in the seventh year of the Western Gaṅga king Śrīpuruśar (Śrīpurusha). Records that a certain Erumai-Eruvāḍi and a certain Kūnarundai-Vaḍugan fell, perhaps in connection with a deer hunt *(mān-vēṭṭai)*. [Mr. Krishna Sastri believes that the king referred to was the W. Gaṅga Śrīpurusha Muttaraśa (765—805 according to Fleet) and Teḷiniyar was a form of *Eḷini* or Yavanika, a title of the Adiyamāns of Tagaḍūr (i.e., Dharmapuri), who had a territory which bordered the Gaṅga territory and who were therefore engaged in frequent raids. He thinks that the capture of Yeruvāyil ("somewhere near Oḍḍapaṭṭi") by Teḷiniyar must have referred to one of these raids. For the epigraphical evidence to prove that the Adiyamāns had the title of *Eḷini* see *Ep. Ind.*, Vol. VI, p. 331. Erumai is evidently Eṟumaināḍu of Tamil literature and Erumaṟaināḍu of the Hoysaḷa records (See *Ep. Carna.* X, Cu. 20). For the detailed history of the Adiyamāns see *Ep. Rep.*, 1911, pp. 58–9 and *Ibid.*, 1906, p. 74.

213. "In the possession of a resident of the village is an undated copper-plate grant recording a gift of lands to the Brāhmans." *Antiquities*, Vol. I, p. 202.

Paṭṭukkāṇampaṭṭi.

214. 254 *of* 1909.—(Tamil.) On the rock near the ruined Śiva temple. A record in the twenty-fifth year of the Chōḷa king Rājarājakēsarivarman *alias* Śrī-Rājarājadēva (I). Records gift of land to the temple of Mahādēva at Nelvāy by Nanni-gāmuṇḍan, son of Erumaiya-nāḷgāmuṇḍan *alias* Vīraśōḷa-gāmuṇḍan of Ariyūr in Puramalaināḍu, while Pañchavan-Brahmādhirāyan was ruling Tagaḍūr-nāḍu, which was granted to him for maintenance *(jivitam)* by the king. [Tagaḍūr-nāḍu was included in Gaṅgavāḍi which was conquered by Rājarāja in or before the fourteenth year of his reign. The inscription shows that it was conferred as a *jaghir* to Brahmādhirāja, who was a *perundaram* of the king. *Perundaram* has been interpreted to be a nobleman or high official. See *S.I.I.*, Vol. II, p. 141, note 1.]

Tirthamalai.

215. 658 *of* 1905.—(Tamil.) On the north and west walls of the central shrine in the Tīrthagirīśvara temple on the hill. A record of the Vijayanagara king Vijaya-Bhūpatirāya (1409—22), son of Vīra Dēvarāya (I) in Ś. 1331, Virōdhin. Mentions Perumalai-nāḍu surrounding the hill (name not clear) on the southern bank of the Peṇṇai river in Nigarili-śōḷamaṇḍalam.

216. 659 *of* 1905.—(Tamil.) On the north wall of the same shrine. An incomplete record of the Vijayanagara king Vīra-Vījayarāya-Uḍaiyār (1409—22), son of Vīra-Dēvarāya-Mahārāja (I) in Ś. 1333, *Khara*. Mentions Tīttamalai.

217. 660 *of* 1905.—(Tamil.) On the south wall of the maṇṭapa in front of the same shrine. A record in the eighth year of the Chōḷa king Tribhuvanachakravartin Rājarājadēva (III ?). Records gift of ornaments. Mentions a chief of Kūḍal in Puramalai-nāḍu, who bore the title Muḍigoṇḍa-Chōḷa-Karkaṭamārāyan.

218. 661 *of* 1905.—(Tamil.) On the same wall. A record in the thirty-fourth year of the Chōḷa king Tribhuvanachakravartin Kulōttuṅga-Chōḷadēva. Records gift of cows and a lampstand for a lamp to the temple at Tīttamalai by a native of Miṇiyūr in Tāyal-nāḍu.

219. 662 *of* 1905.—(Tamil.) On the same wall. A record of the Western Gaṅga (?) king Mallidēva-Mahāraja. Records gift of the village of Ālambāḍi in Āḍaiyūr-nāḍu. The inscription is preceded by the words *svasti śri-Kuvalālapuraparmēśvara Gaṅgakulōtta* in characters which appear to be somewhat older.

220. 663 *of* 1905.—(Tamil.) On the same wall. A record of the Chōḷa king Tribhuvanachakravartin Kulōttuṅga-Chōḷadēva, the date of which is doubtful. Records gift of sixteen cows for a lamp.

221. 664 *of* 1905.—(Tamil.) On the same wall. A record of the Vijayanagara king Vīra-Bukkaṇa-Uḍaiyār (II, 1399—1406), son of Hariyappa-Uḍaiyar (Harihara II), in Ś. 1321, Pramāthin. Records gift of land. Mentions Bukkarāyanpēṭṭai and Avanivēndarāmanallūr.

222. 665 *of* 1905.—(Tamil.) On the north wall of the same maṇṭapa. An incomplete record of the Vijayanagara king Dēvarāya I in Ś. 1325, Subhānu. Built in.

223. 666 *of* 1905.—(Tamil.) On the same wall. A damaged record of the Vijayanagara king Vīra-Dēvarāya-Uḍaiyār (II) in Plavaṅga (i.e., Ś. 1350). Mentions the Mahāpradhāna-Lakkaṇṇa-Uḍaiyār.

224. 667 *of* 1905.—(Telugu.) On the south wall of the Śilai-Nāyaḍu maṇṭapa in the same temple. A record in Ś. 1620, K. 4799, Bahudhānya. Refers to the building of the central shrine and to the setting up of the image of Kāśi-Viśvanātha in it.

225. 668 *of* 1905.—(Vaṭṭeḷuttu.) On a slab placed near the central shrine of the same temple. A damaged record.

226. 669 *of* 1905.—(Tamil.) On the rock to the west of the same shrine. A record in the twenty-ninth year of the Chōḷa king Parakēsarivarman *alias* Uḍaiyar Rājēndra-Chōḷadēva (I). Mentions Kaṛkaḍai-Mahārāya.

227. 670 *of* 1905.—(Tamil.) On the same rock. A record in the twenty-ninth year of the Chōḷa king Parakēsarivarman *alias* Uḍaiyār Rājēndra-Chōḷadēva (I, 1011—43). Records gift of three villages by Uttama-Śōḷa-Puramalaināḍāḷvān, who seems to have been the chief of Rājēndra-Śōḷa-Viriyūr-nāḍu. The donor repaired the temple and constructed the mukha-maṇṭapa. The temple is called Tīrttamalai-Uḍaiyār-Mahādēvar in Puramalai-nāḍu, a subdivision of Tagaḍūr-nāḍu, which was a district of Nigarili-Śōḷa-maṇḍalam.

228. 671 *of* 1905.—(Tamil.) On the same rock. A record of the Chōḷa king Parakēsarivarman *alias* Uḍaiyār Rājēndra-Chōḷa-dēva (1011—43), the date of which is lost. Records the building of the shrines of Kshētrapāla and Chaṇḍēśvara. Mummuḍi-Chōḷa, son of Uttamachchōḷapuramalai Nāḍāḷvān, was the builder.

229. 672 *of* 1905.—(Tamil.) On the same rock. A record in th fourth year of the Chōḷa king Parakēsarivarman. Records gift of gold for a lamp.

230. 673 *of* 1905.—(Tamil.) On the same rock. A record in the fourth year of the Chōḷa king Parakēsarivarman. Records gift of gold for a lamp. Mentions the queen of Mummuḍi-Chōḷa-Kūḍal-āḷvār in this and in the above epigraph.

231. 674 *of* 1905.—(Tamil.) On the same rock. A record in the seventeenth year of the Chōḷa king Tribhuvanachakravartin Kulōttuṅga-Chōḷadēva. Records gift of thirty-two cows for a lamp.

232. 675 *of* 1905.—(Tamil.) On the same rock. A record in the twelfth year of the Chōḷa king Tribhuvanachakravartin Kulōttuṅga-Chōḷadēva. Records gift of land for offerings.

233. 676 *of* 1905.—(Tamil.) On the same rock. A record in the tenth year of the Chōḷa king Kulōttuṅga-Chōḷadēva. Records the appointment of a *pūjāri* at the temple of Tīrttamalai in Tagaḍūr-nāṭṭu-Puramalai-nāḍu, which was a district of Nigarili-Śōḷa-maṇḍalattu-Gaṅganāḍu.

Supplementary Note.

55. The inscription purports to prove the origin of the local Malayāḷi settlers and says: "These hills are assigned by Venuvarāyan, the ruler who owned a lakh of horses of each different colour, as a gift for the celebration of the car and other festivals in propitiation of Karia Perumāḷ and other deities in the nāds of Chinnakalvirāyan and Periakalvirāyan. The people of the seven nāds are herein concerned, and are bound to give effect to the wishes of the donor."

TANJORE DISTRICT.

ARANTĀNGI TALUK.

Arantāṅgi.

1. 409 *of* 1902.—(Tamil.) On the west wall of the Viśvanātha shrine in the fort. A record in the third year of Tribhuvanachakravartin Kōnērinmaikoṇḍān. Records gift of land.

Ponpētti.

Venkayya identifies this place with Ponpaṟṟi, the birthplace of Buddhamitra, the author of the *Virasōḻiyam* which he composed in honour of his patron, the Chōḷa king Vīrarājēndra I (1063—70). See *Ep. Rep.*, 1899, pp. 18–19.

2. 617 *of* 1902.—(Tamil.) On the east wall of the Vīṟṟirunda Perumāḷ temple. A record in Ś. 1294, Paridhāvin, of the Vijayanagara king Kampaṇa Uḍaiyār II (son of Bukka I). Records gift of taxes by the king.

Tiruppunavāśal.

3. 612 *of* 1902.—(Tamil.) On a stone set up near the southern prākāra of the Vriddhapurīśvara temple. A record of the Pāṇḍya king Kōnērinmaikoṇḍān Tribhuvanachakravartin Vikrama-Pāṇḍyadēva, in his seventeenth year, Ś. 1339, corresponding to Wednesday, 12th January 1418. Provides for the repairs of the temple. See *Ep. Ind.*, Vol. VIII, 281. The king came to the throne between 13th January and 27th July, A.D. 1401.

4. 613 *of* 1902.—(Tamil.) On the east wall of the maṇṭapa in front of the same temple. A record in the seventeenth year of the Pāṇḍya king Jaṭāvarman *alias* Vīra-Pāṇḍyadēva. Records gift of land. [Was he the king who ascended the throne in 1253 ?]

5. 614 *of* 1902.—(Tamil.) On the same wall. A record in the fourteenth year of the Pāṇḍya king Jaṭāvarman *alias* Tribhuvanachakravartin Vīra-Pāṇḍyadēva. Records gift of land. [See note to the above epigraph.]

6. 615 *of* 1902.—(Tamil and Vaṭṭeḻuttu.) On the inner side of the north wall of the same maṇṭapa. A record in the thirteenth year of the Pāṇḍya king Jaṭāvarman *alias* Sundara-Pāṇḍyadēva. Mentions Vīra-Pāṇḍyadēva and quotes the fifth year of Kulaśēkharadēva. [It is impossible to say whether the king is Sundara Pāṇḍya I (1251—64) or Sundara Pāṇḍya II (1270— ?) discovered by Diwan Bahadur Swamikannu Pillai or Sundra Pāṇḍya III (1276—90).]

7. 616 *of* 1902.—(Tamil.) In the same place. A record in the seventeenth year of the Pāṇḍya king Māravarman *alias* Tribhuvanachakravartin Sundara-Pāṇḍyadēva, who conquered every country. Records sale of land. [The king referred to is apparently the second of that name, who ascended the throne between June 15, A.D. 1238 and January 18, A.D. 1239.]

KUMBAKŌNAM TALUK.

Aḻagādriputtūr.

7-A. 283 *of* 1908.—(Tamil.) On the north wall of the central shrine in the Svarṇapurīśvara temple. A mutilated record in the seventh year of the Chōḷa king Rājarājakēsarivarman. Records gift of land (1,300 *kuḻis*) for offerings to the temple of Tirupputtūr-uḍaiya-Paramasvāmin at Paradāyakuḍi, a *brahmadēya* in Tirunaṟaiyūr-nāḍu. Refers to the building of the central shrine with stone.

7-B. 284 *of* 1908.—(Tamil.) On the same wall. A damaged record in the twenty-eighth year of the Chōḷa king Rājarājakēsarivarman *alias* Rājarājadēva (I). Records gift of lamps.

7-C. 285 *of* 1908.—(Tamil.) On the south wall of the same shrine. A record in the seventh year of the Chōḷa king Vikrama-Chōḷadēva (1118—35). Records gift of money for a lamp to the temple of Aḻagiyadēva of Tirupputtūr. On the same tier is an unfinished inscription with the usual historical introduction of Vikrama-Chōḷa beginning with the words *pū-mādupuṇara*, etc.

7-D. 286 *of* 1908.—(Tamil.) On the same wall. A mutilated record. Seems to record a gift of a lamp. Mentions Aḻagar-Tirupputtūr; in Kulōttuṅgaśōḷa-vaḷanāḍu.

7-E. 287 *of* 1908.—(Tamil.) On the east wall of the same shrine. A damaged record in the twenty-second year of the Chōḷa king Rājarājakēsarivarman *alias* Rājarājadēva (I). Records gift of land (3 *mās*) for a lamp to the temple of Tirupputtūr Mahādēva in Paradāyakuḍi, a *brahmadēya*, in Tirunaṟaiyūr-nāḍu, a subdivision of Kshatriyaśikhāmaṇi-vaḷanāḍu.

7-F. 288 *of* 1908.—(Tamil.) On the same wall. A record of the Chōḷa king Rājakēsarivarman *alias* Tribhuvanachakravartin Kulōttuṅga-Chōḷadēva (I), the date of which is lost. Records gift of land for offerings.

7-G. 289 *of* 1908.—(Tamil.) On the east and south walls of the same shrine. A record in the fourth year of the Chōḷa king Parakēsarivarman *alias* Rājēndra-Chōḷadēva (I). Records sale of land (6 *mās* for 30 *kāśus*) for offerings to the shrine of Sūryadēva, constructed in the temple by a native of Kallūr in Mēl-Vembanāḍu, a subdivision of Pāṇḍi-nāḍu *alias* Rājarājamaṇḍalam. Mentions Kurugūrmaḍam at the north bank of the tank where the sabhā met. *Ulagaḷanda-kōle* mentioned. [There is a village of the name of Kallūr in this taluk.]

*Dārāśuram.**

The architectural merits of the two shrines here are far greater than those of the Kumbhakōṇam shrines. See Fergusson's *Ind. and East. Arch.*, pp. 367—9.

8. 2 *of* 1915.—(Tamil.) On the north wall of the verandah round the Airāvatēśvara temple. Consists of 108 sections, each containing the name and surname of the Śaivāchārya whose image is sculptured below. See No. 10.

9. 3 *of* 1915.—(Tamil.) On a pillar of the maṇṭapa in front of the central shrine of the Sōmēśvarasvāmin temple in the same taluk. A damaged record in the fifth year of the Chōḷa king Rājarājakēsarivarman (Rājarāja I). Records gift of land for sacred bath, offerings and *śri-bali* to the Āḷvār of Tirusōmīśvaram at Tirukkuḍamūkku (i.e., Kumbhakōṇam), a *dēvadāna* of Vaḍagarai-Pāmbura-nāḍu.

10. 16 *of* 1908.—(Tamil.) On the walls of the central shrine in the Airāvatēśvara temple. Contains the names of Śaiva devotees, with sculptures representing the principal events of their lives. A very interesting epigraph illustrative of the establishment of Śaivite saint worship by the tenth century.

11. 17 *of* 1908.—(Tamil.) On the east wall of the first prākāra of the same temple. A damaged record in the twenty-first year of the Chōḷa king Tribhuvanachakravartin śrī-Rājarājadēva (II ?). The temple is called Rājarājēśvaramuḍaiyār. Arrangements are made for the disposal of fruits grown on the temple garden. [This seems to be the same as *Ins., S. Dts.*, No. 119, p. 248.]

12. 18 *of* 1908.—(Tamil.) On the same wall. A fragmentary record of the Chōḷa king Rājādhirāja II (1171—1186), containing a portion of the historical introduction beginning with the words *kaḍalśūḷnda*.

13. 19 *of* 1908.—(Tamil.) On the same wall. An unfinished record in the twelfth year of the Chōḷa king Rājakēsarivarman *alias* Tribhuvanachakravartin śrī-Rājādhirājadēva (II ?). [This seems to be the same as No. 124 in *Ins., S. Dts.*, p. 249; but the regnal year reads thirteenth.]

14. 20 *of* 1908.—(Tamil.) On the same wall. A record in the eighth year of the Chōḷa king Parakēsarivarman *alias* Tribhuvanachakravartin Śrī-Kulōttuṅga-Chōḷadēva. The temple is called

---

* The Mack. MSS. (as summarized in *Ins., S. Dts.*, pp. 248—50, Nos. 118—128) give eleven inscriptions. Of these three have been noted against the corresponding numbers in the departmental list. Others are given under Nos. 21-A to 21-H.

Rājarāja Īśvaramuḍaiyār. [The king referred is evidently Kulōttuṅga III, 1178—1216.]

15. 21 *of* 1908.—(Tamil.) On the south wall of the same prākāra. A record in the third year of the Pāṇḍya king Māravarman Tribhuvanachakravartin Vīra-Pāṇḍyadēva. Records gift of land for repairs to the temple of Uḍaiyār Rājarāja-Īśvaramuḍaiyār-Nāyanār at Rājarājapuram. [Was this king one of the mediæval Pāṇḍyas or identical with Māravarman Vīra Pāṇḍya Abhirāman Vīramāran Śeliyan Kaliyugarāman Tirunelvēlipperumāḷ who ascended the throne between March and July 1443 and who was joint ruler with Arikēsari, 1422—64? See *Ins.*, *S. Dts.*, p. 248, No. 118.]

16. 22 *of* 1908.—(Tamil.) On the inner gōpura of the same temple, right of entrance. Records in Ś. 1408, expired, Krōdhana, gift of land for providing the requirements of worship in the temple of Irārāśuram (also Rārāśuram).

17. 23 *of* 1908.—(Tamil.) In the same place. A record of the Pāṇḍya king Māravarman Tribhuvanachakravartin Śrī-Vallabhadēva, the date of which is doubtful. Registers provision made for repairs and for celebrating festivals in the temple of Irārāśuram-uḍaiya-Nāyanār. [Was the king the predecessor of the mediæval Pāṇḍya Jaṭāvarman Kulaśēkhara I or identical with the later Iṛandakālameḍutta Śrīvallabha or the great Ativīrarāma? It is evidently the former.]

18. 24 *of* 1908.—(Tamil.) Below the image of a dvārapālaka set up close to the same gōpura, left of entrance. A record of Uḍaiyār Śrī-Vijayarājēndradēva. Records that the image was brought from Kalyāṇapuram by the king after his capture of the place. [The king was evidently Rājādhirāja (I), Jayaṅkoṇḍachōḷa (1018—52), the anointer of heroes at Kalyāṇapura.]

19. 25 *of* 1908.—(Tamil.) On the walls of the outer gōpura of the same temple. These are small labels containing the names of gods, whose images have, in most cases, since disappeared or have been mutilated.

20. 26 *of* 1908.—(Tamil.) On two stones lying in the courtyard of the same temple. Each of them contains a portion of the historical introduction of Kulōttuṅga (I).

21. 27 *of* 1908.—(Tamil.) On a third stone in the same place. The gōpura is called Īgaimūvēndiraiyar-tirukkōpuram.

The following inscriptions have been taken from the *Mack. MSS.* Their exact places in the temple are not given.

21-A. A grant of half *paṇam* by each inhabitant of the village to the God in the tenth year of Vallabha Rāya Mahādēva.

21-B. Grant of 2 *mās* and 3½ *kāṇi* of land for the God by Rājarājadēva in his thirty-first year.

21-C. A grant of 3½ *vēlis* of land by the same king in his second year at "Vayeghanelloor."

21-D. A grant of 2½ *vēlis* of land at "Auyenvama Rāja Poorum" by Pratāpadēvarāya in Ś. 1268, Krōdhi. The date is wrong.

21-E. A grant of 13½ *vēlis* of land at "Taramala Varatadi Colla" by Rājarājadēva in his twenty-second year.

21-F. A grant of 3 *vēlis* and 8 *mās* of land in "Paninaralliyoor" to the Vrishabavāhana festival by Raṅgapati Uḍaiyān in the thirty-third year of Rājarājadēva.

21-G. A record dated in Ś. 1199, Bahudhānya, in the reign of Vīrapratāpa-Dēvarāya. Records the erection of a maṇṭapam and tank at Paṭṭīśvaram and grant of 4 *mās* and 3 *kāṇis* of land to Paṭṭīśvara-Nāyanār. *Ins., S. Dts.*, p. 250, No. 127. Date wrong.

21-H. A record of Vīradēva Mahārāya in Ś. 1137, Dhātu. Records the erection of a pagoda of God Paṭṭīśvara and grant of 9½ *vēlis* of land at "Chundole Poorum" for the repair of the temple. *Ibid.*, No. 128. Date wrong.

Kāvalkūḍam.

21-I. 298 *of* 1911.—(Tamil.) On a stone in the Kaṇkuḍutta Vināyaka temple. A much damaged record. Mentions the Mahāmaṇḍalēśvara Achyutappa Nāyakkar Aiyan (evidently the Tanjore Nāik king who ruled from 1572 to 1614).

Kumbhakōṇam.

The antiquity of Kumbhakōṇam is well recognized, its God Sāraṅgapāṇi or Ārāvamuda having been sung in the *Prabandhas* in the eighth century, but no epigraphical evidences are available to show its antiquity. It has twelve Śaivite and four Vaishṇavite shrines, besides a Brahma temple. The temples are comparatively modern (being the works of the Nāik kings) in outer parts, but ancient, going back to the Chōḷa period at least in inner parts. The Nāgēśvara shrine is famous for the adoration of its deity by the sun and the Chakrapāṇi shrine for the statue of a Tanjore king holding a lamp for the God. The *Śaṅkarāchārya maṭha* is one of the most important historical institutions.

22. 13 *of* 1908.—(Tamil.) On the west wall of the shrine of the goddess in the Nāgēśvara temple. A record in the eighth year of the Pāṇḍya king Mārañjaḍaiyan. Records gift of 138 cows for milk and 100 *kāśu* for two lamps by the king to the temple of Tirukkīḻkkōṭṭattu Bhaṭāra at Tirukkuḍamūkku. [The exact identity of Mārañjaḍaiyan is not known. Tirukkuḍandai Kiḻkkōṭṭam is famous in Śaivite tradition as the place where the sun worshipped Śiva and got back the splendour which he had lost owing to Viśvakarma's curse.]

23. 14 *of* 1908.—(Tamil.) On the north wall of the Sūryanārāyaṇa shrine in the Nāgēśvara temple. A record of the Chōḷa king Rājakēsarin Uḍaiyār Śrī-Vijayarājēndradēva (Rājādhirāja I), in his thirty-sixth year, Makha, Apara, Wednesday, Āyilyam. Records sale of land for 498 *kaḻañju* and lands made rent-free. [See *Ep. Ind.*, Vol. X, p. 121, where Mr. R. Sewell points out that the date corresponds to December 29, A.D. 1053.]

24. 15 *of* 1908.—(Tamil.) On the east wall of the same shrine. An unfinished record in the eighth year of the Chōḷa king Parakēsarivarman *alias* Śrī-Rājēndra-Chōḷadēva (I). Seems to provide for offerings to the shrine of Chandraśēkharadēva.

25. 223 *of* 1911.—(Tamil.) On the north wall of the central shrine in the Nāgēśvara temple. A record in the sixth year of the Chōḷa king . . . sarivarman. Built in at the beginning. Records gift of 96 sheep for a lamp to the temple of Tirukkīḻkōṭṭattu-Paramasvāmi at Tirukkuḍamūkku in Vaḍagarai Pāmbūr-nāḍu, by Iṅgaḷa-Mādēvan Kōdai Māran, a native of Iṅgaḷ-nāḍu.

26. 224 *of* 1911.—(Tamil.) On the same wall. A record in the second year of the Chōḷa king Parakēsarivarman. Records sale of land to a certain Kāḍan Āchchan for 25 *kaḻañju* which he had deposited in the same temple, for maintaining a perpetual lamp. [Mr. Krishna Sastri surmises that the king referred to might be Āditya Karikāla II.]

27. 225 *of* 1911.—(Tamil.) On the same wall. A record in the fifth year of the Chōḷa king Parakēsarivarman (Āditya II ?), " who took the head of the Pāṇḍya." Records sale of land by the assembly of Tirukkuḍamūkku, a *dēvadāna* in Vaḍagarai-Pāmbūr-nāḍu, to the palace woman *(peṇḍāṭṭi)* Periyan Tribhuvana-sundari (a resident) of Paḷaiya-vēḷam at Tañjāvūr in Tañjāvūr-kūṟṟam, for 85 *kaḻañju* of gold which she had deposited, for feeding a Śivayōgin in the temple of Tirukkīḻkōṭṭattu-Paramasvāmi. The land given by Kāḍan Āchchan (see the above epigraph) formed one of the boundaries of this land.

28. 226 *of* 1911.—(Tamil.) On the same wall. A record in the fourth year of the Chōḷa king Parakēsarivarman (Āditya II ?) " who took the head of the Pāṇḍya." Records gift of ninety sheep for a lamp to the temple of Tirukkīḻkōṭṭattu-Paramēśvara by Peṇḍāṭṭi Dēvayan Puḷalakkaṉ *alias* Avaniśikhāmaṇi (a resident) of Kīḻai-vēḷam (quarter) at Tañjāvūr, called after Uḍaiyapirāṭṭiyār Kīḻanaḍigal, the mother of Ānaimēṟṟuñjinār [i.e., Rājāditya who was killed by Bhūtuga II while seated in his elephant and whose mother was Kōkkiḻāṇaḍigaḷ, the queen of Parāntaka I. See *Leyden Grant* in *Tam. and Sans. Ins.*, p. 204 ff. ; the Ātakūr inscription as interpreted by R. Narasimhachar in *J.R.A.S.*, April 1909; and *Mys. Arch. Rep.*, 1911, p. 38.]

29. 227 *of* 1911.—(Tamil.) On the same wall. A record in the third year of the Chōḷa king Rājakēsarivarman. Records sale of land by the assembly of Tirukkuḍamūkkil, to Arayan Kalaṅgāmalai, a Veḷḷāḷa of Tañjāvūr, for feeding a Śivayōgin in the temple of Tirukkīḻkōṭṭattu-Paramasvāmi.

30. 228 *of* 1911.—(Tamil.) On the same wall. A record in the third year of the Chōḷa king Rājakēsarivarman (Gaṇḍarāditya ?). Records gift of ninety sheep for a lamp by Kumāran Tūduvan, one of the *Kaikkōḷas* of Vīraśōḻatteriñja-Kaikkōḷar and a resident of Tañjāvūr. [Vīra Chōḷa was a surname of Parāntaka I and the Kaikkōḷars evidently got the title from him. For similar epithets see Tj. 1397 and 1398.

31. 229 *of* 1911.—(Tamil.) On the same wall. A damaged record in the eighth year of the Chōḷa king Parakēsarivarman. Records gift of ninety-six sheep for a lamp. Mr. Swamikannu Pillai calculates the date to be Thursday, the 30th January, A.D. 979, and so the king must have been Madhurāntaka Uttama Chōḷa who came to the throne in A.D. 969–70.

32. 230 *of* 1911.—(Tamil.) On the same wall. A record in the third year of the Chōḷa king Parakēśarivarman (Āditya II?) "who took the head of the Pāṇḍya." Records sale of land by the assembly of Srī-kuḍandai to Kōilmayilai *alias* Parāntaka-Mūvēndavēḷān of Śirṟiṅgan in Iṅganāḍu, for feeding twenty *apūrvins* versed in the Vēdās and five Śivayōgins in the temple *(śrikōil)* of Tirukkīḻkōṭṭattu Perumāḷ. [Kuḍandai is the name of Kumbhakōṇam by which orthodox Vaishṇavites even now call it.] See No. 35.

33. 231 *of* 1911.—(Tamil.) On the same wall. A record in the fourth year of the Chōḷa king Parakēsarivarman, "who took the head of the Pāṇḍya." Records gift of land by the same person for feeding fifty Brāhmaṇas. See Nos. 26, 27 and 28 above.

34. 232 *of* 1911.—(Tamil.) On the same wall. A record in the twenty-seventh year of the Chōḷa king Madiraikoṇḍa Parakēsarivarman (Parāntaka I). Built in at the end. An inscription to the left of this on the same wall has its beginning built in and records a gift of land for feeding a Śivayōgin and maintaining a lamp in the temple of Tirukkīḻkōṭṭattu-Perumānaḍigaḷ.

35. 233 *of* 1911.—(Tamil.) On the same wall. A record in the third year of the Chōḷa king Parakēsarivarman, "who took the head of the Pāṇḍya." Records sale of land to Kōyilmayilai *alias* Parāntaka Mūvēndavēḷān by the assembly of Tirukkuḍamūkku, which he presented as a *bhaṭṭavritti* to those who expounded *Prabhākaram* in the temple. [Mr. Krishna Sastri identifies the Chōḷa king with Āditya Karikāla II, but it seems that Parāntaka II is more probable. *Prabhākara matha* is one of the famous schools of Mīmāmsa, founded by Prabhākara, a contemporary of Kumarila in the eighth century.]

36. 234 *of* 1911.—(Tamil.) On the same wall. A record in the eighth year of the Chōḷa king Parakēsarivarman. Records gift of ninety-six sheep for a lamp. Mentions Śrī-Uttamaśōḷa-Nambirāṭṭiyār. [Evidently refers to Madhurāntaka Uttamachōḷadēva.]

37. 235 *of* 1911.—(Tamil.) On the west wall of the same shrine. A record in the fortieth year of the Chōḷa king Parakēsarivarman (i.e., Parāntaka I, 906—47) "who took Madirai (Madura) and Īḷam (Ceylon)." Records gift of ninety sheep for a lamp.

38. 236 *of* 1911.—(Tamil.) On the same wall. A damaged record in the fifth year of the Chōḷa king Rājakēsarivarman. Quotes the third year of . . . kēsarivarman and seems to record a gift of seventy *Īḷakkāsu*, for offerings. [Īḷakkāśu = the coin of Ceylon.]

39. 237 *of* 1911.—(Tamil.) On the same wall. A much damaged record of the Chōḷa king Parakēsarivarman, the date of which is doubtful. Records gift of eighty *kaḷañju* of gold for feeding Brāhmaṇas.

40. 238 *of* 1911.—(Tamil.) On the same wall. A much damaged record of the Chōḷa king Madiraikoṇḍa Parakēsarivarman (906-–47), the date of which is lost. Records gift of ninety-six sheep for a lamp to the temple of Tirukkīḻkōṭṭattu-Mahādēva, by a certain Kāri-Viḻupparaiyan.

41. 239 *of* 1911.—(Tamil.) On the same wall. A much damaged record of the Chōḷa king Rājakēsarivarman, the date of which is lost. Records gift of ninety-six sheep for a lamp.

42. 240 *of* 1911.—(Tamil.) On same wall. A much damaged record in the thirteenth year of the Chōḷa king Parakēsarivarman. Records gift of land by Vīranārāyaṇiyār, daughter of . . . and queen *(nambirāṭṭiyar)* of Śrī-Uttamaśōḷar, for providing garlands of flowers to the temple of Tirukkīḻkōṭṭattu-Perumāḷ. [According to Mr. Swamikannu Pillai the date corresponds to Friday, the 9th June A.D. 982 and so the king referred to is Madhurāntaka Uttamachōḷa, whose date of accession was A.D. 969-70.]

43. 241 *of* 1911.—(Tamil.) On the same wall. Records gift of gold for lamps by two private individuals.

44. 242 *of* 1911.—(Tamil.) On the west and south walls of the same shrine. A record in the second year of the Chōḷa king Parakēsarivarman. Records gift of ninety sheep for a lamp by a Kaikkōḷan named Dēvan Rājādittan.

45. 243 *of* 1911.—(Tamil.) On the same walls. A record in the fifth year of the Chōḷa king Parakēsarivarman. Records gift of sheep for lamps.

46. 244 *of* 1911.—(Tamil.) On the same walls. A record in the fifth year of the Chōḷa king Parakēsarivarman. Records gift of ninety-seven sheep for a lamp by a certain Dēvan Nakkan.

47. 245 *of* 1911.—(Tamil.) On the same walls. A much damaged record in the fourth year of the Chōḷa king Parakēsarivarman. Records sale of land by the assembly of Tirukkuḍamūkku for maintaining a lamp in the temple of Tirukkīḻkōṭṭattu-Paramasvāmin in the name of Kāri Kolamban, a Kaikkōḷan. [According to Mr. Swamikannu Pillai the date corresponded to Thursday, the 22nd April, A.D. 975, and so the king referred to is evidently Madhurāntaka Uttamachōḷa whose accession was in A.D. 969–70.]

48. 246 *of* 1911.—(Grantha and Tamil.) On the same walls. A record in the twenty-eighth year of the Chōḷa king Parakēsarivarman. Records gift of money for a lamp by Tanavadi Araṅgan *alias* Pañchavan, a native of Karuvūr in Miḻalai-kūṟṟam, to the temple of Tirukkīḻkōṭṭattu-Bhaṭṭāraka.

49. 247 *of* 1911.—(Tamil.) On the south wall of the same shrine. An incomplete record in the fourth year of the Chōḷa king Parakēsarivarman. Records gift of land for feeding a Brāhmaṇa by a merchant of Nandipuram.

50. 248 *of* 1911.—(Tamil.) On the same wall. A record in the third year of the Chōḷa king Parakēsarivarman. Records gift of 25 *kaḻañju* of gold for a lamp, by Pūvan Kaṇṇan of Neḍumpuṟaiyūr in Malai-nāḍu.

51. 249 *of* 1911.—(Tamil.) On the same wall. A record of the Chōḷa king Madiraikoṇḍa Parakēsarivarman (Parāntaka I), the date of which is lost. Built in at the end and damaged. Records sale of land by the assembly of Tirukkuḍamūkku for feeding two persons in the temple of Tirukkīḻkōṭṭattu-Perumānaḍigaḷ. Mentions Āyirattaḷi in Kiḻār-kūṟṟam, a subdivision of Teṅkarainādu.

52. 250 *of* 1911.—(Tamil.) On the same wall. A record in the thirty-eighth year of the Chōḷa king Madiraikoṇḍa Parakēsarivarman. Records gift of ninety-six sheep for a lamp by a certain Maiñjan Kavaiyan, a native of Aiyyāru in Tirunaṟaiyūr-nāḍu.

53. 251 *of* 1911.—(Tamil.) On the same wall. A record in the second year of the Chōḷa king Parakēsarivarman. Records gift of ninety sheep for a lamp by Kaḍigāvan Kaḷḷān, one of *Uḍaiyār-Vīraśōḻatteriñja-Kaikkōḷar*. See No. 30 above.

54. 252 *of* 1911.—(Tamil.) On the same wall. A record in the fifteenth year of the Chōḷa king Rājakēsarivarman. Records gift of a lamp by Kalayan Māṇikkam, to the temple of Tirukkīḻkōṭṭattu-Perumānaḍigaḷ.

55. 253 *of* 1911.—(Tamil.) On the same wall. A damaged record in the fortieth year of the Chōḷa king Parakēsarivarman (905—47), who took Madirai (Madura) and Īḻam (Ceylon). Records gift of land for providing a lamp and burning incense *(śidāri)* in the temple of Tirukkīḻkōṭṭattu-Perumānaḍigaḷ and for maintaining two lamps in the shrine of Sūryadēvar,

56. 254 *of* 1911.—(Tamil.) On the same wall. A damaged record of the Chōḷa king Madiraikoṇḍa-Parakēsarivarman (906—47), the date of which is lost. Records gift of 105 pieces of gold *(tuḷaipon)* by Villavan Pēraraiyan *alias* Śiḍupayam Pāṇḍan, a native of Kāvalūr which was a *dēvadāna* of Āyirattaḷi in Kiḻār-kūṟṟam a subdivision of Tenkarainādu, for conducting festivals in the same temple.

57. 255 *of* 1911.—(Tamil.) On the same wall. A damaged record in the third year of the Chōḷa king Rājakēsarivarman (Gaṇḍarāditya). Records sale of land in Ariśalūr by the assembly of Tirukkuḍamūkku to the temple of Tirukkīḻkōṭṭattu-Paramasvāmi, for 500 *kaḷañju* of gold, in order to pay a part of 3,000 *kaḷañju* levied upon them as an impost *(daṇḍam)* by Madiraikoṇḍa-Uḍaiyār (i.e., Parāntaka I) in his thirty-eighth year. Mentions the army of the Pāṇḍya (Pāṇḍi-paḍai) and the temple of Jalaśayana. [In *Ep. Rep.*, 1907, p. 73, Venkayya describes the three invasions of Parāntaka I against the Pāṇḍya, in the last of which he conquered Īḻam also. Inscriptions show that this took place in his thirty-seventh year. The present inscription corroborates it. The Pāṇḍipaḍayar has been interpreted to be the army which conquered the Pāṇḍya country.]

58. 256 *of* 1911.—(Tamil.) On the same wall. A much damaged record in the sixth year of the Chōḷa king Parakēsarivarman *alias* Rājēndra-Chōḷadēva (I). Records gift of land for providing offerings to the image of Śelvappirān in the Śrīvimāna (central shrine) of the temple of Tirukkīḻkōṭṭam-Uḍaiyār, by the assembly of Tirukkuḍamūkku in Pāmbūr-nāḍu, a subdivision of Uyyakkoṇḍār-vaḷanāḍu.

59. 257 *of* 1911.—(Tamil.) On the north wall of the maṇṭapa in front of the same shrine. A record in the twenty-second year of the Chōḷa king Tribhuvanachakravartin Rājarājadēva. Records gift of land by a Brāhmaṇa lady, for maintaining certain festivals in the shrine of Maḍandaipāga-Nāyanār, situated in the temple of Tirukkīḻkōṭṭam-Uḍaiyār at Tirukkuḍamūkkil in Pāmbūr-nāḍu, a subdivision of Uyyakoṇḍār-vaḷanāḍu. [This inscription is evidently the same as *Ins., S. Dts.*, p. 195, No. 10. But the donors are given as Nārāyaṇa Ambalattān and "Pramanavooyavundan."]

60. 258 *of* 1911 *.—(Tamil.) On the same wall. A record in the twentieth year (Chitra, Mīna, first lunar fortnight) of the Chōḷa king Rājakēsarivarman *alias* Tribhuvanachakravartin Rājarājadēva. Begins with a new historical introduction *śir-manni-iru-nāngu-diśai*, etc. Records gift of land for repairs and jewels to

---

* The *Mack. List, Ins., S. Dts.*, gives side by side with this another inscription (see No. 12 in p. 195). It is dated Ś. 1482 in the reign of Sadāśiva Ráya and grants 25 *pons* for the offering of cakes to the deity on new-moon days.

the same shrine by a certain Kūttāḍum Tirugñānasambandar Maḍandaipāgan. A gift of land by Kūttāḍum Tirugñānasambandar Māṇikkavāśagan, to the shrine of Kūttāḍum Tirugñānasambandēśvaram-Uḍaiyār built by himself in the temple of Tirukkīḻkōṭṭam-Uḍaiyār, is recorded below the above. [Mr. Swamikannu Pillai calculates the year of the inscription to be 1235-36, and so the king should have been Rājarāja III (1216—48). I have traced this inscription in the *Mack. Lists* to *Ins., S. Dts.*, p. 195, No. 11.]

61. 259 *of* 1911.—(Tamil.) On the same wall. A record of Mahāmaṇḍalēśvara Paṭṭukkaṭṭāri Kōnēridēva-Mahārāja, "lord of Kāñchīpura, the best of towns," in Ś. 1412, Sādhāraṇa. Registers that Timmanan (surnamed) Maḍandaipāga-Koṅgarāyan, son of Śēdirāya-Māṇikkam, was granted food, house and land by the authorities managing the temple of Maḍandaipāga-Nāyanār at Tirukkuḍamūkku, a *brahmadēya* in Pāmburattu-nāḍu, a subdivision of Uyyakkoṇḍārśōḻa-vaḷanāḍu, for the services rendered by him to the temple. [Mr. Krishna Sastri believes that the king might be the same as he who is referred to in the *Kōyiloḻugu* as the successor of Śāḷuva Tirumal Rāja in the Government of the Trichinopoly country, who was an anti-Vaishṇavite. This inscription is given in *Ins., S. Dts.*, p. 194, No. 8, also.]

62. 260 *of* 1911.—(Tamil.) On the same wall. An unfinished record in the thirty-fifth year of the Chōḻa king Tribhuvanachakravartin Tribhuvanavīradēva (Kulōttuṅga III) "who being pleased to take Madurai (Madura), Īḻam (Ceylon), Karuvūr and the crowned head of the Pāṇḍya, was pleased to perform the anointment of victors and heroes." Records that a certain Āḻvār Tiruppurāmbiyam-Uḍaiyān *alias* Sembiyan Pallavaraiyan of Vēlūr had set up an image called Tiruppurāmbiyam-Uḍaiyār in the eastern enclosure of the temple of Tirukkīḻkōṭṭam-Uḍaiyār and presented 17,000 *kaśu* for offerings and lamps to that image and for a *makara-tōraṇa* to Tirukkīḻkōṭṭam-Uḍaiyār. [This inscription is given in *Ins., S. Dts.*, p. 194, No. 9.]

62-A. *C.P. No.* 4 *of* 1915.—A Telugu record of the Penugoṇḍa king Vīrapratāpa Veṅkaṭadēva Mahārāja, dated Ś. 1630, Vikriti, Kārttigai, *śu. di.* 15, Monday, Rōhiṇi. Records grant of land by the Madura Nāik king Vijaya Raṅga Chokkanātha for the maintenance of worship, feeding of Brahmans, etc., in the Śaṅkarāchārya *maṭha* at Jambukēśvaram. For a full account of Vijaya Raṅga Chokkanātha see *Ind. Antq.*, August and September 1917.

62-B. *C.P. No.* 5 *of* 1915.—Records an agreement in the reign of Śrīraṅgadēva Mahārāya in Ś. 1663, Dundubhi, Tai 15, which the servants of Vijaya Raghunātha Rāya Toṇḍaimān with one Bhavāni Veṅkaṭakṛishṇaiya of Conjeeveram regarding the fee (?) due to him from them.

62-C. *C.P. No.* 6 *of* 1915.—A Telugu record in Ś. 1608, Prabhava, Vaiśākha, *śu. di.* 15, Saturday, lunar eclipse. Registers that Mahādēvēndra Sarasvati, pupil of Chandraśēkhara Sarasvati, of the Śaṅkarāchārya-Śārada *maṭha* at Kāñchi, gave to one Rāma-Śāstrilu of the Hoysaṇa-Kannaḍi sect land in the village of Mēlpāka, an annuity of two *varāhas* in the *maṭha*, and certain collections in the Jaghir of Chingleput given to the *maṭha* by Akkanna and Mādanna of Gōlcoṇḍa. [These were the celebrated ministers of Abdulla Kutb Shah and Abul Hassan of Gōlcoṇḍa. For a brief account of them as based on the Dutch journalist Havart see *Ep. Rep.*, 1915, p. 118. Mahādēvēndra Sarasvati was apparently the Āchārya who presided over the *maṭha* from 1703 to 1746 and in whose time the *maṭha* was removed from Conjeeveram first to Uḍaiyārpālaiyam and then, at the instance of Pratāpa Singh of Tanjore and of his minister Dabhir Pant, to Kumbhakōṇam.]

62-D. *C.P. No.* 7 *of* 1915.—A record of Kṛishṇadēva Rāya in Ś. 1450, Virōdhin Vaiśākha, Paurṇami, in Sanskrit. Registers the gift of the village of Udayambākkam in Chingleput Śīma, Kaḷattūr-kōṭṭam to Sadāśiva Sarasvati, a disciple of Chandra-Sēkhara Śarasvati. [In a list of Śaṅkarāchāryas of the Kāmakōṭipīṭha of Conjeeveram, later on removed to Kumbhakōṇam, published by the talented scholar T. S. Narayana Sastri, I find that the fifty-fifth Āchārya was called Chandrachūḍēndra and that he presided over the *maṭha* from 1506 to 1512 and that the fifty-sixth was Sadāśivēndra, who was in charge of the *maṭha* from 1512 to 1538. These are the two Āchāryas apparently referred to in this epigraph.]

62-E. *C.P. No.* 8 *of* 1915.—Registers a grant by Kṛishṇadēva Rāya in Ś. 1444, Svabhānu, Mārgaśīrsha, *śu. di.* 12, of the village of Poḍavūru or Kṛishṇarāyapuram in Śeṅgāḍ Kūṟṟam, Nīrvalūr Nāḍu in Chandragiri Rājya to Chandrachūḍa Sarasvati of Conjeeveram, disciple of Mahādēva Sarasvati. See the above epigraph.

Sundarapperumāḷkōyil.

The following inscriptions are taken from *Mack. MSS.* (*Ins., S. Dts.*, pp. 247–48, Nos. 115—17):—

62-F. On the steps of the spire of Sundararājapperumāḷ temple. Records that in Ś. 1193, Viśvāvasu, Pratāpa Rāyadēva granted two *vēlis* of land for the God. (The date is evidently incorrect.)

62-G. In the same place. Records that in Ś. 1299, Naḷa, Virūpākshadēvarāya gave twelve *vēlis* of land to the God. (Here also the date is evidently a mistake.)

62-H. In the same place. Records that Rājarājadēva gave 4 *mās* and 3½ *kāṇis* of land for a festival of the God in the twenty-first year of his reign.

Svāmimalai.

The Subrahmaṇya shrine of this place, famous as the place where the God instructed His own father in religion and therefore a centre of pilgrimage and vows, has got two inscriptions of the sixteenth century. It has a choultry founded by a Principal Sadr Amiṅ who was cured of a disease by taking a vow in the temple; it has, however, no epigraph in it.

63. 496 *of* 1907. – (Grantha and Tamil.) On the first gōpura of the Subrahmaṇyasvāmi temple, right of entrance. A damaged record of the Vijayanagara king Vīrapratāpa Kṛishṇadēva Mahārāya in Ś. 1436, expired, *Bhava.* The *triśūla* and a peacock are engraved on the top of the inscription.

64. 497 *of* 1907.—(Grantha and Tamil.) In the same place. A record of the Nāyaka king Śevappa Nāyaka (1549—72) in Ś. 1495, expired . . . Refers to the son of Timmappa-Nāyakkar of the *chaturtha gōtra,* who was a native of Neḍuṅgunṟam in Toṇḍamaṇḍalam.

Taṇḍantōṭṭam (near *Kumbhakōṇam*).

65. *C.P. No.* 7 *of* 1912.—(Sanskrit and Tamil.) An incomplete record of Kō-Vijaya. Nandivikramavarman, the son of Hiraṇyavarman, making the gift of the village of Dayāmukhamaṅgalam (named after the donor Dayāmukha) to 308 Brāhmans learned in the Vēdās and Smritis, in the fifty-eighth year of his reign. The village granted was over the forest and uncultivated waste west of Taṇḍantōṭṭam. The record ends with the obligations imposed on the tenants and the exemptions *(parihāras)* as well. [The identity of Nandi Vikramavarman is a question of controversy. The Government Epigraphist believes that it is the so-called Gaṅga Pallava king Nandivarman III. He further points out that amongst the achievements of Nandivarman is mentioned his conquest of a Gaṅga king, and that this king might be Śivamāra II attributed by Dr. Fleet to A.D. 805—810. He cites in proof of this fact the Manne grant of Śivamāran II which says that "his forehead was adorned by a fillet" by the "two ornaments of the Rāshṭrakūṭa and Pallava lineages named Gōvindarāja (i.e., Gōvinda III) and Nandivarman." But Prof. Dubreuil of Pondicherry is of opinion that the donor of the grant was not Nandivarman III, but Nandivarman II or Pallavamalla. He bases this on the ground of palæography and on the fact that we are aware of only one Hiraṇayavarman, viz., the father of Nandivarman II. Nandivarman III, he further argues, must have ruled only for a period of twenty-four years. See his *Pallavas,* 1917, pp. 62–3, for details. It seems to me that the arguments of Prof. Dubreuil are unanswerable and ought to be accepted.]

Tiruchchirai.

66. 612 *of* 1909.—(Tamil.) On a stone built into the tank in front of the Sāranātha-Perumāḷ temple. A mutilated record in the tenth year of the Chōḷa king Parakēsarivarman. Records gift of sheep for a lamp to the temple at Śeṟṟūr, a *dēvadāna* in Śeṟṟūr-kūṟṟam, by a native of Kīramaṅgalam which belonged to Poyyil-kūṟṟam.

67. 613 *of* 1909.—(Tamil.) On another stone in the same place. A fragmentary record of the Chōḷa king Rājēndra-Chōḷa I. Contains a portion of the historical introduction which begins with *tirumanni.*

68. 614 *of* 1909.—(Tamil.) On the south wall of the central shrine in the same temple. Records in Ś. 1566, Tāraṇa, gift of land to the temple of Sāranāthasvāmin and to the shrine of Āḷvār, by a certain Gōvindadāsa for the merit of king Vijaya-Rāghava. [Was the donor the celebrated Gōvinda Dīkshita, minister of Achyutappa Nāyaka (1572—1614)?]

69. 615 *of* 1909.—(Tamil.) On the south wall of the maṇṭapa in front of the central shrine in the Sāra-Paramēśvara temple at Uḍaiyārkōyil, a hamlet of the same village. A record in the seventh year of the Chōḷa king Tribhuvanachakravartin Rājarāja-dēva. Records gift of money for a lamp to the temple of Tiruch-chennēri-Uḍaiyār at Tiruchchirai.

70. 616 *of* 1909.—(Tamil.) On the same wall. A damaged record in the first year of the Chōḷa king Tribhuvanachakra-vartin Rājarājadēva. Records gift of money for a lamp to the temple at Tiruchchirai *alias* Rājasundari-chaturvēdimaṅgalam, by a native of Karivēḍu in Dāmar-kōṭṭam of Jayaṅgoṇḍa-Chōḷamaṇḍalam.

71. 617 *of* 1909.—(Tamil.) On the north wall of the same maṇṭapa. A record in the fifth year of the Chōḷa king Vikrama-Chōḷadēva (1118—35). Built in, at the bottom. Records gift of land to the shrine of the goddess.

72. 618 *of* 1909.—(Tamil.) On the same wall. A record in the fourth year of the Chōḷa king Tribhuvanachakravartin Vikrama-Chōḷadēva (1118—35). Records gift of land to the temple of Tiruch-chennēri Uḍaiyār at Tiruchchirai by the assembly of Vīśalūr.

73. 619 *of* 1909.—(Tamil.) On the same wall. A damaged record in the fifth year of the Chōḷa king Tribhuvanachakravartin Vikrama-Chōḷadēva (1118—35). Built in, at the bottom. Records gift of land by the same assembly.

74. 620 *of* 1909.—(Tamil.) On the same wall. A record in the forty-seventh year of the Chōḷa king Tribhuvanachakravartin Kulōttuṅga-Chōḷadēva (I,? 1070—1118). Records sale of land to the temple of Tiruchchennēri Uḍaiyār at Rājasundari-chaturvēdimaṅgalam, a *brahmadēya* in Śeṟṟūr-kūṟṟam, which was a subdivision of Kulōttuṅga-Chōḷavaḷanāḍu. Another inscription below this is dated in the ninth year of Tribhuvanachakravartin Vikramal Chōḷadēva and records also a sale of land. [The inscription is of fiscal interest. It says that, in accordance with the king's *Śrimukha*, the lands of those who were in two years' arrears of the royal dues during the forty-seventh year of the reign should be sold, and that the lands of certain Brāhmaṇa tenants who had been unable to pay the taxes and left the village were sold to the local temple. See inscriptions at Kōnērirājapuram, Tirumālam, Kūvam and Ukkāl for similar examples.]

75. 621 *of* 1909.—(Tamil.) On the same wall. A record in the fifth year of the Chōḷa king Tribhuvanachakravartin Vikrama-Chōḷadēva (1118—35). Records gift of land to the shrine of the goddess by a certain Ulaguyyavandān, who purchased it from the assembly of Rājasundari-chaturvēdimaṅgalam, a *brahmadēya* in the same district.

Tirubuvanam.

The Government Epigraphist surmises that the village was founded by Kulōttuṅga Chōḷa III who had the title Tribhuvanavīradēva.

76. 159 *of* 1911.—(Tamil.) On the south base of the Raṅganātha-Perumāḷ temple. A damaged record in the tenth year of the Pāṇḍya king Jaṭāvarman Tribhuvanachakravartin Parākrama-Pāṇḍyadēva. Registers a contract between the residents of "the city" of Trubhuvanavīrapura and those of Kulamaṅgala-nāḍu who owned the *ūr-kāval* of that village. [The *ūr-kāval* men take an oath not to be unjust or injure the people in any way and they receive, in return for their duty, a *śēlai* (cloth) on each marriage among the *Kaḷḷar-makkaḷ*. They were to demand no *śēlai* on other marriages than the first.]

77. 160 *of* 1911.—(Tamil.) On the north and west bases of the same temple. A mutilated record in the tenth year of the Pāṇḍya king Jaṭāvarman Tribhuvanachakravartin Parākrama-Pāṇḍyadēva. Refers to a contract similar to that registered in the above epigraph and mentions the chief Uḍaiyār Kulaśekharadēva *alias* Kūpakarāya in whose presence Śēnaipperumāḷ *alias* Kulōttuṅgaśōḷa-varaiyan, agreed to the contract. [Is the king referred to the same as Jaṭāvarman Parākrama who ascended the throne in 1334?]

78. 189 *of* 1907.—(Grantha.) On the south wall of the central shrine in the Kampaharēśvara temple. A damaged record. Mentions Ārya Śrī-Sōmanātha.

79. 190 *of* 1907.—(Grantha.) On the same wall. A record of the Chōḷa king Srī-Kulōttuṅga-Chōḷadēva (III). Registers the building operations of the king.

80. 191 *of* 1907.—(Grantha.) At the entrance into the outer gōpura of the same temple, right side. A record of the Chōḷa king Tribhuvanavīra. [This is a duplicate copy of the above epigraph.]

81. 192 *of* 1907.—(Grantha.) On the same gōpura, left side. A record of the Chōḷa king Śrī-Kulōttuṅga-Chōḷa. [This is also a duplicate copy of No. 79.]

Tirukkalittaṭṭai.

82. 291 *of* 1908.—(Tamil.) On the north wall of the central shrine in the Vēdapurīśvara temple. A record in the seventh year of king Perumāḷ Sundara-Chōḷadēva, "who drove the Pāṇḍya into the forest." Records gift of land for offerings to the temple of Śrīkuḍittiṭṭai-Uḍaiyār in Vaḍagarai-Vēmbaṟṟūr, by the king's general *(sēnāpati)* Pirāntakan Śiriyavēḷār *alias* Tirukkaṟṟaḷi-Pichchan. Edited in *Ep. Ind.*, XII, pp. 120—6, by Mr. K. V. Subrahmanya Ayyar, who points out that Sundara Chōḷa was Parāntaka II.

83. 292 *of* 1908.—(Tamil.) On the same wall. A record in the ninth year of the Chōḷa king Parakēsarivarman *alias* Rājēndra-Chōḷadēva (1012—43). Refers to the remission of taxes on land belonging to the temple of Śrīkuḍīttiṭṭai Paramasvāmin in Vēmbaṟṟūr *alias* Śōḷamārttāṇḍa-chaturvēdimaṅgalam, a *brahmadēya* in Maṇṇinādu, which was a subdivision of Rājēndraśiṅga-vaḷanāḍu, by the assembly of that village, after the receipt of sixty-five *kāśus.* Out of the interest on this the assembly bound itself to pay all taxes. The taxes included, among others, the paddy for *pañchavāriyam* and those on corn, gram, oil, ghee, etc.

84. 293 *of* 1908.—(Tamil.) On the same wall. A record in the ninth year of the Chōḷa king Parakēsarivarman *alias* Rājēndra-Chōḷadēva (I). Refers to a similar transaction by the same assembly. Mentions Rājarāja-Īśvaramuḍaiyār. The chief territorial division is here called Vaḍagarai Rājēndraśiṅgavaḷanāḍu. Amongst the terms figuring in the epigraph may be mentioned *Kaḍikai-madhyastha, Kāraṇattān, Vaikhānasa, Śiva Brāhmaṇa,* etc.

85. 294 *of* 1908.—(Tamil.) On the north wall of the central shrine in the Vēdapurīśvara temple. A record in the eighth year of the Chōḷa king Parakēsarivarman *alias* Rājēndra-Chōḷadēva (I). Registers still another transaction of the same kind. 50 *kāśus* received for taxes on 3⅝ *mā.* (உலகளந்தபடி மும்மாவரை அரைக் காணி.)

86. 295 *of* 1908.—(Tamil.) On the west wall of the same shrine. A record in the twenty-second year of the Chōḷa king Parakēsarivarman. Records gift of land for offerings to the temple of Śrīkuḍittiṭṭai-Perumāḷ by a member of the assembly of Amaninārāyaṇa-chaturvēdimaṅgalam, a *dēvadāna* and a *brahmadēya* in Vaḍagarai (i.e., the northern bank).

87. 296 *of* 1908.—(Tamil.) On the same wall. A record in the second year of the Chōḷa king Parakēsarivarman. Records gift of land for a lamp to the temple of Tirukkuḍittiṭṭai-Perumāḷ in Amaninārāyaṇa-chaturvēdimaṅgalam.

88. 297 *of* 1908.—(Tamil.) On the same wall. A record of the Chōḷa king Rājakēsarivarman, the date of which is lost. Records gift of a silver pot to the temple of Śrīkuḍittiṭṭai Mahādēva at Vēmbaṟṟūr by Śembiyan-Mahādēvi-ppirāṭṭiyār, who gave birth to Uttama-Chōḷadēva. See next epigraph.

89. 298 *of* 1908.—(Tamil.) On the same wall. A record in the third year of the Chōḷa king Rājarājakēsarivarman. Records gift of land for offerings and for the supply of 108 pots of bathing water to the temple of Mahādēva in Amaninārāyaṇa-chaturvēdimaṅgalam by Kiḷānaḍigaḷ, the daughter of Viḷupparaiyar and the queen of Uttama-Chōḷaḍēva (970 ?—85), son of Gaṇḍarādittadēva.

90. 299 *of* 1908.—(Tamil.) On the south wall of the same shrine. An unfinished record in the fourteenth year of the Chōḷa king Rājakēsarivarman. Records gift of money for two lamps by the wife and daughter of Śiriyavēḷār. See No. 82 above.

91. 300 *of* 1908.—(Tamil.) On the same wall. An unfinished record in the fifteenth year of the Chōḷa king Rājakēsarivarman. Records gift of money for two lamps.

92. 301 *of* 1908.—(Tamil.) On the same wall. A record in the twenty-eighth year of the Chōḷa king Rājarājakēsarivarman *alias* Rājarājadēva (I). Records gift of ninety sheep for a lamp by Vēmban Śīruḍaiyār *alias* Mīnavan-mahādēviyār, queen of Rājarājadēva. States that Amaninārāyaṇa-chaturvēdimaṅgalam was situated in Maṇṇi-nāḍu, a subdivision of Vaḍagarai-Rājēndra-siṁha-Valanādu.

93. 302 *of* 1908.—(Tamil.) On the same wall. A damaged record of the Chōḷa king Perumāḷ Sundara-Chōḷadēva *alias* Pon . . . "who drove the Pāṇḍya into the forest," the date of which is lost. Mentions Pirāntakan Śiriyavēḷār, the general referred to in No. 82 above.

94. 303 *of* 1908.—(Tamil.) On the same wall. A record of the Chōḷa king Parakēsarivarman *alias* Rājēndra-Chōḷadēva (I), the date of which is lost. Records the remission of taxes on a land belonging to the temple of Tirukkuḍittiṭṭai-Paramasvāmin in Vēmbaṟṟūr *alias* Śōḷamārttāṇḍa-chaturvēdimaṅgalam, by the assembly of that village. The taxes are *Śittāyya*, *Pañchavāra-ūriḍuvari*, *Veṭṭivēdinai* and other *Śilvaris*. The amount received was 200 *kāśus* and this was for the exemption of the tax on 4½ *mās*.

Tirumayānam.

(Called in orthodox tradition Tirukkaḍavūr Mayānam and famous as the place where Śiva burnt Brahma, adorned himself with his ashes and then revived him. Hence the name Brahmapurīśvara.)

95. 53 *of* 1906.—(Tamil.) On the north wall of the maṇṭapa in front of the central shrine in the Brahmapurīśvara temple. An unfinished record in the thirty-fourth year of Tribhuvanachakravartin Kōnērimaikoṇḍān. Records gift of land for growing water lilies to be offered to the god Tirumayānamuḍaiyār.

96. 54 *of* 1906.—(Tamil.) On the same wall. A record in the twenty-second year of Tribhuvanachakravartin Kōnērinmaikoṇḍān. Records gift of land. In continuation of this is an inscription which appears to be dated in the eleventh year of some unmentioned king. Provision is here made for the maintenance of those who have to play on the *viṇa* and recite the Vēdās and the *Śrirudram.* Mentions the villages of Tiruttoṇḍattogaimaṅgalam and Śivapādaśēkharamaṅgalam. [The inscription is interesting for the mention of the *viṇa* and for the reference to the Śaivite saints. See Cg. 997 and 1006.

97. 55 *of* 1906.—(Tamil.) On the same wall. A record in the ninth year of Tribhuvanachakravartin Kōnērinmaikoṇḍān. Records gift of land. The temple is called Tirumayānamuḍaiyār at Tirukkaḍavūr, a *brahmadēya* in Ākkūr-nāḍu, a district of Jayaṅgoṇḍa-Chōḷa vaḷanādu. Refers to the revenue survey in the sixteenth year of the reign of Kulōttuṅga I, who abolished tolls. [Ākkūr is known in tradition as the place where Śiruppuli Nāyanār became one with the deity.]

98. 56 *of* 1906.—(Tamil.) On the south wall of the same maṇṭapa. A record in the sixth year of the Chōḷa king Tribhuvanachakravartin Vīrarājēndradēva (I or II ?). Records gift of land for a lamp. In continuation of this is an inscription of the eighth year of a Kulōttuṅga.

99. 57 *of* 1906.—(Tamil.) On the same wall. A record in the thirty-fifth year of the Chōḷa king Tribhuvanachakravartin Tribhuvanavīradēva, " who took Madurai, Īḷam (Ceylon), Karuvūr and the crowned head of the Pāṇḍya and was pleased to perform the anointment of heroes and the anointment of victors" (i.e., Kulōttuṅga III). Records gift of land for cultivating water-lilies to be offered to the God Tirumaiyānamuḍaiya-Perumāḷ.

100. 58 *of* 1906.—(Tamil.) On the same wall. A record in the fourteenth year of the Chōḷa king Rājakēśarivarman *alias* Tribhuvanachakravartin Rājādhirājadēva (II, 1171—86), " who was pleased to take Madurai and Īḷam (Ceylon)." Records gift of land. Mentions Tirunīṟṟuch-chōḷamaṅgalam (i.e., the village founded by Tirunīṟṟuchchōḷa or Rājarāja I).

101. 59 *of* 1906.—(Tamil.) On the same wall. A record in the thirty-fifth year of the Pāṇḍya king Kōnērimaikoṇḍān Tribhuvanachakravartin Perumāḷ Kulaśēkharadēva (I, 1268—1308), " who was pleased to take every country." Records gift of land for celebrating a festival called Kulaśēkharan-śandi and for repairs.

102. 60 *of* 1906.—(Tamil.) On the same wall. A record in the thirty-third year of the Chōḷa king Tribhuvanachakravartin Tribhuvanavīradēva (Kulōttuṅga III, 1178—1216), " who took Madurai, Īḷam (Ceylon), Karuvūr and the crowned head of the Pāṇḍya and was pleased to perform the anointment of heroes and the anointment of victors." Records gift of land to the temple of Uḍaiyār Tirumaiyānamuḍaiya-Perumāḷ in Ambanāḍuṭpaḍamēviya Tirukkaḍavūr in Ākkūr-nāḍu, a district of Jayaṅgoṇḍa-Chōḷa-vaḷanāḍu.

103. 61 *of* 1906.—(Tamil.) On the west wall of the same maṇṭapa. A record in the eighth year of the Chōḷa king Tribhuvanachakravartin Kulōttuṅga-Chōḷadēva (III), " who was pleased to take Madurai." Records gift of a lamp to the temple of Uḍaiyār Tirumaiyānamuḍaiya-Perumāḷ at Tirukkaḍavūr in Ākkūr-nāḍu, a district of Jayaṅgoṇḍa-Chōḷa-vaḷanāḍu.

104. 62 *of* 1906.—(Tamil.) On the same wall. A record in the ninth year of the Chōḷa king Tribhuvanachakravartin Kulōttuṅga-Chōḷadēva (III), " who was pleased to take Madura." Records gift of land for a lamp by a native of Kīlvēṅgaināḍu, a district of Rājarāja-vaḷanāḍu.

105. 63 *of* 1906.—(Tamil.) On the same wall. A record in the ninth year of the Chōḷa king Tribhuvanachakravartin Kulōttuṅga-Chōḷadēva (III), " who was pleased to take Madura." Records gift of land for a lamp.

106. 64 *of* 1906.—(Tamil.) On the west wall of the first prākāra of the same temple. A damaged record in the seventeenth year of the Chōḷa king Tribhuvanachakravartin Kulōttuṅga-Chōḷadēva (III ?), " who took Madurai and was pleased to take the crowned head of the Pāṇḍya."

107. 65 *of* 1906.—(Tamil.) On the south wall of the same prākāra. A damaged record in the thirteenth year of the Chōḷa king Tribhuvanachakravartin Kulōttuṅga-Chōḷadēva (III), " who was pleased to take Madurai, Īḷam (Ceylon) and the crowned head of the Pāṇḍya." Stones out of order. Seems to record the appointment of a gardener to look after the temple flower-garden.

Tirumeyñānam (Tirumanjnānam.)

108. 310 *of* 1910.—(Tamil.) On the south wall of the central shrine in the Jñānaparamēśvara temple. A record in the twenty-fourth year of the Chōḷa king Parakēsarivarman *alias* Uḍaiyār Śrī-Rājēndra-Chōḷadēva (I, 1012—53). Built in on both sides. Mentions Śeṟṟūr-kuṟṟam.

109. 311 *of* 1910.—(Tamil.) On the same wall. Built in at the top. Refers to a gift of land to the temple of Brahmīśvaraṭṭu Mahādēva.

110. 312 *of* 1910.—(Tamil.) On the same wall. A record in the fifteenth year of the Chōḷa king Parakēsarivarman. Records sale of land by the assembly of Nālūr, a *brahmadēya* in Śeṟṟūrkūṟṟam.

111. 313 *of* 1910.—(Tamil.) On the same wall. A damaged record in the thirty-sixth year of the Chōḷa king Tribhuvana-chakravartin-Kulōttuṅga-Chōḷadēva. Seems to record a gift of two lamps to the temple of Tirumayānamuḍaiya-Paramasvāmin at Nālūr.

112. 314 *of* 1910.—(Tamil.) On the same wall. A record of the Chōḷa king Parakēsarivarman *alias* Śrī-Rājēndra-Chōḷadēva (I, 1012—53). Built in at the top and the left side. Seems to record a gift of land to the temple of Agastīśvaram-Uḍaiyār at Nālūr.

113. 315 *of* 1910.—(Tamil.) On the same wall. A damaged record. Built in at the top. Seems to record a sale of land.

114. 316 *of* 1910.—(Tamil.) On the west wall of the same shrine. A damaged record in the fifteenth year of the Chōḷa king Parakēsarivarman. Records sale of land to the temple of Tiru-mayānattu-Paramasvāmi by the assembly of Nālūr.

115. 317 *of* 1910.—(Tamil.) On the same wall. A damaged record in the third year of the Chōḷa king Tribhuvanachakravartin Vikrama-Chōḷadēva (1118—35). Records gift of money for a lamp to the temple of Tirumayānam-Uḍaiyār in Nālūr *alias* Vānavan-mādēvi-chaturvēdimaṅgalam in Śeṟṟūr-kūṟṟam, which was a district of Kulōttuṅga-Chōḷa-vaḷanāḍu.

116. 318 *of* 1910.—(Tamil.) On the same wall. A record of the Chōḷa king Parakēsarivarman, the date of which is lost. Records sale of land to the same temple by the assembly of Nālūr.

117. 319 *of* 1910.—(Tamil.) On the same wall. A record in the sixth year of the Chōḷa king Parakēsarivarman. Records sale of land to the temple of Tirukkarkaṭīśvarattu-Perumān at Nālūr by the assembly of that village.

118. 320 *of* 1910.—(Tamil.) On the same wall. A record in the seventh year of the Chōḷa king Rājakēsarivarman. Records gift of land by the assembly of Paḷaiya Śembiyanmahādēvi-chatur-vēdimaṅgalam on the southern bank of the Cauvery.

119. 321 *of* 1910.—(Tamil.) On the north wall of the same shrine. A record in the second year of the Chōḷa king Rājakēsari-varman. Records that the assembly of Nālūr sold the right of collecting the tax called *aṅgāḍi-kkūli* from stalls opened in the bazaar to the temple of Mūlasthānattu-Mahādēva of Tirumayānam. [The fees are specified to be one *nāḻi* in kind in each measurable article of paddy, rice, etc., brought for sale from towns outside Nālūr; one *palam* of articles sold by weight; one *paṟṟu* on each basket of betel leaves; and two nuts on each basketful of areca-nuts.]

120. 322 *of* 1910.—(Tamil.) On the same wall. An incomplete record of the Chōḷa king Rājarāja-Rājakēsarivarman *alias* Śrī-Rājarājadēva (I) in his twenty-fourth year, *makara*, *Aparapaksha*, Viśākha, Friday. Seems to record a gift of land for offerings to the temple of Lakshmi-Rāghavadēva of Tirunārāyaṇa-Viṇṇagar, by a merchant of Nālūr, on the occasion when the assembly of that village met at the big hall called Rājarājan in front of the temple of Sāmaparīśvarattu-Mahādēva.

121. 323 *of* 1910.—(Tamil.) On the same wall. An incomplete record in the forty-third year of the Chōḷa king Tribhuvana-chakravartin Śrī-Kulōttuṅga-Chōḷadēva (I ?). Records sale of land by the assembly of Nālūr to a resident of Vānavanmādēvi-chaturvēdimaṅgalam in Śēṟṟūr-kūṟṟam, which was a subdivision of Kulōttuṅga-Chōḷa-vaḷanāḍu.

122. 324 *of* 1910.—(Tamil.) On the same wall. A damaged record. Seems to record a gift of land to the temple of Tirumayānattu-Paramasvāmi and mentions also the temple of Sāmaparēśvarattu-Perumāḷ.

123. 325 *of* 1910.—(Tamil.) On the same wall. A damaged record in the forty-third year of the Chōḷa king Tribhuvana-chakravartin Śrī-Kulōttuṅga-Chōḷadēva (I ?). Seems to record a gift of land for a lamp.

124. 326 *of* 1910.—(Tamil.) On the same wall. A record in the twenty-third year of the Chōḷa king Rājarāja-Rājakēsarivarman *alias* Śrī-Rājarājadēva (I). Records gift of land for a lamp to the shrine of Kṛishṇa-Veṇṇaikkūttāḍi-aruḷuginṟa-Āḷvār in Tirunārāyaṇa-Viṇṇagar of Nālūr, a *brahmadēya* in Śēṟṟūr-kūṟṟam, which was a district of Kshatriya-śikhāmaṇi-vaḷanāḍu. On this occasion the assembly of Nālūr met at the "big hall" called Gaṇḍarādittan.

125. 327 *of* 1910.—(Tamil.) On the same wall. A damaged record in the fourth year of the Chōḷa king Madiraikoṇḍa-Parakēsarivarman (Parāntaka I). Records gift of land to the temple of Sāmaparēśvarattu-Perumānaḍigaḷ at Nālūr, by the assembly of Akkiramakoṭṭa-chaturvēdimaṅgala, a *brahmadēya* in Teṅkarai-Tirunaṟaiyūr-nāḍu.

126. 328 *of* 1910.—(Tamil.) On the same wall. A damaged record in the sixteenth year of the Chōḷa king Parakēsarivarman. Built in at the end. Seems to record a gift of land by the assembly of Ārurchchēri, a *brahmadēya* in Tirunaṟaiyūr-nāḍu, to the temple of Tirumayānam in Nālūr.

127. 329 *of* 1910.—(Tamil.) On the south wall. A much damaged record of the Chōḷa king Rājakēsarivarman, the date of which is doubtful.

128. 330 *of* 1910.—(Tamil.) On the same wall. A record in the fifteenth year of the Chōḷa king Rājakēsarivarman. Records gift of twelve *Iḷa-kāśu* for twelve lamps, by a merchant of Nalūr, named Nāraṇan Śōḷaḍigaḷ *alias* Tirunāvukkaraiyan, to the temple of Tirumayānattu-Paramēśvara.

129. 331 *of* 1910.—(Tamil.) On the south wall of the maṇṭapa in front of the same shrine. A record in the seventh year of the Chōḷa king Tribhuvanachakravartin Vīrarājēndradēva. Records gift of two lamps by a lady from Śembiyaṅkuḍavāyil *alias* Ālampāḷil to the temple of Tirumayānam-Uḍaiyār. [It is impossible to say whether the king was Vīra Rājēndra I or II. The former ruled from 1063 to 1070 and the latter (same as Kulōttuṅga III) from 1178 to 1216.]

130. 332 *of* 1910.—(Tamil.) On the same wall. A record in the seventeenth year of the Chōḷa king Tribhuvanachakravartin Rājarājadēva (III). Registers a decision of the assembly of Nalūr *alias* Vānavanmādēvi-chaturvēdimaṅgalam, which met at the foot of a tamarind tree. States "that the residents should not do anything against the interests of their village nor against the temple of Tirumayānam-uḍaiyār and similar institutions; that if they did so, they must suffer as the *grāmadrōhins* do and that people who act against this decision should not be allowed the privilege of 'touching Śiva,' etc." Mr. Krishna Sastri believes that the *grāmadrōhins* were evidently the *grāmakaṇṭakas* of the Uttaramallūr inscriptions.

Tirunāgēśvaram * *(Aṇakkuḍi).*

The village is now well known not only for its Nāganāthasvāmi temple but its Uppiliyappan or Tiruviṇṇahar shrine referred to in the Prabandhas.

131. 211 *of* 1911.—(Tamil.) On the north wall of the central shrine in the Nāganāthasvāmin temple. A damaged record in the sixth year of the Chōḷa king Parakēsarivarman *alias* Rājēndra-Chōḷa (I). Provides for a gold jewel worked in gems and pearls, from the accumulated income of a land evidently presented by Aḍigaḷ Achchān, one of the junior elephant mahauts *(Iḷaiyakuñjira-mallar)* in the army of Uḍaiyār-Śrī-Rājēndra-Chōḷadēva commanded by Śōḷamūvēndavēḷār, to the temple of Tirunāgēśvaram Uḍaiyar at Tiruviṇṇagar-Tirunāgēśvaram in Tiraimūr-nāḍu, a subdivision of Uyyakkoṇḍār-vaḷanāḍu. [Tiruviṇṇagar is named after the local God Vishṇu or Uppiliyappa. The great Gōpāla Dēśika, the founder of the *Munitraya* cult of Śri Vaishṇavism is said to be an *avatār* of this God.]

---

* According to Śaivite tradition this place is noted for the worship of Indra. The God's name is Champakāraṇyēśvara and the *tirtha* Indratirtha.

132. 212 *of* 1911.—(Tamil.) On the same wall. A record in the eighth year of the Chōḷa king Parakēsarivarman *alias* Rājēndra-Chōḷa (I). Records gift of forty-eight sheep for half a lamp to the same Mahādēva (Śiva) temple by a palace-woman *(peṇḍāṭṭi)* Tīran Śattiviḍaṅgi for (the merit of) her daughter Araiyan Uttamadāni (a resident) of Uḍaiyār-Ānaimeṟṟuñjinār-vēḷam *alias* Abhimānabhūshana-tterinda-tiruvandikkāppu-vēḷam. Mentions Jananāthapuram in Tiraimūr-nāḍu.

133. 213 *of* 1911.—(Tamil.) On the same wall. A partly damaged record in the fourteenth year of the Chōḷa king Parakēsarivarman *alias* Rājēndra-Chōḷa (I). Built in. Registers jewels, gold and silver vessels, etc., owned by the temple, with the permission of the king which was obtained at the request of a temple servant named Kaṇḍan Kōvalanāḍan. Tirunāgēśvaramuḍaiya Mahādēva is stated to have been situated in Tirukkuḍamūkku in Pāmbūr nāḍu, a subdivision of Uyyakkoṇḍār vaḷanāḍu.

134. 214 *of* 1911.—(Tamil.) On the west wall of the same shrine. A record in the second year of the Chōḷa king Parakēsarivarman *alias* Uḍaiyār Śrī-Rājēndradēva (1050—63). Records that the assembly *(mūla-parudaiyār)* of Tirukkuḍamūkku received 100 *kāśu* from Māṇikkan Māvali *alias* Vikkiramaśiṅga-Pallavaraiyan, a native of Marudam in Veṅkuṉṟa-kōṭṭam, a subdivision of Jayaṅgoṇḍa-chōḷa-maṇḍalam. This money was utilized by them for repairing damages caused by the Kāvēri floods to the irrigation channel. For this, interest at the rate one *kalam* of paddy on each *kāśu* was set apart for providing offerings in the temple of Tirunāgēśvaram Uḍaiyār and for expounding the *Śivadharma* in the assembly hall called Tiruchchiṟṟambalamuḍaiyān built in the temple by the abovementioned Vikkiramaśiṅga-Pallavaraiyan.

135. 215 *of* 1911.—(Grantha and Tamil.) On the south wall of the same shrine. An unfinished and damaged record in the ninth year of the Chōḷa king Rājakēsarivarman (Gaṇḍarāditya). Seems to provide for offerings and mentions Ariñjigaippirāṭṭiyār, a Bāṇa queen and the daughter of prince Arikulakēsari (son of Parāntaka I). Mentions the Simhaḷas (i.e., Ceylon). [The marriage of a Bāṇa king with Parāntaka's granddaughter shows the later friendship of the Bāṇa and the Chōḷa houses.]

136. 216 *of* 1911.—(Tamil.) On the same wall. A record of the Chōḷa king Rājēndra-Chōḷa I. Built in at the right end. Mentions Pāśupatadēva as the name of the image carried about in processions.

137. 217 *of* 1911.—(Tamil.) On the same wall. A record in the thirty-second year of the Chōḷa king Parakēsarivarman *alias* Uḍaiyār Śrī-Rājēndra-Chōḷadēva I. Built in at the right end. It records gift of land to the temple of Tirunāgēśvaramuḍaiya-Mahādēva at Tirukkuḍamūkku in Pāmbūr-nāḍu, a subdivision of Uyyakkoṇḍār-vaḷanāḍu, by Nārakkan Kṛishṇan Rāman of Kēraḷāntaka-chaturvēdimaṅgalam in Vennāḍu, another subdivision of the same vaḷanāḍu. The twenty-fourth and thirty-first years of the king are quoted in the body of the inscription. Mentions also the coin *Rājēndraśōḷan-kāśu* (evidently issued by Rājēndrachōḷa I). It seems that the original area endowed was 9⅛ *mās*, but according to "the *mā* of the twenty-fourth year which contained 128 *kuḷis*" it amounted to 7⅛ *mās*. [Kṛishnan-Rāman was the general of Rājarāja I and superintended the building of the enclosure of the Brihadīśvarasvāmi temple. See *S.I.* Vol. II, p. 139. He also set up an Ardhanāriśvara image in the shrine.]

138. 218 *of* 1911.—(Tamil.) On the same wall. A record in the fourteenth year of the Chōḷa king Rājarāja-Rājakēsarivarman (I). Records of sale of 1½ *vēlis* of land to the same temple by the assembly of Madanamaṅgalam, a *brahmadēya* in Tirunaṟaiyūr-nāḍu. Tiruviṇṇagar Tirunāgēśvaram is stated to have been a *dēvadāna* in Tiraimūr-nāḍu. The cost of the land (6 *mā* and 1 *kāṇi*), viz., 101 *kaḷañju* (of *tuḷaipon*) was the fund formerly deposited for offerings by the princess Ariñjigai-Pirāṭṭiyār, the Bāṇa queen and the daughter of Prince Arikula-kēsari. An introduction of Rājādhirāja beginning with *tingaḷēr taru* is inscribed next to this; but is much damaged and incomplete. [The *tuḷai-pon* is gold after being "burnt, cut, melted, cooled and found current."]

139. 219 *of* 1911.—(Grantha.) On the same wall. A damaged record. Mentions Gaṇḍarāditya, the temple (*harmya*) of Nāga, Madhurāntaka and the latter's mother and two queens. [It seems to be hinted, says Mr. Krishna Sastri, that Gaṇḍarāditya was the builder of the temple.]

140. 220 *of* 1911.—(Tamil.) On the north wall of the first prākāra of the same temple. A record in the nineteenth year of the Chōḷa king Tribhuvanachakravartin Rājarājadēva (II ?). Records gift of land in the hamlet of Śivapādhaśēkharamaṅgalam which was a part of Tirunaṟaiyūr *alias* Pañchavanmahādēvi-chaturvēdimaṅgalam in Tirunaraiyūr-nāḍu, a subdivision of Kulōttuṅga-Chōḷavaḷanāḍu, to the temple of Tirunāgēśvaramuḍaiyār at Tirunāgēśvaram in Uyyakkoṇḍār-vaḷanāḍu. Refers to a *karaiyiḍu* (lease) given to the tenants, by prince Kōsalarāyar.

141. 221 *of* 1911.—(Tamil.) On the south wall of the same prākāra. A much damaged record of the Chōḷa king Parakēsarivarman *alias* Tribhuvanachakravartin Rājarājadēva (II), the date of which is doubtful. Begins with the historical introduction *pūmaruviya-poḷil*, etc., and seems to record a gift of land.

142. 222 *of* 1911.—(Tamil.) On a pillar lying in a maṇṭapa at the end of the street in front of the same temple. A record in the second year of the Chōḷa king Rājakēsarivarman. Records gift of *vāṛāvaikal* (?) collected by the *perunagarattār* of Kumāramārttāṇḍapuram (hamlet of Tirunāgēśvaram) for the renovation of the gōpura and the *tiruchchuṟṟālai* called Kumāramāttāṇḍan in the Milāḍuḍaiyār *paḷḷi* (temple) of that village, which is stated to have been situated in Teṅkarai-Tiraimūr-nāḍu. [The Chōḷa king was evidently Āditya I. The name Kumāra mārttāṇḍapuram reminds one of the Pallava Nandipōttaraiyār who had that title (see No. 199 of 1907). The name Milāḍuḍaiyār *paḷḷi*, again, suggests a Jain shrine. This, together with the Jain images round the shrine of the goddess in the Nāganāthasvāmi temple, shows that this place must have been an early Jain centre. Again Milāḍuḍaiyār is another name for Saint Meypporuḷnāyanār and if we suppose that the *paḷḷi* was a school or *maṭha* built in his honour, the present epigraph can be said to give a clue to his date, i.e., that he was prior to Āditya, I. He was connected with the Chēdi chief of Kīḷiyūr (S. Arcot District). See also *S.I.I.*, Vol. II, p. 166, for a reference to the saint.]

143. 81 *of* 1897.—(Tamil.) On the west wall of the central shrine of the Nāganāthasvāmin temple. A damaged record of the Chōḷa king Kō-Rājarāja-Rājakēsarivarman (I) the date of which is indistinct. Records gift of land.

144. 82 *of* 1897.—(Tamil.) On the same wall. A record in the fourteenth year of the Chōḷa king Kō-Rājarāja-Rājakēsarivarman (I). Records gift of land by a queen.

145. 83 *of* 1897.—(Tamil.) On the north wall of the same shrine. A much damaged record of the Chōḷa king Kō-Parakēsarivarman *alias* Rājēndra-Chōḷadēva (I), the date of which is doubtful.

146. 84 *of* 1897.—(Tamil.) On the south wall of the second prākāra of the same temple. A record in the fourteenth year of Tribhuvanachakravartin Kōnērimēnkoṇḍān. Records gift of land.

Tirunaṟaiyūr.

[This place is known in orthodox literature as Tirunaṟaiyūr-Siddhēśvaram, the place where the Lord was worshipped by Kubēra, Dēvas and Gandharvas. Accordance to the Vaishṇavas it was the place where God Saundarēśvara appeared to Mēdavamuni. It is sung by Tirumaṅgai Āḷvār (*Periya Tirumoḻi* 7-3-1), Gñānasambanda and Sundara Mūrti. See No. 149 below.

147. 156 *of* 1908.—(Tamil.) On the south wall of the central shrine in the Siddhanāthasvāmin temple. A record in the second year of the Chōḷa king Rājakēsarivarman. Records gift of silver vessels and a *chauri* of gold to the temple of Siddhēśvaramuḍaiya-Mahādēva at Tirunaṟaiyūr in Tirunaṟaiyūr-nāḍu by Uḍaiyapiraṭṭiyār Śembiyan Mahādēviyār *alias* Pirāntakan Mādēvaḍigaḷār.

148. 157 *of* 1908.—(Tamil.) On the same wall. A damaged record of the Chōḷa king Rājarājakēsarivarman *alias* Rājarājadēva (I), the date of which is doubtful. Mentions a *dēvadāna* village belonging to the temple of Arumoḷidēva-Īśvara at Paḷaiyāru in Tirunaṟaiyūr-nāḍu, a subdivision of Kshatriyaśikāmaṇi-vaḷanāḍu and Arumoḷidēva-vaḷanāḍu. [Is this Paḷaiyāru the same as the capital of the Chōḷa king Rājēndra Chōḷa I?] See No. 460 below.

149. 158 *of* 1908.—(Tamil.) On the same wall. A record of the Chōḷa king Rājakēsarivarman *alias* Tribhuvanachakravartin Kulōttuṅga-Chōḷadēva (I). Built in at the end. Seems to record a gift of land by the assembly of Tirunaṟaiyūr in Tirunaṟaiyūr-nāḍu, a subdivision of Kulōttuṅga-Chōḷa-vaḷanāḍu. [Tirunaṟaiyūr was the native place of Nambiāṇḍār Nambi, the compiler of the Dēvāram hymns, who, according to literary tradition, was the "contemporary of Abhaya Kulaśēkhara Chōḷa." The latter has not been identified. According to Sundaram Pillai he was Rājarāja I, but it is doubtful. See *Mile-stones in Tam. Lit.*, p. 38.

150. 159 *of* 1908.—(Tamil.) On the same wall. Built in at the beginning. Records gift of land for offerings to the temple of Siddhēśvaramuḍaiya-Mahādēva by queen Pirāntakan Mādēvaḍigaḷār *alias* Śembiyan Mādēviyār, who gave birth to Uttamachōḷadēva. [She was the queen of Gaṇḍarāditya.]

151. 160 *of* 1908.—(Tamil.) On the north wall of the same shrine. A record in the fourth year of the Chōḷa king Rājarājakēsarivarman. Records gift of land for a lamp and for offerings to the same temple.

152. 161 *of* 1908.—(Tamil.) On the same wall. A record in the twenty-sixth year of the Chōḷa king Rājarājakēsarivarman *alias* Rājarājadēva (I). Records gift of money (thirty *kāśu*) for offerings to the image of Kaṅkaladēva in Siddhēśvara by the Śiva Brāhmaṇas of that village. Sixty *kalams* of paddy to be spent.

153. 162 *of* 1908.—(Tamil.) On the same wall. A record in the third year of the Chōḷa king Parakēsarivarman *alias* Rājēndra-Chōḷadēva (I, 1012—43). Records gift of sheep for a lamp to Kaṅkaladēva, the lord of Siddhēśvara at Tirunaṟaiyūr.

154. 163 *of* 1908.—(Tamil.) On the south wall of the maṇṭapa in front of the same shrine. A record in the third year of the Chōḷa king Parakēsarivarman *alias* Tribhuvanachakravartin Vikrama-Chōḷadēva (1118—35). Records gift of land to the temple of Siddhēśvaram-Uḍaiyār at Pañchavanmahādēvi-chaturvēdimaṅgalam, a *brahmadēya* in Tirunaṟaiyūr-nāḍu, which was a subdivision of Kulōttuṅga-Chōḷa-vaḷanāḍu. Mentions Mummuḍi-śōḷa-chaturvēdimaṅgalam, a *brahmadēya* in Tirunaṟaiyūr-nāḍu, a subdivision of Bhūpālakulavalli-vaḷanāḍu, and quotes the sixth year of Chakravartin Kulōttuṅga-Chōḷadēva (I).

155. 164 *of* 1908.—(Tamil.) On the same wall. A record in the third year of the Chōḷa king Parakēsarivarman *alias* Tribhuvanachakravartin Vikrama-Chōḷadēva (1118—35). Records gift of land by purchase for feeding the Mahēśvaras visiting the temple of Siddhēśvaram Uḍaiyār at Tirunaṟaiyūr *alias* Pañchavanmahādēvi Chaturvēdimaṅgalam by a native of Karuppūr in Maṇṇināḍu, a subdivision of Virudarājabhayaṁkara-vaḷanāḍu. [See *Ep. Ind.*, Vol. XI, p. 121, where Prof. Jacobi points out that the exact date is Friday, 4th June, A.D. 1120.]

156. 165 *of* 1908.—(Tamil.) On the same wall. A record in the fifth year of the Chōḷa king Parakēsarivarman *alias* Rājarājadēva (II, 1146—78). Records gift of money for a lamp. [See *Ep. Ind.*, Vol. XI, p. 122, where Prof. Jacobi concludes that the English date should be Friday, 24th November, A.D. 1150, after correcting Saturday into Friday.]

157. 166 *of* 1908.—(Tamil.) On the same wall. A record in the second year of the Chōḷa king . . . chakravartin Kulōttuṅga-chōḷadēva (III, 1178—1216). Records gift of money for a lamp by Ēkavāśagan Kulōttuṅgaśōḷanūr *alias* Vānakōvaraiyar who was a native of Tuṇḍa-nāḍu, a subdivision of Vaḍagarai Muḍigoṇḍa-śōḷa-vaḷanāḍu. [See *Ep. Ind.*, Vol. XI, pp. 123-4, where Prof. Jacobi discusses the details of the date and settles it as Wednesday, 13th February, A.D. 1180.]

158. 167 *of* 1908.—(Tamil.) On the same wall. A record in the twelfth year of the Chōḷa king Parakēsarivarman *alias* Tribhuvanachakravartin Vikrama-Chōḷadēva (1118—35). Records gift of land. [See *Ep. Ind.*, Vol. XI, p. 122, where it is pointed out that the date corresponded to Thursday, 15th May, A.D. 1130.]

159. 168 *of* 1908.—(Tamil.) On the same wall. A record in the second year of the Chōḷa king Tribhuvanachakravartin Rājēndra Chōḷadēva (I ?). Records gift of land. [It is doubtful which of the three Rājēndrachōḷas is referred to here.]

160. 169 *of* 1908.—(Tamil.) On the north wall of the same maṇṭapa. A record in the sixth year of the Chōḷa king Vikrama-Chōḷadēva (1118—35). Records gift of money for a lamp. Mentions Panaiyūr-nāḍu in Kulōttuṅga-Chōḷa-vaḷanāḍu.

161. 170 *of* 1908.—(Tamil.) On the same wall. A record in the second year of the Chōḷa king Parakēsarivarman *alias* Tribhuvanachakravartin Vikrama-Chōḷadēva (1118—35). Records gift of land. [See *Ep. Ind.*, Vol. XI, p. 121, where Prof. Jacobi points out that the date given in the epigraph (Monday, Vaiśākha, Mithuna, Pūrvapaksha 12) is wrong. If the *tithi* is corrected into fourteen and the Nakshattra to Mūla, it would correspond to Monday, 23rd June, A.D. 1119.]

162. 171 *of* 1908.—(Tamil.) On the same wall. A record in the third year of the Chōḷa king Vikrama-Chōḷadēva (1118—35),

Records gift of land. See *Ep. Ind.,* Vol. XI, p. 121. The date is incorrect like the above.

163. 172 *of* 1908.—(Tamil.) On the same wall. A record in the sixth year of the Chōḷa king Tribhuvanachakravartin Rājādhirājadēva (II). Built in at the end. Records a gift of lamp. See *Ep. Ind.,* Vol. XI, p. 123. [Prof. Jacobi equates the date to Thursday, 6th March, A.D. 1169, and further infers that the king should have come to the throne between 7th and 30th March, 1163.]

164. 173 *of* 1908.—(Tamil.) On the same wall. A record in the ninth year of the Chōḷa king Parakēsarivarman *alias* Tribhuvanachakravartin Rājarājadēva (II, ? 1146—78). The bottom of the inscription is lost. Mentions Tribhuvanachakravartin Kōnērinmaikoṇḍān and seems to record a gift of land.

165. 174 *of* 1908.—(Tamil.) On the same wall. A record in the twelfth year of the Chōḷa king Parakēsarivarman *alias* Tribhuvanachakravartin Vikrama-Chōḷadēva (1118—35). Records gift of land for offerings to the shrine of a Piḍāri at Tirunaṟaiyūr.

166. 175 *of* 1908.—(Tamil.) On the same wall. A record in the second year of the Chōḷa king Tribhuvanachakravartin Kulōttuṅga-Chōḷadēva (III). Records gift of money for a lamp. See *Ep. Ind.*, Vol. XI, p. 124, where it is pointed out that the date corresponded to Thursday, 28th February, A.D. 1180.

167. 176 *of* 1908.—(Tamil.) On the north wall of the maṇṭapa in front of the central shrine in the Siddhanāthasvāmin temple. A record in the fifth year of the Chōḷa king Parakēsarivarman *alias* Tribhuvanachakravartin Vīrarājēndradēva II, i.e., Kulōttuṅga III. Records a gift of land by Chāmuṇḍadēva, a native of Māttūr in Kumiḷināḍu, a subdivision, Āmūr-kōṭṭam in Jayaṅgoṇḍa-Chōḷa-maṇḍalam. [The date, according to Prof. Jacobi, is Friday, 18th February, A.D. 1183. *Ep. Ind.*, Vol. XI, p. 124.]

168. 177 *of* 1908.—(Tamil.) On the same wall. A damaged record in the fifth year of the Chōḷa king Parakēsarivarman *alias* Tribhuvanachakravartin Vikrama-Chōḷadēva (1118—35). Built in at the end. Records gift of land for a lamp and for feeding the Śiva-Yōgins.

169. 178 *of* 1908.—(Tamil.) On the same wall. A record in the sixth year of the Chōḷa king Rājakēsarivarman *alias* Tribhuvanachakravartin Vīrarājēndra-Chōḷadēva (II, i.e., Kulōttuṅga III). Records gift of money for a lamp by a native of Tuṇḍa-nāḍu, a subdivision of Muḍigoṇḍaśōḷa-vaḷanāḍu. He is different from the donor mentioned in No. 157. [See *Ep. Ind.*, Vol. XI, p. 124, where the *Navami* of the original date is pointed out to be wrong for *Saptami* and the date then settled as Saturday, 10th September, A.D. 1183.]

170. 179 *of* 1908.—(Tamil.) On the same wall. An unfinished record in the twelfth year of the Chōḷa king Vikrama-Chōḷadēva

(1118—35). Records gift of money for a lamp by a native of Neḍumbulam in Puṟaṅgarambai-nāḍu, a subdivision of Rājēndra-śōḷa-vaḷanāḍu.

171. 180 *of* 1908.—(Tamil.) On the same wall. A record in the fifth year of the Chōḷa king Vikrama-Chōḷadēva (1118—35). Records gift of money (one *kāśu*) for a lamp by the wife of a merchant of Avanināráyaṇapuram.

Tiruppanandāḷ.

The place is now famous for its Śūdra *maṭha* founded in A.D. 1720 by a certain Tillaināyaka Tambirān, a disciple of the central *maṭha* of Dharmapuram and the head of a similar *maṭha* established at Benares in 1580 by another disciple thereof. For the relation between these *maṭhas* and other details see *Tanj. Gazr.*, Vol. I, p. 222.

172. 29 *of* 1914.—(Tamil.) On the east wall of the central shrine in the Aruṇajaṭēśvara temple. A record in the eighth year of the Chōḷa king Parakēsarivarman *alias* Śrī-Rājēndra-Chōḷadēva I. Portions built in. Records gift of ninety-six sheep for a lamp to the temple of Tiruttāṭakēśvaram-Uḍaiyār at Tiruppanandāḷ. [The deity is named after a lady devotee Tāṭakai who adorned the God with garland. The place is also associated with the legend of Kuṅguliyakkalaya Nāyanār.]

173. 30 *of* 1914.—(Tamil.) On the southern entrance into the same shrine, left side. A record in the eighteenth year of the Chōḷa king Rājakēsarivarman. Records gift of ninety sheep for a lamp to the temple of Tiruttāṭakai-Īśvaragarattu-Mahādēva-Bhaṭāra at Tiruppanandāḷ, which was a *dēvadāna* in Vaḍagarai-Maṇṇi-nāḍu, by Kōvan Amudan, a native of Karuppūr in the same Nāḍu. Below this record is a fragment which seems to provide for offerings and a flower garden evidently to the same temple.

174. 31 *of* 1914.—(Tamil.) On the same entrance, right side. A portion of the stone is cut away. Records a gift of land by purchase for offerings to the God Śivalōkaviṭaṅkadēva and the goddess, by Kīrttirājarāja *alias* Rājarāja Gandharva-Mārāyan.

175. 32 *of* 1914.—(Tamil.) On the southern entrance into the same shrine, right side. A record in the twenty-ninth year of the Chōḷa king Madiraikoṇḍa Parakēsarivarman (Parāntaka I). Records gift of ninety sheep for a lamp to the temple of Tiruttaṭākēś-varattu-Mahādēva at Tiruppanandāḷ, a *dēvadāna* in Vaḍagarai-Maṇṇi-nāḍu, by Iṟaiyan Mādēvan of Kumāramaṅgalam in Ambar-nāḍu.

176. 33 *of* 1914.—(Tamil.) On the same entrance, left side. A record in the twenty-ninth year of the Chōḷa king Madiraikoṇḍa Parakēsarivarman (Parāntaka I). Records gift of land for offerings to the same temple by a native of Karambiyam in Eyi-nāḍu.

177. 34 *of* 1914.—(Tamil.) On the south wall of the maṇṭapa in front of the same shrine. Refers to the metallic image of Ksētrapāladēva consecrated by a certain Rājarājakka Tirupamārāyan and registers a gift of land to it for offerings.

178. 35 *of* 1914.—(Tamil.) On the same wall. A record in the twentieth year of the Chōḷa king Tribhuvanachakravartin Kulōttuṅga-Chōḷadēva. Records gift of land for a lamp by a native of Kanni-Kuḷattūr in Pulivala-nāḍu, a subdivision of Kāliyūr-Kōṭṭam in Jayaṅgoṇḍaśōḷa-maṇḍalam.

179. 36 *of* 1914.—(Tamil.) On the north wall of the first prākāra of the same temple. A record of the Pāṇḍya king . . . chakravartin Perumāḷ Kulaśēkharadēva in his second year, Makara, śu. di. 3, Monday, Śravaṇa. Built in at the beginning. Records sale of land to the temple at Tiruppanandāḷ which is said to be a *brahmadēya* in Maṇṇi-nāḍu, a subdivision of Vaḍagarai-Virudarājabhayaṅkara-vaḷanāḍu, by the assembly of the same village. Mr. Swamikannu Pillai is of the opinion that the date intended was probably Monday, 21st December 1237, but it is the first and not the second year of Jaṭāvarman Kulaśēkhara II. See *Ind. Antq.*, 1913, June.

180. 37 *of* 1914.—(Tamil.) On the same wall. A record of the Pāṇḍya king Jaṭāvarman *alias* Tribhuvanachakravartin Perumāḷ Sundara-Pāṇḍyadēva (date lost), Kanyā, śu. di. 8, Sunday, Uttarāshāḍa. Built in at the end. Records gift of land for offerings, etc., on festival days to the temple of Tiruttāṭakēśvaramuḍaiya-Nāyanār at Tiruppanandāḷ by the same assembly. [Was Perumāḷ Sundara Pāṇḍya the son of Māravarman Kulaśēkhara I (1268—1308) who afterwards murdered his father ?]

181. 38 *of* 1914.—(Tamil.) On the same wall. A record of the Pāṇḍya king Māravarman *alias* Tribhuvanachakravartin Vīra-Pāṇḍyadēva, in his twenty-fifth year, Vrischika, śu. di. 14, Sunday, Pushya, corresponding to January 9, A.D. 1278. Records gift of land to the same temple by the residents of the village who purchased it from the village assembly. Mr. Swamikannu Pillai infers from this date that the king began to rule between January 9 and July 13, A.D. 1253, and corrects Kielhorn's version in *Ep. Ind.*, Vol. IX, p. 227.

182. 39 *of* 1914.—(Tamil.) On the same wall. A record in the ninth year of the Chōḷa king Tribhuvanachakravartin Kulōttuṅga-Chōḷadēva (III ?), "who was pleased to take Madurai (Madura)." Records gift of money to the temple of Tiruttāṭaki-Īśvaram-Uḍaiyār at Tiruppanandāḷ in Maṇṇi-nāḍu, a subdivision of Virudarājabhayaṅkara-vaḷanāḍu for bathing the God daily in *Pañcha-gavya.*

183. 40 *of* 1914.—(Tamil.) On the same wall. A record of the Chōḷa king Tribhuvanachakravartin Kulōttuṅga-Chōḷadēva (III) in his eighth year, Makara, śu. di. 2, Wednesday, Śravaṇa (corresponding to December 25, 1185). Built in at the beginning. Records gift of land for offerings to the images of Tirukkaḍavūr Kuṅgiliyakkalaiya-Nāyanār and other Śaiva devotees in the temple at Tiruppanandāḷ by a person bearing the same name. [The Nāyanār is said to have turned the face of the deity to its normal position from which it had previously been diverted by the Lord's desire to save Tāṭakai's shame.]

184. 41 *of* 1914.—(Tamil.) On the same wall. An unfinished record of the Chōḷa king Parakēsarivarman *alias* Tribhuvanachakravartin Kulōttuṅga-Chōḷadēva (III), "who was pleased to take Madurai (Madura)," in his ninth year, Rishabha, ba. di. 10, Monday, Pūrvabhādrapada, corresponding to 4th May, A.D. 1187. Records gift of land to the same temple by the servants of Tirukkāmakkōṭṭamuḍaiya-Periya-Nāchchiyār in this temple.

185. 42 *of* 1914.—(Tamil.) On the same wall. A damaged record of the Vijayanagara king Immaḍi . . . , son of Vīrapratāpa-Dēvarāya-Mahārāya (II), "who was pleased to institute the elephant hunt," in Ś. 1369, Kshaya. Records gift of land for conducting the festival of Mārgaḷi-Tiruvādirai. Mentions a place called Iḍavai *alias* Pāṇḍiyanai-ven-kaṇḍa-śōḷa-chaturvēdimaṅgalam in Maṇṇi-nāḍu. [The epigraph shows that the place was founded by a Chōḷa who defeated a Pāṇḍya at Iḍavai and saw him retreat and this took place in the time of Varaguṇa Pāṇḍya who came to the throne in A.D. 862. See *Ep. Ind.*, Vol. IX, p. 87.]

186. 43 *of* 1914.—(Tamil.) On the east wall of the same prākāra. A record of the Chōḷa king Rājakēsarivarman *alias* Tribhuvanachakravartin Kulōttuṅga-Chōḷadēva (II), the date of which is lost. Records gift of land by purchase. Quotes the fifteenth year of Vikrama-Chōḷadēva (1118—35).

187. 44 *of* 1914.—(Tamil.) On the same wall. A record in the third year of the Chōḷa king Tribhuvanachakravartin Rājarāja (III). Records gift of land to the temple of Tiruvajanīśvaram-Uḍaiyār. The signatories are Vayirādarāyan, Vīrāḍarājan and Toṇḍamān. Refers to the fifteenth year probably of his predecessor.

188. 45 *of* 1914.—(Tamil.) On the south wall of the same prākāra. A record of the Chōḷa king Parakēsarivarman *alias* Tribhuvanachakravartin Rājarājadēva (II, 1146—78) in . . . Makara, ba. di. 10, Monday, Vaiśākha. Records gift of land for opening a road through which the God had to be taken in procession to the river Koḷḷiḍam, on festive occasions.

189. 46 *of* 1914.—(Tamil.) On the same wall. A record in the twenty-ninth year of the Chōḷa king Rājakēsarivarman *alias* Tribhuvanachakravartin Kulōttuṅga-Chōḷadēva (I). Registers the sale by a temple priest of his right of worship on 4½ days in the month to recoup a portion of money which he was unable to pay towards his misappropriation of gold and silver ornaments, bronze utensils, etc., belonging to the temple. The embezzlement, it is stated, was detected in the twenty-eighth year of the king. Reference is also made to similar misappropriations by the same person, detected in the third year of Adhirājēndradēva and in the eighth and twenty-first years of Kulōttuṅga-Chōḷadēva, when the temple treasury was inspected by Rājarāja-Mūvēndavēḷār, Sēnāpati-Pallavarājar and Sēnāpati-Nandiarājar, respectively. The amounts which he had thus to make good were also included in the present sale.

190. 47 *of* 1914.—(Tamil.) On the same wall. This inscription probably refers to the same king as the above. Records in the twenty-ninth year similar sales of the right of worship held by five other temple priests on account of similar misappropriations.

Tiruppurambiyam.

The Śiva temple here is well known in Śaivite tradition. It is said to celebrate the grace of the Lord towards Sunda and Upasunda and the miraculous power of Gñānasambanda in reviving the lover of a Vaṇiga woman who had died of snake bite. Hence the name Sākshīśvara of the deity. The temple is mentioned in the Dēvāram. It is also historically important as the scene of a battle between the Gaṅga Prithvīpati I and Varaguṇa Pāṇḍya, in which the former lost his life. See *Udayēndram Plates of Prithvipati* II (*S.I.I.*, Vol. II, p. 381). It was in Aṇḍāttukūṟṟam in Rājēndrasiṁhavaḷanāḍu.

191. 69 *of* 1897.—(Tamil.) On the south wall of the central shrine of the Sākshīśvara temple. A record in the fourth year of the Chōḷa king Kō-Parakēsarivarman " who cut off the head of the Pāṇḍya." Records gift of land. Built in. [Was the king Parakēsarivarman Sundara Chōḷa, the destroyer of Vīra Pāṇḍya ?]

192. 70 *of* 1897.—(Tamil.) On the same wall. A record in the forty-third year of the Chōḷa king Tribhuvanachakravartin Kulōttuṅga-Chōḷadēva (I). Records gift of land. Built in.

193. 71 *of* 1897.—(Tamil.) On the same wall. A record in the sixteenth year of the Chōḷa king Kō-Rājakēsarivarman. Records gift of land for two lamps.

194. 72 *of* 1897.—(Tamil.) On the same wall. A record in the tenth year of the Chōḷa king Kō-Rājakēsarivarman. Records gift of gold for a lamp.

195. 73 *of* 1897.—(Tamil.) On the same wall. A record in the fifteenth year of the Chōḷa king Kō . . . kēsarivarman. Records gift of a lamp.

196. 74 *of* 1897.—(Tamil.) On the same wall. A record in the seventh year of the Chōḷa king Kō-Rājakēsarivarman. Records gift of a lamp.

197. *75 of* 1897.—(Tamil.) On the same wall. A record in the fourteenth year of the Chōḷa king Madiraikoṇḍa Kō-Rājakēsarivarman. Records gift of cows for a lamp. [Was he the same as Gaṇḍarāditya, the son of Parāntaka I who had the titles of Maduraikoṇḍa and Rājakēsarivarman ?]

198. *76 of* 1897.—(Tamil.) On the same wall. A record in the tenth year of the Chōḷa king Kō-Parakēsarivarman. Records gift of sheep for half a lamp.

199. *77 of* 1897.—(Tamil.) On the same wall. A record in the twenty-first year of the Chōḷa king Madiraikoṇḍa Kō-Parakēsarivarman (Parāntaka I). Records gift of sheep for a lamp.

200. 78 *of* 1897.—(Tamil.) On the same wall. A record in the ninth year of the Chōḷa king Kō-Rājakēsarivarman. Records that certain gold ornaments and a silver vessel were made out of the savings of the temple treasury between the second and ninth years of the king's reign.

201. 79 *of* 1897.—(Tamil.) On the same wall. A record in the sixteenth year of the Chōḷa king Kō-Rājakēsarivarman. Records gift of one and a half lamps.

202. 80 *of* 1897.—(Tamil.) On the north wall of the same shrine. A record in the sixteenth year of the Chōḷa king Kō-Parakēsarivarman *alias* Rājēndra-Chōḷadēva (I). Records a gift of money for ten lamps to the Ādittēśvara temple at Tiruppurāmbiyam.

Tiruvalanjuḻi.

The local temple is well known for its delicately chiselled stone work. Some of the figures are considered to be Jain. See *Tanj. Gazr.*, Vol. I, p. 223, for details. The place was so called because the Kāvēri was prevented from submerging into the nether world by the self-sacrifice of Varagaṇḍa muni.

203. 618 *of* 1902.—(Tamil.) On the south wall of the maṇṭapa in front of the central shrine in the Kapardīśvara temple. A record in the thirty-ninth year of the Chōḷa king Tribhuvanachakravartin Tribhuvanavīradēva, who took Madura, Ceylon, Karuvūr and the crowned head of the Pāṇḍya (i.e., Kulōttuṅga III). Records gift of land. The date corresponded to Wednesday, 25th January A.D. 1217. See *Ep. Ind.*, Vol. VIII, p. 5.

204. 619 *of* 1902.—(Tamil.) On the south wall of the maṇṭapa in front of the central shrine in the same temple. A record in the ninth year of the Chōḷa king Tribhuvanachakravartin Rājādhirājadēva (I ?). Records gift of two lamps.

205. 620 *of* 1902.—(Tamil.) On the same wall. A record in the seventeenth year of the Chōḷa king Rājarāja-Rājakēsarivarman *alias* Rājarājadēva (I). Refers to a grant made in the thirty-eighth year of Madurai-koṇḍa Parakēsarivarman (Parāntaka I).

206. 621 *of* 1902.—(Tamil.) On the same wall. A damaged record in the eighth year of the Chōḷa king Tribhuvanachakravartin Rājādhirājadēva (I ?). Records gift of three lamps.

207. 622 *of* 1902.—(Tamil.) On the same wall. A record in the fourth year of the Chōḷa king Parakēsarivarman *alias* Tribhuvanachakravartin Rājarājadēva (II). Records gift of land for lamps. See *Ep. Ind.*, Vol. VIII, p. 2, where Dr. Kielhorn shows that the English equivalent of the date is Wednesday, 23rd November, A.D. 1149.

208. 623 *of* 1902.—(Tamil.) On the same wall. A damaged record in the fourth year of the Chōḷa king Parakēsarivarman *alias* Tribhuvanachakravartin Vikrama-Chōḷadēva (1118—35).

209. 624 *of* 1902.—(Tamil.) On the same wall. A record in the twenty-first year of the Chōḷa king Rājarāja-Rājakēsarivarman *alias* Rājarājadēva (I). Records that, while staying at Tiruvallam, the king, who bore (as in Tanjore inscriptions) the surname Śivapādaśēkharadēva, confirmed a grant of land made in the twelfth year of Parakēsarivarman.

210. 625 *of* 1902.—(Tamil.) On the north wall of the same maṇṭapa. A record in the eighth year of the Chōḷa king Vikrama-Chōḷadēva (1118—35). Records copy of an inscription of the seventh year of Parakēsarivarman *alias* Uḍaiyār Rājēndradēva (1050—63).

211. 626 *of* 1902.—(Tamil.) On the same wall. A damaged record in the sixteenth year of the Chōḷa king Parakēsarivarman *alias* Tribhuvanachakravartin Rājarājadēva (II). See *Ep. Ind.*, Vol. VIII, p. 263, where Dr. Kielhorn discusses the date of this inscription and concludes that it should be assigned to Wednesday, 11th July, 1162.

212. 627 *of* 1902.—(Tamil.) On the same wall. A damaged record in the eighth year of the Chōḷa king Rājakēsarivarman *alias* Tribhuvanachakravartin Rājādhirājadēva II. See *Ep. Ind.*, Vol. IX, p. 211, where Dr. Kielhorn points out that the date corresponds to Monday, 10th August, A.D. 1170.

213. 628 *of* 1902.—(Tamil.) On the same wall. A record in the twelfth year of the Chōḷa king Parakēsarivarman *alias* Tribhuvanachakravartin Rājarājadēva (II). Records gifts of land to the images of Tirunāvukkaraśudēvar, Tiruvādavūraḍigaḷ (i.e., Māṇikkavāśagar) and Tirukkaṇṇappadēvar. The date corresponded to Wednesday, 26th March, A.D. 1158. *Ep. Ind.*, Vol. VIII, p. 3.

214. 629 *of* 1902.—(Tamil.) On the south wall of the second prākāra of the same temple. A record in the eighth year of the Chōḷa king Tribhuvanachakravartin Rājarājadēva (III). Records gift of land. The corresponding date is Monday, 7th October, 1224. See *Ep. Ind.*, Vol. IV, p. 6.

215. 630 *of* 1902.—(Tamil.) On the same wall. A record in the twelfth year of the Chōḷa king Tribhuvanachakravartin Rājarājadēva (III ?). Partly built in.

216. 631 *of* 1902.—(Tamil.) On the north wall of the Nandimaṇṭapa in the same temple. An incomplete record in the thirty-sixth year of the Chōḷa king Tribhuvanachakravartin Tribhuvanavīradēva, who took Madura, Ceylon, Karuvūr and the crowned head of the Pāṇḍya, i.e., Kulōttuṅga III. The date corresponded to Monday, 14th April, A.D. 1214. See *Ep. Ind.*, Vol. VIII, p. 5.

217. 632 *of* 1902.—(Tamil.) On a stone set up in front of the inner gōpura in the same temple. A record in Śaka (year doubtful) Viśvāvasu. A few syllables of every line are cut away.

218. 633 *of* 1902.—(Tamil.) On the north wall of the Bhairava shrine in the same temple. A record in the twenty-fifth year of the Chōḷa king Rājakēsarivarman *alias* Rājarājadēva (I). Records gifts of ornaments by Rājarājadēva's queen Dantiśakti-Viṭaṅki *alias* Lōkamahādēvi, his daughter Kuṇḍavai, the queen of Vimalādityadēva (the Eastern Chāḷukyan king), and his middle daughter Mādēvaḍigal, to the shrine of Kshētrapāladēva, which had been built by the king.

219. 634 *of* 1902.—(Tamil.) On a stone lying in the garden in the same temple. Records gift of land [to the shrine of Śvētavighnēśvara. [Said in the legends to have been worshipped by Indra.]

Tiruviḍaimarudūr.

Known as Madhyārjunam among the orthodox, this place, prominent in Śaivite legendary lore, is epigraphically very rich. For details of legends, festivals, etc., see *Tanj. Gazr.*, Vol. I, p. 223. From 1798 onward it has been the residence of the descendants of Amir Singh of Tanjore. The *Dēvāram* mentions it as *Iḍaimarudu.* In Chōḷa time it was in Tiṟaimūr-nāḍu in Uyyakkoṇḍa chōḷa-vaḷa-nāḍu. The local epigraphs contain a large number of Rājakēsarivarmans and Parakēsarivarmans who are mostly unidentifiable.

220. 193 *of* 1907.—(Tamil.) On the north wall of the central shrine in the Mahāliṅgasvāmin temple. A record in the tenth year of the Chōḷa king Parakēsarivarman. Records gift of money for a lamp. The money was entrusted to the assembly of Tirunīlaguḍi in Tiraimūr-nāḍu.

221. 194 *of* 1907.—(Tamil.) On the same wall. A record in the fourteenth year of the Chōḷa king Parakēsarivarman. Records a sale of land.

222. 195 *of* 1907.—(Tamil.) On the same wall. A record in the thirty-eighth year of the Chōḷa king Madiraikoṇḍa Parakēsarivarman (Parāntaka I). Mentions Irumuḍiśōḷa-Pallavaraiyar and refers to the *Paḷangāviri-nirōḍu-kāl.*

223. 196 *of* 1907.—(Tamil.) On the same wall. A record of the Chōḷa king Parakēsarivarman, the date of which is damaged. Purchase of land with the gold granted for a lamp by Piḷḷaiyār Uttamaśīliyār. Mentions Mahēndramaṅgalam and Nāṭṭu-vāykkāl. (Uttamaśīli was the son of Parāntaka I, 905—47).

224. 197 *of* 1907.—(Tamil.) On the same wall. A record in the tenth year of the Chōḷa king Rājarājakēsarivarman (Rājarāja I), " who destroyed the ships at Kāndalūr." Records gift of gold flower by a certain Hridayaśiva of Tirupputtūr.

225. 198 *of* 1907.—(Tamil.) On the same wall. A record in the fourth year of the Chōḷa king Parakēsarivarman. Records gift of a gold hand *(hasta)* set with precious stones.

226. 199 *of* 1907.—(Tamil.)· On the same wall· A record in the fourth year of the Chōḷa king Parakēsarivarman. Refers to the inscriptions registering money endowments for lamps to the temple and states that all the stones bearing them were used up when the central shrine was built of stone. Accordingly copies were made of these records, one of which belonged to the reign of the Kāḍupaṭṭigaḷ Nandipōttaraiyar. This king had endowed a lamp called Kumāramāttāṇḍa. Kāḍupaṭṭigaḷ Nandipōttaraiyar was evidently the Pallava king Nandivarman III who must have had the title kumāra-mārttāṇḍa.]

227. 200 *of* 1907.—(Tamil.) On the same wall. A record in the third year of the Chōḷa king Parakēsarivarman *alias* Śrī-Rājēndra-Chōḷadēva (I). Records gift of forty-five sheep for a lamp to burn at night at the gate called Ēkanāyakam-tiruvāśal.

228. 201 *of* 1907.—(Tamil.) On the same wall. A record in the twentieth year of the Chōḷa king Madiraikoṇḍa-Parakēsarivarman (Parāntaka I). Records gift of gold for the green gram offering.

229. 202 *of* 1907.—(Tamil.) On the same wall. An incomplete record in the third year of the Chōḷa king Rājakēsarivarman.

230. 203 *of* 1907.—(Tamil.) On the same wall. A record in the thirty-seventh year of the Chōḷa king Madiraikoṇḍa Parakēsarivarman (Parāntaka I). Records gift of hundred sheep for a lamp by the Manrāḍi Kolli-Pugaḷan.

231. 204 *of* 1907.—(Tamil.) On the same wall. A record in the thirty-seventh year of the Chōḷa king Madiraikoṇḍa Parakēsarivarman (905—47). Records gift of ninety sheep for a lamp.

232. 205 *of* 1907.—(Tamil.) On the same wall. A record in the thirty-seventh year of the Chōḷa king Madiraikoṇḍa Parakēsarivarman (905—47). Records gift of eighty-seven sheep for a lamp.

233. 206 *of* 1907.—(Tamil.) On the north wall of the central shrine in the Mahāliṅgasvāmin temple. A record in the thirty-seventh year of the Chōḷa king Madiraikoṇḍa Parakēsarivarman (905—47). Records gift of ninety sheep for a lamp.

234. 207 *of* 1907.—(Tamil.) On the same wall. A record in the thirty-seventh year of the Chōḷa king Madiraikoṇḍa Parakēsarivarman (905—47). Mentions a certain Kavarāmoḷimādēvan *alias* Toṇḍaraḍippoḍi. [Toṇḍaraḍippoḍi reminds one of the Vaishṇava Āḷvār; but there is nothing to show that the saint is referred to here.]

235. 208 *of* 1907.—(Tamil.) On the same wall. A damaged record in the sixteenth year of the Chōḷa king Parakēsarivarman.

236. 209 *of* 1907.—(Tamil.) On the same wall. A damaged record in the twelfth year of the Chōḷa king Parakēsarivarman.

237. 210 *of* 1907.—(Tamil.) On the same wall. A record in the ninth year of the Chōḷa king Parakēsarivarman. Above this is another damaged inscription.

238. 211 *of* 1907.—(Tamil.) On the same wall. A much damaged record.

239. 212 *of* 1907.—(Tamil.) Mentions Iṅganāṭṭu-Pallavaraiyan and the image of Tiruviḍaimarudil-āḍalviḍaṅgadēvar which he set up. In the body of the inscription the sabhā of Tiraimūr is said to consist of 300 men and the citizens of 400.

240. 213 *of* 1907.—(Tamil.) On the same wall. A partly damaged record in the fourth year of the Chōḷa king Parakēsarivarman. Records gifts of lamps.

241. 214 *of* 1907.—(Tamil.) On the same wall. A record in the fourth year of the Chōḷa king Parakēsarivarman, "who took the head of the Pāṇḍya." The temple is called Tiruviḍaimarudil Āḷvār-kōyil. Mentions Śiṟṟiṅgan-uḍaiyān Kōvil-Mayilai *alias* Parāntaka Mūvēndavēḷān. [Was the king Parāntaka II, Uttama-chōḷa ?]

242. 215 *of* 1907.—(Tamil.) On the same wall. A record in the sixth year of the Chōḷa king Rājakēsarivarman. Records that the Chōḷa queen Vānavanmādēvi came to worship the God.

243. 216 *of* 1907.—(Tamil.) On the same wall. A record in the seventeenth year of the Chōḷa king Rājakēsarivarman. Records the laying out of a jasmine flower-garden.

244. 217 *of* 1907.—(Tamil.) On the north and west walls of the same shrine. A damaged record in the fourteenth year of the Chōḷa king Parakēsarivarman.

245. 218 *of* 1907.—(Tamil.) On the north and west walls of the same shrine. A record in the ninth year of the Chōḷa king whose name is damaged. Records gift of land.

246. 219 *of* 1907.—(Tamil.) On the north, west and south walls of the same shrine. A record in the sixth year of the Chōḷa king Parakēsarivarman. Public sale of land. Mentions Iṅganāṭṭu-Pallavaraiyar and Śiṟṟiṅgan-uḍaiyān Kōyil-Mayilai *alias* Madhurāntaka Mūvēndavēḷān. See Nos. 241 above and 255 below.

247. 220 *of* 1907.—(Tamil.) On the north, west and south walls of the same shrine. A record in the twentieth year of the Chōḷa Parakēsarivarman *alias* Uḍaiyār Śrī-Rājēndra-Chōḷadēva (I). Built in at both ends and mutilated in the middle.

248. 221 *of* 1907.—(Tamil.) On the north, west and south walls of the same shrine. A record in the fourteenth year of the Chōḷa king Parakēsarivarman.

249. 222 *of* 1907.—(Tamil.) On the west wall of the same shrine. A damaged record in the thirty-seventh year of the Chōḷa king Madiraikoṇḍa Parakēsarivarman (Parāntaka I). Seems to record a gift of land for celebrating the *tiruvādiari, śadaiyam* and *amāvāsai* festivals.

250. 223 *of* 1907.—(Tamil.) On the same wall. A much damaged record of the Chōḷa king Madiraikoṇḍa Parakēsarivarman. Seems to record a gift of land.

251. 224 *of* 1907.—(Tamil.) On the same wall. A much damaged record in the twenty-seventh year of the king, whose name is lost. Seems to record a gift of lamps.

252. 225 *of* 1907.—(Tamil.) On the west wall of the central shrine in the Mahāliṅgasvāmin temple. A damaged record in the fourteenth year of the Chōḷa king Parakēsarivarman. Seems to record a gift of gold for a lamp.

253. 226 *of* 1907.—(Tamil.) On the same wall. A mutilated record of the Chōḷa king Parakēsarivarman *alias* Rājēndradēva (I). Only the beginning of the historical introduction is preserved.

254. 227 *of* 1907.—(Tamil.) On the same wall. A record in the twenty-seventh year of the Chōḷa king Madiraikoṇḍa Parakēsarivarman (905—47). Records gift of land. Mentions Kumāramāttāṇḍapuram. See No. 227 above.

255. 228 *of* 1907.—(Tamil.) On the same wall. A record in the fourteenth year of the Chōḷa king Parakēsarivarman. Mentions Śiṟṟiṅgan-uḍaiyān Paṭṭan Kaṇṇan *alias* Iṅganāṭṭu-Pallavaraiyan.

256. 229 *of* 1907.—(Tamil.) On the same wall. Records in the fourteenth year gift of a gold bowl *(maṇḍai)* by a native of Tañjāvūr (Tanjore).

257. 230 *of* 1907.—(Tamil.) On the same wall. A record in the eleventh year of the Chōḷa king Parakēsarivarman. Mentions Veṇṇāṭṭu Varambuśaluḍaiyān Śandirāchchan Śatturugaṇḍan.

258. 231 *of* 1907.—(Tamil.) On the same wall. A record in the eleventh year of the Chōḷa king Parakēsarivarman. Mentions the same person.

259. 232 *of* 1907.—(Tamil.) On the same wall. A mutilated record in the tenth year of the king whose name is lost.

260. 233 *of* 1907.—(Tamil.) On the same wall. A fragment of record of the Chōḷa king. Registers the grant of one *vēli* of land to a person who had to sing *dōśi* songs.

261. 234 *of* 1907.—(Tamil.) On the same wall. A record in the seventh year of the Chōḷa king Parakēsarivarman. Refers to the building of a temple; also to the thirtieth year of Madiraikoṇḍa Parakēsarivarman (905—47).

262. 235 *of* 1907.—(Tamil.) On the south wall of the same shrine. A damaged record in the thirty-first year of the Chōḷa king Madiraikoṇḍa Parakēsarivarman (905—47). Mentions Nalaṅgiḷinallūr-kūṟṟam. Seems to provide for feeding two Brāhmaṇas.

263. 236 *of* 1907.—(Tamil.) On the same wall. A damaged record in the fourteenth year of the Chōḷa king Parakēsarivarman. Records gift of sixty-two cows.

264. 237 *of* 1907.—(Tamil.) On the same wall. A damaged record in the fourth year of the Chōḷa king Parakēsarivarman. Records gift of money for a lamp.

265. 238 *of* 1907.—(Tamil.) On the same wall. A record in the sixteenth year of the Chōḷa king Madiraikoṇḍa Parakēsarivarman (905—47). Records gift by a native of Irumbēḍu Māgaḷūr-nāḍu, a subdivision of Śeṅgāṭṭu-kōṭṭam in Toṇḍai-nāḍu.

266. 239 *of* 1907.—(Tamil.) On the same wall. A record in the second year of the Chōḷa king Rājakēsarivarman. Records gift of eight *Iḷakkāśu* to the shrine of Purāṇa Gaṇapati on the southern side of the Mūlasthāna at Tiruviḍaimarudil by a native of Ēmanallūr, a *brahmadēya* in Vaḍagarai-Maṇṇi-nāḍu.

267. 240 *of* 1907.—(Tamil.) On the same wall. A damaged record in the thirty-seventh year of the Chōḷa king Madiraikoṇḍa Parakēsarivarman (905—47).

268. 241 *of* 1907.—(Tamil.) On the same wall. A record in the twenty-ninth year of the Chōḷa king Madiraikoṇḍa Parakēsarivarman (905—47). Records gift of sheep for a lamp.

269. 242 *of* 1907.—(Tamil.) On the same wall. A record in the third year of the Chōḷa king Rājakēsarivarman. Provides for the supply of tender coconuts to the God.

270. 243 *of* 1907.—(Tamil.) On the same wall. Mentions Toṅgamaṅgalamuḍaiyān, one of the Mūtta-Pirāntaka-aṇukkar.

271. 244 *of* 1907.—(Tamil.) On the same wall. A record in the second year of the Chōḷa king Parakēsarivarman. Mentions the *Śingaḷāntaka-teṟinda-Kaikkōḷar*.

272. 245 *of* 1907.—(Tamil.) On the south wall of the central shrine in the Mahāliṅgasvāmin temple. A record in the seventeenth year of the Chōḷa king Madiraikoṇḍa Parakēsarivarman (905—47). Records gift of paddy by the inhabitants of Tiruviḷai-nāḍu.

273. 246 *of* 1907.—(Tamil.) On the same wall. A record of the Chōḷa king Madiraikoṇḍa Parakēsarivarman (905—47), the date of which is lost. Records gift of ninety-one sheep. Mentions the *Tai-pūśam* festival.

274. 247 *of* 1907.—(Tamil.) On the same wall. A record in the third year of the Chōḷa king Parakēsarivarman. Records gift of a silver *kalaśam* by a native of Tulakkilimaṅgalam in Pāṇḍināḍu.

275. 248 *of* 1907.—(Tamil.) On the same wall. A damaged record in the twelfth year of the Chōḷa king Madiraikoṇḍa Parakēsarivarman (905—47). Records gift of a lamp. Mentions the festival of *Tai-pūśam*. See No. 274 above.

276. 249 *of* 1907.—(Tamil.) On the same wall. A damaged record of the Chōḷa king Parakēsarivarman, "who took the head of the Pāṇḍya," the date of which is lost. Records a gift of land for maintaining the *champaka* flower garden laid out by Tiruveṇkāṭṭu Pichchan. [The king referred to might be Parāntaka II Sundara Chōḷa.] See No. 287 below.

277. 250 *of* 1907.—(Tamil.) On the same wall. A damaged record in the thirty-sixth year of the Chōḷa king Madiraikoṇḍa Parakēsarivarman (905—47). Records gift of gold vessels.

278. 251 *of* 1907.—(Tamil.) On the same wall. A damaged record in the thirty-fourth year of the Chōḷa king Madiraikoṇḍa-Parakēsarivarman (905—47).

279. 252 *of* 1907.—(Tamil.) On the same wall. A record in the thirty-eighth year of the Chōḷa king Madiraikoṇḍa-Parakēsarivarman (905—47). Records gift of a lamp for the merit of Ariñjiyaipirāṭṭiyār. (She was the daughter of Arikulakēsari, the son of Parāntaka I (905—47).

280. 253 *of* 1907.—(Tamil.) On the same wall. A record in the second year of the Chōḷa king Parakēsarivarman. Refers to the putting up of the window, the door, the door-post and the steps in front of the big maṇṭapa by the regiment called *Kaikkōḷa-Perumbaḍai*. The maṇṭapa was called *Tigai Ayirattān-nūṟṟuvar*.

281. 254 *of* 1907.—(Tamil.) On the same wall. A record of the Chōḷa king Rājarāja-Rājakēsarivarman I (985—1013), "who destroyed the ships at Śālai," in his tenth year and two hundred and seventy-eighth day. Records gift of a gold image of Umāsahitar by the queen Pañchavanmahādēvi.

282. 255 *of* 1907.—(Tamil.) On the same wall. A damaged record in the fifth year of the Chōḷa king Parakēsarivarman, "who took the head of the Pāṇḍya." [Was the king intended Parāntaka II Sundara Chōḷa ?]

283. 256 *of* 1907.—(Tamil.) On the same wall. An unfinished record in the fourth year of the Chōḷa king Parakēsarivarman, "who defeated Vīra-Pāṇḍya and took his head." See note to the above.

284. 257 *of* 1907.—(Tamil.) On the same wall. A record in the sixth year of the Chōḷa king Kōnōinmaikoṇḍān. Records a gift in favour of Śirukuḷattūruḍayān Araiyan Pirāntakan *alias* Śembiyan Śōḷiyavaraiyan. The sixth year of Parakēsarivarman is quoted in the body of the inscription.

285. 258 *of* 1907.—(Tamil.) On the same wall. A record in the thirtieth year of the Chōḷa king Madiraikoṇḍa Parakēsarivarman (905—47). Registers an endowment in favour of the drummers *(uvachugaḷ)*. Refers to the agent of the Chōḷa king in Koṅgu. [See the Tiruchenġōḍu inscriptions for Parāntakā's conquests in Koṅgu.]

286. 259 *of* 1907.—(Tamil.) On the same wall. A record in the twenty-fourth year of the Chōḷa king Madiraikoṇḍa Parakēsarivarman (905—47). Records gift of ninety sheep for a lamp by a native of Ānaimaṅgalam in Paṭṭiṇakkūṟṟam.

287. 260 *of* 1907.—(Tamil.) On the same wall. A record in the ninth year of the Chōḷa king Rājakēsarivarman. Refers to the laying out of a *śiruśeṇbuga* flower-garden by Tiruveṇkāṭṭu-Pichchan. See No. 276 above.

288. 261 *of* 1907.—(Tamil.) On the south wall of the central shrine in the Māliṅgasvāmin temple. A record in the nineteenth year of the Chōḷa king Madiraikoṇḍa Parakēsarivarman (905—47). Records gift of gold for a lamp. Mentions the Nampirāṭṭiyār Kōkkiḷān Aḍigaḷ.

289. 262 *of* 1907.—(Tamil.) On the same wall. A record in the eighteenth year of the Chōḷa king Madiraikoṇḍa Parakēsarivarman (905—47). Records gift of gold for a lamp by a merchant of Kumāramāttāṇḍapuram in Teṅkarai-Tiraimūr-nāḍu.

290. 263 *of* 1907.—(Tamil.) On the same wall. Beginning much damaged. Records gift of two lamps.

291. 264 *of* 1907.—(Tamil.) On the same wall. A record in the thirty-second year of the Chōḷa king Rājakēsarivarman *alias* Uḍaiyār Śrī-Rājādhirājadēva (I, 1018—52). Registers an endowment of 2 *vēlis* and 2 *mās* in favour of Araiyan Tiruviḍaimaruduḍaiyān *alias* Mummuḍi-Śōḷa-Nittappēraiyan and his troupe. The grant proper begins with the word *kō-nō-inmai-koṇḍān.* The record says that a daily allowance of 2 *tūṇi* of paddy and annual allowance of 240 *kalams* should be given to the *pāḍavyam-vāsippār* (பாடவ்யம் வாசிப்பார்).

292. 265 *of* 1907.—(Tamil.) On the same wall. A record of the Chōḷa king Uttama-Chōḷa *alias* Parakēsarivarman in Kaliyuga 4083 and in his thirteenth year. Mentions Kañjanūr *alias* Siṁhavishṇu-chaturvēdimaṅgalam, a *brahmadēya* in Vaḍagarai-Nallāṟṟūr-nāḍu.

[The inscription is of unique value in giving the Kali and regnal years together and distinctly proves that Parakēsarivarman Madhurāntaka Uttamachōḷa came to the throne in A.D. 969–70.]

293. 266 *of* 1907.—(Tamil.) On the same wall. A record in the thirteenth year of the Chōḷa king Madiraikoṇḍa Parakēsarivarman (905—47). Records gift of ninety sheep for a lamp by a native of Kaṭṭivayal in Muttūṟṟu-kūṟṟam, a district of Pāṇḍi-nāḍu.

294. 267 *of* 1907.—(Tamil.) On the same wall. Mentions Tirutturutti-Nambi Śrīkaṇṭhar and Śivacharaṇaśēkharan. Close to this is a sculpture representing a liṅga, a worshipper, an attendant and a lampstand.

295. 268 *of* 1907.—(Tamil.) On the east wall of the same shrine. A damaged record of the Chōḷa king Parakēsarivarman, the date of which is doubtful. Records gift of sheep for two lamps.

296. 269 *of* 1907.—(Tamil.) On the same wall. A damaged record of the Chōḷa king Madiraikoṇḍa Parakēsarivarman (905—47), the date of which is lost.

297. 270 *of* 1907.—(Tamil.) On the same wall. Damaged in the beginning. Mentions Kuḍamūkku (Kumbhakōṇam).

298. 271 *of* 1907.—(Tamil.) On the west wall of the maṇṭapa in front of the same shrine. A record of the Vijayanagara king Vīrapratāpa Achyutadēva Mahārāya (1530—42) in Ś. 1456, expired, Jaya. Records gift of a village for the merit of Vasavaṇṇāyaka.

299. 272 *of* 1907.—(Tamil.) On the south base of the same maṇṭapa. A record in the seventh year of the Chōḷa king Parakēsarivarman *alias* Tribhuvanachakravartin Śrī-Vikrama-Chōḷadēva (1118—35). Records gift of the village of Vaṇṇakkuḍi *alias* Tyāgasamudra-chaturvēdimaṅgalam. Refers to a revenue settlement in the thirty-eighth year of Kulōttuṅga I.

300. 273 *of* 1907.—(Tamil.) On the south base of the maṇṭapa in front of the central shrine in the same temple. A record in the seventh year of the Chōḷa king Parakēsarivarman *alias* Tribhuvanachakravartin Śrī-Vikrama-Chōḷadēva (1118—35). Connected with the above epigraph. Mentions Vaṇṇakkuḍi *alias* Tyāgasamudra-chaturvēdimaṅgalam, a *brahmadēya* in Tiraimūr-nāḍu, a subdivision of Uyyakkoṇḍār-vaḷanāḍu. Refers to the revenue survey of the country and to the revenue settlement in the thirty-eighth year of Kulōttuṅga I.

301. 274 *of* 1907.—(Tamil.) On the same base. A mutilated record of the Chōḷa king Parakēsarivarman *alias* Tribhuvanachakravartin Śrī-Vikrama-Chōḷadēva (1118—35), the date of which is lost. Stones out of order. The ninth year of the king is referred to on one of the stones. Seems to record a gift of lamps.

302. 275 *of* 1907.—(Tamil.) On the north base of the same maṇṭapa. A record in the ninth year of the Chōḷa king Parakēsarivarman *alias* Tribhuvanachakravartin Śrī-Vikrama-Chōḷadēva (1118—35). Refers to the shrine of Vikkirama-Śōḷa-Īśvaramuḍaiyār in the temple at Tiruviḍaimarudūr and records the grant of the village of Madhurāntakanallūr *alias* Arindavan-Śāttamaṅgalam under the name Vikramaśōḷanallūr. Mentions the revenue survey and settlement made in the thirty-eighth year of Kulōttuṅga I.

303. 276 *of* 1907.—(Tamil.) On the same base. A record in the tenth year of the Chōḷa king Parakēsarivarman *alias* Tribhuvanachakravartin Śrī-Vikrama Chōḷadēva (1118—35). Records gift of the village of Nallāḍi in Tirunaṟaiyūr-nāḍu, a subdivision of Kulōttuṅga-Śōḷa-vaḷanāḍu. Queen Tribhuvanamuḻuduḍaiyāḷ is mentioned. The king was seated on the couch called Śōḷakōn.

304. 277 *of* 1907.—(Tamil.) On a stone built into the floor of the same maṇṭapa. A fragment of record of the Chōḷa king Parakēsarivarman *alias* Rājēndra-Chōḷadēva I (1012—43), the date of which is lost. Contains a portion of the historical introduction of the king.

305. 278 *of* 1907.—(Tamil.) On a pillar of the same maṇṭapa. A record in the ninth year of the Chōḷa king Rājarāja-Rājakēsarivarman (985—1013). Records gift of ornaments (*iraṭṭaimaṇi, tāli,* etc., weighing nine *kaḻañju* of gold) to the goddess Umābhaṭṭāraki by the Nambirāṭṭiyār Śrī-Pañchavanmādēviyār.

306. 279 *of* 1907.—(Tamil.) On the east wall of the first prākāra of the same temple, right of entrance. A record in the forty-first year of the Chōḷa king Tribhuvanachakravartin Śrī-Kulōṭṭuṅga-Chōḷadēva (I, 1070—1118). Provides for the supply of a bathing water-pot to the temple. The donor was a native of Gaṅgaikoṇḍaśōḷapuram.

307. 280 *of* 1907.—(Tamil.) In the same place. A record in the third year of the Chōḷa king Tribhuvanachakravartin Śrī-Vikrama-Chōḷadēva (1118—35). Records gift of money for supplying periodically an earthen pot by a native of Śembaṅguḍi in Tiruvindaḷūr nāḍu, a subdivision of Rājādhirāja-vaḷanāḍu.

308. 281 *of* 1907.—(Tamil.) On the east wall of the first prākāra of the same temple, right of entrance. A record in the forty-first year of the Chōḷa king Tribhuvanachakravartin Śrī-Kulōttuṅga-Chōḷadēva (I). Records gift of money for a lamp by a native of Gaṅgaikoṇḍaśōḷapuram.

309. 282 *of* 1907.—(Tamil.) In the same place. A record in the seventh year of the Chōḷa king Tribhuvanachakravartin Śrī-Vikrama-Chōḷadēva (1118—35). Records gift of money for a lamp and for a bathing water pot by a native of Śuttamali-chaturvēdi-maṅgalam, a *brahmadēya* in Puraṅgarambai-nāḍu, a subdivision of Rājēndra-Chōḷa-vaḷanāḍu.

310. 283 *of* 1907.—(Tamil.) In the same place, left of entrance. A record in the fifth year of the Chōḷa king Tribhuvanachakravartin Śrī-Vikrama-Chōḷadēva (1118—35). Records gift of money for a lamp and of a lamp-stand by a native of Tiraimūr in Viḷaināḍu, a subdivision of Rājanārāyaṇa-vaḷanāḍu.

311. 284 *of* 1907.—(Tamil.) In the same place. A record in the seventh year of the Chōḷa king Tribhuvanachakravartin Śrī-Vikrama-Chōḷadēva (1118—35). Records gift of money for a lamp and for a bathing water pot by a native of the village mentioned in No. 309 above.

312. 285 *of* 1907.—(Tamil.) In the same place. A record in the tenth year of the Chōḷa king Parakēsarivarman *alias* Tribhuvanachakravartin Śrī-Vikrama-Chōḷadēva (1118--35). Records gift of money for a lamp by a certain Āṇḍapillaiyāṇḍār.

313. 286 *of* 1907.—(Tamil.) In the same place. A record in the fifth year of the Chōḷa king Parakēsarivarman *alias* Uḍaiyār Śrī-Vikrama-Chōḷadēva. Records gift of land for offerings to the image of Māṇikkakkūttar in the stone temple at Tiruviḍaimarudūr and money for a bathing water pot.

314. 287 *of* 1907.—(Tamil.) In the same place. A record in the fourth year of the Chōḷa king Parakēsarivarman *alias* Tribhuvanachakravartin Śrī-Vikrama Chōḷadēva (1118—35). Records gift of village-site land.

315. 288 *of* 1907.—(Tamil.) In the same place. A record in the sixteenth year of the Chōḷa king Parakēsarivarman *alias* Tribhuvanachakravartin Śrī-Kulōttuṅga-Chōḷadēva (III), "who was pleased to take Madurai (Madura) and the crowned head of the Pāṇḍya". Registers an order of the king altering the procession of the God during festivals and arranging the streets of Tiruviḍaimarudūr.

316. 289 *of* 1907.—(Tamil.) In the same place. A mutilated record in the twenty-eighth year of the Chōḷa king Tribhuvanachakravartin Śrī-Kulōttuṅga-Chōḷadēva (III), "who took Madura, Karuvūr and Īḷam (Ceylon) and who was pleased to take the crowned head of the Pāṇḍya." Records gift to the image of Āḷuḍaiya-Piḷḷaiyār set up by Vānadhirājan of the village of Kulōttuṅga-Śōḷanpūṇḍi *alias* Vikramaśōḷan-śūraḷūr in Tiruvaḷundūr-nāḍu, a subdivision of Jayaṅgoṇḍa-Chōḷa-vaḷanāḍu. Refers to the revenue survey in the sixteenth year of Śungandavirtta Kulōttuṅga Chōḷadēva (I). See Nos. 299, 300 and 302 above.

317. 290 *of* 1907.—(Tamil.) In the same place. A record in the third year of the Chōḷa king Tribhuvanachakravartin Śrī-Vikrama Chōḷadēva (1118—35). Records gift of money for a bathing water pot.

318. 291 *of* 1907.—(Tamil.) In the same place. A mutilated record (on Wednesday, Pushya Makara Pūrvapaksha Pañchami) of the twenty-seventh year of the Chōḷa king Tribhuvanachakravartin Śrī-Rājarājadēva (III). Records sale of land. [See *Ep. Ind.*, Vol. X, p. 135, where Mr. R. Sewell points out that the fifth *tithi* is a mistake for the fifteenth and then equates the date to Wednesday, 7th January A.D. 1243.]

319. 292 *of* 1907.—(Tamil.) On the south wall of the same prākāra. A record in the fourth year of the Chōḷa king Vikrama Chōḷa dēva (1118—35). Records gift of money for a bathing water pot by a native of Śāttamaṅgalam in Innamba-nāḍu, a sub-division of Virudarājabhayaṅkara-vaḷanāḍu.

320. 293 *of* 1907.—(Tamil.) On the south wall of the first prākāra of the Mahāliṅgasvāmin temple. A record in the fourth year of the Chōḷa king Vikrama Chōḷadēva (1118—35). Records gift of money for a bathing water-pot by a native of Gaṅgaikoṇḍa-śōḷapuram.

321. 294 *of* 1907.—(Tamil.) On the same wall. A record in the sixth year of the Chōḷa king Vikrama-Chōḷadēva (1118—35). Records gift of money for four lamps by another native of Gaṅgaikoṇḍaśōḷapuram.

322. 295 *of* 1907.—(Tamil.) On the same wall. A record in the fourth year of the Chōḷa king Vikrama-Chōḷadēva (1118—35). Records gift of money for a bathing water pot and for a lamp by the Veḷḷāḷaṅgaṇḍa-Avaiyampukkāṉ *alias* Adalaiyūr-nāṭṭu Pallavaraiyan of Śeṟṟūr in Rājarāja-Pāṇḍināḍu.

323. 296 *of* 1907.—(Tamil.) On the same wall. A damaged record in the fourth year of the Chōḷa king Vikrama-Chōḷadēva (1118—35). Records gift of money.

324. 297 *of* 1907.—(Tamil.) On the same wall. A record in the fourth year of the Chōḷa king Vikrama-Chōḷadēva (1118—35). Records gift of money for two lamps by a native of Uttama-śīli-chaturvēdimaṅgalam in Pāṇḍikulāśani-vaḷanāḍu.

325. 298 *of* 1907.—(Tamil.) On the same wall. A record in the seventh year of the Chōḷa king Tribhuvanachakravartin Śrī-Vikrama-Chōḷadēva (1118—35). Records gift of a cow for a lamp by a woman of Mūlanallūr in Tiraimūr-nāḍu.

326. 299 *of* 1907.—(Tamil.) On the same wall. A record in the seventh year of the Chōḷa king Tribhuvanachakravartin Śrī-Vikrama-Chōḷadēva (1118—35). Records gift of a cow for a lamp by a dancing girl *(dēvar-aḍiyāḷ.)*

327. 300 *of* 1907.—(Tamil.) On the same wall. A record in the twenty-seventh year of the Ghōḷa king Rājakēsarivarman *alias* Chakravartin Śrī-Kulōttuṅga-Chōḷadēva (I?). Records gift of sixty sheep for a lamp and of a lamp-stand.

328. 301 *of* 1907.—(Tamil.) On the same wall. A record in the fourth year of the Chōḷa king Parakēsarivarman *alias* Tribhuvanachakravartin Śrī-Vikrama-Chōḷadēva (1118—35). Records gift of land to the image of Kulōttuṅga-Chōḷīśvaramuḍaiya-Mahādēva set up by Svāmidēvar Śrīkaṇṭhaśiva at Maṅgalakkuḍi, a hamlet of Śōḷamāttāṇḍa-chaturvēdimaṅgalam in Maṇṇi-nāḍu, a subdivision of Virudarāja-bhayaṁkara-vaḷanāḍu for the merit of Uḍaiyār Śrī-Kulōttuṅga-Chōḷadēva (I). [In his list of *Sans. MSS.* in the Tiruviḍaimarudūr library Dr. Hultzsch mentions a Śrīkaṇṭha Śivāchārya who wrote the Vēdāntic work *Brahmamimāmsā bhāshyā* and a Śrīkāṇṭha, a tantric writer who belonged to the Kashmir school, and composed the *Ratnatraya pariksha* about the close of the eleventh century. The present epigraph not improbably refers to the former. See also Prof. Rangacharya's *Des. Cat., Sans. MSS.*, Vol. X, No. 5092, p. 3874--6. The famous Appayya Dīkshita has written a commentary on Śrīkaṇṭha's Bhāshya. See *Ibid.*, p. 3876-7. Śrīkaṇṭha's son was Sōmēśvara or Īśvara Śiva who wrote the *Siddhānta ratnākara.* This Īśvara Śiva was the *guru* of Kulōttuṅga III (1178--1216) and consecrated the temple which he built at Tribhuvanam. The Government Epigraphist surmises that this Īśvara Śiva might be the same as Īśāna Śiva, the author of the *Siddhāntasāra,* but different from his namesake of the Āmardamaṭha who wrote the *Krinākramādyōtikā.*]

329. 302 *of* 1907.—(Tamil.) On the same wall. A record in the third year of the Chōḷa king Parakēsarivarman *alias* Tribhuvana-chakravartin Śrī-Vikrama-Chōḷadēva (1118--35). Records gift of land to the same image set up in the same village, here said to be the eastern hamlet of Śōḷamāttāṇḍa-chaturvēdimaṅgalam in Maṇṇi-nāḍu, a subdivision of Virudarājabhayaṁkara-vaḷanāḍu.

330. 303 *of* 1907.- (Tamil.) On the south wall of the first prākāra of the same temple. A record in the eighth year of the Chōḷa king Rājakēsarivarman *alias* Tribhuvanachakravartin Śrī-Kulōttuṅga-Chōḷadēva (II ?) Records sale of land to a native of Taṇḍattōṭṭam by the sabhā of Kulōttuṅgaśōḷamaṅgalam detached from Kēraḷāntaka-chaturvēdimaṅgalam, a *brahmadēya* in Veṇṇāḍu, a subdivision of Uyyakkoṇḍār-vaḷanāḍu. Refers to the fourth year of Śrī-Vikrama-Chōḷadēva (1118—35). See No. 65 above.

331. 304 *of* 1907.—(Tamil.) On the same wall. A record in the twenty-sixth year of the Chōḷa king Rājakēsarivarman *alias* Chakravartin Śrī-Kulōttuṅga-Chōḷadēva (I). Records gift of 180 sheep for three lamps by the Nambirāṭṭiyār Śirāman Arumoḷinaṅgaiyār *alias* Ēḷulagumuḍaiyār.

332. 305 *of* 1907.—(Tamil.) On the same wall. A record in the thirteenth year of Tribhuvanachakravartin Kōnērinmaikoṇḍān. Refers to the revenue survey in the sixteenth year of Śuṅgandavirtta-Kulōttuṅga-Chōḷadēva I.

333. 306 *of* 1907.—(Tamil.) On the same wall. A record in the thirteenth year of the Chōḷa king Tribhuvanachakravartin Śrī-Kulōttuṅga-Chōḷadēva III, "who took Madura and was pleased to take the crowned head of the Pāṇḍya." Records an addition made to the dancing masters of the temple. The new incumbent had to dance with gestures.

334. 307 *of* 1907.—(Tamil.) On the same wall. A record in the twenty-second year of Tribhuvanachakravartin Kōnērinmai-koṇḍān. Records gift of land to the shrine of the Piḍāri-Yōgirunda-Paramēśvari in the fourth prākāra of the temple.

335. 308 *of* 1907.—(Tamil.) On the same wall. An unfinished record in the ninth year of the Chōḷa king Kulōttuṅga-Chōḷadēva. Mentions Pāṇan-Irumuḍi-Śōḷan Pirān *alias* Aśaiñjalappērayan.

336. 309 *of* 1907.—(Tamil.) On the west wall of the same prākāra. A record in the twenty-first year of Tribhuvanachakravartin Kōnērinmaikoṇḍān. Records gift of land. Mentions Irumara bundūya-Perumāḷchaturvēdimaṅgalam in Uyyakkoṇḍār-vaḷanāḍu and refers to land which had been granted tax-free for the worship of Āḷudaiya-Piḷḷaiyār and Āḷuḍaiya-Nambi (i.e., Saint Sundaramūrti).

337. 310 *of* 1907.—(Tamil.) On the second eastern gōpura of the same temple, right of entrance. A damaged record in the seventh year of the Chōḷa king Tribhuvanachakravartin Śrī-Rājarājadēva (III ?). A few syllables of each line were inaccessible at the end. Mentions Tribhuvanavīra-chaturvēdimaṅgalam.

338. 311 *of* 1907.—(Tamil.) On the same gōpura, left of entrance. A record in the third year of the Pāṇḍya king Māravarman Tribhuvanachakravartin Kulaśēkharadēva. Seems to record a gift of land for temple repairs. [It is doubtful whether the king is the first or second of that name (1268—1308) or (1314—21).]

339. 312 *of* 1907.—(Tamil.) On the third eastern gōpura of the same temple, right of entrance. A much damaged record.

340. 313 *of* 1907.—(Grantha and Tamil.) On the same gōpura left of entrance. A damaged record in the third year of the Pāṇḍya king Vikrama-Pāṇḍya. Seems to record a gift of land for celebrating a festival called Vikkirama-Pāṇḍyan-śandi.

341. 130 *of* 1895.—(Tamil.) On the east wall of the second prākāra of the Mahāliṅgasvāmin temple, right of entrance. A record in the fifth year of the Chōḷa king Kō-Parakēsarivarman *alias* Vikrama-Chōladēva (1118—35). Records gift of land and money.

342. 131 *of* 1895.—(Tamil.) In the same place. A record in the seventh year of the Chōḷa king Tribhuvanachakravartin Vikrama-Chōḷadēva (1118—35). Records gift of money for two lamps.

343. 132 *of* 1895.—(Tamil.) In the same place. A record in the twenty-sixth year and one hundred and seventy-second day of the Chōḷa king Kō-Rājakēsarivarman *alias* Kulōttuṅga-Chōḷadēva (I). Records gift of 120 sheep for two lamps. Mentions the four queens of the king. See *S.I.I.*, Vol. III, No. 72, pp. 155—9. The priests and the local assembly were trustees and undertook to supply per day one *uri* of ghee by the *Ēkanāyaka* measure.

344. 133 *of* 1895.—(Tamil.) On the same wall, left of entrance. A record in the forty-ninth year of the Chōḷa king Tribhuvanachakravartin Kulōttuṅga-Chōḷadēva (I). Records gift of money for a pot.

345. 134 *of* 1895.—(Tamil.) In the same place. A record in the forty-ninth year of the Chōḷa king Tribhuvanachakravartin Kulōttuṅga-Chōḷadēva (I). Records gift of money for a lamp.

346. 135 *of* 1895.—(Tamil.) In the same place. A record in the eighteenth year of Sakalabhuvanachakravartin Kō-Peruñjiṅga-dēva. Records gift of land. See *Ep. Ind.*, Vol. VII, p. 165, where Dr. Kielhorn calculates the exact date to be Friday, the 30th July, A.D. 1249.

347. 136 *of* 1895.—(Tamil.) On the south wall of the same prākāra. A record in the sixth year of the Chōḷa king Vikrama-Chōḷadēva (1118—35). Records gift of money for a lamp.

348. 137 *of* 1895.—(Tamil.) In the same place. A record in the sixth year of the Chōḷa king Vikrama-Chōḷadēva (1118—35). Records gift of money for a lamp by an inhabitant of Conjeeveram.

349. 138 *of* 1895.—(Tamil.) In the same place. A record in the fourth year of the Chōḷa king Kō-Parakēsarivarman *alias* Vikrama-Chōḷadēva (1118—35). Refers to the twenty-fifth year of Kulōttuṅga-Chōḷadēva (I).

350. 139 *of* 1895.—(Tamil.) In the same place. A record in the seventh year of the Chōḷa king Kō-Parakēsarivarman *alias* Vikrama-Chōḷadēva (1118—35).

351. 140 *of* 1895.—(Tamil.) In the same place. A record of the Vijayanagara king Sadāśivadēva-Mahārāya in Ś. 1466, expired, Krōdhin. Records gift of two villages by Rāmarāja-Viṭṭhaladēva-Mahārāja. [He was the conqueror of South India in 1545 and was then Viceroy for about a decade.]

352. 141 *of* 1895.—(Tamil.) In the same place. A record in the ninth year of the Chōḷa king Kō-Rājakēsarivarman *alias* Kulōttuṅga-Chōḷadēva (I ?). Records gift of land.

353. 142 *of* 1895.—(Tamil.) In the same place. A record in the twelfth year of the Chōḷa king Tribhuvanachakravartin Kulōttuṅga-Chōḷadēva III, "who took Madurai and cut off the crowned head of the Pāṇḍya." Records allotment of shares.

354. 143 *of* 1895.—(Tamil.) In the same place. A record in the second year of the Chōḷa king Tribhuvanachakravartin Rājarājadēva. Records gift of land.

355. 144 *of* 1895.—(Tamil.) In the same place. A record in the eighteenth year of Tribhuvanachakravartin Kōnērinmaikoṇḍān. Records gift of land.

356. 145 *of* 1895.—(Tamil.) On the south wall of the maṇṭapa in front of the shrine in the same temple. A record in the fourth year of the Chōḷa king Kō-Parakēsarivarman. Records gift of money for a lamp.

357. 146 *of* 1895.—(Tamil.) On the same wall. A record of the Chōḷa king Madiraikoṇḍa Kō-Parakēsarivarman (905—47), the date of which is doubtful. Records gift of gold.

358. 147 *of* 1895.—(Tamil.) On the south wall of the shrine in the same temple. A record in the thirty-seventh year of the Chōḷa king Madiraikoṇḍa Kō-Parakēsarivarman (Parāntaka I, 905—47). Records gift of land for a lamp.

359. 148 *of* 1895.—(Tamil.) On the same wall. An incomplete record in the sixteenth year of the Chōḷa king Kō-Rājakēsarivarman.

360. 149 *of* 1895.—(Tamil.) On the west wall of the same shrine. A record in the thirty-fifth year of the Chōḷa king Madiraikoṇḍa Kō-Parakēsarivarman (Parāntaka I, 905—47). Records gift of land.

361. 150 *of* 1895.—(Tamil.) On the same wall. A record in the eleventh year of the Chōḷa king Kō-Parakēsarivarman. Records gift of eating vessels.

362. 151 *of* 1895.—(Tamil.) On the same wall. A record in the third year of the Chōḷa king Kō-Parakēsarivarman. Records gift of a lamp.

363. 152 *of* 1895.—(Tamil.) On the north wall of the same shrine. A record in the third year of the Chōḷa king Kō-Rājakēsarivarman. Records gift of paddy.

364. 153 *of* 1895.—(Tamil.) On the same wall. A record of the Chōḷa king Kō-Rājakēsarivarman, the date of which is lost. Records gift of land.

365. 154 *of* 1895.—(Tamil.) On the same wall. A record in the fourth year of the Chōḷa king Kō-Parakēsarivarman "who cut off the head of the Pāṇḍya." Records gift of land. [The king referred to was evidently Parāntaka II, Sundara Chōḷa.]

366. 155 *of* 1895.—(Tamil.) On the same wall. A record in the thirty-fourth year of the Chōḷa king Madiraikoṇḍa Kō-Parakēsarivarman (905—47). Records gift of a lamp.

367. 156 *of* 1895.—(Tamil.) On the same wall. A record in the tenth year of the Chōḷa king Kō-Rājakēsarivarman. Records gift of gold for a lamp.

368. 157 *of* 1895.—(Tamil.) On the same wall. A record in the thirty-seventh year of the Chōḷa king Madiraikoṇḍa Kō-Parakēsarivarman (905—47). Records gift of land.

369. 158 *of* 1895.—(Tamil.) On a pillar in the maṇṭapa surrounding the shrine in the same temple. A record in the fourteenth year of the Chōḷa king Kō-Rājakēsarivarman. Records gift of land.

370. 159 *of* 1895.—(Tamil.) On another pillar in the same place. A record in the sixteenth year of the Chōḷa king Kō-Rāja-rāja-Rājakēsarivarman (I, 985—1013). Records gift of land.

Tiruviśalūr.

One of the 63 North-Kāveri Śaivite centres renowned as the place where a devotee who died of fear of the king was revived by God's grace. It was sung by Tirujñānasambanda, and known in ancient times as Vēmbaṟṟūr or Chōḷamārtāṇḍa-chaturvēdimaṅgalam.

371. 1 *of* 1907.—(Tamil.) On the south wall of the central shrine in the Śivayōganāthasvāmin temple. A record in the fourth year of the Chōḷa king Parakēsarivarman *alias* Śrī-Rājēndra-Chōḷadēva (1011—43). Records gift of a gold fillet to the temple of Tiruviśalūr-Mahādēvar at Vēmbaṟṟūr *alias* Śōḷamārtāṇḍa-chaturvēdimaṅgalam, a *brahmadēya* in Maṇṇi-nāḍu, a subdivision of Vaḍagarai-Rājēndrasiṁha-vaḷanāḍu.

372. 2 *of* 1907.—(Tamil.) On the same wall. A record in the tenth year of the Chōḷa king Rājarājakēsarivarman (I, 985—1013) "who destroyed the ships at Kāndaḷūr-Śālai." Records gift of money for a lamp.

373. 3 *of* 1907.—(Tamil.) On the same wall. A record in the tenth year of the Chōḷa king Rājarājakēsarivarman (Rājarāja I, 985—1013) "who destroyed the ships at Kāndaḷūr-Śālai." Records gift of money for a lamp to the temple of Tiruviśalūr-Perumāḷ at Avaninārāyaṇa-chaturvēdimaṅgalam, a *dēvadāna* and a *brahmadēya*.

374. 4 *of* 1907.—(Tamil.) On the same wall. A record in the second year of the Chōḷa king Parakēsarivarman. Records gift of 96 sheep for a lamp.

375. 5 *of* 1907.—(Tamil.) On the same wall. A record in the third year of the Chōḷa king Rājakēsarivarman. The date is expressed in words. But above the akshara *mu* of *mūnrāvadu*, the numeral 20 seems to be inserted. If this is part of the date, it would be the twenty-third year of the king's reign.

376. 6 *of* 1907.—(Tamil.) On the same wall. A record in the third year of the Chōḷa king Parakēsarivarman. Makes provision for bathing the god.

377. 7 *of* 1907.—(Tamil.) On the same wall. A record in the fourth year of the Chōḷa king Parakēsarivarman. Built in at the end. Records gift of 180 sheep for two lamps.

378. 8 *of* 1907.—(Tamil.) On the same wall. A record of the Chōḷa king Parakēsarivarman. Built in at the end. Records gift of a lamp.

379. 9 *of* 1907.—(Tamil.) On the same wall. A record in the sixth year of the Chōḷa king Parakēsarivarman. Records gift of gold by Śembiyan Kāraikkāḍuḍaiyān *alias* Anniyūraḍigaḷ.

380. 10 *of* 1907.—(Tamil.) On the same wall. A record in the third year of the Chōḷa king Parakēsarivarman. Records gift of a lamp to the temple of Tiruviśalūr-Perumāḷ in Amani-nārāyaṇa-chaturvēdimaṅgalam, a *dēvadāna* and a *brahmadēya* in the country on the northern bank (*vaḍagarai*) of the river Cauvery.

381. 11 *of* 1907.—(Tamil.) On the same wall. A partially damaged record in the fourteenth year of the Chōḷa king Tribhuvanachakravartin Vikrama-Chōḷadēva (1118—35). Makes provision for bathing the god and for sacred garlands.

382. 12 *of* 1907.—(Tamil.) On the same wall. A record in the sixteenth year of the Chōḷa king Madiraikoṇḍa Parakēsarivarman (Parāntaka I). Records gift of 180 sheep for two lamps.

383. 13 *of* 1907.—(Tamil.) An incomplete record in the ninth year of the Chōḷa king Rājakēsarivarman. Records sale of land to a relation of Karugāvūr-kiḷavan Marudan-Paṭṭan *alias* Śōḷavēḷān, son of Śembiyan Kāraikkāḍuḍaiyān.

384. 14 *of* 1907.—(Tamil.) On the same wall. A record in the eighteenth year of the Chōḷa king Parakēsarivarman *alias* Tribhuvanachakravartin-Kulōttuṅga-Chōḷadēva (III), "who was pleased to take Madura and the crowned head of the Pāṇḍya." Records sale of land. The village is called Vēmbaṟṟūr *alias* Edirilišōḷachaturvēdimaṅgalam. See *Ep. Ind.*, Vol. IX, p. 214, where Dr. Kielhorn, after pointing out certain irregularities in the date, fixes it as Saturday, 3rd December, 1196.

385. 15 *of* 1907.—(Tamil.) On the same wall. A record in the third year of the Chōḷa king Parakēsarivarman *alias* Rājēndra-Chōḷadēva (I, 1011—43). Records gift of gold in order to provide *śidāri* for the incense.

386. 16 *of* 1907.—(Tamil.) On the same wall. An incomplete record in the third year of the Chōḷa king Parakēsarivarman. Records gift of land.

387. 17 *of* 1907.—(Tamil.) On the same wall. A record in the thirty-second year of the Pāṇḍya king Varaguṇa-Mahārāja.

Partly covered by a wall. [If this Varaguṇa is the same as he who ascended the throne in A.D. 862, it has to be inferred that he ruled at least till A.D. 894.]

388. 18 *of* 1907.—(Tamil.) On the same wall. A record in the fourth year of the Chōḷa king Parakēsarivarman. Records gift of hundred sheep for a lamp by Nakkan Ariñjigai *alias* Pirāntaka Pallavaraiyan.

389. 19 *of* 1907.—(Tamil.) On the west wall of the same shrine. A record of the Chōḷa king Rājarājakēsarivarman (Rājarāja I) in his fifth year, Sunday, Mūla, Dhanus. Records gift of gold by a queen of Rājarājadēva. See *Ep. Ind.*, Vol. IX, p. 207, where Dr. Kielhorn points out that the date corresponded to Sunday, the 1st December, A.D. 989.

390. 20 *of* 1907.—(Tamil.) On the same wall. An incomplete record in the twenty-eighth year of the Chōḷa king Madiraikoṇḍa-Parakēsarivarman (905—47). Records a gift by a native of Kuḷittaṇḍilai in Kuṟumbūr-nāḍu.

391. 21 *of* 1907.—(Tamil.) On the same wall. A record of the Chōḷa king Parakēsarivarman, the date of which is doubtful. The date is expressed by the symbol for nine followed by that for ten. Records gift of a lamp.

392. 22 *of* 1907.—(Tamil.) On the same wall. A damaged record in the twenty-seventh year of the Chōḷa king Madiraikoṇḍa Parakēsarivarman (905—47).

393. 23 *of* 1907.—(Tamil.) On the same wall. A record in the forty-first year of the Chōḷa king Parakēsarivarman (905—47), "who took Madirai and Īḻam (Ceylon)." Records gift of gold for a lamp.

394. 24 *of* 1907.—(Tamil.) On the same wall. A damaged record in the sixteenth year of the Chōḷa king Madiraikoṇḍa Parakēsarivarman (905—47).

395. 25 *of* 1907.—(Tamil.) On the north wall of the same shrine. A record in the tenth year of the Chōḷa king Parakēsarivarman. Records gift of ninety sheep for a lamp.

396. 26 *of* 1907.—(Tamil.) On the same wall. A record in the tenth year of the Chōḷa king Parakēsarivarman. Records gift of ninety sheep for a lamp.

397. 27 *of* 1907.—(Tamil.) On the same wall. A record in the fifteenth year of the Chōḷa king Madiraikoṇḍa Parakēsarivarman (905—47). Records gift of ninety-three sheep for a lamp.

398. 28 *of* 1907.—(Tamil.) On the same wall. A record of the Chōḷa king Parakēsarivarman *alias* Śrī-Kaṇḍarādittan Śrī-Madhurāntakar (i.e., Madhurāntaka, son of Gaṇḍarāditya). Records gift of ornaments by the king's mother. The king was apparently the same as Uttamachōḷa.

399. 29 *of* 1907.—(Tamil.) On the same wall. A record in the third year of the Chōḷa king Madiraikoṇḍa Parakēsarivarman (905—47). Built in at the beginning. Records gift of sheep for a lamp.

400. 30 *of* 1907.—(Tamil.) On the same wall. A record in the tenth year of the Chōḷa king Parakēsarivarman. Built in at the beginning. Records gift of ninety-three sheep for a lamp.

401. 31 *of* 1907.—(Grantha and Tamil.) On the same wall A record in the twenty-second year of the Chōḷa king Madiraikoṇḍa Parakēsarivarman (905—47). Records gift of ninety-six sheep for a lamp.

402. 32 *of* 1907.—(Tamil.) On the same wall. An unfinished record in the fifth year of the Chōḷa king Parakēsarivarman.

403. 33 *of* 1907.—(Tamil.) On the same wall. A damaged record of the Chōḷa king Madiraikoṇḍa Parakēsarivarman, the date of which is lost. Records gift of ninety sheep for a lamp.

404. 34 *of* 1907.—(Tamil.) On the same wall. An incomplete record in the fourth year of the Chōḷa king Rājakēsarivarman.

405. 35 *of* 1907.—(Tamil.) On the same wall. A record in the twenty-seventh year of the Chōḷa king Madiraikoṇḍa Parakēsarivarman (905—47). Makes provision for the supply of bathing water from the Kāvēri for the god. The temple is called Tiruviśalūr-Mādēvabhaṭṭārakar at Avaninārāyaṇa-chaturvēdimaṅgalam *alias* Vēmbaṟṟūr, a *dēvadāna* and *brahmadēya* on the northern bank *(vaḍagarai)* of the river Kāvēri.

406. 36 *of* 1907.—(Tamil.) On the same wall. A record in the tenth year of the Chōḷa king Parakēsarivarman. Records gift of ninety-six sheep for a lamp.

407. 37 *of* 1907.—(Tamil.) On the same wall. A record in the twelfth year of the Chōḷa king Rājakēsarivarman. Records gift of ninety-six sheep for a lamp by a native of the Pāṇḍya country.

408. 38 *of* 1907.—(Tamil.) On the same wall. A record in the eighteenth year of the Chōḷa king Madiraikoṇḍa Parakēsarivarman (905—47). Records gift of ninety sheep for a lamp.

409. 39 *of* 1907.—(Tamil.) On the same wall. A damaged and incomplete record of the Chōḷa king Madiraikoṇḍa Parakēsarivarman (905—47).

410. 40 *of* 1907.—(Grantha and Tamil.) On the same wall. A record in the fifth year of the Chōḷa king Sundara-Chōḷa. Built in at the beginning.

411. 41 *of* 1907.—(Tamil.). On the south wall of the maṇṭapa in front of the same shrine. A record in the tenth year of the Chōḷa king Rājarājakēsarivarman, "who destroyed the ships at

Kāndaḷūr-Sālai" (985—1013). Records gift of money for feeding two Brāhmaṇas, for scents and for lamps.

412. 42 *of* 1907.—(Tamil.) On the same wall. A record in the twenty-ninth year of the Chōḷa king Rājarājakēsarivarman *alias* Śrī-Rājarājadēva (I). The village is called Vēmbaṟṟūr *alias* Śōḷamāttāṇḍa-chaturvēdimaṅgalam, a *brahmadēya* in Maṇṇi-nāḍu, a subdivision of Rājēndrasiṁha-vaḷanāḍu. Refers to the performance of *tulābhāra* by the king and of *hēmagarbha* by his queen Dantiśakti Viṭaṅkiyār *alias* Lōkamahādēviyār in the temple at Tiruviśalūr.

413. 43 *of* 1907.—(Tamil.) On the west wall of the same maṇṭapa. A record in the twenty-fourth year of the Chōḷa king Rājarājakēsarivarman *alias* Śrī-Rājarājadēva (I, 985—1013). Records a gift of land for offerings at the shrine of Pichchadēva.

414. 44 *of* 1907.—(Tamil.) On the same wall. A record in the twenty-fourth year of the Chōḷa king Rājarājakēsarivarman *alias* Śrī-Rājarājadēva I. Records a gift of land for offerings at the shrine of Pichchadēva. Refers to a revenue survey made some time prior to the date of the inscription.

415. 45 *of* 1907.—(Tamil.) On the north wall of the same maṇṭapa. An incomplete record in the third year of the Chōḷa king Parakēsarivarman *alias* Śrī-Rājēndra-Chōḷadēva (1011—43). Records gift of land for lamps.

416. 46 *of* 1907.—(Tamil.) On the same wall. A record in the third year of the Chōḷa king Parakēsarivarman *alias* Śrī-Rājēndra-Chōḷadēva (1011—43). Records gift of ornaments by the queen of the Pāṇḍya king Śrīvalluvar (i.e., Śrīvallabhadēva).

417. 47 *of* 1907.—(Tamil.) On the same wall. Refers to the foundation of a *maṭha* on the northern bank of the fresh water tank in the temple of Tiruviśalūruḍaiya-Mahādēvar at Śōḷamāṭṭāṇḍa chaturvēdimaṅgalam in Maṇṇi-nāḍu, a subdivision of Virudarājabhayaṅkara-vaḷanāḍu.

418. 48 *of* 1907.—(Tamil.) On the same wall. An incomplete record in the thirtieth year of Kōnērinmaikoṇḍān. The royal order was issued from Kāñchīpuram.

419. 49 *of* 1907.—(Tamil.) On the same wall. A record in the fifth year of the Chōḷa king Kulōttuṅga-Chōḷadēva. Records gift of land.

420. 50 *of* 1907.—(Tamil.) On the north wall of the shrine in the southern side of the same temple. Close to the inscription is a piece of sculpture which seems to represent the person who built the maṇṭapa and whose name was Anantaśivan.

421. 51 *of* 1907.—(Tamil.) On the same wall. A record in the fifth year of the Chōḷa king Parakēsarivarman, "who took the head of the Pāṇḍya." Records gift of gold for a lamp. The temple is called Tiruviśalūr Perumānaḍigaḷ at Amaninārāyaṇa-chaturvēdimaṅgalam, a *dēvadāna* and *brahmadēya* in the country on the northern bank (*vaḍagarai*) of the river Kāvēri. The Government Epigraphist suggests that the king may be Āditya Karikāla, son of Parāntaka II Sundarachōḷa Parakēsarivarman, who took the head of Vīra Pāṇḍya. See *S.I.I.*, Vol. III, p. 21.

422. 52 *of* 1907.—(Tamil.) On the inner gōpura of the same temple, right of entrance. Records that the gōpura as well as the enclosing verandah were built by Vikrama-Chōḷa (1118—35).

423. 314 *of* 1907.—(Tamil.) On the north wall of the central shrine in the Śivayōganāthasvāmin temple. A record in the second year of the Chōḷa king Rājakēsarivarman. Records gift of ninety sheep for a lamp by a native of Peṇṇāgaḍam in Tañjāvūr-kūṟṟam.

424. 315 *of* 1907.—(Tamil.) On the north wall of the central shrine in the same temple. A record in the twenty-third year of the Chōḷa king Madiraikoṇḍa Parakēsarivarman (905—47). Records gift of 190 sheep for two lamps.

425. 316 *of* 1907.—(Tamil.) On the same wall. A record in the twenty-third year of the Chōḷa king Madiraikoṇḍa Parakēsarivarman (905—47). Records gift of ninety sheep for a lamp.

426. 317 *of* 1907.—(Tamil.) On the same wall. A record in the second year of the Chōḷa king Rājakēsarivarman. Records gift of land for feeding a Brāhmaṇa learned in the Vēdas, by Pirāntakan Iruṅgōḷar *alias* Śiriyavēḷār of Koḍumbāḷūr. [The Koḍumbāḷūr chiefs belonged to the Kāḍava tribe and had Irukkuvēḷ or Iḷaṅgō-vēḷ for their family name. See *Ep. Rep.*, 1908, pp. 87—9, for history of Koḍumbāḷūr and its chiefs.]

427. 318 *of* 1907.—(Tamil.) On the same wall. An unfinished record in the fifth year of the Chōḷa king Parakēsarivarman.

428. 319 *of* 1907.—(Tamil.) On the same wall. A record of the Chōḷa king Madiraikoṇḍa Parakēsarivarman (905—47), the date of which is damaged. Records gift of ninety sheep for a lamp by a relation of Kalikēsarin, the son of Kāraikkāḍuḍaiyār.

429. 320 *of* 1907.—(Tamil.) On the same wall. A record in the fourth year of the Chōḷa king Rājakēsarivarman. Records gift of land by Pirāntakan Iruṅgōḷar *alias* Śiriyavēḷār. See No. 426.

430. 321 *of* 1907.—(Tamil.) On the same wall. A record in the thirty-seventh year of the Chōḷa king Madiraikoṇḍa-Parakēsarivarman (905—47). Records gift of forty-five sheep for a lamp.

431. 322 *of* 1907.—(Tamil.) On the same wall. A record in the sixth year of the Chōḷa king Rājakēsarivarman. Records gift of a lamp.

432. 323 *of* 1907.—(Tamil.) On the same wall. A damaged record in the sixth year of the Chōḷa king Rājakēsarivarman. Records gift of a lamp.

433. 324 *of* 1907.—(Tamil.) On the same wall. An unfinished record in the fifth year of the Chōḷa king Parakēsarivarman. Seems to record the gift of a lamp.

434. 325 *of* 1907.—(Tamil.) On the same wall. A damaged record in the third year of the Chōḷa king Rājakēsarivarman. Records gift of land by the queen of Uttama-Chōḷadēva, who seems to have been the daughter of Miḷāḍuḍaiyār.

435. 326 *of* 1907.—(Tamil.) On the same wall. An unfinished record of the Chōḷa king Rājakēsarivarman, the date of which is lost.

436. 327 *of* 1907.—(Tamil.) On the same wall. An unfinished record in the third year of the Chōḷa king Rājakēsarivarman. Close to this is an inscription which mentions the mother of Śrī-Uttama-Chōḷadēva.

437. 328 *of* 1907.—(Tamil.) On the west wall of the same shrine. A much damaged record in the forty-first year of the Chōḷa king Parakēsarivarman (905—47), "who took Madirai and Īḷam (Ceylon)."

438. 329 *of* 1907.—(Tamil.) On the same wall. A record of the Chōḷa king Madiraikoṇḍa Parakēsarivarman (905—47), the date of which is damaged. Records gift of a lamp by a native of Mahēndramaṅgalam, a *brahmadēya* in Teṅkarai Tiraimūr-nāḍu.

439. 330 *of* 1907.—(Tamil.) On the north and west walls of the same shrine. A record in the twenty-fourth year of the Chōḷa king Madiraikoṇḍa Parakēsarivarman. Records sale of land by two natives of Veḷimānallūr in Ūṟṟukkāṭṭukōṭṭam, a subdivision of Toṇḍai-nāḍu.

440. 331 *of* 1907.—(Tamil.) On the south wall of the same shrine. A damaged record in the ninth year of the Chōḷa king Parakēsarivarman. Built in at the end. Records gift of ninety sheep for a lamp.

441. 332 *of* 1907.—(Tamil.) On the same wall. A record of the Chōḷa king Rājakēsarivarman *alias* Rājādhirāja I. Built in at the end. Contains a portion of the historical introduction of the king.

442. 333 *of* 1907.—(Tamil.) On the same wall. A damaged record in the seventeenth year of the Chōḷa king Rājakēsarivarman. Records gift of 300 sheep for three lamps.

443. 334 *of* 1907.—(Tamil.) On the same wall. A record in the thirtieth year of the Chōḷa king Madiraikoṇḍa Parakēsarivarman (905—47). Records gift of ninety sheep for a lamp.

444. 335 *of* 1907.—(Tamil.) On the same wall. A damaged record in the twelfth year of the Chōḷa king Rājakēsarivarman.

445. 336 *of* 1907.—(Tamil.) On the same wall. A record in the twenty-sixth year of the Chōḷa king Madiraikoṇḍa Parakēsarivarman (905—47). Built in at the end. Records gift of ninety sheep for a lamp.

446. 337 *of* 1907.—(Tamil.) On the same wall. A record of the Chōḷa king Parakēsarivarman. Built in at the end. Records gift of sheep.

447. 338 *of* 1907.—(Tamil.) On the south wall of the maṇṭapa in front of the central shrine in the Śivayōganāthasvāmin temple. A damaged record in the second year of the Chōḷa king Parakēsarivarman *alias* Rājēndra-Chōḷadēva (I, 1011—43). Records gift of a lamp.

448. 339 *of* 1907.—(Tamil.) On the same wall. A record in the third year of the Chōḷa king Parakēsarivarman *alias* Śrī-Rājēndra-Chōḷadēva (I, 1011—43). Records gift of lamps.

449. 340 *of* 1907.—(Tamil.) On the same wall. A damaged record in the third year of the Chōḷa king Parakēsarivarman *alias* Śrī-Rājēndra-Chōḷadēva (I, 1011—43). Records gift of a silver pot *(kalaśa)* by a queen.

450. 341 *of* 1907.—(Tamil.) On the same wall. A record in the third year of the Chōḷa king Parakēsarivarman *alias* Śrī-Rājēndra-Chōḷadēva (I, 1011--43). Built in at the end. Refers to the building of the *tiruchchuṟṟālaiyam* and the gōpura. The temple is called Tiruviśalūr-Mahādēvar at Vēmbaṟṟūr *alias* Śrī-Śōḷamattāṇḍa-chaturvēdimaṅgalam, a *brahmadēya* in Maṇṇi-nāḍu, a district of Vaḍagarai Rājēndrasiṁhavaḷanāḍu. The *Valaṅgai* caste is mentioned.

451. 342 *of* 1907.—(Tamil.) On the same wall. A damaged record in the sixth year of the Chōḷa king Rājarājakēsarivarman (I, 985—1013). Mentions an individual belonging to the *Uḍaiyār Kōdaṇḍarāmatanichchēvagam*. Records gift of nine *mās* of land.

452. 343 *of* 1907.—(Tamil.) On the same wall. A record in the fifth year of the Chōḷa king Śrī-Kulōttuṅga-Chōḷadēva. Records gift of a water pot.

453. 344 *of* 1907.—(Tamil.) On the same wall. A record of the Chōḷa king Parakēsarivarman *alias* Śrī-Rājēndra-Chōḷadēva (I, 1011--43), the date of which is damaged. Records gift of 28 *kāśu* for a lamp.

454. 345 *of* 1907.—(Tamil.) On the west and south walls of the same maṇṭapa. An incomplete record of the Chōḷa king Rājakēsarivarman *alias* Uḍaiyār Śrī-Rājādhirājadēva (I) in his thirty-third year and sixty-fifth day.

455. 346 *of* 1907.—(Tamil.) On the west wall of the same maṇṭapa. A record in the ninth year of the Chōḷa king Parakēsarivarman *alias* Rājēndra-Chōḷadēva (1011—43). Records gift of twenty-five *kāśu* for a lamp to the image of Umāsahitar, entitled Aṇḍanāyagar, by a native of Rājarāja-maṇḍalam, i.e., the Pāṇḍya country.

456. 347 *of* 1907.—(Tamil.) On the same wall. A damaged record in the twenty-ninth year of the Chōḷa king Parakēsarivarman *alias* Uḍaiyār Śri-Rājēndra-Chōḷadēva (I, 1011—43). Seems to record a gift of land for a lamp. Refers to the revenue survey of the country, probably that of the reign of Rājarāja I.

457. 348 *of* 1907.—(Tamil.) On the north wall of the same maṇṭapa. A record in the third year of the Chōḷa king Parakēśarivarmaṅ *alias* Śrī-Rājēndra-Chōḷadēva (I, 1011—43). Records gift of land for a lamp by Nakkan Śembiyan Mādēviyār, queen of Rājēndra-Chōḷadēva.

458. 349 *of* 1907.—(Tamil.) On the same wall. A record in the fifth year of the Chōḷa king Parakēsarivarman *alias* Śrī-Rājēndra-Chōḷadēva (I, 1011—43). Built in at the top and middle. Provides for feeding Brāhmaṇas. Refers to a revenue survey and mentions Uruttiran Arumoḷi *alias* Pirudimahādēviyār, queen of Śrī-Rājarājadēva (I). See No. 21 of 1897 at Tanjore.

459. 350 *of* 1907.—(Tamil.) On the same wall. A record in the fourth year of the Chōḷa king Parakēsarivarman *alias* Śrī-Rājēndra-Chōḷadēva (I, 1011—43). Built in at the end. Records gift by Āḷvār Śrī-Pirāntakan Kuṇḍavai-Pirāṭṭiyār while she was in the palace *(kōyil)* at Paḷaiyāru. [Kuṇḍavai Pirāṭṭiyār was the king's aunt, i.e., the elder sister of Rājarāja I and the queen of Vallavaraiyar Vandya dēvar, who survived her brother into the reign of Rājēndra Chōḷa I. Paḷaiyāru is not improbably the place in Tirunaṛaiyūr Nāḍu referred to in No. 148 above.]

460. 351 *of* 1907.—(Tamil.) On the north wall of the maṇṭapa in front of the central shrine in the Śivayōganāthasvāmin emple. A record in the fourth year of the Chōḷa king Parakēsarivarman *alias* Śrī-Rājēndra-Chōḷadēva (I, 1011—43). Built in at the beginning. The donor is the same as in the above. Refers to the third year of Rājēndra-Chōḷadēva. Mentions Śrī-Pirāntaka-chaturvēdimaṅgalam, a *brahmadēya* in Ārkkāṭṭu-kūṟṟam, a subdivision of Pāṇḍikulāśani-vaḷanāḍu.

461. 352 *of* 1907.—(Tamil.) On the east wall of the first prākāra of the same temple, right side. A record of the Chōḷa king Tribhuvanachakravartin Śrī-Kulōttuṅga-Chōḷadēva (III), "who was pleased to take Madura and the crowned head of the Pāṇḍya," the date of which is lost. Refers to Vēmbaṟṟūr *alias* Edirilisōḷa-chaturvēdimaṅgalam as the *dēvādāna* of Rājarājīśvaramuḍaiyār; refers also to a revenue survey of the country.

462. 353 *of* 1907.—(Tamil.) On the same wall. A record in the seventeenth year of the Chōḷa king Tribhuvanachakravartin Śrī-Kulōttuṅga-Chōḷadēva (III), "who was pleased to take Madura and the crowned head of the Pāṇḍya." Records sale of land by a woman. Vēmbaṟṟūr is described as in the above. See *Ep. Ind.*, Vol. X, p. 128, where Mr. Sewell shows that the details of the date given in the epigraph (Kumbha Apara. 1, Saturday Anurādha) indicate January 28th, A.D. 1195, but the nakshattra should be Magha and Pūrvaphalguni and not Anurādha.

463. 354 *of* 1907.—(Tamil.) On the same wall. A damaged record in the seventeenth year of the Chōḷa king Tribhuvana-chakravartin Śrī-Kulōttuṅga-Chōḷadēva (III), "who was pleased to take Madura and the crowned head of the Pāṇḍya." Refers to a revenue survey of the country; seems to register a sale of land.

464. 355 *of* 1907.—(Tamil.) On the second gōpura of the same temple, right of entrance. A fragmentary record of the Vijaya-nagara king Vīra-Kṛishṇadēvarāya-Mahārāya, the date of which is lost. Records the remission by the king of *jōḍi* and *araśupēru* and other taxes in favour of certain Śiva and Vishṇu temples. The revenue remitted amounted to 10,000 varāhas. See S.A. Nos. 163 and 233.

Vēppattūr.

465. 47 *of* 1910.—(Tamil.) On the south wall of the maṇṭapa in front of the central shrine in the Karkaṭēśvara temple. A damaged record in the sixth year of the Chōḷa king Vikrama-Chōḷadēva (1118—35). Records gift of land to a private individual for playing on the *viṇa (viṇaikkāṇi)* in presence of the god Arum-arund-Uḍaiyār at Tirundudēvaṅguḍi in Miḷalai-nāḍu, a subdivision of Virudarājabhayaṁkara-vaḷanāḍu.

466. 48 *of* 1910.—(Tamil.) On the same wall. A much damaged record in the fourth year of the Chōḷa king Vikrama-Chōḷadēva (1118—35). Records gift of money for a lamp.

467. 49 *of* 1910.—(Tamil.) On the north wall of the same maṇṭapa. A record in the sixteenth year of the Chōḷa king Tribhuvanachakravartin Rājarājadēva. Records gift of money for a lamp by Araiyan Śīrāḷadēvan *alias* Rājarāja-Mūvēndavēḷān of Śennimaṅgalam in Tirunaṟaiyūr-nāḍu, a subdivision of Kulōt-tuṅga-Chōḷa-vaḷanāḍu.

468. 50 *of* 1910.—(Tamil.) On the same wall. A damaged record in the sixth year of the Chōḷa king Tribhuvanachakravartin Rājādhirājadēva. Seems to record a gift of lamp and mentions Vēmbaṟṟūr *alias* Ediriliśōḷa-chaturvēdimaṅgalam.

469. 51 *of* 1910.—(Tamil.) On the same wall. A damaged record in the forty-seventh year of the Chōḷa king Rājakēsari-varman *alias* Tribhuvanachakravartin Kulōttuṅga-Chōḷadēva (I). Mentions the hall called Rājēndraśōḷan in the palace at Muḍi-goṇḍaśōḷapuram. Records that Tirundadēvaṅguḍi was a *dēvadāna* of Gaṅgaikoṇḍa-chōḷīśvaram-Uḍaiyār and registers a gift of land.

470. 52 *of* 1910.—(Tamil.) On the same wall. A record of the Chōḷa king Rājakēsarivarman *alias* Tribhuvanachakravartin. Built in, at the beginning. Contains a portion of the historical introduction, refers to the revenue survey of the sixteenth year and records a gift of land for offerings.

471. 53 *of* 1910.—(Tamil.) On the lintel of the entrance into the same maṇṭapa. Mentions that this maṇṭapa was built by Kulōttuṅgaśōḷan (evidently Kulōttuṅga I).

MANNĀRGUDI TALUK.

Kaḷappāḷ.

472. 656 *of* 1902.—(Tamil.) On the south wall of the Aḻagiyanāthasvāmin temple. A record in the fourth year of the Chōḷa king Tribhuvanachakravartin Vīrarājēndra-Chōḷadēva. Records repairs to the central shrine of the temple. [Was it Vīra Rājēndra I (1063—70) or Vīra Rājēndra II, i.e., Kulōttuṅga III, 1178—1216 ?]

473. 657 *of* 1902.—(Tamil.) On the north wall of the same temple. A record in the twenty-third year of Pāṇḍya king Māravarman *alias* Tribhuvanachakravartin Kulaśēkharadēva. Records a gift to the Ādityēśvara temple. [The king was probably the same as he who reigned from 1268 to 1308.]

474. 658 *of* 1902.—(Tamil.) On the north wall of the Kailāśanātha temple in the same village. A record in the twenty-ninth year of the Chōḷa king Tribhuvanachakravartin Tribhuvanavīradēva (i.e., Kulōttuṅga III, 1178—1216) who took Madura, Ceylon, Karuvūr and the crowned head of the Pāṇḍya. Records that the king fixed the revenue from a village at the request of a certain Nandivarman.

475. 659 *of* 1902.—(Tamil.) On the south wall of the same temple. A record in the twenty-seventh year of the Chōḷa king Tribhuvanachakravartin Tribhuvanavīradēva who took Madura, Ceylon, Karuvūr and the crowned head of the Pāṇḍya (i.e., Kulōttuṅga III). Records gift of money for a lamp. According to Kielhorn the date corresponded to Monday, the 17th November. A.D. 1214. *Ep. Ind.*, Vol. VIII, p. 5.

476. 660 *of* 1902.—(Tamil.) On the north wall of the maṇṭapa in front of the Aṉaikātta Perumāḷ temple in the same village. A record in the thirteenth year of the Pāṇḍya Jaṭāvarman *alias* Tribhuvanachakravartin Rājarāja-Sundara-Pāṇḍyadēva (unidentified). Records sale of land to a certain Śokkanāyanār *alias* Vijayagaṇḍa-Gōpāla.

477. 661 *of* 1902.—(Tamil.) On the south wall of the same maṇṭapa. A record in the thirty-fourth year of the Pāṇḍya king

Māravarman *alias* Tribhuvanachakravartin Kulaśēkharadēva (I, 1268—1308). Records gift of land. The date corresponds to Saturday, 8th July, 1301. See *Ep. Ind.*, Vol. VIII, pp. 277-8.

478. 662 *of* 1902.—(Tamil.) On the same wall. An incomplete record in the twenty-third year of the Pāṇḍya king Māravarman *alias* Tribhuvanachakravartin Kulaśēkharadēva (I, 1268—1308). Records gift by Vijayagaṇḍa-Gōpāla.

479. 663 *of* 1902.—(Tamil.) On the same wall. A record in the twenty-third year of the Pāṇḍya king Rājarāja-Sundara-Pāṇḍyadēva. Records sale of land to Vijayagaṇḍa-Gōpāla. See No. 477 above.

Kōṭṭūr.

480. 443 *of* 1912.—(Tamil.) On the south base of the central shrine in the Koḷundīśvara temple. An incomplete record in the seventeenth year of the Chōḷa king Tribhuvanachakravartin Rājarājadēva (III); stone missing at the right end. Records gift of money for a lamp to the temple of Mūlasthānam Uḍaiyār at Kōṭṭūr in Nenmalināḍu, a subdivision of Rājēndraśōḷa-vaḷanādu, by a certain Marudirpirān of Śellūr in Paranḍaiyūr-nāḍu, a subdivision of Rājarāja-vaḷanāḍu.

481. 444 *of* 1912.—(Tamil.) On the same base. A much damaged record of the Chōḷa king Tribhuvanachakravartin Rājādhirājadēva (II), the date of which is lost. Records gift of money for a lamp.

482. 445 *of* 1912.—(Tamil.) On the same base. A much damaged record in the second year of the Chōḷa king Tribhuvanachakravartin Kulōttuṅga-Chōḷadēva (III). Records gift of money for a lamp by Śēkkiḷān Pālaṟāvāyan Kaḷappāḷarāyar of Kunṟattūr in Kunṟattūr-nāḍu, a subdivision of Kulōttuṅgaśōḷa-vaḷanāḍu. [The inscription is of incalculable value in affording the date of Śēkkiḷar's brother Pālaṟāvāyar and thus of the composition of the *Periapurāṇa* some years earlier.]

483. 446 *of* 1912.--(Tamil.) On the north base of the same shrine. A much damaged record in the third year of the Chōḷa king Tribhuvanachakravartin Kulōttuṅga-Chōḷadeva (III). Records gift of money for a lamp by the *maṭhapati* Ṭirumāḷigaippichchar, a native of Tirutturaipūṇḍi in Vaṇḍāḷaivēlūr-kūṟṟam, a subdivision of Rājēndraśōḷa-vaḷanāḍu.

484. 447 *of* 1912.—(Tamil.) On the same base. A much damaged and incomplete record of the Chōḷa king Tribhuvanachakravartin Rājarājadēva III (1216—48). Records gift by a certain Villavarājar.

485. 448 *of* 1912.—(Tamil.) On the south wall of the maṇṭapa in front of the same shrine. A record in the eighteenth year of the

Chōḷa king Tribhuvanachakravartin Rājarājadēva III (1216—48). Built in at the beginning. Seems to record a grant of land to the shrine of Tirujñānamperṟa-Āḷuḍaiya-Piḷḷaiyār, which was set up in the temple of Koḻundāṇḍār.

486. 449 *of* 1912.—(Tamil.) On the same wall. A record of the Chōḷa king Tribhuvanachakravartin Rājādhirājadēva II (1171—86), "who was pleased to take Madurai (Madura) and Īḻam (Ceylon)," in his thirteenth year, Karkaṭaka, śu. di. 6, Tuesday, Anilam (= 29th July, 1175). Records gift of money for a lamp to the temple of Koḻundāṇḍār at Kōṭṭūr by a native of Śuḷḷaṅguḍi, a village in Āvur-kūṟṟam, which was a subdivision of Nittavinōda-vaḷanāḍu.

487. 450 *of* 1912.—(Tamil.) On the same wall. A record in the ninth year of the Chōḷa king Tribhuvanachakravartin Rājarājadēva (III), 1216—48. Records gift of money by the trustees to the shrine of Tirujñānamperṟa-Piḷḷaiyār set up in the temple of Koḻundāṇḍār, by a certain Nāgamaṅgalamuḍaiyān Ambalan-kōyilkoṇḍān. Also records a gift of land to the same shrine by a Brāhmaṇa lady.

488. 451 *of* 1912.—(Tamil.) On the same wall. An unfinished record of the Chōḷa king Rājakēsarivarman *alias* Tribhuvana-chakravartin Rajādhirājadēva (II, 1171—86), "who was pleased to take Madurai (Madura) and Īḻam (Ceylon)," in his thirteenth year Karkaṭaka, śu. di. 7, Saturday, Śōdi (= Sat., 26th July 1175) Mentions the temple of Mūlasthānam Uḍaiyār *alias* Koḻundāṇḍār.

489. 452 *of* 1912.—(Tamil.) On the same wall. A record in the thirteenth year of the Chōḷa king Tribhuvanachakravartin Rājādhirājadēva (II, 1171—86), "who was pleased to take Madurai (Madura) and Īḻam (Ceylon)." Records gift of money for a lamp by Rājēndraśiṅgappallavarāyan of Kīḻiyūr-nāḍu, a subdivision of Pāṇḍikulāśani-vaḷanāḍu.

490. 453 *of* 1912.—(Tamil.) On the same wall. An unfinished record in the fourteenth year of the Chōḷa king Tribhuvana-chakravartin Rājādhirājadēva (II, 1171—86), "who was pleased to take Madurai (Madura) and Īḻam (Ceylon)." Supplies only the name of the king and his regnal year.

491. 454 *of* 1912.—(Tamil.) On the north base of the maṇṭapa. A record of the Chōḷa king Tribhuvanachakravartin Vīrarājēndra-Chōḷadēva (i.e., Kulōttuṅga-Chōḷa III) in his fourth year, Tulā, ba. ḍi. 9, Sunday, Āyilyam (= 4th October 1181). Registers that a water-trough in the temple was to be filled with water in the morning every day and that for this purpose a grant of money was made by a merchant living in the quarter Dharaṇichintāmaṇi-perunderuvu at Gaṅgaikoṇḍaśōḻapuram, to a certain ugachchan of Kōṭṭūr.

492. 455 *of* 1912.—(Tamil.) On a pillar of the same maṇṭapa. A mutilated and incomplete record of the Chōḷa king Kulōttuṅga-Chōḷadēva (III), " who took Madurai (Madura) and was pleased to take the crowned head of the Pāṇḍya." Refers to the worshippers in the temple of Vaikuṇḍattāḷvār at Kōṭṭūr.

493. 456 *of* 1912.—(Tamil.) On another pillar of the same maṇṭapa. A damaged record in the twenty-seventh year of the Chōḷa king Tribhuvanachakravartin Kulōttuṅga-Chōḷadēva (I). Seems to record a grant of paddy to the temple of Pūdi-Viṇṇagar-Āḷvān at Kōṭṭūr in Nenmali-nāḍu, a subdivision of Arumoḷidēva-vaḷanāḍu, by Śivandiram who was a native of Taṇṇīrkunṟam.

494. 457 *of* 1912.—(Tamil.) On detached slabs built into the main gōpura of the same temple. A record in the twenty-sixth year of the Chōḷa king Rājakēsarivarman *alias* Chakravartin Kulōttuṅga-Chōḷadēva (I). Stones missing at the end. Begins with the historical introduction *pugaḻ-mādu*, etc., of Kulōttuṅga I.

495. 458 *of* 1912.—(Tamil.) On detached slabs built into the main gōpura of the same temple. A fragmentary record in the twenty-first year of the Chōḷa king Rājakēsarivarman *alias* Rāja-rājadēva (I). Mentions Nenmali-nāḍu, a subdivision of Arumoḷi-dēva-vaḷanāḍu.

496. 459 *of* 1912.—(Tamil.) On detached slabs built into the main gōpura of the same temple. A fragmentary record of the Chōḷa king Tribhuvanachakravartin Kulōttuṅga-Chōḷadēva (I), in his fiftieth year, Āḍi, 3, Saturday, Pañchami, Śadayam. Mentions Nenmali-nāḍu, a subdivision of Rājēndra-śōḷa-vaḷanāḍu. The date corresponded to Saturday, 28th June 1119. From this Mr. Swamikannu Pillai infers that " the reign must have commenced before the 28th June 1070."

497. 460 *of* 1912.—(Tamil.) On detached slabs built into the main gōpura of the same temple. A fragmentary record in the forty-first year of the Chōḷa king Tribhuvanachakravartin Kulōttuṅga-Chōḷadēva (I). Mentions Nenmali-nāḍu, a subdivision of Rājēndraśōḷa-vaḷanāḍu.

498. 461 *of* 1912.—(Tamil.) On detached slabs built into the main gōpura of the same temple. A fragmentary record in the tenth year of the Chōḷa king Parakēsarivarman. Mentions Nenmali-nāḍu.

499. 462 *of* 1912.—(Tamil.) On a slab set up in a field in the same village. Records in Vrisha gift of land to the temple of Koḷundīśvarasvāmin for the merit of the Mahārāja-Sāheb (evidently the Mahratta king of Tanjore).

500. 463 *of* 1912.—(Tamil.) On a slab set up in a second field in the same village. Records in Śubhakrit gift of land to the same temple during the rule of Dāḷavāy Ānandarāyar Sāheb. See *Ind.*

Antq., September 1917, where I have given an account of the martial exploits of Ānanda Rao.

501. 464 *of* 1912.—(Tamil.) On a third slab set up in a grove in the same village. Records gift of a grove of *iluppai* trees to the same temple for the purpose of providing the sacred bath to the image.

502. 465 *of* 1912.—(Tamil.) On the fourth slab set up in another grove of the same village. Records in Siddhārthi gift of ten *vēlis* of land by Raghunātha-Nāyaka (of Tanjore) (who ascended the throne in 1614 and ruled till about 1632). See *Tanj. Gazr.*, p. 39.

Kōvilveṇṇi.

The Śiva temple of the place is mentioned in the Dēvāram, but the epigraphical evidences concern the Chōḷa dynasty.

503. 396 *of* 1902.—(Tamil.) On the west wall of the Ikshupurīśvara shrine. A record in the seventh year of the Chōḷa king Tribhuvanachakravartin Rājarājadēva III (1216—48). Refers to a gift of land made in the nineteenth year of his immediate predecessor Tribhuvanavīradēva. The English date of the epigraph is Thursday, 13th October A.D. 1222. See *Ep. Ind.*, Vol. VII, p. 175.

504. 397 *of* 1902.—(Tamil.) On the same wall. An incomplete record in the nineteenth year of the Chōḷa king Tribhuvanachakravartin Kulōttuṅga-Chōḷadēva (III), who took Madura and the crowned head of the Pāṇḍya. See *Ep. Ind.*, Vol. VII, p. 173, where Kielhorn discusses the date which is intrinsically wrong and which, he says, was evidently intended for Monday, the 2nd September, A.D. 1196.

505. 398 *of* 1902.—(Tamil.) On the north wall of the same shrine. A record in the ninth year of the Chōḷa king Tribhuvanachakravartin Kulōttuṅga-Chōḷadēva. Records gift of land.

Mannārguḍi.

The epigraphs of this ancient place are interesting as they refer not only to the Chōḷas and Pāṇḍyas but also to the Hoysaḷas. Tradition also connects the place with the latter who, it is said, had a palace here, the present hamlet of Mēlavāśal being called after its western gate. The Jayaṅkoṇḍanātha and Rājarājēśvara shrines were founded by Rājādhirāja I (1018—53) and the Rājagōpāla temple by Kulōttuṅga Chōḷa I (rebuilt by Vijayaraghava Naik of Tanjore). See *Tanj. Gazr.*, Vol. I, p. 227. Mannārguḍi is also a jain centre. Its ancient name was Rājarājachaturvēdimaṅgalam and it belonged to Śuttamalli vaḷanāḍu.

506. 85 *of* 1897.—(Grantha and Tamil.) In the front gōpura of the Jayaṅkoṇḍanātha temple, left of entrance. A record in the third year of the Hoysaḷa king Vīra-Rāmanāthadēva. Records gift of land. [Vīra Rāmanātha was the younger brother of Narasimha III (1254—91) and son of Vīra Sōmēśvara (1234—52) who was left in charge of the southern half of the Hoysaḷa Empire.]

507. 86 *of* 1897.—(Grantha and Tamil.) On the south wall of the central shrine of the same temple. The name of the king is indistinct. Records gift of land.

508. 87 *of* 1897.—(Tamil.) On the north wall of the same shrine. A record in the eighth year of the Pāṇḍya king Kō-Māravarman Parākrama-Pāṇḍyadēva. (Unidentified.) Records gift of land.

509. 88 *of* 1897.—(Tamil.) On the north wall of the maṇṭapa in front of the same shrine. Records description of boundaries.

510. 89 *of* 1897.—(Tamil.) On the east wall of the same maṇṭapa right of entrance. A record in the twelfth year. Provides for the payment of certain dues on arecanuts.

511. 90 *of* 1897.—(Tamil.) On the same wall, left of entrance. A record in the twelfth year of the Pāṇḍya king Kō-Jaṭāvarman *alias* Sundara-Pāṇḍyadēva II (1276—90). Provides for the payment of certain dues on pepper and cloths. See *Ep. Ind.*, Vol. VI, p. 311, where Dr. Kielhorn discusses the date. He points out that the *tithi* is not quite right and arrives at the date Friday, 12th September 1287. As Diwan Bahadur Swamikannu Pillai has discovered another king of this name who came to the throne in 1270, the present king should be termed the *third* of his name and not the second.]

512. 91 *of* 1897.—(Tamil.) On the south wall of the central shrine of the Aṇṇāmalainātha temple. An incomplete record in the twenty-second year of the Chōḷa king Tribhuvanachakravartin Rājēndra-Chōḷadēva III, corresponding to Sunday, 8th May, A.D. 1267. *Ep. Ind.*, Vol. VII, p. 177. The temple is said to have been in Śārigai Kōṭṭai, a hamlet west of Rājādhirājachaturvēdimaṅgalam.

513. 92 *of* 1897.—(Tamil.) On the same wall. Records in the thirty-second year of a certain king a sale of land.

514. 93 *of* 1897.—(Grantha and Tamil.) On the same wall. A record of the Chōḷa king Parakēsarivarman *alias* Rājēndra-Chōḷa (1011—43). Records gift of land.

515. 94 *of* 1897.—(Tamil.) On the north wall of the same shrine. Records gift of land.

516. 95 *of* 1897.—(Tamil.) On the north wall of the maṇṭapa in front of the same shrine. A record in the nineteenth year of the Pāṇḍya king Rājakēsarivarman *alias* Vīra-Pāṇḍyadēva. Resembles Nos. 510 and 511. [The combination of a Chōḷa title with Pāṇḍyan king is very anomalous. Was he the Koṅgu Pāṇḍya who ruled from 1265 to 1281? See Cb. 196 and 197.

517. 96 *of* 1897.—(Tamil.) On the north wall of the central shrine of the Kailāśanāthasvāmin temple. A record in the twenty-second year of the Chōḷa king Tribhuvanachakravartin Rājarāja-dēva. Records a private agreement. [Which is the Rājarāja referred to here ?]

518. 97 *of* 1897.—(Tamil.) On the same wall. A record in the twenty-sixth year of the Hoysaḷa king Vīra-Sōmēśvaradēva (the father of Vīra Rāmanātha and Narasiṁha III, who conquered the Chōḷa country about 1252 and founded Vikramapura there). Records gift of land to an image of the goddess, set up by Mahā-pradhānin Kampaya-Daṇḍanāyaka.

519. 98 *of* 1897.—(Tamil.) On the west and south walls of the same shrine. A record in the twenty-second year of the Chōḷa king Tribhuvanachakravartin Rājarājadēva (III ?). Records a private agreement.

520. 99 *of* 1897.—(Tamil.) On the north wall of the same shrine. An incomplete record in the twenty-second year of the Chōḷa king Tribhuvanachakravartin Rājarājadēva (III ?).

521. 100 *of* 1897.—(Tamil.) On the south wall of the same shrine. A record of the Pāṇḍya king Kō-Māravarman Parākrama-Pāṇḍyadēva, the date of which is indistinct. Records gift of land.

522. 101 *of* 1897.—(Tamil.) On the same wall. A record in the eighth year of the king whose name is doubtful. Records gift of land.

523. 102 *of* 1897.—(Tamil.) In the third gōpura in front of the Rājagōpāla Perumāḷ temple. A record in the twelfth year of Tribhuvanachakravartin Kōnērimēlkoṇḍān. Records gift of land.

524. 103 *of* 1897.—(Tamil.) On the north wall of the central shrine in the same temple. A damaged record in the forty-eighth year of the Chōḷa king Kō-Rājakēsarivarman *alias* Kulōttuṅga-Chōḷadēva (I).

525. 104 *of* 1897.—(Tamil.) On the north, west and south walls of the same shrine. A record in the twenty-second year of the Chōḷa king Tribhuvanachakravartin Rājarājadēva. Records a private agreement.

526. 105 *of* 1897.—(Tamil.) On the west and south walls of the same shrine. A record in the twenty-first year of the Chōḷa king Tribhuvanachakravartin Rājēndra-Chōḷadēva (III). Records gift of land. The date corresponded to Wednesday, 30th June, A.D. 1266. *Ep. Ind.*, Vol. VII, pp. 176–7.

527. 106 *of* 1897.—(Tamil.) On the south wall of the second prākāra of the same temple. Records gift of land.

528. 107 *of* 1897.—(Tamil.) On the west wall of the same prākāra. A fragmentary record in Ś. 1499, expired, Īśvara.

529. 108 *of* 1897.—(Tamil.) On the north wall of the same prākāra. Mentions Achyutappa-Nāyaka; a fragmentary record.

530. 109 *of* 1897.—(Tamil.) In the cellar of the same temple. A record of the Pāṇḍya king Tribhuvanachakravartin Sundara-Pāṇḍyadēva (unidentified) "who took every country." Records gift of land.

Rishiyūr.

531. 473 *of* 1907.—(Tamil.) On the south wall of the Kailāsanātha temple. A record in the twenty-eighth year of the Chōḷa king Śrī-Kulōttuṅga-Chōḷadēva (unidentified). Records gift of money to the temple of Tiruvagattīśuramuḍaiyār. [The king was in all probability Kulōttuṅga III.]

532. 474 *of* 1907.—(Tamil.) On the same wall. A mutilated record of the Chōḷa king Tribhuvanachakravartin . . . Madura, Īḷam (Ceylon), Karuvūr and the crowned head of the Pāṇḍya, the date of which is lost (Kulōttuṅga III, 1178—1216). Records gift of land.

533. 475 *of* 1907.—(Tamil.) On the same wall. A record in the twenty-fifth year of the Chōḷa king Tribhuvanachakravartin Śrī-Kulōttuṅga-Chōḷadēva (III), "who was pleased to take Madura, Īḷam (Ceylon) and the crowned head of the Pāṇḍya and Karuvūr. Records gift of land for a lamp to the temple of Tiruvagattīśuramuḍaiyār at Piḷiśūr in Pāmbuṇikūṟṟam, a subdivision of Śuttamalli-vaḷanāḍu.

534. 476 *of* 1907.—(Tamil.) On the south wall of the same temple. A record in the thirty-third year of the Chōḷa king Tribhuvanachakravartin Tribhuvanavīra-dēva (1178—1216), "who took Madura, Īḷam (Ceylon), Karuvūr and the crowned head of the Pāṇḍya and who was pleased to perform the anointment of heroes and the anointment of victors." Records gift of land by Malaiyappiyarāyan to the temple of Tiruvānaikāvuḍaiyār at Perumūr in Veṇṇikūṟṟam, a subdivision of Śuttamalli-vaḷanāḍu. The donor had married a daughter of Kulōttuṅga-Chōḷa-Vānakōvaraiyar of Kaḷattūr.

Tirukkaḷar.

[Celebrated in Śaivite tradition as the place where Kāḷamuni and Durvāsas worshipped the deity.]

535. 642 *of* 1902.—(Tamil.) On the north wall of the maṇṭapa in front of the central shrine in the Pārijātavanēśvarasvāmin temple. A record in the twenty-fifth year of the Pāṇḍya king Jaṭāvarman *alias* Tribhuvanachakravartin Śrī-Vallabbadēva. Records sale of land to Vijayagaṇḍa-Gōpāla. [Was Śrī Vallabha the contemporary of Māravarman Sundara Pāṇḍya I, 1216—35?]

536. 643 *of* 1902.—(Tamil.) On the same wall. A record in the sixth year of the Chōḷa king Tribhuvanachakravartin Rājarājadēva. Records gift of land.

537. 644 *of* 1902.—(Tamil.) On the east wall of the same maṇṭapa. A record in the third year of the Chōḷa king Tribhuvanachakravartin Kulōttuṅga-Chōḷadēva. Records gift of money for a lamp.

538. 645 *of* 1902.—(Tamil.) On the same wall. Records the building of the maṇṭapa by a certain Karuṇākara of Paḷaiyanūr. [Was he the Karuṇākara Toṇḍamān who was the hero of Jayaṅkoṇḍān's *Kalingattupparaṇi* ?]

539. 646 *of* 1902.—(Tamil.) On the south wall of the same maṇṭapa. A record in the forty-fourth year of the Pāṇḍya king Māravarman *alias* Tribhuvanachakravartin Kulaśēkharadēva (I, ? 1268—1308). Fixes the dues on certain land.

540. 647 *of* 1902.—(Tamil.) On the same wall. An incomplete record of the Chōḷa king Tribhuvanachakravartin Kulōttuṅga-Chōḷadēva (III), who took Madura in his tenth year. Records gift of taxes.

541. 648 *of* 1902.—(Tamil.) On the same wall. A record in the twelfth year of the Chōḷa king Kulōttuṅga-Chōḷadēva. Records gift of money.

542. 649 *of* 1902.—(Tamil.) On the same wall. A record in Śrīmukha, i.e., Ś. 1315, of the Vijayanagara king Vīra-Viruppaṇṇa-Uḍaiyār II, i.e., Virūpāksha I, son of Ariyaṇa-Uḍaiyār (i.e., Harihara II). Records gift of a house-site to a certain Tirunāṭṭupperumāḷ, who had spent 400 *paṇam* for the temple during a famine in the Prajāpati year, i.e., Ś. 1313.

543. 650 *of* 1902.—(Tamil.) On the same wall. A record in the fourth year of the Chōḷa king Tribhuvanachakravartin Kulōttuṅga-Chōḷadēva. Records gift of land.

544. 651 *of* 1902.—(Tamil.) On the same wall. A record in the second year of the Chōḷa king Tribhuvanachakravartin Vīra-Rājēndra-Chōḷadēva. Records gift of money for a lamp.

545. 652 *of* 1902.—(Tamil.) On the same wall. A record in the tenth year of the Chōḷa king Tribhuvanachakravartin Rājādhi-Rājadēva. Records gift of money for a lamp by Karuṇākaradēva of Paḷaiyanūr. See Tj. 538 above.

546. 653 *of* 1902.—(Tamil.) On the same wall. A record in Ś. 1343, Śārvarin, of the Vijayanagara king Vīra-Bhūpati-Uḍaiyar (1409—22). Records gift of a house-site to a private person.

547. 654 *of* 1902.—(Tamil.) On the same wall. A record in Ś. 1304 of the Vijayanagara king Viruppaṇṇa-Uḍaiyar II, i.e., Virūpāksha I (son of Harihara II). Records gift of a house-site to a private person.

548. 655 *of* 1902.—(Tamil.) On the same wall. A damaged record.

549-A—E. Five copper plates in the Pārijātavanēśvara temple now in the Madras Museum. "The first of them is dated in the eighteenth year of Rājēndra Chōḷa I, who ascended the throne in A.D. 1011-12, and opens with the usual historical introduction (திருமன்னிவளர, etc.). The second belongs to the thirty-first year of his successor Rājakēsarivarman *alias* Rājādhirājadēva, "who took by an army the head of Vīra Pāṇḍya, Śerala Śālai and Laṅka," and the third to the twenty-sixth year of Kulōttuṅga Chōḷa III, whose reign commenced in A.D. 1178. The last plate bears two inscriptions of the twenty-eighth year of Kulōttuṅga Chōḷa (III ?) and of the eighteenth year of Rājarāja (III ?)". [*Mad. Ep. Rep.*, 1903, p. 8, para. 17.]

Tiruvirāmiśvaram.

This is Rāmanadīchcharam of the *Dēvāram*. Its antiquity is proved by the early Chōḷa inscriptions. It was known in the time of Rājarāja as Madanamañjari-chaturvēdimaṅgalam *alias* Neḍumaṇal and it was in Nenmalināḍu of Arumoḷitēvavaḷanāḍu. [See No. 586 below and *S.I.I.*, Vol. II, Pt. III, p. 320.]

550. 117 *of* 1911.—(Tamil.) On the south wall of the central shrine in the Rāmanāthēśvara temple. A damaged record in the sixth year of the Chōḷa king Rājakēsarivarman. Records gift of land by purchase.

551. 118 *of* 1911.—(Tamil.) On the same wall. A damaged record in the twenty-ninth year of the Chōḷa king Rājakēsarivarman *alias* Uḍaiyār Śrī-Rājādhirājadēva (I, 1018—52). Records gift of lamp to the temple by a Brāhmaṇa of Tiruvīrāmēśvaram in Madanamañjari-chaturvēdimaṅgalam.

552. 119 *of* 1911.—(Tamil.) On the north wall of the same shrine. An incomplete record in the twelfth year of the Chōḷa king Rājarājakēsarivarman (985—1013), "who destroyed the ships at Śālai." Records gift of money for two lamps to the temple of Tiruvirāmīśvaramuḍaiya-mahādēva at Madanamañjari-chaturvēdimaṅgalam, a *brahmadēya* in Nenmali-nāḍu.

553. 120 *of* 1911.—(Tamil.) On the same wall. A record in the twelfth year of the Chōḷa king Rājarājakēsarivarman (985—1013), "who destroyed the ships at Śālai." Records gift of money for a lamp.

554. 121 *of* 1911.—(Tamil.) On the same wall. A record in the twenty-second year of the Chōḷa king Rājakēsarivarman *alias* Rājarājadēva (985—1013). Records gift of a lamp to the temple of Tiruvirāmīśvarattu-Mahādēva at Madanamañjari-chaturvēdimaṅgalam, a *brahmadēya* in Nenmali-nāḍu which was a subdivision of Arumoḷidēvavaḷanāḍu.

555. 122 *of* 1911.—(Tamil.) On the same wall. A record in the third year of the Chōḷa king Parakēsarivarman *alias* Śrī-Rājēndra-Chōḷadēva (I, 1011—43). Records gift of money for four lamps.

556. 123 *of* 1911.—(Tamil.) On the south wall of the maṇṭapa in front of the same shrine. A mutilated and unfinished record in the thirty-fifth year of the Chōḷa king Rājakēsarivarman *alias* Uḍaiyār Śrī-Vijayarājēndradēva (Rājādhirāja I, 1018—52). Contains only a portion of the historical introduction.

557. 124 *of* 1911.—(Tamil.) On the same wall. A damaged record in the seventh year of the Chōḷa king Parakēsarivarman *alias* Śrī-Rājēndra-Chōḷadēva (I, 1011—43). Seems to record a sale of land for maintaining lamps and for feeding Śivayōgins in the same temple.

558. 125 *of* 1911.—(Tamil.) On the same wall. A record in the fourth year of the Chōḷa king Parakēsarivarman. Records gift of 24 *kāśu* for a lamp.

559. 126 *of* 1911.—(Tamil.) On the same wall. A mutilated record in the seventh year of the Chōḷa king Parakēsarivarman. Records gift of land.

560. 127 *of* 1911.—(Tamil.) On the same wall. A record in the fourteenth year of the Chōḷa king . . . Rājēndra-Chōḷadēva. Records gift of money (ten *kaḻañjus*). The record is incomplete.

561. 128 *of* 1911.—(Tamil.) On the same wall. A record of the Chōḷa king Parakēsarivarman, the date of which is lost. Records gift of money for a lamp by a merchant who was living in the street Vīraśōḷapperunderu at Tañjāvūr.

562. 129 *of* 1911.—(Tamil.) On the same wall. A damaged and mutilated record in the thirteenth year of the Chōḷa king Parakēsarivarman. Registers the distribution of stores for oblations in the temple as settled by a certain Tirumañjuṇapittar.

563. 130 *of* 1911.—(Tamil.) On a same wall. Registers the gift of a lamp. The stone is obviously misplaced and contains only the end of an inscription.

564. 131 *of* 1911.—(Tamil.) On the same wall. A mutilated record. Records gift of a jewel (*paṭṭam*).

565. 132 *of* 1911.—(Tamil.) On the same wall. A mutilated record in the seventh year of the Chōḷa king Rājarājakēsarivarman (985—1013). Records gift of a lamp.

566. 133 *of* 1911.—(Tamil.) On the west wall of the same maṇṭapa. A record in the ninth year of the Chōḷa king Rājarājakēsarivarman (985—1013). Records gift of money for three lamps.

567. 134 *of* 1911.—(Tamil.) On the same wall. A record in the ninth year of the Chōḷa king Parakēsarivarman. Records gift of money for three lamps.

568. 135 *of* 1911.—(Tamil.) On the same wall. A damaged record in the eighth year of the Chōḷa king Rājarājakēsarivarman (985—1013). Records gift of money.

569. 136 *of* 1911.—(Tamil.) On the north wall of the same maṇṭapa. A record in the eleventh year of the Chōḷa king Rājarājakēsarivarman (985—1013). Records gift of land for a lamp, by one of the *gaṇattār* who managed the affairs of the village. See No. 571.

570. 137 *of* 1911.—(Tamil.) On the same wall. A record in the eleventh year of the Chōḷa king Rājarājakēsarivarman (I, 985—1013), " who destroyed the ships at Kāndaḷur Śālai." Records gift of money for three lamps.

571. 138 *of* 1911.—(Tamil.) On the same wall. A mutilated record in the seventeenth year of the Chōḷa king Rājakēsarivarman. Records gift of land for a lamp by one of the *gaṇattār*. See No. 569.

572. 139 *of* 1911.—(Tamil.) On the same wall. A record in the third year of the Chōḷa king Parakēsarivarman *alias* Śrī-Rājēndra-Chōḷadēva (I, 1011—1043). Records gift of money nineteen *kāśus* for three lamps each to burn for 7½ *nāḻikas*.

573. 140 *of* 1911.—(Tamil.) On the same wall. A mutilated record in the eleventh year of the Chōḷa king Rājarājakēsarivarman (I, 985—1013), " who destroyed the ships at Śālai." Seems to record a gift of money for a lamp.

574. 141 *of* 1911.—(Tamil.) On the same wall. A record in the tenth year of the Chōḷa king Rājarājakēsarivarman (985—1013), " who destroyed the ships at Kāndaḷūr-Śālai." Records gift of money (twelve *kāśu*) for a lamp by a Brāhmaṇa lady of Amitravallichaturvēdimaṅgalam, a *brahmadēya* in Avūr-kūṟṟam (which, according to Tanjore inscriptions, supplied Brahmachārins to the temple of that place).

575. 142 *of* 1911.—(Tamil.) On the same wall. A record in the third year of the Chōḷa king Parakēsarivarman *alias* Śrī-Rājēndra-Chōḷadēva (I, 1011—43). Records gifts of land (16 *kuḻis* for a lamp).

576. 143 *of* 1911.—(Tamil.) On the same wall. A mutilated record in the thirteenth year of the Chōḷa king Rājarāja-Rājakēsarivarman (I, 985—1013), " who destroyed the ships at Śālai." Seems to record a gift of land to the temple of Ūrkāṭṭu-Bhagavadēva of Mēr-Pūdamaṅgalam in Nenmali-nāḍu.

577. 144 *of* 1911.—(Tamil.) On the same wall. A damaged record in the sixth year of the Chōḷa king Parakēsarivarman *alias*

Śrī-Rājēndra-Chōḷadēva (I, 1011—43). Seems to record a gift of land.

578. 145 *of* 1911.—(Tamil.) On the same wall. A record in the third year of the Chōḷa king Śrī-Rājēndra-Chōḷadēva (1012—43). Records gift of money for a lamp.

579. 146 *of* 1911.—(Tamil.) On the same wall. A mutilated record in the eighth year of the Chōḷa king Rājarājakēsarivarman (985—1013). Records gift of land for a lamp to the shrine of Brahmīśvara and for offerings to the shrine of Tribhuvanasundara (both of which were perhaps, situated in the same temple) by the cavalier *(kudirikkāra)* Śōbhanayyan.

580. 147 *of* 1911.—(Tamil.) On the same wall. A record in the eleventh year of the Chōḷa king Rājarājakēsarivarman (I, 985—1013), "who destroyed the ships at Śālai." Records gift of land for a lamp by the same person to the temple of Tiruvirāmīśvarattu Mahādēva.

581. 148 *of* 1911.—(Tamil.) On the same wall. A record in the eighth year of the Chōḷa king Rājarāja-Rājakēsarivarman. Records gift of money (three *kāśus*) for a lamp to burn for 7½ *nāḻis* by the wife of one of the *gaṇattār* "who managed the affairs of the village."

582. 149 *of* 1911.—(Tamil.) On the same wall. An unfinished record in the eleventh year of the Chōḷa king Rājarājakēsarivarman (985—1013), "who destroyed the ships at Śālai."

583. 150 *of* 1911.—(Tamil.) On the south wall of the first prākāra in the same temple. A record in the fourth year of the Chōḷa king Chakravartin Vikrama-Chōḷadēva (1118—35). Records gift of land for lamps to the temple of Tiruvirāmīśvaramuḍaiya-Mahādēva by Tēvan Tiruppurambiyamuḍaiyān, a native of Kīḷiyūr.

584. 151 *of* 1911.—(Tamil.) On the same wall. A record in the thirty-fourth year of the Chōḷa king Tribhuvanachakravartin Tribhuvanavīradēva (1178—1216), "who being pleased to take Madurai (i.e., Madura), Īḻam (Ceylon), Karuvūr and the crowned head of the Pāṇḍya was pleased to perform the anointment of heroes and victors." Records gift of land for lamps.

585. 152 *of* 1911.—(Tamil.) On the same wall. A record in the eighth year of the Chōḷa king Tribhuvanachakravartin Rājadhirājadēva (II?). Records gift of money for a lamp by a priest of the temple of Tirutturaippūṇḍi in Vaṇḍāḷai-vēlūr-kūṟṟam in Nenmali-nāḍu, to the temple of Tiruvirāmīśvaram-uḍaiyār in the village of Nedumaṇal-Madanamañjari-chaturvēdimaṅgalam.

586. 153 *of* 1911.—(Tamil.) On the north wall of the same prākāra. A damaged record in the fourteenth year of the Pāṇḍya ing Tribhuvanachakravartin Sundara-Pāṇḍyadēva (unidentified).

Seems to record a gift of land and states that Nedumaṇal was another name of Madanamañjari-chaturvēdimaṅgalam.

587. 154 *of* 1911.—(Tamil.) On the same wall. A damaged record in the twenty-third year of the Chōḷa king Tribhuvana-chakravartin Rājarājadēva (II or III ?). Stones out of order. Seems to record an agreement among the *kuṭumbins* and the *kuḍimakkaḷ* regarding exchange, measuring, etc., of grain.

588. 155 *of* 1911.—(Tamil.) On a stone set up in a field of the same village. In modern characters. Records in Kīlaka gift of land at Taṇṇīrkunnam-māgāṇam, to the God Rāmanāthasvāmin and the Goddess Tirumaṅgai-nāyaki of the temple of Tiruvirāmīś-varam by a certain Arichchandirarāja-Sāyēbu.

MĀYAVARAM TALUK.

Ānatāṇḍavaram.

One of the eighteen villages which form the settlements of the Vāttima Brahmans. Gōpāla Kṛishṇa Aiyar, a native of this place and the author of *Nandanār charitra kirttanai*, lived about the first quarter of the nineteenth century.

589. 297 *of* 1911.—(Tamil.) On a stone in the house of the village munsif. A damaged record in Ś. 1518, Durmukhi. Records gift of a village to the temple of Vinaittīta-Tambirānār (perhaps a temple at Ānatāṇḍavaram) for bathing and oblations, by a native of Puḷḷirukkuvēḷūr (i.e., Vaittīśvaraṅkōvil). See *Maṇimēhalai*, p. 410.

Kuttālam.

590. 477 *of* 1907.—(Tamil.) On the south wall of the central shrine in the Chōḷēśvara temple. A record in the fourth year of the king whose name is not mentioned. Records gift of land. Records an order of Jayadara-Pallavaraiyar. Kuṟṟālam belonged to Jayaṅgoṇḍa-Chōḷa-vaḷanāḍu. Mentions the temple of Vikrama-Chōḷīśvaramuḍaiyār. See No. 592.

591. 478 *of* 1907.—(Tamil.) On the south wall of the central shrine in the Ōṁkārēśvara temple in the same village. A mutilated record of the Chōḷa king Tribhuvanachakravartin . . . Madura, Īḻam (Ceylon) and the crowned head of the Pāṇḍya, the date of which is lost. In a small inscription close to this the name of Ōṁkārēśvaramuḍaiya-Paramasvāmi occurs. [The king referred to is apparently Kulōttuṅga Chōḷa III.]

592. 479 *of* 1907.—(Tamil.) On the same wall. A record in the twenty-fifth year of the Chōḷa king Tribhuvanachakravartin Śrī-Kulōttuṅga-Chōḷadēva III, "who was pleased to take Madura, Īḻam (Ceylon) and the crowned head of the Pāṇḍya." Records gift of land to the temple of Ōṁkārēśvaramuḍaiyār built by Piḷḷai

Jayadara Pallavaraiyar. See *Ep. Ind.*, Vol. X, pp. 129–30, where Mr. Sewell fixes the date on Saturday, 4th January, A.D. 1203. See No. 595 below.

593. 480 *of* 1907.—(Tamil.) On the same wall. A record in the thirty-fifth year of the Chōḷa king Tribhuvanachakravartin Śrī-Kulōttuṅga-Chōḷadēva III, "who was pleased to take Madura, Īḻam (Ceylon) and the crowned head of the Pāṇḍya." Records gift of land. Mentions Pallavanārāyaṇapuram *alias* Ulagamādēvipuram, in Tiruvaḷundūr-nāḍu, a subdivision of Jayaṅgoṇḍachōḷa-vaḷanāḍu. See *Ep. Ind.*, Vol. X, pp. 133-4, where Mr. Sewell fixes the English date on Tuesday, 26th February, A.D. 1213, after correcting the Nakshattra Krittikā into Bharaṇi.

594. 481 *of* 1907.—(Tamil.) On the west wall of the same shrine. A record (mutilated in the middle) of Tribhuvanachakravartin Kōnērimēnkoṇḍān. Seems to record a gift of land.

595. 482 *of* 1907.—(Tamil.) On the north wall of the maṇṭapa in front of the same shrine. A record in the twenty-fifth year of the Chōḷa king Tribhuvanachakravartin Śrī-Kulōttuṅga-Chōḷadēva III, "who was pleased to take Madura, Īḻam (Ceylon) and the crowned head of the Pāṇḍya." Records gift of land to the temple of Ōṁkārēśvaramuḍaiyār built by Araiyan Āḷuḍaiyanāyaganār *alias* Jayadara Pallavaraiyar. Mentions Kāvirinallūr, a *dēvadāna* of the temple of Uḍaiyār Śonnavārariyār at Vīṅgunīrtturutti. See *Ep. Ind.*, Vol. X, p. 129, where Mr. Sewell calculates the English equivalent of the date to be Sunday, March 15th, A.D. 1203.

596. 483 *of* 1907.—(Tamil.) On the same wall. A record in the twenty-ninth year of Tribhuvanachakravartin Kōnērimēnkoṇḍān. Mentions the shrine of Vikkirama-Chōḷīśvaramuḍaiyār at Kulōttuṅga-Śōḷan-Kuṟṟālam in Virudarāja-bhayaṁkara-vaḷanāḍu. Refers to the revenue survey in the sixteenth year of Śuṅganda-vitta-Kulōttuṅga-Chōḷadēva I. The royal order is addressed to Vānadarāyan.

597. 484 *of* 1907.—(Tamil.) On the north and west walls of the Chaṇḍēśvara shrine in the same temple. A record in the twenty-fifth year of the Chōḷa king Tribhuvanachakravartin Śrī-Kulōttuṅga-Chōḷadēva III (1178—1216), "who was pleased to take Madura, Īḻam (Ceylon) and the crowned head of the Pāṇḍya." Records gift of land. Mentions Anapāyapuram in Tiruvaḷandūr-nāḍu, a subdivision of Jayaṅgoṇḍa-Chōḷa-vaḷanāḍu. See *Ep. Ind.*, Vol. X, p. 130, where it is pointed out that the date corresponded to Wednesday, March 19th, A.D. 1203.

598. 485 *of* 1907.—(Tamil.) On the north wall of the central shrine in the Uttaravēdīśvara temple. A record in the ninth year of the Chōḷa king Parakēsarivarmaṇ *alias* Uḍaiyār Śrī-Rājēndra-Chōḷadēva (I, 1011—43). Records sale of land to the temple of Vīṅgunīrttirutturuttiuḍaiya-Mahādēvar.

599. 486 *of* 1907.—(Tamil.) On the same wall. A record in the fifth year of the Chōḷa king Parakēsarivarman *alias* Uḍaiyār Śrī-Rājēndradēva (1050—63). Records gift of money by a native of Gaṅgaikoṇḍa-Chōḷapuram to the temple of Śonnavārarivār at Vīṅgunīrttirutturutti in Tiruvaḷandūr-nāḍu, a subdivision of Jayaṅgoṇḍa-chōḷa-vaḷanāḍu. The endowment was intended for feeding itinerant Śaiva devotees in order to secure success to the arms of the king.

600. 487 *of* 1907.—(Tamil.) On the east wall of the same shrine. A record in the eighth year of the Chōḷa king Parakēsarivarman *alias* Śrī-Rājēndra-Chōḷadēva (I, 1011—43). Records sale of land by the sabhā of Villavan-Mahādēvi-chaturvēdimaṅgalam, a *brahmadēya* in Tiruvaḷundūr-nāḍu, a subdivision of Uyyakkoṇḍār-vaḷanāḍu to the temple of Tirukkaṟṟali-Mahādēva at Vīṅgunīrttirutturutti.

601. 488 *of* 1907.—(Grantha.) On the south wall of the same shrine. The temple is called Kalyāṇālaya.

602. 489 *of* 1907.—(Tamil.) On the north wall of the maṇṭapa in front of the same shrine. A record in the sixth year of the Chōḷa king Tribhuvanachakravartin Śrī-Vikrama-Chōḷadēva (1118—35). Records gift of land by the *sabhā* of Uttama-Chōḷa-chaturvēdimaṅgalam, a *brahmadēya* in Tiruvaḷundūr-nāḍu, a subdivision of Rāyanārāyaṇa-vaḷanāḍu. See *Ep. Ind.*, Vol. X, pp. 123-4, where the date is discussedand surmised to be Thursday, August 19th, A.D. 1123.

603. 490 *of* 1907.—(Tamil.) On the same wall. A record in the fifth year of the Chōḷa king Tribhuvanachakravartin Śrī-Vikrama-Chōḷa-dēva (1118—35). Records gift of land by the *sabhā* of Pūlōgamāṇikka-chaturvēdimaṅgalam, a *brahmadēya* in Virudarājabhayaṁkara-vaḷanāḍu to the temple of Śonnavārarivār at Vīṅgunīrtirutturutti. See *Ep. Ind.*, Vol. X, p. 123, where the details of the date (Simhapūrva 13, Wednesday, Hasta) are shown to be irregular.

604. 491 *of* 1907.—(Tamil.) On the same wall. A record in the third year of the Chōḷa king Tribhuvanachakravartin Śrī-Vikrama-Chōḷadēva (1118—35). Records gift of land by the *sabhā* of Pūlōgamāṇikka-chaturvēdimaṅgalam, *brahmadēya* in Nallāṟūr-nāḍu, a subdivision of Virudarāyabhayaṁkara-vaḷanāḍu, to the temple of Uḍaiyār Śonnavārarivār at Vīṅgunīrtirutturutti in Tiruvaḷundūr-nāḍu, a subdivision of Teṅkarai-Rājanārāyaṇa-vaḷanāḍu. See *Ep. Ind.*, Vol. X, p. 122, where the details of the date (Makara, Apara 7, Monday, Hasta) are shown to be irregular.

605. 492 *of* 1907.—(Tamil.) On the same wall. A record in the eighth year of the Chōḷa king Tribhuvanachakravartin Śrī-Vikrama-Chōḷadēva (1118—35). Records gift of land by the same *sabhā* to the same temple. *Ibid.*, p. 124, where it is shown that the date (Makara, Pūrva 9, Saturday, Anurādha) is irregular.

606. 493 *of* 1907.—(Tamil.) On the same wall. A record of the Vijayanagara king Bhujabala Vīrapratāpa Kṛishṇadēva-Mahārāya in Ś. 1440, expired, Dhātri. Records gift of the proceeds of the taxes *jōḍi* and *śūlavari* amounting to ninety *pon* in favour of the temple of Śonnavārarivār. The gift was made by the king on the occasion of the *māmāṅgam* festival at the request of Basavarasa of Tiruppeyarrūr in Toṇḍaimaṇḍalam.

607. 494 *of* 1907.—(Tamil.) On the south wall of the same maṇṭapa. A damaged record in Ś. 1303, expired, Durmati. Seems to register the remission of certain taxes. Kampaṇa-Uḍaiyār (II) is mentioned about the end of the inscription.

608. 495 *of* 1907.—(Tamil.) On the same wall. A record in the fifteenth year of the Chōḷa king Tribhuvanachakravartin Śrī-Rājēndra-Chōḷadēva. Records sale of a house-site to a *maṭha*. Mentions the temple of Tiruchchattimurramuḍaiyār at Kīḻ-Paḻaiyāru *alias* Rājarājapuram in Kulōttuṅga-Chōḷa-vaḷanāḍu.

Māyavaram.

[Famous in Śaivite tradition as the place where Śiva transformed his wife Pārvati into a mayūra (peahen) for disobedience and then restored her.]

609. 300 *of* 1911.—(Tamil.) On the south wall of the first prākāra of the Mayūranāthasvāmin temple. A damaged and incomplete record in the fourteenth year of the Chōḷa king Rāja-kēsarivarman *alias* Tribhuvanachakravartin Rājādhirājadēva (II), " who took Madurai (Madura) and Īḻam (Ceylon)." Given the latter portion of the historical introduction beginning with *kaḍalśūḻnda*. [For the legend in connexion with the Mayūranāthasvāmi temple see *Tanj. Gazr.*, Vol. I, p. 231.]

610. 301 *of* 1911.—(Tamil.) On the three faces of a pillar set up in the street in front of the same temple. A damaged record in the tenth year of the Pāṇḍya king Jaṭāvarman Tribhuvanachakravartin Sundara-Pāṇḍyadēva. It is not known which of the three Pāṇḍyas of this name is referred to.

611. 371 *of* 1907.—(Tamil.) On the south wall of the first prākāra of the same temple. A record in the twenty-sixth year of the Chōḷa king Tribhuvanachakravartin Śrī-Rājarājadēva (III ?). Records gift of money.

612. 372 *of* 1907.—(Tamil.) In one of the shrines in the northern side of the same temple. A record in the fourteenth year of the Chōḷa king Tribhuvanachakravartin Śrī-Rājarājadēva (III). Records gift of land to the shrine of the goddess called Tiruppaḷḷi-arai-Nāchchiyār in the temple of Tirumaiyilāḍuturai-Uḍaiyār. See *Ep. Ind.*, Vol. X, p. 134, where it is pointed out that the date corresponded to Sunday, October 7, A.D. 1229.

613. 373 *of* 1907.—(Tamil.) On a stone built into the floor in front of the central shrine in the same temple. A fragmentary record.

614. 374 *of* 1907.—(Tamil.) On the north wall of the maṇṭapa in front of the central shrine in the Pañchanādēśvara temple in the same village. A damaged record in the thirty-first year of the king. Seems to record a gift of land.

615. 375 *of* 1907.—(Tamil.) On the same wall. A record in the thirty-second year of Tribhuvanachakravartin Kōnērinmaikoṇḍān. Connected with the above. The temple is described as in No. 617 below.

616. 376 *of* 1907.—(Tamil.) On the same wall. A record in the nineteenth year of the king, whose name is not mentioned. Mentions the Vikkirama-śōḷan-*maḍām* and Kulōttuṅga-Śōḷanallūr *alias* Kulōttuṅga-Śōḷan-Kuṟṟālam. Refers to the twenty-first year of Uḍaiyār Śuṅgandavirttaruḷina Kulōttuṅga-Śōḷadēvar (I, 1070—1118).

617. 377 *of* 1907.—(Tamil.) On the same wall. A record in the nineteenth year of the king. Records gift of land to the image of Tiruvaiyāruḍaiyār set up at Kulōttuṅga Śōḷanallūr *alias* Kulōttuṅga-Śōḷan-Kuṟṟālam in Tiruvaḷundūrnāḍu, a subdivision of Jayaṅgoṇḍachōḷavaḷanāḍu. Refers also to the twenty-first year of Śuṅgandavirttaruḷina Kulōttuṅga-Śōḷadēvar (I, 1070—1118).

618. 378 *of* 1907.—(Tamil.) On the north wall of the maṇṭapa in front of the central shrine in the Pañchanādēśvara shrine. A record in the thirtieth year of Tribhuvanachakravartin Kōnērinmaikoṇḍān. Records gift of land.

619. 379 *of* 1907.—(Tamil.) On the same wall. A record in the thirtieth year of the king whose name is not mentioned. Records gift of land. Refers to the twenty-first year of Uḍaiyār Śuṅgandavirttaruḷina Kulōttuṅga-Śōḷadēvar (I, 1070—1118).

620. 380 *of* 1907.—(Tamil.) On the same wall. A record in the twenty-fifth year of the Chōḷa king Tribhuvanachakravartin Śrī-Kulōttuṅga-Chōḷadēva (III), " who was pleased to take Madurai (Madura), Īḷam (Ceylon), Karuvūr and the crowned head of the Pāṇḍya." Records gift of land to the temple of Uḍaiyār Tiruvayāruḍaiyār at Kulōttuṅga-Śōḷan-Kuṟṟālam in Tiruvaḷundūr-nāḍu, a subdivision of Jayaṅgoṇḍachōḷavaḷanāḍu. See *Ep. Ind.*, Vol. X, p. 130. Date same as that of the next epigraph.

621. 381 *of* 1907.—(Tamil.) On the east wall of the same maṇṭapa. A record in the twenty-fifth year (Makara, Purva 14, Monday) of the Chōḷa king Tribhuvanachakravartin Śrī-Kulōttuṅga-Chōḷadēva (III), " who was pleased to take Madura, Īḷam (Ceylon), Karuvūr and the crowned head of the Pāṇḍyan." Records gift of paddy. Mentions Śivapādaśēkhara-chaturvēdimaṅgalam.

See *Ep. Ind.*, Vol. X, p. 130, where it is pointed out that the date corresponded to Monday, December 30, A.D. 1202 (but the *tithi* 14 ought to be 15).

622. 382 *of* 1907.—(Tamil.) On the same wall. A record in the thirty-third year of the Chōḷa king Tribhuvanachakravartin Tribhuvanavīradēva (Kulōttuṅga III, 1178—1216), "who was pleased to take Madurai (Madura), Īḷam (Ceylon), Karuvūr and the crowned head of the Pāṇḍya and was pleased to perform the anointment of heroes and the anointment of victors." Records gift of land by the *sabhā* of Nallūr-Pudukkuḍi.

623. 383 *of* 1907.—(Tamil.) On the same wall. A record in the twenty-fifth year of the Chōḷa king Tribhuvanachakravartin Śrī-Kulōttuṅga-Chōḷadēva (III), "who was pleased to take Madura, Īḷam (Ceylon), Karuvūr and the crowned head of the Pāṇḍya." Records gift of land. See *Ep. Ind.*, Vol. X, p. 131 and No. 621, above.

624. 384 *of* 1907.—(Tamil.) On the same wall. A record of the Chōḷa king Tribhuvanachakravartin Śrī-Kulōttuṅga-Chōḷadēva (III), "who was pleased to take Madura, Īḷam (Ceylon) and the crowned head of the Pāṇḍya," the date of which is damaged. Records gift of land.

625. 385 *of* 1907.—(Tamil.) On the south wall of the same maṇṭapa. A record in the nineteenth year of the Chōḷa king Tribhuvanachakravartin Śrī-Kulōttuṅga-Chōḷadēva III "who took Madura, Īḷam (Ceylon) and was pleased to take the crowned head of the Pāṇḍya." Records sale of land.

Śoraikkāvūr.

625-A. The Śoraikkāvūr Plates of Virūpāksha. This is a C.P. grant of the Vijayanagara Prince Virūpāksha I or Vīra Virūpaṇa Uḍaiyār II, son of Harihara II, recording the grant of the village of Śiraikkāvūr (near Kuttālam) surnamed Vijaya Sudarśanapuram, to fourteen Brahmans in Ś. 1308 (expired), Kshaya, Paṅguni 25th, corresponding to Wednesday, the 20th March, A.D. 1387. The inscription is interesting for the light it throws on the relation between the Vijayanagar and the Yādava dynasties and on the influence of the important Śrī Vaishṇava families. See *Ep. Ind.*, Vol. III, pp. 298—306.

Tirukkaḍaiyūr.

The temple is well known as the place where Śiva killed the God of Death at the instance of the devotee Mārkaṇḍēya. In literary history this place is important as the birth-place of Abhirāma Bhaṭṭa, the author of *Abhirāmi andādi* (*Abhidhāna chintāmaṇi*, p. 45). There is no epigraph concerning him.

626. 15 *of* 1906.—(Tamil.) On the north wall of the central shrine in the Amritaghaṭēśvara temple. A damaged record in the second year of the Chōḷa king Tribhuvanachakravartin Vikrama-Chōḷadēva (1118—35).

627. 16 *of* 1906.—(Tamil.) On the same wall. A damaged record in the forty-eighth year of the Chōḷa king Rājakēsarivarman *alias* Tribhuvanachakravartin Kulōttuṅga-Chōḷadēva (I).

628. 17 *of* 1906.—(Tamil.) On the east wall of the same shrine. A partly damaged record in the forty-fourth year of the Chōḷa king Rājakēsarivarman *alias* Tribhuvanachakravartin Kulōttuṅga-Chōḷadēva (I). Records gift of a lamp and a lamp-stand. The temple is called Uḍaiyār Śrī-Kālakāladēva at Tirukkaḍayūr. Another much damaged inscription of Kulōttuṅga is also found on the same wall.

629. 18 *of* 1906.—(Tamil.) On the south wall of the same shrine. An incomplete reccrd of the Chōḷa king Rājakēsarivarman *alias* Tribhuvanachakravartin Kulōttuṅga-Chōḷadēva, the date of which is lost. Records gift of a lamp.

630. 19 *of* 1906.—(Tamil.) On the same wall. A very much damaged record of the Chōḷa king Rājakēsarivarman *alias* Tribhuvanachakravartin Kulōttuṅga-Chōḷadēva, the date of which is lost.

631. 20 *of* 1906.—(Tamil.) On the north base of the same shrine. A record in the fifteenth year of the Chōḷa king Parakēsarivarman *alias* Uḍaiyār Śrī-Rājēndra-Chōḷadēva (I, 1011—43). Built in at the end. Records an agreement of the *sabhā* of Paḍaiēviya Tirukkaḍavūr in Ambar-nāḍu, a district of Uyyakkoṇḍārvaḷanāḍu.

632. 21 *of* 1906.—(Tamil.) On the east base of the same shrine. A record in the twenty-third year of the Chōḷa king Rājarāja-Rājakēsarivarman *alias* Śrī-Rājarājadēva (I, 985—1013). The inscription seems to be unfinished and ends abruptly with the word Mummuḍi-Śōḷan. Records sale of land for a lamp.

633. 22 *of* 1906.—(Tamil.) On the same base. A record in the fourteenth year of the Chōḷa king Rājarājakēsarivarman (985—1013). Records gift of land. Mentions the conquest of Śālai, Gaṅgapāḍi, Nuḷambapāḍi, Kaḍigaivaḷi and Veṅgai-nāḍu. The temple is called Śrī-Kālakāladēva at Paḍaiēviya Tirukkaḍavūr in Ambar-nāḍu.

634. 23 *of* 1906.—(Tamil.) On the same base. A damaged record in the fifteenth year of the Chōḷa king Rājarāja-Rājakēsarivarman (I, 985—1013). The *sabhā* of Kaḍavūr gave certain land as *kāṇi* to a person for doing certain services in the temple. Mentions the conquest of Kāndaḷūr-Śālai, Veṅgai-nāḍu. Refers to the shrine called Tiruvīrattānattu-Perumānaḍigaḷ.

635. 24 *of* 1906.—(Tamil.) On the same base. An incomplete record in the thirteenth year of the Chōḷa king Parakēsarivarman *alias* Uḍaiyār Śrī-Rājēndra-Chōḷadēva (1011—43). Mentions Nallūr in Nallūrnāḍu, a district of Nittavinōda-vaḷanāḍu. The conquests extend up to the Gaṅga.

636. 25 *of* 1906.—(Tamil.) On the south base of the same shrine. A damaged record in the twenty-sixth year of the Chōḷa king Rājakēsarivarman *alias* Tribhuvanachakravartin Kulōttuṅga-Chōḷadēva. Registers an agreement of the assembly of Uḷpaḍa-ēviya Tirukkaḍavūr in Ambar-nāḍu, a district of Rājanārāyaṇa-vaḷanāḍu. Mentions Kuṅgiliyakkalaya-Nāyanār.

637. 26 *of* 1906.—(Tamil.) On the same base. A slightly damaged and incomplete record of the Chōḷa king Rājarājakēsari-varman (985—1013) in his sixteenth year, Mithuna, Pañchami, Thursday, Rēvati. Records sale of land.

638. 27 *of* 1906.—(Tamil.) On the same base. An incomplete record in the sixteenth year of the Chōḷa king Rājarājakēsari-varman (i.e., Rājarāja I), Puraṭṭāśi, Monday, Punarvasu. Records sale of land. The village is called Paḍai-ēviya Tirukkaḍavūr in Ambar-nāḍu. See *Ep. Ind.*,Vol. IX, p. 208, where it is shown that the date corresponded to Monday, 23rd September, A.D. 1000.

639. 28 *of* 1906.—(Tamil.) On the north wall of the maṇṭapa in front of the same shrine. A mutilated record of the Pāṇḍya king Māravarman *alias* Tribhuvanachakravartin Kulaśēkharadēva (I, 1268—1308), " who was pleased to take every country," the date of which is lost. Quotes the thirteenth year of the reign of Perumāḷ Sundara-Pāṇḍyadēva (evidently the eldest son and murderer of Kulaśēkhara).

640. 29 *of* 1906.—(Tamil.) On the south wall of the same maṇṭapa. A mutilated record in the seventh year of the Chōḷa king Parakēsarivarman *alias* Tribhuvanachakravartin Vikrama-Chōḷadēva (1118—35). Records gift of money for a lamp.

641. 30 *of* 1906.—(Tamil.) On the same wall. An incomplete record in the sixth year (Vrischika, Mārgaśīrsha, Wednesday) of the Chōḷa king Parakēsarivarman *alias* Tribhuvanachakravartin Vikrama-Chōḷadēva (1118—35). The continuation is covered with chunam. See *Ep. Ind.*, Vol. IX, p. 209, where the date is calculated to be Wednesday, November 7, A.D. 1123.

642. 31 *of* 1906.—(Tamil.) On the west wall of the same maṇṭapa. A record in the fifth year of the Chōḷa king Tribhu-vanachakravartin Rājarājadēva. The shrine is called Uḍaiyār Śrī-Kālakāladēva, at Tirukkaḍavūr in Ākkūr-nāḍu, a district of Jayaṅgoṇḍa-Chōḷa-vaḷanāḍu.

643. 32 *of* 1906.—(Tamil.) On the south wall of the first prākāra of the same temple. A record in the eighteenth year of the Chōḷa king Tribhuvanachakravartin Rājarājadēva. Registers the lamps granted to the temple and the lands reclaimed at Maṇar-kuṇṛu in Erukkāṭṭuchchēri for their maintenanc e. One of the donors is Vēdavanamuḍaiyān Ammaiyappan of Paḷaiyanūr in Mēlmalai-Paḷaiyanūr-nāḍu.

644. 33 *of* 1906.—(Tamil.) On the same wall. A record in the twenty-first year of the Chōḷa king Tribhuvanachakravartin Rājarājadēva. Mentions a document referring to the village, dated in the thirteenth year of Periyadēvar (i.e., Kulōttuṅga III) and quotes the twentieth year of the king. [As Kulōttuṅga III is referred to, the Rājarāja mentioned here should be the third of his name.]

645. 34 *of* 1906.—(Tamil.) On the same wall. A record in the second year of the Chōḷa king Tribhuvanachakravartin Vīra-rājēndra-Chōḷadēva. Records gift of land for lamps to the temple of Uḍaiyār Śrī-Kālakāladēva at Tirukkaḍavūr in Ākkūr-nāḍu, a district of Jayaṅgoṇḍa-Chōḷa-vaḷanāḍu. [Is Vīrarājēndra II, or Kulōttuṅga III, intended ?]

646. 35 *of* 1906.—(Tamil.) On the same wall. A record of the Chōḷa king Tribhuvanachakravartin Rājādhirājadēva, the date of which is lost. Records gift of land for a lamp by a native of Emappērūr in Emappērūr-nāḍu (a subdivision) of Naḍuvil-nāḍu *alias* Rājarājavaḷanāḍu. Another lamp was given by a native of Naḍār in Pāmbura-nāḍu, a district of Uyyakkoṇḍār-vaḷanāḍu (*sic*).

647. 36 *of* 1906.—(Tamil.) On the same wall. A record in the twelfth year of the Chōḷa king Tribhuvanachakravartin Rājādhi-rājadēva (II), " who was pleased to take Madurai and Īḻam (Ceylon). " Records gift of land for a lamp by a native of Pūdalūr in Pūdalūr-vaṭṭam, a district of Pāṇḍikulāśani-vaḷanāḍu.

648. 37 *of* 1906.—(Tamil.) On the same wall. A record in the ninth year of the Chōḷa king Tribhuvanachakravartin Kulōttuṅga-Chōḷadēva (III), " who was pleased to take Madurai." Records gift of land for a lamp by a native of Mūlaṅguḍi in Nallāṟṟūr-nāḍu, a district of Virudarājabhayaṁkara vaḷanāḍu.

649. 38 *of* 1906.—(Tamil.) On the same wall. A record in the ninth year of the Chōḷa king Tribhuvanachakravartin Kulōttuṅga-Chōḷadēva (III, 1186—1216), " who was pleased to take Madurai." Records gift of land at Maṇalkunṟu in Erukkāṭṭuchchēri by a native of Peruṅallūr in Kīḻveṅgai-nāḍu, a district of Rājarāja-vaḷanāḍu.

650. 39 *of* 1906.—(Tamil.) On the same wall. A record in the fourth year of the Chōḷa king Tribhuvanachakravartin Kulōttuṅga-Chōḷadēva. Records gift of land in the same locality by Śekkiḻān Ammai-appan Parāntakadēvan *alias* Karikāla Chōḷa-Pallavaraiyan of Kunṟattūr in Kunṟattūr-nāḍu, a district of Puliyūr-kōṭṭam *alias* Kulōttuṅga-Chōḷa-vaḷanāḍu. [The inscription is very important as it refers to Śekkiḻar of Kunṟattūr who, according to Tamil literary tradition, was the contemporary of Kulōttuṅga II, and author of the *Periapurāṇa*. The poet was rewarded, it is said, by the king with the whole of Toṇḍamaṇḍalam, but as Śēkkiḷār turned an ascetic, the king appointed his brother Pālarāvāya as minister.]

651. 40 *of* 1906.—(Tamil.) On the same wall. A record in the seventeenth year of the Chōḷa king Tribhuvanachakravartin Kulōttuṅga-Chōḷadēva (III, 1178—1216), "who took Madurai and was pleased to take the crowned head of the Pāṇḍya." Records that a certain Svāmidēvar cancelled an order of the king appointing two Śaiva Āchāryas and put in two others who possessed hereditary rights to the office. Mentions the shrine of Kālakāladēva Kūttāḍundēvar, Kulōttuṅga-Chōḷīśvaramuḍaiyār and Vikrama-Chōḷīśvaramuḍaiyār in the temple of Tiruvīrattānamuḍaiyār.

652. 41 *of* 1906.—(Tamil.) On the same wall. A record in the fourteenth year of the Chōḷa king Parakēsarivarman *alias* Tribhuvanachakravartin Rājarājadēva. Records gift of land. The king may be Rājarāja II, but the historical introduction is different.

653. 42 *of* 1906.—(Tamil.) On the same wall. A record in the sixteenth year of the Chōḷa king Parakēsarivarman *alias* Tribhuvanachakravartin Kulōttuṅga-Chōḷadēva (III), "who took Madurai and was pleased to take the crowned head of the Pāṇḍya." Records a gift of land to the image of Rājarāja-Īśvara set up by Araiyan Rājarājadēvar *alias* Vāṇādharāyar.

654. 43 *of* 1906.—(Tamil.) On the same wall. A record in the sixteenth year (Mēsha, Pūrva 8, Thursday, Pushya) of the Chōḷa king Parakēsarivarman *alias* Tribhuvanachakravartin Kulōttuṅga-Chōḷadēva (III), "who was pleased to take Madurai and the crowned head of the Pāṇḍya." Records gift of land to the image of Rājarāja-Īśvara by the *sabhā* of Uḷppaḍamēviya Tirukkaḍavūr in Ambar-nāḍu, a subdivision of Ākkūr-nāḍu, a district of Jayaṅgoṇḍa-Chōḷa-vaḷanāḍu. See *Ep. Ind.*, Vol. IX, p. 213, where it is shown that the date corresponded to 31st March, A.D. 1194. Vīra-Pāṇḍya is said to have taken refuge with his relations in Kollam.

655. 44 *of* 1906.—(Tamil.) On the base of the verandah enclosing the central shrine in the same temple, south side. Records gift of land in the village of Vēḷāṇmaṇai in Kānattūr-nāḍu to the temple of Kālakāladēva at Oḷugamaṅgalam.

656. 45 *of* 1906.—(Tamil.) On the same base. A record in the fourteenth year of the Pāṇḍya king Jaṭāvarman Tribhuvanachakravartin Vīra-Pāṇḍyadēva. Records gift of land. Mentions the forty-first year of the king's predecessor and the shrine of Vikrama-Chōḷīchchuramuḍaiyār. [Is this the king who ascended the throne in A.D. 1253 ?]

657. 46 *of* 1906.—(Tamil.) On the same base. A record in the thirty-fourth year of the Pāṇḍya king Māravarman Tribhuvanachakravartin Kulaśēkharadēva (I? 1268—1308). Records gift of land for forty lamps for the merit of Ulaguḍaiya-Perumāḷ. The country is said to have been in a state of confusion for a long time and the inhabitants to be suffering distress, evidently in consequence of the king's making over a portion of his dominions to his younger brothers. The king resumed the lands and the people returned.

658. 47 *of* 1906.—(Tamil verse.) On the third gōpura of the same temple. A record in Vishaiya (Vrisha ?) of the Vijayanagara king Kṛishṇarāya. A certain Brāhmaṇa named Āpatsahāya of Tirukkaḍavūr repaired the temple. He is said to have taken part in the war against Rāchchūr. The epigraph gives thus an example of a Brahman's military career. For an account of Raichur siege see *Forg. Empe.*, pp. 136–54.

659. 48 *of* 1906.—(Tamil.) On the same gōpura. Records that a native of the Pāṇḍya country presented the *simhāsana* in the bed-room of the God Kālakāladēva.

660. 49 *of* 1906.—(Tamil.) On the same gōpura. A damaged record. Mentions Kāḍavarkōn.

661. 50 *of* 1906.—(Tamil verse.) On the same gōpura. Composed by Kālakāla, king of Ceylon.

662. 51 *of* 1906.—(Tamil.) On the same gōpura. A damaged record of the Pāṇḍya king Perumāḷ-Sundara-Pāṇḍya, the date of which is lost.

663. 52 *of* 1906.—(Tamil.) On the north wall of the Sundarēśvara shrine in the same temple. A record in the tenth year of the Chōḷa king Tribhuvanachakravartin Rājarājadēva. Records gift of land.

*Tirumaṇañjēri.**

664. 1 *of* 1914.—(Tamil.) On the north wall of the central shrine in the Udvāhanāthasvāmin temple. A record in the second year of the Chōḷa king Tribhuvanachakravartin Kulōttuṅga-Chōḷadēva (III). Records gift of money for a lamp to the temple of Tirumaṇañjēri-Uḍaiyār, by a native of Gaṅgaikoṇḍa-śōḷapuram.

665. 2 *of* 1914.—(Tamil.) On the same wall. A record in the twenty-eighth year of the Chōḷa king Rājakēsarivarman *alias* Uḍaiyār Śrī-Rājādhirājadēva I. Records gift of land for feeding annually one thousand devotees including Śivayōgins and tapasvins, in the temple of Tirukkaṟṟaḷi-Mahādēva at Tirumaṇañjēri near Gaṅgaikoṇḍaśōḷa-chaturvēdimaṅgalam in Kurukkaināḍu, a subdivision of Rājēndraśiṅga-vaḷanāḍu, on the occasion of the Paṅguni-uttiram festival.

* One of the holy Saivite centres of the North-Kāvēri region. It has been sung by Jñānasambands and Appar.

666. 3 *of* 1914.—(Tamil.) On the same wall. A damaged record of the Chōḷa king Rājakēsarivarman *alias* Uḍaiyār Śrī-Rājādhirājadēva I in his twenty-seventh year, Rishabha, ba. di. 6, Thursday, Śravaṇa. Registers a gift of land by the *sabhā* of Tirumaṇañjēri to the same temple. The date, according to Mr. Swamikannu Pillai, corresponds to 9th May, A.D. 1045, and "shows that the reign began between May 9, A.D. 1018, and 3rd December 1018, thus reducing Kielhorn's limits by two months."

667. 4 *of* 1914.—(Tamil.) On the same wall. A record of the Chōḷa king Parakēsarivarman *alias* Vikrama-Chōḷadēva (1118—35) in his fifth year Makara, śu. di. 10, Wednesday, Mrigaśira, corresponding to February 7, A.D. 1123. Records gift of land by the great assembly of Karikālaśōḷa-chaturvēdimaṅgalam in Kurukkaināḍu, a subdivision of Vaḍagarai-Virudarājabhayaṅkara-vaḷanāḍu, which had assembled together in the temple of Karikālaśōḷa-Viṇṇagar-Āḻvār situated in the centre of the village.

668. 5 *of* 1914.—(Tamil.) On the north, west and south walls of the same shrine. A record in the eighth year of the Chōḷa king Rājakēsarivarman *alias* Chakravartin Kulōttuṅga-Chōḷadēva I. Records gift of land. States that at the request of Munaiyadaraiyar, the royal secretary *(tirumandira-ōlai)*, Vikkiramaśiṅga-viḻupparaiyar issued the order.

669. 6 *of* 1914.—(Tamil.) On the west wall of the same shrine. A record in the sixteenth year of the Chōḷa king Rājarājakēsarivarman (Rājarāja I). Records gift of 96 sheep for a lamp to the temple of Maṇavāḷapperumāḷ at Tirumaṇañjēri near Viḍēlviḍugu-dēvichaturvēdimaṅgalam which was a *brahmadēya* in Vaḍagarai-Kurukkai-nāḍu, by Māran Tiṭṭai of Ambar, a village in the same nāḍu. *Viḍēlviḍugu* is a title of the Pallava kings, and the place was evidently founded by a Pallava queen.

670. 7 *of* 1914.—(Tamil.) On the same wall. An unfinished record in the ninth year of the Chōḷa king Parakēsarivarman *alias* Rājēndradēva (1050—63). Records gift of a gold diadem to the temple of Tiruverudupāḍi-uḍaiya-Mahādēva at Gaṅgaikoṇḍaśōḷa-chaturvēdimaṅgalam in Kurukkai-nāḍu, a subdivision of Rājādhirājavaḷanāḍu, by Karuṇākaran Muḍigoṇḍaśōḷan *alias* Vaḷavarāja-Mūvēndavēḷān, a native of Koṭṭaiyūr in the same nāḍu.

671. 8 *of* 1914.—(Tamil.) On the same wall. An unfinished record in the fifth year of the Chōḷa king Parakēsarivarman *alias* Chakravartin Vikrama-Chōḷadēva (1118—35). Seems to record a gift of land by the members of the assembly of Gaṅgaikoṇḍaśōḷa-chaturvēdimaṅgalam in Kurukkaināḍu, a subdivision of Virudarājabhayaṅkara-vaḷanāḍu, to the temple of Tirumaṇañjēri-uḍaiya Mahādēva.

672. 9 *of* 1914.—(Tamil.) On the same wall. A record in the sixth year of the Chōḷa king Rājarājakēsarivarman (Rājarāja I).

Registers that, at the command of Uḍaiyapirāṭṭiyār, the mother of Uttama-Chōḷadēva, the *piḍiligai-vāri* Ārūran Kamban *alias* Tirukkaṟṟali-Pichchan of Tirumaṇañjēri gave sixteen *kaḻañju* of gold for sandal paste, offerings, cloth and oil (for lamps) to the God Mahādēva at Tirumaṇañjēri which is here stated to be near the *brahmadēya* of Kaḍalaṅguḍi in Vaḍagarai-Kurukkai-nāḍu. [*Piḍiligai-vāri* has been surmised to be an officer of the temple.]

673. 10 *of* 1914.—(Tamil.) On the west and south walls of the same shrine. Registers an order (fixing the grain emoluments of temple servants) of Uḍaiyapirāṭṭiyār, the officers Kandāḍai-Nambi and Pichchan who constructed the temple at Tirumaṇañjēri and makes provision for the daily expenses in the temple. [Kandāḍai-Nambi reminds one of the Vaishṇava family of the Vādhūlas.

674. 11 *of* 1914.—(Tamil.) On the south wall of the same shrine. A record in the fourth year of the Chōḷa king Parakēsarivarman. Records gift of ninety-six sheep for a lamp, of a lamp-stand and of the stone on which this inscription is engraved, to the temple of Paramasvāmin at Tirumaṇañjēri, by a woman servant *(peṇḍāṭṭi)* attached to the royal kitchen at Tañjāvūr.

675. 12 *of* 1914.—(Tamil.) On the same wall. A record in the seventeenth year of the Chōḷa king Rājarājadēva (III). Records gift of forty-five *kāśu* for a lamp and a lamp-stand made of *tarā*, by a native of Tūṟṟukkuḍi in Paṇaiyūr-nāḍu.

676. 13 *of* 1914.—(Tamil.) On the same wall. Records gift of ninety-six sheep for a lamp by a native of Arkāḍu in Ārkkāṭṭu-kūṟṟam.

677. 14 *of* 1914.—(Tamil.) On the same wall. A record in the fourth year of the Chōḷa king Parakēsarivarman. Records gift of a dish, a trumpet, a hanging lamp, a bell and an image to the same temple by Muṇḍan Araṅgan *alias* Nārppatteṇṇāyira Vanmahēśvara Māyilaṭṭi. It is stated that the stone on which this inscription is engraved was also his gift.

678. 15 *of* 1914.—(Tamil.) On the same wall. Registers the gift of a stone by the residents of Tirūppūkallūr.

679. 16 *of* 1914.—(Tamil.) On the same wall. Records that Māṇavan Maṇṟan *alias* Vīraśeṭṭi presented this stone.

680. 17 *of* 1914.—(Tamil.) On the same wall. Mentions the name of the servant who plays on the pot drum *(kuḍamiḻā)* in the temple of Paramasvāmin at Tirumaṇañjēri.

681. 18 *of* 1914.—(Tamil.) On the same wall. Registers the presentation of a stone to the temple of Tirumaṇañjēri-Āḻvār by a certain Araṅgan Śandirādittan.

682. 19 *of* 1914.—(Tamil.) On the same wall. An incomplete record of the Chōḷa king Parakēsarivarman *alias* Chakravartin

Vikrama-Chōḷadēva (1118—35) in his third year. A portion of the inscription is probably lost.

683. 20 *of* 1914.—(Tamil.) On the same wall. Records gift of the stone by a certain Tāḷi Tiruvaḍikkāri.

684. 21 *of* 1914.—(Tamil.) On the same wall. A record in the second year of the Chōḷa king Rājakēsarivarman. Registers an arrangement made by Uḍaiyapirāṭṭiyār Śembiyan-Mahādēviyār, the mother of Uttama-Chōḷadēva, regarding the various items of expenditure in the temple of Tirukkaṟṟaḷi-Mahādēva at Tirumaṇañjēri, to be met from the income of paddy from the fourteen *vēlis* of land in Mūlanguḍi in Nallāṟṟūr-nāḍu.

685. 22 *of* 1914.—(Tamil.) On the main gōpura of the same temple, left of entrance. States that the gōpura was built by Nallama Nāyakkar of Neḍunguṉṟam.

686. 23 *of* 1914.—(Grantha.) On the second gōpura of the same temple, right of entrance. Quotes certain verses from the *Agnipurāṇa* in praise of the God Udvāhanātha.

687. 24 *of* 1914.—(Tamil.) On the north wall of the central shrine in the Madhyānēśvara temple in the same village. A record of the Pāṇḍya king Jaṭāvarman *alias* Tribhuvanachakravartin Sundara-Pāṇḍyadēva I . . . Sunday, Hasta. Built in at the end. Refers to the eleventh, twelfth and thirteenth years of Kōpperuñjingadēva (1243—80?) and seems to state that a certain person left the village without paying the taxes and concealed himself, but was betrayed by another. The portion dealing with the result is damaged.

688. 25 *of* 1914.—(Grantha and Tamil.) On the same wall. A record of the Pāṇḍya king Jaṭāvarman *alias* Tribhuvanachakravartin Sundara-Pāṇḍya I in his eleventh year, Rishabha (should be *Mithuna*), ba. di. 14, Sunday, Rōhiṇi, corresponding to May 29, A.D. 1261. Commences with the words *samasta-jagad-ādhāra*, etc. Refers to a transaction made in the eleventh year of the reign of Kōpperuñjingadēva (1243—80?) regarding certain lands belonging to the temple of Tiru-Edirkoḷpāḍi Uḍaiyār in Kurukkai-nāḍu, a subdivision of Virudarājabhayaṅkara-vaḷanāḍu.

689. 26 *of* 1914.—(Tamil.) On the same wall. States that provision was made for the worship in and repairs to the temple of Edirkōḷpāḍi-Tambirānār of Tirumaṇañjēri, by a certain Deyvanāyakkan of Arivalam.

690. 27 *of* 1914.—(Tamil.) On the south wall of the same shrine. A record in the third year of the Chōḷa king Tribhuvanachakravartin Kulōttunga-Chōḷadēva (III). Records gift of a night lamp to the temple of Tiru-Edirkoḷpāḍi-Uḍaiyār in Kurukkai-nāḍu, by Araśukkaḍiyān Tirunīlakaṇḍan Śēramāntōḷan of Kīranūr who constructed it of stone.

691. 28 *of* 1914.—(Tamil.) On the same wall. A record in the seventh year of the Chōḷa king Tribhuvanachakravartin Rājarājadēva. Records that the wife of Kaṉṉamaṅgalamuḍaiyār Vīmappiḷḷai and daughter of Puliyūruḍaiyān Ādittadēvan Miḷalai-nāṭṭukkōn gave money and lands for building the shrine of Tirukkāmakkōṭṭam-uḍaiya-Nāchchiyār, a monastery *(guhai)* called after Ālālasundara for the use of Pugaḻivēndar of Pūṇḍi and for offerings, lamps, etc.

Tranquebar.

A history of this place under Danish occupation from the foundation of the fort by Ove Gedde to its purchase by the English is given in *Tanj. Gazr.*, Vol. I, pp. 233—6.

692. 75 *of* 1890.—(Tamil.) On the wall of the Māśilāmaṇīśvara temple. A record in the thirty-seventh year of the Pāṇḍya king Kō-Māravarman Tribhuvanachakravartin Śrī-Kula-śēkharadēva. [Was he the king who ruled from 1268 to 1308 or his namesake who ruled from 1314 to 1321 ?]

693. 76 *of* 1890.—(Tamil.) On a stone built into the floor of the same temple. A record in Ś. 1775 (read 1705) and Kaliyuga 4884, expired, the Śobhakrit year.

694. 77 *of* 1890.—(Tamil.) On a detached stone at the same temple. A record in Prabhava year.

695. A copper plate grant in the Vishṇu temple, dated Ś. 1531 (A.D. 1609). Mr. Sewell's *Antiquities*, Vol. I, p. 273.

Uḍaiyārkōyil.

696. 399 *of* 1902.—(Tamil.) On the south wall of the Karavandīśvara shrine. A record in the sixteenth year of the Chōḷa king Rājakēsarivarman *alias* Tribhuvanachakravartin Kulōttuṅga-Chōḷadēva (I). Records gift of land. See *Ep. Ind.*, Vol. VII, p. 170, where Kielhorn shows that the exact date was Thursday, the 12th March, A.D. 1086.

697. 400 *of* 1902.—(Tamil.) On the same wall. A record in the eighth year of the Chōḷa king Parakēsarivarman *alias* Tribhuvanachakravartin Vikrama-Chōḷadēva (1118—35). Records gift of land.

698. 401 *of* 1902.—(Tamil.) On the same wall. A record in the fourteenth year of the Chōḷa king Rājakēsarivarman *alias* Tribhuvanachakravartin Kulōttuṅga-Chōḷadēva II. Records gift of land for a lamp. See *Ep. Ind.*, Vol. XI, p. 290, where it is pointed out that the date corresponded to Thursday, 10th April 1147.

699. 402 *of* 1902.—(Tamil.) On the same wall. A record in the tenth year of the Chōḷa king Rājakēsarivarman *alias* Tribhuvanachakravartin Rājādhirājadēva. Records gift of land.

700. 403 *of* 1902.—(Tamil.) On the same wall. A record in the thirty-first year of the Chōḷa king Parakēsarivarman *alias* Uḍaiyār Rājēndra-Chōḷadēva (I, 1011—43). Records gift of land. See *Ep. Ind.*, Vol. VII, pp. 169-70, where Dr. Kielhorn calculates the exact date to be Friday, the 23rd July, A.D. 1042.

701. 404 *of* 1902.—(Tamil.) On the west wall of the same shrine. A record in the fifteenth year of the Chōḷa king Parakēsarivarman *alias* Tribhuvanachakravartin Vikrama-Chōḷadēva (1118—1135). Records gift of land for lamps. "The date does not admit of verification." See *Ep. Ind.*, Vol. VII, p. 171.

702. 405 *of* 1902.—(Tamil.) On the north wall of the same shrine. A record in the fourth year of the Chōḷa king Rājakēsarivarman *alias* Tribhuvanachakravartin Kulōttuṅga-Chōḷadēva (II). Records gift of land. See *Ep. Ind.*, Vol. XI, p. 288, where it is pointed out that the date corresponded to Monday, 17th August 1136.

703. 406 *of* 1902.—(Tamil.) On the same wall. A record in the third year of the Chōḷa king Tribhuvanachakravartin Rājēndra-Chōḷadēva. Records gift of land. Dr. Kielhorn gives the English date of the inscription to be Saturday, 20th March, A.D. 1249. See *Ep. Ind.*, Vol. VII, pp. 175-6.

704. 407 *of* 1902. -(Tamil.) On the same wall. A record in the sixth year of the Chōḷa king Parakēsarivarman *alias* Tribhuvanachakravartin Rājarājadēva (II). Records gift of land. See *Ep. Ind.*, Vol. VIII, p. 2, where Dr. Kielhorn points out that the date corresponded to Thursday, 24th January, A.D. 1152.

705. 408 *of* 1902.—(Tamil verse and prose.) On the same wall. A record in the eighteenth year of the Chōḷa king Tribhuvanachakravartin Kulōttuṅga-Chōḷadēva (III) "who took Madura, Ceylon and the crowned head of the Pāṇḍya." Records gift of land.

Vaḻuvūr.

706. 418 *of* 1912.—(Tamil.) On the south wall of the central shrine in the Vīraṭṭānēśvara temple. A partly damaged record in the eleventh year of the Chōḷa king Parakēsarivarman *alias* Tribhuvanachakravartin Rājarājadēva (II). Records gift of money for lamps to the temple of Vīraṭṭānam-Uḍaiyār at Vaḻugūr, a *brahmadēya* in Tiruvaḻundūr-nāḍu which was a district of Jayaṅgoṇḍaśōḷa-vaḷanāḍu. Quotes the sixth year of Periyadēvar Vikrama-Chōḷadēva. [The Government Epigraphist surmises that *Periya Dēvar* may be taken to denote that Vikrama Chōḷa was the father of Rājarāja II.]

707. 419 *of* 1912.—(Tamil.) On the south base of the same shrine. A record of the Chōḷa king Rājarājadēva (II) in his fifteenth year Tulā, ba. di. 10, Tuesday, Āyilyam (=Tuesday, 27th September 1160). Registers gift of money (100 *kāśus*) with lands described for two lamps and two lamp-stands, one of which was given by a native of Śiṟṟārkāḍu in Ārkāṭṭu-kūṟṟam of Pāṇḍyakulāśani-vaḷanāḍu, for the merit of Kuṇḍavvai.

708. 420 *of* 1912.—(Tamil.) On the south wall of the maṇṭapa in front of the same shrine. A record in the third year of the Chōḷa king Parakēsarivarman *alias* Tribhuvanachakravartin-Vīrarājēndradēva (i.e., Kulōttuṅga III). Built in the middle. Records gift of land by purchase for offerings to the image of Vādavūr-Nāyanār set up in the temple of Tiruvīraṭṭānam Uḍaiyār by a native of Mūlaṅguḍi in Vēḷā-nāḍu, a subdivision of Kulōttuṅga-śōḷa-vaḷanāḍu. Records also gift of money for other articles required for worship. See note to the next epigraph.

709. 421 *of* 1912.—(Tamil.) On the same wall. A record of the Chōḷa king Tribhuvanachakravartin Rājādhirājadēva (II) in his fifth year, Karkāṭaka, śu. di. 13, Saturday (=1st July, 1167). Built in the middle. Records gift of money by the same individual for getting the *Tiruvembāvai* recited before the image of Vādavūraḷi-Nāyanār in the temple on Mārgaḷi-Tiruvādirai festival and for also maintaining the festival of Paṅguni. Tiruvādavūrār was the celebrated Māṇikkavāśaga, the contemporary of Varaguṇa Pāṇḍya, in the ninth century and the author of the *Tiruvembāvai*.

710. 422 *of* 1912.—(Tamil.) On the same wall. A record of the Vijayanagara king Vīra-Bokkaṇa-Uḍaiyār (i.e., Bukka II, 1399—1406) in Ś. 1324, Chitrabhānu. Records that certain lands *(paṟṟu)* which had been submerged and lying waste for some years on account of flood in the Kāvēri were brought under cultivation, being granted favourable concessions in the payment of assessment. The lands belonged to Vaḷuvūr in Tiruvaḻundūr-nāḍu, a subdivision of Eḻumuṟi-paṟṟu. See *Ep. Rep.*, 1913, pp. 118-9, for a full summary of the concessions given. The record is very interesting as it illustrates the fiscal policy of the age.]

711. 423 *of* 1912.—(Tamil.) On the same wall. A record in the thirty-third year of the Chōḷa king Parakēsarivarman *alias* Tribhuvanachakravartin Tribhuvanavīradēva (1178—1216) " who being pleased to take Madurai (Madura), Īḻam (Ceylon), Karuvūr and the crowned head of the Pāṇḍya, was pleased to perform the anointment of heroes and the anointment of victors." Built in at the end. Records gift of money by a Brāhmaṇa lady to the shrine of Tiruchchattimuṟṟam-Uḍaiyār consecrated by her in the twenty-ninth year of the king in the temple of Tiru-Vīraṭṭānam-Uḍaiyār at Vaḷugūr, a *brahmadēya* in Tiruvaḻundūr-nāḍu, a subdivision of Jayaṅgoṇḍaśōḷavaḷanāḍu.

712. 424 *of* 1912.—(Tamil.) On the west wall of the same maṇṭapa. A record of the Vijayanagara king Pratāpadēvarāya-Mahārāya (II) in Ś. 1356, Pramādin, Mithuna, . . . 5. Built in at the end. Seems to refer to certain additions made to the temple from the year Śōbhakrit when, apparently, a tank and an irrigation channel were constructed.

713. 425 *of* 1912.—(Tamil.) On the same wall. A record of the Chōḷa king . . . Tribhuvanachakravartin Rājēndra-Chōḷa-dēva (III) in his second year, Dhanus, śu. di. 4, Monday, Tiruvōṇam. Built in the middle. Records gift of money for a lamp. Begins with an unusual historical introduction *pūmaruviya tirumaḍandai*, etc. (the usual introduction being *Bhūmiyumtiruvum*). The money was received by the temple authorities and a land assigned for the amount. The king is said to have established the six systems of religion and been obeyed by all kings including the Śēraḷas.

714. 426 *of* 1912.—(Tamil.) On the north wall of the same maṇṭapa. A record of the Pāṇḍya king Jaṭāvarman Tribhuvanachakravartin Sundara-Pāṇḍyadēva III in his fifth (sixth) year, Makara, śu. di., Wednesday, Śōdi, corresponding to 30th December 1276. Registers that a tenant of the temple having absconded without paying his dues, the amount was recovered from a man who had stood surety for him, by selling his land.

715. 427 *of* 1912.—(Tamil.) On the same wall. A record of the Chōḷa king Parakēsarivarman *alias* Tribhuvanachakravartin Kulōttuṅga-Chōḷadēva (III) in his second year, Rishabha, śu. di. 5th, Thursday, Tiruvōṇam, corresponding to the 15th May 1180. Records gift of money for a lamp to the same temple by a native of Mōḍappākkam in Śurattūr-nāḍu, a subdivision of Puliyūr-kōṭṭam *alias* Kulōttuṅgaśōḷa- vaḷanāḍu in Jayaṅgoṇḍaśōḷa-maṇḍalam.

716. 428 *of* 1912.—(Tamil.) On the same wall. A record of the Chōḷa king Rājakēsarivarman *alias* Tribhuvanachakravartin Rājādhirājadēva (II) in the fifteenth year, Simha, ba. di. 8, Thursday, Rohaṇi, corresponding to 18th August 1177. Records gift of money for purchasing land to maintain a lamp in the temple of Tiruvīraṭṭānam Uḍaiyār at Vaḷugūr, by a native of Tīyaṅguḍi in Tiruvārūrkūṟṟam, a subdivision of Gēyamāṇikka-vaḷanāḍu. The land was situated at Kīraṅguḍi, a hamlet of Vīrarājēndra-chaturvēdimaṅgalam which was a *brahmadēya* in Tiruvaḷundūr-nāḍu. Mentions the sixteenth year of Rājarāja (II).

717. 429 *of* 1912.—(Tamil.) On the north verandah of the first prākāra of the same temple. A record in the fifth year of the Chōḷa king Rājakēsarivarman *alias* Tribhuvanachakravartin Vīrarājēndradēva (i.e., Kulōttuṅga-Chōḷa III). Registers the construction of the shrine of the goddess in the north-west corner of the north verandah by Ēkavāchakan Ulagukaṇviḍutta-perumāḷ *alias* Vānakōvaraiyar, chief of Toṇḍa-nāḍu in Muḍigoṇḍaśōḷa-vaḷanāḍu. Also records a gift of money in the eighth year of the king for purchasing land and maintaining worship in the same shrine.

718. 430 *of* 1912.—(Tamil.) On either side of the entrance into the main gōpura of the same temple. Records in Subhānu the construction of the gōpura and the prākāra wall by Aḷagapperumāḷ-Piḷḷai, son of Gāṅgēyar Gaṇapatināyinār-Piḷḷai of Nallāvūr in Iruṅgōḷappāṇḍi-nāḍu.

719. 431 *of* 1912.—(Tamil.) On the four sides of the same gōpura. Records the gift of Bhikshāṭanamūrti, the main gōpura, the prākāra wall and the street, by the same Aḷagapperumāḷ-Piḷḷai.

720. 432 *of* 1912.—(Tamil.) On a slab set up in a grove in the same village. Records in Durmukha gift of land *(mukkālvaṭṭam, nattam and tiḍal)* in Vaḷavarāyakuppam by the residents of that village including Tambā-Piḷḷai.

NANNILAM TALUK.

Kuḻikkarai.

721. 82 *of* 1911.—(Tamil.) On the south wall of the Kāḷahastīśvara temple. A record in the twenty-eighth year of Tribhuvanachakravartin Kōnērinmaikoṇḍān. Records gift of the brokerage fee *(taragu)* which remained in arrears from the fifth year of the king to the temple of Tirunaṅgāḷīśvaram-Uḍaiyār by the *nagarattār* of Oṭṭakkuḍi (evidently Kuḻikkarai) *alias* Edirilišōḷapuram in Arumoḻidēva-vaḷanāḍu. [Mr. Krishna Sastri identifies the king with Kulōttuṅga III on the ground that the inscription mentions Īśvaraśiva who, we know from inscriptions at Tribhuvanam, was the preceptor of that king.]

722. 83 *of* 1911.—(Tamil.) On the same wall. This stone temple was built by Iṅgaikkuḍaiyār Karuṇākaradēvar *alias* Gurukularāyar.

723. 84 *of* 1911.—(Tamil.) On the same wall. A record of the Chōḷa king Tribhuvanachakravartin Rājēndra-Chōḷadēva III (1245—67). Records gift of land for offerings by the *nagarattār* of the same village to the shrine of the goddess which was built by a certain Śiraikkāvūruḍaiyān Tyāgapperumāḷ.

Śrivāñjiyam.

Though mentioned in the *Dēvāram*, this place has no ancient epigraphs. This is due, most probably, to the vandalism of later repairers. See No. 731 below.

724. 63 *of* 1911.—(Tamil.) On the south wall of the central shrine in the Vāñjīśvara temple. A damaged record in the thirteenth year of the Chōḷa king Tribhuvanachakravartin Rājarājadēva. Built in on the right side. Seems to record gift of lamps.

725. 64 *of* 1911.—(Tamil.) On the same wall. An unfinished record in the third year of the Chōḷa king Tribhuvanachakravartin Rājādhirājadēva. Records gift of money for five lamps to the temple of Tiruvāñjīyadēva of Tiruvāñjiyam in Panaiyūr-nāḍu, a subdivision of Kulōttuṅga-chōḷa-vaḷanāḍu.

726. 65 *of* 1911.—(Tamil.) On the same wall. An unfinished record in the eleventh year of the Chōḷa king Rājakēsarivarman *alias* Tribhuvanachakravartin Rājādhirājadēva (II). Contains only the historical introduction *kaḍalśūḻnda*, etc.

727. 66 *of* 1911.—(Tamil.) On the north wall of the maṇṭapa in front of the same shrine. An unfinished record in the twenty-fourth year of the Chōḷa king Tribhuvanachakravartin Rājarājadēva. Built in at the beginning. It gives a list of lands owned by the temple and its subordinate shrines.

728. 67 *of* 1911.—(Tamil.) On the base of the south verandah in the same temple. An unfinished record in the twenty-second year of the Pāṇḍya king Jaṭāvarman Tribhuvanachakravartin Vīra-Pāṇḍyadēva. Seems to record a sale of land. [The king was not improbably he who came to the throne in A.D. 1253 and who conquered Īḻam, Koṅgu and Śōḻamaṇḍalam and had the anointment of victor at Perumbaṟṟappuliyūr.]

729. 68 *of* 1911.—(Tamil.) On the same base. A record in the tenth year of the Pāṇḍya king Jaṭāvarman Tribhuvanachakravartin Sundara-Pāṇḍyadēva. Built in at the end. Records sale of land to the temple by a native of Rājagambhīra-chaturvēdi-maṅgalam which was a surname of Tiruvāñjiyam. See No. 730.

730. 69 *of* 1911.—(Tamil.) On the same base. A record in the eleventh year of the Pāṇḍya king Jaṭāvarman Tribhuvanachakravartin Sundara-Pāṇḍyadēva. Built in at the end. Records another sale of land by a private individual who is stated to have acquired it as *samskāra-dakshiṇa*. [It is not certain which of the three kings of this name is intended.]

731. 70 *of* 1911.—(Tamil.) On the north wall of the Maṅgaḷāmbā shrine in the same temple. An unfinished record in the eighteenth year of the Chōḷa king Tribhuvanachakravartin Rājarājadēva. Refer to the building of the shrine and the consecration of the goddess in the temple of Tiruvāñjiyamuḍaiya-Nāyanār. On this occasion a gift of land and a house appears also to have been made.

732. 71 *of* 1911.—(Tamil.) On the same wall. A damaged record in the twentieth year of the Chōḷa king Tribhuvanachakravartin Rājarājadēva. Seems to register gifts of lands made to the temple in different years of the king's reign. Mentions Perumbaṟṟappuliyūr and Tiruveḷḷarai.

733. *72 of* 1911.—(Tamil.) On a pillar of the Dakshiṇāmūrti shrine in the same temple. A damaged and mutilated record in the thirty-ninth year of the Chōḷa king Rājakēsarivarman *alias* Tribhuvanachakravartin Kulōttuṅga-Chōḷadēva (I ?). Records gift of land to the goddess Tiruppaḷḷiyarai-Nambiraṭṭiyār who was presented to the temple of Tiruvāñjiyamuḍaiya-Mahādēva by a native of Kōmaṅguḍi.

734. *73 of* 1911.—(Tamil.) On the south wall of the first prākāra of the same temple. A damaged record in the twenty-second year of the Pāṇḍya king Tribhuvanachakravartin Vīra-Pāṇḍyadēva. Seems to record a sale of land to the temple.

735. *74 of* 1911.—(Tamil.) On the north wall of the same prākāra. A much damaged record in the twenty-third year of the Pāṇḍya king Jaṭāvarman *alias* Tribhuvanachakravartin Sundara-Pāṇḍyadēva. Records sale of land to the temple by a native of Śirupanṟūr in Vēḷa-nāḍu.

736. *75 of* 1911.—(Tamil.) On the same wall. A much damaged record in the twelfth year of the Pāṇḍya king Māravarman Tribhuvanachakravartin Sundara-Pāṇḍyadēva (I ?). Records sale of land at Śirupanṟūr by a native of Vaḍa-Kaṇṇamaṅgalam.

737. *76 of* 1911.—(Tamil.) On the same wall. A record in the eleventh year of the Pāṇḍya king Māravarman Tribhuvanachakravartin Sundara-Pāṇḍyadēva. Records sale of land. See the above epigraph.

738. *77 of* 1911.—(Tamil.) On the second inner gōpura of the same temple; left side. A record of the Nāyaka (Tanjore) king Raghunātha-Nāyakkar (1614—?) in Śārvari. Records gift of certain taxes to the dancing girls of Tiruvāñjiyam for the merit of the king's agent Mādayya-Nāyakka-Mallappa Nāyakka.

739. *78 of* 1911.—(Tamil.) On the same gōpura; right side. A damaged record. Seems to refer to the same or a similar gift.

740. *79 of* 1911.—(Tamil.) On a slab set up in a field of the same village. Records in Ś. 1501, Īśvara (wrong) that a certain Perumānayinār Paṇḍāram of Achchuṟṟamaṅgalam, who was a pupil of Aghōraśivāchārya of the Bhikshā-maṭha at Chidambaram, purchased one *vēli* of land at Kunduvāñjēri for his *maṭha*. See Cd. 72.

Tiruchcheṅgāṭṭaṅguḍi.

This place is well known as the native place of Saint Śiruttoṇḍa who was a contemporary of Gñānasambanda, who figures in the *Periapurāṇa*, and who was present in the battle of Vātāpi about 642. See *S.I.I.*, Vol. II, p. 172, for his idol set up at Tanjore. Śaivite tradition connects it with God Gaṇapati's victory over a demon, thereby giving rise to the name of the shrine Gaṇapatīchchuram. It has been sung by Gñānasambanda and Appar.

741. 51 *of* 1913.—(Tamil.) On the north wall of the central shrine in the Uttarāpatīśvara temple. An unfinished record of the Vijayanagara king Vīra-Viruppaṇṇa-Uḍaiyār (II), i.e., Virūpāksha I, son of Vīra-Ariyarāya (Harihara II) in Ś. 1306, Raktākshi. Seems to record a gift of land to the shrine of Gaṇapatīśuram Uḍaiya-Nāyinār and Uttarā-pati-Nāyaka at Tiruchcheṅgāṭṭaṅguḍi in Marugal-nāḍu which was a subdivision of Gēyamāṇikkavaḷa-nāḍu by the chief Sōmaya-Daṇṇāyakkar.

742. 52 *of* 1913.—(Tamil.) On the wall to the left of the dvārapāla images in front of the same shrine. A record of the Vijayanagara king Vīra-Bhūpatirāya-Uḍaiyār (1409—22) in Ś. 1332, Khara. Records gift of a lamp to the temple of Uttarāpati-Nāyaka at Tiruchcheṅgāṭṭaṅguḍi by a native of Pālaiyūr *alias* Malaikiḷānvaḷam in Ūṟṟukkāṭṭu-kōṭṭam, a district of Toṇḍai-maṇḍalam.

743. 53 *of* 1913.—(Tamil.) On the south wall of the maṇṭapa in front of the same shrine. A damaged record in Viśvāvasu. Registers a gift of land and houses to certain merchants connected with the treasury of Uttarāpati-Nāyakar, on their having presented a throne to the temple.

744. 54 *of* 1913.—(Tamil.) On the west wall of the same maṇṭapa. A damaged record in Plavaṅga. Seems to provide for a festival in the same temple by the merchants of the Chōḷa country.

745. 55 *of* 1913.—(Tamil.) On the west wall of the Gaṇa-patīśvara shrine in the same temple. A record in the thirty-second year of the Chōḷa king Rājakēsarivarman *alias* Uḍaiyār Śrī-Rājā-dhirājadēva (I ?). Records sale of land as *iṟaili* to the temple of Gaṇapatīśuram uḍaiya-Mahādēva at Tiruchcheṅgāṭṭaṅguḍi by the assembly of the village Tirukkaṇṇapuram, a *brahmadēya* in Marugal-nāḍu which was a subdivision of Kshatriyaśikhāmaṇi vaḷa-nāḍu. The assembly is stated to have met together in the temple of Piramīśvaramuḍaiya-Mahādēva of their village. Śīrāḷa was the son of Śiruttoṇḍa who was sacrificed to Śiva when he came as a guest of Śiruttoṇḍa. The price of 2,450 *kuḻis* or 1⅜ *nilas* has been given as 115 *kāśus*.

746. 56 *of* 1913.—(Tamil.) On the same wall. A record in the third year of the Chōḷa king Rājakēsarivarman Rājarājadēva (I). Records gift of land for two lamps to the shrine of Śīrāḷadēva at Tiruchcheṅgāṭṭukkuḍi by a certain Veḷḷāḷan Uḷagan Śiṟṟiyan *alias* Tappillā Mūvēndavēḷan.

747. 57 *of* 1913.—(Tamil.) On the same wall. A record in the nineteenth year of the Chōḷa king Rājarāja-Rājakēsarivar-man *alias* Rājarājadēva (I). Records gift of land for feeding the devotees attending the festival of Śittirai Tiruvādirai when the

God Śīrāḷadēvar of Tiruchcheṅgāṭṭukkuḍi in Marugal-nāḍu, a subdivision of Mummuḍiśōḷa-vaḷanāḍu, was taken in procession to the maṇṭapa of Śiruttoṇḍa-Nambi in that temple.

748. 58 *of* 1913.—(Tamil.) On the same wall. A record in the third year of the Chōḷa king Parakēsarivarman *alias* Tribhuvanachakravartin Rājēndra-Chōḷadēva (I). Records gift of land at Īkkāḍu *alias* Perumūr to the temple of Gaṇapatīśvaram-Uḍaiyār of Tiruchcheṅgāṭṭaṅguḍi by a certain Tāyan Tiruchchiṟṟambalamuḍaiyān, for maintaining the same festival.

749. 59 *of* 1913.—(Tamil.) On the north wall of the same shrine. A record in the nineteenth year of the Chōḷa king Rāja-rāja-Rājakēsarivarman *alias* Rājarājadēva (I). Records gift of land (3 *mās*) for the festival *(tiruviḻā)* of Śiruttoṇḍa-Nambi who was a devotee of Śīrāḷadēva of Tiruchcheṅgāttaṅguḍi, by two residents of Marugal. Refers to the " Revenue Survey " made in the seventeenth year of Rājarāja (உலகளந்தநீனடி).

750. 60 *of* 1913.—(Tamil.) On the same wall. A record in the fifth year of the Chōḷa king Parakēsarivarman. Records gift of land by purchase to the temple of Paramēśvara at Tiruchcheṅgāṭṭaṅguḍi by the assembly of Marugal in order to provide for two lamps in that temple.

751. 61 *of* 1913.—(Tamil.) On the same wall. A record of the Chōḷa king Rājadhirāja I. Fragment containing portions of the historical introduction beginning with *tiṅgaḷēr taru.*

752. 62 *of* 1913.—(Tamil.) On the same wall. A record in the eleventh year of the Chōḷa king Parakēsarivarman. Records sale of land for a lamp by the assembly of Marugal.

753. 63 *of* 1913.—(Tamil.) On the west base of the maṇṭapa in front of the same temple. A record of the Chōḷa king Tribhuvanachakravartin Rājarājadēva (III) in his third year, Karkāṭaka (wrong for Rishabha), śu. di. 11, Monday, Attam, corresponding to Monday, 7th May 1218. Built in at the right end. Records gift of land to the shrines of Uttarāpati-Nāyaka and Śiruttoṇḍadēva in the temple of Uttarāpatināyaka by two residents of Maruṅgūr *alias* Rājanārāyaṇachaturvēdimaṅgalam.

754. 64 *of* 1913.—(Tamil.) On the north wall of the same maṇṭapa. A record in the forty-fifth year of the Chōḷa king Tribhuvanachakravartin Kulōttuṅga-Chōḷadēva (III). Records gift of land for providing garlands of red lilies to the two shrines of Gaṇapatīśvaram-Uḍaiyār and Uttarāpati-Nāyaka by the residents of Tiruchcheṅgāṭṭaṅguḍi, a village in Marugal-nāḍu, which was a subdivision of Gēyamāṇikka-vaḷanāḍu.

755. 65 *of* 1913.—(Tamil.) On the same wall. A record of the Chōḷa king Parakēsarivarman *alias* Tribhuvanachakravartin Kulōttuṅga-Chōḷadēva (III), " who took Madurai (Madura) and was pleased to take the crowned head of the Pāṇḍya," in his eleventh year and 175th day, Vrischika, ba. di. 14, Friday, Anilam. Registers that a document connected with the temple of Tiruvirāmanandīśvaram-Uḍaiyār at Tirukkaṇṇapuram, a *brahmadēya* village of Marugal-nāḍu in Gēyamāṇikka-vaḷanāḍu, was engraved on the walls of the temple at Tiruchcheṅgāṭṭaṅguḍi, as the former was evidently not constructed of stone. The record refers to the fifth and tenth years of Periyadēvar Kulōttuṅga-Chōḷadēva in whose time the Tirukkaṇṇapuram temple came into existence. Mr. Swamikannu Pillai points out that eleventh is an error for twenty-second year; that the date corresponds to Friday, 19th November 1199, and that the 175th day shows that the reign began on 23rd May, A.D. 1178.

756. 66 *of* 1913.—(Tamil.) On the same wall. A record of the Chōḷa king Tribhuvanachakravartin Kulōttuṅga-Chōḷadēva (III), "who took Madurai (Madura) and was pleased to take the crowned head of the Pāṇḍya" in his eighteenth year and 330th day. Records gift of land by purchase for laying out a road to carry in procession Śīrāḷapiḷḷaiyār from the maṇṭapa of Śiruttoṇḍadēvar at Tiruchcheṅgāṭṭaṅguḍi to the village of Tiru-Marugal. Refers to the land survey made in the sixteenth year of Kulōttuṅga-Chōḷadēva (I), "who abolished tolls."

757. 67 *of* 1913.—(Tamil.) On the same wall. A record in the eighteenth year and 330th day of the king of the Chōḷa king Tribhuvanachakravartin Kulōttuṅga-Chōḷadēva (III), "who took Madurai (Madura) and was pleased to take the crowned head of the Pāṇḍya." Registers the remission of taxes in favour of the temple, for maintaining the worship of Śīrāḷapiḷḷaiyār. Refers also to the eleventh year of Kulōttuṅga-Chōḷadēva, "who abolished tolls."

758. 68 *of* 1913.—(Tamil.) On the same wall. Records that the grants registered in the above two inscriptions were caused to be made by Savaṇṇachakravartin of Veḷichchēri, by the lady devotee, Alliyaṅgōdai-ammai and Āṇḍār Viḷaṅguḍaiyār Śiruttoṇḍār.

759. 69 *of* 1913.—(Tamil.) On the north base of the same maṇṭapa. A record of the Chōḷa king Tribhuvanachakravartin Rājarājadēva (III), in his twenty-fourth year, Simha, ba. di. 13, Saturday, Pūśam. Records gift of land by Araśūruḍaiyān Tiruchchiṟṟambalamuḍaiyān *alias* Tiruchchiṟṟambala-Pallavaraiyan for providing offerings in the maṇṭapa called Tirumuttuvānēri to the God Uttarāpati-Nāyaka on the occasion when he was to give salvation to his devotee during the festival of *Śittirai-Baraṇi*. [Bhairava was the form in which Śiva came from the north and gave salvation to Śiruttoṇḍa.]

760. 70 *of* 1913.—(Tamil.) On the same base. A record of the Chōḷa king Parakēsarivarman *alias* Tribhuvanachakravartin-

Kulōttuṅga-Chōḷadēva (III), "who was pleased to take Madurai (Madura)," in his tenth year and 123rd day. Built in at the beginning. The king is called Tribhuvanachakravartin Kōnērinmaikoṇḍān. Seems to record the grant of landed property to a certain Rājēndraśōḷa-Achāriyan, who was perhaps the temple architect. The Royal Secretary *(tirumandira-ōlai)* was Rājēndraśiṅga-Mūvēndavēḷan.

761. *71 of* 1913.—(Tamil.) On the same base. An unfinished record of the Chōḷa king Tribhuvanachakravartin, the date of which is lost. Seems to record a gift of land in the villages Tiruveṭṭaikaṭṭaḷai and Dinachintāmaṇi-chaturvēdimaṅgalam for providing offerings on every day of Bharaṇi to the God Uttarāpati.

762. *72 of* 1913.—(Tamil.) On the east, north and west walls of the Vatāpi-Gaṇapati shrine in the same temple. A much damaged record of the Chōḷa king Tribhuvanachakravartin Kulōttuṅga-Chōḷadēva (III), "who was pleased to take Madurai (Madura), Īḷam (Ceylon), Karuvūr and the crowned head of the Pāṇḍya," in his twenty-second year and 130th day. Seems to register a number of lands acquired for constructing the third prākāra of the temple and a street round it. Reference is also frequently made to the reign of Kulōttuṅga-Chōḷa I, "who was pleased to abolish tolls," and to the temple of Vikrama-Chōḷīśvara.

763. *73 of* 1913.—(Tamil.) On the east wall of the same shrine. This wall is the gift of Vaṭṭavārśaḍaiyan Rājasūriyappallavaraiyan of Puduvūr.

764. *74 of* 1913.—(Tamil.) On the second gōpura of the same temple, right of entrance. A record in Ānanda of Paṭṭukkaṭṭāri Kōnēridēva-Mahārāja. Records gift of taxes to the temple of Uttarāpati-Nāyaka at the request of Māḷuvachakravartin for maintaining certain festivals.

765. *75 of* 1913.—(Tamil.) In the same place. A much damaged record of the Vijayanagara king Viruppaṇṇa-Uḍaiyār (II), i.e., Virūpaksha I, son of Vīra-Ariyappa-Uḍaiyār (Harihara II), in Ś. 1306, Raktākshi, Kumbha, ba. di. 10, Sunday, Mūla, corresponding to 5th February 1385. Seems to record a gift of land.

766. *76 of* 1913.—(Tamil.) In the same place, left of entrance. A record in the seventh year of the Pāṇḍya king Tribhuvanachakravartin Parākrama-Pāṇḍyadēva. Records gift of two *vēlis* of land at Maruṅgūr for repairs in the temple of Uttarāpati-Nāyaka. Refers to the Śīrāḷān-Siruttoṇḍan-maḍam in the temple of Gaṇapatīśuramuḍaiya-Nāyanār.

767. *77 of* 1913.—(Grantha and Tamil.) In the same place. A damaged record of the Chōḷa king Parakēsarivarman *alias* Rājādhirājanarapati Rājēndra-Chōḷa (III, 1245—67), "who cut off the heads of two Pāṇḍya kings." Supplies a long list of the Sanskrit *birudas* of the king. Seems to record a gift of land to the God

Uttarāpati-Nāyaka in the temple of Gaṇapatīśvaram-Uḍaiyār for the purpose of the Bharaṇi festival in the months of *Sittirai* and *Arpaśi.* Among the achievements of the king are mentioned his capture of the stronghold of Vīra-Rākshasa, which was called Uttara Laṅka and which Mr. Krishna Sastri surmises to be a place near Rājahmundry in the Gōdāvari delta; his victory over two Pāṇḍyas; and his power over the Karnāṭa king Sōmēśvara of the Hoysaḷa dynasty. Vīra-Rākshasa is said to be the sole hero of the Vaḍugas, and Rājēndra's campaign against him was perhaps due to a general war against Kōpperuñjiṅga who had territory as far as Drākshārāma and who had given a good deal of trouble to Rājarāja III. Rājēndrachōḷa's time was thus one of genuine attempt to revive the Chōḷa greatness. For the relations between Rājēndra and Sōmēśvara see 49 of 1913 at Śivāyam (Trichinopoly district).

768. 78 *of* 1913.—(Tamil.) In the same place. A damaged and unfinished record of the Vijayanagara king Vīra-Viruppaṇṇa-Uḍaiyār II, *i.e.*, Virūpāksha I, in Ś. 1322, Pramādi, Mēsha, ba. di. 12, Friday, Uttiraṭṭādi corresponding to Friday, 2nd May, 1399. Seems to provide for certain festivals in the temple of Uttarāpati-Nāyaka.

769. 79 *of* 1913.—(Tamil.) In the same place. A fragmentary record in Ś. 1394, Nandana, Simha, su. di., Monday, Attam. Seems to record a gift of land by purchase at Paḷūr in Vadagāl Marugal-nāḍu which was a subdivision of Gēyamāṇikka-vaḷanāḍu, for offerings to the temple of Uttarāpati-Nāyaka by a native of Nandīśvaram in Toṇḍaimaṇḍalam.

770. 80 *of* 1913.—(Tamil.) On the west wall of the maṇṭapa in front of the Chūḷikāmbā shrine in the same temple. A record of the Chōḷa king Rājādhirājadēva (II), "who was pleased to take Madurai (Madura) and Īḷam (Ceylon)," in the thirteenth year, Simha, ba. di. 9, Wednesday, corresponding to 24th July 1174. Some stones are missing. Seems to record the sale of four women as *dēvaraḍiyār* to the temple of Tiruvālaṅgāḍuḍaiya-Nāyanār for 700 *kāśu.*

771. 81 *of* 1913.—(Tamil.) On the main gōpura of the same temple, right of entrance. A damaged record in Prajāpati. Seems to record the fees on looms, etc., fixed by an agent of Vīra-Nara-śiṅgarāya-Ayyan.

772. 82 *of* 1913.—(Tamil.) On the same gōpura left of entrance. A record of the Chōḷa king Rājakēsarivarman *alias* Tribhuvanachakravartin Rājādhirājadēva (II), the date of which is lost. Begins with the introduction *kaḍal-śūḻnda,* etc. Refers to a certain Kaḍuvaṇguḍaiyān Araiyan Āṭkoṇḍa-Nāyakan who was perhaps the donor.

Tirukkaṇḍiśvaram (Tirukkoṇḍichchuram).

This is one of the Śaivite centres of the South-Kāvēri region, where Kāmadhēnu worshipped Śiva. Hence the name Paśupatīsvara. It has been sung by Appar.

773. 80 *of* 1911.—(Tamil.) On the south wall of the maṇṭapa in front of the central shrine in the local Paśupatīśvara temple. Dated in Ś. 1439 (A.D. 1517), Iśvara, in the reign of Kṛishṇa dēva Rāya. Records gift of taxes bestowed from Vejavāḍai (Bezwada) in favour of the Tirukkoṇḍīśvara temple on the king's return from the victorious tour in the east. The inscription refers to the capture of the fortress of Udayagiri and of Tirumalai Rāhuttarāya (its governor ?), the subjugation of Vīnukoṇḍa, Nāgārjunakoṇḍa, Koṇḍavīḍu, Koṇḍapalli, Rājamahēndrapura, etc.

Tirukkoḷḷambūdūr.

This place is famous in Śaivite tradition as the scene where Gñānasambanda saved himself and his following from the freshes of the Kāvēri. It is the theme of the *padika* கொட்டமேகமழுங்கொள் ளம்பூதூர் . . .

774. 1 *of* 1899.—(Tamil.) On the south wall of the first prākāra of the Bilvāraṇyēśvara temple. A record in the fourth year of the Chōḷa king Parakēsarivarman *alias* Tribhuvanachakravartin Kōnērimēnkoṇḍān (i.e., Kulōttuṅga III). Records the gift of the village of Kulōttuṅga-śōḷa-Kaḷattūr to a private individual.

775. 2 *of* 1899.—(Tamil.) On the same wall. A record in the thirtieth year of the Chōḷa king Tribhuvanachakravartin Tribhuvanavīradēva (Kulōttuṅga III), "who took Madura, Ceylon, Karuvūr and the crowned head of the Pāṇḍya." Records gift of land for two lamps.

Tirumāḷam.

The place is one of great social interest as the Brahmans of the Prathamaśākha sect generally known as midday Pariahs owe their existence to a religious sacrifice here. See *Tanj. Gazr.*, Vol. I, pp. 237-8, for details.

776. 93 *of* 1910.—(Tamil.) On the south wall of the central shrine in the Māgāḷēśvara temple. A damaged record in the forty-second year of the Chōḷa king Rājakēsarivarman *alias* Chakravartin Śrī-Kulōttuṅga-Chōḷadēva (I ?). Registers an order of the king from his throne Vāṇādhirājan in the hall Rājēndrachōḷan of his palace at Muḍigoṇḍa-Chōḷapuram. Mentions the temple of Ambar-Tirumāgāḷam-Uḍaiyār in Ambar-nāḍu, a subdivision of Uyyakoṇḍār vaḷanāḍu.

777. 94 *of* 1910.—(Tamil.) On the west wall of the same shrine. A record in the forty-second year of the Chōḷa king Rājakēsarivarman *alias* Chakravartin Śrī-Kulōttuṅga-Chōḷadēva (I ?).

Records gift of the village Puravuvarivilagam which was a *dēvadāna* of the temple to a certain Tiruchchirrambala-Nandarājan of Māttūr at the request of Nuḷambarājan.

778. 95 *of* 1910.—(Tamil.) On the north wall of the same shrine. A record in the forty-second year of the Chōḷa king Kulōttuṅga-Chōḷadēva (I). Records gift of the village of Vādaṇḍūr (?), a *dēvadāna* of the temple to a certain Udayamārtāṇḍan of Ambar, at the request of the same chief.

779. 96 *of* 1910.—(Tamil.) On the same wall. A record in the forty-second year of the Chōḷa king Rājakēsarivarman *alias* Tribhuvanachakravartin Śrī-Kulōttuṅga-Chōḷadēva (I). Records gift of the village of Eyinikuḍi, also a *dēvadāna* of the temple, to a certain Śerkaḷān Veḷān Tiruvāykkulamuḍaiyān at the request of the same chief, as previous Kāṇiyāḷas had neglected it so as not to yield even the *Antarāya-kāśu.* "The tenants could neither clear their old arrears nor grow fresh crops on them without breaks."

780. 97 *of* 1910.—(Tamil.) On the same wall. A damaged record in the sixteenth year of the Chōḷa king Parakēsarivarman *alias* Tribhuvanachakravartin Vikrama-Chōḷadēva (1118—35). Records gift of land. See *Ep. Ind.*, Vol. XI, p. 243, where Mr. R. Sewell discusses the date (Āni, Tritīya, Monday, Tiruvōṇa) and shows that the thirteenth year of the king should have been intended and that the date then corresponded to Monday, 25th June 1131. "The date proves that the reign could not have begun before June 16th, A.D. 1118."

781. 98 *of* 1910.—(Tamil.) On the north wall of the maṇṭapa in front of the same shrine. A record in the twenty-seventh year of Tribhuvanachakravartin Kōnērinmaikoṇḍān. Refers to the revenue survey of the sixteenth year of *Śuṅgandavirtta*-Kulōttuṅga-Chōḷadēva (I, 1070—1118), and records a gift of land in Śembaṅguḍi, a village of Ambarnāḍu.

782. 99 *of* 1910.—(Tamil.) On the south wall of the first prākāra of the same temple. Records that this prākāra *(tirumāḷigai)* was built by Vikrama-Chōḷa (1118—35).

783. 100 *of* 1910.—(Tamil.) On the same wall. A record in the tenth year of the Chōḷa king Parakēsarivarman *alias* Tribhuvanachakravartin Vikrama-Chōḷadēva (1118—35). Mentions that in the fifteenth year of Rājēndra-Chōḷadēva (II, i.e., Kulōttuṅga I), the Goddess Umā-Paramēśvari was set up, that a grant of land was made for its maintenance and, as it was neglected, it was renewed in the tenth year of Vikrama Chōḷa by the assembly of Madhurāntaka-chaturvēdimaṅgalam. In continuation of this inscription is another, dated in the fifteenth year of a king whose name is doubtful. It records a gift of land to the shrine of the same Goddess by the residents of Ambar-nagara.

784. 101 *of* 1910.—(Tamil.) At the end of the same record. A record in the fifteenth year of the Chōḷa king Rājēndra-Chōḷadēva. Records gift of land to the same shrine.

785. 102 *of* 1910.—(Tamil.) At the end of the same record. A record in the twelfth year of the Chōḷa king Kulōttuṅga-Chōḷadēva (i.e., Kulōttuṅga II, 1123—46, according to the Government Epigraphist). Records gift of land for offerings to the images of Aṭkoṇḍa-Nāyakar and the goddess, both of which were presented to the temple at Tirumāgāḷam by the ancestors of Amudan Tiruchchiṟṟambalamuḍaiyān *alias* Udayamārttāṇḍa-Mūvēndavēḷān, a native of Śiruvēḷūr in Paṇaiyūr-nāḍu which was a subdivision of Kshatriyaśikhāmaṇi-vaḷanāḍu.

786. 103 *of* 1910.—(Tamil.) On the same wall. A record in the forty-fourth year of the Chōḷa king Rājakēsarivarman *alias* Chakravartin Śrī-Kulōttuṅga-Chōḷadēva (I). Records gift of money for a lamp by Vīra-Vichchādara-Pallavaraiyan, a native of Aṇṇiyūr in Kurukkai-nāḍu, a subdivision of Virudarājabhayaṁkara-vaḷanāḍu.

787. 104 *of* 1910.—(Tamil.) On the same wall. A record in the third year of the Chōḷa king Parakēsarivarman *alias* Tribhuvanachakravartin Vikrama-Chōḷādēva (1118—35). Records gift of land to the shrine of the goddess by certain residents of Śiruvēḷūr in Paṇaiyūr-nāḍu, a subdivision of Kulōttuṅga-Chōḷavaḷanāḍu.

788. 105 *of* 1910.—(Tamil.) On the west wall of the same prākāra. A fragmentary record in the forty-fourth year of the Chōḷa king Kulōttuṅga-Chōḷadēva (I ?). Provides for a lamp.

789. 106 *of* 1910.—(Tamil.) On the north wall of the same prākāra. An incomplete record in the forty-third year (of ?). Records gift of money for a lamp by a native of Kuṇḍavai-chaturvēdimaṅgalam in Muḷaiyūr-nāḍu, a subdivision of Gēyamāṇikkavaḷanāḍu.

790. 107 *of* 1910.—(Tamil.) On the same wall. A record in the fiftieth year of the Chōḷa king Rājakēsarivarman *alias* Tribhuvanachakravartin Śrī-Kulōttuṅga-Chōladēva. Seems to record a gift of land for offerings, to the temple of Ambar-Tirumāgāḷam Uḍaiyār in Ambar-nāḍu, a subdivision of Bhūpālakulavalli-vaḷanāḍu, by certain residents of Śiruvēḷūr.

791. 108 *of* 1910.—(Tamil.) On the same wall. A record in the tenth year of the Chōḷa king Parakēsarivarman *alias* Chakravartin Vikrama-Chōḷadēva (1118—35). Records gift of paddy for offerings to the image of Āṭkoṇḍa-Nāyakar.

792. 109 *of* 1910.—(Tamil.) On the east wall of the same prākāra. A record in the eleventh year of the Chōla king Rājakēsarivarman . . . Kulōttuṅga-Chōḷadēva (II). Records gift of land for a lamp by Dēvargaṇḍan *alias* Rājarāja Paṇaiyūr-nāṭṭu Mūvēndavēḷān, a native of Śiruvēḷūr, and others. See *Ep. Ind.*, Vol. XI, p. 244, where Mr. Sewell calculates the date (Saturday, *Pushya*, second solar day in Dhanus) to be November 27th, A.D. 1143.

793. 110 *of* 1910.—(Tamil.) On the same wall. A damaged record in the second year of the Chōḷa king Parakēsarivarman *alias* Tribhuvanachakravartin. Records gift of money for two lamps.

794. 111 *of* 1910.—(Tamil.) On the same wall. A record in the seventeenth year of Tribhuvanachakravartin Kōnērimēnkoṇḍān. Records that certain lands close to the temple of Mudupagavar which were being enjoyed by a private individual, Rājarāja Pallavarāyan, by mistake, was given back to the temple. [These lands were claimed by the trustees of the temple to be the free-holding of the God from early times. The case was placed before Vēśālipparaiyar for inquiry. Pallavaraiyan stated that he had purchased the lands as *Rājarājapperuvilai* in presence of Vāṇādhirāja, Nuḷambādhirāja, Kachchiyarāya and Paḷandīvarāya when these had assembed in the *Kulōttuṅgaśōḷantiruvāśal* in his palace at Perumbaṟṟapuliyūr and produced documents to prove it. The trustees, on the other hand, produced evidences to show that the temple had purchased these lands in the fourth year of Rājarāja and was in possession till the thirteenth year of the king. Vēśālipparayar and the councillors decided in favour of the trustees.]

795. 112 *of* 1910.—(Tamil.) On the same wall. A record in the seventeenth year of the Chōḷa king Parakēsarivarman *alias* Tribhuvanachakravartin Kulōttuṅga-Chōḷadēva (Kulōttuṅga III, 1186—1216), "who was pleased to take Madurai (Madura) and the crowned head of the Pāṇḍya." Registers the release of the land referred to in the above epigraph. Mentions the fourth year of Rājarājadēva. [Mr. Krishna Sastri points out that as the chiefs mentioned in the inscription were contemporaries of Kulōttuṅga I, Rājarāja should be Rājarāja I.]

796. 113 *of* 1910.—(Tamil.) On a slab lying in the courtyard of the same temple. Records gift of gold for fifty lamps, to the temple of Mahākāḷattu-Mahādēva at Ambar, by a native of Anaṅga-Vallavappāḍi.

797. 114 *of* 1910.—(Tamil.) On another slab lying in the same place. A record in the fourth year of the Chōḷa king Rājakēsarivarman. Records gift of a necklace of pearls and a crown set with gems to the temple of Mahākāḷattu-Mahādēva by Kāripuliyan *alias* Śōḷamārāyan of Paḷuvūr in Kunṟa-kūṟṟam, on the occasion of his celebrating the God's *abhishēka*. [The Government Epigraphist believes that the real meaning of the inscription is that the temple which was known to the *Dēvāram* hymners was "patronised for the first time by an officer of the Chōḷa king." See No. 800 below.]

798. 115 *of* 1910.—(Tamil.) On the third stone in the same place. A record in the fifteenth year of the Chōḷa king Parakēsarivarman. Records gift of ninety sheep for a lamp by Udayamārtāṇḍan, son of Mannamudan, who was a native of Śiruvēḷūr in Paṇaiyūr-vaḷanāḍu.

799. 116 *of* 1910.—(Tamil.) On the fourth stone in the same place. A mutilated record in the eighth year of the Chōḷa king Parakēsarivarman. Records gift of land to the temple of Tirumāgāḷattu Mahādēva at Ambar in Ambar-nāḍu by a certain Vāṇarāyan Araṅgan Mādēvan.

800. 117 *of* 1910.—(Tamil.) On the same stone. A mutilated record in the second year of the Chōḷa king Parakēsarivarman, "who took the head of the Pāṇḍya." Mentions Kāri Puliyan *alias* Śōḷamārāyan of Paḷuvūr in Kuṉṟa-kūṟṟam and the servants of the temple of Ambar-Śrī-Māhakāḷam. [As this Kāri figures in an inscription of a Rājakēsarivarman, it is plain that the Parakēsarivarman of this inscription was the successor of Rājakēsarivarman. They might be Parāntaka II and his predecessor.]

Tirumiyachchūr.

801. 635 *of* 1902.—(Tamil.) On a pillar of the maṇṭapa in front of the Śāntanāyaki shrine in the Mihirāruṇēśvara temple. A record in the ninth year of the Chōḷa king Parakēsarivarman. Records gift of land for two lamps.

802. 636 *of* 1902.—(Tamil.) On the same pillar. A damaged record in the second year of the Chōḷa king Rājakēsarivarman. Records gift of land.

803. 637 *of* 1902.—(Tamil.) On another pillar of the same maṇṭapa. A damaged record of the Chōḷa king Parakēsarivarman, the date of which is doubtful. Records gift of land.

804. 638 *of* 1902.—(Tamil.) On a third pillar of the same maṇṭapa. A record in the fourth year of the Chōḷa king Rājakēsarivarman. Records gift of land for a lamp by a merchant.

805. 639 *of* 1902.—(Tamil.) On the east wall of the maṇṭapa in front of the central shrine in the same temple. A record in the twenty-first year of the Pāṇḍya king Māravarman *alias* Tribhuvanachakravartin Kulaśēkharadēva (I? 1268—1308). Records gift of land.

806. 640 *of* 1902.—(Tamil.) On the inner gōpura of the same temple, left of entrance. A record in the tenth year of the Pāṇḍya king Jaṭāvarman *alias* Tribhuvanachakravartin Śrī-Vallabhadēva. Records gift of land. Was he the contemporary of Māravarman Suṇdara Pāṇḍya I (1216—1235)?

807. 641 *of* 1902.—(Tamil.) On the south wall of the second prākāra of the same temple. An incomplete record in the twenty-eighth year of the Pāṇḍya king Māravarman *alias* Tribhuvanachakravartin Śrī-Vallabhadēva. [It is not improbable that this king was the predecessor of Jaṭāvarman Kulaśēkhara I, 1190–1217.]

Tirunellikkāval.

One of the South-Kāvēri centres of Śaivitism, it has been sung by Gñānasambanda.

807-A. 520 *of* 1904.—(Tamil.) On the north wall of the central shrine in the Amalakēśvara temple. A record in the twenty-first year of the Chōḷa king Tribhuvanachakravartin Rājarājadēva. Records gift of land.

807-B. 521 *of* 1904.—(Tamil.) On the same wall. A damaged and incomplete record in the twentieth year of the Chōḷa king Tribhuvanachakravartin Rājarājadēva. Seems to record a gift of land.

807-C. 522 *of* 1904.—(Tamil.) On the same wall. A mutilated and incomplete record in the twentieth year of the Chōḷa king Tribhuvanachakravartin Rājarājadēva.

807-D. 523 *of* 1904.—(Tamil.) On the same wall. A record in the ninth year of the Chōḷa king Tribhuvanachakravartin Rājarājadēva. The god is called the lord of Tirunellikkā in Arvalakkūṟṟam, a subdivision of Rājēndra-Śōḷa-vaḷanāḍu. Mutilated.

807-E. 524 *of* 1904.—(Tamil.) On the north and east walls of the same shrine. A damaged and mutilated record of the Chōḷa king Tribhuvanachakravartin Rājarājadēva, the date of which is lost.

807-F. 525 *of* 1904.—(Tamil.) On the same walls. A record in the seventh year of the Chōḷa king Tribhuvanachakravartin Vīrarājēndradēva. Records gift of money for a lamp.

807-G. 526 *of* 1904.—(Tamil.) On the south wall of the same shrine. A much damaged record in the thirty-first year of the Chōḷa king Tribhuvanachakravartin Rājarājadēva.

807-H. 527 *of* 1904.—(Tamil.) On the same wall. A mutilated record in the fourth year of the Chōḷa king Tribhuvanachakravartin Rājarājadēva. Records gift of money for lamps.

Tiruppāmburam.

This place which is one of the South-Kāvēri centres of Śaivitism is the theme of a *paḍika* by Tirugñānasambanda.

808. 85 *of* 1911.—(Tamil.) On the south base of the central shrine in the Śēshapurīśvara temple. An incomplete and damaged record in the twenty-seventh year of the Chōla king Tribhuvanachakravartin Kulōttuṅga-Chōḷadēva (III), " who was pleased to take

Madurai (i.e., Madura), Īḷam (Ceylon), Karuvūr and the crowned head of the Pāṇḍya." Refers to an exchange of land.

809. 86 *of* 1911.—(Tamil.) On the same base. A record in the twenty-third year of the Chōḷa king Tribhuvanachakravartin Kulōttuṅga-Chōḷadēva (III, 1186—1216), "who was pleased to take Madurai (i.e., Madura), Īḷam (Ceylon), and the crowned head of the Pāṇḍya." Records that a Veḷḷāḷan of the village sold himself and his two daughters as slaves to the temple of Tiruppāmburam-Uḍaiyār, for a sum of 100 *kāśus,* "as the time was very bad, as paddy was sold at three *nāḷis* per *kāśu,*" and his children in consequence were dying of starvation. The inscription clearly shows that there must have been a famine of a serious character.

810. 87 *of* 1911.—(Tamil.) On the west base of the same shrine. A record in the thirteenth year of the Chōḷa king Rājarājadēva. Records gift of fourteen cows to the temple, by a certain Vāraṇavādīśuramuḍaiyān *alias* Kōśalarāyar of Maṇakkuḍi. The donor provided also for the cows being kept in the cow-shed within the temple, for their fodder and for the cowherd boy that grazed them.

811. 88 *of* 1911.—(Tamil.) On the same base. A record in the fifteenth year of the Chōḷa king Tribhuvanachakravartin Rājēndra Chōḷadēva (unidentified). Records sale of land to the temple.

812. 89 *of* 1911.—(Tamil.) On the same base. A record in the second year of the Pāṇḍya king Jaṭāvarman *alias* Tribhuvanachakravartin Sundara-Pāṇḍyadēva (I, ? 1251—64). Records gift of land.

813. 90 *of* 1911.—(Tamil.) On the same base. An unfinished record in the twenty-second year of the Chōḷa king Tribhuvanachakravartin Rājarājadēva. Records gift of land by a certain Paḷuveṭṭaraiyar of Vāṇavappāḍi, for garlands and sacred bath, to the temple of Tiruppāmburam-Uḍaiyār (at Tiruppāmburam) in Uyyakkoṇḍār-vaḷanāḍu. Refers also to the shrine of the goddess Māmalaiyāṭṭiyār built in the same temple by a native of Peruḷūr.

814. 91 *of* 1911.—(Tamil.) On the north base of the same shrine. A record in the twenty-eighth year of the Chōḷa king Tribhuvanachakravartin Kulōttuṅga-Chōḷadēva (III), "who was pleased to take Madurai (Madura), Īḷam (Ceylon), Karuvūr and the crowned head of the Pāṇḍya." Records gift of land to the shrine of Rājarāja-Vināyaka-Piḷḷaiyār set up on the bank of the river Ariśilāru, by a certain Mīnavan Mūvēndavēḷar. Pāmburam *alias* Kulōttuṅgaśōḷachaturvēdimaṅgalam is stated to have been situated in Pāmbura-nāḍu, a subdivision of Uyyakkoṇḍār-vaḷanāḍu.

815. 92 *of* 1911.—(Tamil.) On the same base. A record in the thirty-fifth year of the Chōḷa king Tribhuvanachakravartin Tribhuvanavīradēva (Kulōttuṅga III), "who being pleased to take Madurai (i.e., Madura), Īḷam (Ceylon), Karuvūr and the crowned head of the Pāṇḍya was pleased to perform the anointment of heroes and victors. Records sale of land to the temple for the worship of Periyadēvar and Nāchchiyār, set up therein by a dancing girl.

816. 93 *of* 1911.—(Tamil.) On the same base. A record in the twenty-third year of the Pāṇḍya king Jaṭāvarman Tribhuvana-chakravartin Sundara-Pāṇḍyadēva (not identified). Records sale of houses and lands belonging to a registered tenant who ran away without paying the taxes, by the friends who stood surety for him, to the temple. The inscription is of interest in the light it throws on one aspect of the village fisc.

817. 94 *of* 1911.—(Tamil.) On the same base. A record in the thirty-fifth year of the Chōḷa king Tribhuvanachakravartin Tribhuvanavīradēva (Kulōttuṅga III), "who having taken (Madura), Īḷam (Ceylon), Karuvūr and the crowned head of the Pāṇḍya, was pleased to perform the anointment of heroes and victors." Refers to the images set up by the dancing girl mentioned in No. 815 and registers certain privileges granted to her by the temple priests.

818. 95 *of* 1911.—(Tamil.) On the same base. Records that this stone temple Pugaḷābharaṇan was built by Pālarāvāyar of Koṟṟamaṅgalam. [Was this Pālarāvāya the brother of Śekkiḷār, the author of the *Periyapurāṇa* ?]

819. 96 *of* 1911.—(Tamil.) On the same base. A record in the thirty-first year of the Chōḷa king Tribhuvanachakravartin Tribhuvanavīra-Chōḷadēva (1178—1216), "who having taken Madurai (i.e., Madura), Īḷam (Ceylon), Karuvūr and the crowned head of the Pāṇḍya, was pleased to perform the anointment of heroes and victors." Records gift of land free of certain taxes to the same temple at the request of a certain Arumoḷi-Brahma-mārāyaṇ. One of the taxes is mentioned to be Kāvērikkarai-vini-yōgam.

820. 97 *of* 1911.—(Tamil.) On the same base. Registers in the thirty-first year the settlement of dues until that year, on certain lands situated at Pāmburam *alias* Kulōttuṅga-Chōḷa-chaturvēdimaṅgalam.

821. 98 *of* 1911.—(Tamil.) On the maṇṭapa in front of the same shrine. Records in Ś. 1644, and Kali. 4824, Śōbhakrit, that Māṇukkōpaṇḍitarayyan agent to Subēdār *(Śupayadār)* Rāgōpaṇḍi-tarayyan, built the vasanta-maṇṭapa. [The Epigraphist points out that this officer should have been an officer of the Tanjore king Serfoji (I 1711—29).]

822. 99 *of* 1911.—(Tamil.) On the base of the central shrine. A record in the twenty-fourth year of the Chōḷa king Tribhuvana-chakravartin Rājarājadēva. Records gift of land for the upkeep of a maṇṭapa built by a certain Dāmōdaran *alias* Śōḷiyādaraiya-vēḷan in the second prākāra of the temple.

Tiruviḻimiḻalai.

The temple is a strong Śaivite centre as it owes its name to the alleged offer of an eye by Vishṇu in place of flower in the course of his worship of Śiva, and as it is connected with the exploits of Gñānasambanda and Appar in the seventh century.

823. 382 *of* 1908.—(Grantha and Tamil.) On the north wall of the central shrine in the Viḷināthasvāmin temple. A damaged record in the sixth year. Seems to record a gift of land for festivities in connexion with the two temples of Tivīḷimiḷalai-Uḍaiyār and the goddess Piḍāriyār. The latter of these was perhaps built in this year.

824. 383 *of* 1908.—(Grantha and Tamil.) On the same wall. A damaged record in the twenty-fourth year of the Chōḷa king Rājakēsarivarman *alias* Chakravartin Kulōttuṅga-Chōḷadēva (I ?). Mentions Tiruvīḷimiḷalai which was a *brahmadēya* in Veṇṇāḍu, a subdivision of Ulaguyyakkoṇḍaśōḷa-vaḷanādu. The donor was perhaps a native of Annavāyil in Śeṟṟūr-kūṟṟam, a district of Kulōttuṅgaśōḷa-vaḷanāḍu.

825. 384 *of* 1908.—(Grantha and Tamil.) On the same wall. Built in at the beginning. Records in the thirty-sixth year (of an unknown king) gift of tiles covered with gold to the temple of Tiruvīḷimiḷalai-uḍaiya-Mahādēva. One of the donors was Vijayarājēndradēvār-Aṇukkiyār Pallavan Paṭṭālinaṅgai.

826. 385 *of* 1908.—(Tamil.) On the same wall. A damaged record in the eighth year of the Chōḷa king Parakēsarivarman *alias* Tribhuvanachakravartin Vikrama-Chōḷadēva (1118—35). Seems to record a gift of land for a lamp, by purchase.

827. 386 *of* 1908.—(Tamil.) On the same wall. A record in the seventh year of the Chōḷa king Tribhuvanachakravartin Kulōttuṅga-Chōḷadēva (III). Records gift of a lamp-stand and a lamp. See *Ep. Ind.*, Vol. XI, p. 125, where Professor Jacobi points out that the details of the date (Makara, Pūrva 14, Thursday, Punarvasu) show that 16th January 1185 is intended, but that Thursday is mistake for Wednesday.]

828. 387 *of* 1908.—(Tamil.) On the same wall. A record in the second year of the Chōḷa king Vikrama-Chōḷadēva. Records gift of money for two lamps. Mentions Āvūr-kūṟṟam, a district in Nittavinōda-vaḷanāḍu.

829. 388 *of* 1908.—(Tamil.) On the same wall. A record in the fifth year of the Chōḷa king Parakēsarivarman *alias* Tribhuvanachakravartin Vikrama-Chōḷadēva (1118—35). Records gift of land for offerings at the request of a native of Āvūr in Āvūr-kūṟṟam.

830. 389 *of* 1908.—(Tamil.) On the same wall. A record in the fifth year of the Chōḷa king Vikrama-Chōḷadēva. Records gift of land in Tattamangalam for feeding Brāhmaṇas, at the request of the same person.

831. 390 *of* 1908.—(Tamil.) On the south wall of the central shrine in the same temple. A record in the forty-fifth year of the Chōḷa king Rājakēsarivarman *alias* Tribhuvanachakravartin Kulōttuṅga Chōḷadēva (I ?). Built in at the end. Refers to the gathering of the assembly of Tiruvīḻimiḻalai to discuss the business of the village *(grāma-kārya).*

832. 391 *of* 1908.—(Tamil.) On the same wall. A record in the seventh year of the Chōḷa king Tribhuvanachakravartin Rājadhi-rājadēva (I or II ?). Records gift of a gold ornament.

833. 392 *of* 1908.—(Tamil.) On the west wall of the same shrine. A record in the twenty-third year of the Chōḷa king Tribhuvanachakravartin Rājēndra-Chōḷadēva. Records gift of land to a *maṭha* at Tiruvīḻimiḻalai Aḻagiya-Tiruchchiṟṟambalam-uḍaiyār-maḍam, by a certain Gñānaśiva who was the disciple of Tiruchchattimuṟṟattu-Mudaliyār of *Tirugñānasambhanda-tirumaḍam* situated to the east of the temples of Tiruchchattimuṟṟamuḍaiya-Nāyanār and Tirukkāmakōṭṭamuḍaiya Periya-Nāchchiyār at Rāja-rājapuram in Tirunaṟaiyūr-nāḍu, a district of Kulōttuṅgachōḷa-vaḷanāḍu.* Tiruchchattimuṟṟam is one of the Śaivite centres south of the Kāvēri, figuring in the legends of Appar.]

834. 393 *of* 1908.—(Tamil.) On the west and south walls of the same shrine. A record in the thirty-first year of the Chōḷa king Rājakēsarivarman *alias* Uḍaiyār Śrī Rājādhirājadēva (I or II ?). It gives a detailed description of the boundaries of Jayaṅgoṇḍa-śōḷanallūr, the *dēvadāna* village of the temple at Tiruvīḻimiḻalai, and refers to a survey of the lands belonging to the temple.

835. 394 *of* 1908.—(Tamil.) On the north wall of the maṇṭapa in front of the same shrine. A record in the tenth year of the Pāṇḍya king Perumāḷ Sundara-Pāṇḍyadēva. Records gift of land. It is not known which of the Sundara Pāṇḍyas is meant.

836. 395 *of* 1908.—(Tamil.) On the same wall. A record in the second year (Dhanus, Apara. 14, Āślēsha, Sunday) of the Pāṇḍya king Jaṭāvarman Tribhuvanachakravartin Sundara-Pāṇḍyadēva (I ?). Records sale of land. See *Ep. Ind.*, Vol. XI, p. 134, where Dr. Jacobi discusses the date and shows that it is not consistent with the known dates of Jaṭāvarman Sundara Pāṇḍya III.

837. 396 *of* 1908.—(Tamil.) On the south wall of the same maṇṭapa. A record of the Vijayanagara king Viruppaṇa-Uḍaiyār II (i.e., Virūpāksha I), son of Vīra-Ariyappa-Uḍaiyār (Haripara II) in Ś. 1307, Krōdhana. Records gift of land for a garden by a merchant of Kāvēripūmpaṭṭaṇam in Rājādhirāja-vaḷanāḍu. [The

* The Tamil poet Śattimuttappulavar belonged to this place.

inscriptions show that this sea-port was still extant in the end of the fifteenth century. Perhaps it was at this time that Paṭṭiṇattu Piḷḷai, the celebrated Tamil saint and psalmist, lived.]

838. 397 *of* 1908.—(Tamil.) On one of the pillars in the same maṇṭapa. Records the name of Ukkal-kīḷān Ediriliśōḷan *alias* Pallavarājan. Two other pillars bear the same name.

839. 398 *of* 1908.—(Grantha and Tamil.) On one of the door posts in the same maṇṭapa. Records gift of a lamp.

840. 399 *of* 1908.—(Tamil.) On the north wall of the first prākāra of the same temple. A record of the Chōḷa king Tribhuvanachakravartin Rājēndra-Chōḷadēva in his twenty-fourth year (in words the date is given as twenty-first). Records sale of land by a native of Tiruveḷundūr-nāḍu in Jayaṅgoṇḍa-śōḷa-vaḷanāḍu to a native of Nerkuppai in Tañjāvūr-kūṟṟam, a subdivision of Pāṇḍyakulāśani-vaḷanāḍu.

841. 400 *of* 1908.—(Tamil.) On the same wall. A record in eleventh year (Kumbha, Apara., Saturday, Mūla) of the Chōḷa king Tribhuvanachakravartin Rājarājadēva (III). Records gift of land by a Brāhmaṇa for the merit of the king. See *Ep. Ind.*, Vol. XI, p. 127 and No. 851 below.

842. 401 *of* 1908.—(Tamil.) On the same wall. A record in the sixth year (Kanyā, Pūrva 6, Friday, Mūla) of the Pāṇḍya king Jaṭāvarman Tribhuvanachakravartin Vīra-Pāṇḍyadēva (1295—1342?). Records gift of land by a native of Periyaṅguḍi in Tirunaṟaiyūr-nāḍu, a subdivision of Kulōttuṅgaśōḷa-vaḷanāḍu. See *Ibid.*, p. 137, where Dr. Jacobi calculates the date to be Friday, the 28th September, A.D. 1302.

843. 402 *of* 1908.—(Tamil.) On the same wall. A record in the second year of the Chōḷa king Tribhuvanachakravartin Rājēndra-Chōḷadēva. Registers a list of lands owned by the Tirunāvukkaraśar-maḍam at Tiruvīḻimiḻalai.

844. 403 *of* 1908.—(Tamil.) On the same wall. A record in the thirty-first year of the Chōḷa king Tribhuvanachakravartin Rājarājadēva (III?). Records gift of land and a house-site to a carpenter *(tachchachēri)* for executing the repairs in the shrines of Ninṟaruḷiya Nāyanār and Neṟivārkuḻali Nāchchiyār in the same temple.

845. 404 *of* 1908.—(Tamil.) On the south wall of the same prākāra. A damaged record of the Chōḷa king Tribhuvanachakravartin Kulōttuṅga-Chōḷadēva (III), "who took Madura and was pleased to take the crowned head of the Pāṇḍya," the date of which is lost. Stones out of order. Seems to record a gift of land.

846. 405 *of* 1908.—(Tamil.) On the same wall. A damaged record in the thirty-seventh year of the Chōḷa king Tribhuvanachakravartin Kulōttuṅga-Chōḷadēva (III) who took Madura,

Karuvūr and Īḷam (Ceylon) and was pleased to take the crowned head of the Pāṇḍya and to perform the anointment of heroes and victors." Appears to record a gift of land for offerings to the shrine of the goddess.

847. 406 *of* 1908.—(Tamil.) On the same wall. A damaged record. Records gift of land for a lamp by a native of Vīrāṇam, a village in Mērka-nāḍu, a subdivision of Virudarājabhayaṅkara vaḷanādu.

848. 407 *of* 1908.—(Tamil.) On the same wall. A damaged record in the twentieth year (Rishabha, Pūrva 10th, Friday, Uttara-Phalguni) of the Chōḷa king Tribhuvanachakravartin Rājarājadēva (III). Registers a lease of land for maintaining lamps. See *Ep. Ind.*, Vol. XI, p. 129, where it is pointed out that the date probably corresponded to Friday, the 16th May, A.D. 1236.

849. 408 *of* 1908.—(Tamil.) On the same wall. A damaged record in the twentieth year of the king.

850. 409 *of* 1908.—(Tamil.) On the same wall. A record in the eleventh year (Dhanus, Pūrva 10th, Monday, Rēvati) of the Chōḷa king Tribhuvanachakravartin Rājarājadēva (III). Records gift of land for offerings to the image of Tiruvādavūrdēvar Māṇikka-vāśaka set up in the third prākāra of the temple at Tiruvīḷimiḷalai. Refers to the thirty-ninth year of Periyadēvar Tribhuvanavīra-dēva (Kulōttuṅga III). See *Ibid.*, p. 128, where the date is pointed out as incorrect and equated to Monday, 30th November 1226, after correcting the month Dhanus into Makara.

851. 410 *of* 1908.—(Tamil.) On the same wall. A record in the twenty-first (Kumbha, Apara, 11th, Saturday, Mūlam) year of the Chōḷa king Tribhuvanachakravartin Rājarājadēva (III). Records gift of land. See *Ibid.*, p. 129, where the date is given as Saturday, 24th January, A.D. 1237, (Kumbha is an error for Makara).

852. 411 *of* 1908.—(Tamil.) On the west wall of the same prākāra. A damaged record in the eighth year (Dhanus, Pūrva 8. Rēvati, Friday) of the Pāṇḍya king Jaṭāvarman Tribhuvana-chakravartin Sundara Pāṇḍyadēva. Seems to record a gift of land for the benefit of the *maṭhas* and minor shrines in the temple at Tiruvīḷimiḷalai. Mentions a certain Nārpatteṇṇāyira Piḷḷai, among the Śaiva devotees. See *Ibid.*, p. 134, where it is shown that the details suit neither of the kings of this name who came to the throne in 1251 and 1276. Can it be the king who came to the throne in A.D. 1270?

853. 412 *of* 1908.—(Tamil.) On the west wall of the first prākāra of the Viḷināthasvāmin temple. A damaged record in the eighteenth year (Kumbha, Pūrva 5th, Wednesday, Uttarāshāḍha) of the Chōḷa king Tribhuvanachakravartin Rājēndra-Chōḷadēva

(III). Appears to record a gift of land by purchase. See *Ep. Ind.*, Vol. XI, p. 132, where Kumbha is pointed out as an error for Tulā and *tithi* 5 for *tithi* 6, and the date is then equated to Wednesday, 10th October, A.D. 1263.

854. 413 *of* 1908.—(Tamil.) On the same wall. A damaged record in the eighteenth year of the Chōḷa king Tribhuvanachakravartin-Rājēndra-Chōḷadēva (III ?). Refers to the construction of a *maṭha* on the northern side of the temple.

855. 414 *of* 1908.—(Tamil.) On the same wall. A damaged record in the ninth year (Tulā, Apara 7, Pushya, Sunday) of the Pāṇḍya king Jaṭāvarman Tribhuvanachakravartin Sundara-Pāṇḍyadēva. Records gift of land, by purchase for the recital of the *Tirumuṟai* hymns in the *Tirukkaikkōṭṭi* which was constructed for that purpose in the temple during the time of king Naraśiṅgadēva. See *Ep. Ind.*, Vol. XI, p. 135, where it is shown that the dates correspond neither to the 'first' (1251—64) nor to the 'second' (in reality the third) (1276—90) of the kings who bore this name. See No. 853 above. The classification of the Śaivite hymns into twelve *Tirumuṟais* is common place knowledge to every student of South Indian Śaivite history.

856. 415 *of* 1908.—(Tamil.) On the east wall of the same prākāra. A damaged record in the third year of the Chōḷa king Tribhuvanachakravartin Kulōttuṅga-Chōḷadēva. Built in at the beginning. Mentions the temple of Tiruvagattīśvaramuḍaiya-Mahādēva at Vaḷavan Anniyūr in Veṇṇāḍu, a subdivision of Uyyakkoṇḍārvaḷanāḍu. Mentions the sixth year of Vikrama-Chōḷadēva (1118—35).

857. 416 *of* 1908.—(Tamil.) On the same wall. A record in the seventeenth year (Karkaṭaka, Apara. 14th, Monday, Punarvasu) of the Chōḷa king Kulōttuṅga-Chōḷadēva (III), "who took Madura and was pleased to take the crowned head of the Pāṇḍya." Records gift of land by purchase to the temple of Tiruchchuvargam Uḍaiyār at Tiruvīḻimiḻalai. See *Ep. Ind.*, Vol. XI, p. 126. The date is irregular.

858. 417 *of* 1908.—(Tamil.) On the same wall. A record in the second year of the Chōḷa king Tribhuvanachakravartin Rājarājadēva (III ?). Records gift of land to the shrine of Tiruvēgambam Uḍaiyār in the first prākāra of the temple. Mentions Anapāyan Śēvūr in Paṇaiyūrnāḍu, a subdivision of Kulōttuṅgaśōḷavaḷanāḍu.

859. 418 *of* 1908.—(Tamil.) On the same wall. A damaged record in the sixteenth year (Kumbha, Pūrva 5, Rēvati, Friday) of the Chōḷa king Tribhuvanachakravartin Kulōttuṅga-Chōḷadēva (III), "who was pleased to take Madura and the crowned head of the Pāṇḍya." Records gift of land by purchase to the shrine of Pārvatīśvaram Uḍaiyār in the first prākāra of the temple at

Tiruvīḷimiḷalai. Mentions the temple of Tiruchchuvargam-Uḍaiyār, whose *dēvadāna* village was Kulōttuṅgaśōḷanallūr. See *Ep. Ind.*, Vol. XI, p. 125, where the date is shown to be Friday, 28th January, A.D. 1194.

860. 419 *of* 1908.—(Tamil.) On the same wall. A damaged record in the second year of the Chōḷa king Tribhuvanachakravartin Rājarājadēva. Built in at the end. Mentions Komāran Kulōttuṅgaśōḷa-chaturvēdimaṅgalam (named after Kulōttuṅga II).

861. 420 *of* 1908.—(Tamil.) On the same wall. A damaged record of the Chōḷa king Rājakēsarivarman *alias* Tribhuvana-chakravartin . . . Built in at the end. Mentions Jayaṅgoṇḍa-śōḷanallūr, a *dēvadāna* village of the temple of Tiruvīḷimiḷala Uḍaiyār and the village Komāran-Kulōttuṅgaśōḷa-chaturvēdimaṅgalam in Tiruvaḷundūr-nāḍu. [Kumara Kulōttuṅga was Kulōttuṅga II, the patron of Poet Oṭṭakkūttar.]

862. 421 *of* 1908.—(Tamil.) On a pillar in the inner verandah of the same temple. A much damaged record of the Chōḷa king Parakēsarivarman *alias* Rājēndra-Chōḷadēva (I, 1011—53) the date of which is doubtful. Mentions *Rājarājan-kāśu.*

863. 422 *of* 1908.—(Tamil.) On another pillar in the same place. A record in the twenty-fourth year of the Chōḷa king Rājarājakēsarivarman *alias* Rājarājadēva (I). Begins with the usual historical introduction. Records gift of paddy (21 *kalams*) by the assembly of Tiruvīḷimiḷalai as interest for 30 *kāśus* received in the *paṇḍāram* for the maintenance of visitors in Aippaśi Tiruvōṇa festival.

864. 423 *of* 1908.—(Tamil.) On the third pillar in the same place. A record in the twenty-second year of the Chōḷa king Rājarājakēsarivarman *alias* Rājarājadēva (I). Records that the assembly of Tiruvīḷimiḷalai, a *dēvadāna* village of the god in Veṇṇāḍu, a subdivision of Uyyakkoṇḍārvaḷanāḍu, made provision for the singing of the *Tirupadiyam* hymns in the temple.

865. 424 *of* 1908.—(Tamil.) On the fourth pillar in the same place. Records that the pillar was the gift of a certain Bhāradvāja Dēvargaḷnāyan. The same is recorded on two other pillars.

866. 425 *of* 1908.—(Tamil.) On one of the steps in front of the Subrahmaṇya shrine in the same temple. A fragmentary record in the eleventh year of the Chōḷa king Kulōttuṅga-Chōḷadēva (III), " who was pleased to take the crowned head of the Pāṇḍya and . . . Mentions Koṟṟamaṅgalam in Puraṅgarambaināḍu, a subdivision of Rājēndraśōḷavaḷanāḍu.

867. 426 *of* 1908.—(Tamil.) On the south and east walls of the Chaṇḍikēśvara shrine in the same temple. A record in the sixth year of the Chōḷa king Rājakēsarivarmam *alias* Tribhuvana-chakravartin Vikrama-Chōḷadēva (1118—35 ?). Stones out of order. Records gift of money for two lamps.

868. 427 *of* 1908.—(Tamil.) On the east wall of the same shrine. A fragmentary record of the thirty-fourth year of the Chōḷa king Rājakēsarivarman *alias* Tribhuvanachakravartin Kulōttuṅga-Chōḷadēva (I ?) Seems to refer to the building of the shrine of Ādichaṇḍēśvaradēva of stone.

869. 428 *of* 1908.—(Tamil.) On the same wall. A damaged and unfinished record of the Vijayanagara king Vīra-Viruppaṇṇa-Uḍaiyār (II), i.e., Virūpāksha I, son of Vīra-Viruppaṇṇa-Uḍaiyār, in Ś. 1310. Mentions Veṇṇāḍu in Uyyakoṇḍar-vaḷanāḍu. [Virūpāksha I was the son of Harihara II and not of his brother Virupaṇṇa Uḍaiyār I; but it is not improbable that he was adopted by his uncle.]

870. 429 *of* 1908.—(Tamil.) On the north of wall of the Gaṇēśa shrine in the same temple. A record in the fifth year of the Chōḷa king Rājakēsarivarman *alias* Tribhuvanachakravartin Rājarājadēva (I). Seems to record a gift of money to an ascetic *(tapasvin)* in the temple of Śivalōkamuḍaiya-Nāyanār, at Jayaṅgoṇḍaśōḷanallūr, the *dēvadāna* village of the temple of Tiruvīḻimiḻalai-Uḍaiyār.

871. 430 *of* 1908.—(Tamil.) On the west wall of the same shrine. A record in the fourth year of the Chōḷa king Tribhuvanachakravartin Kulōttuṅga-Chōḷadēva. Records gift of an ornament by a native of Viḷandai in Merkala-nāḍu, a subdivision of Virudarājabhayaṅkara-vaḷanāḍu.

872. 431 *of* 1908.—(Tamil.) On the small wall. A record in the sixth year of the Chōḷa king Rājakēsarivarman *alias* Tribhuvanachakravartin Vikrama-Chōḷadēva (1118—35). Mentions Vishṇuvardhanapuram, a village in Veṇṇāḍu, a subdivision of Uyyakkoṇḍār-vaḷanāḍu.

873. 432 *of* 1908.—(Tamil.) On the south wall of the same shrine. A damaged record in the tenth year of the Chōḷa-king Parakēsarivarman *alias* Tribhuvanachakravartin Rājarājadēva (II ?). Records gift of a lamp.

874. 433 *of* 1908.—(Tamil.) On the north wall of the Mūlasthānēśvara shrine in the same temple. A record in the twenty-seventh year of the Chōḷa king Tribhuvanachakravartin Kulōttuṅga-Chōḷadēva (III), "who was pleased to take . . . and the crowned head of the Pāṇḍya." Stones out of order. Refers to a sale of land. Another incomplete record of the same king is inscribed at the bottom.

875. 434 *of* 1908.—(Tamil.) On the east wall of the Mūlasthānēśvara shrine in the Viḻiṇāthasvāmin temple. A record in the fifteenth year of the Chōḷa king Tribhuvanachakravartin Kulōttuṅga Chōḷadēva (III), " who was pleased to take Madura and the crowned head of the Pāṇḍya." Refers to certain arrangements in connexion with the irrigation of the temple lands at Jayaṅgoṇḍa-śōḷanallūr in Uyyakkoṇḍārvaḷanāḍu. Mentions Tribhuvana-chakravartin Kōnērinmaikoṇḍān and Kīrtimārtāṇḍapperāru.

876. 435 *of* 1908.—(Tamil.) On the pillar in the Sundara-kuchāmbāḷ shrine in the same temple. A record in the fifteenth year of the Chōḷa king Parakēśarivarman. Records gift of ninety-six sheep for a lamp to the temple of Tiruttānṟōnṟi-bhaṭṭārar at Tiru-maḷalai in Veṇṇāḍu.

877. 436 *of* 1908.—(Tamil.) On the same pillar. A record in the sixth year of the Chōḷa king Parakēsarivarman. Records gift of gold for feeding four Brāhmaṇas in the temple of Tiruttānṟōnṟi-Mahādēva at Tirumaḷalai. The donor was a certain Amara-bhujaṅgan Muppuli *alias* Gaṇḍaragaṇḍa-Pallavaraiyan.

878. 437 *of* 1908.—(Tamil.) On the same pillar. A mutilated record. Records gift of land for a flower garden to the temple of Tiruttānṟōnṟi-bhaṭāra at Tirumaḷalai.

879. 438 *of* 1908.—(Tamil.) On the same pillar. Records gift of a sword *(vāḷ)* called Śrī-Kālakālan by Vāṇiyan Pādan *alias* Arikulakēsari Viḷupparaiyan, to the temple of Tiruvīḷimiḷalai Uḍaiyār.

880. 439 *of* 1908.—(Tamil.) On the same pillar. A record in the third year of the Chōḷa king Parakēsarivarman. Records gift of a silver dish to the temple of Tiruvīḷimiḷalai Uḍaiyār Paramēśvara-bhaṭṭāra.

881. 440 *of* 1908.—(Tamil.) On the second pillar in the same shrine. A damaged record in the thirty-second year of the Chōḷa king Madiraikoṇḍa Parakēsarivarman (Parāntaka I). Records gift of ninety sheep for a lamp to the temple of Tiruvagattīśvarapperu-mānaḍigaḷ.

882. 441 *of* 1908.—(Tamil.) On the third pillar in the same place. A much damaged record in the thirty-eighth year of the Chōḷa king Madiraikoṇḍa-Parakēsarivarman (Parāntaka I). Mentions Pāmburanāḍu.

883. 442 *of* 1908.—(Tamil.) On the same pillar. A record in the fifth year of the Chōḷa king Parakēsarivarman *alias* Rājēndra Chōḷadēva (1011—43). Seems to record gift of a lamp.

884. 443 *of* 1908.—(Tamil.) On the fourth pillar in the same place. A mutilated record. Refers to the setting up of an image of Śrī-Kṛishṇa and seems to record a gift of land for offerings.

885. 444 *of* 1908.—(Tamil.) On the same pillar. A damaged record in the tenth year of the Chōḷa king Parakēsarivarman *alias* Uḍaiyār Śrī Rājēndra-Chōḷadēva (1011—43). Mentions the copper image of Aḷagiya Maṇavāḷa which was caused to be made by the mother of Rājēndraśoḷa Aṇukkappallavaraiyar.

886. 445 *of* 1908.—(Tamil.) On a pillar in the inner gōpura of the same temple, right of entrance. A record in the twelfth year of the Chōḷa king Rājarājakēsarivarman, "who destroyed the ships at Śālai" (Rājarāja I, 785—1013). Records gift of land as *kāṇi* by the assembly of Maḷalai to a servant in the temple Tiruttāṉṟōṉṟi Bhaṭāra.

887. 446 *of* 1908.—(Tamil.) On the same pillar. A record of the Chōḷa king Rājakēsarivarman. The continuation of this record on the west face of the pillar is apparently chiselled off.

888. 447 *of* 1908.—(Tamil.) On another pillar in the same gōpura, left of entrance. An unfinished record in the eighteenth year of the Chōḷa king Rājarājakēsarivarman. Refers to the great assembly of Tirumaḷalai.

889. 448 *of* 1908.—(Tamil.) On the second gōpura in the same temple. A record in the second year of the Pāṇḍya king Jaṭāvarman Tribhuvanachakravartin Sundara-Pāṇḍyadēva. Seems to record a gift by the merchants *(śeṭṭi)* living in the villages belonging to the temple. [It is not known which of the three Jaṭāvarman Sundara Pāṇḍyas is intended.]

890. 449 *of* 1908.—(Tamil and Grantha.) On the third gōpura in the same temple, right of entrance. A record in the twenty-second year of the Chōḷa king Rājarājakēsarivarman *alias* Rājarājadēva (I). Seems to provide for lamps.

NEGAPATAM TALUK.

Ānaimaṅgalam.

890-A. The large Leyden grant (issued by Rājēndrachōḷa (I) and preserved in the Leyden University Museum). It is a record in twenty-one plates and engraved in Chōḷa-Grantha character (like the Tiruppūvaṇam grants). The first five plates are in Sanskrit and the other sixteen in Tamil. The record is of priceless value in illustrating the history of the Chōḷa dynasty. It records the grant of the village of Ānaimaṅgalam in the Paṭṭaṇakūṟṟu division of Kshatriya Śikhāmaṇi vaḷanāḍu by Rājarāja I in the twenty-third year of his reign to the Chūḍāmaṇi padma vihāra at Nāgapattaṇa, built by Śrīmāra Vijayōttuṅgavarman, son of Chūḍāmaṇivarman, king of Kaṭāha (Burma), who was his feudatory. See *Tamil and Sanskrit Ins.*, No. 30, pp. 204—24, where it is edited and translated. For reference to Buddhistic shrines at Negapatam, see the Śrī Vaishṇava *Guruparampara* (where Tirumaṅgai Āḻvār is said to have once robbed the Buddhistic temple), *Ind. Antq.*, Vol. XXII, p. 45 and *Ibid.*, Vol. VII, p. 224 ff. and *Tanj. Gazr.*, p. 248.

890-B. The smaller Leyden grant. Records in Tamil that Rājakēsarivarman Kulōttuṅgachōḷa (I) issued an edict in the twentieth year of his reign to "the crest-jewel of the assembly of earth-rulers" that some lands at Ānaimaṅgalam, Muṇjikkuḍi, etc., were given to the temple by being transferred from the old owners and that various taxes were exempted. See *Tamil and Sanskrit Ins.*, pp. 224—7.

Kivaḷūr.

The local temple (which later on suffered under Lally's vandalism) resembles the Subrahmaṇya shrine of Tanjore and is therefore of architectural interest. The gōpuram, again, is of granite, which is rare in the east of the delta.

891. 515 *of* 1904.—(Tamil.) On the south wall of the central shrine in the Akshayaliṅgēśvara temple. A record in the eighteenth year of the Chōḷa king Tribhuvanachakravartin Rājarājadēva III, corresponding to Sunday, 25th December, 1233. Records gift of land. See *Ep. Ind.*, Vol. VIII, p. 269.

892. 516 *of* 1904.—(Mahrāthi.) On the west wall of the prākāra of the same temple. Records in Ś. 1697, expired, Manmatha, that Tuḷajāja-Rāja (1763—87) of Tanjore built the prākāra wall. [For details about Tulsāji Rāja see *Tanj. Gazr.*, p. 49 ff.]

893. 517 *of* 1904.—(Tamil.) On the south wall of the Sundarakuchāmbā shrine in the same temple. A mutilated* record in the tenth year of the Chōḷa king Tribhuvanachakravartin Rājarājadēva.

Nāgūr.

893-A. Over the tomb in the local mosque. Records that the mosque was built by Pratāpa Singh of Tanjore in eleven days in H. 1171 (A.D. 1757). *Antiquities*, Vol. I, p. 281.

893-B. A C.P. grant in the same place. Records the grant of fifteen villages to the mosque by the same king. *Ibid.*, p. 281.

Negapatam.

See Mr. Sewell's *Antiquities*, Vol. I, p. 281 and *Tanj. Gazr.*, p. 243 f., for detailed accounts of the Antiquities of this place. Dr. Hultzsch mentions in the ancient Kāyārōhaṇasvāmi temple (called Kārōṇa in inscriptions and in the *Periyapurāṇa*), a number of epigraphs alleged to belong to "Rājarāja, Rājēndrachōḷa and other Chōḷa kings," but he gives no details about these. See *Mad. Ep. Rep.*, June 1891, p. 3, para. 6. The following have been taken from *Antiquities* and *Tanj. Gazr.* :—

893-C. In a stone in the wall of the Kailāsanātha temple. Records in Dutch the death of a gentleman in A.D. 1777.

893-D. On a bronze image discovered near the demolished tower of the ancient "China pagoda." A record, according to Dr. Burnell, belonging to the twelfth or early thirteenth century.

---

* In his *Antiquities* Mr. Sewell gives an inscription in Ś. 1637 in this place, recording a grant of lands to the temple by Dukkōji Rāja (Tukkōji, 1728—35).

893-E. On a stone in "a small temple." A Dutch record saying that it was built in 1777 under the auspices of the Governor Reynier Van Vlissingen.

893-F. On a drum in the hands of Mr. C. E. Crighton. "A short inscription in ancient Tamil and Grantha characters." No details given.

893-G. A Telugu silver plate grant (now in the Batavia Museum). Records that Vijaya Rāghava, the last Ṅāik king of Tanjore, gave Negapatam to the Dutch.

893-H. A Tamil silver plate grant in the same place. Records the confirmation of the above grant by the Mahrātha king Ekoji in A.D. 1676.

893-I. On a stone in the old Dutch church. Records its foundation in 1774.

Śikkil.

894. 100 *of* 1911.—(Tamil.) On the south wall of the central shrine in the Kōlavāmana-Perumāḷ temple. A record of Lakkaṇa-Daṇṇāyakka, "Lord of the southern ocean," in Ś. 1366, Rudhirōdgārin. The village Śiṟṟāyanallūr originally granted to the temple of Kōlavāmana-Perumāḷ being found to be "far away," other lands were granted instead at Śikkil in Gēyamāṇikka-vaḷanāḍu. Mentions Veṇṇainallūr in Śikkalnāḍu which was a subdivision *(uśāvaḍi)* of Śōḷamaṇḍalam. See No. 946 below.

895. 101 *of* 1911.—(Tamil.) On the west base of the same shrine. This stone building of the temple was caused to be made by Ayāppiḷḷai, native of Maṅgaḷam.

896. 102 *of* 1911.—(Grantha.) On the south base of the central shrine of the Navanītēśvara temple in the same village. Supplies some information about the *māhātmya* of the place referred to in the Skanda-purāṇa. For the quotation of the verses see *Ep. Rep.*, 1911, pp. 67–68.

897. 103 *of* 1911.—(Tamil and Grantha.) On the same base. It gives the names of the Rishis, the tank and the trees which worshipped the God Pālveṇṇai-Nāyanār at this sacred place. Figures of these devotees are depicted below the record.

898. 104 *of* 1911.—(Tamil.) On the same base. A record of the Vijayanagara king Mahāmaṇḍalēśvara Sadāśivadēva-Mahārāya in Ś. 1482, Raudri. Registers that Jñānaprakāśa-paṇḍāram of Tiruvārūr was appointed supervisor of Śikkal, Vaḍakuḍi, Vōḍachchēri and other temples under orders of Kṛishṇamarasayyan, son of Aḷiya-Rāmarāsayya. [There are four Gñānaprakāśas met with in Tamil literature. One of these was a native of Jaffna. Another lived in the time of Kṛishnadēva Rāya. A third Gñānaprakāśa lived at Tiruvoṟṟiyūr, and the fourth at Tiruvārūr.

The last of these wrote the *Puṭpavidhi*. It is difficult to say to whom the present epigraph refers. See the *Abhidhānachintāmani*, p. 480.]

899. 105 *of* 1911.—(Tamil.) On the west base of the same shrine. A mutilated record of the Vijayanagara king Vīra-pratāpa Achyutadēva-Mahārāya, the date of which is lost. Seems to record a grant of land for lamps and festivals to the shrine of Kumārasvāmin in the temple of Pālveṇṇai Nāyanār at Śikkal.

900. 106 *of* 1911.—(Tamil.) On the same base. Seems to record in Vijaya the gift of the village of Kandasvāmipēṭṭai to the temple by Raṅgapparāja and the residents of the district.

901. 107 *of* 1911.—(Tamil.) On the same base. A record in the fourteenth year of the Pāṇḍya king Jaṭāvarman Tribhuvana-chakravartin Vīra-Pāṇḍyadēva. Built in at the bottom. Seems to record a gift of money tothe temple of Pālveṇṇai-Nāyanār. [Was he the king who came to the throne in 1295 ? See No. 842 above.]

Tirukkāravāśal.

This is the *Śivasthala* Tirukkārāyil, where Indra, Muśukunda and others are said to have worshipped the Lord. It has been sung by Tirugñānasambanda.

902. 451 *of* 1908.—(Tamil.) On a pillar lying in a grove. A mutilated record in the third year of the Chōḷa king Parakēsari-varman *alias* Rājēndra-Chōḷadēva (1011—43). Records gift of land by purchase, for a lamp and for offerings to the temple of Tirukkārāyil-Uḍaiyār.

903. 452 *of* 1908.—(Tamil.) On another pillar in the same place. A record in the twenty-seventh year of the Chōḷa king Rājakēsarivarman *alias* Rājarājadēva (I). Records the construction of the ōlakkamaṇṭapam and mentions Arumoḷidēva-vaḷanāḍu.

904. 453 *of* 1908.—(Tamil.) On the third pillar in the same place. A record in the third year of the Chōḷa king Rājakēsari-varman Mummuḍi-Chōḷadēva (Rājarāja I). Records gift of land 35 *mās* by purchase by the *sabhā* fora lamp to the temple of Mahādēva at Tirukkārāyil, a *brahmadēya* in Puliyūr-nāḍu. Mentions Kīraṅguḍi in Valivala-kūṟṟam.

905. 454 *of* 1908.—(Tamil.) On some of the detached stones lying in the same temple. An incomplete record in the twenty-eighth year (Karkaṭaka, Pūrva 14th, Wednesday, Uttaraphalguni) of the Chōḷa king Tribhuvanachakravartin Rājarājadēva (III). Records gift of land for feeding the persons who recite the *Tirumuṟai* in the *Tirukkaikkōṭṭi* of the temple at Tirukkārāyil by the residents of Mūvūr, a village in Puliyūr-nāḍu, a subdivision of Arumoḷidēva-vaḷanāḍu. See *Ep. Ind.*, Vol. XI, p. 130, where the English date is given as Wednesday, the 22nd July, A.D. 1243 (with some corrections). For the *Tiṟumuṟai* see No. 855 above.

Tēvūr.

This place is one of the South-Kāvēri centres of Śaivitism, sung by Tirugñānasambanda.

906. 518 *of* 1904.—(Tamil.) On the south wall of the maṇṭapa in front of the central shrine in the Dēvapurīśvara temple. A record in the eleventh year of the Pāṇḍya king Jaṭāvarman *alias* Tribhuvanachakravartin Sundara-Paṇḍyadēva III (1276—90). Records gift of land. The temple is called Ādittīśuramuḍaiyār at Tēvūr in Tēvūr-nāḍu, a subdivision of Arumoḷidēva-vaḷanāḍu. The date corresponds to Wednesday, October 29, A.D. 1287. See *Ep. Ind.*, Vol. VIII, p. 279.

907. 519 *of* 1904.—(Tamil.) On the north wall of the same maṇṭapa. An incomplete record of the Vijayanagara king Dēvarāya Mahārāya II, in Ś. 1347, expired, Viśvāvasu. Refers to Bukkaṇa-Uḍaiyār (Bukka II ?) who is called Dēvargaḷ-Nāyan.

Tiruvārūr.

For an account of the legends, the local shrine and other antiquities of this important *Śivasthala* see *Tanj. Gazr.*, pp. 248—50.

908. 73 *of* 1890.—(Grantha.) On the west wall of the second prākāra of the Tyāgarājasvāmin temple. A record of the Chōḷa king Anapāya, i.e., Kulōttuṅga Chōḷa II. See No. 911.

909. 74 *of* 1890.—(Grantha.) On a stone near a well in the first prākāra of the same temple.

910. 164 *of* 1894.—(Tamil.) On the north wall of the second prākāra of the same temple. A record in the fifth year of the Chōḷa king Kō-Parakēsarivarman *alias* Vikrama-Chōḷadēva (1118—1135). Records gift of land. Refers to the *Periapurāṇam* legend of king Manuchōḷa and the calf.

911. 269 *of* 1901.—(Tamil.) On the west wall of the second prākāra of the same temple. A record in the seventh year of the Chōḷa king Rājakēsarivarman *alias* Tribhuvanachakravartin Kulōttuṅga-Chōḷadēva (II). The concluding portion was copied in 1890 (No. 73 of 1890). The inscription is very important for the information it gives that the Kulōttuṅgachōḷa whose inscription begins with the expression பூமன் னுபதுமம் (i.e., Kulōttuṅga II) was Anapāya Chōḷa. This enables us to say at once that Śēkkiḷār, the author of the *Periapurāna*, lived in this reign and not in that of Kulōttuṅga I, as some suppose.

912. 533 *of* 1904.—(Tamil.) On the east wall of the Tyāgarāja shrine in the same temple, left of entrance. A record built in in the twenty-third year of the Chōḷa king Rājakēsarivarman *alias* Tribhuvanachakravartin Kulōttuṅga-Chōḷadēva (I ?), and damaged.

913. 534 *of* 1904.—(Tamil.) On the north wall of the Tyāgarāja shrine in the same temple. A mutilated record in the ninth year of the Chōḷa king Parakēsarivarman *alias* Rājēndradēva (1050—62). Seems to record a sale of land.

914. 535 *of* 1904.—(Tamil.) On a slab built into the floor of the first prākāra, north of the same shrine. Records in Kali. 4818 and Ś. 1639, expired, Hēmalamba, that the Mahrātha king Sarfoji (1711—27) of Tanjore made some repairs to the temple. See *Tanj Gazr.*, p. 44.

915. 536 *of* 1904.—(Tamil.) On another slab built into the floor of the same prākāra, north of the central shrine in the same temple. A damaged record of the Nāyaka king Achyutappa (1572—1614), son of Śevvappa-Nāyaka (1549—72), in Ś. 1482, expired, Rudhirōdgārin (wrong). See *Tanj. Gazr.*, p. 38.

916. 537 *of* 1904.—(Tamil.) On the east wall of the first prākāra of the same temple, right of entrance. A record in the eighth year of the Chōḷa king Parakēsarivarman *alias* Tribhuvanachakravartin Kulōttuṅga-Chōḷadēva (III). Built in at the end. Records gift of land for three lamps.

917. 538 *of* 1904.—(Tamil.) In the same place. A record in the second year of the Chōḷa king Rājakēsarivarman *alias* Tribhuvanachakravartin Rājādhirājadēva (II ?). Records gift of land by a native of Paḷaiyanūr in Mēnmalai-Paḷaiyanūr-nāḍu, a subdivision of Jayaṅgoṇḍa-Chōḷamaṇḍalam. See No. 919.

918. 539 *of* 1904.—(Tamil.) In the same place. A record in the thirty-fifth year of the Pāṇḍya king Māravarman Tribhuvanachakravartin Śrī-vallabhadēva. Built in at the end. Seems to record a gift of land. [Was the king the predecessor of Jaṭāvarman Kulaśēkhara I, 1190—1217 ?]

919. 540 *of* 1904.—(Tamil.) In the same place. A record in the tenth year of the Chōḷa king Rājakēsarivarman *alias* Tribhuvanachakravartin Rājādhirājadēva (II), corresponding to Tuesday, February 27, A.D. 1173. Records gift of land by a native of Paḷaiyanūr different from the donor in No. 917. See *Ep. Ind.*, Vol. IX, pp. 211-2.

920. 541 *of* 1904.—(Tamil.) In the same place. A record in the forty-fourth year of the Chōḷa king Rājakēsarivarman *alias* Tribhuvanachakravartin Kulōttuṅga-Chōḷadēva (I). Records gift of land.

921. 542 *of* 1904.—(Tamil.) In the same place. A record in the ninth year of the Chōḷa king Rājakēsarivarman *alias* Tribhuvanachakravartin Rājādhirājadēva (II). Built in at the end. Records gift of land by the donor in No. 919.

922. 543 *of* 1904.—(Tamil.) In the same place. A record in the fifth year of the Chōḷa king Tribhuvanachakravartin Rājādhirājadēva (II). Built in at the bottom. Refers to an order issued during the ninth year of Vikrama-Chōḷa's reign.

923. 544 *of* 1904.—(Tamil.) On the south wall of the same prākāra. A damaged record in the thirty-fourth year of the Chōḷa king Rājakēsarivarman *alias* Tribhuvanachakravartin Kulōttuṅga-Chōḷadēva (I). Registers lands belonging to the shrine of Ulagīś-varamuḍaiyār at Tiruvārūr.

924. 545 *of* 1904.—(Tamil.) On the same wall. An incomplete record in the sixth year of the Chōḷa king Parakēsarivarman Tribhuvanachakravartin Vikrama-Chōḷadēva (1118—35). Seems to record a gift of land.

925. 546 *of* 1904.—(Grantha and Tamil.) On the west wall of the same prākāra. Records in the second year of the king gift of land.

926. 547 *of* 1904.—(Tamil.) On the same wall. Contains an incomplete introduction beginning with the words *pūmaruviya-poḻil-ēḻum.*

927. 548 *of* 1904.—(Tamil.) On the same wall. Records in the fifteenth year of the king a grant of land to a certain Pūṅgōyil Nambi who sang the *Viraṇukkavijayam* in honour of "our son" Vīra-Śōḷa-Aṇukkar.

928. 549 *of* 1904.—(Tamil.) On the same wall. An incomplete record in the fifteenth year of the Chōḷa king Rājakēsarivarman *alias* Tribhuvanachakravartin Kulōttuṅga-Chōḷadēva (I). The inscription stops with the date.

929. 550 *of* 1904.—(Tamil.) On the same wall. A record in the thirteenth year of the Chōḷa king Tribhuvanachakravartin Kulōttuṅga-Chōḷadēva (III), "who took Madura and the crowned head of the Pāṇḍya." Records gift of land for the requirements of Tikkuniṟainda-Vināyagapiḷḷaiyār set up on the western bank of the fresh water pond.

930. 551 *of* 1904.—(Tamil.) On the same wall. A record in the fortieth year of the Pāṇḍya king Māravarman Tribhuvana-chakravartin Kulaśēkharadēva (I, 1268—1308). Registers gifts of land made in the thirty-second and fortieth years of the king's reign. At the end Ś. 1229, expired (i.e., 1230) is given as the equivalent of the fortieth year. The date corresponded to Monday, 18th March, 1308. See *Ep. Ind.*, Vol. VIII, pp. 276–7.

931. 552 *of* 1904.—(Tamil.) On the same wall. A record in the twelfth year of the Chōḷa king Kulōttuṅga-Chōḷadēva. Refers to the sixteenth year of "the king who abolished tolls" (i.e., Kulōttuṅga I) and records a gift of land for a flower-garden.

932. 553 *of* 1904.—(Tamil.) On the same wall. A record in the tenth year of the Chōḷa king Rājakēsarivarman *alias* Tribhuvanachakravartin Kulōttuṅga-Chōḷadēva. Records that the members of the assembly Rājarāja Brahmamaṅgalam (a *brahmadēya* in Tiruvārūr-kūṟṟam, a subdivision of Gēyamāṇikka-vaḷanāḍu) being assembled in the maṇṭapa called Dēvāśriyan (i.e., Dēvāś raya) exempted from taxes certain lands belonging to the Tiruvārūr temple. See *Ep. Ind.*, Vol. XI, p. 289, where it is pointed out that the date corresponded to Monday, 30th November, A.D. 1142.

933. 554 *of* 1904.—(Grantha and Tamil.) On the north wall of the same prākāra. A record in the twenty-fourth year of the Chōḷa king Tribhuvanavīradēva (Kulōttuṅga III). Registers the redistribution of certain temple lands. The king is described as "the friend of the God."

934. 555 *of* 1904.—(Tamil.) On the same wall. A record in the twentieth year of the Chōḷa king Tribhuvanachakravartin Rājēndra-Chōḷadēva (III). Records gift of land. The date corresponds to Wednesday, the 20th January, A.D. 1266. See *Ep. Ind.*, Vol. VIII, p. 274.

935. 556 *of* 1904.—(Tamil.) On the same wall. A record in the eighth year of the Chōḷa king Parakēsarivarman *alias* Tribhuvanachakravartin Vikrama-Chōḷadēva, corresponding to Tuesday, August 18, 1125. Records gift of money for a lamp by a merchant of Melai-Mārāyapāḍi *alias* Koyyakkuṟu-nāḍu. See *Ep. Ind.*, Vol. VIII, p. 263.

936. 557 *of* 1904.—(Tamil.) On the same wall. A record in the thirteenth year of the Chōḷa king Tribhuvanachakravartin Rājēndra-Chōḷadēva. Records gifts of land to the shrines of Aḻagiya-Tiruchchiṟṟambalamuḍaiyār and Poṟpadikkunāyaga Īśvaramuḍaiyār built in the southern street in front of the temple; to the shrine of Tirumāḷigai-Vināyakapiḷḷaiyār built in this temple in the twentieth year; and to the shrine of Subramaṇya built in the same temple in the twenty-second year.

937. 558 *of* 1904.—(Grantha and Tamil.) On the same wall. Registers the opinions, Nārada, Maskara, Yājñavalkya and other authorities regarding the origin, duties and privileges of certain mixed castes *(anulōma)*. A very interesting epigraph illustrating the social ideas of the age.

938. 559 *of* 1904.—(Tamil.) On the same wall. A record in the thirty-ninth year of the Chōḷa king Tribhuvanavīradēva (Kulottuṅga III). Mentions the temple of Vikrama-Chōḷēśvaramuḍaiyār at Śrī-Mahēśvaranallūr and records a gift of land by a woman who had a relation at Vāḷaippandal in Paḷakunṟa-kōṭṭam, a subdivision of Jayaṅgoṇḍa-Chōḷamaṇḍalam.

939. 560 *of* 1904.—(Tamil.) On the south wall of the second prākāra of the same temple. An incomplete record in the third year of the Chōḷa king Parakēśarivarman *alias* Tribhuvanachakravartin Vikrama-Chōḷadēva (1118—35). Records gift of land.

940. 561 *of* 1904.—(Tamil.) On the same wall. An incomplete record in the forty-ninth year of the Chōḷa king Rājakēsarivarman *alias* Tribhuvanachakravartin Kulōttuṅga-Chōḷadēva (I). Mentions (the maṇṭapa called) Dēvāśriyan.

941. 562 *of* 1904.--(Tamil.) On the same wall. An incomplete record in the third year of the Chōḷa king Rājakēsarivarman *alias* Chakravartin Vikrama-Chōḷadēva. Records gift of land. [Vikramachōḷa was a Parakēsarivarman. The present epigraph is one of the very few which give the title Rājakēsarivarman to him.]

942. 563 *of* 1904.—(Tamil.) On the same wall. A record in the fourth year of the Chōḷa king Parakēsarivarman *alias* Tribhuvanachakravartin Vikrama-Chōḷadēva (1118—35). Built in at the bottom. Records gift of a pond. Date as in the next. (But *Aparapaksham* wrongly given for *Pūrvapaksham*. See *Ep. Ind.*, Vol. VIII, p. 262.

943. 564 *of* 1904.—(Tamil.) On the same wall. An incomplete record in the fourth year of the Chōḷa king Parakēsarivarman *alias* Tribhuvanachakravartin Vikrama-Chōḷadēva. Connected with the previous inscription. Same date as that of the previous one, but the details more correct. Corresponds to Wednesday, 10th May, A.D. 1122. See *Ep. Ind.*, Vol. VIII, p. 262.

944. 565 *of* 1904.—(Tamil.) On the same wall. A mutilated record containing an incomplete introduction of Vikrama-Chōḷa (1118—35).

945. 566 *of* 1904.—(Tamil.) At the entrance into the western gōpura of the same prākāra right side. A record in Ś. 1362, expired, Raudri. Records the building of the gōpura by Nāgarasa, son of Siddharasa, for the merit of the minister Lakkaṇadaṇṇāyakka-Uḍaiyār. See note to the next inscription.

946. 567 *of* 1904.—(Kanarese.) In the same place left side. A record in Ś. 1362, expired, Raudra. A Kanarese copy of the above epigraph. Lakkaṇa-Daṇṇāyaka is here called Dakshiṇa-samudrādhipati, while in the above one the portion occupied by the *biruda* is damaged. For a coin of Lakkaṇa see *Ep. Rep.*, 1905, pp. 58-9. His position in Madura history has been summarized by me in *Ind. Antq.*, 1914 (January).

947. 568 *of* 1904.—(Tamil.) On the north wall of the Achalēśvara shrine in the south-east corner of the second prākāra of the same temple. A mutilated record in the eighth year of the Chōḷa king Parakēsarivarman *alias* Rājēndra-Chōḷadēva (I, 1011—1053).

948. 569 *of* 1904.—(Tamil.) On the same wall. An incomplete record in the second year of the Chōḷa king Rājarājakēsarivarman *alias* Rājarājadēva (I, 985—1013). Records gift of land.

949. 570 *of* 1904.—(Tamil.) On the south wall of the same shrine. An incomplete record in the second year of the Chōḷa king Rājakēsarivarman. Records gift of silver vessels by Uḍaiyapirāṭṭiyār Śembiyan Mahādēviyār for the merit of Śrī-Uttama-Chōḷadēva. [She was the queen of Gaṇḍarāditya and the mother of Madhurāntaka Uttama Chōḷa.]

950. 571 *of* 1904.—(Tamil.) On the same wall. A record in the seventh year of the Chōḷa king Rājarājakēsarivarman. Refers to the building of a shrine of stone in the temple of Tiruvaranēri Āḷvār by Uḍaiyapirāṭṭiyār Śembiyan Mahādēviyār and the setting up of two images in it by the same lady and records that she presented 234 *kāśus* for daily requirements, additions to the temple and repairs.

951. 572 *of* 1904.—(Tamil.) On the west wall of the maṇṭapa in front of the same shrine, right of entrance. A record in the twentieth year of the Chōḷa king Rājakēsarivarman. Records gift of two lamps.

952. 573 *of* 1904.—(Tamil.) In the same place. A record in the thirty-second year of the Chōḷa king Parakēsarivarman (905—947), "who took Madurai." Records gift of gold for a lamp. The characters are comparatively modern.

953. 574 *of* 1904.—(Tamil.) On the same wall, left of entrance. A record in the sixth year of the Chōḷa king Parakēsarivarman. Records gift of gold for a lamp. The characters are comparatively modern.

954. 575 *of* 1904.—(Tamil.) On the north wall of the maṇṭapa in front of the Achalēśvara shrine in the south-east corner of the second prākāra of the same temple. A damaged record in Kīlaka of Vīrabhūpati-Uḍaiyār (1409—22).

955. 576 *of* 1904.—(Sanskrit and Grantha.) On the west wall of the third prākāra of the same temple, left of the gōpura. A mutilated record. Mentions the shrine of Ānandēśvara.

956. 577 *of* 1904.—(Tamil.) On the south wall of the central shrine in the Satyavāchakēśvara temple in the same village. A damaged and incomplete record of the Chōḷa king Rājakēsarivarman *alias* Chakravartin Kulōttuṅga-Chōḷadēva, the date of which is lost. Mentions Tirumaṇḍaḷi-uḍaiya-Mahādēvar.

957. 578 *of* 1904.—(Tamil.) On the same wall. A mutilated record in the forty-eighth year of the Chōḷa king Rājakēsarivarman *alias* Chakravartin Kulōttuṅga-Chōḷadēva (I). Registers allotments for the various requirements.

958. 579 *of* 1904.—(Tamil.) On the north wall of the same shrine. A record mutilated at the end. Contains a portion of the historical introduction of Kulōttuṅga (I). Mentions the temple of Tirumaṇḍaḷi-uḍaiya-Mahādēvar,

Valivalam.

This *Śivasthala* of the South-Kāvēri region has been sung by Gñānasambanda, Sundara and Appar.

959. 108 *of* 1911.—(Tamil.) On the south wall of the central shrine in the Manattuṇai-Īśar temple. A damaged record in the fifth year of the Chōḷa king Tribhuvanachakravartin Rājēndra-Chōḷadēva (III). Registers an exchange of land granted to a certain Ediroppilādār Sōmanāthadēva-Mudaliyār of Tavapperumāḷ-*tirumaḍam*, by the servants of the temple of Uḍaiyār Manattuḷ-Nāyanār.

960. 109 *of* 1911.—(Tamil.) On the west wall of the same shrine. A record in the twentieth year of the Chōḷa king Tribhuvanachakravartin Rājēndra-Chōḷadēva (III). Records gift of land by the resident of Tenviḍaṅgaḷūr, a village in Valivala-kūṟṟam which was a subdivision of Arumoḷidēva-vaḷanāḍu, to Ediroppilādār Sōmanāthadēva-Mudaliyār of *Tiruchcheṟṟimuṟṟam* lineage, who was presiding over the Tavapperumāḷ-*tirumaḍam* situated on the south side of the temple of Manattuḷ-Nāyanār at Valivalam.

961. 110 *of* 1911.—(Tamil.) On the same wall. A record in the third year of the Chōḷa king Tribhuvanachakravartin Kulōttuṅga-Chōḷadēva. Records exchange of land given to the temple of Manattuḷdēva at Valivalam *alias* Ubhayakulaśuddha-chaturvēdimaṅgalam in Valivala-kūṟṟam, a subdivision of Arumoḷidēva-vaḷanādu, for the land taken up to dig a tank called Rājādhirājan-Peruṅguḷam at Kulōttuṅgaśōḷanallūr which was a *dēvadāna* village of the temple.

962. 111 *of* 1911.—(Tamil.) On the same wall. A mutilated record. Records gift of land to the temple of Manattuḷ-Nāyanār in the *dēvadāna* village of Kulōttuṅgaśōḷa-nallūr.

963. 112 *of* 1911.—(Tamil.) On the same wall. A record in the fourteenth year of the Chōḷa king Tribhuvanachakravartin Rajarājadēva (III). Records gift of land which was purchased by some people for 30,000 *kāśus* in a public auction *(rājarājapperuvilai)* at Kulōttuṅgaśoḷanallūr to the same temple. The lands had originally belonged to certain persons who were declared *drōhins* (enemies) of the state.

964. 113 *of* 1911.—(Tamil.) On the same wall. A record in the twelfth year of the Chōḷa king Tribhuvanachakravartin Rājarājadēva. Records that a certain land was declared a *dēvadāna* by planting in it the *tiruchchūlam*.

965. 114 *of* 1911.—(Tamil.) On the north and west walls of the same shrine. A record in the seventh year of the Pāṇḍya king Jaṭāvarman *alias* Tribhuvanachakravartin Sundara-Pāṇḍyadēva. Records sale of land in the village of Kūṟṟūr *alias* Ponmēnda-perumāḷnallūr to the temple of Manattuḷ-Nāyanār at Tiruvalivalam in Valivala-kūṟṟam, a subdivision of Arumoḷidēva-vaḷanāḍu, by the wife of a certain Vayirādarāyan, a native of Pālaikkuruchchi which was a village in Ālattūr-nāḍu, a subdivision of Madhurōdaya-vaḷanāḍu in Pāṇḍimaṇḍalam. [It is not certain as to which of the Jaṭāvarman Sundara Pāṇḍyas is intended.]

966. 115 *of* 1911.—(Tamil.) On the same walls. A record in the seventh year of the Pāṇḍya king Jaṭāvarman *alias* Tribhuvanachakravartin Sundara-Pāṇḍyadēva. Records sale of land in the village of Kulōttuṅgaśōḷanallūr, to the same temple by Vayirādarāyan mentioned in the above epigraph. The subdivision Valivalakūṟṟam is here called *Valivala-vagai.*

967. 116 *of* 1911.—(Tamil.) On the north wall of the same shrine. A record of the Chōḷa king Tribhuvanachakravartin Rājēndra-Chōḷadēva, the date of which is lost. Records sale of land apparently to the *maṭha* of Tirumūladēva by the priests of the temple. Quotes the fourteenth year of Periyadēvar Rājarājadēva. [Tirumūla was not improbably the great Śaivite Siddha and author of the *Tirumūlar-Tirumantra,* whose tradition is connected with Tiruvāvaḍuturai. See *Abhidhānachintāmaṇi,* p. 534, for a short account of his life. His *Tirumantra* forms the tenth *Tirumuṟai.* See No. 855 above.

Pāpanāsam Taluk.

Āḍuturai.

This place, known as Tirukkuraṅgāḍuturai, is connected with Śaivite traditions and is so called because it saw the Lord's grace to Vāli, the monkey lord of Kishkindha, who was slain by Rāma.

968. 356 *of* 1907.—(Tamil.) On the south wall of the central shrine in the Āpatsahāyēśvara temple. A record in the ninth year of the Chōḷa king Rājarājakēsarivarman (I, 985—1013). Records gift of land for lamps. The temple is called Tirukkuraṅgāḍuturai Mahādēvar in Teṅkarai-Tiṟaimūr-nāḍu.

969. 337 *of* 1907.—(Tamil.) On the same wall. A record in the sixteenth year of the Chōḷa king Uttamachōḷadēva *alias* Parakēsarivarman (970—86). Refers to the temples as having been built by the mother of Śrī-Madhurāntakadēva *alias* Śrī-Uttama-chōḷa. [His mother was Śembian Mahādēvi, the wife of Gaṇḍarāditya.]

970. 358 *of* 1907.—(Tamil.) On the same wall. A damaged record in the eighth year of the Pāṇḍya king Māran Śaḍayan. [Was he Jaṭilavarman who incised the Ānaimalai cave inscription and issued the Vēḷvikuḍi grant about A.D. 770 ?]

971. 359 *of* 1907.—(Tamil.) On the same wall. A damaged record. Mentions Maruttuvakkuḍi.

972. 360 *of* 1907.—(Tamil.) On the same wall. A damaged record.

973. 361 *of* 1907.—(Tamil.) On the west wall of the same shrine. A damaged record in the twenty-eighth year of the Chōḷa king Rājakēsarivarman *alias* Chakravartin Śrī-Kulōttuṅga-Chōḷadēva (I ?). Mentions gift of a lamp.

974. 362 *of* 1907.—(Tamil.) On the north wall of the same shrine. A record in the ninth year of the Chōḷa king Rājarājakēsarivarman (985—1013). Records gift of land (8 *mās*, etc.) by Uḍaiyapirāṭṭiyār Pirāntakan Mādēvaḍigaḷār *alias* Śembiyan Mādēviyār, mother of Madhurāntakadēva *alias* Śrī-Uttama-Chōḷa. See No. 969 above.

975. 363 *of* 1907.—(Tamil.) On the same wall. A record in the fourteenth year of the Chōḷa king . . . Śrī-Kulōttuṅga-Chōḷadēva (I ?). Records gift of lamps. Refers to the river Śuṅgandavirttaśōḷa-Pērāru (named evidently after Kulōttuṅga I).

976. 364 *of* 1907.—(Tamil.) On the north wall of the central shrine in the same temple. A damaged record in the sixth year of the Pāṇḍya king Māran Śaḍayan. See No. 970 above.

977. 365 *of* 1907.—(Tamil.) On the same wall. A record in the twenty-ninth year of the Chōḷa king Chakravartin Śrī-Kulōttuṅga-Chōḷadēva (I ?). Records sale of land for a lamp. The village is called Tirukkuraṅgāḍuturai in Tiṟaimūr-nāḍu, a subdivision of Bhūpālakulavalli-vaḷanāḍu. Mentions Śuṅgandavirttān, i.e., perhaps the river mentioned in No. 975.

978. 366 *of* 1907.—(Tamil.) On the south wall of the maṇṭapa, in front of the same shrine. A record in the tenth year of the Chōḷa king Rājakēsarivarman *alias* Tribhuvanachakravartin Śrī-Kulōttuṅga-Chōḷadēva (I ?). Mentions Vēdagōmapuram in Vikramaśōḷa-chaturvēdimaṅgalam.

979. 367 *of* 1907.—(Tamil.) On the same wall. A record of the Chōḷa king Rājakēsarivarman *alias* Tribhuvanachakravartin, the date of which is lost. Records gift of a lamp.

980. 368 *of* 1907.—(Tamil.) On the same wall. A record in the sixteenth year of the Chōḷa king Tribhuvanachakravartin Śrī-Rājarājadēva. Records sale of land. Mentions Śuṅgandavirtta-Śōḷa-Pērāru. See No. 975 above.

981. 369 *of* 1907.—(Tamil.) On the same wall. A record in the second year of the Chōḷa king Tribhuvanachakravartin Śrī-Vīrarājēndradēva. Records gift of money. [The king was evidently Vīra Rājēndra (I), 1063—70.]

982. 370 *of* 1907.—(Tamil.) On the same wall. A damaged record in the fifth year of the Chōḷa king Rājakēsarivarman *alias* Tribhuvanachakravartin Śrī-Kulōttuṅga-Chōḷadēva (I ?). Records gift of a lamp.

Alaṅguḍi (near Nīḍāmaṅgalam).

As the Śiva temple of this village, known as Irumbulai among the orthodox, is mentioned in the *Dēvāram*, it should have existed in the seventh century. The inscriptions, however, belong only to the Chōḷa period.

983. 44 *of* 1891.—(Tamil.) On the south wall of the first prākāra of the Āpatsahāyēśvara temple. A record in the forty-fifth year of the Chōḷa king Kō-Rājakēsarivarman *alias* Kulōttuṅga-Chōḷadēva (I). Refers to the king's invasion of Kaliṅga in A.D. 1111-2 Venkayya points out that this invasion (in which Vikrama Chōḷa took part) was different from the invasion of 1095-6; that the *Kaliṅgattupparaṇi* and *Vikramachōḷan-ulā* refer to this; and that it was against North Kaliṅga in order to assist Anantavarman Chōḍagaṅga against Kaliṅga rebels while the earlier one was against North Kaliṅga invaders of South Kaliṅga. See *Ep. Rep.*, 1905, p. 53. [See also 608 of 1904 at Śrīnivāsanallūr in Trichinopoly district.]

984. 165 *of* 1894.—(Tamil.) On the north wall of the Āpatsahāyēśvara shrine. A record in the eleventh year of the Chōḷa king Kō-Parakēsarivarman *alias* Vikrama-Chōḷadēva (1118—35).

985. 3 *of* 1899.—(Tamil.) On the south wall of the second prākāra of same temple. A record in the eleventh year of the Chōḷa king Rājakēsarivarman *alias* Tribhuvanachakravartin Rājādhirājadēva (II, 1171—86), "who took Madura and Ceylon." Appears to record a fresh settlement of the revenues of the village of Ālaṅguḍi.

986. 4 *of* 1899.—(Tamil.) On the same wall. A damaged record in Ś. 1186. Mentions Kalikāla in line 3.

987. 5 *of* 1899.—(Tamil.) On the south wall of the central shrine of the same temple. A record in the sixth year of the Chōḷa king Parakēsarivarman *alias* Tribhuvanachakravartin Rājarājadēva (II). Kielhorn corrects Mīna into Kumbha and then arrives at the English equivalent, Thursday, 14th February 1152. See *Ep. Ind.*, Vol. VIII, pp. 3-4.

Āṇḍānkōyil.

987-A. 290 *of* 1908.—(Tamil.) On the east, south and west walls of the shrine of the goddess in the Śiva temple. A record in the twenty-second year of the Pāṇḍya king Jaṭāvarman Tribhuvanachakravartin Vīra-Pāṇḍyadēva. Mentions Āṇḍanāyanārkōyil and records the gift of a *maṭha* by a native of Tirupputtūr in Śeṟṟūr-kūṟṟam, a subdivision of Arumoḷidēva-vaḷanāḍu. [Was the king the same as he who ascended the throne in 1253 and who had the *birudas* conqueror of Īḻam, Koṅgu and Śōḻamaṇḍalam and the anointment of victors at Perumbaṟṟappuliyūr?]

987-B. Mr. Sewell mentions a C.P. inscription in the temple, dated Ś. 1711, Saumya (A.D. 1789), recording gifts of land to the temple by the chief of Śivagaṅga. [*Antiquities*, Vol. I, p. 273.]

Aridvāramaṅgalam.

988. 611 *of* 1902.—(Tamil.) On the north wall of the maṇṭapa in front of the central shrine in the Pātāḷīśvara temple. An incomplete record in the tenth year of the Chōḷa king Tribhuvanachakravartin Kulōttuṅga-Chōḷadēva (III) who took Madura. The date is irregular, but Dr. Kielhorn points out that the day intended is Tuesday, 5th January, A.D. 1188. See *Ep. Ind.*, Vol. VIII, p. 4.

Avaḷivanallūr.

Connected in Śaivite legends with Varāhamūrti who is said to have done penance here and got the sight of the Lord. Hence the name Sākshinātha. Sung by Gñānasambanda and Appar.

989. 603 *of* 1902.—(Tamil.) On the south wall of the maṇṭapa in front of the central shrine in the Sākshināthasvāmin temple. An incomplete record in the seventh year of the Chōḷa king Tribhuvanachakravartin Rājēndra-Chōḷadēva (III ?).

990. 604 *of* 1902.—(Tamil.) On the south wall of the central shrine in the same temple. A record in the eighteenth year of the Chōḷa king . . . Chōḷadēva (III ?). Records the setting up of several images by a merchant.

991. 605 *of* 1902.—(Tamil.) On the north wall of the same shrine. A damaged record in the twenty-second year of the Chōḷa king Tribhuvanachakravartin Rājēndra-Chōḷadēva (III), corresponding to Wednesday, 20th April, A.D. 1267. See *Ep. Ind.*, Vol. VIII, p. 7.

992. 606 *of* 1902.—(Tamil.) On the same wall. A damaged record in the nineteenth year of a king, whose name is doubtful.

Āvūr.

Āvūr is Tamil for Paśupatīśvara and is well known in Śaivite tradition as the place where Indra, the Saptarishis and cows worshipped Śiva. It has been celebrated in Gñānasambanda's *padikas*.

993. 81 *of* 1911.—(Tamil.) On the west base of the central shrine in the Paśupatīśvara temple. A record in the third year of the Chōḷa king Tribhuvanachakravartin Rājēndra-Chōḷadēva (III ?). Registers a list of lands owned up to the third year of the king, by the temple of Paśupatīśvaramuḍaiyār at Āvūr in Āvūr-kūṟṟam, which was a subdivision of Nitta-vinōda-vaḷanāḍu.

Irumbudalai.

This village and Melaṭṭūr borrowed money from the Tanjore temple and agreed to supply paddy and watchmen to it.

994. 32 *of* 1910.—(Tamil.) On the south wall of the central shrine in the Trilōkanāthēśvara temple. A fragmentary record. Records gift of paddy to the temple of Tiruvirumbudaluḍaiya-Mahādēva at Manukula-chūḷāmaṇi-chaturvēdimaṅgalam, by the assembly of that village.

995. 33 *of* 1910.—(Tamil.) On a tier running round the base of the same shrine. A record in the twenty-third year of the Chōḷa king Rājarājakēsarivarman *alias* Śrī-Rājarājadēva (I). Stones in disorder and built up-side down. Records gift of paddy for offerings and lamps to the temple of Tiruvirumbudaluḍaiya Mahādēva at Manukulachūḷāmaṇi-chaturvēdimaṅgalam, a *brahmadēya* in Āvūr-kūṟṟam, a subdivision of Nittavinōda-vaḷanāḍu. Mentions the shrine of Amarabhujaṅgadēva.

996. 34 *of* 1910.—(Tamil.) On the north and west tiers of the same base. A record in the sixth year of the Chōḷa king Parakēsari-varman *alias* Tribhuvanachakravartin Vikrama-Chōḷadēva (1118—1135). Stones in disorder. Records a gift of lamp.

Kapistalam.

996-A. On a stone in the Dēvaṅga "pallala" *maṭha.* An effaced record dated in Ś. 1464 in the reign of Achyuta Dēva Rāya. Grant by one "Sarungadavun" to "Dēvaṅga Chaktarroogull" (?). *Ins., S. Dts.*, p. 196, No. 13.

996-B. A C.P. dated in Ś. 1349 in the reign of Vīra Śiṅgarāya Dēva Mahārāya. Records that Mulloo Nāyakan of "Nalloda" village disposed half the village for 125 pagodas to Banume Śeṭṭi. *Ibid.*, No. 14.

996-C. A C.P. in the same place. Records that in Ś. 1351, Vikrama (?), in the reign of the same king, Muttiyappa Nāyakan of (Kṛishṇa vōḍa) village sold half of it for 113 pagodas to Arane Śeṭṭi of Chinnamaṅgalam village. *Ibid.*, No. 15.

Maruttuvakkuḍi.

997. 386 *of* 1907.—(Tamil.) On the north wall of the maṇṭapa in front of the central shrine in the Airāvatēśvara temple. A record in the thirty-ninth year of the Chōḷa king Tribhuvanachakra-vartin Śrī-Tribhuvanavīradēva (Kulōttuṅga III) who took Madura, Īḷam (Ceylon) and Karuvūr and was pleased to take the crowned head of the Pāṇḍya and to perform the anointment of heroes and the anointment of victors. Records gift of land to provide for daily requirements. Refers to the twenty-fifth and twenty-sixth years of the king.

998. 387 *of* 1907.—(Tamil.) On the same wall. A record in the twenty-first year of Tribhuvanachakravartin Kōnērinmaikoṇ-ḍān. The temple is called Uḍaiyār Tiruviḍaikkuḷamuḍaiyār at

Ānaichchūḷ in Tiraimūr-nāḍu, a subdivision of Uyyakkoṇḍār-vaḷanāḍu.

999. 388 *of* 1907.—(Tamil.) On the same wall. A record in the twenty-first year of Tribhuvanachakravartin Kōnērinmaikoṇḍān. Records gift of land. Refers to the fortieth year of some unnamed king.

1000. 389 *of* 1907.—(Tamil.) On the north wall of the maṇṭapa in front of the central shrine in the same temple. A record in the twenty-first year of the king. Records gift of land to provide for the daily requirements of the temple of Tiruviḍaikkuḷamuḍaiyār at Ānaichchūḷ in Tiraimūr-nāḍu, a subdivision of Uyyakkoṇḍār-vaḷanāḍu. Refers to the fortieth year of Tribhuvanavīradēva (Kulōttuṅga III).

1001. 390 *of* 1907.—(Tamil.) On the same wall. A record in the twenty-seventh year of the Chōḷa king Tribhuvanachakravartin Śrī-Kulōttuṅga-Chōḷadēva III, who was pleased to take Madura, Īḷam (Ceylon) and Karuvūr and the crowned head of the Pāṇḍya. Refers to the Revenue survey *(aḷavu)* in the sixteenth year of Śuṅgandavirttaruḷina Kulōttuṅga-Śōḷa-dēva (I).

1002. 391 *of* 1907.—(Tamil.) On the same wall. Records in the twenty-first year of the king (?) gift of land. Refers to the fortieth year of Periyadēva Tribhuvanavīradēva (Kulōttuṅga III). Mentions Tiṟaimūr *alias* Ulaguyyakkoṇḍa-Śōḷa-chaturvēdimaṅgalam in Viḷai-nāḍu, a district of Jayaṅgoṇḍa-Chōḷa-valanāḍu.

1003. 392 *of* 1907.—(Tamil.) On the south wall of the same maṇṭapam. A record in the sixteenth year of the Chōḷa king Tribhuvanachakravartin Śrī-Kulōttuṅga-Chōḷadēva (III), who took Madura and was pleased to take the crowned head of the Pāṇḍya. Records gift of land. Mentions Śivapādaśēkharanallūr, which was a *mēl-vēṭṭappēṟu* and refers to two Jaina temples *(paḷḷi)* at Jananāthapuram called Chēdikulamāṇikkapperumbaḷḷi and Gaṅgarulasundarapperumbaḷḷi.

1004. 393 *of* 1907.—(Tamil.) On the same wall. A record in the tenth year (Karkaṭaka, Pūrva 12, Saturday, Mūlam) of the Chōḷa king Parakēsarivarman *alias* Tribhuvanachakravartin Śrī-Kulōttuṅga-Chōḷadēva III, who was pleased to take Madura. Registers the foundation of a village *(agaram)* called Kulōttuṅga-Śōḷan-Niyāyaparipāla-chaturvēdimaṅgalam by taking land from several villages. See *Ep. Ind.*, Vol. X, p. 127, where it is shown that the date corresponded to Saturday, July 18th, A.D. 1187.

1005. 394 *of* 1907.—(Telugu.) On a stone set up on the bank of the Uyyakkoṇḍān channel near the surplus sluice. A record of the Nāyaka queen, Maṅgammāgāru (1689—1705), the queen of Viśāvantha Nāyani-Chokka-Nāyanivāru in Ś. 1628, current, Tāraṇa. Records the construction of the sluice *(kalingulu)* by a Brāhmaṇa. See *Ind. Antq.*, 1917, p. 156 ff.

Melaṭūr (Milattūr).

1006. 28 *of* 1910.—(Tamil.) On the south wall of the maṇṭapa in front of the central shrine in the Unnatapurīśvara temple. A damaged record in the fourth year of the Chōḷa king Parakēsarivarman *alias* Tribhuvanachakravartin Vikrama-Chōḷadēva (1118—1135). Built in at the end. Mentions Peru-Milaṭṭūr in Kiḷār-kūṟṟam, a subdivision of Nittavinōda-vaḷanāḍu and seems to record a gift of sheep for lamps.

1007. 29 *of* 1910.—(Tamil.) On the same wall. An unfinished record of the Chōḷa king Tribhuvanachakravartin Rājarājadēva, the date of which is lost. The temple is called Tiruvagattīśuram-Uḍaiyār of Peru-Milaṭṭūr in Nittavinōda-vaḷa-nāḍu. Mentions a temple named Vikrama-Chōḷīśuram-Uḍaiyār and appears to record a gift of land.

1008. 30 *of* 1910.—(Tamil.) On the north wall of the same maṇṭapa. A record in the second year (Rishabha, Pūrva 3, Wednesday, Punarvasu) of the Chōḷa king Tribhuvanachakravartin Kulōttuṅga-Chōḷadēva. Records gift of land to the temple of Tiruvagattīśuramuḍaiya-Mahādēva at Peru-Milaṭṭūr, by a native of that village. See *Ep. Ind.*, Vol. XI, p. 246, where Mr. Sewell discusses the date in regard to each of the three kings of this name and finds no satisfactory English equivalent.

1009. 31 *of* 1910.—(Tamil.) On the south wall of the Vighnēśvara shrine in the courtyard of the same temple. A damaged record in the third year of the Chōḷa king Tribhuvanachakravartin Rājādhirājadēva. Records gift of sheep for a lamp.

Muṇiyūr.

1010. 156 *of* 1911.—(Tamil.) On the south wall of the Agastyēśvara temple. A record in the second year of the Chōḷa king Tribhuvanachakravartin Rājarājadēva. Records gift of land to the *guhai* of *Tirujñānasambanda-maḍam* on the south side of the temple of Tiruvagattīśuram-Uḍaiyār at Muṇiyūr in Āvūr-kūṟṟam which was a subdivision of Nittavinōda-vaḷanāḍu, by the assembly of Puttūr *alias* Tribhuvanamādēvi-chaturvēdimaṅgalam, a *brahmadēya* in Vīraśōḷa-vaḷanāḍu of the same territorial division. See No. 1012 and the inscriptions of Nallūr and Valivalam for similar institutions.

1011. 157 *of* 1911.—(Tamil.) On the same wall. A record in the fourth year of the Chōḷa king Tribhuvanachakravartin Rājarājadēva (III). States that some early records which registered grants to the temple of Tiruvagattīśvaram-Uḍaiyār at Muṇiyūr, were engraved on stone with the permission of Udayapperumāḷ Śōḷakōnār. For similar examples of copying old records in renovated temples see Tirumalaivāḍi, Tiruvallam and Siddhaliṅga-maḍam.

1012. 158 *of* 1910.—(Tamil.) On the north wall of the same temple. A record in the twenty-eighth year of the Chōḷa king Tribhuvanachakravartin Rājarājadēva. Records gift of land to the *Tirumuṟai-ttēvarachchelvan-maṭha* on the north side of the Tiruttoṇḍīśuramuḍaiya-Nāyanār temple at Tirukkaḷumalam (in Tirukkaḷumalanāḍu, a subdivision of Rājādhirājavaḷanāḍu, by the residents of Muṇiyūr. See No. 1010 above.

Nālūr.

This place, generally called Tirunālūr Mayānam, is one of the south Kāvēri Śaivite places. It has been sung by Gñānasambanda.

1013. 308 *of* 1910.—(Tamil.) On the door posts at the entrance into the Plāśapurīśvara temple. A partly damaged record in the twenty-fourth year of the Choḷa king Rājakēsarivarman. Appears to record a lease of land and states that the assembly of Nālūr, a *brahmadēya* of Śēṟṟur-kūṟṟam, met in the temple of Vaṇṇakkanār ambalam. Mentions also the village Vaḍa-Śāttaṅguḍi *alias* Kaḷarañjēnda-chaturvēdimaṅgalam.

1014. 309 *of* 1910.—(Tamil.) On the same door posts. A mutilated record in the twenty-second year of the Chōḷa king Madiraikoṇḍa Parakēsarivarman (Parāntaka I). Records gift of ninety sheep for a lamp to the temple of Śamaparēśvarattu-Mahādēva at Nālūr, a *brahmadēya* village in Śēṟṟur-kūṟṟam. The same door-post appears to have contained on it still another inscription of Madiraikoṇḍa-Parakēsarivarman, much damaged.

Nallūr.

One of the Śaivite centres of worship south of the Kāvēri; it has been sung by Gñānasambanda and Appar.

1015. 40 *of* 1911.—(Tamil.) On the south wall of the central shrine in the Kalyāṇasundarēśa temple. A fragmentary record of the twenty-third year of the Chōḷa king . . . kēsarivarman. Seems to record a gift of lamp to the temples of Iḷaṅgōyil-Mahādēva.

1016. 41 *of* 1911.—(Tamil.) On the same wall. A fragmentary record of the tenth year of the Chōḷa king Parakēsarivarman Madhurāntaka Uttama-Chōḷa. Refers to an enquiry into the affairs *(śrikārya)* of the temple of Mahādēva at Nallūr under orders of the king, by a certain Māṇakkuṟṟai-Vīranārāyaṇanār.

1017. 42 *of* 1911.—(Tamil.) On the same wall. A fragmentary record in the fifteenth year of the Chōḷa king Rājakēsarivarman (i.e., Rājarāja I). Contains portions of the historical introduction of Rājarāja I, and refers to a maṇṭapa built by a certain Nārāyaṇan Ēkavīran of Pañchavanmahādēvi-chaturvēdimaṅgalam which appears to have been another name of Nallūr.

1018. 43 *of* 1911.—(Tamil.) On the south wall of the second prākāra of the same temple. A record in the twenty-third year of the Hoysaḷa king Sārvabhaumachakravartin Vīra-Rāmanāthadēva. Records gift of land by a certain Aghōradēva to the temple at Tirunallūr *alias* Pañchavanmahādēvi-chaturvēdimaṅgalam in Nallūr-nāḍu, a subdivision of Nittavinōda-vaḷanāḍu. [The inscription affords a proof of Hoysaḷa domination over Chōḷa dominion in the time of Vīra Rāmanātha. See No. 1038 below.]

1019. 44 *of* 1911.—(Tamil.) On the same wall. An unfinished and damaged record in the fifteenth year of the Chōḷa king Rājarājadēva (III ?). Records sale of a temple land to a certain Ponnan Rājan *alias* Vikkiramaśiṅgadēva of Pāṇḍimaṇḍalam, who was a subordinate of Śōḷakōnār.

1020. 45 *of* 1911.—(Tamil.) On the same wall. An unfinished and damaged record in the fifth year of the Chōḷa king Tribhuvana-chakravartin Rājarājadēva (III ?). Records gift of a lamp to the same temple by a certain Vānakōvaraiyar.

1021. 46 *of* 1911.—(Tamil.) On the same wall. A record in the fourth year of the Chōḷa king Tribhuvanachakravartin Rājēndra-Chōḷa-dēva (III). Records gift of lands clubbed together under certain specified names. [A hamlet called Manukulameḍutta Perumāḷ was evidently named after the king who, we know from No. 1095 below, had that *biruda*.]

1022. 47 *of* 1911.—(Tamil.) On the same wall. A record in the fifth year of the Chōḷa king Tribhuvanachakravartin Rājarājadēva (III ?). Records gift of money for a lamp and of a lamp-stand by the chief mentioned in No. 1020 who bore the titles Tuṇḍanāḍuḍaiyān Ēkavāchakan and Ulagukaṇviḍutta-Perumāḷ.

1023. 48 *of* 1911.—(Tamil.) On the same wall. A record in the twenty-fourth year of the Chōḷa king Tribhuvanachakravartin Rājarājadēva (III ?). It gives a list of all the tax-free lands enjoyed by a temple, the name of which is not clear on the stone.

1024. 49 *of* 1911.—(Tamil.) On the same wall. A record in the twenty-fifth year of the Chōḷa king Tribhuvanachakravartin Rājarājadēva (III ?). Records gift of a *maṭha* to the teacher called Tattanuḍaiyār Īśānadēva, by a lady disciple of his, in accordance with the instructions of her dying husband. Later on, the epigraph registers the grant of an additional land to the same *maṭha*. Īśāna Śiva was a teacher of the Mudaliārs of Māḷigai *maṭham* at Tiruviḍamarudūr and he evidently settled at Nalūr. See Tj. 1010, 1012, etc., for similar *maṭhas*.

1025. 50 *of* 1911.—(Tamil.) On the same wall. A record in the thirtieth year of the Chōḷa king Tribhuvanachakravartin Rājarājadēva. Records sale of land to the temple by a native of Kīḷiyūr in Pāṇḍikulāśani-vaḷanāḍu. In continuation of this inscription is engraved a record of the second year of the same king which refers to the assembly of Rājakēsari-chaturvēdimaṅgalam in Nallūr-nāḍu and to a gift of land for a lamp to the temple of Tirunallūr-Nāyanār.

1026. 51 *of* 1911.—(Tamil.) On the east wall of the same prākāra. A record in the thiry-third year of the Chōḷa king Tribhuvanachakravartin Rājarājadēva. Records gift of land for supplying a garland of red lilies *(śeṅgaḷunir)*.

1027. 52 *of* 1911.—(Tamil.) On the same wall. A damaged record in the twenty-first year of the Chōḷa king Tribhuvanachakravartin Rājarājadēva. Records gift of land for supplying a garland of red lilies *(śeṅgaḷunir)*.

1028. 53 *of* 1911.—(Tamil.) On the same wall. A record in the twenty-ninth year of the Chōḷa king Tribhuvanachakravartin Rājarājadēva. Records gift of paddy for offerings.

1029. 54 *of* 1911.—(Tamil.) On the same wall. A record in the thirteenth year of the Chōḷa king Tribhuvanachakravartin Rājādhirājadēva II, who was pleased to take Madurai, i.e., Madura and Īḷam (Ceylon). Records gift of 200 *kāśus* for two lamps.

1030. 55 *of* 1911.—(Tamil.) On the same wall. A record in the third year of the Chōḷa king Tribhuvanachakravartin Kulōttuṅga-Chōḷadēva. Records gift of land.

1031. 56 *of* 1911.—(Tamil.) On the same wall. A damaged and incomplete record in the eleventh year of the Chōḷa king Tribhuvanachakravartin Rājādhirājadēva (II ?). Records gift of land for offerings.

1032. 57 *of* 1911.—(Tamil.) On the same wall. A damaged record in the fifth year of the Chōḷa king Tribhuvanachakravartin Rājarājadēva (III ?). Records sale of a house-site and a garden for the temple of Agambaḍi-Vināyaka-Piḷḷaiyār.

1033. 58 *of* 1911.—(Tamil.) On the same wall. A record in the fifth year of the Chōḷa king Tribhuvanachakravartin Rājarājadēva (III ?). Records sale of a house and eight coconut trees to the same temple which is stated to have been built by the Agambaḍiyār (i.e., the servants of the temple of Tirunallūr-Nāyanār). [Was the term Agambaḍiyār connected with the Agamuḍaiyār caste ?]

1034. 59 *of* 1911.—(Tamil.) On the same wall. A record in the twenty-ninth year of the Chōḷa king Tribhuvanachakravartin Rājarājadēva. Records gift of land for offerings to the temple of Tirunallūr-Nāyanār.

1035. 60 *of* 1911.—(Tamil.) On the base of the north verandah in the same temple. A mutilated record in the fourth year of the Chōḷa king Tribhuvanachakravartin Rājēndra-Chōḷadēva. Records gift of lands situated in different villages to the same temple.

1036. 61 *of* 1911.—(Tamil.) On the same base. A record in the fifth year of the Chōḷa king Tribhuvanachakravartin Rājēndra-Chōḷadēva. Built in at the bottom. Records gift of land.

1037. 62 *of* 1911.—(Tamil.) On the second gōpura of the same temple; right of entrance. A record in the twenty-sixth year of the Chōḷa king Tribhuvanachakravartin Rājarājadēva. Records gift of land for feeding the Mahēśvaras.

Śūlamaṅgalam.

1038. 292 *of* 1911.—(Tamil.) On the west and south walls of the central shrine in the Krittivāsēśvara temple. A record in the twentieth year of the Hoysaḷa king Vīra-Rāmaṇāthadēva. Records gift of land for offerings to the temple at Śūlamaṅgalam which was a *brahmadēya* in Kiḻāy-kūṟṟam a subdivision of Nittavinōda-vaḷanāḍu. [His capital was Kaṇṇanūr. Mr. Richards, I.C.S., suggests that Dēvar kundāṇi was perhaps his capital above the ghats. See No. 1018 above.]

1039. 293 *of* 1911.—(Tamil.) On the north wall of the maṇṭapa in front of the same shrine. A damaged record in the ninth year of the Pāṇḍya king Tribhuvanachakravartin Sundara-Pāṇḍya-dēva. Records sale of land to the temple of Kari-uritta-Nāyanār at Śūlamaṅgalam by three Brāhmaṇa brothers who were natives of Tirukkuḍandai (i.e., Kumbhakōṇam).

1040. 294 *of* 1911.—(Tamil.) On the south wall of the same maṇṭapa. A record in the twelfth year of the Pāṇḍya king Jaṭāvarman *alias* Tribhuvanachakravartin Parākrama-Pāṇḍyadēva (1334 —?). Records that a certain Tirunāvuḍaiyār of Dānavi-nōdanallūr, a *dēvadāna* village of the goddess in the temple of Tiruvālavāyuḍaiyār in Tayandaṇaṟkuḍināḍu, a subdivision of Pāṇḍimaṇḍalam, set up an image of Tirunāvuḍaiya-Piḷḷaiyār in the temple of Kariyuritta-Nāyanār at Śūlamaṅgalam, a *brahmadēya* in Kiḻār-kūṟṟam of Nittavinōda-vaḷanāḍu, and presented lands for offerings.

1041. 295 *of* 1911.—(Tamil.) On the same wall. An incomplete record in the thirteenth year of the Chōḷa king Tribhuvana-chakravartin Kulōttuṅga-Chōḷadēva (III), "who was pleased to take Madurai (Madura) and the crowned head of the Pāṇḍya." Refers to the assembly of Śūlamaṅgalam and a settlement which it made for the benefit of the temple of Kariyuritta-Nāyanār.

1042. 296 *of* 1911.—(Tamil.) On the same wall. An incomplete record of the Chōḷa king Tribhuvanachakravartin Kulōttuṅga-Choḷadēva III, "who was pleased to take Madurai (Madura), Īḻam (Ceylon), Karuvūr and the crowned head of the Pāṇḍya." Records sale of maid-servants to the temple of Kari-uritta-Kandar at

Śūlamaṅgalam by two accountants of the temple of Tirukkāroṇam-Uḍaiyār at Śōḷakulavallipaṭṭinam, a village in Paṭṭiṇa-kūṟṟam, a subdivision of Gēyamāṇikka-vaḷanāḍu

1042-A. In the inner shrine of Perumbuhutu Īśvara at Paśupatikōvil. Records that Kulōttuṅgadēva granted seventeen *vēlis* of land to the Goddess Prajā Sundari. *Ins., S. Dts.*, p. 258, No. 165.

1042-B. In the same place. A grant by the same king in his twenty-second year of 1,000 *kuḻi* of land. *Ibid.*, No. 166.

1042-C. In the same place. Grant of land by Kō-Parakēsarivarman to Ādi-Chaṇḍēśvara, in his fifteenth year. *Ibid.*, No. 167.

1042-D. In the same place. A gift of land (4 *mās*, 1 *kāṇi* and *muḍi* to the God by the same king in his thirteenth year. *Ibid.*, No. 168.

1042-E. In the same place. Records in the twenty-second year of Kō-Rājakēsarivarman grant of two *vēlis* of wet land and one of dry land to the God. *Ibid.*, No. 169.

Tirukkaḷāvūr (Tirurukkarugāvūr)

This place is well known in Śaivite tradition as the place where the moon and constellations worshipped the Lord and where the Lord fed Saint Sundaramūrti. It has been sung by Gñānasambanda.

1043. 35 *of* 1910.—(Tamil.) On the south wall of the central shrine in the Madhuvanēśvara temple. A record in the sixteenth year of the Chōḷa king Parakēsarivarman. Records gift of land by the village assembly, to the temple of Tirukkarugāvūr Mahādēva.

1044. 36 *of* 1910.—(Tamil.) On the same wall. A record in the fourteenth year of the Chōḷa king Madiraikoṇḍa Parakēsarivarman (905—47). Records gift of land for a lamp by a merchant of Nandipura, to the temple of Paḷakkarugāvūr Mahādēva of Tirukkuḍamūkkil, a *dēvadāna* in Vaḍagarai Pāmburanāḍu.

1045. 37 *of* 1910.—(Tamil.) On the same wall. A record in the thirty-ninth year of the Chōḷa king Madiraikoṇḍa Parakēsarivarman (905—47), "who also took Īḻam (Ceylon)." Records gift of land to the same temple by a servant of queen Villavanmādēviyār.

1046. 38 *of* 1910.—(Tamil.) On the same wall. A record in the twenty-fourth year of the Chōḷa king Madiraikoṇḍa Parakēsarivarman (905—47). Records gift of land for a lamp by a native of Tañjāvūr.

1047. 39 *of* 1910.—(Tamil.) On the same wall. A record in the seventeenth year of the Chōḷa king Madiraikoṇḍa Parakēsarivarman (905—47). Records gift of land for festivals.

1048. 40 *of* 1910.—(Tamil.) On the same wall. A record in the twenty-third year of the Chōḷa king Madiraikoṇḍa-Parakēsarivarman (905—47). Provides for ghee by a native of Uḻundaṉguḍi.

1049. 41 *of* 1910.—(Tamil.) On the same wall. A record of the Chōḷa king Parakēsarivarman, the date of which is lost. Built in at the right end. Records gift of land for offerings and a lamp.

1050. 42 *of* 1910.—(Tamil.) On the west wall of the same shrine. An incomplete record in the twenty-seventh year of the Chōḷa king Madiraikoṇḍa Parakēsarivarman (A.D. 905—47). It gives a list of the lands owned by the temples of Mahādēva, Kāla-Piḍāri and Mahā-Vishṇu at Paḷa-Tirukkarugāvūr.

1051. 43 *of* 1910.—(Tamil.) On the same wall. A record in the eighteenth year of the Chōḷa king Madiraikoṇḍa-Parakēsarivarman (A.D. 905—47). Records gift of land for offerings and a lamp.

1052. 44 *of* 1910.—(Tamil.) On the north wall of the same shrine. A record in the fifth year of the Chōḷa king Parakēsarivarman. It gives a list of lands belonging to the temple; one of the donors was Koṟṟaṅguḍaiyāṉ Araṅgan Kuñjiramallan. The beginning of the historical introduction *(tingaḷēr taru)* of Rājādhirāja I is found below this inscription.

1053. 45 *of* 1910.—(Tamil.) On the same wall. A record in the fifth year of the Chōḷa king Parakēsarivarman. Records gift of land. Mentions the coin *Īḻakkāśu.*

1054. 46 *of* 1910.—(Tamil.) On the same wall. A record in the fifth year of the Chōḷa king Parakēsarivarman. Mentions Tiruvalañjuḻi and Kōyilmayilai *alias* Madhurāntaka-Mūvēndavēḷān and records a gift of land for offerings by Śiṅgan Kaliyan *alias* Uttamaśōḻa-Mūvēndavēḷān of Kommaipākkam.

1055. In the inner shrine of Madhuvanēśvara. Records grant of 4 *mās*, 3½ *kaṇi* and 1 *mundiri* of land to Tilla Nāyanār by Kō-Parakēsarivarman in his eighth year. See *Ins., S. Dts.*, p. 259, No. 170.

1056. A grant of the same king in his thirteenth year. *Ibid.*, No. 171.

1057. In the same place. Grant of thirteen *vēlis* by the same king in his eighth year. *Ibid.*, No. 172.

1058. Grant of two *vēlis* by the same king in his seventeenth year. *Ibid.*, No. 173.

1059. Grant of land for lamps and food by the same king in his twenty-third year. *Ibid.*, No. 174.

1060. Grant of land by the same king in his twenty-first year. *Ibid.*, No. 175.

1061. A similar grant of 4 *mās*, 3½ *kaṇis* and 1 *mundiri* is Vīramaṅgaiyūr by the same king in his thirteenth year. *Ins., S. Dts.*, No. 176.

1062. A grant of ¾ *vēli* by Kō-Rājakēsarivarman in his twenty-fourth year. *Ibid.*, No. 177.

1063. A record by the same king in his seventeenth year for the celebration of the Pushya ceremony. *Ibid.*, No. 178.

1064. A gift of 3 *mās* and 1½ *kaṇi* by the same king in his eighteenth year. *Ibid.*, No. 179.

1065. A gift of 10 *vēlis* of land south of Vīrachōḷa river by Parakēsarivarman in his twenty-third year. *Ibid.*, No. 180.

1066. Gift of land by Rājakēsarivarman in his twenty-first year. *Ibid.*, No. 181.

Tiruppālātturai.

1067. 433 *of* 1912.—(Tamil.) On the south wall of the central shrine in the Kshīravanēśvara temple. A much damaged record in the tenth year of the Chōḷa king Vikrama-Chōḷadēva (1118—35). Records gift of jewels to the temple of Mahādēva at Tiruppālait-turai. [The place figures in Appar's psalms.]

1068. 434 *of* 1912.—(Tamil.) On the west wall of the same shrine. A record in the forty-third year of the Chōḷa king Rājakēsarivarman *alias* Tribhuvanachakravartin Kulōttuṅga-Chōḷadēva (I). Registers that the *dēvudāna* village Tiruchchirrambalanallūr of the temple of Mahādēva at Tiruppālaitturai in Nallūr-nāḍu, a subdivision of Nittavinōda-vaḷanādu, was granted, on account of the low finances of the temple, the remission of the *antarāyapāṭṭam* and other taxes, at the request of Madhurāntakap-paravainaṭṭu-Mūvēndavēḷān. [The epigraph is interesting for the fact that it mentions the introductions of Vīrarājēndra I and Kulōttuṅga I thereby showing that Adhirājēndra (who was the brother-in-law of the Chāḷukya Vikramāditya VI and the rival of Kulōttuṅga I) was ignored. The last year of Vīrarājēndra is moreover (1069-70) the first year of Kulōttuṅga (I). *Ep. Rep.*, 1913, p. 105.]

1069. 435 *of* 1912.—(Tamil.) On a slab built into the west floor of the first prākāra of the same temple. Records in Kīlaka gift of land by the cultivating classes to the temple of Pālavana-nāthasvāmin for conducting the festival in the month of Āḍi.

1070. 436 *of* 1912.—(Tamil.) On a slab fixed into the floor of the north verandah of the same prākāra. Interrupted by the bases of a pillar. Seems to record in Vikrama a gift of land by an agent of Vīra-Naraśiṅgarāya-Nāyaka (evidently the Śāḷuva usurper).

1071. 437 *of* 1912.—(Tamil.) On the west verandah of the same prākāra. A record in the twenty-eighth year of the Chōḷa king Tribhuvanachakravartin Rājarājadēva (III). Records gift of land by purchase in Tiruchchiṟṟambalanallūr and Rājagambhīranallūr, to the shrine of Tirujñānasambandhīśuram-Uḍaiyār which was consecrated by a certain Nīlagaṅgaraiyan, in the east verandah of the temple of Tiruppālattuṟai-Uḍaiyār.

1072. 438 *of* 1912.—(Tamil.) On the second gōpura of the same temple, right of entrance. A much damaged and unfinished record in the fifteenth year of the Chōḷa king Parakēsarivarman *alias* Tribhuvanachakravartin Kulōttuṅga-Chōḷadēva (III), "who having taken Madurai (Madura) was pleased to take the crowned head of the Pāṇḍya."

1073. 439 *of* 1912.—(Tamil.) In the same place. A record in the fourth year of the Chōḷa king Tribhuvanachakravartin Kulōttuṅga-Choḷadēva (III). Records gift of gold for jewels to the shrines of Periyadēvar and Nāchchiyār, concentrated in the temple by Periyadēvanambi of Peṇṇāgaḍam who held proprietary right in the *dēvadāna* villages of Tiruchchiṟṟambala-nallūr and Rājagambhīranallūr.

1074. 440 *of* 1912.—(Tamil.) On the east wall of the first prākāra of the same temple. A damaged and unfinished record of the Chōḷa king Parakēsarivarman *alias* Tribhuvanachakravartin Rājarājadēva (II) in his twelfth year and 264th day. Begins with the introduction *jayamādum nā maruviya*, etc. Seems to record the gift of land *(kāval kāḍu)* in the grove called Kuñjiran *alias* Bhuvanamuḻuduḍaiyāḷ, under the new name Rājagambhīranallūr for worship, etc., in the temple and for maintaining a flower garden. Reference is also made to the "Revenue Survey" *(aḷavu)* of the sixteenth year of Śuṅgandavirttadēva (i.e., Kulōttuṅga I) and to his fortieth year.

1075. 441 *of* 1912.—(Tamil.) On the north wall of the same prākāra. A record of the Chōḷa king Tribhuvanachakravartin Kulōttuṅga-Chōḷadēva (III), "who was pleased to take Madurai (Madura) and the crowned head of the Pāṇḍya," in his twelfth year and ninety-third day. Registers that the re-distribution (கரைக்கூறு) and assignment of lands *(puñjai and nattam)* in the village of Kuladīpanāyakapura were, by the corporate consent of the *Sāḷiya* merchants, permanently engraved on the walls of the temple. The epigraph shows that there was periodical re-distribution of the village lands.

1076. 442 *of* 1912.—(Tamil.) On two detached stones fixed into the same wall. Records gift of land *(Tirunāmattukkāṇi)* in the village of Vēmbakkuḍi which was a *dēvadāna* of the temple of Tiruchchōṟṟuttuṟai-Uḍaiyār, by a certain Kāvērivallavan.

Tiruvaigāvūr.

This place, known in Śaivite tradition as Bilva-vanakshētram, is said to have been the scene of Lakshmi's worship of Śiva. It figures in Gñānasambanda's *Dēvāram.*

1077. 48 *of* 1914.—(Tamil.) On the south wall of the maṇṭapa in front of the central shrine in the Bilvanāthēśvara temple. A record in the twenty-second year of the Pallava king Nandivarmarāja (II or III ?). Records gift of land for offerings and a lamp to the temple of Tiruvaigāvuḍaiya-Mahādēva. States that this is only a copy of a stone inscription.

1078. 49 *of* 1914.—(Tamil.) On the same wall. An unfinished record of the Chōḷa king Parakēsarivarman *alias* Tribhuvanachakravartin Kulōttuṅga-Chōḷadēva (II) in his fifth year. Mentions Moykuḍi in Emapperūrnāḍu, a subdivision of Rājarāja-vaḷanāḍu and the temple of Tiruvaigāvuḍaiyār in Innambar-nāḍu, a subdivision of Vaḍagarai-Vikrama-Śōḷa-vaḷanāḍu. [Mr. Krishna Sastri notes that, while in other epigraphs the king receives the title of Rājakēsarivarman, he receives in this the title of Parakēsarivarman.]

1079. 50 *of* 1914.—(Tamil.) On the same wall. A record in the eleventh year of the Chōḷa king Parakēsarivarman *alias* Tribhuvanachakravartin Rājarājadēva (II). Records gift of thirty *kāśus* for a lamp by a dancing girl *devaradiyāḷ* of the temple of Tiruvaigāvuḍaiyār in Aṇḍattukūṟṟam, a subdivision of Vikrama-Śōḷa-vaḷanāḍu.

1080. 51 *of* 1914.—(Tamil.) On the same wall. A record in the fortieth year of the Chōḷa king Parakēsarivarman *alias* Tribhuvanachakravartin Kulōttuṅga-Chōḷadēva (III ?). States that Pūṇḍi-uḍaiyān Sūriyan Pavaḷakkuṉṟanār *alias* Vaṇṇāḍuḍaiyār of Paravaichchuṟṟupūṇḍi in Rājarāja-vaḷanāḍu petitioned to the king in his thirty-second year and built of stone the central shrine and the maṇṭapa of the temple of Tiruvaigāvuḍaiya-Mahādēva in Aṇḍattukūṟṟam, a subdivision of Ulaguyyavandaśōḷa-vaḷanāḍu, after removing the old brick structure which was dilapidated. He also increased the temple *dēvadāna* by supplementing it with gift of lands in the village of Kaḷappākuḍi, in Viṟaikūṟṟam to meet the additional requirements of the temple. [The Government Epigraphist believes that the king was, in spite of the title Parakēsarivarman, Kulōttuṅga (I).]

1081. 52 *of* 1914.—(Tamil.) On the same wall. A record in the seventh year of the Chōḷa king Tribhuvanachakravartin Rājarājadēva. Records gift of gold for three lamps to the shrine of Tirumaḷigaippiḷḷaiyār, by a native of Paḷavālakkuḍi in Viḷaināḍu which was a subdivision of Jayaṅgoṇḍaśōḷa-vaḷanāḍu.

1082. 53 *of* 1914.—(Tamil.) On the same wall. A damaged record of the Chōḷa king Parakēsarivarman *alias* Tribhuvanachakravartin Rājarājadēva (II) in his seventeenth year. Records gift of money for offerings to the image of Nittavinōdakalyāṇa-Sundaradēva set up in the temple of Tiruvaigāvūr.

1083. 54 *of* 1914.—(Tamil.) On the south and west walls of the same maṇṭapa. A record in the twentieth year of the Chōḷa king Tribhuvanachakravartin Kulōttuṅga-Chōḷadēva (III), "who was pleased to take Madurai (Madura) and the crowned head of the Pāṇḍya." Records gift of paddy by the temple servants to the sacred monastery *(tirukkugai)* of Tirumuḍiyālnaḍandān which was presided over by Nānāndūr-Uḍaiyār Pugaḻivēndar. [Pugaḻivēndar cannot be the poet Pugaḻēndi who was the contemporary of Oṭṭakkootta and Kulōttuṅga (II).]

1084. 55 *of* 1914.—(Tamil.) On the west wall of the same maṇṭapa. An unfinished record of the Chōḷa king Tribhuvana-chakravartin Rājarājadēva in his seventh year. Mentions Tillai-nāyakan Kaṇavadi Nambi *alias* Madhurāntaka Vaṇṇāḍuḍaiyān of Paravaichchuṟṟu-pūṇḍi in Rājarāja-vaḷanāḍu.

1085. 56 *of* 1914.—(Tamil.) On the same wall. A damaged record of the Chōḷa king Tribhuvanachakravartin Rājēndra Chōḷadēva (III) in his fifth year, Mēsha, śu. di. 4th, Monday, Rōhiṇi. Records sale of land. Mentions Vāmaśivamudaliyār of the lineage of the Mudaliyārs of Śelva-Tiruvārūr and the image of Villavanapperumāḷ in this temple. The date, points out Mr. Swamikannu Pillai, corresponded to Monday, 27th March A.D. 1251. He further "shows that the reign began between 28th March and 20th April 1246, which reduces Kielhorn's limits by eight days." See *Ep. Ind.*, Vol. IX, p. 222.

1086. 57 *of* 1914.—(Tamil.) On the north wall of the same maṇṭapa. A record of the Chōḷa king Tribhuvanachakravartin Tribhuvanavīradēva (1178—1216), "who having been pleased to take Madurai (Madura), Īḻam (Ceylon), Karuvūr and the crowned head of the Pāṇḍya was pleased to perform the anointment of heroes and the anointment of victors," in his thirty-third year, Mithuna, ba. di. 9, Monday, Rēvati, corresponding to June 6, A.D. 1211. Records sale of land and two houses for arrears of revenue due on a *dēvadāna* land. The arrears were found out by Piḷḷai-Muṇaiya-daraiyar who was in charge of the temple lands, by auditing the accounts from the twenty-fourth to the thirty-third year.

1087. 58 *of* 1914.—(Tamil.) On the same wall. A record of the Chōḷa king Tribhuvanachakravartin Tribhuvanavīradēva (1178—1216), "who having been pleased to take Madurai (Madura), Īḻam (Ceylon), Karuvūr and the crowned head of the Pāṇḍya, was pleased to perform the anointment of heroes and the anointment of victors" in his thirty-third year, Mithuna, ba. di. 9, Monday, Rēvati. Built in at the bottom. Refers to the *dēvadāna* village Tribhuvana-mādēvichaturvēdimaṅgalam. Registers a similar transaction as in the above epigraph. Date same as in the previous inscription.

1088. 59 *of* 1914.—(Tamil.) On the same wall. A record of the Vijayanagara king Vīrapratāpa Dēvarāya Mahārāya (II), in Ś. 1351, Saumya, Vrischika, ba. di. 10, Monday, Hasta (Oct. 29, A.D. 1429). Registers an agreement entered into by the assembly of Parāntaka-nāḍu, a subdivision of Innambar-nāḍu and the *Valaṅgai* 98 and the *Idangai* 98 *sects* regarding the payment of dues to the king *(rājāgaram).* [This epigraph is one of the most valuable documents for the construction of the financial history of the period. It is analysed in detail in *Mad. Ep. Rep.*, 1915, pp. 106—8, paragragh 44, and it is too long to be quoted here.]

1089. 60 *of* 1914.—(Tamil.) On the east and north walls of the same maṇṭapa. A record of the Chōḷa king Tribhuvanavīradēva, (1178—1216) "who having been pleased to take . . . Karuvūr and the crowned head of the Pāṇḍya, was pleased to perform the anointment of heroes and the anointment of victors," in his thirty-third year, Mithuna, ba. di. 9, Monday, Rēvati. Built in at the beginning. Registers a transaction similar to that of No. 1075 above. The land was sold to the temple of Nittavinōda-Īśvaram Uḍaiyār at Tiruvaigāvūr in Innambar-nāḍu, a subdivision of Vaḍagarai-Vikrama-Śōḷa-vaḷanāḍu. For date see 1086.

PATTUKKŌTTAI TALUK.

Karuṅgāḍu.

1090. 10 *of* 1892.—(Tamil.) On a stone in front of the Māri-Amman temple. A record dated in Vyaya.

Kōvilūr.

1091. 181 *of* 1908.—(Tamil.) On the east wall of the maṇṭapa in front of the central shrine in the Mantrapurīśvara temple. An incomplete record in the twenty-fifth year of the Chōḷa king Tribhuvanachakravartin Kulōttuṅga-Chloadēva (III) "who was pleased to take Madurai, Iḷam (Ceylon) and the crowned head of the Pāṇḍya." Records the gift of a servant to the temple of Uśattāṇa-muḍaiya-Nāyanār by a native of Śelgalūr in Iḍaikkanāḍu, a subdivision of Rājēndra-śōḷa-vaḷanāḍu.

1092. 182 *of* 1908.—(Tamil.) On the same wall. A record in the twenty-sixth year (Kanyā,. Pūrva 8 or 5, Anurādha, Monday) of the Chōḷa king Tribhuvanachakravartin Rājarājadēva. Records gift of land by order of Viḷuppādirājan, a native of Śīṟṟāṟkāḍu in Pāṇḍyakulāśani-vaḷanāḍu. The land granted was in Sundara-śōḷapuram. See *Ep. Ind.*, Vol. XI, p. 130. An irregular date.

1093. 183 *of* 1908.—(Tamil.) On the same wall. A record in the twenty-fifth year of the Chōḷa king . . . Kulōttuṅga-Chōḷadēva, "who was pleased to take . . . " Built in at the bottom and the end. Records gift of land to the temple of

Uśattāṇamuḍaiya-Nāyanār at Uśattāṇam *alias* Kēraḷakulāśani-chaturvēdimaṅgalam, a *brahmadēya* in Puraṅgarambai-nāḍu, a subdivision of Rājēndraśōḷa-vaḷanāḍu.

1094. 184 *of* 1908.—(Tamil.) On the south wall of the same maṇṭapa. A record in the twenty-fourth year of the king Records gift of money for a lamp, by a native of Puduppaṭṭaṇam.

1095. 185 *of* 1908.—(Tamil.) On the same wall. A record in the fourth year of the Chōḷa king Tribhuvanachakravartin Rājēndra-Chōḷadēva (III). Seems to record a gift of paddy to a temple servant by the tenants of the temple lands. [The king had the title of Manukula meḍutta Perumāḷ.]

1096. 186 *of* 1908.—(Tamil.) On the same wall. A record in the tenth year of the Chōḷa king Tribhuvanachakravartin Rājēndra-Chōḷadēva. Records gift of land for offerings to the shrines of Piḷḷaiyār Nāyanār (i.e., Gñānasambanda) and Tirunāvukkaraśu-Nāyanār. Refers to the revenue survey of the thirtieth year.

1097. 187 *of* 1908.—(Tamil.) On the same wall. A record in the fourth year of the Chōḷa king Tribhuvanachakravartin Rājēndra-Chōḷadēva. Records an arrangement entered into by the dancing girls of the temple to burn a lamp in the shrine of Bhuvana-pati-Nāchchiyār built by Ponnambalakūttan *alias* Īrumuḍiśōḷap-pallavaraiyan.

1098. 188 *of* 1908.—(Tamil.) On the same wall. A record in the fourth year of the Chōḷa king Tribhuvanachakravartin Rājēn-dra-Chōḷadēva. Records gift of land for offerings to the image of Bhuvanādhipati-Nāchchiyār by the residents of Mummuḍiśōḷa-puram in Puraṅgarambai-nāḍu, a subdivision of Rājēndra-śōḷa-vaḷanāḍu. Refers to the revenue survey of the thirty-eighth year of Tribhuvanavīradēva (Kulōttuṅga III). This survey "shows the still prosperous condition of the Chōḷa Empire about the end of that king's reign." It is doubtful, however, whether Kulōttuṅga (I) or (III) is intended. See *Ep. Rep.*, 1909, p. 102, for details. See No. 1101 below.

1099. 189 *of* 1908.—(Tamil.) On the same wall. A record in the fifth year and the king's name is lost. Records gift of money (3,000 *kāśus*) and paddy for offerings to the shrine of Bhuvanādhi-pati Nāchchiyār built by Ponnambalakūttan *alias* Īrumuḍiśōḷa Pallavariyan.

1100. 190 *of* 1908.—(Tamil.) On the same wall. Gives a list of *dēvadāna* lands belonging to the temple and their boundaries.

1101. 191 *of* 1908.—(Tamil.) On the same wall. Gives a list of the rent-free lands *(dēvadāna)* possessed by the temple, up to the thirty-eighth year and refers to the fiftieth year of Kulōttuṅga-Chōḷadēva (I) "who was pleased to abolish tolls" and to the eighteenth year of Rājarājadēva. The revenue survey of the thirty-eighth year is also referred to. See 1098 above.

1102. 192 *of* 1908.—(Tamil.) On the north wall of the same maṇṭapa. Records in the twenty-first year (of ?) gift of land for offerings by order of a certain Kāḷiṅgarāya. Mentions Kalyāṇapuraṅgoṇḍaśōḷapuram, among the boundaries. [Kalyāṇapuraṅgoṇḍaśōḷa was Rājādhirāja (I), 1018--1052.]

1103. 193 *of* 1908.—(Tamil.) On the north wall of the maṇṭapa in front of the central shrine in the Mantrapurīśvara temple. A record in the thirtieth year of the Chōḷa king Tribhuvanachakravartin Rājarājadēva (III ?). Records gift of land to the shrine of Subrahmaṇya by the assembly of Peruvāḷvutanda-Perumāḷ-chaturvēdimaṅgalam (i.e., the modern Peruvāḷandān) in Puraṅgarambaināḍu, a subdivision of Rājēndra-śōḷa-vaḷanāḍu.

1104. 194 *of* 1908.—(Tamil.) On the same wall. A record in the fifth year of the Chōḷa king Tribhuvanachakravartin Vikrama-Chōḷadēva (1118—35). Records gift of land. Mentions Śākkānam *alias* Kēraḷakulāśani-chaturvēdimaṅgalam. Perhaps Śākkānam is a mistake for *Śāttaṇam* (i.e., Uśāttaṇam).

1105. 195 *of* 1908.—(Tamil.) On the same wall. A req rd in the twentieth year (Makara, Pūrva 7, Monday, Aśvini) of the Chōḷa king Tribhuvanachakravartin Rājarājadēva (III). Records gift of land by the assembly mentioned in No. 1103, for offerings to the shrine of Tirukkāmakkōṭṭamuḍaiya Periya-Nāchchiyār, set up by prince Purōśaikkuḍaiyār. The gift was made for the health of the king and for the victory of prince Iruṅgōḷar. See *Ep. Ind.*, Vol. XI, 128, where the details of date show the English equivalent to be Monday, 5th January, A.D. 1237, in the twenty-first and not twentieth year of the king.

1106. 196 *of* 1908.—(Tamil.) On the same wall. A record in the twenty-first year of the Chōḷa king Tribhuvanachakravartin Rājarājadēva (III ?). Records gift of land to the same shrine by the assembly of Śuttavalli-chaturvēdimaṅgalam which was in charge of the village duties *(grāma-kārya)* for the health of the king and for the victory of prince Iruṅgōḷar.

1107. 197 *of* 1908.—(Tamil.) On the same wall. A record in the tenth year of the Chōḷa king Tribhuvanachakravartin Rājarājadēva (III ?). Assignment by the assembly of Uśāttāṇam of certain taxes collected on temple lands up to the tenth year for the repair of the temple.

1108. 198 *of* 1908.—(Tamil.) On the same wall. A record in the eleventh year (Rishabha, Pūrva 7, Sunday, Magha) of the Chōḷa king Tribhuvanachakravartin Rājarājadēva (III). Records gift of land, for offerings to the shrine of Sūryadēva in the temple of Uśāttāṇam-Uḍaiyār by the residents of Vikramābharaṇapuram in Umbar-nāḍu. See *Ep. Ind.*, Vol. XI, p. 128, where it is shown that 11 is a mistake for 21 and that then the date corresponds to 3rd May, A.D. 1237.

1109. 199 *of* 1908.—(Tamil.) On the same wall. A record in the thirty-first year (Mēsha, . . . 5, Anurādha, Monday) of the Chōḷa king Tribhuvanachakravartin Rājarājadēva (III). Records gift of land to the same shrine by the residents of Parāntakapuram in Umbar-nāḍu. *Ibid.*, pp. 130–1. A very irregular date.

1110. 200 *of* 1908.—(Tamil.) On the same wall. An unfinished record. Records the boundaries of certain rent-free lands belonging to the temple. Mentions Periyadēvar Vikrama-Chōḷadēva (1118—35).

1111. 201 *of* 1908.—(Tamil.) On the water spout *(gōmukha)* in the south wall of the same maṇṭapa. Records gift of the spout by a certain Vīraśiṅgarāyan.

1112. 202 *of* 1908.—(Tamil.) On the south base of the verandah in the first prākāra of the same temple. A record in the eleventh year of the Chōḷa king Tribhuvanachakravartin Rājēndra-Chōḷadēva (III ?). Records gift of land for worship and repair in the temple of Uśāttāṇamuḍaiya-Nāyanār by order of Paiyūḷān Periyan Aḷagiya-Perumāḷ *alias* Śōḷagaṅgan, evidently one of the king's executive officers.

1113. 203 *of* 1908.—(Tamil.) On the same base. Records in the twenty-second year (of ?) gift of land for the *Tirukkaikkōṭṭi-ōduvār* of the temple, by order of Śokkanāyan *alias* Rājagambhīra Śōḷiyavaraiyan.

1114. 204 *of* 1908.—(Tamil.) On the same base. An unfinished record in the eleventh year of the Chōḷa king Tribhuvanachakravartin Rājēndra-Chōḷadēva. Records gift of duties (in kind) payable on each bullock load *(podi)* of paddy and rice, carried by the road called *Jananāthan-pādai*, as directed by the prince (not named), to the temple of Uśāttaṇamuḍaiya-Nāyanār by order of the villagers of Mummuḍiśōḷapuram.

1115. 205 *of* 1908.—(Tamil.) On the same base. A record in the eleventh year of the Chōḷa king Tribhuvanachakravartin Rājēndra-Chōḷadēva (III ?). Records gift of land by order of Periyan Aḷagiya-Perumāḷ *alias* Śōḷagaṅgan.

1116. 206 *of* 1908.—(Tamil.) On the same base. A record in the twelfth year of the Chōḷa king Tribhuvanachakravartin Rājēndra-Chōḷadēva (III ?). Records gift of land by Ādittadēvan, a native of Veḷḷūr, in Paiyyūrkōṭṭam, a district of Perun-Toṇḍaimaṇḍalam.

1117. 207 *of* 1908.—(Tamil.) On the same base. A record in the thirteenth year of the Chōḷa king Tribhuvanachakravartin Rājēndra-Choḷadēva. Mentions the donor referred to in the above epigraph and his gift. It is here stated that Ādichchadēvan was a native of Vēḷūr in Toṇḍaimaṇḍalam.

1118. 208 *of* 1908.—(Tamil.) On the same base. A record in the eleventh year (Kanyā, Apara. 6, Monday, Rōhiṇi) of the Chōḷa king Tribhuvanachakravartin Rājēndra-Chōḷadēva (III). Records sale of land. Refers to the survey in the thirty-eighth year of Periyadēvar Tribhuvanavīradēva (Kulōttuṅga III). See *Ep. Ind.*, Vol. XI, p. 131. The date corresponded to Monday, 11th September, A.D. 1256; but *Kanyā* is said to be a mistake for *Simha.*

1119. 209 *of* 1908.—(Tamil.) On the west base of the same verandah. An unfinished record of the Chōḷa king Tribhuvanachakravartin Rājēndra-Chōḷadēva (III ?), the date of which is lost. Records gift of land by order of Pallavaraiyan *alias* Rājagambhīra-śōḷa-Pallavaraiyan.

1120. 210 *of* 1908.—(Tamil.) On the same base. A record in the twelfth year of the Chōḷa king Tribhuvanachakravartin Rājēndra-Chōḷadēva (III ?). The writing on one of the stones in the middle of the inscription has been erased by chiselling. Records gift of land for offerings to the image of Pallavanmādēvīśvara-muḍaiya-Nāyanār by order of Vāṇarāya *alias* Śōḷiyavaraiyan.

1121. 211 *of* 1908.—(Tamil.) On the same base. A record in the twelfth year of the Chōḷa king Tribhuvanachakravartin Rājēndra-Chōḷadēva (III ?). Records gift of land for a *maṭha* called *Vāṇarāyan-maḍam* by order of the same person.

1122. 212 *of* 1908.—(Tamil.) On the north base of the verandah in the first prākāra of the Mantrapurīśvara temple. An unfinished record in the tenth year of the Chōḷa king Tribhuvanachakravartin Rājēndra-Chōḷadēva. Records gift of land for offerings by the assembly of Śuttavalli-chaturvēdimaṅgalam in Puraṅgarambai-nāḍu, a subdivision of Rājēndraśōḷa-vaḷanāḍu.

1123. 213 *of* 1908.—(Tamil.) On the same base. A record in the seventeenth year (Rishabha, Pūrva. 3, Sunday, Pushya) of the Chōḷa king Tribhuvanachakravartin Rājēndra-Chōḷadēva (III). Records gift of land for offerings by the great assembly *(peruṅguṟi-mahāsabhai)* of Uśattāṇam. See *Ibid.*, where it is shown that the date corresponded to Sunday, the 21st May, A.D. 1262 (but the *tithi* is 2, it is said, and not 3).

1124. 214 *of* 1908.—(Tamil.) On the same base. An unfinished record in the fourteenth year (Simha, Pūrva. 3, Hasta, Wednesday) of the Pāṇḍya king Jaṭāvarman *alias* Tribhuvanachakravartin Sundara-Pāṇḍyadēva (III). See *Ibid.*, p. 136, where it is shown that the date corresponded to Wednesday, 9th August, A.D. 1290.

1125. 215 *of* 1908.—(Tamil.) On the east, north and west walls of the Chaṇḍēśvara shrine in the same temple. A record in the eighth year (Kumbha, Pūrva. 3, Svāti, Monday) of the Chōḷa king Tribhuvanachakravartin Rājarājadēva (III). Records gift of land for offerings to the image of Pallavanīśvaramuḍaiya-Nāyanār, set up in the temple by Pichchan Pallavarāyan *alias* Śōḷyavaraiyan, a native of Paiyyūr in Paiyyūr-nāḍu. See *Ep. Ind.*, Vol. XI, p. 127, where the date (after some corrections) is equated to 20th February, A.D. 1223.

1126. 216 *of* 1908.—(Tamil.) On the east wall of the first prākāra of the same temple. A damaged record in the twenty-eighth year (Kumbha, Apara. 6, Svāti, Monday) of the Chōḷa king Tribhuvanachakravartin Rājēndra-Chōḷadēva (III). Records gift of land for offerings to the image of Tirujñānampeṟṟa Piḷḷaiyār set up by a merchant of Mummuḍiśōḷapuram. Refers to the revenue survey in the thirty-eighth year of Periyadēvar Tribhuvana-vīradēva (Kulōttuṅga III). See *Ibid.*, p. 132, where it is shown that the date is irregular and that "its nearest approach" is Monday, 14th February, A.D. 1267.

1127. 217 *of* 1908.—(Tamil.) On the same wall. A damaged record in the twelfth year of the Pāṇḍya king Jaṭāvarman *alias* Tribhuvanachakravartin Sundara-Pāṇḍyadēva (I, II or III?). Records gift of land for offerings to an image of Gaṇapati *called* Nambi-Vināyaka-Piḷḷaiyār by the great assembly *(peruṅguṟimahā-sabhai)* of Uśattāṇam.

1128. 218 *of* 1908.—(Tamil.) On the same wall. A damaged record in the ninth year. Records gift of land to *Paripūrṇa-Śivāchārya* who presided over the Kūttāḍu-Nāyanār-maḍam on the western side of the temple. The Śaiva teacher belonged to the lineage *(santāna)* of Tiruchchatti-muṟṟattu-Mudaliyār. See *Mad. Ep. Rep.*, 1909, p. 104. See Tj. 1010, 1012, 1024, etc.

1129. 219 *of* 1908.—(Tamil.) On the south wall of the same prākāra. A damaged record in the fourteenth year. Refers to the gift mentioned in the above inscription.

1130. 220 *of* 1908.—(Tamil.) On the same wall. Records in the eleventh year gift of money for offerings, etc., to the image of Aḷagiya-Tiruchchiṟṟambalamuḍaiya-Nāyanār set up in the temple by Īśana (Śiva)chāriyar who belonged to the lineage of Śaiva teachers mentioned in No. 1128 above.

1131. 221 *of* 1908.—(Tamil.) On the same wall. A record in the second year of the Pāṇḍya king Sundara-Pāṇḍyadēva. Records gift of a grove and a maṇṭapa by order of Rājanārāyaṇa-Viḷupparaiyan. See No. 1127 above where perhaps the same king is referred to.

1132. 222 *of* 1908.—(Tamil.) On the north wall of the same prākāra. A much damaged record in the twenty-sixth year of the Pāṇḍya king Māravarman Tribhuvanachakravartin . . . Pāṇḍyadēva. Seems to record a sale of land.

1133. 223 *of* 1908.—(Tamil.) On the inner gōpura of the same temple. A damaged record in the seventeenth year (Tulā, Pūrva,

14, Aśvini, Friday) of the Chōḷa king Tribhuvanachakravartin Rājēndra-Chōḷadēva (III). Records gift of land for the maintenance of a flower garden. See *Ep. Ind.*, Vol. XI, p. 131, where the date is calculated to be Friday, 27th October, A.D. 1262.

1134. 224 *of* 1908.—(Tamil.) On the same gōpura. A record in the eighteenth year. An unnamed Daṇḍanāyaka granted and confirmed the old scale of worship in the temple.

1135. 225 *of* 1908.—(Tamil.) On the outer gōpura of the same temple. A damaged record in the fourth year of the Pāṇḍya king Perumāḷ Sundara-Pāṇḍyadēva [who "might be the same" as Jaṭāvarman Sundara Pāṇḍya I. See *Ep. Rep.*, 1909, p. 82.]

1136. 226 *of* 1908.—(Tamil.) On the same gōpura. A much damaged record in the fourteenth year of the Pāṇḍya king Jaṭāvarman Tribhuvanachakravartin . . . Pāṇḍyadēva.

1137. 227 *of* 1908.—(Tamil.) On the same gōpura. A much damaged record in the fourteenth year (of?). Mentions the order of Śōḷiyavaraiyan.

Pattukkōṭṭai.

1138. In the ruined fort (now in the Taluk office). A record ascribing the foundation of the fort to Vānaji Paṇḍitar Aiyar Avargaḷ in honour of Shahji Mahārāja in A.D. 1686–7. It says that Shahji "conquered all the Paṭṭukkōṭṭai country inhabited by the Kaḷḷans extending to the south as far as Pāmbanār." [Local tradition, however, attributes the fort to one Paṭṭu Maḷava Rāya. It was garrisoned by the British in 1781 and captured by Haidar subsequently. See *Tanj. Gazr.*, Vol. I, p. 253.]

Śāḷuvanāyakkan-paṭṭaṇam.

1139. On the memorial tower built by Rāja Sarabhōji in 1814, usually called *Manora* by the people. Commemorates the downfall of Napoleon and the success of British arms. [Sarabhōji lived at this place and hence it came to be called Sarabhēndrarājanpaṭṭaṇam.]

SHIYĀLI TALUK.

In his *Antiquities* Mr. Sewell says that there are copper plate grants in the hands of the residents or temples of Kīrnāṅgūr, Maruvattūr, Tiruvālaṅgāḍ and Vaidyēśvarankōvil, but no details of these are available. I have given below such of them as are definite and dated.

Erukkūr.

1140. 299 *of* 1911.—(Tamil.) On a detached stone built into the entrance of the Perumāḷ temple. A fragmentary record in the third year of the Chōḷa king Rājādhirājadēva (I or II?).

Kāvēripaṭṭinam.

This ancient seaport identified with the Kamara of the *Periplus*, the *Chabaris* emporium of Ptolemy and *Charitrapura* of Hiouentsang, ceased to be of importance only about the fifteenth century, in consequence evidently of the silting up of the Kāvēri. It is now a hamlet of fishermen and a place of pilgrimage. For its ancient trade, its splendour, its wealth under Karikālchōḷa, its people, etc., as given in Tamil Literature, see *Tamils 1800 years ago*. To the literary men the place is of interest as the birth-place of *Paṭṭiṇattuppiḷḷai* and to the sociologist as the birth-place of the Nāṭṭukkōṭṭai Cheṭṭi community.

1141. 140 *of* 1910.—(Tamil.) On a slab excavated and now preserved in the Taluk office at Shiyāli. A mutilated record. In modern characters. Mentions the street called after Rāyanārāyaṇa and a tank.

Koṇḍattūr.

1142. A C.P. grant in the possession of a resident of the village, dated in Ś. 1529 (A.D. 1607). *Antiquities*, Vol. I, p. 272.

Śāyāvanam.

This is near the ancient site of Kāvēripaṭṭiṇam. See No. 1151 below which refers to Śāyai in Pukār. It is also referred to in the *Periapurāṇa* in connexion with the legend of Iyarpagai Nāyanār. See *Tanj. Gazr.*, p. 258. For the description of the ancient grandeur of the place see Kaḍialūr Udirankaṇṇanār's *Paṭṭanappālai*.

1143. 261 *of* 1911.—(Tamil.) On the north wall of the prākara in the Śāyāvanēśvara temple. A record in the eighth year of the Chōḷa king Tribhuvanachakravartin Kōnērimēnkoṇḍān (Rājarāja). Records that at the instance of a certain Piḍāran-Nāyakan some *dēvadāna* lands belonging to the temple of Tiruchchāyakāḍ-Uḍaiyar at Kāvērippūmpaṭṭiṇam in Nāṅgūr-nāḍu, a subdivision of Rājādhirāja-vaḷanāḍu, were restored by the king for a flower-garden. henceforward named Rājarājan-tirunandavanam. The royal secretary (*tirumandira-ōlai*) was Paṇḍitaśōḷa-Mūvēndavēḷān. Mentions some other officers of the king as signatories.

1144. 262 *of* 1911.—(Tamil.) On the same wall. A record in the thirty-fifth year of the Chōḷa king Tribhuvanachakravartin Tribhuvanavīradēva (1178—1216), "who was pleased to take Madurai (Madura), Īḷam (Ceylon), Karuvūr and the crowned head of the Pāṇḍya and to perform the anointment of heroes and victors." Registers the distribution of paddy collected by the temple, for offerings and for repairs, under orders of Piḷḷai Ambaruḍaiyār Kāḷiṅgarāyar.

1145. 263 *of* 1911.—(Tamil.) On the same wall. A record in the fifth year of the Chōḷa king Tribhuvanachakravartin Rājarājadēva. Records gift of land for an additional ½ lamp in the temple of Tiruchchāyakāḍ Uḍaiyār, 1½ having been previously provided for in the seventh year of Periyadēvar by a certain Malaimēlmarundu *alias* Vānavan Viḷupparaiyan of Marudamaṅgalam in Tiruvinḓalūr-nāḍu, a subdivision of Rājādhirājavaḷanāḍu.

1146. 264 *of* 1911.—(Tamil.) On the same wall. A record in the eighteenth year of Tribhuvanachakravartin Kōnērinmaikoṇḍan. Registers that certain tenants in the *dēvadāna* villages of the temple did not pay their dues till the seventeenth year of the king and that in the eighteenth year they were made to sell back their holdings to the temple in payment thereof, on the representation made by Vāṇakovaraiyan. The royal secretary was Rājanārāyaṇa Mūvēndavēḷān.

1147. 265 *of* 1911.—(Tamil.) On the same wall. An unfinished record in the fifth year, of the Chōḷa king Tribhuvanachakravartin Vīrarājēndra-Chōḷadēva (II, or Kulōttuṅga III ?). Stones out of order. Mentions Kāvērippūmpaṭṭiṇam in Nāṅgūr-nāḍu, a subdivision of Rājādhirājavaḷanāḍu.

1148. 266 *of* 1911.—(Tamil.) On the west wall of the same prākāra. A damaged record in the thirty-fifth year of the Chōḷa king Tribhuvanachakravartin Tribhuvanavīradēva (178—1216) "who took Madurai (Madura), Īḷam (Ceylon), Karuvūr and the crowned head of the Pāṇḍya and was pleased to perform the anointment of heroes and victors." Lease of a temple land and a house to Uttarāpati-Nāyakan *alias* Tiruchchāyakkāṭṭu-vēḷān, the headman of Vallam, for the supply of 8 *śāyāvana-nāḻi* of pepper every day, to the temple. [The *nāḻi* measure here mentioned was probably a local one but must have been widely in use on account of the commercial importance of the place.]

1149. 267 *of* 1911.—(Tamil.) On the south wall of the same prākāra. A damaged record in the ninth year of the Chōḷa king Parakēsarivarman *alias* Tribhuvanachakravartin Vikrama-Chōḷadēva (1118—35). Begins with the introduction *pūmalai miḍaindu*, etc.

1150. 268 *of* 1911.—(Tamil.) On the same wall. A much damaged record in the twenty-seventh year of the Chōḷa king Tribhuvanachakravartin Kulōttuṅga-Chōḷadēva III, "who was pleased to take Madurai (Madura), Īḷam (Ceylon), Karuvūr and the crowned head of the Pāṇḍya". Records gift of land for presenting rice to Brāhmaṇas.

1151. 269 *of* 1911.—(Tamil verse.) On the same wall. A record in the fifth year of the Chōḷa king Vikrama-Chōḷadēva. Registers that a minister of the Chōḷa king named Mukundayaradipati Tiruchchiṟṟambalavan built a *maṭha* and presented land to it for feeding fifty Brāhmaṇas (of Śāyāvanam) in Pugār-nagar (i.e., Kāvērippūmpaṭṭiṇam).

1152. 270 *of* 1911.—(Tamil verse.) On the same wall. Records gift of land for offerings to the temple of Śāyai-Nāyakar, by a certain Guṇākara.

1153. 271 *of* 1911.—(Tamil.) On the same wall. An unfinished record in the third year of the Chōḷa king Tribhuvanachakravartin Vikrama-Chōḷadēva (1118—35). Mentions a certain Gaṅgaikoṇḍaśōḷaraiyan and the temple of Tiruchchāyakkāḍuḍaiyār.

1154. 272 *of* 1911.—(Tamil.) On the west wall of the central shrine of the Pallavanēśvara temple in the same village. A damaged record in the seventeenth year of the Pāṇḍya king Māravarman Tribhuvanachakravartin Sundara-Pāṇḍyadēva (I or II ?). Built in at the bottom. Seems to record a gift of land to the temple of . . . at Kāvērippūmpaṭṭinam in Rājādhirājavaḷanāḍu.

1155. 273 *of* 1911.—(Tamil.) On a stone set up in the courtyard of the same temple. A record in Ś. 1679 and Kaliyuga 4775, Jaya (wrong). Records gift of land for offerings, festivals, repairs, etc., to the temple of Pallavanīśuram at Kāvērippaṭṭiṇam in Kāvērippūmpaṭṭiṇa-māgāṇam, a subdivision of Tiruchchāyakkāṭṭūr-śīmai, by a certain Rāyarāvuttamiṇḍa and others.

*Shiyali.**

The historic importance of the place lies in its being the birthplace of the great Tirugñānasambanda and in consequence the scene of legends, festivals and commemorations of that saint. See *Tanj. Gazr.*, Vol. I, p. 258.

1156. 123 *of* 1896.—(Tamil.) On the north wall of the Tirugñānasambanda shrine in the Brahmapurīśvara temple. A record in the eleventh year of the Chōḷa king Tribhuvanachakravartin Rājādhirājadēva. Records gift of land for providing offerings to Āḷuḍaiya-Piḷḷaiyār (i.e., Gñānasambanda).

1157. 124 *of* 1896.—(Tamil.) On the south wall of the Brahmapurīśvara shrine in the same temple. A record in the fourteenth year of the Chōḷa king Tribhuvanachakravartin Kulōttuṅga-Chōḷadēva (III), "who was pleased to take Madurai and the crowned head of the Pāṇḍya." Records gift of land.

1158. 125 *of* 1896.—(Tamil.) On the same wall. A record in the ninth year of the Chōḷa king Tribhuvanachakravartin Kulōṭṭuṅga-Chōḷadēva (III), "who was pleased to take Madurai." Quotes an inscription of the sixteenth year of Kulōṭṭuṅga I.

---

* A Tamil work on the local *purāṇa* by Aruṇāchalakkavirāya exists. He died in Ś. 1701. For his life and other works see *Abhidhānachintāmaṇi*, p. 65.

Tirumayilāḍi.

1159. A C.P. grant in the hands of a local ryot, recording a grant of lands by a Sētupati chief. No other details given. *Antiquities*, Vol. I, p. 272.

Tiruveṇkāḍu.

Known in the *Periapurāṇa* as the place of Śiruttoṇḍa's wife. The epigraphs of the village belong to the Chōḷa and Pāṇḍya periods. The inscription 1172 which refers to the Kākatīya Gaṇapati is particularly noteworthy.

1160. 110 *of* 1896.—(Grantha.) On the south wall of the Śvētāraṇyēśvara shrine. A record in the thirty-ninth year of the Chōḷa king Kulōttuṅga Chōḷa I. Records gift of lamp. See *Ep. Ind.*, Vol. V, p. 104, where Dr. Hultzsch edits the inscription.

1161. 111 *of* 1896.—(Tamil.) On the same wall. A record in the twentieth year of the Chōḷa king Kō-Rājarāja-Rājakēsarivarman *alias* Rājarājadēva (I). Records gift of a golden bowl by a queen of Rājarājadēva.

1162. 112 *of* 1896.—(Tamil.) On the same wall. A record in the nineteenth year of the Chōḷa king Kō-Rājarāja-Rājakēsarivarman *alias* Rājarājadēva (I). Records gift of a string of rubies by another queen of his.

1163. 113 *of* 1896.—(Tamil.) On the west wall of the same shrine. A record in the second year of the Chōḷa king Kō-Parakēsarivarman *alias* Vīra-Rājēndradēva. Records gift of several villages. [As the king was a Parakēsari we have to infer that Vīra-Rājēndra II (i.e., Kulōttuṅgachōḷa III) was intended.]

1164. 114 *of* 1896.—(Tamil.) On the north wall of the same shrine. A record in the twenty-ninth year of the Chōḷa king Kō-Rājakēsarivarman *alias* Rājādhirājadēva (I). Records gift of land. The king should be the first of that name, as the second did not rule for such a long period.

1165. 115 *of* 1898.—(Tamil.) On the same wall. A record in the twenty-seventh year of the Chōḷa king Kō-Rājakēsarivarman *alias* Rājarājadēva (I). Beginning built in.

1166. 116 *of* 1896.—(Tamil.) On the same wall. A record in the twenty-seventh year of the Chōḷa king Kō-Rājarājakēsarivarman *alias* Rājarājadēva (I). Records gift of a lamp.

1167. 117 *of* 1896.—(Tamil.) On the same wall. A record in the twenty-eighth year of the Chōḷa king Kō-Rājarājakēsarivarman *alias* Rājarājadēva (I). Records gift of a lamp by the mother of a queen.

1168. 118 *of* 1896.—(Tamil.) On the north wall of the second prākāra of the same temple. A record in the eighth year of the

Chōḷa king Kō-Parakēsarivarman *alias* Kulōttuṅga-Chōḷadēva (III?). Records gift of a lamp.

1169. 119 *of* 1896.—(Tamil.) On the same wall. A record in the twenty-second year of the Chōḷa king Tribhuvanachakravartin Rājarājadēva. Records a sale of land to the temple.

1170. 120 *of* 1896.—(Tamil.) On the same wall. A record in the fifth year of the Pāṇḍya king Kō-Māravarman *alias* Vikrama-Paṇḍya. Records gift of a lamp. [The king was not improbably the same as he who ascended the throne in A.D. 1282 and who had the titles of "the sun to the darkness of the Kēraḷa race," "the submarine fire to the ocean of Chōḷa race" and the conqueror of Vīragaṇḍagōpāla and Gaṇapati.]

1171. 121 *of* 1896.—(Tamil.) On the west wall of the same prākāra, right of entrance. A record in the fifth year of the Chōḷa king Kō-Parakēsarivarman *alias* Vikrama-Chōḷadēva (1118—35). Records gift of land.

1172. 122 *of* 1896.—(Tamil and Grantha.) On the same wall left of entrance. A record in the seventh year of the Pāṇḍya king Vikrama-Pāṇḍyadēva. Records gift of land. The inscription refers to a victory over the Kākatīya king Gaṇapati. See No. 1170 for the identity of the king.

Toṟudūr.

1173. On a stone fixed in the ground north of the village. Records grant of lands to the Śiva temple at Vēlūr in Ś. 1518. *Antiquities*, Vol. I, p. 272.

Vēlūr.

1174. A C.P. grant in the local Śiva temple, dated Ś. 1515. *Ibid.*

TANJORE TALUK.

Būdalūr.

1175. In the inner shrine of the Āpatsahāya temple. Records gift of land at Būdalūr or Girikoṇḍa-chōḷanallūr to the God in the twelfth year of Kōnērinmaikoṇḍān. *Ins., S. Dts.*, p. 255, No. 151.

1175-A. In the same place. Records gift of land bought for 1,048 *paṇams* to the local God in the first year of the reign of Sundara Pāṇḍya. *Ibid.*, No. 152. See No. 1175.

Kaduveli (Candoovalee).

1175-B. On a stone in the pagoda of Ākāśapurīśvara temple. Records that Rājarājadēva gave to the God in his fourteenth year 4 *mās* of land. *Ibid.*, p. 247, No. 111.

Kaḷḷa-Perumbūr.

1176-A. 580 *of* 1904.—(Tamil verse.) On the south wall of the central shrine in the Kailāsanātha temple. A partly damaged record in the twelfth year of the Chōḷa king Kulōttuṅga (III). Records gift of land. The village is called Pirambu.

1176-B. 581 *of* 1904.—(Tamil.) On the west wall of the same shrine. A record in the forty-ninth year of the Chōḷa king (Kulōttuṅga I?). Registers an agreement *(vyavasthā)* by the *sabhā* of Rājasundarichaturvēdimaṅgalam.

1176-C. 582 *of* 1904.—(Tamil.) On the same wall. An incomplete record in the forty-ninth year of the Chōḷa king Rājakēsarivarman *alias* Uḍaiyār Tribhuvanachakravartin Kulōttuṅga-Chōḷadēva (I). Records gift of land to the temple of Śrīkayilāyam *alias* Śrī-Kulōttuṅga-Chōḷa-Īśvaramuḍaiya-Mahādēvar at Rājasundari-chaturvēdimaṅgalam.

1176-D. 583 *of* 1904.—(Tamil.) On the north wall of the same shrine. A record in the nineteenth year of the Chōḷa king Tribhuvanachakravartin Rājarājadēva. Records an agreement by the *sabhā* of the same village dismissing a village accountant who had cheated them and preventing his descendants and relations from writing the accounts of the village.

1176-E. 584 *of* 1904.—(Tamil.) In the gōpura of the same temple, right of entrance. A record in twenty-fifth year of the Chōḷa king Tribhuvanachakravartin Kulōttuṅga-Chōḷadēva (III), "who took Madura, Īḷam (Ceylon) and the crowned head of the Pāṇḍya." Records gift of land. [*Ins., S. Dts.*, p. 240, No. 75, gives this inscription but wrongly attributes it to the forty-fifth in place of twenty-fifth year.]

1176-F. 585 *of* 1904.—(Tamil.) In the same place, left of entrance. A record in the twenty-third year of the Chōḷa king Tribhuvanachakravartin Kulōttuṅga-Chōḷadēva (III), "who took Madura, Īḷam (Ceylon), and the crowned head of the Pāṇḍya." Records gift of land. [The *Mack. MSS.* contain this epigraph. See *Ins., S. Dts.*, p. 241, No. 76.]

*Kaṇḍiyūr.**

The local temple is mentioned in the *Periapurāṇa* (twelfth century). Later on it figured largely in the Karnatic wars (see *Tanj. Gazr.*, Vol. I, p. 263). It was situated, according to the Tanjore inscriptions, in Āyirattaḷi.

---

* The *Mack. MSS.* as summarized in *Ins., S. Dts.*, p. 242, give three inscriptions in this place Nos. 83—5. They are attributed to the seventeenth year of Kō-Rājakēsari, eleventh year of a king of the same name and tenth year of "Côpadêva". No details are given except in the first which records grant of "Vooputtoore" village to Vīrattānes vara.

1177. 13 *of* 1895.—(Tamil.) On the north wall of the central shrine in the Vīraṭṭānēśvara temple. A record in the ninth year of the Chōḷa king Uttama-Chōḷadēva *alias* Kō-Parakēsarivarman. Records gift of a lamp.

1178. 14 *of* 1895.—(Tamil.) On the same wall. A record of the Chōḷa king Madiraikoṇḍa Kō-Parakēsarivarman (905—47), the date of which is lost. Records gift of gold by an inhabitant of Tañjāvūr.

1179. 15 *of* 1895.—(Tamil.) On the same wall. A record in the forty-sixth year of the Chōḷa king Kō-Parakēsarivarman (905—947) "who took Madirai and Ceylon." Records gift of land.

1180. 16 *of* 1895.—(Tamil.) On the same wall. A record in the eleventh year of the Chōḷa king Madiraikoṇḍa Kō-Parakēsarivarman (905—47). Records gift of land.

1181. 17 *of* 1895.—(Tamil.) On the same wall. A record in the twenty-first year of Kō-Vijaya-Nripatuṅgavikramavarman (Cir. A.D. 875). Records gift of lamp.

1182. 18 *of* 1895.—(Tamil.) On the same wall. A mutilated record in the fourth year of the Chōḷa king Kō-Parakēsarivarman "who cut off the head of the Pāṇḍyan." [The king might be Parāntaka (II) Sundara Chōḷa.]

1183. 19 *of* 1895.—(Tamil.) On the east wall of the same shrine. A record in the twenty-sixth year of the Chōḷa king Madiraikoṇḍa Kō-Parakēsarivarman (905—47). Records gift of gold for a lamp.

1184. 20 *of* 1895.—(Tamil.) On the south wall of the same shrine. A record in the tenth year of the Chōḷa king Kō-Parakēsarivarman. Records gift of a lamp.

1185. 21 *of* 1895.—(Tamil.) On the same wall. A record of the Chōḷa king Kō-Parakēsarivarman, the date of which is lost. Records gift of land.

1186. 22 *of* 1895.—(Grantha and Tamil.) On the east wall of the shrine of Maṅgaḷāmbika in the same temple. A record in the sixth year of the Chōḷa king Kō-Parakēsarivarman *alias* Rājēndra-Chōḷadēva I (1011—43). Records gift of land.

1187. 23 *of* 1895.—(Grantha and Tamil.) On the same wall. A record in the thirteenth year of the Chōḷa king Kō-Parakēsarivarman *alias* Rājēndra-Chōḷadēva I (1011—43). Records that a new dancing master was appointed instead of a deceased relative of his.

Karuttaṭṭāṅguḍi.

1188. 42 *of* 1897.—(Tamil.) On the south wall of the central shrine of the Viśishṭhēśvara temple. A record in the tenth year of the Chōḷa king Kō-Parakēsarivarman. Records gift of sheep by Madhurāntakan Kaṇḍarādittan (i.e., Gaṇḍarāditya, son of Madhurāntaka, who ruled from 970 to 986).

1189. 43 *of* 1897.—(Tamil.) On the same wall. Records a private gift.

1190. 44 *of* 1897.—(Tamil.) On the same wall. A record in the third year of the Chōḷa king Kō-Parakēsarivarman *alias* Rājēndra-Chōḷadēva I (1011—43). Records sale of land to the temple.

1191. 45 *of* 1897.—(Tamil.) On the same wall. A record in the third year of the Chōḷa king Kō-Parakēsarivarman *alias* Rājēndra-Chōḷadēva I (1011—43). Records sale of land to the temple.

1192. 46 *of* 1897.—(Tamil.) On the south and west walls of the same shrine. A record in the seventeenth year of the Chōḷa king Kō-Rājarāja-Rājakēsarivarman I (985—1013). Records sale of land.

1193. 47 *of* 1897.—(Tamil.) On the west wall of the same shrine. A fragmentary record in the twenty-fourth year of the Chōḷa king Tribhuvanachakravartin Rājarājadēva.

1194. 48 *of* 1897.—(Tamil.) On the same wall. A record in the twenty-fourth year of the Chōḷa king Kō-Rājarājakēsarivarman *alias* Rājarājadēva I. Records gift of a lamp.

1195. 49 *of* 1897.—(Tamil.) On the north wall of the same shrine. A damaged record in the second year of the Chōḷa king Kō-Parakēsarivarman.

1196. 50 *of* 1897.—(Tamil.) On the same wall. A record in the fifth year of the Chōḷa king Kō-Parakēsarivarman *alias* Rājēndra-Chōḷadēva I (1011—43). Records gift of a gold diadem.

1197. 51 *of* 1897.—(Tamil.) On the east wall of the same shrine, right of entrance. A record in the tenth year of the Chōḷa king Kō-Parakēsarivarman. Records the setting up of the images of two door-keepers, near which the inscription is found.

Kōnērirājapuram.

1198. 450 *of* 1908.—(Tamil.) On the south wall of the central shrine in the Umāmahēśvarasvāmin temple. A record of the Chōḷa king Madhurāntakadēva *alias* Uttama-Chōḷa (970—85). Records that the temple of Tirunallamuḍaiyār was built of stone by Mādēvaḍigaḷār *alias* Śembiyan-Mādēviyār, queen of Gaṇḍarādittadēva and mother of the king. [Gaṇḍarāditya was a Śaivite devotee and writer. His hymns have been included in the ninth *Tirumuṟai.*]

1199. 622 *of* 1909.—(Tamil.) On the south wall of the central shrine in the Umāmahēśvara temple. A damaged record in the eleventh year of the Chōḷa king Parakēsarivarman. Records gift of land for a lamp.

1200. 623 *of* 1909.—(Tamil.) On the same wall. An unfinished record of the Chōḷa king Rājēndra-Chōḷa I. Contains a portion of the historical introduction of the king beginning with *tirumanni.*

1201. 624 *of* 1909.—(Tamil.) On the same wall. A record in the sixth year (Karkaṭaka, Apara. 14, Wednesday, Punarvasu) of the Chōḷa king Rājarāja-Rājakēsarivarman (I). Records gift of land by *sabhā* as *kāṇi* at Pūṅguḍi to two individuals who had to sing the *Tiruppadiyam-hymns* in the temple of Tirunallam-Uḍaiyār. See *Ep. Ind.*, Vol. XI, p. 241, where Mr. R. Sewell gives July 12th, A.D. 1010, as the equivalent of the date.

1202. 625 *of* 1909.—(Tamil.) On the same wall. A damaged record in the fifth year (Mēsha, Pūrva., Hasta, Friday) of the Chōḷa king Parakēsarivarman *alias* Uḍaiyār Śrī-Rājēndradēva (1050—1063). Begins with the historical introduction *tiru maruviya śeṅgōl,* etc. Records sale of about one *mā* of land to temple by the assembly. [If this is correct the accession of the sovereign must have taken place between June 25th and July 12th, A.D. 985.]

1203. 626 *of* 1909.—(Tamil.) On the same wall. Records that the figure on the stone was one of Śāttan Guṇabhaṭṭan *alias* Haracharaṇaśēkharan of Ālattūr who caused this stone temple to be built under orders of Uḍaiya-Piraṭṭiyār, mother of Madhurāntakadēva *alias* Uttama-Chōḷa (970—85). He was evidently raised to the dignity of Rājakēsari-Mūvēndavēḷān in recognition of his services.

1204. 627 *of* 1909.—(Tamil.) On the same wall. A record in the twelfth year of the Chōḷa king Rājarāja-Rājakēsarivarman (Rājarāja I), who destroyed the ships at Śālai. Records gift of a silver image of the god, and a copper image of Chaṇḍēśvara, by Nakkan Nallattaḍigaḷ, one of the members of the *Rājarājatteriñja-Kaikkōḷar* (community), translated by the Epigraphist into "the selected Kaikkōlars of king Rājarāja." Nakkan is said to have been the son of Aṇukkan Mahāmalli, a maid servant (*peṇḍāṭṭi ?*) in the palace (*vēḷam ?*) of Rājakēsarivarman.

1205. 628 *of* 1909.—(Tamil.) On the same wall. A record of the Chōḷa king Parakēsarivarman *alias* Uḍaiyār Śrī-Rājēndradēva (1050—63) in Rishabha, Pūrva, Friday, Tritiya, Tiruvādirai. Refers to the assembly of Tirunallam, a *brahmadēya* in Veṇṇāḍu, a sub-division of Uyyakkoṇḍār-vaḷanāḍu and records a sale of land to the temple of Tirunallamuḍaiya-Mahādēva (97½ *kāśus*).

1206. 629 *of* 1909.—(Tamil.) On the same wall. A record in the twenty-seventh year of the Chōḷa king Rājarājakēsarivarman *alias* Śrī-Rājarājadēva I. Records gift of money for a lamp.

1207. 630 *of* 1909.—(Tamil.) On the same wall. A damaged record in the fourteenth year of the Chōḷa king Parakēsarivarman.

Records gift of land for offerings to a shrine of Gaṇapati at Tirunallam which was a *brahmadēya* in Veṇṇāḍu.

1208. 631 *of* 1909.—(Tamil.) On the same wall. A damaged and unfinished record in the eleventh year of the Chōḷa king Rāja-rāja-Rājakēsarivarman (I, 985—1013), " who destroyed the ships at Kāndaḷūr-Śālai ". Seems to record a gift to the temple of Tirunallamuḍaiya-Mahādēva, by a queen.

1209. 632 *of* 1909.—(Grantha and Tamil.) On the north, west and south walls of the same shrine. A record in the seventeenth year of the Chōḷa king Parakēsarivarman *alias* Uḍaiyār Śrī-Rājēndra-Chōḷadēva (I, 1011—43). Built in in the middle. Refers to the setting up of an image of Kshētrapāla by the queen Arindavan-Mahādēvi.

1210. 633 *of* 1909.—(Tamil.) On the same walls. A much damaged record of the Chōḷa king, the year of which is lost (Mithuna, Apara., Sunday, Trayōdaśi, Aśvati). Built in in the middle. Begins with the historical introduction whose first words are *tirumādar puvi ennum.* The inscription " discloses the name of a temple at Kōnērirājapuram called Madhurāntaki Īśvara, evidently so called after Madhurāntaki ", daughter of Rājēndradēva and queen of Kulōttuṅga Chōḷa I.

1211. 634 *of* 1909.—(Tamil.) On the same walls. A record of the Chōḷa king Parakēsarivarman *alias* Uḍaiyār Śrī-Rājēndradēva (1050—62), in his seventh year, Mēsha, Friday, Dvitiya, Kārttigai. Built in in the beginning. Records a gift of land and mentions that the assembly met in the temple of Madhurāntaki-Īśvara-muḍaiyār.

1212. 635 *of* 1909.—(Tamil.) On the same walls. The beginning of the inscription is built in. Mentions that queen Śembiyan-Mahādēvi, the mother of Madhurāntakadēva *alias* Uttama-Chōḷa, constructed the stone temple at Tirunallam in the name of her husband Gaṇḍarāditya, and made a gift of land for the upkeep of a flower garden and another for feeding 25 Brāhmaṇas in the sixth year of the king in response to a request made by Parakēsari Mūvēndavēḷān, while the king was in his palace at Pichchan kōyil, north of Kaḍambūr. In the eighth year of Parakēsarivarman, he, from his palace in his camp at Paṇaiyūr near Kāraikkāḍu, issued orders to have these gifts entered in books and to regulate the expenses of the temple according to the income of these lands. The interest of the record lies in the completeness of the detail. The chief officers and their titles are mentioned. See *Ep. Rep.*, 1910, p. 87, for details.

1213. 636 *of* 1909.—(Tamil.) On the north wall of the same shrine. A record in the thirty-first year of the Chōḷa king Parakēsarivarman *alias* Uḍaiyār Śrī-Rājēndra-Chōḷadēva I (1011—43). Records gift of paddy to a servant of the temple.

1214. 637 *of* 1909.—(Tamil.) On the same wall. A record in the seventh year of the Chōḷa king Parakēsarivarman *alias* Śrī-Rājēndra Chōḷadēva I (1011—45). Records gift of money (30 *kāśus*) for a lamp by a native of Tiruvāli in Tiruvāli-nāḍu, a subdivision of Vaḍagarai Rājēndra-Chōḷa-vaḷanāḍu. The statement is made that even if the property changes hands by sale or mortgage, the object of the endowment will be done.

1215. 638 *of* 1909.—(Tamil.) On the same wall. A record in the sixth year of the Chōḷa king Uttama-Chōḷa *alias* Parakēsarivarman. Records gift of land for a lamp to the temple of Ādityēś-vara muḍaiya-Mahādēva at Tirunallam.

1216. 639 *of* 1909.--(Tamil.) On the same wall. A damaged record of the fifth year of the Chōḷa king Parakēsarivarman *alias* Śrī-Rājēndra-Chōḷadēva (I). Refers to the third year of the reign and to a gift by Āḷvār Parāntakan Kuṇḍavai-Pirāṭṭiyār and her palace at Paḷaiyāru, referred to elsewhere as the royal home of her nephew. [Kuṇḍavai was the elder sister of Rājarāja I. The Epigraphist believes that all the Tanjore grants previous to the third year of Rājēndrachōḷa I are hers and as the present inscription of the king's fifth year refers to one of her gifts in the third year, it has to be inferred that she died between the third and fifth years of Rājēndrachōḷa I.]

1217. 640 *of* 1909.--(Tamil.) On the same wall. A record of the Chōḷa king Rājakēsarivarman *alias* Vijaya-Rājēndradēva (Rājādhirāja I) in his thirty-sixth year, *Karkaṭaka, Pūrva,* Thursday, *Hasta*. Records sale of land to the temple at Tirunallam by the assembly of Pāvaikkuḍi, a *brahmadēya* in Veṇṇāḍu, a subdivision of Uyyakkoṇḍavaḷanāḍu. The meeting of the *sabhā* took place at the foot of a tree (called Rājēndraśōḷan) on the banks of a canal. [The Government Epigraphist points out that the introduction திங்களேர் தரு shows that the king was Rājādhirāja I. He evidently assumed the title Vijaya Rājēndra after his capture of Kalyāṇa-puram.]

1218. 641 *of* 1909.--(Tamil.) On the same wall. A record in the twelfth year of the Chōḷa king Rājarājakēsarivarman I (985—1013), " who destroyed the ships at Śālai ". Records gift of land to the temple of Tirumūlaṭṭānamuḍaiya Mahādēva at Tirunallam, by Ariñjigaininrān, a native of Vaḍagarai-Maṅgalam in Veṇṇāḍu. Elaborate description of offerings.

1219. 642 *of* 1909.--(Tamil.) On the same wall. A record in the seventh year of the Chōḷa king Parakēsarivarman *alias* Srī-Rājēndra-Chōḷadēva I (1011—43). Records that some drummers of the temple agreed to beat drums and blow horns and conches during the early morning service, in consideration of the money (8 *kāśus*) which they received from a private person (a Veḷḷāḷa).

1220. 643 *of* 1909.—(Tamil.) On the same wall. A record in the eleventh year of the Chōḷa king Tribhuvanachakravartin Rājēndra-Chōḷadēva (I). Records gift of gold ornaments and a silver bugle, by the wife of Vānakōvaraiyar, a native of Kāraikkāḍu, to the god *(Uḍaiyār)* Umaikkunallār. Near Kāraikkāḍu was Paṇayūr which had a camp-palace of the king.

1221. 644 *of* 1909.—(Tamil.) On the same wall. A record in the fifteenth year of the Chōḷa king Rājarāja-Rājakēsarivarman (Rājarāja I). Records gift of money *(7 kāśus)* for a lamp to the temple of Ādityēśvaramuḍaiya-Mahādēva at Tirunallam.

1222. 645 *of* 1909.—(Tamil.) On the same wall. A record in the seventh year of the Chōḷa king Parakēsarivarman *alias* Śrī-Rājēndra Chōḷadēva (I). Records gift of money *(6 kāśus)* for a lamp.

1223. 646 *of* 1909.—(Tamil.) On the south wall of the maṇṭapa in front of the same shrine. A record of the Chōḷa king Rājakēsarivarman *alias* Tribhuvanachakravartin, the date of which is lost. Built in at the ends. Provides for the feeding of the Mahēśvaras.

1224. 647 *of* 1909.—(Tamil.) On the same wall. An unfinished record in the forty-ninth year of the Chōḷa king Rājakēsarivarman *alias* Tribhuvanachakravartin Śrī-Kulōttuṅga-Chōḷadēva (I). Refers to the assembly of Tirunallam, a *brahmadēya* in Vēṇṇāḍu a subdivision of Bhūpāla-kulavalli-vaḷanāḍu and records a decision regarding the resumption of certain temple lands, the tenants of which had deserted the village in consequence of their inability to pay the taxes. The date of the inscription (Wednesday, Pūrvapaksha-Trayōdaśi, Uttaraphalguni, *Mēsha*) corresponds, according to Mr. Sewell, to March 26th, A.D. 1119. This date clearly enables Mr. Sewell to fix the date of Kulōttuṅga's accession in between March 27th and October 8th of A.D. 1070. See *Ep. Ind.*, Vol. XI, pp. 241-2.

1225. 648 *of* 1909.—(Tamil.) On the same wall. A record of the Chōḷa king Rājakēsarivarman *alias* Tribhuvanachakravartin . . . the date of which is lost. Built in at the end and damaged. Contains the historical introduction which commences with the word *viramēṭuṇaiyāga*.

1226. 649 *of* 1909.—(Tamil.) On the same wall. A record in the twentieth year of the Chōḷa king Rājakēsarivarman *alias* Tribhuvanachakravartin Kulōttuṅga-Chōḷadēva. Built in at the beginning. Records gift of money for offerings by a native of Tēvūr in Tēvūr-nāḍu, a subdivision of Vijayarājēndra-vaḷanāḍu.

1227. 650 *of* 1909.—(Tamil.) On the same wall. A record in the fortieth year of the Chōḷa king Rājakēsarivarman *alias* Tribhuvanachakravartin Śrī-Kulōttuṅga-Chōḷadēva (I). Records gift of land by the assembly of Pāvaikkuḍi *alias* Nittavinōda-chaturvēdimaṅgalam, for feeding the Mahēśvaras in the temple at Tirunallam. Another record in continuation which is incomplete at the right end, contains portions of the historical introduction of Vikrama-Chōḷa (1118—35) and provides for the bathing and offerings for the God.

1228. 651 *of* 1909.—(Tamil.) On the north wall of the same maṇṭapa. A record in the thirteenth year of the Chōḷa king Parakēsarivarman *alias* Tribhuvanachakravartin Vikrama-Chōḷadēva (1118—35). Records gift of land for offerings.

1229. 652 *of* 1909.—(Tamil.) On the same wall. A mutilated record in the third year of the Chōḷa king Parakēsarivarman *alias* Tribhuvanachakravartin. Seems to record a gift of land.

1230. 653 *of* 1909.—(Tamil.) On the same wall. A record in the forty-seventh year (Dhanus, Pūrva 1, Monday, Mūla) of the Chōḷa king Rājakēsarivarman *alias* Tribhuvanachakravartin Kulōttuṅga-Chōḷadēva (I). Records sale of land to the temple of Kailāsamuḍaiya-Mahādēva at Tirunallam by the assembly of Pāvaikkuḍi *alias* Nittavinōda-chaturvēdimaṅgalam, a *brahmadēya* in Veṇṇāḍu which was a subdivision of Uyyakkoṇḍār-vaḷanāḍu. See *Ep. Ind.*, Vol. XI, p. 242, where the date is calculated to be Monday, November 26th, A.D. 1117. Mr. Sewell believes that the composer erroneously stated the forty-seventh instead of the forty-eighth regnal year.

1231. 654 *of* 1909.—(Tamil.) On the west wall of the same maṇṭapa. A record in the seventeenth year of the Chōḷa king Tribhuvanachakravartin Kuḷōttuṅga-Chōḷadēva III, "who was pleased to take Madurai (Madura) and the crowned head of the Pāṇḍya". Records gift of jewels to the goddess.

1232. 655 *of* 1909.—(Tamil.) At the entrance into the Naṭarāja shrine in the same temple, right side. A record in the thirty-third year of the Chōḷa king Rājakēsarivarman *alias* Uḍaiyār Śrī-Rājādhirājadēva I, "who took the head of the Vīra-Pāṇḍya, the Śālai of the Chēra and Laṅka (Ceylon)." Records gift of money for a lamp to the temple of Uttamaśōḷa-Viṇṇagar Āḻvār at Tirunallam. [The king was evidently identical with Rājakēsarivarman Rājādhirāja I. See the next epigraph.]

1233. 656 *of* 1909.—(Tamil.) In the same place left side. A record in the thirty-fifth year of the Chōḷa king Rājakēsarivarman *alias* Uḍaiyār Śrī-Vijaya Rājēndradēva. The king is said to have taken the head of the Pāṇḍya, the head of the Chēra, Laṅka (Ceylon) and Raṭṭapāḍi, seven and a half lakhs and to have performed the anointment of victors at Kalyāṇapura. Records the gift of a lamp to a Vaishṇava temple. [The king was evidently identical with Rājakēsarivarman Rājādhirāja I, the conqueror of Kalyāṇapura.]

1234. 657 *of* 1909.—(Tamil.) On the gōpura of the same temple, right of entrance. Records the name of the donor of this gōpura *(vāśal)*, who was a Mudalippiḷḷai of Vaṅgipuram.

1235. 658 *of* 1909.—(Tamil.) On the west wall of the Chaṇḍikēśvara shrine in the same temple. A record in the fifteenth year of the Chōḷa king Chakravartin Kulōttuṅga-Chōḷadēva I. Records that this stone temple of Chaṇḍēśvara was built by Tiṭṭai-Viḷumiyan *alias* Piḷḷai-aḍiyār. Representation of Chaṇḍēśvara worshipping the God Tirunallam-Uḍaiyār is cut on the stone wall, as well as the figure of the builder of the temple.

1236. 659 *of* 1909.—(Tamil.) On the east, north and west walls of the same shrine. A much damaged record of the Chōḷa king Rājakēsarivarman *alias* Chakravartin Śrī-Kulōttuṅga-Chōḷadēva, the date of which is lost. Seems to record a gift of paddy for offerings.

1237. 660 *of* 1909.—(Tamil.) On a pillar in the verandah round the central shrine of the same temple. Records that this Tirunaḍaimāḷigai was built by Arumoḷidēvan *alias* Vayanāṭṭaraiyan of Ādanūr. The same fact is recorded on another pillar of the verandah.

1238. 661 *of* 1909.—(Tamil.) On the east wall of the first prākāra of the same temple. A record in the twenty-fifth year (Mēsha, Apara. 8, Friday, Śravaṇa) of the Chōḷa king Tribhuvanachakravartin Rājarājadēva (III). Appears to record a gift of land for garlands. See *Ep. Ind.*, Vol. XI, p. 249, where the date is pointed out to be April 5th, A.D. 1241.

1239. 662 *of* 1909.—(Tamil.) On the same wall. A record in the sixteenth year (Mīna, Apara. 1, Wednesday, Hasta) of the Chōḷa king Tribhuvanachakravartin Kulōttuṅga-Chōḷadēva III, "who was pleased to take Madurai (Madura) and the crowned head of the Pāṇḍya." Records gift of land to a shrine of Vināyaka-Piḷḷaiyār set up on the south side of the Pugaḷābharaṇa maṇṭapa, in the temple of Tirunalam-Uḍaiyār. See *Ep. Ind.*, Vol. XI, p. 246, where it is pointed out that the date corresponded to March 9th, A.D. 1194.

*Kōviladi.**

The antiquity of the place (which figured largely in the Karnatic wars of the eighteenth century) is evidenced by its inscriptions.

1240. 270 *of* 1901.—(Tamil.) On the east wall of the maṇṭapa in front of the central shrine in the Raṅganātha temple. A record

* The *Mack. MSS.* as summarized in *Ins.*, *S. Dts*, pp. 241–2, Nos. 81–2, give two inscriptions in this place. Of these one is dated in the thirty-first year of Rājarājadēva, and records grant of 1½ *vēli* and 1 *kāṇi* of land in Śuttamalli and the second is an inscription of the fifth year of Sundara Pāṇḍya recording a sale of land (500 *paṇams*) = 2½ *mās* of land).

in the fourteenth year of the Pāṇḍya king Māravarman *alias* Tribhuvanachakravartin Sundara-Pāṇḍyadēva I (1216—35), "who was pleased to present the Chōḷa country." Records gift of money for offerings.

1241. 271 *of* 1901.—(Tamil.) On the north wall of the same maṇṭapa. A damaged record in the twenty-first year of the Chōḷa king Tribhuvanachakravartin Rājarājadēva (III?).

1242. 272 *of* 1901.—(Grantha and Tamil.) On the east wall of the central shrine in the same temple. Records in Ś. 1485 (A.D. 1563), Raktākshin, gifts to the temple by a certain Tātāchārya of Śrīraṅgam.

1243. 273 *of* 1901.—(Tamil.) On the same wall. A record of the Vijayanagara king Sadāśivarāya in Ś. 1467, Krōdhin. Records a gift by Viṭṭhaladēva Mahārāja (his representative in the south and the leader in the campaign of 1545).

1244. 274 *of* 1901.—(Tamil.) On the south wall of the same shrine. Records in Ś. 1393, Khara, a gift for the merit of Dēvarāja, the son of Pokkaraśasāmanta.

1245. 275 *of* 1901.—(Grantha and Tamil.) On the north wall of the maṇṭapa in front of the central shrine in the Divyajñānēśvara temple. A record of the Pāṇḍya king Jaṭāvarman *alias* Sundara-Pāṇḍyādēva (I). Begins with *samasta-jagad-ādhāra*. Built in. Appears to record a sale of land.

1246. 276 *of* 1901.—(Tamil.) On the south wall of the same maṇṭapa. A record in the eleventh year of the Chōḷa king Tribhuvanachakravartin Vikrama-Chōḷadēva (1118—35). Records gift of land.

1247. 277 *of* 1901.—(Tamil.) On the same wall. A record in the forty-fourth year of the Chōḷa king Rājakēsarivarman *alias* Tribhuvanachakravartin Kulōttuṅga-Chōḷadēva (I). Records sale of land.

1248. 278 *of* 1901.—(Tamil.) On the north wall of the central shrine in the same temple. A record in the third year of the Chōḷa king Parakēsarivarman *alias* Rājēndra-Chōḷadēva I (1011—43). Records gift of land.

1249. 279 *of* 1901.—(Tamil.) On the south wall of the same shrine. A record of the Chōḷa king Rājakēsarivarman, the date of which is lost. Records sale of land.

1250. 280 *of* 1901.—(Tamil.) On the west wall of the same shrine. An incomplete record in the second year of the Chōḷa king Rājakēsarivarman.

1251. 281 *of* 1901.—(Tamil.) On the same wall. A record in the third year of the Chōḷa king Rājakēsarivarman. Records gift of land.

Tiruchchennampūṇḍi (near *Kōviladi*).

1252. 282 *of* 1901.—(Tamil.) On the left of the entrance into the Śaḍaiyar temple at Tiruchchennampūṇḍi near the same place. A record in the second year of the Chōḷa king Parakēsarivarman. Records gift of a lamp to the temple of Tirukkaḍaimuḍi-Mahādēva.

1253. 283 *of* 1901.—(Tamil.) On the right of the entrance into the same temple. A record in the eighteenth year of the Pallava king Teḷḷāṟṟerinda Nandipōttaraiyar (i.e., Nandivarman III). Records gift of two lamps to the same temple. [Prof. Dubreuil fixes the date of Nandivarman III between 830 and 850. The poet Perundēvanār of the *Bhāratavenbā* was a contemporary of this king.]

1254. 284 *of* 1901.—(Tamil.) On the north wall of the same temple. A record in the twenty-ninth year of the Chōḷa king Madiraikoṇḍa-Parakēsarivarman (i.e., Parāntaka I). Records gift of gold to the same temple which belonged to Teṅkarai-Iḍaiyāṟṟu-nāḍu.

1255. 285 *of* 1901.—(Tamil.) On the same wall. A damaged record in the thirtieth year of the Chōḷa king Madiraikoṇḍa Parakēsarivarman (A.D. 905—47). Records gift of a lamp.

1256. 286 *of* 1901.—(Tamil.) On the same wall. A record in the thirty-fourth year of the Chōḷa king Madiraikoṇḍa Parakēsarivarman (A.D. 905—47). Records gift of a lamp.

1257. 287 *of* 1901.—(Tamil.) On the south wall of the same temple. A record in the thirty-fourth year of the Chōḷa king Madiraikoṇḍa Parakēsarivarman (A.D. 905—47). Records gift of gold for a lamp to the temple of Tiruchchaḍaimuḍi Mahādēva by Vimalāṅkuśan, an inhabitant of Śāḷakkirāmam in the Pāṇḍya country.

1258. 288 *of* 1901.—(Tamil.) On the same wall. A damaged record in the eighteenth year of the Chōḷa king Madiraikoṇḍa Parakēsarivarman (905—47). Records gift of a lamp. Mentions a certain Vīranārāyaṇa Mūvēndavēḷān. [The chief should have received the title Vīranārāyaṇa from the king himself.]

1259. 289 *of* 1901.—(Tamil.) On the same wall. A damaged record of the Chōḷa king Madiraikoṇḍa Parakēsarivarman (905—47), the date of which is lost. Records gift of a lamp.

1260. 290 *of* 1901.—(Tamil.) On the same wall. A damaged record in the thirty-fifth year of the Chōḷa king Madiraikoṇḍa Parakēsarivarman (905—47).

1261. 291 *of* 1901.—(Tamil.) On the same wall. A damaged record in the twentieth year of the Chōḷa king Madiraikoṇḍa Parakēsarivarman (905—47). Records gift of a lamp.

1262. 292 *of* 1901.—(Tamil.) On the north wall of the maṇṭapa in front of the same temple. A damaged record in the thirty-fifth year of the Chōḷa king Madiraikoṇḍa-Parakēsarivarman (905—47).

1263. 293 *of* 1901.—(Tamil.) On the same wall. A damaged record of the Chōḷa king Madiraikoṇḍa Parakēsarivarman (905--947), the date of which is lost. Appears to record a gift of land.

1264. 294 *of* 1901.—(Tamil.) On the south wall of the same maṇṭapa. A damaged record in the thirty-sixth year of the Chōḷa king Madiraikoṇḍa Parakēsarivarman (905—47). Records gift of gold.

1265. 295 *of* 1901.—(Tamil.) On the same wall. A record in the second year of the Chōḷa king Parakēsarivarman. Records gift of sheep for a lamp to the temple of Tirukkaḍaimuḍi-Mahādēva.

1266. 296 *of* 1901.—(Tamil.) On the same wall. A record in the thirtieth year of the Chōḷa king Madiraikoṇḍa Parakēsarivarman (905--47). Records sale of land. Mentions the temple of Tiruchchaḍaimuḍi-Mahādēva in Teṅgarai-Iḍaiyāṟṟu-nāḍu.

1267. 297 *of* 1901.—(Tamil.) On the same wall. A record in the fourteenth year of the Chōḷa king Madiraikoṇḍa Parakēsarivarman (905—47). Records gift of gold for a lamp to the temple of Tirukkaḍaimuḍi-Mahādēva.

1268. 298 *of* 1901.—(Tamil.) On the same wall. A record in the thirty-seventh year of the Chōḷa king Madiraikoṇḍa Parakēsarivarman (905—47). Records gift of sheep for a lamp.

1269. 299 *of* 1901.—(Tamil.) On the same wall. A damaged record in the seventeenth year of the Chōḷa king Madiraikoṇḍa Parakēsarivarman. Records gift of a lamp.

1270. 300 *of* 1901.—(Tamil.) On a pillar in front of the Śaḍaiyar temple. A record in the second year of the "Gaṅga-Paḷlava king" Vijaya-Nripatuṅga-Vikramavarman (*Circa* 875). Records gift of gold by a Pallava queen to the temple of Tirukkaḍaimuḍi-Mahādēva ; mentions Kachchippēḍu.

1271. 301 *of* 1901.—(Tamil.) On the same pillar. A record in the twenty-second year of "the Gaṅga-Pallava king" Vijaya-Nripatuṅgavarman. Records gift of a lamp to the temple of Tirukkaḍaimuḍi-Mahādēva by a certain Veṭṭuvadiyaraiyar.

1272. 302 *of* 1901.--(Tamil.) On another pillar in front of the same temple. Records gift of gold to the temple of Tirukkaḍaimuḍi Perumānaḍigaḷ.

1273. 303 *of* 1901.—(Tamil.) On a third pillar in the same place. A record in the eighteenth year of "the Gaṅga-Pallava king" Nripatuṅgavarman. Mentions the temple of Tirukkaḍaimuḍi-Perumānaḍigaḷ and the Pallava queen referred to in No. 1270.

Kōvilpattu.

1273-A. On a stone in the pagoda of Vīrakaṇḍēśvara in the village. Records that in the twenty-fifth year of Kulaśēkharadēva the people granted some land in the village to the God. *Ins., S. Dts.*, p. 245, No. 98.

1273-B. In the same place. Records the agreement among certain classes of people for building a maṇṭapam to Uyyakkoṇḍa Nāyanār in the eighth year of Kulaśēkharadēva. *Ibid.*, No. 99.

1273-C. In the same place. A record granting some land to the God by "Tiruchitumbanum" (Tiruchidambaram ?). *Ibid.*, No. 100.

1273-D. In the same place. Records that Kulaśēkharadēva granted in his forty-second year six *vēlis* of land to God Chokkanāyar. *Ibid.*, No. 101.

Niyamam.

1274. 15 *of* 1899.—(Tamil.) On a stone to the left of entrance, in one of the doorways on the south wall of the Airāvatēśvara temple. A mutilated record in the eighteenth year of the Chōḷa king Madiraikoṇḍa Parakēsarivarman (905—47).

1275. 16 *of* 1899.—(Tamil.) A damaged record of the Chōḷa king Rājakēsarivarman, the date of which is lost. Mentions the queen of Nandipōttaraiyar of the Pallavatilaka family. [The king Nandipōttaraiyar was not improbably Nandivarman III and Rājakēsarivarman probably Āditya I; but in this case Āditya should have been in power much earlier than A.D. 880, to which his accession has been generally ascribed.]

Orattanāḍ.

The importance of this place in Mahratta times is evidenced not only by the two epigraphs below, but by the largest and most magnificent choultry of the Tanjore Rājās founded by Muktāmbāḷ, a mistress of Sarabhōji and endowed, at her request, by the British Government with four villages in October 1805.

1276. 166 *of* 1911.—(Nāgari and Marāthi.) On a slab set up on the east side of the village. A record of the Tanjore Marāthi king Chhatrapati Rājāśrī Sarabhōji-Mahārāja (1798—1824) in Ś. 1731, Śukla. Registers that three vēdic sacrifices were caused to be performed under the patronage of the king at Muktāmbāpura, in a *śāla* specially built for the purpose. See note to the next epigraph. For the vicissitudes of Sarabhōji see *Tanj. Gazr.*, Vol. I, pp. 51-2.

1277. 167 *of* 1911.—(Nāgari and Marāthi.) On another slab set up on the west side of the same village. A record of the Tanjore Marātha king Sarabhōji-Mahārāja (1798—1824) in Ś. 1731, Śukla. Registers that two other vēdic sacrifices were caused to be performed on the same day in a hall (*śāla*) built for the occasion. [The sacrifices were (1) Agnishṭhōma performed by Śittappa Dīkshita; (2) the same by Śēsha Jaṭāvallabha; (3) Ādhāna and Prathamātirātra, preceded by Chayana by Veṅkaṭēśvara Dīkshita, son of Mrityuñjaya Vājapēyin; (4) Agnishṭhōma or Sōmayāga by Sāmavēdi Appāsvāmi Dīkshita; and (5) Ādhāna and Prathamātirātra by Rig Vēdi Subrahmaṇya Jaṭāvallabha.]

Śendalai * (or *Mannārsamudram).*

The ancient name of this place was Chandralēkhai-chaturvēdimaṅgalam and that of its temple Perunduṟai. It was in the District of Ārkāṭṭu-kūṟṟam.

1278. 56 *of* 1897.—(Grantha.) In the second gōpura of the Sundarēśvara temple, left of entrance. Mentions a prince Tippa.

1279. 57 *of* 1897.—(Tamil.) In the same place. A record in the tenth year of the Hoysaḷa king Vīra-Rāmanāthadēva. Mentions the Jambukēśvara temple near Trichinopoly. See Tj. 506 above.

1280. 58 *of* 1897.—(Tamil.) On a stone built into the floor of the first prākāra in the same temple. A record in the seventeenth year of the Chōḷa king Kō-Rājakēsarivarman. Records gift of gold.

1281. 59 *of* 1897.—(Tamil.) On the north wall of the central shrine in the same temple. A record in the fourth year of the Chōḷa king Kō-Parakēsarivarman. Records gift of sheep for a lamp.

1282. 60 *of* 1897.—(Tamil.) On the same wall. A record in the forty-fourth year of the Chōḷa king Kulōttuṅga-Chōḷadēva (I). Records gift of land.

1283. 61 *of* 1897.—(Tamil.) On the same wall. A record in the second year of the Chōḷa king Kō-Rājakēsarivarman. Records gift of gold for a lamp.

1284. 62 *of* 1897.—(Tamil.) On the same wall. A record in the third year of the Chōḷa king Kō-Rājakēsarivarman. Records gift of gold for a lamp.

1285. 63 *of* 1897.—(Tamil.) On the west wall of the same shrine. A record in the ninth year of the Chōḷa king Kō-Rājakēsarivarman. Records gift of land. Provides for the recitation of the *Bhārata* in a maṇṭapa.

1286. 64 *of* 1897.—(Tamil.) On the west wall of the same shrine. A record of the Chōḷa king Kō-Parakēsarivarman *alias* Rājēndra Chōḷadēva I. End built in.

---

* The *Mack. MSS.* (*Ins., S. Dts*, p. 241, Nos. 178—80 and p. 255, Nos. 153—5) give six inscriptions in this place. One of them seems to be the same as No. 1285 (but the number of regnal year wrongly given as the 7th). There is an inscription of Rājakēsarivarman. The other three are given under Nos. 1302-A to 1302-C.

1287—1290. 65 *to* 68 *of* 1897.—(Tamil.) On four pillars in the maṇṭapa in front of the same shrine. One record describes the building of a temple of Piḍāri by the Pāṇḍya king Perumbiḍugu-Muttaraiyan *alias* Śuvaran Māran, the son of Iḷaṅgōvadiyaraiyan *alias* Māran Paramēśvaran and grandson of Perumbiḍugu Muttaraiyan *alias* Kuvāvaṉ Māran; and further contains the names of the towns which he destroyed, his surnames and the poets who sang his praise, one of these was Vēḷnamban of Pāchchil near Śrīraṅgam. This king, his father and grandfather seem to be members of a different family from that of the Chinnamanūr plates and their connexion is not known. Venkayya suggests that the king Muttaraiyan who is mentioned in the verses 200 and 296 of the Tamil anthology *Nāladiyār* might be the king mentioned in these inscriptions.

1291. 6 *of* 1899.—(Tamil.) On the south wall of the central shrine of the Sundarēśvara temple. A record in the fourth year of the Chōḷa king Parakēsarivarman, "who took the head of the Pāṇḍya king" (Parāntaka II, Sundara Chōḷa?). Records gift of land for lamps to the temple at Perunduṟai.

1292. 6-*A of* 1899.—(Tamil.) On a stone lying close to the north wall of the same shrine. A record in the seventeenth year of the Chōḷa king Rājakēsarivarman. Records gift of gold for offerings.

1293. 7 *of* 1899.—(Tamil.) On a stone built into the wall of the outer gōpura of the same temple, left of entrance. A fragmentary record in the twelfth year of the Chōḷa king Parakēsarivarman. Mentions Kanakasēnabhaṭāra, probably a Jaina. See Md. 42.

1294. 8 *of* 1899.—(Tamil.) In the Vighnēśvara shrine of the same temple, right of entrance. A record in the fifth year of the Uḍaiyār king Sayaṇa-Uḍaiyār (I or II?). Records the building of the shrine by a Nāyaka.

1295. 9 *of* 1899.—(Tamil.) In the same shrine, left of entrance. A record in the sixteenth year of the Pāṇḍya king Mārañjaḍaiyan. Records gift of gold for a lamp to the temple at Perunduṟai. The king has not been identified.

1296. 10 *of* 1899.—(Tamil.) On the first pillar in the maṇṭapa of the same temple. A record in the tenth year of the Pāṇḍya king Mārañjaḍaiyan. Records gift of land to the Piḍāri temple of Māgaḷam at Niyamam by the servant of a certain Viḍēlviḍugu Muttaraiyan. Venkayya suggests that he must have been anterior to Nandipōttaraiyar.

1297. 11 *of* 1899.—(Tamil.) On the first pillar in the maṇṭapa of the same temple. A record in the twelfth year of the Pallava king Nandipōttaraiyar (i.e., Nandivarman III), "who defeated his enemies at Teḷḷāru." Records gift of land to the same temple by the king (who belonged to the middle of the ninth century).

1298. 12 *of* 1899.—(Tamil.) On the second pillar in the same maṇṭapa. A record in the eighteenth year of the Pāṇḍya king Iḷaṅgo-Muttaraiyar. Records gift of land to the same temple, apparently by the king. See 61 of 1895 at Tiruchchāṟṟuṟai for another inscription of this king. Iḷaṅgo Muttaraiyan might be the son of Perumbuḍugu, suggests Venkayya. See *Ep. Rep.*, 1899, p. 7, paragraph 20.

1299. 13 *of* 1899.—(Tamil.) On the fourth pillar in the same place. A damaged record in the eighteenth year of the Chōḷa king Rājakēsarivarman. Records gift of gold for a lamp to the same temple.

1300. 14 *of* 1899.—(Tamil.) On the base of the south wall of the central shrine of the same temple. A record of the Chōḷa king Parakēsarivarman (905—47), "who took Madura and Ceylon". Built in.

1300-A. On a stone in the gate of the Sundarēśvara temple. Records that in Ś. 1440, Pramādi, one Veṅkaṭarāya Mudali of Kāvēripākkam, granted 38 *vēlis* of land in Vellore, 4¾ *vēlis* in Karūr and other places to God Chokkanāyanār. See *Ins., S. Dts.*, p. 255, No. 153.

1300-B. In the same place. Records in year Prajōtpatti, grant of land for the Pushya festival by Pratāpa Kṛishṇa Rāya. *Ibid.*, No. 154.

1300-C. Records grant of 17 *vēlis* of land by "Tarmayutt" Uḍaiyār in Ś. 1433, in the reign of Pratāpa Kṛishṇa Rāya. *Ibid.*, p. 155.

Tanjore (General).

1301. *C.P. No.* 5 *of Mr. Sewell's List.*—(Tamil.) Records grant by Āṇḍavarāyar Vaṇaṅgāmuḍi Toṇḍamān to certain members of his family. [They belonged to Pāpanāḍu.]

1302. *C.P. No.* 6 *of Mr. Sewell's List.*—(Tamil and Telugu.) Records grant by seventy-four artisans in Ś. 1640 (A.D. 1718), "while Rājādhirāja Ēkoji's sons, Sarfoji and Dukkoji, were reigning as kings" to a Gaṇēśa temple "on the west road from Rāmēśvaram",—the other boundaries being very vaguely given.

1303. *C.P. No. 7 of Mr. Sewell's List.*—Records a deed of sale of some lands in Ś. 1581, A.D. (1659) by Vijaya Aruṇāchala Vaṇaṅgāmuḍi Toṇḍamān, son of Āṇḍavarāyar Vaṇaṅgāmuḍi Toṇḍamān to Andōni Muttu Tēvar, son of Koṭṭa Rāyappa Tēvar.

1303-A. The Tanjore Sanskrit and Kanarese spurious plates of the W. Gaṅga Ari-varma-Mahārājādhirāja (now in the British Museum). Ari-varma was the son of Mādhava I, who was the son of Koṅgaṇivarma of the Jāhnavēya family and Kaṇvāyana gōtra. The date is given, but irregular, according to Dr. Kielhorn. See

Ind. Antq., Vol. VIII, p. 212; *Ibid.*, Vol. XXIV, p. 10, No. 166, and Kielhorn's *Southern List*, No. 108..

1304. 65 *of* 1888.—(Tamil and Grantha.) On the north and west walls of *garbhagriha* of the Brihadīśvara temple, second tier. A record in the twenty-sixth year and twentieth day of Kō-Rāja-kēsarivarman *alias* Rājarājadēva (I). The king issued orders that the gifts made by him, his elder sister (Kuṇḍaviyār) and his queens should be recorded on the walls of the temple he built. See *S.I.I.*, Vol. II, No. 1, pp. 1—14.

1305. 66 *of* 1888.—(Tamil and Grantha.) On the west wall of *garbhagriha*, second tier. A record in the twenty-fifth year of Kō-Rājakēsarivarman *alias* Rājarājadēva. *Ibid.*, No. 2, pp. 14—20. Enumerates the gifts of gold vessels and ornaments by Kuṇḍaviyār.

1306. 67 *of* 1888.—(Tamil and Grantha.) On the south wall of *garbhagriha*, first and second tiers. A record in the fifteenth year of Kō-Parakēsarivarman *alias* Uḍaiyār Rājēndra-Choḷa-dēva (I, 1011—43).

1307. 68 *of* 1888.—(Tamil and Grantha.) On the south wall of *garbhagriha*, first tier. Records dated in the sixth and tenth years of Kō-Parakēsarivarman *alias* Uḍaiyār Rājēndra-Chōḷadēva regarding the interest to be paid to temple by certain villagers for a sum of money contributed by several donors and by the temple treasury. The inscription is valuable for throwing light on the prices and rate of interest in that age. *Ibid.*, Nos. 9, 10, 11, 12, 13, 14, 15, 16, 17, 18 and 19, pp. 90—105.

1308. 69 *of* 1888.—(Tamil and Grantha.) On the south wall of *garbhagriha*, second tier. A record in the twenty-ninth year of Kō-Rājakēsarivarman *alias* Rājarājadēva I. Specifies the revenue in paddy, in gold and in money which a number of villages had to pay to the temple. These had been assigned by the king till the twenty-ninth year of his reign. The inscription is of value for the construction of the fiscal history of the land. *Ibid.*, No. 4, pp. 42—53.

1309. 70 *of* 1888.—(Tamil and Grantha.) On the east wall, second tier. A record in the third year of Kō-Parakēsari-varman *alias* Uḍaiyār Rājēndra-Śōḷa-dēva (I, 1011—43).

1310. 71 *of* 1888.—(Tamil and Grantha.) On the north wall, second tier. A record of Kō-Rājakēsarivarman *alias* Rājarāja-dēva I, the date of which is lost. Contains a description of thirty ornaments made partly of gold and jewels from the temple treasury and partly of pearls given by the king. *Ibid.*, No. 3, pp. 21—42.

1311. 72 *of* 1888.—(Tamil and Grantha.) On the north wall, third tier. A record in the fifth year of Tribhuvanachakravartin Kō-nērinmai-koṇḍān. Records an order of the king by which certain lands which had been wrongfully sold during the third and fourth years of his reign were restored to the temple. *S.I.I.*, Vol. II, No. 21, pp. 109—112.

1312. 73 *of* 1888.—(Tamil and Grantha.) On the south wall, first tier. A record of Śāḷuva Tirumalaidēva in Ś. 1377, expired, by which a number of villages are exempted from taxes (e.g., *pradhānijōḍi, kāraṇikhajōḍi, talayārikkam*, dues on animals, trees, tanks, etc. *Ibid.*, No. 23, pp. 117—9.

1313. 74 *of* 1888.—(Tamil and Grantha.) On the south wall, first and second tiers. A record in the thirty-fifth year of Tribhuvanachakravartin Kōnērinmaikoṇḍān. Records the grant of the village of Śuṅgamtavirttachōḷanallūr (suburb of Tanjore) in 108 shares to Brahmans and the local deity by a feudatory Sāmantanārāyaṇa. The inscription is singularly valuable for the fiscal terms it uses. See *Ibid.*, No. 22, pp. 112 –7.

1314. 75 *of* 1888.—(Tamil and Grantha.) On the south wall, second tier. A record in the twenty-ninth year of Kō-Rājakēsarivarman *alias* Rājarājadēva I, describing the gifts made till that year by Āḻvār Parāntakan Kuṇḍavaiyār. See *Ibid.*, No. 6, pp. 68—77. The inscription, like the others of the series, is of incalculable value in the light it throws on currency, weights and measures, rate of interest, prices, etc.

1315. 76 *of* 1888.—(Tamil and Grantha.) On the south wall of Chaṇḍēśvara shrine. A record in the second year of Uḍaiyār Rājēndra-Śōḷa-dēva I (1011—43). Records the weight of the four water-pots of gilt copper presented by Ādittan Sūryan Tennavan Mūvēndavēḷan of Poygai-nāḍu. See *Ibid.*, No. 60, pp. 246-7.

1316. 77 *of* 1888.—(Tamil and Grantha.) Round the base of Chaṇḍēśvara shrine. A record of Kō-Rājakēsarivarman *alias* Rājarājadēva I, the date of which is lost. See *Ibid.*, No. 59, pp. 236—45. Describes the diadem and girdles of God Rājarājēśvara. Elaborate details.

1317. 78 *of* 1888.—(Tamil and Grantha.) Inside gōpura, left of entrance. A record in the twenty-ninth year of Kō-Rājakēśarivarman *alias* Rājarājadēva I, to the effect that two sums of money were deposited by Kāḍan Gaṇapati, a *śirudanam* servant of the king, with the inhabitants of a bazaar at Tanjore and of certain villages for supplying (for the cost of the interest) cardamom seeds, champaka buds and khaskhas roots for scenting the *abhiśhēka* water of two deities. *Ibid.*, No. 24, pp. 121—4. Also No. 25, pp. 125-6.

1318. 79 *of* 1888.—(Tamil and Grantha.) Inside gōpura, right of entrance. A record in the twenty-ninth year of Kō-Rājakēsarivarman *alias* Rājarājadēva (I). Records two deposits of money by Ādittan Sūryan Tennavan Mūvēndavēḷān, the *śrīkārya* of the Rājarājēśvara temple, with the people of a village, the interest of which, paid in paddy in the first case and in money in the second, was to be devoted for certain needs. *S.I.I.*, Vol. II, No. 26, pp. 126—31.

1319. 80 *of* 1888.—(Tamil and Grantha.) Inside gōpura, right of entrance. A record in the twenty-ninth year of Uḍaiyār Rājarāja-dēva I. Records that an officer of the king (Kārāyil-eḍutta-pādam) deposed 50 *kāśus* with the *sabhā* of a village (Perunaṅgaimaṅgalam) the interest on which (6¼ *kāśus*) was to be used for purchasing camphor for a sacred lamp. *Ibid.*, No. 27, pp. 131—2. Also No. 28 *ibid.*

1320. 81 *of* 1888.—(Tamil and Grantha.) Inside prākāra, east, first niche. A record in the twenty-ninth year of Uḍaiyār Rājarāja-dēva I. Records that an officer of Rājarāja named *Irāyiravan* Pallavayan *alias* Mummaḍi-chōḷa-pōśan set up a copper image of Chaṇḍēśvaradēva and presented ornaments. *Ibid.*, No. 55, pp. 222—4.

1321. 82 *of* 1888.—(Tamil and Grantha.) Inside gōpura, east, second niche. A record in the twenty-ninth year of Uḍaiyār Rājarāja-dēva I. Records the setting up of the image of Sūryadēva by a *śirudanam* servant, Kōvan Aṇṇāmalai *alias* Kēraḷāntaka Viḷupparayan, and presentation of ornaments. *Ibid.*, No. 56, pp. 224—7.

1322. 83 *of* 1888.—(Tamil and Grantha.) Inside gōpura, east, second pillar. A record in the twenty-ninth year of Uḍaiyār Rājarāja-dēva I. Describes a number of copper images made by the king till his twenty-ninth year to represent scenes from the life of Chaṇḍēśvara and the lord of his heart. *Ibid.*, No. 29, pp. 134—7.

1323. 84 *of* 1888.—(Tamil and Grantha.) Inside gōpura, east, third pillar. A record in the twenty-ninth year of Uḍaiyār-Rāja-rāja-dēva I.

1324. 85 *of* 1888.—(Tamil and Grantha.) Inside prākāra, south, first pillar. A record in the twenty-ninth year of Rājarāja-dēva I. Gives the dimensions of a copper image of Pañchadēha (Śiva with five bodies) set up by the king. *Ibid.*, No. 30, pp. 137–8.

1325. 86 *of* 1888.—(Tamil and Grantha.) Inside gōpura, south, third pillar. A record of Uḍaiyār Rājarāja-dēva I. *Ibid.*, No. 31, p. 139. Records that the enclosure was built by the order of the king under the superintendence of the General Kṛishṇa Rāma.

1326. 87 *of* 1888.—(Tamil and Grantha.) Inside gōpura, south, fourth pillar. A record in the twenty-ninth year of Uḍaiyār Raja-rājadēva I. Describes a group of copper images of Śiva, Pārvati, their two sons, etc., set up by Vēḷān Ādittan Parāntaka Pallavaraiyan, a *perundanam* servant of the king. *S.I.I.*, Vol. II, No. 32, pp. 139—41.

1327. 88 *of* 1888.—(Tamil and Grantha.) Inside gōpura, south, sixth pillar. A record in the twenty-ninth year of the king, whose name is lost (evidently Rājarāja I).

1328. 89 *of* 1888.—(Tamil and Grantha.) Inside gōpura, south, eighth pillar. No details given.

1329. 90 *of* 1888.—(Tamil and Grantha.) Inside prākāra, south, ninth pillar. A record in the twenty-ninth year of Uḍaiyār-Rājarāja-dēva.

1330. 91 *of* 1888.—(Tamil and Grantha.) Inside prākāra, south niche. A record in the twenty-ninth year of Uḍaiyār Rājarāja-dēva. *Ibid.*, No. 33, pp. 141–2. Same as 1323 above.

1331. 92 *of* 1888.—(Tamil and Grantha.) Inside prākāra south, tenth pillar. Records that Lōkamahādēvi, a queen of Rājarāja, set up a copper image of Pichchadēvar and presented a number of ornaments. *Ibid.*, No. 34, pp. 142—5. Also No. 35 which records a deposit of money in favour of Pichchadēva by certain officers of the king.

1332. 93 *of* 1888.—(Tamil and Grantha.) Inside prākāra, west first pillar. A record in the twenty-ninth year of Uḍaiyār-Rājarājadēva I. Records that Aravaṇai Malari Kēśava, the *śrikārya-kaṅkāṇi Nāyaka* of the temple, gave an *Īḻapariśu* spittoon (*paḍikkam*), weighing sixty-nine *palas* and costing three *kāśus*. *Ibid.*, pp. 149–50.

1333. 94 *of* 1888.—(Tamil and Grantha.) Inside prākāra, west, second pillar. A record in the third year of Uḍaiyār Rājēndra-Śōḻa-dēva (I, 1011—43).

1334. 95 *of* 1888.—(Tamil and Grantha.) Inside prākāra, west, third pillar. A record in the twenty-ninth year of Uḍaiyār Rājarājadēva I.

1335. 96 *of* 1888.—(Tamil and Grantha.) Inside prākāra, west, fourth pillar. A record in the twenty-ninth year of Uḍaiyār-Rājarājadēva I.

1336. 97 *of* 1888.—(Tamil and Grantha.) Inside prākāra, west, first niche. A record in the twenty-ninth year of Uḍaiyār-Rājarāja-dēva I.

1337. 98 *of* 1888.—(Tamil and Grantha.) Inside prākāra, west, first niche. A record in the twenty-ninth year of the king, whose name is not mentioned. Records that Aravaṇai mālari Kēśava, the *śrikārya-kaṅgāṇi Nāyakā*, gave a spittoon weighing sixty-nine *palas* and costing three *kaśus*. *Ibid.*, No. 36, pp. 149—54. Also No. 37 recording Rājarāja's deposit of 360 *kāśus* with four bazaars at Tanjore for paying out interest, one hundred and fifty plantains daily (54,000 in the year). The cost of the plantain is one *kāśu* for 1,200. So the total cost would be forty-five *kāśus*, which is the usual interest on three hundred and sixty *kāśus*. Also No. 38 of *ibid.* which describes the setting up of seven images, among which were those of Gñānasambanda, Appar and Sundaramūrti, pp. 152—61.

1338. 99 *of* 1888.—(Tamil and Grantha.) Inside prākāra, west, fifth and sixth pillars. A record in the twenty-ninth year of Uḍaiyār Rājarājadēva (I). Records that Kṛishṇa Rāma, the commander who built the enclosure, set up an image of Ardhanārīśvara and presented ornaments. *S.I.I.*, Vol. II, No. 39, pp. 161—6.

1339. 100 *of* 1888.—(Tamil and Grantha.) Inside prākāra, west, seventh and eighth pillars. A record in the third year of Kō-Parakēsarivarman *alias* Rājēndra-Chōḷadēva (I). Records the setting up of a copper image by Ādittan Sūryan (see No. 1318 above). The image represented Milāḍuḍaiyar or Meypporuḷnāyanār whose career (narrated in the *Periapurāṇa*) is referred to. *Ibid.*, No. 40, pp. 166—9.

1340. 101 *of* 1888.—(Tamil and Grantha.) Inside prākāra, west, second niche. A record in the third year of Uḍaiyār Rājēndra-śōḷa-dēva (I), which describes gifts of two lamps and one stand for sacred ashes made to the four images of Gñānasambanda Appar, Sundaramūrti and Periya Perumāḷ (Brihadīśvara). See No. 1337 above. *Ibid.*, No. 41, p. 169.

1341. 102 *of* 1888.—(Tamil and Grantha.) Inside prākāra, west, second niche and ninth pillar. A record in the twenty-ninth year of Uḍāiyār Rājarāja-dēva (I). Says that Rājarāja's queen Lōkamahādēvi set up the images of Āḍavallār and his consort, and presented ornaments. *Ibid.*, No. 42, pp. 169—72.

1342. 103 *of* 1888.—(Tamil and Grantha.) Inside prākāra, west, tenth pillar. A record in the tenth year of Uḍaiyār Rājarāja-dēva, saying that his queen Abhīmānavalli set up the images of Śiva, Brahma and Vishṇu as a boar to illustrate the *Aruṇāchala-māhātmya*. *Ibid.*, No. 44, pp. 174—7.

1343. 104 *of* 1888.—(Tamil and Grantha.) Inside prākarā, west, third niche. A record of Uḍaiyār Rājarājadēva (I). *Ibid.*, No. 45. Same as 1323 and 1329.

1344. 105 *of* 1888.—(Tamil and Grantha.) Inside prākāra, west, third niche, eleventh and twelfth pillars and fourth niche. A record in the twenty-ninth year of Uḍaiyār Rājarājadēva (I), saying that queen Chōḷa Mahādēvi set up images of Śiva, Umā and Gaṇapati, and presented ornaments. *Ibid.*, No. 46, pp. 178—90.

1345. 106 *of* 1888.—(Tamil and Grantha.) Inside prākāra, west, thirteenth pillar. A record in the twenty-ninth year of

Uḍaiyār Rājarājadēva (I). Records that an officer of the king set up a copper image of Bhriṅgīśa. *S.I.I.*, Vol. II, No. 47, pp. 190—93.

1346. 107 *of* 1888.—(Tamil and Grantha.) Inside prākāra, west, fifth niche and fourteenth pillar. A record in the twenty-ninth year of Uḍaiyār Rājarājadēva I. Records that queen Trailōkya Mahādēvi set up the images of Kalyāṇasundara, Umā, Vishṇu, Brahmā, etc., and presented ornaments to the first two. *Ibid.*, No. 48, pp. 193—98.

1347. 108 *of* 1888.—(Tamil and Grantha.) Inside prākāra, north, first pillar. A record in the twenty-ninth year of Uḍaiyār Rājarājadēva (I), regarding the setting up of a copper image of Subrahmaṇya. See *Ibid.*, No. 49, pp. 198-99.

1348. 109 *of* 1888.—(Tamil and Grantha.) Inside prākāra, north, second pillar. A record in the twenty-ninth year of Uḍaiyār Rājarājadēva I. Describes the images of Dakshiṇāmūrti and other deities set up by the king. See *Ibid.*, No. 50, pp. 199—202.

1349. 110 *of* 1888.—(Tamil and Grantha.) Inside prākāra, north, third pillar. A record of Uḍaiyār Rājarājadēva I. Built in.

1350. 111 *of* 1888.—(Tamil and Grantha.) Inside prākāra, first niche, fourth and fifth pillars and second niche. A record in the twenty-ninth year of Uḍaiyār Rājarājadēva (I), saying that queen Pañchavan Mahādēvi set up the images of Tañjayaḷagar, Umā and Gaṇapati and presented ornaments. The inscription has been edited in *Ibid.*, No. 51, pp. 203—17. An elaborate document on the jewellery of the age.

1351. 112 *of* 1888.—(Tamil and Grantha.) Inside prākāra, north, sixth pillar. A record in the twenty-ninth year of Uḍaiyār Rājarājadēva (I). *Ibid.*, No. 52, pp. 217-18. Records the setting up of a copper image of Mahā Vishṇu.

1352. 113 *of* 1888.—(Tamil and Grantha.) Inside prākāra, north, seventh pillar. A record in the twenty-ninth year of Uḍaiyār Rājarājadēva I. Records the erection by queen Pañchavan Mahādēvi of a copper image of Patañjalidēva (half man and half snake). *Ibid.*, No. 53, pp. 218—20.

1353. 114 *of* 1888.—(Tamil and Grantha.) Inside prākāra, north base. A record in the tenth year of Kō-Parakēsarivarman *alias* Rājēndra-Chōḷadēva (I, 1012—53). Records that a sum of 120 *kāśus* was deposited with the assembly of Perumakkaḷūr by a number of officers in favour of Chandraśēkhara and his consort and that the *sabhā* undertook to pay 15 *kāśus* every year as interest. *Ibid.*, No. 54, pp. 220—22.

1354. 52 *of* 1890.—On the north wall of the *garbhagriha* of the same temple. A record in the twenty-ninth year of the Chōḷa king Kō-Rājakēsarivarman *alias* Rājarājadēva (I).

1355. 53 *of* 1890.—In the base of the west verandah of the same temple. *S.I.I.*, Vol. II, No. 43, pp. 172—74. Records the setting up of the images of Kshētrapāladēva, Bhairava, Śiruttoṇḍa and his wife and son.

1356. 35 *of* 1891.—(Tamil.) On the east wall of the *garbha-griha* of the Tanjore temple. A record of the Vijayanagara king Dēvarāya II in Ś. 1368, expired, Kshaya. The beginning of every line is built in. Describes a few gold and silver ornaments which were presented to the temple by a certain Vallabhadēva, apparently a military officer of the king. *Ibid.*, No. 71, pp. 338—40.

1357. 36 *of* 1891.—(Tamil.) On the west wall of the Brihannāyaki shrine. A record on the three-hundred and thirty-fourth day in the second year of Kōnērinmaikoṇḍān, saying that he built the shrine of Ulagamuḻududaiya Nāchchiyār and presented to it eleven *vēlis* of land at Koṭṭagarkuḍi or Ulagāṇḍanāyaki-nallūr. See *Ibid.*, No. 61, pp. 246–47.

1358. 37 *of* 1891.—(Tamil.) On the outside of the north wall of the enclosure of the Tanjore temple, first inscription. An obliterated record in the fifteenth year of the Chōḷa king Kō-Rājakēsarivarman *alias* Kulōttuṅga-Chōḷadēva (I)—the only record of this king in the Tanjore temple. Unfinished inscription. The donor was apparently Arumoḷinaṅgai, the queen of Vīra Rājēndradēva (1064—70). See *Ibid.*, No. 58, pp. 229—36.

1359. 38 *of* 1891.—(Tamil.) On the west wall of the Brihannāyaki shrine in the Tanjore temple. Records gift of the remnants of sacred offerings to the inhabitants of Puliyūr, who, at the instance of Mallappa Nāyakkar, constructed the Mūrtiamma maṇṭapa adjoining the Brihannāyaki shrine. *Ibid.*, No. 62, pp. 247–48.

1360. 39 *of* 1891.—(Tamil.) On the outside of the north wall of the enclosure of the Tanjore temple, second inscription. A record in the twenty-ninth year of the Chōḷa king Kō-Rājakēsarivarman *alias* Rājarājadēva I. First two lines only copied. Contains a list of shepherds who had to supply ghee for temple lamps from the milk of a number of cattle either presented to the temple or purchased from its funds. See *Ibid.*, No. 63, pp. 249—51.

1361. 40 *of* 1891.—(Tamil.) On the outside of the north wall of the enclosure of the Tanjore temple, third inscription. A record of the Chōḷa king Rājarājadēva I. First two lines only copied. *Ibid.*, No. 64, pp. 251–52.

1362. 41 *of* 1891.—(Tamil.) On the outside of the north wall of the enclosure of the Tanjore temple, fourth inscription. A record in the twenty-ninth year of the Chōḷa king Kō-Rājakēsarivarman *alias* Rājarājadēva I. End not copied. Records an order of the king assigning a daily allowance of paddy to each of 48 persons appointed to recite the *Tiruppadiyam* in the temple and to two persons who had to accompany the others on drums. *S.I.I.*, Vol. II, No. 65, pp. 252—59.

1363. 42 *of* 1891.—(Tamil.) On the outside of the north wall of the enclosure of the Tanjore temple, fifth inscription. A record in the twenty-ninth year of the Chōḷa king Kō-Rājakēsarivarman *alias* Rājarājadēva I. End not copied. A very long inscription, recording the king's order assigning the produce of a certain land to a number of men who performed various services in the temple and 400 women (evidently dancing girls) transferred to the Tanjore temple from other temples in the Chōḷa country. Each received one or more shares, each of which consisted of a *vēli* of land, which was calculated at 100 *kalams* of paddy. The inscription is of great interest and value as the names of those figuring in it are of historic interest and as a good knowledge of temple establishments is given. See *Ibid.*, No. 66, pp. 259—303.

1364. 43 *of* 1891.—(Tamil.) On the outside of the east wall of the enclosure of the Tanjore temple, left of entrance. A record of a Chōḷa king (whose name is not clear). Professes to be the continuation of an inscription to the right of the entrance, which is now obliterated. Gives a list of villages which had to supply watchmen for the temple. *Ibid.*, No. 57, pp. 227—29. Gives a number of nāḍus. See 1368.

1365. 55 *of* 1893.—(Tamil.) On the outside of the north wall of the enclosure of the Tanjore temple. A record in the sixth year of the Chōḷa king Kō-Parakēsarivarman *alias* Rājēndradēva (1050—63). Invasion of Iraṭṭapāḍi and conquest of Āhavamalla mentioned. [Records that the king assigned a daily allowance of paddy to a troop of actors who had to perform the drāma *Rājarājēśvara-nāṭaka* on the occasion of the Vaikāśi festival. *Ibid.*, No. 67, pp. 303—7.]

1366. 56 *of* 1893.—(Tamil.) On the outside of the north wall of the enclosure of the Tanjore temple. A record in the fourth year of the Chōḷa king Kō-Parakēsarivarman *alias* Vikrama-Chōḷa-dēva (1118—35). Records that the king assigned an allowance to a person who used to check and measure the supplies of paddy which, according to the numerous inscriptions, were delivered into the temple stores. Refers to the king's viceroyalty in the north in the earlier period. *Ibid.*, No. 68, pp. 307—12.

1367. 57 *of* 1893.—(Tamil.) On the outside of the east wall of the enclosure of the Tanjore temple, right of entrance. A record in the twenty-ninth year of the Chōḷa king Kō-Rājakēsari-varman *alias* Rājarājadēva I. Consists of a list of villages which had to supply treasurers, servants and accountants to the Rāja-rājēśvara temple in accordance with the king's order. *Ibid.*, No. 69, pp. 312—28.

1368. 58 *of* 1893.—(Tamil.) On the outside of the east wall of the enclosure of the Tanjore temple, right of entrance. A record in the twenty-ninth year of the Chōḷa king Kō-Rājakēsarivarman *alias* Rājarājadēva I, giving a list of the villages in the Chōḷa country which had to supply watchmen for the temple. *S.I.I.*, Vol. II, No. 70, pp. 328—38. This is the earlier part of No. 1364 above.

1369. 20 *of* 1897.—(Tamil.) On the outside of the north enclosure of the Rājarājēśvara temple. A record in the twenty-ninth year of the Chōḷa king Kō-Rājakēsarivarman *alias* Rājarājadēva I. Records gift in the shape of money, she-buffaloes, cows and ewes by the king's officers, and other individuals and groups of men for burning lamps in the temple. *Ibid.*, No. 94, pp. 436—58.

1370. 21 *of* 1897.—(Tamil.) On the same wall. A record in the twenty-ninth year of the Chōḷa king Kō-Rājakēsarivarman *alias* Rājarājadēva (I). Records gift of cattle to various shepherds by Rājarājadēva for the supply of ghee for lamps to the Rājarājēśvara temple. *Ibid.*, No. 95, pp. 458—97.

1371. 22 *of* 1897.—(Tamil.) On the second gōpura of the same temple, right of entrance. A record of the Nāyaka king Achyutappa-Nāyaka (1572--1614), son of Śevvappa-Nāyaka, in Ś. 1499, expired, Bahudhānya. Records grant of exemption from taxes to the goldsmiths of Tanjore. *Ibid.*, No. 97, pp. 498-9.

1372. 23 *of* 1897.—(Tamil.) In the same place. A mutilated record in the third year of the Chōḷa king Tribhuvanachakravartin Rājarājadēva (III). Records a political compact entered into by three chiefs of the Chōḷa country to be faithful to the king and to stand by each other. *Ibid.*, No. 96, pp. 497-98. The compact shows that the country was disturbed by internal dissensions and Tanjore was not free from them.

1373. 24 *of* 1897.—(Tamil.) In the same place. A record in the twenty-ninth year of the Chōḷa king Kō-Rājakēsarivarman *alias* Rājarājadēva (I, 985—1013). Records the gift, by the priest Īśānaśiva Paṇḍita, of eight copperpots and of one receptacle for sacred ashes, in the second year of Rājēndra Chōḷa (I, 1011—43). A ninth pot was presented by Pavana-Piḍāran, the Śaiva āchārya of the temple, in the third year of Rājēndra-Chōḷadēva. The *tulākkōl* is mentioned. *Ibid.*, No. 90, pp. 413—5.

1374. 25 *of* 1897.—(Tamil.) On a pillar of the south enclosure of the same temple. A record in the twenty-ninth year of the Chōḷa king Kō-Rājakēsarivarman *alias* Rājarājadēva. Records a gift. Published in *ibid.*, No. 32.

1375. 26 *of* 1897.—(Tamil.) On another pillar of the same enclosure. A record in the twenty-ninth year of the Chōḷa king Kō-Rājakēsarivarman *alias* Rājarājadēva (I). Records that a native of Nallūr *alias* Pañchavanmādevichaturvēdimaṅgalam in Nallūrnāḍu, a district of Nittavinōda-vaḷanāḍu, set up a copper image of Durgā-Paramēśvari and presented a number of ornaments to it. *S.I.I.*, Vol. II, No. 79, pp. 395—400.

1376. 27 *of* 1897.—(Tamil.) On another pillar of the same enclosure. A record in the twenty-ninth year of the Chōḷa king Kō-Rājakēsarivarman *alias* Rājarājadēva (I). Records that Prithvīmahādēviār, a queen of Rājarājadēva, set up a copper image of Śrīkaṇṭhamūrtigaḷ, and presented some ornaments to it. See *ibid.*, No. 80, pp. 400–1.

1377. 28 *of* 1897.—(Tamil.) On another pillar of the same enclosure. A record in the twenty-ninth year of the Chōḷa king Kō-Rājakēsarivarman *alias* Rājarājadēva (I). Records that the son of an officer of Rājarājadēva set up a copper image of the goddess Kāḷa-Piḍāri. Four different varieties of Piḍāri are mentioned, namely, Punnaitturainaṅgai, Poduvagai-ūr-uḍaiyāḷ, Kuduraivaṭṭam-uḍaiyāḷ and Tiruvāḷ-uḍaiyāḷ. *Ibid.*, No. 81, pp. 401–2.

1378. 29 *of* 1897.—(Tamil.) On the base of the same enclosure. A record in the seventh year of the Chōḷa king Kō-Parakēsarivarman *alias* Rājēndra-Chōḷadēva I (1011—43). Records an endowment in money in favour of the image of Śrīkaṇṭhamūrtigaḷ set up by Prithvīmahādēviār, queen of Rājarājadēva. *Ibid.*, Nos. 82 and 83, pp. 402--5.

1379. 30 *of* 1897.—(Tamil.) On a pillar of the west enclosure of the same temple. A record in the twenty-ninth year of the Chōḷa king Kō-Rājakēsarivarman *alias* Rājarājadēva I. Records the setting up of seven copper images of the God Gaṇapati by king Rājarājadēva viz, two in the dancing posture, one big and the other small; three of varying heights comfortably seated; and two in the standing posture. *Ibid.*, No. 84, pp. 405--7.

1380. 31 *of* 1897.—(Tamil.) On another pillar of the same enclosure. A record in the third year of the Chōḷa king Kō-Parakēsarivarman *alias* Rājēndra-Chōḷadēva I (1011—43). Records the gift of copper, zinc and bell metal vessels to the image of Gaṇapatiyār set up in the principal temple. The image was known as Ālaiyattu-Piḷḷaiyār. *Ibid.*, No. 85, pp. 407—9.

1381. 32 *of* 1897.—(Tamil.) On another pillar of the same enclosure. A record in the twenty-ninth year of the Chōḷa king Kō-Rājakēsarivarman *alias* Rājarājadēva (I). Records gift to the shrine of Gaṇapatiyār in the *parivārālaya* made by king Rājarāja and by Ādittan Sūryan, of ornaments to the same image. *Ibid.*, No. 86, pp. 409—11.

1382. 33 *of* 1897.—(Tamil.) On another pillar of the same enclosure. A record in the twenty-ninth year of the Chōḷa king Kō-Rājakēsarivarman *alias* Rājarājadēva I. Records gift of ornaments made to the Gaṇapatiyār shrine in the principal temple by a servant of king Rājarājadēva named Madhurāntakan Parāntakan, a native of Marudūr in Śeṟṟūr-kūṟṟam in Kshattriya-Śikhāmaṇi vaḷanāḍu. *S.I.I.*, Vol. II, No. 87, pp. 411-12.

1383. 34 *of* 1897.—(Tamil.) On another pillar of the same enclosure. A record in the twenty-ninth year of the Chōḷa king Kō-Rājakēsarivarman *alias* Rājarājadēva I. Records the gift of a bell-metal dish to the shrine of Gaṇapatiyār in the enclosure hall by a servant of Rājarājadēva. *Ibid.*, No. 88, p. 412. The donor was a native of Kāmadamaṅgalam in Purakkiḷiyūrnāḍu and evidently employed in the department for assessing tax on endowments (*tiṇaikaḷanāyakam*).

1384. 35 *of* 1897.—(Tamil.) On a niche of the same enclosure. A record in the twenty-ninth year of the Chōḷa king Kō-Rājakēsarivarman *alias* Rājarājadēva (I). Records gift of ornaments to the same image. *Ibid.*, No. 89, pp. 412-13.

1385. 36 *of* 1897.—(Tamil.) On the north wall of the maṇṭapa in front of the central shrine of the same temple. A record in the twenty-ninth year of the Chōḷa king Kō-Rājakēsarivarman *alias* Rājarājadēva (I). Records gift of *silver* vessels. This is the only inscription which records gift of *silver* and not gold vessels. See *Ibid.*, No. 91, pp. 415—24.

1386. 37 *of* 1897.—(Tamil.) On the south wall of the same maṇṭapa. A record in the twenty-ninth year of the Chōḷa king Kō-Rājakēsarivarman *alias* Rājarājadēva. Records the assignment to the Tanjore temple of certain villages in Toṇḍaināḍu Pāṇḍināḍu, Gaṅgapāḍi, Nuḷambapāḍi, Malaināḍu and Īḷam (Ceylon). *Ibid.*, No. 92, pp. 424—28.

1387. 38 *of* 1897.—(Tamil.) On the same wall. A record in the twenty-ninth year of the Chōḷa king Kō-Rājakēsarivarman *alias* Rājarājadēva (I). Records the jewels and ornaments presented by the king out of the treasures seized from the Chēras and Pāṇḍyas and out of his own treasures. *Ibid.*, No. 93, pp. 428—36.

1388. 39 *of* 1897.—(Tamil.) On the gōpura in front of the Toppuḷ-Piḷḷaiyār temple. A record of the Vijayanagara king Achyutadēva-Mahārāya in Ś. 1454, expired, Nandana. Records gift of land by Taṭṭapa-Nāyaka, son of Kōnappa-Nāyaka.

1389. 40 *of* 1897.—(Tamil.) On the west and south walls of the shrine of the Rājagōpala-Perumāḷ temple. A record of the Vijayanagara king Achyutadēva-Mahārāya in Ś. 1461, expired, Viḷambin. Records the foundation of the temple.

1390. 41 *of* 1897.—(Grantha.) On the north wall of the same shrine. An incomplete genealogy of the Vijayanagara kings.

1391. 274 *of* 1911.—(Tamil.) On a pillar of the kitchen in the Brihadīśvara temple. The beginning and end of this inscription are lost. Gives the measurements of certain images made of alloy (called *tara*) and set with jewels. These were evidently meant to be placed in the temple.

1392. 275 *of* 1911.—(Tamil.) On another pillar built into a wall of the same kitchen. A record of the Chōḷa king Uḍaiyār Śrī-Rājarājadēva (I). The face now exposed refers to one of the five-bodied images (*pañchadēhamūrti*) of copper, placed in the temple of Rājarājēśvaramuḍaiyār by the king, until his twenty-ninth year.

*Tillasthānam.**

This is the well-known Neyttānam of the *Periyapurāṇa* and the inscriptions, where Sarasvati is said to have worshipped the Lord. It figures in the *Dēvāram* of Gñānasambanda and Appar.

1393. 276 *of* 1911.—(Tamil.) On the west wall of the central shrine in the Ghritasthānēśvara temple. A damaged record. Records a gift of thirty *kaḻañju* of gold for a lamp, by a certain Śembiyan Īkkāṭṭu-vēḷān *alias* Pariśaikiḷān Maravan Nakkan.

1394. 277 *of* 1911.—(Tamil.) On the same wall. A damaged record in the second year of the Chōḷa king Parakēsarivarman. Records gift of twenty-five *kaḻañjus* of gold for a lamp to the temple at Tiruneyttānam by a certain Koṟṟan Arumoḷi *alias* Vānavan Pēraraiyan. The land purchased for this amount bordered on that of Naṅgai Varaguṇa-Perumānār, which was also purchased on account of a lamp.

1395. 278 *of* 1911.—(Tamil.) On the south wall of the same shrine. An unfinished record in the third year of the Chōḷa king Rājakēsarivarman. Apparently records gifts by Kūttan Nikaḷaṅkan, a member of *Samarakēsari-teriñja-Kaikkōḷar* and by another of *Vikramaśiṅga-teriñja-Kaikkōḷar,* to the temple of Mahādēva at Tiruneyttānam, a *dēvadāna* in Kīḻpilāṟu of Poygainādu. See No. 228 of 1911 at Kumbakōnam for a similar epithet to the Kaikkōḷars.

1396. 279 *of* 1911.—(Tamil.) On the same wall. An unfinished record in the third year of the Chōḷa king Rājakēsarivarman. Apparently records a gift to the same temple on behalf of Mallan Araiyan, one of *Samarakēsari-teriñja-Kaikkōḷar*.

1397. 280 *of* 1911.—(Tamil.) On the same wall. A record in the eleventh year of the Chōḷa king Rājakēsarivarman (I, 985—1013), "who destroyed the ships at Kāndalūr-Śālai." Built in at the right end. Seems to record a gift of gold for offerings in the same temple, ninety *kaḻañjus*.

---

* The *Mack. MSS.* (as summarized in *Ins., S. Dts.*, pp. 245—7, Nos. 102—10) give nine inscriptions. Of these three have been noted against the corresponding epigraphs in the departmental list. Others are given under Nos. 1439-A to 1439-F.

1398. 281 *of* 1911.—(Tamil.) On the same wall. A record in the eighteenth year of the Chōḷa king Madiraikoṇḍa-Parakēsarivarman (Parāntaka I). Built in at the right end and damaged. Records gift of gold for a lamp. Mentions Koṅgapperuvaḷi. [Shows Parāntaka's connexion with Koṅgu country. See 457 of 1911 at Kōlār.]

1399. 282 *of* 1911.—(Tamil.) On the same wall. A record in the seventeenth year of the Chōḷa king Rājakēsarivarman. Records gift of gold for a lamp to the temple of Mahādēva by Kuṇavan-Puttaḍi, a native of Kumārapāḍi in Paidāvūr-nāḍu, a subdivision of Kalattūr-kōṭṭam. [*Ins., S. Dts.*, p. 247, No. 110.]

1400. 283 *of* 1911.—(Tamil.) On the same wall. A record in the eleventh year of the Chōḷa king Rājakēsarivarman. Records gift of two gold forehead plates *(paṭṭam)* to the temple at Tirunettānam by Āyan Kāmakkōdanallūr, the superintendent of temple affairs.

1401. 284 *of* 1911.—(Tamil.) On the same wall. A record in the fourteenth year of the Chōḷa king Rājakēsarivarman. Records gift of thirty *kaḻañjus* of gold for a lamp, by Naṅgai Śāttaperumānār, a concubine of Śōḷa-Perumānaḍigal. The assembly of Tiruneyattānam used this amount for constructing a bathing hall (*namanamaṇṭapa*) to Tirunettānattu-Mahādēva, assigning, instead, some temple land for maintaining the charity.

1402. 285 *of* 1911.—(Tamil.) On the same wall. A record in the fourteenth year of the Chōḷa king Rājakēsarivarman. Records gift of ninety-six sheep for a lamp by a certain Vaḷavakōn Pēraraiyar to the temple of Tirunettānattu-Mahādēva (at Tirunettānam), a *dēvadānu* in Poygaināḍu.

1403. 286 *of* 1911.—(Tamil.) On the same wall. A record of the Chōḷa king Rājakēsarivarman, " who extended (his territory to) Toṇḍaināḍu (i.e., Āditya I as the Tiruvālaṅgāḍu plates show). Records gift of 100 sheep for a lamp to the temple of Tiruneyattānattu Mahādēva by Kaḍamba Mādēvi, wife of Vikki-Aṇṇan, the chief of Koḍumbāḷūr, on whom was bestowed the title Śembiyan Tamiḷavēḷ, together with other distinguishing marks of dignity, by the Chōḷa king and by the Chēra (Śēramān) Sthānu-Ravi. The marks of royal dignity included the fly-whisk, palanquin, drum, bugle, elephants, etc. The inscription is of value for the light it throws on the relations between the Chēras and Chōḷas. The Government Epigraphist surmises that Sthānu-Ravi was identical with Kōkkaṇḍan Ravi of the Chandrāditya family referred to in Veḷḷalūr inscriptions. It was this alliance which made Parāntaka I marry the daughter of the Kēraḷa king. The Sthānu-Ravi of the Koṭṭayam plates was later. See *Ep. Ind.*, Vol. IV, p. 293.

1404. 287 *of* 1911.—(Tamil.) On the same wall. A record in the thirteenth year of the Chōḷa king Rājakēsarivarman. Records gift of fifty *kaḻañju* of gold for two lamps to the same temple, by Tennavan Pirudimārāśan *alias* Kaṭṭi Oṟṟiyūran and by Varaguṇa Perumānār, queen of Parāntaka-Iḷaṅgōvеḷār. [The Government Epigraphist points out that the last-mentioned chief or Bhūti Vikramakēsarin was the contemporary of Āditya Karikāla II, on the ground that both claim to have conquered a Vīra Pāṇḍya.]

1405. 288 *of* 1911.—(Tamil.) On the same wall. A damaged record of the Chōḷa king Madiraikoṇḍa-Parakēsarivarman (905—47), the date of which is lost. Records gift of paddy for offerings by Kaṇṇanārāyaṇan, a native of Muṇḍaṅguḍi.

1406. 289 *of* 1911.—(Tamil.) On the same wall. A damaged record of the Chōḷa king Madiraikoṇḍa-Parakēsarivarman (905—947) in his thirty-second year. Records gift of gold for a lamp by Kākkan Naṅgāḷi of Tirunettānam. [See *Ins.*, *S. Dts.*, p. 245, No. 102.]

1407. 290 *of* 1911.—(Tamil.) On the same wall. A record in the fourteenth year of the Chōḷa king Madiraikoṇḍa Parakēsarivarman (Parāntaka I). Records gift of ninety sheep for a lamp by a native of Parāntakapuram in Koṅga-nāḍu. See No. 1398 above. [See *Ibid.*, p. 246, No. 104.]

1408. 291 *of* 1911.—(Tamil.) At the entrance into the gōpura of the same temple. A record in the second year of the Chōḷa king Tribhuvanachakravartin Rājādhirājadēva. Records sale of land to the temple of Tirunettānam-Uḍaiyār at Tirunettānam in Poygai-nāḍu (a subdivision) of Rājarāja-vaḷanāḍu, by two residents of the same village.

1409. 24 *of* 1895.—(Tamil.) On the south wall of the maṇṭapa in front of the central shrine in the Ghritasthānēśvara temple. An incomplete record in the third year of the Chōḷa king Kō-Rājakēsarivarman.

1410. 25 *of* 1895.—(Tamil.) On the same wall. A record in the forty-fourth year of the Chōḷa king Madiraikoṇḍa Kō-Parakēsarivarman (905—47). Records that a son of his deposited for a lamp 40 Ceylon *kaḻañjus* which were equal to 20 current *kaḻañjus*. Dr. Hultzsch infers that the Ceylon *kaḻañju* was equal to 10 *mañjāḍi* while the Chōḷa one to 20 *mañjāḍis*. This relation between the gold weights of the two regions is corroborated by 156 of 1895 at Tiruviḍaimarudūr (Tj. 367 above).

1411. 26 *of* 1895.—(Tamil.) On the same wall. A record in the eighth year of the Chōḷa king Kō-Parakēsarivarman. Records gift of gold for a lamp.

1412. 27 *of* 1895.—(Tamil.) On the same wall. A record in the sixth year of the Chōḷa king Kō-Parakēsarivarman. Records gift of gold for two lamps by a drummer of the temple.

1413. 28 *of* 1895.—(Tamil.) On the same wall. A record in the seventh year of the Chōḷa king Kō-Parakēsarivarman. Records gift of a lamp.

1414. 29 *of* 1895.—(Tamil.) On the same wall. A record of the Chōḷa king Parakēsarivarman, the date of which is doubtful. Records gift of gold for a lamp.

1415. 30 *of* 1895.—(Tamil.) On the same wall. An incomplete record in the tenth year of the Chōḷa king Kō-Parakēsarivarman *alias* Vikrama-Chōḷadēva (1118—35).

1416. 31 *of* 1895.—(Tamil.) On the base of the same wall. A record in the twenty-fifth year of the Chōḷa king Madiraikoṇḍa-Kō-Parakēsarivarman (Parāntaka I, A.D. 905—47).

1417. 32 *of* 1895.—(Tamil.) On the north wall of the same maṇṭapa. Private document in archaic characters.

1418. 33 *of* 1895.—(Tamil.) On the same wall. A record in the twenty-seventh year of the Chōḷa king Madiraikoṇḍa-Kō-Parakēsarivarman (905—47). Records gift of a lamp by a merchant.

1419. 34 *of* 1895.—(Tamil.) On the south wall of the shrine in the same temple. A record in the seventeenth year of the Chōḷa king Kō-Rājakēsarivarman. Records gift of gold for a lamp.

1420. 35 *of* 1895.—(Tamil.) On the same wall. A record in the eleventh year of the Chōḷa king Kō-Rājakēsarivarman. Records gift of gold for ornaments.

1421. 36 *of* 1895.—(Tamil.) On the same wall. A record in the fourteenth year of the Chōḷa king Kō-Rājakēsarivarman. Records gift of gold for a lamp by a dancing girl.

1422. 37 *of* 1895.—(Tamil.) On the same wall. A record in the fourteenth year of the Chōḷa king Kō-Rājakēsarivarman. Records gift of a lamp.

1423. 38 *of* 1895.—(Tamil.) On the same wall. A record in the eighth year of the Chōḷa king Kō-Rājakēsarivarman. Gift by Ādittan Kaṇṇaradēva, the king's son. Dr. Hultzsch points out that the king Ādittan referred to (as the father of Kaṇṇara) was the father of Parāntaka I. Kaṇṇara, he says, should be either Parāntaka or a brother of his. Some of the similar archaic inscriptions of Rājakēsarivarman in this place are ascribed by Dr. Hultzsch to Āditya I.

1424. 39 *of* 1895.—(Tamil.) On the same wall. A record in the fifteenth year of the Chōḷa king Kō-Rājakēsarivarman. Records gift of a lamp by an inhabitant of Tañjāvūr.

1425. 40 *of* 1895.—(Tamil.) On the same wall. A record in the tenth year of the Chōḷa king Kō-Parakēsarivarman. Records gift of a lamp.

1426. 41 *of* 1895.—(Tamil.) On the same wall. A record in the seventeenth year of the Chōḷa king Kō-Rājakēsarivarman. Records gift of a lamp by his queen.

1427. 42 *of* 1895.—(Tamil.) On the same wall. A record in the seventeenth year of the Chōḷa king Kō-Rājakēsarivarman. Records gift of gold for a lamp by another queen of his.

1428. 43 *of* 1895.—(Tamil.) On the same wall. A record in the thirty-fifth year of the Chōḷa king Madiraikoṇḍa-Parakēsarivarman (905—47). Records gift of gold for a lamp.

1429. 44 *of* 1895.—(Tamil.) On the base of the same wall. A record in the thirty-fourth year of the Chōḷa king Madiraikoṇḍa-Kō-Parakēsarivarman. Records gift of a lamp by his queen.

1430. 45 *of* 1895.—(Tamil.) In the same place. A record in the third year of the Chōḷa king Kō-Parakēsarivarman. Partly built in. Gift by Muḷḷūr-naṅgai, the king's mother-in-law. See 125 of 1895 as Tirupparaṇam (where she is mentioned).

1431. 46 *of* 1895.—(Tamil.) On the west wall of the same shrine. A record in the eighteenth year of the Chōḷa king Kō-Rājarāja-Rājakēsarivarman (I). Records sale of land.

1432. 47 *of* 1895.—(Tamil.) On the base of the same wall. A record in the sixth year of the Chōḷa king Kō-Parakēsarivarman. Records gift of gold for a lamp.

1433. 48 *of* 1895.—(Tamil.) On the north wall of the same shrine. A fragmentary record of the Chōḷa king Kō-Parakēsarivarman *alias* Rājēndradēva (1050—63).

1434. 49 *of* 1895.—(Tamil.) On the base of the same wall. A record in the eleventh year of the Chōḷa king Kō-Parakēsarivarman. Records gift of a lamp at a solar eclipse.

1435. 50 *of* 1895.—(Tamil.) At the entrance of the maṇṭapa in front of the same shrine. A fragmentary record of the Chōḷa king Kō-Rajakēsarivarman *alias* Rājādhirājadēva (I or II ?).

1436. 51 *of* 1895.—(Tamil.) On the gateway of the same shrine, right of entrance. A record in the fourth year of the Pāṇḍya king Kō-Mārañjaḍaiyan. Records gift of a lamp for the spiritual merit of Varaguṇa-Mahārāja, the Pāṇḍyan king who ascended the throne in A.D. 862. See *Ep. Ind.*, Vol. IX, p. 84.

1437. 52 *of* 1895.—(Tamil.) In the same place, left of entrance. A record in the tenth year of the Pallava king Tellāṟeṟinda Nandipōttaraiyar (Nandivarman III). Records gift of gold for a lamp.

1437-A. On a stone in the pagoda of "Nayadiapper ?." God in the village. Gift of ten *pons* in the reign of Maduraikoṇḍa Koppakēsari (905—47), in his fifteenth year. *Ins., S. Dts.*, p. 245, No. 103.

1437-B. In the same pagoda. Records a gift of some land by the same king in his twenty-second year. *Ins., S. Dts.*, p. 245, No. 105.

1437-C. A record of Kō-Parakēsarivarman in his twentieth year endowing ¼ *padi* of ghee. *Ibid.*, No. 106.

1437-D. A grant of Rājarājadēva in his second year of some land. *Ibid.*, No. 107.

1437-E. A grant of land by the same king in his twenty-fifth year. *Ibid.*, No. 108.

1437-F. A grant by "Cōpadēvur" in his fourth year of three *vēlis* of land. *Ibid.*, No. 109.

Tiruchchātturai.

[This is the Śōrrutturai or Tiruchchōrrutturai of the *Periapurāṇam* and the inscriptions, celebrated by the three Śamayāchāryas of Śaivitism. The department gives twelve epigraphs in this place, but the *Mack. MSS.* (*Ins., S. Dts.*, pp. 234—9) give 27. Of these two are evidently the same as 1442 and 1447. The rest I have given under Nos. 1449-A—1449-X.]

1438. 53 *of* 1895.—(Tamil.) On the south wall of the maṇṭapa in front of the shrine in the Ōdanavanēśvara temple. A record in the sixth year of the Chōḷa king Kō-Rājakēsarivarman. Records gift of fifty lamps by Rājarājadēva.

1439. 54 *of* 1895.—(Tamil.) On the same wall. A record in the ninth year of the Chōḷa king Kō-Rājarājakēsarivarman (I). Gift by a headman of Poygai nāḍu who figures frequently in the donations of Rājarāja (I) and Rājēndra Chōḷa (I).

1440. 55 *of* 1895.—(Tamil.) On the same wall. A record in the seventh year of the Chōḷa king Kō-Rājarājadēva (I) *alias* Kō-Rājakēsarivarman. Records gift of land.

1441. 56 *of* 1895.—(Tamil.) On the same wall. A record in the seventh year of the Chōḷa king Kō-Rājakēsarivarman. Records gift of gold for a lamp by a merchant.

1442. 57 *of* 1895.—(Tamil.) On the south wall of the same shrine. A record in the thirty-second year of the Chōḷa king Parakēsarivarman. Records gift of gold for a lamp by a native of the Pāṇḍya country. [This seems to be the same as *Ins., S. Dts.*, p. 235, No. 48.]

1443. 58 *of* 1895.—(Tamil.) On the base of the same wall. A record in the nineteenth year of the Chōḷa king Kō-Rājakēsarivarman. Records gift of two conches.

1444. 59 *of* 1895.—(Tamil.) In the same place. A record of the Chōḷa king Kō-Rājakēsarivarman, the date of which is doubtful. Records gift of a lamp.

1445. 60 *of* 1895.—(Tamil.) In the same place. A record in the tenth year of the Chōḷa king Kō-Parakēsarivarman. Records gift of gold for a lamp.

1446. 61 *of* 1895.—(Tamil.) On the west wall of the same shrine. Records gift of gold for a lamp. In archaic characters.

1447. 62 *of* 1895.—(Tamil.) On the north wall of the same shrine. A record in the third year of the Chōḷa king Kō-Parakēsarivarman. Records gift of a lamp. [This seems to be the same as *Ins., S. Dts.*, p. 235, No. 47.]

1448. 63 *of* 1895.—(Tamil.) On the same wall. A record in the eleventh year of the Chōḷa king Madiraikoṇḍa Kō-Parakēsarivarman (905—47). Records gift of gold for a lamp.

1449. 64 *of* 1895.—(Tamil.) On the north wall of the maṇṭapa in front of the same shrine. An incomplete record in the fifteenth year of the Chōḷa king Kō-Rājarāja-Rājakēsarivarman (I).

1449-A. On a stone in the temple of Tolayādaśelvar. A damaged grant of Kōnērinmaikoṇḍān. *Ibid.*, p. 234, No. 41.

1449-B. In the same place. A grant of land to the dancing girls of the temple by Kulōttuṅgachōḷa in his twentieth year. *Ibid.*, No. 42.

1449-C. In the same place. A grant of land to the God by Kulōttuṅgachōḷa in his fifth year. *Ibid.*, No. 43.

1449-D. In the same place. Records that Kāri Rājarāja Uḍayār erected a pagoda to the God Nāyanār during his reign. *Ibid.*, No. 44.

1449-E. On a stone in the pagoda of Tolayādaśelvar. A grant of 3 *vēlis*, 10½ *mās* and 31¼ *kuḷis* of land in the village of Munyalanellore to the God and Goddess in the thirty-second year of the reign of Kulōttuṅgachōḷadēva. *Ibid.*, No. 45.

1449-F. In the same place. A grant of 1 *vēli* of land to the God Ādi-Chaṇḍēśvara in the reign of Koppakēsari (Kō-Parakēsari). *Ibid.*, No. 46.

1449-G. In the same place. A grant of a portion of land to the Gōd in the thirtieth year of the reign of Tirukonda (?) Koppakēsari (Kō-Parakēsari). *Ibid.*, No. 49.

1449-H. In the same place. A grant of the village of Tirupoliyore (Tiruppuliyūr ?) as a free gift to the God Mahādēva in the eleventh year of Kō-Rājakēsari. *Ibid.*, No. 50.

1449-I. In the same place. A grant of 15 *kaḷañjus* of gold for the lamp of the God Mahādēva in the twelfth year of the reign of Kō-Rājakēsari. *Ibid.*, No. 51.

1449-J. In the same place. Grant of a lamp-stand to the God Nāyanār in the thirtieth year of the reign of Kō-Rājakēsari. *Ibid.*, No. 52.

1449-K. In the same place. Records gift of lamps by Kō-Parakēsari in his seventh year. *Ibid.*, No. 53.

1449-L. In the same place. Records gift of a lamp-stand by Nalamallūr-Dēvar in the eleventh year of Kō-Parakēsarivarman. *Ins., S. Dts.*, p. 234, No. 54.

1449-M. In the same place. Records gift of lamp by Kō-Parakēsarivarman in his thirteenth year. *Ibid.*, No. 55.

1449-N. In the same place. Records that Śrī "Cuntalava Bhuttur" gave some land to the God in the third year of Kō-Rājakēsarivarman. *Ibid.*, No. 56.

1449-O. In the same temple. A record of Kō-Parakēsarivarman in his seventh year. *Ibid.*, No. 57.

1449-P. In the same place. Grant of land by Rājarājadēva in his seventh year. *Ibid.*, No. 58.

1449-Q. In the same temple. Grant of land in the village of Śinga-Pārthivēndranellore by Kulōttuṅgachōḷadēva in his tenth year. *Ibid.*, No. 59.

1449-R. In the same temple. Records gift of ninety goats at ¼ measure of ghee for lamp by Kō-Parakēsarivarman in his third year. *Ibid.*, No. 60.

1449-S. In the same temple. A gift of land by Rājarājadēva in his fourth year. *Ibid.*, No. 61.

1449-T. In the same temple. A gift of Kulōttuṅgachōḷadēva in his thirty-second year. *Ibid.*, No. 62.

1449-U. In the same place. Gift of land north of Kulōttuṅgan canal by Maduraikoṇḍa Kō-Parakēsarivarman (905—97) in his twenty-second year. *Ibid.*, No. 63.

1449-V. In the same place. Records gift of 4 *mās* and 2½ *kāṇis* of land by Kō-Parakēsarivarman in his fourth year. *Ibid.*, No. 64.

1449-W. In the same place. Records grant of 2 *vēlis* of dry land to God Mahādēva in the fourth year of Rājarājakēsarivarman (I, 985—1013). *Ibid.*, No. 65.

1449-X. In the same place. Records allowance of 15 *kāśus* for the God by Kō-Rājakēsari in his third year. *Ibid.*, No. 66.

1449-Y. In the same place. Records grant of 2 *vēlis* and ½ *kāṇi* of land in the twentieth year of Rājarājadēva by himself. *Ibid.*, No. 67.

1449-Z. In the same place. Records grant of 13 *vēlis* and ½ *kāṇi* of land to the God in the twenty-first year of Rājarājadēva. *Ibid.*, No. 68.

Tirukkānūr.

One of the north Kāvēri centres of Śaiviṭism; it is famous as the place where Śiva appeared before Umā in the form of fire. It has been sung by Gñānasambanda and Appar.

1450. 161 *of* 1911.—(Tamil.) On the south wall of the central shrine in the Ikshupurīśvara temple. A seriously damaged record of the forty-first year of the Pāṇḍya king Māravarman *alias* Tribhuvanachakravartin Kulaśēkharadēva (1268—1308), "who was pleased to take all countries." Mentions the temple at Phaṇipati-maṅgala *alias* Karikālachōḷa-chaturvēdimaṅgalam in Poygaiyūr-nāḍu, a subdivision of Vaḍagarai-Rājarāja-vaḷanāḍu.

1451. 162 *of* 1911.—(Tamil.) On one of the door-posts at the entrance into the same shrine. Records that this door-post was the gift of a certain Periyan Appan *alias* Uttamaśōḷa-nāḍāḷvān who owned the *kāval* of this village.

1452. 163 *of* 1911.—(Tamil.) On the other door-post at the same entrance. An unfinished record in the fourth year of the Chōḷa king Rājādhirājadēva (I or II?). Mentions the temple of Karikālchōḷīśvaramuḍaiya-Mahādēva.

1453. 164 *of* 1911.—(Tamil.) On a stone built into the gōpura of the same temple. A fragmentary record in the sixth year of the Chōḷa king Rājakēsarivarman *alias* Uḍaiyār Śrī-Vīrarājēndradēva (1063--70). Mentions the assembly of Ālaiyūr, a *brahmadēya* in Poygai-nāḍu, which was a subdivision of Vaḍagarai-Rājēndraśiṅga-vaḷanāḍu and seems to refer to a temple of Vishṇu *(tiru-mēṟkōyil)* in the village.

1454. 165 *of* 1911.—(Tamil.) On another stone built into the same gōpura. A fragmentary record in the third year of the Chōḷa king Uḍaiyār Śrī-Adhirājēndradēva. Records a gift of land and a house by the same assembly to the Vishṇu temple of Maṇavāḷa-Āḷvār at Ālaiyūr. Mentions also the channel called Vīrarājēndra-dēvar-vāykkāl [named after Adhirājēndra's immediate predecessor Vīra Rājēndra (I), 1064—70. Adhirājēndra was the brother-in-law of the Western Chāḷukyan Vikramāditya VI and the victim of Kulōttuṅga Chōḷa I's ambition].

*Tirukkāṭṭuppaḷḷi.**

This place (which figured largely in the Karnatic wars) is described in *Tanj. Gazr.*, Vol. I, p. 275).

1455. 52 *of* 1897.—(Tamil.) On the west wall of the Saundara-nāyaki shrine in the Agnīśvara temple. A record in the seventh year of the Pāṇḍya king Kō-Māravarman Sundara-Pāṇḍyadēva

* The summary of the Mack. Inscriptions (*Ins., S. Dts.*, pp. 239-40, Nos. 70-1 and p. 254, Nos. 146--50) gives seven inscriptions in this place: (1) An epigraph of Sundara Pāṇḍya Dēva which records a grant of land to Agnēśvara; (2) one of Kulōttuṅga Chōḷa, recording grant of land by the people of Tirukkāṭṭuppaḷḷi in his eleventh year; (3) a grant of the fee of one *paṇam* on each marriage by Virūpāksha Rāya in S. 1387; (4) A grant of land at Chintāmaṇi-chaturvēdimaṅgalam by Śembiyan Pallavaraiyan and (5) a damaged grant in the fourteenth year of Vikrama Chōḷa; and (6-7) two others which have been identified above.

(I, 1216--35) who presented the Chōḷa country. Records the building of the shrine of the goddess. See *Ep. Ind.*, Vol. VI, p. 304, where Dr. Kielhorn points out that the equivalent of the date of this epigraph (Monday, day of Pushya, Rishabha, Mīna 9) is Monday, 13th March, A.D. 1223.

1456. 53 *of* 1897.—(Tamil.) On the same wall. A record in the thirteenth year of Tribhuvanachakravartin Kōnērimēnkoṇḍān. Records gift of land (*vēli*) to the goddess. See *Ins., S. Dts.*, p. 254, No. 148.

1457. 54 *of* 1897.—(Tamil.) On a pillar in the maṇṭapa in front of the same shrine. A record in the thirteenth year of the Chōḷa king Kō-Rājarājakēsarivarman (I, 985--1013). Records gift of land.

1458. 55 *of* 1897.—(Tamil.) In the second gōpura of the same temple, left of entrance. A record in Vikrama of the Vijayanagara king Tirumalaidēva-Mahādhirāja (1567--78). Records gift of land. [This inscription is given in *Ins., S. Dts.*, p. 254, No. 147. It says that the village Karayāḍi was granted by Sāḷuva Tirumala Dēva.]

Tiruppayanam.

The following inscriptions have been taken entirely from *Ins., S. Dts.*, pp. 229 to 234, Nos. 17 to 40 :—

1458-A. 123 *of* 1895.—(Tamil.) On the south wall of the shrine in the Āpatsahāyēśvara temple. A record in the seventeenth year of the Chōḷa king Kō-Rājakēsarivarman. Records gift of a lamp by his queen.

1458-B. 124 *of* 1895.—(Tamil.) On the same wall. A record in the twentieth year of the Chōḷa king Kō-Rājakēsarivarman. Records gift of a lamp.

1458-C. 125 *of* 1895.—(Tamil.) On the same wall. A record in the third year of the Chōḷa king Kō-Parakēsarivarman. Records gift of a lamp.

1458-D. 126 *of* 1895.—(Tamil.) On the west wall of the same shrine. A record in the sixth year of the Chōḷa king Kō-Parakēsarivarman. Records gift of a lamp.

1458-E. 127 *of* 1895.—(Tamil.) On the same wall. A record in the eleventh year of the Chōḷa king Madiraikoṇḍa Parakēsarivarman (905—47). Records gift of gold for a lamp.

1458-F. 128 *of* 1895.—(Tamil.) On the same wall. A record in the ninth year of the Chōḷa king Kō-Rājarāja-Rājakēsarivarman (905—47). Records gift of gold ornaments.

1458-G. 129 *of* 1895.—(Tamil.) On the same wall. A record in the thirty-first year of the Chōḷa king Madiraikoṇḍa Kō-Parakēsarivarman (905—47). Records gift of land by the nurse of the Chōḷa king Parāntaka (I).

1459-A. On a stone in the inner shrine of the local Āpatsahāya temple. Records that the people of the village gave in the fourth year of Vikramachōḷa, besides some grain for daily consumption, ¼ *paṇam* per each bag of paddy for the daily worship and lighting expense in the temple.

1459-B. In the same place. Records grant of ninety-five goats in the eighth year of Kō-Parakēsarivarmaṇ.

1459-C. In the same place. Records grant of 20 *kaḻañjus* of gold for a light in the reign of Maduraikoṇḍa Kō-Parakēsarivarman (905—47).

1459-D. In the same place. Records grant of 6 *vēlis* of land in the fourteenth year of Rājarājakēsari.

1459-E. In the same place. Records grant of ghee per day in the eighth year of Kō-Parakēsarivarman for a lamp.

1459-F. On the stone in the pagoda of Āpatsahāya temple. Records purchase and grant of some land to God Mahādēva in the eighth year of Kō-Parakēsarivarman.

1459-G. In the same place. Records that Chēdirāya appointed in the thirty-first year of Kōnērinmaikoṇḍān one Dakshiṇāmūrti as priest.

1459-H. On a stone in the same temple. Records that a Vēḷān gave in the twentieth year of Rājarājadēva some land to God Parvatēśvara in the village of Purakkuḍi.

1459-I. In the same place. Records that Kulōttuṅgachōḷadēva granted some land in the village of Mūlapāḍi in his seventeenth year to God Tripura-Liṅgēśvara.

1459-J. In the same place. Records that in the fourth year of the reign of Baladēva, the inhabitants of "Tanoutt" village allowed 11½ *pons* to God Ādi-Chaṇḍēśvara.

1459-K. In the same place. Records that Rājarājadēva granted in the third year of his reign to the God 32¾ *vēlis* and 4 *mās* of land.

1459-L. In the same place. Records that Kōnērinmaikoṇḍān gave 7 *vēlis* of land in the village of Vīramānkuḍi in his fourteenth year to the Goddess.

1459-M. In the same place. A grant of 1 *mā* of land to the temple by Rājarājadēva in the thirtieth year of his reign.

1459-N. In the same place. Records that in the thirty-second year of the reign of Tribhuvanavīra (Kulōttuṅga Chōḷa III) some land was sold at Sindinellore for 15,500 *kāśu* and given to the Goddess.

1459-O. In the same place. Records that Maḷavarāya give in the thirtieth year of Rājarājadēva 32 *vēlis* and ½ *mā* of land for the God and Goddess.

1459-P. In the same place. Records an allowance for ghee to the God by Rājakēsari in his fourth year.

1459-Q. In the same temple. A damaged grant of Tribhuvanarāja (Kulōttuṅga III ?) in his seventh year.

1459-R. In the same place. A grant of lamp in the seventh year of Kō-Parakēsarivarman.

1459-S. On a stone in the same temple. Records gift of 4 *mās*, 3 *kāṇis* and 1 *mundiri* of land to God Āpatsahāya by Rājarājadēva in the fourth year of his reign.

1459-T. In the same place. A grant of 2½ *mās* and 1 *mundiri* of land at Tirumalavāḍi for a flower garden in the third year of Kulōttuṅga-Chōḷa.

1459-U. In the same place. Records gift of 43 gold *kāśus* to God Mahādēva for a lamp by Maḷavarāya in the thirty-second year of Kō-Parakēsarivarman.

1459-V. In the same temple. Records gift of forty "*Vira kāśus*" to the God by Vīrappa in the seventeenth year of Kō-Rājakēsarivarman.

1459-W. In the same place. Records that Viruppuḍaiyān erected a stone maṇṭapa in the twentieth year of Kō-Rājakēsarivarman.

1459-X. On a stone in the same temple. Records grant of 3½ *vēlis* and ½ *kāni* of land to the God in the thirty-second year of Kulōttuṅgachōḷa by Vīra-Bhūpati Uḍaiyār.

Tiruppūndurutti.

The temple of this place is mentioned in the *Dēvāram* of Appar. It is the scene of a tradition which says that Appar and Gñānasambanda met.

1460. 166 *of* 1894.—(Tamil.) On the north wall of the Pushpavanēśvara temple. A record in the seventh year of the Pāṇḍya king Kō-Jaṭāvarman *alias* Sundara-Pāṇḍyadēva (I, 1251—64). Records gift of land. [The exact date of the inscription (Sunday, Hasta, Aparapaksha, Trayōdaśi, Kanyā), according to Kielhorn, is Sunday, 7th October 1257, but the month should be Tuḷā and not Kanyā.]

1460-A. On a stone in the temple. Records that Vijayarāya Mahārāja (i.e., Vīra Vijaya or Bukka III) granted some land to God Chaṇḍēśvara in Ś. 1346, Krōdhi. *Ins., S. Dts.*, p. 242, No. 86.

1460-B. In the same place. Records a grant of land to the same in Ś. 1336, Manmada, in the reign of Vīrabhūpati Uḍaiyār (Bukka III). *Ibid.*, No. 87.

1460-C. In the same temple. Records the gift of some *nañja* land to God Pushpavanēśvara in the tenth year of a Chōḷa king. *Ibid.*, p. 243, No. 88.

1460-D. In the same place. Records gift of land in the thirtieth year by Maduraikoṇḍa Chōḷadēva (Parāntaka I, 905—47 ?). *Ibid.*, No. 89.

1460-E. In the same place. Gift of land in the twentieth year of Dēvarāya Chōḷa. *Ins., S. Dts.*, p. 243.

1460-F. In the same place. Records in Ś. 1454, Nandana, in the reign of Achyutadēva Mahārāya, the exemption of the tax on pasturage of the village of Tiruppūnturutti as well as the weavers of Kaṇḍiyūr. *Ibid.*, No. 91.

1460-G. In the same temple. A damaged record of "Nauvenda Areyanayaner." *Ibid.*, No. 92.

1460-H. In the same temple. Records gift of 425 *kuḻis* of land to the God and Goddess in the seventh year of the reign of Sundarapāṇḍyadēva. *Ibid.*, p. 244, No. 93.

1460-I. In the same temple. Grant of ten *kāśus* to the God Mahādēva by Kāviriyār in the reign of Maduraikoṇḍa-Chōḷa. *Ibid.*, No. 94.

1460-J. In the same place. A grant of thirty *kaḻañjus* of gold to God Mahādēva for a lamp in the reign of "Cochadabeenkasari." *Ibid.*, No. 95.

1460-K. In the same place. Records that Śiṅgappa built a maṇṭapam in Ś. 1487, Krōdhi. *Ibid.*, No. 96.

1460-L. On a stone situated in the north bank of the Paḷaiyār. Records that in Ś. 1693, Khara, Tulasi Mahārāja (1763—87) granted 4,800 *kuḻis* of land in Paḷayār village to God Pushpavanēśvara at Tiruppūnturutti. *Ibid.*, No. 97.

*Tiruvēdikkuḍi.**

This is the Vēdikkuḍi of the *Periapurāṇam* and the theme of the *paḍi* kas of Gñānasambanda and Appar.

1461. 65 *of* 1895.—(Tamil.) On the north wall of the shrine in the Vēdapurīśvara temple. A record in the twenty-fifth year of the Chōḷa king Kō-Rājakēsarivarman. Records gift of gold.

1461-A. 66 *of* 1895.—(Tamil.) On the same wall. A record in the third year of the Chōḷa king Kō-Parakēsarivarman. Records gift of gold for a lamp.

1462. 67 *of* 1895.—(Tamil.) On the same wall. A record in the nineteenth year of the Chōḷa king Kō-Rājakēsarivarman. Records gift of gold for a lamp.

1463. 68 *of* 1895.—(Tamil.) On the base of the same wall. A record in the fifth year of the Chōḷa king Kō-Rājakēsarivarman. Records gift of thirty lamps by Rājarājadēva.

1464. 69 *of* 1895.—(Tamil.) On the base of the west wall of the same shrine. An incomplete record in the twenty-fifth year of the Chōḷa king Kō-Rājakēsarivarman.

---

* The List of *Mack. Ins.* as given in *Ins., S. Dts.* (p. 262, Nos. 182—9), gives eight epigraphs in this place. I give them under Nos. 1464-A—1464-H.

1464-A. A record of Rājarājakēsarivarman in his twenty-first year granting land to Mahādēva. *Ins., S. Dts.*, p. 262, No. 182.

1464-B. A grant of 2 *mās* and ½ *kāṇi* of land and 15 *kaḷañju* of gold by Kō-Parakēsarivarman in his eleventh year. *Ibid.*, No. 183.

1464-C. A record of the seventh year of Kulōttuṅga-Chōḷa relating grant of 4 *mās*, 12 *kāṇi* and 1 *mundiri* of land to the temple. *Ibid.*, No. 184.

1464-D. A similar gift of the same king in his eleventh year. *Ibid.*, No. 185.

1464-E. A grant of 13 *vēlis* for the Pushya festival by king Rājarājadēva in his thirteenth year. *Ibid.*, No. 186.

1464-F. A record of the second year of Kulaśēkharadēva relating grant of 13 *vēlis* of land for the worship of the God. *Ibid.*, No. 187.

1464-G. Records grant of two brass lamp-stands by Kō-Rājakēsarivarman "Tirumalladēva" in his eleventh year. *Ibid.*, No. 188.

1464-H. Records grant of 2 *vēlis* of land for the Vrishaba festival by Kulōttuṅgadēva in the thirty-second year of his reign. *Ibid.*, No. 189.

*Tiruvaiyāṟu.**

For an account of this most important stronghold of Śaiviṭism, see *Tanj. Gazr.*, Vol. I, pp. 276--9.

1465. 213 *of* 1894.—(Tamil.) On the east wall of the Dakshiṇakailāsa shrine in the Pañchanādēśvara temple. A record in the third year of the Chōḷa king Kō-Parakēsarivarman *alias* Rājēndradēva (1050—63).

1466. 214 *of* 1894.—(Grantha.) On the same wall. A record of the Chōḷa king Parakēsarivarman *alias* Rājēndra-Chōḷa (1011—1043).

1467. 215 *of* 1894.—(Tamil.) On the east wall of the maṇṭapa in front of the Uttarakailāsa shrine in the same temple, right of entrance. A record in the twenty-ninth year of the Chōḷa king Kō-Rājakēsarivarman *alias* Rājarājadēva (I).

1468. 216 *of* 1894.—(Tamil.) In the same place, left of entrance. A record in the fourth year of the Chōḷa king Kō-Parakēsarivarman *alias* Rājēndra-Chōḷadēva (I).

1469. 217 *of* 1894.—(Tamil.) On the south wall of the same shrine. A record in the twenty-second year of the Chōḷa king Kō-Rājarāja-Rājakēsarivarman *alias* Rājarājadēva (I). Records gift of a lamp.

---

* The List of *Mack. MSS.* (as given in *Ins., S. Dts.*) gives twenty inscriptions in this place. See page 267-ff., Nos. 190—209. I have not given the corresponding numbers.

1470. 218 *of* 1894.—(Tamil.) On the same wall. A record in the twenty-first year of the Chōḷa king Kō-Rājarājakēsarivarmaṇ *alias* Rājarājadēva (I). Records gift of two lamps.

1471. 219 *of* 1894.—(Tamil.) On the base of the same wall. A record in the twenty-first year of the Chōḷa king Kō-Rāja-kēsarivarman *alias* Rājarājadēva (I).

1472. 220 *of* 1894.—(Tamil.) On the west wall of the same shrine. A record in the third year of the Chōḷa king Kō-Para-kēsarivarman *alias* Rājēndra-Chōḷadēva (I).

1473. 221 *of* 1894.—(Tamil.) On the north wall of the same shrine. A record in the thirty-second year of the Chōḷa king Kō-Rājakēsarivarman *alias* Rājādhirājadēva I (1018—52).

1474. 222 *of* 1894.—(Tamil.) On the base of the north, west and south walls of the same shrine. A record in the twenty-fourth year of the Chōḷa king Kō-Rājarājakēsarivarman *alias* Rājarāja-dēva (I). Records gift of gold ornaments and vessels.

1475. 223 *of* 1894.—(Tamil.) On the base of the south wall of the Pañchanādēśvara shrine in the same temple. A record in the twenty-first year of the Chōḷa king Madiraikoṇḍa-Kō-Para-kēsarivarman (905—47). Records gift of a lamp.

1476. 224 *of* 1894.—(Tamil.) On the west wall of the same shrine. A record in the tenth year of the Chōḷa king Kō-Rāja-kēsarivarman. Records gift of land.

1477. 225 *of* 1894.—(Tamil.) On the base of the same wall. A record in the twenty-second year of the Chōḷa king Madirai-koṇḍa Kō-Parakēsarivarman (905—47). Records gift of a lamp by a queen.

1478. 226 *of* 1894.—(Tamil.) In the same place. A record of the Chōḷa king Madiraikoṇḍa Kō-Parakēsarivarman (905—47), the date of which is lost. Records gift of a lamp by queen Chōḷa-śikhāmaṇi.

1479. 227 *of* 1894.—(Tamil.) On the north wall of the same shrine. A record in the sixteenth year of the Chōḷa king Madiraikoṇḍa Kō-Parakēsarivarman (905—47). Records gift of a lamp.

1480. 228 *of* 1894.—(Tamil.) On the same wall. A record of the Chōḷa king Kō-Rājakēsarivarman, the date of which is lost. Records gift of land for a lamp.

1481. 229 *of* 1894.—(Tamil.) On the same wall. A record in the ninth year of the Chōḷa king . . . sarivarman. Records gift of gold for a lamp.

1482. 230 *of* 1894.—(Tamil.) On the same wall. A record in the ninth year of the Chōḷa king Kō-Rājakēsarivarman. Records gift of a lamp.

1483. 231 *of* 1894.—(Tamil.) On a stone built into the maṇṭapa surrounding the same shrine. An incomplete record in the fourth year of the Chōḷa king Kō-Parakēsarivarman. Records gift of land by a merchant of Tañjāvūr.

1484. 232 *of* 1894.—(Tamil.) On another stone in the same place. A fragmentary record in the fortieth year of the Chōḷa king Kō-Parakēsarivarman (905—47), "who took Madirai and Ceylon."

1485. 233 *of* 1894.—(Tamil.) On the same stone. An incomplete record in the thirty-ninth year of the Chōḷa king Kō-Parakēsarivarman (905—47), "who took Madirai and Ceylon." Records gift of a lamp.

1486. 234 *of* 1894.—(Tamil.) On the south wall of the maṇṭapa in front of the same shrine. A record in the third year of the Chōḷa king Kō-Parakēsarivarman. Records gift of land for three lamps.

1487. 235 *of* 1894.—(Tamil.) On the same wall. A record in the seventeenth year of the Chōḷa king Kō-Rājakēsarivarman. Records gift of land for two lamps. Partly built in.

1488. 236 *of* 1894.—(Tamil.) On the same wall. A record in the twenty-first year of the Chōḷa king Kō-Rājakēsarivarman. Records gift of land for a lamp. Partly built in.

1489. 237 *of* 1894.—(Tamil.) On the same wall. A record in the twenty-sixth year of the Chōḷa king Kō-Rājakēsarivarman. Records gift of a lamp by an inhabitant of Tañjāvūr.

1490. 238 *of* 1894.—(Tamil.) On the same wall. A record in the nineteenth year of the Chōḷa king Kō-Rājakēsarivarman. Records gift of a lamp by a queen. Partly built in.

1491. 239 *of* 1894.—(Tamil.) On the same wall. A record in the nineteenth year of the Chōḷa king Kō-Rājakēsarivarman. Records gift of a lamp by a queen. Partly built in.

1492. 240 *of* 1894.—(Tamil.) On the same wall. A record of the Chōḷa king Kō-Parakēsarivarman "who cut off the head of Vīra Pāṇḍya." Records gift of a lamp. Partly built in. The king was evidently Parāntaka II, Sundara Chōḷa, the son of Ariñjaya and father of Āditya II Karikāla.

1493. 241 *of* 1894.—(Tamil.) On the same wall. An incomplete record in the thirty-first year of the Chōḷa king Madiraikoṇḍa Kō-Parakēsarivarman (905—47).

1494. 242 *of* 1894.—(Tamil.) On the same wall. A record in the fourteenth year of the Chōḷa king Kō-Madiraikoṇḍa Parakēsarivarman (905—47). Records gift of gold for a lamp by a queen.

1495. 243 *of* 1894.—(Tamil.) On the same wall. A record in the twenty-fifth year of the Chōḷa king Kō-Rājakēsarivarman. Records gift of gold for a lamp.

1496. 244 *of* 1894.—(Tamil.) On the same wall. A record in the seventeenth year of the Chōḷa king Kō-Rājakēsarivarman. Records gift of gold for a lamp, by a dancing girl of the king.

1497. 245 *of* 1894.—(Tamil.) On the same wall. A record of the Chōḷa king Kō-Rājakēsarivarman, the date of which is doubtful. Records gift of land for a lamp.

1498. 246 *of* 1894.—(Tamil.) On the same wall. A record in the second year of the Chōḷa king Kō-Parakēsarivarman. Records gift of a lamp.

1499. 247 *of* 1894.—(Tamil.) On the same wall. A record in the twenty-fifth year of Chōḷa king-Kō-Rājakēsarivarman. Records gift of gold for a lamp by a merchant.

1500. 248 *of* 1894.—(Tamil.) On the same wall. A record in the thirty-first year of the Chōḷa king Madiraikoṇḍa Kō-Parakēsarivarman (905—47). Records gift of a silver lamp and of land by a queen.

1501. 249 *of* 1894.—(Tamil.) On the same wall. A record in the sixteenth year of the Chōḷa king Kō-Rājakēsarivarman. Records gift of land for a lamp.

1502. 250 *of* 1894.—(Tamil.) On the same wall. A record in the twelfth year of the Chōḷa king Kō-Rājakēsarivarman. Records gift of a lamp by a queen.

1503. 251 *of* 1894.—(Tamil.) On the same wall. A record in the twentieth year of the Chōḷa king Kō-Rājakēsarivarman. Records gift of land for a lamp by the nurse of Kaṇṇaradēva (Kṛishṇa III of the Rashtrakūṭa dynasty ?).

1504. 252 *of* 1894.—(Tamil.) On the same wall. A record of the Chōḷa king Kō-Parakēsarivarman, the date of which is indistinct. Records gift of a lamp.

1505. 253 *of* 1894.—(Tamil.) On the east wall of the second prākāra, left of entrance. A record of Vīra Sāvaṇa Uḍaiyār, son of "Vīra Mukkaṇa Uḍaiyār" (i.e., Bukkaṇa Uḍaiyār, i.e., Bukka II), dated Ś. 1303 (expired), Durmati. See *Ins., S. Dts.*, p. 267, No. 209. The latter says that 19 *vēlis* of land were granted for the Pushya festival.

1506. 254 *of* 1894.—(Tamil.) On the south wall of the third prākāra. A record of the second year of Kō-Jaṭāvarman Sundara Pāṇḍya I, making a gift of land. The exact date was Thursday, 27th March, A.D. 1253. See *Ep. Ind.*, Vol. VI, p. 306.

1507. 255 *of* 1894.—(Tamil.) On the west wall of the same prākāra. A record of Dēvarāya II (1422—49) of Vijayanagar, dated Ś. 1351 (expired), Saumya.

1508. 256 *of* 1894.—(Tamil.) On a stone north of the Uttara Kailāsa shrine. A record of Sadāśiva Rāya, dated in Ś. 1480 (expired), Siddhārtin. *Ins., S. Dts.*, p. 267, No. 208.

Tiṭṭe (Tittaya).

1508-A. On a stone in the Vasishṭēśvara pagoda. (Tamil.) Records grant of one *vēli* of land for the celebration of the Uttarabhadra festival in the local temple by Kulottuṅga-chōḷa in his eleventh year. *Ins., S. Dts.*, p. 256, No. 151.

1508-B. In the same place. Records grant of 10½ *mās* of land by the same king in his thirteenth year. *Ibid.*, No. 158.

1508-C. In the same place. Gift of two *vēlis* of land for the Vrishaba festival by the same king in his eighteenth year. *Ibid.*, No. 159.

TIRUTTURAIPPŪNDI TALUK.

Agattiyanpaḷḷi.

1509. 504 *of* 1904.—(Tamil.) On the south wall of the central shrine in the Agastyēśvara temple. A damaged record in the fifteenth year of the Pāṇḍya king Māravarman Tribhuvanachakravartin Vīra-Pāṇḍyadēva. Seems to record a gift of land. [Was he the king who ruled from 1253 to 1278 ?]

1510. 505 *of* 1904.—(Tamil.) On the south base of the same shrine. A record in the second year of the Chōḷa king Tribhuvanachakravartin Rājarājadēva (III). Records gift of 1,500 *kāśus* for a lamp. The date corresponds to Monday, 29th January, A.D. 1218. See *Ep. Ind.*, Vol. VIII, p. 267.

1511. 506 *of* 1904.—(Tamil.) On the north wall of the same shrine. A record in the thirty-first year of the Pāṇḍya king Māravarman Tribhuvanachakravartin Kulaśēkharadēva (1268—1308). Records gift of land in order to celebrate a festival in the temple for the recovery of the king from some illness.

1512. 507 *of* 1904.—(Tamil.) On the north base of the same shrine. A record in the fifth year of the Pāṇḍya king Māravarman Tribhuvanachakravartin Kulaśēkharadēva (1268—1308). Records gift of money.

Kōḍikkarai.

1513. 1 *of* 1909.—(Nāgari and Marāthi.) On a slab near the Siddharāśramam on the seashore. A record of the Tanjore (Marātha) king Tuḷajā Mahārāja (1763--87), son of Pratāpasiṁha Mahārāja. Refers to Nānā-Gōsāvi, son of Sētubāvasvāmi, styled Advaitāgrēsara, who was probably the spiritual guru of the king. See *Tanj. Gazr.*, Vol. I, p. 49.

Kōḍiyakkāḍu.

1514. 508 *of* 1904.—(Tamil.) On the west wall of the Amritaghaṭēśvara temple. A record in the fourteenth year of the Chōḷa king Tribhuvanachakravartin Rājarājadēva. Built in at the end. Seems to record the gift of a lamp.

1515. 509 *of* 1904.—(Tamil.) On the north wall of the same temple. A mutilated record of the Pāṇḍya king . . . Tribhuvanachakravartin Sundara-Pāṇḍya, the date of which is lost.

1516. 510 *of* 1904.—(Tamil.) On the same wall. A mutilated record in the eighteenth year of the Pāṇḍya king Jaṭāvarman Tribhuvanachakravartin Kōnērinmaikoṇḍān. Mentions the temples of Tirukkōḍikkuḷagar and Tiruvagattiyānpaḷḷi.

1517. 511 *of* 1904.—(Tamil.) On the same wall. An incomplete record in the fifth year of the Pāṇḍya king Jaṭāvarman *alias* Tribhuvanachakravartin Parākrama-Pāṇḍya. Records gift of money for a lamp. The king was probably the same as he who ascended the throne in 1334.

1518. 512 *of* 1904.—(Tamil.) On the same wall. An incomplete record in the thirty-ninth year of the Pāṇḍya king Jaṭāvarman Tribhuvanachakravartin Kulaśēkharadēva (I, 1190—1217, or II, 1239—51 ?).

1519. 513 *of* 1904.—(Tamil.) On the same wall. A mutilated record in the thirty-second year of the Chōḷa king Tribhuvanachakravartin Rājēndra-Chōḷadēva (I ?). Seems to record a gift of land.

1520. 514 *of* 1904.—(Tamil.) On the same wall. A mutilated record in the thirty-second year of the Chōḷa king Tribhuvanachakravartin Rājēndra-Chōḷadēva (I ?). Records gift of land.

1521. A single plate in the possession of the temple priest. It is "a modern record which mentions 'Rājarājēndra Śōsharājargaḷ.' The first three lines of the inscription which contains the date are written in comparatively small characters and might be a subsequent addition. The date given is Ś. 1208, corresponding to Kali. 4374 and the cyclic year *Jaya*. Ś. 1208 actually corresponded to Kali. 4387 and to the cyclic year *Pārthiva* which would be nine years earlier than *Jaya*. The alphabet employed in the inscription is quite modern and may belong roughly to the seventeenth century. It is hardly necessary to add that "Rājēndra-Śōsharājargaḷ" is not the name of any particular Chōḷa king but is perhaps a faint reminiscence of Kulōttuṅga I, one of whose *birudas* was Rājarājēndra." (*Mad. Ep. Rep.*, 1905, p. 54, paragraph 21.)

Tiruttenġūr.

1522. 528 *of* 1904.—(Tamil.) On the south wall of the central shrine in the Rajatagirīśvara temple. A record in the thirty-first year of the Pāṇḍya king Māravarman *alias* Tribhuvanachakravartin Kulaśēkharadēva (I, 1268—1308). Records that provision was made for the celebration of a festival called Māḷavan-śandi after a certain Māḷavachchakravartin, son of Naraśiṅgadēvar.

1523. 529 *of* 1904.—(Tamil.) On the same wall. A record in the twentieth year of the Chōḷa king Tribhuvanachakravartin

Rājarājadēva. Refers to the thirtieth year of Tribhuvanavīradēva (1178—1216) and records a gift of 4,000 *kāśus* for a lamp.

1524. 530 *of* 1904.—(Tamil.) On the same wall. A record in the thirty-eighth year of the Chōḷa king Tribhuvanachakravartin Tribhuvanavīradēva (Kulōttuṅga III, 1178—1216) who took Madura, Karuvūr, Īḻam (Ceylon) and the crowned head of the Pāṇḍya and performed the anointment of victors and the anointment of heroes. The God is called Tiruveḷḷiyaṅgunṟamuḍaiyār.

1525. 531 *of* 1904.—(Tamil.) On the north wall of the same shrine. A record in the twelfth year of the Chōḷa king Tribhuvanachakravartin Rājēndra-Chōḷadēva III, corresponding to Monday, July 19, A.D. 1257. Records a remission of the tax on oil. See *Ep. Ind.*, Vol. VIII, p. 273.

1526. 532 *of* 1904.—(Tamil.) On the same wall. A partly damaged record in the twenty-fifth year of the Chōḷa king Tribhuvanachakravartin Rājarājadēva (III?). Records gift of land to those who had to supply oil to the temple lamps.

Tirutturaippūṇḍi.

•**1527.** 466 *of* 1912.—(Tamil.) On the north wall of the maṇṭapa in front of the central shrine of the Marundīśvara temple. A record of the Chōḷa king Tribhuvanachakravartin Rājarājadēva (III) in his eleventh year, Rishabha, ba. di. 14, Saturday, Kārttigai, corresponding to 15th May, 1227. Registers grant of land and a tank called Murukkaṅguḷam by the residents of the *dēvadāna* village of Śattamaṅgalam and those living in the Paḷḷichchandam (i.e., property of Jain temple) portion of the same village. The land was to be utilized as a flower garden for the God at Tirutturaippūṇḍi in Vaṇḍāḷai-vēḷūr-kūṟṟam, a subdivision of Rājēndraśōḷa-vaḷanāḍu. Mentions also the temple of Kulōttuṅgaśōḷīśvaram-Uḍaiyār at Śattamaṅgalam.

1528. 467 *of* 1912.—(Tamil.) On the same wall. A record of the Chōḷa king Tribhuvanachakravartin Rājarājadēva (III) in his twelfth year Tulā, śu. di. 7, Monday, Uttirāḍam (= Monday, 18th October 1227). Registers that a tank for the temple of Tirutturaippūṇḍi-Uḍaiyār was dug at Śōḷanmarutinallūr which was a hamlet of Śuttavallichaturvēdimaṅgalam, a *brahmadēya* in Puraṅgarambai-nāḍu, which was a subdivision of Rājēndraśōḷa-vaḷanāḍu, by a merchant of Kulōttuṅgaśōḷa-pattaṇa. The same merchant also granted land for a maṇṭapa. Mentions the members of the village assembly who were doing executive work in the village, for that year.

1529. 468 *of* 1912.—(Tamil.) On the same wall. A record in the twenty-eighth year of the Chōḷa king Tribhuvanachakravartin Rājarājadēva (III). Records gift of money for two lamps.

1530. 469 *of* 1912.—(Tamil.) On the same wall. Records in the twentieth year and one hundred and seventy-eighth day (of ?) gift of money for a lamp by the accountant of Kulōttuṅgaśōḷa-chaturvēdimaṅgalam, a village in Puraṅgarambai-nāḍu.

1531. 470 *of* 1912.—(Tamil.) On the same wall. A record in the twenty-sixth year of the Chōḷa king Tribhuvanachakravartin Rājarājadēva (III). Records gift of money for a lamp by a lady of Iraiyamaṅgalam for the merit of her sons.

1532. 471 *of* 1912.—(Tamil.) On the same wall. A partly damaged record in the second year of the Chōḷa king Tribhuvana-chakravartin Rājarājadēva (III). Registers that a *guhai* was constructed for a Śaiva teacher called Tiruchchiṟṟambalamuḍaiya-Mudaliyār, who came to Tirutturaippūṇḍi and who was requested by people to stay there and that land was granted for feeding strangers that might visit the *guhai*. The teacher is stated to have died in the twenty-fourth year of Periyadēvar (Kulōttuṅga III, 1186—1216), two years later, when there was "a crusade against monasteries of this type" (குகையிடிகலகம்) and when the monastic property was confiscated. One Hridayadēva is then said to have succeeded. The Epigraphist surmises that the crusade might have been due to Brahmanical instigation.

1533. 472 *of* 1912.—(Tamil.) On the same wall. A record in the seventeenth year of the Chōḷa king Tribhuvanachakravartin Rājarājadēva (III). Records gift of land for offerings to the temple of Tirutturai-Nāyanār by the members of the assembly who were doing "the year's work *(samvatsaragrāmakārya)* of that village."

1534. 473 *of* 1912.—(Tamil.) On the same wall. A record of the Chōḷa king Tribhuvanachakravartin Rājarājadēva (III), in his seventeenth year, Rishabha, ba. di. 5, Saturday, Uttirāḍam and three hundred and sixteenth day. Records gift of land for offerings by the *mahājanās* of Koṟṟamaṅgalam, a hamlet of Śuttavalli-chaturvēdimaṅgalam in Puraṅgarambai-nāḍu, which was a sub-division of Rājēndraśōḷa-vaḷanāḍu. The date (which contains the error Rishabha for Tulā) corresponds, according to Mr. Swami-kannu Pillai, to 30th September 1233 and the three hundred and sixteenth day "implies that the reign began on 17th June."

1535. 474 *of* 1912.—(Tamil.) On the north base of the same maṇṭapa. A record in the tenth year of the Chōḷa king Tri-bhuvanachakravartin Rājēndra-Chōḷadēva (III). Records gift of land by a native of Vīranārāyaṇa-chaturvēdimaṅgalam, a *taniyūr* in Vaḍagarai-Virudarāja-bhayaṅkara-vaḷanāḍu, to an image of Śiva which he had set up in the north verandah of the first prākāra of the temple.

1536. 475 *of* 1912.—(Tamil.) On the south wall of the same maṇṭapa. A record of the Chōḷa king Tribhuvanachakravartin Rājarājadēva (III) in his seventh year, Karkaṭaka, su. di. 3, Monday,

Ayilyam, corresponding to 13th June 1222. Records sale of land at Śōlanmārutinallūr, a hamlet of Śuttamalli-chaturvēdimaṅgalam, by the members of the *samvatsaragrāmakārya* of that village, for digging a sacred tank for the temple of Tirutturaippūṇḍi-Uḍaiyār. [The lands connected with the tank were declared tax-free *(irai-ili)*. The document is signed by fifty persons who evidently formed the village assembly. The privileges of the *iraili* lands are defined.]

1537. 476 *of* 1912.—(Tamil.) On the same wall. A record in the eighteenth year and one hundred and fifty-seventh day of the Chōḷa king Tribhuvanachakravartin Kōnērinmaikoṇḍān (Rājarāja III). Registers that certain *dēvadāna* lands were made tax free in the village of Śāttamaṅgalam in Vaṇḍāḷaivēḷūr-kūṟṟam. The royal secretary *(tirumandira-ōlai)* was Rājēndraśiṅga-Muvēnda-vēḷān.

1538. 477 *of* 1912.—(Tamil.) On the same wall. A record in the eleventh year of the Chōḷa king Tribhuvanachakravartin Rāja-rājadēva (III). Records gift of land by purchase at Pūśālaṅguḍi in Ārvala-kūṟṟam, a subdivision of Rājēndraśōḷa-vaḷanāḍu, for building a brick *maṭha* at Śelva-Tiruvārūr, by a Śaiva devotee of Tirutturaippūṇḍi called Pālarāvayan. The *maṭha* was presided over by Nētradēva. [Was Pālarāvāya, the brother of Śekkiḷār ?]

1539. 478 *of* 1912.—(Tamil.) On the same wall. A record in the eighteenth year of the Chōḷa king Tribhuvanachakravartin Rājarājadēva (III). Records gift of land at Uttamaśōḷapuram to the temple of Tirutturaippūṇḍi-uḍaiya-Nāyanār, by a certain Vaṇtoṇḍa-Mudaliyār.

1540. 479 *of* 1912.—(Tamil.) On the west wall of the same maṇṭapa. A record in the nineteenth year of the Chōḷa king Tribhuvanachakravartin Rājarājadēva (III). Records gift of land at Āriyanāṟṟūr in Puraṅgarambai-nāḍu, a subdivision of Rājēndra-śōḷavaḷanāḍu.

1541. 480 *of* 1912.—(Tamil.) On the same wall. A record of the Chōḷa king Tribhuvanachakravartin Rājarājadēva (III) in his thirtieth year, Kanni, śu. di. 5, Sunday, Uttiraṭṭādi. Records gift of money for providing one rice offering three (every day) in the same temple.

1542. 481 *of* 1912.—(Tamil.) On the north wall of the Gaṇēśa shrine in the same temple. An unfinished record in the thirtieth year of the Chōḷa king Tribhuvanachakravartin Rājarājadēva (III). Records gift of money for lamps and rice offerings.

1543. 482 *of* 1912.—(Tamil.) On the same wall. A record of the Chōḷa king Tribhuvanachakravartin Rājarājadēva (III) in his second year, Dhanus (should be Makara), ba. di. 11, Monday, Anilam. Records gift of money for a lamp. The date corresponded to 22nd January 1218.

1544. 483 *of* 1912.—(Tamil.) On the same wall. A record in the third year of the Chōḷa king Tribhuvanachakravartin Rājēndra-Chōḷadēva (III). Records gift of money for maintaining the festival Āḍippūram in the shrine of the goddess.

1545. 484 *of* 1912.—(Tamil.) On the south wall of the Mahāgaṇapati shrine in the same temple. A damaged record of the Chōḷa king Tribhuvanachakravartin Rājēndra-Chōḷadēva (III) in his third year. Records gift of land for maintaining coconut garden laid out in the third prākāra of the temple.

1546. 485 *of* 1912.—(Tamil.) On the north and west bases of the Navagraha shrine in the same temple. A record of the Chōḷa king Tribhuvanachakravartin Kulōttuṅga-Chōḷadēva III, "who took Madurai (Madura) and was pleased to take the crowned head of the Pāṇḍya" in his eighteenth year, Vrischika, śu. di. 15, Saturday, Rōhiṇi, corresponding to the 18th November 1195. Records gift of land by the residents of Śattamaṅgalam.

1547. 486 *of* 1912.—(Tamil.) On the main gōpura of the same temple, right of entrance. A record in the twenty-third year of the Pāṇḍya king Jaṭāvarman Tribhuvanachakravartin Śrīvallabhadēva. Registers that certain fees which were being collected from the temple were granted to the same temple for maintaining a special service called *Vāḷvāśikāṭṭiṉān-śandi.* [Was Śrīvallabha the contemporary of Māravarman Sundara Pāṇḍya I, 1216—35 ?]

1548. 487 *of* 1912.—(Tamil.) On the same gōpura. A record of the Vijayanagara king Vīrapratāpa Dēvarāya-Mahārāya in Ś. 1392, Vikriti, Simha, śu. di. 13, Saubhāgyayōga, Thursday, Magha. Records that Paḷḷigoṇḍa-Perumāḷ Pratāpadēvarāya Maḷavarāyar remitted all taxes on the lands owned by the temple. The several items of taxation are specified.

1549. 488 *of* 1912.—(Tamil.) On the bronze pot *pañchamukha-vādya* preserved in the same temple. Records the gift of this pot-drum *(kuḍa-viḷā)* by the chief artisan *(taṭṭār)* Mallāṇḍār *alias* Śōḷakōnār.

Vēdāraṇyam.

In literary history Vēdāraṇyam is known as the native place of Parañjōti Munivar, the son of Mīnākshi Sundara Dēśika, and the author of the monumental *Tiruviḷayāḍal-purāṇa.* For his life-career see *Abhidhāna chintāmani*, p. 637. His date has been one of controversy, but he evidently belonged to the thirteenth century.

1550. 415 *of* 1904.—(Tamil.) On the south wall of the central shrine in the Vēdāraṇyēśvara temple. A record in the fourth year of the Chōḷa king Tribhuvanachakravartin Kulōttuṅga-Chōḷadēva, corresponding to Thursday, 11th March 1182. Records gift of gold for a lamp by a certain Gaṅgaikoṇḍān Rājarājadēva *alias*

Pottappichchōḷar to the temple at Tirumaṛaikkāḍu in Kunṛūr-nāḍu, a subdivision of Umbala-nāḍu. See *Ep. Ind.*, Vol. VIII, p. 264.

1551. 416 *of* 1904.—(Tamil.) On the same wall. A record in the twenty-ninth year of the Chōḷa king Tribhuvanachakravartin Kulōttuṅga Chōḷadēva III, "who took Madura, Īḷam (Ceylon) and the crowned head of the Pāṇḍya". Records gift of money for a lamp.

1552. 417 *of* 1904.—(Tamil.) On the same wall. A damaged record in the fifteenth year of the Chōḷa king Tribhuvanachakravartin Kulōttuṅga-Chōḷadēva III, "who took Madura and the crowned head of the Pāṇḍya". Records the gift of a lamp.

1553. 418 *of* 1904.—(Tamil.) On the south wall of the maṇṭapa in front of the same shrine. A damaged record in the ninth year of the Chōḷa king Tribhuvanachakravartin Rājēndra-Chōḷadēva III. Records gift of land for a lamp. Dr. Kielhorn calculates the date to be Tuesday, the 12th January, 1255. See *Ibid.*, Vol. VIII, p. 273.

1554. 419 *of* 1904.—(Tamil.) On the same wall. A record in the fourth year of a Chōḷadēva. Records gift of money for a lamp by a certain Vīraśingapanmar.

1555. 420 *of* 1904.—(Tamil.) On the same wall. A record in the fifth year of the Chōḷa king Tribhuvanachakravartin Rājarājadēva. Built in at the beginning. Records gift of money for lamps. At the bottom is an inscription of Kulōttuṅga III, which is also partly built in.

1556. 421 *of* 1904.—(Tamil.) On the same wall. A record in the sixth year of the Chōḷa king Tribhuvanachakravartin Rājēndra-Chōḷa-dēva. Records an order of Vāṇadarāyan.

1557. 422 *of* 1904.—(Tamil.) On the north wall of the same maṇṭapa. A record in the second year of the Chōḷa king Rājakēsarivarman *alias* Tribhuvanachakravartin Kulōttuṅga-Chōḷadēva (I ?). Records that the king granted to a certain individual the privilege of singing the *Tiruppadiyam* hymns in the temple and the emoluments connected therewith.

1558. 423 *of* 1904.—(Tamil.) On the same wall. A record in the fourth year of the Chōḷa king Tribhuvanachakravartin Rājēndra-Chōḷadēva (III), corresponding to Wednesday, 5th January 1250. Records gift of land for a lamp. The Śaiva Brāhmaṇas of the *Muppaduvaṭṭam* of the temple took charge of the land. See *Ibid.*, p. 272.

1559. 424 *of* 1904.—(Tamil.) On the same wall. A mutilated record in the seventeenth year of the Chōḷa king Tribhuvanachakravartin Rājarājadēva. Records gift of jewels to the temple.

1560. 425 *of* 1904.—(Tamil.) On the same wall. A damaged record in the twenty-third year of the Chōḷa king Rājakēsarivarman *alias* Tribhuvanachakravartin Kulōttuṅga-Chōḷadēva (I or II ?).

1561. 426 *of* 1904.—(Tamil.) On the same wall. A record in the twentieth year of the Chōḷa king Tribhuvanachakravartin

Kulōttuṅga-Chōḷadēva III, "who took Madura, Īḷam (Ceylon) and the crowned head of the Pāṇḍya." Built in at the end. Records gift of fifty sheep for a lamp.

1562. 427 *of* 1904.—(Tamil.) On the same wall. An incomplete record in the thirty-second year of the Chōḷa king Tribhuvanachakravartin Tribhuvanavīradēva (1178—1216), "who took Madurai, Karuvūr and the crowned head of the Pāṇḍya and performed the anointment of heroes and the anointment of victors," i.e., Kulōttuṅga III. The date corresponds to Monday, the 21st December, A.D. 1209. *Ep. Ind.*, Vol. VIII, p. 266.

1563. 428 *of* 1904.—(Tamil.) On the north wall of the maṇṭapa in front of the central shrine in the same temple. A record in the thirty-fifth year of the Chōḷa king Tribhuvanavīradēva (Kulōttuṅga III). Records gift of money for a lamp.

1564. 429 *of* 1904.—(Tamil.) On the same wall. A record in the twenty-seventh year of the Chōḷa king Tribhuvanachakravartin Rājarājadēva (III ?). Records gift of land for a lamp.

1565. 430 *of* 1904.—(Tamil.) On the same wall. A record in the twentieth year of the Chōḷa king Tribhuvanachakravartin Kulōttuṅga-Chōḷadēva (III), "who took Madurai, Īḷam (Ceylon) and the crowned head of the Pāṇḍya." Records gift of money for a lamp. At the bottom is an incomplete and damaged inscription of the twentieth year of the same king. The date corresponds to Sunday, the 3rd May, A.D. 1198. See *Ibid.*, p. 265.

1566. 431 *of* 1904.—(Tamil.) On the same wall. A record in the twenty-seventh year of the Chōḷa king Tribhuvanachakravartin Rājarājadēva. Records gift of land.

1567. 432 *of* 1904.—(Tamil.) On the same wall. A damaged record in the twenty-second year of the Chōḷa king Tribhuvanachakravartin Rājarājadēva. Records gift of land.

1568. 433 *of* 1904.—(Tamil.) On a pillar within the same maṇṭapa. An incomplete record in the thirty-third year of the Chōḷa king Madiraikoṇḍa Parakēsarivarman (905—47).

1569. 434 *of* 1904.—(Tamil.) On the same pillar. A record in the thirty-fifth year of the Chōḷa king Madiraikoṇḍa Parakēsarivarman (905—47). Records gift of ninety sheep for a lamp.

1570. 435 *of* 1904.—(Tamil.) On another pillar in the same place. A record in the thirtieth year of the Chōḷa king Madiraikoṇḍa Parakēsarivarman (905—47). Records the gift of six *iḻakkāśu** for a lamp.

* The currency of Ceylon coins in the mainland need occasion no surprise when we remember the position of Vēdāraṇya and the commercial intercourse between the mainland and the island. A very late poet Gaṇapati Kurukkaḷ who had a number of disciples in the surrounding district; took advantage of this to sing the whole *Skāndapurāṇa* in songs which could be sung by the sailors.

1571. 436 *of* 1904.—(Tamil.) On the same pillar. A record in the ninth year of the Chōḷa king Parakēsarivarman. Records gift of ninety sheep for a lamp.

1572. 437 *of* 1904.—(Tamil.) On the same pillar. A record in the fifteenth year of the Chōḷa king Rājarāja-Rājakēsarivarman (I, 985—1013). Records gift of ninety sheep for a lamp.

1573. 438 *of* 1904.—(Tamil.) On the same pillar. A damaged record in the eighth year of the Chōḷa king Parakēsarivarman.

1574. 439 *of* 1904.—(Tamil.) On the same pillar. A record in the twenty-second year of the Chōḷa king Rājakēsarivarman *alias* Rājarājadēva I. Records gift of land.

1575. 440 *of* 1904.—(Tamil.) On the same pillar. A record in the sixth year of the Chōḷa king Rājarājakēsarivarman (985—1013). Records gift of ninety sheep for a lamp.

1576. 441 *of* 1904.—(Tamil.) On the same pillar. A record in the ninth year of the Chōḷa king Rājarājakēsarivarman (985—1013). Records gift of money. Mentions Muttūṟṟu-kūṟṟam in Pāṇḍi-nāḍu.

1577. 442 *of* 1904.—(Tamil.) On the same pillar. A damaged record in the sixth year of the Chōḷa king Rājakēsarivarman.

1578. 443 *of* 1904.—(Tamil.) On the same pillar. A damaged record of the Chōḷa king Parakēsarivarman, the date of which is lost.

1579. 444 *of* 1904.—(Tamil.) On a third pillar in the same place. A record in the twentieth year of the Chōḷa king Madiraikoṇḍa Parakēsarivarman (905—47). Records gift of gold.

1580. 445 *of* 1904.—(Tamil.) On the same pillar. A record in the twenty-eighth year of the Chōḷa king Madiraikoṇḍa Parakēsarivarman (905—47). Records gift of ninety sheep for a lamp by Arunidi-Kaliyan of Marudūr, an officer of Śrī-Parakēsarivarman.

1581. 446 *of* 1904.—(Tamil.) On the same pillar. A record of the Chōḷa king Madiraikoṇḍa-Parakēsarivarman (905—47), the date of which is lost. Records gift of ninety sheep.

1582. 447 *of* 1904.—(Tamil.) On the same pillar. A record in the twenty-fourth year of the Chōḷa king Madiraikoṇḍa-Parakēsarivarman (905—47). Records gift of land.

1583. 448 *of* 1904.—(Tamil.) On the same pillar. A record in the sixth year of the Chōḷa king Parakēsarivarman. Records gift of ninety sheep for a lamp.

1584. 449 *of* 1904.—(Tamil.) On the same pillar. A record in the twenty-seventh year of the Chōḷa king Madiraikoṇḍa-Parakēsarivarman (905—47). Records gift of sheep for a lamp.

1585. 450 *of* 1904.—(Tamil.) On a fourth pillar in the same place. A record in the twentieth year of the Chōḷa king Madiraikoṇḍa-Parakēsarivarman (905—47). Records gift of ninety sheep for a lamp.

1586. 451 *of* 1904.—(Tamil.) On a fourth pillar in the same place. A record in the eighteenth year of the Chōḷa king Madiraikoṇḍa Parakēsarivarman (905—47). Records gift of ninety sheep for a lamp.

1587. 452 *of* 1904.—(Tamil.) On a fourth pillar in the same place. A record in the twenty-fifth year of the Chōḷa king Madiraikoṇḍa Parakēsarivarman (905—47). Records gift of ninety sheep for a lamp.

1588. 453 *of* 1904.—(Tamil.) On a fourth pillar in the same place. A record in the thirteenth year of the Chōḷa king Madiraikoṇḍa Parakēsarivarman (905—47). Records gift of gold.

1589. 454 *of* 1904.—(Tamil.) On a fourth pillar in the same place. A record in the eighteenth year of the Chōḷa king Madiraikoṇḍa Parakēsarivarman. Records gift of sheep ninety for a lamp.

1590. 455 *of* 1904.—(Tamil.) On a fourth pillar in the same place. A record in the thirtieth year of the Chōḷa king Madiraikoṇḍa Parakēsarivarman (905—47). Records gift of ninety sheep for a lamp.

1591. 456 *of* 1904.—(Tamil.) On a fourth pillar in the same place. A record in the twenty-seventh year of the Chōḷa king Madiraikoṇḍa Parakēsarivarman (905—47). Records gift of 180 sheep for two lamps.

1592. 457 *of* 1904.—(Tamil.) On a fourth pillar in the same temple. A mutilated record in the thirty-second year of the Chōḷa king Madiraikoṇḍa Parakēsarivarman (905—47).

1593. 458 *of* 1904.—(Tamil.) On a fourth pillar in the same place. A damaged record in the thirteenth year of the Chōḷa king Madiraikoṇḍa Parakēsarivarman (905—47).

1594. 459 *of* 1904.—(Tamil.) On a fourth pillar in the same place. A record in the fifth year of the Chōḷa king Parakēsarivarman. Records gift of ninety sheep for a lamp.

1595. 460 *of* 1904.—(Tamil.) On the south wall of the Tyāgarāja shrine in the same temple. A record in the sixteenth year of the Chōḷa king Tribhuvanachakravartin Rājēndra-Chōḷadēva (III), corresponding to Monday, 1st May, 1262. Records gift of land for meeting the expenses of two festivals called *Tiruvikkiraman-śandi*. See *Ep. Ind.*, Vol. VIII, p. 273.

1596. 461 *of* 1904.—(Tamil.) On a pillar in the maṇṭapa in front of the same shrine. A mutilated record in the sixteenth year of the Chōḷa king Rājarāja-Rājakēsarivarman (I, 985—1013).

1597. 462 *of* 1904.—(Tamil.) On the same pillar. A damaged record in the nineteenth year of the Chōḷa king Rājakēsarivarman *alias* Rājarājadēva (985—1013).

1598. 463 *of* 1904.—(Tamil.) On the same pillar. A damaged record in the fourteenth year of the Chōḷa king Parakēsarivarman.

1599. 464 *of* 1904.—(Tamil.) On the same pillar. Records in the sixteenth year of the king gift of land.

1600. 465 *of* 1904.—(Tamil.) On the second pillar in the maṇṭapa in front of the Tyāgarāja shrine in the same temple? A record of the Chōḷa king Madiraikoṇḍa Parakēsarivarman (905—47), the date of which is lost. Records gift of ninety sheep for a lamp.

1601. 466 *of* 1904.—(Tamil.) On the third pillar in the same maṇṭapa. A partly damaged record in the third year of the Chōḷa king Rājakēsarivarman. Records gift of ninety sheep for a lamp.

1602. 467 *of* 1904.—(Tamil.) On the same pillar. A record in the eighth year of the Chōḷa king Rājakēsarivarman. Records gift of a lamp.

1603. 468 *of* 1904.—(Tamil.) On the fourth pillar in the same maṇṭapa. A partly damaged record in the seventeenth year of the Chōḷa king Madiraikoṇḍa Parakēsarivarman (905—47). Records gift of a lamp.

1604. 469 *of* 1904.—(Tamil.) On the same pillar. A partly damaged record in the twenty-eighth year of the Chōḷa king Madiraikoṇḍa Parakēsarivarman (905—47). Records gift of ninety sheep.

1605. 470 *of* 1904.—(Tamil.) On the fifth pillar in the same maṇṭapa. A mutilated record in the fifteenth year of the Chōḷa king Rāja-Rājakēsarivarman (985—1013). Records gift of 180 sheep for two lamps.

1606. 471 *of* 1904.—(Tamil.) On the sixth pillar in the same maṇṭapa. A damaged record in the twentieth year of the Chōḷa king Rājakēsarivarman.

1607. 472 *of* 1904.—(Tamil.) On the same pillar. A record in the sixth year of the Chōḷa king Parakēsarivarman. Records gift of ninety sheep for a lamp.

1608. 473 *of* 1904.—(Tamil.) On the seventh pillar in the same maṇṭapa. A record in the nineteenth year of the Chōḷa king Madiraikoṇḍa Parakēsarivarman (905—47). Records gift of two lamps.

1609. 474 *of* 1904.—(Tamil.) On the same pillar. A record in the sixth year of the Chōḷa king Parakēsarivarman. Records gift of ninety sheep. Damaged at the end.

1610. 475 *of* 1904.—(Tamil.) On the same pillar. A damaged record in the ninth year of the Chōḷa king Parakēsarivarman.

1611. 476 *of* 1904.—(Tamil.) On a pillar in the maṇṭapa in front of the Rāmanāthēśvara shrine in the same temple. A record of the Chōḷa king Madiraikoṇḍa Parakēsarivarman (905—47), the date of which is doubtful. Records gift of ninety sheep for a lamp.

1612. 477 *of* 1904.—(Tamil.) On the same pillar. An incomplete record in the twenty-seventh year of the Chōḷa king Rājakēsarivarman.

1613. 478 *of* 1904.—(Tamil.) On the same pillar. A record in the thirtieth year of the Chōḷa king Madiraikoṇḍa Parakēsarivarman (905—47). Records gift of 180 sheep for two lamps.

1614. 479 *of* 1904.—(Tamil.) On the same pillar. A record in the fifteenth year of the Chōḷa king Madiraikoṇḍa Parakēsarivarman (905—47). Records gift of ninety sheep for a lamp.

1615. 480 *of* 1904.—(Tamil.) On the same pillar. A record in the fifteenth year of the Chōḷa king Madiraikoṇḍa Parakēsarivarman (905—47). Records gift of 180 sheep for two lamps.

1616. 481 *of* 1904.—(Grantha.) On the second pillar in the same maṇṭapa. Records the gift of ninety sheep for a lamp by a certain Kalikēsarin.

1617. 482 *of* 1904.—(Tamil.) On the same pillar. A record in the thirteenth year of the Chōḷa king Madiraikoṇḍa Parakēsarivarman (905—47). Records gift of ninety sheep for a lamp by the same donor.

1618. 483 *of* 1904.—(Tamil.) On the same pillar. A record in the tenth year of the Chōḷa king Rājakēsarivarman. Records gift of ninety sheep for a lamp.

1619. 484 *of* 1904.—(Tamil.) On the same pillar. A record in the eighth year of the Chōḷa king Parakēsarivarman. Records gift of ninety sheep for a lamp.

1620. 485 *of* 1904.—(Tamil.) On the same pillar. A record in the seventh year of the Chōḷa king Madiraikoṇḍa Parakēsarivarman (905—47). Records gift of a lamp.

1621. 486 *of* 1904.—(Tamil.) On the same pillar. A record in the thirty-second year of the Chōḷa king Madiraikoṇḍa Parakēsarivarman (905 -47). Records gift of ninety sheep for a lamp.

1622. 487 *of* 1904.—(Tamil.) On the same pillar. A record in the twenty-sixth year of the Chōḷa king Rājakēsarivarman. Records gift of 180 sheep for two lamps.

1623. 488 *of* 1904.—(Tamil.) On the same pillar. A damaged record of the Chōḷa king Parakēsarivarman (905—47), "who took Madurai and Īḷam (Ceylon)," the date of which is indistinct.

1624. 489 *of* 1904.—(Tamil.) In the second gōpura of the same temple, left of entrance. A record of the Vijayanagara king Prabhushi (for Prauḍha) Dēvarāya Mahārāya (1449--65) in Ś. 1386, expired, Tāraṇa. Records sale of land.

1625. 490 *of* 1904.—(Tamil.) In the same place. A mutilated record of the Vijayanagara king Vīrapratāpa Dēvamahārāya in Ś. (date lost), cyclic year (doubtful). Seems to record a gift of land.

1626. 491 *of* 1904.—(Mahrāthi.) On a slab built into the floor in front of the same gōpura. Mentions the Mahrātha kings Pratāpasiṁha-Mahārāja and his son Tuḷaja-Mahārāja (1763—87) of Tanjore. See *Tanj. Gazr.*, Vol. I, p. 49.

1627. 492 *of* 1904.—(Tamil.) On the south wall of the first prākāra of the same temple. A partly damaged record in the thirty-third year of the Chōḷa king Tribhuvanachakravartin Rājēndra-Chōḷadēva (III ?). Records gift of land.

1628. 493 *of* 1904.—(Tamil.) On the same wall. A partly damaged record of the Chōḷa king Tribhuvanachakravartin Rājarājadēva (III ?) the date of which is lost. Records gift of land for a lamp.

1629. 494 *of* 1904.—(Tamil.) On the west wall of the same prākāra. A record in the eighteenth year of the Chōḷa king Tribhuvanachakravartin Rājēndra-Chōḷadēva (III). Records gift of land. Dr. Kielhorn discussing the details of the date, points out that *Aparapaksha* is a mistake for *Pūrvapaksha* and that the English equivalent is Wednesday, 2nd January 1264. See *Ep. Ind.*, p. 274.

1630. 495 *of* 1904.—(Tamil.) On the same wall. A record in the twenty-seventh year of the Chōḷa king Tribhuvanachakravartin Rājarāja-dēva (III). Records gift of land. An irregular date. See *Ibid.*, p. 271.

1631. 496 *of* 1904.—(Tamil.) On the west wall of the first prākāra of the same temple. A record in the nineteenth year of the Chōḷa king Tribhuvanachakravartin Rājarājadēva (III). Built in at the beginning. Records gift of land for a lamp. The date corresponds to Sunday, 11th June, A.D. 1234. *Ibid.*, p. 269.

1632. 497 *of* 1904.—(Tamil.) On the north wall of the same prākāra. A record in the twenty-first year of the Chōḷa king Tribhuvanachakravartin Rājēndra-Chōḷadēva (III ?). Records gift of land.

1633. 498 *of* 1904.—(Tamil.) On the same wall. A record in the fourteenth year of the Chōḷa king Tribhuvanachakravartin Rājādhirājadēva (II ?). Records gift of land for a lamp.

1634. 499 *of* 1904.—(Tamil.) On the same wall. A record in the third year of the Chōḷa king Tribhuvanachakravartin Rājarājadēva (III). Records a sale of five men and five women and their relations *(vargattār)* for 1,000 *kāśus* by a certain Ariyan Pichchan *alias* Ediriḷiśōḷa-Gaṅgaināḍāḷvān who was evidently the police officer of the district. He says that the five men were his slaves and "had been made over to the temple as slaves by his master *(mudaliyār)*."

1635. 500 *of* 1904.—(Tamil.) On the same wall. A record in the eighth year of the Chōḷa king Tribhuvanachakravartin Rājarāja-dēva (III ?). Records gift of land for a lamp.

1636. 501 *of* 1904.—(Tamil.) On the same wall. A partly damaged record in the thirtieth year of the Chōḷa king Tribhuvanachakravartin Rājarājadēva (III ?). Refers to an invasion of Śiṅgaṇṇa Daṇḍanāyaka and to the rebuilding of the temple of Kōḍikkuḷagar. See 498 of 1902 at Tiruvaṇṇāmalai where a Siṁhaṇa Daṇḍanātha is referred in the fifth year of Rājēndra Chōḷa III (i.e., 1250-51), but it is doubtful whether the two are identical.

1637. 502 *of* 1904.—(Tamil.) On the same wall. A damaged record in the twenty-fourth year of the Chōḷa king Tribhuvanachakravartin Rājarājadēva (III). Records a sale of two women by the same man as is mentioned in No. 1634 above.

1638. 503 *of* 1904.—(Tamil.) On the same wall. A record in the twelfth year of the Chōḷa king Tribhuvanachakravartin Rājēndra-Chōḷadēva (III ?). Records gift of land.

1639. *C.P. No.* 40 *of Mr. Sewell's List.*—(Tamil.) Records a document in Ś. 1418 (A.D. 1496), Krōdhi, by which the temple authorities at the Vēdāraṇya temple of the God Chaṇḍīśvara granted certain privileges to a priest.